Readings in Juvenile Delinquency

D. C. Heath and Company Lexington, Massachusetts Toronto

Readings in Juvenile Delinquency

DEAN G. ROJEK
University of Georgia

GARY F. JENSEN
University of Arizona

Published simultaneously in Canada.

Printed in the United States of America.

International Standard Book Number: 0-669-03763-X

Library of Congress Catalog Card Number: 81-81603

Preface

It is important that students learn to grapple for the truth in the same way that social scientists do. Even though the so-called experts do not all agree, decisions still have to be made, and social policy must be implemented. Thus, most of the ten sections of this book have been developed around a "point-counterpoint" theme, intended to challenge students by presenting differing perspectives and thereby to encourage a critical evaluation of each reading. Our selections are articles that have made important contributions to the study of delinquency. They are a representative sample of concise, straightforward, and hopefully provocative discussions.

The book is intended for use in undergraduate and graduate courses in juvenile delinquency and criminology. We see as a major innovation the fact that each of the ten distinct sections is a self-contained study unit with an introduction and a concluding summary. Each introduction serves as a mini-lecture for the material that follows and prepares the reader to understand the nature of the argument in the readings. Each summary reexamines the basic thrust of the readings and helps the student draw conclusions.

The ten sections into which the readings are divided represent the major topics in the study of delinquency. Section One, which serves as an introduction, immediately confronts the student with the differing images of the juvenile delinquent projected by the mass media. Section Two examines the origins of the juvenile justice system and highlights the debate on the effectiveness of this social invention. In Section Three, the student is introduced to some of the most problematic areas in delinquency. There are different data bases, different jurisdictional ingredients, and ultimately different conclusions regarding the relationship of basic demographic variables to delinquency. Sections Four and Five deal with the theoretical explanations of delinquency: Section Four addresses the question of physiological and psychological causes, while Section Five looks at the major sociological explanations. The impact of adolescent contextual variables—for example, the family, school, religion, and media—is discussed in Section Six. The debate between the labeling and deterrence schools is presented in Section Seven. Sections Eight and Nine focus on the treatment of juvenile offenders. In Section Eight we examine the issue of institutionalization, while in Section Nine we consider the concept of diversion. Finally, Section Ten tackles the complex issue of prevention and the dilemma of social policy in resolving the problem of delinquency.

There are many people to whom we are indebted for stimulating our interest and for aiding us in this particular endeavor. However, there is one person who deserves a special acknowledgment. Janet Jensen assisted us in many tasks, ranging from typing to doing a critical assessment of our final product. She passed away while this book was in its final stage of preparation. Words are incapable of expressing the magnitude of our loss. We dedicate this book to her memory.

Dean G. Rojek
Gary F. Jensen

Contributors

Suzanne S. Ageton
Ronald L. Akers
Gary L. Albrecht
David Bakan
Donald J. Black
Scott Briar
Bruce Bullington
Robert L. Burgess
Stephen A. Cernkovich
William J. Chambliss
Albert K. Cohen
Lawrence E. Cohen
Delbert S. Elliott
Maynard L. Erickson
Jack P. Gibbs
Peggy C. Giordano
Eleanor Glueck
Sheldon Glueck
Martin Gold
John Hagan
Bill Haney
Timothy F. Hartnagel
Paul C. Higgins
Paul S. Higgins
Michael J. Hindelang
Travis Hirschi
Frederick W. Howlett
Gary F. Jensen
Daniel Katkin
Lloyd W. Klemke
James R. Kluegel
Marvin D. Krohn
Lonn Lanza-Kaduce
Jeffrey Leon
Paul Lerman
Jennie J. McIntyre
Donal E.J. MacNamara
Anne Rankin Mahoney
Robert Martinson
David Matza
Robert K. Merton
Walter B. Miller
Mark Phillips
Irving Piliavin
Anthony Platt
Kenneth Polk
Marcia Radosevich
Albert J. Reiss, Jr.
Gerald D. Robin
Dean G. Rojek
Herman Schwendinger
Julia R. Schwendinger
B.F. Skinner
James Sprowls
Suzanne K. Steinmetz
Murray A. Straus
Gresham M. Sykes
James J. Teevan, Jr.
Terence P. Thornberry
Bernard A. Thorsell
Charles R. Tittle
Jackson Toby
Wayne J. Villemez

Contents

Readings in Juvenile Delinquency

SECTION ONE

Delinquency as a Social Problem

"Half of all serious crimes in the United States are committed by youths 10 to 17!" " 'Kiddie crime,' as it's sometimes called, includes murder, rape, armed robbery, violent assault, mugging, robbery, arson, vandalism—hardly 'kid stuff.' " "Virtually all adult criminals were juvenile offenders. IF ONLY THEY COULD HAVE BEEN STOPPED THEN!" These statements appear in promotional advertisements for the award-winning film *Scared Straight,* which documents a controversial "get-tough" program designed to "scare" juvenile offenders "straight." A *Time* magazine article published in the late 1970s dramatizes the problem similarly, referring to "the youth crime plague." The article maintains that kids are literally "getting away with murder."

There is some truth to these claims. Young people do account for a disproportionate share of arrests in Federal Bureau of Investigation statistics. They do commit a large proportion of those crimes against persons and property that attract public and media attention. Adults with arrest records are likely to have run afoul of the law as juveniles. The reason we do not wholeheartedly endorse the claims is that, in the process of dramatizing juvenile delinquency, they give a biased and misleading representation of the problem.

Contrary to the image conveyed in the statements above, it can be and has been argued that the most "serious" crimes in the United States are more likely to be committed by adults than by persons ten to seventeen and that adult-dominated crime is of greater economic and social cost than all juvenile offenses combined. For example, price fixing is an adult offense estimated to cost 10 billion dollars a year. So-called white-collar crime, also perpetrated primarily by adults, is estimated to cost over ten times the loss attributable to robbery, burglary, larceny, and auto theft (Jensen and Rojek,

1980). Add to these the cost of organized crime and the total is staggering. In economic terms, adult crime is considerably more consequential than juvenile crime.

Of course, the seriousness of crime is not adequately measured in financial terms. It is difficult to assign physical and mental suffering a value in terms of dollars and cents. But can we conclude that the amount of suffering attributable to juvenile crime is greater than that attributable to adult-dominated crime? Persons aged ten to seventeen do commit violent acts, but their contribution to arrest statistics for murder, rape, and assault is not particularly high, given the proportion of the total population they constitute. Arrests for these three crimes peak at age twenty-one and are dominated by young adults. Arrests for violent offenses against the family, such as child and spouse abuse, peak at age twenty-four.

On the other hand, juveniles are greatly overrepresented in arrest statistics for any crime involving direct theft of property (robbery, burglary, larceny, motor vehicle theft) or attack on property (vandalism, arson). They are also greatly overrepresented in arrest statistics for robbery. Robbery is an offense involving violence or the threat of violence, and the high robbery rate among juveniles is a major component of our dramatic image of youth delinquency. In fact, some criminologists argue, "Robbery is the best indicator of the type of crime most feared by the public" (Conklin, 1972:4). Adults engage in robbery as well, but their targets are different. Adults are more likely than juveniles to rob commercial establishments (including taxicab operations), while juveniles are more likely than adults to steal from people on the streets and snatch purses. Juveniles also tend to choose older victims than do adult robbers.

Thus, the view of juvenile delinquency as a particularly severe problem appears to reflect far more than actual economic loss, which is less for juvenile crime than for crime attributable to adults. It reflects more than the measure of suffering attributable to criminal violence. The attacks by the young on their elders for what appears to be relatively minor economic gain is particularly disturbing to adults and provides the basis for our frightening view of juvenile delinquency.

We should be careful, however, not to confuse the dramatic with the typical. For example, studies of gangs in the 1960s and 1970s show that, although there has been an increase in attacks on the elderly, the typical victims of gang attacks are only rarely the weak and the defenseless (Miller, 1966, 1975). Moreover, robbery accounts for only about 2 percent of arrests of persons under eighteen. Juvenile gang attacks on the weak and defenseless are disturbing but insignificant as a component of the delinquency problem.

In their article "The Delinquent Nobody Knows," Bill Haney and Martin Gold attack the traditional image of the delinquent presented by the news media. The delinquent nobody knows turns out to be the delinquent everybody knows, because most teenagers violate the juvenile or criminal code at one time or another. This does not mean that everyone commits equal numbers of offenses or equally serious offenses, but rather that the pool of candidates for possible official processing is quite large. Moreover, it is more difficult to pin down a distinct social background characterizing delinquents when self-admissions of delinquency are substituted for official police or court records. When self-admissions are used, race and social class do not differentiate well, and even differences by gender appear muted. The emphasis in Haney and Gold's article is on the most commonly seen characteristics of youthful delinquents.

But what of the relationship between adult criminality and juvenile delinquency? The statement quoted previously, "If only they could have been stopped then!" implies an inevitable connection between delinquency and adult crime that can best be broken by the reduction of juvenile delinquency. We should carefully examine this point of view. It is based on a narrow conception of crime and ignores the fact that the most costly form of crime (white-collar offenses) may involve people who are not likely to have acquired delinquency records as juveniles. Moreover, while there is a definite correlation between acquiring a juvenile record and participating in adult crime, it is far from perfect. It is probably safe to conclude that most adolescents involved in delinquency *do not* become criminals as adults. It should also be noted that the relationship between adult crime and juvenile delinquency is quite complex. There is, for example, a "generational" continuity to illegal behavior (Goode, 1972: 34). Children whose parents break the law are themselves more likely to break the law. Children who come to believe that people get away with breaking the law are themselves more likely to break the law. In short, the involvement of adults in crime may directly or indirectly cause delinquency. Consequently, a reduction in adult crime might be as effective as the traditional "nip-it-in-the-bud" response.

The third and final article in this section, "The Saints and the Roughnecks," was chosen because it elaborates on several of the ideas we have discussed and suggests lines of reconciliation between conflicting images of delinquency and delinquents as problems. By comparing two groups of boys involved in delinquent activities, William Chambliss illustrates that some types of illegal activities and the participants in those activities are ignored or tolerated while others are not. The total harm done may be the same but public reaction may differ considerably, and the probability of one group's becoming a "problem" is greater than the other's. Moreover, from the observations and descriptions of the two groups of boys and of what happens to each, we get a much more realistic view than if selected dramatic examples had been used. Comparing and contrasting all three articles should provide an idea of the ordinary and extraordinary dimensions of delinquency and suggest important questions concerning the common responses to it.

REFERENCES

Conklin, J. E. 1972. *Robbery and the Criminal Justice System.* Philadelphia: J. B. Lippincott.

Goode, E. 1972. *Drugs in American Society.* New York: Alfred A. Knopf.

Jensen, G. F., and D. G. Rojek. 1980. *Delinquency: A Sociological View.* Lexington, Massachusetts: D. C. Heath.

Miller, W. B. 1966. "Violent Crimes in City Gangs." *Annals of the American Academy of Political and Social Science* 364 (March): 97–112.

——. 1975. *Violence by Youth Gangs and Youth Groups as a Crime Problem in Major American Cities.* Washington, D.C.: U.S. Government Printing Office.

The Youth Crime Plague

Chicago. Johnny, 16, who had a long record of arrests for disorderly conduct, simple battery and aggravated assault, lured a motorist into an alley. He drew a .22-cal. pistol and shot the driver six times, killing him. Johnny was arrested yet again, but he was released because witnesses failed to show up in court. Today he is free.

New Orleans. Steven, 17, was first arrested for burglary when he was eleven and diagnosed as psychotic. But he kept escaping from the state hospital and was seized for 22 different crimes, including theft and attempted murder. Just four days after he was charged with robbery and attempted murder, he was arrested for raping and murdering a young nurse.

Hartford. Touché, 19, who earned his nickname by his dexterity with a switchblade, has been in trouble since he was eleven; he started fires, snatched pocketbooks, stole cars, burglarized homes, slashed and shot people. When a pal was locked up in Connecticut's Meriden Home for Boys, Touché broke in with a gun and freed him. Touché was placed in a specially built cell in Meriden because he had escaped from the institution 17 times.

Wilmington. Eric, 16, who had escaped conviction for a previous mugging charge, pleaded guilty to knocking down an 86-year-old woman and stealing her purse. Three months later, the woman is still hospitalized and is not expected to walk again. Eric was released into the custody of his father. Since then, he has been charged with three burglaries. Says Detective James Strawbridge: "He's going to kill somebody some day, and he's still out there."

Houston. Lawrence was 15 when he was charged with murdering two brothers in his neighborhood: Kenneth Elliott, 11, and Ronald Elliott, 12. Lawrence tied up Kenneth, castrated him and stabbed him twice in the heart. Then he cut off the boy's head, which he left about 50 feet from the body. He also admitted killing Ronald, whose body was never found, in similar fashion. Like all other offenders in juvenile facilities in Texas, Lawrence was released from prison when he turned 18.

People have always accused kids of getting away with murder. Now that is all too literally true. Across the U.S., a pattern of crime has emerged that is both perplexing and appalling. Many youngsters appear to be robbing and raping, maiming and murdering as casually as they go to a movie or join a pickup baseball game. A new, remorseless, mutant juvenile seems to have been born, and there is no more terrifying figure in America today.

More than half of all serious crimes* in the U.S. are committed by youths aged ten to 17. Since 1960, juvenile crime has risen twice as fast as that of adults. In San Francisco, kids of 17 and under are arrested for 57% of all felonies against people (homicide, assault, etc.) and 66% of all crimes against property. Last year in Chicago, one-third of all murders were committed by people aged 20 or younger, a 29% jump over 1975. In Detroit, youths commit so much crime that city officials were forced to impose a 10 p.m. curfew last year for anyone 16 or under.

Though offenders come from every ethnic group and environment, most are nonwhite kids whose resentments are honed and hardened in the slums. Usually they are victims themselves, abused or abandoned by parents who tend to have a history of crime, chronic alcoholism or emotional disturbances. About half of the violent juvenile crime is committed by black youths, and a large but indeterminate amount by Hispanics. Especially in ghettos of big cities, the violent youth is the king of the streets.

When he is caught, the courts usually spew him out again. If he is under a certain age, 16 to 18 depending on the state, he is almost always taken to juvenile court, where he is treated as if he were still the child he is supposed to be. Even if he has murdered somebody, he may be put away for only a few months. He is either sent home well before his term expires or he escapes, which, as the kids say, is "no big deal." Small wonder that hardened juveniles laugh, scratch, yawn, mug and even fall asleep while their crimes are revealed in court.

A New York teen-ager explained in a WCBS radio interview how he started at the age of twelve to rob old women. "I was young, and I knew I wasn't gonna get no big time. So, you know, what's to worry? If you're doin' wrong, do it while you're young, because you won't do that much time."

Another boy, 15, recalled why he shot a "dude": "Wasn't nothin'. I didn't think about it. If I had to kill him, I just had to kill him. That's the way I look at it, 'cause I was young. The most I could have got then is 18 months."

In Miami, Edward Robinson, 15, was accused of raping a housewife at knife point, even while police surrounded the home. "What you gonna do to me?" he sneered. "Send me to youth hall? I'll be out in a few hours." That taunt landed him in adult court. But his case was an exception. Most juvenile criminals are precluded from effective punishment. Says Andrew Vogt, executive director of Colorado's District Attorneys' Association: "In effect, we have created a privileged class in society."

That privileged class keeps enlisting ever younger members. Partly this is a response to juvenile laws. Older kids employ younger confederates—who tend to get off easily if caught—to push drugs, commit robberies and sometimes murder. In New Haven, two brothers, Ernest Washington, 16, and Erik, 14, along with four other kids, were arrested for robbing and killing a Yale student. Since Erik was underage, he confessed that he had pulled the trigger. He told New Haven Prosecutor Michael Whalen: "The most you're going to give me is two years." Erik, in fact, was bound over to adult court. At his trial last month, guess what? Erik denied doing the shooting. It did not help. He was convicted and sentenced to 15 years to life. Says Whalen: "He showed no awareness of conscience or remorse. He grinned like crazy. He probably figures that prison is not a hell of a lot worse than other places he's been."

Aside from this sort of calculation, kids seem to be developing a taste for sadism earlier in life. William S. White,

*Murder, rape, aggravated assault, robbery, burglary, larceny, motor vehicle theft.

From *Time*, (July 11, 1977), pp. 18–20, 25–28. Reprinted by permission from *Time*, The Weekly Newsmagazine; copyright Time Inc., 1977.

presiding judge of the Cook County, Ill., juvenile court, thinks that a lower limit may have been reached: "I don't expect a six-year-old to be committing homicides." Don't be too sure. In Washington, D.C., a six-year-old boy siphoned gasoline out of a car and poured it over a sleeping neighbor. Then he struck a match and watched the man go up in flames.

More girls are getting involved in violent crime. From 1970 to 1975, the arrest rate of girls under 18 for serious offenses climbed 40%, *v.* 24% for boys. In 1975, 11% of all juveniles arrested for violent crimes were female. Last month Chicago police finally caught a gang of six girls, aged 14 to 17, after they had terrorized elderly people for months. Their latest crime: the brutal beating of a 68-year-old man. "I was amazed," says Police Lieut. Lawrence Forberg. "They were indignant toward their victims, and none of them shed any tears. This is the first time I've encountered young girls this tough."

The Killing Costs

Youthful criminals prey on the most defenseless victims. The very young, the old, the lame, sick and blind are slugged, slashed and shot. They have retreated with broken limbs and emotional scars behind triple-locked doors. Many never venture out at night; some do not even risk the streets during the day. In confinement, their anguish is not heard. Often poor and not well educated, they do not know where to turn or how to complain.

So what's new? ponders the director of a juvenile facility in New York. The old folks have been assailed for years. The kids, he insists, have a "value system" of their own that should be respected. They are rebels, by his murky reckoning, against a society that does not give them a chance. One peculiar value is demonstrated by a teen-ager who prowls Manhattan's Upper East Side in search of eyes to gouge. To date, he has made known attempts on a bus driver, a journalist, an Egyptian tourist, the son of former Manhattan Democratic Party Leader Edward Costikyan and others. He was never locked up because he was underage.

Elizabeth Griffith, 84, a black woman, was beaten in her New York City apartment by two black teen-agers. "I didn't feel the blows because I was so numb from the choking," she recalled. "The big one hollered, 'Hit her!' and the little one would come over and hit me again. And I looked at the little one and said, 'Shame on you.' I saw death and I was dead, and I started to call the Lord. I was thinking to myself, 'What a nightmare, oh, what a nightmare!' " A nightmare shared by innumerable others who cannot count on the basic minimum of a supposedly civilized society: personal safety. Says Jim Wilson, a black homicide detective in Harlem: "Anybody should be able to go out on the streets any time he wants."

Analysts tirelessly—and correctly—say that unemployment, slum housing, inadequate schools and the pathology of the ghetto contribute to the spreading scourge of youth crime. But the reverse is also true: the ripple effects of crime eventually overwhelm a city and destroy its *élan*. People are frightened away from downtown, reducing business for stores, theaters, restaurants. In their place, thick as weeds, sprout porno houses, massage parlors and gambling havens, where criminals thrive.

Crime is decimating communities like Harlem. Says William Lundon, a homicide detective: "It's as if there were a cancer out there, with the doctor operating every day." To ward off robberies, Harlem merchants—almost all of them blacks—often stay open 24 hours a day. But the longer they are around, the more chance there is that they will be assaulted. One all-night grocer, a genial man in his 60s who was shot in the stomach by robbers, lives permanently in the Alamo. Thieves managed to break through solid steel sheets over his windows; 20 cases of beer were lugged out through the skylight. "I couldn't have whipped my people into doing that," says the grocer in disbelief. Increasingly, Harlem businessmen are giving up in despair, contributing to the steady spiral of decline. In Queens, N.Y., a dozen plants employing some 1,000 people threatened for a while to relocate unless action was taken against the youth gangs that continually robbed them. The

---

CRIPPLERS IN THE WAR ZONE

Frightening enough when they are alone or in pairs, youths in a gang are a formidable engine of mayhem. Today's urban gangs commit roughly 25% of the juvenile crime, and they are better organized than ever, more heavily armed and less queasy about the blood they spill.

Particularly in the ghetto, the gang gives a kid the structured life he has never had at home or anywhere else. The peer pressure to enlist is almost irresistible. Rico, 17, joined a Puerto Rican gang in Chicago for "protection, man, protection. I was a skinny little kid, and I was tired of having hassles. You don't last long if you don't belong to a club. You can always count on having someone stand up for you." A 14-year-old boy who committed frequent robberies in Central Falls, R.I., and once smashed 350 windowpanes in a factory says he was lured into crime because "I felt out of place. If you stand around when the other kids are doing that stuff, you feel like a pussy. I didn't want to be a pussy."

Nothing pussyfooted about the average gang or "click," as some kids like to call it. At the top of the heap is the "prez," who, if he wants to stay there, had better respond to every threat and challenge. The "veep" supervises internal affairs, especially dues and initiation rituals; the "war counselor" plans the "rip-offs" and "gang-hits" and commands the "gestapo" squads, which consist of the enforcers; the "armorer" keeps the weapons functioning in a safe place such as an abandoned building or a girl friend's apartment. Even automatic and semiautomatic firearms—like M-16s and M-15s—can be bought or stolen. Also available for bigger bashes are hand grenades many decibels above the zip guns of the old days.

The great numbers in a gang seem to suppress the last vestige of conscience. In New York City, members of a gang sat on either side of a man on the subway, stuck him with knives from both sides, robbed him and kept him propped up until they disembarked. To finish off rival mobs, gangs have invaded hospitals in The Bronx, and once were repelled from an operating room by a surgeon wielding a scalpel.

Seattle even has a one-family gang: seven brothers, eleven to 20, who have been arrested 192 times in the past nine years. Enough of the boys are always at liberty to keep up the family tradition. Says Seattle Police Sergeant Dick Ramon: "The frightening thing is that they're going to continue producing misery for years and years."

In Los Angeles one gang is called the Cripplers (with a special auxiliary for girls known as Crippettes), because a member is initiated only after furnishing evidence that he has physically injured somebody. In what is close to a war zone, ghetto residents often eat and sleep on the floor to avoid the stray bullets whizzing through their windows. Joe, 17, a former Crip who has gone straight because he is tired of "hustlin'," says he was always stalking a rival gang member or a potential robbery victim. "Whenever I was shootin' [had a gun], I had someone in mind. If I couldn't get him, I'd get his partner or a substitute." He regrets a murder for which he was never prosecuted. "I took someone's life," Joe reminisces. "He could be on the earth, makin' babies and havin' fun."

kids were so sure of not being punished that they even announced to the executives when they would strike next.

Schools are blamed, often justly, for not equipping children with the most elementary skills. But the schools in many cities have turned into criminal dens where the distraught teacher spends most of the time trying to keep order. The FBI reports that last year some 70,000 teachers were assaulted in U.S. schools and the cost of vandalism reached $600 million. Every school day an estimated 200,000 New York City kids are truant. At least some are fleeing the danger in the classroom. At a state legislative hearing this month, Felix Davila, 16, testified that he stayed away from school because gangs terrorized teachers and shoved girls into bathrooms where they were sexually molested or forced to take drugs. Miguel Sanchez, 16, told the committee that a gang called the Savage Nomads runs his school. "All they do is rape people, mug people. I got out."

The Elusive Causes

It takes a diligent search through history to discover another society that has been as vulnerable to its youthful predators. During the early days of the Industrial Revolution in England, gangs of rapacious children roamed the streets, filling passers-by with dread. But the youngsters' crimes had a clear purpose: destitute, they would kill for food.

Obviously, a relationship still exists between poverty and crime. But the connection is rather tenuous. The great majority of poor kids do not commit crimes. The persistent offenders may come from a ghetto, but they often have more money than the people they rob. Some earn enough from selling drugs and mugging to buy all they want and then some. Explains a juvenile thief: "You know, they don't wanta be wearin' the same old sneakers every day. They wanta change like, you know, they wanta pair of black sneakers." After buying sneakers, gobs of junk food, flashy clothes, a car and, of course, guns, what else does a growing boy need? Nothing, maybe, except kicks. Mugging is like "playing a game," says a youth who attends a school for problem kids in Manhattan. "Kids do it for the fun of it."

One kid, 14, and another, 17, pistol-whipped a woman carrying two bags of groceries to her home in Miami. As she lapsed into a fatal coma on the sidewalk, they continued to kick her, then walked off leaving the groceries. In Washington, two teen-age boys went to the home of a 100-year-old minister and asked for some water. When he let them in, one kid tried to garrote him and then the other slit his throat; somehow he survived. During a robbery in the same city, in which three men were killed and one was seriously wounded, a 15-year-old armed with a machete flailed away, as prosecutors described it, in "wanton, aimless destruction."

How can such sadistic acts—expressions of what moral philosophers would call sheer evil—be explained satisfactorily by poverty and deprivation? What is it in our society that produces such mindless rage? Was the 19th century French criminologist Jean Lacassagne right when he observed that "societies have the criminals they deserve"? Or has the whole connection between crime and society been exaggerated?

Some of the usual explanations seem pretty limp. Yes, America is a materialistic society where everyone is encouraged to accumulate as much as possible. Francis Maloney, commissioner of the department of children and youth in New Haven, notes that "merchants are upset about shoplifting. Well, all the goods are there on the rack to be taken. If you're trying to entice me with the tourist trap, the kid who hasn't money is going to take advantage too. We contribute to the offenses that are committed."

Yes, television glorifies violence and, yes, America is "permissive." In Madison, Wis., Dane County Judge Archie Simonson released a rapist, 15, into the custody of his family. Madison, the judge explained, is a sexually permissive community where women wear see-through blouses. The kid was only reacting "normally," said the judge, though the 16-year-old victim was wearing an unprovocative sweater. But surely these and similar arguments, which go to any length to hold society and not the individual accountable, are glib and shallow.

More serious analysts point to the fact that, historically, rapid economic expansion and ethnically mixed populations have produced crime—hence the waves of violence in the U.S. in the middle and late 19th century. Another factor that historically has been accompanied by crime, points out Sociologist Marvin Wolfgang, is individual freedom. Some experts today argue that juvenile crime is spreading because everyone is pushing what he considers his "rights" to the utmost limits. Standards are lowered and blurred; any behavior, however deviant, finds its instant defenders. The traditional and constraining institutions of family, church and school have lost much of their authority. Says LaMar Empey, a University of Southern California criminologist who specializes in youth: "The 1960s saw the dissipation of the traditional controls of society. There was much more freedom of activity in all spheres, and it was inevitable that there would be more crime. Also, the admission that we had a racist society gave some people an excuse to attack that society without guilt."

Most important is the breakdown in the family. "The old saws about the family are true," says Judge Seymour Gelber, who hears 1,000 delinquency cases a year in Dade County, Fla. "We look for quick solutions, but family stability is the long-term answer." Adds Detective Ellen Carlyle: "The parents don't seem to care. They turn to the police and say, 'Here's my problem. Take care of it.' But they must start caring for their children in infancy."

Gelber notes that blacks commit 75% of the violent crime in Dade County, though they constitute only 15% of the population. But Cubans make up a third of the county's population and account for only 12% of the violent crime. The judge believes the strong Cuban family structure explains this difference. Adds Juan Clark, a sociologist at Miami-Dade Community College: "Like the Chinese, the Cubans have close-knit families with more supervision. There are more three-generation families, and, customarily, middle- and upper-middle-class women do not work." But the stress of exile, as well as modern influences, is beginning to weaken Cuban families; gangs are forming and committing crimes.

For eleven years, Ned O'Gorman, a poet, has run a nursery school in Harlem where no kid is considered too far gone to be accepted. But O'Gorman claims few permanent successes; early parental influence is hard to shake. "The rate of failure," he says, "the return to the cycle that has been their lot and their families' lot forever, is enormous." By the time some youngsters reach O'Gorman at age three or four, their lives have been blighted by what can only euphemistically be called child abuse. Not only is the child cuffed around, but because of neglect, he risks being burned up in his bed, drowning in the bathtub, falling out the window. "In his eyes," says O'Gorman, "is the fixed stare of the blasted spirit."

Charles King, the black director of the Phoenix School, which provides therapy and schooling for 30 problem kids on Manhattan's Upper West Side, thinks that inconsistency of family treatment is more damaging to children than unrelieved harshness. First the parent strikes the kid, then lavishes gifts on him. The bewildered child has no way of telling right from wrong. He remains largely illiterate because no one talks to him. "His language," says King, "is not made to communicate, to establish relationships. It's rejection and rejection, it's the hell with it. The child learns that the only way to be heard is to kick somebody in the teeth. With violence, he suddenly becomes a being."

The Failed System

The juvenile-justice system, a sieve through which most of these kids come and go with neither punishment nor rehabilitation, has become a big part of the problem. The system evolved over the past several decades on the theory that there is no such thing as a bad boy, or at least none beyond salvage. However horrendous his crime, he is still fit for rehabilitation, given time and patience. If he is underage, he is usually not photographed and rarely fingerprinted. Records of his crimes are kept confidential and then destroyed after he becomes a legal adult. He is thus reborn with a *tabula rasa*—no evidence whatsoever of his misconduct. James Higgins, a juvenile judge in New Haven, reflects the attitude of many apologists for the system. "We treat delinquency," he says, "as a civil inquiry into the doings of a child. The court does not consider the child a criminal—irresponsible, perhaps, but not a criminal."

When a cherubic lad of nine was brought into a Washington, D.C., court for crippling an old woman by pushing her down a flight of stairs, the judge told the prosecutor: "I'm sorry, but nothing you can say will convince me that child is guilty." Complains Robert M. Ross, a former assistant corporation counsel in Washington: "Some judges and prosecutors have told me they thought a third to half of all juvenile cases could be solved simply by sitting the kid down and giving him a stern lecture." That attitude might have served well in the halcyon days of Huck Finn and Penrod, when pranks were the principal business before the courts. Says Judge Gelber: "The juvenile courts weren't conceived for the brutal act. They were created with the image of Middle America."

Aside from the shaky assumptions on which it rests, the juvenile court is notoriously inefficient *(see box following page)*. Judges consider assignment to it not a plum but the pits. "I would rather die than preside in Family Court," says New York Criminal Court Judge Eve Preminger. "It's completely unrewarding." Cases are backed up in the overburdened, understaffed system. Complainants and witnesses, who are nervous to begin with and sometimes threatened by the offenders, become exasperated with waiting and walk out. Case dismissed.

Even if the case proceeds, the deck is stacked in favor of the defendant. A juvenile may not be able to read or write, but he can recite his *Miranda* rights* without pausing for breath. When he is arrested, his main effort—and his lawyer's—is to get the case thrown out on some legal technicality, and he often succeeds. In a San Francisco police squad room, the cops toss darts at an unusual board. Its rings are labeled: *Investigate further, Admonish, Cite,* and the bull's-eye is *Complaint withdrawn.* Police Lieut. George Rosko sums up the whole juvenile process: "It fosters the kid's belief that he can beat the system. He goes through the court, comes back to the neighborhood, and he's a hero."

Most of the youths are routinely released into their parents' custody. They are supposed to be on probation, but overworked probation officers can hardly give them much attention. Sometimes parents call the court and cannot even find out the name of the officer assigned to their child. In Providence, young criminals are often given a rent allowance and sent out to make it on their own. One boy, 17, made it all the way to a flophouse alongside winos, junkies and prostitutes. He enjoyed the homelike atmosphere; if forced to move, he told social workers, he would return to prostituting himself at the train station.

When even juvenile authorities decide a youngster is just too dangerous to release, nobody is quite sure what to do with him. Should he be sent to a prison-like facility or a more open work camp or juvenile home? The costs of correctional programs can be astronomical. New York State spends some $15,000 a year for every kid in an "open" facility; a small, experimental psychiatric program costs $50,000 a year for each youth.

The results have been mixed in states like Arizona, California and Connecticut, where authorities have been farming out the inmates of large juvenile prisons to smaller, barless camps and homes. Recidivism has not declined among the hard-core cases, although some of the halfway houses that deal mostly with nonviolent youngsters in a community setting have been effective. When several large detention centers in New York were closed on the grounds that rehabilitation works better in smaller places, many youths were sent to a forestry camp outside Ithaca; soon they burned down the camp.

The toughest kids manage to resist the most earnest efforts at rehabilitation. Robert Watts, a youth officer in Boston, describes a typical failure with a 16-year-old boy: "We gave him everything—intensive education, group sessions, counseling, forestry, experimental camp, acting in plays. We thought we had turned the corner with him." So he was given a twelve-hour pass—only to disappear until he was booked for robbing a bank and stealing two cars.

Juvenile authorities try to find jobs for offenders, but legitimate employment often cannot match what crime pays. One 16-year-old, who spends the day in a school for delinquents in Manhattan and the night pushing drugs in Harlem, has taken in as much as $1,000 in four hours ($600 is turned over to the distributor). He spends it almost as fast as he earns it, but he boasts: "Right now, I got $1,200 in the bank. That ain't nothin' to what other people got. They have $10,000 to $20,000."

Steps Toward Cure

No programs for juveniles are likely to work unless the law is first enforced. It is estimated that 10% of the youngsters who tangle with the law are incorrigible offenders. By now, even many liberals concede that this hard core must be put under some kind of permanent constraint until age, if nothing else, finally mellows them.

Phoenix Director King feels that no violent juvenile should be released until he appreciates the enormity of what he has done. King cites the case of a 16-year-old girl whose crime—murder—was explained to her over and over again. Finally, she made the connection between her mind and her hands—instruments of death. At that point, she broke down sobbing and gradually began to mend. But most of the killers remain remorseless and even bored by talk of their crimes.

If society is to be protected from the violent young, respect for punishment must be restored. Youngsters should know just what to expect if they commit a particular crime. An adult crime—like armed robbery, rape or murder—deserves adult treatment. Yet in many states, a juvenile cannot be tried in adult court for any offense. Says Harlem Detective Wilson: "There are no ifs, ands or buts about it, the laws have to be changed. The idea was to protect kids who had minor skirmishes with the law from getting a record. This kind of treatment was not made for 14- and 15-year-old kids who are killers."

The evidence suggests that a tougher policy toward violent youths reduces crime. This may seem obvious, but it was long doubted by many social scientists. Since Bronx courts this year started handing out stiffer, five- to ten-year sentences for robbery of elderly people, arrests for the offense have dropped 40%.

*From the 1966 U.S. Supreme Court ruling that before a suspect can be interrogated, police must inform him of his rights to remain silent and to obtain a lawyer. More recently, the court has ruled that a youth's confession is invalid unless it is made in the presence of a parent or other "friendly adult."

GAMES IN KIDDIE COURT

Young toughs call it "kiddie court" because of its leniency; so do policemen and prosecutors. New York City Family Court, governed by strict laws designed to protect children and served by slack bureaucracies, primarily handles domestic disputes, but it is also where the kid criminals between seven and 15 are sent. TIME *Bureau Chief Laurence I. Barrett watched delinquency proceedings in the Manhattan branch. His report:*

Opened only last year, the $28 million black granite building in Lower Manhattan resembles a modern free-form museum or college library. Inside, the light, airy waiting area could be mistaken for an airport lounge. There are no juries or casual spectators at the confidential proceedings, so the small courtrooms look like corporate conference chambers. Only the black robe and elevated bench maintain tradition.

The vocabulary would baffle courtroom buffs. There are "contacts" rather than arrests, "fact findings" instead of trials, "findings" in place of convictions. If guilt is established, the judge may order a "placement," not a sentence.

Few cases get that far. The city probation department screens out petty cases and releases most first offenders immediately after "contact." But tracing the child's arrest record is often difficult. Neither the court nor probation maintains a citywide data bank, though probation hopes to have a computerized system working by winter. Says Administrative Judge Joseph Williams: "You could have a youngster taken in here today who was picked up yesterday in Queens and last week in Brooklyn. We wouldn't necessarily know about the previous cases."

Unlike the regular district attorneys who handle suspects aged 16 and over, prosecutors in Family Court have no investigative staff to follow through in collecting evidence. Getting witnesses to cooperate is a major problem. One of the ugliest open cases at the moment involves a twelve-year-old boy accused of stabbing an adult. The child is a "chicken," or male prostitute, and his victim was a "chicken hawk," his homosexual customer. After being wounded in his own bathtub, the man called police and signed a complaint. Stitched up and calmed down, he now wants to forget the whole thing. The boy remains free.

So do hundreds of other youngsters, even after the court has ordered otherwise. In an "intake part"—a court that, among other things, determines whether a kid should be held or paroled pending a hearing—Judge Phillip Thurston calls for the next docket number. It involves a 15-year-old, already being held on a narcotics charge, who had been remanded to a privately run shelter. Now he is to have a new hearing on a car theft. There is an awkward silence after the judge asks, "Well, where is he?" Papers are shuffled, and a probation officer announces: "Judge, he wasn't sent down. He disappeared a few days ago. He's a chronic absconder."

A boy comes in with his sister, mother and Legal Aid Society lawyer. Most of the kids hustled through intake are black or Hispanic and poorly dressed; this one is Chinese and wears expensive boots. The boy, just 14, was picked up carrying a loaded .38 revolver. The judge explains that a formal hearing will be held in three weeks. He does not even ask the boy what he was doing with a gun. Probation recommends parole in the custody of the mother and the judge routinely grants it. The kid is now free to buy another gun.

In Judge Louis Otten's courtroom, a full hearing is to begin. The charge is sexual abuse of a 13-year-old girl by three boys aged twelve, 13 and 15. The older two have had previous "contacts." A petition, or formal accusation, has been drawn. Many hours of work—and taxpayers' dollars—already have gone into the proceeding. But Otten dismisses the case. He has no choice; the victim's mother decided that her daughter should not appear. The boys grin as they leave.

In the next case, a 14-year-old suspect is up for brandishing a loaded pistol in school. The main witness, a teacher, is present. But a police department ballistics specialist —whose testimony is essential under the rules to establish whether the pistol was operable—has failed to appear. The judge riffles through the dossier and says: "He didn't show up in May, either." Otten reschedules the case for July, but the teacher will be on vacation. They settle on Sept. 19, and Otten warns that the case will be dropped if there is one more delay. The boy goes home.

Occasionally a youngster is found guilty. Judge Aileen Haas Schwartz presides over one such rarity. A black 14-year-old with a record was one of two kids accused of forcible theft of bicycles from two younger white children. The suspect has previously been accused of mugging an 85-year-old woman, but that incident was "A.C.D.'d"—adjourned in contemplation of dismissal. The accomplice in the bike case, having no previous "contacts," has been let off. The case is clear-cut; both victims are in court ready to testify. One claims to have been struck and knocked down, but there was no injury. The suspect and his lawyer agree to an "admission" —the euphemism for a guilty plea—but only to third-degree grand larceny, a lesser offense than robbery and assault.

ALAN E. COBER

JUVENILE AT HEARING IN FAMILY COURT IN MANHATTAN

Schwartz then explains—slowly and carefully—the suspect's rights and makes sure he understands the admission and its implications. Looking bored, he nods silently. Sentencing, or "disposition," requires still another hearing at a future date. Before that can occur, a full probation report must be made on the child's background. That can take months. "This one should be done on an urgent basis," Schwartz says. The boy goes home.

Larry Schwartzstein, chief prosecutor in Manhattan Family Court, speaks with studied bitterness. "I have kids tell me to my face that we can't do anything to them. They think it's a game. Witnesses are deathly afraid of reprisals. They feel that the court is more interested in the criminal than the victim." Last November Schwartzstein won a finding against a 15-year-old who had slashed an actor to death. Schwartzstein hopes to get a disposition hearing within two weeks —eight months after the manslaughter finding—if the probation department is finished with its investigation. Meanwhile, the small killer is free on parole.

After stronger juvenile laws were enacted and violent repeaters were finally jailed in New Orleans, teen-age homicides declined from 29 in 1973 to five in 1975. Says District Attorney Harry Connick: "If you take a career criminal off the streets, his peers get the message. They do not want to follow him."

In Memphis, the cases heard in juvenile court declined from 16,191 in 1975 to 14,174 last year; in this year's first quarter, they were down another 16%. "We are not afraid to use the word punish," says Juvenile Judge Kenneth A. Turner, who encourages the press to publish the names and addresses of youthful lawbreakers. Speaking of first offenders, he says, "Every dog is entitled to one bite." But he also warns them, "If you come back again, you'd better bring your toothbrush because we keep our word." That word means jail for the second serious offense. Explains Turner: "Rather than simply emphasize the needs of the child, we also figure we have a paramount duty to protect society."

Atlanta has one of the most rapidly declining juvenile-crime rates in the country—along with some of the strictest judges. Chief Judge Tom Dillon insists that offenders be tried within ten days after they are indicted. "A child's memory is short," says Dillon. "The sooner facts are presented after the offense has occurred, the better it is for everyone, most of all for the child."

With hard-core juveniles isolated, it will be easier to deal with the more manageable majority of delinquents: runaways, truants, vandals, petty thieves. Most do not have to be confined, and they should never be put in the same jails or homes with rapists and murderers. When all types of criminals are mixed in the same place, the lesser offenders come under the influence of the hard core and emerge more dangerous and violent.

Some juvenile courts make the punishment fit the crime precisely. The thief is forced to make restitution; he may go to work for the person whose property he has stolen or destroyed, or he may take some other job until the money is paid back. In Seattle, lesser offenders are put to work in hospitals, state and local agencies and community service projects. When restitution has been made, they are eligible for full-time jobs with social service programs. In Memphis, Judge Turner occasionally orders parents to subsidize their child in some correctional institution. Says he: "That puts more responsibility on parents to keep their kids out of trouble."

Next to enforcing the law, nothing is more important than mobilizing the support of the community to fight crime. Like guerrillas, criminals have to live off the land; if it is not congenial, they will move elsewhere. In Memphis, some 900 concerned adults have volunteered to help with probation by befriending and advising problem youths. "The role model is a tremendous factor in youth crime," declares Judge Gelber. "The potential for great change is there. If a pimp can get to a kid, so can Walt Frazier."

A growing number of black leaders, including Chicago's Jesse Jackson and New York Mayoral Candidate Percy Sutton, are trying to organize blacks in community crusades against crime. Last week people in Harlem led police to two youths who had used a sawed-off shotgun to kill a taxi driver. Says Lewis Mitrano, assistant district attorney in Philadelphia: "The black community is increasingly supporting the efforts of police because it's the black community that suffers most from youth crime and violence. This attitude has done more to combat crime than all the federal funds that have gone into social projects, important as they are."

The social programs that seem to work best are those that aim to reassert the youths' individual responsibility. "It's a cop-out to blame their problems on anything but themselves," declares Michael Major, 30, director of a youth program in Providence called Junction, which has had a better than 50% success record in getting its kids out of crime; the usual success rate is much lower. Among the many roads to self-reliance, Major has chosen scouting. As he puts it, "Any blue-eyed kid from suburbia has support from his parents and money for camping equipment. Inner-city kids don't, but we help make the experience happen. That stuff about 'On my honor, I will do my best' is beautiful—if you can make it a reality for inner-city children."

The same philosophy guides Youth Development Center No. 3, which houses some 50 juveniles in a brownstone complex in Brooklyn. The kids are drilled in their responsibilities by resident counselors. The non-Freudian therapy does not permit them to blame society, family, school or friends—only themselves. They have a free will, they are told, which they should exercise.

The message came across to at least one 13-year-old boy: "I got to face up to reality," he says. "Some of the brothers in here want to play the part of the fool, saying that being here is everybody's fault but their own. But where I am is me, nobody else."

The Juvenile Delinquent Nobody Knows

Bill Haney and Martin Gold

A juvenile delinquent runs with a gang, lives in a slum, and is likely a member of a minority group. Right? Not necessarily. Two sizeable studies surface the middle-class, white delinquent, and suggest youthful lawbreakers are less likely to repeat criminal acts if they're never caught and fed through our juvenile justice system.

THE JUVENILE DELINQUENT leans against the lamppost, cigarette in hand and leer on face. His gang controls this part of the black ghetto, so he is, for the moment, safe. He and his buddies plan their crimes carefully, for crime gives them kicks and macho points. The boy's parents don't know or care what he does out on the streets; his father ran out years ago, and his weary mother has lost control of the boy.

We all know this juvenile delinquent. His image has been drummed into us from Hollywood movies, Government commissions, scholarly reports. In one sense it is handy to have a commonly accepted image; it provides a symbol for people to hurl accusations at or to rally around. There is only one thing wrong. Despite all the care and ink lavished on him by so many for so long, the delinquent is a myth.

Verbose Machinery

The stereotype has emerged from the profile of youths who are *caught and referred to court*, and the police, in turn, tend to catch and refer those who fit the stereotype. Everyone has assumed that *detected* delinquency accurately reflects *undetected delinquent behavior*. This assumption, we have learned, is largely wrong. The official records are highly misleading. Delinquency is not confined to lower-class black males, or to lower-class white males. It is just that middle-class kids are more likely to be overlooked, or that their parents can afford to buy them out of trouble, or that their actions are interpreted as "hijinks" rather than offenses. Further, only a tiny percent of all delinquent acts are ever discovered. And in spite of a vigorous and verbose legal machinery, catching a delinquent does little to stop his or her illegal acts. To the contrary, getting caught makes adolescents *more* likely to commit delinquent acts.

In 1967 Gold and Jay Williams conducted the first National Survey of Youth, assisted by Myrtle Blum. It was the first of a series intended to gauge periodically whether there is any change in the frequency, seriousness, or nature of delinquent behavior in the United States. The 847 teenagers surveyed represented all Americans 13 to 16 years old. The lengthy interviews took place outside of their homes and out of earshot of parents, usually in community centers, libraries, or churches. In addition to this group, we had interviewed a sample of 522 teen-agers from Flint, Michigan, in 1961.

Delinquent Acts

Our definition of *delinquent* behavior includes both an individual's motives and a community's norms. A delinquent act is one that is illegal, and one the individual knows is illegal when he commits it. Actually, we did not settle for mere technical illegality; for example, we did not count smoking tobacco as delinquent even though it is illegal for juveniles to do so almost everywhere. But that law is never enforced and teen-agers know it. Our respondents admitted to a wide range of delinquent acts:

Percent of Respondents Who Committed Each Offense at Least Once in the Three Years Prior to the Interview

Offense	*Flint Sample* (Boys)	*National Sample* (Boys)	*Flint Sample* (Girls)	*National Sample* (Girls)
trespass	50	54	23	27
drinking	55	43	43	29
theft	60	54	30	31
threatened assault	20	49	7	31

From *Psychology Today* (September 1973), pp. 49–55. Reprinted from *Psychology Today* Magazine,

	Flint Sample	*National Sample*	*Flint Sample*	*National Sample*
Offense	*Boys*		*Girls*	
truancy	30	43	17	34
property destruction	27	48	6	25
entering	38	42	23	33
assault	11	39	2	15
false I.D.	10	31	2	27
gang fight	23	34	5	14
fraud	3	23	1	15
concealed weapon	13	12	1	1
hitting parents	2	9	2	11
UDAA[b]	10	7	3	3
runaway	6	6	6	5
drugs	a	2	a	2
arson	*	1	0	0
extortion	8	1	1	0
armed robbery	6	0	0	0

*–under one percent
a–not asked of Flint sample
b–unauthorized driving away of an automobile

Boys are significantly more delinquent than girls, as official records suggest. Males were exclusively reponsible for stealing a part of a car or some gasoline and for armed robbery. They were mostly accountable for concealing weapons and driving away a car without the owner's permission. Yet nearly equal proportions of boys and girls committed other offenses: striking a parent, running away from home. Even so, these two offenses, when combined with fornication, account for only 11 percent of girls' delinquency. This demonstrates that the assumption that running away, incorrigibility and fornication are typical of "female-style" delinquency is wrong. Boys do their share of these offenses, and girls do their share of stealing, truancy, and other delinquencies.

The question of the honesty of the respondents is critical if we are to argue the merits of self-reports over official records. Some adolescents may exaggerate wildly to impress interviewers with their exploits; others may conceal offenses about which they are embarrassed or apprehensive. To counter this problem, we did a special validation study.

We obtained information on the delinquent behavior of 125 teen-agers who were unaware that we already knew what they had done. We chose these 125 on the basis only of first-hand testimony from peers who had actually witnessed their delinquent acts, or who had been told of them by the offenders themselves. The interviewers did not know whether their respondents were in this validation sample, which corresponded to the larger sample in social status, race, sex, and so on.

Majority of Truth-Tellers

We compared what the 125 validating respondents told us with what we knew about them from our informants. Overall, we classified 72 percent as "truth-tellers"; that is, they confessed to everything the informants had reported or to more recent or more serious offenses. About 17 percent were outright liars and the remaining 11 percent gave questionable information. (Even with this validation, we still had no idea of the extent to which loners are truth-tellers or concealers. A person who commits his delinquent acts alone and tells no one else could not have fallen into this validation sample.)

Another validation check confirmed our belief that self-reports provide fairly accurate information. In a recent set of confidential interviews, 17 teen-agers on probation were asked whether they had committed a delinquent act since being on probation. They were obviously aware that if the authorities found out, they could be sent to a state reformatory. Even so, 15 of the 17 confessed to at least one serious delinquent act.

Convinced of the study's reliability, we constructed two measures of delinquent behavior:

1. An index of *frequency,* or the number of illegal offenses a respondent admitted.
2. An index of *seriousness,* devised by Thorsten Sellin and Marvin Wolfgang of the University of Pennsylvania, which rates each delinquent act according to its severity. For example, authorities may react to one offense with a scolding, and treat another with immediate arrest and full engagement of legal machinery.

Both indexes mark *degrees* of delinquent behavior. The indexes make no arbitrary distinction, as official records do, between "delinquents" and "nondelinquents." We viewed the respondents as more or less delinquent, from those 20 percent who committed no illegal acts to those who committed serious crimes often. This approach permits a more realistic assessment of the role that delinquency plays for adolescents.

Most teen-agers, and adults, do not realize how rarely someone is caught for a delinquent act. In the Flint study, 433 of the 522 respondents admitted to 2,490 delinquent acts, yet

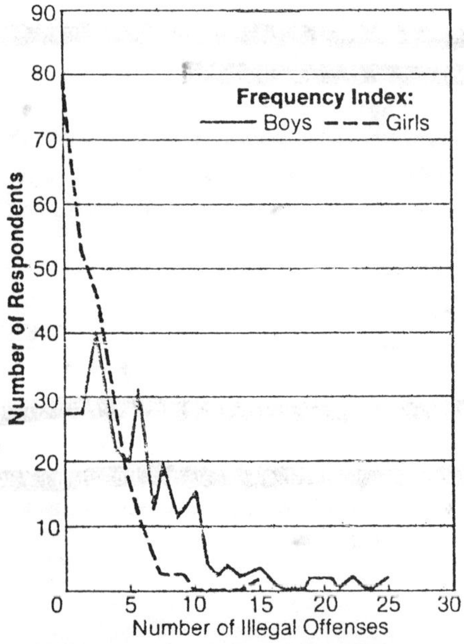

Delinquency Is a Matter of Degree, and Most Teen-agers Are Not Very Delinquent.

only 47 adolescents and their 80 offenses made it into police records. That is, only three percent of the delinquencies committed were detected. But 65 percent of the respondents set the odds of getting caught at an illegal act at seven to three; more than 80 percent placed the odds at better than 50-50. Such data suggest that adolescents exaggerate the risks of delinquency, and also that fear of apprehension is not nearly so effective in restraining delinquent behavior as supposed. Teen-agers who accurately projected little risk were among the least delinquent.

Another common belief is that delinquents are caught because they want to be caught, that this is indeed the reason they behave delinquently to begin with. We found that the common reaction to getting caught was not satisfaction but rather resentment and surprise. Fully 95 percent of the discovered offenses occurred because the police or a passerby chanced to happen along. Naturally, frequent offenders are most likely to be caught; but since the overall chances of apprehension are small, frequency of offense is only slightly related to having an official record. Once frequency is taken into account, the seriousness of a youth's behavior adds little or nothing to his chances of acquiring a police record.

Boy in Trouble:

Milestones in a Labyrinth

On the golf course next to the reform school a man wedges his ball out of a sand trap. The cafeteria empties out and the kids amble back across campus to class. In their long hair and jeans and tie-dye shirts they are a motley, but altogether familiar-looking crew. They monkey around. There's no rush to get back to work. They look like any other adolescents. What sets them apart from their peers is mysterious. They have records, but that only means they got caught.

"I lie in bed at night and I just can't picture myself doing all that stuff," Mike Richards says. "Mike Richards" is a pseudonym; the boy is very real. In 1969 he and a friend ran away. They hung out not far from their parents' homes in Escondido in Southern California, stealing food and clothes until the police picked them up for petty larceny, burglary, and possession of stolen property. Ten months later Mike got caught stealing mail out of mailboxes. Seven months after that he got caught again, stealing a bottle of Gallo wine from a grocery store. A month later he was arrested again, for burglary and malicious mischief. Three weeks later he broke into a trailer, then bashed in the speedometers on two tractors. In the next year Mike was picked up three more times, culminating in his arrest for shoplifting and assaulting the department-store guard who tried to stop him. Now at the ripe old age of 15, he is a popular boy at the reform school that the juvenile court committed him to, known by the Homburg hat he wears everywhere.

He also wears low-slung jeans and a coil of chain on his left wrist. He is big for his age, a likable kid with a crooked nose. He has a slow, pleasant grin, but something deters the stranger from looking too close. Mike radiates trouble, horrible trouble. The instinctive reaction is to shun real contact with the boy.

Mike's file in the reform-school office further documents his disastrous educational experience, his confinements in Juvenile Hall awaiting disposition after each arrest, his sorry conversations with social workers, psychologists, probation officers trying to help him. Mike's version of his story gibes with the record, except that in his version the arrests are milestones in a labyrinth.

He's been on the run from home a lot, he says. "I stay with friends. I sleep in their closets. For a while I stayed with a friend whose parents are rich and have a ranch. They didn't ask any questions." He ran away from school, the vocational school he tried after he was expelled from regular school. "It was a pretty good school, but we took advantage of it. We were stoned all the time. We used to climb a hill in back of the school and throw rocks at it." While awaiting trial, he ran away. "I heard a friend of mine had died. I wanted to make his funeral. I got out, but I was too late. That night I slept by his grave."

To the citizen who sees himself as an outlaw when he runs a red light, Mike's stories are fairy tales. He had a girl friend at the reform school until she was taken away to a mental hospital. "She slashed her wrists. She had a horse that she loved. But her parents figured she was here, so they sold it. It broke her heart. . . . I got a letter from her, though, and she says she's doing better."

Mike volunteers no information about his parents. None. They celebrate their silver wedding anniversary this year. Mr. Richards is an electrical engineer. Mrs. Richards, with little formal education, is a voracious reader. They have seven children. They have lived in Escondido for years.

Mike talks willingly only about one person, his brother Ron, 21. Ron has gotten in scrapes with the law, but nothing serious. "He's stopped getting in trouble. One time after he got in trouble, my Mom started crying and he couldn't face it."

Mike originally planned to hitchhike to San Francisco after reform school. But that was impractical, he realizes, and now he plans to live with Ron in Escondido, get a job, and buy a motorcycle. His other friends are scattered.

Mike as no real explanation for his behavior. "My brother and I did the same things. I just started younger," he says. Pressed for an explanation, he switches off. He gets lost. He cocks his head peculiarly. When he recovers, he describes plans to build a parakeet cage. His file says he is good with his hands. He himself tells of his interest in birds and varmints. Pressed again for an explanation, Mike takes the first opportunity to flee. Mr. and Mrs. Richards have no real explanation for their son's behavior either. He has always been hard to control, they say.

The authorities have several explanations for Mike's behavior. They have diagnosed a looping problem characteristic of dyslexia, a hyperkinetic problem, perceptual problems and impaired hearing. Also, they suggest he has a rather schizoid personality and a tendency to act out. In short, they say, he is neurologically handicapped and emotionally disturbed. Labels, like the general label juvenile delinquent, beat back the terror of Mike's life for us, but don't help Mike much.

—Peter Koenig

Counterproductive Justice

The consequences of getting caught are contrary to societal interests. Gold and Williams compared a group of apprehended offenders with a carefully matched group of unapprehended offenders. They matched 35 pairs on sex, race, age, and number and kind of offenses. The findings completely contradict the aims of our reform machinery. In 20 of the 35 pairs, the apprehended member subsequently committed *more* offenses than did his unapprehended match. Five pairs later committed an equal number of delinquent acts. In only 10 of the 35 pairs did the unapprehended control commit more offenses. Whatever it is that the authorities do once they have caught a youth, it seems to be worse than doing nothing at all, worse even than never apprehending the offender. Getting caught encourages rather than deters further delinquency.

We have searched for a typology of offenses. Is an adolescent who commits one kind of offense, such as theft, more likely to commit other thefts rather than assault? Do various delinquent acts tend to cluster? The answer is no. Teen-agers simply do not specialize. This was true among those who had committed at least two offenses and among the most delinquent half of both the Flint and national samples. We couldn't type them. Among the 100 most delinquent, the *fewest* different offenses was four. These offenses ranged from assault to theft in one case, from running away to calculated fraud in another case.

One of our most striking findings contradicted the commonly held belief, which official data indicate, that delinquent behavior is predominantly a lower-class, particularly "slum," problem. We measured social status by the father's occupation, or, in the absence of a father, by the mother's occupation. (We designate status as "higher" or "lower" in accordance with Otis Dudley Duncan's scale of prestige of occupations in the United States.) We found no strong relationship between social status and delinquent behavior. The only statistically reliable relationship in the national sample was that between the social status of *white boys* and the seriousness of their delinquent behavior. That is, higher status white boys reported somewhat more serious delinquent behavior than did their lower status peers. The former committed more thefts, stole more cars, and assaulted more people. Social status seemed to exert no effect whatsoever on the delinquent behavior of girls.

The two popular images of the delinquent are the gang member and the troubled loner. The sociological view is that a boy in a gang asserts the values of his subculture through frequent and serious delinquent behavior, which integrates his personal needs with his social environment. By contrast, the psychiatric view sees a boy alone, troubled and disorganized, committing symbolic acts of aggression. Some of our respondents fit one view or the other; most fit neither.

Four-hundred and thirty-three Flint teen-agers committed 2,490 delinquent acts; a substantial majority of these acts occurred in the company of others. Indeed, offenders committed only 25 percent of the acts alone, and one fourth of these loners soon told someone else what they had done. The lone offenses tend to be impulsive ones, such as striking a parent, running away from home, and threatening assault.

Thus we considered a true lone delinquent to be one who committed delinquent acts relatively frequently—in about the highest fourth of the sample—and who committed at least half of his offenses by himself. In the Flint sample, this criterion would mean that a loner would have admitted to five or more offenses during the past three years, and committed at least three of them alone. Out of 522 teen-agers, we found only 11 who fit that description, nine boys and two girls.

Companions in Crime

Usually, then, delinquent acts are shared experiences, but not gang experiences. Of offenses committed by young people in the Flint sample, 41 percent were with one other person, 23 percent with two others, 15 percent with three others, nine percent with four others, and only 12 percent with five or more others. Offender and companions were of the same sex 78 percent of the time. The only delinquent acts to break the unisexual pattern were drinking, presenting false identification, and, obviously, fornication, all of which usually occur in connection with dating or parties.

We defined a gang delinquent as a frequent offender who had committed more than half of his or her offenses with a *most frequent companion.* Again, only 11 Flint teen-agers met this criterion. Of these, seven were boys, four were girls, and collectively they confessed to 134 offenses, some 54 more than the 11 loners admitted.

This small number of gang members casts doubt on the importance of the stable delinquent gang in understanding delinquency. In fact, we find it most significant that neither loner nor gang member is a type that includes many young people. By far the most common pattern was for delinquent behavior to occur as a "pickup" game in the company of shifting numbers of friends.

We wondered next what characteristics were related to a teen-ager's disposition to companionate delinquency. We found three, all opposite to expectation and stereotype about gangs:

—The *least* delinquent adolescents committed a *larger* proportion of their acts with their most frequent companions.

—Children of *white-collar* workers more often engaged in delinquent behavior with the same friends than did children of blue-collar workers.

—*Girls* were more likely to have a constant companion in delinquency than were boys.

We found no evidence in the Flint study that academic performance has any effect at all on delinquency among girls. A stronger factor in predicting a girl's delinquency was her perception of her friends' delinquency. When a girl saw her friends as highly delinquent, she was herself more than twice as delinquent as girls who did not so describe their friends.

The reverse was true for Flint boys. Whether or not boys believed their friends to be delinquent, they were delinquent more seriously and more frequently if their grades were poor. There is undoubtedly a strong interplay at work among academic performance, choice of friends, and other factors; we cannot say which are causes and which are results. We can speculate that poor grades foster delinquent behavior in boys because, in this society, the consequences of poor grades are more serious for boys than for girls.

School work and delinquent behavior are both "performances," and if a boy does poorly at school he may turn for self-affirmation to delinquent friends and delinquent pursuits.

The Father Factor

Delinquent behavior may also be an assertion of independence from parents and teachers, as well as a means of earning applause and acceptance from peers.

The relationship that adolescents have with their fathers is an important correlate of delinquent behavior, but it is not true, as many courts believe, that a stepfather is better than no father at all. On the contrary, both for boys and for girls, being raised by a stepfather as well as the natural mother was conducive to more frequent and more serious delinquent behavior. A plausible but unproved theory is that the stepfather introduces new sources of rivalry and hostility, which outweigh his ability to control the adolescent.

But single-parent (broken) homes did not always produce more delinquent youngsters than intact homes. Boys being raised only by their mothers were among the least delinquent in the Flint and national samples. On the other hand, boys with delinquent friends and poor grades were usually highly delinquent, whether their homes were broken or intact. Similarly for girls, having delinquent friends was more important than intactness of the home in predicting their delinquency. Girls who had highly delinquent friends were likely to be more delinquent, and they came equally from intact and broken homes. The only difference occurred among girls, those with less-delinquent friends. In this group, twice as many came from broken as from intact homes.

Parents knew far more about the delinquent behavior of their children than did the police; they learned of about one quarter of their children's offenses, compared with the three percent that became known to the authorities. Respondents voluntarily confessed 11 percent of their offenses to their parents, girls confiding more often than boys and the less delinquent being more likely to volunteer a confession. Parents discovered some offenses more or less accidentally and authorities told them about a few.

But few parents who were informed did much to help their children. In 40 percent of the instances in which they had an opportunity to react, their children said that absolutely nothing was done. Typically, they got the impression that their parents did not care. But in an equal number of instances the parent's response was to scold or to punish. Only five percent of the time, the teen-agers said, did their parents discuss the matter calmly with them. The other 15 percent responded with behavior we could not easily classify.

Older boys and girls commit more delinquencies. Girls showed a steady increase in frequency with age, and older teen-age girls were slightly more inclined to commit more serious acts than younger girls. There was a sharp increase in frequency of delinquency in boys from 13 to 14 and then a more gradual increase. Fourteen- and 15-year-old boys committed more serious acts than either 13- or 16-year olds did. As might be expected, the kinds of offenses that teen-agers commit change significantly with age. For example, the most frequent offenses of the 16-year-old boys in the Flint and national samples were truancy and drinking, offenses which were not in the top rank among 13- to 15-year olds.

Someone Else

Even the most delinquent teen-agers characterized their own friends as being *less* delinquent than *teen-agers* in *general.* No matter how frequent or serious their offenses, they did not see themselves and their friends as the town's toughest, meanest, and most rebellious teen-agers. This finding challenges the "delinquency subculture" theory. The classic "hood" is always somebody else, not them, not known to them. The stereotype of teen-ager as hoodlum has become so widely accepted in American society that nearly all young people from ages 13 to 16 subscribe to it as unquestioningly as do a high percentage of adults.

The Slum Myth

In 1967, the Presidential Commission on Law Enforcement and Administration of Justice endorsed one of the most common features of the delinquent stereotype—that delinquent behavior is predominantly a lower-class phenomenon. "There is still no . . . reason to doubt that delinquency, and especially the most serious delinquency, is committed disproportionately by slum and lower-class youth." Our research finds this statement completely wrong.

The consequences of our continuing to believe such falsehoods are dangerous to individual adolescents and to society. Such an erroneous perception makes it more difficult for even the most well-meaning white officials to ensure that nonwhites receive equal treatment. White authorities now tend to be lenient with a white boy, interpreting his behavior as a tolerable, sowing-his-wild-oats brand of delinquency. But they become fearful and hard-nosed with a black adolescent who coincides with their image of The Delinquent.

Misdirected Programs

The mythical American Delinquent casts a shadow over what might loosely be termed the delinquency-prevention industry. He dominates the juvenile courts and obscures the reality important to researchers, law-enforcement officials, social workers, the courts, the media, and the public. As a result, current treatment and prevention programs are, in a word, misdirected. Starting with false assumptions about who commits delinquent acts, they aim the wrong programs at the wrong groups. Expensive programs grind away without making progress, operating too far from reality to touch the right lives in the right ways. A first step toward improving a system that, despite good intentions and dedication, serves so inadequately, is to put myths to rest. Somewhere beyond The Delinquent is a person with a real problem that is both his and ours.

The Saints and the Roughnecks

William J. Chambliss

Eight promising young men—children of good, stable, white upper-middle-class families, active in school affairs, good pre-college students—were some of the most delinquent boys at Hanibal High School. While community residents and parents knew that these boys occasionally sowed a few wild oats, they were totally unaware that sowing wild oats completely occupied the daily routine of these young men. The Saints were constantly occupied with truancy, drinking, wild driving, petty theft and vandalism. Yet not one was officially arrested for any misdeed during the two years I observed them.

This record was particularly surprising in light of my observations during the same two years of another gang of Hanibal High School students, six lower-class white boys known as the Roughnecks. The Roughnecks were constantly in trouble with police and community even though their rate of delinquency was about equal with that of the Saints. What was the cause of this disparity? the result? The following consideration of the activities, social class and community perceptions of both gangs may provide some answers.

THE SAINTS FROM MONDAY TO FRIDAY

The Saints' principal daily concern was with getting out of school as early as possible. The boys managed to get out of school with minimum danger that they would be accused of playing hookey through an elaborate procedure for obtaining "legitimate" release from class. The most common procedure was for one boy to obtain the release of another by fabricating a meeting of some committee, program or recognized club. Charles might raise his hand in his 9:00 chemistry class and asked to be excused—a euphemism for going to the bathroom. Charles would go to Ed's math class and inform the teacher that Ed was needed for a 9:30 rehearsal of the drama club play. The math teacher would recognize Ed and Charles as "good students" involved in numerous school activities and would permit Ed to leave at 9:30. Charles would return to his class, and Ed would go to Tom's English class to obtain his release. Tom would engineer Charles' escape. The strategy would continue until as many of the Saints as possible were freed. After a stealthy trip to the car (which had been parked in a strategic spot), the boys were off for a day of fun.

Over the two years I observed the Saints, this pattern was repeated nearly every day. There were variations on the theme, but in one form or another, the boys used this procedure for getting out of class and then off the school grounds. Rarely did all eight of the Saints manage to leave school at the same time. The average number avoiding school on the days I observed them was five.

Having escaped from the concrete corridors the boys usually went either to a pool hall on the other (lower-class) side of town or to a cafe in the suburbs. Both places were out of the way of people the boys were likely to know (family or school officials), and both provided a source of entertainment. The pool hall entertainment was the generally rough atmosphere, the occasional hustler, the sometimes drunk proprietor and, of course, the game of pool. The cafe's entertainment was provided by the owner. The boys would "accidentally" knock a glass on the floor or spill cola on the counter—not all the time, but enough to be sporting. They would also bend spoons, put salt in sugar bowls and generally tease whoever was working in the cafe. The owner had opened the cafe recently and was dependent on the boys' business which was, in fact, substantial since between the horsing around and the teasing they bought food and drinks.

THE SAINTS ON WEEKENDS

On weekends the automobile was even more critical than during the week, for on weekends the Saints went to Big Town—a large city with a population of over a million 25 miles from Hanibal. Every Friday and Saturday night most of the Saints would meet between 8:00 and 8:30 and would go into Big Town. Big Town activities included drinking heavily in taverns or nightclubs, driving drunkenly through the streets, and committing acts of vandalism and playing pranks.

By midnight on Fridays and Saturdays the Saints were usually thoroughly high, and one or two of them were often so drunk they had to be carried to the cars. Then the boys drove around town, calling obscenities to women and girls; occasionally trying (unsuccessfully so far as I could tell) to pick girls up; and driving recklessly through red lights and at high speeds with their lights out. Occasionally they played "chicken." One boy would climb out the back window of the car and across the roof to the driver's side of the car while the car was moving at high speed (between 40 and 50 miles an hour); then the driver would move over and the boy who had just crawled across the car roof would take the driver's seat.

Searching for "fair game" for a prank was the boys' principal activity after they left the tavern. The boys would drive alongside a foot patrolman and ask directions to some street. If the policeman leaned on the car in the course of answering the question, the driver would speed away, causing him to lose his balance. The Saints were careful to play this prank only in an area where they were not going to spend much time and where they could quickly disappear around a corner to avoid having their license plate number taken.

Construction sites and road repair areas were the special province of the Saints' mischief. A soon-to-be-repaired hole in the road

From *Society*, Vol. 11, No. 1 (November/December 1973), pp. 341–355. Published by permission of Transaction, Inc., from *Society*, Vol. 11, No. 1.

inevitably invited the Saints to remove lanterns and wooden barricades and put them in the car, leaving the hole unprotected. The boys would find a safe vantage point and wait for an unsuspecting motorist to drive into the hole. Often, though not always, the boys would go up to the motorist and commiserate with him about the dreadful way the city protected its citizenry.

Leaving the scene of the open hole and the motorist, the boys would then go searching for an appropriate place to erect the stolen barricade. An "appropriate place" was often a spot on a highway near a curve in the road where the barricade would not be seen by an oncoming motorist. The boys would wait to watch an unsuspecting motorist attempt to stop and (usually) crash into the wooden barricade. With saintly bearing the boys might offer help and understanding.

A stolen lantern might well find its way onto the back of a police car or hang from a street lamp. Once a lantern served as a prop for a reenactment of the "midnight ride of Paul Revere" until the "play," which was taking place at 2:00 AM in the center of a main street of Big Town, was interrupted by a police car several blocks away. The boys ran, leaving the lanterns on the street, and managed to avoid being apprehended.

Abandoned houses, especially if they were located in out-of-the-way places, were fair game for destruction and spontaneous vandalism. The boys would break windows, remove furniture to the yard and tear it apart, urinate on the walls and scrawl obscenities inside.

Through all the pranks, drinking and reckless driving the boys managed miraculously to avoid being stopped by police. Only twice in two years was I aware that they had been stopped by a Big City policeman. Once was for speeding (which they did every time they drove whether they were drunk or sober), and the driver managed to convince the policeman that it was simply an error. The second time they were stopped they had just left a nightclub and were walking through an alley. Aaron stopped to urinate and the boys began making obscene remarks. A foot patrolman came into the alley, lectured the boys and sent them home. Before the boys got to the car one began talking in a loud voice again. The policeman, who had followed them down the alley, arrested this boy for disturbing the peace and took him to the police station where the other Saints gathered. After paying a $5.00 fine, and with the assurance that there would be no permanent record of the arrest, the boy was released.

The boys had a spirit of frivolity and fun about their escapades. They did not view what they were engaged in as "delinquency," though it surely was by any reasonable definition of that word. They simply viewed themselves as having a little fun and who, they would ask, was really hurt by it? The answer had to be no one, although this fact remains one of the most difficult things to explain about the gang's behavior. Unlikely though it seems, in two years of drinking, driving, carousing and vandalism no one was seriously injured as a result of the Saints' activities.

THE SAINTS IN SCHOOL

The Saints were highly successful in school. The average grade for the group was "B," with two of the boys having close to a straight "A" average. Almost all of the boys were popular and many of them held offices in the school. One of the boys was vice-president of the student body one year. Six of the boys played on athletic teams.

At the end of their senior year, the student body selected ten seniors for special recognition as the "school wheels"; four of the ten were Saints. Teachers and school officials saw no problem with any of these boys and anticipated that they would all "make something of themselves."

How the boys managed to maintain this impression is surprising in view of their actual behavior while in school. Their technique for covering truancy was so successful that teachers did not even realize that the boys were absent from school much of the time. Occasionally, of course, the system would backfire and then the boy was on his own. A boy who was caught would be most contrite, would plead guilty and ask for mercy. He inevitably got the mercy he sought.

Cheating on examinations was rampant, even to the point of orally communicating answers to exams as well as looking at one another's papers. Since none of the group studied, and since they were primarily dependent on one another for help, it is surprising that grades were so high. Teachers contributed to the deception in their admitted inclination to give these boys (and presumably others like them) the benefit of the doubt. When asked how the boys did in school, and when pressed on specific examinations, teachers might admit that they were disappointed in John's performance, but would quickly add that they "knew that he was capable of doing better," so John was given a higher grade than he had actually earned. How often this happened is impossible to know. During the time that I observed the group, I never saw any of the boys take homework home. Teachers may have been "understanding" very regularly.

One exception to the gang's generally good performance was Jerry, who had a "C" average in his junior year, experienced disaster the next year and failed to graduate. Jerry had always been a little more nonchalant than the others about the liberties he took in school. Rather than wait for someone to come get him from class, he would offer his own excuse and leave. Although he probably did not miss any more classes than most of the others in the group, he did not take the requisite pains to cover his absences. Jerry was the only Saint whom I ever heard talk back to a teacher. Although teachers often called him a "cut up" or a "smart kid," they never referred to him as a troublemaker or as a kid headed for trouble. It seems likely, then, that Jerry's failure his senior year and his mediocre performance his junior year were consequences of his not playing the game the proper way (possibly because he was disturbed by his parents' divorce). His teachers regarded him as "immature" and not quite ready to get out of high school.

THE POLICE AND THE SAINTS

The local police saw the Saints as good boys who were among the leaders of the youth in the community. Rarely, the boys might be stopped in town for speeding or for running a stop sign. When this happened the boys were always polite, contrite and pled for mercy. As in school, they received the mercy they asked for. None ever received a ticket or was taken into the precinct by the local police.

The situation in Big City, where the boys engaged in most of their delinquency, was only slightly different. The police there did not know the boys at all, although occasionally the boys were stopped by a patrolman. Once they were caught taking a lantern from a construction site. Another time they were stopped for running a stop sign, and on several occasions they were stopped for speeding. Their behavior was as before: contrite, polite and penitent. The urban police, like the local police, accepted their demeanor as sincere. More important, the urban police were convinced that these were good boys just out for a lark.

THE ROUGHNECKS

Hanibal townspeople never perceived the Saints' high level of delinquency. The Saints were good boys who just went in for an occasional prank. After all, they were well dressed, well mannered and had nice cars. The Roughnecks were a different story. Although the two gangs of boys were the same age, and both groups engaged in an equal amount of wild-oat sowing, everyone agreed that the not-so-well-dressed, not-so-well-mannered, not-so-rich boys were heading for trouble. Townspeople would say, "You can see the gang members at the drugstore, night after night, leaning against the storefront (sometimes drunk) or slouching around inside buying cokes, reading magazines, and probably stealing old Mr. Wall blind. When they are outside and girls walk by, even respectable girls, these boys make suggestive remarks. Sometimes their remarks are downright lewd."

From the community's viewpoint, the real indication that these kids were in for trouble was that they were constantly involved with the police. Some of them had been picked up for stealing, mostly small stuff, of course, "but still it's stealing small stuff that leads to big time crimes." "Too bad," people said. "Too bad that these boys couldn't behave like the other kids in town; stay out of trouble, be polite to adults, and look to their future."

The community's impression of the degree to which this group of six boys (ranging in age from 16 to 19) engaged in delinquency was somewhat distorted. In some ways the gang was more delinquent than the community thought; in other ways they were less.

The fighting activities of the group were fairly readily and accurately perceived by almost everyone. At least once a month, the boys would get into some sort of fight, although most fights were scraps between members of the group or involved only one member of the group and some peripheral hanger-on. Only three times in the period of observation did the group fight together: once against a gang from across town, once against two blacks and once against a group of boys from another school. For the first two fights the group went out "looking for trouble"—and they found it both times. The third fight followed a football game and began spontaneously with an argument on the football field between one of the Roughnecks and a member of the opposition's football team.

Jack had a particular propensity for fighting and was involved in most of the brawls. He was a prime mover of the escalation of arguments into fights.

More serious than fighting, had the community been aware of it, was theft. Although almost everyone was aware that the boys occasionally stole things, they did not realize the extent of the activity. Petty stealing was a frequent event for the Roughnecks. Sometimes they stole as a group and coordinated their efforts; other times they stole in pairs. Rarely did they steal alone.

The thefts ranged from very small things like paperback books, comics and ballpoint pens to expensive items like watches. The nature of the thefts varied from time to time. The gang would go through a period of systematically shoplifting items from automobiles or school lockers. Types of thievery varied with the whim of the gang. Some forms of thievery were more profitable than others, but all thefts were for profit, not just thrills.

Roughnecks siphoned gasoline from cars as often as they had access to an automobile, which was not very often. Unlike the Saints, who owned their own cars, the Roughnecks would have to borrow their parents' cars, an event which occurred only eight or nine times a year. The boys claimed to have stolen cars for joy rides from time to time.

Ron committed the most serious of the group's offenses. With an unidentified associate the boy attempted to burglarize a gasoline station. Although this station had been robbed twice previously in the same month, Ron denied any involvement in either of the other thefts. When Ron and his accomplice approached the station, the owner was hiding in the bushes beside the station. He fired both barrels of a double-barreled shotgun at the boys. Ron was severely injured; the other boy ran away and was never caught. Though he remained in critical condition for several months, Ron finally recovered and served six months of the following year in reform school. Upon release from reform school, Ron was put back a grade in school, and began running around with a different gang of boys. The Roughnecks considered the new gang less delinquent than themselves, and during the following year Ron had no more trouble with the police.

The Roughnecks, then, engaged mainly in three types of delinquency: theft, drinking and fighting. Although community members perceived that this gang of kids was delinquent, they mistakenly believed that their illegal activities were primarily drinking, fighting and being a nuisance to passersby. Drinking was limited among the gang members, although it did occur, and theft was much more prevalent than anyone realized.

Drinking would doubtless have been more prevalent had the boys had ready access to liquor. Since they rarely had automobiles at their disposal, they could not travel very far, and the bars in town would not serve them. Most of the boys had little money, and this, too, inhibited their purchase of alcohol. Their major source of liquor was a local drunk who would buy them a fifth if they would give him enough extra to buy himself a pint of whiskey or a bottle of wine.

The community's perception of drinking as prevalent stemmed from the fact that it was the most obvious delinquency the boys engaged in. When one of the boys had been drinking, even a casual observer seeing him on the corner would suspect that he was high.

There was a high level of mutual distrust and dislike between the Roughnecks and the police. The boys felt very strongly that the police were unfair and corrupt. Some evidence existed that the boys were correct in their perception.

The main source of the boys' dislike for the police undoubtedly stemmed from the fact that the police would sporadically harass the group. From the standpoint of the boys, these acts of occasional enforcement of the law were whimsical and uncalled for. It made no sense to them, for example, that the police would come to the corner occasionally and threaten them with arrest for loitering when the night before the boys had been out siphoning gasoline from cars and the police had been nowhere in sight. To the boys, the police were stupid on the one hand, for not being where they should have been and catching the boys in a serious offense, and unfair on the other hand, for trumping up "loitering" charges against them.

From the viewpoint of the police, the situation was quite different. They knew, with all the confidence necessary to be a policeman, that these boys were engaged in criminal activities. They knew this partly from occasionally catching them, mostly from circumstantial evidence ("the boys were around when those tires were slashed"), and partly because the police shared the view of the community in general that this was a bad bunch of boys. The best the police could hope to do was to be sensitive to the fact that these boys were engaged in illegal acts and arrest them whenever there was some evidence that they had been involved. Whether or not the boys had in fact committed a particular act in a particular way was not especially important. The police had a broader view: their job was to stamp out these kids' crimes; the tactics were not as important as the end result.

Over the period that the group was under observation, each member was arrested at least once. Several of the boys were arrested a number of times and spent at least one night in jail. While most were never taken to court, two of the boys were sentenced to six months' incarceration in boys' schools.

THE ROUGHNECKS IN SCHOOL

The Roughnecks' behavior in school was not particularly disruptive. During school hours they did not all hang around together, but tended instead to spend most of their time with one or two other members of the gang who were their special buddies. Although every member of the gang attempted to avoid school as much as possible, they were not particularly successful and most of them attended school with surprising regularity. They considered school a burden—something to be gotten through with a minimum of conflict. If they were "bugged" by a particular teacher, it could lead to trouble. One of the boys, Al, once threatened to beat up a teacher and, according to the other boys, the teacher hid under a desk to escape him.

Teachers saw the boys the way the general community did, as heading for trouble, as being uninterested in making something of themselves. Some were also seen as being incapable of meeting the academic standards of the school. Most of the teachers expressed concern for this group of boys and were willing to pass them despite poor performance, in the belief that failing them would only aggravate the problem.

The group of boys had a grade point average just slightly above "C." No one in the group failed either grade, and no one had better than a "C" average. They were very consistent in their achievement or, at least, the teachers were consistent in their perception of the boys' achievement.

Two of the boys were good football players. Herb was acknowledged to be the best player in the school and Jack was almost as good. Both boys were criticized for their failure to abide by training rules, for refusing to come to practice as often as they should, and for not playing their best during practice. What they lacked in sportsmanship they made up for in skill, apparently, and played every game no matter how poorly they had performed in practice or how many practice sessions they had missed.

TWO QUESTIONS

Why did the community, the school and the police react to the Saints as though they were good, upstanding, nondelinquent youths with bright futures but to the Roughnecks as though they were tough, young criminals who were headed for trouble? Why did the Roughnecks and the Saints in fact have quite different careers after high school—careers which, by and large, lived up to the expectations of the community?

The most obvious explanation for the differences in the community's and law enforcement agencies' reactions to the two gangs is that one group of boys was "more delinquent" than the other. Which group *was* more delinquent? The answer to this question will determine in part how we explain the differential responses to these groups by the members of the community and, particularly, by law enforcement and school officials.

In sheer number of illegal acts, the Saints were the more delinquent. They were truant from school for at least part of the day almost every day of the week. In addition, their drinking and vandalism occurred with surprising regularity. The Roughnecks, in contrast, engaged sporadically in delinquent episodes. While these episodes were frequent, they certainly did not occur on a daily or even a weekly basis.

The difference in frequency of offenses was probably caused by the Roughnecks' inability to obtain liquor and to manipulate legitimate excuses from school. Since the Roughnecks had less money than the Saints, and teachers carefully supervised their school activities, the Roughnecks' hearts may have been as black as the Saints', but their misdeeds were not nearly as frequent.

There are really no clear-cut criteria by which to measure qualitative differences in antisocial behavior. The most important dimension of the difference is generally referred to as the "seriousness" of the offenses.

If seriousness encompasses the relative economic costs of delinquent acts, then some assessment can be made. The Roughnecks probably stole an average of about $5.00 worth of goods a week. Some weeks the figure was considerably higher, but these times must be balanced against long periods when almost nothing was stolen.

The Saints were more continuously engaged in delinquency but their acts were not for the most part costly to property. Only their vandalism and occasional theft of gasoline would so qualify. Perhaps once or twice a month they would siphon a tankful of gas. The other costly items were street signs, construction lanterns and the like. All of these acts combined probably did not quite average $5.00 a week, partly because much of the stolen equipment was abandoned and presumably could be recovered. The difference in cost of stolen property between the two groups was trivial, but the Roughnecks probably had a slightly more expensive set of activities than did the Saints.

Another meaning of seriousness is the potential threat of physical harm to members of the community and to the boys themselves. The Roughnecks were more prone to physical violence; they not only welcomed an opportunity to fight; they went seeking it. In addition, they fought among themselves frequently. Although the fighting never included deadly weapons, it was still a menace, however minor, to the physical safety of those involved.

The Saints never fought. They avoided physical conflict both inside and outside the group. At the same time, though, the Saints frequently endangered their own and other people's lives. They did so almost every time they drove a car, especially if they had been drinking. Sober, their driving was risky; under the influence of alcohol it was horrendous. In addition, the Saints endangered the lives of others with their pranks. Street excavations left unmarked were a very serious hazard.

Evaluating the relative seriousness of the two gangs' activities is difficult. The community reacted as though the behavior of the Roughnecks was a problem, and they reacted as though the behavior of the Saints was not. But the members of the community were ignorant of the array of delinquent acts that characterized the Saints' behavior. Although concerned citizens were unaware of much of the Roughnecks' behavior as well, they were much better informed about the Roughnecks' involvement in delinquency than they were about the Saints'.

VISIBILITY

Differential treatment of the two gangs resulted in part because one gang was infinitely more visible than the other. This differential visibility was a direct function of the economic standing of the families. The Saints had access to automobiles and were able to remove themselves from the sight of the community. In as routine a decision as to where to go to have a milkshake after school, the Saints stayed away from the mainstream of community life. Lacking transportation, the Roughnecks could not make it to the edge of town. The center of town was the only practical place for them to meet since their homes were scattered throughout the town and any noncentral meeting place put an undue hardship on some members. Through necessity the Roughnecks congregated in a crowded area where everyone in the community passed frequently, including teachers and law enforcement officers. They could easily see the Roughnecks hanging around the drugstore.

The Roughnecks, of course, made themselves even more visible by making remarks to passersby and by occasionally getting into fights on the corner. Meanwhile, just as regularly, the Saints were either at the cafe on one edge of town or in the pool hall at the other edge of town. Without any particular realization that they were making themselves inconspicuous, the Saints were able to hide their time-wasting. Not only were they removed from the mainstream of traffic, but they were almost always inside a building.

On their escapades the Saints were also relatively invisible, since they left Hanibal and travelled to Big City. Here, too, they were mobile, roaming the city, rarely going to the same area twice.

DEMEANOR

To the notion of visibility must be added the difference in the responses of group members to outside intervention with their activities. If one of the Saints was confronted with an accusing policeman, even if he felt he was truly innocent of a wrongdoing, his demeanor was apologetic and penitent. A Roughneck's attitude was almost the polar opposite. When confronted with a threatening adult authority, even one who tried to be pleasant, the Roughneck's hostility and disdain were clearly observable. Sometimes he might attempt to put up a veneer of respect, but it was thin and was not accepted as sincere by the authority.

School was no different from the community at large. The Saints could manipulate the system by feigning compliance with the school norms. The availability of cars at school meant that once free from the immediate sight of the teacher, the boys could disappear rapidly. And this escape was well enough planned that no administrator or teacher was nearby when the boys left. A Roughneck who wished to escape for a few hours was in a bind. If it were possible to get free from class, downtown was still a mile away, and even if he arrived there, he was still very visible. Truancy for the Roughnecks meant almost certain detection, while the Saints enjoyed almost complete immunity from sanctions.

BIAS

Community members were not aware of the transgressions of the Saints. Even if the Saints had been less discreet, their favorite delinquencies would have been perceived as less serious than those of the Roughnecks.

In the eyes of the police and school officials, a boy who drinks in an alley and stands intoxicated on the street corner is committing a more serious offense than is a boy who drinks to inebriation in a nightclub or a tavern and drives around afterwards in a car. Similarly, a boy who steals a wallet from a store will be viewed as having committed a more serious offense than a boy who steals a lantern from a construction site.

Perceptual bias also operates with respect to the demeanor of the boys in the two groups when they are confronted by adults. It is not simply that adults dislike the posture affected by boys of the Roughneck ilk; more important is the conviction that the posture adopted by the Roughnecks is an indication of their devotion and commitment to deviance as a way of life. The posture becomes a cue, just as the type of the offense is a cue, to the degree to which the known transgressions are indicators of the youths' potential for other problems.

Visibility, demeanor and bias are surface variables which explain the day-to-day operations of the police. Why do these surface variables operate as they do? Why did the police choose to disregard the Saints' delinquencies while breathing down the backs of the Roughnecks?

The answer lies in the class structure of American society and the control of legal institutions by those at the top of the class structure. Obviously, no representative of the upper class drew up the operational chart for the police which led them to look in the ghettoes and on streetcorners—which led them to see the demeanor of lower-class youth as troublesome and that of upper-middle-class youth as tolerable. Rather, the procedure simply developed from experience—experience with irate and influential upper-middle-class parents insisting that their son's vandalism was simply a prank and his drunkenness only a momentary "sowing of wild oats"—experience with cooperative or indifferent, powerless, lower-class parents who acquiesced to the laws' definition of their son's behavior.

ADULT CAREERS OF THE SAINTS AND THE ROUGHNECKS

The community's confidence in the potential of the Saints and the Roughnecks apparently was justified. If anything, the community members underestimated the degree to which these youngsters would turn out "good" or "bad."

Seven of the eight members of the Saints went on to college immediately after high school. Five of the boys graduated from college in four years. The sixth one finished college after two years in the army, and the seventh spent four years in the air force before returning to college and receiving a B.A. degree. Of these seven college graduates, three went on for advanced degrees. One finished law school and is now active in state politics, one finished medical school and is practicing near Hanibal, and one boy is now working for a Ph.D. The other four college graduates entered submanagerial, managerial or executive training positions with larger firms.

The only Saint who did not complete college was Jerry. Jerry had failed to graduate from high school with the other Saints. During his second senior year, after the other Saints had gone on to college, Jerry began to hang around with what several teachers described as a "rough crowd"—the gang that was heir apparent to the Roughnecks. At the end of his second senior year, when he did graduate from high school, Jerry took a job as a used-car salesman, got married and quickly had a child. Although he made several abortive attempts to go to college by attending night school, when I last saw him (ten years after high school) Jerry was unemployed and had been living on unemployment for almost a year. His wife worked as a waitress.

Some of the Roughnecks have lived up to community expectations. A number of them were headed for trouble. A few were not.

Jack and Herb were the athletes among the Roughnecks and their athletic prowess paid off handsomely. Both boys received unsolicited athletic scholarships to college. After Herb received his scholarship (near the end of his senior year), he apparently did an about-face. His demeanor became very similar to that of the Saints. Although he remained a member in good standing of the Roughnecks, he stopped participating in most activities and did not hang on the corner as often.

Jack did not change. If anything, he became more prone to fighting. He even made excuses for accepting the scholarship. He told the other gang members that the school had guaranteed him a "C" average if he would come to play football—an idea that seems far-fetched, even in this day of highly competitive recruiting.

During the summer after graduation from high school, Jack attempted suicide by jumping from a tall building. The jump would certainly have killed most people trying it, but Jack survived. He entered college in the fall and played four years of football. He and Herb graduated in four years, and both are teaching and coaching in high schools. They are married and have stable families. If anything, Jack appears to have a more prestigious position in the community than does Herb, though both are well respected and secure in their positions.

Two of the boys never finished high school. Tommy left at the end of his junior year and went to another state. That summer he was arrested and placed on probation on a manslaughter charge. Three years later he was arrested for murder; he pleaded guilty to second degree murder and is serving a 30-year sentence in the state penitentiary.

Al, the other boy who did not finish high school, also left the state in his senior year. He is serving a life sentence in a state penitentiary for first degree murder.

Wes is a small-time gambler. He finished high school and "bummed around." After several years he made contact with a bookmaker who employed him as a runner. Later he acquired his own area and has been working it ever since. His position among the bookmakers is almost identical to the position he had in the gang; he is always around but no one is really aware of him. He makes no trouble and he does not get into any. Steady, reliable, capable of keeping his mouth closed, he plays the game by the rules, even though the game is an illegal one.

That leaves only Ron. Some of his former friends reported that they had heard he was "driving a truck up north," but no one could provide any concrete information.

REINFORCEMENT

The community responded to the Roughnecks as boys in trouble, and the boys agreed with that perception. Their pattern of deviancy was reinforced, and breaking away from it became increasingly unlikely. Once the boys acquired an image of themselves as deviants, they selected new friends who affirmed that self-image. As that self-conception became more firmly entrenched, they also became willing to try new and more extreme deviances. With their growing alienation came freer expression of disrespect and hostility for representatives of the legitimate society. This disrespect increased the community's negativism, perpetuating the entire process of commitment to deviance. Lack of a commitment to deviance works the same way. In either case, the process will perpetuate itself unless some event (like a scholarship to college or a sudden failure) external to the established relationship intervenes. For two of the Roughnecks (Herb and Jack), receiving college athletic scholarships created new relations and culminated in a break with the established pattern of deviance. In the case of one of the Saints (Jerry), his parents' divorce and his failing to graduate from high school changed some of his other relations. Being held back in school for a year and losing his place among the Saints had sufficient impact on Jerry to alter his self-image and virtually to assure that he would not go on to college as his peers did. Although the experiments of life can rarely be reversed, it seems likely in view of the behavior of the other boys who did not enjoy this special treatment by the school that Jerry, too, would have "become something" had he graduated as anticipated. For Herb and Jack outside intervention worked to their advantage; for Jerry it was his undoing.

Selective perception and labeling—finding, processing and punishing some kinds of criminality and not others—means that visible, poor, nonmobile, outspoken, undiplomatic "tough" kids will be noticed, whether their actions are seriously delinquent or not. Other kids, who have established a reputation for being bright (even though underachieving), disciplined and involved in respectable activities, who are mobile and monied, will be invisible when they deviate from sanctioned activities. They'll sow their wild oats—perhaps even wider and thicker than their lower-class cohorts—but they won't be noticed. When it's time to leave adolescence most will follow the expected path, settling into the ways of the middle class, remembering fondly the delinquent but unnoticed fling of their youth. The Roughnecks and others like them may turn around, too. It is more likely that their noticeable deviance will have been so reinforced by police and community that their lives will be effectively channelled into careers consistent with their adolescent background.

SECTION ONE

Summary

As we noted in the introduction to this section, each selection presents a different image of delinquency. The *Time* article focuses on a rare but disturbing dimension of the delinquency problem and conveys a "get-tough," "nip-it-in-the-bud" philosophy. The youth crime plague is depicted as a problem involving nonwhite slum youths who prey on defenseless victims. But the Haney and Gold article argues that such images projected by the media are biased and do not accurately reflect the distribution of serious delinquent behavior. Haney and Gold show delinquency to be more widely distributed than official statistics indicate; delinquency looms as a more serious problem than police statistics imply, though one not easily attributable to specific categories of American youth.

Haney and Gold also suggest that getting caught encourages further delinquency. This finding may or may not be inconsistent with the get-tough orientation of the *Time* article. To juvenile offenders, the consequences of getting caught may be the realization that the juvenile court is going to do little or nothing to them: such an interpretation might lead to further delinquency. Another outcome of getting caught might be changes in the social relationships or the self-conceptions of juvenile offenders, likewise culminating in further delinquency; from this perspective, exposure to a "tougher" system might increase delinquency even more. Whichever interpretation one prefers, both suggest that contact with the system does not serve its intended functions. However, in the first instance, the problem could conceivably be solved through a get-tough policy. In the second, the suggested solution might be to leave juveniles alone as much as possible.

Chambliss's article illustrates the difficulty of assessing the seriousness of the delinquency problem and the different views of the problem in a community. Differential reactions to the Saints and the Roughnecks did reflect differences in the activities of the two groups, but other considerations were involved as well, such as the two groups' visibility and demeanor, and public bias. In short, conceptions of delinquency as a problem are not based entirely on objective assessments. Rather, visible activities carried out by certain groups in certain ways are more amenable to dramatization than others. This observation applies to the dramatization of juvenile as compared to adult crime as well as to public conceptions of different delinquent activities.

Subsequent readings will return to many of the issues raised by the comparison of these three selections. How do images of delinquency vary when we use police statistics instead of interview data or the observations of groups of youths? Are some categories of youths really more likely to engage in delinquent activities than others? Does exposure to the juvenile justice system propel youths into delinquent careers? Can the problem be approached through tinkering with the justice system? The reader may be frustrated by the lack of simple answers. But then we are not dealing with a simple problem.

SECTION TWO

The Social History of Delinquency

Unlike the adult criminal justice system, whose roots go back to antiquity, the juvenile justice system is a product of very modern times. The notion of a trial by jury, the principle of judicial precedent, and the concept of an adversary system of justice date back to the twelfth and thirteenth centuries in criminal justice history, whereas the concepts first associated with the juvenile court, such as probation, treatment, and status offenses, came into vogue at the turn of the twentieth century. Indeed, the terms *adolescent, delinquent,* and even *childhood* are of relatively recent vintage. Thus, the study of the history of juvenile delinquency encompasses a rather narrow time span, despite the indisputably enduring vitality of crime as a human act.

One might assume that the events leading up to the creation of the juvenile court are relatively simple and straightforward. However, in attempting to reconstruct what Anthony Platt (1974) refers to as "the invention of delinquency," one must consider a number of critical social factors. First and foremost is the sheer brutal fact of a high death rate among infants and young children prior to modern times, which resulted in a pronounced lack of attention to childhood. John Gillis (1974) points out that before the modern age, the vast majority of young people died before the age of twenty. Various childhood maladies that we barely make mention of today, such as measles, smallpox, and diptheria, as well as malnutrition, were at one time so serious that the chances of survival beyond childhood were extremely problematic. The meteoric rise in the world's population began only some three or four centuries ago, when basic improvements in sanitation, food production, and, later on, medical knowledge raised the life span from twenty-five or thirty years to the current estimate of some seventy-five, and reduced infant and childhood mortality rates to a level at which survival was expected. What originally took perhaps 98,000 years—for the population to reach a level of 200 million people (estimated population at 1 A.D.)—is now accomplished in just two years!

The grim reality of disease and death made life cheap and childhood almost unknown. Childhood as a phase in the life cycle was not culturally defined until relatively late in human social history. Philippe Ariès (1962), in examining the literature, art, and language of Western countries, concluded that childhood received little attention from our ancestors: he noted that many languages of old did not even include words to describe it. A natural response to the reality of childhood mortality, beyond a certain degree of unconcern for children, was a pronounced lack of interest in child-rearing techniques. Furthermore, the practice of age grading—the delineation of age categories such as childhood, adolescence, and young adulthood—was illogical when the total expected life span was only a few decades. But as the survival rate for children began to change in the twelfth and thirteenth centuries, Ariès detected a subtle cultural response. For example, family portraits that originally depicted children as miniature adults began to show them as distinctly different individuals. They came to be portrayed in attire that distinguished them from adults and in activities that indicated dependence and immaturity. Childhood and child-rearing practices began to take on some semblance of importance. Children were born not to die but to be nurtured, protected, and educated. What began to emerge was the concept of childhood as a critically important stage in human development that was qualitatively different from adulthood.

Accompanying the basic change in survival rates for the young were cultural adaptations that further enhanced the unique position of children. Ariès pointed out that education during the Dark Ages, from the sixth century to the twelfth century, was virtually nonexistent. The little formal education that was carried out was limited to the training of religious clerics. But with the advent of the Renaissance, beginning in about the fifteenth century, the intellectual stagnation of the previous era was swept aside in a rebirth of the arts, literature, and science. While education was not directed exclusively toward children, the notion that children needed to be prepared for adult life became popular, and a formal education was mandatory for well-bred children.

A second important social change that brought attention to childhood was the emergence of the nuclear family. Prior to the advent of industrialization, families were commonly "extended," with two or more family units living communally. With the gradual trend toward urbanization, industrialization, and increased productivity, families took on more of a nuclear configuration, consisting solely of parents and their children. Children occupied a more visible position in the nuclear family, and child rearing became an important family function. The Puritans in Colonial America enacted laws that supported and defended the primacy of the family to such an extent that parents who failed to teach their children reading skills or a trade were brought before the authorities (Bremner, 1970). By the early 1800s, there began to emerge a literature on child rearing that promoted the view that childhood was a distinct period of life and emphasized the family's critical role in educating and disciplining children.

A third major catalyzing force in the "discovery" of childhood was the transition in societal orientation from agrarian to industrialized. In agrarian settings, the social stratification system was relatively undifferentiated and the occupational choices were few. Children generally assumed the occupational roles of their parents. But as societies evolved into highly stratified and industrialized economies, the occupational structures became far more complex, and children assumed occupational roles different from those of their parents. Children became displaced from the work force as labor-intensive productivity was replaced by mechanized productivity. The results were the delayed entry of the young into the labor force and, because industrialization demanded long periods of formal training, the advent of compulsory education, coupled with legislation prohibiting child labor (Coleman, 1974). Thus, the advance of industrialization led to the prolongation of childhood and the popularization of the concept of the "formative period of life."

Finally, there is evidence to suggest that democracy itself, or what Tocqueville (1945) referred to as that "noble experiment," had a significant impact on the discovery of childhood. Thomas Jefferson argued that democracy could survive only with literate citizens who participated in the affairs of government through the electoral process. He viewed the education of the young as the path to citizenship. The Jacksonian period represented a concerted attack on elitism, out of which emerged a seminal discussion of "general education" as a way of enhancing democratic principles (Katz, 1973). Again, the focus was on children as the standard-bearers of the promise of democracy. But it was Horace Mann who saw education as "the great equalizer of the conditions of men" and brought public education to full fruition. Since all children were educable, education could provide for the poorest child a chance to succeed equal to that of the richest. Under the tutelage of Mann, the Massachusetts Board of Education argued that the dangers of a rigid system of social stratification could be overcome only when "the children of the rich and the poor, of the honored and the unknown, meet together on common ground. . . . No foundation will be laid in our social life for the brazen walls of caste; and our political life, which is but the outgrowth of the social, will pulsate in harmony with it and so be kept true to the grand ideals of the fathers and founders of the republic" (Twenty-Ninth Annual Report of the Massachusetts Board of Education, 1866).

Children symbolized the future of the democratic state. Unlike any other political regime, America adopted a youth orientation that amounted to a veneration of the young. The Founding Fathers, thoroughly imbued with the philosophy of the Enlightenment, envisioned unlimited progress for future generations of children. However, for America's destiny to be fulfilled, children had to be inculcated with the values and beliefs of the new nation. Seen in this light, childhood was exalted to a position linked to America's political destiny, and the cult of childhood became an American trademark

(Skolnick, 1973).

The three discussions that follow were selected to elucidate further the consequences of the "creation" of this stage of life we refer to as childhood. In the first selection, David Bakan (1971) traces the origin of the concept of adolescence. According to Bakan, the notion of a period of life called adolescence was added to the concept of childhood in response to the profound social changes that took place in America following the Civil War. The idea of adolescence represented a prolongation of childhood that was needed by the increasingly industrial society. In the second reading, Anthony Platt (1974), using a different set of lenses, examines the same time period in American history and concludes that social policies directed toward children were made to serve the best interests of corporate capitalism. The child-saving movement, as interpreted by Platt, represented a form of social control designed to protect the existing social structure. In the third selection, John Hagan and Jeffrey Leon (1977) challenge Platt's interpretation of history. In reexamining the development of the juvenile court, Hagan and Leon do not find evidence that children became the pawns of industrialists. Each of the three selections is intended to sensitize us to the complex origins of the concept of childhood and the controversy that surrounds the development of the juvenile court.

REFERENCES

Ariès, P. 1962. *Centuries of Childhood.* Translated by Robert Baldick. New York: Alfred A. Knopf.

Bakan, D. 1971. "Adolescence in America: From Idea to Social Fact." *Daedalus* (Fall): 979–95.

Bremner, R. H., et al., eds. 1970. *Children and Youth in America: A Documentary History.* 2 vols. Cambridge, Mass.: Harvard University Press.

Coleman, J. S., et al. 1974. *Youth: Transition to Adulthood.* Chicago: University of Chicago Press.

de Tocqueville, A. 1945. *Democracy in Action.* Edited by Phillips Bradley. New York: Alfred A. Knopf.

Gillis, J. R. 1974. *Youth and History.* New York: Academic Press.

Hagan, J., and J. Leon. 1977. "Rediscovering Delinquency: Social History, Political Ideology, and the Sociology of Law." *American Sociological Review* 42 (August): 587–98.

Katz, M. 1968. *The Irony of School Reform.* Cambridge, Mass.: Harvard University Press.

Platt, A. 1974. "The Triumph of Benevolence: The Origins of the Juvenile Justice System in the United States." In Richard Quinney, ed, *Criminal Justice in America,* pp. 356–89. Boston: Little, Brown.

Skolnick, A. 1973. *The Intimate Environment: Exploring Marriage and the Family.* Boston: Little, Brown.

Adolescence in America: From Idea to Social Fact

David Bakan

The Idea of Adolescence

Often a technical term is invented in order to create a social condition and a social fact; such has been true with respect to the term "adolescence." The idea of adolescence as an intermediary period in life starting at puberty and extending to some period in the life cycle unmarked by any conspicuous physical change but socially defined as "manhood" or "womanhood" is the product of modern times. The *Oxford English Dictionary* traces the term to the fifteenth century. Prior to that, if we follow the thought of Philip Aries,[1] the notion of childhood hardly existed, let alone the idea of the prolongation of childhood beyond puberty, as the term adolescence suggests.

Meaningful ascription of serious role characteristics for this period of life occurs, perhaps for the first time, in Rousseau's *Émile*, in which he characterized the period of adolescence as being beyond the earlier period of weakness of childhood and as a second birth. "We are born, so to speak, twice over; born into existence, and born into life; born a human being and born a man."[2] His aim was explicitly to prolong childhood, including the condition of innocence, as long as possible.

Although *Émile* has had considerable influence since its publication, the conversion of the idea of adolescence into a commonly accepted social reality was largely associated with modern urban-industrial life. Rousseau may have *invented* adolescence, as maintained by Musgrove,[3] but the notion as it is commonly understood in contemporary thought did not prevail prior to the last two decades of the nineteenth century and was "on the whole an American discovery."[4] The idea received an important stamp of reality from G. Stanley Hall in his monumental two-volume work on *Adolescence*, which he proudly presented to the reader as "essentially the author's first book" in 1904.[5] In point of fact he had introduced the idea as a special stage of development earlier.[6] In *Adolescence* he complained that we in America, because of our history, "have had neither childhood nor youth, but have lost touch with these stages of life because we lack a normal developmental history . . . Our immigrants have often passed the best years of youth or leave it behind when they reach our shores, and their memories of it are in other lands. No country is so precociously old for its years."[7] The giving of social reality to adolescence would, as it were, youthen the nation.

By reviewing some of the history, I will attempt to show in this essay that the invention or discovery of adolescence in America was largely in response to the social changes that accompanied America's development in the latter half of the nineteenth and the early twentieth century, and that the principal reason was to prolong the years of childhood. Adolescence was added to childhood as a second childhood in order to fulfill the aims of the new urban-industrial society which developed so rapidly following the Civil War.

Historical Background

From the days of the early settlement of America to the second half of the nineteenth century, America suffered a chronic labor shortage. It sought to overcome this labor shortage through slavery, the encouragement of immigration, and industrialization. The incompatibility of slavery and industrialization plagued America during much of its early history, and that incompatibility remained until the Civil War, the Emancipation Proclamation, and the Thirteenth Amendment resolved it in favor of industrialization. But with the development of urban-industrial society, the nation became possessed of new contradictions characteristic of modern technological society, most serious among them the presence of a large number of persons who were mature by historical standards but immature in the new context.

The country changed dramatically during the second half of the nineteenth century. In 1880 the railroad network was completely integrated; there was no longer a frontier; the number of cities that had populations of more than 8,000 almost doubled in the decade from 1880 to 1890. By the year 1900 more than a third of the population was living in cities and more than half the population of the North Atlantic area lived in cities of more than 8,000 persons. In 1890 more than a third of the American population were people of foreign parentage. The question of property was becoming increasingly salient, as testified to by the proliferation of criminal laws designed to protect property rights—a not unimportant fact when we consider the question of juvenile delinquency, because most juvenile crimes are crimes against property, such as burglary, larceny, robbery, and auto theft.

The low level of "morality" of the new occupants of the burgeoning cities was a matter of frequent comment. Drinking, sexual immorality, vagrancy, and crime were not only intrinsically threatening to orderliness, but were also particularly distressing influences on the young. The rapid breeding, the continuing threat of "street Arabs," evoked a strong cry that the state intercede in restraining and training the young. In an address before the American Social Science Association in 1875, the influential Mary Carpenter said

From *Daedalus* (Fall 1971), pp. 979–995. Reprinted by permission of *Daedalus*, Journal of the American Academy of Arts and Sciences, Vol. 100, No. 4, 1971, Cambridge, Mass.

that if the parents of the young fail in their duty, then the whole society suffers; it was therefore the duty of the state to intercede and "stand *in loco parentis* and do its duty to the child and to society, by seeing that he is properly brought up."[8] Not the least of the dangers was the presence of un-American ideas and ideologies brought by the new immigrants, which were considered threatening to the basic fiber of American life. Even private education, as compared with public education, was regarded as a threat, the fear being that the children would not be sufficiently socialized and "Americanized." The Ku Klux Klan, for example, took a firm stand against private education.

As a result of these conditions, three major social movements developed, all of which conspired to make a social fact out of adolescence: compulsory (and characteristically public) education, child labor legislation, and special legal procedures for "juveniles." By the explicit citation of a precise chronological age, the legislation associated with these three areas essentially removed the vagueness of all previous ideas of the time at which adolescence terminates. Thus adolescence became the period of time between pubescence, a concrete biological occurrence, and the ages specified by law for compulsory education, employment, and criminal procedure.

There is no doubt that these movements were strongly motivated, at least on the conscious level, by humanitarian considerations. The rhetoric in defense of these three types of law was always cast in terms of the benefit and the saving quality that they would have for the young. The presumption that the various child welfare laws were principally created for the benefit of youth must, however, be confronted with the fact that there has been only a small degree of legal attention to the serious problem of child abuse in our society. The so-called "battered child" was not discovered until the late 1940's and early 1950's, and to this day appropriate protective and social support legislation is still quite negligible in contrast to the magnitude of the problem and the frequency of cases of cruelty to children.[9] The confluence of humanitarian considerations with the major economic, social, and political forces in the society needs to be clearly recognized. Indeed, the recognition of these underlying forces may help us to understand some of the failures to fulfill humanitarian aims and the disabilities which currently prevail with respect to that period of life that we call adolescence.

Compulsory Education

In the late nineteenth century, public compulsory education for children between six and eighteen, characteristically to age sixteen, was introduced widely in the United States. English common law had given parents virtually complete control over the education of the child, a principle prevalent in colonial America and throughout most of our early history. However, the general legal position later became that: "The primary function of the public school . . . is not to confer benefits upon the individual as such." Rather "the school exists as a state institution because the very existence of civil society demands it. The education of youth is a matter of such vital importance to the democratic state and to the public weal that the state may do much, may go very far indeed, by way of limiting the control of the parent over the education of his child."[10]

In the case of a father who had violated the compulsory attendance law, the court stated in its opinion:

> The course of study to be pursued in the public schools of our state is prescribed either by statute or by the school authorities in pursuance thereof. These schools include not only elementary schools, but high schools as well . . . A parent, therefore, is not at liberty to exercise a choice in that regard, but, where not exempt for some lawful reason, must send his child to the school where instruction is provided suitable to its attainments as the school authorities may determine.[11]

It has been held that even a competent parent may not engage in domestic education on the following grounds:

> We have no doubt many parents are capable of instructing their own children, but to permit such parents to withdraw their children from the public schools without permission from the superintendent of schools, and to instruct them at home, would be to disrupt our common school system and destroy its value to the state.[12]

At the same time the school authorities have been granted virtually complete discretionary powers with respect to suspension, expulsion, and punishment.[13] Such power rests in the hands of school authorities even in cases where the pupil has violated no rules. In one case, for example, a pupil was expelled for general misbehavior. In holding that the board of education had power to expel the pupil, the court said:

> It matters not whether rules have been announced by either the directors or teachers. If the conduct of the pupil is such as reasonably to satisfy such school officers that the presence of that pupil is detrimental to the interests of the school, then the power of expulsion is conferred.[14]

Thus, it has turned out that the power of the state in America is such that it can, through its officials, not only compel school attendance, but also bar a pupil access to educational resources. Certainly there have been numerous legislative acts and court actions which would qualify particular cases. However, the total thrust of the various steps that have been taken since the middle of the nineteenth century has been in the direction of increasing the power of the state rather than protecting the rights of young people and their parents.

At the same time as the legal power of school authorities over pupils and their parents has been great, the schools have been derelict in the teaching of law—instruction which some regard as essential for people living in a democracy. In a society that is heavily dependent for its functioning on law, it is important that an appreciation of law, how it works, and its limits be taught in the public schools. One critic of this aspect of American education, in discussing the matter of education on due process, indicates that it is taught as though it applies only to criminals and that it fails to reflect itself in procedural fairness in school disciplinary matters. The idea of freedom of the press is characteristically not brought to bear in connection with school newspapers. "One of the difficult problems," he laconically comments, "is whether [proposed] law courses will be permitted to ventilate these issues, given the anxiety about them."[15]

Although from time to time there have been steps to increase the knowledge of law among educators, the emphasis has been on the kind of legal knowledge that an educator might require to deal with relationships of the school to outside institutions and individuals rather than on teaching law to students. One article along these lines, for example, deals with the legal structure of education, pupil personnel policies, control of pupil conduct, staff personnel policies, curricula, and liability. Illustrations are that: physical education coordinators should be expert in the law of liability for pupil injuries; guidance teachers should be familiar with compulsory education laws and their enforcement; curriculum coordinators should understand the legal position of parents in relation to school studies and activities; business administrators should understand contract law; personnel administrators should understand the legal aspects of employing and discharging teachers; and teachers of the history or philosophy of education should be acquainted with the relevant judicial opinions.[16]

Child Labor

The movement to restrict child labor in the United States also provided a definition of the termination of adolescence. Though there is a considerable amount of variation from state to state, the laws with respect to employment give specific minimum ages for definitions of maturity of different kinds: eighteen, minimum age for work in "hazardous occupations"; under eighteen, eight-hour day and forty-hour week; under eighteen, employment certificate required; under sixteen, limited hours of night work; sixteen, minimum age for factory work and employment during school hours; fourteen, minimum age for work outside of school hours. These are fairly typical laws governing age and employment.

The regulation of child labor has been one of the most controversial issues in this country since the nineteenth century. The harm to children from work in factories has been stridently declaimed. On the other hand, the virtues of work, the harm associated with idleness, and even the economic discriminatory effect of such legislation have also been consistently indicated. As an example, Senator Alexander Wiley, in questioning the representative of the American Federation of Labor before a Senate subcommittee to investigate juvenile delinquency said: "To me when I see the youth of this country in idleness, walking the streets of the cities, [I feel] we are meeting a challenge to our common sense because we know idleness breeds not only crime but everything else."[17] There have been repeated charges that the legal regulation of child labor is partly responsible for the widespread unemployment among young people, particularly Negroes.[18]

Adolescents in the labor force were a common occurrence throughout American history. In 1832 about 40 per cent of the factory workers in New England were children. Starting a few years after the Civil War the major historical trend of a chronic labor shortage began to reverse itself, with ever-increasing evidences of labor surplus. With the changes in the kinds of work needed in the growing cities in the second half of the nineteenth century, an increasing proportion of females sought gainful employment. Indeed, the possibility of a close relationship between the various movements in connection with "child saving" and female employment has been seriously suggested.[19] Labor began to organize. The Knights of Labor, the precursor of the American Federation of Labor, was founded in 1869. In 1885 it had a membership of 100,000; a year later it could boast a membership of 730,000. Virtually from its founding, the Knights of Labor began its campaign for the prohibition of child labor. In spite of its efforts, child labor increased. The participation rate of youth between the ages of ten and fifteen in the labor force increased until 1900 and then began to decline. Indeed, in the decade which ended in 1900, the number of child laborers in the canneries, glass industry, mines, and so forth in the South tripled. The effort to control the labor supply in the United States was evident also in legislation to restrict immigration. In 1882 the Chinese Exclusion Act, barring immigration of Chinese laborers, was passed and was followed by other laws which severely restricted immigration.

Among employers there was a polarization. On the one hand there were certainly those employers who were in favor of having access to the cheap labor of young people and new immigrants; on the other hand the nature of industrial requirements was changing rapidly in favor of more skilled, and especially more reliable, workers. One of the most serious interferences with the reliability of labor was alcohol, and the prohibition movement grew simultaneously with the efforts to remove young people from the labor market and to restrict immigration. The prohibition movement gained increasing support from industrial leaders, "who were not unaware of the economic implications of the trade in intoxicants."[20]

The belief, common during the early part of the nineteenth century, that the children of the poor should work and that education of the children of the poor was filled with social danger tended to decline in the course of the century. The enlightened leaders of industry, taking ever longer views of history, recognized the dependence of industry on the existence of a reasonably educated labor force, educated not only with respect to knowledge and skill, but also with respect to bureaucratic subordination and reliable work habits.[21] At the same time, organized labor sought not only reforms in the conditions of child labor, but also education for their own children, to increase the likelihood of vertical social mobility. The continuing interest of both industry and labor in the education of the young is evidenced by the clear agreement on this on the part of both the National Association of Manufacturers and organized labor.[22]

One of the classic conflicts in connection with child labor was that between the textile manufacturers of the North and those in the South. The northern manufacturers charged that the South had a competitive advantage from its greater use of young workers.[23] Among the factors that eventually led to a resolution of the conflict was the later discovery, resulting in part from the changed nature of manufacture and experience of some restrictive legislation, that, as the *Textile World Journal* in 1918 put it: "The labor of children under fourteen years of age is not only inefficient in itself, but tends to lower the efficiency of all departments in which they are employed; also children of fourteen to sixteen years, worked on a short time basis, are scarcely less efficient and have a disorganizing effect in the departments where they are utilized. Because of these facts, and entirely apart from humanitarian considerations, large numbers of southern mills will not re-employ children of these ages."[24]

Juvenile Delinquency

Quite analogous to the "invention of adolescence," as Musgrove put it, was the "invention of delinquency," as Anthony M. Platt puts it in his book on the history of the notion of delinquency in the United States.[25] The humane motivation associated with the development of the notion of the juvenile delinquent was the desire to remove young people from the rigidities and inexorabilities associated with criminal justice and to allow wider discretionary powers to authorities in dealing with juveniles. The new legal apparatus was intended to separate young offenders from older offenders, and to provide corrective rather than punitive treatment. The first Juvenile Court Act was passed by the Illinois legislature in 1899 and brought together for single consideration cases of dependency, neglect, and delinquency. The hearings under the act were to be informal, the records were to be confidential, the young people were to be detained separately from adults. The aims were to be investigation and prescription rather than the determination of guilt or innocence. Lawyers were to be unnecessary. The definition of the "juvenile delinquent" in the various laws which multiplied after the model legislation in Illinois now vary for the upper limit from sixteen to twenty-one. The United States Children's Bureau had recommended nineteen, and this has been followed in about two-thirds of the states.[26]

Although the juvenile acts tended to free the courts from the obligation of imposing punishments associated with the criminal codes, they also had the effect of suspending the fundamental principle of legality, that one may not be punished for an offense unless a definite law in effect at the time when the act in question was committed has been broken. Considerations of due process were not obligatory. Guilt did not have to be established beyond a reasonable doubt. Among the acts reported under the heading of juvenile delinquency may be found the following: immoral conduct around schools, association with vicious or immoral persons, patronizing public pool rooms, wandering about railroad yards, truancy, incorrigibility, absenting self from home without consent, smoking cigarettes in public places, begging or receiving alms (or in street for purposes of).[27] As Harvey Baker of the Boston juvenile court put it in 1910:

> The court does not confine its attention to just the particular offense which brought the child to its notice. For example, a boy who comes to court for such a trifle as failing to wear his badge when selling papers may be held on probation for months because of difficulties at school; and a boy who comes in for playing on the street may . . . be committed to a reform school because he is found to have habits of loafing, stealing or gambling which can not be corrected outside.[28]

Questions have been raised as to whether the procedures of such courts adequately protect the rights of young offenders and whether they are consistent with constitutional rights.[29] In some states corrective legislation has been attempted by providing for legal defense of persons who come under the jurisdiction of the juvenile courts. However, the evidence is that this is not common. Indeed, treatment by officials tends to be more kindly toward young persons who admit guilt and indicate that they will mend their ways than toward those who are defensive or those whose parents are defensive.[30] The failure of the juvenile court to achieve its avowed objectives is notorious.

Suggestions that the aim of the juvenile court is to introduce a middle-class child-rearing orientation to the courtroom are apparent in the opinion of Judge Ben Lindsey of Denver, one of the pioneers in the juvenile court movement, and in the findings of Melvin L. Kohn. In an introduction to a book called *Winning the Boy* by Lilburn Merrill, Lindsey stressed the importance of "character," rather than the act itself.

> You have not really a safe citizen until there comes into the boy's heart the desire to do right because it is right . . . I ask the boy why he will not steal again and he invariably replies, "Because I will get in jail." He is afraid of jail; he is not afraid to do wrong . . . Conscience is the moral director; without it character is impossible, and character is the greatest need, for it means that the pure in heart shall see and know and act the truth, as surely as they shall see God.[31]

Kohn has been able to show, on the basis of comparative data which he has collected, that there are differences in corrective actions between working-class and middle-class parents. Working-class parents tend to punish the external consequences of an action, as contrasted with middle-class parents who tend to punish on the basis of intention, rather than the action itself.[32] The latter mode is clearly suggested in Judge Lindsey's comment. Thus one way of interpreting the development of juvenile delinquency practices is as an effort to bring middle-class child-rearing practices into play, even when they involved the suspension of the principle of legality.

The legal disability of those who come under the juvenile laws is not limited to a small minority of youth in our society. "Statutes often define juvenile delinquency so broadly as to make virtually all youngsters delinquent . . . Rough estimates by the Children's Bureau, supported by independent studies, indicate that one in every nine youths—one in every six male youths—will be referred to juvenile court in connection with a delinquent act (excluding traffic offenses) before his 18th birthday."[33] As soon as the young person gains what may be called the animal sufficiency that comes with puberty, and may enter public places without an attendant, he becomes subject to extraordinary powers of the state until the legal definition of his maturity comes into being. This power of the state differs dramatically from the power of the state over adults in our society. The great discrepancy between adult justice and juvenile justice and the legal vulnerability of juveniles has been one of the major factors associated with the conversion of the idea of adolescence into the social fact of adolescence.

The Study of Adolescence

Starting with the work of G. Stanley Hall, adolescence became the subject of a considerable amount of investigation. There can be no doubt about the value of such investigation—indeed, this may be attested to by the essays in this volume. Nonetheless, this body of literature articulated with the cultural forces in the society at large. Although the intention of people like Hall to draw attention to an extremely important age period significant to the history of civilization generally, and the United States in particular, and thereby to create greater concern with proper development at that stage, was meritorious, there was another effect which needs to be pointed out. By stressing, for example, the presumptive emotional instability and unformed nature of people of that age—the work of Margaret Mead and others suggests that such phenomena of adolescence may be extrinsic rather than intrinsic[34]—Hall and others tended to put a gloss of psychopathology on this age period. Since it has long been a principle in our society that persons regarded as psychologically pathological are to be relieved of rights,[35] the effect of this literature has been to serve the general disability of persons under legal ages. In this way, the workers in the field of adolescence have tended to conspire, certainly unwittingly, with some of the forces depriving adolescents of their rights.

The Promise

A major factor which has sustained the social fact of adolescence in our society has been the belief, so pervasive in our success-oriented culture, in "the promise." The promise is that if a young person does all the things he is "supposed to do" during his adolescence, he will then realize success, status, income, power, and so forth in his adulthood.

A study by Arthur L. Stinchcombe[36] may help us to understand the operation of the promise. He studied the attitudes, behavior, and perceptions of the labor market among high school students, and found a direct and dramatic relationship between the images of the future that the students have and their rebellious attitudes and behavior. His data bear out the hypothesis "that high school rebellion, and expressive alienation, are most common among students who do not see themselves as gaining an increment in future status from conformity in high school."[37] In elaborating on the dynamics of the hypothesis, he writes: "When a student realizes that he does not achieve status increment from improved current performance, current performance loses meaning. The student becomes hedonistic because he does not visualize achievement of long-run goals through current self-restraint. He reacts negatively to a conformity that offers nothing concrete. He claims autonomy from adults because their authority does not promise him a satisfactory future."[38] Stinchcombe's hypothesis is derived from considerations of the legitimacy of bureaucratic authority as developed by Max Weber. Among the interesting derivations Stinchcombe makes from the hypothesis is an explanation of the difference between the sexes in various categories of expressive alienation. Girls are less likely to be rebellious because they perceive at least the possibility of marriage as a viable "career." He points out that the relatively high delinquency rate among Negroes is associated with the perception of the employment discrimination against Negro adult males.

As the credibility of the promise declines, the willingness of young people to accept the varieties of disabilities of adolescence equally declines. The profoundly pervasive metaphor of appropriate behavior in adolescence as a form of capital investment for the realization of returns in the future necessarily falters in cogency as the likelihood of such returns declines. The problems of order in the schools, juvenile delinquency, and other forms of expressive alienation cannot readily be solved by making small changes in the schools, Stinchcombe says.[39] It would appear that the schools cannot promise much because the society cannot promise much.

A study by William Westley and Frederick Elkin[40] of young

people in an upper-class suburb of Montreal in 1951 attempted to explode the notion of the adolescent period as being one of storm and stress, nonconformity, gang formation, struggle for emancipation, and the like. The data collected in that place and time indicated considerably greater harmony and positive social adjustment by conventional standards than one might expect. However, the characterization of these young people would clearly indicate that they expected that the promise would be fulfilled. The typical youth in the study "internalizes aspirations for a professional or business career; he learns the expected patterns of language and breeding; he learns to resolve disputes by peaceable means; he learns to defer many immediate gratifications for the sake of future gains."[41]

The major question in our society today is whether, for youth of *all* social classes, the promise has continued credibility. Unemployment among manual workers is increasingly patent. The public service advertisements directed at potential drop-outs to remain in school in order to get better jobs later are met with increasing cynicism.[42] The poor acceptance rates of college students into the labor market predicted in the early sixties[43] are rapidly materializing. Even for scientists with Ph.D.'s the possibilities for employment are extremely dismal.[44] And few young people are ignorant of the fact that a career in "free enterprise" is virtually impossible without access to capital.[45] The idyllic vision of Erik Erikson that adolescence "can be viewed as a *psychosocial moratorium* during which the individual through free role experimentation may find a niche in some section of his society, a niche which is firmly defined and yet seems to be uniquely made for him,"[46] must increasingly be viewed cynically if that niche in life is contingent upon an appropriate niche in the labor force.

One of the likely consequences of these trends will be a strong move on the part of youth and their parents to dissolve the social fact of adolescence and to remove the historical disabilities which have been created by the state and sustained by the promise. Albert K. Cohen, in 1965, indicated that he thought it was sad that youth accepted their disabilities without protest.[47] The picture soon changed. Jerry Farber's critique of what he calls America's "Auschwitz" educational system, "The Student as Nigger," originally published in 1967 in the Los Angeles *Free Press,* quickly became one of the most widely distributed underground documents in history—reprinted, reduplicated, recopied many times by student groups all over America and Canada.[48] A national clearing house of anti-public school thought has been formed in Washington, D.C., which puts out a regular biweekly newsletter called *FPS* (*the letters don't stand for anything*). Ellen Lurie has written what is fast becoming a standard manual for parents seeking to reduce state control over their children's education in the public schools.[49] This book is consistent with the United Nations Universal Declaration of Human Rights, adopted in 1948, that "Parents have a prior right to choose the kind of education that shall be given to their children."[50] The crime statistics mount at an exponential rate. Demonstrations become ever more strident. The "underground revolution"[51] gets new recruits daily.

The future? My assignment was to discuss history. The future must be left to time and other occasions.[52]

References

1. P. Aries, *Centuries of Childhood* (New York: Knopf, 1962).
2. Jean Jacques Rousseau, *Émile,* trans. Barbara Foxley (New York: Dutton, 1966; originally published 1762), pp. 128, 172.
3. F. Musgrove, *Youth and the Social Order* (Bloomington, Ind.: Indiana University Press, 1964). Musgrove titles one of his chapters "The Invention of the Adolescent," pp. 33-57.
4. John Demos and Virginia Demos, "Adolescence in Historical Perspective," *Journal of Marriage and the Family,* 31 (1969), 632-638, 632.
5. G. Stanley Hall, *Adolescence: Its Psychology and Its Relations to Physiology, Anthropology, Sociology, Sex, Crime, Religion, and Education* (New York: D. Appleton and Company, 1904).
6. G. Stanley Hall, "The Moral and Religious Training of Children," *Princeton Review* (January 1882), pp. 26-48.
7. Hall, *Adolescence,* p. xvi.
8. As cited in Grace Abbot, ed., *The Child and the State* (Chicago: University of Chicago Press, 1938), II, 372.
9. See M. G. Paulsen, "The Law and Abused Children," in R. E. Helfer and C. H. Kempe, *The Battered Child* (Chicago: University of Chicago Press, 1968), pp. 175-207; and D. Bakan, *Slaughter of the Innocents: A Study of the Battered Child Phenomenon* (San Francisco: Jossey-Bass, 1971; Toronto: Canadian Broadcasting Corp., 1971).
10. Newton Edwards, *The Courts and the Public Schools: The Legal Basis of School Organization and Administration,* rev. ed. (Chicago: University of Chicago Press, 1955), p. 24.
11. *Miller* v. *State,* 77 Ind. App. 611, 134 N. E. 209, as cited by Edwards, *The Courts and the Public Schools,* p. 524.
12. *State* v. *Counort,* 69 Wash. 361, 124 Pac. 910, 41 L.R.A. (N.S.) 95, as cited by Edwards, *The Courts and the Public Schools,* p. 522.
13. Edwards, *The Courts and the Public Schools,* pp. 601ff.
14. *State* v. *Hamilton,* 42 Mo. App. 24, as cited by Edwards, *The Courts and the Public Schools,* p. 603.
15. Alex Elson, "General Education in Law for Non-Lawyers," in The American Assembly, Columbia University, *Law in a Changing America* (Englewood Cliffs, N.J.: Prentice-Hall, 1968), pp. 183-191, 189.
16. E. E. Reutter, Jr., "Essentials of School Law for Educators," in Harold J. Carter, ed., *Intellectual Foundations of American Education* (New York: Pitman Publishing Corporation, 1965), pp. 216-225.
17. *Juvenile Delinquency: Hearings before the Subcommittee to Investigate Juvenile Delinquency,* Senate, 1955 (New York: Greenwood Press, 1968), p. 86.
18. See, for example, the effort to counter these charges by H. M. Haisch of the U.S. Department of Labor: H. M. Haisch, "Do Child Labor Laws Prevent Youth Employment?" *Journal of Negro Education,* 33 (1964), 182-185.
19. "Although child saving had important symbolic functions for preserving the prestige of middle-class women in a rapidly changing society, it also had considerable instrumental significance for legitimizing new career openings for women. The new role of social worker combined elements of an old and partly fictitious role—defender of family life—and elements of a new role—social servant. Social work and philanthropy were thus an affirmation of cherished values and an instrumentality for women's emancipation." Anthony M. Platt, *The Child Savers: The Invention of Delinquency* (Chicago: University of Chicago Press, 1969), p. 98.
20. John Allen Krout, *The Origins of Prohibition* (New York: Russell and Russell, 1967), p. 302.
21. For an analysis of relations between education and industry see John Galbraith, *The New Industrial State* (Boston: Houghton Mifflin, 1967).
22. See Charles R. Sligh, Jr., "Views on Curriculum," *Harvard Educational Review,* 4 (1957), 239-245; Walter P. Reuther, "What the Public Schools Should Teach," *Harvard Educational Review,* 4 (1957), 246-250.
23. Stephen B. Wood, *Constitutional Politics in the Progressive Era: Child Labor and the Law* (Chicago: University of Chicago Press, 1968), p. 9.
24. Cited by Wood, *Constitutional Politics,* p. 172.
25. Anthony M. Platt, *The Child Savers: The Invention of Delinquency* (Chicago: University of Chicago Press, 1969).
26. Robert W. Winslow, ed., *Juvenile Delinquency in a Free Society: Selec-*

tions from the President's Commission on Law Enforcement and Administration of Justice (Belmont, Calif.: Dickenson Publishing Company, 1968), pp. 119-120.

27. Winslow, *Juvenile Delinquency*, pp. 166-167.

28. Cited in Platt, *The Child Savers*, p. 142.

29. See Lewis Mayer, *The American Legal System* (New York: Harper and Row, 1964), pp. 146-149.

30. Winslow, *Juvenile Delinquency*, pp. 140, 150.

31. Cited in Bernard Wishy, *The Child and the Republic: The Dawn of Modern American Child Nurture* (Philadelphia: University of Pennsylvania Press, 1968), p. 134.

32. M. L. Kohn, "Social Class and Parent-Child Relationships: An Interpretation," *American Journal of Sociology*, 68 (1963), 471-480; M. L. Kohn, "Social Class and the Exercise of Parental Authority," *American Sociological Review*, 24 (1959), 352-366; M. L. Kohn, *Class and Conformity: A Study in Values* (Homewood, Ill.: Dorsey Press, 1969).

33. Winslow, *Juvenile Delinquency*, p. 2.

34. Margaret Mead, *Coming of Age in Samoa* (New York: W. Morrow and Co., 1928).

35. See Thomas S. Szasz, *Law, Liberty and Psychiatry* (New York: Macmillan, 1963).

36. Arthur L. Stinchcombe, *Rebellion in a High School* (Chicago: Quadrangle Books, 1964).

37. *Ibid.*, p. 49; see especially chaps. 3 and 4, pp. 49-102, titled "The Labor Market and Rebellion I; II."

38. *Ibid.*, pp. 5-6.

39. *Ibid.*, passim.

40. William A. Westley and Frederick Elkin, "The Protective Environment and Adolescent Socialization," in Martin Gold and Elizabeth Douvan, eds., *Adolescent Development: Readings in Research and Theory* (Boston: Allyn and Bacon, 1969), pp. 158-164; reprinted from *Social Forces*, 35 (1957), 243-249.

41. *Ibid.*, p. 158.

42. See, for example, the stress on the employment advantages of school in the *National Stay-in-School Campaign Handbook for Communities* (Washington, D.C.: Government Printing Office, 1957). The campaign was sponsored jointly by the Department of Labor, Department of Health, Education and Welfare, and Department of Defense.

43. J. Folger and C. Nam, "Trends in Education in Relation to the Occupational Structure," *Sociology of Education*, 38 (1964), 19-33; R. Havighurst and B. Neugarten, *Society and Education*, 2d ed. (Boston: Allyn and Bacon, 1962).

44. Allan Cartter, "Scientific Manpower for 1970-1985," *Science*, 172 (1971), 132-140.

45. Such has been the case at least since 1885 when Andrew Carnegie, the great exponent of the idea that any able and energetic young man could "rise to the top," told a group of students that "There is no doubt that it is becoming harder and harder as business gravitates more and more to immense concerns for a young man without capital to get a start for himself." Cited in H. J. Perkinson, *The Imperfect Panacea: American Faith in Education, 1865-1965* (New York: Random House, 1968), p. 120. Ironically, one of the few spheres in which "free enterprise," with relatively little capital and high returns on investment, is still possible is in the illegal merchandising of drugs.

46. Erik H. Erikson, "The Problem of Ego Identity," in Gold and Douvan, *Adolescent Development*, p. 19; reprinted from *Identity and the Life Cycle* (New York: International Universities Press, 1959).

47. In his foreword to Musgrove, *Youth and the Social Order*, p. xix: "Do they really believe that all preparation for life must, in the nature of things, take for its model the process of becoming a thirty-second degree Mason?"

48. Jerry Farber, *The Student as Nigger* (New York: Pocket Books, 1970).

49. Ellen Lurie, *How to Change the Schools: A Parents' Action Handbook on How to Fight the System* (New York: Vintage Books, 1970).

50. Article 26-3.

51. Naomi Feigelson, ed., *The Underground Revolution: Hippies, Yippies and Others* (New York: Funk and Wagnalls, 1970).

52. Since the time that I wrote this the amendment reducing the voting age to eighteen has been ratified. I am of the opinion that it will have important consequences bearing on the considerations in this essay.

The Triumph of Benevolence: The Origins of the Juvenile Justice System in the United States

Anthony Platt

The Child-Saving Movement

Although the modern juvenile justice system can be traced in part to the development of various charitable and institutional programs in the early nineteenth century,[1] it was not until the close of the century that the modern system was systematically organized to include juvenile courts, probation, child guidance clinics, truant officers, and reformatories. The child-saving movement—an amalgam of philanthropists, middle-class reformers and professionals—was responsible for the consolidation of these reforms.[2]

The 1890s represented for many middle-class intellectuals and professionals a period of discovery of "dim attics and damp cellars in poverty-stricken sections of populous towns" and "innumerable haunts of misery throughout the land."[3] The city was suddenly discovered to be a place of scarcity, disease, neglect, ignorance, and "dangerous influences." Its slums were the "last resorts of the penniless and the criminal"; here humanity reached the lowest level of degradation and despair.[4] These conditions were not new to American urban life and the working class had been suffering such hardships for many years. Since the Haymarket Riot of 1886, the centers of industrial activity had been continually plagued by strikes, violent disruptions, and widespread business failures.

What distinguished the late 1890s from earlier periods was the recognition by some sectors of the privileged classes that far-reaching economic, political and social reforms were desperately needed to restore order and stability. In the economy, these reforms were achieved through the corporation which extended its influence into all aspects of domestic and foreign policies so that by the 1940s some 139 corporations owned 45 percent of all the manufacturing assets in the country. It was the aim of corporate capitalists to limit traditional laissez-faire business competition and to transform the economy into a rational and interrelated system, characterized by extensive long-range planning and bureaucratic routine.[5] In politics, these reforms were achieved nationally by extending the regulatory powers of the federal government and locally by the development of commission and city manager forms of government as an antidote to corrupt machine politics. In social life, economic and political reforms were paralleled by the construction of new social service bureaucracies which regulated crime, education, health, labor and welfare.

The child-saving movement tried to do for the criminal justice system what industrialists and corporate leaders were trying to do for the economy—that is, achieve order, stability and control while preserving the existing class system and distribution of wealth. While the child-saving movement, like most Progressive reforms, drew its most active and visible supporters from the middle class and professions, it would not have been capable of achieving significant reforms without the financial and political support of the wealthy and powerful. Such support was not without precedent in various philanthropic movements preceding the child-savers. New York's Society for the Reformation of Juvenile Delinquents benefited

[1] For discussions of earlier reform movements, see Pickett, *loc. cit.* and Sanford J. Fox, "Juvenile Justice Reform: An Historical Perspective," 22 *Stanford Law Review,* (June, 1970), pp. 1187–1239.

[2] The child-saving movement was broad and diverse, including reformers interested in child welfare, education, reformatories, labor and other related issues. This paper is limited primarily to child-savers involved in anti-delinquency reforms and should not be interpreted as characterizing the child-saving movement in general.

[3] William P. Letchworth, "Children of the State," National Conference of Charities and Correction, *Proceedings* (St. Paul, Minnesota, 1886), p. 138.

[4] R. W. Hill, "The Children of Shinbone Alley," National Conference of Charities and Correction, *Proceedings* (Omaha, 1887), p. 231.

[5] William Appleman Williams, *The Contours of American History* (Chicago: Quadrangle Books, 1966), especially pp. 345–412.

From Richard Quinney, ed., *Criminal Justice in America* (Boston: Little Brown, 1974), pp. 366–384. Reprinted by permission of the author.

in the 1820s from the contributions of Stephen Allen, whose many influential positions included Mayor of New York and president of the New York Life Insurance and Trust Company.[6] The first large gift to the New York Children's Aid Society, founded in 1853, was donated by Mrs. William Astor.[7] According to Charles Loring Brace, who helped to found the Children's Aid Society, "a very superior class of young men consented to serve on our Board of Trustees; men who, in their high principles of duty, and in the obligations which they feel are imposed by wealth and position, bid fair hereafter to make the name of New York merchants respected as it was never before throughout the country."[8] Elsewhere, welfare charities similarly benefited from the donations and wills of the upper class.[9] Girard College, one of the first large orphanages in the United States, was built and furnished with funds from the banking fortune of Stephen Girard;[10] and the Catholic bankers and financiers of New York helped to mobilize support and money for various Catholic charities.[11]

The child-saving movement similarly enjoyed the support of propertied and powerful individuals. In Chicago, for example, where the movement had some of its most notable successes, the child-savers included Louise Bowen and Ellen Henrotin who were both married to bankers;[12] Mrs. Potter Palmer, whose husband owned vast amounts of land and property, was an ardent child-saver when not involved in the exclusive Fortnightly Club, the elite Chicago Woman's Club or the Board of Lady Managers of the World's Fair;[13] another child-saver in Chicago, Mrs. Perry Smith, was married to the vice-president of the Chicago and Northwestern Railroad. Even the more radically-minded child-savers came from upper-class backgrounds. The fathers of Jane Addams and Julia Lathrop, for example, were both lawyers and Republican senators in the Illinois legislature. Jane Addams' father was one of the richest men in northern Illinois, and her stepbrother, Harry Haldeman, was a socialite from Baltimore who later amassed a large fortune in Kansas City.[14]

The child-saving movement was not simply a humanistic enterprise on behalf of the lower classes against the established order. On the contrary, its impetus came primarily from the middle and upper classes who were instrumental in devising new forms of social control to protect their privileged positions in American society. The child-saving movement was not an isolated phenomenon but rather reflected massive changes in productive relationships, from laissez-faire to monopoly capitalism, and in strategies of social control, from inefficient repression to welfare state benevolence.[15] This reconstruction of economic and social institutions, which was not achieved without conflict within the ruling class, represented a victory for the more "enlightened" wing of corporate leaders who advocated strategic alliances with urban reformers and support of liberal reforms.[16]

Many large corporations and business leaders, for example, supported federal regulation of the economy in order to protect their own investments and stabilize the marketplace. Business leaders and political spokesmen were often in basic agreement about fundamental economic issues. "There was no conspiracy during the Progressive Era," notes Gabriel Kolko. "There was basic agreement among political and business leaders as to what was the public good, and no one had to be cajoled in a sinister manner."[17] In his analysis of liberal ideology in the Progressive era, James Weinstein similarly argues that "few reforms were enacted without the tacit approval, if not the guidance, of the large corporate interests." For the corporation executives, liberalism meant "the responsibility of all classes to maintain and increase the efficiency of the existing social order."[18]

Progressivism was in part a businessmen's movement and big business played a central role in the Progressive coalition's support of welfare reforms. Child labor legislation in New York, for example, was supported by several groups, including upper-class industrialists who did not depend on cheap child labor. According to Jeremy Felt's history of that movement, "the abolition of child labor could be viewed as a means of driving out marginal manufacturers and tenement operators, hence increasing the consolidation and efficiency of business."[19] The rise of compulsory education, another welfare state reform, was also closely tied to the changing forms of industrial production and social control. Charles Loring Brace,

6 Pickett, *op. cit.*, pp. 50–55.

7 Committee on the History of Child-Saving Work, *History of Child-Saving in the United States* (National Conference of Charities and Correction, 1893), p. 5.

8 Charles Loring Brace, *The Dangerous Classes of New York and Twenty Years' Work Among Them* (New York: Wynkoop and Hallenbeck, 1880), pp. 282–83.

9 Committee on the History of Child-Saving Work, *op. cit.*, pp. 70–73.

10 *Ibid.*, pp. 80–81.

11 *Ibid.*, p. 270.

12 For more about these child-savers, see Anthony Platt, *The Child-Savers: The Invention of Delinquency*, (Chicago: University of Chicago Press, 1969), pp. 75–100.

13 Louise C. Wade, *Graham Taylor: Pioneer for Social Justice, 1851–1938* (Chicago: University of Chicago Press, 1964), p. 59.

14 G. William Domhoff, *The Higher Circles: The Governing Class in America* (New York: Random House, 1970), p. 48 and Platt, *op. cit.*, pp. 92–98.

15 "The transformation in penal systems cannot be explained only from changing needs of the war against crime, although this struggle does play a part. Every system of production tends to discover punishments which correspond to its productive relationships. It is thus necessary to investigate the origin and fate of penal systems, the use or avoidance of specific punishments, and the intensity of penal practices as they are determined by social forces, above all by economic and then fiscal forces." Georg Rusche and Otto Kirchheimer, *Punishment and Social Structure*, (New York: Russell & Russell, 1968), p. 5.

16 See, for example, Gabriel Kolko, *The Triumph of Conservatism: A Reinterpretation of American History, 1900–1916* (Chicago: Quadrangle Books, 1967); James Weinstein, *The Corporate Ideal in the Liberal State, 1900–1918* (Boston: Beacon Press, 1969); Samuel Haber, *Efficiency and Uplift: Scientific Management in the Progressive Era, 1890–1920* (Chicago: University of Chicago Press, 1964); and Robert H. Wiebe, *Businessmen and Reform: A Study of the Progressive Movement* (Cambridge: Harvard University Press, 1962).

17 Kolko, *op. cit.*, p. 282.

18 Weinstein, *op. cit.*, pp. ix, xi.

19 Jeremy P. Felt, *Hostages of Fortune: Child Labor Reform in New York State* (Syracuse: Syracuse University Press, 1965), p. 45.

writing in the mid-nineteenth century, anticipated the use of education as preparation for industrial discipline when, "in the interests of public order, of liberty, of property for the sake of our own safety and the endurance of free institutions here," he advocated "a strict and careful law, which shall compel every minor to learn and read and write, under severe penalties in case of disobedience."[20] By the end of the century, the working class had imposed upon them a sterile and authoritarian educational system which mirrored the ethos of the corporate workplace and was designed to provide "an increasingly refined training and selection mechanism for the labor force."[21]

While the child-saving movement was supported and financed by corporate liberals, the day-to-day work of lobbying, public education and organizing was undertaken by middle-class urban reformers, professionals and special interest groups. The more moderate and conservative sectors of the feminist movement were especially active in anti-delinquency reforms.[22] Their successful participation derived in part from public stereotypes of women as the "natural caretakers" of "wayward children." Women's claim to the public care of children had precedent during the nineteenth century and their role in child rearing was paramount. Women, generally regarded as better teachers than men, were more influential in child-training and discipline at home. The fact that public education also came more under the direction of women teachers in the schools served to legitimize the predominance of women in other areas of "child-saving."[23]

The child-saving movement attracted women from a variety of political and class backgrounds, though it was dominated by the daughters of the old landed gentry and wives of the upper-class nouveau riche. Career women and society philanthropists, elite women's clubs and settlement houses, and political and civic organizations worked together on the problems of child care, education and juvenile delinquency. Professional and political women's groups regarded child-saving as a problem of women's rights, whereas their opponents seized upon it as an opportunity to keep women in their "proper place." Child-saving became a reputable task for any woman who wanted to extend her "housekeeping" functions into the community without denying anti-feminist stereotypes of woman's nature and place.[24]

For traditionally educated women and daughters of the landed and industrial gentry, the child-saving movement presented an opportunity for pursuing socially acceptable public roles and for restoring some of the authority and spiritual influence which many women felt they had lost through the urbanization of family life. Their traditional functions were dramatically threatened by the weakening of domestic roles and the specialized rearrangement of the family.[25] The child-savers were aware that their championship of social outsiders such as immigrants, the poor and children, was not wholly motivated by disinterested ideals of justice and equality. Philanthropic work filled a void in their own lives, a void which was created in part by the decline of traditional religion, increased leisure and boredom, the rise of public education, and the breakdown of communal life in large, crowded cities. "By simplifying dress and amusements, by cutting off a little here and there from our luxuries," wrote one child-saver, "we may change the whole current of many human lives."[26] Women were exhorted to make their lives useful by participating in welfare programs, by volunteering their time and services, and by getting acquainted with less privileged groups. They were also encouraged to seek work in institutions which were "like family-life with its many-sided development and varied interests and occupations, and where the woman-element shall pervade the house and soften its social atmosphere with motherly tenderness."[27]

While the child-saving movement can be partly understood as a "symbolic crusade"[28] which served ceremonial and status functions for many women, it was by no means a reactionary and romantic movement, nor was it supported only by women and members of the old gentry. Child-saving also had considerable instrumental significance for legitimizing new career openings for women. The new role of social worker combined elements of an old and partly fictitious role–defender of family life–and elements of a new role–social servant. Social work and professional child-saving provided new opportunities for career-minded women who found the traditional professions dominated and controlled by men.[29] These child-savers

---

[20] Brace, *op. cit.*, p. 352.

[21] David K. Cohen and Marvin Lazerson, "Education and the Corporate Order," 8 *Socialist Revolution,* (March–April, 1972), p. 50. See, also Michael B. Katz, *The Irony of Early School Reform: Educational Innovation in Mid-Nineteenth Century Massachusetts,* (Cambridge: Harvard University Press, 1968), and Lawrence A. Cremin. *The Transformation of the School: Progressivism in American Education, 1876–1957,* (New York: Vintage, 1961).

[22] It should be emphasized that child-saving reforms were predominantly supported by more privileged sectors of the feminist movement, especially those who had an interest in developing professional careers in education, social work and probation. In recent years, radical feminists have emphasized that "we must include the oppression of children in any program for feminist revolution or we will be subject to the same failing of which we have so often accused men: of not having gone deep enough in our analysis, of having missed an important substratum of oppression merely because it didn't directly concern *us*." Shulamith Firestone, *The Dialectic of Sex: The Case for Feminist Evolution,* (New York: Bantam, 1971), p. 104.

[23] Robert Sunley, "Early Nineteenth Century American Literature on Child-Rearing," in Margaret Mead and Martha Wolfenstein (Eds.), *Childhood in Contemporary Cultures* (Chicago: University of Chicago Press, 1955), p. 152; see, also, Orville G. Brim, *Education for Child-Rearing* (New York: Free Press, 1965), pp. 321–49.

[24] For an extended discussion of this issue, See Platt, *loc. cit.* and Christopher Lasch, *The New Radicalism in America, 1889–1963: The Intellectual as a Social Type,* (New York: Alfred A. Knopf, 1965), pp. 3–68.

[25] Talcott Parsons and Robert F. Bales, *Family, Socialization and Interaction Process* (Glencoe, Illinois: Free Press, 1955), p. 3–33.

[26] Clara T. Leonard, "Family Homes for Pauper and Dependent Children," Annual Conference of Charities, *Proceedings* (Chicago, 1879), p. 175.

[27] W. P. Lynde, "Prevention in Some of its Aspects," *Ibid.*, pp. 165–166.

[28] Joseph R. Gusfield, *Symbolic Crusade, loc. cit.*

[29] See, generally, Roy Lubove, *The Professional Altruist: The Emergence of Social Work as a Career, 1880–1930* (Cambridge: Harvard University Press, 1965).

were members of the emerging bourgeoisie created by the new industrial order.

It is not surprising that the professions also supported the child-saving movement, for they were capable of reaping enormous economic and status rewards from the changes taking place. The clergy had nothing to lose (but more of their rapidly declining constituency) and everything to gain by incorporating social services into traditional religion. Lawyers were needed for their technical expertise and to administer new institutions. And academics discovered a new market which paid them as consultants, elevated them to positions of national prestige and furnished endless materials for books, articles and conferences. As Richard Hofstadter has noted:

The development of regulative and humane legislation required the skills of lawyers and economists, sociologists and political scientists, in the writing of laws and in the staffing of administrative and regulative bodies. Controversy over such issues created a new market for the books and magazine articles of the experts and engendered a new respect for their specialized knowledge. Reform brought with it the brain trust.[30]

While the rank and file reformers in the child-saving movement worked closely with corporate liberals, it would be inaccurate to simply characterize them as lackeys of big business. Many were principled and genuinely concerned about alleviating human misery and improving the lives of the poor. Moreover, many women who participated in the movement were able to free themselves from male domination and participate more fully in society. But for the most part, the child-savers and other Progressive reformers defended capitalism and rejected socialist alternatives. Most reformers accepted the structure of the new industrial order and sought to moderate its cruder inequities and reduce inharmonies in the existing system.[31] Though many child-savers were "socialists of the heart" and ardent critics of society, their programs were typically reformist and did not alter basic economic inequalities.[32] Rhetoric and righteous indignation were more prevalent than programs of radical action.

The intellectual and professional communities did little to criticize Progressive reforms, partly because so many benefited from their new role as government consultants and experts, and partly because their conception of social change was limited and elitist. As Jackson Wilson observed, many intellectuals in the Progressive movement were "interested in creating a system of government which would allow the people to rule only at a carefully kept distance and at infrequent intervals, reserving most real power and planning to a corps of experts and professionals."[33] Those few reformers who had a genuine concern for liberating the lives of the poor by considering socialist alternatives were either coopted by their allies, betrayed by their own class interests, or became the prisoners of social and economic forces beyond their control.[34]

Images of Crime and Delinquency

The child-saving reformers were part of a much larger movement to readjust institutions to conform to the requirements of corporate capitalism and the modern welfare state. As the country emerged from the depressions and industrial violence of the late nineteenth century, efforts were made to rescue and regulate capitalism through developing a new political economy, designed to stabilize production and profits. The stability and smooth functioning of this new order depended heavily on the capacity of welfare state institutions, especially the schools, to achieve cultural hegemony and guarantee loyalty to the State. As William Appleman Williams has commented, "it is almost impossible to overemphasize the importance of the very general—yet dynamic and powerful—concept that the country faced a fateful choice between order and chaos."[35] In order to develop support for and legitimize the corporate liberal State, a new ideology was promoted in which chaos was equated with crime and violence, and salvation was to be found in the development of new and more extensive forms of social control.

The child-savers viewed the "criminal classes" with a mixture of contempt and benevolence. Crime was portrayed as rising from the "lowest orders" and threatening to engulf "respectable" society like a virulent disease. Charles Loring Brace, a leading child-saver, typified popular and professional views about crime and delinquency:

As Christian men, we cannot look upon this great multitude of unhappy, deserted, and degraded boys and girls without feeling our responsibility to God for them. The class increases: immigration is pouring in its multitudes of poor foreigners who leave these young outcasts everywhere in our midst. These boys and girls . . . will soon form the great lower class of our city. They will influence elections; they may shape the policy of the city; they will assuredly, if unreclaimed, poison society all around them. They will help to form the great multitude of robbers, thieves, and vagrants, who are now such a burden upon the law-respecting community. . . .[36]

This attitude of contempt derived from a view of criminals as less-than-human, a perspective which was strongly influenced and aggravated by nativist and racist ideologies.[37] The "criminal class" was variously described as "creatures" living in "burrows," "dens," and "slime"; as "little Arabs" and "foreign childhood that floats along the streets and docks of the city—vagabondish, thievish, familiar with the vicious ways and

[30] Hofstadter, *op. cit.*, p. 155.

[31] Williams, *op. cit.*, p. 373 and Weinstein, *op. cit.*, p. 254.

[32] Williams, *op. cit.*, pp. 374, 395–402.

[33] R. Jackson Wilson, "United States: the Reassessment of Liberalism," *Journal of Contemporary History* (January, 1967), p. 96.

[34] Ralph Miliband, *The State in Capitalist Society*, (New York: Basic Books, 1969), pp. 265–277.

[35] Williams, *op. cit.*, p. 356.

[36] Committee on the History of Child-Saving Work, *op. cit.*, p. 3.

[37] See, generally, John Higham, *Strangers in the Land: Patterns of American Nativism, 1860–1925* (New York: Atheneum, 1965).

places of the town";[38] and as "ignorant," "shiftless," "indolent," and "dissipated."[39]

The child-savers were alarmed and frightened by the "dangerous classes" whose "very number makes one stand aghast," noted the urban reformer Jacob Riis.[40] Law and order were widely demanded:

The "dangerous classes" of New York are mainly American-born, but the children of Irish and German immigrants. They are as ignorant as London flashmen or costermongers. They are far more brutal than the peasantry from whom they descend, and they are much banded together, in associations, such as "Dead Rabbit," "Plug-ugly," and various target companies. They are our enfant perdus, *grown up to young manhood. . . . They are ready for any offense or crime, however degraded or bloody. . . . Let but Law lift its hand from them for a season, or let the civilizing influences of American life fail to reach them, and, if the opportunity offered, we should see an explosion from this class which might leave this city in ashes and blood.*[41]

These views derived considerable legitimacy from prevailing theories of social and reform Darwinism which, *inter alia,* proposed that criminals were a dangerous and atavistic class, standing outside the boundaries of morally regulated relationships. Herbert Spencer's writings had a major impact on American intellectuals and Cesare Lombroso, perhaps the most significant figure in nineteenth century criminology, looked for recognition in the United States when he felt that his experiments on the "criminal type" had been neglected in Europe.[42]

Although Lombroso's theoretical and experimental studies were not translated into English until 1911, his findings were known by American academics in the early 1890s, and their popularity, like that of Spencer's works, was based on the fact that they confirmed widely-held stereotypes about the biological basis and inferior character of a "criminal class." A typical view was expressed by Nathan Allen in 1878 at the National Conference of Charities and Correction: "If our object is to prevent crime in a large scale, we must direct attention to its main sources—to the materials that make criminals; the springs must be dried up; the supplies must be cut off."[43] This was to be achieved, if necessary, by birth control and eugenics. Similar views were expressed by Hamilton Wey, an influential physician at Elmira Reformatory, who argued before the National Prison Association in 1881 that criminals had to be treated as a "distinct type of human species."[44]

Literature on "social degradation" was extremely popular during the 1870s and 1880s, though most such "studies" were little more than crude and racist polemics, padded with moralistic epithets and preconceived value judgments. Richard Dugdale's series of papers on the Jukes family, which became a model for the case-study approach to social problems, was distorted almost beyond recognition by anti-intellectual supporters of hereditary theories of crime.[45] Confronted by the evidence of Darwin, Galton, Dugdale, Caldwell and many other disciples of the biological image of behavior, many child-savers were compelled to admit that "a large proportion of the unfortunate children that go to make up the great army of criminals are not born right."[46] Reformers adopted and modified the rhetoric of social Darwinism in order to emphasize the urgent need for confronting the "crime problem" before it got completely out of hand. A popular proposal, for example, was the "methodized registration and training" of potential criminals, "or these failing, their early and entire withdrawal from the community."[47]

Although some child-savers advocated drastic methods of crime control—including birth control through sterilization, cruel punishments, and life-long incarceration—more moderate views prevailed. This victory for moderation was related to the recognition by many Progressive reformers that short-range repression was counter-productive as well as cruel and that long-range planning and amelioration were required to achieve economic and political stability. The rise of more benevolent strategies of social control occurred at about the same time that influential capitalists were realizing that existing economic arrangements could not be successfully maintained only through the use of private police and government troops.[48] While the child-savers justified their reforms as humanitarian, it is clear that this humanitarianism reflected their class background and elitist conceptions of human potentiality. The child-savers shared the view of more conservative professionals that "criminals" were a distinct and dangerous class, indigenous to working-class culture, and a threat to "civilized" society. They differed mainly in the procedures by which the "criminal class" should be controlled or neutralized.

Gradually, a more "enlightened" view about strategies of control prevailed among the leading representatives of professional associations. Correctional workers, for example, did not want to think of themselves merely as the custodians of a

---

[38] Brace, *op. cit.,* pp. 30, 49; Bradford Kinney Peirce, *A Half Century with Juvenile Delinquents* (Montclair, New Jersey: Patterson Smith, 1969, originally published 1869), p. 253.

[39] Nathan Allen, "Prevention of Crime and Pauperism," Annual Conference of Charities, *Proceedings* (Cincinnati, 1878), pp. 111–24.

[40] Jacob A. Riis, *How the Other Half Lives* (New York: Hill and Wang, 1957, originally published in 1890), p. 134.

[41] Brace, *op. cit.,* pp. 27, 29.

[42] See, for example, Lombroso's comments in the Introduction to Arthur MacDonald, *Criminology* (New York: Funk and Wagnalls, 1893).

[43] Allen, *loc. cit.*

[44] Hamilton D. Wey, "A Plea for Physical Training of Youthful Criminals," National Prison Association, *Proceedings* (Boston: 1888), pp. 181–93. For further discussion of this issue, see Platt, *op. cit.,* pp. 18–28 and Arthur E. Fink, *Causes of Crime: Biological Theories in the United States, 1800–1915* (New York: A. S. Barnes, 1962).

[45] Richard L. Dugdale, *The Jukes: A Study in Crime, Pauperism, Disease, and Heredity* (New York: G. P. Putnam's Sons, 1877).

[46] Sarah B. Cooper, "The Kindergarten as Child-Saving Work," National Conference of Charities and Correction, *Proceedings* (Madison, 1883), pp. 130–38.

[47] I. N. Kerlin, "The Moral Imbecile," National Conference of Charities and Correction, *Proceedings* (Baltimore, 1890), pp. 244–50.

[48] Williams, *op. cit.,* p. 354.

pariah class. The self-image of penal reformers as "doctors" rather than "guards," and the medical domination of criminological research in the United States at that time facilitated the acceptance of "therapeutic" strategies in prisons and reformatories.[49] Physicians gradually provided the official rhetoric of penal reform, replacing cruder concepts of social Darwinism with a new optimism. Admittedly, the criminal was "pathological" and "diseased," but medical science offered the possibility of miraculous cures. Although there was a popular belief in the existence of a "criminal class" separated from the rest of humanity by a "vague boundary line," there was no good reason why this class could not be identified, diagnosed, segregated, changed and incorporated back into society.[50]

By the late 1890s, most child-savers agreed that hereditary theories of crime were overfatalistic. The superintendent of the Kentucky Industrial School of Reform, for example, told delegates to a national conference on corrections that heredity is "unjustifiably made a bugaboo to discourage efforts at rescue. We know that physical heredity tendencies can be neutralized and often nullified by proper counteracting precautions."[51] E. R. L. Gould, a sociologist at the University of Chicago, similarly criticized biological theories of crime as unconvincing and sentimental. "Is it not better," he said, "to postulate freedom of choice than to preach the doctrine of the unfettered will, and so elevate criminality into a propitiary sacrifice?"[52]

Charles Cooley, writing in 1896, was one of the first American sociologists to observe that criminal behavior depended as much upon social and economic circumstances as it did upon the inheritance of biological traits. "The criminal class," he observed, "is largely the result of society's bad workmanship upon fairly good material." In support of this argument, he noted that there was a "large and fairly trustworthy body of evidence" to suggest that many "degenerates" could be converted into "useful citizens by rational treatment."[53]

Although there was a wide difference of opinion among experts as to the precipitating causes of crime, it was generally agreed that criminals were abnormally conditioned by a multitude of biological and environmental forces, some of which were permanent and irreversible. Strictly biological theories of crime were modified to incorporate a developmental view of human behavior. If, as it was believed, criminals are conditioned by biological heritage and brutish living conditions, then prophylactic measures must be taken early in life. "We must get hold of the little waifs that grow up to form the criminal element just as early in life as possible," exhorted an influential child-saver. "Hunt up the children of poverty, of crime, and of brutality, just as soon as they can be reached."[54] Efforts were needed to reach the criminals of future generations. "They are born to crime," wrote the penologist Enoch Wines, "brought up for it. They must be saved."[55] New institutions and new programs were required to meet this challenge.

Juvenile Court and the Reformatory System

The essential preoccupation of the child-saving movement was the recognition and control of youthful deviance. It brought attention to, and thus "invented" new categories of youthful misbehavior which had been hitherto unappreciated. The efforts of the child-savers were institutionally expressed in the juvenile court which, despite recent legislative and constitutional reforms, is generally acknowledged as their most significant contribution to progressive penology. There is some dispute about which state first created a special tribunal for children. Massachusetts and New York passed laws, in 1874 and 1892 respectively, providing for the trials of minors apart from adults charged with crimes. Ben Lindsey, a renowned judge and reformer, also claimed this distinction for Colorado where a juvenile court was, in effect, established through an educational law of 1899. However, most authorities agree that the Juvenile Court Act, passed by the Illinois legislature in the same year, was the first official enactment to be recognized as a model statute by other states and countries.[56] By 1917, juvenile court legislation had been passed in all but three states and by 1932 there were over 600 independent juvenile courts throughout the United States.[57]

The juvenile court system was part of a general movement directed towards developing a specialized labor market and industrial discipline under corporate capitalism by creating new programs of adjudication and control for "delinquent," "dependent" and "neglected" youth. This in turn was related to augmenting the family and enforcing compulsory education in order to guarantee the proper reproduction of the labor force. For example, underlying the juvenile court system was the concept of *parens patriae* by which the courts were authorized to handle with wide discretion the problems of "its least fortunate junior citizens."[58] The administration of juvenile

[49]Fink, *op. cit.*, p. 247.

[50]See, for example, Illinois Board of State Commissioners of Public Charities, *Second Biennial Report* (Springfield: State Journal Steam Print, 1873), pp. 195–96.

[51]Peter Caldwell, "The Duty of the State to Delinquent Children," National Conference of Charities and Correction, *Proceedings* (New York, 1898), pp. 404–10.

[52]E. R. L. Gould, "The Statistical Study of Hereditary Criminality," National Conference of Charities and Correction, *Proceedings* (New Haven, 1895), pp. 134–43.

[53]Charles H. Cooley, "'Nature' v. 'Nurture' in the Making of Social Careers," National Conference of Charities and Correction. *Proceedings* (Grand Rapids, 1896), pp. 399–405.

[54]Committee on the History of Child-Saving Work, *op. cit.*, p. 90.

[55]Enoch C. Wines, *The State of Prisons and of Child-Saving Institutions in the Civilized World*, (Cambridge: Harvard University Press, 1880).

[56]Helen Page Bates, "Digest of Statutes Relating to Juvenile Courts and Probation Systems," 13 *Charities* (January, 1905), pp. 329–36.

[57]Joel F. Handler, "The Juvenile Court and the Adversary System: Problems of Function and Form," 1965 *Wisconsin Law Review* (1965), pp. 7–51.

[58]Gustav L. Schramm, "The Juvenile Court Idea," 13 *Federal Probation* (September, 1949), p. 21.

justice, which differed in many important respects from the criminal court system, was delegated extensive powers of control over youth. A child was not accused of a crime but offered assistance and guidance; intervention in the lives of "delinquents" was not supposed to carry the stigma of criminal guilt. Judicial records were not generally available to the press or public, and juvenile hearings were typically conducted in private. Court procedures were informal and inquisitorial, not requiring the presence of a defense attorney. Specific criminal safeguards of due process were not applicable because juvenile proceedings were defined by statute as civil in character.[59]

The judges of the new court were empowered to investigate the character and social background of "predelinquent" as well as delinquent children; they concerned themselves with motivation rather than intent, seeking to identify the moral reputation of problematic children. The requirements of preventive penology and child-saving further justified the court's intervention in cases where no offense had actually been committed, but where, for example, a child was posing problems for some person in authority, such as a parent or teacher or social worker.

The role model for juvenile court judges was doctor-counselor rather than lawyer. "Judicial therapists" were expected to establish a one-to-one relationship with "delinquents" in the same way that a country doctor might give his time and attention to a favorite patient. Juvenile courtrooms were often arranged like a clinic and the vocabulary of its participants was largely composed of medical metaphors. "We do not know the child without a thorough examination," wrote Judge Julian Mack. "We must reach into the soul-life of the child."[60] Another judge from Los Angeles suggested that the juvenile court should be a "laboratory of human behavior" and its judges trained as "specialists in the art of human relations." It was the judge's task to "get the whole truth about a child" in the same way that a "physician searches for every detail that bears on the condition of the patient."[61] Similarly, the judges of the Boston juvenile court liked to think of themselves as "physicians in a dispensary"[62].

The unique character of the child-saving movement was its concerns for predelinquent offenders—"children who occupy the debatable ground between criminality and innocence"—and its claim that it could transform potential criminals into respectable citizens by training them in "habits of industry, self-control and obedience to law."[63] This policy justified the diminishing of traditional procedures and allowed police, judges, probation officers and truant officers to work together without legal hindrance. If children were to be rescued, it was important that the rescuers be free to pursue their mission without the interference of defense lawyers and due process. Delinquents had to be saved, transformed and reconstituted. "There is no essential difference," noted a prominent child-saver, "between a criminal and any other sinner. The means and methods of restoration are the same for both."[64]

The juvenile court legislation enabled the state to investigate and control a wide variety of behaviors. As Joel Handler has observed, "the critical philosophical position of the reform movement was that no formal, legal distinctions should be made between the delinquent and the dependent or neglected."[65] Statutory definitions of "delinquency" encompassed (1) acts that would be criminal if committed by adults; (2) acts that violated county, town, or municipal ordinances; and (3) violations of vaguely worded catch-alls—such as "vicious or immoral behavior," "incorrigibility," and "truancy"—which "seem to express the notion that the adolescent, if allowed to continue, will engage in more serious conduct."[66]

The juvenile court movement went far beyond a concern for special treatment of adolescent offenders. It brought within the ambit of governmental control a set of youthful activities that had been previously ignored or dealt with on an informal basis. It was not by accident that the behavior subject to penalties—drinking, sexual "license," roaming the streets, begging, frequenting dance halls and movies, fighting, and being seen in public late at night—was especially characteristic of the children of working-class and immigrant families. Once arrested and adjudicated, these "delinquents" became wards of the court and eligible for salvation.

It was through the reformatory system that the child-savers hoped to demonstrate that delinquents were capable of being converted into law-abiding citizens. Though the reformatory was initially developed in the United States during the middle of the nineteenth century as a special form of prison discipline for adolescents and young adults, its underlying principles were formulated in Britain by Matthew Davenport Hill, Alexander Maconochie, Walter Crofton and Mary Carpenter. If the United States did not have any great penal theorists, it at least had energetic administrators—like Enoch Wines, Zebulon Brockway and Frank Sanborn—who were prepared to experiment with new programs.

The reformatory was distinguished from the traditional penitentiary in several ways: it adopted a policy of indeterminate sentencing; it emphasized the importance of a country-side location; and it typically was organized on the "cottage" plan as opposed to the traditional congregate housing found in penitentiaries. The ultimate aim of the reformatory was

[59] Monrad G. Paulsen, "Fairness to the Juvenile Offender," 41 *Minnesota Law Review* (1957), pp. 547–67.

[60] Julian W. Mack, "The Chancery Procedure in the Juvenile Court," in Jane Addams (Ed.), *The Child, the Clinic and the Court* (New York: New Republic, 1925), p. 315.

[61] Miriam Van Waters, "The Socialization of Juvenile Court Procedure," 21 *Journal of Criminal Law and Criminology* (1922), pp. 61, 69.

[62] Harvey H. Baker, "Procedure of the Boston Juvenile Court," 23 *Survey* (February, 1910), p. 646.

[63] Illinois Board of State Commissioners of Public Charities, *Sixth Biennial Report* (Springfield: H. W. Rokker, 1880), p. 104.

[64] Frederick H. Wines, "Reformation as an End in Prison Discipline," National Conference of Charities and Correction, *Proceedings* (Buffalo, 1888), p. 198.

[65] Joel F. Handler, *op. cit.*, p. 9.

[66] Joel F. Handler and Margaret K. Rosenheim, "Privacy and Welfare: Public Assistance and Juvenile Justice," 31 *Law and Contemporary Problems* (1966), pp. 377–412.

reformation of the criminal, which could only be achieved "by placing the prisoner's fate, as far as possible, in his own hand, by enabling him, through industry and good conduct to raise himself, step by step, to a position of less restraint. . . ."[67]

Based on a crude theory of rewards and punishments, the "new penology" set itself the task of re-socializing the "dangerous classes." The typical resident of a reformatory, according to one child-saver, had been "cradled in infamy, imbibing with its earliest natural nourishment the germs of a depraved appetite, and reared in the midst of people whose lives are an atrocious crime against natural and divine law and the rights of society." In order to correct and reform such a person, the reformatory plan was designed to teach the value of adjustment, private enterprise, thrift and self-reliance. "To make a good boy out of this bundle of perversities, his entire being must be revolutionized. He must be taught self-control, industry, respect for himself and the rights of others."[68] The real test of reformation in a delinquent, as William Letchworth told the National Conference of Charities and Correction in 1886, was his uncomplaining adjustment to his former environment. "If he is truly reformed in the midst of adverse influences," said Letchworth, "he gains that moral strength which makes his reform permanent."[69] Moreover, reformed delinquents were given every opportunity to rise "far above the class from which they sprang," especially if they were "patient" and "self-denying."[70]

Reformation of delinquents was to be achieved in a number of different ways. The trend from congregate housing to group living represented a significant change in the organization of penal institutions. The "cottage" plan was designed to provide more intensive supervision and to reproduce, symbolically at least, an atmosphere of family life conducive to the re-socialization of youth. The "new penology" also urged the benefits of a rural location, partly in order to teach agricultural skills, but mainly in order to guarantee a totally controlled environment. This was justified by appealing to the romantic theory that corrupt delinquents would be spiritually regenerated by their contact with unspoiled nature.[71]

Education was stressed as the main form of industrial and moral training in reformatories. According to Michael Katz, in his study on nineteenth-century education, the reformatory provided "the first form of compulsory schooling in the United States."[72] The prominence of education as a technique of reform reflected the widespread emphasis on socialization and assimilation instead of cruder methods of social control. But as Georg Rusche and Otto Kirchheimer observed in their study of the relationship between economic and penal policies, the rise of "rehabilitative" and educational programs was "largely the result of opposition on the part of free workers," for "wherever working-class organizations were powerful enough to influence state politics, they succeeded in obtaining complete abolition of all forms of prison labor (Pennsylvania in 1897, for example), causing much suffering to the prisoners, or at least in obtaining very considerable limitations, such as work without modern machinery, conventional rather than modern types of prison industry, or work for the government instead of for the free market."[73]

Although the reformatory system, as envisioned by urban reformers, suffered in practice from overcrowding, mismanagement, inadequate financing and staff hiring problems, its basic ideology was still tough-minded and uncompromising. As the American Friends Service Committee noted, "if the reformers were naive, the managers of the correctional establishment were not. Under the leadership of Zebulon R. Brockway of the Elmira Reformatory, by the latter part of the nineteenth century they had co-opted the reformers and consolidated their leadership and control of indeterminate sentence reform."[74] The child-savers were not averse to using corporal punishment and other severe disciplinary measures when inmates were recalcitrant. Brockway, for example, regarded his task as "socialization of the anti-social by scientific training while under completest governmental control."[75] To achieve this goal, Brockway's reformatory became "like a garrison of a thousand prisoner soldiers" and "every incipient disintegration was promptly checked and disinclination of individual prisoners to conform was overcome."[76] Child-saving was a job for resolute professionals who realized that "sickly sentimentalism" had no place in their work."[77]

"Criminals shall either be cured," Brockway told the National Prison Congress in 1870, "or kept under such continued restraint as gives guarantee of safety from further depredations."[78] Restraint and discipline were an integral part of the "treatment" program and not merely expediencies of administration. Military drill, "training of the will," and long hours of tedious labor were the essence of the reformatory system and the indeterminate sentencing policy guaranteed its smooth operation. "Nothing can tend more certainly to secure the most hardened and desperate criminals than the present system of short sentences," wrote the reformer Bradford Kinney Peirce in 1869.[79] Several years later, Enoch Wines was able to report that "the sentences of young offenders are wisely regulated for their amendment; they are not absurdly shortened as if they signified only so much endurance of vindictive suffering."[80]

---

[67]From a report by Enoch Wines and Theodore Dwight to the New York legislature in 1867, quoted by Max Grünhut, *Penal Reform* (Oxford: Clarendon Press, 1948), p. 90.

[68]*Peter Caldwell, "The Reform School Problem,"* National Conference of Charities and Correction, *Proceedings* (St. Paul, 1886), pp. 71–76.

[69]Letchworth, *op. cit.*, p. 152.

[70]Committee on the History of Child-Saving Work, *op. cit.*, p. 20.

[71]See Platt, *op. cit.*, pp. 55–66.

[72]Katz, *op. cit.*, p. 187.

[73]Rusche and Kirchheimer, *op. cit.*, pp. 131–132.

[74]American Friends Service Committee, *op. cit.*, p. 28.

[75]Zebulon R. Brockway, *Fifth Years of Prison Service* (New York: Charities Publication Committee, 1912), p. 393.

[76]*Ibid.*, pp. 310, 421.

[77]*Ibid.*, pp. 389–408.

[78]*Ibid.*

[79]Peirce, *op. cit.*, p. 312.

[80]Enoch Wines, *op. cit.*, p. 81.

Since the child-savers professed to be seeking the "best interests" of their "wards" on the basis of corporate liberal values, there was no need to formulate legal regulation of the right and duty to "treat" in the same way that the right and duty to punish had been previously regulated. The adversary system, therefore, ceased to exist for youth, even as a legal fiction.[81] The myth of the child-saving movement as a humanitarian enterprise is based partly on a superficial interpretation of the child-savers' rhetoric of rehabilitation and partly on a misconception of how the child-savers viewed punishment. While it is true that the child-savers advocated minimal use of corporal punishment, considerable evidence suggests that this recommendation was based on managerial rather than moral considerations. William Letchworth reported that "corporal punishment is rarely inflicted" at the State Industrial School in Rochester because "most of the boys consider the lowering of their standing the severest punishment that is inflicted."[82] Mrs. Glendower Evans, commenting on the decline of whippings at a reform school in Massachusetts, concluded that "when boys do not feel themselves imprisoned and are treated as responsible moral agents, they can be trusted with their freedom to a surprising degree."[83] Officials at another state industrial school for girls also reported that "hysterics and fits of screaming and of noisy disobedience, have of late years become unknown. . . ."[84]

The decline in the use of corporal punishment was due to the fact that indeterminate sentencing, the "mark" or "stage" system of rewards and punishments, and other techniques of "organized persuasion" were far more effective in maintaining order and compliance than cruder methods of control. The chief virtue of the "stage" system, a graduated system of punishments and privileges, was its capacity to keep prisoners disciplined and submissive.[85] The child-savers had learned from industrialists that persuasive benevolence backed up by force was a far more effective device fo social control than arbitrary displays of terrorism. Like an earlier generation of penal reformers in France and Italy, the child-savers stressed the efficacy of new and indirect forms of social control as a "practical measure of defense against social revolution as well as against individual acts."[86]

Although the child-saving movement had far-reaching consequences for the organization and administration of the juvenile justice system, its overall impact was conservative in both spirit and achievement. The child-savers' reforms were generally aimed at imposing sanctions on conduct unbecoming "youth" and disqualifying youth from the benefit of adult privileges. The child-savers were prohibitionists, in a general sense, who believed that social progress depended on efficient law enforcement, strict supervision of children's leisure and recreation, and enforced education. They were primarily concerned with regulating social behavior, eliminating "foreign" and radical ideologies, and preparing youth as a disciplined and devoted work force. The austerity of the criminal law and penal institutions was only of incidental concern; their central interest was in the normative outlook of youth and they were most successful in their efforts to extend governmental control over a whole range of youthful activities which had previously been handled locally and informally. In this sense, their reforms were aimed at defining, rationalizing and regulating the dependent status of youth.[87] Although the child-savers' attitudes to youth were often paternalistic and romantic, their commands were backed up by force and an abiding faith in the benevolence of government.

The child-saving movement had its most direct impact on the children of the urban poor. The fact that "troublesome" adolescents were depicted as "sick" or "pathological," imprisoned "for their own good," addressed in paternalistic vocabulary, and exempted from criminal law processes, did not alter the subjective experiences of control, restraint and punishment. It is ironic, as Philippe Ariès observed in his historical study of European family life, that the obsessive solicitude of family, church, moralists and administrators for child welfare served to deprive children of the freedoms which they had previously shared with adults and to deny their capacity for initiative, responsibility and autonomy.[88]

The child-savers' rhetoric of benevolence should not be mistaken for popular, democratic programs. Paternalism was a typical ingredient of most reforms in the Progressive era, legitimizing imperialism in foreign policy and extensive state control at home. Even the corporate rich, according to William Appleman Williams, "revealed a strikingly firm conception of a benevolent feudal approach to the firm and its workers" and "were willing to extend—to provide in the manner of traditional beneficence—such things as new housing, old age pensions, death payments, wage and job schedules, and bureaus charged with responsibility for welfare, safety, and sanitation."[89] But when benevolence failed—in domestic institutions such as schools and courts or in economic policies abroad—government officials and industrial leaders were quick to resort to massive and overwhelming force.[90]

This is not to suggest that the child-savers and other Pro-

---

[81] On informal cooperation in the criminal courts, see Jerome H. Skolnick, "Social Control in the Adversary System," 11 *Journal of Conflict Resolution,* (March, 1967), pp. 52–70.

[82] Committee on the History of Child-Saving Work, *op, cit.,* p. 20.

[83] *Ibid.,* p. 237.

[84] *Ibid.* p. 251.

[85] Rusche and Kirchheimer, *op. cit.,* pp. 155–156.

[86] *Ibid.,* p. 76. For a similar point, see American Friends Service Committee, *op. cit.,* p. 33.

[87] See, generally, Frank Musgrove, *Youth and the Social Order* (London: *Routledge and Kegan Paul,* 1964).

[88] Philippe Ariès, *Centuries of Childhood: A Social History of Family Life* (New York: Vintage Books, 1965).

[89] Williams, *op. cit.,* p. 382.

[90] On benevolence and repression in foreign policy, see Felix Greene, *The Enemy: What Every American Should Know about Imperialism* (New York Vintage Books, 1971). For examples of domestic repression, see William Preston, Jr., *Aliens and Dissenters: Federal Suppression of Radicals, 1903-1933* (New York: Harper Torchbooks, 1966) and Jacobus tenBroek, Edward N. Barnhart and Floyd W. Matson, *Prejudice, War and the Constitution* (Berkeley: University of California Press, 1968).

gressive movements did not achieve significant reforms. They did in fact create major changes. In the arena of criminal justice they were responsible for developing important new institutions which transformed the character of the administration of juvenile justice. But these reforms, to use André Gorz's distinctions, were "reformist" rather than "structural":

> *[S]tructural reform . . . does not mean a reform which rationalizes the existing system while leaving intact the existing distribution of powers; this does not mean to delegate to the (capitalist) State the task of improving the system.*
>
> *Structural reform is by definition a reform implemented or controlled by those who demand it. Be it in agriculture, the university, property relations, the region, the administration, the economy, etc., a structural reform* always *requires the creation of new centers of democratic power. Whether it be at the level of companies, schools, municipalities, regions, or of the national Plan, etc., structural reform always requires a* decentralization *of the decision making power, a* restriction on the powers of State or Capital, *an* extension of popular power, *that is to say, a victory of democracy over the dictatorship of profit.*[91]

By this definition, then, the child-saving movement was a "reformist reform." It was not controlled by those whom it was supposed to benefit; it did not create new centers of democratic power; it extended and consolidated the powers of the state; and it helped to preserve existing economic and political relationships.

---

[91] André Gorz, *Strategy for Labor: A Radical Proposal* (Boston: Beacon Press, 1964), p. 8.

*Rediscovering Delinquency: Social History, Political Ideology and the Sociology of Law**

John Hagan
Indiana University and University of Toronto

Jeffrey Leon
University of Toronto

This paper examines a Marxian social historical approach to the study of legal evolution. The emergence of the Marxian perspective and the logic of its premises are reviewed. Using Canadian delinquency legislation as an historical example, it is found that the Marxian perspective assumes a great deal that is unconfirmed (e.g., that this legislation serves the teleologically inferred "basic interests" of an ambiguously identified "ruling class"), asserts other things that are wrong or misleading (that this legislation increased imprisonment, "invented" new categories of youthful misbehavior, created a "specialized labor market" and increased "industrial discipline"), and ignores much that an organizational analysis helps to reveal (that the emergence of probation work as an organizational concern was the prime factor in the development of Canadian delinquency legislation). Implications of these findings are considered.

It is now common to begin sociological discussions of deviance by reaffirming the shift, in the 1960s, from studying the antecedents of rule-breaking behavior to a concern with the origins of legal norms and the statuses that may or may not follow their violation. Equally noteworthy, however, is an increasingly apparent shift from studying the entrepreneurial and organizational origins of legal norms (e.g., Becker, 1963; Gusfield, 1963; Lemert, 1970; Dickson, 1968) and their enforcement (e.g., Wheeler, 1968; Reiss, 1971; Blumberg, 1967), to a more monotheistic focus in the 1970s on class conflict as the independent variable of concern (Taylor et al., 1973; Quinney, 1975a; Chambliss, 1973; Platt, 1975).

Several recent papers have questioned the accuracy of class conflict propositions about normative dissensus (Rossi et al., 1974) and the enforcement process (Hagan, 1974; Chiricos and Waldo, 1976). These studies have helped stimulate a clarification and reformulation of propositions (Turk, 1976). At the same time, however, the presumed strength of a Marxian conflict perspective continues to be a class-based, social historical approach to the study of legal evolution (Platt, 1973:30; Chambliss, 1974:8, Taylor et al., 1973:266). This paper reviews recent developments in the sociology of law and critically examines the theoretical and empirical usefulness of the class conflict approach, using the origins of juvenile delinquency legislation in Canada as its data.

Conflict, Consensus, and the Sociology of Law

It is still less than a decade since most sociologists adopted a rather agnostic view of the "conflict-consensus debate." (For discussion of this debate see Chambliss and Seidman, 1973; Hills, 1971; Chambliss, 1973; Hagan, 1977.) Chambliss (1969: 8) expressed a common view when he reasoned that a "resolution of this debate . . . would be premature"; that "in many cases there is no conflict . . ."; and that "the influence of interest groups . . . is but one aspect of the processes which determine the emergence and focus of the legal norms" (Chambliss, 1969:10). However, two years later, Chambliss (Chambliss and Seidman, 1971:19) finds the literature far more conclusive: "Indeed, the empirical studies . . . make it quite clear that the value-consensus model is . . . incapable of accounting for the shape and character of the legal system. . . ."

Similarly, Quinney's (1969:1970) early work contained pluralistic themes and a restrained optimism about legal

*Authorship is alphabetized and does not reflect seniority or priority; the authors share equal responsibility for this paper.

From *American Sociological Review,* Vol. 42 (August 1977), pp. 587–598. Reprinted by permission of the American Sociological Association and the authors.

change. Perhaps nostalgically, Quinney (1969:5) noted that criminal prosecutions emerged in Athens, in the sixth century B.C., and that "this step protected . . . the lower class of Athens from aggression by the rich and powerful." Furthermore, Quinney (1970:41) conceded that "groups . . . similar in power may well check each others' interests . . ." and that "interest groups receive their individual claims in return for allowing other groups to press for their interests." At this stage, he was a reformed pluralist, denying the assumption that a diversity of interests typically is resolved through compromise, but acknowledging that a plurality of interests operate, and clinging to the Poundian hope that "the public interest may become an ideal fulfilled . . ." (Quinney, 1970: 42; cf. Pound, 1943).

The "New Criminologists" (Taylor et al., 1973:265-6) responded by arguing that "the view of law as . . . in the hands of 'powerful interest groups,' does not take us far enough. . . ." Quinney (1975b:193) soon agreed that "from the evidence of radical scholarship, government and business are inseparable." Thus, "whilst pluralists may suggest that there are diverse and conflicting interests among groups in the upper class, what is ignored is the fact that members of the ruling class work within a common framework . . ." (Quinney, 1975:194). Taylor et al. (1975:3) endorse Quinney's new position as a "move to a Marxist economism."

The key proposition in this new Marxian perspective on law creation is that "The criminal law is . . . first and foremost a reflection of the interests and ideologies of the governing class . . ." (Chambliss, 1974:37; see also Quinney, 1975b:192). Chambliss (1974:37) comes closest to identifying this "ruling class," but is ultimately unable to decide "whether that class is private industry or state bureaucracy." Instead, he offers the contradictory conclusion that "government bureaucracies may, in the last analysis, be controlled by those who influence the society's economic resources . . ., but they also have a life and a force of their own . . ." (1974:27). Assuming these two possibilities were not mutually exclusive, which they are, undermining the notion of a *single* ruling class, some significant questions would remain unanswered. For example, how much of private industry and state bureaucracy is to be included within the "ruling class"? How diverse and extensive can these groupings be and still be considered a single "ruling class"? To what extent is there conflict within and between private industries and state bureaucracies? And, under what conditions do various industrial or bureaucratic groups prevail?

Quinney's response to such questions is to argue that "in contrast to pluralist theory, radical theory notes that the *basic interests,* in spite of *concrete differences,* place the elite into a distinct ruling class" (1975b:194, emphasis added). A difficulty with this argument is that "basic interests" are not identified with sufficient specificity to allow a predictive test of legal control strategies presumed to follow from these interests. Thus, one "Marxist criminologist" includes "direct release" as evidence of an "integrative control" used to perpetuate "state capitalism" (Spitzer, 1975:647-9). Unfortunately, this type of conceptualization encourages tautologous theorizing and, in a manner similar to functionalist formulations of the past, engages the fallacy of affirming the consequences. Thus, discussions of "interests served," like those of "functions performed," characteristically are retrospective in form, reasoning teleologically from selected consequences to presumed motivations (cf. Rock, 1974:598; Hirst, 1972).

A different type of evidence sometimes offered in support of class conflict propositions consists of information on the backgrounds and contacts of persons active in lawmaking. For example, Chambliss (1974:21) regards the fact that "legislatures, appellate court judges, and committee members are drawn largely from upper-class members of society . . ." as evidence of what Schattschneider (1960) calls the "mobilization of bias." However, since the membership of a class itself can be in conflict and since membership in one class need not exclude the possibility of siding with another (Mintz et al., 1976:316, 317), the use of this "guilt by membership" argument often amounts to a genetic fallacy and the tendency to argue *ad hominem.*

Finally, Chambliss and Quinney give little empirical attention to the actual level of conflict, consensus or apathy that may accompany the operation of interests, ignoring that the pursuit of these interests may occur with the explicit or tacit support of those affected (Hopkins, 1975:616). The issue is whether "class interests" operate as causes or whether, in many instances, the association with assumed effects may be spurious.

Where the active pursuit of class interests can be tested for its influence in the presence or absence of consensus, a scientific purpose can be served. It is, however, the recent extension of the Marxian perspective beyond its scientific base that concerns us. Quinney (1973:594) argues that "ideas are to be put at the service of the community . . ., and we ourselves must engage in people's struggles." Our concern is that this ideological mission is based on a perspective that is (1) prone to logical errors, (2) largely unconfirmed, (3) often unconfirmable and (4) possibly quite frequently false.

The Social History of American Delinquency Legislation

The patterns observed in the development of a Marxist theory of law creation are repeated in Anthony Platt's analysis of the origins of American juvenile delinquency legislation. Platt's original work, *The Child Savers,* is grounded in a theoretical tradition (Ranulf, 1938; Gusfield, 1963; cf. Platt, 1969:3,7) that focused on middle-class interests: "Child-saving may be understood as a crusade which served symbolic and ceremonial functions for native, middle-class Americans" (Platt, 1969:98). The culmination of this "symbolic crusade" was the Illinois Juvenile Court Act of 1899, and Platt adopted a partially pluralist stance in explaining that "its success was due in large measure to the fact that it was *widely* sponsored and in turn satisfied *diverse* interest groups" (1969:134, emphasis added). At this point, Platt's most pressing concerns were that "the juvenile court system . . . 'invented' new categories of youthful deviance . . ." (1969:145), that the child-savers "recommended increased imprisonment . . ." (1969:135), and therefore that "'delinquents' were increasingly committed to institutions . . ." (1969:145).

Four years later, Platt (1973:26) argues that "ideology is healthy and should be made explicit," and concludes that "the problem with *The Child Savers* is that . . . [it] focuses too much attention on the middle-class reformers. . . ." Platt reasons anew that the impetus for delinquency legislation flowed from close and compromising links between members of the middle and upper classes (1974:369), and that "the juvenile court system was part of a general movement directed towards developing a specialized labor market and industrial discipline under corporate capitalism by creating new programs of adjudication and control . . ." (1974:377).

Evidence for this new, class-interested Marxian theory is the same as that presented in Platt's (1969:ch. 3) original account and is similar in type to that proposed by Chambliss and Quinney. Descriptions of a "new penology" are offered, but no evidence is provided that passage of juvenile court legislation resulted in an increase in the number of juveniles incarcerated, that the industrial elite benefited significantly as a result of this incarceration, or that the "ruling class" played any direct role in the passage of this legislation. Instead, the primary evidence presented engages a genetic fallacy of the type we previously associated with the "mobilization of bias" argument. Thus, the main body of information consists of a cataloguing of the class backgrounds and backings of persons involved in the child-saving movement. Platt (1969:367–8) concludes that this movement "would not have been capable of achieving significant reforms without the financial and political support of the wealthy and powerful" and that "Even the more radically-minded child-savers came from upper-class backgrounds." What is lacking in this account is any concrete evidence that this sponsorship was a *causal* factor that operated independently of widespread support for the ensuing legislation.

Summarizing, Platt's primary concerns are that links between middle-class reformers and upper-class sponsors resulted in the wealthy and powerful using the passage of American delinquency legislation to "invent" new forms of youthful misbehavior and increase imprisonment, all in the larger interest of "developing a specialized labor market and industrial discipline under corporate capitalism." Alternatively, we have argued that this Marxian perspective on the origins of American delinquency legislation is either unconfirmed or unconfirmable, plagued by logical errors and, therefore, quite possibly false. In the following section, these conclusions are tested anew with historical information on the origins of Canadian delinquency legislation.

The Social History of Canadian Delinquency Legislation

This part of our analysis is based on historical data drawn from a variety of sources: historical accounts written by participants in, and observers of the child-saving movement; personal correspondence and accounts drawn from the archives of leading advocates of delinquency legislation; proceedings of conferences concerned with child welfare; reports of government commissions; legislative debates; and statistics drawn from the Toronto Juvenile Court. Particular attention is given to an extensive correspondence between the two leading advocates of delinquency legislation in Canada: J.J. Kelso and W.L. Scott.

Our analysis focuses on entrepreneurial interests and activities leading to the emergence of the juvenile court, the organizational development of this court, and the objective consequences of this process (Becker, 1963; Dickson, 1968). Of particular concern is the manner in which the entrepreneurial interests of individuals are aggregated and polarized into organizational issues (Lemert, 1970). Weber reminds us that these organizational issues can be directed to various ends: "bureaucracy as such is a precision instrument which can put itself at the disposal of quite varied—purely political as well as purely economic, or any other sort—of interests . . ." (Gerth and Mills, 1946:231). Thus, Platt's Marxian position is only one among the possibilities entertained by Weber. With this in mind, we will consider first the link proposed by Platt between class interests in social control and the coercive consequence of increased juvenile imprisonment.

Data available for the City of Toronto[1] do not support Platt's position. In the year preceding juvenile court operations, 123 juveniles were sent to industrial schools; 71 were sent to such schools in the first year of juvenile court proceedings (City of Toronto, 1912:14). More detailed information on other forms of institutionalization (including a working-boys home, two hospitals and a training school) is available from the court reports of succeeding years (see Appendix 1). Here again, no consistent pattern of increase is apparent, and at no time during the forty-year period does the *total* institutionalized population exceed the number sent to industrial school alone in the year before court operations began.[2] In the following historical discussion, we will see that the inaccuracy of Platt's position derives from a misrepresentation of legal developments that preceded delinquency legislation in Canada. Furthermore, we will find little evidence, either in personal correspondence or in public documents, that members of the industrial elite expressed an active economic interest in the passage of delinquency legislation. The activities of other individuals and interest groups, particularly those involved with the probation movement (cf. Schultz, 1973), will be considered, but the involvement of the "ruling class" seems to have been peripheral at most. We discuss three periods that preceded the passage of delinquency legislation:

[1] In the following, emphasis is placed on the development of a system of juvenile justice in Ottawa and Toronto, and the Province of Ontario, as well as on the federal level. Much of the federal legislation was anticipated and first implemented in Ontario, where many of the most influential child-savers lived. As a result of limitations in resources, the provisions of this Act allowed that it not take immediate effect in some cities and provinces; therefore, dates of implementation varied. Toronto was among the first Canadian cities to establish a Juvenile Court in 1912 (Ontario Law Reform Commission, 1974).

[2] This finding is consistent with less comprehensive figures reported by Scott (1906–1908) for Ottawa and in his correspondence with provincial officials in many other parts of Canada.

an initial period in which lengthy stays in reformatories, replaced sentences spent in common gaols; a second period during which treatment-focused industrial schools began to replace reformatories; and a third period when organized probation emerged as a new treatment strategy influential in the development of delinquency legislation.

The child-savers focused first on juveniles convicted as criminals. Two acts were passed in 1857: *An Act for Establishing Prisons for Young Offenders* and *An Act for the More Speedy Trial and Punishment of Young Offenders.* The first directed the construction of "reformatory prisons," while the second provided for summary trial procedures and increased powers to discharge juveniles in order "to avoid the evils of their long imprisonment previously to trial." Thus, as early as 1857 in Canada, there were provisions for special institutions and trial procedures for juveniles.

In 1874, Ontario passed *An Act Respecting Industrial Schools,* intending to provide residential institutions that would be less severe than reformatories and to which "neglected, uncontrolled, and delinquent" children could be sent. Subsequent to this legislation, J. J. Kelso, a crusading news reporter who later became Ontario's Superintendent of Neglected and Dependent Children, emerged as a key "moral entrepreneur" (cf. Becker, 1963) in the Canadian child-saving movement. In 1887, Kelso brought together the Toronto Humane Society for "better laws, better methods, [and] the development of the humane spirit in all affairs of life" (Kelso, 1911:17; Hodgins, 1888).

Generally consistent with such principles, Ontario passed *An Act for the Protection and Reformation of Neglected Children* in the following year. Provisions of this act allowed that "the Lieutenant-Governor may . . . appoint . . . commissioners . . . to hear and determine complaints against juvenile offenders . . ." and that "their cases be disposed of . . . separately from other offenders. . . ." However, this act also authorized the courts to commit neglected children to industrial schools. Kelso consistently tempered this approach by arguing that "the aim . . . is not to steal children from their parents . . ., but by every available means to make the home and family all it ought to be" (Province of Ontario, 1895). It took Kelso several years to translate these views into law.

In 1890, two additional statutes were enacted in Ontario (*An Act Respecting the Custody of Juvenile Offenders* and *An Act Respecting the Commitment of Persons of Tender Years*), each of which further restricted the use of reformatories and expanded the use of industrial schools for selected children. In 1891, a Commission of Inquiry into the Prison and Reformatory System of Ontario (Province of Ontario, 1891) completed a report that seemed to forecast the shape of things to come. In addition to dealing with institutional reforms, the Commission recommended that magistrates grant discharges to first offenders convicted of trivial offenses and that various powers be given to probation officers.

Later the same year, the Commission's chairman and one of its most prominent members joined Kelso in Toronto to organize a public meeting at which the Children's Aid Society and Fresh Air Fund was founded, with Kelso as President. A letter announcing the goals of this meeting signaled a growing interest in an important organizational innovation: "The appointment of a probation officer to ascertain and submit to the court full particulars of each child brought up for trial, and to act in the capacity of the child's next friend" (see Kelso, 1911:69).

As reform efforts gathered momentum, a theme of professionalism emerged: "What is needed," wrote Kelso (n.d. (a):20), "is personal service, the complete organization of charitable forces, harmony of action, and the appointment of trained and experienced workers. . . ." Gradually, persons involved in the movement seemed to develop an interest in their own positions in an emerging bureaucracy. The influence of this emerging interest group on the legislative process is suggested in Kelso's comment to the Sixth Canadian Conference of Charities and Corrections that "we have as much if not more law than we can assimilate, and the governments are ready to give new measures whenever they are asked to do so . . ." (Proceedings, 1903–1909:21).

The legislation of this period was particularly useful in setting the organizational base for probation work. The first *Criminal Code of Canada* was passed in 1892, providing for separate trials of persons under sixteen where it was "expedient and practicable" to do so; and, in 1893, at the urging of Kelso and others, the Ontario legislature enacted a comprehensive *Children's Protection Act* giving explicit recognition and authority to Children's Aid Societies. The latter act specifically stipulated that it was the duty of the court to notify the Executive Officer of the Children's Aid Society (if one existed in the county) prior to initiating proceedings against a boy under twelve or a girl under thirteen; this officer was then to investigate the charges, inquire into the child's family environment, and report back to the court with his findings. These procedures were reaffirmed in the following year with a federal *Act Respecting Arrest, Trial and Imprisonment of Youthful Offenders.*

In a short Commons debate of this act, the Minister of Justice and Attorney General noted that "a great many magistrates from motives of humanity" were already conducting separate trials for juveniles (Canada, 1894, June 24:4940–1). A magistrate in the Toronto Police Court later confirmed this, noting that "in 1892 we instituted the Children's Court. . . . We set apart a small room in the lower part of City Hall . . ., and I was accustomed to go down to that room to try all charges against children . . ." (Denison, 1920: 254). These developments, and Kelso's role in them, became the basis for claims that the juvenile court had a Toronto origin and was therefore a "Canadian enterprise" that had been appropriated by "American social workers."[3] Thus, Kelso later expressed his concern to Scott that "our Ontario work should not be overlooked as I advocated the Children's

[3]For example, these claims are made in a 1933 Toronto newspaper article titled "Juvenile Court had Toronto Origin" (see Hagan, 1977:21). These claims (as contrasted, for example, with those made for New York and Massachusetts) are less important for their factual accuracy than for their indication of close connections between Canadian and American child-saving efforts.

Court here twenty years ago, gave addresses in Chicago and elsewhere in favor of it and got the law (the Children's Protection Act) passed here in 1893" (Scott, 1906-1908: 12/27/1906; 7/4, 8/1907). One address to which Kelso refers was given in Chicago on October 11, 1893 (Proceedings, 1893; see, also, 1895). Kelso notes that "Judge Hurd consulted with me as to the drafting of the Juvenile Court following my address,"[4] and that a much discussed extract from this speech appeared in the *Chicago Tribune* the following day (cf. Flexner and Baldwin, 1914:3-4). Kelso's view was that ". . . of course, the Denver and Chicago courts have far outstripped us but at the same time we gave them the inspiration that led to their present success (Scott, 1906-1908: 12/27/1906).

In 1903, a subsection was added to the Ontario *Children's Protection Act,* specifying that without being convicted of a provincial offense, persons under sixteen could be placed by a judge under the care of a probation officer, who would report periodically "concerning the progress and welfare of the child." The idea of a probation *system* "to help the children before they become criminally disposed" was increasingly discussed (Kelso, 1907:107). Kelso gave this top priority: "We want to bring about what is called the Probation System, following the children up from their first offense . . ." (Proceedings, 1903:21). The assumption behind this proposal was that imprisonment frequently could be avoided: "Whenever there is an offense there is a cause behind it and our children's court and probation system should be able to reach that cause and . . . remove it for the safety and protection of the children in the home" (Department of Neglected and Dependent Children, 1907:15).

To this point, we have focused on J. J. Kelso as the central "moral entrepreneur" in the advocacy of probation and delinquency legislation. However, he was joined in this pursuit by a "professional" (cf. Becker, 1963:152) counterpart, W. L. Scott, Local Master for the Supreme Court of Ontario and President of the Ottawa Children's Aid Society. Kelso and Scott vocalized three primary concerns. First, additional funds were needed to elevate "philanthropic work to the status of a profession and to encourage University graduates to become specialists in social and moral reform work" (Proceedings, 1907:8). Second, it was claimed that probation officers were now hampered in their work by a lack of "legislative recognition" (Scott, 1906-1908:1/2/1907). And, third, there was a perceived need for special judges: "The Children's Court should undoubtedly be . . . conducted by specially selected persons . . ." (Kelso, 1908:164).

Drafted by Scott and others in response to these concerns, the federal *Juvenile Delinquents Act* was introduced first in the Speech from the Throne in 1906, reintroduced to the Senate in 1907 and eventually passed in 1908. A "juvenile delinquent" was defined broadly by this act as any child under sixteen who violated any federal or provincial statute, or municipal by-law, or who was liable by any other act to committal to an industrial school or juvenile reformatory. Thus, this act consolidated various previously illegal behaviors into a new category called "delinquency," but it did not add any behaviors to those already specified under existing statutes and by-laws. It would be misleading to conclude, as Platt does for the United States, that Canadian delinquency legislation " 'invented' new categories of youthful misbehavior."[5]

The act did, however, give juvenile courts exclusive primary jurisdiction in cases of delinquency. It also provided for the formation of a voluntary Juvenile Court Committee to consult with and advise probation officers, or to appoint an officer where remuneration was available and an officer was not already appointed under provincial authority. Furthermore, probation officers were assigned powers of a constable, with their duties including: conducting investigations, being present and representing the interests of the child in court, furnishing the court with such assistance and information as required, and taking charge of any child before or after trial, as directed by the court.

Discussions of these and other provisions of the act mainly involved two groups. The ultimately successful group included those who advocated treatment and prevention through probation and a special court; they distributed copies of the bill, circulated petitions, and invited such speakers as Judge Lindsay, of the Denver Juvenile Court, and Mrs. Schoff, of the Philadelphia Mother's Union, to address various gatherings. The opposition included police officers and magistrates who already assumed organizational responsibilities for children and who, therefore, had a very immediate interest to protect (see Scott 1906-1908:3/7, 3/15/1907). This group advocated a more "punitive" approach to delinquency. Particularly vehement in this view were several police officials, including Inspector Archibald and Police Magistrates Denison and Kingsford, associated with the Toronto Children's Court. The debate was often bitter, with Archibald, in a report circulated to gain support for the police position, charging that the new proposals:

work upon the sympathies of philanthropic men and women for the purpose of introducing a jelly-fish and abortive system of law enforcement, whereby the judge or magistrate is expected to come down to the level of the incorrigible street

---

[4]This comment is found in Kelso's (n.d.(b):19) handwriting at the bottom of a page of an article by Hurly on "The History of the Illinois Juvenile Court Law."

[5]Sixteen years later, *An Act to Amend the Juvenile Delinquents Act,* 1924, proposed the addition of an omnibus clause—"or who is guilty of sexual immorality or any other form of vice"—to the definition of a juvenile delinquent. However, by this time, such omnibus clauses had been a part of legal definitions of neglect for more than thirty years. It is sometimes argued that such clauses define as delinquent behaviors that are most common among underclass youth. However, this alone cannot count as support for a Marxian class conflict perspective, since the underclass may agree with such legal definitions. The latter possibility is supported by the findings of Black and Reiss (1970) that black complainants are more likely than whites to insist on the arrest of blacks accused of delinquency. Perhaps most significantly, however, the same Marxian theorists (e.g., Liazos, 1974) who claim underclass behaviors are defined differentially by law as delinquent, also cite self-report studies reporting an absence of relationship between social class and delinquent behavior. Probably the safest conclusion is the vague statutory clauses like those defining delinquency depend most heavily for their consequences on the discretion of those who must interpret and enforce them: citizens, the police and prosecutors.

Arab and assume an attitude absolutely repulsive to British subjects. The idea seems to be that by profuse use of slang phraseology he should place himself in a position to kiss and coddle a class of perverts and delinquents who require the most rigid disciplinary and corrective methods to ensure the possibility of their reformation. (Archibald, 1907:5)

In response, Scott (1906-1908:3/19/1907) labeled Archibald a "person of very limited intelligence," while Kelso (Scott 1906-1908:5/14/1907) called him "self-opinionated" and opposed to those who failed to treat him with "deference." Scott (5/2/1907) concluded that the members of the Toronto Police Department felt the new proposals were intended to supplant them and were therefore a reflection on their past work. Moreover, Archibald's particularly negative attitude was said to be based on the fact that he "had prepared all the legislation on the subject during the last forty years and . . . is apparently deeply offended that anyone else should have usurped this prerogative" (Scott, 1906-1908 4/16/1907).

Scott (1908:894) went on to campaign successfully for the *Juvenile Delinquents Act,* emphasizing in his arguments "that probation is the only effective method for dealing with young offenders." Thus, when the bill was reintroduced to the Senate in May, 1908, Senator Coffey referred to "the differences of view as to the means and methods whereby the best results may be achieved," and explicitly dismissed the position of Inspector Archibald as being characterized by an outmoded "spirit of rigidity and severity" (Canada, 1907-8: 975-7). Although some objectives were raised in the House of Commons by those concerned with the legal rights of children, the temper of the ensuing debate probably is summarized best by one member of Parliament who observed that the act "is to be laughed through as a joke" (Canada, 1907-8:1240-1). The legislation was passed, but this did not end the organizational search for support. The following years brought a succession of minor revisions and extensions of the original legislation, concerted efforts to secure appropriate provincial legislation creating the newly authorized juvenile courts, and continued efforts to obtain sufficient funds from various levels of government to employ probation officers (Proceedings, 1909; Scott, 1952).

The consequences of the entrepreneurial activities we have described are illustrated in the statistical records of the Toronto Juvenile and Family Court (see Appendix 1). Probation officers in this court predominated in both their number and scale of activities. Thus, while the number of *official* occurrences recorded by the Juvenile Court actually was lower in 1952 than in 1912, during this period the number of probation officers increased from 4 to 14, and the number of occurrences handled *unofficially* by probation officers escalated more than 900 percent, from 735 to 6,574 cases. The Probation Department apparently did this in a manner the Toronto Police Department seemed initially to fear, that is, by attracting their own new cases and refusing to refer them either to the police or court. Thus, the Probation Department publically proclaimed that "it is our aim, as far as possible, to settle through the Probation Department all difficulties without making them court cases" (City of Toronto, 1920:5), while also annually advising that "we again, as many times before, earnestly solicit those having problems of various kinds, within the jurisdiction of the Court, coming and allowing us to assist before these problems become too acute so as to require official action" (City of Toronto, 1933:9). Specifically, the Probation Department offered social and clinical investigations in all such cases, leading to dramatic increases in the number of interviews counted annually into the Court Reports. This aspect of the court's work was augmented in 1929 with increased jurisdiction over family matters, followed by increasing rates of court referrals and support actions in succeeding years. In this way, *the social work of the Probation Department steadily increased, without simultaneous increases in the number of adolescents institutionalized or placed on probation.* Thus, in those years when official delinquency actually declined, the Probation Department was quick to observe optimistically "that while we had a decrease in delinquency . . . we had an increase of the numbers who came of their own free will to get help. If it is safe to draw an observation from this fact, it would be reasonable to assume that the non-official effort of the court is reducing its official acts" (City of Toronto, 1933:9). This conclusion was, of course, self-serving; the long term effect on children of this increase in non-official activity remains unclear.

Discussion and Conclusions

The conflict that surrounded the *Juvenile Delinquents Act* in Canada was less about normative definition than about the organizational arrangements under which violators of the norm would be processed. More specifically, it was supporters of the police and advocates of probation who quarreled most about the organizational procedures to be followed. J. J. Kelso, a moral entrepreneur who rose from news reporter to a high position in the child-care bureaucracy, collaborated with W. L. Scott, a professional counterpart and philanthropist who occupied an administrative position in the Ontario Supreme Court, to engineer a legislative movement whose organizational goal became the prevention of delinquency through juvenile probation work. Opposition came from representatives of existing police organizational interests whose more punitive philosophy was reflected in writing prior legislation and their current activities in handling juveniles. Advocates of probation prevailed in the passage of delinquency legislation in 1908, and the consequences of these efforts became apparent in the organizational composition and activities of the new Juvenile Court in Toronto: the handling of *unofficial* occurrences by probation officers dramatically increased, while the level of *official activity* showed some signs of decline.

Whether the eventual success of advocates of probation served the basic interests of the ruling elite is unknown, and probably unknowable, for the various reasons discussed above; however, little influence of the industrial elite was revealed in the personal correspondence and public documents of the

Appendix 1. City of Toronto Juvenile and Family Court Statistics, 1912,[a] 1920, and at Two-Year Intervals to 1952

Year	1912	1920	1922	1924	1926	1928	1930	1932	1934	1936	1938	1940	1942	1944	1946	1948	1950	1952
Court Staff																		
Judges[b]	1	1	1	1	1	1	2	2	2	2	2	2	2	5	4	4	4	5
Probation Officers[c]	5	7	7	6	6	6	11	12	12	12	10	10	13	14	14	15	15	15
Clerical Staff	1	5	5	6	5	5	7	7	7	7	8	8	8	8	8	9	10	9
Psychiatrists & Psychologists	0	0	0	1	1	1	1	1	2	1	1	1	1	1	1	1	2	2
Other	0	0	0	0	1	1	2	2	2	2	2	2	2	2	2	2	2	3
Total	7	13	13	14	14	14	23	24	25	24	23	23	26	30	29	31	33	34
Probation Department Statistics																		
Interviews	–	–	2976	2814	3643	4651	10624	9984	9789	8547	9547	9895	11711	–	–	–	–	–
Occurrences	725	955	1753	1243	1636	1701	4127	4021	3962	4780	3415	3488	3800	4732	7336	6574	–	–
Percent Referred to Court	20.7	7.9	6.0	4.5	2.9	1.8	2.7	1.1	3.2	5.3	6.8	10.2	13.1	13.0	10.3	–	–	–
Court Dispositions																		
Probation	769	733	731	877	350	207	304	99	425	629	488	486	544	415	316	387	418	345
Fines	202	77	92	245	228	94	28	28	13	15	29	31	80	111	30	14	17	18
Suspended Sentence & Adjournments[d]	387	679	764	971	1596	2105	1584	846	780	520	416	479	805	413	216	227	280	273
Institutionalized	85	78	43	61	34	49	71	30	44	46	53	50	85	120	67	71	72	97
Dismissed & Withdrawn	105	83	132	66	21	38	56	34	15	28	48	59	107	99	56	39	70	79
Other[e]	191	59	43	77	52	45	74	7	10	0	60	73	72	56	55	12	33	15
Total	1744	1709	1805	2298	2281	2538	2122	1483	1287	1238	1094	1178	1693	1214	740	750	890	827
Support Actions	–	–	–	–	–	–	756	586	510	435	411	689	880	1089	1349	1202	1167	1310

[a] Juvenile court work began in 1912 in Toronto; reports were not issued from 1913–1919; reports ceased in 1952. Dashes indicate years for which specific types of data were not recorded.
[b] Includes commissioners, judges and magistrates.
[c] Includes probation officers, social investigators and social workers.
[d] Includes commitments to industrial schools, Working Boys Home, Orillia Hospital, Ontario Hospital and training schools.
[e] Includes cases pending, remanded, wards of Children's Aid Society, home placements and transfers to higher courts.

key proponents of this legislation. Moreover, in contrast to Platt's account of the passage of delinquency legislation in the United States, no evidence was found in the Canadian data that institutionalization increased as a result of such legislation, or that this legislation was useful in developing a "specialized labor market" or "industrial discipline."

Part of Platt's (1974:389) argument proceeds from a basic Marxian assumption that "as the contradictions (of capitalism) become more apparent and the control system more unsuccessful, the methods of coercion become similarly more explicit and more desperate." It is apparently for this reason that Platt places such great emphasis on the role of the "New Penology" in the emergence of delinquency legislation. In contrast, the argument of this paper is that it was an emphasis on probation work, and not imprisonment, that led to this new legislation. Thus, although this legislation substantially changed the operations of the juvenile and criminal courts, probably with consequences both good and bad, intended and unintended (cf. Hagan, 1975), the overall effect was not to intensify a formal and explicit system of coercion, but rather to reinforce and increasingly intervene in informal systems of social control, particularly the family. These findings raise the possibility that assumed contradictions in the economic sphere may have only marginal significance for the juvenile justice system, or that these assumed contradictions need not necessarily lead to more explicit methods of social coercion. In any case, this paper provides a considerably different account of the origin of delinquency legislation than is offered by Platt, and it is an account which encourages a reconsideration of the conditions under which this version of a Marxian, class conflict perspective can be usefully applied.

References

Archibald, D. 1907. Report on the Treatment of Neglected Children in Toronto. Toronto: Arcade.

Becker, Howard. 1963. *Outsiders.* New York: Free Press.

Black, Donald, and Albert Reiss. 1970. "Police control of juveniles." *American Sociological Review* 25:63–77.

Blumberg, Abraham. 1967. *Criminal Justice.* Chicago: Quadrangle Books.

Canada. 1894. Commons Debates. Ottawa: Queen's Printer.

_____. 1907–1908. Senate Debates. Ottawa: Queen's Printer.

Chambliss, William. 1969. *Crime and the Legal Process.* New York: McGraw-Hill.

_____. 1973. "Functional and conflict theories of crime." MSS Modular Publications 17:1–23.

_____. 1974. "The state, the law and the definition of behavior as criminal or delinquent." Pp. 7–42 in Daniel Glaser, ed., *Handbook of Criminology.* Indianapolis: Bobbs-Merrill.

Chambliss, William, and Robert Seidman. 1971. *Law, Order and Power.* Reading, Ma.: Addison-Wesley.

Chiricos, Theodore, and Gordon Waldo. 1976. "Socioeconomic status and criminal sentencing: an empirical assessment of a conflict proposition." *American Sociological Review* 40:753–72.

City of Toronto. 1912–1952. Annual Reports of the Juvenile Courts of the City of Toronto. Toronto.

Denison, G. T. 1920. *Recollections of a Police Magistrate.* Toronto: Musson.

Department of Neglected and Dependent Children. 1907. Fourteenth Report of the Department of Neglected and Dependent Children. Toronto: Warwick.

Dickson, Donald. 1968. "Bureaucracy and morality: an organizational perspective on a moral crusade." *Social Problems* 16:143–56.

Flexner, Bernard, and Roger Baldwin. 1914. *Juvenile Courts and Probation.* New York: Century.

Gerth, H., and C. W. Mills. 1946. *From Max Weber.* New York: Oxford University Press.

Gusfield, Joseph. 1963. *Symbolic Crusade.* Urbana: University of Illinois Press.

Hagan, John. 1974. "Extra-legal attributes and criminal sentencing: an assessment of a sociological viewpoint." *Law and Society Review* 8:357–83.

_____. 1975. "The social and legal construction of criminal justice: a study of the pre-sentencing process." *Social Problems* 22:620–37.

_____. 1977. *The Disreputable Pleasures.* Toronto: McGraw-Hill Ryerson.

Hills, Stuart. 1971. *Crime, Power and Morality.* Toronto: Chandler.

Hirst, P. Q. 1972. "Marx and Engels on law, crime and morality." *Economy and Society* 1:28–56.

Hodgins, J. G., ed. 1888. *Aims and Objects of the Toronto Humane Society.* Toronto: Briggs.

Hopkins, Andrew. 1975. "On the sociology of criminal law." *Social Problems* 22:608–19.

Kelso, J. J. 1907. "Delinquent children: some improved methods whereby they may be prevented from following a criminal career." *Canadian Law Review* 6:106–10.

_____. 1908. "Children's court." *Canadian Law Times and Review* 26:163–6.

_____. 1909. *Helping Erring Children.* Toronto: Warwick.

_____. 1911. *Early History of the Humane and Children's Aid Movement in Ontario, 1886–1893.* Ontario: King's Printer.

_____. n.d.(a) "Can slums be abolished or must we continue to pay the penalty." Toronto.

_____. n.d.(b) J. J. Kelso Papers. Ottawa: Public Archives.

Lemert, Edwin. 1970. *Social Action and Legal Change.* Chicago: Aldine.

Liazos, Alexander. 1974. "Class oppression: the function of juvenile justice." *Insurgent Sociologist* 5:2–24.

Mintz, Beth, Peter Freitag, Carol Hendricks, and Michael Schwartz. 1976. "Repression and criminal justice in capitalist America." *Sociological Inquiry* 46:95–106.

Ontario Law Reform Commission. 1974. *Report on Family Law,* Part V, *Family Courts.* Toronto: Queen's Printer.

Platt, Anthony. 1969. *The Child Savers.* Chicago: University of Chicago Press.

_____. 1973. "Dialogue with Anthony Platt." *Issues in Criminology* 8:19–33.

_____. 1974. "The triumph of benevolence: the origins of the juvenile justice system in the United States." Pp. 356–89 in Richard Quinney, ed., *Criminal Justice in America.* Boston: Little, Brown.

_____. 1975. "Prospects for a radical criminology in the U.S.A." Pp. 95–112 in Ian Taylor, Paul Walton and Jock Young, ed., *Critical Criminology.* London: Routledge and Kegan Paul.

Pound, Roscoe. 1943. "A survey of social interests." *Harvard Law Review* 57:1–39.

Proceedings

1893. *Proceedings of the Waif-Saving Congress.* Chicago, Illinois.

1895. *Proceedings of the 22nd National Conference of Charities and Corrections.* New Haven, Connecticut.

1903–1909. *Proceedings of the Canadian Conference of Charities and Corrections.* Ottawa, Ontario.

Province of Ontario. 1891. *Report of the Commissioners Appointed to Enquire into the Prison and Reformatory System in Ontario.*

_____. 1895. *Annual Report of the Superintendent of Neglected and*

Dependent Children.
Quinney, Richard. 1969. *Crime and Justice in Society.* Boston: Little, Brown.
_____. 1970. *The Social Reality of Crime.* Boston: Little, Brown.
_____. 1973. "Review of the 'New Criminology.'" *Sociological Quarterly* 14:589–9.
_____. 1975a. *Criminology.* Boston: Little, Brown.
_____. 1975b. "Crime control in capitalist society: a critical philosophy." Pp. 181–212 in Ian Taylor, Paul Walton and Jock Young, eds., *Critical Criminology.* London: Routledge and Kegan Paul.
Ranulf, Svend. 1938. *Moral Indignation and Middle Class Psychology.* Copenhagen: Levin and Monksgard.
Reiss, Albert. 1971. *The Police and the Public.* New Haven: Yale University Press.
Rock, Paul. 1974. "Comment on Mugford." *Sociological Quarterly* 15:597–8.
Rossi, Peter, Emile Waite, Christine Bose, and Richard Berk. 1974. "The seriousness of crimes: normative structure and individual differences." *American Sociological Review* 39:224–37.
Schattschneider, E. E. 1960. *The Semi-Sovereign People.* New York: Holt, Rinehart and Winston.
Schultz, J. L. 1973. "The cycle of juvenile court history." *Crime and Delinquency* 19:457–76.
Scott, W. L. 1906–1908. *W. L. Scott Papers.* Ottawa: Public Archives.
_____. 1908. "The *Juvenile Delinquents Act.*" *Canadian Law Times and Review* 28:892–904.
_____. 1952. *The Juvenile Court in Law.* Ottawa: Canadian Welfare Council.
Spitzer, Steven. 1975. "Toward a Marxian theory of deviance." *Social Problems* 22:638–51.
Taylor, Ian, Paul Walton, and Jock Young. 1973. *The New Criminology.* London: Routledge and Kegan Paul.
_____. 1975. *Critical Criminology.* London: Routledge and Kegan Paul.
Turk, Austin. 1976. "Law, conflict, and order: from theorizing to theories." *Canadian Review of Sociology and Anthropology:* In press.
Wheeler, Stanton, ed. 1968. *Controlling Delinquents.* New York: Wiley.

SECTION TWO

Summary

It ought to be now apparent that the creation of the first juvenile court in 1899 was but one feature in the changing landscape of nineteenth-century America. There can be no denial of the fact that the so-called invention of a juvenile justice system was in response to a host of social pressures converging around the perceived need to counsel and direct children. However, the forces at work in the nineteenth century were so complex and convoluted that we now are faced with the burden of trying to unravel social history and follow a particular line of development from its initial starting point. Depending on the kind of glasses a viewer wears, or more properly the philosophical presuppositions an investigator applies to historical facts, objectivity may become blurred. In the development of the juvenile court can be found a classic example of historical events lending themselves to a multitude of interpretations and contradictory conclusions.

Bakan's (1971) essay seems to suggest that the creation of the concept of adolescence had a certain Janus-headed quality: humanitarian concern for the needs of children coupled with a desire for the advancement of the power of the state. His discussion of the social movements that culminated in compulsory education, the juvenile justice system, and child labor legislation contains elements of both progressive liberalism and staunch conservatism. His concluding discussion of "the promise" is an intriguing social control technique. The credibility of some future payoff for the deferring of immediate gratification looms as a critical ingredient in the perpetuation of the existence of adolescence. But one is left with the clear impression that adolescents may not be putting much faith in society's standards of success. Rebellion, alienation, and delinquency may be the symptoms of distrust and disbelief. Bakan suggests that as social conditions change, traditional responses or social institutions may have to be modified. Could it be that much of the juvenile justice system is an artifact from a previous era, inappropriate for the twenty-first century?

The Platt (1974) versus Hagan and Leon (1977) debate represents two opposing views of the basic intent of the juvenile justice system. Clearly Platt's depiction of the childsaving movement represents a Marxist interpretation of social history. From this perspective, the events preceding the appearance of the first juvenile court, and the ultimate creation of a separate judicial system for juveniles, exemplify capitalist oppression and exploitation. The juvenile court emerges as a tool of the upper classes to punish and purge "wayward" children who oppose the established order. The evidence Platt presents challenges the humanitarian and progressive image of the juvenile court.

Hagan and Leon (1977) attempt to test Platt's theory by tracing the development of the juvenile court in Canada. They examine the social history surrounding Canadian delinquency legislation, along with the records of court activity, and find little support for Platt's thesis. For Hagan and Leon, the crucial test is whether the juvenile court emerges as a punishment-oriented institution. What they find is that probation rather than institutionalization has become the hallmark of the juvenile court. They conclude that Platt's assertion that the juvenile court benefits the ruling class cannot be substantiated.

The inevitable question we are now confronted with is which view is correct. Other investigators who have examined the series of events leading to the creation of the juvenile court are cautious not to reject Platt but observe that his perspective "probably does not do justice to the events of history" (Empey, 1978: 93). Schlossman (1977), in examining the origins of the juvenile court in Milwaukee, finds prevention and probation to be the basic ingredients in the genesis of that system. However, Schlossman admits that the juvenile court movement is quite diverse and suggests that the social conditions Platt observed in Chicago may have differed from those that existed in Milwaukee. Finestone (1976) also argues that the juvenile court is primarily concerned with treatment in the community but that with persistent recidivism, commitment to reform schools becomes the standard treatment approach. Finestone (1976: 48) concludes, "The old punitive attitudes toward offenders lingered just below the surface." Hence, Platt's observations are not totally incorrect.

The annoying realization is that there may be threads of truth running through two opposing versions of history. What we need to struggle with is the blindspots we inadvertently create by a wholehearted endorsement of a certain philosophical stance. Yet while polarizing lenses filter out certain light waves, they accentuate colors of the spectrum that were previously subdued. The events leading to the development of the juvenile court are composed of a multiplicity of interacting forces. It is difficult enough to tease out and isolate a single social event, but when the full array of forces pushing and pulling at a social system is examined, the result may be total confusion. In the language of physics, we may be confronted with the dilemma of the Heisenberg effect: any attempt to measure the speed of a subatomic particle distorts its direction, while any attempt to determine the particle's direction affects its speed. In other words, you can determine a particle's speed or direction, but you cannot isolate both at the same time. The Heisenberg principle may be applicable to other dimensions of reality. It may be that we can chip away at reality and understand it in a piecemeal fashion but that a fully objective view of social history still eludes us.

REFERENCES

Bakan, D. 1971. "Adolescence in America: From Idea to Social Fact." *Daedalus* (Fall): 979–95.

Empey, L. T. 1978. *American Delinquency: Its Meaning and Construction.* Homewood, Ill.: Dorsey Press.

Finestone, H. 1976. *Victims of Change.* Westport, Conn.: Greenwood Press.

Hagan, J., and J. Leon. 1977. "Rediscovering Delinquency: Social History, Political Ideology and the Sociology of Law." *American Sociological Review* 42 (August): 587–98.

Platt, A. 1974. "The Triumph of Benevolence: The Origins of the Juvenile Justice System in the United States." In Richard Quinney, ed., *Criminal Justice in America*, pp. 356–89. Boston: Little, Brown.

Schlossman, S. L. 1977. *Love and the American Delinquent.* Chicago: University of Chicago Press.

SECTION THREE

Measuring Delinquency

In examining the various ways we can measure juvenile delinquency, we encounter one area of delinquency research that is embroiled in controversy and confusion. What began as a simple counting task has evolved into debates of prejudice, discrimination, data juggling, and statistical gobbledygook. Social scientists have struggled with ways of gathering accurate and meaningful facts in the area of crime and delinquency, but the task is so complex and so subject to value judgments that we need to be extremely cautious in accepting crime statistics on their face value. This is not to say that we know nothing about the volume of crime and delinquency but rather that, as in the case of the proverbial iceberg, there is more beneath the surface than meets the eye.

Probably the best-publicized set of crime statistics is the so-called official statistics gathered from law enforcement agencies. Since 1930, the Federal Bureau of Investigation has had the responsibility of compiling a nationwide report on crime. In its Uniform Crime Reports (UCR), the FBI collects information on the number of arrests and crimes reported to state and local law enforcement agencies throughout the United States. It is important to note that the FBI has no authority to compel law enforcement agencies to report these data. Further, UCR data do not include any information from federal law enforcement agencies. However, despite these shortcomings, UCR statistics represent input from 13,000 law enforcement agencies, representing 95 percent of the total national population. While UCR figures are simply a sample of the total volume of crime in the United States and virtually ignore certain categories, such as federal offenses, organized crime, and white-collar crime, they still remain one of the best national sources of crime statistics.

Total reliance on UCR data produces considerable uneasiness among sociologists. For example, Sutherland and Cressey (1978: 29) argue that "statistics about crime and delinquency are probably the most unreliable and most difficult of all social statistics." A major part of the controversy centers on the submerged portion of the iceberg, or what Biderman and

Reiss (1967) refer to as "the dark figure of crime." A large percentage of all criminal violations go undetected by police and local citizens. In other instances, crime is detected but not reported, or is reported but not acted upon. Finally, this "dark figure" entails variations in the processing of offenders from one jurisdiction to another by police and the courts, as well as differing reactions to deviance by the community itself. The net result is that despite the impressive array of tables in the UCR, we need to assess critically how these data are gathered, categorized, and presented. For example, breaking and entering in one state may be simple trespassing in another. An upsurge in crime from one year to the next may simply be the product of a different recording procedure. Even the graphic accounting in the UCR of law enforcement officers killed in the line of duty is dimmed when one realizes that there is a far higher risk of an individual's being killed in many other fields, such as farming, mining, and construction work.

The need for another source of criminal statistics led to the development in the mid-1950s of a technique known as the self-report survey. Unlike official statistics that are subject to filtering and manipulation by agents and agencies, the self-report method goes directly to individuals and asks them to reveal their deviant activities. One of the most dramatic findings was that upwards of 90 percent of all delinquent activities were going undetected or unacted upon by law enforcement agents (Erickson and Empey, 1963). In another study, Martin Gold (1970) reported that while nearly every juvenile had broken the law, truancy and drinking probably were the most common forms of delinquency, though a wide array of self-reported property crimes, such as larceny, property destruction, and burglary, were quite common. Self-report studies also pointed out that while girls committed far fewer offenses than boys, the pattern of female delinquency paralleled that of boys (Jensen and Eve, 1976).

Probably the most notable finding in self-report research was that the relationship between social class and delinquent behavior was either nonexistent or too small to be of any consequence (Empey and Erickson, 1966). It had been alleged that official statistics were blatantly biased against the lower classes and certain minority groups. Middle- and upper-class kids could often "beat the rap" when they came into conflict with legal authorities, with the result of a gross overrepresentation of lower-class juveniles in official statistics. In fact, some self-report studies uncovered the fact that higher-status boys commit more arson, auto theft, grand theft, and breaking and entering than lower-status boys. The deference accorded self-report findings ultimately produced a pervasive sense of distrust for official statistics. In due time, virtually all research was based exclusively on self-report findings, and official statistics were ignored, if not ridiculed.

Just when it appeared that this issue was resolved, new evidence arose in defense of official statistics. Uniform Crime Report statistics do not record any information on a person's social class. They do record age, race, sex, and geographic locale, but there is no basic information on an individual's educational background, occupation or income level. While official statistics show blacks to be overrepresented in arrest data, self-report findings have revealed that blacks do tend to commit more serious delinquent acts than whites. Williams and Gold (1972), using a nationwide sample of youth, found that black males were more seriously delinquent than white males. Specifically, assaults, burglary, and theft were higher for black youth than white youth.

A third data bank was created in the late 1960s with the introduction of victimization surveys. Like self-report studies, victimization surveys go directly to the general population and inquire about people's experiences as victims of crime. The specific crimes on which victimization data are gathered are roughly equivalent to the Part I Index Crimes found in the Uniform Crime Reports. They are divided into three categories: (1) crimes against persons (rape, robbery, assault, and personal larceny); (2) crimes against households (burglary, household larceny, and motor vehicle theft; and (3) crimes against commercial establishments (burglary and robbery). The Bureau of the Census has been conducting nationwide victimization surveys based on a sample of 60,000 households (covering 136,000 individuals) and 15,000 businesses.

The most glaring finding of victimization surveys has been that the Uniform Crime Reports statistics have vastly underestimated the volume of crime in the United States. While UCR data have shown a total of 10.9 million crimes reported to the police, victimization data have revealed a total of 40.3 million crimes, or a discrepancy of 4 to 1. In general, only 30 percent of all personal crimes have been reported to the police, ranging from a high of 88.6 percent for motor vehicle theft to a low of 14.4 percent for larceny under $50. However, victimization data have supported the findings from the UCR regarding the concentration of crime in urban areas, the enormously higher involvement of males than females, the higher percentage of youths as offenders, and, most significantly, the overrepresentation of blacks as offenders. Victimization data, while looking at crime from a totally different perspective, produce virtually the same picture as the Uniform Crime Reports. What now emerges is the beginning of a reconsideration of self-report surveys and, buoyed by the findings of victimization surveys (Hindelang, 1978), an increased faith in the UCR.

Unfortunately, we are not out of the woods on this matter of gathering and interpreting crime statistics. Whichever data source we use—the UCR, self-report research, or victimization surveys—each represents a sample of the total volume of crime and delinquency. Many theories of delinquency were formulated before reliable data were collected, and other theories were based exclusively on one source of data. The state of the controversy at the present time serves as a warning that before jumping to conclusions, we need to triangulate our findings with multiple sources of data and grapple with inconsistencies when they occur.

The six articles that follow were selected to illuminate the salient aspects of this recurring controversy. Each discussion gives us a partial glimmer of delinquency viewed from a different perspective. While the conclusions are somewhat different, there is unanimous agreement that only by cautiously whittling away at the blurred image of delinquency can we hope to achieve a sharper focus.

REFERENCES

Biderman, A. J., and A. J. Reiss, Jr. 1967. "On Exploring the Dark Figure of Crime." *Annals of the American Academy of Political and Social Science* 374 (November): 1–15.

Empey, L. T., and M. L. Erickson. 1966. "Hidden Delinquency and Social Status." *Social Forces* 45 (June): 546–54.

Erickson, M. L., and L. T. Empey. 1963. "Court Records, Undetected Delinquency and Decision-Making." *The Journal of Criminal Law, Criminology and Police Science* 54 (December): 456–69.

Gold, M. 1970. *Delinquent Behavior in an American City*. Monterey, Calif.: Brooks/Cole.

Hindelang, M. J. 1978. "Race and Involvement in Common Law Personal Crimes." *American Sociological Review* 43 (February): 93–109.

Jensen, G. F., and R. Eve. 1976. "Sex Differences in Delinquency: An Examination of Popular Sociological Explanations." *Criminology* 13 (February): 427–48.

Sutherland, E. H., and D. R. Cressey. 1978. *Criminology*. Philadelphia: J. B. Lippincott.

Williams, J. R., and M. Gold. 1972. "From Delinquent Behavior to Official Delinquency." *Social Problems* 20 (Fall): 209–29.

Social Class and Criminality*

Charles R. Tittle and Wayne J. Villemez
Florida Atlantic University

ABSTRACT

Social class variations in self-reported criminality are examined using data from a comprehensive sample of adults in three states. The results prove to be contrary to any current theories concerning the relationship between social class and deviance, particularly the most popular ones that postulate an inverse relationship between the two. But it is shown that these findings are actually consistent with the bulk of previous research which shows the relationship to be problematic. The extant evidence seems to mandate reconceptualization of theories of deviance to minimize social class as a variable.

Social class has always been a fundamental variable in sociological study of crime/delinquency, and practically every theory has given socioeconomic status a prominent explanatory role. Although several patterns of relationship between class and crime have been theorized (Hirschi, b), the most popular explanations assume an inverse relationship between class position and criminality (A. Cohen, a; Gove; Merton; Miller). And despite some skepticism (see Box and Ford; Empey, for summaries), the belief has persisted for a long time that the bulk of evidence actually demonstrates such a relationship (Bytheway and May; Cressey, 157; Rossides, 443; Wheeler, 213). So firm is this belief that at least one recent book has been written to account for the "diverse empirical findings that link social inequality and deviant behavior, particularly in American Society" (Hewitt, 3). Further, even though some writers, sobered by the results of some self-report studies, are now careful to limit their generalizations to statements about social class and "officially recorded" crime or delinquency (Cohen and Short, 110–1; Reid, 66–7), confidence that at least that relationship has been established is almost universal (Hood and Sparks, 54).

Yet, the literature concerning this issue is unconvincing. For one thing, methodological weaknesses render much of the evidence problematic. Some frequently cited studies report the relationship between class and crime for ecological areas rather than for individuals (Chilton; Lander; Shaw and McKay; Slatin), and several ostensibly relevant investigations have not in fact employed indicators of individual socioeconomic status (B. Cohen; Conger and Miller; Garrett and Short; Meade; Wolfgang et al.). For example, the massive work by Wolfgang and his associates used as a measure of a boy's family status the median income of the census tract in which he lived rather than the boy's actual family income. Although they reveal a lot about contextual effects, tract characteristics may not be good proxies for individual status characteristics. Finally, some of the research is weakened by crude measurement of either social class (Hardt and Peterson; Polk et al.) or crime/delinquency (Stinchcombe), many studies have been limited to only one racial/sexual category (Empey and Erickson; Reiss and Rhodes), samples have often been less than comprehensive (Erickson; Morris), and in several instances analysis has been primitive or attenuated (Conger and Miller; Winslow; Won and Yamamoto).

But even if methodological shortcomings are disregarded and all the studies that focus on individual socioeconomic status are considered in the aggregate, the results prove to be unimpressive. Of 49 research reports we were able to locate,[1] only 24 (49%) report a general negative relationship between socioeconomic status and crime/delinquency,[2] while 19 (39%) find no class gradient,[3] and 6 (12%) report an inverse association only for some specific subcategory of individuals within a sample.[4] In addition, many of the associations that have been measured are quite small or are inconsistent.

Furthermore, those studies based on official police or court data are less consistent than has usually been assumed. For one thing, such studies are actually not very numerous. Despite frequent reference (without citation) in the literature to "many studies," we were able to find only 16 investigations that used official police or court delinquency figures and only 7 studies examining official arrest or conviction data for adults. Of these 23, 15 (65%) do report a negative relationship,[5] but 6 (26%) find no consistent class variation,[6] and 2 (8%) detect class variation only for some specific subcategory of individuals.[7] Thus the weight of evidence drawn from studies using official statistics does favor the class hypothesis, but the case is scarcely compelling.

Moreover, evidence from self-report studies, which many people believe are less biased, severely challenge the class hypothesis. Of 26 such investigations only 9 (35%) find a general negative relationship between status and crime/delinquency,[8] while 13 (50%) find no significant class variation,[9] and 4 (15%) find a negative relationship only for some specific subcategory of individuals in the sample.[10] Overall, then, it appears that

*This research was supported by NSF Grant GS–31744.

1. Studies that examine both official law enforcement statistics and self-report data are counted as two pieces of research.
2. Arnold; Belson; Bonger; Conger and Miller; Douglas et al.; Gold (2); Gould; Green; Hardt and Peterson; Havighurst et al.; Hollingshead (a); Kelly; Kelly and Pink; Kvaraceus; McDonald; Morris; Reiss and Rhodes (2); Walberg et al.; Warner and Lunt; Winslow; Wolf; Wolfgang et al.
3. Akers; Berger and Simon; Casparis and Vaz; Christie et al.; Clark and Wenninger; B. Cohen; Dentler and Monroe; Erickson (2); Empey and Erickson; Garrett and Short; Hirschi (a); Meade; Nye et al.; Pine; Polk et al.; Stark and McEvoy; Vaz (a); Won and Yamamoto.
4. Cameron; Hardt and Peterson; Stinchcombe; Voss; Williams and Gold (2).
5. Bonger; Conger and Miller; Douglas et al.; Gold; Gould; Green; Hardt and Peterson; Havighurst et al.; Hollingshead (a); Kvaraceus; Morris; Reiss and Rhodes; Warner and Lunt; Wolf; Wolfgang et al.
6. B. Cohen; Erickson; Garrett and Short; Meade; Polk et al.; Won and Yamamoto.
7. Cameron; Williams and Gold.
8. Arnold; Belson; Gold; Kelly; Kelly and Pink; McDonald; Reiss and Rhodes; Walberg et al.; Winslow.
9. Akers; Berger and Simon; Casparis and Vaz; Christie et al.; Clark and Wenninger; Dentler and Monroe; Empey and Erickson; Erickson; Hirschi (a); Nye et al.; Pine; Stark and McEvoy; Vaz (a).
10. Hardt and Peterson; Stinchcombe; Voss; Williams and Gold.

the purported relationship between social class and criminality is in fact problematic.

Not only is the general evidence tenuous, but there is a glaring deficiency in the types of extant research. Of the 49 research reports we examined, 41 (84%) are studies of juvenile misconduct, and of the 26 that analyze self-reported crime/delinquency by social class, only 1 has included adults. In fact, to our knowledge, there are in the entire literature only 2 studies of self-reported deviance among adults, and both are extremely limited in applicability. The Wallerstein and Wyle research does not include a breakdown by socioeconomic status, and the Stark and McEvoy study concerns only acts of violence. Furthermore, victimization surveys reveal only the age, sex, and race of offenders, and only then for those crimes in which there is a direct victim—offender contact (Skogan, 16). To balance out the picture, then, there is a clear need for self-report research that uses subjects of various ages, that is based on comprehensive samples, and that uses data concerning a variety of criminal acts. This paper is designed to fill that gap.

Methods

Data for the study were extracted from a large survey conducted in 1972 of the populations aged 15 and over in New Jersey, Iowa, and Oregon. These states were selected to represent variations in degree of urbanization and industrialization, and to minimize bias due to cultural variables such as exceptional age or ethnic concentrations. The sample of 1,993 was selected by area probability techniques combined with random selection of respondents within each sampled household, and two callbacks were mandated. All areas in the three states were included and stratified on the basis of density. Response rates were normal for large surveys. Seventy-four percent of all eligible households were screened and 77 percent of the screened households yielded completed interviews for a total response rate of 57 percent of all eligible households. One-hour interviews were conducted by professional interviewers representing National Analysts, Inc.

Associations between the independent variables of social class and social mobility and twelve indicators of criminality were examined under a variety of control conditions.

SOCIAL CLASS

Two separate indexes of social class were constructed. One represents a combination of family income, occupation, and education of the individual or the head of the household in which the individual lived.[11] A five-category additive index of status was developed as follows. First, raw scores for each of the three components were collapsed into four categories following the rule of marginal equalization. Each of these categories was then assigned a score from one to four. Occupations were collapsed as follows: laborers = one; skilled blue-collar workers, foremen, and craftsmen = two; clerical, sales, and other white-collar workers = three; and professional or managerial workers = four. Educational categories were derived by assigning a score of one to those with less than a high school education, a two to those with a high school diploma, a three to those with one to three years of college, and a four to those with college degrees or higher education. Income was scored: one for incomes less than $7,000 per year, two for $7,001 to $10,000 per year, three for $10,001 to $13,000 per year, and four for those over $13,000 per year.[12] Scores for each of these three class indicators were then summed to produce a total individual score ranging from three to twelve. Finally, the summed scores were collapsed into five classes that were most nearly equal in number (or three in the case of nonwhites) and each individual's position was designated by a number ranging from one to five.

This final index includes in the highest class (9%) those individuals who are high white collar, have educations of at least some college, and who generally have incomes greater than $13,000 per year.[13] The second highest class (19%) is composed of persons who are high and low white-collar workers, who have been educated for at least twelve years, and who generally report family incomes in excess of $10,000 per year. Class three respondents (26%) are predominantly high blue-collar workers (and a few lower white collar), most have high school educations, and most have incomes between $7,000 and $10,000 per year. Of those included in the second from the lowest class (31%) all are blue collar, only about one-third are high school graduates, and over half live on incomes of less than $7,000. Finally, the lowest class individuals (17%) are entirely lower blue collar; only a few have completed high school, and they survive on an income of less than $7,000 per year.

Obviously, this composite index, like all others, is somewhat arbitrary, although we have attempted to minimize subjectivity by following the rules of equalization. We are well aware of the long and controversial history of status measurement, and make no special claims for this simple additive index. The crucial test for any measure of "status" or "social class" is whether it reflects the distribution of persons or groups of persons in the status hierarchy being investigated (Hollingshead, b:567). Since students of crime generally have in mind that type of inequality most clearly signalled by income, education, and occupation when they discuss "class" as a correlate or determinant of individual non-conformity, our index is appropriate for the research problem. If we were researching the effect of "class" on the outcome of apprehension or on the structure of the law we might need an index that more directly reflects power or prestige. But our focus is the criminality of the individual. Therefore this index follows theoretical mandates, and it is faithful to previous research which has universally used the same type of indicators and combination of indicators in investigating the problem, albeit usually in less sophisticated form.

Moreover, we have heeded the caveat of Haug and Sussman concerning placement of status inconsistent individuals, and have structured the index to minimize such inconsistency. Finally, as a check on the validity of our measure (and following the recommendation of Haug and Sussman) we repeated the analyses using occupation alone as the class indicator. Similar findings with the composite index and with occupation by itself suggests that both are tapping the same "class" dimension. Thus the index used here passes every test of adequacy that we know about, and it appears to be an improvement over the class measures used in most other investigations of the class–crime issue.

SOCIAL MOBILITY

Mobility is indexed by comparing the occupational level of the respondent or the head of the respondent's household with the occupation of the head of the respondent's household when he was growing up. Since a broad measure of mobility was desirable, both occupation of origin and of destination were first collapsed into the four occupational categories noted above, and then mobility ascertained. Those whose destination status exceeded origin status were designated "up-mobile"; if origin exceeded destination, the individual was classified as "down-mobile"; and "stables" were those of equal origin and destination status.

CRIMINALITY

Six different criminal acts were considered: (1) "taking something that does not belong to you worth about $5," (2) "taking something that does not belong to you worth about $50," (3) "gambling illegally," (4) "cheating on your income tax," (5) "physically harming somebody on purpose," and (6) "smoking marijuana." Respondents registered the frequency with which they had done each of these acts over the past five years ("past offenses"), and they estimated the probability that they would engage in the behavior in the future ("If you were in a situation tomorrow where you had an extremely strong desire or need to [behavior], what are the chances that you actually would do it?"). The report of past offenses is assumed to indicate the criminality that has already been expressed while the estimate of future probability is designed to assess individual willingness to express criminality in action should the occasion arise. Our objective in employing the future probability measure was to neutralize class variation in the utility of the behavior by asking all individuals to imagine extremely strong desire or

---

11. Occupation is that at which the individual is currently employed or if unemployed that at which s/he was previously employed. Occupation for those not in the labor force (students, housewives) is designated as the occupation of the head of the household.

12. These sample percentages as of 1972 compare with the 1970 Census figures for the three states as follows. Occupation (from highest to lowest): Sample—34%, 18%, 32%, 17%; Census—27%, 25%, 30%, 18%. Education: Sample—14%, 13%, 37%, 36%; Census—14%, 13%, 37%, 36%. Income: Sample—25%, 16%, 19%, 39%; Census—23%, 17%, 18%, 42%.

13. While some of the individual components of a particular social class may appear at first blush to be inconsistent, it should be remembered that each status represents a combination of characteristics. Thus a modest occupation may be counter-balanced by a high education or income. Likewise a relatively low income cut off ($13,000 plus, which is characteristic of 25% of the population of these three states) differentiates the elite 9 percent who are designated high-status because some of those individuals with much higher incomes had modest occupations and educations, and a few who had only about $13,000 income were high in occupation and education (such as professor). Moreover, we did a separate analysis using only occupation as our status indicator to guard against some unusual distortion.

need, and then to record willingness to commit the offense.

Reports of past offenses were recorded in the following categories: (1) never, (2) 1 or 2 times, (3) 3–5 times, (4) 6–10 times, (5) 11–25 times, (6) 26–50 times, (7) more than 50 times. Estimates of future probability were made using a five-category response matrix with only the two extremes (almost no chance and excellent chance) and the middle category (50–50, even chance) named to give the impression of a continuum as well as a set of categories (see Tittle and Villemez for evidence that such a procedure is desirable). Analysis of incidence assumed any admission of these criminal acts over the past five years or any estimated probability of future violation to be indicative of criminality. Analysis of frequency of admitted offense used break points of three or more and six or more offenses over the past five years while analyses of strength of criminality used estimates of 50 percent and greater than 50 percent.

ANALYSIS

Differences among the social classes in past offenses and future probabilities are measured by the X^2 test. Any differences with 5 percent or lower probabilities of occurring by chance are considered statistically significant. The magnitude of association between class and each of the dependent variables is measured with a linear (gamma) as well as non-linear (eta) statistic. In addition, class variations in the measures of criminality were graphed and compared to determine if repetitive patterns of variation could be detected.

VALIDITY

We believe that self-report data are superior to official statistics for assessing the distribution of crime or ciminal tendencies among the social classes. Since much of the criminality of higher-status persons may be less visible than that of lower-status individuals (Chambliss, 167–69), and since several class linked variables influence the probability that there will be official intervention even when crime is known (Piliavin and Briar; Reiss), it is very likely that official criminal statistics distort the true relationship between social class and criminality. Specifically, the observed (or assumed) negative relationship between class and deviance reflected in official statistics probably tells more about differential power in avoiding detection and intervention than about behavior itself. Thus self-report data are advantageous in that they eliminate any effect of biases in official records. Moreover, these self-report data would seem to be more useful than any previously reported, because they are more extensive, the sample is more comprehensive than others, and the quality of the data appears to be good.

But, all self-report data, including these, may suffer from serious biases (Vaz, b:112–3). People may not recall important things, they may misunderstand what is being asked, they may deliberately conceal information that is threatening or which reflects socially undesirable characteristics, or they may exaggerate traits that are role confirming. While we cannot corroborate the evidence directly, we are optimistic that such contaminants have had minimal effect on the quality of these data. For one thing, the candor of the respondents is encouraging. Even with a complete adult sample, there was considerable admission of criminality, and variations among the offenses is about what would be expected impressionistically. Consider: (1) 21 percent admitted having stolen something worth $5 within the past five years, while 23 percent reported that they might do so tomorrow, (2) 7 percent reported having stolen something worth $50, and 13 percent projected some chance in the future, (3) 32 percent of the sample said they had gambled illegally while 40 percent said they might do so if in a favorable situation, (4) 12 percent admitted they had cheated on their income tax in the last half decade, and 23 percent reported some chance that they would, (5) 11 percent were guilty of assault and 14 percent were admitted potential assaulters, and (6) 15 percent confessed marijuana use in the past five years while 20 percent reported some probability that they would use it in the future.

Furthermore, comparison with FBI statistics is reassuring. Since victimization surveys (Ennis, 8–9) and other evidence (Cameron, 123; Price) suggest that official statistics underrepresent the amount of criminal behavior, one would expect valid self-report data to reveal more crime than actually became known to the police. To determine if this is the case, the survey data for those acts which correspond most closely to FBI index categories (theft of $50 and assault) were extrapolated for a five-year period. Since the survey data were reported in categories (never, 1–2, 3–5, 6–10, 11–25, 26–50, and 50+) for a time period covering the entire past five years, extrapolation required an assumption that the midpoint of each category was representative of the specific number of crimes that the respondent was admitting. These figures were then weighted so as to represent the total crimes of the population which was sampled and the final figures were compared with the total FBI data for the same five-year period. The results show that (1) in Oregon approximately twice as many felonious thefts were reported in the survey as were known to the police, and that approximately 70 times as many assaults were admitted, (2) in Iowa there were 4 times as many felonious thefts and 200 times as many assaults self-reported as were known officially, and (3) in New Jersey about 13 times as many felonious thefts and about 100 times as many assaults were self-reported as were known to the police. Of course, some of these differences could be because our categories of offense do not correspond exactly to those used by the FBI, particularly in the case of assault. Although "physically harming somebody on purpose" was considered by the respondents in this survey to be the most serious of the six offenses with 89 percent rating it "very serious," it is still probably a less restrictive and serious offense than that used by the FBI. Moreover, the subjects could have been exaggerating, although the tendency is to underreport serious crimes such as theft (Clark and Tifft), and there is reason to believe that interviewers constrain bragging (Gold). Nevertheless, these comparisons reveal patterns that would be expected from valid self-report data.

Thus, the data appear to be generally adequate. However, the possible presence of the contaminants mentioned above is especially serious in this study if they differentially affect the quality of response among those in various social classes. Some might argue that higher-status persons have better memories and better understanding of questions or that they are more honest than people of lesser statuses (in fact, the same theories that predict an inverse relationship between deviance and social class would also predict an inverse relationship between dishonesty and social class). If this were true, the result would, of course, be a serious underreporting of criminal acts by lower-status individuals. And when the relationship between class and criminality is examined, a "real" negative association would be disguised as no association at all or as a positive one.

We have no way of knowing if biases affect the classes differentially. We do believe, however, that the pattern of results casts doubt on that argument. First, it would seem that if lower-status individuals were underreporting while the higher-status weren't, then the higher classes would consistently admit an equal or greater amount of deviance than those of lesser statuses, especially for the offenses that are most threatening or socially undesirable. As the reader will shortly see, the distribution of admitted offenses follows no particular pattern. In some instances, the lowest reported deviance is among those of high statuses, and in some instances among those of middle status, and in others among the low status. Moreover, this lack of pattern prevails for the offense of felonious theft (the most threatening and undesirable) as well as gambling (the least threatening and undesirable). Because of this, we believe the results both challenge theoretical argument and that they negate the possibility of artifactual findings.

Results

Tables 1 and 2 present, for each of four race/sex categories, the evidence concerning variations among status groupings in admissions of having committed each of the six crimes within the past five years and in estimates of the probabilities that each of the acts would be committed "tomorrow" if the individual were in a situation where s/he had a great desire or need to do so. The figures show that (1) in most cases there are no significant differences at all among the status groups; (2) where significant differences among the groupings are revealed, the variations are opposite in direction to those generally assumed, and (3) there are consistent *patterns* of status variation across the six offenses only when nonwhite females estimate the future probability of crime, and then the pattern is not what most theories would lead us to expect.

Of the 48 relationships measured, only 9 (19%) show differences significant at the .05 level or better. These include admissions of illegal gambling, cheating on income tax, and smoking marijuana and estimates of the probability of engaging in those acts in the future among white males; admissions of having committed assault and smoked marijuana among nonwhite males; and estimates of the future probability of illegal gambling among white females. But in every one of these instances the association between status and criminality is positive in direction rather than negative, and in only one instance (admissions of having smoked marijuana among nonwhite males) is the association monotonic. For example, the white male status groupings do differ significantly in admissions

Table 1. PERCENT OF THOSE AT EACH SES LEVEL ADMITTING HAVING COMMITTED OFFENSES WITHIN THE PAST FIVE YEARS OR ADMITTING SOME PROBABILITY OF FUTURE OFFENSE, BY SEX AND TYPE OF OFFENSE—WHITES ONLY

	SES								
	(Highest) 5	*4*	*3*	*2*	*(Lowest) 1*	*N*	*Significance†*	*gamma*	*eta*
MALE									
Past Offenses									
$5 Theft	19	36	29	31	25	745		−.01	.11
$50 Theft	4	10	8	12	7	745		−.08	.08
Gamble	38	54	50	48	36	740	*	.05	.12
Tax Cheat	16	22	19	13	7	744	*	.20	.12
Assault	14	17	17	12	14	743		.07	.07
Marijuana	16	25	19	13	24	744	*	.04	.12
Future Probability									
$5 Theft	29	27	36	24	25	747		.07	.10
$50 Theft	20	13	19	15	15	748		.04	.07
Gamble	55	58	54	47	38	748	*	.17	.12
Tax Cheat	36	39	34	23	19	749	*	.24	.16
Assault	25	19	24	18	14	748		.12	.09
Marijuana	30	34	23	17	25	748	*	.17	.14
N ∓	89	134	203	227	96	749			
FEMALE									
Past Offense									
$5 Theft	10	13	14	14	16	1004		−.09	.04
$50 Theft	3	3	2	5	6	1006		−.23	.08
Gamble	16	19	26	20	20	1004		.00	.07
Tax Cheat	11	10	4	7	7	1005		.08	.08
Assault	4	8	6	8	9	1004		−.09	.05
Marijuana	15	11	13	9	11	1005		.07	.05
Future Probability									
$5 Theft	16	18	20	19	16	1006		.03	.04
$50 Theft	9	8	11	8	8	1006		.03	.05
Gamble	38	37	40	30	25	1006	*	.16	.12
Tax Cheat	18	24	19	14	13	1005		.17	.10
Assault	7	7	10	10	7	1005		−.01	.04
Marijuana	24	19	19	13	13	1006		.16	.09
N ∓	67	206	259	292	181	1006			

∓ + approximate; it varies from offense to offense depending upon response rate.
† = an asterisk indicates significance at the .05 level or better by X^2.

Table 2. PERCENT OF THOSE AT EACH SES LEVEL ADMITTING HAVING COMMITTED OFFENSES WITHIN THE PAST FIVE YEARS OR ADMITTING SOME PROBABILITY OF FUTURE OFFENSE, BY SEX AND TYPE OF OFFENSE—NONWHITES ONLY

	SES						
	(Highest) 3+	*2*	*(Lowest) 1*	*N*	*Significance†*	*gamma*	*eta*
MALE							
Past Offenses							
$5 Theft	43	32	41	69		.07	.10
$50 Theft	30	9	18	69		.34	.23
Gamble	57	32	47	69		.20	.21
Tax Cheat	23	9	6	69		.52	.22
Assault	27	0	12	69	*	.54	.33
Marijuana	43	18	12	69	*	.56	.31
Future Probability							
$5 Theft	17	32	29	68		−.25	.16
$50 Theft	21	9	24	68		.01	.16
Gamble	55	32	59	68		.04	.23
Tax Cheat	24	23	24	68		.02	.01
Assault	28	14	18	68		.25	.15
Marijuana	38	23	35	68		.10	.14
N ∓	30	22	17	69			
FEMALE							
Past Offense							
$5 Theft	11	26	26	64		−.27	.16
$50 Theft	6	16	15	64		−.26	.13
Gamble	17	37	26	64		−.11	.17
Tax Cheat	28	17	15	63		.26	.14
Assault	11	16	15	64		−.09	.05
Marijuana	22	22	18	63		.08	.04
Future Probability							
$5 Theft	17	26	15	64		.08	.13
$50 Theft	11	21	11	64		.05	.13
Gamble	22	53	30	64		−.04	.26
Tax Cheat	28	32	23	63		.10	.08
Assault	6	26	7	64		.06	.27
Marijuana	17	21	7	64		.29	.17
N ∓	18	19	27	64			

∓ + approximate; it varies from offense to offense depending upon response rate.
† = an asterisk indicates significance at the .05 level or better by X^2.

of illegal gambling (Table 1, row 3), but the association is +.05. Thus 36 percent of the lowest-status white males admit illegal gambling in the past five years, but 38 percent of the highest-status also admit having done so, and 54 percent of the next to highest-status white males confess having gambled illegally. Moreover, although the variation in admitted marijuana use among nonwhite males (Table 2, row 6) is a monotonic 12 percent, 18 percent, 43 percent, the greatest admitted use is among the highest status rather than the lowest.

Finally, only one of the eight sets of data shows a similar pattern of status variation across all offenses, and for no offense is the pattern of status variation similar for all race/sex categories as it should be if social status is a key determinant. Among nonwhite females there is a curvilinear (although nonsignificant for each specific crime) pattern in which estimates of the probability of future crime for all six acts is greatest among those in the middle-status group (Table 2, rows 20–25). For example, 11 percent of the lowest- and highest-status nonwhite females estimate that they would steal something worth $50 if "tomorrow" they were in a favorable situation, while 21 percent of the middle-status women project some probability of committing the crime (Table 2, row 21). Similarly, 7 percent of the lowest and 6 percent of the highest-status nonwhite women estimate that they would physically harm somebody on purpose if in a favorable situation in the future while 26 percent of the middle-status women make this estimate (Table 2, row 24). But note that the highest estimates are not among the lowest-status as most theories would predict, but rather they are made by the middle group.

The data, then, are completely contrary to expectations of an inverse relationship between social class and crime. Indeed, they are inconsistent with any existing theory linking social class to deviance. Although other theories are rarely clearly formulated, various theoretical arguments imply particular relationships between social status and criminality (see Hirschi, b). For example, many social scientists and humanitarians assume that poverty or other conditions of lower-class life are the causes of crime (President's Commission). Therefore, it is expected that the greatest incidence of criminality will be among those in the lowest status. By implication other social classes will have few criminal tendencies and variations among them will be minimal. The picture is one of an extremely skewed distribution. But examination of the data in Tables 1 and 2 shows that the greatest criminal proneness is not concentrated in the lowest statuses. Only 5 of 48 distributions are so characterized.

Other theories emphasize that social rules are made by certain elite groups. These groups formulate behavioral standards to their own advantage, making deviant those acts that non-elites are most likely to practice (Chambliss and Seidman; Quinney). The implication of such arguments is a distribution in which those of the highest class will have lower rates of crime while those of other classes will have higher rates but with little variation among themselves. Again the findings are contrary. Only 12 of 48 distributions show the lowest incidence in the highest class, and in those cases variations among the other classes are substantial.

Still other theories lead one to expect a positive relationship between social status and criminality (Kohn; Sorokin and Lunden; Veblen). One argument is that the more highly placed an individual is in a system, the more likely he is to have developed a hardened conscience, to be motivated to commit unacceptable acts to maintain his position, and to view himself as above the moral and legal constraints that affect others. Kohn's thesis, on the other hand, is that limited education and constrained job conditions lead to restricted autonomy and an overemphasis on conformity among those of lower status. Thus the higher one's status, the greater the likelihood that he will be self-directing and able to overcome the constraints of normative obedience. But the data do not bear out an expectation that the higher the social class, the greater the criminality. As we have already seen, only 9 of 48 associations are positive and statistically significant, and only 1 of them is monotonic.

Finally, some maintain that lower- and upper-status individuals will both exhibit high criminality with the middle-status people remaining at a low level. For example, Homans (357–8) argues that the lower-status person has nothing to lose while the upper-status individual can take risks without jeopardizing his status. The middle-status person, on the other hand, has something to lose by deviance, but he does not have secure enough status to risk anything. The projected relationship between class and criminality is therefore curvilinear with the lowest incidence of criminality among those in the middle statuses. But, this pattern is found in only 8 of 48 tests.

Clearly, then, these data call into question the significance of social status as a determinant or predictor of the incidence of criminal behavior, and in particular they challenge the argument that criminality is negatively related to socioeconomic status. In fact, although the evidence does not favor any of the five theoretical predictions, the strongest support is for a positive association between class and crime while the weakest support is found for an inverse relationship. The data do show that in 17 of 48 distributions (35%) either those in the lowest status have the greatest deviance or those in the highest status have the least deviance. Although this suggests some possible class linkage at the extremes, the inconsistency in these concentrations as well as variations among the other statuses negates any hypothesis of negative association.

As a precaution against artifactual findings, we examined the relationship between socioeconomic status and criminality using only occupation as an indicator of class. It is conceivable that our measure of socioeconomic status, which combines income, occupation, and education, somehow distorts a relationship that others have found with simpler measures. So, we classified respondents into four occupational levels (three in the case of nonwhites) and redid the entire analysis. This alternative procedure produced conclusions almost exactly the same as those reached using the composite measure.[14]

Still, some theorists maintain that it is the experience of life as one grows up that determines the probability of crime (see for example, Glueck and Glueck). And since one's early life experiences are presumably influenced by socioeconomic status (Bronfenbrenner; Hewitt), then one might expect that the status of an individual's childhood household would be predictive of adult criminality although socioeconomic status as an adult might not be. Therefore we examined the relationship between the occupational status of the head of the childhood household and our measures of criminality. These analyses produced results consistent in every way with the earlier ones. The only repetitive pattern found was a curvilinear relationship between status and deviance across all offenses among nonwhite males. But contrary to theoretical expectations, the middle group reported the highest incidence of deviance, not the lowest.[15]

It is possible, of course, that the findings would be different if other variables were taken into account. Hirschi suggests that since socioeconomic status usually changes with age, the relationship between status and criminality may be of one type for some age groups but of another type for other ages. And some researchers maintain that the size or heterogeneity of social milieux as well as the consistency between personal status and the status of others in the social context may influence whether there is status variation in crime/delinquency (Clark and Wenninger; Harry). To test these possibilities, we examined our data for whites, controlling age, place and size of residence, and consistency of respondent status with neighborhood characteristics. Only whites were used because the number of nonwhites within some of the subcategories is too small to permit meaningful conclusions. Age was broken down into four categories: 15–24, 25–44, 45–64, and 65 plus; size of place was categorized as: under 10,000, 10,000–49,999, 50,000–249,999, and 250,000 or more; and the data were analysed separately for each of the three states. In addition, analyses were performed for subgroups representing: (1) those who lived in residences that were judged by the interviewer to be about the same in value as most of those in the area, (2) those who lived in residences more valuable than most in the area, and (3) those who lived in residences less valuable than the norm.

Introduction of these control variables does not alter the conclusions in any way. For no subcategory of age, size or place of residence, or neighborhood/personal status consistency do we find clear evidence of an inverse relationship between socioeconomic status and our measures of the incidence of criminality. Moreover, we find no evidence supporting any of the other postulated relationships between social status and deviance. For example, consider Tables 3 and 4 which show class variations in reported offenses among white males and females respectively for each age category. Although criminality declines with each age group for both males and females, only 3 of the 48 distributions show a significant difference among the SES levels in reported offenses, and in only 20 of 48 instances do the data tend to vary in an inverse direction (gamma = .05 or greater). Although there is a pattern of negative variation in five of six instances among adult females aged 25–44 only three are statistically significant and only two are monotonic . Moreover, for only one subcategory (females aged 65+) is there evidence of a consistent pattern suggested by some other theory. In that instance five of six cases concentrate all offenders in the lowest category. But, given the small number of offenders in that age group (1 out of 131 for five of six offenses), this pattern is meaningless. In a similar fashion the data in other control conditions confirm the original conclusions.

The data considered so far prove to be completely nonsupportive of all current theories about social class and criminality, particularly the most popular ones that postulate an inverse relationship. But those data concern only the admitted incidence of offenses and *any* estimated probability of future incidence. It is possible that a test using frequency of offenses or using a more demanding level of estimated probability of incidence would show patterned class differences. After all, some researchers have found seriousness of offense to be class related, and many would argue on theoretical grounds that classes should differ at least in the frequency with which they do criminal things.

Therefore we compared the socioeconomic status grouping in terms of the percent who admitted at least three offenses within the past five years, and also in terms of the percent who admitted more than five offenses within that time period. In addition, we compared the groups with respect to the percent who estimated the probability of future offenses to be at least 50 percent, and also the percent estimating the probability of future offense to be greater than 50 percent. Table 5 reports the results for whites only (separate analysis for nonwhites was impossible because of small *N*s) using the criteria of three or more admitted offenses and 50 per-

Table 3. PERCENT OF THOSE AT EACH SES LEVEL ADMITTING HAVING COMMITTED OFFENSES WITHIN THE PAST FIVE YEARS, BY AGE—WHITE MALES ONLY

	SES								
	(Highest) 5	*4*	*3*	*2*	*(Lowest) 1*	*N*	*Significance†*	*gamma*	*eta*
15–24									
$5 Theft	23	62	58	57	57	169		−.09	.19
$50 Theft	0	18	19	24	18	169		−.17	.15
Gamble	31	50	57	49	61	168		−.12	.15
Tax Cheat	8	18	23	12	11	169		.12	.15
Assault	38	30	35	26	36	168		.03	.10
Marijuana	54	59	44	35	64	169		.04	.22
25–44									
$5 Theft	25	34	33	44	38	245		−.18	.13
$50 Theft	9	8	7	15	0	245		−.13	.13
Gamble	50	67	58	68	50	244		−.09	.14
Tax Cheat	24	29	25	23	12	245		.08	.07
Assault	12	17	15	16	12	246		−.03	.04
Marijuana	19	20	19	15	38	244		.02	.10
45–64									
$5 Theft	19	18	12	12	19	205		.08	.09
$50 Theft	3	7	6	3	6	205		.05	.08
Gamble	34	52	44	36	31	203		.08	.13
Tax Cheat	16	15	14	8	12	205		.17	.09
Assault	6	7	14	3	6	204		.15	.16
Marijuana	3	0	8	2	6	206		−.01	.15
65+									
$5 Theft	0	15	0	5	4	122		.07	.19
$50 Theft	0	8	0	5	2	122		.07	.14
Gamble	12	15	21	30	20	121		−.06	.13
Tax Cheat	0	15	5	5	2	122		.33	.18
Assault	0	8	0	0	2	122		.08	.18
Marijuana	0	8	0	0	2	122		.08	.18
N∓	85	139	201	226	96	747			

∓ + approximate; it varies from offense to offense depending upon response rate.
† = an asterisk indicates significance at the .05 level or better by X^2.

14. Data can be provided on request.
15. Data can be provided on request.

Table 4. PERCENT OF THOSE AT EACH SES LEVEL ADMITTING HAVING COMMITTED OFFENSES WITHIN THE PAST FIVE YEARS, BY AGE—WHITE FEMALES ONLY

	SES								
	(Highest) 5	*4*	*3*	*2*	*(Lowest) 1*	*N*	*Significance†*	*gamma*	*eta*
15–24									
$5 Theft	22	32	37	25	47	204		−.07	.17
$50 Theft	11	10	2	9	12	206		−.13	.15
Gamble	22	32	23	24	28	206		.02	.07
Tax Cheat	11	16	3	8	12	206		.05	.16
Assault	11	21	15	21	22	205		−.08	.08
Marijuana	44	34	37	28	38	205		.05	.09
25–44									
$5 Theft	11	11	12	19	36	374	*	−.30	.19
$50 Theft	3	3	3	6	16	374	*	−.38	.17
Gamble	20	18	37	22	39	374	*	−.13	.19
Tax Cheat	11	11	6	11	23	374		−.13	.13
Assault	6	8	5	6	19	374		−.18	.15
Marijuana	17	11	9	5	19	374		.12	.15
45–64									
$5 Theft	5	6	0	8	4	287		−.01	.14
$50 Theft	0	0	0	2	2	287		−.66	.11
Gamble	10	16	16	19	18	287		−.09	.06
Tax Cheat	10	6	3	5	2	287		.27	.11
Assault	0	2	2	2	4	287		−.32	.07
Marijuana	0	0	2	4	2	287		−.44	.11
65+									
$5 Theft	0	0	0	0	2	131		—[a]	.09
$50 Theft	0	0	0	0	2	131		—	.09
Gamble	0	0	5	5	8	130		−.34	.10
Tax Cheat	0	0	0	0	2	130		—	.09
Assault	0	0	0	0	2	130		—	.09
Marijuana	0	0	0	0	2	131		—	.09
N∓	66	205	255	290	180	996			

∓ + approximate; it varies from offense to offense depending upon response rate.
† = an asterisk indicates significance at the .05 level or better by X^2.
[a] = gammas are meaningless with this distribution of data.

cent estimated probability of future offense (results using the other criteria are similar).

Examination of the figures shows that our previous conclusions are sustained when the criteria are frequency of offense and *high* probability of future incidence. Only 6 of the 24 distributions show statistically significant differences among the socioeconomic groupings. Of these, only one is inverse; and it is not monotonic. Five of the significant associations are positive, but again none is monotonic and none are large (mean gamma equals .18). None of the distributions show the greatest concentration at the bottom; 5 do show the lowest concentration at the top, but variation among the other status groupings is substantial. Finally, 4 of the distributions are curvilinear but in all instances the curve bulges outward rather than inward as theoretically postulated. Hence these additional data further demonstrate the absence of any consistent association between socioeconomic status and criminality that has been postulated by any theory. And since the weakest evidence is found for the hypothesis of a negative relationship between social class and crime, this popular assumption is most severely challenged.

Although the data do not show a relationship between class and criminality, it is still possible that movement from one socioeconomic status to another during one's life cycle is predictive of criminality. But based on current theory, it is impossible to generate consistent predictions about the nature of the relationship between mobility and crime. According to anomie theory, deviance results from the inability to achieve success goals. Since the upwardly mobile are ostensibly successful goal achievers and downwardly mobiles are failures, one might be tempted to hypothesize the lowest incidence of crime among the upwardly mobile and the greatest among the downwardly mobile, with those remaining at the same class position exhibiting a moderate amount of nonconformity. And indeed the only two studies of mobility and deviance that we know about have demonstrated just such a relationship (Pine; Robins et al.), although longitudinal data in one showed that the direction of causality is opposite to that postulated by the theory.

But if one recognizes that aspiration for success is a key variable in the theory (Elliott; Stinchcombe), then predictions are not so straightforward. Those who are upwardly mobile may still perceive themselves as failures, if their aspirations were for even greater movement and they may be innovators anyway. Similarly those who are downwardly mobile may have aspired for no higher position, and consequently may not experience a conflict between goals and means. Following this logic, the upwardly mobiles may be expected to have low incidence of crime only if they have achieved as much as they aspired to, and the downwardly mobile would be expected to have higher incidences of crime only if their positions represent thwarted aspirations. Furthermore, those who remain at the same position may actually perceive themselves as failures, especially in a culture that emphasizes upward movement.

If this were not complex enough, other theories lead to even more specific expectations. Bohlke, for example, argues that modern individuals may be mobile but lack the value orientations that led to mobility in an earlier era. Under these conditions movement in the class structure is likely to result in social rejection by those already at a particular class level (cf. Ellis and Lane) producing family stress and stifling appropriate socialization into the new value system. Consequently those of blue-collar origins who move upward without a change in values are likely to be more criminal while those who move upward with a value change are likely to be less criminal than others. Likewise those of white-collar origins who move downward or remain stable, but who have middle-class values will be more criminal than others while those of white-collar origins who move upward with a value change will be less criminal than others. And, to add further confusion some argue that deviance results from weak social attachments (Hirschi, a), and since mobility is assumed to weaken social bonds (Ellis and Lane), one would imagine that both the upward and downward mobiles would exhibit greater deviance than the stables. In short, theoretical prediction of criminality on the basis of movement within the class hierarchy alone is impossible. And given the many findings in the stratification literature that show no independent mobility effects on other types of behavior (e.g., Hodge and Treiman; Jackman; Vorwaller) one would not expect to find any independent effects of mobility on criminality in these data.

Nevertheless, because many people assume a negative relationship between upward mobility and deviance (Robins et al.) and because some evidence of such a relationship does exist, we report data in Tables 6 and 7 concerning generational occupational mobility and our measures of self-reported criminality. These data are completely contrary to an expectation of a negative relationship between upward mobility and criminality. Only 5 of 48 distributions (10%) show significant differences among those with different mobility statuses, and four of these reflect generally positive associations. In fact 37 of the 48 measured associations (77%) are in a positive direction. This is shown by the fact that in 26 out of 48 instances (54%) the greatest incidence of criminality is among the upwardly mobile, while in 29 of 48 instances (60%), the lowest incidence is among the downwardly mobile.

Thus, although the data do not show impressive differences of statistical significance, they do seem to form a suggestive pattern, albeit one which is contrary to the patterns reported in other studies, and one which is unpredictable from any current theory. Those who remain at the same position as their fathers or who move upward tend to be more criminal than those who are downwardly mobile. It is worth noting in this regard that nonwhite males appear to exhibit this pattern more dramatically than any of the other categories. Although none of the associations are statistically significant, all 12 of the associations for nonwhite males are positive and in every instance considerably exceed in magnitude those for the other categories. It appears, therefore, that the tendency for the upwardly mobiles and stables to be more criminalistic than the downwardly mobile is especially strong, at least in its consistency across offenses for nonwhite men. It could be that for these individuals crime is a path of upward mobility or at least a way of maintaining the status they already enjoy. Although, of course, the data could mean that status is so important for nonwhite men that its improvement or maintenance creates motivations toward crime. In any case the data suggest that for some subcategories of individuals change in status may bear some relationship to criminality.

Discussion

These findings not only weaken the proposition that those of lesser status are more criminally inclined than those more highly placed, but they also

Table 5. PERCENT OF THOSE AT EACH SES LEVEL ADMITTING HAVING COMMITTED AT LEAST THREE OFFENSES WITHIN THE PAST FIVE YEARS OR ADMITTING AT LEAST 50 PERCENT PROBABILITY OF FUTURE OFFENSE, BY SEX AND TYPE F OFFENSE—WHITES ONLY

	SES								
	(Highest) 5	*4*	*3*	*2*	*(Lowest) 1*	*N*	*Significance†*	*gamma*	*eta*
MALE									
Past Offenses									
$5 Theft	4	14	10	8	6	745		.09	.10
$50 Theft	0	2	3	0	0	745		.28	.11
Gamble	28	40	39	36	27	740		.04	.10
Tax Cheat	6	11	7	5	1	744	*	.27	.12
Assault	2	4	7	3	7	743		.10	.10
Marijuana	10	18	12	09	14	744		.07	.10
Future Probability									
$5 Theft	22	16	25	15	16	747		.10	.11
$50 Theft	14	8	10	11	8	748		.03	.06
Gamble	44	48	43	37	28	748	*	.17	.13
Tax Cheat	20	19	24	12	12	749	*	.18	.14
Assault	18	10	16	12	9	748		.11	.09
Marijuana	23	29	19	13	22	748	*	.15	.14
N ∓	88	133	202	226	96	745			
FEMALE									
Past Offense									
$5 Theft	3	1	2	5	3	1004		−.24	.08
$50 Theft	0	0	0	1	1	1006		−.68	.08
Gamble	6	9	17	14	10	1004	*	−.03	.11
Tax Cheat	0	2	1	3	2	1005		−.18	.07
Assault	2	1	1	3	2	1004		−.19	.08
Marijuana	9	7	6	6	7	1005		.05	.04
Future Probability									
$5 Theft	7	11	14	14	13	1006		−.09	.06
$50 Theft	6	4	7	6	7	1006		−.07	.05
Gamble	29	28	33	23	19	1006	*	.14	.11
Tax Cheat	15	14	10	9	9	1005		.14	.06
Assault	7	4	7	6	4	1005		.03	.05
Marijuana	18	14	15	12	10	1006		.11	.06
N∓	68	206	259	291	181	1005			

∓ + approximate; it varies from offense to offense depending upon response rate.
† = an asterisk indicates significance at the .05 level or better by X^2.

Table 6. PERCENT OF VARIOUS MOBILITY STATUSES WHO ADMIT HAVING COMMITTED OFFENSES WITHIN THE PAST FIVE YEARS AND WHO ADMIT SOME PROBABILITY OF FUTURE OFFENSE, BY SEX AND TYPE OF OFFENSE—WHITES ONLY

	MOBILITY						
	Up	*Stable*	*Down*	*N*	*Significance†*	*gamma*	*eta*
MALE							
Past Offenses							
$5 Theft	32	26	25	656		.11	.07
$50 Theft	7	10	8	656		−.03	.04
Gamble	53	44	41	651		.14	.09
Tax Cheat	19	14	15	655		.07	.05
Assault	14	14	12	654		.05	.02
Marijuana	14	18	14	656		−.02	.06
Future Probability							
$5 Theft	30	29	24	656		.09	.05
$50 Theft	16	17	14	657		.06	.03
Gamble	56	51	45	657		.12	.07
Tax Cheat	36	29	24	658	*	.18	.10
Assault	22	21	16	657		.13	.07
Marijuana	22	24	19	657		.06	.05
N ∓	171	304	181	656			
FEMALE							
Past Offense							
$5 Theft	8	18	13	795	*	−.13	.12
$50 Theft	3	5	3	797		.01	.05
Gamble	22	23	20	795		.03	.03
Tax Cheat	9	8	7	796		.07	.02
Assault	5	9	5	795		.01	.08
Marijuana	10	15	08	796	*	.06	.10
Future Probability							
$5 Theft	16	22	17	797		−.01	.07
$50 Theft	9	10	8	797		.01	.02
Gamble	42	38	28	797	*	.18	.11
Tax Cheat	21	19	16	796		.10	.05
Assault	6	10	11	796		−.19	.07
Marijuana	18	18	14	797		.09	.05
N∓	222	345	228	795			

∓ + approximate; it varies from offense to offense depending upon response rate.
† = an asterisk indicates significance at the .05 level or better by X^2.

seem to suggest that social class is almost irrelevant for criminality. If there is no pattern at all by which status is associated with criminality, then one must conclude that social class really isn't worth the theoretical attention it has received. But such a conclusion may be premature. Although we found little evidence that social class or movement between classes makes any difference in predicting criminality, there are reasons to reserve judgment about the general import of social class.

First, we did not consider all types of deviance or criminality. Perhaps the status groupings would have shown clear patterns of differentiation had we analyzed such offenses as burglary, auto theft, expense account padding, or assault with deadly weapons. Indeed, some might argue that the offenses considered in this study do not provide a fair test of the class hypothesis since they are relatively less serious. But two observations weaken that position. For one thing, the offenses we included were perceived to be quite serious by the respondents. Eighty-nine percent viewed the offense corresponding to our category of assault as being "very serious" with less than one-half of one percent thinking it "not at all serious." Eighty percent viewed $50 theft as very serious while less than 1 percent perceived it as minor, and 66 percent judged income tax cheating to be very serious with less than 3 percent seeing it as trivial. Furthermore, 63 percent considered $5 theft to be very serious and only 4 percent believed it minor, while 60 percent thought marijuana smoking to be extremely serious and 11 percent thought it not to be serious at all. And even illegal gambling, the least serious offense in the minds of our respondents was judged very serious by 40 percent and minor by only 17 percent. But more important, within the range of offenses we examined there is no tendency for the class/criminality relationship to be any more marked for those offenses perceived by the respondents to be more serious than for those considered less serious.

Nevertheless, caution is called for because there could be class variation for some offenses that we did not include. Moreover, broad categories of offense like theft of something worth $50 may actually mask certain kinds of class differences. For example, higher-status people could conceivably steal in subtler and less visible ways relative to lower-status people who might commit property crimes in more open and identifiable contexts. Similarly, high-status people may gamble illegally but within familiar primary group contexts while lower-status people may gamble in impersonal contexts that overlap with general criminal subcultures.

Second, our class distinctions are not rooted in particular communities, but rather are general in character. Thus they may have little meaning in specific neighborhoods where the individuals live. In some places clear and widely recognized status distinctions may exist that do not necessarily correspond to the general classifications that we have made or to those in other places. Perhaps social class does predict deviance in those contexts where general status distinctions are clear although it may be irrelevant when comparisons across communities are made or where the differentiations between categories do not reflect community standards.

Third, socioeconomic status may be important only in interaction with other variables. Just as social mobility would be expected to produce crime only if things like aspirations are simultaneously taken into account, so it may be that social class makes a difference only when it is considered in conjunction with variables like individual perception of rank. Indeed, many would argue that class is important primarily as a subjective phenomenon.

Fourth, as noted earlier, one must be cautious in accepting self-report data at face value. Although we believe these data to be minimally contaminated by differential error, we cannot be absolutely sure. And until it can somehow be determined that the social classes are equally likely to distort, forget, or deliberately conceal information, we believe that a healthy measure of reserve is called for.

Finally, although people within the socioeconomic categories used here do not seem to differ in their propensities toward the specific criminal

Table 7. PERCENT OF VARIOUS MOBILITY STATUSES WHO ADMIT HAVING COMMITTED OFFENSES WITHIN THE PAST FIVE YEARS AND WHO ADMIT SOME PROBABILITY OF FUTURE OFFENSE, BY SEX AND TYPE OF OFFENSE—NONWHITES ONLY

	MOBILITY						
	Up	*Stable*	*Down*	*N*	*Significance*†	*gamma*	*eta*
MALE							
Past Offenses							
$5 Theft	44	29	33	52		.15	.13
$50 Theft	31	19	7	52		.50	.24
Gamble	56	48	40	52		.20	.12
Tax Cheat	19	14	13	52		.13	.06
Assault	19	14	7	52		.33	.14
Marijuana	38	33	7	52		.48	.29
Future Probability							
$5 Theft	27	29	13	51		.23	.16
$50 Theft	27	19	13	51		.14	.07
Gamble	67	43	40	51		.33	.23
Tax Cheat	27	29	13	51		.23	.16
Assault	27	24	7	51		.40	.21
Marijuana	40	33	20	51		.29	.17
N ∓	16	21	15	52			
FEMALE							
Past Offense							
$5 Theft	22	10	23	42		−.08	.17
$50 Theft	11	5	15	42		−.20	.16
Gamble	33	15	31	42		−.02	.20
Tax Cheat	44	5	8	41	*	.64	.45
Assault	11	10	15	42		−.14	.07
Marijuana	33	10	8	41		.50	.28
Future Probability							
$5 Theft	33	5	23	42		.09	.31
$50 Theft	33	5	23	42		.09	.31
Gamble	33	35	31	42		.04	.04
Tax Cheat	33	15	23	42		.12	.17
Assault	11	10	15	42		−.15	.08
Marijuana	0	15	15	42		−.41	.19
N ∓	9	20	13	42			

∓ + approximate; it varies from offense to offense depending upon response rate.
† = an asterisk indicates significance at the .05 level or better by X^2.

acts considered, they might well differ in the extent to which they have been or might be apprehended and punished, in their beliefs as to whether these acts are morally acceptable, and in the ways in which the acts occur (with others or alone, etc.).

Thus, it is clearly too soon to reject the class variable. Nevertheless, the findings do mandate serious rethinking of the issue of social class and criminality. After all, these results are, in fact, consistent with the bulk of previous research which actually demonstrates that the relationship between class and crime/delinquency is problematic. Yet most sociologists cling to the belief that social class is intimately linked with crime. Indeed, this is so widely taken for granted that hardly anyone bothers to treat it as controversial. Even those who recognize the inconsistency of the available evidence, often do no more than pay lip service and then fall back into discussion implying the great importance of social class (e.g., Vaz, b:105–21).

We believe it is time to question just how vital social class is as a determinant or consequence of crime. It seems to us that the variables of importance in most current theories of deviance can easily be conceptualized as operating independently of social class. For example, it is quite plausible to imagine that people of all classes can experience inconsistency between goals and means which is relative to their aspirations rather than to their actual positions. Similarly, in an age of mass communication and widespread deviance, it is not too hard to believe that differential association with definitions favorable toward deviance is pretty equally distributed across the class spectrum. And one can easily apply interaction, identity, psychodynamic, and deterrence theories (see A. Cohen, b) to all socioeconomic groups.

Furthermore, there is reason to question the general viability of social class for analyzing any phenomena in a mass consumption society. Many authors have noted the confused and overlapping nature of statuses in modern times (Cuber and Kenkel; Giddens; Jackson and Curtis; Landecker; Pfautz; Stone and Form) and students of stratification today rarely discuss class or status distinctions in attitudes or behavior. Thus it seems that the prominence of social class in sociological theories of deviance may be an instance of cultural lag.

Conclusions

Research concerning social class and crime/delinquency reveals that the relationship between the two is problematic despite widespread belief to the contrary. Moreover, analysis of data, from a three state survey, concerning variations among socioeconomic groupings in self-reports of crime and criminal propensity fails to reveal any consistent class linkage. In fact, the findings contradict all current theories about the relationship between social class and criminality. Hence the evidence would seem to make it imperative that sociologists surrender their general faith in the efficacy of the class variable for understanding deviance, and that they seek to reconceptualize theories of crime/deviance to minimize social class.

References

Akers, R. L. 1964. "Socioeconomic Status and Delinquent Behavior: A Retest." *Journal of Research in Crime and Delinquency* 1(January):38–46.

Arnold, W. R. 1965. "Continuities in Research: Scaling Delinquent Behavior." *Social Problems* 13(Summer):59–66.

Belson, William A. 1975. *Juvenile Theft: The Causal Factors*. London: Harper & Row.

Berger, A. S., and W. Simon. 1974. "Black Families and the Moynihan Report: A Research Evaluation." *Social Problems* 22(December):145–61.

Bohlke, R. H. 1961. "Social Mobility, Stratification Inconsistency and Middle Class Delinquency." *Social Problems* 8(Spring):351–63.

Bonger, William Adrian. 1916. *Criminality and Economic Conditions*. Boston: Little, Brown.

Box, S. and J. Ford. 1971. "The Facts Don't Fit: On the Relationship Between Social Class and Criminal Behavior." *The Sociological Review* 19(February):31–52.

Bronfenbrenner, U. 1958. "Socialization and Social Class Through Time and Space." In E. E. Maccoby, T. M. Newcomb, and E. L. Hartley (eds.), *Readings in Social Psychology*. New York: Holt.

Bytheway, W. R., and D. R. May. 1971. "On Fitting the 'Facts' of Social Class and Criminal Behavior: A Rejoinder to Box and Ford." *The Sociological Review* 19 (November):585–607.

Cameron, Mary Owen. 1964. *The Booster and the Snitch*. Glencoe: Free Press.

Casparis, J., and E. W. Vaz. 1974. "Social Class and Self-Reported Delinquent Acts Among Swiss Boys." *International Journal of Comparative Sociology* 14(1–2):47–58.

Chambliss, William J. 1975. *Criminal Law in Action*. Santa Barbara: Hamilton.

Chambliss, William J., and Robert B. Seidman. 1971. *Law, Order and Power*. Reading: Addison Wesley.

Chilton, R. J. 1964. "Continuity in Delinquency Area Research: A Comparison of Studies for Baltimore, Detroit, and Indianapolis." *American Sociological Review* 29(February):71–83.

Christie, N., J. Andenaes, and S. Skirbekk. 1965. "A Study of Self-Reported Crime."In *Scandanavian Studies in Criminology. Vol. 1*. London: Tavistock.

Clark, J. P., and L. L. Tifft. 1966. "Polygraph and Interview Validation of Self-Reported Deviant Behavior." *American Sociological Review* 31(August):516–23.

Clark, J. P., and E. P. Wenninger. 1962. "Socioeconomic Class and Area as Correlates of Illegal Behavior Among Juveniles." *American Sociological Review* 27 (December):826–34.

Cohen, Albert K. a:1955. *Delinquent Boys: The Culture of the Gang*. New York: Free Press.

———. b:1966. *Deviance and Control*. Englewood Cliffs: Prentice-Hall.

Cohen, A. K., and J. F. Short, Jr. 1971. "Crime and Juvenile Delinquency." In Robert K. Merton and Robert Nisbet (eds.), *Contemporary Social Problems*. New York: Harcourt Brace Jovanovich.

Cohen, B. 1969. "The Delinquency of Gangs and Spontaneous Groups." In Marvin Wolfgang and Thorsten Sellin (eds.), *Delinquency: Selected Studies*. New York: Wiley.

Conger, John Janeway, and Wilbur C. Miller. 1966. *Personality, Social Class, and Delinquency*. New York: Wiley.

Cressey, Donald R. 1966. "Crime." In Robert K. Merton and Robert Nisbet (eds.), *Contemporary Social Problems*. New York: Harcourt Brace & World.

Cuber, John, and William Kenkel. 1954. *Social Stratification in the United States*. New York: Appleton-Century Crofts.

Dentler, R. A., and L. J. Monroe. 1961. "Social Correlates of Early Adolescent Theft." *American Sociological Review* 26(October):733–43.

Douglas, J. W. B., J. M. Ross, W. A. Hammond, and D. G. Mulligan. 1966. "Delinquency and Social Class." *British Journal of Criminology* 6(July):294–302.

Elliott, D. S. 1962. "Delinquency and Perceived Opportunity." *Sociological Inquiry* 32 (Spring):216–27.

Ellis, R. A., and W. C. Lane. 1967. "Social Mobility and Social Isolation: A Test of Sorokin's Dissociative Hypothesis." *American Sociological Review* 32(April): 237–

53.
Empey, Lamar T. 1967. "Delinquency Theory and Recent Research." *Journal of Research in Crime and Delinquency* 4(January):28–42.
Empey, L. T., and M. L. Erickson. 1966. "Hidden Delinquency and Social Status." *Social Forces* 44(June):546–54.
Ennis, Phillip. 1967. *Criminal Victimization in the United States: A Report of a National Survey*. Washington: Government Printing Office.
Erickson, M. 1973. "Group Violations, Socioeconomic Status and Official Delinquency." *Social Forces* 52(September):41–52.
Garrett, M., and J. F. Short, Jr. 1975. "Social Class and Delinquency: Predictions and Outcomes of Police-Juvenile Encounters." *Social Problems* 22(February): 368–83.
Giddens, Anthony. 1973. *The Class Structure of the Advanced Societies*. New York: Harper & Row.
Glueck, Sheldon, and Eleanor Glueck. 1934. *One Thousand Juvenile Delinquents*. Cambridge: Harvard University Press.
Gold, M. 1966. "Undetected Delinquent Behavior." *Journal of Research in Crime and Delinquency* 3(January):27–46.
Gould, L. C. 1969. "Juvenile Entrepreneurs." *American Journal of Sociology* 74(May): 710–19.
Gove, Walter R. (ed.). 1975. *The Labelling of Deviance: Evaluating a Perspective*. New York: Wiley.
Green, E. 1970. "Race, Social Status, and Criminal Arrest." *American Sociological Review* 35(June):476–90.
Hardt, R. H., and S. J. Peterson. 1968. "Neighborhood Status and Delinquency Activity as Indexed by Police Records and a Self-Report Survey." *Criminologica* VI(May):37–47.
Harry, Joseph. 1974. "Social Class and Delinquency: One More Time." *Sociological Quarterly* 15(Spring):294–301.
Haug, M. R., and M. B. Sussman. 1971. "The Indiscriminate State of Social Class Measurement." *Social Forces* 49(June):549–63.
Havighurst, Robert J., Paul Hoover Bowman, Gordon P. Liddle, Charles V. Matthews, and James V. Pierce. 1961. *Growing Up in River City*. New York: Wiley.
Hewitt, John P. 1970. *Social Stratification and Deviant Behavior*. New York: Random House.
Hirschi, Travis. a:1969. *Causes of Delinquency*. Berkeley: University of California Press.
______. b:1972. "Social Class and Crime." In Gerald W. Thielbar and Saul D. Feldman (eds.). *Issues in Social Inequality*. Boston: Little, Brown.
Hodge, R. W., and D. J. Treiman. 1966. "Occupational Mobility and Attitudes Towards Negroes." *American Sociological Review* 31(February):93–102.
Hollingshead, A. B. a:1947. "Selected Characteristics of Classes in a Middle Western Community." *American Sociological Review* 12(August):385–95.
______. b:1971. "Commentary on the Indiscriminate State of Social Class Measurement." *Social Forces* 49(June):563–68.
Homans, George C. 1961. *Social Behavior: Its Elementary Forms*. New York: Harcourt, Brace & World.
Hood, Roger, and Richard Sparks. 1970. *Key Issues in Criminology*. New York: McGraw-Hill.
Jackman, M. R. 1972. "Social Mobility and Attitude Toward the Political System." *Social Forces* 50(June):462–72.
Jackson, E. F., and R. F. Curtis. 1968. "Conceptualization and Measurement in the Study of Social Stratification." In H. M. Blalock and A. B. Blalock (eds.). *Methodology in Social Research*. New York: McGraw-Hill.
Kelly, D. 1975. "Status Origins, Track Position, and Delinquent Involvement: A Self-Report Analysis." *The Sociological Quarterly* 16(Spring):264–71.
Kelly, D., and W. T. Pink. 1975. "Status Origins, Youth Rebellion, and Delinquency: A Reexamination of the Class Issue." *Journal of Youth and Adolescence* 4(December):339–47.
Kohn, Melvin L. 1969. *Class and Conformity: A Study in Values*. Homewood: Dorsey.
Kvaraceus, W. C. 1944. "Juvenile Delinquency and Social Class." *Journal of Educational Sociology* 18(September):51–54.
Landecker, W. S. 1960. "Class Boundaries." *American Sociological Review* 25(December):868–77.
Lander, Bernard. 1954. *Towards an Understanding of Juvenile Delinquency*. New York: Columbia University Press.
McDonald, Lynn. 1969. *Social Class and Delinquency*. Hamden, Conn.: Archon.
Meade, A. 1973. "Seriousness of Delinquency, the Adjudicative Decision and Recidivism—A Longitudinal and Configuration Analysis." *Journal of Criminal Law and Criminology* 64(December):478–85.
Merton, Robert K. 1968. *Social Theory and Social Structure*. Glencoe: Free Press.
Miller, W. B. 1958. "Lower Class Culture as a Generating Milieu of Gang Delinquency." *Journal of Social Issues* 14(#3):5–19.
Morris, Terrence. 1957. *The Criminal Area*. London: Routledge & Kegan Paul.
Nye, F. I., J. F. Short, Jr., and V. J. Olson. 1958. "Socioeconomic Status and Delinquent Behavior." *American Journal of Sociology* 63(January):381–89.
Pfautz, H. W. 1953. "The Current Literature on Social Stratification: Critique and Bibliography." *American Journal of Sociology* 58(January):391–418.
Piliavin, I., and S. Briar. 1964. "Police Encounters with Juveniles." *American Journal of Sociology* 70(September):206–14.
Pine, G. J. 1965. "Social Class, Social Mobility and Delinquent Behavior." *Personnel and Guidance Journal* XLIII(April):770–74.
Polk, K., D. Frease, and F. L. Richmond. 1974. "Social Class, School Experience, and Delinquency." *Criminology* 12(May):84–96.
President's Commission on Law Enforcement and Administration of Justice. 1967. *The Challenge of Crime in a Free Society*. Washington: Government Printing Office.
Price, J. E. 1966. "A Test of the Accuracy of Crime Statistics." *Social Problems* 14(Fall):214–21.
Quinney, Richard. 1975. *Criminology*. Boston: Little, Brown.
Reid, Sue Titus. 1976. *Crime and Criminology*. Hinsdale: Dryden.
Reiss, Albert J. 1971. *The Police and the Public*. New Haven: Yale University Press.
Reiss, A. J., and A. L. Rhodes. 1961. "The Distribution of Juvenile Delinquency in the Social Class Structure." *American Sociological Review* 26(October):720–32.
Robins, L. N., H. Gyman, and P. O'Neal. 1962. "The Interaction of Social Class and Deviant Behavior." *American Sociological Review* 27(August):480–92.
Rossides, Daniel W. 1976. *The American Class System*. Boston: Houghton Mifflin.
Shaw, Clifford R., and Henry D. McKay. 1969. *Juvenile Delinquency and Urban Areas*. Chicago: University of Chicago Press.
Skogan, Wesley G. (ed.) 1976. *Sample Surveys of Victims of Crime*. Cambridge: Ballinger.
Slatin, G. T. 1969. "Ecological Analysis of Delinquency: Aggregation Effects." *American Sociological Review* 34(December):854–907.
Sorokin, Pitirim A., and Walter A. Lunden. 1959. *Power and Morality*. Boston: Porter Sargent.
Stark, R., and J. McEvoy, III. 1970. "Middle-Class Violence." *Psychology Today* 4(November):52–54. ff.
Stinchcombe, Arthur L. 1964. *Rebellion in a High School*. Chicago: Quadrangle Books.
Stone, G. P., and W. H. Form. 1953. "Instabilities in Status: The Problem of Hierarchy in the Community Study of Status Arrangements." *American Sociological Review* 18(April):149–62.
Tittle, C. R., and W. J. Villemez. 1976. "Category/Continuum Thought Styles and Survey Research." *Sociological Focus* 9(January):1–10.
Vaz, Edward W. a:1966. "Self-Reported Juvenile Delinquency and Socioeconomic Status." *The Canadian Journal of Criminology and Corrections* 8(January):20–27.
______. b:1976. *Aspects of Deviance*. Scarborough, Ontario: Prentice-Hall.
Veblen, Thorsten. 1953. *The Theory of the Leisure Class*. New York: Merton.
Vorwaller, D. J. 1970. "Social Mobility and Membership in Voluntary Organizations." *American Journal of Sociology* 75(January):481–95.
Voss, H. L. 1966. "Socioeconomic Status and Reported Delinquent Behavior." *Social Problems* 13(Winter):314–24.
Walberg, H. J., E. Gee Yeh, and S. Mooney Paton. 1974. "Family Background, Ethnicity, and Urban Delinquency." *Journal of Research in Crime and Delinquency* 11(January):80–87.
Wallerstein, J. S., and C. S. Wyle. 1947. "Our Law-Abiding Lawbreakers." *Probation* 25(April):107–12, ff.
Warner, W. Lloyd, and Paul S. Lunt. 1941. *The Social Life of a Modern Community*. New Haven: Yale University Press.
Wheeler, S. 1966. "Delinquency and Crime." In Howard S. Becker (ed.) *Social Problems: A Modern Approach*. New York: Wiley.
Williams, J. R., and M. Gold. 1972. "From Delinquent Behavior to Official Delinquency." *Social Problems* 20(Fall):209–29.
Winslow, R. W. 1967. "Anomie and Its Alternatives: A Self-Report Study of Delinquency." *The Sociological Quarterly* 8(Autumn):468–80.
Wolf, P. 1962. "Crime and Social Class in Denmark." *British Journal of Criminology* 13:5–17.
Wolfgang, Marvin E., Robert M. Figlio, and Thorsten Sellin. 1972. *Delinquency in a Birth Cohort*. Chicago: University of Chicago Press.
Won, G., and G. Yamamoto. 1968. "Social Structure and Deviant Behavior: A Study of Shoplifting." *Sociology and Social Research*. 53(October):44–55.

Police Control of Juveniles

Donald J. Black
Yale Law School

Albert J. Reiss, Jr.
University of Michigan

This paper begins by defining deviance as behavior in a class for which there is a probability *of sanction subsequent to its detection—a control approach. It proceeds to an analysis of detection and sanctioning differentials in the policing of juveniles. Thus, it explores situational properties besides rule-violative behavior that generate a social control response. The data derive from a three-city observation study of uniformed patrolmen in the field. Findings from the study permit propositions to the following effect: Most police-juvenile contacts are initiated by citizens; the great majority pertain to minor legal matters; the probability of arrest is very low; it increases with the legal seriousness of alleged offenses; police sanctioning reflects the manifest preferences of citizen complainants; Negro juveniles have a comparatively high arrest rate, but evidence is lacking that the police are racially oriented; situational evidence is an important factor in police sanctioning practices; and the sanction probabilities are higher for unusually respectful and disrespectful juveniles. Some implications of these propositions are ventured.*

CURRENT theory on deviant behavior and social control inquires very little into either the organized processes by which deviance is detected or the patterns by which deviance is sanctioned, countenanced, or ignored once it is found out. Despite a ground swell of concern with *social reactions* to deviant behavior—the core of the labeling approach to deviance—the sociology of social control remains a conceptually retarded body of knowledge. One way of drawing detection and sanctioning differentials into the analytical bounds of theory is to define deviance in terms of the probability of a control response. Thus, *individual or group behavior is deviant if it falls within a class of behavior for which there is a probability of negative sanctions subsequent to its detection.*[1] For any form of behavior to be classified as deviant, the probability of negative sanctions must be above zero when the behavior is detected. The greater the probability of sanction, the more appropriate is the classification as deviant.[2] Therefore, whether or not a given form of behavior is deviant and the extent to which it is deviant are empirical questions.

Detection and sanctioning involve separate probabilities. Some forms of deviance, such as those that arise in private places, have extremely low probabilities of detection. Types of deviance that rarely are detected may nonetheless have very high sanction probabilities. In other cases the converse may be true. Furthermore, the particular probabilities of detection and sanctioning may be closely tied to particular types of deviance. In the case of homicide, for example, the probability of detection is high, as is the probability of some form of negative sanction. The probability of official detection of incest surely is low, while the likelihood of sanctioning may be high when incest is detected. Public drunkenness would seem to have a high detection but a low sanctioning probability. Analogous probabilities could be calculated for types of deviance that fall within jurisdictions other than the criminal law.[3]

A control approach, as here propounded, implies three basic types of deviance: (1) undetected deviance, (2) detected, unsanctioned deviance, and (3) sanctioned deviance.[4] These are the three conditions under which empirical instances of deviant behavior appear in relation to control systems. An instance of undetected deviance occurs if an act or a behavior pattern occurs for which there would be a probability of sanction *if it were detected.* Undetected marijuana-smoking is deviant, for example, since there is a probability of negative sanction when an instance of this *class* of behavior is discovered. When a clearly drunken person is encountered on the street by a policeman

* The research reported in this paper was supported by Grant Award 006, Office of Law Enforcement Assistance, United States Department of Justice, under the Law Enforcement Assistance Act of 1965, as well as by grants from the National Science Foundation and the Russell Sage Foundation. Maureen Mileski, Stanton Wheeler and Abraham S. Goldstein made helpful comments on earlier drafts of the paper.

[1] This conceptualization consciously bears the imprint of Max Weber's work. For example, he defines "power" as "the probability that one actor within a social relationship will be in a position to carry out his own will despite resistance, regardless of the basis on which this probability rests" (Parsons, 1964:152). Weber defines "law" as follows: ". . . An order will be called *law* when conformity with it is upheld by the probability that deviant action will be met by physical or psychic sanctions aimed to compel conformity or to punish disobedience, and applied by a group of men especially empowered to carry out this function" (Parsons, 1964:127). Cf. the translation of this definition in Max Rheinstein (1966:5).

[2] This does not, of course, preclude a probability of positive sanctions for the behavior. Some forms of deviant behavior are encouraged by subcultures that bestow positive sanctions for behavior which is handled as deviant in the wider community. One interesting but untouched problem in deviant behavior theory is that of the relative effects of joint probabilities of positive and negative sanctions in producing behavior of a given class.

[3] One consequence of following this approach is that a control system can be examined from the standpoint of the deviant who is concerned with calculating his *risks* in the system. Oliver Wendell Holmes (1897) proposed this perspective as an aproach to the legal system: "If you want to know the law and nothing else, you must look at it as a bad man, who cares only for the material consequences which such knowledge enables him to predict, not as a good one, who finds his reasons for conduct, whether inside the law or outside of it, in the vaguer sanctions of conscience."

[4] The definition of deviance presented above excludes what may appear to be the fourth logical possibility, i.e., undetected, sanctioned deviance.

From *American Sociological Review,* Vol. 35 (February 1970), pp. 63–77. Reprinted by permission of the American Sociological Association and the authors.

but is not arrested, an instance of detected, unsanctioned deviance has taken place. The third type, sanctioned deviance, is self-explanatory.

An elaboration of the analytical distinctions necessary in a control approach would exceed the bounds of this discussion. However, two additional elementary distinctions must be noted. A distinction must be made between official, or formal, detection and sanctioning, on the one hand, and informal detection and sanctioning, on the other. Any approach to deviant behavior that does not inquire into the relations between official and informal control systems is incomplete. In other words, the notion of "social control of deviant behavior" should always have an organizational or system reference. Secondly, it is important to distinguish between the detection of deviant acts and the detection of persons who commit these acts. The general conditions under which persons are linked to deviant acts is a problem for investigation. Informal as well as official control systems involve detective work and the pursuit of evidence.

It should not be surmised from the foregoing that a sociology of the deviance-control process consists solely in the analysis of detection and sanctioning processes. Such would be an overly narrow conception of the subject matter, as well as a distorted analytical description of how control systems operate. The foregoing is oriented mainly to the *case-by-case* responses of control systems to deviant behavior. The framework is not geared to the analysis of control responses that by-pass the problems of detection and sanctioning altogether. For instance, it ignores totally symbolic social control responses, such as may sometimes be found in the enactment of rules where there is no attempt to detect or sanction violations of those rules (Arnold, 1935; Gusfield, 1963). It also neglects the preventive aspects of social control. For example, control systems sometimes take measures to limit opportunities for deviant behavior by constraining the actions of all members of a social category, a tactic illustrated by curfew ordinances, occupational licensing laws, food stamp requirements for welfare recipients, and preventive detention of felony suspects. Thus, an emphasis upon detection and sanctioning differentials should not deflect interest from other important properties of social control systems.

This paper presents findings on citizen and police detection of juvenile deviance and on the sanctioning of juveniles through arrest in routine police work. It makes problematic situational conditions that increase the probability of sanction subsequent to the detection of violative behavior. Put another way, it makes problematic conditions (besides rule-violative behavior itself) that give rise to differentials in official sanctioning. It is a study of law-in-action. Since all of the data pertain to police encounters with alleged delinquents, the relationship between undetected and detected delinquency is not treated.

THE METHOD

The findings reported here derive from systematic observation of police-citizen transactions conducted during the summer of 1966. Thirty-six observers—persons with law, law enforcement, and social science backgrounds—recorded observations of routine patrol work in Boston, Chicago, and Washington, D.C. The observer training period comprised one week and was identical across the three cities. The daily supervision system also was similar across the cities. The observers rode in scout cars or, less frequently, walked with patrolmen on all shifts on all days of the week for seven weeks in each city. To assure the inclusion of a large number of police-citizen encounters, we gave added weight to the times when police activity is comparatively high (evening watches, particularly weekend evenings).

No attempt was made to survey police-citizen encounters in all localities within the three cities. Instead, police precincts in each city were chosen as observation sites. The precincts were selected so as to maximize observation in lower socio-economic, high crime rate, racially homogeneous residential areas. This was accomplished through the selection of two precincts each in Boston and Chicago and four precincts in Washington, D.C. The findings pertain to the behavior of uniformed patrolmen rather than to that of policemen in specialized divisions such as juvenile bureaus or detective units.[5]

The data were recorded by the observers in "incident booklets," forms much like interview schedules. One booklet was filled out for every incident that the police were requested to handle or that they themselves noticed while on patrol.[6] A total of 5,713 of these incidents were observed and recorded. This paper concerns only those 281 encounters that include one or more juvenile suspects among the participants.

THE CONTEXT

Although large police departments invariably have specialized divisions for handling incidents that involve juveniles, the great majority of juvenile encounters with policemen occur with general duty, uniformed patrolmen, rather than with "youth officers." Youth officers receive most of their cases on a referral basis from members of the uniformed patrol division.[7] Usually these referrals enter the police system as arrests of juveniles by uniformed patrolmen. It will be seen, however, that uniformed patrolmen arrest only a small fraction of the legally liable juvenile suspects with whom they have encounters in the field. Youth bureau officers, then, determine what proportion of those arrested will be referred to juvenile court. The outputs of the patrol division thus become the inputs for the youth bureau, which in turn forwards its outputs as inputs to the court.[8] By the time a juvenile is institutionalized, therefore, he has been judged a delinquent at several stages. Correspondingly, sanctions are levied at several stages; institutionalization is the final stage of a sanctioning *process,* rather than *the* sanction for juvenile deviance.

After the commission of a deviant act by a juvenile, the first stage in the elaborate process by which official rates of delinquency are produced is detection. For the police, as for most well-differentiated systems of social control, detection is largely a matter of organizational mobilization, and mobilization is the process by which incidents come to the initial attention of agents of the police organization. There are two basic types of mobilization of the police: *citizen-initiated,* or "reactive" mobilizaztion, and *police-initiated,* or "proactive" mobilization, depending upon who makes the original decision that police action is appropriate. An example of a citizen-initiated mobilization occurs when a citizen phones the police to report an event and the radio dispatcher sends a patrol car to handle the call. A typical police-initiated mobilization takes place when a policeman observes and acts upon what he regards as a law violation or, as in the case of a "stop-and-frisk," a "suspicious" person or situation.

Popular and even sociological conceptions of the police err through an over-reliance on proactive imagery to characterize police operations. Although some specialized divisions of municipal police departments, such as traffic bureaus and vice units, do depend primarily upon proactive mobilization for their input of cases, in routine patrol work

[5] Very little research on the police has dealt with the routine work of the uniformed patrol division. For a review of investigations on the police see Bordua and Reiss (1967). A recent exception is James Q. Wilson (1968); his study, however, relies primarily upon official statistics.

[6] These booklets were not filled out in the presence of the policemen. In fact, the officers were told that our research was not concerned with police behavior but, rather, that we were concerned *only* with citizen behavior toward the police and the kinds of problems citizens make for the police. In this sense the study involved systematic deception.

[7] In two of the cities investigated, however, aggressive youth patrols ("gang dicks") are employed in the policing of juveniles. Most youth officers spend much of their time behind their desks dealing with referrals and work relatively little "on the street."

[8] Most research on the control of juveniles begins at stages beyond the police field encounter. (Examples are Goldman, 1963; Terry, 1967; McEachern and Bauzer, 1967; Cicourel, 1968; Wheeler, 1968.)

the great majority of incidents come to police attention through the citizen-initiated form of mobilization. The crime detection function is lodged mainly in the citizenry rather than in the police. Moreover, most police work with juveniles also arises through the initiative of citizen complainants. In this sense, the citizen population in good part draws the boundaries of its own official rate of juvenile delinquency.[9]

TABLE 1. PERCENT OF POLICE ENCOUNTERS WITH JUVENILE SUSPECTS ACCORDING TO TYPE OF MOBILIZATION AND RACE OF SUSPECT, BY TYPE OF INCIDENT

Type of Incident	Citizen-Initiated: Negro	Citizen-Initiated: White	Police-Initiated: Negro	Police-Initiated: White	All Citizen-Initiated	All Police-Initiated	All Encounters
Felony	10	..	10	..	5	5	5
Misdemeanor: Except Rowdiness	18	11	5	14	15	9	13
Misdemeanor: Rowdiness	62	77	40	33	69	37	60
Traffic Violation	1	..	26	28	*	27	8
Suspicious Person	..	1	17	22	*	19	6
Non-Criminal Dispute	8	12	2	3	10	3	8
Total Percent	99	101	100	100	99	100	100
Total Number	(109)	(94)	(42)	(36)	(203)	(78)	(281)

* .5% or less.

DETECTION OF JUVENILE DEVIANCE

Observation of police encounters with citizens netted 281 encounters with suspects under 18 years of age, here treated as juveniles.[10] The great majority of the juveniles were from blue-collar families.[11] Of the 281 police-juvenile encounters, 72% were citizen-initiated (by phone) and 28% were initiated by policemen on patrol. Excluding traffic violations, these proportions become 78% and 22%, respectively. The mobilization of police control of juveniles is then overwhelmingly a reactive rather than a proactive process. Hence it would seem that the moral standards of the citizenry have more to do with the definition of juvenile deviance than do the standards of policemen on patrol.[12]

Moreover, the incidents the police handle in citizen-initiated encounters differ somewhat from those in encounters they bring into being on their own initiative. (See Table 1.) This does not mean, however, that the standards of citizens and policemen necessarily differ; the differences between incidents in reactive and proactive police work seem to result in large part from differences in detection opportunities, since the police are limited to the surveillance of public places (Stinchcombe, 1963). For example, non-criminal disputes are more likely to occur in private than in public places; they account for 10% of the police-juvenile contacts in citizen-initiated work but for only 3% of the proactive encounters. On the other hand, the "suspicious person" is nearly always a police-initiated encounter. Traffic violations, too, are almost totally in the police-initiated category; it is simply not effective or feasible for a citizen to call the police about a "moving" traffic violation (and nearly all of these cases were "moving" rather than "standing" violations). In short, there are a number of contingencies that affect the detection of juvenile deviance in routine policing.

A broader pattern in the occasions for police-juvenile transactions is the overwhelming predominance of incidents of minor legal significance. Only 5% of the police encounters with juveniles involve alleged felonies; the remainder are less serious from a legal standpoint. Sixty per cent involve nothing more serious than juvenile rowdiness or mischievous behavior, the juvenile counterpart of "disorderly conduct" or "breach of the peace" by adults. This does not mean that the social significance of juvenile deviance is minor for the citizens who call the police or for the police themselves. It should be noted, moreover, that these incidents do not necessarily represent the larger universe of juvenile deviance, since (1) in many cases the juvenile offender is not apprehended by the police, and (2) an unknown number of delinquent acts go undetected. Nonetheless, these incidents represent the inputs from which uniformed patrolmen produce juvenile arrests and thus are the relevant base for analyzing the conditions under which juveniles are sanctioned in police encounters.

Another pattern lies in the differences between Negro and white encounters with policemen. In the aggregate, police encounters with Negro juveniles pertain to legally more serious incidents, owing primarily to the differential in felony encounters (see Table 1). None of the encounters with white juveniles involved the allegation of a felony, though this was true of 10% of the transactions with Negro juveniles in both citizen- and police-initiated encounters. Apart from this difference between the races, however, the occasions for encounters with Negro and white juveniles have many similarities.

It might be noted that the data on the occasions for police-juvenile encounters do not in themselves provide evidence of racial discrimination in the selection of juveniles for police attention. Of course, the citizen-initiated encounters cannot speak to the issue of discriminatory *police* selection. On the other hand, if the police tend to stop a disproportionate number of Negroes on the street in minor incident situations, we might infer the presence of discrimination. But the findings in Table 1 do not provide such evidence. Likewise, we might infer police discrimination if a higher proportion of the total Negro encounters is police-initiated than that of the total white encounters. Again the evidence is lacking: police-initiated encounters account for 28% of the total for both Negro and white juveniles. More data would be needed to assess adequately the issue of police selectivity by race.

INCIDENTS AND ARREST

Of the encounters patrol officers have with juvenile suspects, only 15% result in arrest.[13] Hence it is apparent that by a large

[9] Even in proactive police work, police initiative may be in response to citizen initiative. Proactive police units often are highly dependent upon citizen intelligence, though the dependence usually is once removed from the field situation (see Skolnick, 1966). For example, citizens occasionally provide the police with intelligence about *patterned* juvenile behavior, such as complaints provided by businessmen about recurrent vandalism on their block or recurrent rowdiness on their corner. These may lead the police to increase surveillance in an attempt to "clean up" the area.

[10] The relatively rare police encounters with suspects of mixed age status—adults and juveniles together—are excluded from this analysis. Further, it should be emphasized that the unit of analysis here is the encounter rather than the individual juvenile. Many encounters include more than one suspect.

[11] It sometimes is difficult for a field observer to categorize a citizen according to social class status. During the observation period two broad categories were used, blue-collar and white-collar, but observers occasionally were unable to make the judgment. The precincts sampled were mainly populated by lower status citizens; so, not surprisingly, the vast majority of the citizen participants were labeled blue-collar by the observers. This majority was even larger for the suspects involved. Consequently, there are not enough white-collar suspect cases for separate analysis. However, the small number of juveniles of ambiguous social class status are combined with the blue-collar cases in this analysis.

[12] Some police-citizen conflict may be generated when citizens view the police as reluctant to respond to their definitions of deviance. Citizens regard this as "police laxity" or "underenforcement." This complaint has lately been aired by some segments of the Negro community.

[13] The concept of arrest used here refers only to transportation of a suspect to a police station, not to the formal booking or charging of a suspect with a crime. This usage follows Wayne R. LaFave (1965).

margin most police-juvenile contacts are concluded in the field settings where they arise.[14] These field contacts, 85% of the total, generally are not included in official police statistics on reported cases of juvenile delinquency, and thus they represent the major invisible portion of the delinquency control process. In other words, if these sample data are reasonably representative, the probability is less than one-in-seven that a policeman confronting a juvenile suspect will exercise his discretion to produce an official case of juvenile delinquency. A high level of selectivity enters into the arrest of juveniles. This and subsequent sections of the paper seek to identify some of the conditions which contribute to that selection process.

TABLE 2. PERCENT OF POLICE ENCOUNTERS WITH JUVENILE SUSPECTS ACCORDING TO TYPE OF INCIDENT AND RACE OF SUSPECT, BY FIELD DISPOSITION

Field Disposition	Type of Incident and Race of Suspect														
	Felony		Misdemeanor: Ex. Rowdiness		Misdemeanor: Rowdiness		Traffic Violation		Suspicious Person		Non-Criminal Dispute		All Negro	All White	All Encounters
	N	W	N	W	N	W	N	W	N	W	N	W			
Arrest	73	..	36	20	13	8.	8	..	..	(1)	..	..	21	8	15
Release-in-Field	27	..	64	80	87	92	92	100	(7)	(8)	100	100	80	92	85
Total Percent	100	..	100	100	100	100	100	100	..	..	100	100	101	100	100
Total Number	(15)	..	(22)	(15)	(85)	(84)	(12)	(10)	(7)	(9)	(10)	(12)	(151)	(130)	(281)

A differential in police dispositions that appears at the outset of the analysis is that between Negroes and whites. The overall arrest rate for police-Negro encounters is 21%, while the rate for police-white encounters is only 8%. This difference immediately raises the question of whether or not racial discrimination determines the disposition of juvenile suspects. Moreover, Table 2 shows that the arrest rate for Negroes is also higher within specific incident categories where comparisons are possible. The race difference, therefore, is not merely a consequence of the larger number of legally serious incidents that occasion police-Negro contacts.

Apart from the race difference, Table 2 reveals that patrol officers make proportionately more arrests when the incident is relatively serious from a legal standpoint. The arrest rate for Negro encounters is twice as high for felonies as it is for the more serious misdemeanors, and for encounters with both races the arrest rate for serious misdemeanors doubles the rate for juvenile rowdiness. On the other hand, policemen rarely make arrests of either race for traffic violations or for suspicious person situations. Arrest appears even less likely when the incident is a noncriminal dispute. The disposition pattern for juvenile suspects clearly follows the hierarchy of offenses found in the criminal law, the law for adults.

It is quite possible that the legal seriousness of incidents is more important in encounters between *patrol* officers and juveniles than in those between *youth* officers and juveniles. As a rule, the patrol officer's major sanction is arrest, arrest being the major formal product of patrol work. By contrast, the youth officer has the power to refer cases to juvenile court, a prosecutorial discretion with respect to juveniles that patrolmen in large departments usually do not have. Whether he is in the field or in his office, the juvenile officer plays a role different from that of the patrolman in the system of juvenile justice. For this reason alone, the factors relating to the disposition of juveniles may differ between the two. The youth officer may, for example, be more concerned with the juvenile's past record,[15] a kind of information that usually is not accessible to the patrolman in the field setting. Furthermore, past records may have little relevance to a patrol officer who is seeking primarily to order a field situation with as little trouble as possible. His organizational responsibility ends there. For his purposes, the age status of a suspect may even be irrelevant in the field. Conversely, the youth officer may find that the juvenile court or his supervisor expects him to pay more attention to the juvenile's record than to the legal status of a particular incident. In short, the contingencies that affect the sanctioning of juveniles may vary with the organizational sources of the discretion of sanction.

SITUATIONAL ORGANIZATION AND ARREST

Apart from the substance of police encounters—the kinds of incidents they involve—these encounters have a social structure. One element in this structure is the distribution of situational roles played by the participants in the encounter. Major situational roles that arise in police encounters are those of suspect or offender, complainant, victim, informant, and bystander.[16] None of these roles necessarily occurs in every police encounter.

In police encounters with suspects, which account for only about 50% of all police-citizen contacts,[17] particularly important is the matter of whether or not a citizen complainant participates in the situational action. A complainant in search of justice can make direct demands on a policeman with which he must comply. Likewise a complainant is a witness of the police officer's behavior; thus he has the ability to contest the officer's version of an encounter or even to bring an official complaint against the officer himself. In these respects as well as others, the complainant injects constraints into police-suspect confrontations. This is not to deny that the complainant often may be an asset to a policeman who enters a preexisting conflict situation in the field. The complainant can provide what may be otherwise unavailable information to a situationally ignorant patrolman. The patrol officer is a major intelligence arm of modern police systems, but he, like other policemen, must live with a continual dependence upon citizens for the information that it is his allotted responsibility to gather. Furthermore, when a suspect is present in the field situation, the information provided by a complainant, along with his willingness to stand on his word by signing a formal complaint, may be critical to an arrest in the absence of a police witness.

The relationship between arrest and the presence of a complainant in police-juvenile encounters is shown in Table 3. It is apparent that this relation between situational organization and disposition differs according to the suspect's race. Particularly interesting

[14] The arrest rate for adult suspects is somewhat higher than that for juvenile suspects. For findings on the policing of adults see Donald J. Black (1968: 170–262). The present analysis is similar to that followed in Black's study.

[15] In a study of youth bureau records, it was found that past record was an important factor in the referral of juveniles to the probation department and to the juvenile court (Terry, 1967). Past record was also found to be an important factor in the sanctioning decisions of youth officers in the field (Piliavin and Briar, 1964).

[16] For a discussion of the pivotal roles of lay persons in the control of mentally ill persons, see Erving Goffman's discussion of the complainant's role in the hospitalization of the offender (1961:133–146).

[17] Less than 50% of the citizen-initiated encounters involve a suspect. Police-initiated encounters, by contrast, typically do result in police-suspect interaction. However, almost nine-in-ten encounters patrol officers have with citizens are initiated by citizens. In the modal police encounter, the major citizen participant is a complainant (Black, 1968:45, 92, and 156).

TABLE 3. PERCENT OF POLICE ENCOUNTERS WITH JUVENILE SUSPECTS ACCORDING TO SITUATIONAL ORGANIZATION AND RACE OF SUSPECT, BY FIELD DISPOSITION. (TABLE EXCLUDES FELONIES, TRAFFIC VIOLATIONS, AND NON-CRIMINAL DISPUTES.)

	Situational Organization and Race of Suspect						
	Suspect Only		Complainant and Suspect				
Field Disposition	Negro	White	Negro	White	All Suspect Only	All Complainant and Suspect	All Encounters
Arrest	14	10	21	8	11	16	13
Release-in-Field	86	90	79	92	89	84	87
Total Percent	100	100	100	100	100	100	100
Total Number	(66)	(93)	(48)	(26)	(159)	(74)	(233)

is the finding that when there is no citizen complainant in the encounter the race difference in arrest rates narrows to the point of being negligible—14% versus 10% for encounters with Negro and white juveniles respectively. By contrast, when a complainant participates, this difference widens considerably to 21% versus 8%. This latter difference is all the more striking since felony situations and traffic and noncriminal dispute situations, which may be regarded as confounding factors, are excluded from the tabulation.

It also should be noted that as far as the major citizen participants are concerned, each of these encounters is racially homogeneous. The comparatively rare, mixed race encounters are excluded from these computations. Thus the citizen complainants who oversee the relatively severe dispositions of Negro juveniles are themselves Negro. The great majority of the police officers are white in the police precincts investigated, yet they seem somewhat more lenient when they confront Negro juveniles alone than when a Negro complainant is involved. Likewise, it will be recalled (Table 3) that the arrest difference between Negro and white juveniles all but disappears when no complainant is involved. These patterns complicate the question of racial discrimination in the production of juvenile arrests, given that a hypothesis of discrimination would predict opposite patterns. Indeed, during the observation period a strong majority of the policemen expressed anti-Negro attitudes in the presence of observers (Black and Reiss, 1967:132–139). It might be expected that if the police were expressing their racial prejudices in discriminatory arrest practices, this would be more noticeable in police-initated, typically by the complainants them-by citizens. But the opposite is the case. All of the encounters involving a citizen complainant in this sample were citizen-initiated typically by the complainants themselves. Proactive police operations rarely involve complainants. To recapitulate: the police are particularly likely to arrest a Negro juvenile when a citizen enjoins them to handle the incident and participates as a complainant in the situational action, but this is not characteristic of police encounters with white juveniles. Finally, it is noteworthy that Negro juveniles find themselves in encounters that involve a complainant proportionately more than do white juveniles. Hence, the pattern discussed above has all the more impact on the overall arrest rate for Negro juveniles. Accordingly, the next section examines the role of the complainant in more detail.

THE COMPLAINANT'S PREFERENCE AND ARREST

If the presence of a citizen complainant increases the production of Negro arrests, then the question arises as to whether this pattern occurs as a function of the complainant's mere presence, his situational behavior, or something else. In part, this issue can be broached by inquiring into the relationship between the complainant's behavioral preference for police action in a particular field situation and the kind of disposition the police in fact make.[18]

Before examining this relationship, however, it should be noted that a rather large proportion of complainants do not express clear preferences for police action such that a field observer can make an accurate classification. Moreover, there is a race differential in this respect. Considering only the misdemeanor situations, the Negro complainant's preference for action is unclear in 48% of the police encounters with Negro juveniles, whereas the comparable proportion drops to 27% for the encounters with white complainants and juveniles. Nevertheless, a slightly larger proportion of the Negro complainants express a preference for arrest of their juvenile adversaries—21%, versus 15% for whites. Finally, the complainant prefers an informal disposition in 31% of the Negro cases and in 58% of the white cases. Thus white complainants more readily express a preference for police leniency toward juvenile suspects than do Negro complainants.

Table 4 suggests that white juveniles benefit from this greater leniency, since the police show a quite dramatic pattern of compliance with the expressed preferences of complainants. This pattern seems clear even though the number of cases necessitates caution in interpretation. In not one instance did the police arrest a juvenile when the complainant lobbied for leniency. When a complainant explicitly expresses a preference for an arrest, however, the tendency of the police to comply is also quite strong. Table 4 includes only the two types of misdemeanor, yet the Negro arrest rate when the complainant's preference is arrest (60%) climbs toward the rate of arrest for felonies (73%, Table 2). In no other tabulation does the arrest rate for misdemeanors rise so high. Lastly, it is notable that when the complainant's preference is unclear, the arrest rate falls between the rate for complainants who prefer arrest and those who prefer an informal disposition.

These patterns have several implications. First, it is evident that the higher arrest rate for Negro juveniles in encounters with complainants and suspects is largely a consequence of the tendency of the police to comply with the preferences of complainants. This tendency is costly for Negro juveniles, since Negro complainants are relatively severe in their expressed preferences when they are compared to white complainants vis-à-vis white juveniles. Furthermore, it will be remembered that it is in encounters with this situational organization rather than in those with suspects alone that the race differential is most apparent. Given the prominent role of the Negro complainant in the race differential, then, it may be inappropriate to consider this pattern an instance of discrimination on the part of policemen. While police behavior follows the same *patterns* for Negro and white juveniles, differential *outcomes* arise from differences in *citizen* behavior (cf. Werthman and Piliavin, 1967).

Another implication of these findings is more general, namely, that the citizen complainant frequently performs an adjudicatory function in police encounters with juveniles. In an important sense the patrol officer abdicates his discretionary power to the complainant. At least this seems true of the encounters that include an expressive or relatively aggressive complainant among the participants. To say that the complainant often can play the role of judge in police encounters is tantamount to saying that the moral standards of citizens often can affect the fate of juvenile suspects. Assuming that the moral standards of citizens vary across social space, i.e., that there are moral subcultures, then it follows that police dis-

[18] Jerome Hall (1952:317–319) suggests several propositions concerning the probability of criminal prosecution. One of Hall's propositions is particularly relevant in the present context: "The rate of prosecution varies directly in proportion to the advantage to be gained from it by the complainant or, the rate is in inverse proportion to the disadvantages that will be sustained by him."

TABLE 4. PERCENT OF POLICE ENCOUNTERS WITH JUVENILE SUSPECTS THAT INVOLVE A CITIZEN COMPLAINANT ACCORDING TO RACE OF SUSPECT AND COMPLAINANT'S PREFERENCE, BY FIELD DISPOSITION. (TABLE EXCLUDES FELONIES, TRAFFIC VIOLATIONS, AND NON-CRIMINAL DISPUTES.)

	Race of Suspect and Complainant's Preference								
	Negro			White					
Field Disposition	Prefers Arrest	Prefers Informal Disposition	Preference Unclear	Prefers Arrest	Prefers Informal Disposition	Preference Unclear	All Negro Encounters	All White Encounters	All Encounters
Arrest	60	. . .	17	(1)	. . .	(1)	21	8	16
Release-in-Field	40	100	83	(3)	100	(6)	79	92	84
Total Percent	100	100	100	. . .	100	. . .	100	100	100
Total Number	(10)	(15)	(23)	(4)	(15)	(7)	(48)	(26)	(74)

TABLE 5. PERCENT OF POLICE ENCOUNTERS WITH JUVENILE SUSPECTS ACCORDING TO MAJOR SITUATIONAL EVIDENCE AND RACE OF SUSPECT, BY FIELD DISPOSITION. (TABLE EXCLUDES FELONIES AND TRAFFIC VIOLATIONS.)

	Major Situational Evidence and Race of Suspect										
	Police Witness		Citizen Testimony		No Evidence		Not Ascertained				
Field Disposition	N	W	N	W	N	W	N	W	All Negro Encounters	All White Encounters	All Encounters
Arrest	16	10	22	14	. . .	4	(2)	. . .	15	9	12
Release-in-Field	84	90	78	86	100	96	(7)	(2)	85	91	88
Total Percent	100	100	100	100	100	100	. . .	. . .	100	100	100
Total Number	(57)	(69)	(36)	(21)	(22)	(28)	(9)	(2)	(124)	(120)	(244)

positions of juvenile suspects in part reflect that moral diversity. To this degree policemen become the unwitting custodians of those moral subcultures and thereby perpetuate moral diversity in the larger community. Assuming the persistence of this pattern of police compliance, then it would seem that police behavior is geared, again unwittingly, to moral change. As the moral interests of the citizenry change, so will the pattern of police control. Earlier it was noted that most police encounters with juveniles come into being at the beckoning of citizens. Now it is seen that even the handling of those encounters often directly serves the moral interests of citizens.[19]

SITUATIONAL EVIDENCE AND ARREST

Another variable that might be expected to affect the probability of arrest is the nature of the evidence that links a juvenile suspect to an incident. In patrol work there are two major means by which suspects are initially connected with the commission of crimes: the observation of the act itself by a policeman and the testimony by a citizen against a suspect. The primary evidence can take other forms, such as a bloodstain on a suspect's clothing or some other kind of physical "clue," but this is very unusual in routine patrol work. In fact, the legally minor incidents that typically occasion police-juvenile contacts seldom provide even the possibility of non-testimonial evidence. If there is neither a policeman who witnesses the incident nor a citizen who gives testimony concerning it, then ordinarily there is no evidence whatever in the field setting. Lastly, it should be emphasized that the concept of evidence as used here refers to "situational evidence" rather than to "legal evidence." Thus it refers to the kind of information that appears relevant to an observer in a field setting rather than to what might be acceptable as evidence in a court of law.

In about 50% of the situations a police officer observes the juvenile offense, excluding felonies and traffic violations. Hence, even though citizens initially detect most juvenile deviance, the police often respond in time to witness the behavior in question. In roughly 25% of the situations the policeman arrives too late to see the offense committed but a citizen gives testimonial evidence. The remaining cases, composed primarily of non-criminal disputes and suspicious person situations, bear no evidence of criminal conduct. In a heavy majority of routine police-juvenile encounters, the juvenile suspect finds himself with incriminating evidence of some sort. The low arrest rate should be understood in this context.

On the other hand, it should not be forgotten that these proportions pertain to misdemeanor situations and that the arrests are all arrests without a formal warrant. The law of criminal procedure requires that the officer witness the offense before he may make a misdemeanor arrest without warrant. If the officer does not observe the offense, he must have a signed complaint from a citizen. Such is the procedural law for adults. The law for juveniles, however, is in flux as far as questions of procedure are concerned.[20] It is not at all clear that an appellate court would decide on a juvenile's behalf if he were to appeal his case on the grounds that he was arrested for a misdemeanor even though the arresting officer neither witnessed the act nor acquired a formal complaint from a citizen. Even so, it might be expected that the rate of arrest would be higher in encounters where the act is witnessed by a policeman, if only because these would seem to be the situations where the juvenile suspect is maximally and unambiguously liable. But this expectation is not supported by the observation data (see Table 5).

In Table 5 it is shown that in "police witness" situations the arrest rate is no higher but is even slightly, though insignificantly, lower than the rate in "citizen testimony" situations. It is possible that some or all of these arrests where the major situational evidence lies with the testimony of a citizen would be viewed as "false" ar-

[19] Paul Bohannan (1967) notes that a core function of legal institutions is to *re*institutionalize the normative standards of nonlegal institutions. In other words, the legal process represents an *auxiliary* control resource for *other* normative systems. (Also see Bohannan, 1968.)

The patterned compliance of the police with citizens may be understood partly as an instance of the reinstitutionalization function of the legal process. Police control of juveniles, for example, is partly a matter of reinforcement of the broader institution of authority based upon age status. The police support adult authority; in parent-child conflicts the police tend to support parental authority.

[20] This has been all the more the case since the U.S. Supreme Court decision in 1967, *In re Gault*, 387 U.S. 1. The *Gault* decision is a move toward applying the same formal controls over the processing of juvenile suspects as are applied in the adult criminal process. For an observation study of juvenile court encounters see Norman Lefstein, *et al.* (1969). This study includes a discussion of constitutional issues relating to the processing of juveniles.

It might be added that from a social control standpoint, neither police deviance from procedural law, in the handling of juveniles or adults, nor the low rate of detection and sanctioning of this deviance should be surprising. Rarely can a law of any kind be found without deviance, and equally rare is the detection rate or sanctioning rate for any form of legal deviance near the 100% level. Curiously, however, social scientists seem to take for granted low enforcement of substantive law, while they take low control of deviance by the agents of law, such as policemen, to be an empirical peculiarity. Much might be gained from an approach that would seek to understand both forms of legal deviance and control with the same analytical framework. Moreover, substantive control and procedural control can be profitably analyzed in terms of their inter-relations (cf. Llewellyn, 1962:22). Procedural control of the police—for example, limitations on their power to stop-and-frisk—can decrease detection and sanctioning probabilities for certain forms of substantive deviance, such as "possession of narcotics."

rests if they involved adult suspects, though this legal judgment cannot be made with certainty. It is conceivable, for example, that some citizen complainants signed formal complaints at the police station subsequent to the field encounters.

The low arrest rate in "police witness" situations is striking in itself. It documents the enormous extent to which patrolmen use their discretion to release juvenile deviants without official sanction and without making an official report of the incident. Official statistics on juvenile delinquency vastly underestimate even the delinquent acts that policemen witness while on patrol. In this sense the police keep down the official delinquency rate.[21] One other implication of the low arrest rate should be noted. Because the vast majority of police-juvenile contacts are concluded in field settings, judicial control of police conduct through the exclusion of evidence in juvenile courts is potentially emasculated. Police control of juveniles—like that of adults (Reiss and Black, 1967)—may be less prosecution-oriented than the law assumes. In other words, much about the policing of juveniles follows an informal-processing or harassment model rather than a formal-processing model of control.[22] From a behavioral standpoint, law enforcement generally is not a legal duty of policemen.

On the other hand, the importance of situational evidence should not be analytically underestimated. Table 5 also shows that the police very rarely arrest juveniles when there is no evidence. In only one case was a juvenile arrested when there was no situational evidence in the observer's judgment; this was a suspicious person situation. In sum, then, even when the police have very persuasive situational evidence, they generally release juveniles in the field; but, when they do arrest juveniles, they almost always have evidence of some kind. When there is strong evidence against a suspect, formal enforcement becomes a privilege of the police officer. This privilege provides an opportunity for discriminatory practices (Davis, 1969:169–176).

THE SUSPECT'S DEFERENCE AND ARREST

A final factor that can be considered in its relation to the situational production of juvenile arrests is the suspect's degree of deference toward the police. Earlier research on police work suggests a strong association between situational outcomes and the degree of respect extended to policemen by suspects, namely, the less respectful the suspect, the harsher the sanction (Piliavin and Briar, 1964; Westley, 1955). In this section it is shown that the observation data on police-juvenile contacts draw a somewhat more complex profile of this relationship than might have been anticipated.

Before the findings on this relationship are examined, however, it should be noted that the potential impact of the suspect's deference on juvenile dispositions in the aggregate is necessarily limited. Only a small minority of juveniles behave at the extremes of a continuum going from very deferential or very respectful at one end to antagonistic or disrespectful at the other. In most encounters with patrolmen the outward behavior of juvenile suspects falls between these two extremes: the typical juvenile is civil toward police officers, neither strikingly respectful nor disrespectful. The juvenile suspect is civil toward the police in 57% of the encounters, a rather high proportion in view of the fact that the degree of deference was not ascertained in 16% of the 281 cases. The juvenile is very deferential in 11% and antagonistic in 16% of the encounters. Thus if disrespectful juveniles are processed with stronger sanctions, the subpopulation affected is fairly small. The majority of juvenile arrests occur when the suspect is civil toward the police. It remains to be seen, however, how great the differences are in the probability of arrest among juveniles who display varying degrees of deference.

The relationship between a juvenile suspect's deference and his liability to arrest is relatively weak and does not appear to be unidirectional. Considering all of the cases, the arrest rate for encounters where the suspect is civil is 16%. When the suspect behaves antagonistically toward the police, the rate is higher—22%. Although this difference is not wide, it is in the expected direction. What was not anticipated, however, is that the arrest rate for encounters involving very deferential suspects is also 22%, the same as that for the antagonistic group. At the two extremes, then, the arrest rate is somewhat higher.

Table 6 shows the arrest rates of suspects, excluding felony situations, according to their race and degree of deference toward police. The bi-polar pattern appears in the encounters with Negro juveniles, though in the encounters with white juveniles it does not. In fact, the number of cases where a white juvenile is extreme at one end or the other, particularly where he is very deferential, is so small as to render the differences insignificant. Likewise there is a case problem with the Negro encounters, but there the differences are a little wider, especially between the encounters where the suspect is civil as against those where the suspect is antagonistic. Overall, again, the differences are not dramatic for either race.

Because of the paucity of cases in the "very deferential" and "antagonistic" categories, the various offenses, with one exception, cannot be held constant. It is possible to examine only the juvenile rowdiness cases separately. In those encounters the arrest rates follow the bipolar pattern: 16% for very deferential juveniles, 11% for civil juveniles, and 17% for the encounters where a juvenile suspect is antagonistic or disrespectful. When felony, serious misdemeanor, and rowdiness cases are combined into one statistical base, the pattern is again bipolar: 26%, 18%, and 29% for the very deferential, civil, and antagonistic cases respectively.

Nothing more than speculation can be offered to account for the unexpectedly high arrest rate for juveniles who make an unusually great effort to behave respectfully toward policemen. First, it might be suggested that this finding does not necessarily conflict with that of Piliavin and Briar (1964), owing to an important difference between the coding systems employed. Piliavin and Briar use only two categories, "cooperative" and "uncooperative," so the "very deferential" and "civil" cases presumably fall into the same category. If this coding system were employed in the present investigation, the bipolar distribution would disappear, since the small number of "very deferential" cases would be absorbed by the larger number of "civil" cases and the combined rate would remain below the rate for the "antagonistic" cases. This, then, is one methodological explanation of the discrepancy in findings between the two investigations.

One substantive interpretation of the pattern itself is that juveniles who are and who know themselves to be particularly liable to arrest may be especially deferential toward the police as a tactic of situational self-defense. After all, the notion that one is well-advised to be polite to policemen if one is in trouble is quite widespread in the community. It is a folk belief. These findings might suggest that this tactic is by no means fool-proof. In any event the data do not provide for a test of this interpretation. It would seem that a good deal more research is needed pertaining to the relations between situational etiquette and sanctioning.

[21] Citizens do not necessarily perceive the "delinquency problem" as a function of official delinquency rates and are probably more concerned with what they know about patterns of *victimization* in their communities or neighborhoods. Many citizens may be inclined more to a folk version of the control approach than a labeling approach to delinquency. Their very concern about "the problem" may be partly a dissatisfaction with the existing detection and sanctioning probabilities they divine about juvenile deviance.

[22] Michael Banton (1964:6–7) makes a distinction between "law officers," whose contacts with citizens tend to be of a punitive or inquisitory character, and "peace officers," who operate within the moral consensus of the community and are less concerned with law enforcement for its own sake. He suggests that patrol officers principally are peace officers, whereas detectives and traffic officers, for example, are more involved in law enforcement as such. Banton's distinction has been elaborated by Bittner (1967) and Wilson (1968). Except when patrolmen handle felony situations involving juveniles, the policing of juveniles is mainly a matter of maintaining peace.

TABLE 6. PERCENT OF POLICE ENCOUNTERS WITH JUVENILE SUSPECTS ACCORDING TO THE SUSPECT'S RACE AND DEGREE OF DEFERENCE TOWARD THE POLICE, BY FIELD DISPOSITION. (TABLE EXCLUDES FELONIES.)

	Race and Suspect's Degree of Deference								
	Negro				White				
Field Disposition	Very Deferential	Civil	Antagonistic	Not Ascertained	Very Deferential	Civil	Antagonistic	Not Ascertained	All Encounters
Arrest	20	15	24	...	10	9	13	12	12
Release-in-Field	80	85	76	100	90	91	87	100	88
Total Percent	100	100	100	100	100	100	100	100	100
Total Number	(20)	(72)	(21)	(23)	(10)	(76)	(23)	(21)	(266)

OVERVIEW

This paper examines findings on the official detection and sanctioning of juvenile deviance. It begins with a conception of deviance that emphasizes sanctioning *probabilities,* thereby linking the empirical operation of social control systems to the analytical definition of deviant behavior itself. In the present investigation, the central concern is to specify situational conditions that affect the probability of sanction by arrest subsequent to the mobilization of policemen in field settings. It is a control approach to juvenile deviance. Simultaneously it is a study of interaction between representatives of the legal system and juveniles—a study of law-in-action.

Several major patterns appear in the finding from the observation research. It would seem wise to conclude with a statement of these patterns in propositional form. Observation of police work in natural settings, after all, is hardly beyond an exploratory phase.

I: Most police encounters with juveniles arise in direct response to citizens who take the initiative to mobilize the police to action.

II: The great bulk of police encounters with juveniles pertain to matters of minor legal significance.

III: The probability of sanction by arrest is very low for juveniles who have encounters with the police.

IV: The probability of arrest increases with the legal seriousness of alleged juvenile offenses, as that legal seriousness is defined in the criminal law for adults.

V: Police sanctioning of juveniles strongly reflects the manifest preferences of citizen complainants in field encounters.

VI: The arrest rate for Negro juveniles is higher than that for white juveniles, but evidence that the police behaviorally orient themselves to race as such is absent.

VII: The presence of situational evidence linking a juvenile to a deviant act is an important factor in the probability of arrest.

VIII: The probability of arrest is higher for juveniles who are unusually respectful toward the police and for those who are unusually disrespectful.

Collectively the eight propositions, along with the corollary implications suggested in the body of the analysis, provide the beginning of an empirical portrait of the policing of juveniles. At some point, however, a descriptive portrait of this kind informs theory. This paper proceeds from a definition of deviance as any class of behavior for which there is a probability of negative sanction subsequent to its detection. From there it inquires into factors that differentially relate to the detection and particularly the official sanctioning of juveniles. Hence it inquires into properties that generate a control response. This strategy assumes that sanctioning probabilities are contingent upon properties of social situations besides rule-violative behavior. Since deviance is defined here in terms of the probability of sanction, it should now be apparent that the referent of the concept of deviance may include whatever else, besides rule-violative behavior, generates sanctioning. The present analysis suggests that sanctioning is usually contingent upon a configuration of situational properties. Perhaps, then, deviance itself should be treated theoretically as a configuration of properties rather than as a unidimensional behavioral event. A critical aspect of the sociology of deviance and control consists in the discovery of these configurations. More broadly, the aim is to discover the social organization of deviance and control.

The topic at hand embraces a good deal more than police encounters with juveniles. There is a need for information about other contexts of social control, studies of other detection and sanctioning processes. There is a need for comparative analysis. What is the role of the complainant upon comparable occasions? Is a complainant before a policeman analogous to an interest group before a legislature? Little is known about the differences and similarities between legal and nonlegal systems of social control. What is the effect of evidence in non-legal contexts? How is a policeman before a suspect like a psychiatrist before a patient or a pimp before a whore? Are there varieties of procedural control over the sanctioning process in non-legal contexts? To what extent are other legal processes responsive to moral diversity in the citizen population? The intricacies of social control generally are slighted in sociology. Correspondingly the state of the general theory of deviance and control is primitive.

REFERENCES

Arnold, Thurman N.
1935 The Symbols of Government. New Haven, Connecticut: Yale University Press.

Banton, Michael.
1964 The Policeman in the Community. London: Tavistock Publications Limited.

Bittner Egon.
1967 "The police on skid-row: A study of peace-keeping." American Sociological Review 32 (1967):699–715.

Black, Donald J.
1968 Police Encounters and Social Organization: An Observation Study. Unpublished Ph.D. Dissertation, Department of Sociology, University of Michigan.

Black, Donald J. and Albert J. Reiss, Jr.
1967 "Patterns of behavior in police and citizen transactions." Pp. 1–139 in President's Commission on Law Enforcement and Administration of Justice, Studies in Crime and Law Enforcement in Major Metropolitan Areas, Field Surveys III, Volume 2. Washington, D.C.: U.S. Government Printing Office.

Bohannon, Paul.
1967 "The differing realms of the law." Pp. 43–56 in P. Bohannon (ed.), Law and Warfare: Studies in the Anthropology of Conflict. Garden City, New York: The Natural History Press.
1968 "Law and legal institutions." Pp. 73–78 in David L. Sills (ed.), International Encyclopedia of the Social Sciences, Volume 9. New York: The MacMillan Company and the Free Press.

Bordua, David J. and Albert J. Reiss, Jr.
1967 "Law enforcement." Pp. 275–303 in Paul Lazarsfeld, William Sewell, and Harold Wilensky (eds.), The Uses of Sociology. New York: Basic Books.

Cicourel, Aaron V.
1968 The Social Organization of Juvenile Justice. New York: John Wiley and Sons, Inc.

Davis Kenneth Culp.
1969 Discretionary Justice: A Preliminary Inquiry. Baton Rouge, Louisiana: Louisiana State University Press.

Goffman, Erving.
1961 Asylums: Essays on the Social Situation of Mental Patients and Other Inmates. Garden City, New York: Anchor Books.

Goldman, Nathan.
1963 The Differential Selection of Juvenile Offenders for Court Appearance. New York: National Council on Crime and Delinquency.

Gusfield, Joseph R.

1963 Symbolic Crusade: Status Politics and the American Temperance Movement. Urbana, Illinois: University of Illinois Press.

Hall, Jerome.
1952 Theft, Law and Society. Indianapolis, Indiana: The Bobbs-Merrill Company. (Second Edition.)

Holmes, Oliver Wendell.
1897 "The path of the law." Harvard Law Review 10 (1897):457–478.

LaFave, Wayne R.
1965 Arrest: The Decision to Take a Suspect into Custody. Boston, Massachusetts: Little, Brown and Company.

Lefstein, Norman, Vaughan Stapleton, and Lee Teitelbaum.
1969 "In search of juvenile justice: Gault and its implementation." Law and Society Review 3 (1969):491–562.

Llewellyn, Karl N.
1962 Jurisprudence: Realism in Theory and Practice. Chicago, Illinois: University of Chicago Press.

McEachern, A. W. and Riva Bauzer.
1967 "Factors related to disposition in juvenile police contacts." Pp. 148–160 in Malcolm W. Klein (ed.), Juvenile Gangs in Context. Englewood Cliffs, New Jersey: Prentice-Hall, Inc.

Parsons, Talcott (ed.).
1964 Max Weber: The Theory of Social and Economic Organization. New York: The Free Press.

Piliavin, Irving and Scott Briar.
1964 "Police encounters with juveniles." American Journal of Sociology 70 (1964):206–214.

Reiss, Albert J., Jr. and Donald J. Black.
1967 "Interrogation and the criminal process." The Annals of the American Academy of Political and Social Science 374 (1967): 47–57.

Rheinstein, Max (ed.).
1966 Max Weber on Law in Economy and Society. Cambridge, Massachusetts: Harvard University Press.

Skolnick, Jerome H.
1966 Justice Without Trial: Law Enforcement in Democratic Society. New York: John Wiley and Sons, Inc.

Stinchcombe, Arthur L.
1963 "Institutions of privacy in the determination of police administrative practice." American Journal of Sociology 69 (1963): 150–160.

Terry, Robert M.
1967 "The screening of juvenile offenders." Journal of Criminal Law, Criminology and Police Science 58 (1967):173–181.

Werthman, Carl and Irving Piliavin.
1967 "Gang members and the police." Pp. 56–98 in David J. Bordua (ed.), The Police: Six Sociological Essays. New York: John Wiley and Sons, Inc.

Westley, William A.
1955 "Violence and the police." American Journal of Sociology 59 (1955):34–41.

Wheeler, Stanton (ed.).
1968 Controlling Delinquents. New York: John Wiley and Sons, Inc.

Wilson, James Q.
1968 Varieties of Police Behavior: The Management of Law and Order in Eight Communities. Cambridge, Massachusetts: Harvard University Press.

Determinants of Juvenile Court Dispositions: Ascriptive and Achieved Factors in Two Metropolitan Courts *

Lawrence E. Cohen
University of Illinois, Urbana

James R. Kluegel
University of California, Riverside

This paper examines the impact of stereotypical and discriminatory factors on the severity of dispositions accorded juveniles in two courts, Denver and Memphis, which differed in their orientation to juvenile justice and in regional location. Because the conclusions of earlier research on juvenile justice decision making are affected by inadequate data-analytic techniques, this study analyzes multivariate relationships among qualitative variables using Goodman's method of log linear analysis to investigate possible sources of bias in the severity of disposition for 6,894 male juveniles. Little support is found for the argument that race or social class bias directly affects the dispositions in these two courts. The implications of this research for understanding the prior pattern of contradictory findings and for the general issue of bias in the juvenile justice system are discussed.

According to a number of recent assessments, the contemporary American juvenile justice system incorporates biases which virtually ensure that specific youths, particularly minority group members and those of lower socioeconomic status, will be the objects of discriminatory treatment (Cicourel, 1968; Platt, 1969; Martin, 1970; Schur, 1973). This charge takes several forms, but in essence the contention is that certain youths are more likely to be accorded harsh treatment, not necessarily due to the nature of the offenses for which they are charged, or due to a prior history of delinquency involvement, but rather because they fit the preconceived notions or stereotypes of the delinquent which court officials have formulated. Such youths are thought to be systematically treated more harshly by social control agents than are other juveniles (presumably, those who do not fit the control agents' stereotype of a delinquent), who may often be released without official court intervention.

Martin (1970:3–4) for example, contends, that:

> In effect, the juvenile justice labeling process works to single out adolescents from groups culturally alien to those in power. Those singled out, because of their powerlessness, are ill-equipped to stop the process or to intervene in it effectively to prevent themselves from having various and sundry tags imposed upon them by police, judges, probation officers, psychiatrists, and others who are employed as agents of the juvenile justice system.

Martin (1970:4) maintains that once the child's case is brought to the attention of the juvenile court, it is handled by probation officers and judges whose social and cultural characteristics are decidedly middle class, and that this fact makes it difficult for these functionaries to be objective when judging the behavior of lower-class youths.

Edwin Schur (1973:121) expounds further on the process by which stereotyping is likely to work against youths from certain disadvantaged segments of our society, regardless of the offenses with which they are charged:

> The philosophy of the juvenile court—with its thoroughgoing social investigation of the alleged delinquent, and its relative lack of concern with the particular offense—virtually ensures that stereotypes will influence judicial dispositions.

Schur (1973:125–6) subsequently identifies those juveniles whom he believes to be the most likely recipients of differential treatment from agents of the juvenile court because they are believed to be "delinquency-prone:"

> In our society, lower-class children more than middle-class ones, black children more than white ones, and boys more than girls, face high probabilities (i.e., run a special "categorical risk" in the actuarial sense) not only of engaging in rule-violation in the first

* This project was supported by Grant No. 72-SS-99-006, awarded to the Criminal Justice Research Center (Albany, New York) by the Statistics Division, National Criminal Justice Information and Statistics Service, Law Enforcement Assistance Administration, U.S. Department of Justice. Views or opinions stated in this paper are those of the authors and do not necessarily represent the official position or policies of the U.S. Department of Justice. The authors wish to thank Eliot Smith for helpful comments and suggestions on an earlier draft of this paper.

From *American Sociological Review,* Vol. 43 (April 1978), pp. 162-176. Reprinted by permission of the American Sociological Association and the authors.

place, but also of becoming enmeshed in official negative labeling processes.

While few would deny that lower-class and minority group members are overrepresented at the various stages of the criminal justice process, the issue is whether that overrepresentation reflects stereotyping or bias in the system, or whether it is attributable to such group members' greater proportional involvement in offenses or possession of prior criminal or delinquent records which might justify severe treatment. This issue is further complicated in the area of juvenile court decision making by differences in orientation followed by various juvenile courts around the country, and by the methodological inadequacies of the studies which attempt to assess the criteria upon which dispositions are accorded in these courts.

The findings of the more rigorous empirical studies have been less than conclusive with respect to the role of stereotyping and discrimination in juvenile court decision making.[1] For example, Terry's (1967) study of the Racine, Wisconsin Juvenile Court indicates that no class or race effects are evident when statistical controls are applied to his data. The severity of disposition in the Racine Court was most strongly related to the juvenile's prior offense record and the seriousness of the offense for which the youth was charged. Arnold's (1971) study of a middle-sized southern city, on the other hand, suggests that evidence of discriminatory treatment against blacks was apparent both before and after controls were added to his analysis, but that no substantial differences in treatment could be observed among the various social classes. Finally, Thornberry's (1973) analysis of dispositions in the Philadelphia Juvenile Courts reports that race and class significantly affect the treatment meted out, with black and lower-class male youths being systematically accorded more severe treatment, even with controls for prior record and seriousness of offense added to the analysis.

One possible explanation for this pattern of contradictory findings may lie in the approaches to juvenile justice taken by different courts. Different courts might well adhere to different orientations or philosophies concerning the treatment of juvenile offenders. For example, due to the impact of recent Supreme Court decisions, some juvenile courts have developed systems which pay greater attention to due process guarantees for juveniles (see, for example, in re Gault, 387 U.S. 1, 1967; *Kent* v. *United States*, 383 U.S. 541, 1966; and in re Winship, 397 U.S. 358, 1970). It has been suggested that bias is less apt to occur in courts committed to the due process model, for, as Herbert Packer (1966: 39) has noted, this model of processing has the effect of:

> "Judicializing" each stage of the criminal process, of enhancing the capacity of the accused to challenge the operation of the process, and of equalizing the capacity of all persons to avail themselves of the opportunity for challenge so created.

Hirschi (1975: 191), on the other hand, has recently characterized the traditional therapeutic juvenile court model and summarized the views of many regarding this model's hypothesized effect on juvenile court processing:

> As everyone knows, the (traditional) juvenile justice system was explicitly constructed to give the kindly agents of the state a relatively free hand in dealing with the problems of children. This system was authorized to take into account the needs of the child, his or her probable future behavior, and so on through a long list of considerations that would seem to allow or even require bias or discrimination on the part of officials.

While the possible effect of court differences in the approach to juvenile justice should be considered in accounting for the contradictory findings of previous studies, we must consider as well the possibility that differences in the techniques of analysis have contributed to the variation in the reported results. In our judgment, none of these studies has utilized a data-analytic technique which allows for an adequate treatment of the issue of bias in the juvenile court.

As we have previously noted, the issue of bias as it is usually treated in the empirical literature involves the question of whether extra-legal factors (i.e., race, class, etc.) lead to differential treatment of juvenile cases when relevant legal factors are controlled for (i.e., seriousness of offense, prior record, etc.). To adequately treat this issue, relevant legal variables must be introduced simultaneously into the analysis. An analysis should also allow estimation of the magnitude of the bias, should it be demonstrated that bias is present. In both of these respects the literature cited above is in our judgment deficient, or at least ambiguous. Terry's (1967) multivariate findings, for example, were obtained through the applications of control variables introduced one or two at a time, but not all at once. The simultaneous introduction of several statistical controls may substantially alter the results of one's analysis. In addition, Terry used a single "average" Kendall's tau_b correlation coefficient to summarize the magnitude of the relationships occurring within the subclassifications of his control variables. Thus the average tau he obtained may have been insensitive to possible interaction effects within the various levels of the control variable utilized. Arnold's (1971) multivariate findings, on the other hand, are largely dependent on what he terms a "total consideration score" compiled from his independent variables. However, the procedure by which he constructs this multivariate index is of questionable validity.[2] Finally, Thornberry's (1973) failure to assess the magnitude of the presumed relationships in his data has apparently led him to conclusions which are not justified. Wellford (1975:338–9) effectively demonstrates that when a measure of association (instead of the percentage differences employed by Thornberry) is utilized to assess the strength of the relationships reported by Thornberry, "the data reflect the minimal contribution of race and SES to criminal justice decision making." Thus, methodological inadequacies and failures to consider the effect of court differences in previous studies call for further empirical assessment of the nature and extent of bias in the treatment of juvenile offenders.

This paper is an attempt to address the issue of stereotyping and discrimination in our juvenile justice system by:

(1) utilizing a more appropriate and rigorous system for the analysis of multivariate relationships among qualitative variables, including statistical interactions (Goodman's method of log linear analysis; see Goodman, 1972 and 1973, for a general discussion of log linear analysis, and Burke and Turk, 1975, for an application of this method to the sentencing of adult offenders); and
(2) comparing treatment accorded in two courts differing in orientation to juvenile justice, which allows us to assess intercourt differences.

The Data

The data employed in this study were gathered from completed case history records compiled for all male juveniles

---

[1] Discrimination or bias is generally considered present in these studies if minorities and lower-class juveniles are more likely to have had their offenses handled officially by the court and/or more likely to have been incarcerated in a training institution than were nonminorities and nonlower-class youths.

[2] Arnold's "Total Consideration Score" is an ad hoc procedure employed to control simultaneously for the effects of several independent variables on juvenile dispositions. Arnold presents no logical justification for the weighting procedure used in compiling this score. In addition, the cell frequencies in the devised categories are so small that they lead to questions regarding the stability of these findings under replication.

(excluding dependency, neglect, and traffic cases) referred to the Denver (Colorado), and Memphis (Tennessee) juvenile courts between January 1, and December 31, 1972—a total of 2,465 cases from Denver and 4,429 cases from Memphis.[3] The comparability of the data permits the assessment of court variations in the handling of juvenile offenders. Both courts have their own judges who deal exclusively with juvenile cases and, in addition, the courts have comparable administrative structures to handle the variety of functions which they perform (for a complete description of the administrative structures of these courts and a preliminary analysis of these and other data see Cohen, 1975).

Though there are similarities in the structure of these two respective juvenile courts, there is an important difference in the overall orientation of the court personnel within these two centralized bureaucracies toward the youths who come to their attention. The Denver facility is considerably more due process oriented.[4] The personnel of the Denver facility exhibited an overriding concern for and attention to procedural rights of youths, and the court functions were structured in ways designed to safeguard these rights. The overall orientation of the Memphis facility, on the other hand, resembles more closely the traditional therapeutic model for juvenile courts (i.e., one in which the proper course of action should be taken "in the best interest of the child"). Therapeutic concerns were voiced more often and more emphatically by personnel of the Memphis Court than by personnel of the Denver Court.[5] As we have previously indicated, such differences in orientation are thought by many to contribute to differential treatment of suspected offenders.

In addition to orientation differences, these courts are located in different regions of the country. Thus, we are comparing a nonsouthern court with a due process orientation with a southern court with a more traditional approach to the treatment of juvenile offenders. Previous empirical research conducted in southern courts, both adult and juvenile, has concluded that racial bias was present in the sentencing of apprehended offenders (Johnson, 1941; Garfinkel, 1949; Bullock, 1961; Arnold, 1971). If philosophical and/or regional differences between courts account for differential handling of offenders, they should be readily detectable in our data.

The case records from these two courts permit us to consider the influence on juvenile dispositions of such extra-legal factors as race and social class, and the legal factors of prior record and type of offense. In addition, we have information on a variable whose influence has not been previously studied. In this study we shall label this variable as "Present Activity." The variable designates whether the child is active (working and/or in school), or is idle—that is, not working or in school. Certain observers (Platt, 1969; Cicourel, 1968) have noted the possible relevance of variables of this type to the issue of stereotyping and middle-class bias among juvenile court officials.[6]

Race and Prior Record are dichotomous variables contrasting whites vs. nonwhite youths and those with no prior record vs. those with prior record.[7] Social Class is based on parental yearly income, and is composed of three categories: (1) less than $5,000 yearly income; (2) $5,000 to $9,999; and (3) $10,000 or more. Five categories of offense type will be employed: (1) Miscellaneous, (2) Status, (3) Alcohol or Drug, (4) Property, and (5) Violent.[8] The effects of these variables and of differences due to court orientations on severity of disposition will be assessed. The dependent variable, Severity of Disposition, has three categories which may be ranked from least to most severe.[9] The least severe disposition is informal adjustment; the most severe is incarceration in a juvenile institution or case waived to an adult court for adjudication. Intermediate in level of severity is formal probation. In this paper we refer to these categories as "least," "moderately," and "most severe" dispositions, respectively.

Methods

Although the focus of research on juvenile dispositions primarily has been on the issue of race and class bias, we shall not restrict our attention solely to the question of whether the hypothesis of race and class bias can be supported. Instead, we shall direct our analysis to the more general question of how the six factors of race, class, present activity, prior record, offense type and court orientation appear to influence the severity of disposition accorded adjudicated juveniles. We maintain a principal focus on race and class bias, but at the same time we believe that the analysis of data such as these can offer more general information about the role of legal and extra-legal factors in the disposition process.

To examine these data we employ Goodman's (1972) framework for log linear analysis. Log linear is well suited for the analysis of data pertaining to issues

---

[3] There were approximately 9,700 eligible cases (males, not dependency, neglect, or traffic cases) from these two courts before cases with incomplete information on any of the variables were excluded. A comparison of those cases with missing data to cases without revealed no systematic differences between the two groups in the marginals of all variables. Under our inspection it appears that incomplete cases are largely attributable to random errors of record keeping.

[4] The Denver Juvenile Court is certainly one of the most due process oriented juvenile tribunals in the country; it adheres largely to the model practiced in adult criminal courts. For example, the Denver court requires that the police adhere to a probable cause standard for arrest before any child can be adjudicated as a delinquent. If a child is to be detained for any length of time exceeding 24 hours prior to his adjudication, the Denver Juvenile Court permits the posting of bail. Whenever a child's case is to be adjudicated before a formal court hearing, the court requires that the youth be represented by an attorney and permits (and even encourages) the use of plea bargaining during the adjudication process. Finally, if the attempt at plea bargaining is unsuccessful, the court permits the child (or his parents, guardian, or attorney) to choose between a bench or jury trial. The Memphis court, on the other hand, while complying with Supreme Court mandates, prefers to follow the more traditional therapeutic concerns of the juvenile court and does not utilize plea bargaining, jury trials, or many other characteristics of the due process model followed by the Denver court.

[5] One clear example emphasizing the different orientations of these two courts is the proportion of status offenses processed. Approximately 40% of the cases processed in Memphis in 1972 were status offenses as compared with only 10% in Denver. In the therapeutic court the legal definition of delinquency is quite broad in order to "help" all children regardless of the seriousness of their misconduct. The due process model, however, fearing the abuse of power, demands more precise rules for defining the type of conduct which may result in the finding of delinquency. Our field work and interviews with court functionaries indicate a very clear difference in attitude between agents of the two courts with respect to the type of behavior the court should focus attention upon. Hence, it is probable that the difference in the proportion of status offenses processed in these two courts reflect a difference in orientation rather than a difference in the behavior of juveniles within these jurisdictions.

[6] An extensive preliminary analysis of these data indicated that certain variables available for use in the analysis had no substantial direct or indirect effect on the severity of accorded disposition in either court. These variables (age of the juvenile, family intactness, type of agency or individual making the court referral) were thus excluded from the present analysis.

[7] Individuals of Spanish heritage are classified as nonwhite in this study.

[8] The categorization of type or seriousness of offense was determined by grouping all possible offenses for which youths may be referred in each court into a smaller number of generic categories, and then having probation officers and juvenile judges charged with decision making at both courts rank these categories from least to most severe. There was nearly unanimous agreement among raters both within and between courts on the order of ranking of offense severity. The rankings and the various acts which comprise each category from least to most severe are presented in Appendix A.

[9] The measure of severity of final disposition was compiled by asking probation officers and juvenile court judges from both courts to rank all possible disposition alternatives into different levels of severity. The alternatives available in both courts, and the subjective estimates as to their severity were quite similar. The categories and their proportional frequency of occurrence for both courts are presented in the Appendix (Table B).

of criminal justice (Burke and Turk, 1975). Specifically, log linear analysis provides a means for examining the relationships among sets of qualitative (categorical) variables. Since many dependent variables of interest to criminologists cannot be intervally scaled properly, regression analysis and other forms of the general linear model cannot be readily applied.

Two different approaches to the analysis of the association among a set of variables can be taken within Goodman's (1972) framework. The confirmatory approach calls for the a priori specification of hypothesized models to account for the association among a set of variables. A second approach is exploratory, and involves examining a series of different models with the intent of finding the best fitting one. We find the second approach to be more consistent with the aim of answering the general question of how the six factors measured in this study influence dispositions. Furthermore, this exploratory process provides the same information for the assessment of possible race and class bias which would be obtained if we were to use the more restrictive confirmatory approach, focusing exclusively on hypotheses pertaining to the issue of bias.

Consequently, in our analysis we will examine the general impact of the six legal and extra-legal factors on dispositions. Following this analysis we will assess the specific implications of these general findings for the issue of bias in the treatment of juvenile offenders.

Goodman's (1972) framework includes three procedures which we employ in examining the influence of our set of legal and extra-legal factors on severity of disposition. First, we use a procedure for testing the fit of hierarchical models with the aim of finding a model which most parsimoniously accounts for the association among this set of variables. Second, we apply a procedure for assessing the independent (net) contribution of each factor to the total association. Third, we present estimated effect parameters which provide information on both the sign of the relationship between variables and the relative changes of being accorded different types of dispositions.

Analysis

The starting point for our analysis was the construction of a seven-way contingency table, consisting of 720 cells, for the variables of Race (R), Parental Income (I), Present Activity (A), Offense Type (O), Prior Record (P), Court (C), and Severity of Disposition (D). Under the most general or saturated model (Goodman, 1972) the cell frequencies from this table can be expressed as:

Table 1. Likelihood Ratio χ^2 Values for Selected Models Pertaining to the Association Among Race (R), Parental Income (I), Court (C), Present Activity (A), Prior Record (P), Type of Offense (O) and Severity of Disposition (D)

Model	Fitted Marginals	Degrees of Freedom	Likelihood Ratio χ^2	P
1	All 4-Way Interactions	284	165.42	$>.5$
2	All 3-Way Interactions	501	418.50	$>.5$
3	All 2-Way Interactions	649	1557.94	$<.001$
4	Model 3 + [IAR] [IRC] [APD] [AOR] [POC] [ROC] [IRC] [OPD] [OCD]	607	641.28	$>.163$

$$G_{ijklmno}=\theta+\lambda^{R}_{i}+\lambda^{I}_{j}+\lambda^{A}_{k}+\lambda^{O}_{l}+\lambda^{P}_{m}+\lambda^{C}_{n}+\lambda^{D}_{o}$$

$$+\lambda^{RI}_{ij}+\ldots+\lambda^{CD}_{no} \quad \text{(Total:21 Two Variable Effects)}$$

$$+\lambda^{RIA}_{ijk}+\ldots+\lambda^{PCD}_{mno} \quad \text{(Total:35 Three-way Interactions)}$$

$$+\lambda^{RIAO}_{ijkl}+\ldots+\lambda^{OPCD}_{lmno} \quad \text{(Total:35 Four-Way Interactions)}$$

$$+\lambda^{RIAOP}_{ijklm}+\ldots+\lambda^{AOPCD}_{klmno} \quad \text{(Total:21 Five-Way Interactions)}$$

$$+\lambda^{RIAOPC}_{ijklmn}+\ldots+\lambda^{IAOPCD}_{jklmno} \quad \text{(Total:7 Six-Way Interactions)}$$

where λ equals the log linear effect parameter (log odds ratio). The superscripts refer to the variables and the subscripts refer to the categories of the variables. The values of $G_{ijklmno}$ are the log of the frequencies in each of the 720 cells of the seven-way cross tabulation.[10] Single superscripted λ's correspond to the effect of the marginals of each variable. Double superscripted λ's represent the two variable or main effects.[11] Triple or higher superscripted λ's designate interaction effects of the order corresponding to the number of superscripts.

The terms of this model involving severity of disposition (those including D) give the partial associations among the six factors and disposition. Our principal interest is in these terms. The virtue of the saturated model lies in the ability to examine both the main effects of each factor and all the possible ways in which these factors may interact to influence disposition. However, the large number of terms involving severity of disposition makes the presentation and interpretation of the estimated parameters for these terms from the saturated model unwieldy. To simplify matters we use a procedure, described below, for testing the fit of progressively simpler hierarchical models to find a more parsimonious model which adequately accounts for the association among the variables in our seven-way contingency table.

The likelihood ratio χ^2 values for tests of the goodness of fit of selected models examined in our search procedure are presented in Table 1. We began our search by examining the statistical significance of the effect parameters estimated under the saturated model. This inspection revealed that a model excluding all five, six, and seven-way interactions would adequately fit (Model 1). The likelihood ratio χ^2 shows that we clearly cannot reject the null hypothesis that Model 1 fits the observed cell frequencies. We then attempted to achieve further simplification by using a step down procedure, deleting one order of effects with each step. Model 2 is a model with all four-way interactions and above deleted. Model 3 has all three-way and higher order interactions excluded.[12] Model 2 fits the data while Model 3 does not, indicating that the most parsimonious model includes at least one three-way interaction.

Since many of the 35 three-way interactions included in Model 2 may not be statistically significant, it is possible to achieve further simplification by finding a model which includes a smaller subset of the three-way interactions. We examined several such models and selected Model 4 as the most parsimonious model incorporating three-way interactions.[13] Model 4 specified that we can best understand

[10] θ is a constant added to insure that the cell entries sum to the total sample size (Goodman, 1972: 1043).

[11] Consistent with analysis of variance terminology, throughout this paper we use the term "main effect" to label what Goodman calls a two variable interaction in his framework.

[12] Note that because the models estimated are hierarchical, if any interaction of a set of factors is included in a model, lower order interactions consisting of subsets of these factors must also be included.

[13] To obtain the final model we began with an examination of the effect parameters for Model 2 to see which terms among the three-way interactions might be reasonably deleted on the basis of their statistical significance. These terms were deleted and the χ^2 for the resultant model supported the hypothesis that this simplified model fits the data. We were left with twelve remaining terms, and we estimated several models deleting subsets of these twelve terms. The final model selection was made because the deletion of any of the nine terms in Model 4 resulted in significant increment to the χ^2 value for the model.

Table 2. Likelihood Ratio χ^2 Values for Models Used to Calculate Goodman's Coefficient of Partial Determination

Model	Fitted Marginals	Degrees of Freedom	Likelihood Ratio χ^2	p
5	Model 4—OPD	615	727.20	<.001
6	Model 4—OCD	615	766.83	<.001
7	Model 4—APD	609	692.65	<.001
8	Model 3—CD	651	1671.89	<.001
9	Model 3—RD	651	1559.08	<.001
10	Model 3—OD	657	2092.56	<.001
11	Model 3—PD	651	1742.12	<.001
12	Model 3—AD	651	1611.72	<.001
13	Model 3—ID	653	1567.66	<.001

Table 3. Values of the Coefficient of Partial Determination and Likelihood Ratio χ^2 for Factors Affecting Severity of Dispositions

Factor	Comparison	Degrees of Freedom	Likelihood Ratio χ^2	Coefficient of Partial Determination	p
[OPD]	Model 5—Model 4	8	85.92	.119	<.001
[OCD]	Model 6—Model 4	8	125.55	.180	<.001
[APD]	Model 7—Model 4	2	51.37	.077	<.001
[CD]	Model 8—Model 3	2	113.95	.070	<.001
[RD]	Model 9—Model 3	2	1.11	.002	>.500
[OD]	Model 10—Model 3	8	534.62	.327	<.001
[PD]	Model 11—Model 3	2	184.18	.115	<.001
[AD]	Model 12—Model 3	2	53.78	.031	<.001
[ID]	Model 13—Model 3	4	9.72	.006	<.050

Table 4. Effect of Parameters (λ's) for the Severity of Disposition*

	Types of Disposition		
Main Effects	Least Severe	Moderately Severe	Most Severe
Race [RD]			
White	.041	−.001	−.040
Nonwhite	−.041	.001	.040
Parental Income [ID]			
Low	.088	−.031	−.057
Medium	.031	−.015	−.016
High	−.118	.045	.073
Offense Type [OD]			
Alcohol & Drugs	.096	.060	−.156
Status	.296	−.126	−.070
Property	−.195	.385	−.190
Violent	−.448	−.079	.527
Miscellaneous	.252	−.241	−.011
Court [CD]			
Denver	.111	.072	−.183
Memphis	−.111	−.072	.183
Prior Record [PD]			
No	.136	.061	−.197
Yes	−.136	−.061	.197
Present Activity [AD]			
Active	.217	.159	−.376
Idle	−.217	−.159	.376

* Parameters for the main effects of Race [RD], Parental Income [ID], Offense Type [OD], Court [CD], Prior Record [PD], Present Activity [AD]. Least Severe=unofficial disposition; Moderately Severe=formal probation; Most Severe=institutionalization or waived to adult court.

the effect of the six factors of race, social class, present activity, prior record, offense type, and court on severity of disposition by considering only their six main effects and the three interaction effects of present activity by prior record [APD], prior record by offense type [OPD], and offense type by court [OCD].

As a second step we apply Goodman's procedure for assessing the relative magnitude of effects. This procedure calls for the estimation of models deleting the term of interest. These models (5–13) are presented in Table 2. The comparison of a χ^2 value of such a model with the χ^2 value for a model including the term of interest can be used to construct what Goodman (1972:1056–8) calls a "coefficient of partial determination." The larger the value of this coefficient, the greater the relative magnitude of an effect. The rank order of these coefficients is indicative of the relative importance of a factor.[14]

In Table 3 we present the values of the coefficient of partial determination for each of the terms of Model 4 which involve type of disposition. From this table we see that the two variables with the strongest net impact on the severity of disposition accorded are offense type and prior record. This observation applies for both the main and interaction effects involving these variables. Also we can see that the partial associations of race and dispositions, and income and dispositions make very small relative contributions to the total association. In fact Table 3 shows that the main effect of race on dispositions is nonsignificant at conventional levels.[15]

As the third and final step we examine the effect parameters (λ coefficients) for the relationships between the six factors and dispositions. To simplify presentation these coefficients are arrayed in two tables. Table 4 contains values of the λ coefficients for the main effects of each variable. In Table 5 we present λ coefficients for the three-way interactions involving severity of disposition specified in Model 4.

The coefficients (λ's) found in these tables reflect comparisons with the average or overall probability of individuals being accorded the three types of dispositions. A positive coefficient indicates that, controlling for all other independent variables, there is greater than average chance that individuals falling in the designated category of a variable will be accorded the specified disposition. A negative coefficient indicates a less than average chance, and a coefficient equal to zero shows no difference from the average.

From Table 4 we again see that race has virtually no independent effect on dispositions, and that income has a significant but small effect. Further, it should be noted that the relationship between income and type of disposition is in the opposite direction of that suggested by the conventional

[14] We speak of relative importance of a factor only in the sense of its direct effect controlling for all other factors. As Duncan (1970) notes, to assess relative importance of a factor in terms of its total impact one must also consider indirect effects via an hypothesized model.

[15] The test for the significance of an individual partial term is based on the value of the likelihood ratio χ^2 generated by the model comparisons specified in Table 2.

view of class bias. Controlling for all other factors, higher income youth run a slightly less than average chance of being accorded the least severe disposition (λ = −.118), while lower income juveniles experience a slightly higher than average chance of receiving favorable treatment.

The relationships between prior record, present activity, offense type, court and dispositions all involve three-way interactions. A three-way interaction (e.g., APD) means that the relationship between two variables differs across levels of the third variable. The λ coefficients for three-way interactions specify the difference between the main effect of a variable and its effect within the different categories of a third variable. For example, the coefficient for the interaction of the categories no prior record and active specifies that we add the value .198 (from Table 5) to the main effect parameter for the category of no prior record on the relative chance of being accorded an unofficial disposition (λ = .136, from Table 4). The resultant value (.334) gives the impact of being in the category no prior record on the relative chance of obtaining an unofficial disposition among juveniles who are active.

Inspecting the main effects of present activity [AD] and prior record [PD], and the three-way interaction [APD], we obtain the following information about how these two variables influence dispositions. First, juveniles who are idle have a greater than average probability of being accorded the most severe disposition (λ = .376 and a less than average probability of obtaining the least severe disposition (λ= −.217). Second, the λ coefficients for the main effect of prior record show that, in general, having no prior record increases the likelihood of being given the least severe disposition (λ = .136) and decreases the likelihood of being given the most severe disposition (λ = −.197).

The three-way interaction [APD] indicates that the influence of prior record differs by category of present activity. The coefficients for this three-way interaction show that juveniles who are active receive less severe dispositions than would be expected on the basis of the main effect of prior record alone. Conversely, they also show that juveniles who are idle receive more severe dispositions than would be expected on the basis of the main effect of prior record alone.

The results of this analysis show that the variable of court affects dispositions in two ways. First, the coefficients for the main effect of court [CD] demonstrate that, controlling for all other factors, juveniles brought before the Memphis court are more likely to be accorded the most severe disposition, and less likely to be accorded the least severe disposition than are juveniles adjudicated in Denver.

Table 5. Effect Parameters for the Three-Way Interactions of Severity of Disposition with Present Activity by Prior Record [APD], Offense Type by Court [OCD], and Offense Type by Prior Record [OPD]

	Types of Disposition		
	Least Severe	Moderately Severe	Most Severe
[APD]			
Active, No Prior Record	+.198	−.041	−.157
Active, Prior Record	+.198	−.041	−.157
Idle, No Prior Record	−.198	+.041	+.157
Idle, Prior Record	−.198	+.041	+.157
[OCD]			
Denver, Miscellaneous	+.040	−.074	+.034
Denver, Status	−.437	−.034	+.471
Denver, Alcohol & Drug	+.251	−.148	−.103
Denver, Property	+.266	−.023	−.243
Denver, Violent	−.120	+.279	−.159
Memphis, Miscellaneous	−.040	+.074	−.034
Memphis, Status	+.437	+.034	−.471
Memphis, Alcohol & Drug	−.251	+.148	+.103
Memphis, Property	−.266	+.023	+.243
Memphis, Violent	+.120	−.279	+.159
[OPD]			
No Prior Record, Miscellaneous	−.146	+.062	+.084
No Prior Record, Status	+.267	−.191	−.076
No Prior Record, Alcohol & Drug	−.154	+.037	+.117
No Prior Record, Property	+.155	+.145	−.300
No Prior Record, Violent	−.122	+.070	+.052
Prior Record, Miscellaneous	+.146	−.062	−.084
Prior Record, Status	−.267	+.191	+.076
Prior Record, Alcohol & Drug	+.154	−.037	−.117
Prior Record, Property	−.155	−.145	+.300
Prior Record, Violent	+.122	−.070	−.052

Second, the influence of court is also shown in its interaction with the offense category.

In general, as indicated by the main effect of offense type [OD], youths adjudicated for offenses conventionally thought to be the most serious (property and violent offenses) incur the highest risks of being given either the moderately severe or most severe dispositions. But, there is also a difference between the two courts in the effect of offense category. The coefficients for the three-way interaction [OCD] reveal that, with the exception of status offenders, apprehended juveniles in Memphis are likely to receive a more severe disposition for the same type of offense than apprehended juveniles in Denver.

Finally, the coefficients for the three-way interaction of offense type by prior record by disposition [OPD] indicate that the effect of offense type on disposition depends upon the category of prior record. The value of the coefficients for [OPD] show that this interaction principally involves status and property offenses. They further demonstrate that, on the one hand, if an individual apprehended for a status or property offense has no prior record, he is likely to receive more lenient treatment than would be expected on the basis of the main effects of offense category and prior record. On the other hand, if an individual apprehended for a status or property offense has a prior record, he is likely to receive a more severe disposition than would be expected on the basis of the pertinent main effects.

Discussion

We turn now to the implications of our findings for the issues of race and class bias and the differences in court orientations for the dispositions given to juvenile offenders. To assess the implications for race and class bias we must first consider what criteria should be used in drawing conclusions about the existence of this phenomenon. Three criteria are suggested here:

(1) the existence of a direct effect of race or class such that nonwhites and/or lower income groups receive more severe dispositions, controlling for legal factors such as offense and prior record;

(2) the existence of interaction effects involving race or class and legal factors—such that lower class and/or nonwhite juveniles receive more severe dispositions for the same category of legal factors; and

(3) the existence of indirect effects of

race and/or class through other factors considered to be stereotypical in nature.

The first two of these criteria are relatively straightforward, being either explicitly or implicitly employed in prior research. The third criteria, however, requires further explication. Schur (1973), as previously noted, argues that lower-class and nonwhite juveniles run a higher actuarial risk of being labeled "delinquency-prone." If race and class have no indirect effect on dispositions, but have an indirect effect through their relationship to the chance of being labeled as delinquency prone, then one could conclude that evidence of bias has been demonstrated by the third criterion.

Our analysis has uncovered no evidence of race or class bias of the type specified in criteria (1) and (2) listed above. Race has no significant association nor interaction effect with legal factors on dispositions. Parental income does not interact with legal factors in its effect on dispositions. Although there is a direct effect of parental income on disposition, the direction of this relationship is opposite to the direction hypothesized in the usual argument regarding the effect of class on treatment. Further, our analysis has shown that the total impact of this variable is quite small.

The factor of present activity is relevant to the third criterion for the existence of race or class bias. Present activity seems best interpretable as an indicator of a stereotypical perception by a court official that the juvenile is delinquency-prone. Of particular interest in this respect is the interaction of present activity with prior record. It appears that if a juvenile is idle, he receives a different type of disposition than if he legitimately is engaged in the activities of going to school and/or working at a job.

Our analysis shows that the apparently stereotypical factor of present activity has an effect on disposition by way of its interaction with prior record. To demonstrate that an indirect effect resulting in unfavorable treatment of lower-class or nonwhite youths exists, it is also necessary to demonstrate that these groups do indeed run a higher risk of being found in the categories of present activity and prior record which lead to the most severe dispositions. Information pertaining to this question can be found in Tables 6 and 7, which show the frequency distributions of race and parental income by present activity by prior record. From these tables we can see that nonwhites and lower-income youths do run a slightly higher risk of being in the category which incurs the most severe dispositions (idle with a prior record). Correspondingly, these groups run a lower risk of being in the category which stands the best chance of receiving a favorable disposition (active with no prior record).

Given this pattern, however, an interpretation of bias is not an unequivocal matter. From Table 6 one can see that apprehended nonwhites differ little from apprehended whites in their probability of being idle. One can see also in Table 7 that lower-income youths do differ from higher-income youths in the percent idle, but it should be noted that this difference is not as marked as the difference among income groups in the percent who have a prior record. Thus, in accounting for the disproportionate tendency of nonwhite and lower-income youths to be found in the high risk category of present activity by prior record (and to be absent from the low risk category of these same variables), differences among these groups in the percentage who have a prior record are of greater importance than the differences in present activity.

It appears, then, that the greater risk run by nonwhites and lower-income youths of being labeled as "delinquency prone" does not stem as much from differences in present activity as from differences in prior record. Since prior record is generally accorded the status of a legal factor, one can question the categorization of the indirect effect of race and class through the interaction of present activity by prior record as a type of race or class bias in juvenile dispositions.

Earlier in this paper we raised the question as to whether differences in the approach to juvenile justice taken by different courts might influence the degree of bias shown. Contrary to suggested differences in the potential for bias between a due process and a therapeutic court, no difference was found. Although the two courts differ in their philosophical or legal orientations, this difference has no effect on race or class bias. Instead it appears to center about the overall severity of dispositions and the influence of the different offense types for which juveniles were referred to the court. In our analysis, juveniles referred in Memphis (the therapeutic court) were, on the whole, more likely to be given a severe disposition, and more likely to be given a more severe disposition for the same type of offense than juveniles in Denver (the due process oriented court). Whatever discretionary power is granted under the therapeutic model, then, seems to be manifested in a greater proportion of severe dispositions accorded, but not in the de-

Table 6. Frequency Distributions of Race by Present Activity by Prior Record

	Race					
	White			Nonwhite		
	Present Activity			Present Activity		
Prior Record	Idle	Active	Total	Idle	Active	Total
No	96 (4.2)[a]	1,142 (50.1)	1,238 (54.3)	103 (2.2)	1,565 (33.9)	1,668 (36.1)
Yes	204 (9.0)	835 (36.7)	1,039 (45.7)	583 (12.6)	2,366 (51.2)	2,949 (63.8)
Total	300 (13.2)	1,977 (86.8)	2,277 (100.0)	686 (14.8)	3,931 (85.1)	4,617 (99.9)

[a] Percent of grand total

Table 7. Frequency Distributions of Parental Income by Present Activity by Prior Record

	Parental Income								
	Less than $5,000			$5,000–$9,999			$10,000 +		
	Present Activity			Present Activity			Present Activity		
Prior Record	Idle	Active	Total	Idle	Active	Total	Idle	Active	Total
No	76 (2.3)[a]	1,146 (34.2)	1,122 (36.5)	86 (3.5)	968 (39.4)	1,054 (42.9)	37 (3.4)	593 (54.6)	630 (58.0)
Yes	461 (13.7)	1,671 (49.8)	2,132 (63.5)	267 (10.9)	1,133 (46.2)	1,400 (57.1)	59 (5.4)	397 (36.6)	456 (42.0)
Total	537 (16.0)	2,817 (84.0)	3,354 (100.0)	353 (14.4)	2,101 (85.6)	2,454 (100.0)	96 (8.8)	990 (91.2)	1,086 (100.0)

[a] Percent of grand total

gree of bias shown towards blacks and lower-class youths.

In sum, our analysis offers little support for the argument that race or class bias directly affect the dispositions given to juveniles in the Denver or Memphis juvenile courts. Rather, we found that the disposition process is most strongly influenced by prior record and type of offense in these two courts with different approaches to juvenile justice and from different regions of the country.

Conclusion

Our evidence suggests that offense and prior record are the major determinants of the severity of disposition accorded in the two courts studied. On the basis of these findings are we justified in concluding that the juvenile justice system of these two jurisdictions are unbiased in all aspects of their treatment of adjudicated juveniles? The answer to this question is, of course, no. However, these findings do necessitate the qualifications of the widespread accusations that race and class discrimination permeate the juvenile justice system.

Any discussion of bias in the criminal justice system must ultimately address both the issue of the point at which bias occurs and the issue of how bias is defined. Clearly, bias may appear at stages prior to a youth's referral to the juvenile court. It is possible that race and class bias occur when police and other agents decide which juveniles to refer to the court. Our data do not permit an assessment of this possibility. These data do indicate, however, that once the youth is referred to the court, prior record and offense, not race and class, are the major determinants of severity of accorded disposition.

The conclusion that bias does or does not exist in these juvenile courts depends ultimately on one's definition of bias. The criteria generally used to define the existence of bias in previous studies are based on the assumption that prior record and seriousness of offense are appropriate criteria on which to base decisions. We have followed the same approach here. Whether or not these criteria are indeed appropriate factors which should be considered when deciding the fate of juveniles is an ideological, not an empirical matter.

Some contend that the criteria utilized to make decisions in the criminal justice system are themselves biased in favor of white middle-class persons. That is, the law is seen as the embodiment of middle-class norms and the acts which represent infractions of these norms are associated with minority group or lower-class status. Hence, the norms and life styles of many minority and lower-class group members are seen as especially conducive to behavior which may lead to imprisonment or frequent contact with social control agents. While such speculation is plausible, these issues cannot be empirically addressed in this paper. Here, *given* a set of laws or statutes defining criminal or delinquent conduct, we examine the question of possible differential treatment of minority and majority group members.

At the outset of this paper we raised the issue of whether contradictory findings in prior research are attributable to the influence of possible court differences in juvenile justice approach, or to methodological inadequacies in these studies. On the basis of our research, we suggest that the best explanation of these findings lies in their lack of methodological rigor. Although it is possible that the courts studied in prior research are different from the two studied here and that the earlier findings are accurate, we find this argument to be unconvincing. The two courts we have studied represent nearly polar positions on the continuum of possible court differences. On the one hand, the Memphis court is subject to potentially biasing factors of both region (the South) and orientation toward juvenile justice (therapeutic model), while the Denver court is characterized by factors that are thought to offer the least potential for bias (nonsouthern region, due process orientation). The lack of demonstrated bias in the extreme cases examined here at least suggests that differences in court orientation could not have accounted for the contradictory findings of previous research.

Even though we believe that the two courts studied here give us a broader base for generalization than previous single court studies, further research is called for. In addition to sampling polar cases, future research should provide for a sample of courts from other points on the spectrum of juvenile courts and should employ data-analytic techniques (like log linear analysis) which allow for a rigorous assessment of the relationships among variables in the juvenile dispositions process. Finally, future research should attempt to consider factors thought to be related to juvenile dispositions which are not reported in the case history records used here. Some of the possible factors absent from our data and perhaps related to these decisions could be the child's demeanor, attitudes, and apparent contribution.

REFERENCES

Arnold, William R.
1971 "Race and ethnicity relative to other factors in juvenile court dispositions." American Journal of Sociology 77:211–7.

Bullock, Henry A.
1961 "Significance of the racial factor in the length of prison sentence." Journal of Criminal Law, Criminology, and Police Science 52:411–7.

Burke, Peter J. and Austin T. Turk
1975 "Factors affecting postarrest disposition: a model for analysis." Social Problems 22:313–21.

Cicourel, Aaron V.
1968 The Social Organization of Juvenile Justice. New York: Wiley.

Cohen, Lawrence E.
1975 "Delinquency dispositions: an empirical analysis of processing decisions in three juvenile courts." U.S. Department of Justice, National Criminal Justice Information and Statistics Service. Washington, D.C.: U.S. Government Printing Office.

Duncan, Otis Dudley
1970 "Partials, partitions, and paths." Pp. 38–47 in E. Borgatta (ed.), Sociological Methodology. San Francisco: Jossey-Bass.

Garfinkel, Harold
1949 "Research notes on inter- and intra-racial homicides." Social Forces 27:369–81.

Goodman, Leo A.
1972 "A general model for the analysis of surveys." American Journal of Sociology 77: 1035–86.
1973 "Causal analysis of data from panel studies and other kinds of surveys." American Journal of Sociology 78:1135–91.

Hirschi, Travis
1975 "Labeling theory and juvenile delinquency: an assessment of the evidence." Pp. 181–203 in W. Gove (ed.), The Labelling of Deviance. New York: Halsted.

Johnson, Guy B.
1941 "The Negro and crime." The Annals of the American Academy of Political and Social Science 271:93–104.

Martin, John J.
1970 Toward a Political Definition of Delinquency. U.S. Department of Health, Education, and Welfare. Washington, D.C.: U.S. Government Printing Office.

Packer, Herbert L.
1966 "The courts, the police and the rest of us." Journal of Criminal Law, Criminology and Police Science 57:238–43.

Platt, Anthony
1969 The Child Savers: The Invention of Delinquency. Chicago: University of Chicago Press.

Schur, Edwin
1973 Radical Non-Interventions: Rethinking the Delinquency Problem. Englewood Cliffs: Prentice-Hall.

Terry, Robert M.
1967 "The screening of juvenile offenders." Journal of Criminal Law, Criminology and Police Science 58:173–81.

Thornberry, Terrence P.
1973 "Race, socioeconomic status and sentencing in the juvenile justice system." Journal of Criminal Law and Criminology 64:90–8.

Wellford, Charles
1975 "Labeling theory and criminology: an assessment." Social Problems 22:332–45.

APPENDIX

Table A. Severity Ranking of Offense Categories from Least to Most Severe

Offense	Denver N	Denver %	Memphis N	Memphis %
1. *Miscellaneous Offenses:* disturbance, malicious mischief, filthy language, loitering, other	400	(16.2)	272	(6.1)
2. *Status Offenses:* behavior or condition injurious to self or others, truancy, runaway, beyond parental control, curfew	257	(10.4)	1748	(39.5)
3. *Drug and Alcohol Offenses:* marijuana possession, use or sale of marijuana, possession or sale of narcotics, possession or sale of dangerous drugs, inhaling toxic vapors, drunkenness, possession of liquor	351	(14.2)	365	(8.2)
4. *Property Offenses:* burglary, breaking and entering, auto theft, theft, fraud, forgery, shoplifting, arson, joyriding	1198	(48.6)	1709	(38.6)
5. *Violent Offenses:* assault, aggravated assault, battery, manslaughter, murder, robbery, kidnapping, forcible rape	259	(10.5)	335	(7.6)
	2465	(100%)	4429 6894	(100%)

Table B. Proportional Frequency of Severity of Dispositions

	Dispositions		Denver		Memphis
Least Severe:	Case adjusted at juvenile court by probation officer or judge. The juvenile in effect is counseled and the matter then closed. Also known as "informal adjustment."		71.0%		64.8%
Moderately Severe:	Formal supervised probation.		25.8%		27.6%
Most Severe:	Case waived to adult court for adjudication or child incarcerated in juvenile institution.		3.2%		7.6%
		2465	(100.0%)	4429	(100.0%)

Race, Socioeconomic Status and Sentencing in the Juvenile Justice System

Terence P. Thornberry*

Racial and social class discrimination in the administration of justice has long been of theoretical and empirical interest to criminologists. Although many theoretical works assume that such discrimination exists, Terry has pointed out that this assumption has been made "... even though empirical research dealing with these issues is relatively sparse and poorly conceived." [1] For example, Lemert states that "Members of minority groups, migrants, and persons with limited economic means are often the ... scapegoats of the frustrated police in our local communities." [2] Clinard makes a similar assumption: "It is a generally established fact that the Negroes, as well as Spanish speaking peoples, on the whole, are arrested, tried, convicted, and returned to prison more often than others who commit comparable offenses." [3] Sutherland and Cressey, without data, assert:

> (a) Negroes are more liable to arrest than whites ... (c) Negroes have a higher conviction rate than whites. (d) Negroes are often punished more severely than whites, but this is not true for all crimes. (e) Whites are most likely to receive probation and suspended sentences. (f) Negroes receive pardons less often than do whites.[4]

The purpose of the present study is to examine empirically the validity of this assumption using data from the juvenile justice system in Philadelphia. The basic question to be answered is: Do blacks and members of a low socioeconomic strata (SES) receive more severe dispositions than whites and members of a high SES?

The answer is not simple for there are legal variables to be considered. The principles of Anglo-Saxon justice should not permit nonlegal variables like race and social class to affect the severity of dispositions. Legal variables, however, such as the seriousness of the offense and the number of previous offenses committed by the defendant, may be expected to have a decisive effect on the disposition.

The fact that blacks and lower SES subjects are more likely to be recidivists and to commit serious offenses[5] suggests that these legal variables should be controlled in any attempt to examine the effect of race and socioeconomic status. Otherwise, to find that blacks and lower SES subjects receive more severe dispositions may only reflect the fact that they are indeed more serious offenders. Conclusions about the relationship between social characteristics and dispositions should only be made when these legal variables are held constant.

Previous Work[6]

Terry conducted a study based on a sample of all the cases of delinquent behavior that occurred between 1958 and 1962 in a midwestern community with a population of 100,000.[7] Terry ranked the dispositions according to the severity that the police, the probation department and the juvenile court could give an individual, and then correlated them with a number of independent variables. Although the dispositions in the jurisdiction that Terry studied are slightly different from the dispositions used in Philadelphia, their rank order in terms of severity are quite similar to the scheme employed here.

The most important finding in Terry's study concerns the nonlegal variables of race and SES. In zero-order relationships race and SES were consistently, but not very strongly, related to the severity of the dispositions; but after the number of previous offenses and the seriousness of the offense were controlled, the weak relationships that did exist vanished. "The evidence indicates that the severity of the disposition is not a function of the degree of minority status of the juvenile offender or his socioeconomic status."[8] Age, however, was significantly and positively related to the severity of dispositions, and when the legal variables were controlled, this relationship remained. The legal variables, on the other hand, were strongly related to the severity of dispositions.

> Only one of the major hypotheses is completely and consistently supported at the three stages of the legal-judicial system.... The severity of the societal reaction is a function, at least in part, of the amount of deviance [previous offenses] engaged in by the offender. Also relevant, but less clearly so, [is] the degree of deviation [the seriousness of the offense] ...[9]

None of the other legal or nonlegal variables that Terry studied were significantly or consistently

---

* Research Associate in Sociology, University of Pennsylvania and Assistant Criminology Editor of the *Journal*. The author would like to express his thanks to Drs. Marvin E. Wolfgang, Frank J. Cannavale and Robert A. Silverman for their critical reading of earlier drafts of this article.

[1] Terry, *Discrimination in the Handling of Juvenile Offenders by Social Control Agencies*, 1967 J. Research in Crime and Delinquency 218, 219.

[2] E. Lemert, Social Pathology: A Systematic Approach to the Theory of Sociopathic Behavior 311 (1951).

[3] M. Clinard, The Sociology of Deviant Behavior 550–51 (1963).

[4] E. Sutherland & D. Cressey, Principles of Criminology 286 (1960). These passages are meant to be illustrative of the more general acceptance of this assumption and certainly do not exhaust the case. Further examples and references concerning this question can be found in Terry, *supra* note 1, at 219–20.

[5] *See* M. Wolfgang, R. Figlio & T. Sellin, Delinquency in a Birth Cohort Ch. 5–6 (1972).

[6] Because of the differences between the adult and juvenile court systems, only studies dealing with the latter will be reviewed. Since the present study is based on official police records, only studies based on similar data are considered. Observational studies, like Piliavin and Briar's, will not be treated because of methodological differences. *See* Piliavin, Irving & Briar, *Police Encounters with Juveniles*, 70 Am. J. Soc. 206 (1964).

[7] Terry, *supra* note 1, and *The Screening of Juvenile Offenders*, 58 J. Crim. L.C. & P.S. 173 (1967) [hereinafter cited as *Screening*]. The same study is the basis of two articles.

[8] Terry, *supra* note 1, at 228.

[9] *Screening*, *supra* note 7, at 179.

From *Journal of Criminal Law and Criminology*, Vol. 64, 1973, pp. 90–98. Reprinted by special permission of the *Journal of Criminal Law and Criminology*, related to the dependent variable of dispositions, with the sole exception of the number of adult offenders involved in a given offense. "... [I]t seems to be a safe conclusion that legalistic variables play a significant role in the process at all of the stages considered." [10] The same cannot be said for the nonlegal variables, however. With the exception of age, they were not strongly related to dispositions, and with the introduction of the legal variables as controls the relationship vanished.

A number of other studies have arrived at similar conclusions. McEachern and Bauzer examined patterns of police referrals to the juvenile court in Santa Monica, California.[11] No relationship between race and disposition was found. "The proportions of petitions requested for the three ethnic categories used in this analysis are .28 for Negroes, .27 for Mexican-Americans, and .26 for Angloes." [12] Thus, even when the legal variables were ignored, ethnic group membership did not affect the referral practices of the police. As in Terry's study, McEachern and Bauzer found the legal variables to be most strongly related to dispositions. Delinquents who committed serious offenses, who had a greater number of previous offenses, and who were on probation when arrested were far more likely to be referred to the juvenile court than their counterparts.

An earlier study conducted by Goldman closely parallels the work of McEachern and Bauzer, for it is also concerned with the manner in which the police referred cases to the juvenile court.[13] In general, black children were more likely than white children to be referred to the juvenile court. For example, 6.1 per cent of all the cases involved black delinquents but the blacks "... constituted 11.4 per cent of those referred to the juvenile court." [14] Although the black children were more likely to be referred to juvenile court, they were also more likely to commit more serious offenses and to have had a greater amount of previous contact with the police. Although the legal variables were not held constant, the author suggests that they tend to explain the relationship. "It must be noted that all of the Negro children who were referred to court were involved in instances of serious offenses ..." [15]

Shannon used an ecological approach to investigate the referral behavior of the police in three communities of Madison, Wisconsin.[16] One area was predominantly lower class, another predominantly middle class but with some working class sections, and the third was a mixture of middle and "high class" sections. As would be expected, the lower class had a disproportionately high referral rate to the juvenile court, while the higher class area had a disproportionately low rate. The referral rate in the middle class area was about the same as the expected rate. When Shannon controlled for the seriousness of the offense committed, the relationship between social class and dispositions was eliminated. Delinquents from the lower class area committed more serious offenses than delinquents from the other areas. "This means that ... juveniles engaging in comparable types of delinquent behavior receive pretty much the same treatment from the Madison police." [17]

Hohenstein examined the referral practices of the police in Philadelphia, basing his analysis on 504 delinquent events committed in 1960.[18] These 504 events constitute a ten per cent sample of all the index offenses committed in 1960, as defined by Sellin and Wolfgang.[19] Using predictive attribute analysis to examine the data, Hohenstein found that "three important factors were involved in determining the disposition decision: (1) the attitude of the victim, (2) the previous record of the offender, and (3) the seriousness of the present event." [20] The most striking finding was that the attitude of the victim was the most important variable involved. Regardless of the amount of recidivism or the seriousness of the event, when the victim did not favor prosecution, the offender was almost always given the least serious disposition available. However, when the victim was in favor of prosecution, the offender was usually arrested. Relative to nonlegal variables, Hohenstein found race to be virtually unrelated to dispositions and the age of the offender was totally unrelated.[21] The legal variables of seriousness, recidivism, and the attitude of the victim, however, were found to relate to dispositions.

In general, the preceeding research shows that when legal variables such as the seriousness of the offense and the number of previous offenses committed are held constant, the nonlegal variables of race and SES have been found not to affect disposition decisions. Terry's concluding remarks can be used to summarize this body of literature:

> While our research has focused on only some of the many variables that may be relevant in [disposing of juvenile offenders], it seems to be a safe conclusion that legalistic variables play a significant role in the process at all of the stages considered.[22]

Clearly, the findings of these previous studies do not support the assumptions of Lemert, Clinard and others. Given the findings of the research reported to date, blacks and low SES subjects are not more likely than their counterparts to be treated more severely in the juvenile justice system when recidivism and the seriousness of the offense are held constant.

The studies discussed serve two functions: first, to limit the number of variables to be examined; and second, to form hypotheses. The present research deals only with the variables that were previously found to be most significantly related to dispositions: race, SES, number of previous offenses, and the seriousness of the offense. Other analyzed variables were generally found to be unrelated to dispositions. For example, Terry found that variables such as the number of individuals involved in the offense, the delinquency rate of the area of residence, the degree of involvement with offenders of the opposite sex did not affect the severity of dispositions given by legal agencies. The hypotheses which may be formed are:

1. Blacks and delinquents from the low SES receive more severe dispositions than their counterparts.
2. Juveniles who commit serious offenses and have many previous offenses also receive more severe dispositions.
3. When legal variables are held constant, nonlegal variables are unrelated to disposition decisions.

Methodology

To test these hypotheses data collected by Wolfgang, Figlio and Sellin were used.[23] This study gathered information on all males who were born in 1945 and who lived in Philadelphia at least from the ages of ten through seventeen years. By using the records of a variety of agencies, primarily the schools of Philadelphia, the cohort study delimited a population of 9,945 boys. Of this cohort, 3,475 boys were found to have committed at least one delinquent act, and it is this group of delinquents who were analyzed in the present study. After delimiting the cohort population, a search was made by Wolfgang *et al.* through the files of the Philadelphia Police Department for all *officially* recorded delinquent acts committed by the cohort subjects. There were 10,214 delinquent events, with final dispositions recorded for 9,601 cases.[24]

Measurement of the dependent variable, the severity of legal dispositions, is relatively clear-cut because it is a legal variable already defined by the penal code of Pennsylvania. According to police records, the dispositions that can be given to a juvenile in Philadelphia are the following:

1. *Remedial arrest:* handled entirely by the police. In this case, the juvenile is almost always taken to the police station and detained for an hour or so. His case is not forwarded to any other legal agency (e.g., the courts), but his parents or legal guardians are notified and the case is often referred to the city's Department of Welfare. The offense, however, is listed in his police file. (6515)[25]
2. *Discharged:* cases referred by the police but dismissed at the first juvenile court hearing or after a court continuance, unaccompanied by probation. (590)
3. *Adjusted:* cases dismissed at the juvenile court, either by a juvenile court judge or a member of the court staff after the case is adjusted, but without the use of probation. (748)

---

[10] *Id.* at 181.

[11] McEachern & Bauzer, *Factors Related to Disposition in Juvenile Police Contacts* in JUVENILE GANGS IN CONTEXT 148 (M. Klein & B. Myerhoff eds. 1964).

[12] *Id.* at 150.

[13] N. Goldman, Police Reporting of Offenders to Juvenile Court 11 (mimeographed paper on file with author).

[14] *Id.* at 2.

[15] *Id.* at 3.

[16] Shannon, *Types and Patterns of Delinquency Referral in a Middle-Sized City*, 4 BRIT. J. DELINQUENCY 24 (1963).

[17] *Id.* at 33.

[18] Hohenstein, *Factors Influencing the Police Disposition of Juvenile Offenders*, in DELINQUENCY: SELECTED ESSAYS 138 (T. Sellin & M. Wolfgang eds. 1969).

[19] T. SELLIN & M. WOLFGANG, THE MEASUREMENT OF DELINQUENCY (1964).

[20] Hohenstein, *supra* note 18, at 146.

[21] This study did not contain information on SES.

[22] *Screening*, *supra* note 7, at 181.

[23] M. WOLFGANG, R. FIGLIO, & T. SELLIN, *supra* note 5. The writer wishes to express his deep appreciation to these authors for their generous cooperation in the present research.

[24] For a variety of reasons, information on the dispositions of the other 613 offenses was missing or incomplete.

[25] The number following each definition refers to the number of cohort offenses that received such disposition.

4. *Fine and/or restitution:* cases in which the juvenile pays a fine, makes restitution to the victim, or both. (20)
5. *Probation:* cases in which the juvenile court sentences the individual to a certain period of time on probation. (1074)
6. *Institutionalization:* cases in which the juvenile court sentences the individual to spend a certain period of time in a correctional institution. (654)

Because of the similarity of some categories and the small frequencies in others, these six dispositions have been collapsed into the following four:

Remedial arrest	6,515	67.9%
Adjusted (Adjusted and Discharged)	1,338	13.9%
Probation (Probation and Fine and/or Restitution)	1,094	11.4%
Institutionalization	654	6.8%
Total	9,601	100.0%

Data are presented so as to allow examination of differential disposition at each of the major stages of the juvenile justice system: the police, intake hearings by the juvenile court's probation department, and hearings by the juvenile court itself. The major decision for the police is whether to treat a juvenile leniently by giving him a remedial arrest, or to treat him more severely by referring him to the juvenile court. We shall compare the percentage of cases given remedial arrests with the percentage of cases referred to the court. At the level of the intake hearing the major decision is whether to adjust the case, the more lenient option, or to refer the case for a formal juvenile court hearing. The comparison is between the adjusted category and the referred category—the sum of the cases given a sentence of probation or institutionalization. Finally, the major decision for the juvenile court judge concerns probation which is the lenient alternative, or institutionalization, the severe alternative. These two dispositions will be compared. In sum, the following comparisons are made: (1) for the police—remedial vs. referral; (2) for the intake process—adjusted vs. referral; (3) for the juvenile court—probation vs. institutionalization.

Race and Disposition

As can be seen in Table 1, black offenders are more likely than white offenders to receive a more severe disposition at each of the three stages. The police, for example, give a remedial disposition to 78.8 per cent of the white juveniles, but to only 59.2 per cent of the blacks. At the intake hearing the racial differences are not as great, but are still in the same direction. Blacks are less likely (41.8%) than whites (47.1%) to have their cases adjusted, but are more likely (58.2%) than whites (52.9%) to be referred for a court hearing. At the stage of the court hearing the differences are of the same magnitude as the differences observed at the police level. For example, 42.3 per cent of the blacks are sent to correctional institutions, but only 24.4 per cent of whites are handled in this fashion.

The race of the juvenile makes a difference in the way he is handled by the juvenile justice system. However, this difference may be explained by such legal variables as the seriousness of the offense and the subject's previous record. Before controlling for these variables, their relationship to the dependent variable must be determined. Table 2 presents the relationship between the seriousness of the offense and the severity of disposition. At all three stages the more serious the offense, the more severe the disposition. The differences between seriousness of offense and type of disposition are greatest at the police level and least at the juvenile court level.

When the amount of recidivism is used as the independent variable, as in Table 3, similar differences are observed. The expected relationship is present at all three stages and the differences are strong at all stages. At the police level, for example, remedial disposition for first offenders occurs in 79.6 per cent of the cases, while offenders with three or more previous offenses are given remedial dispositions in only 54.2 per cent of the cases. At the juvenile court level first offenders are sent to an institution in 14.0 per cent of the cases, but 50.0 per cent of the juveniles with three or more previous offenses are institutionalized. These two legal variables are strongly associated with disposition decisions as would be expected from previous studies. The task now is to see if they explain the relationship between race and disposition.

In Table 4 the racial differences are presented, holding constant the seriousness of the offense. The striking finding is that racial differences are still quite apparent even when the influence of the seriousness of the offense is controlled. In only one of the six comparisons, the intake stage for high seriousness offenses, does the difference come close to disappearing, and even here blacks are less likely than whites (36.5% vs. 38.4%) to have their cases adjusted. In the other five comparisons the differences are relatively large. Taking the juvenile court stage as one example, we see that for offenses with a low seriousness score, 39.2 per cent of blacks are institutionalized compared to only 15.2 per cent of whites. For the more serious offenses, 42.8 per cent of blacks are institutionalized, but only 25.6 per cent of whites are so treated. Racial differences observed in the zero-order relationship are not explained by the seriousness of the offense.

If the first and third columns and the second and fourth columns in Table 4 are compared, we observe the relationship between seriousness and dispositions when race is held constant. From these comparisons it is clear that the seriousness of the offense plays a major role in determining the severity of the disposition. Both black and white subjects are more likely to receive a severe disposition when they commit serious offenses. This fact is true at all three stages of the juvenile justice system. Race and seriousness tend to interact in relation to dispositions. Thus, for all three stages, white subjects who committed offenses of low seriousness are most likely to receive a lenient disposition while black subjects who committed a high seriousness offense are least likely to receive a lenient disposition.

This finding should not obscure the major result

TABLE 1

Disposition by Race

Disposition	Race		Total
	Black	White	
Remedial %	59.2	78.8	67.9
Referral %	40.8	21.2	32.1
	(5362)*	(4239)	(9601)
Adjusted %	41.8	47.1	43.4
Referral %	58.2	52.9	56.6
	(2186)	(900)	(3086)
Probation %	57.7	75.6	62.6
Institution %	42.3	24.4	37.4
	(1272)	(476)	(1748)

* In this and all subsequent tables the numbers upon which the percentages are based are presented in parentheses.

TABLE 2

Disposition by Seriousness

Disposition	Seriousness*		Total
	Low	High	
Remedial %	88.0	37.3	67.9
Referral %	12.0	62.7	32.1
	(5782)	(3819)	(9601)
Adjusted %	65.4	37.0	43.4
Referral %	34.6	63.0	56.6
	(691)	(2395)	(3086)
Probation %	66.5	62.0	62.6
Institution %	33.5	38.0	37.4
	(239)	(1509)	(1748)

* Seriousness is measured by the Sellin-Wolfgang index. See footnote 19. A low seriousness score is less than 1 and a high score is 1 or more.

TABLE 3

Disposition by Number of Previous Offenses

Disposition	Number of Previous Offenses			Total
	None	1 or 2	3+	
Remedial %	79.6	69.6	54.2	67.9
Referral %	20.4	30.4	45.8	32.1
	(3404)	(2912)	(3285)	(9601)
Adjusted %	57.0	47.0	34.9	43.4
Referral %	43.0	53.0	65.1	56.6
	(696)	(886)	(1504)	(3086)
Probation %	86.0	73.8	50.0	62.6
Institution %	14.0	26.2	50.0	37.4
	(299)	(470)	(979)	(1748)

TABLE 4

Disposition by Seriousness and Race

Disposition	Seriousness			
	Low		High	
	Black	White	Black	White
Remedial %	83.9	92.3	30.0	50.4
Referral %	16.1	7.7	70.0	49.6
	(2909)	(2873)	(2453)	(1366)
Adjusted %	61.4	73.9	36.5	38.4
Referral %	38.6	26.1	63.5	61.6
	(469)	(222)	(1717)	(678)
Probation %	60.8	84.5	57.2	74.4
Institution %	39.2	15.5	42.8	25.6
	(181)	(58)	(1091)	(418)

TABLE 5

Disposition by Number of Previous Offenses and Race

Disposition	Number of Previous Offenses: None		1 or 2		3+	
	Black	White	Black	White	Black	White
Remedial %	70.6	86.0	62.7	77.6	50.2	64.8
Referral %	29.4	14.0	37.3	22.4	49.8	35.2
	(1426)	(1978)	(1564)	(1347)	(2371)	(914)
Adjusted %	56.9	57.2	46.6	47.7	34.1	37.9
Referral %	43.1	42.8	53.4	52.3	65.9	62.1
	(420)	(276)	(584)	(302)	(1182)	(322)
Probation %	84.5	88.1	71.2	79.1	46.1	65.5
Institution %	15.5	11.9	28.8	20.9	53.9	34.5
	(181)	(118)	(312)	(158)	(779)	(200)

TABLE 6

Disposition by Seriousness, Number of Previous Offenses and Race

Disposition	Seriousness of Offense: Low						High					
	None		1 or 2		3+		None		1 or 2		3+	
	Black	White	Black	White	Black	White	Black	White	Black	White	Black	White
Remedial %	90.7	94.9	86.6	92.2	77.6	86.1	44.1	65.2	34.4	47.0	19.5	28.8
Referral %	9.3	5.1	13.4	7.8	22.4	13.9	55.9	34.7	65.6	53.0	80.5	76.2
	(809)	(1388)	(849)	(911)	(1251)	(574)	(617)	(590)	(716)	(436)	(1120)	(340)
Adjusted %	73.3	81.7	67.5	73.2	55.7	67.5	53.3	48.8	41.5	39.4	27.4	28.1
Referral %	22.7	18.3	32.5	26.8	44.3	32.5	46.7	51.2	58.5	60.6	72.6	71.9
	(75)	(71)	(114)	(71)	(280)	(80)	(345)	(205)	(470)	(231)	(902)	(242)
Probation %	80.0	84.6	75.7	89.5	53.2	80.8	85.1	88.6	70.5	78.2	44.7	63.2
Institution %	20.0	15.4	24.3	10.5	46.8	19.2	14.9	11.4	29.5	22.3	55.3	36.8
	(20)	(13)	(37)	(19)	(124)	(26)	(161)	(105)	(275)	(139)	(655)	(174)

TABLE 7

Disposition by SES

Disposition	SES*: Low	High	Total
Remedial %	63.2	78.5	67.9
Referral %	36.9	21.5	32.1
	(6657)	(2944)	(9601)
Adjusted %	42.2	47.6	43.4
Referral %	57.7	52.4	56.6
	(2452)	(634)	(3086)
Probation %	60.5	71.4	62.6
Institution %	39.5	28.6	37.4
	(1416)	(332)	(1748)

* The measurement of this variable is based upon the median income of the census tract of residence for each subject. For a detailed discussion of the measurement of this variable see the work of Wolfgang, Figlio & Sellin cited in footnote 23.

of Table 4. Even when the seriousness of the offense is held constant, blacks are more likely than whites to receive a more severe disposition at all three stages of the juvenile justice system. This finding refutes the hypothesis based on the results of previous studies. Unlike the other studies, the seriousness of the offense does not explain the relationship between race and disposition.

This finding is essentially the same when the number of previous offenses is held constant as in Table 5. At the police level, blacks are considerably less likely than whites to receive a remedial disposition, regardless of their previous record. At the intake hearing, however, the situation is somewhat different. For the three categories of the control variable, the rates are approximately equal, but in all three cases the small differences that do exist are in the same direction as the differences found when the seriousness of the offense was held constant. At the juvenile court level, blacks are again more likely than whites to be treated severely, especially as the number of previous offenses increases. Although the difference is not great for first offenders (15.5% vs. 11.9% institutionalized), it is sizeable (53.9% vs. 34.5% institutionalized) for those who committed three or more previous offenses. In general, the number of previous offenses does not explain differential dispositions by race.

Finally, racial differences can be examined while both major legal variables are simultaneously controlled as in Table 6. When this is done, racial differences are still clearly observable. At the police level the differences are sizeable, and in all six comparisons blacks are less likely than whites to receive a remedial disposition. The situation for the juvenile court is quite similar. Again the differences are relatively large and all in the same direction. In all six comparisons blacks are more likely to be institutionalized and less likely to be put on probation than are whites. At the intake hearing the results are not as consistent. When dealing with offenses that have a low seriousness score the results are consistent with the findings concerning the police and juvenile court levels. Regardless of the number of previous offenses, blacks are more likely than whites to receive a severe disposition, i.e., to be referred to the juvenile court. On the other hand, when dealing with offenses with a high seriousness score, there are very small differences between the races, and in two of the three comparisons whites are treated more severely than blacks. For example, for first offenders who committed serious offenses, blacks receive an adjusted disposition in 53.3 per cent of the cases, whereas whites do so in 48.8 per cent of the cases.

In conclusion, the data reveal that blacks are treated more severely than whites throughout the juvenile justice system. At the levels of the police and juvenile court there are no deviations from this finding, even when the seriousness of the offense and the number of previous offenses are simultaneously held constant. At the level of the intake hearing this conclusion is generally supported.

Socioeconomic Status and Dispositions

The relationship between SES and the severity of the disposition is quite similar to that observed when race was the independent variable. As can be seen in Table 7, members of the low SES are more likely than members of the high SES to receive a severe disposition at each of the three stages of the juvenile justice system. As was true with race, differences in disposition by SES are greater at the levels of the police and the juvenile court than at the intake hearing level; but at all three levels they are clearly observable. The question now becomes: Do these differences remain when the legal variables are held constant?

Because the analysis of SES is similar to that of race, tables in which the seriousness of the offense and the number of previous offenses are controlled separately are not presented here.[26] The patterns are almost identical to those in Tables 4 and 5.

When these two variables are controlled simultaneously, as in Table 8, SES differences are still present. Dealing first with the level of the police, we see that in all six comparisons the low SES subjects are less likely than the high SES subjects to be given a remedial disposition. These differences are greatest when the offense committed had a high seriousness score, but even for offenses with a low seriousness score the differences conform to the same pattern.

The findings for the intake hearing level, however, are not as consistent. In two of the six comparisons, those involving high seriousness offenses with no previous offenses or with one or two previous offenses, the pattern of the previous results is reversed. In these two cases the low SES subjects are more likely than the high SES subjects to be treated leniently. On the other hand, in the other four comparisons the reverse is true, since the low SES subjects are less likely to be treated leniently.

[26] These tables may, however, be requested from the author.

TABLE 8

DISPOSITION BY SERIOUSNESS, NUMBER OF PREVIOUS OFFENSES AND SES

Disposition	Seriousness of Offense											
	Low						High					
	None		1 or 2		3+		None		1 or 2		3+	
	Lower SES	Higher SES	Lower SES	Higher SES	Lower SES	Higher SES	Lower SES	Higher SES	Lower SES	Higher SES	Lower SES	Higher SES
Remedial %	91.0	96.2	88.3	91.8	79.8	81.8	49.0	65.3	36.2	47.4	20.5	28.2
Referral %	9.0	3.8	11.7	8.2	20.2	18.2	51.0	34.7	63.8	52.6	79.5	71.8
	(1208)	(989)	(1151)	(609)	(1423)	(402)	(804)	(403)	(860)	(289)	(1211)	(252)
Adjusted %	76.8	78.9	68.1	74.0	54.7	72.6	52.4	49.3	41.9	37.5	26.9	30.9
Referral %	23.1	21.0	31.8	26.0	45.3	27.4	47.6	50.7	58.1	62.5	73.1	69.1
	(108)	(38)	(135)	(50)	(287)	(73)	(410)	(140)	(549)	(152)	(963)	(181)
Probation %	80.0	87.5	79.1	84.6	56.2	70.0	85.6	88.8	74.0	69.5	46.4	60.8
Institution %	20.0	12.5	20.9	15.4	43.8	30.0	14.4	11.2	26.0	30.5	53.6	39.2
	(25)	(8)	(43)	(13)	(130)	(20)	(195)	(71)	(319)	(95)	(704)	(125)

At the court level, the data are consistent with the previous results of this study. In five of the six comparisons, low SES subjects are less likely to be put on probation and more likely to be institutionalized than high SES subjects.

The findings with respect to SES are remarkably similar to those concerning race. At the levels of the police and the juvenile court the low SES subjects are treated consistently more severely than their counterparts, even when both legal variables are simultaneously controlled. At the level of the intake hearing the results are similar, but not as pronounced. When both legal variables are controlled simultaneously, and when the offense had a high seriousness score, the low SES subjects are not more likely to be treated more severely than the high SES subjects. However, this is the only deviation from the general pattern of the results. Thus, the third hypothesis—that the legal variables can explain the relationship between SES and dispositions—should be rejected.

Discussion

We have noted that a number of earlier studies found that racial and social class disparities in dispositions could generally be explained by legal variables such as the seriousness of the offense and the number of previous offenses committed. That is, when the seriousness of the offense or the degree of recidivism were held constant, blacks did not receive more severe dispositions than whites, and low SES subjects did not receive more severe dispositions than high SES subjects.

An analysis of comparable data for the Philadelphia birth cohort, however, yields findings that are quite different. With the earlier studies, we found that both the legal and nonlegal variables are related to dispositions. But unlike the previous studies, the present study shows that when the two legal variables were held constant, the racial and SES differences did not disappear. Blacks and low SES subjects were more likely than whites and high SES subjects to receive severe dispositions. Although these differences were more noticeable at the levels of the police and the juvenile court than at the level of the intake hearing, they are generally observable at all three levels.

Furthermore, both sets of variables are related to the severity of dispositions and neither set "explains away" the other. When race and SES were held constant, serious offenders and recidivists still received more severe dispositions than minor offenders and first offenders. However, as we have noted, the effect of the nonlegal variables did not disappear when the legal variables were held constant. The two sets of variables tended to interact in relation to dispositions. Using race and seriousness to illustrate this interaction, we see that the most lenient dispositions were associated with white, minor offenders, and the most severe dispositions were associated with black, serious offenders.

The most important finding, however, in relation to the previous research done in this area, is that the nonlegal variables are still related to the severity of the dispositions received, even when the legal variables are held constant. Why this happens in the birth cohort data and not in the previous studies is not readily apparent. The different nature of the surveys, cross-sectional vs. cohort, should not explain it because the cohort data have been treated in a cross-sectional fashion in this paper. Nor can other plausible factors explain this disparity. All the studies were conducted in urban areas; data were collected during similar time periods (the late 1950's and early 1960's); they used comparable measures of the major variables; and they employed a valid sample of the juvenile delinquency cases occurring in the cities in which the studies were conducted.

One other possible reason should be discussed. Only two legal variables were controlled in the present study—seriousness and recidivism. Perhaps if other variables such as the demeanor of the youth, the "quality" of the juvenile's home, and the attitude of the victim were controlled, racial and SES differences would be eliminated. These items were not tested in this study. However, the other studies controlled only for seriousness and recidivism and concluded that race and SES were not related to dispositions. Thus, although the absence of these other variables limits the scope of these findings, it does not explain the discrepancy between this study and the previous ones.

Finally, the present findings should be related to the assumption often found in the theoretical realms of criminology, namely, that blacks and members of the low SES are treated more harshly than whites and high SES subjects in the juvenile justice system. Clearly, the findings of the present study are in agreement with that assumption. But to conclude that this study confirms the assumption would perhaps be to make a generalization beyond the scope of the data. This study should, however, be used as another piece of evidence in the more general process of confirming or disconfirming that assumption.

*Reconciling Race and Class Differences in Self-Reported and Official Estimates of Delinquency**

Delbert S. Elliott and Suzanne S. Ageton
Behavioral Research Institute, Boulder

This paper addresses the general question of whether or not the satisfactory resolution of the methodological criticisms of self-report research will result in greater consistency between self-reported and official data with respect to the race and class distributions of delinquent behavior. We review the specific methodological criticisms of self-report delinquency (SRD) research; discuss the use of a new SRD measure in a national youth study; compare the race/class findings of this study with previous SRD research and with official arrest data; and examine the epidemiological and theoretical implications of these findings. Both class and race differentials are found in this study. It appears likely that the differences between these findings and those in earlier SRD studies are a result of differences in the specific SRD measures used. Additionally, these findings suggest a logical connection between SRD and official measures, and they provide some insight into the mechanism whereby official data produce more extreme race and class (as well as age and sex) differences than do self-report measures. The results of this study also have implications for previous tests of theoretical propositions which used self-report delinquency data. In short, prior self-report measures may not have been sensitive enough to capture the theoretically important differences in delinquency involvement.

Problems of conceptualization, definition, and measurement continue to plague researchers interested in the epidemiology and etiology of delinquency. While most would acknowledge the conceptual distinction between delinquent behavior and official responses to delinquent behavior, these distinctions are not clearly maintained in the measurement of delinquency or in the interpretation and analysis of specific delinquency data. This problem is clearly illustrated in the current controversy over the validity of self-reported (as compared with official) estimates of the incidence and distribution of delinquency in the general adolescent population. Put simply, there are those who argue that police and arrest records provide more accurate and reliable estimates of the social correlates of delinquent behavior than do self-report surveys; others hold the opposite view.

Self-report measures of delinquency provide a different picture of the incidence and distribution of delinquent behavior than do official arrest records. Both types of data indicate significant age and sex differentials, but the magnitude of these differences is much smaller with self-reported data than with official arrest data (Williams and Gold, 1972; Gold and Reimer, 1974; Elliott and Voss, 1974; Illinois Institute for Juvenile Research, 1973; Bachman et al., 1970; 1971; 1978).

At the center of the controversy, however, is the fact that self-report studies generally find no differences in delinquent behavior by class or race (Gold and Reimer, 1974; Elliott and Voss, 1974; Williams and Gold, 1972; Hirschi, 1969; Bachman et al., 1970; 1971; 1978; Illinois Institute for Juvenile Research, 1973), while studies relying upon police and court data report significant differences by both class and race (Wolfgang et al., 1972; Elliott and Voss, 1974; Williams and Gold, 1972; Gordon, 1976; West, 1973; Short and Nye, 1957–1958).

To date, attempts to reconcile this apparent discrepancy between official and self-reported findings have taken one of two approaches. Most recently, researchers have challenged the strength of the empirical evidence for the class differential in official data. Tittle and Villemez (1977) and Tittle et al. (1978) reviewed earlier published research findings and concluded that the class differences in official data are not clearly established and

* Address all communications to: Delbert S. Elliott, Director; Behavioral Research Institute; 2305 Canyon Boulevard; Boulder, Colorado 80302.

This study was supported by the Center for Studies of Crime and Delinquency, NIMH (MH27552), and the National Institute for Juvenile Justice and Delinquency Prevention, LEAA (78-JN-AX-0003). We gratefully acknowledge the assistance of Judy Beth Berg-Hansen in the preparation of the manuscript.

From *American Sociological Review,* Vol. 45 (February 1980), pp. 95–110. Reprinted by permission of the American Sociological Association and the authors.

that the widespread belief in an inverse relationship between class and crime is not based upon sound empirical research findings. Hindelang et al. (1978) have also concluded that police records of juvenile offenses are not strongly or even moderately related to socioeconomic status.[1] On the other hand, the race differential in official data has not been seriously challenged, to our knowledge.

The second and most frequent approach has been to challenge the methodological adequacy of the self-report technique and the adequacy of self-report research. Specifically, critics of self-report research contend:

(1) There are problems inherent in the method itself which make it inaccurate and unreliable. These problems include deliberate falsification, inaccurate recall, and forward and backward telescoping.
(2) There are problems with the construction of measures used in self-report research and with the procedures for administering the measures. These problems concern the lack of representativity in items, item overlapping, imprecise response sets, and the lack of anonymity of respondents.
(3) There are problems with generalizing from self-report studies, due to the almost exclusive reliance upon small, unrepresentative samples.

This paper is concerned with this second approach to reconciling official and self-reported findings with respect to class and race. We will not deal with those problems inherent in the self-report method itself, except to note that available research seems to support both the validity and reliability of the method (Nye and Short, 1956; Erickson and Empey, 1963; Hirschi, 1969; Gold, 1966; Dentler and Monroe, 1961; Hardt and Bodine, 1965; Hardt and Hardt, 1977; Farrington, 1973; Elliott and Voss, 1974; Clark and Tifft, 1966). Instead, we will deal with the correctable problems, i.e., the construction of measures and their administration, as well as representativity and sample size. The general question we will address here is whether or not the satisfactory resolution of these methodological issues in the construction and administration of self-report measures will result in greater consistency between self-reported and official data. More specifically, will the satisfactory resolution of these problems produce race and class differentials in self-reported estimates of delinquent behavior?

[1] Hindelang et al. (1978) have also recently studied the extent to which sex and race are differentially related to self-reported and official records of delinquency, and some of their conclusions with regard to the race discrepancy will be cited later.

The discussion that follows will focus on: (1) the methodological criticisms of previous self-report delinquency (SRD) research; (2) the use of a new SRD measure in a national youth study; (3) a comparison of the race/class findings of this study with previous SRD research and with official arrest data; and (4) the epidemiological and theoretical implications of these findings.

PROBLEMS WITH SRD RESEARCH

Instrument Construction

Much of the controversy over self-report measures involves problems with instrument construction. Primarily, criticism centers on three issues: (1) the question of the representativeness of items employed in SRD measures; (2) problems of item overlap; and (3) limited or ambiguous response sets.

The major criticism concerns the unrepresentativity of the items selected (Hindelang et al., 1975; Nettler, 1974; Farrington, 1973). Trivial and nonserious offenses (e.g., cutting classes and disobeying parents) are often overrepresented, while serious violations of the criminal code (e.g., burglary, robbery, and sexual assault) are frequently omitted. In addition, many SRD measures tend to overrepresent certain behavioral dimensions (e.g., theft) to the exclusion of other relevant delinquent acts. As a result of such selection processes, most existing SRD measures have a restricted focus and do not represent the full range of delinquent acts; this limits the appropriateness of these scales as general measures of delinquent behavior.

Another problem is the overlapping nature of items often included in SRD measures, which results in inaccurate estimates of frequency due to duplicate counts of certain events. For example, many SRD measures include a "shoplifting" item, a "theft under $5" item, and a "theft $5–50" item. A single theft event could logically be reported on two of these items. The presence of both a "cutting school" and a "cutting class" item represents another form of measurement redundancy since cutting school necessarily involves cutting classes. This problem is not easily overcome, since a given behavioral event in fact may involve more than a single offense. Nevertheless, item overlapping creates a potential source of error in estimating the volume of delinquent behavior from SRD measures.

The type of response sets typically employed with SRD measures has been another source of criticism. One major concern has been the frequent use of normative response categories such as "often," "sometimes," and "occasionally." This type of response set is open to wide variations in interpretation by respondents, and precludes any precise count of the actual number of acts committed.

Other response sets used to estimate the number of behaviors (e.g., "never," "once or twice," and "three times or more") have been challenged on the grounds that they are not precise categories for numerical estimation, and that numerical estimates based upon such categories may severely truncate the true distribution of responses. With the above set, for example, any number of behaviors in excess of two is collapsed into a single "high" category. While this procedure may allow for some discrimination between youth at the low end of the frequency distribution, it clearly precludes any discrimination at the high end. Thus, a youth involved in three shoplifting offenses during the specified period receives the same "score" as a youth involved in 50 or 100 shoplifting events during the period. This limited set of categorical responses appears particularly problematic when the reporting period involves a year or more and when such items as using marijuana; drinking beer, wine or liquor; and carrying a concealed weapon are included in the SRD measure.

Administration Procedures

The manner in which the measures are administered is also a problematic area for self-report delinquency research. Here the issue concerns: (1) anonymous vs. identified respondents, and (2) questionnaire vs. interview formats.

Many researchers have argued that anonymity has to be guaranteed or youth will not admit certain offenses—probably the more serious, stigmatizing ones. Research on this question suggests that there is slightly more reporting of offenses under conditions of anonymity, but that anonymous/identified differences are slight and statistically insignificant (Corey, 1937; Christie, 1965; Kulik et al., 1968). These findings have led Dentler (as cited in Hardt and Bodine, 1965) to comment that the necessity for anonymity is overemphasized, and that it may in fact lead to reduced involvement by respondents and careless or facetious answers.

On the matter of interview vs. questionnaire formats, the discussion again involves the issue of anonymity, and the belief that self-administered questionnaires are more likely to produce accurate responses than personal interviews. One recent self-report delinquency research study compared results from structured interviews and self-administered check lists, where anonymity was guaranteed under both conditions (Krohn et al.,

1974). While seven of the eight offenses were admitted more often under check-list conditions than under interview conditions, none of the differences was significant at the .05 level. Even when education, sex, class, and IQ were controlled, no significant differences were obtained.

Some researchers, most notably Gold (1966), have argued that the interview format has significant advantages for delinquency research in that it permits clarification of specific behaviors and, consequently, the ability to more correctly classify illegal acts. In general, however, there is still controversy over the effects of specific administration procedures when the research is directed toward illegal or socially disapproved behaviors.

Sampling Design and Generality

Another problematic area for self-report delinquency research is that of the generality of findings. Here the question focuses primarily on the adequacy of the sampling designs for: (1) inferences to the adolescent population, and (2) comparisons with official data.

In most cases, SRD measures have been administered to small, select samples of youth, such as high school students in a particular local community or adolescents processed by a local juvenile court. The samples are rarely probability samples, and generalizations (about the adolescent populations sampled) cannot be made with any known degree of accuracy. Only two published studies involve national probability samples.[2]

A further concern is that few cohort studies using normal populations have incorporated a self-report measure in their instruments. This means that the age and sex gradients of SRD measures are not known, a critical fact if this measurement approach is to become more refined and useful. Furthermore, since the studies using self-report measures have almost always been cross-sectional ones, little is known about the dynamics of self-reported behavior over time.

Finally, Empey (1978) notes that national self-report studies have not been conducted on an annual basis and, as a result, it is not possible to discern trends across time or to make direct comparisons with other standard delinquency data such as the Uniform Crime Reports (UCR) or the National Crime Panel (NCP).

[2] These are Gold's 1967 and 1972 National Surveys of Youth and the Youth in Transition Study (Bachman et al., 1970; 1971; 1978). Both studies are limited by a restricted set of SRD items and truncated response sets. The Youth in Transition Study also has problems associated with overlapping reporting periods for its reported SRD measures.

THE NATIONAL YOUTH SURVEY

We will now report on a national youth study in which we have attempted to deal with the previously noted methodological criticisms of self-report delinquency research. Our aim will be to see if these improvements in the quality of self-report research have any impact on self-report findings relative to findings from official data.

The National Youth Survey involves a five-year panel design with a national probability sample of 1,726 adolescents aged 11–17 in 1976.[3] The total youth sample was selected and initially interviewed between January and March, 1977, concerning their involvement in delinquent behavior during the calendar year 1976. The second survey was completed between January and March, 1978, to obtain delinquency estimates for the calendar year 1977. The third, fourth, and fifth surveys will also be conducted between each January and March of the years 1979, 1980, and 1981.

The data reported herein are taken from the first survey, completed in 1977. The estimates presented are thus for delinquent behavior during the calendar year 1976.

Construction of New SRD Measure

In constructing the SRD measure for this study, we attempted to obtain a representative set of offenses. Given our interest in comparing SRD and UCR estimates, we began by listing offenses included in the UCR. Any specific act (with the exception of traffic violations) involving more than 1% of the reported juvenile arrests for 1972–1974 is included in the SRD measure.

In addition to the list of specific offenses, the UCR contains a general category, "all other offenses," which often accounts for a high proportion of the total juvenile arrests. To cover the types of acts likely to fall within this general category, and to increase the comprehensiveness of the measure, two general selection criteria were used to choose additional items. First, items which were theoretically relevant to a delinquent lifestyle or subculture as discussed in the literature were selected for inclusion in this measure (Cohen, 1955; Cloward and Ohlin, 1960; Miller, 1958; 1966; Yablonsky, 1962; Short and Strodtbeck, 1965). Thus, additional items—such as gang fighting, sexual intercourse, and carrying a hidden weapon—are included. Second, a systematic review of existing SRD measures was undertaken to locate items that tapped specific dimensions of delinquent behavior not previously included.

[3] The National Youth Survey is funded by the Center for Studies of Crime and Delinquency, NIMH (MH27552), and the National Institute for Juvenile Justice and Delinquency Prevention, LEAA (78-JN-AX-0003). Current funding covers the first three of the five projected annual surveys. The first survey was funded solely by NIMH, the second and third by NIMH and LEAA jointly.

We believe the resulting set of 47 items to be both more comprehensive and more representative of the conceptual universe of delinquent acts then found in prior SRD measures used in major, large-scale studies. The item set includes all but one of the UCR Part I offenses (homicide is excluded); 60% of Part II offenses; and a wide range of "other" offenses—such as delinquent lifestyle items, misdemeanors, and some status offenses. The vast majority of items involve a violation of criminal statutes. (See Appendix A.)

Two separate response sets are being used. Respondents initially are asked to indicate how many times during the past year they committed each act. If an individual's response to this open-ended question involves a frequency of 10 or more, interviewers then ask the youth to select one of the following categorical responses: (1) once a month, (2) once every 2–3 weeks, (3) once a week, (4) 2–3 times a week, (5) once a day, or (6) 2–3 times a day.[4] A comparison of the two response sets indicates high agreement between frequency estimates given in direct response to the open-ended question and frequency estimates based upon the implied frequency associated with the midpoint of the category selected.[5]

A specific attempt was also made to eliminate as much overlap in items as possible. None of the items contains a necessary overlap as in "cutting school" and "cutting class." Although some possible overlap remains, we do not feel it constitutes a serious problem with this SRD measure.

The SRD measure asks respondents to indicate how many times, "from Christmas a year ago to the Christmas just past," they committed each offense. The recall period is thus a year, anchored by a specific reference point relevant to most youth. The use of a one-year period which

[4] The categorical response set has led to the identification of some highly episodic events, e.g., 20 shoplifting offenses, all occurring within a two-month period during the summer (an initial response of 20; a categorical response 2–3 times a week, and an interviewer probe revealing that the offenses all occurred during the summer).

[5] The only exception involves the last two (high frequency) categories. At this end of the frequency continuum, estimates based upon the midpoint of the category are substantially higher than the frequency response given directly. The open-ended frequency measure thus appears to provide a more conservative estimate of number of delinquent acts, and the estimates reported here are based upon this response.

coincides almost precisely with the calendar year allows for direct comparison with UCR data, NCP victimization data, and some prior SRD data. It also avoids the need to adjust for seasonal variations, which would be necessary if a shorter time period were involved.

Administration Procedures

For the present study, the research design (a longitudinal panel design) precludes a guarantee of anonymity. Therefore, our major concern is to guarantee respondents that their answers will be confidential. This assurance is given verbally as well as being contained in the written consent form signed by all youth and their parents. In addition, a Certificate of Confidentiality from the Department of Health, Education, and Welfare guarantees all respondents that the data and the interviewers will be protected from legal subpoena.

The interview format was selected over the self-administered questionnaire format for several reasons. First, we share Gold's belief that the interview situation (if properly structured to protect confidentiality) can insure more accurate, reliable data. Second, the necessity of securing informed consents from all subjects and the complexity of the present research require, in our judgment, a personal contact with the respondents. Once this contact is made, it seems logical to use the interviewer to facilitate the data collection process and to improve the quality of the data obtained. Finally, some of our previous research suggests that the differences in responding to SRD items in a questionnaire as opposed to an interview format are not significant (Elliott et al., 1976).

The Sample

The 1977 National Youth Survey employed a probability sample of households in the continental United States based upon a multistage, cluster sampling design. The sample contained 2,375 eligible youth aged 11–17 in 1976. Of these, 1,726 (73%) agreed to participate in the study and completed interviews in the 1977 survey.[6] A comparison of the age, sex, and race of eligible youth not interviewed with participating youth indicates that the loss rate from any particular age, sex, or racial group appears to be proportional to that group's representation in the population. Further, with respect to these characteristics, participating youth appear to be representative of the total 11 through 17-year-old youth population in the United States as established by the U.S. Census Bureau (Huizinga, 1978).

Summary of New Measure

In sum, the current SRD measure addresses many of the central criticisms of prior SRD measures.[7] It is more representative of the full range of delinquent acts than were prior SRD measures and involves fewer overlapping items; it also employs a response set which provides better discrimination at the high end of the frequency continuum and is more suited to estimating the actual number of behaviors committed. The choice of a one-year time frame with a panel design involving a one-year time lag is based upon both conceptual and practical concerns. Compared with the other SRD measures, the measure involves a moderate recall period, captures seasonal variations, and permits a direct comparison with other self-report and official measures which are reported annually. And, finally, the study involves a national probability sample of youth aged 11–17.

ANALYSIS OF DATA

Subscales

An earlier paper (Ageton and Elliott, 1978) presented design effects and estimates of the frequency of each specific item on the SRD measure with .95 confidence intervals for the total sample and by age, sex, race, and class. The analysis in this paper focuses upon the total SRD measure and a set of specific subscales. The frequency estimates are based upon the open-ended response set, which provides slightly more conservative frequency estimates than does the categorical response set.

The subscales are based upon Glaser's (1967) offense typology. This particular classification scheme was selected because it offers a logical categorization of offense types while permitting a clear distinction between serious and nonserious crimes.

Glaser's typology encompasses four major types of crime: (1) predatory crimes, (2) illegal service crimes, (3) public disorder crimes, and (4) crimes of negligence. With the exception of category four, all Glaser's types were used.[8]

Furthermore, Glaser acknowledges an additional category called status crimes to encompass those behaviors which at special times and/or for particular classes of people have been illegal. The status crimes category in this national youth study includes all behaviors in the SRD measure which are illegal only when the individual involved is a minor.

In addition, a separate category entitled hard drug use was created to distinguish this type of drug involvement from that of alcohol and/or marijuana use, which are subsumed within the status crimes category and public disorder crimes category, respectively.

Finally, within the predatory crimes category, a distinction was made between crimes against persons and crimes against property. This differentiation separates violent crimes against people from other serious offenses which do not involve confrontation with another person.

Thus, the final offense typology is composed of the following six subscales:

(1) predatory crimes against persons (sexual assault, aggravated assault, simple assault, and robbery);
(2) predatory crimes against property (vandalism, burglary, auto theft, larceny, stolen goods, fraud, and joyriding);
(3) illegal service crimes (prostitution, selling drugs, and buying/providing liquor for minors);
(4) public disorder crimes (carrying a concealed weapon, hitchhiking, disorderly conduct, drunkenness, panhandling, making obscene phone calls, and marijuana use);
(5) status crimes (runaway, sexual intercourse, alcohol use, and truancy);
(6) hard drug use (amphetamines, barbiturates, hallucinogens, heroin,

[6] At each stage, the probabilities of selection were established to provide a self-weighting sample. Seventy-six primary sampling units were selected, with probability of selection being proportional to size. This sampling procedure resulted in the listing of 67,266 households, of which approximately 8,000 were selected for inclusion in the sample. All 11- through 17-year-old youth living in the selected households were eligible respondents for the study. The selected households generated a total of 2,375 eligible youth. Of these, 649 (27%) did not participate in the study due to (1) parental refusal, (2) youth refusal, or (3) the youth being considered inappropriate for inclusion in the study (e.g., severely mentally retarded). In general, based upon a comparison with 1976 U.S. Census Bureau estimates, the resulting sample of participating youth does appear representative of American youth with respect to age, sex, and race (U.S. Bureau of the Census, 1977). For a detailed description of the sample, see Huizinga, 1978, and Ageton and Elliott, 1978.

[7] While we are concerned with the issues of validity and reliability of the self-report method, we will not deal with these issues here beyond reporting that: (1) we are obtaining data on official police contacts for each respondent and intend to compare self-reports of delinquent behavior with official records of police contact and arrest; and (2) the reliability (internal consistency) of the new SRD measure is quite high (Alpha = .91) for the 1977 survey. We are planning further validity tests with these data, but have nothing to report, yet.

[8] Category Four, crimes of negligence, was excluded because it contains predominantly automobile infractions which were not included in the SRD measure.

Table 1. Mean Frequency of Self-Reported Delinquency by Race and Class

	Total Self-Reported Delinquency			Predatory Crimes Against Persons		Predatory Crimes Against Property		Illegal Service		Public Disorder		Hard Drug Use		Status Offenses	
	N	$\bar{X}$	SD	$\bar{X}$	SD	$\bar{X}$	SD	$\bar{X}$	SD	$\bar{X}$	SD	$\bar{X}$	SD	$\bar{X}$	SD
RACE															
White	1357	46.79	161.37	7.84	58.42	8.93	42.87	1.85	22.36	14.98	62.37	1.26	14.03	14.84	49.21
Black	259	79.20	277.38	12.96	76.59	20.57	106.27	1.71	22.83	16.50	67.78	.18	1.35	16.19	53.94
F		6.68		1.50		8.79		.09		.13		1.55		.16	
Probability		≤.01		NS		≤.001		NS		NS		NS		NS	
CLASS															
Lower	717	60.42	220.24	12.02	72.68	13.50	78.60	2.19	30.29	14.32	58.75	1.20	14.64	14.27	46.54
Working	509	50.63	186.19	8.04	67.12	9.40	38.68	1.36	10.92	16.21	78.92	.73	4.02	14.47	42.36
Middle	494	50.96	79.88	3.32	11.31	7.25	23.17	1.56	14.07	13.81	42.44	1.37	15.68	15.66	58.33
F		2.94		3.11		1.94		.25		.22		.35		.13	
Probability		≤.05		≤.05		NS		NS		NS		NS		NS	

and cocaine).

Table 1 presents the mean frequency of self-reported delinquency by race[9] and class[10] for the total SRD measure and for each of the subscales. The statistical tests involve a one-way analysis of variance on these means.[11]

Race and Class Differentials

Unlike most previous self-report studies, we find significant race differences for total SRD and for predatory crimes against property. Blacks report significantly higher frequencies than do whites on each of these measures. In both cases, the differences in means are substantial. With respect to total offenses, blacks report three offenses for every two reported by whites. For crimes against property, blacks report more than two offenses for every offense reported by whites.

While there is a substantial difference in mean scores on the crimes against persons scale, it is not statistically significant. The difference in the total SRD score appears to be primarily the result of the very high level of property crimes reported by blacks.

We also observe a class differential for total SRD and for predatory crimes against persons. For total SRD scores, the difference is between lower socioeconomic status youth and others; i.e., there does not appear to be any difference between working- and middle-class group means.

The differences are greater, and the trend is more linear, for the crimes against persons scale means than for total SRD. Lower-class youth report nearly four times as many offenses as do middle-class youth and one-and-one-half times as many as working-class youth. There is also a substantial class difference in the mean number of crimes against persons, but this difference is not statistically significant. There are clearly no substantial differences in means for any of the remaining subscales.

A two-way analysis of variance (race × class) was also completed with the total SRD measure and each of the subscales. In every case, the direct effects observed in the one-way analysis of variance were replicated and no significant interaction effects were observed.

COMPARISONS WITH PRIOR STUDIES

Our basic concern in this analysis will now be to ascertain: (1) the comparability of the general findings reported here with other SRD findings, and (2) the extent to which these findings might offer some insight into the discrepancy between self-report and official measures of delinquency.

While we have not reported findings from this study relative to the age and sex distribution of delinquent behavior, they are generally consistent with those from other large-scale self-report studies (Hirschi, 1969; Williams and Gold, 1972; Illinois Institute for Juvenile Research, 1973; Gold and Reimer, 1974; Elliott and Voss, 1974). However, the findings relative to the distribution by race and class are not consistent with these earlier studies, none of which report significant differences in the mean frequencies of self-reported offenses by race or class.[12]

In this study, the black/white differential in total offenses is nearly 2:1; and for predatory crimes, over 2:1. Class differences in total offenses are significant and, while the differences are not large, they are in the traditionally expected direction, with lower-class youth reporting higher frequencies. The trend in the previously referenced self-report studies is generally in the opposite direction.

In this study, class differences are clearer on the predatory crimes against persons scale than for total SRD scores; the trend is more linear, in the expected direction, and of greater magnitude (lower:middle = 3:1).

In an effort to determine if this basic difference in findings is due to the differences in the SRD measures employed,

[9] Because of the small number of Mexican-American respondents (N = 72) and some obvious clustering effects for this ethnic group, the accuracy of the estimates of variances is questionable, and we have not included this group in the analysis. The same situation holds for the residual "other" category (N = 32). Comparisons are, thus, limited to whites (Anglos) and blacks.

[10] The social class measure employed in this analysis is the Hollingshead two-factor index (Hollingshead and Redlich, 1958) as applied to the principal wage earner in each youth's family. Hollingshead Classes I and II—involving primarily professional managerial occupations and college level educations—are collapsed to make the "middle" class category. Class III—primarily owners of small businesses, clerical workers, and persons in sales occupations and skilled manual occupations, with high school or some college work completed—constitutes the "working" class category.

Classes IV and V—primarily semiskilled persons and those in unskilled manual occupations with high school or lower levels of education—make up the "lower" class category.

[11] It should also be noted that the statistical tests are based upon a simple random sample design. The effect of our departure from this design is probably in the direction of inflating the F values. However, the design effects are small, suggesting that the effect of this departure is not a serious one. For example, the average design effects on items in the total SRD measure are as follows: Males = 1.13; Females = 1.12; 11–12-year-olds = 1.14; 13–15-year-olds = 1.08; 16–17-year-olds = 1.05; Middle Class = 1.05; Working Class = 1.22; Lower Class = 1.09; Whites = 1.14 and Blacks = 1.15. Further, unless otherwise specified, statistical significance refers to probabilities ≤ .05. Because of our sample sizes, the statistical tests employed are rather powerful. An examination of Table 1 indicates very large variances and, even when significant differences in means are found, it is clear that the distributions being compared overlap substantially.

[12] Williams and Gold (1972) report a white/black race differential for seriousness of self-reported delinquency behavior, but no difference in frequency. They also report a significantly higher seriousness for higher socioeconomic status (SES) boys, but no differences in frequency by SES. We have not considered seriousness here but, to the extent that our predatory crime subscales reflect the more serious offenses, our data would support the race differential and contradict the direction of the class differential in seriousness as reported by Williams and Gold.

we undertook several additional analyses. We "re-scored" the frequency estimates in two ways to approximate the frequency ranges used in the earlier studies. Since our focus is upon those scales where significant class and race differences are observed, our discussion will be limited to the total self-report measure and the two predatory subscales.

First, a comparison of the proportions of youth reporting one or more offenses on each of these scales reveals no statistically significant class or racial differences. Second, all frequencies of three and above on each item in the SRD measure were re-scored as a 3 to approximate the frequency ranges used in the Richmond Youth Study (Hirschi, 1969), the Delinquency and Dropout Study (Elliott and Voss, 1974), and the 1967 and 1972 National Surveys of Youth (Williams and Gold, 1972; and Gold and Reimer, 1974). Frequency scores on items were then summed across items to generate new scale frequencies and means. With one exception, an analysis of race and class differences on these frequency scores reveals no significant differences. The one exception involves a small (but significant) class difference on the predatory crimes against persons scale.[13] The class differential in this case is in the same direction but substantially smaller than that observed with the original scoring.

These two analyses indicate that the extended frequency range used in this study does, in fact, contribute to the difference in findings relative to race and class. Had we used the proportion of youth committing one or more offenses, or a 0–3 range similar to that used in the 1967 and 1972 National Surveys of Youth, our conclusions relative to class and race differences would have been similar to those reported for the earlier self-report studies.

High-Frequency Offenders

Since the above analyses indicate that differences were not occurring at the low end of the frequency distribution (with one exception), we examined race and class differences at several points along the original frequency distribution, with a particular interest in the high end of the frequency continuum. The results of this analysis are presented in Table 2.

The data in Table 2 indicate that the original differences, by both race and class, are due in large part to the relative differences at the high end of the frequency continuum. For example, at the low end of the frequency distribution, the white/black ratios are close to 1:1; but at the high end of the continuum the ratios are greater than 1:2.[14] For class, the lower-class to middle-class ratios at the low end are again close to 1:1; but at the high end the ratio is 2:1 for total SRD and over 3:1 for predatory crimes against persons.

Table 2. Percentage of Respondents Reporting Specific Levels of Delinquency by Race and Class

Number of Offenses Reported	Total Self-Reported Delinquency				
	Race		Class		
	White %	Black %	Lower %	Working %	Middle %
0–24	71.8	67.6	71.7	72.3	70.9
25–49	11.0	8.1	10.6	9.4	11.5
50–199	13.1	15.4	11.4	14.4	14.4
200+	4.1	9.8	6.3	3.9	3.2
	Predatory Crimes Against Property		Predatory Crimes Against Persons		
	Race		Class		
Number of Offenses Reported	White %	Black %	Lower %	Working %	Middle %
0–4	70.6	70.7	77.3	80.0	84.6
5–29	24.1	22.7	18.2	16.1	13.8
30–54	3.4	2.4	1.7	2.1	.8
55+	1.9	4.2	2.8	1.8	.8

Not only are the relative *proportions* of blacks and lower-class youth higher at the high end of the frequency continuum but also, within the high category, blacks and lower-class youth report substantially higher *frequencies* than do whites and middle-class youth.

Lower-class youth in the high category on the total SRD measures (scores ⩾ 200) report over one-and-one-half times as many offenses as do middle-class youth in this category. On the predatory crimes against persons scale, lower-class youth in the high category (scores ⩾ 55) report nearly three times as many offenses as do middle-class youth in this category. Among those in the high category on the predatory property scale, blacks report over one-and-one-half times as many offenses as do whites.

The one exception to the above generalization is that blacks and whites within the high category on the total SRD measure have approximately the same mean frequencies. The black/white differential on this measure thus appears to be more simply the result of differences in proportions of blacks and whites in the high category.

In any case, blacks and lower-class youth are found disproportionately among high frequency offenders. Prior self-report measures were unable to detect this differential involvement because they used response sets which are sensitive to differences only at the low end of the frequency continuum. We thus conclude that the use of open-ended frequency responses does, in fact, contribute to our finding both class and race differentials.

Range of Offenses in SRD Measure

We also believe that the broader range of offenses included in our SRD measure has some effect on these findings. An item-by-item analysis indicates that the particular set of items included in a measure can have a major impact on observed ethnic and class differentials. For example, the predatory crimes against persons scale includes four types of offenses: sexual assault, aggravated assault, simple assault, and robbery. Mean frequencies, by race, on the three types of assault offenses are as follows:

Offense Type	Whites	Blacks	Ratio
Sexual Assault	.03	.15	1:5
Aggravated Assault	.12	.50	1:4
Simple Assault	2.07	1.05	2:1
Total Assault	2.22	1.70	1:1

With respect to all three types of assault, these data indicate a major difference in frequency, by race. They suggest that measures which include only simple assault items do not have a proper representation of assault items. Given the tendency of prior self-report studies to exclude the more serious assault items, findings from such studies are likely to minimize the racial differences regarding assaultive behavior.

Even when all three types of assault are represented, an analysis involving a summary assault measure would obscure, in this case, important differences by type of assault. For example, the magnitude of sexual and aggravated assault offenses is so small, compared with that of simple assault offenses, that the inclusion of the latter in a summary measure conceals major differences in the other items and even reverses the direction of the differential.

While assault items have been used for illustrative purposes, we believe the problem to be a general one. The inclusion of both very high and very low frequency items in a single measure may obscure important differences, often differences in seriousness. This is because nonserious offenses tend to be reported frequently, while serious offenses are reported infrequently.

[13] Mean frequencies were as follows: Lower = 2.02; Working = 1.74; Middle = 1.38.

[14] For purposes of discussion, the low end of the frequency distribution refers to total SRD scores ⩽ 24 and predatory crime against persons and property scores ⩽ 4. The high end refers to total SRD scores ⩾ 200 and predatory crimes against persons and property scores ⩾ 55.

Table 3. Mean Standardized Scores for Selected Scales by Race and Class

	Total Self-Reported Delinquency	Predatory Crimes Against Persons	Predatory Crimes Against Property
RACE			
White	−.2452	−.0860	−.0072
Black	1.5317	.4038	−.0117
F	3.870	8.179	.001
Probability	≤.05	≤.005	NS
CLASS			
Lower	.7375	.2194	−.0905
Working	.1131	−.0746	.1501
Middle	−1.3341	−.2486	−.080
F	3.771	5.159	1.975
Probability	≤.02	≤.006	NS

Weighting SRD Items

For some purposes, it may be instructive to weight each item so that its potential contribution to the total score is the same as that of any other item. In this case, no single high frequency item can dominate the overall score. One procedure for accomplishing this weighting is to transform item frequency scores into standard scores and then add them into a total scale score. This transformation was performed, and the results are presented in Table 3.

With respect to class differences, this transformation confirms the earlier findings observed with raw frequencies. Significant class differences are observed for total SRD scores and predatory crimes against persons scores, but not for predatory crimes against property scores. In both cases, the significance levels are higher when item scores are transformed into standard scores prior to summing.

With regard to racial differences, the black/white difference on the total SRD measure remains, but it is weaker than that observed with raw frequency scores. More importantly, with this transformation the race difference on the predatory property crimes scale (observed earlier) is not replicated. There is essentially no black/white difference in property crimes when separate property offenses are adjusted so as to have the same magnitudes. This change suggests that the higher raw frequency predatory property scale mean for blacks is largely the result of higher frequencies on selected offense items. A review of item specific means confirms that this is indeed the case.

The mean number of vandalism offenses reported by blacks is over three times that of whites, and their mean number of evading payment offenses is over five times that of whites. These two nonserious offenses are relatively high frequency offenses for all youth. The individual item means for blacks are equal to or lower than those of whites on all serious offenses (felonies) included in this scale. Further, with one exception (family theft), means for blacks on all theft items are equal to or lower than those of whites. Thus, the initial racial differences on predatory property offenses are the result of large differences in vandalism (property destruction) and evading payment offenses, and not differences in theft offenses or serious property offenses.

Whereas there are no statistically significant racial differences in predatory crimes against persons offenses when unadjusted frequencies are used, the use of standard scores results in significant differences, with blacks reporting significantly higher scores. The direction of the racial differential is the same as that observed with the use of unadjusted frequencies, but the differential is stronger and statistically significant when standard scores are used.

As noted earlier in the discussion of specific assault items, simple assault is a relatively high frequency offense compared with the other offenses against persons, and whites report substantially higher frequencies than blacks on this offense. On the more serious offenses against persons, magnitudes are relatively low, but blacks report substantially greater frequencies than do whites on most of these items. The only exception involves robbery; here, the black and white means are identical. The transformation of item scores thus results in a greater racial differential than that observed with unadjusted frequencies.

The review and analysis of prior SRD studies by Hindelang et al. (1978) led them to conclude that racial differentials increase with the severity of the offense. The data in our National Youth Survey provide only partial support for that generalization. With respect to offenses against persons, the black/white differential is indeed greater for serious (as compared with nonserious) offenses. However, with respect to property offenses this is not the case. In fact, the opposite is true; i.e., the differential is greater for nonserious property offenses.

When unadjusted item scores are used, there are no significant class by race interactions on any of the self-reported delinquency scales. With the transformation to standard item scores, a significant class by race interaction is observed on the predatory crimes against persons measure. The results of the two-way analysis of variance are presented in Table 4.

Main effects are observed for both race and class. For whites, the major class difference is between middle-class youth and others (as was the case with unadjusted frequency scores). For blacks, the differences between lower-, working-, and middle-class youth are relatively greater,

Table 4. Two-Way Analysis of Variance: Mean Predatory Crimes Against Persons Scale Scores (Standardized) by Race and Class

	CLASS			
RACE	Lower	Working		Middle
White	.013	−.030		−.267
Black	.828	−.253		−.143
Main Effects	Sum of Squares	DF	F	Significance Level
Race	39.818	1	6.256	≤.01
Class	45.149	2	3.547	≤.03
Interaction				
Race x Class	40.944	2	3.216	≤.04

but the major difference is between lower-class youth and others. Working-class black youth report relatively fewer offenses against persons than do middle-class blacks, but this difference is not great. The interaction effect appears to be primarily the result of the relatively higher mean score for lower-class black youth. This analysis suggests a relatively high involvement of lower-class black youth in serious offenses against persons.

IMPLICATIONS OF FINDINGS

Item Selection and Response Sets

Three major points need to be considered relative to the selection and analysis of items in a self-report measure. First, it is critical that the items selected be representative of the offense areas to be covered. Special attention should be directed to this selection process, since the inclusion (or exclusion) of specific items appears to have implications for research findings, at least with regard to the social correlates of delinquent behavior.

Second, when attempting to make incidence estimates, it is important that response sets reflect the total frequency range. In this study, significant class and race differences were found only at the high end of the frequency range and, in most cases, would not have been observed had the traditional response sets been employed.

Third, from both theoretical and epidemiological perspectives, there is a danger in summarizing items into general categories. The present data indicate that using summary measures may obscure important differences by type of offense, and suggest that a more accurate picture is obtained by employing offense specific as well as summary measure analyses.[15]

It seems clear, from our data presentation and discussion, that the criticism of

[15] While summary measures are reported herein, offense-specific analyses were presented in a previous paper (Ageton and Elliott, 1978).

many SRD measures is well-founded; and, further, that generalizations about the social correlates of "delinquent behavior" as derived from measures with a limited response set and item representativity may be very misleading and are probably unwarranted. In addition, the way in which specific items are combined into summary measures has some bearing upon outcomes, and caution must be exercised in the interpretation of general summary measures.

Relationship between SRD and Official Data

In sum, it appears likely that the differences between the findings reported here and those from earlier self-report studies are, in fact, the result of differences in the specific SRD measures employed. The findings also suggest a logical connection between self-report and official measures of delinquency which, at least in part, accounts for the observed differences in the class and race distributions of these two measures.

The consistent findings of earlier self-report studies have led many sociologists and criminologists to the conclusion that race and class differences in arrests are primarily the result of processing biases and have little or no basis in behavior (Turk, 1969; Quinney, 1970; Williams and Gold, 1972; Taylor et al., 1974). The findings from the 1977 National Youth Survey suggest some behavioral basis for the observed class and race differences in official processing. In this sense, the National Youth Survey data are more consistent with official arrest data than are data from most prior self-report studies.

Further, these findings provide some insight into the mechanism whereby official actions produce exaggerated race and class (as well as age and sex) differences in delinquent behavior when compared with self-reported differences in normal adolescent populations. On both logical and empirical grounds, it seems reasonable to argue that the more frequent and serious offenders are more likely to be arrested (Short and Nye, 1957–1958; Erickson and Empey, 1963; Illinois Institute for Juvenile Research, 1973; Elliott and Voss, 1974; Empey, 1978), and that the youth population represented in official police statistics is not a representative sample of all youth.

Self-report studies are capturing a broader range of persons and levels of involvement in delinquent behavior than are official arrest statistics. Virtually all youth report some delinquent activity on self-report measures, but for the vast majority the offenses are neither very frequent nor very serious. Police contacts, on the other hand, are most likely to concern youth who are involved in either very serious or very frequent delinquent acts. Police contacts with youth thus involve a more restricted segment of the general youth population.

The findings discussed previously indicate that race and class differences are more extreme at the high end of the frequency continuum, that part of the delinquency continuum where police contacts are more likely.[16] In fact, at this end of the frequency continuum, self-report and official correlates of delinquent behavior are relatively similar. While we do not deny the existence of official processing biases, it does appear that official correlates of delinquency also reflect real differences in the frequency and seriousness of delinquent acts.

The results of this self-report delinquency study also have implications for previous tests of theoretical propositions which used SRD data. Stated simply, earlier self-report measures may not have been sensitive enough to capture the theoretically important differences in delinquency involvement. Given the truncated frequency distributions and the restricted behavioral range of earlier self-report measures, the only distinctions possible were fine gradations between relatively nondelinquent youth.

For example, earlier distinctions were typically among (1) youth with no reported offenses; (2) those with one or two offenses; and (3) those with three or more offenses. Given the extensive frequency distribution observed in this study, there is reason to question whether or not such a trichotomy would capture meaningful distinctions among offending youth. The most significant difference may not be between the nonoffender and the one-time offender, or even between the one-time and multiple-time offender. Equal or greater significance may be found between those reporting over (or under) 25 nonserious offenses, or between those reporting over (or under) five serious offenses.[17]

The ability to discriminate more fully among many levels and types of involvement in delinquent behavior introduces much more variance into the delinquency measure. That ability also allows for the identification of more extreme groups of offenders, and that identification may be particularly relevant for tests of theoretical propositions.

[16] Although we have not presented the data here, age and sex differences are also greater at the high end of the SRD frequency continuum.

[17] For example: for 1976, 5–10% of the most frequent offenders reported over 200 total offenses each, including over 30 serious offenses against persons.

APPENDIX A

SELF-REPORTED DELINQUENCY AND DRUG-USE ITEMS AS EMPLOYED IN THE NATIONAL YOUTH SURVEY

How many times in the last year have you:

1. purposely damaged or destroyed property belonging to your *parents* or other family *members*.
2. purposely damaged or destroyed property belonging to a *school*.
3. purposely damaged or destroyed *other property* that did not belong to you (not counting family or school property).
4. stolen (or tried to steal) a *motor vehicle*, such as a car or motorcycle.
5. stolen (or tried to steal) something worth more than $50.
6. knowingly bought, sold or held stolen goods (or tried to do any of these things).
7. thrown objects (such as rocks, snowballs, or bottles) at cars or people.
8. run away from home.
9. lied about your age to gain entrance or to purchase something; for example, lying about your age to buy liquor or get into a movie.
10. carried a hidden weapon other than a plain pocket knife.
11. stolen (or tried to steal) things worth $5 or less.
12. attacked someone with the idea of seriously hurting or killing him/her.
13. been paid for having sexual relations with someone.
14. had sexual intercourse with a person of the opposite sex other than your wife/husband.
15. been involved in gang fights.
16. sold marijuana or hashish ("pot," "grass," "hash").
17. cheated on school tests.
18. hitchhiked where it was illegal to do so.
19. stolen money or other things from your *parents* or *other members of your family*.
20. hit (or threatened to hit) a *teacher* or other adult at school.
21. hit (or threatened to hit) one of your *parents*.
22. hit (or threatened to hit) other *students*.
23. been loud, rowdy, or unruly in a public place (disorderly conduct).
24. sold hard drugs, such as heroin, cocaine, and LSD.
25. taken a vehicle for a ride (drive) without the owner's permission.
26. bought or provided liquor for a minor.
27. had (or tried to have) sexual relations with someone against their will.
28. used force (strong-arm methods) to get money or things from other *students*.
29. used force (strong-arm methods) to get money or things from a *teacher* or other adult at school.
30. used force (strong-arm methods) to get money or things from *other people* (not students or teachers).
31. avoided paying for such things as movies, bus or subway rides, and food.
32. been drunk in a public place.

33. stolen (or tried to steal) things worth between $5 and $50.
34. stolen (or tried to steal) something at school, such as someone's coat from a classroom, locker, or cafeteria, or a book from the library.
35. broken into a building or vehicle (or tried to break in) to steal something or just to look around.
36. begged for money or things from strangers.
37. skipped classes without an excuse.
38. failed to return extra change that a cashier gave you by mistake.
39. been suspended from school.
40. made obscene telephone calls, such as calling someone and saying dirty things.

How often in the last year have you used:

41. alcoholic beverages (beer, wine and hard liquor).
42. marijuana—hashish ("grass," "pot," "hash").
43. hallucinogens ("LSD," "Mescaline," "Peyote," "Acid").
44. amphetamines ("Uppers," "Speed," "Whites").
45. barbiturates ("Downers," "Reds").
46. heroin ("Horse," "Smack").
47. cocaine ("Coke").

REFERENCES

Ageton, Suzanne S. and Delbert S. Elliott
1978 The Incidence of Delinquent Behavior in a National Probability Sample of Adolescents. Project Report Number 3. HEW Grant Number MH27552, The Dynamics of Delinquent Behavior: A National Survey. Boulder: Behavioral Research Institute.

Bachman, Jerald G., Swayzer Green, and Ilona D. Wirtanen
1970 Youth in Transition: Vol. II. Ann Arbor: Institute for Social Research, University of Michigan.
1971 Youth in Transition: Vol. III. Ann Arbor: Institute for Social Research, University of Michigan.

Bachman, Jerald G., Patrick O'Malley, and Jerome Johnston
1978 Youth in Transition: Vol. VI. Ann Arbor: Institute for Social Research, University of Michigan.

Christie, Nils
1965 Summary of His Report to the Conference. Pp. 1–3 in Robert H. Hardt and George E. Bodine, Development of Self-Report Instruments in Delinquency Research: A Conference Report. Syracuse: Syracuse University Youth Development Center.

Clark, John P. and Larry L. Tifft
1966 "Polygraph and interview validation of self-reported deviant behavior." American Sociological Review 31:516–23.

Cloward, Richard A. and Lloyd E. Ohlin
1960 Delinquency and Opportunity. Glencoe, Ill.: Free Press.

Cohen, Albert K.
1955 Delinquent Boys: The Culture of the Gang. Glencoe, Ill.: Free Press.

Corey, Stephen M.
1937 "Signed versus unsigned questionnaires." Journal of Educational Psychology 28:144–8.

Dentler, Robert A. and Lawrence J. Monroe
1961 "Social correlates of early adolescent theft." American Sociological Review 26:733–43.

Elliott, Delbert S. and Harwin Voss
1974 Delinquency and Dropout. Lexington, Mass.: D. C. Heath.

Elliott, Delbert S., Suzanne S. Ageton, Margaret Hunter, and Brian Knowles
1976 Research Handbook for Community Planning and Feedback Instruments (Revised). Vol. 1. Prepared for the Office of Youth Development, Department of Health, Education, and Welfare, HEW-OS-74-308. Boulder: Behavioral Research and Evaluation Corporation.

Empey, LaMar T.
1978 American Delinquency. Homewood, Ill.: Dorsey.

Erickson, Maynard L. and LaMar T. Empey
1963 "Court records, undetected delinquency and decision-making." Journal of Criminal Law, Criminology and Police Science 54:456–69.

Farrington, David P.
1973 "Self-reports of deviant behavior: predictive and stable?" Journal of Criminal Law and Criminology 64:99–110.

Glaser, Daniel
1967 "National goals and indicators for the reduction of crime and delinquency." Annals of the American Academy of Political and Social Science 371:104–26.

Gold, Martin
1966 "Undetected delinquent behavior." Journal of Research in Crime and Delinquency 3:27–46.

Gold, Martin and David J. Reimer
1974 Changing Patterns of Delinquent Behavior among Americans 13 to 16 Years Old—1972. Report Number 1 of the National Survey of Youth, 1972. Ann Arbor: Institute for Social Research, University of Michigan.

Gordon, Robert A.
1976 "Prevalence: the rare datum in delinquency measurement and its implications for the theory of delinquency." Pp. 201–84 in Malcolm W. Klein (ed.), The Juvenile Justice System. Beverly Hills: Sage.

Hardt, Robert H. and George E. Bodine
1965 Development of Self-Report Instruments in Delinquency Research: A Conference Report. Syracuse: Syracuse University Youth Development Center.

Hardt, Robert H. and Sandra Peterson-Hardt
1977 "On determining the quality of the delinquency self-report method." Journal of Research in Crime and Delinquency 14:247–61.

Hindelang, Michael J.
1978 "Race and involvement in common law personal crimes." American Sociological Review 43:93–109.

Hindelang, Michael J., Travis Hirschi, and Joseph G. Weis
1975 Self-Reported Delinquency: Methods and Substance. Proposal Submitted to the National Institute of Mental Health, Department of Health, Education, and Welfare, MH27778.
1978 Social Class, Sex, Race and the Discrepancy between Self-Reported and Official Delinquency. Grant Number MH27778-03, Center for Studies of Crime and Delinquency, National Institute of Mental Health, Department of Health, Education, and Welfare.

Hirschi, Travis
1969 Causes of Delinquency. Berkeley: University of California.

Hollingshead, August B. and Frederick C. Redlich
1958 Social Class and Mental Illness. New York: Wiley.

Huizinga, David
1978 Description of the National Youth Sample. Project Report Number 2. HEW Grant Number MH27552, The Dynamics of Delinquent Behavior: A National Survey. Boulder: Behavioral Research Institute.

Illinois Institute for Juvenile Research
1973 Juvenile Delinquency in Illinois. Chicago: Illinois Department of Mental Health.

Krohn, Marvin, Gordon P. Waldo, and Theodore G. Chiricos
1974 "Self-reported delinquency: a comparison of structured interviews and self-administered checklists." Journal of Criminal Law and Criminology 65:545–53.

Kulik, James A., Kenneth B. Stein, and Theodore R. Sarbin
1968 "Disclosure of delinquent behavior under conditions of anonymity and nonanonymity." Journal of Consulting and Clinical Psychology 32:506–9.

Miller, Walter B.
1958 "Lower class culture as a generating milieu of gang delinquency." Journal of Social Issues 14:5–19.

Miller, Walter B.
1966 "Violent crimes in city gangs." Annals of the American Academy of Political and Social Science 364:97–112.

Nettler, Gwynn
1974 Explaining Crime. New York: McGraw-Hill.

Nye, F. Ivan and James F. Short, Jr.
1956 "Scaling delinquent behavior." American Sociological Review 22:326–31.

Quinney, Richard
1970 The Social Reality of Crime. Boston: Little, Brown.

Short, James F., Jr., and F. Ivan Nye
1957–1958 "Reported behavior as a criterion of deviant behavior." Social Problems 5:207–13.

Short, James F., Jr., and Fred L. Strodtbeck
1965 Group Process and Gang Delinquency. Chicago: University of Chicago.

Taylor, Ian, Paul Walton, and Jock Young
1974 The New Criminology. New York: Harper and Row.

Tittle, Charles R. and Wayne J. Villemez
1977 "Social class and criminality." Social Forces 56:474–502.

Tittle, Charles R., Wayne J. Villemez, and Douglas A. Smith
1978 "The myth of social class and criminality." American Sociological Review 43:643–56.

Turk, Austin
1969 Criminality and the Legal Order. Chicago: Rand McNally.

U.S. Bureau of the Census
1977 Population Estimates and Projections. Series P-25, No. 643.

West, D. J.
1973 Who Becomes Delinquent? London: Heinemann.

Wolfgang, Marvin, Robert Figlio, and Thorsten Sellin
1972 Delinquency in a Birth Cohort. Chicago: University of Chicago.

Williams, Jay R. and Martin Gold
1972 "From delinquent behavior to official delinquency." Social Problems 20:209–29.

Yablonsky, Lewis
1962 The Violent Gang. New York: MacMillan.

*A Comparative Analysis of Male and Female Delinquency**

Stephen A. Cernkovich and Peggy C. Giordano
Bowling Green State University

The historically dominant and generally accepted view is that males are much more likely than females to commit delinquent acts, and that when females deviate their misconduct is significantly less serious than that of males. This paper examines the recent contention that the delinquent behavior of males and females is more similar than assumed. Self-report questionnaires were administered in 1977 to a sample of 822 male and female adolescents selected from two urban high schools in a large midwestern state. Following Hindelang (1971), we concentrate on the types of delinquent acts most frequently reported, as well as the extent of involvement in these acts. While males tend to commit most offenses more frequently than females, the pattern of delinquency is virtually identical for the two groups. This uniformity holds for race-sex subgroups, although there are more similarities in delinquency within racial groups than within sex groups.

Criminological theory and research have focused predominantly on males, virtually excluding any systematic examination of females. Undoubtedly, this was due largely to the historically persistent orientation that female deviation is so infrequent and innocuous compared to that of males, that to study it was unproductive at best and useless at worst. The assumption has been that patterns of sex-role socialization and restrictions placed upon females limit their involvement in delinquency or at least in serious persistent misconduct.

Only recently has the study of female crime and delinquency begun to be taken seriously. This sudden interest is partly a function of the belief, still unsubstantiated, that the women's liberation movement has had a significant impact on female involvement in deviant activities (Adler, 1975; Simon, 1975). As a result of this reorientation, many criminologists now assume that patterns of female delinquency have changed significantly over the past few years, both in terms of increased frequency and versatility of involvement (Adler, 1975; Noblit and Burcart, 1976). Some others have not been willing to make such an assumption, however, and are skeptical about the validity of data used to support claims of increasing female delinquency rates (Steffensmeier, 1978; Steffensmeier and Jordan, 1978). Thus, there are two views which can be identified: (1) that, as reflected in the official statistics, female participation in delinquency has increased significantly, especially in areas that have been considered "masculine" crimes; and (2) that not much has changed. This view suggests that any increase in female delinquency reflected in official statistics is merely an artifact of data collection methodologies, or of changes in the behavior of official agents of control rather than changes in the behavior of females.

Unfortunately this debate has remained at a rhetorical level, with little recent data brought to bear on it. This is not to say that data are unavailable or that proponents of the two perspectives do not refer to many studies as support for their positions. Generally, impressionistic evidence (cf. Adler, 1975), official sources of data (cf. Simon, 1975), or resurrected self-report studies from the mid-1960s and early 1970s (cf. Datesman, et al., 1975), are the basis for these arguments. The use of such data, however, has resulted in an incomplete and sometimes misleading profile of female delinquency. We will not review all previous studies, or engage in a detailed examination of the relative usefulness of the data sources, but we shall review the major conclusions drawn from these studies because often they are the only bases for current understandings about female delinquency.

Most studies show that males commit more delinquent

*Revision of a paper presented at the 1977 meetings of the International Sociological Association Research Committee for the Sociology of Deviance and Social Control (August 9–11), Dublin. This study was supported by PHS Research Grant No. MH 29095-01, NIMH, (Center for Studies of Crime and Delinquency) and a Faculty Research Grant from Bowling Green State University. Stephen Cernkovich's address is: Department of Sociology, Bowling Green State University, Bowling Green, Ohio 43402.

From *The Sociological Quarterly,* Vol. 20 (Winter 1979), pp. 131–145. © *The Sociological Quarterly.*

acts than do females, especially serious crimes. While male delinquency includes a wide variety of offenses, female delinquency often is shown to be limited to a much narrower range of activities (Vedder, 1954; Wattenberg and Saunders, 1954; Shaclay, 1965; Doleschal, 1970; Gold, 1970; Jongman and Smale, 1972; Strouse, 1972; Haggart, 1973). Researchers argue that overt-aggressive delinquency and property crimes are more characteristic of male offenders, while female misbehavior is largely limited to incorrigibility (Barker and Adams, 1962; Forer, 1970; Vedder and Somerville, 1970), various sex offenses (Vedder, 1954; Barker and Adams, 1962; O'Reilly, et al., 1968; Vedder and Somerville, 1970; Chesney-Lind, 1973; Datesman, et al., 1975), running away from home (Barker and Adams, 1962; Forer, 1970; Vedder and Somerville, 1970; Chesney-Lind, 1973), truancy (Forer, 1970; Vedder and Somerville, 1970; Miller, 1973), and shoplifting (Adler, 1975).

Official statistics are frequently used to make or support such arguments. For example, the 1975 FBI Uniform Crime Reports indicates that the male/female arrest ratio (for those under 18 years of age) is 3.72 for all crimes, 8.39 for violent crimes, and 4.05 for property crimes. The ratios are significantly smaller for such offenses as prostitution (0.32), offenses against the family (1.70), and larceny-theft (2.37), all of which are considered traditional "female offenses." Even though these recent official statistics are used to indicate considerably greater percentage increases for females than for males in almost every offense category (Adler, 1975), the male/female ratio continues to show significantly more male involvement, particularly in the serious offense categories.

Such data notwithstanding, some researchers argue that females may be more versatile in their delinquent involvement than official records and early self-report studies suggest. For example, Hindelang (1971) found, consistent with official data, a greater *frequency* of self-reported acts by males, but surprisingly, that the *patterns* of delinquent involvement were virtually identical for males and females. Males and females commit roughly the same types of offenses, the only difference between the sexes is that males commit them more often.

As a result of such studies and the large percentage increase in female arrests reflected in the official statistics, some criminologists have suggested that the behavior of males and females is converging, at least in terms of the versatility of delinquency involvement and in some cases even the frequency. Such contentions are often made, however, without the benefit of *comprehensive* or *recent* supporting evidence. The use of official records, impressionistic evidence, or the resurrection of pre-1970 data to substantiate (or to invalidate) assumptions of increasing levels of female delinquency is incomplete at best, and tells us little about present-day patterns.

As a result, an up-to-date profile is essential so that a reasonable estimation of the frequency, nature, and versatility of female delinquency can be established. While Hindelang's (1971) research is an excellent foundation, it has become dated (the study was done in 1968). Nonetheless, it remains a valuable example of the type of basic information needed to conduct informed research. We will use his work as a model from which to proceed in the presentation, analysis, and discussion of our data. The reader is cautioned, however, that although there is similarity with Hindelang's earlier research, methodological and sampling differences in the two studies prohibit any systematic comparison.

The remainder of this paper will focus on a comparative analysis of male and female self-reported delinquency involvement. The goals of the analysis are threefold: (1) to examine the frequency of adolescent self-reported involvement in a wide variety of delinquent offenses, (2) to determine the degree of specialization or versatility of involvement in these offenses, and (3) to compare males and females, in general and by race, along these dimensions in order to isolate similarities and differences in their delinquent involvement. To the extent that basic data which specify the nature, extent, and patterning of delinquency is (or should be) the point of departure for researchers, both in identifying research questions and in guiding theory construction, it is essential that these data be as representative as possible. Many of the data currently used do not meet this criterion. In addition to providing a comparative assessment of male and female delinquency involvement, our analysis seeks to augment the existing data to allow for a more comprehensive understanding of female delinquency.

Sample Characteristics and Operationalization of Variables

Our data were obtained from anonymous self-report questionnaires which were administered to a 1977 sample of 822 students in two midwestern urban high schools. The questionnaires were administered during regularly scheduled, small-sized classes. Participation was voluntary, and the students were given the options of refusing to participate in the study, or of omitting those sections of the schedule which they found to be threatening or objectionable. All students agreed to participate.

While the sample is not random, it was selected to maximize variations along important demographic dimensions. One of the high schools selected is a lower-status inner-city school, the other a higher-status suburban school. The mean age of the subjects is 16.68 years. Females constitute 56.5 percent of the sample. Forty-eight percent of the subjects are white, the remaining non-whites being predominantly black (43 percent of the total sample). Warner's et al. (1949) seven-point Revised Occupational Scale (recoded so that "1" represents the lowest status category, "7" the highest) yielded the following socioeconomic distribution: 1 = 11.8 percent, 2 = 17.9 percent, 3 = 15.3 percent, 4 = 14.9 percent, 5 = 12.4 percent, 6 = 17.6 percent, and 7 = 10.1 percent, with a mean of 3.92 and a standard deviation of 1.92.

These demographic characteristics remain virtually the same for males and females. For the male sub-sample, 46.8 percent are white, the remaining non-whites being predominantly black (45.4 percent of the total male sub-sample). For the females, 49.1 percent are white, the remaining non-whites again being predominantly black (41.1 percent of the total female sub-sample). The mean age is 16.72 for males, 16.65 for females. The Warner et al. socioeconomic distribution for the two sub-samples differ slightly. Males: 1 = 11.6 percent, 2 = 17.5 percent, 3 = 11.9 percent, 4 = 16.5 percent, 5 = 10.9 percent, 6 = 21.1 percent, and 7 = 10.5 percent, with a mean of 4.03 and a standard deviation of 1.94. Females: 1 = 11.7 percent, 2 = 18.3 percent, 3 = 18.0 percent, 4 = 13.7 percent, 5 = 13.7 percent, 6 = 14.9 percent, and 7 = 9.7 percent, with a mean of 3.83 and a standard deviation of 1.90.

In evaluating the analysis to follow, the reader is cautioned about a possible race-class bias in the data. The socioeconomic distribution is skewed toward the higher statuses for whites (mean = 4.82) and toward the lower statuses for non-whites (mean = 2.84). The problem is minimized somewhat, however, by the fact that neither race nor class are significantly related to delinquency at the zero-order. The same holds true for the relationship between class and delinquency, controlling for race. The relationship between race and delinquency, controlling for class (as a trichotomy), produces one small although significant relationship, with middle-class whites tending to be slightly more delinquent than middle-class non-whites.

Delinquency involvement is measured by a combination of items selected from the Short-Nye (1957) and Sellin-Wolfgang (1964) self-report inventories. Individual items were selected to maximize the seriousness range of the behaviors. A total of thirty-six personal, property, and victimless/status offense items are included in the scale. The coding scheme for self-reported involvement in each of these acts is as follows: "very often" = 3, "several times" = 2, "once or twice" = 1, and "never" = 0.

Two observations regarding the use of self-report data in this study are appropriate. First, while measurement of a wide variety of delinquent acts is important in any self-report analysis, it is crucial in the present investigation. Traditionally, it has been assumed that males and females differ greatly in the *type* and *seriousness* of the delinquent acts they commit. While many of the minor forms of misbehavior included in the questionnaire (e.g., disobeying parents, running away from home, being placed on school probation, defying parents' authority to their face) would be considered only marginally delinquent by many researchers, the fact remains that it is these types of activities which are argued to be the most characteristic forms of delinquency among females. Any analysis which seeks to determine the scope and nature of female delinquency involvement must consider these relatively innocuous, benign acts, as well as the more serious, clearly delinquent acts. This becomes even more essential because many of these less serious forms of misbehavior are often combined in a residual "all other offenses except traffic" category in most official records, prohibiting specific offense analysis. An accurate and complete assessment of female delinquency demands information on a broad range of delinquent acts. The scale items included here reflect this necessity to specify the full range of female delinquency involvement.

The second observation concerns the general utility and validity of self-report data. While we recognize the limitations of such data, we would argue that a self-report profile is essential for broadening existing baseline data on female delinquency. There has been an overreliance on official statistics in the study of female delinquency, and in drawing distinctions between males and females. Although official data are not without merit, they are confounded by untold biases and to establish a valid female profile is extremely problematic. It is impossible, for example, to separate the biasing effects of differential processing, an acute problem in the case of female offenders. Official statistics simply give no indication of the extent to which arrest or court referral rates are influenced by such factors as the over- and under-processing of females depending on the offense committed, fluctuations in the orientation of criminal justice personnel regarding the extent to which they desire to equalize the treatment of male and female offenders, and various other legal and extra-legal considerations (Chesney-Lind, 1973, 1974, 1977; Anderson, 1976; Armstrong, 1977; Conway and Bogdan, 1977). If race is introduced as a variable, the reliability and validity of official data are further confounded (cf. Piliavin and Briar, 1964; Black and Reiss, 1970). We suggest that both official and self-report data are necessary for an informed and comprehensive understanding of female delinquency. While self-report data also have actual and potential sources of bias (cf. Nettler, 1978:97-117), we contend that they add new and valuable information about delinquency involvement not evident from official sources. In this sense, we use self-reports for the purpose they were originally intended, as both an alternative and a supplement to official statistics.

Analysis and Findings

Dimensions of male and female involvement in all thirty-six delinquent acts included on the questionnaire are in Table 1. It is clear, and not surprising, from an examination of the "Percent Engaging in Act One or More Times" columns of Table 1, that more males than females report engaging in the various delinquent acts. Exceptions include disobeying parents, running away from home, defying parents' authority, and, surprisingly, using hard drugs. Over half of both the males and females report participation in truancy, disobeying parents, petty theft, sexual intercourse, drinking alcohol, smoking marijuana, gambling, and disturbing the peace, all relatively minor offenses from a legal standpoint. The relatively benign nature of these acts notwithstanding, there is a good deal of similarity in the kinds of acts both sexes report.

The male/female ratios of those reporting involvement in the thirty-six acts are also reported in Table 1, and these data address more directly the issue of degree of uniformity in patterns of delinquency involvement. The largest ratios (indicating a greater percentage of males than of females reporting involvement) include theft of car parts, robbery, car theft, sex for money, burglary-unoccupied, and burglary-occupied. (It is surprising of course that more males than females report involvement in "sex for money." In accounting for a similar finding, Hindelang (1971:527) notes that ". . . Gold (1970) has found that females of high school age tend to underreport

Table 1. Male and Female Self-Reported Delinquency Involvement

Delinquent Act	Percent Engaging in Act One or More Times			Frequency of Delinquency Involvement Male		Female		
	Male	Female	Ratio	Mean	SD	Mean	SD	t-Value[a]
1. Drive Car Without Permission	41.7	25.4	1.64	.64	.89	.35	.68	4.89*
2. Skip School	81.7	80.8	1.01	1.54	1.01	1.55	1.00	−.11
3. Disobey Parents	89.6	93.6	0.96	1.66	.87	1.79	.83	−2.12***
4. Attack Someone With Fists	47.8	25.1	1.90	.68	.83	.34	.66	6.30*
5. Run Away from Home	16.0	16.1	0.99	.21	.54	.20	.51	.25
6. School Probation/ Suspension/Expulsion	31.8	26.6	1.19	.43	.70	.37	.68	1.18
7. Defy Parents' Authority	40.7	42.1	0.97	.52	.71	.60	.82	−1.54
8. Theft (less than $2.00)	66.5	58.2	1.14	.95	.86	.79	.80	2.61*
9. Use Weapon to Attack Someone	11.6	6.6	1.76	.16	.49	.09	.35	2.48*
10. Use Fake ID	34.8	26.5	1.31	.53	.83	.44	.83	1.58
11. Sex With Opposite Sex	77.7	62.0	1.25	1.72	1.14	1.23	1.13	6.00*
12. Gang Fight	38.9	14.5	2.68	.50	.70	.19	.50	6.86*
13. Drink Alcohol	82.8	72.6	1.14	1.77	1.08	1.48	1.10	3.75*
14. Smoke Marijuana	67.2	58.7	1.14	1.46	1.24	1.33	1.25	1.51
15. Theft ($2.00–$50.00)	33.9	26.0	1.30	.47	.76	.36	.70	2.10#
16. Use Hard Drugs	14.8	19.3	0.77	.25	.65	.32	.74	−1.50
17. Sell Marijuana	35.2	19.5	1.80	.67	1.01	.32	.71	5.44*
18. Car Theft	5.5	1.1	5.00	.09	.43	.02	.18	2.97*
19. DWI-Liquor	38.1	21.8	1.75	.70	1.01	.34	.73	5.41*
20. Property destruction of Under $10.00	36.6	16.1	2.27	.44	.65	.19	.47	5.95*
21. DWI-Marijuana	40.4	21.8	1.85	.78	1.08	.41	.86	5.04*
22. Gamble	85.3	60.8	1.40	1.70	1.03	.96	.97	10.02*
23. Burglary-Occupied	9.7	2.3	4.22	.15	.51	.03	.24	3.89*
24. Sell Hard Drugs	11.6	9.5	1.22	.18	.53	.15	.52	.69
25. Robbery	5.0	0.9	5.55	.08	.37	.01	.15	2.80*
26. Theft (over $50.00)	12.7	4.6	2.76	.16	.47	.06	.32	3.31*
27. Disturb the Peace	71.6	68.9	1.04	1.11	.91	.98	.82	1.96##
28. Property Destruction of over $10.00	20.3	5.9	3.44	.26	.58	.08	.37	4.78*
29. Sex with Same Sex	4.2	3.3	1.27	.09	.45	.06	.33	1.01
30. Burglary-Unoccupied	16.5	3.7	4.46	.20	.51	.05	.27	4.94*
31. DWI-Hard Drugs	11.7	7.2	1.62	.18	.54	.12	.47	1.71
32. Extortion	13.6	8.3	1.64	.22	.62	.11	.41	2.84*
33. Theft of Car Parts	20.4	3.2	6.37	.27	.60	.04	.22	6.66*
34. Joyride	18.1	6.1	2.97	.25	.59	.08	.32	4.81*
35. Sex for Money	5.3	1.1	4.82	.08	.36	.02	.22	2.54*
36. Carry Weapon	34.3	17.1	2.01	.53	.86	.27	.67	4.59*

[a]Significance levels are meaningless for these data because they are based on a non-random sample. They are reported here for heuristic and descriptive rather than inferential purposes. The symbols for level of probability are: * = .01, ** = .02, *** = .03, # = .04, ## = .05.

having had sexual intercourse while Clark and Tifft (1966) have found that male college students tend to overreport heterosexual adventures." We suspect that this argument is valid in interpreting the meaning of male/female self-reported participation in the "sex for money" behavioral item.) The ratios are smallest (indicating a comparable percentage of males and females reporting involvement) for using hard drugs, disobeying parents, defying parents' authority, running away from home, truancy, and disturbing the peace. The overall ratio for all thirty-six acts is 2.18, compared to Hindelang's (1971) ratio of 2.56, and the 1975 Uniform Crime Reports overall ratio of 3.72. Although comparison with the Hindelang and official figures indicates a greater male-female similarity in our sample, a large portion of this similarity is due to a high percentage of both sexes' involvement in relatively innocuous, benign behaviors. When many of the more serious offenses are examined, the male-female gap begins to widen.

But most of the ratios obtained are considerably smaller than those revealed in arrest rates for males and females under 18 years of age. For example, the 1975 Uniform Crime Reports indicates male/female arrest ratios of 12.24 for robbery, 4.94 for aggravated assault, 18.98 for burglary, 2.37 for larceny-theft, 12.53 for auto theft, 13.92 for carrying weapons,

19.28 for gambling, and 11.54 for driving while under the influence of alcohol. Comparisons of those ratios with ours suggest that official statistics may be useful indicators of the *legal processing* of juveniles but they are not accurate indices of the *real* extent and nature of delinquency involvement. They nevertheless continue to be used for this purpose (cf. Simon, 1975; Noblit and Burcart, 1976; Steffensmeier and Jordan, 1978). While the official data give the impression of significantly different patterns of delinquency involvement by males and females, our self-report data suggest quite the opposite. A comparison of the rank-ordering of the percent of males and females reporting involvement in each of the thirty-six acts yields a Spearman coefficient (Blalock, 1972:416–18) of 0.90, suggesting high correspondence between the misbehavior of males and females.

This aspect of the analysis, however, deals only with the percentage of males and females who report involvement in each act. It reveals nothing about the *extent* of that involvement. Because the frequency of delinquent behavior is an important variable in the determination of arrest rates, it is instructive to know something about levels of involvement for males and females. The higher arrest rate for males may reflect the fact that they are more persistent offenders than females. The extent of delinquency involvement is presented in the second half of Table 1 which shows the mean frequency of male/female participation in each of the thirty-six delinquent acts.

These data indicate that almost 28 percent (10/36) of the male-female differences in extent of involvement are statistically non-significant. This is an important departure from everyday thinking and from the official statistics which suggest significant male-female differences in virtually every offense category. We find no significant sex differences for truancy, running away from home, school probation/suspension/expulsion, defying parents' authority, using a fake ID, smoking marijuana, using hard drugs, selling hard drugs, sex with the same sex, and driving while under the influence of hard drugs. Especially interesting is the comparison of truancy and running away from home. Males and females are thought to differ considerably in their involvement in these offenses. Our data do not support this view. These offenses clearly are neither restricted to females nor are they the dominant areas of specialization for female offenders.

Small but statistically significant, male-female differences characterize the remaining twenty-six acts. Only one of the reported t-values, however, is impressive (gambling). The large sample size no doubt contributes to the statistical significance of what are otherwise substantively small differences in the frequency of male and female delinquency involvement. Both males and females have high rates of involvement (whether there are significant sex differences or not) in truancy, disobeying parents, intercourse, drinking alcohol, and smoking marijuana (males also have a comparatively high rate for gambling). Similarly, both groups evidence low rates of involvement in car theft, burglary-occupied, robbery, sex with the same sex, and sex for money (males have comparatively low rates for use of weapons and theft greater than \$50.00, while females also infrequently are involved in theft of car parts and burglary-unoccupied).

These data reveal a striking male-female uniformity in delinquency involvement. A rank-order comparison of mean involvement rates yields a coefficient of 0.91, indicating, as was the case for percent reporting involvement, considerable similarity between males and females. As was the case in Hindelang's (1971) data, what seems to differentiate male and female delinquents is their *frequency of involvement,* not the *type of acts* in which they engage. The acts most frequently committed are virtually identical for males and females, tending to be the less serious, victimless/status offenses. Similarly, the acts least frequently engaged in by both males and females are the more serious personal and property offenses, although males tend to engage in these more often than females do.

Because of the significance of this overall similarity it is important to determine the degree to which the uniformities persist in separate examinations by race. The rationale for this stage of the analysis is two-fold: (1) the composition of our sample creates the possibility that the findings reported in Table 1 may be confounded by race, and (2) previous work on female delinquency has revealed interesting racial variations (cf. Adler, 1969; Katzenelson, 1975; Giordano, 1976). The data for this analysis are presented in Table 2 which reveals uniformities even more pronounced than the data in Table 1. Looking first at sex differences within racial categories, these data show that for white males and females, 16 of the 36 (44 percent) frequency of involvement differences are not significant statistically. With the exception of theft (\$2.00–\$50.00), robbery, and extortion, this reflects comparable rates of male and female involvement in victimless, drug-related, or relatively minor offenses. Significant sex differences tend to be for offenses which are more serious personal and property offenses. In every case, males report higher levels of involvement in these acts than females report. The overall mean level of involvement across thirty-six offenses is 22.36 for the white males and 16.94 for the white females. This reflects the fact that while there is an overall uniformity, males commit more offenses, particularly the more serious ones, than females commit.

The same pattern characterizes non-whites. Non-white males report an average of 21.19 delinquent acts, while non-white females report 14.46. Twelve of the thirty-six (33 percent) differences are non-significant, and tend again to be isolated to relatively minor offenses (exceptions are using a weapon to attack someone and car theft). The offenses for which there are significant male-female differences, while including some minor, victimless/status offenses, tend to be offenses of a more serious variety. With the single exception of disobeying parents, non-white males report significantly greater levels of involvement than do non-white females. As was the case with the white sub-sample, the males in the non-white group tend to be more persistent than females in their delinquency, particularly in misbehavior of a serious nature.

Turning to racial differences within sex categories, these data show a remarkable uniformity in the delinquency of white and non-white males. There are no significant differences

Table 2. Frequency of Delinquency Involvement by Sex and Race

	Male				Female							
	A White		B Non-White		C White		D Non-white		t-Value[a]			
Delinquent Act	Mean	SD	Mean	SD	Mean	SD	Mean	SD	AB	CD	AC	BD
1. Drive Car Without Permission	.61	.84	.66	.94	.38	.66	.32	.69	−.49	.91	2.98*	3.96*
2. Skip School	1.48	1.06	1.61	.95	1.56	1.06	1.55	.95	−1.11	.14	−.69	.62
3. Disobey Parents	1.95	.75	1.38	.90	1.94	.79	1.63	.84	6.28*	4.01*	.05	−2.84*
4. Attack Someone With Fists	.65	.79	.71	.88	.26	.58	.41	.73	−.60	−2.35**	5.44*	3.69*
5. Run Away from Home	.21	.55	.21	.54	.23	.51	.16	.48	.05	1.67	−.41	1.00
6. School Probation/ Suspension/Expulsion	.32	.65	.52	.74	.31	.68	.42	.69	−2.53*	−1.64	.16	1.35
7. Defy Parents' Authority	.73	.76	.32	.59	.88	.86	.32	.65	5.44*	7.78*	−1.82	.04
8. Theft (less than $2.00)	1.03	.84	.87	.87	.79	.79	.80	.82	1.72	−.14	2.89*	.83
9. Use Weapon to Attack Someone	.12	.46	.21	.52	.03	.21	.14	.44	−1.54	−3.54*	2.51*	1.30
10. Use Fake ID	.62	.89	.45	.76	.46	.86	.40	.80	1.83	.76	1.68	.54
11. Sex with Opposite Sex	1.44	1.13	2.01	1.07	1.10	1.14	1.36	1.10	−4.59*	−2.46*	2.93*	5.66*
12. Gang Fight	.44	.68	.56	.71	.11	.35	.26	.60	−1.62	−3.24*	5.54*	4.41*
13. Drink Alcohol	1.90	1.06	1.65	1.08	1.77	1.10	1.19	1.02	2.06≠	5.74*	1.17	4.28*
14. Smoke Marijuana	1.41	1.27	1.52	1.20	1.40	1.31	1.26	1.18	−.80	1.17	.07	2.09≠
15. Theft ($2.00-$50.00)	.44	.73	.51	.79	.38	.70	.34	.70	−.80	.62	.78	2.15***
16. Use Hard Drugs	.38	.78	.12	.45	.48	.88	.17	.53	3.74*	4.58*	−1.15	−1.00
17. Sell Marijuana	.65	1.02	.70	.99	.42	.81	.20	.56	−.42	3.39*	2.31**	5.74*
18. Car Theft	.09	.44	.09	.41	.01	.07	.03	.24	.04	−1.61	2.51*	1.68
19. DWI-Liquor	.80	1.08	.60	.94	.53	.88	.16	.50	1.81	5.60*	2.64*	5.55*
20. Property Destruction of Under $10.00	.57	.72	.31	.54	.28	.55	.08	.31	3.65*	4.71*	4.24*	4.65*
21. DWI-Marijuana	.87	1.14	.69	1.02	.58	1.00	.23	.64	1.53	4.45*	2.59*	4.96*
22. Gamble	1.78	.98	1.62	1.07	.93	.90	.98	1.03	1.39	−.51	8.68*	5.73*
23. Burglary-Occupied	.14	.46	.17	.56	.03	.22	.03	.22	−.66	.14	2.65*	3.08*
24. Sell Hard Drugs	.26	.63	.09	.40	.21	.58	.08	.44	2.99*	2.59*	.85	.10
25. Robbery	.04	.28	.11	.45	.01	.07	.02	.20	−1.55	−1.29	1.72	2.22***
26. Theft (over $50.00)	.14	.44	.19	.50	.04	.19	.09	.41	−.96	−1.76	2.75*	2.01≠
27. Disturb the Peace	1.27	.93	.94	.87	1.07	.79	.89	.84	3.21*	2.31**	2.17***	.55
28. Property Destruction of Over $10.00	.20	.48	.32	.68	.07	.35	.10	.40	−1.79	−.79	3.00*	3.62*
29. Sex with Same Sex	.07	.38	.10	.52	.04	.30	.07	.37	−.49	−.74	.82	.63
30. Burglary-Unoccupied	.18	.46	.22	.55	.05	.29	.04	.25	−.67	.24	3.31*	3.76*
31. DWI-Hard Drugs	.25	.63	.11	.42	.21	.62	.02	.18	2.33**	4.34*	.61	2.52*
32. Extortion	.12	.49	.33	.72	.04	.26	.18	.51	−3.01*	−3.39*	1.83	2.30**
33. Theft of Car Parts	.26	.54	.28	.66	.06	.29	.01	.12	−.31	2.29**	4.29*	5.10*
34. Joyride	.23	.55	.27	.64	.08	.30	.06	.31	−.59	.68	3.18*	3.80*
35. Sex for Money	.07	.34	.09	.38	.02	.22	.02	.22	−.54	.17	1.49	2.07≠
36. Carry Weapon	.53	.84	.54	.87	.19	.57	.34	.74	−.07	−2.38**	4.45*	2.30**

[a]The symbols for level of probability are: * = .01, ** = .02, *** = .03, ≠ = .04.

between the two groups for twenty-five of the thirty-six (69 percent) acts. Of the few differences that are significant, whites report greater levels of involvement in disobeying parents, defying parents' authority, drinking alcohol, using hard drugs, property destruction of under $10.00, selling hard drugs, disturbing the peace, and driving while under the influence of hard drugs. Non-white males report higher rates of participation in school probation/suspension/expulsion, sex with the opposite sex, and extortion. In spite of these differences, white and non-white males show almost identical patterns of delinquent involvement. The mean rate of delinquency across all thirty-six acts is 22.36 for the white males, 21.19 for the non-white males.

Similarly, the data in Table 2 reveal that among females, whites engage in slightly more delinquency than do non-whites. The overall mean frequency for white females is 16.94, while for non-whites it is 14.46. Closer inspection of specific delinquent acts, however, suggests that such a comparison is somewhat misleading. Mean frequency of involvement differences between white and non-white females are non-significant for eighteen of the thirty-six (50 percent) acts. Most of these are relatively minor, victimless/status offenses. Exceptions include theft ($2.00–$50.00), car theft, burglary-occupied, robbery, theft (over $50.00), property destruction over $10.00, and burglary-unoccupied.

This uniformity notwithstanding, a distinctive pattern emerges for the eighteen acts in which there are statistically significant differences. Non-white females report higher levels of involvement in fist fighting, using a weapon to attack someone, sex with the opposite sex, gang fighting, extortion and carrying weapons. The common characteristic of these offenses, with the exception of sexual intercourse, is that they are all personal, potentially violent offenses. White females report greater rates of participation in disobeying parents, defying parents' authority, drinking alcohol, using hard drugs, selling marijuana, driving while under the influence of alcohol, property destruction of under $10.00, driving while under the influence of marijuana, selling hard drugs, disturbing the peace, driving while under the influence of hard drugs, and theft of car parts. While white females report a greater overall mean level of involvement in delinquency, this is largely a function of their higher rates of participation in relatively minor or drug-related offenses. Non-white females, while reporting less overall delinquency than whites, have higher involvement rates in the more serious, personal offenses.

In order to examine these patterns further a series of rank order correlations (based on mean frequency of involvement in the thirty-six delinquent acts) were computed. The average correlation of 0.87 indicates that there is a great deal of similarity among all four sub-groups, and does not support many of the racial and sex differences suggested by official data. Interestingly, these rank orders also show *that there are more similarities within racial groups than within sex groups* (see Katzenelson, 1975, for similar findings). White females are more similar in their delinquency involvement to white males (0.96) than to non-whites, female (0.84) or male (0.81). Non-white females' delinquency more closely approximates that of non-white males (0.88) than that of whites, female (0.84) or male (0.84). While important, these differences should not be allowed to obscure the overall similarity among the sub-groups. The *pattern* of delinquency is almost identical for all four groups. Significant differences appear primarily on the basis of *frequency* of involvement.

Summary and Conclusion

As if to compensate for an historical omission, criminologists have initiated an intense study of the female offender. Aside from the effect of the women's liberation movement, the most hotly debated issue, and one important reason for the increased focus on female deviance, centers around answering a number of related questions: What are the basic similarities and differences between male and female delinquency? Has there been a real increase in female involvement in delinquent activities? If so, what is the nature of this increase? Have females moved beyond involvement in relatively specific, less serious offenses, to participation in what traditionally have been considered "masculine crimes?" For the most part, answers to questions such as these have been based on impressionistic, resurrected pre-1970 self-report data, or official sources of data. There is an increased awareness, however, that the problems and limitations inherent in these data have retarded our basic understanding of female deviance, and that we need valid, more comprehensive baseline data from which research and theory construction can proceed.

Our major findings are that (1) with the exception of a few minor offenses, more males than females report engaging in each of the thirty-six delinquent acts; (2) the overall male-female ratio for percent reporting involvement in each of the delinquent offenses is 2.18, considerably smaller than both Hindelang's (1971) self-report ratio of 2.56, and the official arrest ratio of 3.72; (3) when mean frequency of involvement in each of the delinquent acts is examined, almost twenty-eight percent of the male/female differences are shown to be non-significant, and there is considerable uniformity between males and females; (4) while there are virtually no important differences between white and non-white males, a distinctive pattern emerges for the females in that white, more than non-white females report participation in more delinquent acts overall and in relatively minor and drug-related offenses, while non-white more than white females report significantly more involvement in the more serious, personal offenses; and (5) rank order correlations indicate more uniformities in frequency type of delinquency involvement within racial groups than within sex groups.

The focus of this research has been largely descriptive but the findings have several etiological implications. Much criticism has been directed at the stereotypic and oversimplified explanations which have dominated theoretical thinking on female crime and delinquency. A particular model's stress on "personal maladjustments," "women's liberation," or some other factor as the dominant causal ingredient, however, is not as critical as the fact that many of these explanations are based on incomplete and often biased data. *A priori* assumptions are made about the nature of female deviance which often extend far beyond the validity and generalizability of available data.

It is clear from the findings presented here that many of these assumptions are inaccurate. It is equally clear that subsequent research and theory-construction must first establish an up-to-date profile of female delinquency, and must consider fully the entire range and complexity of females' involvement. Accurate theory must be based on empirical reality, but the development of accurate theory continues to suffer because some scholars rush to print with the causes of delinquency before they know what it is they should be explaining.

References

Adler, Freda. 1969. *The Female Offender in Philadelphia.* Unpublished Ph.D. Dissertation. University Park: University of Pennsylvania.

_____ . 1975. *Sisters in Crime.* New York: McGraw-Hill.

Anderson, Etta A. 1976. "The 'chivalrous' treatment of the female offender in the arms of the criminal justice system: a review of the literature." *Social Problems* 23:350–57.

Armstrong, Gail. 1977. "Females under the law–'protected' but unequal." *Crime and Delinquency* 23:109–20.

Barker, Gordon H., and William T. Adams. 1962. "Comparison of the delinquencies of boys and girls." *Journal of Criminal Law, Criminology and Police Science* 53:470–75.

Black, Donald J., and Albert J. Reiss, Jr. 1970. "Police control of juveniles." *American Sociological Review* 35:63–77.

Blalock, Hubert M. Jr. 1972. *Social Statistics.* 2d Ed. New York: McGraw-Hill.

Chesney-Lind, Meda. 1973. "Judicial enforcement of the female sex role: the family court and the female delinquent." *Issues in Criminology* 8:51–69.

_____ . 1974. "Juvenile delinquency: the sexualization of female crime." *Psychology Today* 8:43–46.

_____ . 1977. "Judicial paternalism and the female status offender: training women to know their place." *Crime and Delinquency* 23: 121–30.

Clark, John P., and Larry L. Tifft. 1966. "Polygraph and interview validation of self-reported deviant behavior." *American Sociological Review* 31:516–23.

Conway, Allan, and Carol Bogdan. 1977. "Sexual delinquency: the persistence of a double standard." *Crime and Delinquency* 23:132–35.

Datesman, Susan K., Frank R. Scarpitti, and Richard M. Stephenson. 1975. "Female delinquency: an application of self and opportunity theories." *Journal of Research in Crime and Delinquency* 12:107–23.

Doleschal, Eugene. 1970. "Review: hidden crime." *Crime and Delinquency Literature* 2:546–72.

Forer, Lois G. 1970. *No One Will Listen: How Our Legal System Brutalizes the Poor.* New York: John Day.

Giordano, Peggy C. 1976. "Changing sex roles and females' involvement in delinquency." Paper read at the meeting of the Midwest Sociological Society, St. Louis, April 21–24.

Gold, Martin. 1970. *Delinquent Behavior in an American City.* Belmont, California: Brooks/Cole.

Haggart, Joy Reeve. 1973. "Women and crime." *Humboldt Journal of Social Relations* 1:42–47.

Hindelang, Michael J. 1971. "Age, sex, and the versatility of delinquent involvements." *Social Problems* 18:522–35.

Jongman, R. W., and G. J. A. Smale. 1972. "Unrecorded delinquency among female students." *Tijdschrift Voor Criminologie* 14:1–11.

Katzenelson, Susan. 1975. "The female offender in Washington, D. C." Paper read at the meeting of the American Society of Criminology, Toronto, October 30–November 2.

Miller, Walter B. 1973. "The Molls." *Society* 11:32–35.

Nettler, Gwynn. 1978. *Explaining Crime.* 2d Ed. New York: McGraw-Hill.

Noblit, George W., and Janie M. Burcart. 1976. "Women and crime: 1960–1970." *Social Science Quarterly* 56:650–57.

O'Reilly, Charles, Frank Cizon, John Flanagan, and Steven Pflanczer. 1968. "Sentenced women in a county jail." *American Journal of Corrections* 30:23–25.

Piliavin, Irving, and Scott Briar. 1964. "Police encounters with juveniles." *American Journal of Sociology* 70:206–14.

Sellin, Thorsten, and Marvin E. Wolfgang. 1964. *The Measurement of Delinquency.* New York: John Wiley.

Shaclay, Cockbern E. 1965. "Sex differentials in juvenile delinquency." *British Journal of Criminality* 5:289–308.

Short, James F. Jr., and F. Ivan Nye. 1957. "Reported behavior as a criteria of deviant behavior." *Social Problems* 5:207–13.

Simon, Rita James. 1975. *The Contemporary Woman and Crime.* Rockville, Maryland: National Institute of Mental Health: Crime and Delinquency Issues.

Steffensmeier, Darrell. 1978. "Crime and the contemporary woman: an analysis of changing levels of female property crime, 1960–75." *Social Forces* 57:566–84.

Steffensmeier, Darrell J., and Charlene Jordan. 1978. "Changing patterns of female crime in rural America, 1962–75." *Rural Sociology* 43:87–102.

Strouse, Jean. 1972. "To be minor and female." *Ms.* (August): 70–75, 116.

Uniform Crime Reports for the United States. 1975. Clarence M. Kelley, Director. Federal Bureau of Investigation, U.S. Department of Justice. Washington, D.C.: U.S. Government Printing Office.

Vedder, Clyde B. 1954. *The Juvenile Offender.* New York: Doubleday.

Vedder, Clyde B., and Dora B. Somerville. 1970. *The Delinquent Girl.* Springfield, Illinois: Charles C. Thomas.

Warner, W. Lloyd, Marchia Meeker, and Kenneth Eells. 1949. *Social Class in America.* Chicago: Science Research Associates.

Wattenberg, William, and Frank Saunders. 1954. "Sex differences among juvenile offenders." *Sociology and Social Research* 39:24–31.

SECTION THREE

Summary

The preeminent position that social class has enjoyed as a crucial variable in our understanding of crime and delinquency has been seriously challenged. While many of the major sociological theories of deviant behavior are predicated on the importance of socioeconomic status, research findings are not totally supportive of this traditional assumption. Two issues immediately come to view: (1) the notion that delinquency is concentrated in the lower economic classes and (2) the allegation that there is an administrative bias against persons of lower socioeconomic status at various points in the criminal justice process. Research findings on the first question of crime as a lower-class phenomenon have pointed out that law-violating behavior exists throughout the social hierarchy. When differences are detected between the lower class and the middle or upper, they are not as dramatic as has been commonly assumed. The second question of differential processing is far more problematic. There is not unanimous agreement that discriminatory practices occur or do not occur. This difference of opinion may reflect the fact that law enforcement practices and procedures are not uniform throughout the United States. Inconsistency is even more acute in matters relating to the juvenile court, where the lack of prescribed procedures and clearly enunciated statutes results in widespread variances from one jurisdiction to another.

Another important distinction may be in the separation of social class from other demographic characteristics, such as age, sex, race, and ethnicity. It may be that social class is unimportant, but distinctions between males and females, younger and older adolescents, and white and nonwhite youths should not necessarily be ruled out as insignificant. These ascriptive attributes are far more visible than social class, and a finding of no relationship between social class and delinquency does not rule out other differences.

The article by Charles Tittle and Wayne Villemez clearly demonstrates the tenuous position that social class occupies in the study of crime and delinquency. Whether social class is measured in terms of income, occupation, or education, their findings lend no support to an inverse relationship between social class and crime. Second, social mobility, whether seen in terms of an individual's moving up, down, or remaining the same on the social stratification ladder, does not appear to be an important determinant for deviant behavior. However, there is some indication that downward mobility is associated with less deviant behavior than upward mobility or no mobility at all. This finding is unexplained by any theory of crime or delinquency. Hence, Tittle and Villemez call for a reformulation of theories of deviance that minimizes the importance of social class.

The article by Donald Black and Albert Reiss introduces a number of contextual factors in attempting to unravel the sanctioning of deviant behavior. A major consideration is how the police are mobilized. In the discussion of the notion of reactive mobilization, it is clear that the community itself emerges as the principal "detective" in uncovering crime. The community's reaction to delinquent behavior looms as a key energizing force in the juvenile justice system. The police do not operate as an autonomous agency but rather respond to the needs, perceptions, and perhaps even the prejudices of the local community. The Black and Reiss discussion may partially explain the discrepancies between Terence Thornberry's findings and those of Lawrence Cohen and James Kluegel.

Looking specifically for evidence that race and social class are related to the severity of disposition, Cohen and Kluegel have examined the dispositions given to juveniles in two different court settings. They find no evidence that these two factors are related in any way to the ultimate disposition of juvenile offenders. Thornberry, on the other hand, using the city of Philadelphia as his focus, finds that race and social class are related to juvenile court dispositions. Further, in a reanalysis of these same data in a more recent publication, using the same technique as Cohen and Kluegel, Thornberry has arrived at exactly the same conclusion as he did in his 1973 study (Thornberry, 1979). The question is, who is right? Each of these articles concludes on the same cautionary note: we need further research. But in light of Black and Reiss's discussion, these inconsistencies may be more real than imaginary.

The Delbert Elliott and Suzanne Ageton article focuses on the apparently contradictory findings of official statistics and self-report surveys. Elliott and Ageton argue that the domain of behaviors "captured" in official statistics is not necessarily the same as those measured in self-report surveys. When self-report data are shifted toward more serious offenses that are more representative of UCR data, Elliott and Ageton find differences by race and social class. What Elliott and Ageton are able to demonstrate is that when all forms of delinquency are considered together, a masking effect occurs that dilutes racial or class differences. However, by creating more meaningful categories of delinquent activity, we can detect differences. Additionally, the use of a broader range of delinquent behaviors further enhances the sharpness of these differences.

The painful question we must now confront is whether or not social class and race are related to delinquency. Thornberry, Elliot, and Ageton would most likely vote "yes," while Tittle, Villemez, Cohen, and Kluegel would probably vote "no." Black and Reiss appear to say "maybe," depending on the characteristics of the local citizens more than on the juvenile justice system itself. One problem we face is that we do not have a common definition of *delinquency*. Is it the range of behaviors measured by self-report surveys or official statistics? The precise meaning of *delinquency* differs not only from one self-report to another but from one jurisdiction to another in official statistics. Hence, there may be a lot of "apples and oranges" in these comparisons.

A second problem is that assessing the importance of social class has to do with the way the findings are interpreted. For example, many studies find that blacks are more often involved in serious delinquent behavior than whites. But does this mean that race *explains* or *predicts* delinquency? A higher rate of involvement for blacks in criminal activity does not necessarily mean that race is a powerful explanatory variable in the prediction of delinquent behavior. In examining all the possible correlates of delinquency, one needs to keep a wary eye on the analytic method and the interpretation of the findings.

Finally, the article by Stephen Cernkovich and Peggy Giordano questions the traditional image of female delinquents as being somehow "different" from male delinquents. For some, female delinquency entails primarily petty offenses, while others see a significant convergence between male and female delinquency in the past decade, and still others suggest that there never was nor is any significant difference in deviant activity between two sexes. Cernkovich and Giordano find that males do report more delinquent involvement than females but that the overall pattern for both sexes is quite similar. In other words, the difference is measured in terms of degree rather than kind. Further analysis reveals that for most status offenses and drug-related offenses, the differences were not statistically significant. Even greater similarity for males and females results when the sample is grouped into whites and nonwhites. There is a very high degree of similarity among males and females by racial group, but the pattern of delinquency is similar for the four racial groups. Cernkovich and Giordano conclude that female delinquency is not such an oddity that it should be treated differently from male delinquency. Whether this recent characterization of the female offender is the product of better data collection or represents a significant change in the status of women is not totally clear.

These six discussions are intended to highlight a controversial area in the study of delinquency. Race, sex, and social class are major variables in delinquency research. The debate will undoubtedly continue until data can be collected and analyzed that specifically address these issues. As stated in each of these articles, we need to exercise a great deal of caution in accepting any single study, and we must continue to search for consistent patterns or similar findings among a wide array of research endeavors.

SECTION FOUR

The Search for Physiological and Psychological Causes

Any fan of old horror movies is no doubt familiar with scenes wherein an otherwise normal person injects himself with a criminal's blood and is driven to murder and mayhem, or wherein a dead criminal's hand is grafted onto the arm of an injured concert pianist, who subsequently strangles everyone within his range. Such movies are filled with allusions to "the criminal mind," "compulsion," "psychopaths," "depravity," and "disease." Criminality is viewed as a product of something basically different about the offender's biological makeup, so powerful that it can infect others and compel them to commit horrible crimes.

While students of crime causation reject the view that criminality can be passed on to others through transfusions or grafts, the idea that some people are born criminals has been advocated in a variety of forms in the history of criminology. An Italian physician, Cesare Lombroso, one of the most influential scholars in the early development of criminology as a scientific discipline, argued that about 40 percent of criminals were genetic throwbacks to more primitive humans (1911). A similar position was advocated by E. A. Hooton (1939), a Harvard anthropologist, in the late 1930s. However, their work had serious methodological shortcomings, and the safest conclusion at present is that there is no evidence of a born criminal type.

Nevertheless, the possibility that there are genetic, physical, or organic characteristics that differentiate offenders from nonoffenders has not been totally dismissed. In the study of delinquency, the characteristic that has received the most attention is body build. William Sheldon, a physician and professor of psychology, arguing that the body should be the starting point for the understanding of personality and behavior, began searching for differences in the "somatotypes" of delinquent boys. A person's somatotype was measured by the predominance of different types of tissue. A person characterized by a predominance of skin, appendages, and nervous tissue was high in "ectomorphy." A person with a preponderance of structures associated with digestion and the assimilation of food was high in "endomophy," while an individual characterized by a predominance of bone, muscle, and connective tissue was high in "mesomorphy." Sheldon did not make any predictions about what type would be unusually common among delinquent boys. Comparing measurements of boys from 200 wards of a home for delinquents in Boston between 1939 and 1942 with measurements of 4,000 college students, Sheldon found the delinquent boys to be primarily mesomorphic, or "on the hefty and meaty side." Based on his research, Sheldon advocated the compilation of biological records to determine which individuals were "biologically best."

William Sheldon's work had serious shortcomings, the most obvious problem stemming from the samples compared. The discovery of differences between a select college sample and youths in a home for delinquent boys may reflect differential selection due to the institutions involved. Moreover, the assumption that different body types are connected with a personality or temperament that subsequently affects behavior was never tested. Body type might come to be associated with delinquency if certain builds were to make participation in some activities easy or if recruitment into some types of delinquent activities were affected by physical attributes.

William Sheldon (1949) was not the only researcher to find differences in body type between delinquent youths and supposedly nondelinquent control groups. The first reading in this section summarizes the results of a much better designed study by Sheldon Glueck and Eleanor Glueck, which examined the physical, psychological, and sociological characteristics of 500 youths with delinquent records and 500 nondelinquent youths in the Boston area in the late 1940s. The groups compared were matched as closely as possible in terms of age, ethnicity, intelligence, and residence. The results for body build, health, intelligence, psychiatric makeup, and personality structure were summarized in highlights of their larger work, which was entitled *Unraveling Juvenile Delinquency*.

A more recent analysis of the relationship between intelligence and delinquency is presented in Travis Hirschi and Michael Hindelang's article, which presents a revisionist view of the issue. It is revisionist in the sense that sociologists have tended to dismiss intelligence as a correlate of crime and delinquency and to cite selectively those sources that suggest such a dismissal. Hirschi and Hindelang's reanalysis suggests that intelligence is a significant correlate and that the important issue is to explain the manner in which that significance is generated.

Perspectives based on the assumption that a considerable number of people who break the law are fundamentally different types of human beings have been supplanted by other views. These emphasize that biological characteristics may encourage crime under certain conditions, and attribute human problems to experiences that anyone could encounter in the course of his or her life. The search for differences in the psychological makeup of offenders that supposedly reflect the combined influence of heredity and environment is represented in the Glueck selection and continued in the article by Michael Hindelang on the relationship between self-reports of delinquency and scores on personality inventories commonly used for psychological assessments. Hindelang's work improves on previous psychological research because it does not rely on a comparison of officially processed delinquents with a control sample of youths thought to be nondelinquent. Rather, he examines the ability of the inventories to predict involvement in delinquency based on what students say they have been doing. Moreover, he can test a number of arguments to the effect that any relationships found are due to other variables, such as social class, gender, and age.

There are different types of psychological theories, and many prominent psychologists feel that the search for personality differences is a fruitless approach to either understanding or changing human behavior. Rather than explain human behavior in terms of an individual's mental characteristics or personality traits, some psychologists advocate concentrating on external stimuli and their impact on observable behavior. The most famous modern proponent of this view, B. F. Skinner, argues that if a behavioral approach is adopted, we can both study human behavior more scientifically and identify those aspects of the environment that can be modified to change behavior. To a behaviorist, personality traits are merely characteristics attributed to individuals on the basis of behavior (i.e., answering questions, reacting to inkblots, and so on): they do not explain the behavior itself or any conduct associated with those traits. Rather, the explanation rests with the world external to the individual. The selection from B. F. Skinner's *Beyond Freedom and Dignity* illustrates the conflict among proponents of the various psychological schools of thought.

While Skinner and others have advocated a behavioral approach to explaining human conduct in general, two sociologists, Robert Burgess and Ronald Akers, have specifically rewritten a classic statement on the learning of criminal behavior in terms of "operant theory," a kind of learning theory advocated by behaviorists. From this perspective, the learning process resulting in delinquency can be described in terms of contingencies of reinforcement and punishment as individuals interact with their environments. For our purposes, we include their article here because the focus is on the learning process experienced by individuals who come to participate in delinquency and crime. The study identifies the basic learning mechanisms involved and does not specify the distribution of such experiences in society. Sociologists have played a key role in specifically expanding learning theories to cover deviant behavior, but the basic behavioral theory drawn on was developed by psychologists.

REFERENCES

Hooton, E. A. 1939. *Crime and the Man*. Cambridge, Mass.: Harvard University Press.

Lombroso, C. 1911. *Crime: Its Causes and Remedies.* Boston: Little, Brown.

Sheldon, W. H. 1949. *The Varieties of Delinquent Youth.* New York: Harper and Row.

Some Highlights of Unraveling Juvenile Delinquency: *Characteristics of Delinquents and Nondelinquents*

Sheldon Glueck and Eleanor Glueck

INTRODUCTORY

In seeking the answer to the question why some children of families subjected to the pressures of underprivileged urban regions develop a tendency to antisocial behavior while others manage to comply essentially with the rules of society and law, one must not confine the inquiry to a study of intellectual and personality traits. Such characteristics do not express themselves in a human vacuum. They are at least partially anchored in bodily constitution; they are not all due to life's experiences. The bodily constitution is, moreover, not only basic but first in point of time in the history of the individual.

While it is risky to generalize about the exact participation of heredity and environment in the end-product of human personality and character, it may safely be said that bodily constitution embraces the more fixed and permanent core of the human being (anatomically and physiologically); and in essential structure it is probably determined genetically, although affected, also, by early intra- or extra-uterine environmental influences.

But, in addition to body type, certain findings from psychologic (especially Rorschach) and psychiatric tests and interviews are relevant to an adequate assessment of the two sets of youths we are concerned with. For details and supporting data the reader is referred to *Unraveling Juvenile Delinquency* and two derivative works: *Physique and Delinquency*[1] and *Family Environment and Delinquency*.[2] In the present work we present a bare outline of the materials as part of the necessary briefing preliminary to setting forth the data of the follow-up investigations of the two sets of human beings under comparison.

BODY BUILD

Do our delinquents differ significantly in physical composition from the nondelinquents? And, if so, how?[3]

Comparison of the physiques of the 500 delinquents and 500 nondelinquents disclosed certain findings that cannot be ignored in any comprehensive analysis of the etiologic roots involved in delinquency, just as the under-the-roof culture of the two sets of boys cannot be ignored. First, as a group, the law-violating boys have sturdier bodies than the law-abiding ones. Second, their bodily structure is more harmonious. Third, they are generally somewhat more masculine. Most important, if one reflects on the anthropologic findings regarding bodily indices and physique types, one is forced to the conclusion that the majority of persistent juvenile delinquents tend to be of the *mesomorphic* (muscular, well-knit) type. This is important not only in itself but because the various physique types into which human beings can be classified[4] tend to be related to certain traits and factors which can be plotted along a biosocial continuum.[5] When certain characteristics especially conducive to the commission of antisocial acts are found, for example, to characterize mesomorphs, this constitutional type *and* the related traits must somehow be involved in etiology, though several stages removed from the acts of persistent delinquency. To illustrate: it was found that the mesomorphic physique type is more highly characterized by such traits suitable to aggressive acts as physical strength, energy, insensitivity, the tendency to express tensions and frustrations in action; and the mesomorphic type was also found to be relatively free from such *inhibitions* to antisocial adventures as feelings of inadequacy, marked submissiveness to authority, emotional instability, and the like.[6]

It is not unreasonable to assume that the basic reason for the excess of mesomorphs among delinquents may be that boys of predominantly mesomorphic physique are endowed with traits that equip them especially for a delinquent role when under the pressure of malign sociocultural conditions, while endomorphs (to cite a body type in which the incidence of delinquents and nondelinquents in our

Reprinted by permission of the publishers from *Delinquents and Nondelinquents in Perspective* by Sheldon and Eleanor Glueck (Cambridge, Mass: Harvard University Press, 1968), pp. 18–28.

samples is similar), being less energetic and less likely to act out their drives, have a lower *delinquency potential* than mesomorphs. True, other traits investigated, such as aggressiveness, adventurousness, acquisitiveness — although etiologically involved in the end-product of delinquency — do not vary significantly in incidence among body types. Nevertheless, boys who possess certain other characteristics, such as excessive energy and a tendency to act out tensions, frustrations, feelings of aggression, thirst for adventure, acquisitive impulses, and the like, are especially prone to delinquency, particularly if they live in the exciting and culturally deprived regions of underprivileged urban areas.

But there are other characteristics of the two sets of boys we are discussing that may also be relevant to etiology.

HEALTH

No clinical study of delinquents is deemed complete without a physical examination, but the reason for requiring exploration into the health of maladjusted youth is not always clear. It is obvious that there may be endocrinologic and other deficiencies related to symptoms of fatigue, irritability, and the like; or sensory or muscular handicaps, which have not only a physiologic but a psychologic significance for attitude and behavior. Apart from this, there are special emotional attributes, such as the frequently alluded to "inferiority complex," with its overcompensatory reactive behavior, which may be significant in analyzing the roots of maladjustment and delinquency.

At all events, the aim in *Unraveling Juvenile Delinquency* was to leave no stone unturned in the baffling search for the roots and dynamics of causation.[7] Summarizing the chief findings of the medical examination which was given to both groups of boys by a competent physician-psychiatrist on the staff,[8] it was found that the view that delinquents are in poorer health than nondelinquents from similar general environments is not justified; little difference was discovered on standard physical examination between the two groups.

With respect to their health as infants and young children, no differences between the two sets of boys were revealed from careful inquiry of their mothers and consultation of early medical records, except for the two important facts that a considerably higher proportion of the delinquents were reported to have been enuretic and extremely restless (hyperkinetic) children. In their susceptibility to disease and infection and their immunity to contagious diseases, the two groups resembled each other.

More significant, and in harmony with the low incidence of ectomorphs among the delinquents, a *lower* percentage of them than of the control group of nondelinquents were found to have various neurologic handicaps (63.7% vs. 72.7%).

Although there is no over-all difference between the two groups in observable evidences of functional deviations, a few differences in the incidence of certain of these deviations might be mentioned: tics and ambidexterity are less prevalent among the delinquents (3.0% vs. 8.4%), while extreme nailbiting is more characteristic of them (21.4% vs. 15.6%).

INTELLIGENCE

It will be recalled that at the outset of the inquiry into the differences and similarities between the 500 delinquent boys and 500 nondelinquents we matched the two groups, pair by pair, in respect to *general* (global) intelligence. The 500 pairs encompassed a wide range of intelligence quotients. Thus, 140 of the delinquents and 152 of the nondelinquents had an I.Q. of 100 or over on the Wechsler-Bellevue Full Scale Intelligence Test; at the other end of the scale, 359 of the former and 346 of the latter ranged downward in I.Q. from 99 to 60. The average intelligence quotient of the two groups was 92 for the delinquents and 94 for the nondelinquents.[9]

Yet the two sets of boys could well differ in respect to the specific skills and abilities that enter into the composition of global intelligence, and it was indeed found that there were differences in respect to the *composition* of global intelligence. These were determined through application of the Wechsler-Bellevue Test and, in part, of the Rorschach Test. It was found that the delinquent group was somewhat more apt in those intellectual tasks in which the approach to meaning is by direct physical relationships with a minimal dependence on intermediate symbols or abstract thinking. This may in part explain their inferior school achievement and their more general dislike of the usual classroom tasks. Also, the delinquents were found to be more erratic in their intellectual capacities than the more consistent and steady nondelinquents.

While the two groups tend to resemble each other in many of the more qualitative and creative expressions of intelligence (such as originality, intuition, phantasy), they differ somewhat in others which would seem to be closely associated with capacity or incapacity to make adequate conventional adjustments to the demands of social life. Thus, fewer delinquents than nondelinquents have adequate powers of observation and fewer show a potential capacity for objective interests; and to a greater extent than the control group, the delinquents are unrealistic thinkers, lack "common sense," and are unmethodical in approaching their problems. Reflection upon these differences, especially the ones involving the deeper intellectual tendencies of the two groups, suggests that such strivings are the ones which are especially interwoven with deep-rooted emotional dynamics. They are, therefore, the very mental tendencies likely to be involved not only in ability to cope with ordinary school tasks but also in the general processes of socialization and adjustment to the realistic demands of life.

PSYCHIATRIC SIZE-UP

To the experienced and skillful psychiatrist, children often reveal their emotional stresses and strains much more readily than do adults. Through long experience in interviewing boys, the psychiatric member of our staff had developed a special flair for gaining quick and sympathetic rapport with the boys.

The aim of this portion of the inquiry was to obtain as objective an estimate of the emotional make-up of the 500 delinquent and 500 nondelinquent boys as could be revealed by the psychiatrist's diagnostic art. Therefore, following the original plan of the research to avoid possible circular reasoning, the psychiatrist, in interviewing the boys, did not have access to data about them from other areas of the inquiry.

Briefly, the lawbreakers were found to function on a less efficient level and were less stable emotionally than the nondelinquents. At the same time, they were more dynamic and energetic; more aggressive, adventurous, suggestible, and stubborn. This combination is likely to result in inability or unwillingness to abide by the law's restrictions; for such boys were much inclined to impulsive, unreflective discharge of their energy drives, thereby breaking through the bonds imposed upon them by societal custom and law but not adequately internalized by them. Certain sources of motivation can get such boys into troublesome conflict with society's codes. The delinquents were, for example, much more inclined than the other boys to immediate indulgence of their appetities and were more eager to acquire material possessions.

To such a system of internal forces, which impels toward self-centered satisfaction of impulse irrespective of the prohibitions of custom and law, should be added the finding that basic personality orientations among the delinquents made it more difficult for them to conform to acceptable standards. As a group, they were found to be less conventional than the law-abiding boys, and not nearly so conscientious in achieving their goals. They were also, as already noted, less realistic in facing situations; less practical in considering the feasibility of a contemplated course of conduct; far less critical of themselves and, correspondingly, more self-centered.

Moreover, as we have seen, there is much more in the family background of the delinquents than of the nondelinquents that is stress-producing, so that a far higher proportion of them than of the other boys displayed emotional tensions arising from faulty father–son or mother–son relationships. More of the delinquents than of the boys of the control group had marked conflicts arising out of faulty adjustment of their problems of sexual identification, out of poor relations with companions, out of inability to make a satisfactory compromise between ambition and reality, and out of feelings of inferiority. Significantly, the delinquents tended to resolve their mental struggles through "acting out" their difficulties (extroversive behavior), the nondelinquents through turning them inward (introversion).

These psychiatric findings, so obviously related to the mechanisms tending to inadequate and improper social adjustment, are in general harmony with those revealed independently by the other avenues of exploration. Standing alone, they are highly suggestive hints — though not complete explanations — of why one set of boys inclined to persistent delinquency, while the other, in similar external environmental settings, managed somehow to get along acceptably. When fitted into the total picture, they gain significantly in etiologic relevancy. They tend not only to show that there is much more to the causal explanation of delinquency than indiscriminate and nondiscriminating attribution of etiology to "living in slums," or the "deprivation of opportunity," or other generalized external cultural matrices, but they tend also to confirm, in many respects, the findings derived from the deep-probing Rorschach personality-character tests.

PERSONALITY-CHARACTER STRUCTURE

It is often taken for granted that the way a person gets along in life is almost wholly dependent on his "brains,' that is, his intelligence. But probings of the mainsprings of conduct and social relations tend more and more to stress the role of temperamental and emotional forces in the development of personality and character[10] and the channeling of conduct. Intelligence is of course a powerful instrument of adaptation and for the solution of life's problems; but the way a person *employs* his intellect depends a great deal on the deeper dynamics of the organism — the ebb and flow of feelings, the trends, thrusts, and tensions of emotion that pull the levers behind the scenes of personality and character. So it becomes of the utmost importance to obtain insights into the subsurface forces that influence individual make-up and behavior tendencies. To some extent this has been done in the foregoing section on the psychiatric diagnoses of the boys. There are other techniques for plumbing the depths of psychic structure and dynamics: psychoanalysis, hypnoanalysis, narcoanalysis and others. A systematic and relatively simple means, however, is furnished by a number of "projective tests," including the Rorschach Test, selected at the time our research was decided upon as most suited to the purpose.

In earlier pages, in which the bodily types of delinquents and nondelinquents were compared, the concern was with biologic and essentially hereditary traits, and with a great variety of sociocultural forces that played upon the basic organism of the boys. Now we shall draw in the dynamic emotional moorings of personality and character revealed by the Rorschach Test. For the personality and characterial traits revealed by such a test are, in a sense, the admixtures of the interplay of original endowment and repeated experiences, particularly those of the first few affectively charged years of life.

The Rorschach Test consists of ten symmetrical ink-blots (most of them black, some colored) which look as if they had been made by throwing drops of ink on a paper and folding it in the middle, this resulting in a design often reminiscent of a butterfly. Through long clinical employment of the test on various groups of persons in different countries, its significance has been found to be fairly dependable in revealing the inner mental life; it has established its value as a prober of personality and character. The subject's reaction to the blots is projected out of the depths of his personality without his being able successfully to disguise his inner feelings and emotional attitudes. These responses are then scored according to a standard scheme and interpreted by a skilled psychologist, in respect to *apperception* — that is, the subject's general size-up of the blots, the *quality* of his reactions, and their *content*.[11] The subject is scored on these various aspects of his responses in accordance with established standards, and his score is tabulated to yield a Rorschach *psychogram*, which provides a panoramic view of his temperamental-emotional topography, including both surface and subsurface features. In other words, the diagnosis is not based upon any single response; it is the patterning of responses that is significant. The Rorschach Test thus projects the deeper, often subconscious, elements of mental activity in such a manner that to the expert they reveal highly significant features of structure, tensions, and dynamics of personality and character.

Briefly summarizing the results of comparisons of the delinquents and the control group in respect to the Rorschach Test, the first category is that of basic attitudes toward authority and society; and in the traits here encompassed, it was found that the delinquents were markedly distinguishable from the law-abiding boys by their unwillingness or inability to tame their natural impulses toward self-indulgent behavior in order to bring their drives into line with the authoritative demands of the home, the school, and the larger society. While only slightly more self-assertive than the nondelinquents, the boys who got into trouble were found to be far more socially defiant, far less submissive, and more ambivalent, to authority.

In regard to feelings of insecurity, anxiety, inferiority, frustration, a significantly higher proportion of the delinquents than of the control group were found to be subject to feelings of not being recognized or appreciated, and of resentment. However, the delinquents as a group had an appreciably *lower* incidence of other handicapping emotional attitudes, such as feelings of anxiety or insecurity, of helplessness, of fear of failure.

Surprisingly little difference was found between the two groups in the degree to which they felt unwanted or unloved, or not taken care of, or not being taken seriously. It may be that, in the rough and tough milieu in which the two sets of boys lived, such feelings are quite common among children. While this situation is to be deplored and ought certainly to be coped with in a responsible society, the similar incidence among delinquents and nondelinquents of such emotional attitudes makes it unlikely that they have any close causal relationship to persistent delinquency, although they may act as differentiative catalytic agents when other psychologic factors are brought into play.

With respect to kindliness and hostility, it was found that the delinquent boys were markedly less cooperative in their relationships with those with whom they were closely associated; a substantially greater proportion of them than of the nondelinquents had conscious or unconscious hostile impulses; they were more suspicious of the motives of others; they were more destructive. And more of the delinquents than of the nondelinquents were armed with an exaggeratedly defensive attitude toward life.

As to traits subsumed under the heading of dependence and independence, it was found that the delinquents felt far less dependent than did the nondelinquents; they were less conforming, far less conventional, and more confident of their ability to handle their own problems.

As to the goals of strivings, it was found that the law violators as a group were more narcissistic, more orally receptive (parasitic), and more destructive-sadistic (cruel) than the boys who conformed to the legal order. Correlatively, the delinquents were far less masochistic (self-punishing) than the law-abiding boys.

With respect to certain general qualities of personality, the delinquents again were found to possess qualities which made it difficult for them to adapt to society's prohibitions. They were considerably more impulsive and vivacious than the law-abiding boys, less self-controlled, and they tended to act out their emotional tensions.

Finally, it was apparent that there were some differences between delinquents and nondelinquents in the extent and nature of mental abnormality or pathology.[12] A somewhat higher proportion of the lawbreakers than of the law-abiding youngsters were found to have a mental abnormality of one kind or another (51.4% vs. 44.3%). Many more delinquents than boys in the control group were described by the Rorschach analysis as "poorly adjusted, asocial, poorly adapted," or "primitive," apart from their acts of delinquency (16.9% vs. 5.9%). On the other hand, neither definite psychoses nor disturbances of the central nervous system played a significant role in the lives of these two sets of boys. Although it is often claimed that many delinquents are "psychopathic"[13] or show marked trends toward such a condition, only 7.3% of the delinquents and 0.4% of the nondelinquents were so diagnosed.[14]

Severe neuroticism was found to exist in only 3.2% of the delinquents and 5.1% of the other boys. However, mild neuroticism (a condition in which the neurosis does not prevent the individual from quite efficient and not too painful social adaptation) was found among 16.3% of the former and 23.2% of the latter; and youths with distinct neurotic trends but not classifiable in the two former categories amounted to 5.1% among the delinquents and 7.5% among the nondelinquents. Totaling the boys diagnosed as markedly or mildly neurotic, or with neurotic trends, it becomes clearer that there is less neuroticism among the delinquents than among the control group (24.6% vs. 35.8%).

To summarize the findings of the Rorschach Test, it is clear that the delinquents possessed to an excessive degree certain traits and tendencies likely to interfere with adequate and wholesome adjustment to the requirements of the social order. In much greater proportion than their nondelinquent counterparts they were defiant, and they were ambivalent toward or nonsubmissive to authority. They were more resentful. They were far more hostile, suspicious, and destructive. The goals of their drives were to a far greater extent both parasitic and destructive-sadistic. They were definitely more impulsive and less self-controlled. They were far less cooperative and markedly less conventional in their ideas, feelings, and behavior than the nondelinquents.

Some of the traits possessed in excess by the delinquents are of a kind which, if guided into socially acceptable channels, are far from undesirable. Such characteristics as a tendency to "act out" their difficulties (extroversion), greater freedom from fear of failure and defeat, and less dependence on others, might, under proper circumstances and influential guidance, be assets rather than liabilities.

SUMMARY

The variations in physique type and derivative traits, and the marked differences in incidence of so many of the personality-character traits of boys growing up in underprivileged urban areas should convince the reader that, while the study of environmental pressures is important, examination of how and why different children respond to these external pressures is indispensable. It is not alone exposure to unwholesome environmental experiences that can explain delinquency, but rather what these experiences mean, selectively, in the shaping of personality and character and the canalizing or sublimating of primitive impulses.

If one reflects on the differences between the two groups of boys in their basic character traits, it becomes apparent that these variations are not altogether haphazard but tend to fall into a general, meaningful personality pattern, despite the fact that there are hints here and there of subpatterns. Among the delinquents, they form themselves into a cluster of associated energy-expressing and emotion-discharging characteristics of the uninhibited, untamed, unreflective child; and there is little mystery about the "causes" of persistent maladapted behavior when one considers the ease with which modern urban conditions supply the theater of action for boys of this nature.

However, one must not ignore the familial backgrounds which helped to differentiate between the two sets of boys. All these influences contribute to the distinction between the two, and one would make a serious mistake to reach for some simple general abstraction to account for this.

Notes

1. Sheldon and Eleanor Glueck (New York: Harper, 1956; New York: Kraus Reprint, 1965).

2. Sheldon and Eleanor Glueck (London: Routledge & Kegan Paul; Boston: Houghton Mifflin, 1962).

3. As a basis for this part of the original inquiry, full-length photographs (front, side, rear) of the 500 delinquents and 500 nondelinquents were taken. (For detailed method of taking the photographs and of analyzing them anthropologically, see *Unraveling Juvenile Delinquency*, Appendix C, p. 307, prepared by Carl C. Seltzer.) The reader is reminded that our delinquents and nondelinquents were originally matched in accordance with their ethnic origins (Italian delinquent with Italian nondelinquent, Irish with Irish, Greek with Greek, etc.). This precludes the possibilty that any dfferences in the physique of delinquents and that of nondelinquents are due to basic differences in racial stock.

4. Dominance of the *mesomorphic* component among the delinquents is shown by the fact that, while 60.4% of that group could be so classified, only 30.8% of the nondelinquents were mesomorphic. Dominance of the *ectomorphic* component among the *nondelinquents* was found in the fact that while 39.4% of such boys were so classifiable, only 14.4% of the delinquents were. The numbers involved in the other somatotypes (*endomorphic* and *balanced*) were small. See *Unraveling Juvenile Delinquency*, p. 193.

5. Glueck, *Physique and Delinquency*.

6. *Ibid*., chap. XI.

7. One of the lines of investigation we wanted to carry out was to compare the electroencephalograms of the two sets of boys; but when *Unraveling* was begun the standards of the indications of this type of inquiry had not yet been sufficiently worked out for the "normal."

8. Dr. Bryant E. Moulton, previously with the Judge Baker Guidance Center of Boston.

9. See *Unraveling Juvenile Delinquency*, Table IV-7 and Appendix B. Dr. David Wechsler, originator of the test, regarded this as a very close match.

10. These two concepts are often related, combined, or used interchangeably in the literature, stemming largely, we suppose, from the difficulty of dividing personality and character patterns into their constituent traits and of determining the typical affinities of individual traits to temperamental and characterial types. It is clarifying if one conceives personality to be the totality of physical, temperamental, affective, and intellectual make-up of an individual. Personality is neutral so far as character is concerned; character is personality plus the ingredients of ethico-religious, parental, and other ideals or goals that typically guide or dictate an individual's conduct. A man may have a strong or weak personality, and a judgment of his personality would be similar regardless of his parental inculcation of one or another set of values and regardless of his ethical views or religious convictions. A man may have a good or bad character, and the judgment as to this depends upon the extent to which his actions typically conform to a set of ethical or religious standards within which he is judged. However, character type is related more or less to the nature of personality structure.

11. In regard to apperception, responses are noted and evaluated as being to the *whole* blot, to *details*, and the like. In respect to quality, three types of basic mental responses are set down: *form*, *movement*, and *color*. In regard to content, the subject may, for example, recognize the form of an animal, or a human being, or an object, a landscape, some anatomical pattern, or some abstract design. Originality and banality of his responses also are noted and integrated into the total personality size-up.

12. These diagnoses were corroborated by independent classifications made by the staff psychiatrist. See *Unraveling Juvenile Delinquency*, p. 242, n. 8.

13. The Rorschach experts used this term to designate all marked mental and emotional deviations that did not clearly belong in any one of the other diagnostic groupings.

14. The telltale marks that justify an incontrovertible diagnosis of psychopathic personality — difficult to ascertain even in adulthood — may not be fully apparent in boyhood.

Intelligence and Delinquency: A Revisionist Review

Travis Hirschi and Michael J. Hindelang
State University of New York, Albany

Recent research on intelligence and delinquency suggests that (1) the relation is at least as strong as the relation of either class or race to official delinquency; (2) the relation is stronger than the relation of either class or race to self-reported delinquency. In an analysis of the history of the research on the IQ-delinquency relation, we trace the developments leading to the current textbook position that IQ is not an important factor in delinquency. This position, which came into vogue about forty years ago and is still held by many sociologists, has its roots in: (1) a medical to sociological paradigm shift in this century; (2) the failure of subsequent research to substantiate the early exorbitant claims that low IQ was a necessary and sufficient condition for illegal behavior; (3) early negative reviews of research on this question by Sutherland and others; (4) reservations about the validity of the measurement of both IQ and delinquency; (5) erroneous interpretation of research findings; (6) speculation regarding factors which might account for the relation. It is noted that many currently prominent sociological theories of delinquency implicitly or explicitly use IQ as a crucial theoretical element. We show that IQ has an effect on delinquency independent of class and race, and we argue that this effect is mediated through a host of school variables.

Few groups in American society have been defended more diligently by sociologists against allegations of difference than ordinary delinquents. From the beginning, the thrust of sociological theory has been to deny the relevance of individual differences to an explanation of delinquency, and the thrust of sociological criticism has been to discount research findings apparently to the contrary. "Devastating" reviews of the research literature typically meet with uncritical acceptance or even applause, and new theories and "new criminologies" are constructed in a research vacuum, a vacuum that may itself claim research support.

A major source of this stance toward individual differences is the notion widely held in the field of deviance that "kinds of people" theories are non- or even anti-sociological. Most of the major theorists in the area (Sutherland, Merton, Cohen, Becker) have more or less explicitly argued this point, and efforts to bring criminology "up-to-date" with the rest of sociology frequently imply that interest in individual differences is an outmoded relic of the field's positivistic past (e.g., Matza, 1964; Taylor et al, 1973). Another source of this stance toward difference is frankly moral. According to Liazos (1972), who provides extensive documentation, sociologists repeatedly assert that deviants are "at least as good as anyone else." If Liazos' analysis is any guide, we may assume it is easy to confuse the moral-evaluative "as good as" with the empirical "the same as." For example, Liazos goes on to argue that the repeated assertion that " 'deviants' are *not different* may raise the very doubts we want to dispel." Sociologists have observed for some time that, "always and everywhere, *difference* is the occasion and excuse for ignoring the equal claims of others" (Ross, 1901:25). They therefore feel duty-bound, it seems, to protect delinquents from those who would justify abusing them on these grounds.

Among the many possible individual differences between delinquents and nondelinquents, none is apparently more threatening to the integrity of the field and to its moral commitments than IQ. To the standard list of scientific and moral arguments against IQ, the sociological student of crime and delinquency can add the weight of a half-century struggle against biological theories and the predatory social ethic they are alleged to foster. In fact, the single argument against IQ developed within criminology is sufficiently simple and persuasive that the standard list need not be invoked. At the time criminology became a subfield of sociology, marked differences in IQ between delinquents and nondelinquents were pretty much taken for granted, and a major task confronting those wishing to claim the field for the sociological perspective was to call these alleged differences into question. This task was successfully accomplished. IQ, it was confidently suggested, doesn't matter (see Sutherland, 1924:108). Today, textbooks in crime and delinquency ignore IQ or impatiently explain to the reader that IQ is no longer taken seriously by knowledgeable students simply because no differences worth considering have been revealed by research.

As we shall show, the textbooks are wrong.[1] IQ is an important correlate of delinquency. It is at least as important as social class or race. This fact has straightforward implications for sociological theorizing and research, most of which

[1] In a more general treatment of the measurement and correlates of delinquency, Gordon (1976) independently reaches conclusions about the importance of IQ that are very close to those reported here.

From *American Sociological Review,* Vol. 42 (August 1977), pp. 571–587. Reprinted by permission of the American Sociological Association and the authors.

has taken place within the context of official denial of IQ differences. Its implications for social policy are variably straightforward and are, in any event, strictly irrelevant to questions of the current impact of IQ on delinquency: the actual relation between IQ and delinquency must be the standard against which all arguments, including our own, are judged.

The Current Textbook View

Many textbooks do not even mention IQ (e.g., Gibbons, 1970; Bloch and Geis, 1962). Most, however, introduce the subject and then argue against its significance. The basic position is that there are no differences in IQ between delinquents and nondelinquents. The research and reviews most frequently cited in support of this conclusion are now over forty years old (e.g., Murchison, 1926; Sutherland, 1931; Zeleny, 1933). The tendency to rely on summaries provided by other textbooks, especially, in this case, those written by psychologists, is much in evidence.

Despite the selectivity of textbook summaries of the evidence, most of them leave the reader with the distinct impression that IQ may be a very important cause of delinquency after all. Few textbook writers seem able to resist additional arguments that have the effect of undercutting their basic position:

> It is now generally recognized that so-called intelligence tests tend to measure the degree to which the individual has assimilated and internalized middle-class values rather than intelligence.
>
> We could anticipate that a feeble-minded individual would be more readily incarcerated than other individuals. (Haskell and Yablonsky, 1974:216)
>
> It is not mental deficiency per se which results in crime; rather the inability of a mentally deficient person to make adequate social adjustments. . . . (Johnson, 1968:173)
>
> Although a higher percentage of delinquent children come from the ranks of the mental defective, particularly from those of borderline intelligence, it is not the mental deficiency per se but the inability of the child to make adequate school or social adjustments that usually results in delinquency. (Sutherland and Cressey, 1974:174, quoting Coleman, 1950)
>
> The great proportion of persons with low intelligence scores undoubtedly are nondeviants, whereas there are large numbers of persons with above normal intelligence who are. (Clinard, 1968:170)

All of these arguments take for granted a negative correlation between IQ and delinquency. The "middle-class values" interpretation of IQ tests suggests that scores on these tests may well be the strongest predictor of delinquency available. The "not per se" argument asserts that the relation is, in fact, causal in the usual meaning of the term—i.e., nonspurious. The "more readily incarcerated" view contradicts the "not per se" argument by suggesting a direct link between IQ and, at least, official delinquency. And the "great proportion" argument asserts only that the relation is not perfect. Still, the current view, simply stated, is that IQ makes no difference. This view is not supported by the results of research.

Recent Research on Official Delinquency

At least half a dozen recent studies permit examination of the effects of IQ on official delinquency. These studies have been conducted in diverse settings, they rely on a variety of measures of IQ and of delinquency, and they all employ some measure of control for the effects of such variables as social class and race. All of them show IQ to be an important predictor of official delinquency.[2]

How strong is this effect? Since social class and race are considered important correlates of official delinquency by almost everyone, they should provide a sufficiently stringent criterion and be available for comparison. Further, since both class and race are frequently used to discount the effects of IQ, this comparison will provide evidence relative to the common argument that IQ effects are merely a by-product of race and class effects.

IQ, Social Class and Official Delinquency

Reiss and Rhodes (1961) examined the juvenile court records of more than 9,200 in-school *white* boys in Davidson County, Tennessee. Using three-category divisions on occupational status of the head of household and on IQ, they found that the rate (per 100) of court adjudication ranged from 5.7 in the high to 9.6 in the low status groups, and from 4.8 in the high to 10.3 in the low IQ groups. In other words, the rate of adjudication in the lowest occupational group was 1.7 times that of the highest occupational group, while the rate of the adjudication in the lowest IQ group was 2.1 times that of the highest IQ group.[3] Since the distributions of occupational status and IQ were roughly comparable, in the Davidson County data IQ is more important than social class as a predictor of official delinquency among white boys.

Table 1. Percent Committing Two or More Official Delinquent Acts by IQ (Stanford Binet) and Race[a]

	IQ				
	0–19	20–39	40–59	60–79	80–99
White males	22.6 (204)	25.6 (282)	14.6 (309)	8.4 (341)	6.2 (403)
Black males	38.2 (429)	36.2 (273)	26.2 (153)	19.7 (71)	19.0 (42)

[a] IQ scores are shown as percentiles. Gammas, calculated on the entire range of delinquency scores (0–4), are –.31 for whites and –.16 for blacks.

Hirschi (1969) examined the police records of over 3,600 boys in Contra Costa County, California. Since previously published analyses do not directly compare the effects of social class and IQ, we have reanalyzed these data, with the results shown in Tables 1 and 2 (for details of data collection, see Hirschi, 1969:35–46).

In these data, the effect of IQ on official delinquency is stronger than that of father's education. Among whites, the gamma for the relationship between IQ and delinquency is –.31, while the comparable gamma for father's education is –.20; among blacks, the gammas are –.16 and –.05, respectively. Although the data are not shown, a composite measure of family status which includes employment and welfare status, presence of the father, and education and occupation of the parents shows results comparable to those for father's education in both racial categories. For whites, the gamma is –.18; for blacks, it is –.09. When the effects of this measure of family status and IQ are examined *simultaneously* within racial groups, the results are consistent with the zero-order relations. Both family status and IQ are independently related to official delinquency; the superiority of IQ in comparison with family status, however measured, is especially noticeable among blacks.

Wolfgang et al. (1972) obtained IQ scores on 8,700 of the 10,000 boys in their Philadelphia cohort. They do not present measures of association for these IQ scores and delinquency, nor do they show tabular material in which IQ is treated as an independent variable. They do, however, present average IQ scores by number of contacts with the police in groups homogeneous on class and race. The differences in average scores between chronic offenders and nondelinquents range from nine IQ points among high socioeconomic status nonwhites to fourteen IQ points among low socioeconomic

[2] Unless otherwise noted, all references to "the relation between IQ and delinquency" assume an inverse correlation.

[3] When father's occupational status was dichotomized and IQ trichotomized, the two variables were shown to have independent effects, with some tendency toward interaction: the effects of occupational status were more marked as IQ decreased, which also says that the effects of IQ were more marked for blue-collar than for white-collar boys.

Table 2. Percent Committing Two or More Official Delinquent Acts by Father's Education and Race[a]

Race	Father's Education: Less than High School Grad.	High School Graduate	Trade or Business	Some College	College Graduate
White Males	17.7 (356)	14.3 (485)	13.4 (82)	8.0 (201)	7.8 (306)
Black Males	33.8 (343)	34.4 (209)	42.1 (57)	30.8 (123)	19.1 (84)

[a] Gammas, calculated on the entire range of delinquency scores (0–4), are –.20 for whites and –.05 for blacks.

Table 3. Percent Committing Two or More Official Delinquent Acts by IQ and Race[a]

Race	IQ: Low	High
White males	24.3 (486)	9.4 (1053)
Black males	37.6 (702)	23.3 (266)

[a] IQ scores dichotomized at the 40th percentile.

status whites (Wolfgang et al., 1972:62, 93). Again, although no direct comparison with social class is possible, the Philadelphia data reveal a strong relation between IQ and delinquency independent of class.[4]

West (1973:84) followed 411 London boys over a ten-year period and "compared the delinquent and non-delinquent groups on the prevalence of low IQ in just the same way [he] compared them on other factors such as poverty, large families, or criminal parents." The relation between IQ and delinquency in West's data is substantial. While one-quarter of those with IQ scores of 110 or more had a police record, the same was true of one-half of those with IQ scores of 90 or less. Even more impressively, while only one in fifty boys with an IQ of 110 or more was a recidivist, one in five of those with an IQ of 90 or less fell in this category. West (1973:84–5) concludes from his thorough analysis that "low IQ was a significant precursor of delinquency to much the same extent as other major factors." Although he reports a stronger relation between family income and delinquency than that typically reported in American studies, IQ was able to compete with it on equal terms and to survive when family income and several other measures of family culture were controlled by a matching procedure.

It should be noted that the striking differences in delinquency produced by IQ in West's data reflect a difference in IQ of about 12 points between nondelinquents and recidivists—a difference that falls within the range of the race- and SES-specific differences calculated from the Wolfgang et al. data. West's data agree with those of Wolfgang et al. that the IQ effect is largely attributable to multiple offenders (recidivists), which may explain the relatively weak performance of IQ in studies of self-reported delinquency.

IQ, Race and Official Delinquency

Comparison of the effects of race and IQ is more difficult than the class-IQ comparison because of a greater paucity of data or, at least, of appropriately analyzed data. There can be no doubt that IQ is related to delinquency within race categories. All of the studies mentioned are consistent on this point. The relative strength of the two variables is, however, open to question.

The multiple regression analysis using number of offenses as the dependent variable presented by Wolfgang et al. (1972:275–9) includes both race and IQ. Unfortunately for present purposes, it also includes highest grade completed and number of school moves, variables which account for the bulk of the explained variance in this measure of delinquency. Thus, the fact that race places third behind these school variables and IQ accounts for virtually nothing cannot be taken as direct evidence of their relative importance. We know that IQ is strongly related to delinquency in the Wolfgang data independent of race. We know, too, that IQ is strongly related to the school variables (r=.468 for highest grade completed) that, in variance terms, do most of the work. Therefore, we know that if these intervening variables were excluded from the analysis, the proportion of variance accounted for by IQ would increase substantially.

In the Contra Costa data, IQ and race have virtually identical effects on official delinquency. For illustration, we compare a dichotomous measure of IQ with the two categories of race in Table 3.

Measures of association between IQ and delinquency and between race and delinquency reflect the percentage differences in Table 3: race and IQ are virtually identical in their ability to predict delinquency. For race, r=.26; for IQ, r=.27.

The findings of McCord and McCord (1959:66, 203) from the Cambridge-Sommerville Youth Study are sometimes cited (e.g., West, 1973:91) as showing "no connection between low IQ and delinquency." Although in the McCords' data those in the lowest IQ group (80 or below) did have an intermediate rate of conviction during the follow-up period,[5] within the normal range of IQ scores (above 80) there was a monotonic decrease in rates of conviction from almost one-half in the 81–90 IQ group to one-quarter in the 110 or more IQ group. Because those in the lowest IQ group are only ten percent of the sample, the McCords' data, too, show an inverse relation between IQ and official misconduct.

Such problems of interpretation do not arise in Short and Strodtbeck's (1965) study of gang delinquency in Chicago. They report that gang boys scored lower on "all six intelligence measures" than non-gang boys in the same (lower) class; this difference held for white and black respondents alike.

Toby and Toby (1961) found "intellectual status" to be a significant forerunner of delinquency independent of socioeconomic status. And Reckless and Dinitz (1972) found that their teacher-nominated "good" boys had IQs from 8 to 12 points higher than their teacher-nominated "bad" boys in a class-homogeneous area.[6]

All in all, it seems reasonable to conclude on the basis of currently available data that IQ is related to official delinquency and that, in fact, it is as important in predicting official delinquency as social class or race. We know of no current research findings contrary to this conclusion.

Self-Reported Delinquency

A significant consequence of the no-IQ-difference position was that it helped set the stage for extensive use of self-report methods of measuring delinquent behavior. This position explicitly asserts that delinquents are as likely as others to possess the various skills reflected by IQ tests. If, however, the assumption of

[4] Wolfgang et al. used the Philadelphia Verbal Ability Test. The typical IQ test has a standard deviation of 15.

[5] Our figures are for the experimental and control groups combined (McCord and McCord, 1959:66, 203). Strictly speaking, the McCord data apply to adult criminality as well as juvenile delinquency, since the average age of their subjects was 27 at the time data on convictions were obtained.

[6] The Toby-Toby and Reckless-Dinitz studies may be marginal to the question of IQ effects. However, this concern would carry greater weight if their results were contrary to research focusing directly on the IQ question.

equal ability is unfounded, the measurement of delinquent behavior by the self-report method may be confounded with IQ, i.e., those most likely to commit delinquent acts may be least able to report adequately on their behavior. The self-report method, especially questionnaires,[7] therefore does not provide an unambiguous test of the hypothesis that IQ is related to delinquent behavior.

In any event, most studies do find a relation between IQ and self-reported delinquency, but this relation is less robust than that found in official data. At one extreme, West (1973:158) found that 28.4 percent of the worst quarter of his sample on self-reported delinquency had low IQs, as compared to 16.6 percent in the remaining three-quarters—a difference only slightly smaller than his finding for official delinquency.

Weis (1973), too, found differences as strong as those typically reported when delinquency is measured by official data. In his study in a white upper-middle-class community near San Francisco, Weis collected Wechsler-Bellevue IQ scores and self-reports of delinquency for 255 male and female eleventh-grade students. One of the clusters emerging from his analysis was a property deviance scale that included items on theft, burglary, shoplifting and vandalism. When these scores were trichotomized, Weis found that 27 percent of those with IQ scores of less than 110, and 49 percent of those with IQ scores of 110 or more, had low scores on the property deviance scale. He found a similar difference (23% versus 41%) on a social deviance scale that included items on marijuana, alcohol and gambling.[8]

More typical of self-report studies, however, are the relations from the Contra Costa data shown in Table 4. Among white males, twice the proportion in the lowest as in the highest IQ group report involvement in two or more of a possible six delinquent acts; among black males the comparable ratio is 3:2.

Whatever the strength of the relations in Table 4, we believe they should be evaluated by comparison with social class and race. As Table 4 shows, race has no impact on self-reported delinquency—a finding consistent with much of the self-report literature (e.g., Williams and Gold, 1972). The same literature has consistently revealed a weaker relation of social class (e.g., Nye et al., 1958; Akers, 1964) to self-reported delinquency than that found in Table 4. The weight of the evidence is that IQ is more important than race and social class. The voluminous criticisms advanced against self-report delinquency research—with an eye to rescuing social class—presumably would have the same or even greater consequences for IQ. For example, the heavy reliance on in-school populations, the overabundance of minor offenders, and the dependence on subject cooperation may work to attenuate the relationship between social class and delinquency. If so, there is reason to believe that these factors would also depress the relation between self-reported delinquency and IQ. In fact, Hirschi (1969:46) reports that among those with the highest grades in English who had no police records, 79 percent cooperated with the self-report survey, while among those with the lowest grades in English who had police records, only 38 percent cooperated. More importantly, not only did grades in English and official delinquency substantially affect cooperation with the self-report survey, the two factors were found to interact: low ability boys with police records were disproportionately unlikely to appear in the self-report sample. Since official delinquents are likely to be "self-report" delinquents (if sampled), the number of self-reported delinquents in the sample is considerably depressed, especially at the low end of the ability scale.

Table 4. Percent Committing Two or More Self-Reported Delinquent Acts by IQ and Race [a]

Race	Low IQ				High IQ
White males	24 (196)	26 (270)	20 (302)	19 (336)	12 (396)
Black males	27 (393)	26 (257)	19 (149)	19 (68)	18 (39)

[a] IQ scores are grouped in percentiles as in Table 1. Gammas, calculated on the entire range of delinquency scores (0–6), are –.15 for whites and –.07 for blacks.

In short, however delinquency is measured, IQ is able to compete on at least equal terms with class and race, the major bases of most sociological theories of delinquency. At the same time, a relation between IQ and delinquency is routinely denied in sociological textbooks.

Implications for Theory

Our original purpose in introducing theory was frankly argumentive: we expected to find theorists struggling with a conflict between their own logic and the erroneous "results of research" on IQ. In short, we expected to find that they had often been led astray by the anti-IQ climate of criminology.

Actual examination of currently influential theories required revision of our plans. In most cases, theorists were not paying all that much attention to the "results of research." *We* had been led astray by the naive textbook assumption that theory organizes research and research tests and modifies theory. In the case of IQ, however, it would be more accurate to say that theory opposes research and research ignores theory.

Theories from the period (Merton, 1938; Sutherland and Cressey, 1974) when most researchers considered low IQ a strong correlate of delinquency ignore this variable,[9] while theories from the period when IQ was almost universally considered irrelevant predict either very strong negative (Cohen, 1955) or weak but important positive relations (Cloward and Ohlin, 1960) with delinquency. And a theoretical tradition (labeling) spanning both periods has managed to take a position opposite to research in both of them. Although all of these theories have been heavily researched, investigators have paid little or no attention to their views regarding IQ.

Since it is difficult to argue with those who agree, we will briefly show that resistence to consideration or inclusion of IQ does not characterize any current theory; that, on the contrary, several important theories require a relation between IQ and delinquency. Explicit recognition of this fact would only increase their scope, the plausibility of their claims, and their consistency with research findings.

The best example is Cohen's (1955) effort to relate social class to delinquency by way of differential experience in the educational system. In Cohen's theory, children differentially prepared or qualified encounter a school system that treats all comers alike. Children inadequately "prepared" for success in school find the experience painful and are likely, as a consequence, to turn to delinquency. The place of IQ in this process would seem obvious and, in fact, Cohen (1955:102–3) could not be more explicit on this question:

> It may be taken as established that ability, as measured by performance in conventional tests of intelligence, varies directly with social class. . . . The conventional tests do test for abilities that are highly prized by middle-class people, that are fostered by middle-class socialization, and that are especially important for further achievement in the academic world and in middle-class society. In short, *the results of these tests are one important index of the ability of the child to meet middle-class expectations,* to do the kinds of things that bring rewards in the middle-class world. (emphasis added)

---

[7] Early warnings that the questionnaire method is especially limited by the high rates of illiteracy among delinquents (Erickson and Empey, 1963) have gone essentially unheeded.

[8] For details of data collection, see Weis (1973). The data reported in the text cannot be found in Weis' dissertation. We are grateful to him for making them available to us.

[9] The Gluecks reported periodically throughout the thirties that their delinquents were "burdened with feeblemindedness" (e.g., Glueck and Glueck, 1934).

In Cohen's theory, intelligence intervenes between social class and delinquency or it is at least an important indicator of the social class of the *child*. In either case, IQ should be more strongly related to delinquency than such indirect measures of the ability of the child to meet middle-class expectations as "*father's* occupation."

Cohen's views on the interchangeability of IQ and class illustrate how the former could have been used to extend the scope of his theory beyond the confines of "lower-class delinquency." The situation facing the middle-class child with low IQ may not be all that different from the situation facing the lower-class child and, if such a situation explains the delinquency of one of them, it may explain the delinquency of the other as well. If both lower- and middle-class delinquency can be explained by the same mechanism, Cohen's reliance on a separate mechanism for middle-class boys (Cohen, 1955:162–9) is inexplicable or is, at the very least, theoretically and empirically inelegant.

If a zero relation between IQ and delinquency would falsify Cohen's theory, it would virtually falsify the theory of Cloward and Ohlin (1960) as well, but for quite different reasons. Cloward and Ohlin (1960:111) suggest a positive relation between intelligence and delinquency:

> Some persons who have experienced a marked discrepancy between aspirations and achievements may look outward, attributing their failure to the existence of unjust or arbitrary institutional arrangements which keep men of ability and ambition from rising in the social structure. Such persons do not view their failure as a reflection of personal inadequacy but instead blame a cultural and social system that encourages everyone to reach for success while differentially restricting access to the success-goals. In contrast to this group there are individuals who attribute failure to their own inadequacies—to a lack of discipline, zeal, intelligence, persistence, or other personal quality.

In other words, the lower-class boy with a high IQ whose talents go unrecognized and unrewarded is a prime candidate for delinquency.

On the basis of available evidence, Cloward and Ohlin are wrong. For present purposes, however, the point is that their theory requires research on the IQ of juvenile offenders and is enduring testimony to the dangers in the view that IQ need be "no longer seriously considered" by criminologists.[10]

At first glance, labeling theory would seem to be an exception to our argument that IQ is important, since this theory puts no stock in the notion that individual differences may act as causes of delinquent behavior. In one of the first efforts by a labeling theorist to neutralize individual-difference research, Tannenbaum (1938:6) focused special attention on IQ, arguing that "whatever 'intelligence' is, it has no demonstrated relationship to crime." As labeling theory has "progressed," however, as it has become more closely associated with the conflict perspective according to which "society organizes itself for the protection of the ruling classes against the socially inferior" (Doleschal and Klapmuts, 1973:622), it has tended more and more to recognize that it too is dependent on individual differences. The generally low IQ of official delinquents is now accepted by labeling theorists and is used as evidence *for* their view that the system discriminates against or creates the disadvantaged (Doleschal and Klapmuts, 1973:612, 616; Polk and Schafer, 1972:34–54).

If labeling theorists argue that discrimination produces the relation between IQ and delinquency, then the mechanism that connects IQ to delinquency is the bone of contention between labeling and conventional theories—not the fact of a relation itself. We will return to the mechanism question.

Perhaps the only major theory strictly silent on the question of IQ is Sutherland's "differential association" (Sutherland and Cressey, 1974:75–7). Sutherland (1931) played a major role in constructing the current position of criminology on IQ. He rejoiced in its alleged failure to discriminate between delinquents and nondelinquents, and his influential text continues to belittle "mental testers" to the present day. Even so, differential association has nothing to fear from intelligence. This theory faintly suggests a positive association among those exposed to the delinquent culture (as does any theory that emphasizes the need to learn crime), but it really cannot be used to predict even the sign of the relation in the general population. If the theory cannot predict the sign of this relation, it is, nonetheless, capable of accounting for any relation between IQ and delinquency that might be revealed by research.

A final set of theories might be grouped under the heading of "social control" (for a convenient summary, see Nettler, 1974). These theories focus on a broad range of causal variables, and they are relatively open to individual differences, to the idea that "in learning to conduct ourselves, some of us need more lessons than others" (Nettler, 1974:232). Although none of them may now consider IQ of central importance, most suggest a negative association, and none would have difficulty absorbing this variable. In fact, for those sociologically-oriented control theories that emphasize "stakes in conformity" (e.g., Toby, 1957), IQ is of obvious importance.

Most sociological theories, then, have been saying for some time that IQ should be related to delinquency for the same reason that social class is, or should be related to it. Given the theoretical overlap of IQ and social class, the contrast in how the research community has reacted to their varying fates would be hard for an outsider to understand.

The finding that social class was unrelated to self-reported delinquency produced a large volume of follow-up research. The "finding" that IQ was unrelated to any measure of delinquency was, in contrast, accepted without so much as a murmur of protest. The literature on IQ contains none of the "what may have gone wrong" kinds of methodological critiques so often encountered in efforts to save social class. Instead, it is marked by considerable speculative ingenuity directed against an established relation. The extent to which this relation has been established may be revealed by a review of the history of IQ testing as it applies to delinquency and crime.

History

As a cause of delinquency, IQ got off to a very strong start in the first years of this century. The notion that "imbeciles" and "idiots" would be unable to resist criminal impulses or, for that matter, even to distinguish right from wrong, was a straightforward extension of Lombroso's then prestigious theory of the born or biologically defective criminal. Initial research did nothing to dampen enthusiasm for this idea. Goring (1972:255) in Great Britain reported that criminals "as a class, are highly differentiated mentally from the law abiding classes," and Goddard (1914:7) in the United States concluded that "probably from 25% to 50% of the people in our prisons are mentally defective and incapable of managing their affairs with ordinary prudence." In the period 1910–1914, the "percentage feebleminded" in fifty studies of institutionalized delinquents had a median value of 51 (Sutherland, 1931:358). Since it was then assumed that the proportion feebleminded in the general population was less than one percent (Goring used an estimate of .46 percent), the conclusion that faulty intelligence was the "single most important cause of crime" followed, or at least seemed to follow directly from the evidence.

If we follow the fate of IQ through mainstream criminology, we discover that its day was very brief. Less than two decades after Goring estimated .6553 as a

[10] Although Merton (1938) ignores IQ and its "success" implications, IQ is obviously relevant to any opportunity theory.

"minimum value" for the correlation between mental defectiveness and crime, Sutherland (1931) was poking fun at the absurdities of the "mental testers."[11] His negative review of their research was so influential that the "modern" or "recent" position on IQ described by today's textbooks appears to have been firmly established at that time, i.e., forty-five years ago.

Sutherland's stance is not difficult to understand. As Savitz (1972:xviii) has reminded us, the medical profession seized power in criminology before the end of the nineteenth century and still maintained a preeminent position in the early days of intelligence testing—both Goring and Goddard were physicians. A short time later, however, criminology had become a subfield of sociology. Given this shift in disciplinary dominance, an equivalent paradigm shift is now pretty much accepted as a logical necessity. "Intelligence" was a central element of the "old" paradigm. It just had to go. And go it did.

The history of IQ in research findings is not so quickly or easily told. The initial claims about the proportion of feebleminded delinquents were excessively high because—as Merrill (1947:159) has pointed out—researchers were basing their cutting point on children in institutions for the mentally deficient. The logic of this procedure went something like this: if no child in an institution for the feebleminded has a mental age in excess of twelve, then a mental age of twelve or less is sufficient to classify a person feebleminded. There was nothing especially silly about this procedure, it merely made the mistake of assuming that the same procedure would not also classify a large portion of the general population feebleminded. As it became apparent that a too-large portion of the general population would be classified feebleminded, the mental age requirement was first abruptly and then gradually lowered, with the result that the proportion feebleminded among delinquents also first abruptly and then gradually declined. Sutherland (1931) called attention to this twenty-year trend—which, in fact, continued for another 30 years (Woodward, 1955; Caplan, 1965)—and allowed his readers to conclude that it would continue until the initial claims of difference between delinquents and nondelinquents had no foundation in fact.

The most direct evidence against an IQ difference resulted from the extensive testing of the draft army in World War I. Murchison (1926) and Tulchin (1939) reported that the distribution of intelligence in the draft army was virtually identical to the distribution among adult prisoners. Without including details of the investigation, Murchison also reported that the prisoners in a certain midwestern institution were more intelligent than the guards, an anecdotal fact even now more widely quoted than the results of many carefully conducted studies showing important differences in favor of the intelligence hypothesis. Although Sutherland (1931:364) acknowledged that "serious questions have been raised regarding the validity of these tests and the validity of using the draft army as a sample of the general population," he carefully noted that "the consistency in results is a fact that cannot be overlooked."

By the late 1920s and early 1930s, the evidence was sufficiently mixed that summaries of the research literature were arriving at variant conclusions. Thomas and Thomas (1928:365) concluded from their review of the same literature examined by Sutherland that important differences between delinquents and nondelinquents on IQ were "beyond question." They reached this conclusion by focusing on the many studies reporting such differences and by discounting the draft-army research as being so clearly out of line as to be suspect. In 1935, Chassell published an extensive review of research on this question. Her general conclusion, based on nearly 300 studies:

> Undoubtedly the relation between morality and intellect in the general population is considerably higher than usually found in restricted groups. Nevertheless, it is hardly probable that this relation is high. Expressed in correlational terms, the relation in the general population may therefore be expected to fall below .70. (Chassell, 1935:470)[12]

As IQ tests improved, the average score of samples of delinquents also improved until, with the advent of the Revised Stanford Binet and the Wechsler-Bellevue scales in the late 1930s, they were obtaining an average IQ of about 92 (Merrill, 1947; Woodward, 1955; Caplan, 1965). With the advent of these improved tests about 35 years ago, the marked trends and occasional fluctuations of earlier research apparently came to an end. Since that time, it has been reasonable to expect that samples of delinquents would differ from the general population by about eight IQ points. This conclusion has been accepted by Woodward (1955) and Caplan (1965) in major reviews of the literature and is generally consistent with the more recent research reviewed in this paper.

The question, then, is how a reliable eight IQ point difference was converted to the no-difference conclusion of the textbooks. One possibility is that an eight IQ point difference was not seen as theoretically or practically important. This possibility is easily disputed: no modern reviewer has questioned the importance of a difference of this magnitude.[13] Assuming that ten percent of the population is delinquent, this difference would produce a correlation (Yule's Q) between IQ and delinquency of about −.4.

The neglect of IQ after a reliable and important difference had been established may be traced to the initial plausibility of an unusual number of counter-arguments. These arguments are so numerous and diverse that we can hope to deal with them only generally and briefly.

The Spuriousness Argument

Scholarly reviews of the literature have made much of the hypothesis that the low IQs of delinquents are a spurious consequence of differences in class or culture. Against the estimated eight IQ point difference between delinquents and nondelinquents, Woodward (1955) assembles a good deal of material suggesting the possibility that cultural factors are at work: the children of professionals differ from those of unskilled manual workers by about 20 IQ points; average IQ scores are low in *areas* with high delinquency rates;[14] children in large families have low IQ scores and are more likely to be delinquent; overcrowding is related both to low IQ and to delinquency; finally, studies based on sib-sib comparisons (such as Healy and Bronner, 1936) and on other methods of control for cultural factors "tend to support the contention that complete control *would* eliminate the difference between delinquents and non-

[11] Sutherland summarized about 350 studies conducted between 1910 and 1928 noting downward trends in the proportion feebleminded in delinquent and criminal groups, as well as inconsistencies in the results. "In those early days of mental testing the influence of Goddard was very great; he had asserted that the more expert the mental tester the larger the proportion of delinquents he would find to be feebleminded. Many of the testers attempted to demonstrate their superiority in that manner." "Consequently a report regarding the proportion of a delinquent group feebleminded is of primary significance in locating the mental tester upon a scale of mental testing methods. In this sense the psychometric tests of delinquents throw more light upon the intelligence of the mental testers than upon the intelligence of delinquents." (Sutherland, 1931:358–62).

[12] Present-day researchers would not be so modest about a correlation of .70! Chassell's caution may be indicative of the standards against which empirical relations were judged in the early days of quantitative research. These standards may account for the ease with which reviewers were able to reject IQ as a "significant" causal variable (see also footnote 1).

[13] Caplan (1965:104) refers to this eight-point difference as a "first class" relationship. As noted below, however, he cautions the reader that cultural factors be taken into account before it is accepted as genuine.

[14] This is an example of what might be called the reverse ecological fallacy: because IQ and delinquency are related at the ecological level, it is *unlikely* that they are related at the individual level.

delinquents" (Woodward, 1955:289; emphasis added).[15] As we have seen, the evidence says otherwise. Differences by class and race do not account for IQ differences between delinquents and nondelinquents. These differences remain pronounced within groups homogeneous on these variables. If there exists a cultural correlate of both IQ and delinquency strong enough to account for the relation between them, it has not yet been identified.

Ten years after Woodward's influential review (see Wootten, 1959:302), Caplan (1965) was unable to find additional research material bearing directly on her cultural hypothesis. His conclusions about the effects of IQ are, however, if anything, more skeptical than Woodward's, because he is able to cite an additional source of concern.

Arguments Focusing on the Measurement of Delinquency

The advent of the self-report method helped Caplan (1965:120–1) call into question the measures of delinquency upon which the original findings of IQ differences were based. Once again, the evidence against IQ was inferential rather than direct: if official data measure delinquency imperfectly, then imperfections in measurement rather than the phenomenon itself may account for the observed relation. And, indeed, few have been able to resist ascribing IQ differences between officially identified delinquents and nondelinquents to the ability of the bright delinquent to avoid detection or to differential response of officials to high and low IQ adolescents (e.g., Sutherland, 1931; Doleschal and Klapmuts, 1973; Stark, 1975).

Both the differential detection and differential reaction hypotheses require that IQ have a direct or independent effect on official delinquency.[16] Such direct effect hypotheses compete with intervening variable hypotheses and may be directly tested when the latter are available. A competing hypothesis widely mentioned in the literature (e.g., Short and Strodtbeck, 1965:238; West, 1973:44) is that IQ affects delinquency through school performance. If IQ has the direct effect suggested by the differential detection and reaction hypotheses, nothing consequent to IQ can explain the zero-order relation. Two studies bear on this question. When Wolfgang et al. removed by statistical adjustment the effects of such intervening variables as highest grade completed, the relation between IQ and such "detection" measures as number of offenses virtually vanished (Wolfgang et al., 1972:275–9). (We have replicated this finding with the Contra Costa County data.) Taking a somewhat different approach, West (1973:217) also was able to reduce the relation between IQ and official delinquency below the significant level by matching on peer and teacher ratings on "troublesomeness." These ratings were made at ages eight and ten, well before the delinquent acts recorded by officials. Once again, then, *the differential ability to avoid detection and the differential official reaction on the basis of IQ arguments are not supported by available evidence.* (The tests of the official reaction hypothesis are limited by available data to reactions by the police.)

Tests of these and related direct effect hypotheses[17] at the same time identify the mechanism linking IQ to delinquency. This mechanism, the data suggest, is performance in and attitudes toward the school. That school variables are strong enough to account for the impact of IQ should come as no surprise. Their significance for delinquency is nowhere in dispute and is, in fact, one of the oldest and most consistent findings of delinquency research (e.g., Thrasher, 1963; Gold, 1970; Hindelang, 1973; Weis, 1973). What should come as a surprise is the easy acceptance of the no-difference-on-IQ conclusion, since the consequences of IQ differences are generally accepted as major predictors of delinquency. This brings us to the most troublesome of the arguments against IQ effects.

Arguments Focusing on the Measurement or Meaning of IQ

The facts we have presented compete with a wide variety of counter-arguments that focus on the meaning or measurement of IQ: "anybody can learn anything" (Eckland, 1967:174–5, quoting Faris, 1961:838), "it is impossible to make intelligence part of any respectable theory" (ASR referee, 1975), "so-called intelligence tests measure only 'test intelligence' and not innate intelligence" (Clinard, 1968:170), and "mainly they [IQ tests] measure the socioeconomic status of the respondent" (Chambliss and Ryther, 1975:373). Excellent discussions of many of these issues are available in the sociological literature (Eckland, 1967; Gordon, 1975). We will deal only with those counter-hypotheses that have a direct bearing on the relation between IQ and delinquency and that can be addressed to some extent using data already presented.

The cultural bias of IQ tests. The argument against IQ tests most frequently encountered in the sociological literature is that these tests are biased against low-income and minority group children. Specific test items (e.g., "What color are rubies?") are often presented to show the obviousness of this bias (Chambliss and Ryther, 1975:373). Since the groups said to be discriminated against by IQ tests are the same groups with high rates of delinquency, the cultural bias hypothesis is certainly plausible. In form, it is identical to the traditional cultural hypothesis previously encountered and may be tested using the same data. These data show that the bias hypothesis is inadequate: important differences in IQ between delinquents and nondelinquents *within* race and class categories cannot be explained by argument or evidence that these tests are biased in favor of middle-class whites.

The stability of test scores. To the extent that IQ test scores are unstable and subject to subtle social influence, the meaning of a correlation between IQ and delinquency is open to question. It may be that reaction to the misbehavior of the child influences his IQ, that the low IQ child today may be the high IQ child tomorrow, and so on. These possibilities are summarized in assertions that "the scores are highly unstable through time" (Polk and Schafer, 1972:195). Unfortunately for such assertions, they are not consistent with the evidence: the IQs of children at

[15] Healy and Bronner (1936) controlled cultural factors by matching 105 delinquents with their same sex, nondelinquent sib nearest in age and then comparing IQ test scores. Although they found an IQ difference in favor of the nondelinquents, this difference was not statistically significant and was not interpreted as practically or theoretically significant by them. (Thirty-four percent of the delinquents and 26 percent of the nondelinquents had IQs under 90.)

The difficulty with this widely cited study (e.g., Wootton, 1959) is that its design makes the outcome a statistical necessity. Pushing the logic of Healy and Bronner's matching procedure one step further, we would compare identical twins raised together, only one of whom was delinquent. Since the correlation between the IQs of identical twins raised together is about .87, a figure "nearly as high . . . the correlation between two parallel tests for the same individual" (Eckland, 1967:177), we would be asking whether errors in IQ measurement are related to delinquency. By the same token, knowing that the "control" is a brother or sister reared in the same household tells us a good deal about what to expect in the way of IQ (in most studies the sib-sib correlation is in the neighborhood of .55), and there is little reason to expect the original relation to survive with anything like its "natural" magnitude.

[16] Contrary to the "intelligence per se is not a cause . . ." arguments with which it is often paired, the differential detection argument suggests that, in fact, intelligence per se *is* a cause of delinquency—when delinquency is measured by official records.

[17] Other very old direct effect hypotheses are that IQ differences stem from (1) the inability of the unintelligent to understand distinctions between right and wrong or (2) their inability to foresee and appreciate the consequences of their acts. These hypotheses assume that low IQ children are more likely to be delinquent, regardless of the social consequences (e.g., school difficulties) of their lack of IQ. Again, current data do not appear to support hypotheses of this form.

four or five years of age have a correlation of about .7 with their IQs at age 17 (Bloom, 1964); after age ten, test-retest correlations (regardless of the number of years between the tests) fall between the test's reliability and the square of its reliability (Jensen, 1969:18). For that matter, the ability of IQ tests to predict delinquency at some period far removed from their administration is inconsistent with the gross implications of the instability argument.

A fall-back position for those who would argue instability is that these scores *could be* manipulated by simple and straightforward shifts in the environment of the child:

> We may treat people differently out of ignorance or prejudice, but the result is the same as if the supposed differences were real. Studies have shown that school children seen as liable to be educationally backward become educationally backward and that, vice versa, children seen as educationally capable become educationally capable. (Taylor et al., 1973:142; see also Polk and Schafer, 1972:46; Schur, 1973:164)

The study cited in support of such arguments is Rosenthal and Jacobson, *Pygmalion in the Classroom* (1968). In this study, students in grades K through 5 in one elementary school were given group-administered IQ tests at the end of the 1964 academic year. The following fall, a random 20 percent of the students were identified to their teachers as students expected to show unusual intellectual gains during the academic year. In May, 1965, all students were re-tested on the same IQ test. Although both the experimental and the control subjects showed IQ gains, the experimental group showed a 3.8 point greater gain, with the bulk of this gain coming in the first and second grades. On the basis of these results, Rosenthal and Jacobson (1968:98) conclude that favorable expectations of teachers "can be responsible for gains in their pupils' IQ's and, for the lower grades, that these gains can be quite dramatic."

Unfortunately, *Pygmalion* has problems. Snow (1969:197) asserts that the study "stands as a casebook example of many of Darrell Huff's (*How to Lie with Statistics*) admonitions to data analysts" and that it "fails to come close to providing an adequate demonstration of the phenomenon" (the effects of teacher expectations on IQ scores). Thorndike (1968:708) begins his similarly negative review with what has turned out to be a prophetic statement:

> In spite of anything I can say, I am sure it (*Pygmalion in the Classroom*) will become a classic—widely referred to and rarely examined critically. Alas, it is so defective technically that one can only regret that it ever got beyond the eyes of the original investigators!

Thorndike concludes that "the basic data . . . are so untrustworthy that any conclusions based upon them must be suspect." And, indeed, this too was prophetic. Elashoff and Snow (1971) report that *none of nine attempts to replicate the effects of teacher expectations on IQ scores has been successful*. One would think that this would be enough to put an end to the "Rosenthal effect." However, Beeghley and Butler (1974:750) still maintain that the effects of teacher expectations on IQ "have been forcefully demonstrated by Rosenthal and Jacobson," and they muddy the waters by citing two "replications" of *Pygmalion*. In the first, "changes in intellectual functioning were not expected" by the investigators themselves (Meichenbaum et al., 1969:307) and in fact, as far as we can determine, IQ was not even a variable in the study. In the second, the author summarizes a variety of research results and concludes the findings do not "provide any direct proof that teacher expectations can influence pupil performance" (Pidgeon, 1970:126). Ironically—for a study which Beeghley and Butler purport to be a replication of *Pygmalion*—Pidgeon (1970:126) notes that the Rosenthal and Jacobson study "would bear repetition, providing conditions could be found for employing a more satisfactory research design." As of now, it is clear that no labeling or expectation effects of the sort alleged by Rosenthal and Jacobson (and widely cited in the crime and delinquency literature) have been established.

Conclusions

The assertion that IQ affects the likelihood of delinquent behavior through its effect on school performance is consistent with available data. The corollary descriptive assertion that delinquents have lower IQs than nondelinquents is firmly established. Both of these assertions are inconsistent with the "no-IQ-difference" view of the textbooks. They are clearly inconsistent with the image of the delinquent in much sociological writing on the subject, and those planning prevention and treatment programs would do well to take them into account.[18]

Interestingly enough, most modern theories of delinquency assume (and some explicitly state) that IQ affects delinquency. That their views have been ignored by researchers testing them speaks to the depth of the concern that individual differences are both non-sociological and positively dangerous. In this sense, IQ is doubly significant in that it represents an entire class of variables traditionally ignored by sociological students of crime and delinquency. Variables in this large residual category (virtually everything beyond class, culture, and official processing) will not lose their status as alternative hypotheses simply by being ignored, and they will continue to restrict and even embarrass sociological theory until some effort is made to incorporate them.

For that matter, IQ is a poor example of a variable that may require modification of sociological perspectives. As of now, there is no evidence that IQ has a direct impact on delinquency. The police bias, differential ability to avoid detection, and inability to appreciate moral distinctions hypotheses are not consistent with current data. If the mechanism linking IQ to delinquency is school performance and adjustment, then IQ does not lead away from the arena in which sociological theories have focused their quest for the antecedents of delinquency; rather, it helps illuminate the social processes occurring there.

[18] See Nettler (1974:162–5). The range of treatment programs affected by these differences is considerably broader than is usually imagined: "The frequent mental dullness . . . and reading and writing disabilities of a larger proportion of delinquents *make them poor risks for industrial training* (Shulman, 1951:781, emphasis added).

REFERENCES

Akers, Ronald L.
1964 "Socio-economic status and delinquent behavior: a retest." Journal of Research on Crime and Delinquency 1:38–46.

Beeghley, Leonard and Edgar W. Butler
1974 "The consequences of intelligence testing in public schools before and after desegregation." Social Problems 21:740–54.

Bloch, Herbert A. and Gilbert Geis
1962 Man, Crime and Society. New York: Random House.

Bloom, B.A.
1964 Stability and Change in Human Characteristics. New York: Wiley.

Caplan, Nathan S.
1965 "Intellectual functioning" Pp. 100–38 in Herbert C. Quay (ed.), Juvenile Delinquency. Princeton: Van Nostrand.

Chambliss, William J. and Thomas E. Ryther
1975 Sociology: The Discipline and Its Direction. New York: McGraw-Hill.

Chassell, Clara F.
1935 The Relation between Morality and Intellect. New York: Teachers College, Columbia University.

Clinard, Marshall B.
1968 Sociology of Deviant Behavior. New York:

Holt, Rinehart and Winston.

Cloward, Richard E. and Lloyd E. Ohlin
1960 Delinquency and Opportunity. New York: Free Press.

Cohen, Albert K.
1955 Delinquent Boys: The Culture of the Gang. New York: Free Press.

Coleman, James C.
1950 Abnormal Psychology and Modern Life, Glenview, Il.: Scott, Foresman.

Doleschal, Eugene and Nora Klapmuts
1973 "Toward a new criminology." Crime and Delinquency Literature: 607–26.

Eckland, Bruce K.
1967 "Genetics and sociology: a reconsideration." American Sociological Review 32:193–4.

Elashoff, J. and R. Snow
1971 *Pygmalion* Reconsidered. Worthington, Oh.: Jones

Erickson, Maynard L. and LaMar T. Empey
1963 "Court records, undetected delinquency and decision-making." Journal of Criminal Law, Criminology and Police Science 54:456–69.

Faris, Robert E. L.
1961 "The ability dimension in human society." American Sociological Review 26:835–43.

Gibbons, Don C.
1970 Delinquent Behavior. Englewood Cliffs, N.J.: Prentice-Hall.

Glueck, Sheldon and Eleanor Glueck
1934 Five Hundred Delinquent Women. New York: Knopf.

Goddard, Henry H.
1914 Feeble-Mindedness: Its Causes and Consequences. New York: Macmillan.

Gold, Martin
1970 Delinquent Behavior in an American City. Belmont, Ca.: Brooks/Cole.

Gordon, Robert A.
1975 "Examining labeling theory: the case of mental retardation." Pp. 83–146 in Walter Gove (ed.), The Labelling of Deviance. New York: Wiley.
1976 "Prevalence: the rare datum in delinquency measurement and its implications for the theory of delinquency." Pp. 201–84 in Malcolm W. Klein (ed.), The Juvenile Justice System. Beverly Hills, Ca.: Sage.

Goring, Charles
[1913] 1972 The English Convict. Montclair, N.J.: Patterson Smith

Haskell, Martin R. and Lewis Yablonsky
1974 Crime and Delinquency. Chicago: Rand McNally

Healy, William and Augusta F. Bronner
1936 New Light on Delinquency and Its Treatment. New Haven: Yale University Press.

Hindelang, Michael J.
1973 "Causes of delinquency: a partial replication and extension." Social Problems 20:471–87.

Hirschi, Travis
1969 Causes of Delinquency. Berkeley: University of California Press.

Jensen, A. R.
1969 "How much can we boost I.Q. and scholastic achievement?" Harvard Educational Review 39:1–123.

Johnson, Elmer
1968 Crime, Correction and Society. Homewood, Il.: Dorsey Press.

Liazos, Alexander
1972 "The poverty of the sociology of deviance: nuts, sluts, and preverts." Social Problems 20:103–20.

McCord, William and Joan McCord
1959 Origins of Crime: A New Evaluation of the Cambridge-Somerville Study. New York: Columbia Press.

Matza, David
1964 Delinquency and Drift. New York: Wiley.

Meichanbaum, Donald H., Kenneth S. Bowers and Robert R. Ross
1969 "A behavioral analysis of teacher expectancy effect." Journal of Personality and Social Psychology 13:306–16.

Merrill, Maud A.
1947 Problems of Child Delinquency. Boston: Houghton Mifflin.

Merton, Robert K.
1938 "Social structure and anomie." American Sociological Review 3:672–82.

Murchison, Carl
1926 Criminal Intelligence. Worcester, Ma.: Clark University Press.

Nettler, Gwynn
1974 Explaining Crime. New York: McGraw-Hill.

Nye, F. Ivan, James F. Short, Jr. and Virgil J. Olson
1958 "Socio-economic status and delinquent behavior." American Journal of Sociology 63:381–9.

Pidgeon, Douglas
1970 Expectation and Pupil Performance.' London: National Foundation for Educational Research in England and Wales.

Polk, Kenneth and Walter E. Schafer
1972 Schools and Delinquency. Englewood Cliffs, N.J.: Prentice-Hall.

Reckless, Walter C. and Simon Dinitz
1972 The Prevention of Delinquency. Columbus: Ohio State University Press.

Reiss, Albert J. and Albert L. Rhodes
1961 "The distribution of juvenile delinquency in the social class structure." American Sociological Review 26:720–32.

Rosenthal, R. and Lenore Jacobson
1968 Pygmalion in the Classroom. New York: Holt, Rinehart and Winston.

Ross, Edward A.
1901 Social Control. New York: Macmillan.

Savitz, Leonard D.
1972 "Introduction." Pp. v–xx in Gina Lombroso-Ferrero, Criminal Man. Montclair, N.J.: Patterson Smith.

Schur, Edwin M.
1973 Radical Non-Intervention: Rethinking the Delinquency Problem. Englewood Cliffs, N.J.: Prentice-Hall.

Short, James F., Jr. and Fred L. Strodtbeck
1965 Group Process and Gang Delinquency. Chicago: University of Chicago Press.

Shulman, Harry M.
1951 "Intelligence and delinquency." Journal of Criminal Law and Criminology 41:763–81.

Snow, R.
1969 "Unfinished Pygmalion." Contemporary Psychology 14:197–9.

Stark, Rodney
1975 Social Problems. New York: CRM/Random House.

Sutherland, Edwin H.
1924 Criminology. Philadelphia: Lippincott.
1931 "Mental deficiency and crime," Pp. 357–75 in Kimball Young (ed.), Social Attitudes. New York: Holt, Rinehart and Winston.

Sutherland, Edwin H. and Donald R. Cressey
[1939] 1974 Principles of Criminology. Philadelphia: Lippincott

Tannenbaum, Frank
1938 Crime and the Community. Boston: Ginn.

Taylor, Ian, Paul Walton and Jock Young
1973 The New Criminology. New York: Harper.

Thomas, William I. and Dorothy Swaine Thomas
1928 The Child in America. New York: Knopf.

Thorndike, R. L.
1968 "Review of R. Rosenthal and L. Jacobson, 'Pygmalion in the Classroom.' " American Educational Research Journal 5:708–11.

Thrasher, F.
[1927] 1963 The Gang. Chicago: University of Chicago press.

Toby, Jackson
1957 "Social disorganization and stake in conformity: complementary factors in the predatory behavior of hoodlums." Journal of Criminal Law, Criminology and Police Science 48:12–7.

Toby, Jackson and Marcia L. Toby
1961 Low School Status as a Predisposing Factor in Subcultural Delinquency. New Brunswick, N.J.: Rutgers University. Mimeo.

Tulchin, Simon H.
1939 Intelligence and Crime. Chicago: University of Chicago Press.

Weis, Joseph
1973 Delinquency among the Well-to-Do. Unpublished Ph.D. dissertation. University of California, Berkeley.

West, D. J.
1973 Who Becomes Delinquent? London: Heinemann.

Williams, Jay and Martin Gold
1972 "From delinquent behavior to official delinquency." Social Problems 20:209–29.

Wolfgang, Marvin, Robert M. Figlio and Thorsten Sellin
1972 Delinquency as a Birth Cohort. Chicago: University of Chicago Press.

Woodward, Mary
1955 "The role of low intelligence in delinquency." British Journal of Delinquency 5:281–303.

Wootton, Barbara
1959 Social Science and Social Pathology. New York: Macmillan.

Zeleny, Leslie D.
1933 "Feeblemindedness and criminal conduct." American Journal of Sociology 38:564–78.

The Relationship of Self-Reported Delinquency to Scales of the CPI and MMPI

Michael J. Hindelang*

Reviews of studies of personality attributes of delinquents and criminals have shown that the Minnesota Multiphasic Personality Inventory (MMPI) and the California Psychological Inventory (CPI) have quite consistently differentiated offenders from non-offenders.[1] Of the studies reviewed by Scheussler and Cressey and Waldo and Dinitz, those using the MMPI have been successful 30 out of 33 times, while those using the CPI have been successful 8 out of 8 times in discriminating offenders from non-offenders.

Hathaway, Monachesi, and their associates have exhaustively studied the relationship of the MMPI to police and court records of delinquents.[2] In a 1960 study, Hathaway, Monachesi and Young, examined the MMPI profiles of more than 11,000 adolescents who had been tested as ninth grade pupils in the 1953–1954 academic year.[3] As had been found in previous studies, high scores on certain combinations of the Psychopathic Deviate, the Schizophrenia, and the Hypomania Scales, tends to be associated with high rates of delinquency. Hence, these scales of the MMPI have been referred to by Hathaway, *et al.*, as *Excitory Scales*. The boys who scored high on the *Excitory Scales* had delinquency rates 20 percent greater than the average rate in the male sample; among the girls, those who scored high on the *Excitory Scales* had delinquency rates 50 percent higher than the average rate in the female sample. These findings are typical of those using the MMPI.[4]

Gough has done extensive research in the area of delinquency in connection with his development and validation of the CPI. In 1960, he reported the results of studies using 41 samples of subjects who completed his Socialization Scale, which is a subscale of the CPI.[5] Groups of both male and female respondents were classified on the basis of whether their behavior in the past had been designated as asocial or not. For example, the asocial group included high school disciplinary problems, reformatory inmates, county jail inmates, prison inmates, etc.; the non-asocial group included nominated high school "best citizens," medical school applicants, etc. It was found that among the males the mean difference between the former (less socialized $N = 1295$) and the latter (more socialized, $N = 9001$), as measured by the Socialization Scale, was significant at the .001 level; the point-biserial correlation coefficient was .73 ($p < .001$). Similarly, among the females the mean difference between the less socialized ($N = 784$) and the more socialized ($N = 9776$) groups was significant at the .001 level; the point-biserial correlation coefficient was .78 ($p < .001$).

In 1965, Gough reported results of cross-cultural comparisons of delinquents and non-delinquents with respect to their scores on the Socialization Scale which was administered in eight languages, in ten countries, to 21,772 non-delinquent and 5052 delinquent males and females.[6] For both sexes, in all comparisons, delinquents and non-delinquents differed at the .001 level. Furthermore, none of the non-delinquent sample means overlapped with the delinquent sample means.

In spite of the abundance of studies using the MMPI and the CPI in connection with delinquency and criminality, virtually all of these studies have used "official" offenders—i.e., those having police and/or court records.[7] Although studies of social characteristics of offenders have widely used self-report delinquency techniques to supplement or complement official records,[8] research into personality characteristics of offenders has more rarely used self report delinquency instruments.[9] Since it has been estimated that more than ninety percent of delinquent activities do not result in official action[10], it seems probable that "official" delinquents are a rather select sample of those engaging in delinquent activities. It is, therefore, important to determine whether previous findings

* Assistant Professor of Criminal Justice, State University of New York at Albany.

[1] Scheussler & Cressey, *Personality Characteristics of Criminals*, 55 AM. J. SOCIOLOGY 297–304 (1950). Waldo & Dinitz, *Personality Attributes of the Criminal: An Analysis of Research Studies, 1960-1965*, 4 J. RESEARCH IN CRIME & DELINQUENCY 185–202 (1967).

[2] S. HATHAWAY & E. MONACHESI, ANALYZING AND PREDICTING JUVENILE DELINQUENCY WITH THE MMPI (1953). S. HATHAWAY & E. MONACHESI, ADOLESCENT PERSONALITY AND BEHAVIOR (1963). Hathaway, Monachesi, & Young, *Delinquency Rates and Personality*, 51 J. CRIM. L.C. & P.S. 433–40 (1960).

[3] *Id.*

[4] *See* Scheussler & Cressey, *supra* note 1; Waldo & Dinitz, *supra* note 1, for a more inclusive bibliography.

[5] Gough, *The Theory and Measurement of Socioliza-tion*, 24 J. CONSULTING PSYCHOLOGY 23–30 (1960).

[6] Gough, *Cross Cultural Validation of a Measure of Asocial Behavior*, 17 PSYCHOLOGICAL REPORTS 397 (1965).

[7] *See* F. Scarpitti, A FOLLOW-UP STUDY OF THE "GOOD" BOY IN A HIGH DELINQUENCY AREA, 1959 (unpublished thesis at Ohio State University), for an exception. Although Scarpitti, Murray, Dinitz & Reckless, *The "Good" Boy in a High Delinquency Area: Four Years Later*, 25 AM. SOCIOLOGICAL REV. 555–8 (1960), and Dinitz, Scarpitti & Reckless, *Delinquency Vulnerability: A Cross-Group and Longitudinal Analysis*, 27 AM. SOCIOLOGICAL REV. 515–17 (1962), report having administered CPI and self-report delinquency scales, they do not report the relationship between the two.

[8] Vaz, *Juvenile Delinquency in the Middle-Class Youth Culture*, in MIDDLE CLASS JUVENILE DELINQUENCY 131–47 (E. Vaz ed. 1967); Clark & Tifft, *Polygraph and Interview Validation of Self-Reported Delinquent Behavior*, 31 AM. SOCIOLOGICAL REV. 516–23 (1966); Goode, *Multiple Drug Use Among Marijuana Smokers*, 17 SOCIAL PROBLEMS (1969); Hirshci & Stark, *Hellfire and Delinquency*, 17 SOCIAL PROBLEMS 202–13 (1969); Jensen, *Crime Doesn't Pay: Correlates of a Shared Misunderstanding*, 17 SOCIAL PROBLEMS 189–201 (1969).

[9] M. Hindelang, PERSONALITY ATTRIBUTES OF SELF-REPORTED DELINQUENTS, 1969 (unpublished Ph.D. dissertation in University of California at Berkeley Library); Siegman, *Personality Variables Associated with Admitted Criminal Behavior*, 26 J. CONSULTING PSYCHOLOGY 199 (1962).

[10] Erickson & Empey, *Class Position, Peers and Delinquency*, 49 SOCIOLOGY & SOCIAL RESEARCH 260–82 (1965).

From *Journal of Criminal Law and Criminology*, Vol. 63, 1972, pp. 75–81. Reprinted by special permission of the *Journal of Criminal Law and Criminology*, © 1972 by Northwestern University School of Law, Vol. 63, No. 1.

using subscales of the MMPI and the CPI are replicated when youths who engage in delinquencies but who have generally not come to the attention of the authorities are used as subjects. In addition, it may in fact be the case that contact with the authorities somehow *results* in the formation of the personality attributes that these scales tap. Finally, in past research "delinquency" has been viewed as unidimensional and undifferentiated, since researchers have generally not examined the relationship of the MMPI and the CPI sub-scales to types of delinquent activities.

It is the aim of the present research to examine the relationship of some of the MMPI and CPI sub-scales to self-reported delinquency. Specifically, the Psychopathic Deviate (PD) Scale from the MMPI and the Socialization (SO), Self Control (SC), and Responsibility (RE) Scales[11] from the CPI were administered to high school respondents as part of a larger battery of tests which also included a self-report index of delinquent behavior. Two samples of male subjects from Catholic high schools in generally middle-class areas of Oakland and Berkeley, California were chosen for study.[12]

In both schools, the author was introduced to the students as a researcher from the University of California who was interested in finding out about the attitudes and activities of high school students. The subjects of the research consisted of all those present and willing to cooperate on the day of testing—approximately ninety percent of those enrolled at the time of the study. The subjects were asked to respond to questions anonymously and they were assured that their responses would be considered confidential.

For all subjects, the mean age was 15.3 years with a standard deviation of 2.3 years; the ethnic breakdown was seventy-five percent Caucasian, seventeen percent Negro, six percent Mexican-American, and two percent Oriental.

Using Turner's (1964) occupational prestige scale, it was found that the respondents' fathers' occupations had the following distribution: two percent unskilled laborers and service workers, seven percent semi-skilled laborers, twelve percent skilled laborers and foremen, twenty-five percent clerical workers and salesclerks, fourteen percent small business owners and managers and retail salesmen, seven percent semi-professionals, fourteen percent business agents and managers, fourteen percent professionals, and five percent large business owners and officials.

Table 1 displays, in part, the twenty-six delinquent activities that made up the self-reported delinquency questionnaire. The respondents were asked to indicate the number of times in the last year that they had engaged in each activity. For each activity, if the number of times that the activity had been engaged in was between zero and eight inclusive, the respondent was given a score equal to that number; if the respondent indicated that he had engaged in the activity nine or more times, he was given a score of nine. As an index of overall delinquent involvement, a simple sum was taken across all twenty-six delinquent activities and has been designated Total Delinquent Involvement.

Table 1 presents the correlation coefficients which show the relationship of the personality and background characteristics to the delinquent activities.[13] These correlation coefficients should be interpreted in light of the knowledge that the distributions of the delinquent activities are generally J-shaped rather than normal. That is, most of the respondents engaged in a given act zero times, some of the respondents engaged in the act once, fewer yet engaged in an act twice, and so on; this J-shape has been found to characterize delinquent involvement in past research.[14] The fact that these dependent variables are not distributed normally has the consequence that the range of the correlation coefficient is severely restricted.[15]

From Table 1, it can be seen that the occupational prestige score of the respondent's father—as measured by the Turner (1964) Scale—is unrelated to his delinquent involvement. Also the number of years of father's education is quite uniformly unrelated to the delinquent activities; the two exceptions are the slight relationships between father's education and heroin use and between father's education and shaking down others for money. Ethnicity likewise is unrelated to the bulk of delinquent activities; compared to Caucasian, non-Caucasians are more likely to shake down others for money, visit a prostitute, and force their sexual attentions on a girl against her will. Age, too, is unrelated to most delinquent activities. However, as age increases so does involvement in drinking, drag racing, driving under the influence, using false identification and cutting school; glue sniffing is inversely related to age.

An examination of the relationship of the personality attributes to the delinquent activities, indicates that these variables are substantially more strongly related to the delinquent activities than are the demographic variables. The socialization and self-control scales are the most strongly related to the dependent variables; their mean correlation coefficient across the twenty-six delinquent activities is $-.27$. On the other hand, the mean correlation coefficients across the twenty-six delinquent activities are less than .04 for age, ethnicity, father's education, and father's occupational prestige score. The personality variables, relative to the demographic variables, appear to be substantially more strongly related to the dependent variables.

The correlations of the CPI subscales with each other indicate that they are not independent; although correlations of the Psychopathic Deviate scale with the CPI subscales cannot be determined from the present study since they were not administered to the same sample, one can use as an estimate of this relationship correlations published by Gough,[16] where he found that the correlations of the Psychopathic Deviate Scale with the Socialization, Responsibility and Self-control scales were .23, .04, and $-.10$ respectively. Using these correlations in conjunction with the remaining correlations from the present study, the estimated multiple correlations of the MMPI and CPI subscales with the delinquent activities appear in Table 1 in the column labeled R. As can be seen from Table 1, the multiple correlation coefficients are of generally moderate strength. The multiple correlation coefficient is strongest for the relationship between the personality scales and total delinquent involvement ($R = .69$, $p < .01$).

By using a cluster analysis technique[17] it is possible to examine the relationship of the independent variables to types of delinquent behavior. Tryon and Bailey's BC TRY package of computer programs allows the researcher to "define" clusters of delinquent activities.[18] In the present study, the following clusters were composed of the activities indicated. Cluster 1: Fighting (individual fist fighting, group fist fighting, individual weapon fighting, gang weapon fighting, and carrying a concealed weapon); Cluster 2: Soft Drug Use (drinking, getting drunk, using marijuana, and driving under the influence); Cluster 3: Malicious Destruction (doing property damage of less than $10.00, and doing property damage of more than

[11] The PD, SO and RE scales were selected for use since past research had indicated that they were strongly related to officially recorded delinquency. *See* Hathaway, Monachesi and Young, *supra* note 2; Gough, *supra* note 5.

The SC scale was selected because of its theoretical relevance. *High* scores on the PD scale show an absence of deep emotional response, an inability to profit from experience, a lack of responsibility, immaturity, and a disregard of social mores.

The SO scale assesses the degree of social maturity, integrity and rectitude which the individual has attained. A *low* score indicates that an individual is stubborn, undependable, deceitful in dealing with others and ostentatious in behavior. The RE scale identifies persons of conscientious, responsible and dependable disposition and temperament. A *low* score indicates an individual is immature, moody, dogmatic and undercontrolled. The SC scale measures the degree and adequacy of self-regulation and self-control and freedom from impulsivity and self-centeredness. A *low* score indicates that an individual is impulsive, shrewd, uninhibited, aggressive and pleasure-seeking. H. GOUGH, CALIFORNIA PSYCHOLOGICAL INVENTORY MANUAL (1957). Since time considerations prohibited administering all *personality* instruments to all respondents, the PD scale was administered to 245 students at one school and the SO, RE, and SC scales were administered to 337 students at the second school.

[12] At the time the data were collected, May, 1968, it was not possible to gain access to San Francisco Bay Area public schools. Although using Catholic school respondents represents a severe sampling restriction, it is somewhat comforting to note Hirschi and Selvin's 1969 finding that religious belief and church attendance generally are not related to delinquent involvement.

[13] For the purpose of analysis, enthnicity was dichotomized into Caucasian and non-Caucasian groups. Caucasian groups were assigned a score of zero and non-Caucasian groups a score of 1. Table 1, therefore, gives the point-biserial 0 correlation coefficients rather than the Pearson correlation coefficients to show the relationships between ethnicity and the other variables. The scoring on the PD scale was also reversed so that a low score would be in the psychopathic direction as in the SO, SC and RE scales where low scores mean a lack of socialization, self control and responsibility, respectively.

[14] M. GOLD, DELINQUENCY IN AN AMERICAN CITY (1970); Hindelang, *supra* note 9.

[15] Using a formula provided by Carroll, the maximum possible positive Pearson product-moment correlation coefficient for joint distributions of personality variables and delinquent activities similar to these (see Hindelang, 1969) was found to be .50. Because of this severe restriction in the range of the correlation coefficient, the sampling distributions (which are based on the ideal full range—from $-.100$ to $+1.00$—of possible correlation coefficients) from which the significance levels in standard tables have been calculated, are inappropriate. Since no simple solution to this problem exists, however, the standard table values will be used, but it should be borne in mind that our significance tests may be quite conservative.

[16] *See generally* GOUGH, *supra* note 11.

[17] R. TYRON & D. BAILEY, CLUSTER ANALYSIS (1970).

[18] The restrictions in the range of the correlation coefficients is somewhat reduced for the clusters since the distributions of the cluster scores are less markedly J-shaped than are the distributions for the individual delinquency items.

$10.00); Cluster 4: Theft (thefts less than $10.00), and thefts greater than $10.00); Cluster 5: Drug Use (sniffing glue, using LSD, methedrine or mescaline, and using heroin). Table 2 presents the correlations of the background and personality variables with the five clusters of delinquent activities. Once again it can be seen that the demographic variables account for much less of the variance than do the personality variables. With the exception of the relationship between age and soft drug use, the demographic variables are virtually unrelated to the clusters of delinquent activities. The Responsibility scale is most closely related to the clusters ($\bar{r}$ = .43) followed by the Socialization scale ($\bar{r}$ = .41), the Psycopathic Deviate scale ($\bar{r}$ = .40), and the self-control scale ($\bar{r}$ = .24). The multiple correlation coefficients appear in the column labeled R. The multiple correlations of the delinquent behaviors with the personality variables are somewhat invariant across clusters with soft drug use being the most predictable cluster and fighting the least predictable cluster.

Finally, because the relationships between the personality variables and the clusters of delinquent activities may still be partially masked by the non-normal distributions of the latter, non-parametric H tests were used. For each of the four scales, the respondents were divided into high, medium, and low scoring groups;[19] this trichotomizing allows one to test for non-linear relationships. The results presented in Table 3 clearly show monotonic patterns of moderate strength which are rather consistent across clusters; across all clusters the Responsibility scale shows the greatest differentiation, and the Self-Control scale shows the least differentiation.

These data support the conclusion that the Psychopathic Deviate, Socialization, Responsibility and Self-Control Scales are related to self-reported delinquent involvement. As an individual scores in a more psychopathic, a less socialized, a less responsible, or a less controlled direction, he is more likely to be involved in delinquent activities. It is interesting to note that even widely varying clusters of the delinquent activities are similarly related to the four scales. Father's education, race, and age have been found by other researchers to be moderately related to officially detected offenses and less related to self-reported offenses.[20] Herein, these demographic variables are virtually unrelated to reported delinquency. Although there was a good sampling of father's educational and occupational levels, an adequate (five year) range of ages, and a substantial proportion (twenty-two percent) of non-Caucasians, a more inclusive sampling of respondents and of delinquent activities may be required for the relationships to manifest themselves, if, in fact, they exist.

TABLE 1

CORRELATION COEFFICIENTS SHOWING THE RELATIONSHIP OF THE DEMOGRAPHIC AND PERSONALITY VARIABLES TO SELF REPORTED DELINQUENT BEHAVIORS

	Father's Occupational Prestige	Father's Education	Ethnicity	Age	PD	SO	RE	SC	R
Psychopathic Deviate (PD)	.04	.06	−.08	−.12	1.00	X	X	X	X
Socialization (SO)	.07	.15	−.10	−.03	X	1.00	.56	.25	X
Responsibility (RE)	.05	.14	−.08	−.01	X	.56	1.00	.33	X
Self Control (PD)	.05	.01	.08	.05	X	.25	.33	1.00	X
Theft less than $10	.01	−.04	−.04	−.10	−.32	−.32	−.38	−.23	.51
Theft greater than $10	−.02	.04	.05	.05	−.37	−.26	−.27	−.18	.47
Property destruction causing less than $10 damage	.00	−.03	.05	.07	−.25	−.24	−.28	−.22	.40
Property destruction causing greater than $10 damage	−.09	−.07	−.01	.07	−.35	−.25	−.32	−.14	.47
Drinking alcohol	−.07	−.09	−.11	.19	−.34	−.42	−.39	−.28	.57
Getting drunk	.03	−.04	−.05	.09	−.27	−.40	−.38	−.19	.24
Engaging in fist-fights with an individual	−.06	−.05	.10	.00	−.22	−.19	−.22	−.28	.39
Engaging in gang fist-fights	.08	−.06	.12	.02	−.18	−.26	−.23	−.14	.32
Carrying a concealed weapon	.03	−.07	.02	.05	−.19	−.30	−.31	−.24	.40
Engaging in fights with an individual with a weapon	.01	−.02	.11	.06	−.18	−.20	−.25	−.13	.32
Engaging in gang fights with weapons	−.01	−.04	.07	.07	−.24	−.26	−.31	−.10	.39
Engaging in illegal gambling	−.04	−.04	.07	.09	−.05	−.17	−.16	−.09	.20
Using marijuana	.05	.03	.02	.07	−.30	−.43	−.36	−.23	.52
Sniffing glue	.03	.02	.06	−.30	−.21	−.16	−.16	−.16	.30
Using LSD, Methedrine, or Mescaline	.03	−.05	−.01	.00	−.29	−.20	−.23	−.01	.36
Using Heroin	.01	.16	.08	−.04	−.13	−.12	−.13	−.08	.20
Shaking down others for money	−.02	.17	.24	.00	−.24	−.09	−.17	−.12	.32
Visiting a prostitute	−.01	.02	.17	−.01	−.14	−.14	−.14	−.18	.24
Forcing sexual attention on a girl against her will	−.09	.01	.16	−.01	−.22	−.14	−.18	−.14	.30
Engaging in promiscuous sexual activity	−.09	.06	.03	.02	−.12	−.28	−.14	−.17	.32
Drag racing on street in excess of speed limit by 20 MPH	−.03	.03	−.06	.18	−.23	−.23	−.25	−.17	.36
Driving while strongly under influence of alcohol or drugs	−.02	.01	−.05	.26	−.28	−.26	−.18	−.11	.36
Being involved in hit and run accidents	−.06	−.01	.02	−.03	.05	−.16	−.14	−.08	.20
Cheating on exams	−.10	−.04	−.03	.08	−.21	−.22	−.31	−.21	.39
Using false ID to pose as older person	.02	−.03	−.05	.15	−.23	−.34	−.26	−.20	.41
Cutting school	−.04	−.06	−.05	.14	−.19	−.32	−.30	−.25	.41
Total	−.03	−.05	.01	.10	−.41	−.51	−.50	−.33	.69
$\bar{r}$	−.02	−.02	.03	.04	−.24	−.27	−.27	−.18	.38

Correlation coefficients involving Pd scores are based on $N_1 = 245$, those involving So, Re, and Sc scores are based on $N_2 = 337$, those involving demographic variables are based on $N_1 + N_2 = 582$. For N_1, when $r \geq .163$, $p < .01$. For N_2, when $r \geq .139$, $p < .01$. For $N_1 + N_2$, when $r \geq .107$, $p < .01$.

TABLE 2

CORRELATION COEFFICIENTS SHOWING THE RELATIONSHIP OF THE DEMOGRAPHIC AND PERSONALITY VARIABLES TO THE OBLIQUE CLUSTER DOMAINS OF DELINQUENT ACTIVITIES*

	Father's Education	Ethnicity	Age	PD	SO	RE	SC	R
Cluster 1: Fighting (.79)	−.08	.13	.09	−.32	−.32	−.39	−.22	.54
Cluster 2: Soft Drug Use (.82)	−.01	−.08	.22	−.43	−.53	−.46	−.28	.69
Cluster 3: Malicious Destruction (.74)	−.04	.04	.09	−.41	−.32	−.39	−.24	.58
Cluster 4: Theft (.71)	.05	.04	.03	−.46	−.41	−.46	−.29	.66
Cluster 5: Drug Use (.67)	.01	.03	.00	−.39	−.45	−.45	−.24	.59
$\bar{r}$	−.02	.03	.09	−.40	−.41	−.43	−.24	.61

* Reliabilities of the cluster scores appear in parentheses.

[19] In all cases, those falling more than .6 of a standard deviation above the mean were assigned to the high group; those falling more than .6 of a standard deviation below the mean were assigned to the low group, those remaining were assigned to the middle group. A similar procedure was used with father's education and age but these variables failed to show any significant relationships to the clusters.

[20] *See generally* GOLD, *supra* note 14; Shout & Nye, *Reported Problems as a Criterion of Deviant Behavior*, 5 SOCIAL PROBLEMS 207 (1957).

TABLE 3

H-Tests Results Showing the Relationship of Low, Medium, and High Scorers on the Personality Variables to the Clusters of Delinquent Activities*

	Low	Medium	High	*p*	W**
Cluster 1: Fighting					
Pd	197.82	183.21	155.16	.00036	.25
So	184.34	158.10	128.68	.00002	.27
Re	195.50	150.67	128.50	.00001	.30
Sc	184.96	157.79	135.88	.00025	.24
Cluster 2: Soft Drug Use					
Pd	211.11	176.43	145.59	.00001	.35
So	210.84	150.48	115.29	.00001	.43
Re	203.34	157.30	110.48	.00001	.38
Sc	194.50	159.26	125.65	.00001	.32
Cluster 3: Malicious Destruction					
Pd	207.08	178.77	153.57	.00001	.32
So	187.68	150.82	134.09	.00004	.25
Re	199.39	150.98	125.66	.00001	.32
Sc	194.89	151.60	137.09	.00001	.29
Cluster 4: Theft					
Pd	201.42	182.82	149.51	.00004	.30
So	195.17	155.02	120.23	.00001	.34
Re	216.69	147.41	112.10	.00001	.44
Sc	194.79	154.38	135.72	.00001	.28
Cluster 5: Drug Use					
Pd	201.18	177.91	154.76	.00009	.28
So	214.49	158.73	133.69	.00001	.37
Re	216.05	162.80	124.48	.00001	.38
Sc	182.45	151.09	122.69	.00001	.29

* Scores on the dependent variables are given in mean ranks.

** This statistic is the square root of the ratio of the explained to the unexplained variance; it varies between zero and 1.00.

Summary

Because the demographic variables are unrelated to the dependent variables, it can be said that the relationships between the four personality subscales and the clusters of delinquent involvement have been shown not to be spurious as a function of the demographic variables. In addition, since sex has been held constant, the relationships cannot be spurious as a function of sex. Therefore, when the effects of father's education and occupation, and the race, sex, and age of the respondent have been controlled, the relationships between the personality variables and the delinquent activities maintain. This is dissonant with Volkman's finding that none of the MMPI subscales differentiated[21] twenty-seven delinquents from twenty-seven non-delinquents who were matched on race, age, father's occupation and intelligence; these findings also cast doubt upon his suggestion that previously obtained relations between MMPI subscales and delinquency may have been spurious due to a failure to control age, race, and social class. The findings of the present study indicate that those engaging in a wide range of delinquent activities, relative to those not engaging in these delinquent activities are more stubborn, undependable, and deceitful in dealing with others (SO); the former are immature, moody, and undercontrolled (RE), more impulsive, shrewd, uninhibited, aggressive, and pleasure-seeking (SC), and show an absence of deep emotional response, an inability to profit from experience, and a disregard of social mores (PD).

[21] Volkman, *A Matched Personality Comparison of Delinquent and Non-delinquent Juveniles*, 6 Social Problems 238 (1958). Although the Hypochondriasis scale did differentiate between the two groups, the non-delinquents scored in the more disturbed direction. It should be pointed out that Volkman's findings were generally in the direction hypothesized by Hathaway and Monachesi, and that his lack of significant results was largely due to his small sample size.

A Technology of Behavior

B. F. Skinner

Twenty-five hundred years ago it might have been said that man understood himself as well as any other part of his world. Today he is the thing he understands least. Physics and biology have come a long way, but there has been no comparable development of anything like a science of human behavior. Greek physics and biology are now of historical interest only (no modern physicist or biologist would turn to Aristotle for help), but the dialogues of Plato are still assigned to students and cited as if they threw light on human behavior. Aristotle could not have understood a page of modern physics or biology, but Socrates and his friends would have little trouble in following most current discussions of human affairs. And as to technology, we have made immense strides in controlling the physical and biological worlds, but our practices in government, education, and much of economics, though adapted to very different conditions, have not greatly improved.

We can scarcely explain this by saying that the Greeks knew all there was to know about human behavior. Certainly they knew more than they knew about the physical world, but it was still not much. Moreover, their way of thinking about human behavior must have had some fatal flaw. Whereas Greek physics and biology, no matter how crude, led eventually to modern science, Greek theories of human behavior led nowhere. If they are with us today, it is not because they possessed some kind of eternal verity, but because they did not contain the seeds of anything better.

It can always be argued that human behavior is a particularly difficult field. It is, and we are especially likely to think so just because we are so inept in dealing with it. But modern physics and biology successfully treat subjects that are certainly no simpler than many aspects of human behavior. The difference is that the instruments and methods they use are of commensurate complexity. The fact that equally powerful instruments and methods are not available in the field of human behavior is not an explanation; it is only part of the puzzle. Was putting a man on the moon actually easier than improving education in our public schools? Or than constructing better kinds of living space for everyone? Or than making it possible for everyone to be gainfully employed and, as a result, to enjoy a higher standard of living? The choice was not a matter of priorities, for no one could have said that it was more important to get to the moon. The exciting thing about getting to the moon was its feasibility. Science and technology had reached the point at which with one great push, the thing could be done. There is no comparable excitement about the problems posed by human behavior. We are not close to solutions.

It is easy to conclude that there must be something about human behavior which makes a scientific analysis, and hence an effective technology, impossible, but we have not by any means exhausted the possibilities. There is a sense in which it can be said that the methods of science have scarcely yet been applied to human behavior. We have used the instruments of science; we have counted and measured and compared; but something essential to scientific practice is missing in almost all current discussions of human behavior. It has to do with our treatment of the causes of behavior. (The term "cause" is no longer common in sophisticated scientific writing, but it will serve well enough here.)

Man's first experience with causes probably came from his own behavior: things moved because he moved them. If other things moved, it was because someone else was moving them, and if the mover could not be seen, it was because he was invisible. The Greek gods served in this way as the causes of physical phenomena. They were usually outside the things they moved, but they might enter into and "possess" them. Physics and biology soon abandoned explanations of this sort and turned to more useful kinds of causes, but the step has not been decisively taken in the field of human behavior. Intelligent people no longer believe that men are possessed by demons (although the exorcism of devils is occasionally practiced, and the daimonic has reappeared in the writings of psychotherapists), but human behavior is still commonly attributed to indwelling agents. A juvenile delinquent is said, for example, to be suffering from a disturbed personality. There would be no point in saying it if the personality were not somehow distinct from the body which has got itself into trouble. The distinction is clear when one body is said to contain several personalities which control it in different ways at different times. Psychoanalysts have identified three of these personalities—the ego, superego, and id—and interactions among them are said to be responsible for the behavior of the man in whom they dwell.

Although physics soon stopped personifying things in this way, it continued for a long time to speak as if they had wills, impulses, feelings, purposes, and other fragmentary attributes of an indwelling agent. According to Butterfield, Aristotle argued that a falling body accelerated because it grew more jubilant as it found itself nearer home, and later authorities supposed that a projectile was carried forward by an impetus, sometimes called an "impetuosity." All this was eventually abandoned, and to good effect, but the behavioral sciences still appeal to comparable internal states. No one is surprised to hear it said that a person carrying good news walks more rapidly because he feels jubilant, or acts carelessly because of his impetuosity, or holds stubbornly to a course of action through sheer force of will. Careless references to purpose are still to be found in both physics and biology, but good practice has no place for them; yet almost everyone attributes human behavior to intentions, purposes, aims, and goals. If it is still possible to ask whether a machine can show purpose, the question implies, significantly, that if it can it will more closely resemble a man.

Physics and biology moved farther away from personified causes when they began to attribute the behavior of things to essences, qualities, or natures. To the medieval alchemist, for example, some of the properties of a substance might be due to the mercurial essence, and substances were compared in what might have been called a "chemistry of individual differences." Newton complained of the practice in his contemporaries: "To tell us that every species of thing is endowed with an occult specific quality by which it acts and produces manifest effects is to tell us nothing." (Occult qualities were examples of the hypotheses Newton rejected when he said "Hypotheses non fingo," though he was not quite as good as his word.) Biology continued for a long time to appeal to the *nature* of living things, and it did not wholly abandon vital forces until the twentieth century. Behavior, however, is still attributed to human nature, and there is an extensive "psychology of individual differences" in which people are compared and described in terms of traits of character, capacities, and abilities.

Almost everyone who is concerned with human affairs—as political scientist, philosopher, man of letters, economist, psychologist, linguist, sociologist, theologian, anthropologist, educator, or psychotherapist—continues to talk about human behavior in this prescientific way. Every issue of a daily paper, every magazine, every professional journal, every book with any bearing whatsoever on human behavior will supply examples. We are told that to control the number of people in the world we need to change *attitudes* toward children, overcome *pride* in size of family or in sexual potency, build some *sense of responsibility* toward offspring, and reduce the role played by a large family in allaying *concern* for old age. To work for peace we must deal with the *will to power* or the *paranoid delusions* of leaders; we must remember that wars begin in the *minds* of men, that there is something suicidal in man—a *death instinct* perhaps—which leads to war, and that man is aggressive by *nature*. To solve the problems of the poor we must inspire *self-respect*, encourage *initiative*, and reduce *frustration*. To allay the disaffection of the young we must provide a *sense of purpose* and reduce feelings of *alienation* or *hopelessness*. Realizing that we have no effective means of doing any of this, we ourselves may experience *a crisis of belief* or a *loss of confidence*, which can be corrected only by returning to a *faith in man's inner capacities*. This is staple fare. Almost no one questions it. Yet there is nothing like it in modern physics or most of biology, and that fact may well explain why a science and a technology of behavior have been so long delayed.

It is usually supposed that the "behavioristic" objection to ideas, feelings, traits of character, will, and so on concerns the stuff of which they are said to be made. Certain stubborn questions about the nature of mind have, of course, been debated for more than twenty-five hundred years and still go unanswered. How, for example, can the mind move the body? As late as 1965 Karl Popper could put the question this way: "What we want is to understand how such nonphysical things as *purposes, deliberations, plans, decisions, theories, tensions*, and *values* can play a part in bringing about physical changes in the physical world." And, of course, we also want to know where these nonphysical things come from. To that question the Greeks had a simple answer: from the gods. As Dodds has pointed out, the Greeks believed that if a man behaved foolishly, it was because a hostile god had planted ἄτη (infatuation) in his breast. A friendly god might give a warrior an extra amount of μένος, with the help of which he would fight brilliantly. Aristotle thought there was something divine in thought, and Zeno held that the intellect *was* God.

We cannot take that line today, and the commonest alternative is to appeal to antecedent physical events. A person's genetic endowment, a product of the evolution of the species, is said to explain part of the workings of his mind and his personal history the rest. For example, because of (physical) competition during the course of evolution people now have (nonphysical) feelings of aggression which lead to (physical) acts of hostility. Or, the (physical) punishment a small child receives when he engages in sex play produces (nonphysical) feelings of anxiety which interfere with his (physical) sexual behavior as an adult. The nonphysical stage obviously bridges long periods of time: aggression reaches back into millions of years of evolutionary history, and anxiety acquired when one is a child survives into old age.

The problem of getting from one kind of stuff to another could be avoided if everything were either mental or physical, and both these possibilities have been considered. Some philosophers have tried to stay within the world of the mind arguing that only immediate experience is real, and experimental psychology began as an attempt to discover the mental laws which governed interactions among mental elements. Contemporary "intrapsychic" theories of psychotherapy tell us how one feeling leads to another (how frustration breeds aggression, for example), how feelings interact, and how feelings which have been put out of mind fight their way back in. The complementary line that the mental stage is really physical was taken, curiously enough, by Freud, who believed that physiology would eventually explain the workings of the mental apparatus. In a similar vein, many physiological psychologists continue to talk freely about states of mind, feelings, and so on, in the belief that it is only a matter of time before we shall understand their physical nature.

The dimensions of the world of mind and the transition from one world to another do raise embarrassing problems, but it is usually possible to ignore them, and this may be good strategy, for the important objection to mentalism is of a very different sort. The world of the mind steals the show. Behavior is not recognized as a subject in its own right. In psychotherapy, for example, the disturbing things a person does or says are almost always regarded merely as symptoms, and compared with the fascinating dramas which are staged in the depths of the mind, behavior itself seems superficial indeed. In linguistics and literary criticism what a man says is almost always treated as the expression of ideas or feelings. In political science, theology, and economics, behavior is usually regarded as the material from which one infers attitudes, intentions, needs, and so on. For more than twenty-five hundred years close attention has been paid to mental life, but only recently has any effort been made to study human behavior as something more than a mere by-product.

The conditions of which behavior is a function are also neglected. The mental explanation brings curiosity to an end. We see the effect in casual discourse. If we ask someone, "Why did you go to the theater?" and he says, "Because I felt like going," we are apt to take his reply as a kind of explanation. It would be much more to the point to know what has happened when he has gone to the theater in the past, what he heard or read about the play he went to see, and what other things in his past or present environments might have induced him to go (as opposed to doing something else), but we accept "I felt like going" as a sort of summary of all this and are not likely to ask for details.

The professional psychologist often stops at the same point. A long time ago William James corrected a prevailing view of the relation between feelings and action by asserting, for example, that we do not run away because we are afraid but are afraid because we run away. In other words, what we feel when we feel afraid is our behavior—the very behavior which in the traditional view expresses the feeling and is explained by it. But how many of those who have considered James's argument have noted that no antecedent event has in fact been pointed out? Neither "because" should be taken seriously. No explanation has been given as to why we run away *and* feel afraid.

Whether we regard ourselves as explaining feelings or the behavior said to be caused by feelings, we give very little attention to antecedent circumstances. The psychotherapist learns about the early life of his patient almost exclusively from the patient's memories, which are known to be unreliable, and he may even argue that what is important is not what actually happened but what the patient remembers. In the psychoanalytic literature there must be at least a hundred references to felt anxiety for every reference to a punishing episode to which anxiety might be traced. We even seem to prefer antecedent histories which are clearly out of reach. There is a good deal of current interest, for example, in what must have happened during the evolution of the species to explain human behavior, and we seem to speak with special confidence just because what actually happened can only be inferred.

Unable to understand how or why the person we see behaves as he does, we attribute his behavior to a person we cannot see, whose behavior we cannot explain either but about whom we are not inclined to ask questions. We probably adopt this strategy not so much because of any lack of interest or power but because of a longstanding conviction that for much of human behavior there *are* no relevant antecedents. The function of the inner man is to provide an explanation which will not be explained in turn. Explanation stops with him. He is not a mediator between past history and current behavior, he is a *center* from which behavior emanates. He initiates, originates, and creates, and in doing so he remains, as he was for the Greeks, divine. We say that he is autonomous—and, so far as a science of behavior is concerned, that means miraculous.

The position is, of course, vulnerable. Autonomous man serves to explain only the things we are not yet able to explain in other ways. His existence depends upon our ignorance, and he naturally loses status as we come to know more about behavior. The task of a scientific analysis is to explain how the behavior of a person as a physical system is related to the conditions under which the human species evolved and the conditions under which the individual lives. Unless there is indeed some capricious or creative intervention, these events must be related, and no intervention is in fact needed. The contingencies of survival responsible for man's genetic endowment would produce tendencies to *act* aggressively, not feelings of aggression. The punishment of sexual behavior changes sexual *behavior*, and any feelings which may arise are at best by-products. Our age is not suffering from anxiety but from the accidents, crimes, wars, and other dangerous and painful things to which people are so often exposed. Young people drop out of school, refuse to get jobs, and associate only with others of their own age not because they feel alienated but because of defective social environments in homes, schools, factories, and elsewhere.

We can follow the path taken by physics and biology by turning directly to the relation between behavior and the environment and neglecting supposed mediating states of mind. Physics did not advance by looking more closely at the jubilance of a falling body, or biology by looking at the nature of vital spirits, and we do not need to try to discover what personalities, states of mind, feelings, traits of character, plans, purposes, intentions, or the other perquisites of autonomous man really are in order to get on with a scientific analysis of behavior.

A Differential Association-Reinforcement Theory of Criminal Behavior

Robert L. Burgess and Ronald L. Akers
University of Washington

Introduction

In spite of the body of literature that has accumulated around the differential association theory of criminal behavior,[1] it has yet to receive crucial empirical test or thorough restatement beyond Sutherland's own revision in 1947. Recognizing that the theory is essentially a learning theory, Sutherland rephrased it to state explicitly that criminal behavior is learned as any behavior is learned. In Cressey's two revisions of the textbook, the theory has been deliberately left unchanged from Sutherland's revision. Thus, the theory as it stands now is postulated upon the knowledge of the learning process extant 20-25 years ago.[2]

Sutherland, himself, never was able to test directly or find specific empirical support for his theory, but he was convinced that the two-edged theory —(1) genetic, differential association and (2) structural, differential social organization—accounted for the known data on the full range of crimes, including conventional violations and white-collar crimes.[3] The theory has received some other empirical support,[4] but negative cases have also been found.[5] The attempts to subject the theory to empirical test are marked by inconsistent findings both within the same study and between studies, as well as by highly circumscribed and qualified findings and conclusions. Whether the particular researcher concludes that his findings do or do not seem to support the theory, nearly all

---

1 By 1960, Cressey had collected a 70-item bibliography on the theory; see Edwin H. Sutherland and Donald R. Cressey, *Principles of Criminology,* 6th ed., Chicago: J. B. Lippincott Co., 1960, p. vi. He has presented an exhaustive review of the mistaken notions, criticisms, attempted reformulations, and empirical tests of the theory contained in a sizable body of literature. Donald R. Cressey, "Epidemiology and Individual Conduct: A Case from Criminology," *Pacific Sociological Review,* 3 (Fall, 1960), pp. 47-58. For more recent literature see Donald R. Cressey, "The Theory of Differential Association: An Introduction," *Social Problems,* 8 (Summer, 1960), pp. 2-5. James F. Short, Jr., "Differential Association as a Hypothesis: Problems of Empirical Testing," *Social Problems,* 8 (Summer, 1960), pp. 14-25. Henry D. McKay, "Differential Association and Crime Prevention: Problems of Utilization," *Social Problems,* 8 (Summer, 1960), pp. 25-37. Albert J. Reiss, Jr., and A. Lewis Rhodes, "An Empirical Test of Differential Association Theory," *The Journal of Research in Crime and Delinquency,* 1 (January, 1964), pp. 5-18. Harwin L. Voss, "Differential Association and Reported Delinquent Behavior: A Replication," *Social Problems,* 12 (Summer, 1964), pp. 78-85. Siri Naess, "Comparing Theories of Criminogenesis," *The Journal of Research in Crime and Delinquency,* 1 (July, 1964), pp. 171-180. C. R. Jeffery, "Criminal Behavior and Learning Theory," *The Journal of Criminal Law, Criminology and Police Science,* 56 (September, 1965), pp. 294-300.

2 The original formal statement appeared in Edwin H. Sutherland, *Principles of Criminology,* 3rd ed., Philadelphia: J. B. Lippincott Co., 1939, pp. 4-8. The terms, "systematic" and "consistency" along with some statements referring to social disorganization and culture conflict were deleted in the revised theory. Two sentences stating that criminal behavior is learned were added and the terms "learned" and "learning" were included in other sentences. The modalities of duration, priority, and intensity were added. The revised theory is in Sutherland and Cressey, *op. cit.,* pp. 77-79. For Cressey's discussion of why he left the theory in its 1947 form see *ibid.,* p. vi.

3 *Ibid.,* pp. 77-80. Edwin H. Sutherland, *White Collar Crime,* New York: Holt, Rinehart and Winston, 1961, pp. 234-256 (originally published 1949). See also Cressey's "Foreword," *ibid.,* p. x.

4 John C. Ball, "Delinquent and Non-Delinquent Attitudes Toward the Prevalence of Stealing," *The Journal of Criminal Law, Crimonology and Police Science,* 48 (September-October, 1957), pp. 259-274. James F. Short, "Differential Association and Delinquency," *Social Problems,* 4, (January, 1957), pp. 233-239. Short, "Differential Association with Delinquent Friends and Delinquent Behavior," *Pacific Sociological Review,* 1 (Spring, 1958), pp. 20-25. Short, "Differential Association as a Hypothesis," *op. cit.* Voss, *op. cit.* Donald R. Cressey, "Application and Verification of the Differential Association Theory," *The Journal of Criminal Law, Criminology and Police Science,* 43 (May-June, 1952), pp. 47-50. Cressey, *Other People's Money,* Glencoe, Ill.: The Free Press, 1953, pp. 147-149. Glaser, *op. cit.,* pp. 7-10.

5 Marshall Clinard, *The Black Market,* New York: Rinehart Co., 1952, pp. 285-329. Marshall Clinard, "Rural Criminal Offenders," *American Journal of Sociology,* 50 (July, 1944), pp. 38-45. Edwin M. Lemert, "An Isolation and Closure Theory of Naive Check Forgery," *The Journal of Criminal Law, Criminology and Police Science,* 44, (September-October, 1953), pp. 293-307. Reiss and Rhodes, *op. cit.* Cressey, "Application and Verification of the Differential Association Theory," *op. cit.,* pp. 51-52. Cressey, *Other People's Money, op. cit.,* pp. 149 151. Glaser, *op. cit.,* pp. 12 13.

From *Social Problems,* Vol. 14 (Fall 1966), pp. 128–147. Reprinted with the permission of the Society of Social Problems and the authors.

have indicated difficulty in operationalizing the concepts and recommend that the theory be modified in such a way that it becomes more amenable to empirical testing.

Suggested theoretical modifications have not been lacking, but the difficulty with these restatements is that they are no more readily operationalized than Sutherland's.[6] One recent paper, however, by DeFleur and Quinney,[7] offers new promise that the theory can be adequately operationalized. They have presented a detailed strategy for making specific deductions for empirical testing. But while they have clarified the problems in the derivation and generation of testable hypotheses from differential association, they still see its empirical validation as a very difficult, though not impossible task.

Regardless of the particular criticisms, the exceptions taken, and the difficulties involved in testing and reformulating the theory that have been offered, few take exception to the central learning assumptions in differential association. If we accept the basic assumption that criminal behavior is learned by the same processes and involves the same mechanisms as conforming behavior, then we need to recognize and make use of the current knowledge about these processes and mechanisms. Neither the extant statement of the theory nor the reformulations of it make explicit the nature of the underlying learning process involved in differential association. In short, no major revisions have been made utilizing established learning principles.

That this type of revision of the theory is needed has been recognized and some criticism of differential association has revolved around the fact that it does not adequately portray the process by which criminal behavior is learned. But as Cressey explains:

> It is one thing to criticise the theory for failure to specify the learning process accurately and another to specify which aspects of the learning process should be included and in what way.[8]

Sutherland, of course, was as interested in explaining the "epidemiology" of crime as in explaining how the individual comes to engage in behavior in violation of the law and insisted that the two explanations must be consistent.[9] Differential social organization (normative conflict) has been successful in "making sense" of variations in crime rates. But differential association has been less successful in explicating the process by which this differential organization produces individual criminality. This seems to be due not to the lack of importance of associations for criminal behavior but:

> . . . rather to the fact that the theory outran the capacity of either psychology or social psychology to give adequate, scientific answers to the question of why there are such qualitative (selective) differences in human association.[10]

It now appears, however, that there is a body of verified theory which is adequate to the task of accurately specifying this process. Modern learning theory seems capable of providing insights into the problem of uniting structural and genetic formulations. While sociologists know a great deal about the structure of the environment from which deviants come, we know very little about the determining variables operating within this environment. The burden of criminological theory today is to combine knowledge of structural pressures with explanations of "why only *some* of the persons on whom this pressure is exerted become non-conformists."[11]

It is for this reason that the recent effort by C. R. Jeffery to re-examine differential association in light of modern learning theory marks a new departure in the abundance of thinking and writing that has characterized the intellectual history of this theory.[12]

In spite of their intricate axiomatization of the theory, DeFleur and Quinney, for example, recognize that even they have left the learning process in differential association unspecified. But, they note, "modern reinforcement learning theory would handle this problem. . . ."[13] This is precisely what Jeffery proposed to do and to the extent that this objective is served by discussing learning theory and criminal behavior together, he is at least partially successful. However, Jeffery does not in fact make it clear just how Sutherland's differential association theory may be revised. His explanation incorporates differential reinforcement:

> . . . [A] criminal act occurs in an environment in which in the past the actor has been reinforced for behaving in this manner, and the aversive consequences attached to the behavior have been of such a nature that they do not control or prevent the response.[14]

This statement, as it stands, bears no obvious or direct relation to Sutherland's differential association, and nowhere else does Jeffery make it clear how differential reinforcement is a reformulation of differential association. Jeffery does discuss modern learning principles, but he does not show how these principles may be incorporated within the framework of Sutherland's theory, nor how these principles may lead to explanations of past empirical findings.

Jeffery's theory and his discussion of criminal behavior and learning theory remains not so much incorrect as unconvincing. His presentation of learning principles is supported wholly by reference to experiments with lower organisms and his extension to criminal behavior is mainly through anecdotal and illustrative material. The potential value and impact of Jeffery's article is diminished by not calling attention to the already large and growing body of literature in experimental behavioral science, especially evidence using human subjects, that has direct implications for differential association theory. We are basically in agreement with Jeffery that learning theory has progressed to the point where it seems likely that differential association can be restated in a more sophisticated and testable form in the language of modern learning theory. But that restatement must be attempted in a thorough fashion before we can expect others to

[6] See Daniel Glaser, "Criminality Theories and Behavioral Images," *American Journal of Sociology,* 61 (March, 1956), pp. 433-444. Glaser, "Differential Association and Criminological Prediction," *op. cit.,* pp. 10-13. Naess, *op. cit.,* pp. 174-179.

[7] Melvin DeFleur and Richard Quinney, "A Reformulation of Sutherland's Differential Association Theory and a Strategy for Empirical Verification," *Journal of Research in Crime and Delinquency,* 3 (January, 1966), p. 13.

[8] Cressey, "Epidemiology and Individual Conduct," *op. cit.,* p. 54.

[9] Sutherland and Cressey, *op. cit.,* p. 80. Albert K. Cohen, Alfred R. Lindesmith, and Karl F. Schuessler (eds.), *The Sutherland Papers,* Bloomington: Indiana University Publications, Social Science Series, No. 15, 1956, pp. 5-42. That Sutherland intended an explanation of the two-fold problem of rates of crime and individual criminal behavior is, of course, the basic point of Cressey's paper, "Epidemiology and Individual Conduct," *op. cit.*

[10] George B. Vold, *Theoretical Criminology,* New York: Oxford University Press, 1958, p. 198.

[11] Cressey, "The Theory of Differential Association," *op. cit.,* p. 5.

[12] Jeffery, *op. cit.*

[13] DeFleur and Quinney, *op. cit.,* p. 3.

[14] *Ibid.,* p. 295.

accept it. Jeffery begins to do this and his thoughts are significant, but they do not take into account the theory as a whole.

The amount of empirical research in the social psychology of learning clearly has shown that the concepts in learning theory are susceptible to operationalization. Therefore, applying an integrated set of learning principles to differential association theory should adequately provide the revision needed for empirical testing. These learning principles are based on literally thousands of experimental hours covering a wide range of the phylogenetic scale and more nearly constitute empirically derived *laws* of behavior than any other set of principles. They enable the handling of a great variety of observational as well as experimental evidence about human behavior.

It is the purpose of this paper to take the first step in the direction to which Jeffery points. A restatement of the theory, not an alternative theory, will be presented, although, of necessity, certain ideas not intrinsic to differential association will have to be introduced and additions will be made to the original propositions. It should be pointed out that DeFleur and Quinney have been able to demonstrate that Sutherland's propositions, when stated in the form of set theory, appear to be internally consistent. By arranging the propositions in axiomatic form, stating them in logical rather than verbal symbols, they have brought the theoretical grammar up to date.[15] Such is not our intention in this paper, at all. We recognize and appreciate the importance of stating the propositions in a formal, deductive fashion. We do feel, however, that this task is, at the present time, subsidiary to the more urgent task of: (1) making explicit the learning process, as it is now understood by modern behavioral science, from which the propositions of differential association can be derived; (2) fully reformulating the theory, statement by statement, in light of the current knowledge of this learning process; and (3) helping criminologists become aware of the advances in learning theory and research that are directly relevant to an explanation of criminal behavior.[16] No claim is made that this constitutes a final statement. If it has any seminal value at all, that is, if it provokes a serious new look at the theory and encourages further effort in this direction, our objective will have been served.

Differential Association and Modern Behavior Theory

In this section the nine formal propositions in which Sutherland expressed his theory will be analyzed in terms of behavior theory and research and will be reformulated as seven new propositions. (See Table 1.)

I. "Criminal behavior is learned." VIII. "The process of learning criminal behavior by association with criminal and anti-criminal patterns involves all of the mechanisms that are involved in any other learning."

Since both the first and eighth sentences in the theory obviously form a unitary idea, it seems best to state them together. Sutherland was aware that these statements did not sufficiently describe the learning process,[17] but these two items leave no doubt that differential association theory was meant to fit into a general explanation of human behavior and, as much is unambiguously stated in the prefatory remarks of the theory: an "explanation of criminal behavior should be a specific part of a general theory of behavior."[18] Modern behavior theory as a general theory provides us with a good idea of what the mechanisms are that are involved in the process of acquiring behavior.[19]

According to this theory, there are two major categories of behavior. On the one hand, there is reflexive or *respondent* behavior which is behavior that is governed by the stimuli that elicit it. Such behaviors are largely associated with the autonomic system. The work of Pavlov is of special significance here. On the other hand, there is *operant* behavior: behavior which involves the central nervous system. Examples of operant behavior include verbal behavior, playing ball, driving a car, and buying a new suit. It has been found that this class of behavior is a function of its past and present environmental consequences. Thus, when a particular operant is followed by certain kinds of stimuli, that behavior's frequency of occurrence will increase in the future. These stimuli are called reinforcing stimuli or reinforcers[20] and include food, money, clothes, objects of various sorts, social attention, approval, affection and social status. This entire process is called positive reinforcement. One distinguishing characteristic of operant behavior as opposed to respondent behavior, then, is that the latter is a function of its antecedent stimuli, whereas the former is a function of its antecedent environmental consequences.

Typically, operant and respondent behaviors occur together in an individual's everyday behavior, and they interact in extremely intricate ways. Consequently, to fully understand any set of patterned responses, the investigator should observe the effects of the operants on the respondents as well as

15 DeFleur and Quinney, *op. cit.*

16 Our main concern here, of course, is with the nine statements of the theory as a genetic explanation of the process by which the individual comes to engage in illegal behavior. We do not lose sight of the fact, however, that this must be integrated with explanations of the variation and location of crime.

17 Cressey, 1960, *op. cit.*, p. 54.

18 Sutherland and Cressey, *op. cit.*, p. 75.

19 It should be mentioned at the outset that there is more than one learning theory. The one we will employ is called Behavior Theory. More specifically, it is that variety of behavior theory largely associated with the name of B. F. Skinner. (*Science and Human Behavior*, New York: Macmillan, 1953.) It differs from other learning theories in that it restricts itself to the relations between observable, measurable behavior and observable, measurable conditions. There is nothing in this theory that denies the existence, or importance, or even the inherent interest of the nervous system or brain. However, most behavioral scientists in this area are extremely careful in hypothesizing intervening variables or constructs, whether they are egos, personalities, response sets, or some sort of internal computers. Generally they adopt the position that the only real value of a construct is its ability to improve one's predictions. If it does not, then it must be excluded in accordance with the rule of parsimony.

20 It has been said by some that a tautology is involved here. But there is nothing tautological about classifying events in terms of their effects. As Skinner, *op. cit.*, pp. 72-73, has noted, this criterion is both empirical and objective. There is only one sure way of telling whether or not a given stimulus event is reinforcing to a given individual under given conditions and that is to make a direct test: observe the frequency of a selected behavior, then make a stimulus event contingent upon it and observe any change in frequency. If there is a change in frequency then we may classify the stimulus as reinforcing to the individual under the stated conditions. Our reasoning would become circular, however, if we went on to assert that a given stimulus strengthens the behavior *because* it is reinforcing. Furthermore, not all stimuli, when presented, will increase the frequency of the behavior which *produced* them. Some stimuli will increase the frequency of the behavior which *removes* them, still others will neither strengthen nor weaken the behavior which produced them. See Robert L. Burgess, Ronald L. Akers, "Are Operant Principles Tautological?" *The Psychological Record,* 16 (July, 1966), pp. 305-312.

TABLE 1
A DIFFERENTIAL ASSOCIATION-REINFORCEMENT THEORY OF CRIMINAL BEHAVIOR

Sutherland's Statements	*Reformulated Statements*
1. "Criminal behavior is learned." 8. "The process of learning criminal behavior by association with criminal and anti-criminal patterns involves all of the mechanisms that are involved in any other learning."	1. Criminal behavior is learned according to the principles of operant conditioning.
2. "Criminal behavior is learned in interaction with other persons in a process of communication."	2. Criminal behavior is learned both in nonsocial situations that are reinforcing or discriminative and through that social interaction in which the behavior of other persons is reinforcing or discriminative for criminal behavior.
3. "The principal part of the learning of criminal behavior occurs within intimate personal groups."	3. The principal part of the learning of criminal behavior occurs in those groups which comprise the individual's major source of reinforcements.
4. "When criminal behavior is learned, the learning includes (a) techniques of committing the crime, which are sometimes very complicated, sometimes very simple; (b) the specific direction of motives, drives, rationalizations, and attitudes."	4. The learning of criminal behavior, including specific techniques, attitudes, and avoidance procedures, is a function of the effective and available reinforcers, and the existing reinforcement contingencies.
5. "The specific direction of motives and drives is learned from definitions of the legal codes as favorable or unfavorable."	5. The specific class of behaviors which are learned and their frequency of occurrence are a function of the reinforcers which are effective and available, and the rules or norms by which these reinforcers are applied.
6. "A person becomes delinquent because of an excess of definitions favorable to violation of law over definitions unfavorable to violation of law."	6. Criminal behavior is a function of norms which are discriminative for criminal behavior, the learning of which takes place when such behavior is more highly reinforced than noncriminal behavior.
7. "Differential associations may vary in frequency, duration, priority, and intensity."	7. The strength of criminal behavior is a direct function of the amount, frequency, and probability of its reinforcement.
9. "While criminal behavior is an expression of general needs and values, it is not explained by those general needs and values since noncriminal behavior is an expression of the same needs and values."	9. (Omit from theory.)

the effects of the respondents on the operants. The connections between operant and respondent behaviors are especially crucial to an analysis of attitudes, emotional and conflict behaviors.

In everyday life, different consequences are usually contingent upon different classes of behavior. This relationship between behavior and its consequences functions to alter the rate and form of behavior as well as its relationship to many features of the environment. The process of operant reinforcement is the most important process by which behavior is generated and maintained. There are, in fact, six possible environmental consequences relative to the Law of Operant Behavior. (1) A behavior may produce certain stimulus events and thereby increase in frequency. As we have indicated above, such stimuli are called positive reinforcers and the process is called positive reinforcement. (2) A behavior may remove, avoid, or terminate certain stimulus events and thereby increase in frequency. Such stimuli are termed negative reinforcers and the process, negative reinforcement. (3) A behavior may produce certain stimulus events and thereby decrease in frequency. Such stimuli are called aversive stimuli or, more recently, punishers.[21] The entire behavioral process is called positive punishment. (4) A behavior may remove or terminate certain stimulus events and thereby decrease in frequency. Such stimuli are positive reinforcers and the process is termed negative punishment. (5) A behavior may produce or remove certain stimulus events which do not change the behavior's frequency at all. Such stimuli are called neutral stimuli. (6) A behavior may no longer produce customary stimulus events and thereby decrease in frequency. The stimuli which are produced are neutral stimuli, and the process, extinction. When a reinforcing stimulus no longer functions to increase the future probability of the behavior which produced it, we say the individual is satiated. To restore the reinforcing property of the stimulus we need only deprive the individual of it for a time.[22]

The increase in the frequency of occurrence of a behavior that is reinforced is the very property of reinforcement that permits the fascinating variety and subtlety that occur in operant as opposed to respondent behavior. Another process producing the variety we see in behavior is that of *conditioning*. When a primary or unconditioned reinforcing stimulus such as food is repeatedly paired with a neutral stimulus, the latter will eventually function as a reinforcing stimulus as well. An illustration of this would be as follows. The milk a mother feeds to her infant is an unconditioned reinforcer. If the food is repeatedly paired with social attention, affection, and approval, these latter will eventually become reinforcing as will the mother herself as a stimulus object. Later these *conditioned reinforcers* can be used to strengthen other behaviors by making these reinforcers contingent upon those new behaviors.

Differential reinforcement may also alter the form of a response. This process is called *shaping* or *response differentiation.* It can be exemplified by a child learning to speak. At first, the parent will reinforce any vocalization, but as time wears on, and as the child grows older, the parent will differentially reinforce only those responses which successfully approximate certain criteria. The child will be seen to proceed from mere grunts to "baby-talk" to articulate speech.[23]

[21] N. H. Azrin and D. F. Hake, "Conditioned Punishment," *Journal of the Experimental Analysis of Behavior,* 8 (September, 1965), pp. 279-293.

[22] See Jacob L. Gewirtz and Donald M. Baer, "Deprivation and Satiation of Social Reinforcers as Drive Conditions," *Journal of Abnormal and Social Psychology,* 57, 1958, pp. 165-172.

[23] This seems to be the process involved in learning to become a marihuana user. By successive approximations, the user learns (from others) to close on the appropriate techniques and effects of using marihuana. See Howard S. Becker, *Outsiders,* Glencoe, Ill.: The Free Press, 1963, pp. 41-58.

Of course, organisms, whether pigeons, monkeys or people, do not usually go around behaving in all possible ways at all possible times. In short, behavior does not occur in a vacuum; a given behavior is appropriate to a given situation. By appropriate we mean that reinforcement has been forthcoming only under certain conditions and it is under these conditions that the behavior will occur. In other words, differential reinforcement not only increases the probability of a response, it also makes that response more probable upon the recurrence of conditions the same as or similar to those that were present during previous reinforcements. Such a process is called *stimulus control* or *stimulus discrimination.* For example, a child when he is first taught to say "daddy" may repeat it when any male is present, or even, in the very beginning, when any adult is present. But through differential reinforcement, the child will eventually only speak the word "daddy" when his father is present or in other "appropriate" conditions. We may say that the father, as a stimulus object, functions as a discriminative stimulus (S^D) setting the occasion for the operant verbal response "daddy" because in the past such behavior has been reinforced under such conditions.

It has also been discovered that the pattern or schedule of reinforcement is as important as the amount of reinforcement. For example, a *fixed-interval* schedule of reinforcement, where a response is reinforced only after a certain amount of time has passed, produces a lower rate of response than that obtained with reinforcement based on a *fixed-ratio* schedule where a response is reinforced only after a certain number of responses have already been emitted. Similarly a response rate obtained with a fixed-ratio schedule is lower than that obtained with a *variable-ratio* schedule, where reinforcement occurs for a certain proportion of responses randomly varied about some central value. A schedule of reinforcement, then, refers to the response *contingencies* upon which reinforcement depends. All of the various schedules of reinforcement, besides producing lawful response characteristics, produce lawful extinction rates, once reinforcement is discontinued. Briefly, behavior reinforced on an intermittent schedule takes longer to extinguish than behavior reinforced on a continuous schedule.

This concept, schedules of reinforcement, is one the implications of which are little understood by many behavioral scientists, so a few additional words are in order. First of all, social reinforcements are for the most part intermittent. One obvious result of this fact is the resistance to extinction and satiation of much social behavior, desirable as well as undesirable. This is not peculiar to human social behavior, for even lower organisms seldom are faced with a continuous reinforcement schedule. Nevertheless, reinforcements mediated by another organism are probably much less reliable than those produced by the physical environment. This is the case because social reinforcement depends upon behavioral processes in the reinforcer which are not under good control by the reinforcee. A more subtle, though essentially methodological, implication of this is that because most social behaviors are maintained by complex intermittent schedules which have been shaped over a long period of time, a social observer, newly entering a situation may have extreme difficulty in immediately determining exactly what is maintaining a particular behavior or set of behaviors. Nor can the individual himself be expected to be able to identify his own contingencies of reinforcement.[24]

An important aspect of this theory is the presentation of the general ways that stimuli and responses can be formed into complex constellations of stimulus-response events. Although the basic principles are simple and must be separated to distinguish and study them, in actual life the principles function in concert, and consist of complex arrays and constellations.[25] Such complexity can be seen in the fact that single S-R events may be combined into sequences on the basis of conditioning principles. That is, responses can be thought to have stimulus properties. In addition, more than one response may come under the control of a particular stimulus. Thus, when the stimulus occurs, it will tend to set the occasion for the various responses that have been conditioned to it. These responses may be competitive, that is, only one or the other can occur. When this is so, the particular response which does occur may also depend upon other discriminative stimuli present in the situation that control only one or the other response. Finally, while some of the stimuli to which an individual responds emanate from the external environment, social and otherwise, some come from his own behavior. An individual is, then, not only a source of responses, he is also a source of some stimuli—stimuli that can effect his own behavior.

The most general behavioral principle is the Law of Operant Behavior which says that behavior is a function of its past and current environmental consequences. There have been numerous studies with children[26] as well as adults[27] which indicate that individual behavior conforms to this law. Of much more interest to sociologists is an experiment designed by Azrin and Lindsley in 1956[28] to investigate cooperative social behavior. Their study demonstrated that cooperative behavior could be developed, maintained, eliminated and reinstated solely through the manipulation of the contingency between reinforcing stimuli and the cooperative response. This basic finding has received much subsequent support. It has also been demonstrated that not only cooperative behavior, but also competitive behavior and leading and following behavior are a function of their past and present consequences.

Another of the behavioral principles we mentioned was that of stimulus discrimination. A discriminative stimulus is a stimulus in the presence of which a particular operant response is reinforced. Much of our behavior has come under the control of certain environmental, including social stimuli because in the past it has been reinforced in the presence of those stimuli. In an experiment by Donald Cohen,[29] a normal 13-year-old boy named Justin, when placed under identical experimental conditions emitted different be-

[24] Cressey encountered this problem in trying to get trust violators to reconstruct past associations. Cressey, *Other People's Money, op. cit.*, p. 149.

[25] Arthur Staats, "An Integrated-Functional Learning Approach to Complex Human Behavior," *Technical Report 28,* Contract ONR and Arizona State University, 1965.

[26] See, for example, S. W. Bijou and P. T. Sturges, "Positive Reinforcers for Experimental Studies with Children—Consumables and Manipulatables," *Child Development,* 30, 1959, pp. 151-170.

[27] J. G. Holland, "Human Vigilance," *Science,* 128, 1959, pp. 61-67; Harold Weiner, "Conditioning History and Human Fixed-Interval Performance," *Journal of the Experimental Analysis of Behavior,* 7 (September, 1964), pp. 383-385.

[28] N. H. Azrin and O. R. Lindsley, "The Reinforcement of Cooperation Between Children," *The Journal of Abnormal and Social Psychology,* 52 (January, 1956).

[29] Donald J. Cohen, "Justin and His Peers: an Experimental Analysis of a Child's Social World," *Child Development,* 33, 1962.

haviors depending upon whether his partner was his mother, brother, sister, friend, or a stranger. The results of this investigation demonstrated that Justin's social behavior was differentially controlled by reinforcement; but it also demonstrated that his behavior was different depending upon the social stimuli present, thus reaffirming the principle of stimulus discrimination. In other words, the dynamic properties of his social behavior, whether cooperative, competitive, leading or following, were controlled by his previous extra-experimental history with his teammates, although the experimenter could change those behaviors by experimentally altering the contingencies of reinforcement. It is, of course, almost a truism to say that an individual behaves differently in the presence of different people. The significance of this experiment, however, is that the investigator was able to isolate the determining variables and the principles by which they operated to produce this common phenomenon.

While this is by no means a complete survey of the relevant experimental tests of the behavioral principles outlined above, it may serve to point out that many forms of "normal" social behavior function according to the Law of Operant Behavior. But what about "deviant" behavior? Can we be sure these same principles are operating here? Unfortunately there have been no studies which attempt to test directly the relevance of these behavioral principles to criminal behavior. But there have been several experimental investigations of deviant behaviors emitted by mental patients. For example, in a study by Ayllon and Michael,[30] it was shown that the bizarre behaviors of psychotics functioned according to these learning principles. In this particular study various behavioral problems of psychotic patients were "cured" through the manipulation of reinforcement contingencies. Such principles as extinction, negative and positive reinforcement, and satiation were effectively utilized to eliminate the unwanted behaviors.[31] This study was one of the first experimental tests of the contention that not only conforming but also many unusual, inappropriate, or undesirable behaviors are shaped and maintained through social reinforcement. In another experiment Isaacs, Thomas, and Goldiamond[32] demonstrate that complex adjustive behaviors can be operantly conditioned in long-term psychotics by manipulating available reinforcers.

In yet another investigation,[33] the personnel of a mental hospital ward for schizophrenics recorded the behavior of the patients and provided consequences to it according to certain pre-established procedures. Without going into the many important details of this long investigation, we may note that in each of the six experiments that were carried out, the results demonstrate that reinforcement was effective in maintaining desired performances, even though these were "back-ward" psychotics who had resisted all previous therapy, including psychoanalysis, electroshock therapy, lobotomies and so forth.

> In each experiment, the performance fell to a near zero level when the established response-reinforcement relation was discontinued. . . . The standard procedure for reinforcement had been to provide tokens . . . [exchanged] for a variety of reinforcers. Performance decreased when this response-reinforcement relation was disrupted (1) by delivering tokens independently of the response while still allowing exchange of tokens for the reinforcers (Exp II and III), (2) by discontinuing the token system entirely but providing continuing access to the reinforcers (Exp IV), or (3) by discontinuing the delivery of tokens for a previously reinforced response while simultaneously providing tokens for a different, alternative response (Exp I and VI). Further, the effectiveness of the reinforcement procedure did not appear to be limited to an all-or-none basis. Patients selected and performed the assignment that provided the larger number of tokens when reinforcement was available for more than one assignment (Exp V).[34]

Again, we cannot review all of the relevant literature, yet perhaps the three investigations cited will serve to emphasize that many forms of deviant behavior are shaped and maintained by various contingencies of reinforcement.[35] Given this experimental evidence we would amend Sutherland's first and eighth propositions to read: I. *Criminal behavior is learned according to the principles of operant conditioning.*

II. "Criminal behavior is learned in interaction with other persons in the process of communication."

As DeFleur and Quinney have noted, the major implication of this proposition is that symbolic interaction is a necessary condition for the learning of criminal behavior.[36] Of direct relevance to this is an experiment designed to test the relative significance of verbal instructions and reinforcement contingencies in generating and maintaining a certain class of behaviors.[37] In brief, the results indicated that behavior could not be maintained solely through verbal instructions. However, it was also discovered that it was an extremely arduous task to shape a set of complex behaviors without using verbal instructions as discriminative stimuli. Behavior was quickly and effectively developed and maintained by a combination of verbal instructions *and* reinforcement consequences. Symbolic interaction is, then, not enough, contingencies of reinforcement must also be present.

From the perspective of modern behavior theory, two aspects of socialization are usually considered to distinguish it from other processes of behavioral change: (1) Only those behavioral changes occurring through learning are considered relevant; (2) only the changes in behavior having their origins in interaction with other persons are considered products of socialization.[38] Sutherland's theory may, then, be seen to be a theory of differential socialization since he, too, restricted himself to learning having its origin in interaction with other persons. While social learning is, indeed, important and even predominant,

---

[30] T. Ayllon and J. Michael, "The Psychiatric Nurse as a Behavioral Engineer," *Journal of the Experimental Analysis of Behavior,* 2, 1959, pp. 323-334.

[31] There is, of course, no intention on our part to equate "mental" illness or similarly severe behavior problems with criminal behavior. The only connection that we are making is that both may be seen to function according to the same basic behavioral principles and both may be in opposition to established norms.

[32] W. Isaacs, J. Thomas, and I. Goldiamond, "Application of Operant Conditioning to Reinstate Verbal Behavior in Psychotics," *Journal of Speech and Disorders,* 25, 1960, pp. 8-12.

[33] T. Ayllon and N. Azrin, "The Measurement and Reinforcement of Behavior of Psychotics," *Journal of the Experimental Analysis of Behavior,* 8 (November, 1965), pp. 357-383.

[34] *Ibid.,* p. 381.

[35] See also J. J. Eysenck (ed.), *Experiments in Behaviour Therapy,* New York: Pergamon Press, The Macmillan Company, 1964. L. Krasner and L. Ullman, *Research in Behavior Modification,* New York: Holt, Rinehart and Winston, 1965. L. Ullman and L. Krasner, *Case Studies in Behavior Modification,* New York: Holt, Rinehart and Winston, 1964.

[36] DeFleur and Quinney, *op. cit.,* p. 3.

[37] T. Ayllon and N. Azrin, "Reinforcement and Instructions with Mental Patients," *Journal of the Experimental Analysis of Behavior,* 7, 1964, pp. 327-331.

[38] Paul E. Secord and Carl W. Backman, *Social Psychology,* New York: McGraw-Hill, 1964.

it certainly does not exhaust the learning process. In short, we may learn (and, thus, our behavior would be modified) without any direct contact with another person. As such, Sutherland's theory may be seen to suffer from a significant lacuna in that it neglected the possibility of deviant behavior being learned in nonsocial situations. Consequently, to be an adequate theory of deviant behavior, the theory must be amended further to include those forms of deviant behavior that are learned in the absence of social reinforcement. Other people are not the only source of reinforcement although they are the most important. As Jeffery[39] has aptly noted, stealing is reinforcing in and by itself whether other people know about it and reinforce it socially or not. The same may be said to apply to many forms of aggressive behaviors.[40]

There are many studies which are relevant to social interaction and socialization on the one hand, and Sutherland's second proposition on the other. For example, in a study by Lott and Lott[41] it was found that when child A was reinforced in the presence of child B, child A would later select child B as a companion. The behavior of selecting child B was not the behavior that was reinforced. The experimental conditions simply paired child B with positive reinforcement. In accordance with the principle of conditioning, child B had become a conditioned positive reinforcer. As such any behavior which produced the presence of child B would be strengthened, such behaviors, for example, as verbal responses requesting child B's company. Thus, as Staats[42] has noted, the results of this study indicate that the concepts of reinforcing stimuli and group cohesion are related when analyzed in terms of an integrated set of learning principles.

Glaser[43] has attempted to reformulate Sutherland's differential association theory in terms of social identification. It should be recognized, however, that identification as well as modeling and imitative behavior (which are usually associated with identification) comprise just one feature of the socialization process. Furthermore, such behavior may be analyzed quite parsimoniously with the principles of modern behavior theory. For example, in a study by Bandura and Ross,[44] a child experienced the pairing of one adult with positive reinforcers. Presumably this adult would become a conditioned reinforcer. And indeed, later it was found that the child imitated this adult more than he did an adult who was not paired with positive reinforcers. That is, the one adult, as he became a stronger reinforcer, had also become a stronger S^D for imitating or following behavior. Thus, Bandura's and Ross's results demonstrate that imitating or following behavior is at least in part a function of the reinforcing value of people as social stimuli.

> On the basis of these results it is suggested that a change in the reinforcing value of an individual will change his power as a stimulus controlling other people's behavior in various ways. An increase in the reinforcing value of an individual will increase verbal and motor approach, or companionable responses, respectful responses, affectionate behavior, following behavior, smiling, pleasant conversation, sympathetic responses and the like.[45]

The relevance of these studies is that they have isolated some of the determining variables whereby the behavior of one person is influenced or changed by the behavior of another as well as the principles by which these variables operate. We have, of course, only scratched the surface. Many other variables are involved. For instance, not all people are equally effective in controlling or influencing the behavior of others. The person who can mediate the most reinforcers will exercise the most power. Thus, the parent, who controls more of his child's reinforcers, will exercise more power than an older sibling or the temporary "baby sitter." As the child becomes older and less dependent upon the parent for many of his reinforcers, other individuals or groups such as his peers may exercise more power. Carrying the analysis one step further, the person who has access to a large range of aversive stimuli will exert more power than one who has not. Thus a peer group may come to exercise more power over a child's behavior than the parent even though the parent may still control a large share of the child's positive reinforcers.

In addition to the reinforcing function of an individual or group, there is, as seen in the Cohen and the Bandura and Ross studies, the discriminative stimulus function of a group. For example, specific individuals as physical stimuli may acquire discriminative control over an individual's behavior. The child in our example above is reinforced for certain kinds of behaviors in the presence of his parent, thus the parent's presence may come to control this type of behavior. He is reinforced for different behaviors in the presence of his peers, who then come to set the occasion for this type of behavior. Consequently this proposition must be amended to read: II. *Criminal behavior is learned both in nonsocial situations that are reinforcing or discriminative, and through that social interaction in which the behavior of other persons is reinforcing or discriminative for criminal behavior.*

III. "The principal part of the learning of criminal behavior occurs within intimate personal groups."

In terms of our analysis, the primary group would be seen to be the major source of an individual's social reinforcements. The bulk of behavioral training which the child receives occurs at a time when the trainers, usually the parents, possess a very powerful system of reinforcers. In fact, we might characterize a primary group as a generalized reinforcer (one associated with many reinforcers, conditioned as well as unconditioned). And, as we suggested above, as the child grows older, groups other than the family may come to control a majority of an individual's reinforcers, e.g., the adolescent peer group.

To say that the primary group is the principal molder of an individual's behavioral repertoire is not to ignore social learning which may occur in other contexts. As we noted above, learning from social models can be adequately explained in terms of these behavioral principles. The analysis we employed there can also be extended to learning from the mass media and from "reference" groups. In any case, we may alter this proposition to read:

---

[39] Jeffery, *op. cit.*

[40] For some evidence that aggressive behavior may be of a respondent as well as an operant nature, see N. Azrin, R. Hutchinson, and R. McLaughlin, "The Opportunity for Aggression as an Operant Reinforcer during Aversive Stimulation," *Journal of the Experimental Analysis of Behavior,* 8 (May, 1965), pp. 171-180.

[41] B. E. Lott and A. J. Lott, "The Formation of Positive Attitudes Toward Group Members," *The Journal of Abnormal and Social Psychology,* 61, 1960, pp. 297-300.

[42] Arthur Staats, *Human Learning,* New York: Holt, Rinehart and Winston, 1964, p. 333.

[43] Glaser, "Criminality Theories and Behavioral Images," *op. cit.*

[44] A. Bandura, D. Ross, and S. Ross, "A Comparative Test of the Status Envy, Social Power and the Secondary Reinforcement Theories of Identification Learning," *Journal of Abnormal and Social Psychology,* 67, 1963, pp. 527-534.

[45] Staats, 1964, *op. cit.,* p. 333.

III. *The principal part of the learning of criminal behavior occurs in those groups which comprise the individual's major source of reinforcements.*

IV. "When criminal behavior is learned, the learning includes (a) techniques of committing the crime, which are sometimes very complicated, sometimes very simple; (b) the specific direction of motives, drives, rationalizations, and attitudes."

A study by Klaus and Glaser[46] as well as many other studies[47] indicate that reinforcement contingencies are of prime importance in learning various behavioral techniques. And, of course, many techniques, both simple and complicated, are specific to a particular deviant act such as jimmying, picking locks of buildings and cars, picking pockets, short- and big-con techniques, counterfeiting and safe-cracking. Other techniques in criminal behavior may be learned in conforming or neutral contexts, e.g., driving a car, signing checks, shooting a gun, etc. In any event, we need not alter the first part of this proposition.

The second part of this proposition does, however, deserve some additional comments. Sutherland's major focus here seems to be motivation. Much of what we have already discussed in this paper often goes under the general heading of motivation. The topic of motivation is as important as it is complex. This complexity is related to the fact that the same stimulus may have two functions: it may be both a reinforcing stimulus and a discriminative stimulus controlling the behavior which is followed by reinforcement.[48] Thus, motivation may be seen to be a function of the processes by which stimuli acquire conditioned reinforcing value and become discriminative stimuli. Reinforcers and discriminative stimuli here would become the dependent variables; the independent variables would be the conditioning procedures previously mentioned and the level of deprivation. For example, when a prisoner is deprived of contact with members of the opposite sex, such sex reinforcers will become much more powerful. Thus, those sexual reinforcers that are available, such as homosexual contact, would come to exert a great deal of influence and would shape behaviors that would be unlikely to occur without such deprivation. And, without going any further into this topic, some stimuli may be more reinforcing, under similar conditions of deprivation, for certain individuals or groups than for others. Furthermore, the satiation of one or more of these reinforcers would allow for an increase in the relative strength of others.

Much, therefore, can be learned about the distinctive characteristics of a group by knowing what the available and effective reinforcers are and the behaviors upon which they are contingent. Basically, we are contending that the nature of the reinforcer system and the reinforcement contingencies are crucial determinants of individual and group behavior. Consequently, a description of an individual's or group's reinforcers, and an understanding of the principles by which reinforcers affect behavior, would be expected to yield a great deal of knowledge about individual and group deviant behavior.

Finally, the rationalizations which Cressey identifies with regard to trust violators and the peculiar extensions of "defenses to crimes" or "techniques of neutralization" by which deviant behavior is justified, as identified by Sykes and Matza,[49] may be analyzed as operant behaviors of the escape or avoidance type which are maintained because they have the effect of avoiding or reducing the punishment that comes from social disapproval by oneself as well as by others. We may, therefore, rewrite this proposition to read: IV. *The learning of criminal behavior, including specific techniques, attitudes, and avoidance procedures, is a function of the effective and available reinforcers, and the existing reinforcement contingencies.*

V. "The specific direction of motives and drives is learned from definitions of the legal codes as favorable or unfavorable."

In this proposition, Sutherland appears to be referring, at least in part, to the concept "norm" which may be defined as a statement made by a number of the members of a group, not necessarily all of them, prescribing or proscribing certain behaviors at certain times.[50] We often infer what the norms of a group are by observing reaction to behavior, i.e., the sanctions applied to, or reinforcement and punishment consequences of, such behavior. We may also learn what a group's norms are through verbal or written statements. The individual group member also learns what is and is not acceptable behavior on the basis of verbal statements made by others, as well as through the sanctions (i.e., the reinforcing or aversive stimuli) applied to his behavior (and other norm violators) by others.

Behavior theory specifies the place of normative statements and sanctions in the dynamics of acquiring "conforming" or "normative" behavior. Just as the behavior and even the physical characteristics of the individual may serve discriminative functions, verbal behavior, and this includes normative statements, can be analyzed as S^D's. A normative statement can be analyzed as an S^D indicating that the members of a group ought to behave in a certain way in certain circumstances. Such "normative" behavior would be developed and maintained by social reinforcement. As we observed in the Ayllon-Azrin study[51] of instructions and reinforcement contingencies, such verbal behavior would not maintain any particular class of behaviors if it were not at least occasionally backed by reinforcement consequences. Extending their analysis, an individual would not "conform" to a norm if he did not have a past history of reinforcement for such conforming behavior. This

[46] D. J. Klaus and R. Glaser, "Increasing Team Proficiency Through Training," Pittsburg: American Institute of Research, 1960.

[47] See Robert L. Burgess, "Communication Networks and Behavioral Consequences," forthcoming.

[48] A central principle underlying this analysis is that reinforcing stimuli, both positive and negative, elicit certain respondents. Unconditioned reinforcers elicit these responses without training, conditioned reinforcers elicit such responses through respondent conditioning. Staats and Staats (*Complex Human Behavior,* New York: Holt, Rinehart and Winston, 1964) have characterized such respondents as "attitude" responses. Thus, a positive reinforcer elicits a positive attitude. Furthermore, these respondents have stimulus characteristics which may become discriminative stimuli setting the occasion for a certain class of operants called "striving" responses for positive reinforcers and escape and/or avoidance behaviors for negative reinforcers. These respondents and their attendant stimuli may be generalized to other reinforcing stimuli. Thus, striving responses can be seen to generalize to new positive reinforcers since these also will elicit the respondent responses and their characteristic stimuli which have become S^D's for such behavior.

[49] Cressey, *Other People's Money, op. cit.,* pp. 93-138. G. M. Sykes and David Matza, "Techniques of Neutralization: A Theory of Delinquency," *American Sociological Review,* 22 (December, 1957), pp. 664-670.

[50] George C. Homans, *Social Behavior: Its Elementary Forms,* New York: Harcourt, Brace and World, 1961.

[51] Ayllon-Azrin, 1964, *op. cit.*

is important, for earlier we stated that we can learn a great deal about a group by knowing what the effective reinforcers are and the behaviors upon which they are contingent. We may now say that we can learn a great deal about an individual's or a group's behavior when we are able to specify, not only what the effective reinforcers are, but also what the rules or norms are by which these reinforcers are applied.[52] For these two types of knowledge will tell us much about the types of behavior that the individual will develop or the types of behaviors that are dominant in a group.

For example, it has often been noted that most official criminal acts are committed by members of minority groups who live in slums. One distinguishing characteristic of a slum is the high level of deprivation of many important social reinforcers. Exacerbating this situation is the fact that these people, in contrast to other groups, lack the behavioral repertoires necessary to produce reinforcement in the prescribed ways. They have not been and are not now adequately reinforced for lawful or normative behavior. And as we know from the Law of Operant Reinforcement, a reinforcer will increase the rate of occurrence of any operant which produces it. Furthermore, we would predict that given a large number of individuals under similar conditions, they are likely to behave in similar ways. Within such groups, many forms of social reinforcement may become contingent upon classes of behaviors which are outside the larger society's normative requirements. Norms and legal codes, as discriminative stimuli, will only control the behavior of those who have experienced the appropriate learning history. If an individual has been, and is, reinforced for such "normative" behavior, that behavior will be maintained in strength. If he has not been, and is not now reinforced for such behaviors they would be weak, if they existed in his repertoire at all. And, importantly, the reinforcement system may shape and maintain another class of behaviors which do result in reinforcement and such behaviors may be considered deviant or criminal by other members of the group. Thus we may formulate this proposition to read: V. *The specific class of behaviors which are learned and their frequency of occurrence are a function of the reinforcers which are effective and available, and the rules or norms by which these reinforcers are applied.*

[52] Staats and Staats, *op. cit.*

VI. "A person becomes delinquent because of an excess of definitions favorable to violation of law over definitions unfavorable to violation of law."

This proposition is generally considered the heart of Sutherland's theory; it is the principle of differential association. It follows directly from proposition V, and we must now refer back to that proposition. In proposition V, the use of the preposition "from" in the phrase, "learned from definitions of the legal codes as favorable or unfavorable," is somewhat misleading. The meaning here is not so much that learning results *from* these definitions as it is that they form part of the *content* of one's learning, determining which direction one's behavior will go in relation to the law, i.e., law-abiding or lawbreaking.

These definitions of the law make lawbreaking seem either appropriate or inappropriate. Those definitions which place lawbreaking in a favorable light in a sense can be seen as essentially norms of evasion and/or norms directly conflicting with conventional norms. They are, as Sykes and Matza and Cressey note, "techniques of neutralization," "rationalizations," or "verbalizations" which make criminal behavior seem "all right" or justified, or which provide defenses against self-reproach and disapproval from others.[53] The principle of negative reinforcement would be of major significance in the acquisition and maintenance of such behaviors.

This analysis suggests that it may not be an "excess" of one kind of definition over another in the sense of a cumulative ratio, but rather in the sense of the relative amount of discriminative stimulus value of one set of verbalizations or normative statements over another. As we suggested in the last section, normative statements are, themselves, behaviors that are a function of reinforcement consequences. They, in turn, may serve as discriminative stimuli for other operant behaviors (verbal and nonverbal). But recall that reinforcement must be forthcoming, at least occasionally, before a verbal statement can continue as a discriminative stimulus. Bear in mind, also, that behavior may produce reinforcing consequences even in the absence of any accompanying verbal statements.

[53] Sykes and Matza, *op. cit.*, Cressey, *Other People's Money*, *op. cit.*, pp. 93-138; Donald R. Cressey, "The Differential Association Theory and Compulsive Crimes," *Journal of Criminal Law, Criminology and Police Science*, 45 (May-June, 1954), pp. 29-40; Donald R. Cressey, "Social Psychological Foundations for Using Criminals in the Rehabilitation of Criminals," *Journal of Research in Crime and Delinquency*, 2 (July, 1965), pp. 45-59. See revised proposition IV.

In other terms, a person will become delinquent if the official norms or laws do not perform a discriminative function and thereby control "normative" or conforming behavior. We know from the Law of Differential Reinforcement that that operant which produces the most reinforcement will become dominant if it results in reinforcement. Thus, if lawful behavior did not result in reinforcement, the strength of the behavior would be weakened, and a state of deprivation would result, which would, in turn, increase the probability that other behaviors would be emitted which are reinforced, and such behaviors would be strengthened. And, of course, these behaviors, though common to one or more groups, may be labelled deviant by the larger society. And such behavior patterns, themselves, may acquire conditioned reinforcing value and, subsequently, be enforced by the members of a group by making various forms of social reinforcement, such as social approval, esteem, and status contingent upon that behavior.

The concept "excess" in the statement, "excess of definitions favorable to violation of law," has been particularly resistant to operationalization. A translation of this concept in terms of modern behavior theory would involve the "balance" of reinforcement consequences, positive and negative. The Law of Differential Reinforcement is crucial here. That is, a person would engage in those behaviors for which he had been reinforced most highly in the past. (The reader may recall that in the Aylon-Azrin study with schizophrenics, it was found that the patients selected and performed those behaviors which provided the most reinforcers when reinforcement was available for more than one response.) Criminal behavior would, then, occur under those conditions where an individual has been most highly reinforced for such behavior, and the aversive consequences contingent upon the behavior have been of such a nature that they do not perform a "punishment function."[54]

[54] This, then, is essentially differential reinforcement as Jeffery presents it. We have attempted to show how this is congruent with differential association. Further, while Jeffery ignores the key concepts of "definitions" and "excess" we have in-

This leads us to a discussion of proposition VII. But, first, let us reformulate the sixth proposition to read: VI. *Criminal behavior is a function of norms which are discriminative for criminal behavior, the learning of which takes place when such behavior is more highly reinforced than noncriminal behavior.*

VII. "Differential associations may vary in frequency, duration, priority, and intensity."

In terms of our analysis, the concepts frequency, duration, and priority are straightforward enough. The concept *intensity* could be operationalized to designate the number of the individual's positive and negative reinforcers another individual or group controls, as well as the reinforcement value of that individual or group. As previously suggested the group which can mediate the most positive reinforcers and which has the most reinforcement value, as well as access to a larger range of aversive stimuli, will exert the most control over an individual's behavior.

There is a good reason to suspect, however, that Sutherland was not so much referring to differential associations with other persons, as differential associations with criminal *patterns.* If this supposition is correct, then this proposition can be clarified by relating it to differential contingencies of reinforcement rather than differential social associations. From this perspective, the experimental evidence with regard to the various schedules of reinforcement is of major importance. There are three aspects of the schedules of reinforcement which are of particular importance here: (1) the *amount* of reinforcement: the greater the amount of reinforcement, the higher the response rate; (2) the *frequency* of reinforcement which refers to the number of reinforcements per given time period: the shorter the time period between reinforcements, the higher the response rate; and (3) the *probability* of reinforcement which is the reciprocal of responses per reinforcement: the lower the ratio of responses per reinforcement, the higher the rate of response.[55]

Priority, frequency, duration, and intensity of association with criminal persons and groups are important to the extent that they insure that deviant behavior will receive greater amounts of reinforcement at more frequent intervals or with a higher probability than conforming behavior. But the frequency, probability, and amount of reinforcement are the crucial elements. This means that it is the coming under the control of contingencies of reinforcement that selectively produces the criminal definitions and behavior. Consequently, let us rewrite this proposition to read: VII. *The strength of criminal behavior is a direct function of the amount, frequency, and probability of its reinforcement.*

IX. "While criminal behavior is an expression of general needs and values, it is not explained by those general needs and values since noncriminal behavior is an expression of the same needs and values."

In this proposition, Sutherland may have been reacting, at least in part, to the controversy regarding the concept "need." This controversy is now essentially resolved. For, we have finally come to the realization that "needs" are unobservable, hypothetical, fictional inner-causal agents which were usually invented on the spot to provide spurious explanations of some observable behavior. Futhermore, they were inferred from precisely the same behavior they were supposed to explain.

While we can ignore the reference to needs, we must discuss values. Values may be seen as reinforcers which have salience for a number of the members of a group or society. We agree with Sutherland to the extent that he means that the nature of these general reinforcers do not necessarily determine which behavior they will strengthen. Money, or something else of general value in society, will reinforce any behavior that produces it. This reinforcement may depend upon noncriminal behavior, but it also may become contingent upon a set of behaviors that are labelled as criminal. Thus, if Sutherland can be interpreted as meaning that criminal and noncriminal behavior cannot be maintained by the same set of reinforcers, we must disagree. However, it may be that there are certain reinforcing consequences which only criminal behavior will produce, for the behavior finally shaped will depend upon the reinforcer that is effective for the individual. Nevertheless, it is the reinforcement, not the specific nature of the reinforcer, which explains the rate and form of behavior. But since this issue revolves around contingencies of reinforcement which are handled elsewhere, we will eliminate this last proposition.

Concluding Remarks

The purpose of this paper has been the application of the principles of modern behavior theory to Sutherland's differential association theory. While Sutherland's theory has had an enduring effect upon the thinking of students of criminal behavior, it has, till now, undergone no major theoretical revision despite the fact that there has been a steady and cumulative growth in the experimental findings of the processes of learning.

There are three aspects of deviant behavior which we have attempted to deal with simultaneously, but which should be separated. First, how does an individual *become* delinquent, or how does he learn delinquent behavior? Second, what *sustains* this delinquent behavior? We have attempted to describe the ways in which the principles of modern behavior theory are relevant to the development and maintenance of criminal behavior. In the process, we have seen that the principle of differential reinforcement is of crucial importance. But we must also attend to a third question, namely, what sustains the pattern or *contingency* of reinforcement? We only have hinted at some of the possibly important variables. We have mentioned briefly, for example, structural factors such as the level of deprivation of a particular group with regard to important social reinforcers, and the lack of effective reinforcement of "lawful" behavior[56] and the concomitant failure to develop the appropriate behavioral repertoires to produce reinforcement

corporated them into the reformulation. These definitions, viewed as verbalizations, become discriminative stimuli; and "excess" operates to produce criminal behavior in two related ways: (1) verbalizations conducive to law violation have greater discriminative stimulus value than other verbalizations, and (2) criminal behavior has been more highly reinforced and has produced fewer aversive outcomes than has law abiding behavior in the conditioning history of the individual.

[55] R. T. Kelleher and L. R. Gollub, "A Review of Positive Conditioned Reinforcement," *Journal of the Experimental Analysis of Behavior* (October, 1962), pp. 543-597. Because the emission of a fixed ratio or variable ratio of responses requires a period of time, the rate of responding will indirectly determine the frequency of reinforcement.

[56] Robert K. Merton, *Social Theory and Social Structure,* Glencoe, Ill.: The Free Press, pp. 161-195. For a more complete discussion of social structure in terms relevant to this paper, see Robert L. Burgess and Don Bushell, Jr., *Behavioral Sociology,* Parts IV and V, forthcoming, 1967.

legally.[57] We have also suggested that those behaviors which do result in reinforcement may, themselves, gain reinforcement value and be enforced by the members of the group through the manipulation of various forms of social reinforcement such as social approval and status, contingent upon such behaviors.[58] In short, new norms may develop and these may be termed delinquent by the larger society.

There are many other topics that are of direct relevance to the problem of deviant behavior which we have not been able to discuss given the requirements of space. For instance, no mention has been made of some outstanding research in the area of punishment. This topic is, of course, of prime importance in the area of crime prevention. To illustrate some of this research and its relevance, it has been found experimentally that the amount of behavior suppression produced by response-contingent aversive stimuli is a direct function of the intensity of the aversive stimulus, but that a mild aversive stimulus may produce a dramatic behavior-suppression if it is paired with reinforcement for an alternative and incompatible behavior. Furthermore, it has been discovered that if an aversive stimulus is repeatedly paired with positive reinforcement, and reinforcement is not available otherwise, the aversive stimulus may become a discriminative stimulus (S^D) for reinforcement and, consequently, not decrease the behavior's frequency of occurrence.

There are, in conclusion, numerous criteria that have been used to evaluate theories. One such set is as follows:

(1) The amount of empirical support for the theory's basic propositions.

(2) The "power" of the theory, i.e., the amount of data that can be derived from the theory's higher-order propositions.

(3) The controlling possibilities of the theory, including (a) whether the theory's propositions are, in fact, *causal* principles, and (b) whether the theory's propositions are stated in such a way that they suggest possible *practical* applications.

What dissatisfaction there has been with differential association can be attributed to its scoring low on these criteria, especially (1) and (3). We submit that the reformulated theory presented here answers some of these problems and better meets each of these criteria. It is our contention, moreover, that the reformulated theory not only specifies the conditions under which criminal behavior is learned, but also some of the conditions under which deviant behavior in general is acquired. Finally, while we have not stated our propositions in strictly axiomatic form, a close examination will reveal that each of the later propositions follow from, modify, or clarify earlier propositions.

[57] *Ibid.*, and Richard A. Cloward, "Illegitimate Means, Anomie, and Deviant Behavior," *American Sociological Review*, 24 (April, 1959), pp. 164-177.

[58] Albert K. Cohen, *Delinquent Boys: The Culture of the Gang*, Glencoe, Ill.: The Free Press, 1955 .

SECTION FOUR

Summary

There is wide consensus that delinquent behavior is primarily learned behavior—that children are not born delinquent. No one has discovered physical, physiological, or genetic traits that automatically propel youths into delinquency. Moreover, no one has found a particular set of physical characteristics to justify the consideration of delinquent youths as biologically inferior, genetically abnormal, or in any way "diseased" or ill compared to other youths. However, there may be physical, genetic, or physiological traits that differentiate *to some degree*, such as body build. This finding should not suggest that youths with a particular build are propelled into delinquency by mysterious inner forces. As the Gluecks argue, certain traits may simply facilitate involvement in delinquency under some conditions, while under others they may be associated with quite conventional and widely approved accomplishments. We also have to recognize that differences noted in studies of delinquent youths may stem from a link between certain physical characteristics and the likelihood of official processing. If youths with a certain physique are thought to be dangerous or threatening, they may have a greater chance of acquiring a record than less threatening youths engaged in the same activity.

Performance on intelligence tests and on various psychological assessments is related to delinquent behavior. But the relationships do not necessarily support arguments concerning genetic versus environmental causes of delinquency, because the controversy over genetic and environmental determination of intelligence-test performance and personality has not been settled. Moreover, there is an ongoing debate about what intelligence tests and personality tests measure. Intelligence tests have been criticized for assessing skills necessary for success or achievement in some environments but not others. Poor performance on these tests is associated with poor performance in school, and poor school performance is a significant correlate of delinquency. Delinquent youth may be very skilled in other senses.

Certain personality tests differentiate between delinquents and nondelinquents, but for several reasons they have not contributed much to the explanation of delinquency. First, some of the questions posed ostensibly to assess "personality" are actually measures of delinquency. The MMPI calls for responses to statements whereby the test-taker admits to various types of delinquency. Observed correlations between test scores and delinquency may mean no more than that youths who say they break rules are more likely to break rules. To deem people who engage in antisocial or aggressive conduct antisocial or aggressive personalities merely substitutes a new word for the phenomenon to be explained. The substitution does not add to our understanding of causes of the conduct, and such substitutions have not been demonstrated to make a difference in our dealing with criminal or delinquent behavior. Compared with nondelinquent youths, delinquent youths are less likely to accept the law as morally binding, are less attached to their parents and teachers, and are less committed to conventional goals. Words like *primitive, poorly adjusted, impulsive,* and *mentally abnormal* do not explain their behavior. To paraphrase B. F. Skinner, these words do not denote clearly identifiable conditions "of which behavior is a function."

On the other hand, if assessments of attitudes, feelings, and social relationships were (1) to avoid merely substituting vague words for the behavioral patterns of interest and (2) to identify the specific characteristics of a youth's social world that correlate with delinquent behavior, then they could tell us something new and potentially useful. If delinquency is related to attitudes toward legal institutions, then further attention should be directed to the elucidation of what in the delinquent's interaction with the law generates such a relationship. If attitudes toward teachers and school make a difference, then attention could be directed toward the conditions at school of which delinquent behavior is a function. In sum, personality research would be more useful if it avoided explaining behavior with vague concepts and instead sought to connect specific tensions with specific institutions.

The fact that many sociologists as well as psychologists are comfortable with behaviorism reflects a common tendency to view most human behavior as learned behavior. Every major sociological theory of crime and delinquency is based on the assumption that criminal as well as conventional behavior is learned, and that other people are particularly crucial to the process. However, the fact that both sociologists and psychologists are comfortable with this assumption does not mean that there are no differences between psychological and sociological perspectives, nor that all sociological theories are in accord on other issues. While psychologists have been most concerned with discovering basic principles of learning, sociologists have sought to identify those features of the social world that affect involvement in deviant and conventional learning processes. Concepts introduced in the following section, such as social disorganization, lower-class culture, anomie, and structural strain, refer to aspects of society that sociologists have described in the attempt to identify the social conditions affecting the distribution of learning experiences.

SECTION FIVE

Sociological Perspectives

Over the last decade, sociological study of the causes of juvenile delinquency has concentrated on theory testing. Sociologists have been especially interested in assessing the relative merits of three different kinds of sociological explanations: status frustration or "strain" theories, cultural conflict theories, and social control theories. While each explanation has roots in classic treatises on sociological theory, each has been expressed in popular interpretations of adolescent deviance as well.

For example, the following statement concerning the problems of alcohol use in Sweden can be classified as a strain theory of juvenile drinking.

Swedes are generally a calm, controlled people. But a recent report by their Board of Education has them stunned.

The report says that two out of three 12-year-olds in Sweden drink regularly.

A survey of 14,000 children in the 11–17 age bracket reveals that many of these kids turn to crime to finance liquor-buying, which is both expensive and state-run in Sweden. A bottle of Scotch costs $20 in Stockholm.

One of the most shocking revelations is that among 16-year-old girls, drinking is more prevalent than among boys. One such girl in five classifies herself as a hard drinker, frequently downing half a bottle in one sitting.

Many of these Swedish girls finance their drinking through prostitution. Police report that some girls start selling themselves at age 12.

According to Dr. Ingrid Blomberg of the Organization for Alcohol and Narcotic Information, the pressure to achieve high grades in school is what drives the Swedish kids to drink.

"The root causes are many," she concedes. "But to my mind the rise in drinking correlates to the rise in home pressures for success. Children are told over and over again that if they don't make the highest marks at school, they will have no chance for a successful future. They drink to face the exams, and if they do less than well on them, they drink to forget their poor performance."

The key characteristics of a strain theory are clearly represented in this statement. Pressure to succeed coupled with limited success results in frustration and ultimately leads to some form of deviance. The strain theory has been very prominent in the sociology of delinquency and is referred to under a variety of other names: opportunity theory, status frustration theory, illicit means theory, anomie theory, and subcultural theory. Sociologists who have been major proponents of this kind of theory include Robert Merton (1957), Albert Cohen (1955), and Richard Cloward and Lloyd Ohlin (1960). An article by Merton and selections from Cohen's *Delinquent Boys* are included in the readings.

A second variety of sociological theory presumes that there are differences among categories of people in their definitions of right and wrong conduct. Thus, some people can run afoul of the law by merely attempting to live up to standards of acceptable conduct in their own special world. This point of view is reflected in a *Time* magazine article, "The American Underclass:"

Their bleak environment nurtures values that are often at radical odds with those of the majority. . . . Thus the underclass minority produces a highly disproportionate number of the nation's juvenile delinquents, school dropouts, drug addicts and welfare mothers, and much of the adult crime, family disruption, urban decay and demand for social expenditures.

The key word here that justifies classifying this statement as an example of cultural conflict theory is *values*. It is not merely that the "underclass" is different, but also that its values are at odds with majority values; hence, the underclass is disproportionately prone to conduct viewed as deviant by more advantaged Americans. Sociologists associated with this kind of theory include Edwin Sutherland and Donald Cressey (1978), George Vold (1958), Marvin Wolfgang and Franco Ferracuti (1967), and Walter Miller (1958). An article by Walter Miller that clearly contrasts the cultural deviance perspective with the strain perspective is reprinted in this section.

A third variety of sociological theory, social control theory, emphasizes the role that bonds to conventional people, values, and institutions play in maintaining law-abiding conduct. Lawbreaking is interpreted as a product of the absence or weakening of such bonds. Interpretations of delinquency that concentrate on the failure of schools, family, church, and neighborhood to involve, inspire, or control the young fit this mold. For example, a *Time* magazine article entitled "Crime: Why and What to Do" concludes the discussion of causes with the following statement:

It seems clear that some of the old values and restraints have been battered by recent upheavals—war, riots, assassinations, racial strife, situational ethics, the youth rebellion. As disillusionment sets in, fewer and fewer Americans look to the churches, schools or Washington for moral leadership. Stern observers of today's widespread ethical torpor tend to agree with the 19th century French criminologist Jean Lacassagne: "A society gets the criminals it deserves."

The emphasis is not on the motivation for breaking the law but on the failure of society to prevent lawbreaking.

The social control perspective is advocated in the article by Scott Briar and Irving Piliavin and has been promoted by sociologists such as Travis Hirschi (1969), Walter Reckless (1973), Albert Reiss (1951), and Jackson Toby (1957). Briar and Piliavin question both strain and cultural deviance theory. Rather than searching for some broad structural source of motivation, they focus on the strength of commitments to conformity as the key to understanding delinquency. The motives for delinquency are viewed as common, diverse, and episodic—thus, as inadequate for explaining delinquency. The explanation of who does and does not deviate rests with the strength of barriers rather than motives that we may all have at one time or another. The focus on barriers instead of motives is the basis for references to commitment or control theories as "amotivational" theories.

While not specifically advancing a social control theory, the fifth selection in this section illustrates some of the features of this perspective in contrast to strain and cultural deviance theories. The latter emphasize "contracultural" or "subcultural" values and definitions that facilitate or require delinquent activity. David Matza and Gresham Sykes argue that the values stressed in such theories are depicted as in opposition to "the world of the middle-class" when they are actually part of a complex and often contradictory set of values shared by all segments of society. Delinquency is viewed not as stemming from oppositional values but rather as a reflection of the marginal status of American youth, whose behavior is more akin to that of a leisure class than a deviant subculture.

In one form or another, these three theories of delinquency have dominated sociological discourse, and a considerable amount of research has been devoted to testing them. It is impossible to represent all of that research here, but we have included three selections that have a bearing on some of the key ideas associated with each perspective. Michael Hindelang tests social control theory and points out its strengths and weaknesses. Paul Lerman examines the relationship between values and delinquency and does not find the type of oppositional values or conflicting codes suggested by strain or cultural deviance theory. Finally, Travis Hirschi considers the relationship between measures of frustrated ambition and delinquency and finds little support for strain theory.

The final selection is both a presentation and a test of a brand of theory referred to as social learning theory. It is different from the other three kinds of theories and has been included here because it is advocated by a prominent sociologist, Ronald Akers. Akers and others have argued that it is the best general theory and that other theories can be restated in similar terms. However, the theory does not make any claims about many of the issues that distinguish the three competing sociological theories, such as the existence of distinct value systems, structural strain, and subcultures. Social learning theory focuses on the one assumption that all sociological perspectives share: that delinquency is best understood as learned behavior. The learning involves differential association, differential reinforcement, definitions, and imitation. No claims are made about the criminogenic nature of social arrangements in America. The theory does tell us a great deal about the processes involved when one's social and cultural environment operates to facilitate delinquency.

REFERENCES

Cloward, R. A., and L. E. Ohlin. 1960. *Delinquency and Opportunity*. New York: Free Press.

Cohen, A. K. 1955. *Delinquent Boys*. New York: Free Press.

Hirschi, T. 1969. *Causes of Delinquency*. Berkeley: University of California Press.

Miller, W. 1958. "Lower Class Culture as a Generating Milieu of Gang Delinquency." *Journal of Social Issues* 14: 5–19.

Reckless, W. C. 1973. *The Crime Problem*. Englewood Cliffs, N.J.: Prentice-Hall.

Reiss, A. J., Jr. 1951. "Delinquency as the Failure of Personal and Social Controls." *American Sociological Review* 16: 196–207.

Sutherland, E. H., and D. R. Cressey. 1978. *Criminology*, 10th ed. Philadelphia: J. B. Lippincott.

Toby, J. 1957. "Social Disorganization and Stake in Conformity: Complementary Factors in the Predatory Behavior of Hoodlums." *Journal of Criminal Law, Criminology and Police Science* 48: 2–17.

Vold, G. B. 1958. *Theoretical Criminology*. New York: Oxford University Press.

Wolfgang, M. E., and F. Ferracuti. 1967. *The Subculture of Violence*. London: Tavistock Publications Ltd.

Social Structure and Anomie

Robert K. Merton
Harvard University

There persists a notable tendency in sociological theory to attribute the malfunctioning of social structure primarily to those of man's imperious biological drives which are not adequately restrained by social control. In this view, the social order is solely a device for "impulse management" and the "social processing" of tensions. These impulses which break through social control, be it noted, are held to be biologically derived. Nonconformity is assumed to be rooted in original nature.[1] Conformity is by implication the result of an utilitarian calculus or unreasoned conditioning. This point of view, whatever its other deficiences, clearly begs one question. It provides no basis for determining the nonbiological conditions which induce deviations from prescribed patterns of conduct. In this paper, it will be suggested that certain phases of social structure generate the circumstances in which infringement of social codes constitutes a "normal" response.[2]

The conceptual scheme to be outlined is designed to provide a coherent, systematic approach to the study of socio-cultural sources of deviate behavior. Our primary aim lies in discovering how some social structures *exert a definite pressure* upon certain persons in the society to engage in nonconformist rather than conformist conduct. The many ramifications of the scheme cannot all be discussed; the problems mentioned outnumber those explicitly treated.

Among the elements of social and cultural structure, two are important for our purposes. These are analytically separable although they merge imperceptibly in concrete situations. The first consists of culturally defined goals, purposes, and interests. It comprises a frame of aspirational reference. These goals are more or less integrated and involve varying degrees of prestige and sentiment. They constitute a basic, but not the exclusive, component of what Linton aptly has called "designs for group living." Some of these cultural aspirations are related to the original drives of man, but they are not determined by them. The second phase of the social structure defines, regulates, and controls the acceptable modes of achieving these goals. Every social group invariably couples its scale of desired ends with moral or institutional regulation of permissible and required procedures for attaining these ends. These regulatory norms and moral imperatives do not necessarily coincide with technical or efficiency norms. Many procedures which from the standpoint of *particular individuals* would be most efficient in securing desired values, e.g., illicit oil-stock schemes, theft, fraud, are ruled out of the institutional area of permitted conduct. The choice of expedients is limited by the institutional norms.

To say that these two elements, culture goals and institutional norms, operate jointly is not to say that the ranges of alternative behaviors and aims bear some constant relation to one another. The emphasis upon certain goals may vary independently of the degree of emphasis upon institutional means. There may develop a disproportionate, at times, a virtually exclusive, stress upon the value of specific goals, involving relatively slight concern with the institutionally appropriate modes of attaining these goals. The limiting case in this direction is reached when the range of alternative procedures is limited only by technical rather than institutional considerations. Any and all devices which promise attainment of the all important goal would be permitted in this hypothetical polar case.[3] This constitutes one type of cultural malintegration. A second polar type is found in groups where activities originally conceived as instrumental are transmuted into ends in themselves. The original purposes are forgotten and ritualistic adherence to institutionally prescribed conduct becomes virtually obsessive.[4] Stability is largely ensured while change is flouted. The range of alternative behaviors is severely limited. There develops a tradition-bound, sacred society characterized by neophobia. The occupational psychosis of the bureaucrat may be cited as a case in point. Finally, there are the intermediate types of groups where a balance between culture goals and institutional means is maintained. These are the significantly integrated and relatively stable, though changing, groups.

An effective equilibrium between the two phases of the social structure is maintained as long as satisfactions accrue to individuals who conform to both constraints, viz., satisfactions from the achievement of the goals and satisfactions emerging directly from the institutionally canalized modes of striving to attain these ends. Success, in such equilibrated cases, is twofold. Success is reckoned in terms of the product and in terms of the process, in terms of the outcome and in terms of activities. Continuing satisfactions must derive from sheer *participation* in a competitive order as well as from eclipsing one's competitors if the order itself is to be sustained. The occasional sacrifices involved in institutionalized conduct must be compensated by socialized rewards. The distribution of statuses and roles through competition must be so organized that positive incentives for conformity to roles and adherence to status obligations are provided *for every position* within the distributive order. Aberrant conduct, therefore, may be viewed as a symptom of dissociation between culturally defined aspirations and socially structured means.

Of the types of groups which result from the independent variation of

[1] E.g., Ernest Jones, *Social Aspects of Psychoanalysis*, 28, London, 1924. If the Freudian notion is a variety of the "original sin" dogma, then the interpretation advanced in this paper may be called the doctrine of "socially derived sin."

[2] "Normal" in the sense of a culturally oriented, if not approved, response. This statement does not deny the relevance of biological and personality differences which may be significantly involved in the *incidence* of deviate conduct. Our focus of interest is the social and cultural matrix; hence we abstract from other factors. It is in this sense, I take it, that James S. Plant speaks of the "normal reaction of normal people to abnormal conditions." See his *Personality and the Cultural Pattern*, 248, New York, 1937.

[3] Contemporary American culture has been said to tend in this direction. See André Siegfried, *America Comes of Age*, 26–37, New York, 1927. The alleged extreme(?) emphasis on the goals of monetary success and material prosperity leads to dominant concern with technological and social instruments designed to produce the desired result, inasmuch as institutional controls become of secondary importance. In such a situation, innovation flourishes as the *range of means* employed is broadened. In a sense, then, there occurs the paradoxical emergence of "materialists" from an "idealistic" orientation. Cf. Durkheim's analysis of the cultural conditions which predispose toward crime and innovation, both of which are aimed toward efficiency, not moral norms. Durkheim was one of the first to see that "contrairement aux idées courantes le criminel n'apparait plus comme un être radicalement insociable, comme une sorte d'elément parasitaire, de corps étranger et inassimilable, introduit au sein de la société; c'est un agent régulier de la vie sociale." See *Les Règles de la Méthode Sociologique*, 86–89, Paris, 1927.

[4] Such ritualism may be associated with a mythology which rationalizes these actions so that they appear to retain their status as means, but the dominant pressure is in the direction of strict ritualistic conformity, irrespective of such rationalizations. In this sense, ritual has proceeded farthest when such rationalizations are not even called forth.

From *American Sociological Review,* Vol. 3 (October 1938), pp. 672–682. Reprinted by permission of the *American Sociological Review* and the author.

the two phases of the social structure, we shall be primarily concerned with the first, namely, that involving a disproportionate accent on goals. This statement must be recast in a proper perspective. In no group is there an absence of regulatory codes governing conduct, yet groups do vary in the degree to which these folkways, mores, and institutional controls are effectively integrated with the more diffuse goals which are part of the culture matrix. Emotional convictions may cluster about the complex of socially acclaimed ends, meanwhile shifting their support from the culturally defined implementation of these ends. As we shall see, certain aspects of the social structure may generate countermores and antisocial behavior precisely because of differential emphases on goals and regulations. In the extreme case, the latter may be so vitiated by the goal-emphasis that the range of behavior is limited only by considerations of technical expediency. The sole significant question then becomes, which available means is most efficient in netting the socially approved value?[5] The technically most feasible procedure, whether legitimate or not, is preferred to the institutionally prescribed conduct. As this process continues, the integration of the society becomes tenuous and anomie ensues.

Thus, in competitive athletics, when the aim of victory is shorn of its institutional trappings and success in contests becomes construed as "winning the game" rather than "winning through circumscribed modes of activity," a premium is implicitly set upon the use of illegitimate but technically efficient means. The star of the opposing football team is surreptitiously slugged; the wrestler furtively incapacitates his opponent through ingenious but illicit techniques; university alumni covertly subsidize "students" whose talents are largely confined to the athletic field. The emphasis on the goal has so attenuated the satisfactions deriving from sheer participation in the competitive activity that these satisfactions are virtually confined to a successful outcome. Through the same process, tension generated by the desire to win in a poker game is relieved by successfully dealing oneself four aces, or, when the cult of success has become completely dominant, by sagaciously shuffling the cards in a game of solitaire. The faint twinge of uneasiness in the last instance and the surreptitious nature of public delicts indicate clearly that the institutional rules of the game *are known* to those who evade them, but that the emotional supports of these rules are largely vitiated by cultural exaggeration of the success-goal.[6] They are microcosmic images of the social macrocosm.

Of course, this process is not restricted to the realm of sport. The process whereby exaltation of the end generates a *literal demoralization*, i.e., a deinstitutionalization, of the means is one which characterizes many[7] groups in which the two phases of the social structure are not highly integrated. The extreme emphasis upon the accumulation of wealth as a symbol of success[8] in our own society militates against the completely effective control of institutionally regulated modes of acquiring a fortune.[9] Fraud, corruption, vice, crime, in short, the entire catalogue of proscribed behavior, becomes increasingly common when the emphasis on the *culturally induced* success-goal becomes divorced from a coordinated institutional emphasis. This observation is of crucial theoretical importance in examining the doctrine that antisocial behavior most frequently derives from biological drives breaking through the restraints imposed by society. The difference is one between a strictly utilitarian interpretation which conceives man's ends as random and an analysis which finds these ends deriving from the basic values of the culture.[10]

Our analysis can scarcely stop at this juncture. We must turn to other aspects of the social structure if we are to deal with the social genesis of the varying rates and types of deviate behavior characteristic of different societies. Thus far, we have sketched three ideal types of social orders constituted by distinctive patterns of relations between culture ends and means. Turning from these types of *culture patterning*, we find five logically possible, alternative modes of adjustment or adaptation *by individuals* within the culture-bearing society or group.[11] These are schematically presented in the following table, where (+) signifies "acceptance," (−) signifies "elimination" and (±) signifies "rejection and substitution of new goals and standards."

	Culture Goals	Institutionalized Means
I. Conformity	+	+
II. Innovation	+	−
III. Ritualism	−	+
IV. Retreatism	−	−
V. Rebellion[12]	±	±

Our discussion of the relation between these alternative responses and other phases of the social structure must be prefaced by the observation that persons may shift from one alternative to another as they engage in different social activities. These categories refer to role adjustments in specific situations, not to personality *in toto*. To treat the development of this process in various spheres of conduct would introduce a complexity unmanageable within the confines of this paper. For this reason, we shall be concerned primarily with economic activity in the broad sense, "the production, exchange, distribution and consumption of goods and services" in our competitive society, wherein wealth has taken on a highly symbolic cast. Our task is to search out some of the factors which exert pressure upon individuals to engage in certain of these logically possible alternative responses. This choice, as we shall see, is far from random.

In every society, Adaptation I (conformity to both culture goals and means) is the most common and widely diffused. Were this not so, the stability and continuity of the society could not be maintained. The mesh of expectancies which constitutes every social order is sustained by the modal behavior of its members falling within the first category. Conventional role behavior oriented toward the basic values of the group is the rule rather than the exception. It is this fact alone which permits us to speak of a human aggregate as comprising a group or society.

Conversely, Adaptation IV (rejection of goals and means) is the least common. Persons who "adjust" (or maladjust) in this fashion are, strictly speaking, *in* the society but not *of* it. Sociologically, these constitute the true "aliens." Not sharing the common frame of orientation, they can be included within the societal population merely in a fictional sense. In this category are *some* of the activities of psychotics, psychoneurotics, chronic autists, pariahs, outcasts, vagrants, vagabonds, tramps, chronic drunkards and drug addicts.[13] These have relinquished, in certain spheres of activity, the culturally defined goals, involving complete aim-inhibition in the polar case, and their adjustments are not in accord with institutional norms. This is not to say that in some cases the source of their behavioral adjustments is not in part the very social structure which they have in effect repudiated nor that their very existence within a social area does not constitute a problem for the socialized population.

This mode of "adjustment" occurs, as far as structural sources are con-

[5] In this connection, one may see the relevance of Elton Mayo's paraphrase of the title of Tawney's well known book. "Actually the problem *is not that of the sickness of an acquisitive society; it is that of the acquisitiveness of a sick society.*" *Human Problems of an Industrial Civilization*, 153, New York, 1933. Mayo deals with the process through which wealth comes to be a symbol of social achievement. He sees this as arising from a state of anomie. We are considering the unintegrated monetary-success goal as an element in producing anomie. A complete analysis would involve both phases of this system of interdependent variables.

[6] It is unlikely that interiorized norms are completely eliminated. Whatever residuum persists will induce personality tensions and conflict. The process involves a certain degree of ambivalence. A manifest rejection of the institutional norms is coupled with some latent retention of their emotional correlates. "Guilt feelings," "sense of sin," "pangs of conscience" are obvious manifestations of this unrelieved tension; symbolic adherence to the nominally repudiated values or rationalizations constitute a more subtle variety of tensional release.

[7] "Many," and not all, unintegrated groups, for the reason already mentioned. In groups where the primary emphasis shifts to institutional means, i.e., when the range of alternatives is very limited, the outcome is a type of ritualism rather than anomie.

[8] Money has several peculiarities which render it particularly apt to become a symbol of prestige divorced from institutional controls. As Simmel emphasized, money is highly abstract and impersonal. However acquired, through fraud or institutionally, it can be used to purchase the same goods and services. The anonymity of metropolitan culture, in conjunction with this peculiarity of money, permits wealth, the sources of which may be unknown to the community in which the plutocrat lives, to serve as a symbol of status.

[9] The emphasis upon wealth as a success-symbol is possibly reflected in the use of the term "fortune" to refer to a stock of accumulated wealth. This meaning becomes common in the late sixteenth century (Spenser and Shakespeare). A similar usage of the Latin *fortuna* comes into prominence during the first century B.C. Both these periods were marked by the rise to prestige and power of the "bourgeoisie."

[10] See Kingsley Davis, "Mental Hygiene and the Class Structure," *Psychiatry*, 1928, I, esp. 62–63; Talcott Parsons, *The Structure of Social Action*, 59–60, New York, 1937.

[11] This is a level intermediate between the two planes distinguished by Edward Sapir; namely, culture patterns and personal habit systems. See his "Contribution of Psychiatry to an Understanding of Behavior in Society," *Amer. J. Sociol.*, 1937, 42:862–70.

[12] This fifth alternative is on a plane clearly different from that of the others. It represents a *transitional* response which seeks to *institutionalize* new procedures oriented toward revamped cultural goals shared by the members of the society. It thus involves efforts to *change* the existing structure rather than to perform accommodative actions *within* this structure, and introduces additional problems with which we are not at the moment concerned.

[13] Obviously, this is an elliptical statement. These individuals may maintain some orientation to the values of their particular differentiated groupings within the larger society or, in part, of the conventional society itself. Insofar as they do so, their conduct cannot be classified in the "passive rejection" category (IV). Nels Anderson's description of the behavior and attitudes of the bum, for example, can readily be recast in terms of our analytical scheme. See *The Hobo*, 93–98, *et passim*, Chicago, 1923.

cerned, when both the culture goals and institutionalized procedures have been assimilated thoroughly by the individual and imbued with affect and high positive value, but where those institutionalized procedures which promise a measure of successful attainment of the goals are not available to the individual. In such instances, there results a twofold mental conflict insofar as the moral obligation for adopting institutional means conflicts with the pressure to resort to illegitimate means (which may attain the goal) and inasmuch as the individual is shut off from means which are both legitimate *and* effective. The competitive order is maintained, but the frustrated and handicapped individual who cannot cope with this order drops out. Defeatism, quietism and resignation are manifested in escape mechanisms which ultimately lead the individual to "escape" from the requirements of the society. It is an expedient which arises from continued failure to attain the goal by legitimate measures and from an inability to adopt the illegitimate route because of internalized prohibitions and institutionalized compulsives, *during which process the supreme value of the success goal has as yet not been renounced.* The conflict is resolved by eliminating *both* precipitating elements, the goals and means. The escape is complete, the conflict is eliminated and the individual is a socialized.

Be it noted that where frustration derives from the inaccessibility of effective institutional means for attaining economic or any other type of highly valued "success," that Adaptations II, III and V (innovation, ritualism and rebellion) are also possible. The result will be determined by the particular personality, and thus, the *particular* cultural background, involved. Inadequate socialization will result in the innovation response whereby the conflict and frustration are eliminated by relinquishing the institutional means and retaining the success-aspiration; an extreme assimilation of institutional demands will lead to ritualism wherein the goal is dropped as beyond one's reach but conformity to the mores persists; and rebellion occurs when emancipation from the reigning standards, due to frustration or to marginalist perspectives, leads to the attempt to introduce a "new social order."

Our major concern is with the illegitimacy adjustment. This involves the use of conventionally proscribed but frequently effective means of attaining at least the simulacrum of culturally defined success,—wealth, power, and the like. As we have seen, this adjustment occurs when the individual has assimilated the cultural emphasis on success without equally internalizing the morally prescribed norms governing means for its attainment. The question arises, Which phases of our social structure predispose toward this mode of adjustment? We may examine a concrete instance, effectively analyzed by Lohman,[14] which provides a clue to the answer. Lohman has shown that specialized areas of vice in the near north side of Chicago constitute a "normal" response to a situation where the cultural emphasis upon pecuniary success has been absorbed, but where there is little access to conventional and legitimate means for attaining such success. The conventional occupational opportunities of persons in this area are almost completely limited to manual labor. Given our cultural stigmatization of manual labor, and its correlate, the prestige of white collar work, it is clear that the result is a strain toward innovational practices. The limitation of opportunity to unskilled labor and the resultant low income can not compete *in terms of conventional standards of achievement* with the high income from organized vice.

For our purposes, this situation involves two important features. First, such antisocial behavior is in a sense "called forth" by certain conventional values of the culture *and* by the class structure involving differential access to the approved opportunities for legitimate, prestige-bearing pursuit of the culture goals. The lack of high integration between the means-and-end elements of the cultural pattern and the particular class structure combine to favor a heightened frequency of antisocial conduct in such groups. The second consideration is of equal significance. Recourse to the first of the alternative responses, legitimate effort, is limited by the fact that actual advance toward desired success-symbols through conventional channels is, despite our persisting open-class ideology,[15] relatively rare and difficult for those handicapped by little formal education and few economic resources. The dominant pressure of group standards of success is, therefore, on the gradual attenuation of legitimate, but by and large ineffective, strivings and the increasing use of illegitimate, but more or less effective, expedients of vice and crime. The cultural demands made on persons in this situation are incompatible. On the one hand, they are asked to orient their conduct toward the prospect of accumulating wealth and on the other, they are largely denied effective opportunities to do so institutionally. The consequences of such structural inconsistency are psychopathological personality, and/or antisocial conduct, and/or revolutionary activities. The equilibrium between culturally designated means and ends becomes highly unstable with the progressive emphasis on attaining the prestige-laden ends by any means whatsoever. Within this context, Capone represents the triumph of amoral intelligence over morally prescribed "failure," when the channels of vertical mobility are closed or narrowed[16] *in a society which places a high premium on economic affluence and social ascent for* all *its members.*[17]

This last qualification is of primary importance. It suggests that other phases of the social structure besides the extreme emphasis on pecuniary success, must be considered if we are to understand the social sources of antisocial behavior. A high frequency of deviate behavior is not generated simply by "lack of opportunity" or by this exaggerated pecuniary emphasis. A comparatively rigidified class structure, a feudalistic or caste order, may limit such opportunities far beyond the point which obtains in our society today. It is only when a system of cultural values extols, virtually above all else, certain *common* symbols of success *for the population at large* while its social structure rigorously restricts or completely eliminates access to approved modes of acquiring these symbols *for a considerable part of the same population,* that antisocial behavior ensues on a considerable scale. In other words, our egalitarian ideology denies by implication the existence of noncompeting groups and individuals in the pursuit of pecuniary success. The same body of success-symbols is held to be desirable for all. These goals are held to *transcend class lines,* not to be bounded by them, yet the actual social organization is such that there exist class differentials in the accessibility of these *common* success-symbols. Frustration and thwarted aspiration lead to the search for avenues of escape from a culturally induced intolerable situation; or unrelieved ambition may eventuate in illicit attempts to acquire the dominant values.[18] The American stress on pecuniary success and ambitiousness for all thus invites exaggerated anxieties, hostilities, neuroses and antisocial behavior.

This theoretical analysis may go far toward explaining the varying correlations between crime and poverty.[19] Poverty is not an isolated variable.

[14] Joseph D. Lohman, "The Participant Observer in Community Studies," *Amer. Sociol. Rev.*, 1937, 2:890–98.

[15] The shifting historical role of this ideology is a profitable subject for exploration. The "office-boy-to-president" stereotype was once in approximate accord with the facts. Such vertical mobility was probably more common then than now, when the class structure is more rigid. (See the following note.) The ideology largely persists, however, possibly because it still performs a useful function for maintaining the *status quo.* For insofar as it is accepted by the "masses," it constitutes a useful sop for those who might rebel against the entire structure, were this consoling hope removed. This ideology now serves to lessen the probability of Adaptation V. In short, the role of this notion has changed from that of an approximately valid empirical theorem to that of an ideology, in Mannheim's sense.

[16] There is a growing body of evidence, though none of it is clearly conclusive, to the effect that our class structure is becoming rigidified and that vertical mobility is declining. Taussig and Joslyn found that American business leaders are being *increasingly* recruited from the upper ranks of our society. The Lynds have also found a "diminished chance to get ahead" for the working classes in Middletown. Manifestly, these objective changes are not alone significant; the individual's subjective evaluation of the situation is a major determinant of the response. The extent to which this change in opportunity for social mobility has been recognized by the least advantaged classes is still conjectural, although the Lynds present some suggestive materials. The writer suggests that a case in point is the increasing frequency of cartoons which observe in a tragi-comic vein that "my old man says everybody can't be President. He says if ya can get three days a week steady on W.P.A. work ya ain't doin' so bad either." See F. W. Taussig and C. S. Joslyn, *American Business Leaders*, New York, 1932; R. S. and H. M. Lynd, *Middletown in Transition*, 67 ff., chap. 12, New York, 1937.

[17] The role of the Negro in this respect is of considerable theoretical interest. Certain elements of the Negro population have assimilated the dominant caste's values of pecuniary success and social advancement, but they also recognize that social ascent is at present restricted to their own caste almost exclusively. The pressures upon the Negro which would otherwise derive from the structural inconsistencies we have noticed are hence not identical with those upon lower class whites. See Kingsley Davis, *op. cit.*, 63; John Dollard, *Caste and Class in a Southern Town*, 66 ff., New Haven, 1936; Donald Young, *American Minority Peoples*, 581, New York, 1932.

[18] The psychical coordinates of these processes have been partly established by the experimental evidence concerning *Anspruchsniveaus* and levels of performance. See Kurt Lewin, *Vorsatz, Wille und Bedurfnis*, Berlin, 1926; N. F. Hoppe, "Erfolg und Misserfolg," *Psychol. Forschung*, 1930, 14:1–63; Jerome D. Frank, "Individual Differences in Certain Aspects of the Level of Aspiration," *Amer. J. Psychol.*, 1935, 47:119–28.

[19] Standard criminology texts summarize the data in this field. Our scheme of analysis may serve to resolve some of the theoretical contradictions which P. A. Sorokin indicates. For example, "not everywhere nor always do the poor show a greater proportion of crime . . . many poorer countries have had less crime than the richer countries . . . The [economic] improvement in the second half of the nineteenth century, and the beginning of the twentieth, has not been followed by a decrease of crime." See his *Contemporary Sociological Theories*, 560–61, New York, 1928. The crucial point is, however, that poverty has varying social significance in different social structures, as we shall see. Hence, one would not expect a linear correlation betweem crime and poverty.

It is one in a complex of interdependent social and cultural variables. When viewed in such a context, it represents quite different states of affairs. Poverty as such, and consequent limitation of opportunity, are not sufficient to induce a conspicuously high rate of criminal behavior. Even the often mentioned "poverty in the midst of plenty" will not necessarily lead to this result. Only insofar as poverty and associated disadvantages in competition for the culture values approved for *all* members of the society is linked with the assimilation of a cultural emphasis on monetary accumulation as a symbol of success is antisocial conduct a "normal" outcome. Thus, poverty is less highly correlated with crime in southeastern Europe than in the United States. The possibilities of vertical mobility in these European areas would seem to be fewer than in this country, so that neither poverty *per se* nor its association with limited opportunity is sufficient to account for the varying correlations. It is only when the full configuration is considered, poverty, limited opportunity and a commonly shared system of success symbols, that we can explain the higher association between poverty and crime in our society than in others where rigidified class structure is coupled with *differential class symbols of achievement.*

In societies such as our own, then, the pressure of prestige-bearing success tends to eliminate the effective social constraint over means employed to this end. "The-end-justifies-the-means" doctrine becomes a guiding tenet for action when the cultural structure unduly exalts the end and the social organization unduly limits possible recourse to approved means. Otherwise put, this notion and associated behavior reflect a lack of cultural coordination. In international relations, the effects of this lack of integration are notoriously apparent. An emphasis upon national power is not readily coordinated with an inept organization of legitimate, i.e., internationally defined and accepted, means for attaining this goal. The result is a tendency toward the abrogation of international law, treaties become scraps of paper, "undeclared warefare" serves as a technical evasion, the bombing of civilian populations is rationalized,[20] just as the same societal situation induces the same sway of illegitimacy among individuals.

The social order we have described necessarily produces this "strain toward dissolution." The pressure of such an order is upon outdoing one's competitors. The choice of means within the ambit of institutional control will persist as long as the sentiments supporting a competitive system, i.e., deriving from the possibility of outranking competitors and hence enjoying the favorable response of others, are distributed throughout the entire system of activities and are not confined merely to the final result. A stable social structure demands a balanced distribution of affect among its various segments. When there occurs a shift of emphasis from the satisfactions deriving from competition itself to almost exclusive concern with successful competition, the resultant stress leads to the breakdown of the regulatory structure.[21] With the resulting attenuation of the institutional imperatives, there occurs an approximation of the situation erroneously held by utilitarians to be typical of society generally wherein calculations of advantage and fear of punishment are the sole regulating agencies. In such situations, as Hobbes observed, force and fraud come to constitute the sole virtues in view of their relative efficiency in attaining goals,—which were for him, of course, not culturally derived.

It should be apparent that the foregoing discussion is not pitched on a moralistic plane. Whatever the sentiments of the writer or reader concerning the ethical desirability of coordinating the means-and-goals phases of the social structure, one must agree that lack of such coordination leads to anomie. Insofar as one of the most general functions of social organization is to provide a basis for calculability and regularity of behavior, it is increasingly limited in effectiveness as these elements of the structure become dissociated. At the extreme, predictability virtually disappears and what may be properly termed cultural chaos or anomie intervenes.

This statement, being brief, is also incomplete. It has not included an exhaustive treatment of the various structural elements which predispose toward one rather than another of the alternative responses open to individuals; it has neglected, but not denied the relevance of, the factors determining the specific incidence of these responses; it has not enumerated the various concrete responses which are constituted by combinations of specific values of the analytical variables; it has omitted, or included only by implication, any consideration of the social functions performed by illicit responses; it has not tested the full explanatory power of the analytical scheme by examining a large number of group variations in the frequency of deviate and conformist behavior; it has not adequately dealt with rebellious conduct which seeks to refashion the social framework radically; it has not examined the relevance of cultural conflict for an analysis of culture-goal and institutional-means malintegration. It is suggested that these and related problems may be profitably analyzed by this scheme.

---

[20] See M. W. Royse, *Aerial Bombardment and the International Regulation of War*, New York, 1928.

[21] Since our primary concern is with the socio-cultural aspects of this problem, the psychological correlates have been only implicitly considered. See Karen Horney, *The Neurotic Personality of Our Time*, New York, 1937, for a psychological discussion of this process.

Delinquent Boys: The Culture of the Gang

Albert K. Cohen

The Content of the Delinquent Subculture

The common expression, "juvenile crime," has unfortunate and misleading connotations. It suggests that we have two kinds of criminals, young and old, but only one kind of crime. It suggests that crime has its meanings and its motives which are much the same for young and old; that the young differ from the old as the apprentice and the master differ at the same trade; that we distinguish the young from the old only because the young are less "set in their ways," less "confirmed" in the same criminal habits, more amenable to treatment and more deserving, because of their age, of special consideration.

The problem of the relationship between juvenile delinquency and adult crime has many facets. To what extent are the offenses of children and adults distributed among the same legal categories, "burglary," "larceny," "vehicle-taking," and so forth? To what extent, even when the offenses are legally identical, do these acts have the same meaning for children and adults? To what extent are the careers of adult criminals continuations of careers of juvenile delinquency? We cannot solve these problems here, but we want to emphasize the danger of making facile and unproven assumptions. If we assume that "crime is crime," that child and adult criminals are practitioners of the same trade, and if our assumptions are false, then the road to error is wide and clear. Easily and unconsciously, we may impute a whole host of notions concerning the nature of crime and its causes, derived from our knowledge and fancies about adult crime, to a large realm of behavior to which these notions are irrelevant. It is better to make no such assumptions; it is better to look at juvenile delinquency with a fresh eye and try to explain what we see.

What we see when we look at the delinquent subculture (and we must not even assume that this describes *all juvenile* crime) is that it is *non-utilitarian, malicious* and *negativistic.*

We usually assume that when people steal things, they steal because they want them. They may want them because they can eat them, wear them or otherwise use them; or because they can sell them; or even–if we are given to a psychoanalytic turn of mind–because on some deep symbolic level they substitute or stand for something unconsciously desired but forbidden. All of these explanations have this in common, that they assume that the stealing is a means to an end, namely, the possession of some object of value, and that it is, in this sense, rational and "utilitarian." However, the fact cannot be blinked–and this fact is of crucial importance in defining our problem–that much gang stealing has no such motivation at all. Even where the value of the object stolen is itself a motivating consideration, the stolen sweets are often sweeter than those acquired by more legitimate and prosaic means. In homelier language, stealing "for the hell of it" and apart from considerations of gain and profit is a valued activity to which attach glory, prowess and profound satisfaction. There is no accounting in rational and utilitarian terms for the effort expended and the danger run in stealing things which are often discarded, destroyed or casually given away. . . .

If stealing itself is not motivated by rational, utilitarian considerations, still less are the manifold other activities which constitute the delinquent's repertoire. Throughout there is a kind of *malice* apparent, an enjoyment in the discomfiture of others, a delight in the defiance of taboos itself. Thrasher quotes one gang delinquent:

We did all kinds of dirty tricks for fun. We'd see a sign, "Please keep the streets clean," but we'd tear it down and say, "We don't feel like keeping it clean." One day we put a can of glue in the engine of a man's car. We would always tear things down. That would make us laugh and feel good, to have so many jokes.

The gang exhibits this gratuitous hostility toward non-gang peers as well as adults. Apart from its more dramatic manifestations in the form of gang wars, there is keen delight in terrorizing "good" children, in driving them from playgrounds and gyms for which the gang itself may have little use, and in general in making themselves obnoxious to the virtuous. The same spirit is evident in playing hookey and in misbehavior in school. The teacher and her rules are not merely something onerous to be evaded. They are to be *flouted*. There is an element of active spite and malice, contempt and ridicule, challenge and defiance, exquisitely symbolized, in an incident described to the writer by Mr. Henry D. McKay, of defecating on the teacher's desk.

All this suggests also the intention of our term "negativistic." The delinquent subculture is not only a set of rules, a design for living which is different from or indifferent to or even in conflict with the norms of the "respectable" adult society. It would appear at least plausible that it is defined by its "negative polarity" to those norms.

* * *

Some Attempts at Explanation

The literature on juvenile delinquency has seldom come to grips with the problem of accounting for the content and spirit of the delinquent subculture. To say that this content is "traditional" in certain areas and is "handed down" from generation to generation is but to state the problem rather than to offer a solution. Neither does the "social disorganization" theory come to grips with the facts. This theory holds that the delinquent culture flourishes in the "interstitial areas" of our great cities. These are formerly "good" residential areas which have been invaded by industry and commerce, are no longer residentially attractive, and are inhabited by a heterogeneous, economically depressed and highly mobile population with no permanent stake in the community. These people lack the solidarity, the community spirit, the motivation and the residential stability necessary for organization, on a neighborhood basis, for the effective control of delinquency. To this argument we may make two answers. First, recent research has revealed that many, if not most, such "interstitial" and "slum" areas are by no means lacking in social organization. To the observer who has lived in them, many such areas are anything but the picture of chaos and heterogeneity which we find drawn in the older literature. We find, on the contrary, a vast and ramifying network of informal associations among like-minded people, not a horde of anonymous families and individuals, strangers to one another and rudely jostling one another in the struggle for existence. The social organization of the slum may lack the spirit and the objectives of organization in the "better" neighborhoods, but the slum is not necessarily a jungle. In the "delinquency area" as elsewhere, there is an awareness of community, an involvement of the individual in the lives and doings of the neighborhood, a concern about his reputation among his neighbors. The organization which exists may indeed not be adequate for the effective control of delinquency and for the solution of other social problems, but the qualities and defects of organization are not to be confused with the absence of organization. However, granting the absence of community pressures and concerted action for the repression of delinquency, we are confronted by a second deficiency in this argument. It is wholly negative. It accounts for the presence of delinquency by the absence of effective constraints. If one is disposed to be delinquent, the absence of constraint will facilitate the expression of these impulses. It will not, however, account for the presence of these impulses. The social disorganization argument leaves open the question of the origin of the impulse, of the peculiar content and spirit of the delinquent subculture.

Another theory which has enjoyed some vogue is the "culture conflict" theory. According to this view, these areas of high mobility and motley composition are lacking in cultural unity. The diverse ethnic and racial stocks have diverse and incongruent standards and codes, and these standards and codes are in turn inconsistent with those of the schools and other official representatives of the larger society. In this welter of conflicting cultures, the young person is confused and bedevilled. The adult world presents him with no clear-cut and authoritative models. Subject to a multitude of conflicting patterns, he respects none and assimilates none. He develops no respect for the legal order because it represents a culture which finds no support in his social world. He becomes delinquent.

From the recognition that there exists a certain measure of cultural diversity it is a large step to the conclusion that the boy is confronted by such a hodge-podge of definitions that he can form no clear conception of what is "right" and "wrong." It is true that some ethnic groups look more tolerantly on certain kinds of delinquency than others do; that some even encourage certain minor forms of delinquency such as picking up coal off railroad tracks; that respect for the courts and the police are less well established among some groups and that other cultural differences exist. Nonetheless, it is questionable that there is any ethnic or racial group which positively encourages or even condones stealing, vandalism, habitual truancy and the general negativism which characterizes the delinquent subculture. The existence of culture conflict must not be allowed to obscure the important measure of consensus which exists on the essential "wrongness" of these activities, except under special circumstances which are considered mitigating by this or that ethnic subculture. Furthermore, if we should grant that conflicting definitions leave important sectors of conduct morally undefined for the boy in the delinquency area, we must still explain why he fills the gap in the particular way he does. Like the social disorganization theory, the culture conflict theory is at best incomplete. The delinquent subculture is not a fund of blind, amoral, "natural" impulses which inevitably well up in the absence of a code of socially acquired inhibitions. It is itself a positive code with a definite if unconventional moral flavor, and it demands a positive explanation in its own right.

Another view which currently commands a good deal of respect we may call the "illicit means" theory. According to this view our American culture, with its strongly democratic and equalitarian emphasis, indoctrinates all social classes impartially with a desire for high social status and a sense of ignominy attaching to low social status. The symbols of high status are to an extraordinary degree the possession and the conspicuous display of economic goods. There is therefore an unusually intense desire for economic goods diffused throughout our population to a degree unprecedented in other societies. However, the means and the opportunities for the legitimate achievement of these goals are distributed most unequally among the various segments of the population. Among those segments which have the least access to the legitimate channels of "upward mobility" there develop strong feelings of deprivation and frustration and strong incentives to find other means to the achievement of status and its symbols. Unable to attain their goals by lawful means, these disadvantaged segments of the population are under strong pressure to resort to crime, the only means available to them.

This argument is sociologically sophisticated and highly plausible as an explanation for adult professional crime and for the property delinquency of some older and semi-professional juvenile thieves. Unfortunately, it fails to account for the non-utilitarian quality of the subculture which we have described. Were the participant in the delinquent subculture merely employing illicit means to the end of acquiring economic goods, he would show more respect for the goods he has thus acquired. Furthermore, the destructiveness, the versatility, the zest and the wholesale negativism which characterizes the delinquent subculture are beyond the purview of this theory. None of the theories we have considered comes to grips with the data: the distinctive content of the delinquent subculture.

* * *

The Bottom of the Heap: Problems of the Working-Class Boy

What is it about the structure of American society that produces, in certain sectors of that society, a subculture of a certain distinctive content? We do not believe that there is any simple answer to that question. We believe that it is necessary, in order to arrive at a satisfactory solution, to discover those combinations of personality and situation which yield the problems of adjustment to which the delinquent subculture is an appropriate response, and to show how these personalities and situations are generated by the life-conditions in those sectors in which that subculture prevails. . . .

First and most obviously, the working class child shares the social class status of his parents. In the status game, then, the working-class child starts out with a handicap and, to the extent that he cares what middle-class persons think of him or has internalized the dominant middle-class attitudes toward social class position, he may be expected to feel some "shame . . . ."

Furthermore, people of status tend to be people of power and property. They have the means to make more certain that their children will obtain respect and other rewards which have status significance even where title in terms of deserving middle-class conduct is dubious. . . .

One of the situations in which children of all social levels come together and compete for status in terms of the same set of middle-class criteria and in which working-class children are most likely to be found wanting is in the school. American educators are enamored of the idea of "democracy" as a goal of the schools. An examination of their writings reveals that "democracy" signifies "the fullest realization of the individual's potentialities," "the development of skills to an optimal level," "the development of character and abilities which can be admired by others," "preparation for effective participation in the adult vocational world." Despite reservations such as "with due regard to individual differences," this conception of "democratic" education implies that a major function of the schools is to "promote," "encourage," "motivate," "stimulate," in brief, reward middle-class ambition and conformity to middle-class expectations. However sincerely one may desire to avoid odious comparisons and to avoid, thereby, injury to the self-esteem of those who do not conform to one's expectations, it is extremely difficult to reward, however subtly, successful conformity without at the same time, by implication, condemning and punishing the non-conformist. That same teacher who prides himself on his recognition and encouragement of deserving working-class children dramatizes, by that very show of pride, the superior merit of the "college-boy" working-class child to his less gifted or "corner-boy" working-class classmates.

* * *

Research on the kinds of behavior which teachers regard as the most "problematical" among their pupils gives results consistent with our expectations. The most serious problems, from the standpoint of the teacher, are those children who are restless and unruly, who fidget and squirm, who annoy and distract, who create "discipline" problems. The "good" children are the studious, the obedient, the docile. It is precisely the working-class children who are most likely to be "problems" because of their relative lack of training in order and discipline, their lack of interest in intellectual achievement and their lack of reinforcement by the home in conformity to the requirements of the school. Both in terms of "conduct" and in terms of academic achievement, the failures in the classroom are drawn disproportionately from the lower social class levels. . . .

* * *

In summary, it may confidently be said that the working-class boy, particularly if his training and values be those we have here defined as working-class, is more likely than his middle-class peers to find himself at the bottom of the status hierarchy whenever he moves in a middle-class world, whether it be of adults or of children. To the degree to which he values middle-class status, either because he values the good opinion of middle-class persons or because he has to some degree internalized middle-class standards himself, he faces a problem of adjustment and is in the market for a "solution."

What the Delinquent Subculture Has to Offer

The delinquent subculture, we suggest, is a way of dealing with the problems of adjustment we have described. These problems are chiefly status problems: certain children are denied status in the respectable society because they cannot meet the criteria of the respectable status system. The delinquent subculture deals with these problems by providing criteria of status which these children can meet.

* * *

It is a plausible assumption . . . that the working-class boy whose status is low in middle-class terms cares about that status, that this status confronts him with a genuine problem of adjustment. To this problem of adjustment there are a variety of conceivable responses, of which participation in the creation and the maintenance of the delinquent subculture is one. Each mode of response entails costs and yields gratifications of its own. The circumstances which tip the balance in favor of the one or the other are obscure. One mode of response is to desert the corner-boy for the college-boy way of life. To the reader of Whyte's *Street Corner Society* the costs are manifest. It is hard, at best, to be a college-boy and to run with the corner-boys. It entails great effort and sacrifices to the degree that one has been indoctrinated in what we have described as the working-class socialization process; its rewards are frequently long-deferred; and for many working-class boys it makes demands which they are, in consequence of their inferior linguistic, academic and "social" skills, not likely ever to meet. Nevertheless, a certain proportion of working-class boys accept the challenge of the middle-class status system and play the status game by the middle-class rules.

Another response, perhaps the most common, is what we may call the "stable corner-boy response." It represents an acceptance of the corner-boy way of life and an effort to make the best of a situation. If our reasoning is correct, it does not resolve the dilemmas we have described as inherent in the corner-boy position in a largely middle-class world, although these dilemmas may be mitigated by an effort to disengage oneself from dependence upon middle-class status-sources and by withdrawing, as far as possible, into a sheltering community of like-minded working-class children. Unlike the delinquent response, it avoids the radical rupture of good relations with even working-class adults and does not represent as irretrievable a renunciation of upward mobility. It does not incur the active hostility of middle-class persons and therefore leaves the way open to the pursuit of some values, such as jobs, which these people control. It represents a preference for the familiar, with its known satisfactions and its known imperfections, over the risks and the uncertainties as well as the moral costs of the college-boy response, on the one hand, and the delinquent response on the other.

What does the delinquent response have to offer? Let us be clear, first, about what this response is and how it differs from the stable corner-boy response. The hallmark of the delinquent subculture is the explicit and wholesale repudiation of middle-class standards and the adoption of their very antithesis. *The corner-boy culture is not specifically delinquent.* Where it leads to behavior which may be defined as delinquent, e.g., truancy, it does so not because nonconformity to middle-class norms *defines* conformity to corner-boy norms but because conformity to middle-class norms *interferes with* conformity to corner-boy norms. The corner-boy plays truant because he does not like school, because he wishes to escape from a dull and unrewarding and perhaps humiliating situation. But truancy is not defined as intrinsically valuable and status-giving. The member of the delinquent subculture plays truant because "good" middle-class (and working-class) children do not play truant. Corner-boy resistance to being herded and marshalled by middle-class figures is not the same as the delinquent's flouting and jeering of those middle-class figures and active ridicule of those who submit. The corner-boy's ethic of reciprocity, his quasi-communal attitude toward the property of in-group members, is shared by the delinquent. But this ethic of reciprocity does not sanction the deliberate and "malicious" violation of the property rights of persons outside the in-group. We have observed that the differences between the corner-boy and the college-boy or middle-class culture are profound but that in many ways they are profound differences in emphasis. We have remarked that the corner-boy culture does not so much repudiate the value of many middle-class achievements as it emphasizes certain other values which make such achievements improbable. In short, the corner-boy culture temporizes with middle-class morality; the full-fledged delinquent subculture does not.

It is precisely here, we suggest, in the refusal to temporize, that the appeal of the delinquent subculture lies. Let us recall that it is characteristically American, not specifically working-class or middle-class, to measure oneself against the widest possible status universe, to seek status against "all comers," to be "as good as" or "better than" anybody—anybody, that is, within one's own age and sex category. As long as the working-class corner-boy clings to a version, however attenuated and adulterated, of the middle-class culture, he must recognize his inferiority to working-class and middle-class college-boys. The delinquent subculture, on the other hand, permits no ambiguity of the status of the delinquent relative to that of anybody else. In terms of the norms of the delinquent subculture, defined by its negative polarity to the respectable status system, the delinquent's very nonconformity to middle-class standards sets him above the most exemplary college boy.

* * *

This interpretation of the delinquent subculture has important implications for the "sociology of social problems." People are prone to assume that those things which we define as evil and those which we define as good have their origins in separate and distinct features of our society. Evil flows from poisoned wells; good flows from pure and crystal fountains. The same source cannot feed both. Our view is different. It holds that those values which are at the core of "the American way of life," which help to motivate the behavior which we most esteem as "typically American," are among the major determinants of that which we can stigmatize as "pathological." More specifically, it holds that the problems of adjustment to which the delinquent subculture is a response are determined, in part, by those very values which respectable society holds most sacred. The same value system, impinging upon children differently equipped to meet it, is instrumental in generating both delinquency and respectability.

Lower Class Culture as a Generating Milieu of Gang Delinquency

Walter B. Miller

The etiology of delinquency has long been a controversial issue, and is particularly so at present. As new frames of reference for explaining human behavior have been added to traditional theories, some authors have adopted the practice of citing the major postulates of each school of thought as they pertain to delinquency, and going on to state that causality must be conceived in terms of the dynamic interaction of a complex combination of variables on many levels. The major sets of etiological factors currently adduced to explain delinquency are, in simplified terms, the physiological (delinquency results from organic pathology), the psychodynamic (delinquency is a "behavioral disorder" resulting primarily from emotional disturbance generated by a defective mother-child relationship), and the environmental (delinquency is the product of disruptive forces, "disorganization," in the actor's physical or social environment).

This paper selects one particular kind of "delinquency" [1]—law-violating acts committed by members of adolescent street corner groups in lower class communities—and attempts to show that the dominant component of motivation underlying these acts consists in a directed attempt by the actor to adhere to forms of behavior, and to achieve standards of value as they are defined within that community. It takes as a premise that the motivation of behavior in this situation can be approached most productively by attempting to understand the nature of cultural forces impinging on the acting individual as they are perceived *by the actor himself*—although by no means only that segment of these forces of which the actor is consciously aware—rather than as they are perceived and evaluated from the reference position of another cultural system. In the case of "gang" delinquency, the cultural system which exerts the most direct influence on behavior is that of the lower class community itself—a long-established, distinctively patterned tradition with an integrity of its own—rather than a so-called "delinquent subculture" which has arisen through conflict with middle class culture and is oriented to the deliberate violation of middle class norms.

The bulk of the substantive data on which the following material is based was collected in connection with a service-research project in the control of gang delinquency. During the service aspect of the project, which lasted for three years, seven trained social workers maintained contact with twenty-one corner group units in a "slum" district of a large eastern city for periods of time ranging from ten to thirty months. Groups were Negro and white, male and female, and in early, middle, and late adolescence. Over eight thousand pages of direct observational data on behavior patterns of group members and other community residents were collected; almost daily contact was maintained for a total time period of about thirteen worker years. Data include workers' contact reports, participant observation reports by the writer—a cultural anthropologist—and direct tape recordings of group activities and discussions.[2]

Focal Concerns of Lower Class Culture

There is a substantial segment of present-day American society whose way of life, values, and characteristic patterns of behavior are the product of a distinctive cultural system which may be termed "lower class." Evidence indicates that this cultural system is becoming increasingly distinctive, and that the size of the group which shares this tradition is increasing.[3] The lower class way of life, in common with that of all distinctive cultural groups, is characterized by a set of focal concerns—areas or issues which command widespread and persistent attention and a high degree of emotional involvement. The specific concerns cited here, while by no means confined to the American lower classes, constitute a distinctive *patterning* of concerns which differs significantly, both in rank order and weighting from that of American middle class culture. The following chart presents a highly schematic and simplified listing of six of the major concerns of lower class culture. Each is conceived as a "dimension" within which a fairly wide and varied range of alternative behavior patterns may be followed by different individuals under different situations. They are listed roughly in order of the degree of *explicit* attention accorded each, and, in this sense represent a weighted ranking of concerns.

[1] The complex issues involved in deriving a definition of "delinquency" cannot be discussed here. The term "delinquent" is used in this paper to characterize behavior or acts committed by individuals within specified age limits which if known to official authorities could result in legal action. The concept of a "delinquent" individual has little or no utility in the approach used here; rather, specified types of *acts* which may be committed rarely or frequently by few or many individuals are characterized as "delinquent."

[2] A three year research project is being financed under National Institutes of Health Grant M-1414, and administered through the Boston University School of Social Work. The primary research effort has subjected all collected material to a uniform data-coding process. All information bearing on some seventy areas of behavior (behavior in reference to school, police, theft, assault, sex, collective athletics, etc.) is extracted from the records, recorded on coded data cards, and filed under relevant categories. Analysis of these data aims to ascertain the actual nature of customary behavior in these areas, and the extent to which the social work effort was able to effect behavioral changes.

[3] Between 40 and 60 per cent of all Americans are directly influenced by lower class culture, with about 15 per cent, or twenty-five million, comprising the "hard core" lower class group—defined primarily by its use of the "female-based" household as the basic form of child-rearing unit and of the "serial monogamy" mating pattern as the primary form of marriage. The term "lower class culture" as used here refers most specifically to the way of life of the "hard core" group; systematic research in this area would probably reveal at least four to six major subtypes of lower class culture, for some of which the "concerns" presented here would be differently weighted, especially for those subtypes in which "law-abiding" behavior has a high overt valuation. It is impossible within the compass of this short paper to make the finer intracultural distinctions which a more accurate presentation would require.

From *Journal of Social Issues,* Vol. 14, 1958, pp. 5–19. Reprinted by permission of the Society for the Psychological Study of Social Issues.

CHART 1
FOCAL CONCERNS OF LOWER CLASS CULTURE

Area	Perceived Alternatives (state, quality, condition)	
1. *Trouble:*	law-abiding behavior	law-violating behavior
2. *Toughness:*	physical prowess, skill; "masculinity"; fearlessness, bravery, daring	weakness, ineptitude; effeminacy; timidity, cowardice, caution
3. *Smartness:*	ability to outsmart, dupe, "con"; gaining money by "wits"; shrewdness, adroitness in repartee	gullibility, "con-ability"; gaining money by hard work; slowness, dull-wittedness, verbal maladroitness
4. *Excitement:*	thrill; risk, danger; change, activity	boredom; "deadness," safeness; sameness, passivity
5. *Fate:*	favored by fortune, being "lucky"	ill-omened, being "unlucky"
6. *Autonomy:*	freedom from external constraint; freedom from superordinate authority; independence	presence of external constraint; presence of strong authority; dependency, being "cared for"

The "perceived alternatives" represent polar positions which define certain parameters within each dimension. As will be explained in more detail, it is necessary in relating the influence of these "concerns" to the motivation of delinquent behavior to specify *which* of its aspects is oriented to, whether orientation is *overt* or *covert, positive* (conforming to or seeking the aspect), or *negative* (rejecting or seeking to avoid the aspect).

The concept "focal concern" is used here in preference to the concept "value" for several interrelated reasons: (1) It is more readily derivable from direct field observation. (2) It is descriptively neutral—permitting independent consideration of positive and negative valences as varying under different conditions, whereas "value" carries a built-in positive valence. (3) It makes possible more refined analysis of subcultural differences, since it reflects actual behavior, whereas "value" tends to wash out intracultural differences since it is colored by notions of the "official" ideal.

Trouble: Concern over "trouble" is a dominant feature of lower class culture. The concept has various shades of meaning; "trouble" in one of its aspects represents a situation or a kind of behavior which results in unwelcome or complicating involvement with official authorities or agencies of middle class society. "Getting into trouble" and "staying out of trouble" represent major issues for male and female, adults and children. For men, "trouble" frequently involves fighting or sexual adventures while drinking; for women, sexual involvement with disadvantageous consequences. Expressed desire to avoid behavior which violates moral or legal norms is often based less on an explicit commitment to "official" moral or legal standards than on a desire to avoid "getting into trouble," e.g., the complicating consequences of the action.

The dominant concern over "trouble" involves a distinction of critical importance for the lower class community—that between "law-abiding" and "non-law-abiding" behavior. There is a high degree of sensitivity as to where each person stands in relation to these two classes of activity. Whereas in the middle class community a major dimension for evaluating a person's status is "achievement" and its external symbols, in the lower class, personal status is very frequently gauged along the law-abiding-non-law-abiding dimension. A mother will evaluate the suitability of her daughter's boyfriend less on the basis of his achievement potential than on the basis of his innate "trouble" potential. This sensitive awareness of the opposition of "trouble-producing" and "non-trouble-producing" behavior represents both a major basis for deriving status distinctions, and an internalized conflict potential for the individual.

As in the case of other focal concerns, which of two perceived alternatives—"law-abiding" or "non-law-abiding"—is valued varies according to the individual and the circumstances; in many instances there is an overt commitment to the "law-abiding" alternative, but a covert commitment to the "non-law-abiding." In certain situations, "getting into trouble" is overtly recognized as prestige-conferring; for example, membership in certain adult and adolescent primary groupings ("gangs") is contingent on having demonstrated an explicit commitment to the law-violating alternative. It is most important to note that the choice between "law-abiding" and "non-law-abiding" behavior is still a choice *within* lower class culture; the distinction between the policeman and the criminal, the outlaw and the sheriff, involves primarily this one dimension; in other respects they have a high community of interests. Not infrequently brothers raised in an identical cultural milieu will become police and criminals respectively.

For a substantial segment of the lower class population "getting into trouble" is not in itself overtly defined as prestige-conferring, but is implicitly recognized as a means to other valued ends, e.g., the covertly valued desire to be "cared for" and subject to external constraint, or the overtly valued state of excitement or risk. Very frequently "getting into trouble" is multi-functional, and achieves several sets of valued ends.

Toughness: The concept of "toughness" in lower class culture represents a compound combination of qualities or states. Among its most important components are physical prowess, evidenced both by demonstrated possession of strength and endurance and athletic skill; "masculinity," symbolized by a distinctive complex of acts and avoidances (bodily tatooing; absence of sentimentality; non-concern with "art," "literature," conceptualization of women as conquest objects, etc.); and bravery in the face of physical threat. The model for the "tough guy"—hard, fearless, undemonstrative, skilled in physical combat—is represented by the movie gangster of the thirties, the "private eye," and the movie cowboy.

The genesis of the intense concern over "toughness" in lower class culture is probably related to the fact that a significant proportion of lower class males are reared in a predominantly female household, and lack a consistently present male figure with whom to identify and from whom to learn essential components of a "male" role. Since women serve as a primary object of identification during pre-adolescent years, the almost obsessive lower class concern with "masculinity" probably resembles a type of compulsive reaction-formation. A concern over homosexuality runs like a persistent thread through lower class culture. This is manifested by the institutionalized practice of baiting "queers," often accompanied by violent physical attacks, an expressed contempt for "softness" or frills, and the use of the local term for "homosexual" as a generalized pejorative epithet (e.g., higher class individuals or upwardly mobile peers are frequently characterized as "fags" or "queers"). The distinction between "overt" and "covert" orientation to aspects of an area of concern is especially important in regard to "toughness." A positive overt evaluation of behavior defined as "effeminate" would be out of the question for a lower class male; however, built into lower class culture is a range of devices which permit men to adopt behaviors and concerns which in other cultural milieux fall within the province of women, and at the same time to be defined as "tough" and manly. For example, lower class men can be professional short-order cooks in a diner and still be regarded as "tough." The highly intimate circumstances of the street corner gang involve the recurrent expression of strongly affectionate feelings towards other men. Such expressions, however, are disguised as their opposite, taking the form of ostensibly aggressive verbal and physical interaction (kidding, "ranking," roughhousing, etc.).

Smartness: "Smartness," as conceptualized in lower class culture, involves the capacity to outsmart, outfox, outwit, dupe, "take," "con" another or others, and the concomitant capacity to avoid being outwitted, "taken," or duped oneself. In its essence, smartness involves the capacity to achieve a valued entity—material goods, personal status—through a maximum use of mental agility and a minimum use of physical effort. This capacity has an extremely long tradition in lower class culture, and is highly valued. Lower class culture can be characterized as "non-intellectual" only if intellectualism is defined specifically in terms of control over a particular body of formally learned knowledge involving "culture" (art, literature, "good" music, etc.), a generalized perspective on the past and present conditions of our own and other societies, and other areas of knowledge imparted by formal educational institutions. This particular type of mental attainment is, in general, overtly disvalued and frequently associated with effeminancy; "smartness" in the lower class sense, however, is highly valued.

The lower class child learns and practices the use of this skill in the street corner situation. Individuals continually practice duping and outwitting one another through recurrent card games and other forms of gambling, mutual exchanges of insults, and "testing" for mutual "con-ability." Those who demonstrate competence in this skill are accorded considerable prestige. Leadership roles in the corner group are frequently allocated according to demonstrated capacity in the two areas of "smartness" and "toughness"; the ideal leader combines both, but the "smart" leader is often accorded more prestige than the "tough" one—

reflecting a general lower class respect for "brains" in the "smartness" sense.[4]

The model of the "smart" person is represented in popular media by the card shark, the professional gambler, the "con" artist, the promoter. A conceptual distinction is made between two kinds of people: "suckers," easy marks, "lushes," dupes, who work for their money and are legitimate targets of exploitation; and sharp operators, the "brainy" ones, who live by their wits and "getting" from the suckers by mental adroitness.

Involved in the syndrome of capacities related to "smartness" is a dominant emphasis in lower class culture on ingenious aggressive repartee. This skill, learned and practiced in the context of the corner group, ranges in form from the widely prevalent semi-ritualized teasing, kidding, razzing, "ranking," so characteristic of male peer group interaction, to the highly ritualized type of mutual insult interchange known as "the dirty dozens," "the dozens," "playing house," and other terms. This highly patterned cultural form is practiced on its most advanced level in adult male Negro society, but less polished variants are found throughout lower class culture—practiced, for example, by white children, male and female, as young as four or five. In essence, "doin' the dozens" involves two antagonists who vie with each other in the exchange of increasingly inflammatory insults, with incestuous and perverted sexual relations with the mother a dominant theme. In this form of insult interchange, as well as on other less ritualized occasions for joking, semi-serious, and serious mutual invective, a very high premium is placed on ingenuity, hair-trigger responsiveness, inventiveness, and the acute exercise of mental faculties.

Excitement: For many lower class individuals the rhythm of life fluctuates between periods of relatively routine or repetitive activity and sought situations of great emotional stimulation. Many of the most characteristic features of lower class life are related to the search for excitement or "thrill." Involved here are the highly prevalent use of alcohol by both sexes and the widespread use of gambling of all kinds—playing the numbers, betting on horse races, dice, cards. The quest for excitement finds what is perhaps its most vivid expression in the highly patterned practice of the recurrent "night on the town." This practice, designated by various terms in different areas ("honky-tonkin' "; "goin' out on the town"; "bar hoppin' "), involves a patterned set of activities in which alcohol, music, and sexual adventuring are major components. A group or individual sets out to "make the rounds" of various bars or night clubs. Drinking continues progressively throughout the evening. Men seek to "pick up" women, and women play the risky game of entertaining sexual advances. Fights between men involving women, gambling, and claims of physical prowess, in various combinations, are frequent consequences of a night of making the rounds. The explosive potential of this type of adventuring with sex and aggression, frequently leading to "trouble," is semi-explicitly sought by the individual. Since there is always a good likelihood that being out on the town will eventuate in fights, etc., the practice involves elements of sought risk and desired danger.

Counterbalancing the "flirting with danger" aspect of the "excitement" concern is the prevalence in lower class culture of other well established patterns of activity which involve long periods of relative inaction, or passivity. The term "hanging out" in lower class culture refers to extended periods of standing around, often with peer mates, doing what is defined as "nothing," "shooting the breeze," etc. A definite periodicity exists in the pattern of activity relating to the two aspects of the "excitement" dimension. For many lower class individuals the venture into the high risk world of alcohol, sex, and fighting occurs regularly once a week, with interim periods devoted to accommodating to possible consequences of these periods, along with recurrent resolves not to become so involved again.

Fate: Related to the quest for excitement is the concern with fate, fortune, or luck. Here also a distinction is made between two states—being "lucky" or "in luck," and being unlucky or jinxed. Many lower class individuals feel that their lives are subject to a set of forces over which they have relatively little control. These are not directly equated with the supernatural forces of formally organized religion, but relate more to a concept of "destiny," or man as a pawn of magical powers. Not infrequently this often implicit world view is associated with a conception of the ultimate futility of directed effort towards a goal: if the cards are right, or the dice good to you, or if your lucky number comes up, things will go your way; if luck is against you, it's not worth trying. The concept of performing semi-magical rituals so that one's "luck will change" is prevalent; one hopes that as a result he will move from the state of being "unlucky" to that of being "lucky." The element of fantasy plays an important part in this area. Related to and complementing the notion that "only suckers work" (Smartness) is the idea that once things start going your way, relatively independent of your own effort, all good things will come to you. Achieving great material rewards (big cars, big houses, a roll of cash to flash in a fancy night club), valued in lower class as well as in other parts of American culture, is a recurrent theme in lower class fantasy and folk lore; the cocaine dreams of Willie the Weeper or Minnie the Moocher present the components of this fantasy in vivid detail.

The prevalence in the lower class community of many forms of gambling, mentioned in connection with the "excitement" dimension, is also relevant here. Through cards and pool which involve skill, and thus both "toughness" and "smartness"; or through race horse betting, involving "smartness"; or through playing the numbers, involving predominantly "luck," one may make a big killing with a minimum of directed and persistent effort within conventional occupational channels. Gambling in its many forms illustrates the fact that many of the persistent features of lower class culture are multi-functional—serving a range of desired ends at the same time. Describing some of the incentives behind gambling has involved mention of all of the focal concerns cited so far—Toughness, Smartness, and Excitement, in addition to Fate.

Autonomy: The extent and nature of control over the behavior of the individual—an important concern in most cultures—has a special significance and is distinctively patterned in lower class culture. The discrepancy between what is overtly valued and what is covertly sought is particularly striking in this area. On the overt level there is a strong and frequently expressed resentment of the idea of external controls, restrictions on behavior, and unjust or coercive authority. "No one's gonna push *me* around," or "I'm gonna tell him he can take the job and shove it. . . ." are commonly expressed sentiments. Similar explicit attitudes are maintained to systems of behavior-restricting rules, insofar as these are perceived as representing the injunctions, and bearing the sanctions of superordinate authority. In addition, in lower class culture a close conceptual connection is made between "authority" and "nurturance." To be restrictively or firmly controlled is to be cared for. Thus the overtly negative evaluation of superordinate authority frequently extends as well to nurturance, care, or protection. The desire for personal independence is often expressed in such terms as "I don't need *nobody* to take care of me. I can take care of myself!" Actual patterns of behavior, however, reveal a marked discrepancy between expressed sentiment and what is covertly valued. Many lower class people appear to seek out highly restrictive social environments wherein stringent external controls are maintained over their behavior. Such institutions as the armed forces, the mental hospital, the disciplinary school, the prison or correctional institution, provide environments which incorporate a strict and detailed set of rules defining and limiting behavior, and enforced by an authority system which controls and applies coercive sanctions for deviance from these rules. While under the jurisdiction of such systems, the lower class person generally expresses to his peers continual resentment of the coercive, unjust, and arbitrary exercise of authority. Having been released, or having escaped from these milieux, however, he will often act in such a way as to insure recommitment, or choose recommitment voluntarily after a temporary period of "freedom."

Lower class patients in mental hospitals will exercise considerable ingenuity to insure continued commitment while voicing the desire to get out; delinquent boys will frequently "run" from a correctional institution to activate efforts to return them; to be caught and returned means that one is cared for. Since "being controlled" is equated with "being cared for," attempts are frequently made to "test" the severity or strictness of superordinate authority to see if it remains firm. If intended or executed rebellion produces swift and firm punitive sanctions, the individual is reassured, at the same time that he is complaining bitterly at the injustice of being caught and punished. Some environmental milieux, having been tested in this fashion for the "firmness" of their coercive sanctions, are rejected, ostensibly for being too strict, actually for not being strict enough. This is frequently so in the case of "problematic" behavior by lower class youngsters in the public schools, which generally cannot command the coercive controls implicitly sought by the individual.

A similar discrepancy between what is overtly and covertly desired is found in the area of dependence-independence. The pose of tough rebellious independence often assumed by the lower class person frequently

[4] The "brains-brawn" set of capacities are often paired in lower class folk lore or accounts of lower class life, e.g., "Brer Fox" and "Brer Bear" in the Uncle Remus stories, or George and Lennie in "Of Mice and Men."

conceals powerful dependency cravings. These are manifested primarily by obliquely expressed resentment when "care" is not forthcoming rather than by expressed satisfaction when it is. The concern over autonomy-dependency is related both to "trouble" and "fate." Insofar as the lower class individual feels that his behavior is controlled by forces which often propel him into "trouble" in the face of an explicit determination to avoid it, there is an implied appeal to "save me from myself." A solution appears to lie in arranging things so that his behavior will be coercively restricted by an externally imposed set of controls strong enough to forcibly restrain his inexplicable inclination to get in trouble. The periodicity observed in connection with the "excitement" dimension is also relevant here; after involvement in trouble-producing behavior (assault, sexual adventure, a "drunk"), the individual will actively seek a locus of imposed control (his wife, prison, a restrictive job); after a given period of subjection to this control, resentment against it mounts, leading to a "break away" and a search for involvement in further "trouble."

Focal Concerns of the Lower Class Adolescent Street Corner Group

The one-sex peer group is a highly prevalent and significant structural form in the lower class community. There is a strong probability that the prevalence and stability of this type of unit is directly related to the prevalence of a stabilized type of lower class child-rearing unit—the "female-based" household. This is a nuclear kin unit in which a male parent is either absent from the household, present only sporadically, or, when present, only minimally or inconsistently involved in the support and rearing of children. This unit usually consists of one or more females of child-bearing age and their offspring. The females are frequently related to one another by blood or marriage ties, and the unit often includes two or more generations of women, e.g., the mother and/or aunt of the principal child-bearing female.

The nature of social groupings in the lower class community may be clarified if we make the assumption that it is the *one-sex peer unit* rather than the two-parent family unit which represents the most significant relational unit for both sexes in lower class communities. Lower class society may be pictured as comprising a set of age-graded one-sex groups which constitute the major psychic focus and reference group for those over twelve or thirteen. Men and women of mating age leave these groups periodically to form temporary marital alliances, but these lack stability, and after varying periods of "trying out" the two-sex family arrangement, gravitate back to the more "comfortable" one-sex grouping, whose members exert strong pressure on the individual *not* to disrupt the group by adopting a two-sex household pattern of life.[5] Membership in a stable and solidary peer unit is vital to the lower class individual precisely to the extent to which a range of essential functions—psychological, educational, and others, are not provided by the "family" unit.

The adolescent street corner group represents the adolescent variant of this lower class structural form. What has been called the "delinquent gang" is one subtype of this form, defined on the basis of frequency of participation in law-violating activity; this subtype should not be considered a legitimate unit of study per se, but rather as one particular variant of the adolescent street corner group. The "hanging" peer group is a unit of particular importance for the adolescent male. In many cases it is the most stable and solidary primary grroup he has ever belonged to; for boys reared in female-based households the corner group provides the first real opportunity to learn essential aspects of the male role in the context of peers facing similar problems of sex-role identification.

The form and functions of the adolescent corner group operate as a selective mechanism in recruiting members. The activity patterns of the group require a high level of intra-group solidarity; individual members must possess a good capacity for subordinating individual desires to general group interests as well as the capacity for intimate and persisting interaction. Thus highly "disturbed" individuals, or those who cannot tolerate consistently imposed sanctions on "deviant" behavior cannot remain accepted members; the group itself will extrude those whose behavior exceeds limits defined as "normal." This selective process produces a type of group whose members possess to an unusually high degree both the *capacity* and *motivation* to conform to perceived cultural norms, so that the nature of the system of norms and values oriented to is a particularly influential component of motivation.

Focal concerns of the male adolescent corner group are those of the general cultural milieu in which it functions. As would be expected, the relative weighting and importance of these concerns pattern somewhat differently for adolescents than for adults. The nature of this patterning centers around two additional "concerns" of particular importance to this group—concern with "belonging," and with "status." These may be conceptualized as being on a higher level of abstraction than concerns previously cited, since "status" and "belonging" are achieved *via* cited concern areas of Toughness, etc.

Belonging: Since the corner group fulfills essential functions for the individual, being a member in good standing of the group is of vital importance for its members. A continuing concern over who is "in" and who is not involves the citation and detailed discussion of highly refined criteria for "in-group" membership. The phrase "he hangs with us" means "he is accepted as a member in good standing by current consensus"; conversely, "he don't hang with us" means he is not so accepted. One achieves "belonging" primarily by demonstrating knowledge of and a determination to adhere to the system of standards and valued qualities defined by the group. One maintains membership by acting in conformity with valued aspects of Toughness, Smartness, Autonomy, etc. In those instances where conforming to norms of this reference group at the same time violates norms of other reference groups (e.g., middle class adults, institutional "officials"), immediate reference group norms are much more compelling since violation risks invoking the group's most powerful sanction: exclusion.

Status: In common with most adolescents in American society, the lower class corner group manifests a dominant concern with "status." What differentiates this type of group from others, however, is the particular set of criteria and weighting thereof by which "status" is defined. In general, status is achieved and maintained by demonstrated possession of the valued qualities of lower class culture—Toughness, Smartness, expressed resistance to authority, daring, etc. It is important to stress once more that the individual orients to these concerns *as they are defined within lower class society;* e.g., the status-conferring potential of "smartness" in the sense of scholastic achievement generally ranges from negligible to negative.

The concern with "status" is manifested in a variety of ways. Intra-group status is a continued concern, and is derived and tested constantly by means of a set of status-ranking activities; the intra-group "pecking order" is constantly at issue. One gains status within the group by demonstrated superiority in Toughness (physical prowess, bravery, skill in athletics and games such as pool and cards), Smartness (skill in repartee, capacity to "dupe" fellow group members), and the like. The term "ranking," used to refer to the pattern of intra-group aggressive repartee, indicates awareness of the fact that this is one device for establishing the intra-group status hierarchy.

The concern over status in the adolescent corner group involves in particular the component of "adultness," the intense desire to be seen as "grown up," and a corresponding aversion to "kid stuff." "Adult" status is defined less in terms of the assumption of "adult" responsibility than in terms of certain external symbols of adult status—a car, ready cash, and, in particular, a perceived "freedom" to drink, smoke, and gamble as one wishes and to come and go without external restrictions. The desire to be seen as "adult" is often a more significant component of much involvement in illegal drinking, gambling, and automobile driving than the explicit enjoyment of these acts as such.

The intensity of the corner group member's desire to be seen as "adult" is sufficiently great that he feels called upon to demonstrate qualities associated with adultness (Toughness, Smartness, Autonomy) to a much greater degree than a lower class adult. This means that he will seek out and utilize those avenues to these qualities which he perceives as available with greater intensity than an adult and less regard for their "legitimacy." In this sense the adolescent variant of lower class culture represents a maximization or an intensified manifestation of many of its most characteristic features.

Concern over status is also manifested in reference to other street corner groups. The term "rep" used in this regard is especially significant, and has broad connotations. In its most frequent and explicit connotation, "rep" refers to the "toughness" of the corner group as a whole relative to that of other groups; a "pecking order" also exists among the several corner groups in a given interactional area, and there is a common perception that the safety or security of the group and all its members depends on maintaining a solid "rep" for toughness vis-a-vis other groups. This motive is most frequently advanced as a reason for involvement in

[5] Further data on the female-based household unit (estimated as comprising about 15 per cent of all American "families") and the role of one-sex groupings in lower class culture are contained in Walter B. Miller, Implications of Urban Lower Class Culture for Social Work. *Social Service Review*, 1959, *33*, No. 3.

gang fights: "We *can't* chicken out on this fight; our rep would be shot!"; this implies that the group would be relegated to the bottom of the status ladder and become a helpless and recurrent target of external attack.

On the other hand, there is implicit in the concept of "rep" the recognition that "rep" has or may have a dual basis—corresponding to the two aspects of the "trouble" dimension. It is recognized that group as well as individual status can be based on both "law-abiding" and "law-violating" behavior. The situational resolution of the persisting conflict between the "law-abiding" and "law-violating" bases of status comprises a vital set of dynamics in determining whether a "delinquent" mode of behavior will be adopted by a group, under what circumstances, and how persistently. The determinants of this choice are evidently highly complex and fluid, and rest on a range of factors including the presence and perceptual immediacy of different community reference-group loci (e.g., professional criminals, police, clergy, teachers, settlement house workers), the personality structures and "needs" of group members, the presence in the community of social work, recreation, or educational programs which can facilitate utilization of the "law-abiding" basis of status, and so on.

What remains constant is the critical importance of "status" both for the members of the group as individuals and for the group as a whole insofar as members perceive their individual destinies as linked to the destiny of the group, and the fact that action geared to attain status is much more acutely oriented to the fact of status itself than to the legality or illegality, morality or immorality of the means used to achieve it.

Lower Class Culture and the Motivation of Delinquent Behavior

The customary set of activities of the adolescent street corner group includes activities which are in violation of laws and ordinances of the legal code. Most of these center around assault and theft of various types (the gang fight; auto theft; assault on an individual; petty pilfering and shoplifting; "mugging"; pocketbook theft). Members of street corner gangs are well aware of the law-violating nature of these acts; they are not psychopaths, nor physically or mentally "defective"; in fact, since the corner group supports and enforces a rigorous set of standards which demand a high degree of fitness and personal competence, it tends to recruit from the most "able" members of the community.

Why, then, is the commission of crimes a customary feature of gang activity? The most general answer is that the commission of crimes by members of adolescent street corner groups is motivated primarily by the attempt to achieve ends, states, or conditions which are valued, and to avoid those that are disvalued within their most meaningful cultural milieu, through those culturally available avenues which appear as the most feasible means of attaining those ends.

The operation of these influences is well illustrated by the gang fight—a prevalent and characteristic type of corner group delinquency. This type of activity comprises a highly stylized and culturally patterned set of sequences. Although details vary under different circumstances, the following events are generally included. A member or several members of group A "trespass" on the claimed territory of group B. While there they commit an act or acts which group B defines as a violation of its rightful privileges, an affront to their honor, or a challenge to their "rep." Frequently this act involves advances to a girl associated with group B; it may occur at a dance or party; sometimes the mere act of "trespass" is seen as deliberate provocation. Members of group B then assault members of group A, if they are caught while still in B's territory. Assaulted members of group A return to their "home" territory and recount to members of their group details of the incident, stressing the insufficient nature of the provocation ("I just *looked* at her! Hardly even said anything!"), and the unfair circumstances of the assault ("About *twenty* guys jumped just the *two* of us!"). The highly colored account is acutely inflammatory; group A, perceiving its honor violated and its "rep" threatened, feels obligated to retaliate in force. Sessions of detailed planning now occur; allies are recruited if the size of group A and its potential allies appears to necessitate larger numbers; strategy is plotted, and messengers dispatched. Since the prospect of a gang fight is frightening to even the "toughest" group members, a constant rehearsal of the provocative incident or incidents and the essentially evil nature of the opponents accompanies the planning process to bolster possibly weakening motivation to fight. The excursion into "enemy" territory sometimes results in a full scale fight; more often group B cannot be found, or the police appear and stop the fight, "tipped off" by an anonymous informant. When this occurs, group members express disgust and disappointment; secretly there is much relief; their honor has been avenged without incurring injury; often the anonymous tipster is a member of one of the involved groups.

The basic elements of this type of delinquency are sufficiently stabilized and recurrent as to constitute an essentially ritualized pattern, resembling both in structure and expressed motives for action classic forms such as the European "duel," the American Indian tribal war, and the Celtic clan feud. Although the arousing and "acting out" of individual aggressive emotions are inevitably involved in the gang fight, neither its form nor motivational dynamics can be adequately handled within a predominantly personality-focused frame of reference.

It would be possible to develop in considerable detail the processes by which the commission of a range of illegal acts is either explicitly supported by, implicitly demanded by, or not materially inhibited by factors relating to the focal concerns of lower class culture. In place of such a development, the following three statements condense in general terms the operation of these processes:

1. *Following cultural practices which comprise essential elements of the total life pattern of lower class culture automatically violates certain legal norms.*
2. *In instances where alternate avenues to similar objectives are available, the non-law-abiding avenue frequently provides a relatively greater and more immediate return for a relatively smaller investment of energy.*
3. *The "demanded" response to certain situations recurrently engendered within lower class culture involves the commission of illegal acts.*

The primary thesis of this paper is that the dominant component of the motivation of "delinquent" behavior engaged in by members of lower class corner groups involves a positive effort to achieve states, conditions, or qualities valued within the actor's most significant cultural milieu. If "conformity to immediate reference group values" is the major component of motivation of "delinquent" behavior by gang members, why is such behavior frequently referred to as negativistic, malicious, or rebellious? Albert Cohen, for example, in *Delinquent Boys* (Glencoe: Free Press, 1955) describes behavior which violates school rules as comprising elements of "active spite and malice, contempt and ridicule, challenge and defiance." He ascribes to the gang "keen delight in terrorizing 'good' children, and in general making themselves obnoxious to the virtuous." A recent national conference on social work with "hard-to-reach" groups characterized lower class corner groups as "youth groups in conflict with the culture of their (*sic*) communities." Such characterizations are obviously the result of taking the middle class community and its institutions as an implicit point of reference.

A large body of systematically interrelated attitudes, practices, behaviors, and values characteristic of lower class culture are designed to support and maintain the basic features of the lower class way of life. In areas where these differ from features of middle class culture, action oriented to the achievement and maintenance of the lower class system may violate norms of middle class culture and be perceived as deliberately non-conforming or malicious by an observer strongly cathected to middle class norms. This does not mean, however, that violation of the middle class norm is the dominant component of motivation; it is a by-product of action primarily oriented to the lower class system. The standards of lower class culture cannot be seen merely as a reverse function of middle class culture—as middle class standards "turned upside down"; lower class culture is a distinctive tradition many centuries old with an integrity of its own.

From the viewpoint of the acting individual, functioning within a field of well-structured cultural forces, the relative impact of "conforming" and "rejective" elements in the motivation of gang delinquency is weighted preponderantly on the conforming side. Rejective or rebellious elements are inevitably involved, but their influence during the actual commission of delinquent acts is relatively small compared to the influence of pressures to achieve what is valued by the actor's most immediate reference groups. Expressed awareness by the actor of the element of rebellion often represents only that aspect of motivation of which he is explicitly conscious; the deepest and most compelling components of motivation—adherence to highly meaningful group standards of Toughness, Smartness, Excitement, etc.—are often unconsciously patterned. No cultural pattern as well-established as the practice of illegal acts by members of lower class corner groups could persist if buttressed primarily by negative, hostile, or rejective motives; its principal motivational support, as in the case of any persisting cultural tradition, derives from a positive effort to achieve what is valued within that tradition, and to conform to its explicit and implicit norms.

Delinquency, Situational Inducements, and Commitment to Conformity

Scott Briar and Irving Piliavin
University of California, Berkeley

In recent years a theory of delinquency, the delinquent subculture thesis, has been advanced which has had an enormous influence on delinquency prevention and control programs throughout the United States. In the present paper we will show: first, that the subculture thesis, and the general class of theories of which it is a part, are unable to account satisfactorily for crucial aspects of the phenomena of delinquency; and second, that these phenomena can be better explained by an alternative class of formulations currently categorized as social control theories, when these theories are modified in ways suggested below.

The subculture theory of delinquency along with some of the theories it is intended to supersede—such as psychoanalytic theory and the adolescent rebellion thesis—belong to the class of what may be termed motivational theories of delinquency. These theories regard the illegal acts of delinquents as the product of some enduring disposition or combination of dispositions unique to these youths. While motivational theories differ widely on the nature and precise etiology of these dispositions, they follow a common logic regarding the development of these dispositions and their role in delinquent behavior. In brief, these dispositions are seen as: (1) deriving from certain interpersonal and/or social conditions which delinquents experience; (2) essentially permanent aspects of the personality and/or value framework of delinquent boys; and (3) forces which propel them into illegal behavior.

Despite their numerous differences, however, all motivational theories of delinquency have incurred common problems. First, the etiological factors they postulate do not operate uniformly. That is, many boys subjected to experiences which presumably should give rise to delinquency-producing dispositions do not acquire them. Second, many boys who exhibit these dispositions do not appear among identified delinquents. Third, the great majority of identified delinquents apparently become law-abiding in late adolescence and early adulthood—a fact which motivational theories of delinquency cannot explain, with their assumptions on the enduring nature of delinquency-producing dispositions. Fourth, even if we grant, despite the above problems,[1] that delinquent behavior is in some fashion and to some degree a product of enduring dispositions, we still face the unexplained fact that only a small portion of boys who are members of delinquent gangs or who are designated delinquent by juvenile courts have those characteristics predicted for them by contemporary motivational theories of delinquency. Finally, motivational theories of delinquency do not account for the well documented fact that the vast majority of boys engage in delinquent behavior to some degree.

To avoid the above problems, defenders of these theories have (1) indicated that various factors may mitigate the influence of delinquency-producing dispositions, (2) suggested that forces other than those so far identified may also lead boys to commit illegal acts, and (3) argued that the delinquent behavior of so-called non-delinquents is accidental, prankish, or otherwise understandable in terms not applicable to true delinquents.[2] These arguments, however, imply a cumbersome multi-factor theory of delinquency whose obvious defects have led some theorists to doubt whether etio-

[1] Presumably these problems can be dealt with by the introduction of additional factors which either augment or constrain the influence of those factors considered basic to the development of delinquent-producing dispositions and/or the operation of the dispositions themselves. However, to our knowledge, no systematic effort has been made to identify these ancillary conditions and their operation.

[2] This interpretation is not shared by Bloch and Niederhoffer who, in acknowledging the universality of delinquent behavior, attribute it to adolescent identity crisis. But as Cloward and Ohlin point out, this view of delinquency fails to account for apparent differentials in illegal activities among various identifiable adolescent subgroupings. Herbert Bloch and Arthur Niederhoffer, *The Gang: A Study in Adolescent Behavior* (New York: Philosophical Library, 1958), p. 17; Richard A. Cloward and Lloyd E. Ohlin, *Delinquency and Opportunity* (Glencoe, Ill.: The Free Press, 1960), pp. 50-55.

From *Social Problems,* Vol. 13, No. 1, 1965, pp. 35-45. Reprinted with the permission of the Society of Social Problems and the authors.

logical explanations of the phenomena are in fact possible.[3]

Situationally Induced Motives to Deviate

Those who argue for a radical distinction between delinquent and non-delinquent traits attempt to justify it on the basis of the apparent differentials in the frequency of various types of delinquent activity among "delinquents" (or a particular class of delinquents) and "non-delinquents." Having established such differentials, these theorists argue that the infractions of "delinquents" are different in origin from those of "non-delinquents." More concise and less questionable, however, is the assumption that the delinquent acts of both non-delinquents and delinquents are conditioned largely by common factors. This assumption provides the basic premise for the formulation to follow.

Because delinquent behavior is typically episodic, purposive, and confined to certain situations,[4] we assume that the motives for such behavior are frequently episodic, oriented to short-term ends, and confined to certain situations. That is, rather than considering delinquent acts as solely the product of long term motives deriving from conflicts or frustrations whose genesis is far removed from the arenas in which the illegal behavior occurs, we assume these acts are prompted by short-term situationally induced desires experienced by all boys to obtain valued goods, to portray courage in the presence of, or be loyal to peers, to strike out at someone who is disliked, or simply to "get kicks."[5]

The influence of currently experienced situations on individuals' attitudes and behaviors has been emphasized in numerous sociological and social-psychological studies. In brief, these studies indicate that situational factors can confront actors with conflicts, opportunities, pressures, and temptations which may influence the actors' actions and views. Many of these studies, especially those conducted under "real-life" conditions, have focused on highly patterned situations of long duration, such as the social structure of an industrial plant, a hospital ward, or a housing project.[6] On the other hand, several theoretical writings,[7] material from some case studies,[8] and a large number of experimental studies in social psychology indicate that situationally induced stimuli of relatively short duration also can affect, to varying extents, the values and behaviors of those exposed to these stimuli. In the words of Lewin:

> It is a simple fact, but still not sufficiently recognized in psychology and sociology, that the behavior of a person depends above all upon his momentary position. Often, the world looks very different before and after an event which changes the region in which a person is located.[9]

But even granting that short-term situationally induced stimuli can influence individuals, we question whether or not such stimuli are sufficient to effect deviant behavior. There is some evidence to suggest that they are. Cressey, for example, has shown that the criminal violation of financial trust can be viewed as a narrow goal-oriented response to a situationally induced financial problem:

> Trusted persons become trust violators when they conceive of themselves as having a financial problem which is non-sharable, have the knowledge or awareness that this problem can be secretly resolved by violation of the position of financial trust, and are able to apply to their own conduct in that situation verbalizations which enable them to adjust their conceptions of themselves as trusted persons with their conceptions of themselves as users of the entrusted funds or property.[10]

Additional support for the notion that situationally induced stimuli of short duration can lead to illegal behavior is provided by self-reports from gang members.

> When we were shoplifting we always made a game of it. For example we might gamble on who could steal the most caps in a day, or who could steal in the presence of a detective and then get away. This was the best part of the game. . . . It was the fun I wanted, not the hat.[11]
>
> I was walkin' uptown with a couple of friends, and we run into Magician and them there. They asked us if we wanted to go to a fight, and we said "Yes." When they asked me if I wanted to go to a fight, I couldn't say, "No." I mean I could say, "No," but for old-time's sake, I said, "Yes."[12]
>
> You see, man, it's not that I'm against anyone else, I'm just "all for me." Our stealing did have a utilitarian motive. Sometimes we stole something we actually liked and wanted and stealing always proved we had guts. . . . [But] most of the time I didn't even have stealing on my mind. . . .
>
> What have we done? We're just trying to have some fun. We don't want to be

---

[3] David Matza, *Delinquency and Drift* (New York: John Wiley & Sons, 1964), pp. 33-67.

[4] Borrowing from Kohn and Williams, we define a situation as ". . . a series of interactions, located in space and time, and perceived by the participants as an event: in this usage 'situation' is a delimiting term, cutting out from the flow of experience a particular series of interpersonal actions which are seen by the participants as a describable event, separable from preceding and succeeding events, constraining the participants to act in particular ways and having its own unique consequences." Melvin L. Kohn and Robin M. Williams, "Situational Patterning in Intergroup Relations," *American Sociological Review,* 21 (April, 1956), p. 164.

[5] We are suggesting here that the situations which delinquents find tempting and exciting are similar, in spirit, to those which attract the non-delinquent. As Matza has pointed out, the teen-age culture is "a conventional version of the delinquent tradition. Here we find an emphasis on fun and adventure: a disdain for scholastic effort; the more or less persistent involvement in 'tolerated' status offenses like drinking, gambling, occasional truancy, 'making out' in the sense of sexual conquest, driving cars before the appropriate age, smoking, swearing, and staying out late. . . . Aggression is considerably tempered, but there is a persistent concern with the credentials on [sic] masculinity and femininity." David Matza, "Subterranean Traditions of Youth," *Annals of the American Academy of Political and Social Science,* 338 (November, 1961), p. 116.

[6] See for example: Leon Festinger, Stanley Schachter, and Kurt Back, *Social Pressures in Informal Groups* (New York: Harper, 1950); Morton Deutsch and Mary E. Collins, *Interracial Housing: A Psychological Evaluation of a Social Experiment* (Minneapolis: Univ. of Minnesota Press, 1951); Neal Gross, Ward S. Mason, Alexander W. McEachern, *Explorations in Role Analysis* (New York: John Wiley & Sons, 1958); Kurt Lewin, Ronald Lippett, and Ralph K. White, "Patterns of Aggressive Behavior in Experimentally Created 'Social Climates,'" *Journal of Social Psychology* 10 (1939), pp. 271-299; Seymour Lieberman, "The Effects of Changes in Roles on the Attitudes of Role Occupants," *Human Relations,* 9 (1950), pp. 385-403; Alvin Gouldner, *Patterns of Industrial Bureaucracy* (Glencoe, Ill.: The Free Press, 1954); Peter G. Garabedian, "Social Roles and Processes of Socialization in the Prison Community," *Social Problems* 11 (Fall, 1963), pp. 139-152; Alfred Stanton and Morris Schwartz, *The Mental Hospital* (New York: Basic Books, 1954); Peter Blau, "Structural Effects," *American Sociological Review,* 25 (1960), pp. 178-193.

[7] Kurt Lewin, *Field Theory in Social Science* (New York: Harper & Brothers, 1951); George C. Homans, *Social Behavior: Its Elementary Forms* (New York: Harcourt, Brace and World, 1961), pp. 46-47, 51-82.

[8] Gouldner, *op. cit.,* pp. 83-85; Kohn and Williams, *op. cit.,* pp. 164-174.

[9] Lewin, *op. cit.,* p. 137.

[10] Donald R. Cressey, "The Criminal Violation of Financial Trust," *American Sociological Review,* 15 (December, 1950), p. 742.

[11] Clifford R. Shaw, "Juvenile Delinquency—A Group Tradition," *Bulletin of the State University of Iowa,* No. 23, N.S. No. 700, 1933, p. 8.

[12] Lewis Yablonsky, *The Violent Gang* (New York: Macmillan, 1962), p. 13.

like those middle class guys. We are no mamma's boys.[13]

Thus, there is considerable basis for assuming that the immediate situation in which a youth finds himself can play an important role in his decision to engage in delinquent behavior. Obviously, however, this is not to say that the situation offering inducement or pressure to a youth to deviate will necessarily lead him to take such action. For one thing, situationally induced motives vary in intensity. Furthermore, their expression depends on a variety of contingencies, such as the ease with which the motivated behavior can be carried out, the risks involved, and the press or attractiveness of other activities.[14] Finally, whether or not the motives to deviate are situationally induced, the behavioral expression of them depends on the degree to which the individuals experiencing the motives also experience constraints against that behavior.

Constraints on Deviance: The Concept of Commitment

Three dominant views can be identified in motivational theories of delinquency regarding (1) the nature of the influences which constrain individuals from engaging in delinquent behavior, and (2) the conditions under which these influences are neutralized.

In delinquent sub-culture theories, the basic constraint against the exercise of deviant motives is allegiance to the dominant values of the larger society. Depending on the particular theorist, a youth's freedom from this constraint entails allegiance to an oppositional system of values by means of either a type of reaction formation,[15] a more or less rational process of decision-making,[16] or socialization to a cultural tradition differing from that of the larger society.[17]

A second type of constraint involves internalization of parental prohibitions and demands—in other words, the development of a super-ego. Freedom from this constraint is seen largely as the product of parental failure to socialize children properly. Such failure may result from a variety of conditions, ranging from parental failure to articulate conventional values to lack of the kind of familial atmosphere in which such values, even if articulated, can be incorporated by children.[18]

There are, however, important limitations in these two formulations of the constraining influences on deviant behavior. For one thing, empirical studies have failed to find a strong oppositional or autonomous value system among delinquent gang youth as predicted by delinquent sub-culture theorists.[19] Moreover, considerable evidence indicates that moral concerns, such as would be expected from the operation of the super-ego, are neither the only nor necessarily the major factors in constraining persons from engaging in or legitimizing illegal behavior.[20]

A third formulation of the constraints against delinquency, deriving from the writings of social control theorists, overcomes these limitations to some extent. This formulation stresses the importance of social institutions such as the family, the school, and law enforcement as instruments of control on the delinquent motives of boys. Presumably all boys are subject to these motives;[21] however, they express them in overt behavior only when, for whatever reason, the controlling potential of these institutions is not realized. A considerable literature has developed attempting to specify the conditions under which this occurs. Thus the absence of family controls has been linked to parental rejection, ineffectuality, and neglect;[22] and the deficiency of controls within the school has been traced, among other things, to its failure to be oriented to the capabilities and interests of students.[23] But while social control theory can account for much delinquency, it, too, suffers limitations, since the nature of the processes by which social control is exercised and the sequential patterning of these processes have not been specified. Thus, for example, social control theories are ambiguous regarding the relationship between "inner controls" and external (or social) controls; moreover, they are unable to account for some of the phenomena of delinquency, such as the eventual conventionalization of many delinquent boys.

These problems can be eliminated by viewing the central processes of social control as "commitments to conformity." By this term we mean not only fear of the material deprivations and punishments which might result from being discovered as an offender but also apprehension about the deleterious consequences of such a discovery on one's attempts to maintain a consistent self image, to sustain valued relationships, and to preserve current and future statuses and activities. A youth with strong commitments to conformity is less likely to engage in deviant acts than is one for whom these commitments are minimal, given that both experience motives to deviate in the same degree. The cumulative strength of one's various commitments is not to be equated with motives to deviate. Commitment refers instead to the *probability* that such motives will be acted upon when they are experienced. Even persons with strong commitments to conformity experience motives to

[13] Comments of an ex-gang leader as quoted in Sophia M. Robinson, *Juvenile Delinquency* (New York: Holt, Rinehart and Winston, 1960), pp. 134-137.

[14] It should be emphasized, however, that while many situational contingencies of this sort fall in the class of phenomena often considered "accidental," these events do not occur randomly. For example, boys living in slums are more likely to encounter experiences which can evoke motives to deviate in certain ways than are their middle class counterparts. To illustrate: the slum youth is more likely to find drunks sleeping in doorways, to see wares displayed in open counters on the sidewalk, to meet adult criminals, and to come under police surveillance than is the youth living in a middle class neighborhood.

[15] Albert K. Cohen, *Delinquent Boys: The Culture of the Gang* (Glencoe, Ill.: The Free Press, 1955).

[16] Richard A. Cloward and Lloyd E. Ohlin, *op. cit., passim.*

[17] Walter Miller, "Lower Class Culture as a Generating Milieu of Gang Delinquency," *Journal of Social Issues,* 14, No. 3 (1958), pp. 5-19.

[18] Kate Friedlander, *The Psychoanalytic Approach to Juvenile Delinquency* (New York: International Universities Press, 1947).

[19] Robert A. Gordon, James F. Short, Jr., Desmond S. Cartwright, and Fred L. Strodtbeck, "Values and Gang Delinquency: A Study of Street-Corner Groups," *American Journal of Sociology,* 69 (1963), pp. 109-128.

[20] Solomon Rettig and Harve E. Rawson, "The Risk Hypothesis in Predictive Judgements of Unethical Behavior," *Journal of Abnormal and Social Psychology,* 66 (March, 1963), pp. 243-248; Helen Merrell Lynd, *On Shame and the Search for Identity* (New York: Harcourt, Brace, and Co., 1958); David P. Ausubel, "Relationships Between Shame and Guilt in the Socializing Process," *Psychological Review,* 62 (1955), pp. 378-390; Justin Aronfreed, "The Nature, Variety, and Social Patterning of Moral Responses to Transgression," *Journal of Abnormal and Social Psychology,* 63 (1961), pp. 223-240.

[21] However, it must be admitted that the nature of these motives is not well articulated by social control theorists.

[22] F. Ivan Nye, *Family Relationships and Delinquent Behavior* (New York: John Wiley & Sons, 1958); William McCord and Joan McCord, *Origins of Crime* (New York: Columbia University Press, 1959).

[23] Jackson Toby and Marcia L. Toby, *Low School Status as a Predisposing Factor in Subcultural Delinquency* (New Brunswick, N.J.: Rutgers University, no date, mimeographed); Cohen, *op. cit.,* pp. 112-116.

engage in criminal acts, and they may perform such acts when their commitments do not appear to be threatened (for example, under conditions of low visibility) or when the motives to deviate are very strong.

The role of commitments of the type discussed here is not new to sociological or psychological discussion. For example, Goode has stated that interpersonal commitments are fundamentally important in understanding conformity within modern urban society.

> . . . in a secularized society, with perhaps weak commitment to norms or role emotion, role or norm conformity may depend far more on the greater sensitivity of ego to alter's response than it does in other types of societies. This is not to assert that high sensitivity is inversely correlated with high intensity of role commitment or emotion. Rather when there is low intensity there must be a correlative increase of sensitivity to "alter opinion" or to "community opinion" (outsiders related to alter and ego) if role obligations are to be met generally.[24]

A more general formulation of the concept of commitment has been put forth recently by Becker.

> First, the individual is in a position in which his decision with regard to some particular line of action has consequences for other interests and activities not necessarily related to it. Second, he has placed himself in that position by his own prior actions. A third element is present though so obvious as not to be apparent: the committed person must be aware . . . (of these other interests) and must recognize that his decision in this case will have ramifications beyond it.[25]

The applicability of this formulation for socially disapproved as well as conventional behaviors is suggested by one of Becker's examples:

> A middle class girl can find herself committed to a consistently chaste line of behavior by the sizable bit of her reputation that middle class culture attaches to virginity for females. A girl who is a member of a social class where virginity is less valued could not be committed in this way; and except for a few puritanical enclaves in our society, boys cannot acquire commitments of this kind at all, for male virginity has little value. . . .[26]

If commitments to, or stakes in, conformity play an important role in determining a youth's capability for deviance, they also are significant in at least two other respects. First, they affect the stance the youth takes *vis-à-vis* adult authority figures. The boy with high commitments to conformity is by definition committed to maintaining and achieving desired statuses as well as to obtaining the approval of those whose love and protection he regards as important. Those aims, however, will also lead this youth to defer to the judgments of adult authorities, to accord these adults respect during social intercourse, and to be fearful, contrite, and ashamed when they confront him with his misdeeds. The low stake boy, however, is less likely to manifest these attributes. Because the disapproval of these adults entails less cost for him than for the high stake youth, he is not as constrained to defer to or show respect for adults.

Secondly, stakes in conformity will influence the youth's choice of friends. Those boys who have high stakes will tend not to befriend peers whose stakes are low since the latter are more likely to "get into trouble." Boys with low stakes, on the other hand, will tend to avoid those who are "chicken" and to seek out those with congruent interests and freedom to act. These processes are not different logically from those involved in the formation of most youth groups. Just as athletes, daters, and music lovers cluster together,[27] so do those with similar commitments to conformity.[28]

Acquiring or losing stakes in conformity does not take place only through a sudden or cataclysmic event, nor is it an irreversible process. Boys who for a considerable period have had high commitments to maintaining a conventional appearance, and whose deviance is rare and circumspect, may, for a variety of reasons, gradually have these commitments reduced and become more active and visible in their illegal activities. Conversely, many of those whose stakes in conformity have been low may encounter experiences which serve to increase their stakes, leading them in turn to more conventional behavior.

Some Bases for Commitments to Conformity

A variety of conditions can serve as bases for the development of commitments to conformity, including, among others, belief in God, affection for conventionally behaving peers, occupational aspirations, ties to parents, desire to perform well in school, and fear of the material deprivations and punishments associated with arrest. Among the most important, if not, in fact, the most important of these conditions is the relationship of the youth to his parents. In most families, parental sanctions and the withdrawal of love implied in their use are effective instruments for maintaining parental authority. Because of his dependence on and affection for his parents, the child conforms to their expectations in order to obtain their approval. In some families, however, parents fail to exercise authority. The punitive parent who does not reward conformity with affection thereby may undermine the basis for voluntary compliance by his child.[29] The parent who is overwhelmed by current responsibilities and problems may ignore his children, leaving them to fend for themselves and to define alone their relations with the outside world. Some parents who love their children and who are loved by them may caution their children against many things but then fail to enforce these expectations. They thus behave toward their children more as friends and siblings than as authorities, and their desires, therefore, are compromised because control is not exercised. Finally, some parents are unable to be effective authorities because they lack the economic and social statuses which their children equate with legitimate authorities.[30] The unemployed male, for example, may be seen as inferior not only by his peers but by his children, thus undermining his claim to parental authority. These examples obviously do not exhaust the various conditions which can lead chil-

[24] William J. Goode, "Norm Commitment and Conformity to Role-Status Obligations," *American Journal of Sociology,* 66 (November, 1960), pp. 246-258.

[25] Howard S. Becker, "Notes on the Concept of Commitment," *American Journal of Sociology* 66, (July, 1960), pp. 35-36. See also Howard S. Becker, "Personal Change in Adult Life," *Sociometry,* 27 (1964), pp. 40-53.

[26] Becker, "Notes on the Concept of Commitment," *op. cit.,* p. 39.

[27] James S. Coleman, *The Adolescent Society* (New York: The Free Press, 1962), pp. 173-219.

[28] This argument derives from that of Merton and Lazerfeld on value homophyly. Paul F. Lazersfeld and Robert K. Merton, "Friendship as Social Process" in Monroe Berger, Theodore Abel, and Charles H. Page (eds.), *Freedom and Control in Modern Society* (New York: Van Nostrand, 1954), pp. 18-66.

[29] While the threat of severe physical punishment and material deprivation can constrain the child's behavior at home, it is not as likely to control his behavior in other social contexts as less severe parental sanctions. Moreover, severe punishment may lower the child's reliance on parental guidance. Albert Bandura and Richard H. Walters, *Adolescent Aggression* (New York: Ronald Press, 1959); Albert Bandura and Richard H. Walters, *Social Learning and Personality Development* (New York: Holt, Rinehart and Winston, 1963).

[30] Donald G. McKinley, *Social Class and Family Life* (New York: The Free Press, 1964), pp. 92-93, 152-191.

dren to develop autonomy from parental expectations. Moreover, these conditions do not necessarily represent steady states. Parents who are fully able to cope with infants and toddlers may be far less capable of dealing with more active, less dependent, and more perceptive school-age children. Also, a variety of crises and tragedies may vitiate parents' competence to operate as adult authorities, regardless of the adequacy with which they formerly performed these tasks.

It is likely that failure to develop conformity commitments through the desire to satisfy parental expectations reduces the probability that the youth will develop such commitments in other social contexts. As a case in point, the desire to achieve in school is in many instances the product of parents' expectations that their child perform well in the classroom and of the child's concern for fulfilling these expectations.[31] Should either or both of these conditions be lacking, then the chances of developing commitments based on academic aspirations are reduced. Similar considerations hold in the conformity commitments arising from fear of the consequences of arrest. Most youth regard arrest as a fearful experience because they believe, among other things, that (1) it can alter their public image adversely, and (2) it exposes them to punishment, deprivation, and the moral indignation of parents, friends, and officials. Those youths, then, whose behavior is not governed by parental evaluations, lack an important basis for developing concern about the consequences of arrest.

Nevertheless, the failure of children to develop commitments to conformity through a desire to fulfill parental expectations need not necessarily preclude the development of such commitments in other ways. For example, the desire to achieve in school, which can provide a potent incentive for conventional behavior, may develop in response to praise from teachers, respect from friends, and the anticipation of future pay-offs for school achievement, even in the absence of strong commitments to perform in accord with parental expectations. Furthermore, loss of commitments in arenas outside the home may precede and lead to loss of commitments within the family. Again, using the school as an example, some youths with high commitments to parental expectations may nevertheless be disinterested in and perform poorly in school or may be apprehended as offenders. If as a result they experience severe and enduring parental criticism, their commitments to parental authority may diminish.

Congruence with Empirical Data on Delinquency

As noted above, little evidence is available which provides a direct test of the basic propositions in the model presented here. However, we can examine the congruence between this model and what is known empirically about delinquency. Obviously, even if considerable congruence is found, it cannot be interpreted as a demonstration of the validity of these propositions; nevertheless, it does suggest their plausibility.

First, the conditions for lack of commitment to conformity are more prevalent among lower class than middle class youth. "The lower class individual is more likely to have been exposed to punishment, lack of love, and a general atmosphere of tension and aggression since early childhood."[32] Furthermore, his parents devote less time to supervising his activities,[33] are less trusting of him,[34] and are less likely to be viewed by him as legitimate authorities.[35] Consequently, and consistent with empirical findings, the lower class youth, lacking these bases for commitment, will engage in more frequent, more visible, and more severely punished delinquent behavior than their middle class peers.

Second, since this formulation does not regard delinquent acts as the product of enduring motives, nor as completely determined by stable characteristics of boys and their situations, it is consistent with the observation that delinquent behavior is an episodic and typically noncompulsive activity.[36]

Third, the present framework can account for the fact that virtually all middle class and lower class boys engage in some delinquent activities and that some middle class boys are serious delinquents while many lower class boys are not. As indicated earlier, even boys with strong commitments to their parents' expectations, who perform well and aspire to good performance in school, and who fear the punishments associated with arrest and detention, will commit delinquent acts if the rewards are sufficient, visibility is low, and the act can be rationalized or justified so as not to denigrate the youth's self-image.[37] Furthermore, in some middle class families, parent-child relationships are not always so benign as to rule out the possibility that parental authority will fail to be acknowledged. Nor are lower class parents uniformly so punishing, rejecting, or incapable that they fail, even in high delinquency areas, to be effective authority figures *vis-à-vis* their children. Similar considerations apply to childrens' commitments to academic performance and fear of the consequences ensuing from arrest and detention.

Fourth, this formulation explains the evident reduction in delinquent activities among late adolescents and young adults. Specifically, during these years some delinquents obtain jobs;

---

[31] David C. McClelland, John W. Atkinson, Russell A. Clark and Edgar L. Lowell, *The Achievement Motive* (New York: Appleton-Century-Crofts, 1953); McKinley, *op. cit.*, p. 96.

[32] Seymour Martin Lipset, "Democracy and Working-class Authoritarianism," *American Sociological Review,* 24 (August, 1959), p. 495. See, too, Urie Bronfenbrenner, "Socialization and Social Class Through Time and Space," in Eleanor E. Maccoby, Thomas M. Newcomb, and E. L. Hartley (eds.), *Readings in Social Psychology* (New York: Holt, 1958), pp. 400-425, and Genevieve Knupfer, "Portrait of the Underdog," *Public Opinion Quarterly,* 11 (Spring, 1947), pp. 103-114.

[33] Eleanor E. Maccoby, "Effects Upon Children of Their Mothers' Working," in Norman W. Bell and Ezra Vogel (eds.), *A Modern Introduction to the Family* (Glencoe, Ill.: The Free Press, 1960), pp. 521-533.

[34] Ivan Nye, "Adolescent-Parent Adjustment—Socio-Economic Level as a Variable," *American Sociological Review,* 16 (June, 1951), pp. 341-349; George Psathas, "Ethnicity, Social Class, and Adolescent Independence from Parental Control," *American Sociological Review,* 22 (August, 1957), pp. 415-423.

[35] McKinley, *op. cit.*, pp. 92-93, 156-157; Albert Reiss, "Delinquency as the Failure of Personal and Social Controls," *American Sociological Review,* 16 (April, 1951), pp. 196-207.

[36] David Matza, *op cit.*, pp. 22, 26-30.

[37] Sykes and Matza have pointed out that such "techniques of neutralization" are used by so-called confirmed delinquents. Their use by other youths who offend seems therefore quite probable. [Greshman M. Sykes and David Matza, "Techniques of Neutralization: A Theory of Delinquency," *American Sociological Review,* 22 (December, 1957), pp. 664-670.] Moreover, as Matza points out in *Delinquency and Drift* (*op. cit.*, pp. 90-91) "the delinquent by using these techniques of neutralization, is able to consider himself not responsible for his acts, a self-conception which is confirmed, perhaps surpassed by views held in certain quarters of conventional society." In this way, the delinquent is able to preserve an image of himself as an essentially law-abiding person who is being treated unfairly. This at least suggests that the delinquent does not necessarily see himself as more delinquent than the so-called non-delinquent.

others marry; and for all, the penalties for offending behavior greatly increase. Such events increase commitments to conformity. Furthermore, insofar as employment takes boys off the streets and provides them with money, they are less likely to experience motives to commit illegal acts for gain.

Fifth, the group nature of many delinquent activities and the norms of these groups are not nearly as compelling as some theorists have assumed.[38] This is not to suggest that the expectations of gang members do not influence individuals considerably, nor that those delinquent gang members with more than minimal commitments to conformity will not forego these commitments on occasion in response to the demands of their peers. On the other hand, adolescents in general frequently give priority to peer expectations over those emanating from other sources.[39] What is distinctive about delinquent gang members is that a greater proportion of their activities involve illegal acts. This can be accounted for by the argument that members of delinquent gangs, at the time of their recruitment, already lack strong commitments to conformity.[40]

Sixth, the model provides a conceptual basis for understanding the hostile and/or coolly indifferent and unconcerned demeanor which many delinquent boys display toward adult authority figures such as teachers, police, and correctional workers.[41] The boy with a high stake in conformity is by definition committed to meeting conventional expectations in order to maintain and achieve desired statuses as well as to obtain the approval of those whose love and protection he regards as important. These aims, however, will also lead this youth to defer to the judgments of adult authorities, to accord these adults respect during social intercourse and to be fearful, contrite and ashamed when they confront him with his misdeeds. The low stake boy, however, is less likely to manifest these attributes. Because the approval of these adults carries for him less significance than for the high stake youth, he is not as constrained to defer to or show respect for adults.[42]

Finally, the present model permits a more complete explanation of the phenomenon known as secondary deviance. The theory of secondary deviance holds that the experience of being labeled and treated as a deviant has self-fulfilling consequences.

> [Branding and] treating a person as though he were generally deviant . . . sets in motion several mechanisms which conspire to shape the person in the image people have of him.
>
> Put . . . generally, the point is that the treatment of deviants denies them the ordinary means of carrying on the routines of everyday life open to most people. Because of this denial the deviant must of necessity develop illegitimate routines.[43]

Secondary deviance theory, however, has not been able to account for the fact that many boys who are labeled delinquent by the courts apparently do not continue their deviant behavior. An explanation of this phenomenon consistent with the thesis of this paper is that the effects of labeling a youth delinquent are a function of his preexisting commitments to conformity. For the high stake boy, arrest is likely to lead to a reconfirmation of conventional behavior. He will "toe the line" more rigorously in order to (1) regain and maintain the respect and affection of those who expect him to behave conventionally and (2) increase his chances of achieving conventional goals. For the low stake boy, however, arrest may remove one of the few remaining constraints against his exercise of deviant behavior. That is, for the boy who is not committed to parental expectations of conformity and who has little interest in school achievement, etc., one of the few bases for his conformity may be his fear of the experiences he will go through during arrest, trial, and incarceration. But typically these experiences are not as depriving as anticipated, and in encountering them the low stake boys may find they need not be feared. For these boys, then, this source of commitment to conformity has, in effect, been reduced, and the probability of their committing further delinquencies is enhanced.

Conclusion

The formulation presented in this paper is essentially a probabilistic one. It views delinquency as the product of commitments to conformity, situationally induced motives to deviate, and a variety of contingencies. This framework is consistent with the empirical data on delinquency and, in fact, accounts for some aspects of this phenomena—such as its presence among most youth and its decline in early adulthood—which are not accounted for by other theoretical models.

For example, one implication of Cloward and Ohlin's delinquent subculture thesis is that lower class boys will reduce their delinquent activities if they perceive that opportunities for employment will be provided them when they become adults. In our view, however, employment opportunities do not become a salient influence on the day to day behavior of delinquent boys until they develop commitments and needs that make full-time work a valued activity. Moreover, such commitments ordinarily do not occur until late adolescence and early adulthood. Younger boys, those in the age group with the highest rate of delinquent behavior, are not affected by job market conditions; rather, their behavior is influenced, as we have argued above, by more mundane situational considerations. For these boys, therefore, it is necessary to provide bases for conformity commitments which are more immediately relevant than future employment opportunities. While a variety of such bases could be developed, one suggestion by way of example would involve the use of money wages to boys on the condition that they keep out of trouble. The effectiveness of such wages would not depend on long-term efforts by professionals in order to develop boys' aspirations and alleviate their interpersonal problems; consequently, if such wages are effective at all, their impact should be immediate. In any event, the idea of paying boys to conform is sufficiently intriguing to merit study and experimentation.

---

38 Matza, *op. cit.,* pp. 38-40.

39 James S. Coleman, *The Adolescent Society* (New York: The Free Press, 1961), pp. 138-141, 172; Joseph Stone and Joseph Church, *Childhood and Adolescence* (New York: Random House, 1957), pp. 288-292.

40 Albert Cohen considers this possibility but rejects it in favor of the notion that the offenses of delinquent gang members are group compelled. No empirical evidence is given, however, for his conclusions. Albert K. Cohen, *op. cit.,* pp. 31-32.

41 Irving Piliavin and Scott Briar, "Police Encounters with Juveniles," *American Journal of Sociology* 70, (September, 1964), pp. 206-214; Frederic M. Thrasher, *The Gang,* abridged edition (Chicago: University of Chicago Press, 1963), pp. 270-273.

42 It is important to note in this regard that delinquents do respect and work well for some teachers and that they do not hate all policemen. The attributes of liked and respected officials are discussed in Carl Werthman and Irving Piliavin, "Delinquency and Alienation from Authority" (in process).

43 Howard Becker, *Outsiders* (New York: The Free Press, 1963), pp. 34-35.

Juvenile Delinquency and Subterranean Values

David Matza
University of California, Berkeley

Gresham M. Sykes
Dartmouth College

Current explanations of juvenile delinquency place a heavy stress on the delinquent's deviance, not only with regard to his behavior but also with regard to his underlying values. It can be argued, however, that the delinquent's values are far less deviant than commonly portrayed and that the faulty picture is due to an erroneous view of the middle-class value system. A number of supposedly delinquent values are closely akin to those embodied in the leisure activities of the dominant society. To view adolescents in general and delinquents in particular as members of the last leisure class may help us explain both the large amount of unrecorded delinquency and the occurrence of delinquency throughout the class structure.

CURRENT explanations of juvenile delinquency can be divided roughly into two major types. On the one hand, juvenile delinquency is seen as a product of personality disturbances or emotional conflicts within the individual; on the other hand, delinquency is viewed as a result of relatively normal personalities exposed to a "disturbed" social environment—particularly in the form of a deviant sub-culture in which the individual learns to be delinquent as others learn to conform to the law. The theoretical conflict between these two positions has been intensified, unfortunately, by the fact that professional pride sometimes leads psychologists and sociologists to define the issue as a conflict between disciplines and to rally behind their respective academic banners.

Despite many disagreements between these two points of view, one assumption is apt to elicit common support. The delinquent, it is asserted, is deviant; not only does his behavior run counter to the law but his underlying norms, attitudes, and values also stand opposed to those of the dominant social order. And the dominant social order, more often than not, turns out to be the world of the middle class.

We have suggested in a previous article that this image of delinquents and the larger society as antagonists can be misleading.[1] Many delinquents, we argued, are essentially in agreement with the larger society, at least with regard to the evaluation of delinquent behavior as "wrong." Rather than standing in opposition to conventional ideas of good conduct, the delinquent is likely to adhere to the dominant norms in belief but render them ineffective in practice by holding various attitudes and perceptions which serve to neutralize the norms as checks on behavior. "Techniques of neutralization," such as the denial of responsibility or the definition of injury as rightful revenge, free the individual from a large measure of social control.

This approach to delinquency centers its attention on how an impetus to engage in delinquent behavior is translated into action. But it leaves unanswered a serious question: What makes delinquency attractive in the first place? Even if it is granted that techniques of neutralization or some similar evasions of social controls pave the way for overt delinquency, there remains the problem of the values or ends underlying delinquency and the relationship of these values to those of the larger society. Briefly stated, this paper argues that (a) the values behind much juvenile delinquency are far less deviant than they are commonly portrayed; and (b) the faulty picture is due to a gross over-simplification of the middle-class value system.

THE VALUES OF DELINQUENCY

There are many perceptive accounts describing the behavior of juvenile delinquents and their underlying values, using methods ranging from participant observation to projective tests.[2] Although there are some important differences of opinion in the interpretation of this material, there exists a striking consensus on actual substance. Many divisions and sub-divisions are possible, of course, in classifying these behavior patterns and the values on which they are based, but three major themes emerge with marked regularity.

First, many observers have noted that delinquents are deeply immersed in a rest-

[1] Gresham M. Sykes and David Matza, "Techniques of Neutralization," *American Sociological Review*, 22 (December, 1957), pp. 664–670.

[2] Frederic M. Thrasher, *The Gang*, Chicago: University of Chicago Press, 1936; Clifford R. Shaw and Maurice E. Moore, *The Natural History of a Delinquent Career*, Chicago: University of Chicago Press, 1931; Albert K. Cohen, *Delinquent Boys: The Culture of the Gang*, Glencoe, Ill.: The Free Press, 1955; Albert K. Cohen and James F. Short, "Research in Delinquent Subcultures," *Journal of Social Issues*, 14 (1958), pp. 20–37; Walter B. Miller, "Lower Class Culture as a Generating Milieu of Gang Delinquents," *Journal of Social Issues*, 14 (1958), pp. 5–19; Harold Finestone, "Cats, Kicks, and Color," *Social Problems*, 5 (July, 1957), pp. 3–13; Solomin Kobrin, "The Conflict of Values in Delinquent Areas," *American Sociological Review*, 16 (October, 1951), pp. 653–661; Richard Cloward and Lloyd Ohlin, "New Perspectives on Juvenile Delinquency," (unpublished manuscript); Dale Kramer and Madeline Karr, *Teen-Age Gangs*, New York: Henry Holt, 1953; Stacey V. Jones, "The Cougars—Life with a Delinquent Gang," *Harper Magazine*, (November, 1954); Harrison E. Salisbury, *The Shook-Up Generation*, New York: Harper and Brothers, 1958; William C. Kvaraceus and Walter B. Miller, editors, *Delinquent Behavior: Culture and the Individual*, National Education

From *American Sociological Review*, Vol. 26 (October 1961), pp. 712–719. Reprinted by permission of the American Sociological Association and the authors.

less search for excitement, "thrills," or "kicks." The approved style of life, for many delinquents, is an adventurous one. Activities pervaded by displays of daring and charged with danger are highly valued in comparison with more mundane and routine patterns of behavior. This search for excitement is not easily satisfied in legitimate outlets such as organized recreation, as Tappan has indicated. The fact that an activity involves breaking the law is precisely the fact that often infuses it with an air of excitement.[3] In fact, excitement or "kicks" may come to be defined with clear awareness as "any act tabooed by 'squares' that heightens and intensifies the present moment of experience and differentiates it as much as possible from the humdrum routines of daily life."[4] But in any event, the delinquent way of life is frequently a way of life shot through with adventurous exploits that are valued for the stimulation they provide.

It should be noted that in courting physical danger, experimenting with the forbidden, provoking the authorities, and so on, the delinquent is not simply enduring hazards; he is also creating hazards in a deliberate attempt to manufacture excitement. As Miller has noted, for example, in his study of Roxbury, for many delinquents "the rhythm of life fluctuates between periods of relatively routine and repetitive activities and sought situations of greater emotional stimulation."[5] The excitement, then, that flows from gang rumbles, games of "chicken" played with cars, or the use of drugs is not merely an incidental by-product but may instead serve as a major motivating force.

Second, juvenile delinquents commonly exhibit a disdain for "getting on" in the realm of work. Occupational goals involving a steady job or careful advancement are apt to be lacking, and in their place we find a sort of aimless drifting or grandiose dreams of quick success. Now it takes a very deep faith in the maxims of Benjamin Franklin—or a certain naiveté, perhaps—to believe that hard work at the lower ranges of the occupational hierarchy is a sure path to worldly achievement. The delinquent is typically described as choosing another course, rationally or irrationally. Chicanery or manipulation, which may take the form of borrowing from social workers or more elaborate modes of "hustling;" an emphasis on "pull," frequently with reference to obtaining a soft job which is assumed to be available only to those with influential connections: all are seen as methods of exploiting the social environment without drudgery, and are accorded a high value. Simple expropriation should be included, of course, in the form of theft, robbery, and the rest; but it is only one of a variety of ways of "scoring" and does not necessarily carry great prestige in the eyes of the delinquent. In fact, there is some evidence that, among certain delinquents, theft and robbery may actually be looked down upon as pointing to a lack of wit or skill. A life of ease based on pimping or the numbers game may be held out as a far more admirable goal.[6] In any event, the delinquent is frequently convinced that only suckers work and he avoids, if he can, the regimen of the factory, store, and office.

Some writers have coupled the delinquent's disdain of work with a disdain of money. Much delinquent activity, it is said, is non-utilitarian in character and the delinquent disavows the material aspirations of the larger society, thus protecting himself against inevitable frustration. Now it is true that the delinquent's attacks against property are often a form of play, as Cohen has pointed out, rather than a means to a material end.[7] It is also true that the delinquent often shows little liking for the slow accumulation of financial resources. Yet rather than saying that the delinquent disdains money, it would seem more accurate to say that the delinquent is deeply and constantly concerned with the problem of money in his own way. The delinquent wants money, probably no less than the law-abiding, but not for the purposes of a careful series of expenditures or some long-range objective. Rather, money is frequently desired as something to be squandered in gestures of largesse, in patterns of conspicuous consumption. The sudden acquisition of large sums of money is his goal—the "big score"—and he will employ legal means if possible and illegal means if necessary. Since legal means are likely to be thought of as ineffective, it is far from accidental that "smartness" is such an important feature of the delinquent's view of life: "Smartness involves the capacity to outsmart, outfox, outwit, dupe . . ."[8]

A third theme running through accounts of juvenile delinquency centers on aggression. This theme is most likely to be selected as pointing to the delinquent's alienation from the larger society. Verbal and physical assaults are a commonplace, and frequent reference is made to the delinquent's basic hostility, his hatred, and his urge to injure and destroy.

The delinquent's readiness for aggression is particularly emphasized in the analysis of juvenile gangs found in the slum areas of large cities. In such gangs we find the struggles for "turf," the beatings, and the violent feuds which form such distinctive elements in the portrayal of delinquency. As Cloward and Ohlin have pointed out, we can be led into error by viewing these gang delinquents as typical of all delinquents.[9] And Bloch and Niederhoffer have indicated that many current notions of the delinquent gang are quite worn out and require reappraisal.[10] Yet the gang delinquent's use of violence for the maintenance of "rep," the proof of "heart," and so on, seems to express in extreme form the idea that aggression is a demonstration of toughness and thus of masculinity. This idea runs through much delinquent activity. The concept of *machismo,* of the path to manhood through the ability to take it and hand it out, is foreign to the average delinquent only in name.

In short, juvenile delinquency appears to be permeated by a cluster of values that can be characterized as the search for kicks, the disdain of work and a desire for the big score, and the acceptance of aggressive toughness as proof of masculinity. Whether these values are seen as pathological expressions of a distorted personality or as the traits of a delinquent sub-culture, they are taken as indicative of the delinquent's deviation from the dominant society. The delinquent, it is said, stands apart from the dominant society not only in terms of his illegal behavior but in terms of his basic values as well.

DELINQUENCY AND LEISURE

The deviant nature of the delinquent's values might pass unquestioned at first glance. Yet when we examine these values a bit more closely, we must be struck by their similarity to the components of the code of the "gentleman of leisure" depicted by Thorstein Veblen. The emphasis on daring and adventure; the rejection of the prosaic discipline of work; the taste for luxury and conspicuous consumption; and the respect paid to manhood demonstrated through force—all find a prototype in that sardonic picture of a leisured elite. What is *not* familiar is the mode of expression of these values, namely, delinquency. The quality of the values is obscured by their context. When "daring" turns out to be acts of daring by adolescents directed against adult figures of accepted authority, for example, we are apt to see only the flaunting

Association of the United States, 1959; Herbert A. Bloch and Arthur Neiderhoffer, *The Gang,* New York: Philosophical Library, 1958; Beatrice Griffith, *American Me,* Boston: Houghton Mifflin, 1948; Sheldon Glueck and Eleanor Glueck, *Unraveling Juvenile Delinquency,* New York: Commonwealth Fund, 1950.

3 Paul Tappan, *Juvenile Delinquency,* New York: McGraw-Hill, 1949, pp. 148–154.

4 Finestone, *op. cit.*

5 Miller, *op. cit.*

6 Finestone, *op. cit.*

7 Cohen, *op. cit.*

8 Miller, *op. cit.*

9 Cloward and Ohlin, *op. cit.*

10 Bloch and Niederhoffer, *op. cit.*

of authority and not the courage that may be involved. We suspect that if juvenile delinquency were highly valued by the dominant society—as is the case, let us say, in the deviance of prisoners of war or resistance fighters rebelling against the rules of their oppressors—the interpretation of the nature of delinquency and the delinquent might be far different.[11]

In any event, the values of a leisure class seem to lie behind much delinquent activity, however brutalized or perverted their expression may be accounted by the dominant social order. Interestingly enough, Veblen himself saw a similarity between the pecuniary man, the embodiment of the leisure class, and the delinquent. "The ideal pecuniary man is like the ideal delinquent," said Veblen, "in his unscrupulous conversion of goods and services to his own ends, and in a callous disregard for the feelings and wishes of others and of the remoter effects of his actions."[12] For Veblen this comparison was probably no more than an aside, a part of polemical attack on the irresponsibility and pretentions of an industrial society's rulers. And it is far from clear what Veblen meant by delinquency. Nonetheless, his barbed comparison points to an important idea. We have too easily assumed that the delinquent is deviant in his values, opposed to the larger society. This is due, in part, to the fact that we have taken an overly simple view of the value system of the supposedly law-abiding. In our haste to create a standard from which deviance can be measured, we have reduced the value system of the whole society to that of the middle class. We have ignored both the fact that society is not composed exclusively of the middle class and that the middle class itself is far from homogeneous.[13]

In reality, of course, the value system of any society is exceedingly complex and we cannot solve our problems in the analysis of deviance by taking as a baseline a simplicity which does not exist in fact. Not only do different social classes differ in their values, but there are also significant variations within a class based on ethnic origins, upward and downward mobility, region, age, etc. Perhaps even more important, however, is the existence of subterranean values—values, that is to say, which are in conflict or in competition with other deeply held values but which are still recognized and accepted by many.[14] It is crucial to note that these contradictions in values are not necessarily the opposing viewpoints of two different groups. They may also exist within a single individual and give rise to profound feelings of ambivalence in many areas of life. In this sense, subterranean values are akin to private as opposed to public morality. They are values that the individual holds to and believes in but that are also recognized as being not quite *comme il faut*. The easier task of analysis is to call such values deviant and to charge the individual with hypocrisy when he acts on them. Social reality, however, is somewhat more intricate than that and we cannot take the black and white world of McGuffey's Readers as an accurate model of the values by which men live.

Now the value of adventure certainly does not provide the major organizing principle of the dominant social order in modern, industrial society. This is especially true in the work-a-day world where so much activity is founded on bureaucratization and all that it implies with regard to routinization, standardization, and so on. But this is not to say that the element of adventure is completely rejected by the society at large or never appears in the motivational structure of the law-abiding. Instead, it would appear that adventure, i.e., displays of daring and the search for excitement, are acceptable and desirable but only when confined to certain circumstances such as sports, recreation, and holidays. The last has been frequently noted in the observation that conventions are often viewed as social events in which conventional canons of conduct are interpreted rather loosely. In fact, most societies seem to provide room for Saturnalias in one form or another, a sort of periodic anomie in which thrill-seeking is allowed to emerge.

In other words, the middle class citizen may seem like a far cry from the delinquent on the prowl for "thrills," but they both recognize and share the idea that "thrills" are worth pursuing and often with the same connotation of throwing over the traces, of opposing "fun" to the routine. As members of the middle class—and other classes—seek their "kicks" in gambling, nightclubbing, the big night on the town, etc., we can neither ignore their use of leisure nor claim that it is based on a markedly deviant value. Leisure class values have come increasingly to color the activities of many individuals in the dominant society, although they may limit their expression more sharply than does the delinquent. The search for adventure, excitement, and thrills, then, is a subterranean value that now often exists side by side with the values of security, routinization, and the rest. It is not a deviant value, in any full sense, but it must be held in abeyance until the proper moment and circumstances for its expression arrive. It is obvious that something more than the delinquent's sense of appropriateness is involved, but it is also clear that in many cases the delinquent suffers from bad timing.

Similarly, to characterize the dominant society as being fully and unquestioningly attached to the virtue of hard work and careful saving is to distort reality. Notions of "pull" and the soft job are far from uncommon and the individual who entertains such notions cannot be thrust beyond the pale merely because some sociologists have found it convenient to erect a simplified conception of *the* work values of society. As Chinoy and Bell, and a host of other writers have pointed out, the conditions of work in modern society have broken down earlier conceptions of work as a calling and there are strong pressures to define the job as a place where one earns money as quickly and painlessly as possible.[15] If the delinquent carries this idea further than many of society's members might be willing to do, he has not necessarily moved into a new realm of values. In the same vein it can be argued that the delinquent's attachment to conspicuous consumption hardly makes him a stranger to the dominant society. Just as Riesman's "inside dopester," Whyte's "organization man," and Mills' "fixer" have a more authentic ring than an obsolete Weberian image in many instances, the picture of the delinquent as a spender seems more valid than a picture of him as an adolescent who has renounced material aspirations. The delinquent, we suggest, is much more in step with his times. Perhaps it is too extreme to say with Lowenthal[16] that "the idols of work have been replaced by the idols of leisure," but it appears unquestionable that we are witnessing a compromise

[11] Merton's comments on in-group virtues and out-group vices are particularly germane. The moral alchemy cited by Merton might be paraphrased to read:

I am daring
You are reckless
He is delinquent

Cf. Robert K. Merton, *Social Theory and Social Structure,* Glencoe, Ill.: The Free Press, 1957, pp. 426–430.

[12] T. Veblen, *The Theory of the Leisure Class,* The Modern Library, 1934, pp. 237–238.

[13] Much of the current sociological analysis of the value systems of the different social classes would seem to be based on a model which is closely akin to an out-moded portrayal of race. Just as racial groups were once viewed as a clustering of physical traits with no overlapping of traits from one group to the next (e.g., Caucasians are straight-haired, light-skinned, etc., whereas Negroes are kinky-haired, dark-skinned, etc.), so now are the value systems of social classes apt to be seen as a distinct grouping of specific values which are unique to the social class in which they are found. The model of the value systems of the different social classes we are using in this paper is more closely allied to the treatment of race presently used in anthropology, i.e., a distribution of frequencies. Most values, we argue, appear in most social classes; the social classes differ, however, in the frequency with which the values appear.

[14] Robert S. Lynd, *Knowledge for What,* Princeton: Princeton University Press, 1948.

[15] Daniel Bell, *Work and Its Discontents,* Boston: Beacon Press, 1956. Ely Chinoy, *Automobile Workers and the American Dream,* Garden City, N. Y.: Doubleday and Company, 1955.

[16] Leo Lowenthal, "Historical Perspectives of Popular Culture," in Bernard Rosenberg and David M. White, editors, *Mass Culture: The Popular Arts in America,* Glencoe, Ill.: The Free Press, 1957.

between the Protestant Ethic and a Leisure Ethic. The delinquent conforms to society, rather than deviates from it, when he incorporates "big money" into his value sytem.[17]

Finally, we would do well to question prevalent views about society's attitudes toward violence and aggression. It could be argued, for one thing, that the dominant society exhibits a widespread taste for violence, since fantasies of violence in books, magazines, movies, and television are everywhere at hand. The delinquent simply translates into behavior those values that the majority are usually too timid to express. Furthermore, disclaimers of violence are suspect not simply because fantasies of violence are widely consumed, but also because of the actual use of aggression and violence in war, race riots, industrial conflicts, and the treatment of delinquents themselves by police. There are numerous examples of the acceptance of aggression and violence on the part of the dominant social order.

Perhaps it is more important, however, to recognize that the crucial idea of aggression as a proof of toughness and masculinity is widely accepted at many points in the social system. The ability to take it and hand it out, to defend one's rights and one's reputation with force, to prove one's manhood by hardness and physical courage—all are widespread in American culture. They cannot be dismissed by noting the equally valid observation that many people will declare that "nice children do not fight." The use of aggression to demonstrate masculinity is, of course, restricted by numerous prohibitions against instigating violence, "dirty" fighting, bullying, blustering, and so on. Yet even if the show of violence is carefully hedged in by both children and adults throughout our society, there is a persistent support for aggression which manifests itself in the derogatory connotations of labels such as "sissy" or "fag."[18]

In short, we are arguing that the delinquent may not stand as an alien in the body of society but may represent instead a disturbing reflection or a caricature. His vocabulary is different, to be sure, but kicks, big-time spending, and rep have immediate counterparts in the value system of the law-abiding. The delinquent has picked up and emphasized one part of the dominant value system, namely, the subterranean values that coexist with other, publicly proclaimed values possessing a more respectable air. These substerranean values, similar in many ways to the values Veblen ascribed to a leisure class, bind the delinquent to the society whose laws he violates. And we suspect that this sharing of values, this bond with the larger social order, facilitates the frequently observed "reformation" of delinquents with the coming of adult status.[19] To the objection that much juvenile behavior other than simply delinquent behavior would then be analyzed as an extension of the adult world rather than as a product of a distinct adolescent subculture we can only answer that this is precisely our thesis.

DELINQUENCY AND SOCIAL CLASS

The persistence of the assumption that the juvenile delinquent must deviate from the law-abiding in his values as well as in his behavior can be traced in part, we suspect, to the large number of studies that have indicated that delinquents are disproportionately represented in the lower classes. In earlier years it was not too difficult to believe that the lower classes were set off from their social superiors in most attributes, including "immorality," and that this taint produced delinquent behavior. Writers of more recent vintage have avoided this reassuring error, but, still holding to the belief that delinquency is predominantly a lower class phenomenon, have continued to look for features peculiar to certain segments of the lower class that would create values at variance with those of the rest of society and which would foster delinquency.

Some criminologists, however, have long expressed doubts about the validity of the statistics on delinquency and have suggested that if all the facts were at hand the delinquency rate of the lower classes and the classes above them would be found to be far less divergent than they now appear.[20] Preferential treatment by the police and the courts and better and more varied means for handling the offender may have led us to underestimate seriously the extent to which juvenile delinquency crops up in what are euphemistically termed "relatively privileged homes."

Given the present state of data in this field, it is probably impossible to come to any firm conclusion on this issue. One thing, however, seems fairly clear: juvenile delinquency does occur frequently in the middle and upper classes and recent studies show more delinquency in these groups than have studies in the past. We might interpret this as showing that our research methods have improved or that "white-collar" delinquency is increasing—or possibly both. But in any event, the existence of juvenile delinquency in the middle and upper classes poses a serious problem for theories which depend on status deprivation, social disorganization, and similar explanatory variables. One solution has been to change horses in the middle of the stratification system, as it were, shifting from social environment to personality disturbances as the causative factor as one moves up the social ladder. Future research may prove that this shift is necessary. Since juvenile delinquency does not appear to be a unitary phenomenon we might expect that no one theoretical approach will be adequate. To speak of juvenile delinquency in general, as we have done in this paper, should not obscure the fact that there are different types of delinquency and the differences among them cannot be ignored. Yet it seems worthwhile to pursue the idea that some forms of juvenile delinquency—and possibly the most frequent—have a common sociological basis regardless of the class level at which they appear.

One such basis is offered, we believe, by our argument that the values lying behind much delinquent behavior are the values of a leisure class. All adolescents at all class levels are to some extent members of a leisure class, for they move in a limbo between earlier parental domination and future integration with the social structure through the bonds of work and marriage.[21] Theirs is an anticipatory leisure, it is true, a period of freedom from the demands for self-support which allows room for the schooling enabling them to enter the world of work. They thus enjoy a temporary leisure by sufferance rather than by virtue of a permanent aristocratic right. Yet the leisure status of adolescents, modified though it may be by the discipline of school and the lack of wealth, places them in relationship to the social structure in a manner similar to that of an elite which consumes without producing. In this situation, disdain of work, an emphasis on personal qualities rather than technical skills, and a stress on the manner and extent of consumption all can flourish. Insofar, then, as these values do lie behind delinquency, we could expect delinquent behavior to be prevalent among all adolescents rather than confined to the lower class.

CONCLUSION

This theory concerning the role of leisure in juvenile delinquency leaves unsolved, of course, a number of problems. First, there is the question why some adolescents convert subterranean values into seriously devi-

[17] Arthur K. Davis, "Veblen on the Decline of the Protestant Ethic," *Social Forces*, 22 (March, 1944), pp. 282–286.

[18] Albert Bandura and Richard Haig Walters, *Adolescent Aggression*, New York: Ronald Press, 1959, ch. 3.

[19] See, for example, William McCord, Joan McCord and Irving K. Zola, *Origins of Crime*, New York: Columbia University Press, 1959, p. 21.

[20] Milton L. Barron, *The Juvenile in Delinquent Society*, New York: Alfred A. Knopf, 1954.

[21] Reuel Denney, *The Astonished Muse*, Chicago: University of Chicago Press, 1957. See also Barbara Wooton, *Social Science and Social Pathology*, New York: Macmillan, 1959; Arthur L. Porterfield, *Youth in Trouble*, Austin, Tex.: Leo Potishman Foundation, 1946.

ant behavior while other do not. Even if it is granted that many adolescents are far more deviant in their behavior than official records would indicate, it is clear that there are degrees of delinquency and types of delinquency. This variation cannot be explained simply on the basis of exposure to leisure. It is possible that leisure values are typically converted into delinquent behavior when such values are coupled with frustrations and resentments. (This is more than a matter of being deprived in socio-economic terms.) If this is so, if the delinquent is a sort of soured sportsman, neither leisure nor deprivation will be sufficient by itself as an explanatory variable. This would appear to be in accordance with the present empirical observations in the field. Second, we need to know a good deal more about the distribution of leisure among adolescents and its impact on their value systems. We have assumed that adolescents are in general leisured, i.e., free from the demands for self-support, but school drop-outs, the conversion of school into a tightly disciplined and time-consuming preparation for a career, the facilities for leisure as opposed to mere idleness will all probably have their effect. We suspect that two variables are of vital importance in this area: (a) the extent of identification with adult symbols of work, such as the father; and (b) the extent to which the school is seen as providing roles to enhance the ego, both now and in the future, rather than as an oppressive and dreary marking of time.

We conclude that the explanation of juvenile delinquency may be clarified by exploring the delinquent's similarity to the society that produced him rather than his dissimilarity. If his values are the subterranean values of a society that is placing increasing emphasis on leisure, we may throw new light on Taft's comment that the basic values in our culture are accepted by both the delinquent and the larger society of which he is a part.[22]

[22] Donald R. Taft, *Criminology*, New York: Macmillan, 1950.

Causes of Delinquency: A Partial Replication and Extension

Michael J. Hindelang
State University of New York, Albany

Focusing primarily on urban males, Hirschi (1969) presents research findings which are generally consistent with the propositions of his control theory. In an effort to examine the extent to which Hirschi's basic research results can be replicated, groups of rural male and female students in grades six through 12 of one school were asked to respond to a self-report delinquency questionnaire and a series of items which Hirschi used to test propositions of his control theory. Indicators of "attachment" to parents and the school; "commitment" to, and "involvement" in, conventional activities; and "belief," were found to be related to reported delinquent involvement among these rural respondents to about the same extent as among Hirschi's urban males. However, his findings that attachment to peers and attachment to parents are *positively* related (to each other) and attachment to peers and reported delinquent involvement are *negatively* related, were not replicated; rather, the former relationship was found to be nearly orthogonal and the latter variables were found to be positively related.

The disjunction of major theoretical and research efforts in the area of delinquency has been an impediment to the understanding of the phenomenon of juvenile delinquency. With the publication of Causes of Delinquency, Hirschi (1969) clearly reversed a two decade trend in criminology by assembling and integrating a major theory of delinquency causation which presents, examines, and is generally supported by research findings generated by the theorist himself. This empirical-theoretical approach has several decided advantages over that taken by most other major delinquency theorists whose works have emerged in the past two decades. First, by virtue of the fact that the theory has been tempered by research findings of the author, the theory is more likely to withstand further empirical testing;[1] thus such theories can be propagated within the discipline with some assurance that they are at least somewhat concordant with the "real" world. Second, because many (if not all) of the propositions of such a theory will have been operationalized by the theorist himself, there is less chance of ambiguity in subsequent testing and interpretation of the theory. Finally, by means of an integrated theory/research approach, the proliferation of theories that may exist for decades without systematic empirical examination, and the accretion of research findings which are essentially atheoretical, is reduced.

Although the grounded theoretical approach has these and other advantages to offer, it has disadvantages as well. When both the theoretical perspective and the empirical analysis of that perspective are carried out in a single effort, this lack of independence must be viewed cautiously; that is, independent verification would seem to address the potential criticism that the theory is merely *post hoc* speculation[2] or that the theorist/researcher has only presented results which support his hypotheses. In addition, although the theory may have considerable generality, the initial testing may involve a rather restrictive sampling of cases for which the theory may have been constructed; namely, the sample used to verify the theory may have temporal and geographical specificity as well as

[1] The extent to which theories in the delinquency area have been shaped by the theorist's research is not always clear from the presentation of the theoretical perspective itself. Miller's (1958) paper, for example, notes that his theoretical perspective is based upon extensive systematic observations; because he does not present data therein, however, it is impossible to determine how great the leap from his data to his theoretical perspective is. More qualitative research strategies are obviously intrinsically more difficult to report efficiently and to integrate with a theoretical perspective.

[2] One should, in the view of the author, be much more cautious in regard to *ad hoc* speculation! At least *post hoc* speculation has empirical bounds where *ad hoc* speculation has few (if any) empirical bounds.

From *Social Problems,* Vol. 21, 1973, pp. 471–487. Reprinted with the permission of the Society of Social Problems and the author.

restrictions on other important parameters (e.g., age, sex, class, etc.) which imply a need for an extension of the empirical examination of the theoretical propositions involved.

Hirschi's Causes of Delinquency examines the extent to which deductions from his control theory hold for white, male adolescents in an urban California county in 1964. The present study is a quasi-replicative effort which extends the analyses to male and female adolescents in a rural New York State community in 1971. It is a quasi-replication in two senses. First, the scope of Hirschi's reported results made his study impossible to replicate fully; resources available for the present study were insufficient to do so. Second, some of the questions used in the present study (as noted below), although actually very similar to Hirschi's—and in a conceptual vein virtually identical to his—differed slightly from his questions; this situation arose from the fact that the results reported here are part of a larger series of investigations being conducted by the author for which the agreement of questions over time within this series was deemed more essential than absolute agreement with the questions used by Hirschi.

The central aim of the present study is to investigate the extent to which Hirschi's research findings hold for rural males and females in an East Coast locale. Since the emphasis here is on whether his *basic research results* can be replicated within the groups studied, issues of causal ordering, higher order relationships, alternative explanations, and the plausibility of Hirschi's deductions will not be examined here. Thus, the present work is not a critical appraisal of Hirschi's control theory; that effort is underway and will be reported elsewhere.

The subjects of the present research were drawn from grades six through 12 in one school in a rural area of Upstate New York. The county in which the school studied is located has no towns with a population greater than 4,400 and has a population density of 39 inhabitants per square mile; the county in which Hirschi's study was carried out (Contra Costa County, California) has a city with a population of 85,200 and has a density of 756 inhabitants per square mile.

The subjects of the present study were assembled in the auditorium of their school in groups of about 200. All regular teaching and administrative staff left the auditorium, and a research team advised the students that their cooperation was being sought in a survey of the attitudes, beliefs, and behaviors of adolescents. The respondents were told that the information which they provided would be anonymous and confidential. Virtually all of the students present in the school on the day that the survey was administered were present in the auditorium. These 978 students produced 941 questionnaires that were at least useable—i.e., a majority of the questions asked were answered; non-response for particular items can be gauged by noting the n's involved in the individual tables below.

It is obviously not possible to give an adequate presentation of Hirschi's theory and the reasoning he employs in deducing his hypotheses in his book-length work, within these few pages. Therefore, the presentation of his position here should be viewed as a thumbnail sketch; the serious reader will, of course, consult Hirschi (1969) for clarification and expansion of his views. Briefly, his control theory postulates that delinquent behavior becomes more probable as the individual's bond to society weakens. The bond has several components: attachment (caring about others, their opinions, and expectations), commitment (time, energy, and self invested in conventional behaviors), involvement (engrossment in conventional activities), and belief (attribution of moral validity to conventional norms). Hirschi views these components as generally positively associated and as having some independent effects on the likelihood that an individual will engage in delinquent behavior. His general argument, then, is that as elements of the bond become weakened, delinquency becomes possible, although not necessary (Hirschi, 1969:16-34).

The bulk of Hirschi's analyses (and all of his results reported below) focuses on his group of approximately 1300 white males, who are rather evenly distributed among grades seven through 12 (1969:236). The rural males and females studied here are evenly split by sex; also 98 percent of the rural subjects are white. Both the rural males and the rural females are nearly evenly distributed among grades six through 12, although grades 11 and 12 have slightly smaller proportions than the lower grades. Hirschi's white males have the following distribution by father's occupation: 13 percent unskilled labor, 14 percent semi-skilled labor, 35 percent skilled labor-foreman-merchant, 13 percent white collar, and 25 percent professional and executive (1969:69); the respective father's occupation figures for the rural subjects are: eight percent, 12 percent, 31 percent, five percent, and 44 percent.[3] Thus the two groups are virtually equivalent racially; the rural group has a greater range on grade and has somewhat more prestigious father's occupations.[4]

Hirschi's major dependent variable was his "recency index" (1969:54-63), which is composed of several questions regarding involvement in delinquent behaviors.[5] His questions include "have you ever taken little things (worth less than $2) that did not belong to you?"; "Have you ever taken things of some value (between $2 and $50) that did not belong to you?"; "Have you ever taken things of large value (worth over $50) that did not belong to you?"; "Have you ever taken a car for a ride without the owner's permission?"; "Have you ever banged up something that did not belong to you on purpose?"; "Not counting fights you may have had with a brother or sister, have you ever

[3] The rural males and females were classified according to Turner's (1964) criteria. The category "professional and executive" encompasses Turner's five highest categories: small business owners and managers, semiprofessionals, business agents and managers, and professionals. Turner's categories were so grouped to parallel as nearly as possible those used by Hirschi.

[4] According to Turner's criteria, "farmers" are small business owners, which accounts for the large proportion of rural respondents in the highest occupational category.

[5] Hirschi makes extensive use of officially recorded delinquent acts as well; the relationships of his independent variables to officially recorded delinquent acts and the relationships of his independent variables to his recency index, were generally consistent. Information on officially known delinquency was not collected for the rural males and females studied here.

TABLE 1
RECENCY SCORE DISTRIBUTIONS FOR HIRSCHI'S MALES (HM),[a] THE RURAL MALES (RM), AND THE RURAL FEMALES (RF)
(IN PERCENT)

	Recency Score									
	0	1	2[b]	3	4	5	6	7	8	
HM	56	25	19							100 (1303)
RM	26	24	19	11	8	5	2	3	2	100 (441)
RF	57	21	14	4	2	2	0	0	0	100 (445)

[a] These results for Hirschi's males are derived from his Table A-2 (1969:237).
[b] For Hirschi's males this category is actually "two *or* more."

beaten up on anyone or hurt anyone on purpose?" Maintaining consistency with a series of my past research efforts resulted in self-reported delinquency questions which were somewhat different from Hirschi's. The questions used in the present study were "How many times in the last year have you . . .":[6] "Stolen something worth less than $10"; "Stolen something worth $10-$50"; "Stolen something worth more than $50"; "Taken a car for a ride without the owner's permission"; "Destroyed property (less than $10 damage)"; "Destroyed property (more than $10 damage)"; "Been in fist fights." Following Hirschi (1969: 62), if the subject reported never having participated in the act or having participated in it only more than a year ago, the subject was given a score of zero for that act; if the subject reported having participated in the act one or more times in the past year he was given a score of one for that act. The recency index is a simple sum across all acts. It is clear that both sets of questions cover the same ground; however, because Hirschi used some limiting phrases and fewer questions, it may be expected that his questions will generate lower recency index scores. In reporting his results, Hirschi trichotomizes his recency index scores into the categories of zero, one, and two, or more; Table 1 shows the marginal distributions of the recency index scores for Hirschi's subjects and the subjects of the present research. Whether the difference between Hirschi's white males (HM) and the rural males (RM) of the present study is an artifact of method—either in construction of the recency index or due to the fact that Hirschi's subjects were asked to give their names[7]—or reflects an actual difference, is impossible to ascertain; given that the rural males appear to be *more* delinquent than Hirschi's males—a finding opposite to rural-urban comparisons of official delinquency rates as well as rural-urban comparisons of self-reported delinquency[8]—it is more likely that the difference is artifactual. For this reason, and to make comparisons across Hirschi's males, the rural males, and the rural females easier to interpret throughout the remainder of the paper, it was decided to trichotomize the rural males and rural females such that the proportions falling into the low, medium, and high categories of the recency index corresponded as closely as possible to the respective proportions of Hirschi's males. Among the rural males, the low category contains those with recency scores of 0 and 1; the medium category contains those with scores of 2 and 3; the high category contains those with scores of 4 or more. Among the rural females, Hirschi's cutting points were used: the low category contains those with recency scores of 0; the medium category contains those with scores of 1; and the high category contains those with scores of 2 or more. In spite of the discrepancy between the cutting points used for the rural males and those used by Hirschi, the general nature of his control theory and the linearity of his hypotheses seem to indicate that this analytic decision is reasonable.[9]

Attachment to Parents

One of the most basic propositions of Hirschi's control theory is that the bond of affection for conventional others is a major deterrent to illegal behavior (1969:83). He argues that when parental attachment is strong, parental values (presumed to be "anti-criminal") are more readily accepted. Table 2 addresses this issue with the responses to the question, "Would you like to be the kind of person your father is?" It can be seen from this table that the results for the rural males closely parallel Hirschi's results. He finds that 64 percent of those who answer "in every way" to this question compared to 41 percent of those who answer "not at all" to the question, score low on the recency index; the respective figures for the rural males are 61 percent and 36 percent. The results for the females are weaker. Sixty-five percent of those who answer "in every

[6] Hirschi's alternative answers to each of his recency questions included: A. No, never; B. More than a year ago; C. During the last year; D. During the last year and more than a year ago. Although the questions used in the present study asked respondents to report the *number* of times they engaged in each act in the last year, it was possible to score them in such a way that had Hirschi's alternatives been used, the same results would have been obtained. For his recency index, Hirschi gives alternatives A and B a weight of zero and alternatives C and D a weight of one. In the present study the answer "zero times" to the question "In the last year how many times have you. . . ." implies either Hirschi's A or B alternative and, hence, is given a weight of zero; an answer of greater than zero to the question "in the last year how many times have you. . . ." implies either Hirschi's C or D alternative and, hence, is given a weight of one.

[7] Kulik, Stein, and Sarbin (1968) found that responses to self-reported delinquency items under conditions of anonyminity elicit more self-reported acts than under conditions of non-anonyminity. Although there is a change in the absolute amount of delinquency reported under anonymous versus non-anonymous conditions, the rank order of subjects under the two conditions is only minimally affected.

[8] E.g., see Clark and Wenninger (1962). Since rural versus urban delinquency is not the subject of this paper, whether the differences in reported delinquency between Hirschi's males and the rural males are artifactual, is of limited concern here. If the self-report items used here are good indicators of the phenomenon which Hirschi's theory hopes to explain, the fact that they are not identical to the items he used should not be at issue.

[9] Separate analyses using Hirschi's cutting points (zero, one, two or more) for both the rural males and the rural females, revealed relationships essentially the same as those reported below.

way" and 48 percent of those who answer "not at all," score low on the recency index. Perhaps this indicates that attachment to the parent of the same sex—a boy's attachment to his father and a girl's attachment to her mother—is what is crucial in deterring delinquency. However, Hirschi's data do not support such a notion. Although he does not present tabular results for the analogous question concerning affection for mother, Hirschi does report (1969:92) that among his males the relation between affection for mother and self-reported delinquency is stronger than the relation between affection for father and self-reported delinquency. This tendency is confirmed among the rural males; 79 percent of those who answer "in every way" but only 36 percent of those who answer "not at all" score low in self-reported delinquency. Among the rural females, attachment to mother is associated about the same as is attachment to father with self-reported delinquency. Thus, rather than cross-sex child-parent attachment being important, it seems that parental attachment—whether to mother or father—is more of a deterrent to delinquency for males than for females. Among the rural groups as well, then, attachment to parents is related to reported delinquent involvement, as Hirschi predicts.

Attachment to the School

Control theory postulates that attachment to the school is similarly related to delinquency. Specifically, those who do poorly in school reduce their interest in school and, hence, are free —to the extent of their reduced attachment to, commitment to, and involvement in school-related activities—to commit delinquent acts (Hirschi, 1969:120-124). If this hypothesis is correct, Hirschi suggests it should be the case that perceived academic ability is related to delinquent behavior, not only because objective school performance is likely to be closely associated with perceived ability, but also because those who see themselves as able to do well in school will probably find school tolerable and relevant to future needs (1969:117). To test this notion, the respondents were asked to rate their academic ability in relation to other students in their school. Table 3 shows that the general hypothesis receives some support in all three groups studied; the effect is most noticeable in the highest portion of the recency index and in the comparison of the "below average" respondents and all others. In the group of males studied by Hirschi, 13 percent of those rating themselves "among the best" and 35 percent of those rating themselves "below average" score high on the recency index; the respective figures are 13 percent vs. 29 percent for the rural males, and 16 percent vs. 40 percent for the rural females.

Since Hirschi argues that the link of ability and performance with delinquency is through one's bond to the school (1969:120), it should be the case that bond to the school is also related to delinquency. He assesses bond to the school with the question, "In general, do you like or dislike school?" (like/neither like or dislike/dislike). Liking school is related to self-reported delinquent involvement for all three groups. Among Hirschi's males the relationship is the strongest; 68 of those who report liking school, but only 33 percent of those who report disliking school report no delinquent involvement. Among the rural males and females the relationships are similar but weaker: 63 percent of the rural males who report liking school and 45 percent of the rural males who report disliking school, report low delinquent involvement; while 67 percent of the rural females who report liking school and 41 percent of the rural females who report disliking school, report low delinquent involvement. The data show that both perceived ability and the bond to school itself are associated with reported delinquent involvement. In both cases, the differences are largest for Hirschi's males, next largest for the rural females, and smallest for the rural males.

Lastly, in connection with the school, in order to assess attachment to a conventional figure, respondents were asked, "Do you care what teachers think of you?" (a lot/some/not much). Hirschi's findings with urban males hold for both rural males and rural females. Among those who report caring "a lot" what teachers think of them, 70 percent of the rural males and 67 percent of the rural females report low delinquent involvement, while among those who report caring "not much," 35 percent of the rural males and 42 percent of the rural females report low delinquent involvement; Hirschi had found 66 percent and 36 percent, respectively. In terms of school related variables, the bond with the teacher seems most closely associated with self-reported delinquent involvement.

Attachment to Peers

Hirschi points out (1969:98) that both differential association theory and control theory predict that the delinquent behavior of one's own friends is strongly related to one's own delinquent behavior. Table 4 shows that this expectation is confirmed for Hirschi's subjects and for the rural males and females studied here; although among the rural males there are some slight reversals among adjacent categories. Eighty percent of the rural males who report having no close friends picked up by the police score low on reported delinquent involvement, while 26 percent of the rural males who report having four or more friends picked up by the police, score low on reported delinquent involvement; the relationship is somewhat weaker among the rural females, for whom comparable figures are 73 percent and 31 percent, respectively.

Hirschi notes (1969:139-141) that it has been argued (e.g., Coleman, 1961) that attachment to peers and attachment to parents are inversely related; Hirschi's control theory argues the opposite—that attachment to peers and attachment to parents are directly related to each other and that both are inversely related to delinquency. He goes on to suggest that close ties to peers not only fail to substitute for close ties to parents but also fail to provide substitute satisfaction for social mobility; in fact, contrary to the picture painted by many theorists, boys who are most attached to their peers are also most achievement oriented (Hirschi 1969:144). Table 5 shows Hirschi's results among urban males in support of his position; as attachment to mother increases, so does attachment to peers. However, this table also shows results dissonant with both Coleman's and Hirschi's hypotheses; namely, among the rural females, attachment to mother and attachment to

TABLE 2
SELF-REPORTED DELINQUENCY BY IDENTIFICATION WITH FATHER[a]
(IN PERCENT)

Recency Index	*Would you like to be the kind of person your father is?* In Every Way HM	RM	RF	In Most Ways HM	RM	RF	In Some Ways HM	RM	RF	In Just A Few Ways HM	RM	RF	Not At All HM	RM	RF
Low	64	61	65	65	61	59	58	51	59	48	50	55	41	36	48
Medium	21	28	28	24	28	28	25	35	31	30	20	25	22	31	27
High	16	12	8	11	11	14	17	15	21	22	25	25	38	33	24
	101	101	101	100	100	101	100	100	101	100	100	100	101	100	99
	(121)	(51)	(40)	(404)	(103)	(80)	(387)	(141)	(116)	(172)	(56)	(92)	(138)	(55)	(95)

[a] These results for Hirschi's males are taken from his Table 20 (1969:92).

TABLE 3
SELF-REPORTED DELINQUENCY BY PERCEIVED ACADEMIC ABILITY[a]
(IN PERCENT)

Recency Index	*How do you rate yourself in school ability compared with other students in your school?* Among Best HM	RM	RF	Above Average HM	RM	RF	Average HM	RM	RF	Below Average HM	RM	RF
Low	67	58	57	56	59	63	57	49	54	36	47	27
Medium	20	30	28	27	26	20	23	33	25	29	24	33
High	13	13	16	16	16	17	20	18	20	35	29	40
	100	101	101	99	101	100	100	100	100	100	100	100
	(135)	(87)	(51)	(379)	(97)	(88)	(619)	(175)	(241)	(84)	(21)	(15)

[a] Excluded from this table are 21 rural males and 23 rural females who answered that they did not know. The results for Hirschi's males are taken from his Table 31 (1969:118).

TABLE 4
SELF-REPORTED DELINQUENCY BY FRIENDS, CONTACTS WITH THE POLICE[a]
(IN PERCENT)

Recency Index	*Have any of your close friends ever been picked up by the police?* No HM	RM	RF	One HM	RM	RF	Two HM	RM	RF	Three HM	RM	RF	Four or More HM	RM	RF
Low	73	80	73	51	54	50	41	57	39	32	22	38	25	26	31
Medium	20	17	21	27	33	24	37	24	21	24	74	25	30	37	32
High	7	3	6	21	13	26	21	19	39	44	3	38	45	37	37
	100	100	100	99	100	100	99	100	99	100	100	101	100	100	100
	(520)	(152)	(214)	(164)	(61)	(76)	(99)	(37)	(33)	(62)	(27)	(16)	(208)	(134)	(90)

[a] These results for Hirschi's males are taken from his Table 24 (1969:99).

peers are essentially independent, and among the rural males there is only a slight positive association between parental and peer attachment.

Hirschi also hypothesized and found that the greater the peer attachment, the lower the reported delinquent involvement. Table 6 shows that contrary to his hypothesis and results, among the rural males and rural females, there is a generally *direct* relationship between the extent of reported identification with friends and the extent of self-reported delinquency. Hirschi found that 64 percent of those who reported identifying most closely ("in most ways") with their friends reported low delinquent involvement, while 47 percent of those who reported identifying least closely ("Not at all") with their friends reported low delinquent involvement. The results for the rural males and females are virtual mirror images of Hirschi's results. Among the rural males, for example, of those who report identifying most closely with their friends, 49 percent report low delinquent involvement while 67 percent of those identifying least closely with their friends report low delinquent involvement. Thus, in the area of peer attachment we find the first substantial divergence from Hirschi's results. It would seem that these data for the rural subjects show a greater consistency with more traditional views (e.g., Cohen, 1955) than with Hirschi's control theory regarding the association of peer attachment and delinquency. One implication of this finding is that "attachment," as an element of a theory to explain delinquent involvement in a rural area may not be viewed as simply unidimensional; that is, more specifica-

TABLE 5
ATTACHMENT TO MOTHER BY ATTACHMENT TO FRIENDS[a]
(IN PERCENT)

"Would you like to be the kind of person your mother is?"	*"Would you like to be the kind of person your best friends are?"* In Most Ways			In a Few Ways			Not At All		
	HM	RM	RF	HM	RM	RF	HM	RM	RF
In every or most ways	47	28	30	23	21	29	18	21	22
In some ways	31	27	22	41	31	29	29	27	28
In a few ways	12	10	20	23	19	23	26	16	19
Not at all	10	25	28	14	30	20	28	36	30
	100	100	100	101	101	101	101	100	99
	(330)	(87)	(88)	(710)	(243)	(243)	(152)	(75)	(89)

[a] These results for Hirschi's males are taken from his Table 41 (1969:142).

TABLE 6
SELF-REPORTED DELINQUENCY BY IDENTIFICATION WITH BEST FRIENDS[a]
(IN PERCENT)

Recency Index	*Would you like to be the kind of person your best friends are?* In Most Ways			In A Few Ways			Not At All		
	HM	RM	RF	HM	RM	RF	HM	RM	RF
Low	64	49	55	54	54	56	47	67	63
Medium	21	33	19	26	29	26	26	21	16
High	15	18	26	19	17	17	27	12	21
	100	100	100	99	100	99	100	100	100
	(353)	(89)	(84)	(748)	(239)	(234)	(160)	(72)	(86)

[a] These results for Hirschi's males are taken from his Table 44 (1969:146).

tion regarding the characteristics of those to whom one is attached may be necessary before consistent relationships will emerge.[10]

Commitment to Conventional Activities

Hirschi argues that aspirations to achieve conventional goals—rather than being a source of motivation to delinquency as strain theory suggests—constrain delinquency, since delinquent behavior not only fails to assist one in attaining conventional goals, but in fact acts as a means of precluding the attainment of conventional goals (1969:162). He further suggests that many adolescents with low educational aspirations, in effect complete their education without simultaneously being able to begin their occupational careers; when this occurs, they are bound neither to an educational nor to an occupational career. Adolescents caught in this situation—where they are still only guaranteed the freedoms of children—tend to develop attitudes, and behave in ways, appropriate only to adults; the result is a high rate of delinquency (1969:163).

These "adult" behaviors include smoking, drinking, and dating. It is Hirschi's contention that involvement in such behaviors reflects an orientation toward adult activities which is related to involvement in illegal behaviors. "To claim the right to act contrary to the wishes of adults is to express contempt for [adult] expectations, which as we have repeatedly stressed, is to free oneself for the commission of delinquent acts" (1969:166). For example, among those who report having begun to smoke before age 13, 25 percent of Hirschi's males, 28 percent of the rural males, and 30 percent of the rural females score low on reported delinquent involvement; among those who report not smoking, the percents scoring low on reported delinquent involvement are 65 percent, 68 percent, and 71 percent for the three groups, respectively. Hirschi also reports (without giving tabular results) that drinking is more strongly related to delinquency than smoking and that dating is also strongly related to delinquency. Combining these three items into an index in Table 7 shows that their effects are additive and strongly related to reported delinquent involvement in all three groups. Among the rural males, for instance, only 16 percent of those who do not smoke, drink, and date score medium or high on reported delinquent involvement, while 73 percent of those who smoke, drink, and date score medium or high on reported delinquent involvement. That this index is substantially related to delinquent involvement is clear; as Hirschi also notes, however, why the index is related to reported delinquent involvement to this extent is not. His notion that early involvement in these "adult" behaviors reflects an orientation conducive to delinquency is plausible; the source of this orientation is open to question.

The other side of the coin of involvement in "adult" activities is engrossment in activities reflecting a commitment to the conventional student status. Two measures of the extent of commitment to academic activities are the amount of effort spent on homework (discussed below under involvement) and the importance that the respondent personally attaches to getting good grades. Table 8 shows that the reported importance attached to getting good grades is similarly related to the extent of reported delinquent involvement in the three groups. Among those who report viewing grades as being very important to themselves personally, 64 percent of Hirschi's urban males, 66 percent of the rural males, and 65 percent of the rural females report low delinquent involvement; among those who report viewing grades as completely unimportant personally, 21 percent of the urban males, 41 percent of the rural males, and 39 percent of the rural females report low delinquent involvement. It seems, then, that those who have a stake in school performance—an investment which delinquent behavior may jeopardize and with which delinquent behavior may be incompatible—are, as control theory postulates, less inclined to engage in delinquent activities.

[10] Hirschi devotes some attention to this notion, in another connection, when he examines the effect of attachment to conventional verus unconventional parents on reported delinquent involvement (1969:95-96).

TABLE 7
PERCENT SCORING MEDIUM OR HIGH ON REPORTED DELINQUENT INVOLVEMENT BY INDEX OF INVOLVEMENT IN ADULT ACTIVITIES[a]

Index Score[b]																	
0			1			2			3			4			5		
HM	RM	RF	HM	RM	RF	HM	RM	RF	HM	RM	RF	HM	RM	RF	HM	RM	RF
25	16	20	40	29	27	61	46	28	62	54	42	65	48	62	78	73	73
(35)	(106)	(128)	(270)	(38)	(52)	(73)	(41)	(25)	(149)	(65)	(66)	(17)	(31)	(16)	(154)	(122)	(135)

[a] These results for Hirschi's males are taken from his Table 57 (1969:168).
[b] If the student smokes or drinks, he was given a score of 2 on the index. If he dates, he was given a score of 1. The scores on the index may thus be interpreted as follows: 0 = Does not smoke, drink, or date; 1 = Dates but does not drink or smoke; 2 = Smokes or drinks, but does not date; 3 = Smokes or drinks, and dates; 4 = Smokes and drinks, but does not date; 5 = Smokes, drinks, and dates (Hirschi 1969:168).

TABLE 8
SELF-REPORTED DELINQUENCY BY PERCEIVED IMPORTANCE OF GETTING GOOD GRADES[a]

Recency Index	*How important is getting good grades to you personally?* Very Important			Somewhat Important			Fairly Important			Completely Unimportant		
	HM	RM	RF	HM	RM	RF	HM	RM	RF	HM	RM	RF
Low	64	66	65	53	47	53	44	45	52	21	41	39
Medium	23	26	23	28	34	31	24	29	19	21	28	11
High	13	8	12	20	19	17	32	25	29	58	31	50
	100	100	100	101	100	101	100	99	100	100	100	100
	(674)	(144)	(185)	(409)	(146)	(137)	(176)	(75)	(75)	(38)	(32)	(28)

[a] These results for Hirschi's males are taken from his Table 94 (1969:224).

Involvement in Conventional Activities

In Hirschi's (1969:191) view:

> The school does more than prepare students for the future. It acts also as a holding operation; it attempts to engross and involve students in activities that are or may be essentially irrelevant to their occupational futures. If it succeeds, the student's delinquency potential may be less than would be expected from his status prospects.

One facet of involvement in school activities is time spent on homework. In general, there is a monotonic increase in the proportion of those scoring medium or high on reported delinquent involvement as the number of hours per day spent on homework decreases from one and one-half hours to one hour, to one-half hour, and to less than one-half hour. The respective percents falling into the four "hours spent" categories are: Hirschi's males, 34, 48, 52, 64; rural males, 39, 40, 55, 53; rural females 35, 45, 45, 67. As can be seen, the pattern and the magnitude of the relationship is similar for Hirschi's males and the rural females, while it is weaker, with a slight reversal, for the rural males.

In addition to the academic aspects of school activities, there are various non-academic school activities which control theory predicts will be inversely associated with delinquent involvement. To assess involvement in school-related non-academic activities the respondents were asked: "Are you very active in school activities (like playing sports, belonging to clubs, etc.)?" Table 9 shows that for both the rural males and rural females the relationship between reported involvement in school activities and reported involvement in delinquent activities is slightly non-linear; in addition, the largest differentiation is between the category "not active at all" and the other three categories. Finally, the effect of reported involvement in school activities is most manifest in the highest portion of the reported delinquent involvement dimension; among those who report being very active in school activities, 14 percent of the rural males and 18 percent of the rural females score high on self-reported delinquent involvement; while among those who report being not active at all, 37 percent of the rural males and 46 percent of the rural females score high on self-reported delinquent involvement. Although the results in Table 9 give some support to Hirschi's proposition, these results for involvement in school-related activities are not as supportive as are the results for attachment to the school or involvement in academic activities.

Belief

Control theory postulates that delinquent behavior does not result from beliefs which require delinquency but instead that delinquency is made possible by the absence of beliefs that forbid delinquency (Hirschi, 1969:198). Specifically it is Hirschi's position that attachment to parents generates a wider concern for the approval of persons in positions of authority and ultimately a belief that societal norms bind one's conduct. Thus, attachment to conventional others and belief in the moral validity of their rules are not independent (1969:200).

Table 10 contains items which Hirschi uses to tap several aspects of belief. He begins by suggesting that respect for the police is another measure of attachment to conventional others, which is also closely related to respect for the law; therefore, control theory predicts that lack of respect for the police should be related to delinquent involvement for both of these reasons. The data show considerable

TABLE 9
SELF-REPORTED DELINQUENCY BY INVOLVEMENT IN SCHOOL ACTIVITIES
(IN PERCENT)

Recency Index	*Are you very active in school activities (like playing sports, belonging to clubs, etc.)?*[a] Very Active RM	Very Active RF	Somewhat Active RM	Somewhat Active RF	Not Very Active RM	Not Very Active RF	Not Active At All RM	Not Active At All RF
Low	55	54	56	61	49	61	44	38
Medium	31	28	30	26	35	14	20	16
Highs	14	18	14	13	16	26	37	46
	100	100	100	100	100	101	101	100
	(156)	(146)	(155)	(178)	(74)	(74)	(41)	(37)

[a] Although Hirschi asked about involvement in school activities (Hirschi, 1969:253) he does not present a cross-tabulation of the results.

consistency between Hirschi's findings and those of the present study. Among Hirschi's males, 29 percent of those who strongly agree that they have a lot of respect for the police and 66 percent of those who strongly disagree score medium or high on reported delinquent involvement. Among the rural males, 19 percent of those who strongly agree with the statement and 76 percent of those who strongly disagree score medium or high on reported delinquent involvement.

The second belief component examined in Table 10 more directly addresses the beliefs of the respondents with respect to violation of the law—the extent of agreement or disagreement with the statement "It is all right to get around the law if you can get away with it." Hirschi suggests that agreement with this statement indicates acceptance of a definition favorable to violation of the law. Control theory views such an acceptance as freeing (but not constraining) the individual to violate the law when he views it to his advantage to do so (1969:202). Here again there is close agreement among the results of all three groups. Seventy percent of Hirschi's males and 76 percent of the rural males who strongly agree with the statement, but only 29 percent of Hirschi's group and 33 percent of the rural males who strongly disagree score medium or high on reported delinquent involvement.

The remaining items in Table 10 are used by Hirschi to tap Sykes and Matza's (1957:666) five techniques of neutralization—"unrecognized extension[s] of defenses to crimes, in the form of justifications for deviance that are seen as valid by the delinquent but not by the legal system." These techniques of neutralization, they argue, free delinquents to violate norms to which delinquents subscribe.

Sykes and Matza propose that if one believes his actions are due to forces outside of his control, he may believe that he is not responsible—and, hence, not culpable—for those actions. The item "Most criminals should not be blamed for the things they've done" is used to examine the relationship of denial of responsibility to reported delinquent involvement. From Table 10 it is clear that the relationship is slight for Hirschi's males, and small as well as inconsistent for the rural males and females. A second item to measure denial of responsibility ("I can't seem to stay out of trouble no matter how hard I try") gives stronger and more consistent results for all three groups. Among the females, for example, 78 percent of those who strongly agree with the statement but only 24 percent of those who strongly disagree report medium or high delinquent involvement.[11]

Denial of injury, another technique of neutralization, involves the delinquent's defining his acts such that they do not really cause anyone serious harm (Hirschi, 1969:208). Responses to the statement "Most things people call delinquency don't really hurt anyone" were used to determine whether denial of injury is related to reported delinquent involvement. The results for this item in Table 10 show that all three groups produce strikingly similar results: those most strongly agreeing with the statement report most delinquent involvement and those most strongly disagreeing report least delinquent involvement.

Denial of the victim as a technique of neutralization involves the argument that the victim somehow deserves to be victimized or at least contributes to his own victimization. The relationship of reported delinquent involvement to the item "The man who leaves his keys in the car is as much to blame for its theft as the man who steals it" is shown in Table 10. In none of the three groups is this item consistently or strongly related to reported delinquent involvement. Denial of the victim, as measured by this question, does not emerge in any of the groups as control theory predicts it should.

The final technique of neutralization reported by Hirschi involves condemning the condemners—reducing one's relative culpability by indicting "respectable" others. Hirschi uses the item "Policemen try to give all kids an even break" to determine whether reported delinquent involvement is related to condemnation of the condemners (1969:211). The lowest portion of Table 10 shows a moderate relationship between agreement with the item and reported delinquent involvement for all three groups. Among the rural males, for example, 29 percent of those in strong agreement with the item as compared with 63 percent of those in strong disagreement report medium or high delinquent involvement.

Overall, Hirschi's results with his belief items are replicated very closely within both the rural males and females—both those results which support control theory and those which do not. The techniques of neutralization receive mixed reviews; one indicator of denial of responsibility and the indicator of denial of the victim proved unrelated to reported delinquent involvement; while the remaining pur-

[11] In explaining his results, Hirschi notes that this relationship may simply be a reflection of accurate reporting about past behaviors. He further notes that time ordering is a question which plagues the concept of techniques of neutralization and suggests that neutralizations resulting from earlier acts may be causes of later acts (1969:207-81).

TABLE 10
PERCENT SCORING MEDIUM OR HIGH ON SELF-REPORTED DELINQUENCY BY HIRSCHI'S BELIEF ITEMS[a]

Strongly Agree			Agree			Undecided[b] No Opinion			Disagree			Strongly Disagree		
HM	RM	RF	HM	RM	RF	HM	RM	RF	HM	RM	RF	HM	RM	RF
I have a lot of respect for the (Richmond[a]) police														
29	19	31	38	41	34	54	48	48	59	60	63	66	76	77
(273)	(67)	(63)	(496)	(115)	(181)	(325)	(129)	(122)	(98)	(62)	(40)	(89)	(47)	(26)
It's alright to get around the law if you can get away with it														
70	76		68	72	62	54	52	49	45	30	35	29	33	34
(49)	(25)	(13)	(93)	(78)	(66)	(219)	(101)	(101)	(493)	(115)	(152)	(426)	(100)	(100)
Most criminals shouldn't be blamed for the things they've done														
51			51	48	51	48	58	41	44	43	49	39	40	34
(49)	(11)	(7)	(105)	(35)	(35)	(177)	(99)	(90)	(503)	(138)	(185)	(449)	(134)	(113)
I can't seem to stay out of trouble no matter how hard I try														
63	69	78	66	68	63	49	55	55	44	34	42	25	22	24
(46)	(55)	(32)	(104)	(75)	(52)	(176)	(83)	(62)	(621)	(119)	(137)	(251)	(88)	(142)
Most things people call delinquency don't really hurt anyone														
72	70		55	57	56	43	49	41	38	38	41	31	35	29
(78)	(20)	(13)	(232)	(80)	(60)	(432)	(157)	(176)	(376)	(121)	(128)	(164)	(20)	(47)
The man who leaves his keys in the car is as much to blame for its theft as the man who steals it														
44	49	41	42	47	46	49	46	54	46	44	42	37	43	
(391)	(122)	(152)	(461)	(154)	(180)	(131)	(43)	(31)	(211)	(56)	(52)	(102)	(46)	(15)
Police try to give kids an even break														
35	29		42	39	27	39	43	45	55	52	48	58	63	59
(260)	(24)	(17)	(460)	(109)	(104)	(255)	(113)	(130)	(194)	(119)	(120)	(117)	(55)	(62)

[a] These results for Hirschi's males are taken from his Tables 78, 80, 82, 83, 84, 85, 86 (1969:201-211).
[b] Hirschi's "neutral" point was "undecided." The "neutral" point used for the questions used in the present study was "no opinion." As was the case with the questions constituting the recency index, this terminological difference resulted from an attempt to maintain consistency within a series of research efforts by this author. The difference between "undecided" and "no opinion" may not be trivial; however, since each of these alternatives was placed between "agree" and "disagree" along a continuum, the effect was probably not substantial.

ported indicators of techniques (denial of injury, condemning the condemners, and one indicator of denial of responsibility) showed consistent moderate relationships to reported delinquent involvement in all three groups.

SUMMARY AND CONCLUSIONS

As noted at the outset, the aim of this analysis has been limited; namely, to determine the degree to which the bivariate relationships found and reported by Hirschi in Causes of Delinquency hold for groups of rural males and females in Upstate New York.

With one major exception, the overall correspondence between his results and the results here is substantial. Attachment to parents, teachers, and the school; commitment to "adult" activities and conventional activities; involvement in school-related activities; and all of the belief items produce results very similar to those produced by Hirschi.[12]

The one exception, of course, is in the area of peer attachments, which generated two tables contrary to Hirschi's hypotheses and results: attachment to mother and attachment to peers were not substantially related (Hirschi postulates a positive relationship); reported delinquent involvement and attachment to peers were found to be *directly*, rather than inversely, related.

The independence of parental and peer attachments does not constitute a direct challenge to the principles of control theory; the problem created by this orthogonality is, rather, relatively minor. Greater difficulty is generated by the finding that, among the rural groups, peer-attachments are directly related to delinquent involvement. As suggested above, this may indicate that Hirschi's control theory will have to be more specific about attachment to peers. That is, the theory may need to be reconceptualized in terms of attachment to conventional and unconventional peers.

As with the relationships which support control theory, it may be that the relationship between peer attachment and delinquent involvement which contradicts control theory, will disappear or be reversed when other variables are controlled. Questions relating to the direct effects of the variables examined, causal sequences, and the possible interpretations of these findings are beyond the scope of the present work.

12 It should be clear, of course, that not all of Hirschi's results are consonant with the predictions of control theory—for example, one indicator of denial of responsibility ("Most criminals should not be blamed for the things they've done") and the indicator of denial of the victim do not relate to reported delinquency as predicted.

REFERENCES

Clark, John and Eugene Wenninger
1962 "Socio-economic class and areas as correlates of illegal behavior among juveniles." American Sociological Review 27:826-34.

Coleman, James C.
1961 The Adolescent Society. New York: The Free Press.

Hirschi, Travis
1969 Causes of Delinquency. Berkeley: Univ. California Press.

Kulik, James A., Kenneth B. Stein, and Theodore R. Sarbin
1968 "Disclosure of delinquent behavior under conditions of anonymity and nonanonymity." Journal of Consulting and Clinical Psychology 32:506-509.

Miller, Walter B.
1958 "Lower class culture as a generating milieu of gang delinquency." The Journal of Social Issues 14:5-19.

Sykes, Gresham M. and David Matza
1957 "Techniques of neutralization: A theory of delinquency." American Sociological Review 22:664-670.

Turner, Ralph H.
1964 The Social Context of Ambition. San Francisco: Chandler Publishing Co.

*Individual Values, Peer Values, and Subcultural Delinquency**

Paul Lerman
Columbia University School of Social Work

It is difficult to evaluate competing theories of subcultural delinquency when the dependent variable differs from one theory to another. Descriptive issues must, therefore, be resolved before explanatory issues are engaged. Shared values, language, and behavior are basic "elements" of the subculture; this article focuses on theoretical and empirical issues involved in describing subcultural values. Various formulations are evaluated with the use of data. The use of "tension states" in sociological theories is questioned in favor of values competing for the allegiance of youths.

For many years, sociologists have stressed the importance of understanding the peer aspects of the bulk of adolescent delinquency. Since the publication of Cohen's *Delinquent Boys*,[1] this kind of juvenile misconduct has been referred to as "subcultural delinquency." Currently there are various theoretical writings that attempt to describe and explain this phenomenon.[2] It is difficult, however, to evaluate these theories when the dependent variable differs from one to another. There exists a need to describe subcultural delinquency adequately so that the object of the explanation is similar for all theories. Descriptive issues must, therefore, be resolved before explanatory issues are engaged. This article is an attempt to translate theoretical disagreements into new empirical issues that can be resolved with data. In the main, only descriptive issues will be addressed.

In earlier articles[3] we provided evidence in support of the view that the minimal "elements" comprising a subcultural pattern consisted of language, values, and behavior. From this perspective, a subculture is hypothesized to exist if indicators of illegal behavior are significantly related to and consonant with shared symbols, i.e., argot and values. Specifically, this implies the following:

1. Values are deviant from the actor's point of view and can be shared with peers;
2. Linguistic usage is demonstrated by knowledge of argot words used in speaking rather than in writing;
3. Youths scoring high on shared deviant values also score high on argot knowledge, and there is a sense of consonance about the relationship;
4. Youths classified by both their knowledge of argot and shared deviant values can be categorized as *high in shared symbols;* these youths are the most likely to report consonant illegal acts and to be noticed by the police;
5. The interrelationship of deviant values, argot, and illegal behavior constitutes the minimal subpattern that must be demonstrated if a subculture can be posited to exist, and all three variables have to be simultaneously related;
6. The cultural and social boundaries of a deviant youth culture have distinct referents, and the social unit of a subculture is most accurately described as a network of pairs, triads, groups with names, and groups without names.

With each of the "elements" of a subculture there are distinctive issues that can be examined. In the next section we will discuss some of the issues generated by focusing on "values"; data will then be presented relevant to these issues. The findings reported are based on a survey of youths residing in randomly selected households in a portion of New York City's Lower East Side. The original target group consisted of 706 boys and girls aged 10 to 19 years; interviews were completed with 555 youngsters, a rate of 79 percent.

Processing of the entire sample through the official police files disclosed that interviewed boys, even with age controlled, were as likely to be "delinquent" as their non-

* Adapted from Paul Lerman, *Issues in Subcultural Delinquency*, unpublished doctoral dissertation, Columbia University, 1966. The study was conducted under the auspices of the Columbia University School of Social Work, Mobilization for Youth Research Project, Dr. Richard A. Cloward, Project Director. It was funded by the National Institute of Mental Health (Contract MH-01178).

[1] Albert K. Cohen, *Delinquent Boys*, Glencoe, Ill.: Free Press, 1955.

[2] In addition to the previously cited work by Cohen, the following are major statements: Albert K. Cohen and James F. Short, Jr., "Research in Delinquent Subcultures," *Journal of Social Issues*, 14 (Summer, 1958), pp. 20–37; Walter B. Miller, "Lower Class Culture as a Generating Milieu of Gang Delinquency," *ibid.*, pp. 5–19; Richard A. Cloward and Lloyd E. Ohlin, *Delinquency and Opportunity*, Glencoe, Ill.: Free Press, 1960; and David Matza and Gresham M. Sykes, "Juvenile Delinquency and Subterranean Values," *American Sociological Review*, 26 (October, 1961), pp. 712–720.

[3] Paul Lerman, "Argot, Symbolic Deviance and Subcultural Delinquency," *American Sociological Review*, 32 (April, 1967), pp. 209–224; "Gangs, Networks, and Subcultural Delinquency," *American Journal of Sociology*, 73 (July, 1967), pp. 63–72; and the reply to the critical comments of James F. Short, Jr., concerning "Gangs, Networks and Subcultural Delinquency," *American Journal of Sociology*, 73 (January, 1968), pp. 515–517.

From *American Sociological Review*, Vol. 33, 1968, pp. 219–235. Reprinted by permission of the American Sociological Association and the author.

cooperative peers.[4]

Distinguishing Between the Actor's and the Observer's Point of View. In describing patterns of values, it is important to recognize that they can be assessed from either the actor's or the observer's frame of reference. But if one adopts the observer's point of view, how does one avoid the danger that the values inferred will be operationally of little relevance to the actor? If one adopts the actor's point of view, how does one avoid the danger of not being able to infer patterns of values?

This is the central concern in Miller's criticism of Cohen's formulation of the "spirit" of subcultural delinquency. To Cohen, the illegal actions of youths are stimulated by "non-utilitarian," "malicious," and "negativistic" values.[5] From Miller's point of view, these values are not those of the youthful actor but those of adult observers.[6] He argues that youths have certain "focal concerns" which impart quite different meanings to their illegal behavior. It is not necessary to accept Miller's list of "focal concerns" or to agree that these concerns form a lower-class pattern transmitted by adults; these are issues that can be settled empirically. However, it does seem useful to remember that judgments concerning values can vary; therefore, it is important to know who the value-definer is.

In assessing illegal behavior, it may be necessary for us to accept definitions based on the actual operating (discretionary) criteria of the police. In assessing non-standard values, we have no official system to use as a conventional benchmark. Each theorist can set up his own idealized conception of standard values—without, however, any guarantee that the actors will feel fairly presented. For example, a recent study attempted to apply Cohen's characterization of deviant values in a survey using youthful respondents (including officially known delinquents). The authors concluded: ". . . The study design operationalized each of these characteristics of the subculture but the measures generally failed to achieve sufficient discrimination to isolate such a subtype." [7]

In this study, we attempted to offset potential observer bias by asking survey respondents to indicate what they regarded as the most important of several "deviant" and "conforming" value statements. An attempt was made to present the items in a neutral manner. Values presumed to be deviant referred to toughness, "kicks," outsmarting others, making a "fast buck," keeping one's mouth shut to the cops, and connection with a racket; conforming values referred to school and work. If the actors and the observer operated within a similar framework with regard to classifying values, the conforming values should have received the largest proportion of responses as "the most important."

Our approach differs from the Cloward-Ohlin approach to "delinquent norms" [8] in that we do not assume that those who are classified as guided by "deviant values" are also interested in violating legal codes. Violation of legal statutes may in many instances be a tolerated consequence of pursuing desired ends. In other words, boys are not *required* to act illegally on behalf of their values; however, they may tolerate illegal behavior if it is consonant with their values.[9]

Shared Values and Individual Values. A major assumption of the subcultural theorists is that the youthful actors share a common set of values. One empirical test of this assumption might require that values be measured from the perspective of the individual and that of his associates. Assessing individual values is not difficult, but measuring the values of the individual's companions poses problems. In this survey we inferred friends' values from the respondent's report of the abilities (values) admired by his associates. To the degree that the individual's value choices and his perceptions of his friends' values are congruent, it is possible to regard the peer values as shared.

THE CONTENT OF DEVIANT VALUES: VERSATILE OR SPECIALIZED?

In the past few years sociological theorists have debated whether the male delinquent subculture is one or many.[10] Do given neighborhoods tend to specialize in certain types of deviant pattern, or is subcultural delinquency versatile in orientation at the outset, with possible differentiation by age?

The findings on illegal behavior (not reported here) strongly support the contention that, in terms of age sequence, a variety of types of action are quite compatible.[11] Analyses of argot responses, both within an age-grade and between ages, also support the view of versatile deviance.[12] Regarding shared values, the findings should be consonant with those of the behavior and argot analyses. Although major theorists might agree with this assumption, they differ on the values they deem important and on which values "go together."

According to Cloward and Ohlin,[13] delinquent subcultures can be categorized by whether the "dominant orientation" stresses "heart," "kicks," or "scores." Bopping youngsters value "heart," and engage in gang conflicts to maintain their "rep" and to defend their "turf" from invaders. Drug-using "retreatists" seek "kicks" through a "high" via "the needle," eschew violence, and steal only to support their "habit." Criminalistic youth disdain work and seek to "score" by a disciplined, rational approach to conventional crime, or by exploiting their "connections" with the "syndicate." All three types devalue school as well as work, although this is not stressed as part of the explicit characterizations.

Cohen and Short,[14] on the other hand, suggest that subcultures are *not* specialized at the outset but may become so at a later age. In value terms, undifferentiated youth subcultures can be characterized as malicious, hedonistic, negativistic, non-utilitarian, and autonomous. When these values are stripped of invidious connotations, the subcultures can be redefined as aggressive, thrill-seeking, tending to disobey adult rules, and regarding play or kicks as an end. The characterization "autonomous" can be accepted as is, since it is non-invidious to the actor. Cohen also suggests that delinquent boys are ambivalent about school and work, and not alienated from the dominant value system.

Miller,[15] a trained anthropologist, attempts to avoid such invidious terms as "malicious" and "retreatist." He hypothesizes that the values of deviant youths in low-income areas are no different from the values of adults in those milieus. Youth is merely a time when the everyday "focal concerns" of lower-class culture are enacted in an exaggerated fashion by slum boys. These focal concerns are: fatalism, toughness, keeping

[4] Although this finding is important, it is still possible that the non-interviewed boys would have responded differently to the survey's questions. The non-interviewed boys tend to be older; within this age-range they also tend to come from the economically more advantaged households of this low-income area, as well as from non-minority backgrounds. The relationships discussed in this paper are not affected by measures of social class and minority-group status; age, however, is a potent variable. Analysis of the relationship between age and official police contact among boys indicates that the non-interviewed respondents yield a positive, strong relationship—as do the interviewed boys. We assume, therefore, that the *relationships* presented in the following tables hold for both the interviewed and the non-interviewed portion of the sample. For further details about the neighborhood, the sample, and a copy of the questionnaire used, see *A Proposal for the Prevention and Control of Delinquency by Expanding Opportunities,* New York: Mobilization for Youth, Inc., Dec. 9, 1961, Appendices R4, R5.

[5] Cohen, *op. cit.*

[6] Miller, *op. cit.*

[7] Albert J. Reiss, Jr., and Albert L. Rhodes, "Delinquency and Social Class Structure," *American Sociological Review,* 26 (1961), p. 730.

[8] Cloward and Ohlin, *op. cit.*

[9] For a parallel point of view regarding values see David Matza, *Delinquency and Drift,* New York: John Wiley and Sons, 1964, esp. pp. 37–40.

[10] See Cohen and Short, *op. cit.;* and Cloward and Ohlin, *op. cit.,* pp. 161–186.

[11] Paul Lerman, *Issues in Subcultural Delinquency,* unpublished doctoral dissertation, Columbia University, 1966, Chap. 3.

[12] Lerman, "Argot, Symbolic Deviance, and Subcultural Delinquency," *op. cit.*

[13] *Op. cit.*

[14] *Op. cit.*

[15] *Op. cit.*

out of trouble, smartness, autonomy, and excitement. For Miller, and for Cohen as well, toughness, excitement, and autonomy are part of a larger pattern; Cloward and Ohlin use only toughness and excitement, but these are perceived as independent dominant patterns.

One of the broadest attempts to link deviant youth values and the less idealistic everyday values held by many adults in the larger society is the work of Matza and Sykes.[16] They hypothesize that "the delinquent has picked up and emphasized one part of the dominant value system," namely, "the subterranean values that coexist with other, publicly proclaimed values possessing a more respectable air." The "cluster of values" permeating delinquent subcultures are: the search for kicks, disdain for work, desire for the "big score," and acceptance of aggressive toughness as proof of masculinity. Matza and Sykes suggest that these values, when examined more closely, are strikingly similar to the code of the "gentleman of leisure," as portrayed by Thorstein Veblen, with its emphasis on daring and adventure, rejection of the prosaic discipline of work, taste for luxury and conspicuous consumption, and respect paid to manhood demonstrated through force.

The areas of agreement and contention among these theorists will become clearer when we examine the eight value items that were actually used in this study to measure individual and shared orientations.

1. *The ability to keep one's mouth shut to the cops.* This value is implicit in Cloward and Ohlin as cross-cutting all three subcultures; it is explicit in Miller's framework as part of the concern for keeping out of trouble; it is probably implicit in the thinking of both Cohen and Matza-Sykes.

2. *The ability to be hard and tough.* This value is explicitly found in all four theories, but Cloward and Ohlin treat it independently as an aspect of the "conflict" subculture.

3. *The ability to find kicks.* This value also is explicit in all the theories, but Cloward and Ohlin treat it independently in the "retreatist" subculture.

4. *The ability to make a "fast buck."* This value is at variance with Cohen's non-utilitarian approach; it is implicit in Miller's work; Matza-Sykes and Cloward-Ohlin explicitly refer to making a "big score," but the latter treat this value independently in the "criminal" subculture.

5. *The ability to outsmart others.* Matza and Sykes, borrowing explicitly from Miller, conceive of this value as part of the disdain for work; for Cohen it is in contradiction to an emphasis on hedonism and non-utilitarianism; it is restrictively used by Cloward and Ohlin in summarizing the "cool" drug user.[17]

6. *The ability to make connections with a racket.* This value is central to the Cloward-Ohlin description of the criminal type; it plays a part in the Matza-Sykes elaboration of the disdain for work, where they emphasize making a score in the numbers or by pimping; this kind of rationalistic approach to illegal gain is, of course, at variance with Cohen; it appears to be irrelevant to Miller's concerns.

7. *The ability to get good grades.* Cohen suggests that delinquent youths are ambivalent toward this value, whereas Cloward-Ohlin and Miller claim flatly that delinquent boys reject school; Matza and Sykes do not utilize school in their conception of subterranean values, although they imply that differential commitment to school may be related to a strong attraction to subterranean values.

8. *The ability to do well in the job world.* Again Cohen suggests that youths are ambivalent in this regard; the other theorists are quite explicit about youthful alienation from the world of work.

The first six items listed are intended as deviant; the last two are conventional. Except for item 6, the deviant orientations are not explicitly illegal. Worded so as to avoid invidious or unlawful connotations, these items can be used to provide information regarding the types of values that are regarded as part of a pattern by theorists. For example, we could question the creditability of the descriptive models offered by Cohen and by Cloward and Ohlin if the following results were obtained:

1. All of the first six values were interrelated (thus implying a versatile combination of items deemed incompatible by Cohen and regarded as independent entities by Cloward-Ohlin);

2. Boys scoring high on the six interrelated values were also more likely to engage in illegal behavior (thus implying that orientations do not have to be explicitly "delinquent" or in direct opposition to the middle-class ethic); and

3. A majority of boys at all ages were attracted, in some degree, to these interrelated values (thus implying that delinquent actors differ from their peers in the *degree* to which they cherish youthful values, and not in the content of their values).

If these three results were obtained, then the deviant value perspectives advanced by Miller and Matza-Sykes would gain in creditability. This seems paradoxical, since Miller views these orientations as part of broader lower-class focal concerns while Matza and Sykes argue that they are extensions of unofficial, subterranean values permeating all sectors of society (albeit in varying degree). Although the present sample may not contain the broad cross-section of youths necessary to test these competing viewpoints, an assessment will be attempted.

Categorizing actors by their individual and shared orientations toward school and the job world can also be useful in assessing the theorists' descriptions. If youths who score high on deviant values are alienated from school and work, then all theorists except Cohen gain in creditability. If, however, youths who score high on deviant values also share orientations toward school or work that are neither totally accepting nor totally rejecting, then the Cohen thesis of ambivalence regarding dominant values is supported. A finding that deviant youths are ambivalent toward, rather than alienated from, school or work would cause the most difficulty for the Miller and Cloward-Ohlin models; Miller posits that lower-class culture is distinctively different from the dominant value orientations, and Cloward and Ohlin view alienation and repudiation of "legitimate means to success" as precursors to involvement in a deviant youth culture.

Sex Differences. The findings concerning illegal behavior and argot, reported in previous articles, have indicated clear differences between the sexes. The sharing of deviant values should also, therefore, be related to sex. The findings that boys and girls differ in this respect would not only lend creditability to the measures of values but also highlight the fact that the values refer mainly to *masculine* interests.

Age Differences and Value Consistency. Analysis of self-reports of misconduct indicates that all but two of the ten most often admitted items of misbehavior had a relatively early age of onset. However, older boys engage in a greater number of misbehaviors with greater frequency and greater behavioral consistency.[18] This suggests that not only can peer support of behavior via shared values be hypothesized to occur at an early age; it is also likely that older boys will reveal a more consistent pattern of shared values. Such an increase in value consistency would be in harmony with the behavioral data and with general developmental differences between adolescents and younger boys.

A basic age difference in cognitive functioning has been noted in the child-development literature, but has apparently been overlooked by subcultural theorists. Ausubel, for example, notes, "In comparison with childhood, the cognitive life of adolescence is considerably more dominated by symbol-

[16] *Op. cit.*

[17] First portrayed by Harold Finestone in "Cats, Kicks, and Color," *Social Problems,* 5 (July, 1957), pp. 3–13.

[18] Lerman, *Issues in Subcultural Delinquency, op. cit.,* Chap. 3.

ization and abstraction. . . ."[19] He comments that this increased level of cognitive functioning has profound implications for the value and behavior consistency of individuals:

> Growth in cognitive capacity alone accounts for several significant changes in character organization. For one thing, moral concepts, like all other concepts, become more abstract. This enables moral behavior to acquire greater generality and consistency from situation to situation, since abstraction presupposes the identification of essential common elements. Hartshorne and May, for example, using objective tests of character traits, found a significant trend with increasing age toward greater consistency of moral behavior. . . .[20]

Other psychologists have also concluded that adolescents are capable of being more abstract and consistent in their cognitions than younger children. Kuhlen, for example, explicitly links the ability to conceptualize abstractly to actual behavioral consistency:

> It would be expected that, as age increases and broader concepts of honesty are developed, individuals would tend to become more consistent in their behavior; that is, they would tend to operate honestly (or dishonestly) in a broader variety of situations, and prediction of them would be easier. . . .[21]

However, Kuhlen adds, even at the level of individual functioning there has been "little systematic research on the matter."

Regarding greater value consistency for ideas shared by peers, the literature is virtually silent. Yet if consistency in shared values is dependent on the ability of individuals to engage in more abstract cognitive behavior, then a fully elaborated subculture cannot be evolved and sustained without such a development. In short, we suggest that *full participation in a shared way of life is not likely to occur until the actor has reached an adolescent level of cognitive growth.* The anthropologist's notions about "culture pattern" and the sociologist's assumptions about a "strain toward consistency" are most relevant and appropriate when a sufficient number of individuals have reached an abstract and consistent cognitive level of functioning. Tribal initiation rites, for example, may symbolize the attainment of this cognitive as well as sexual maturity.

Perceptions of Peer Orientations toward Illegal Behavior. Theories of subcultural delinquency assume that peers offer the individual actors not only value support but also behavioral support through their examples of illegal conduct. Therefore, merely showing that *individual* misconduct is more likely to occur in a climate of shared deviant values is not a conclusive basis for accepting a subcultural approach. It is important also to demonstrate that different shared-value climates provide a differential likelihood that *peers* are also engaged in illegal behavior.

One way of testing the existence of peer misbehavior is to ask respondents to indicate agreement or disagreement with the statement: "Most teenagers you know are tempted to break the law." A logical inference from this result would be that the differential beliefs about peer temptations are related to actual differences among respondents in the behavior of their associates.

Depending on their associates, youths ought to be in a differential social position to perceive actual differences in behavior; on the basis of their differential perceptions, they ought to differentially *believe* that their associates are likely to be tempted. Although the statement is in the form of a belief (it is doubtful whether youths perceive the temptations *per se*), it seems reasonable to assume that different social realities yield variations in perceptions of misbehavior; this, in turn, would give rise to different rates of agreement with this statement of belief.

This line of analysis might lend credence to the views of Sykes and Matza concerning a "technique of neutralization" used by delinquent actors to fend off invidious definitions from adults. These authors have suggested that blaming outside forces—denying personal responsibility—is a potent means of escaping guilt definitions:

> From a psychodynamic viewpoint, this orientation toward one's own actions may represent a profound alienation from self, but it is important to stress the fact that interpretations of responsibility are cultural constructs and not merely idiosyncratic beliefs.[22]

Sykes and Matza offer no evidence concerning the shared "constructs," but the outcome of the analysis of shared values and beliefs about peer temptation can be of help in this regard. Although our analysis is not meant to suggest that belief about peer temptation is *actually* used as a technique of neutralization, it is possible to infer under which condition this technique *might* be so used. If there are differences among value climates regarding belief in peer temptations, then it seems likely that this technique would not be a personal idiosyncrasy but would have peer support. That the technique would be based on a probable shared perception would remove it even further from the realm of strictly individualistic interpretations. As anthropologists have long known, what seems to be a "psychological defense" to outside observers may be shared perceptual reality to the participants.[23]

INDIVIDUAL VALUES: EMPIRICAL FINDINGS

The Actor's Perception of Deviant Values. Respondents were presented with the list of eight "abilities" and asked to choose the one they most admired now and the one they had "looked up to" most two or three years ago. The list, as we have noted, included six deviant and two conforming values.

Regarding the ability most admired *now,* both boys and girls clearly indicated by their choices that they were sensitive to the value connotations of the question. As a matter of fact, the boys seemed so eager to present themselves in a favorable light that they differed only slightly from the girls in the percentage choosing any of the deviant values (15 percent vs. 8 percent). The major value difference between boys and girls concerned the choice of doing well in school: 64 percent of the girls and 54 percent of the boys regarded this as the most admirable ability.

As might be expected, more respondents were willing to admit attraction to one of the deviant values in the past. The selection of a deviant value increased from 15 percent to 26 percent for boys and from 8 percent to 13 percent for girls when they were asked which ability they had admired most "two or three years ago." The conforming value of good grades remained the dominant choice for both sexes, but girls exceeded boys by a wider margin (71 percent vs. 51 percent).

The shift in the time perspective of the question elicited differences between boys and girls in the rank ordering of the values. For boys, school ranked first at both times, but the second most admired choice "two or three years ago" was one of the deviant values, whereas success in the job world ranked second "now." For girls, too, school ranked first at both times, but deviant values and the job world competed virtually equally as the second most admired ability in the recent past. Although there is little doubt that deviant abilities appear in a less favorable light than good grades, it is also evident that *both* deviant values and the job world are capable of attracting youth away from their dominant choice, school success. This value competition becomes more apparent in an analysis of age differences.

Estimating Age Differences in Attraction to Values. In order to understand the relative "pull" of the three types of value orientation competing for the allegiance of youth, particularly boys, a developmental perspective is

[19] David P. Ausubel, *Theory and Problems of Adolescent Development,* New York: Grune and Stratton, 1954, p. 285.

[20] *Ibid.*, p. 249.

[21] Raymond G. Kuhlen, *The Psychology of Adolescent Development,* New York: Harper, 1952, p. 426.

[22] Gresham M. Sykes and David Matza, "Techniques of Neutralization: A Theory of Delinquency," *American Sociological Review,* 22 (December, 1957), pp. 664–670.

[23] One of the earliest and clearest statements of this point of view can be found in Ruth Benedict, "Anthropology and the Abnormal," *Journal of General Psychology,* 10 (1934), pp. 59–79: reprinted in M. Fried, ed., *Readings in Anthropology,* Vol. II, New York: T. Y. Crowell, 1956, pp. 497–514.

TABLE 1. ABILITY BOYS ADMIRED MOST TWO OR THREE YEARS AGO, BY AGE

	Age			
Ability Admired 2 or 3 Years Ago	10–11	12–13	14–15	16–19
Good Grades	63%	52%	47%	41%
Job Success	10	12	23	30
A Deviant Ability	18	31	27	29
DK or NA *	9	5	3	0
N=	(67)	(84)	(62)	(63)

* Don't know or no answer.

TABLE 2. RELATIONSHIP BETWEEN ABILITY BOYS ADMIRED MOST TWO OR THREE YEARS AGO AND NOW, BY AGE

	Ability Admired 2 or 3 Years Ago					
	10–13 Years			14–19 Years		
Ability Admired Now	Deviant	Grades	Job	Deviant	Grades	Job
Deviant	42%	9%	0%	29%	9%	6%
Grades	34	81	47	34	71	15
Job	24	9	53	37	20	79
N=	(38)	(86)	(17)	(35)	(55)	(33)

quite useful. Using their self-perceptions in the recent past, Table 1 presents the nature of this competition for four age-groups of boys.

As age increases, school declines in attraction, and attraction to the job world increases. However, the appeal of the job world even at 16–19 years does not match that of school success at any age. At the younger ages, deviant values considerably outrank the job world in appeal; in fact, the biggest increase in attraction to deviant values takes place around the age when the appeal of good grades decreases the most, age 12–13. Thus it appears that attraction to deviant values has an early age of onset, as do the most admitted behavior activities.

Assuming that attraction to deviant values is related to illegal behavior, an important question concerning value competition can be posed: Does the decrease in the attraction of school success precede the increase in the attraction of deviant values? If so, then we can describe the dynamic relationship among conforming values, deviant values, and illegal behavior more aptly and also begin to erect a model of explanation in accord with empirical facts. Comparison of the relative stability of the competing value orientations should be of assistance in descriptive and explanatory analysis.

Stability of Value Choices. One means of testing the relative stability of competing value orientations is to cross-tabulate past and present value choices (Table 2). Those choices that are the most stable are likely to represent values that have been internalized for a relatively long time.

At the younger age-range the responses involving good grades are most stable (81 percent), the job world is next in stability (53 percent), and deviant choices are the least stable (42 percent). This suggests that attraction to school is the value that appears earliest in time. This inference is also supported by the fact that none of the respondents who chose job success in the recent past moved to a present choice of a deviant value.

At the older age-range, the deviant responses are not only the least stable but are less stable than for the younger boys (29 percent vs. 42 percent). The good-grades choices are still relatively stable, but less so than for the younger boys (71 percent vs. 81 percent). For this group, job choices are the most stable. Since this value replaces school as the most stable, and the deviant-value choice decreases in stability, we can infer that at the older age attraction to the job world is a more relevant independent variable. This interpretation is supported by the fact that the highest proportion of older boys whose past choices were deviant now choose job success. The percentages of boys who previously made deviant choices but now choose good grades are the same for the two age groups.

The findings concerning stability of attraction suggest that, on an individual level, the world of relevant choices is perceived quite differently by the two age-ranges. At the younger age-range, school is the major counter-attraction to a deviant choice. As the prospect of entering the job world looms closer, older boys may perceive employment as an additional counter-attraction to a deviant choice. Furthermore, at the older age-range, boys who formerly made deviant choices are capable of shifting to this new, more stable value orientation.

If individual attractions were the only operative variable, then widening conforming attractions might serve as an effective counterpoise to a choice of deviant values. However, like-minded peers associate together and produce socialization experiences that limit individual choices. Before exploring some of the consequences of sharing values with peers, we will consider the relationship of individual values and illegal behavior, to provide assurance that the value choices are relevant.

Individual Value Choices and Illegal Behavior. In Table 3 boys are grouped by age and classified into three types: (1) youths guided by a stable good-grades orientation, i.e., youths who choose good grades both now and two or three years ago; (2) youths guided by a stable job orientation or a mixed conforming orientation; and (3) youths guided by a deviant-value orientation, stable or unstable.

The results of Table 3, particularly for the older boys, suggest that attraction to a deviant value as "most important," either in the past or at present, is strongly related to the number of deviant acts reported. That is, boys who chose a deviant value were most likely to admit having committed deviant acts at some time in their lives. Among the younger boys, those attracted to a deviant value differ from those with a stable attraction to grades in the number of deviant acts reported, particularly when the last two behavior categories are collapsed (43 percent vs. 25 percent), but there is virtually no difference between the "deviant choice" and "stable job and mixed" categories (43 percent vs. 41 percent). This finding suggests that at the younger age-range the lack of a stable grade orientation in itself is likely to be related to illegal behavior. In a sense, at this age-range failure to choose good grades consistently may be no less deviant a response than direct attraction to one of the deviant values.

At the older age-range, the behavior differences between those who are or have been attracted to a deviant value and those who favor the other choices are quite clear (60 percent vs. 18 percent and 5 percent at the 4+ category). Although boys who are attracted to a job or to a combination of conforming values are likely to report a higher number of illegal acts than the stable-good-grades boys, they report far fewer than those who are attracted to a deviant choice. Their behavior profile, it is interesting to note, is not very different from that of the younger boys whose orientation is similarly conforming. Apparently a youthful adherence to *any* conforming value—even if the focus shifts—tends to discourage involvement in illegal behavior at an older age.

SHARED VALUES: EMPIRICAL FINDINGS

Our analysis of individual values utilized data elicited by presenting individuals with a forced choice concerning admired abilities.

TABLE 3. RELATIONSHIP OF INDIVIDUAL VALUE-CHOICE TYPES AND BEHAVIOR SUMMARY, BY AGE (BOYS ONLY)

	Individual Value Choices					
	10–13 Years			14–19 Years		
Life-History Acts Reported *	Stable Grades	Stable Job and Mixed	Any Deviant Choice	Stable Grades	Stable Job and Mixed	Any Deviant Choice
None	16%	4%	2%	3%	7%	2%
Lying–1	58	56	55	65	50	19
2–3	17	30	28	28	25	19
4+	8	11	15	5	18	60
N=	(75)	(27)	(46)	(39)	(44)	(42)

* The self-reports are of a life-history variety, since boys were asked if they had ever done any of a list of activities. Those classified as "none" were unwilling to report that they had "ever told a lie"; the "lying–1" classification refers to boys who admitted to lying and/or one other act; the "2–3" category refers to lying and 2 or 3 other acts; and "4+" refers to lying plus 4 or more acts. Elimination of the "none" category would not affect the findings.

TABLE 4. ASSESSMENT OF PEER VALUES BY SEX AND AGE

Ability Admired by Peers "a Lot" or "Some"	10–13 Years		14–19 Years	
	Boys	Girls	Boys	Girls
1. Being Hard and Tough	70%	34%	66%	35%
2. Keeping Mouth Shut to Cops	63	41	66	38
3. Outsmarting Others	62	44	60	44
4. Different Kicks	61	44	62	54
5. Fast Buck	55	29	53	38
6. Connections with Rackets	21	10	21	16
N=	(151)	(147)	(125)	(132)

TABLE 5. PRODUCT-MOMENT CORRELATION COEFFICIENTS OF ABILITIES ADMIRED BY PEERS, BOYS ONLY (N=276) *

	Keep Mouth Shut to Cops	Hard and Tough	Kicks	Fast Buck	Out-smart Others	Connections with Rackets
Keep Mouth Shut to Cops	...	.44	.34	.29	.27	.32
Hard and Tough	...	...	.36	.33	.27	.33
Kicks	...	...	...	.28	.31	.29
Fast Buck	...	...	...	...	.29	.22
Outsmart Others	...	...	...	...	...	.27
Connections with Rackets	...	...	...	...	...	...

* The probability is less than 0.001 that any specific intercorrelation might occur by chance alone.

TABLE 6. RELATIONSHIP BETWEEN PEER-VALUE INDEX AND BEHAVIOR SUMMARY, BY AGE (BOYS ONLY)

	Peer-Value Index					
	10–13 Years			14–19 Years		
Life-History Acts Reported	Low	Medium	High	Low	Medium	High
None	17%	4%	8%	4%	5%	3%
Lying Only	27	27	19	23	15	13
1	29	36	25	33	24	19
2–3	21	22	28	29	22	19
4+	6	10	19	12	34	47
N=	(48)	(67)	(36)	(52)	(41)	(32)

In studying shared values, we asked respondents to indicate whether their group or crowd admired each deviant ability listed "a lot," "some," or "not at all"; they were not asked to choose which ability was most admired by associates or to evaluate the appeal of deviant vs. conforming values. Since youths as well as adults tend to associate with like-minded persons, it can be inferred that respondents share the degree of value attraction estimated for their intimate peers. In this sense, peer values are likely to be shared values. This assumption can be tested by comparing respondents' individual values with their responses regarding peers. If the relationship is strong, we can conclude that the estimates of the strength of peer attraction to values also refer to the degree to which the respondent shares this attraction. To be attracted to a value with others, of course, is not equivalent to assessing it as most important. These distinctions, and the underlying reasoning, should be kept in mind in the analyses that follow.

The Attraction of Peer Values. The extent to which youth are attracted to the listed values can be assessed by combining the "some" and "a lot" responses for each ability. When this is done, even with age controlled, it is readily apparent that males view these items as attractive *peer* values. Table 4 demonstrates that each deviant ability other than the "connections" one is capable of eliciting more than a 50-percent response of attraction on the part of males.

In comparing boys and girls, it should be remembered that the question did not specify the sex of the peer-friends of respondents. Even though older girls probably associate with boys much more than do girls under 13, there is a surprising similarity between the two age-ranges of females. The major difference appears to be the increased attraction to kicks on the part of associates of the older girls; this is the only value for girls that goes above 51 percent, and it is also quite close to the rate for males. At the older ages, the search for kicks, licit and illicit, may be the common meeting ground for boys and girls.

The biggest value difference between younger boys and girls is in the attraction to being tough and hard. Although the attraction of this ability for boys declines with age, it continues to rank fairly high, whereas for girls at both age-ranges it ranks near the bottom of the list. Being tough and hard is, of course, a value that is quite consonant with the aggressive early-age activities of boys.

In summary, the evidence indicates that associates of both boys and girls have at least some attraction to the deviant values listed, and that there is a strong difference by sex. The values refer mainly to masculine interests. Controlling for age discloses only minor differences for boys. A majority of males perceive that their *friends* appreciate values which, on an *individual* basis, were chosen as if the actors were sensitive to their deviant connotation.

Peer-Value Patterns. To ascertain whether peer values are independent of one another or form a versatile pattern, each item was intercorrelated with every other item, and coefficients were computed (Table 5). The analysis indicates that for males *all* the peer values are intercorrelated in a statistically significant manner and thus cohere as one versatile pattern. The approaches of Matza-Sykes and Miller receive support from these findings. Although Cohen hypothesized a versatile pattern of values, he did not appreciate that the search for a "fast buck" and the

TABLE 7. RELATIONSHIP BETWEEN INDIVIDUAL VALUE CHOICES AND PEER-VALUE INDEX (BOYS ONLY)

Current Peer-Value Index	Individual Value Choices: Stable Conforming	Deviant 2–3 Years Ago, Conforming Now	Deviant Now
	%	%	%
Low	46	23	10
Medium	37	45	38
High	17	32	52
N=	(185)	(47)	(41)

pursuit of "kicks" are compatible in the minds of youth. Cloward and Ohlin recognized the important content of the peer values, but erred in describing them as independent.

These peer values were ordered into an index by weighting "a lot" answers as 2, "some" as 1, and "not at all" as zero, and assigning a score to each respondent. "Don't know" and "no answer" responses were arbitrarily weighted as 1. There were very few such responses, and they do not appreciably influence the resulting measure.

After the sample was scored, the distribution was divided roughly into thirds on the basis of the boys' scores. This procedure yielded a "low" group (scores 0–3) comprised of 36 percent of the boys; a "medium" group (scores 4–6) of 39 percent; and a "high" group (7 or more) of 25 percent. The relevance of the index is indicated by its relationship to the life-history behavior summary. Table 6 summarizes the results by age, for boys only.

The relationship between peer values and the behavior summary exists regardless of age, but there is obviously an age factor. The greatest increase in delinquent behavior with age occurs for boys who score medium and high on peer values. Similar results are obtained if past-year self-reports are used as the behavioral measure (data not shown).

The boys who do not admit even to lying do not materially affect the results. Closer analysis indicates that only about one half of these boys can be classified as associating with hyperconformists (i.e., as having low peer-value scores), and that about one fifth have peers with high deviant values (i.e., high peer-value scores). This indicates that as a group they cannot be dismissed merely as hyperconformists, as suggested by Dentler and Monroe.[24]

Peer Values and Individual Values. Data support the expectation that a boy who chooses a deviant ability will be supported by peers who are attracted to similar values. Peer values appear to be shared values, since 50 percent of the boys who choose a deviant value associate with peers who are high in deviant values, as compared to 19 percent of the boys choosing good grades and 21 percent choosing job success. Age does not alter the relationship; even at the younger age-range (10–13 years), individuals choosing a deviant ability tend to associate with peers who share their values to a high degree.

Although the *proportion* of youths guided by conforming (individual) choices who score high on the peer-value index is much smaller than that of the deviant choosers, there appears to be a large *number* of these boys. If we compare the youths who are guided by conforming choices "now" but who were attracted to deviant abilities "two to three years ago" with boys in the stable conforming category, an interesting finding results. Boys who were attracted to a deviant ability in the past on an individual basis but who now perceive themselves as conforming tend to continue their rejection of peers who are low on peer values (Table 7).

In their unwillingness to associate with boys who are low on peer values, these "reformed" deviants appear to stand midway between the stable conformers and the current deviants. The interpretation that youths tend to seek associates whose current individual values are similar to theirs should be amended to account for the influence of past values. Youths who held deviant values in the past probably associated with peers who shared those values; socialization through association with like-minded peers appears to influence choice of friends in the future—even though individual values may begin to change.

Peer Values and Police Contact. As an important subcultural element, peer values could also be expected to be related to contacts with the police. Table 8 summarizes these findings by age for boys. The relationship between police contact and peer values is consistently large for the older boys, regardless of the measure of police contact used. For the younger boys the relationship is insignificant. Examining age differences in the consistency of peer-value patterns may help to account for age differences in the relationship between peer values and police contact.

Age Differences and Peer-Value Patterns. All subcultural models appear to assume implicitly either (1) that adolescence is characterized by increased attraction to deviant values or (2) that adolescents are guided by new deviant values. The findings reported here indicate that adolescence is not characterized by growth in either individual or peer attraction to deviant values. The findings also indicate that the deviant values of adolescents are not new. In this respect, the findings are consonant with our knowledge that delinquency is not an exclusively adolescent phenomenon.

As we have pointed out, a major difference between adolescents and their younger counterparts is the greater propensity toward symbolic behavior and cognitive consistency with age. To be consonant with the findings concerning the greater relationship between values and indices of illegal behavior at the older age-range, there should also be findings that values form a more consistent pattern during this developmental period. The evidence bears out this expectation, as well as clarifying the versatility-specialization issue.

In Table 5 findings were presented concerning the inter-item coefficients of peer values for all boys, regardless of age. In Table 9 the same items have been intercorrelated for boys, but with *age controlled.* At the younger age-range, all of the coefficients are in a positive direction, but only three of the six items can be regarded as forming a significant pattern. Starting with the highest intercorrelated items of "keep mouth shut to cops" and "hard and tough," the only other item associated with these two core values is enjoying "kicks." For the older boys, however, not only is the coefficient higher for every pair of items, but *all* of the coefficients are at least 0.29. Older boys are decidedly more consistent in their values shared with peers.

The greater consistency in value patterns

TABLE 8. RELATIONSHIP OF PEER-VALUE INDEX AND INDICES OF POLICE CONTACT, BY AGE (BOYS ONLY)

Police-Contact Measures	Peer-Value Index: 10–13 Years: Low	Medium	High	14–19 Years: Low	Medium	High
Presence in Police Files	8%	6%	6%	6%	20%	34%
Stopped by Police (Self-Reports)	6	6	11	10	15	31
Index of Police Contact *	10	13	14	12	29	50
N=	(48)	(67)	(36)	(52)	(41)	(32)

* The "index of police contact" refers to whether boys had an official record in the files of the New York City Police Department and/or admitted to having been stopped by the police for one of the self-report items. It therefore represents the sum of the two measures used with duplications eliminated.

[24] Robert A. Dentler and Laurence J. Monroe, "Early Adolescent Theft," *American Sociological Review,* 26 (October, 1961), pp. 733–744.

at the older age-range is consonant with the findings that age is related to an increase in the frequency of illegal behavior, the persistence of behavior patterns, the number of illegal acts, and the likelihood of police contact. The relative absence of peer-value specialization is also consonant with the versatile content of the behavior patterns. Viewed from the perspective of age-sequence, the fact that the peer values refer to the *present* suggests that the behavior patterns are likely to be versatile in content *within a given age-period*.[25]

Conforming Abilities Admired by Peers. On an *individual* level, the relative instability of deviant choices, as well as the dominant preferences for conforming abilities, indicates that adult-sponsored institutional areas are capable of attracting slum youths to a greater degree than values associated with illegal behavior.

On a *peer* level, the evidence is that deviant values are attractive to a majority of youths and their associates. Youths differed mainly on the degree to which their friends emphasized these peer values. Analysis of peer support for conforming values reveals similar findings. Only 9 to 10 percent of the boys report that their friends are completely negative concerning school or work.

Cohen's contention that many slum boys are "ambivalent" toward—not alienated from—school and the job world is apparently closer to the mark than the position of any of the other theorists. However, Cohen underestimated the appeal and versality of deviant values and failed to realize that they compete for the allegiance of pre-adolescent as well as older boys. An analysis of the interaction of peer orientations toward school and deviant values will suggest how this competition can be described.

Table 10 categorizes two age-groups of boys by their perception of their peers' admiration for good grades and their peer-value index scores. The responses of "some" and "not at all" were compared to the "a lot" responses. The school variable is treated as independent on the basis of the findings relating to value stability.

The table clearly reveals that association with peers who are ambivalent toward the rewards of school is likely to lead to association with peers who are attracted to deviant values. Although the relationship is strong

TABLE 9. PRODUCT-MOMENT CORRELATION COEFFICIENTS OF PEER VALUES FOR TWO AGE-RANGES (BOYS ONLY)

	Keep Mouth Shut to Cops	Hard and Tough	Kicks	Fast Buck	Outsmart Others	Connections* with Rackets
	10–13 Years (N=151)					
Keep Mouth Shut to Cops	...	.40	.31	.15	.21	.32
Hard and Tough	...	...	.27	.21	.12	.16
Kicks	...	...	...	.19	.23	.15
Fast Buck	...	...	...	...	.17	.33
Outsmart Others	...	...	...	...	...	.21
Connections with Rackets	...	...	...	...	...	...
	14–19 Years (N=125)					
Keep Mouth Shut to Cops	...	.52	.39	.38	.30	.42
Hard and Tough	...	...	.46	.39	.42	.54
Kicks	...	...	...	.42	.40	.42
Fast Buck	...	...	...	...	.43	.46
Outsmart Others	...	...	...	...	...	.29
Connections with Rackets	...	...	...	...	...	...

* All coefficients with "Connections" employ a biserial coefficient because of the small numbers involved; the two categories are "lot-some" vs. "not at all."

at both ages, there is a greater polarization of peer values at the older age range. Greater consistency among peer values is accompanied by increased consonance between deviant and ambivalent school values.

The importance of assessing the peer orientation toward school in depicting the distribution of peer-value index scores is further highlighted by considering the interaction effect of individual value choices (past and present) and peer orientations toward good grades. Peer orientation toward school is strongly related to both the individual and the peer indices of values.

Table 11 categorizes male youth by both classifications and their relationship to attraction toward shared deviant values (all ages included).

It is readily apparent that individual attraction to conforming values (past or present) is *not* the sole condition for the selection of friends who rank low on the peer-value index, but is coupled with association with peers who support attraction to school rewards. In contrast, individual attraction to conforming values, when coupled with association with peers who are ambivalent toward school rewards, yields a peer-value index profile similar to that yielded by a deviant individual choice plus association with peers who admire good grades.

Since individuals who chose a deviant ability were also rejecting a conforming ability (mainly school), in a sense their association with peers who are ambivalent toward school provides support for their rejection of a conforming value. It is not surprising, therefore, that those who reject a conforming ability and associate with ambivalent peers are likely to have the highest score on the peer-value index. In the everyday world of competing values there tends to be an incompatibility between achievement and peer values.

In this section we have stressed the importance of peer support for school achievement in understanding the value competition confronting youth. Peer support for the job world does not seem to be so important, since boys with friends who admire the job world "a lot" are no less likely to be attracted to a deviant individual value (past/present) than are boys who see their peers as only slightly or not at all attracted to job success. Therefore, it appears safe to conclude that for boys in this sample, low admiration of the job world is probably not part of a *shared* outlook that encompasses deviant values. Low peer orientation toward good grades, on the other hand, tends to be a consistent part of a shared value orientation.

Belief in Peer Temptations and Shared Values. The foregoing analyses have provided strong evidence that individual choices are associated with perception of peer values and hence that perceived peer orientations are likely to be shared by the respondents. Evidence was also presented that youth who score high on the peer-value index are likely to report the highest number of illegal acts, particularly at the older ages. In order to buttress the inference that associates of the respondents are likely to be providing behavioral as well as value support for the actions of individuals, we propose an additional line of analysis. Boys high on the peer-value index should be more likely to indicate agreement with the statement "Most people you know are tempted to break the law."

The data shown in Table 12 suggest that peer values are supportive of illegal behavior for friends as well as self. The relationship is consistent for all ages. It should also be

[25] A similar conclusion regarding behavior was reached by James F. Short, Jr., and Fred L. Strodtbeck, *Group Process and Gang Delinquency,* Chicago: University of Chicago Press, 1965, p. 13. Their studies of gangs in low-income areas of Chicago used reports of gang workers as primary sources of data. The respondents of our survey are also mainly lower-class youths; in addition, the sample included a variety of ethnic groups that could have yielded the Cloward-Ohlin ideal types. For a detailed discussion of the specialization issue, using the variables of argot, shared peer values, and ethnicity, see Lerman, "Argot, Symbolic Deviance, and Subcultural Delinquency," *op. cit.,* pp. 218–220.

TABLE 10. RELATIONSHIP OF PEER ADMIRATION OF GOOD GRADES AND PEER-VALUE INDEX, BY AGE (BOYS ONLY)

	Good Grades Admired by Peers			
	10–13 Years		14–19 Years	
Peer-Value Index	A Lot	Ambivalent	A Lot	Ambivalent
Low	43%	21%	55%	27%
Medium	38	48	35	30
High	18	31	9	43
	—	—	—	—
N=	(76)	(71)	(65)	(60)

TABLE 11. RELATIONSHIP OF INDIVIDUAL VALUE CHOICES AND PEER-VALUE INDEX FOR BOYS WHOSE PEERS ADMIRE GOOD GRADES

	Good Grades Admired by Peers			
	Conforming Individual Values		Deviant Individual Values	
Peer-Value Index	A Lot	Ambivalent	A Lot	Ambivalent
Low	55%	34%	28%	11%
Medium	36	37	41	43
High	9	29	31	46
	—	—	—	—
N=	(109)	(73)	(32)	(56)

TABLE 12. AGREEMENT WITH "MOST PEOPLE YOU KNOW ARE TEMPTED TO BREAK THE LAW," BY PEER-VALUE INDEX AND AGE (BOYS ONLY)

	Peer-Value Index		
Age	Low	Med.	High
10–13 Years	29%	40%	58%
	N=(48)	(67)	(36)
14–19 Years	21%	44%	53%
	N=(52)	(41)	(32)

noted that a majority of the "high" boys at both age-ranges believe that people they know are tempted to break the law. This suggests that boys sharing deviant values to a high degree are likely to perceive more lawbreaking and therefore believe that "most people" they know are tempted in this direction.

This belief may also be used as a "technique of neutralization" vis-à-vis official definers of illegal acts.[26] The fact that the belief is related to shared values indicates that it is supported by others and is therefore a "cultural construct." It is also probable that youth high on peer values would use this peer-supported means of warding off invidious definitions. The early appearance of this belief indicates that young boys are also perceiving illegal behavior. This supports the findings of early age of onset.

SUMMARY AND CONCLUSIONS

In a pluralistic society, the worlds of school, work, and peers compete for the allegiance of youth; the consequences of this competition are relevant for understanding both individual value choices and shared peer values. The findings bearing on this competition among value orientations can be summarized as follows:

1. Although all youth report the ability to get good grades as the most important value choice both now and in the recent past, boys are less attracted to this conforming value than are girls, and they are more likely to be attracted to a deviant value.

2. Attraction to a deviant value begins early, increases at 12–13 years of age, and then may persist as a counter-attraction to school and work.

3. On an individual level, attraction to a deviant value is the least stable and is likely to shift to a conforming value.

4. With increasing age, the job world tends to replace school as the most stable value orientation.

5. There is a greater attraction to deviant values on a peer level than on an individual level; this attraction appears to be relatively constant for all ages, but it does not outrank attraction to good grades and the job world.

6. Youths attracted to a deviant value—either past or present—are most likely to seek out peers who are supportive of this orientation.

7. High admissions of life-history acts of misbehavior are most likely to occur among older boys (a) who are or have been attracted to a deviant value (and rejecting of school or work) and (b) whose associates support deviant values and are ambivalent toward good grades.

8. There are no new peer values in adolescence, nor is there an increase in attraction to peer values; rather, it is the increase in patterned consistency that distinguishes older from younger age-groups. This increased consistency in value patterns accounts in part for the relationship between age and illegal behavior.

9. With increased age, peer values that tend to be shared values are more likely to be a versatile than a specialized pattern; they also tend to symbolize masculine interests.

10. Ambivalent peer reactions toward good grades or the job world are related to high scores on the peer-value index, as well as to each other; analysis of the two conforming orientations discloses that reaction to school is more closely related to a shared value pattern.

11. Youths who share peer values are more likely to believe that most people they know are tempted to break the law. This suggests that peers lend behavioral as well as value support to one another.

These findings enable us to evaluate some of the descriptions posited by major theorists of delinquency. The data support Miller's contention that the focal concerns of lower-class youths are versatile in content and patterned with some differences by sex and age. Whatever the attractiveness of peer values in other strata of society, there is little doubt that slum youths perceive that their friends are attracted by an array of versatile deviant values. Miller's view of a distinctively lower-class culture is opened to doubt, however, by the reluctance of slum youth to publicly reject the values of school and work. Ambivalence toward good grades and the job world suggests that slum youths are not totally deaf to the messages of the dominant interest groupings; they appear to be more open to the blandishments of the job world, however, than to the attraction of school values.

Cohen's description of the delinquent subculture is correct in its emphasis on versatility but incorrect in specifying the content of the values that yield versatility. Only at the younger age-range is there an emphasis on toughness and non-utilitarian "kicks." At the older age-range, the subculture does not become specialized (as Cohen and Short posited in a later article); rather, there is a compatibility between "kicks" and utilitarian concerns (the "fast buck" and "connections") as well as inclusion of the rationalistic value of "outsmarting others." Since five of the six peer values are attractive in some degree to a majority of youths, it is *not* necessary to posit an opposition to middle-class values on the part of slum youths; nor is it necessary to assume that these youths share a similar means of defending themselves psychologically via a "reaction formation" against these values. Cohen, though, is the only theorist to stress correctly that slum youths are ambivalent, not rejecting, in their attitude toward the adult-dominated worlds of school and work.

Cloward and Ohlin utilize all of the value orientations in their tripartite typology but err in assuming that youths are specialized in their value patterns. The compatibility of the various values at the older age-ranges suggests, in fact, that the orientation of youths becomes *more* versatile with age. The fact that increased consistency in the versatile value pattern leads to an increase in illegal behavior suggests, too, that this model's stress on explicit prescriptions in behalf of delinquent behavior is not necessary; attraction to peer values is a matter of degree, and these values are not explicitly illegal (except for connection with a racket). The alienation of their ideal role types is probably overdrawn, since slum youths are not openly rejecting of the worlds of school and work but ambivalent, differing from their conforming peers in degree rather than kind.

[26] See Matza and Sykes, *op. cit.*

Matza and Sykes provide the broadest framework for understanding peer-value patterns. The nonconforming values they select are versatile and consistently patterned, particularly at the older age. However, they appear to underestimate the degree to which "subterranean values" are dominated by masculine interests and are therefore more likely to be shared by males than by females. It also seems likely that to regard these values as non-public may miss the point; these values *are* public for youth, but they are not the *ideal* values set forth by adult mentors. Matza and Sykes are supported in their views about shared techniques of neutralization; they appear to have erred, however, in believing that outright disdain for work is a necessary part of the pattern.

There are other sociologists, not treated at length in this article, whose theoretical perspectives fit in well with the lines of analysis pursued here. Bordua, an important critic of Cohen, Cloward-Ohlin, and Miller, exhibits a keen awareness of the usefulness of employing developmental differences and value competition.[27] He, too, is willing to entertain the idea that peer values are potentially attractive to youngsters. Once this perspective is accepted, it is no longer necessary to posit that enactment of deviance must be preceded by a "tension state." Youthful sin, like youthful virtue, can also be fun.

The idea that values are in competition for the allegiance of youths is, of course, also compatible with classical culture-conflict theory.[28] However, in a traditional conflict of conduct codes, it appears that one of the codes *prescribes* explicitly illegal behavior while the other *proscribes* it. The peer values that we emphasize are not explicitly illegal; they do not require illegal behavior. Youngsters may "drift" in and out of delinquent episodes in the company of peers. Given an attraction to these values, situational variables—as described by Short and Strodtbeck—may play a critical role in triggering actual delinquent episodes.[29]

If there is a "pull" toward the "garden-variety" values of toughness, kicks, and making a fast buck, then the search for evidence of "reaction formations" and "strains" may be futile. We might more profitably address the conditions that make these kinds of values so attractive that linguistic and behavioral deviance will occur with a greater frequency. Toby has highlighted one condition that is quite congruent with our data: youth who are unwilling or unable to maintain a consistent commitment to achieving success in school are most likely to be unduly attracted to realizing peer values.[30] Efforts to understand how this adult-sponsored commitment is effectively transmitted and supported could add to our knowledge of all youth, not just the wayward and the disadvantaged.

---

[27] David J. Bordua, "Some Comments on Theories of Group Delinquency," *Sociological Inquiry,* 32 (Spring, 1962), pp. 245–260; and "Delinquent Subcultures: Sociological Interpretations of Gang Delinquency," *Annals,* 338 (November, 1961), pp. 119–136.

[28] See Solomon Kobrin, "The Conflict of Values in Delinquency Areas," *American Sociological Review,* 16 (October, 1951), pp. 653–661; and Thorsten Sellin, *Culture Conflict and Crime,* New York: Social Science Research Council, 1938.

[29] James F. Short, Jr., and Fred L. Strodtbeck, *op. cit.,* pp. 185–198 and 248–264.

[30] Jackson Toby's work has consistently had this kind of focus. See the following: Larry Karacki and Jackson Toby, "The Noncommitted Adolescent: Candidate for Gang Socialization," *Sociological Inquiry,* 32 (Spring, 1962), pp. 203–215; Jackson Toby and Marcia L. Toby, *Low School Status as a Predisposing Factor in Subcultural Delinquency,* New Brunswick, N.J.: Rutgers University, n.d., mimeo; Jackson Toby, "Hoodlum or Businessman: An American Dilemma," in Marshall Sklare, ed., *The Jews: Social Patterns of an American Group,* Glencoe, Ill.: Free Press, 1958, pp. 542–550; and Jackson Toby, "Affluence and Adolescent Crime," in *Task Force Report: Juvenile Delinquency and Youth Crime,* President's Committee on Law Enforcement and administration of Justice, Washington: Government Printing Office, Appendix H, pp. 132–145. For a discussion of the work of Toby, see Lerman, *Issues in Subcultural Delinquency, op. cit.,* Chaps. 8, 9.

Commitment to Conventional Action

Travis Hirschi

Commitment to Education

Delinquents in Haulburg had high middle-class aspirations. . . . Jackie, aged twenty-one years, continued to express an interest in going to medical school and becoming a surgeon, although he had not gone to college or even completed high school.[12]

"I mean, if something comes up and I can't finish school, I'm gonna go to college. I don't care what comes up." [13]

At least since Merton's "Social Structure and Anomie," aspirations have played a large part in explanations of delinquent behavior. In their simplest form, the hypotheses stemming from Merton's work are opposite to those emerging from a control perspective. Irving Spergel, for example, suggests: "Delinquents may be under more direct and greater pressure from ambitious and upwardly mobile parents or from parents who are particularly dissatisfied with their own status in life, and nondelinquents may have been less baldly and forcefully exposed to general cultural pressures for success." [14] From the Mertonian perspective, a solution to the problem of delinquency would be somehow to bring the adolescent's aspirations into line with his realistic expectations, to synchronize what he wishes to be with what he can be, given his limited academic competence and/or social structural obstacles. From the perspective of control theory, such "cooling out" would remove a major element of social control, leaving the adolescent all the more free to commit delinquent acts.[15]

As the quotations at the beginning of this section suggest, there are many problems in measuring the intensity of aspirations. In the present case, however, the problem is not serious, since the higher the aspiration the less likely the child is to be delinquent, and it is not necessary to convert weak and unrealistic aspirations into the motive force behind delinquent behavior. As Table 59 makes clear, the higher the student's educational aspirations, whether he be white or Negro, the less likely he is to commit delinquent acts (by both the self-report and official measures).

Table 59 / Percent Committing One or More Delinquent Acts by Educational Aspirations,[a] by Race

	White Boys		Negro Boys	
Educational Aspirations	Self-Reported Acts	Official Acts	Self-Reported Acts	Official Acts
Less than college	56 (172)	33 (181)	56 (231)	47 (248)
Some college	47 (240)	23 (246)	51 (145)	38 (155)
College graduation	40 (825)	14 (837)	38 (315)	36 (328)

[a] The item is: "How much schooling would you like to get eventually?"

Aspiration levels in the sample are high and compare with previous research in this area.[16] Forty-five percent of the Negro boys and 66 percent of the white boys in the analyzed sample want to graduate from college. Unfortunately for the anomie hypothesis, however, educational expectations in the sample are virtually as high as aspirations (even among Negroes). If we take such minor discrepancies as the difference between a desire to graduate from college and the expectation of attaining only some college as sufficient to produce delinquency, 19 percent of the white boys may be classified as suffering from a condition of anomie. If we divide aspirations and expectations between college and no college, only 5 percent desire more education than they expect to get. Frustrated educational aspirations therefore cannot be an important antecedent of delinquency in the present sample. Even if true, then, the anomie hypothesis with respect to educational aspirations is largely

[12] Irving Spergel, *Racketville, Slumtown, Haulburg* (Chicago: The University of Chicago Press, 1964), p. 99.

[13] A male Negro student in Richmond, quoted in Alan B. Wilson, "Educational Consequences of Segregation in a California Community," mimeographed, Survey Research Center, Berkeley, 1966, p. 60.

[14] *Racketville, Slumtown, Haulburg*, pp. 94–95.

[15] Strain theorists of course rarely advocate this solution to the discrepancy between aspirations and expectations, advocating instead the removal of barriers to opportunity. Durkheim, in contrast, tended to stress the moral value of poverty (Emile Durkheim, *Suicide* [New York: The Free Press, 1951], especially pp. 246–254).

[16] James F. Short, Jr., and Fred L. Strodtbeck, *Group Process and Gang Delinquency* (Chicago: University of Chicago Press, 1964), p. 111; Ralph H. Turner, *The Social Context of Ambition* (San Francisco: Chandler, 1964), pp. 42–44. For an analysis of sources of educational aspirations in the present data, see Wilson, "Educational Consequences of Segregation," Chapter 8.

From *Causes of Delinquency* (Berkeley: University of California Press, 1969), pp. 170–186. Reprinted by permission of the University of California Press.

Table 60 / Percent Committing One or More Delinquent Acts by Educational Aspirations and Educational Expectations

	Self-Reported Acts		
	Educational Aspirations		
Educational Expectations	College Graduate	Some College	Less than College
College graduate	39 (607)	— (6)	— (5)
Some college	42 (174)	44 (196)	— (12)
Less than college	58 (29)	63 (33)	56 (151)

	Official Acts		
	Educational Aspirations		
Educational Expectations	College Graduate	Some College	Less than College
College graduate	12 (616)	— (6)	— (6)
Some college	18 (177)	18 (200)	— (12)
Less than college	13 (29)	49 (35)	33 (159)

irrelevant, there being insufficient variation on the independent variable to account for more than a small fraction of the variation in delinquency.

Yet the issue of frustrated aspirations is of such theoretical significance that it cannot be dismissed merely by pointing to the small portion of the sample whose aspirations appear to be frustrated. In Table 60 we examine the joint effects of educational aspirations and expectations. On the basis of Table 60, it is safe to say that discrepancies in educational aspirations and expectations are not important in the causation of delinquency for two reasons: few boys in the sample have aspirations greatly in excess of their expectations; and, *those boys whose aspirations exceed their expectations are no more likely to be delinquent than those boys whose aspirations and expectations are identical.*

The solid relation between educational expectations and delinquency evident in Table 60 recalls a question raised some time ago: Why, if social class is related to the variables presumably causing delinquency, is social class itself unrelated to delinquency? Much research shows that the higher the family's socioeconomic status, the more likely the child is to expect to attain higher education. The present data are no exception (Table 61).

Father's education is strongly related to educational expectations. Educational expectations are reasonably strongly related to delinquency. Yet, as has been shown, there is no relation between father's education and delinquency in the present sample. What accounts for the zero relation between father's education and delinquency? In an attempt to answer this question, we examine the relation between father's education and delinquency within groups whose educational expectations are the same (Table 62).

Table 61 / Percent Expecting to Graduate from College by Father's Education

College Graduate	Some College	High School Graduate	Less than High School Graduation
79 (290)	59 (186)	45 (531)	30 (326)

Table 62 / Average Number of Self-Reported Delinquent Acts by Educational Expectations and Father's Education

	Educational Expectations		
Father's Education	Graduate College	Some College	No College
College graduate	.61 (229)	1.20 (45)	1.23 (16)
Some college	.59 (110)	.86 (55)	.83 (21)
High school graduate	.55 (240)	.81 (178)	.98 (113)
Less than high school graduation	.66 (100)	.86 (128)	1.05 (98)

The two groups in the sample with the highest rates of delinquency are sons of college graduates not expecting to graduate from college. If these boys had committed delinquent acts at the same rate as boys with equivalent educational expectations, there would be a weak but consistent negative relation between father's education and delinquency in the sample as a whole.[17]

These results are similar to findings reported by Stinchcombe. In his sample, the sons of lower middle-class parents doing poorly in school were more likely to be "rebellious" than the sons of working-class parents doing equally poorly in school. This helped account for the fact that the lower middle-class children were as likely to be rebellious as the working-class children in the sample as a whole.[18]

Stinchcombe in effect turned strain theory on its head and argued that the middle-class boy, not the lower-class boy, doing poorly in school suffers from a discrepancy between aspirations and expectations and is thus forced into delinquency. Table 62 appears to support Stinchcombe's argument. (The empirical relation is trivial, as it was in Stinchcombe's data. However, it is customary at this point to note that the relation has theoretical significance.)[19] Father's education is probably a better measure of pressure to succeed than an item asking what the student would *like* to do, since the college-educated father is highly likely to desire at least as much education for his son. Thus it would be possible to argue on the basis of Table 62 that most middle-class parents are able to protect their children from delinquency by assuring them access to

[17] The average number of delinquent acts per boy for the four groups separated on the basis of father's education *would* be (from less than high school to college graduate): .86, .73, .70, and .67.

[18] *Rebellion*, pp. 134–169.

[19] This custom is pernicious. We should note that the empirical relation has significance for theory. Theories should choke rather than thrive on such relations.

Table 63 / Average Number of Self-Reported Delinquent Acts by Grade-Point Average in English and Family Status

	Grade-Point Average—English		
Family Status	0–49	50–79	80–99
Lower	.92 (83)	.67 (94)	.57 (66)
Semi-skilled and skilled manual	1.06 (127)	.70 (148)	.62 (135)
White collar	1.23 (36)	.98 (52)	.60 (55)
Professional	.92 (42)	.79 (61)	.59 (128)

Table 64 / Average Number of Self-Reported Delinquent Acts by Parental Pressure and Educational Expectations

"How much education do you expect to get?"	"Do your parents want you to go to college?" They Insist	Very Much	Other [a]
No college	.52 (30)	1.02 (87)	1.08 (140)
Some college	.68 (56)	.84 (283)	.99 (91)
College graduation	.66 (218)	.56 (444)	.39 (30)

[a] This includes: "I think they want me to go but we don't talk about it"; "They don't care one way or the other"; "No, they don't want me to go"; and "Don't know." Over half of those in this category responded, "I think they want me to go."

higher education; that, however, if for any reason (perhaps because the child is not academically qualified) the middle-class parent is unable to assure access to higher education, his emphasis on such education returns to haunt him: his child is more likely to be delinquent than the child who has not been led to value something he cannot have. In effect, then, the advantages enjoyed by the middle-class parent are cancelled by disadvantages, and there is no overall relation between social class and delinquency.

Stinchcombe used father's occupation rather than education, and grade-point average rather than educational expectations. Since grades and father's occupation are available in the present data, and are related to each other and to delinquency in the same manner as in Stinchcombe's data, let us see if his finding is directly replicable in the present sample (Table 63).

Although Table 63 does not show the effect as clearly as Table 62, if Stinchcombe's procedure is followed and the line drawn between white-collar and manual workers, the results are similar: middle- and lower middle-class children doing poorly in school are more likely to be delinquent than working-class children doing equally poorly in school. The differences are very small, but again they appear to help explain the lack of an overall relation between social class and delinquency.

When data agree with a strain hypothesis, such a hypothesis is likely to be more persuasive than alternative hypotheses that also fit the data. In the present case we could give this relation to strain theory without serious damage, since the effect of the apparent strain is very small and applies only to a small minority of the sample (between 5 and 18 percent, depending on the measure used and the definition of "high-expectation" classes). Once again, however, the logic of strain theory is so removed from that of control theory that we should not grant it a victory without examining alternative hypotheses congruent with control theory logic.

One such hypothesis is that these results are statistical or social artifacts. Suppose, let us say, that some causal variable has the same effect on delinquency within each social class. Further suppose that those lowest on this variable are most likely to be delinquent. Now, within any given social class, *the larger the proportion* we take from the low end of the causal variable, *the lower the rate of delinquency.* Thus some method of statistical classification or social selection which isolates the lowest 21 percent of the sons of college graduates and the lowest 70 percent of the sons of those not finishing high school (see Table 61) might very well show a higher rate of delinquency among the sons of college graduates—even though they are no more likely to be delinquent than the sons of those with less education having the same values of the causal variable. (Note that at this point there is no reason to question the validity of the measure of delinquency. We add little to the strength of the claim that a discrepancy between felt parental expectations and actual academic achievement is the cause of the relatively high rate of delinquency by showing that these boys are more delinquent by other measures.)

Instead of attempting to determine whether the positive relation between social class and delinquency among those doing poorly in school and among those not expecting to graduate from college is spurious, let us examine data bearing directly on the parental pressure hypothesis. The students were asked whether their parents wanted them to go to college. If we combine responses to this question with educational expectations, we get evidence bearing directly on the hypothesis that high parental expectations combined with low actual expectations produces pressure resulting in delinquency.

Straightforward interpretation of Table 64 is impossible because parental pressure and educational expectations interact in their effects on delinquency. In order to make sense of such interactions, it is necessary to question the apparent meaning of the indicators or the quality of the data. Nevertheless, the major implication of the parental pressure hypothesis is certainly disconfirmed by Table 64. Among those *not* planning to graduate from college, the greater the apparent parental pressure to attend college, the lower the rate of delinquency. It may be, to question the indicator, that among those with relatively small expectations parental "pressure" is actually parental "interest," and that the boys are simply basing their expectations on a realistic evaluation of their own interests and abilities. In any event, undue parental pressure does not appear to account for the high delinquency rate of those whose educational expectations are limited.

If the parental pressure hypothesis is to find any support in these data, it must come from an unlikely source: from among those who expect to graduate from college. In this group, the greater the apparent parental pressure, the higher the rate of delinquency. Rather than speculate on the meaning of this finding, I will report the outcome of further analysis within the group expecting to graduate from college. Among those getting good grades (the majority of those expecting to graduate from college), the relation again reverses—that is, the greater the apparent parental pressure, the lower the rate of delinquency. Among those whose grades are not so good, the greater the apparent parental pressure, the higher the rate of delinquency. And we have again uncovered a small group whose delinquency could be interpreted as resulting from a condition of strain. I am forced to agree with Stinchcombe: "Almost always there were some results that could be tentatively interpreted as supporting the [strain] hypothesis, provided enough *ad hoc* assumptions and interpretations were made." [20]

Educational expectations are more strongly related to delinquency than educational aspirations, reflecting perhaps a greater reality component in the former.[21] For that matter, the concept

[20] *Rebellion*, p. 156.

[21] See James F. Short, Jr., "Gang Delinquency and Anomie," *Anomie and Deviant Behavior*, ed. Marshall B. Clinard (New York: The Free Press, 1964), pp. 108–111. Short's data show that educational adjustment is more strongly related to delinquency than are educational aspirations. They also show that educational aspirations are negatively related to delinquency, regardless of educational adjustment.

of commitment itself implies that the person has something *invested* in a line of activity: the mere wish to be "something or somebody" is not enough to affect behavior seriously unless the person supports or has supported his words with deeds. The value system the strain theorist sees as feeding the ranks of delinquency also suggests more than that the individual idly aspire to wealth, fame, or success. It may *say* "Be a king in your dreams," but it frowns on dreamers. Thus the unemployed twenty-one-year-old high school dropout who "aspires" to be a surgeon represents not the embodiment of these values, but their absence. The test is not that a man have lofty ambitions, but that he strive mightily. And by this test there is undoubtedly greater variation in the extent to which the values have been "internalized" or the "cultural goal" maintained than is true at the level of verbalized "success aspirations."

Those committed to educational success as evidenced by current efforts should be least likely, according to control theory, to commit delinquent acts. Several items in the questionnaire tap this kind of commitment. For example, "I try hard in school" and "How important is getting good grades to you personally?" both suggest commitment to education at least partially independent of educational aspirations,[22] and they are certainly more relevant to current activities than such aspirations. Since a third item, "Whatever I do, I try hard," is strongly related to the school achievement items, it was combined with them to produce an index of achievement orientation. Table 65 shows the relation between achievement orientation and self-reported delinquency. It is clear from this table that the ambitious, the strivers, are much less likely than the nonambitious to have committed delinquent acts.

Table 65 / Self-Reported Delinquency by Achievement Orientation
(in percent)

Self-Reported Acts	Index of Achievement Orientation 0	1	2	3	4	5	6
None	26	46	55	57	69	75	80
One	27	27	26	29	22	15	10
Two or more	46	27	19	14	9	10	10
Totals	99	100	100	100	100	100	100
	(91)	(184)	(226)	(247)	(241)	(100)	(50)

The data in this chapter could be taken as showing that boys who reject the education game and desire instead the accouterments of success within the lower-class style of life are most likely to become delinquent, as suggested by a Cloward–Ohlin hypothesis.[23] Cloward and Ohlin hypothesize that the boy who desires material success but not the middle-class life style is more likely to be delinquent than the boy who desires neither. If education is the means to the middle-class style of life, and if "cars" and "dames" are symbols of material success within the lower-class culture, then these data suggest that delinquents are boys who reject the former and desire the latter.[24]

This conclusion is unacceptable, however, since it suggests two things antithetical to control theory logic: (1) that the truly nonaspiring are less likely to be delinquent than those who maintain an interest in a quasi-legitimate goal (materialistic success); (2) that delinquency is a means to a quasi-legitimate goal and that the desire to reach this goal produces delinquency. It is difficult to disentangle the Cloward–Ohlin hypothesis from the adult status hypothesis, according to which, it will be recalled, the boy rejects education, takes up the symbols of adult status (cars and dames), and becomes a delinquent: both predict the same relations between the two kinds of aspirations and delinquency. The difference enters with respect to the meaning of the relation between adoption of lower-class success symbols (symbols of adult status) and delinquency.

There is, to be sure, some difficulty in the operationalization of aspirations of "success within the lower-class life style." As Bordua has commented: "If they [lower-class boys] aspire to large (how large?) incomes *within* the style of the lower-class life they clearly aspire to the impossible and, indeed—except through some type of crime—the almost unimaginable. They seem to be as much the victims of misinformation as of injustice."[25] If the Cloward–Ohlin theory is taken on their own terms, we should attempt to find boys who aspire to wealth but not to education and compare them with boys who aspire to neither wealth nor education. (True to the strain theory tradition, some legitimate—in this case quasi-legitimate—aspiration is behind delinquent behavior.) Unfortunately, no measure of income aspirations is available on the present questionnaire. Tangential measures of the relative importance of life style as opposed to income, however, appear to support the Cloward–Ohlin hypothesis. Boys agreeing with the statement, "The only reason to have a job is for money," are more likely to be delinquent than those disagreeing with this statement (Table 66).

Once again, however, this relation would obtain if money were a universal aspiration that remains when other aspirations are stripped away. The important test of the Cloward–Ohlin as opposed to the control theory hypothesis involves a comparison of the delinquency rates of those who desire money only with those who, in effect, desire nothing very badly.[26] The item used in Table 66 ("The only reason to have a job is for money") seems a reasonable measure of "crass materialism." What can we use to measure the second dimension of the Cloward–Ohlin typology, the strength of the desire for money? A second measure of ambition, one not tied to education, is available. Students agreeing to the statements: "You should not expect too much out of life" and "An easy life is a happy life," and who see money as the only

22 In fact, in the present sample, those expecting less than a college education have a slightly higher average achievement orientation than those expecting some college (as opposed to those expecting to graduate from college).

23 Richard A. Cloward and Lloyd E. Ohlin, *Delinquency and Opportunity* (New York: The Free Press, 1960), pp. 94–97.

24 Short and Strodtbeck have shown that delinquents and nondelinquents evaluate elements of the middle-class life style equally highly. For example, they all tend to think that "working for good grades in school" is a good thing. At this level, then, the Cloward–Ohlin hypothesis is false. However, when, as in the present case, we get closer to the boys' actual commitment to these values, the differences between delinquents and nondelinquents are large. See *Group Process*, pp. 47–76.

25 David J. Bordua, "Sociological Perspectives," *Social Deviancy Among Youth, The Sixty-Fifth Yearbook of the National Society for the Study of Education*, ed. William W. Wattenberg (Chicago: University of Chicago Press, 1966), pp. 78–102.

26 The "corner boys," according to Cloward and Ohlin, "are not strongly oriented toward social mobility in any sphere" and are, as a result, less likely to be delinquent than those desiring material success (*Delinquency and Opportunity*, p. 97). Insofar as these distinctions are useful and meaningful, control theory would suggest that those not oriented to any kind of social mobility would be most likely to be delinquent.

Table 66 / Percent Committing Two or More Delinquent Acts by Purpose of Job

"The only reason to have a job is for money."				
Strongly Agree	Agree	Undecided	Disagree	Strongly Disagree
32 (98)	26 (239)	18 (242)	17 (476)	6 (193)

reason for having a job, cannot be said to be strongly motivated toward either the middle-class life style or toward wealth; students disagreeing with these statements come very close to fitting the Cloward–Ohlin picture of the delinquent: they want wealth more than other things, and whatever they want, they want with some force. Is the latter or the former more likely to be delinquent (Table 67)? [27]

In three of the four family-status groups, the delinquency rate is lower among ambitious seekers of money. In the group lowest in family status, although the relation between ambition and delinquency is in the direction predicted by the Cloward–Ohlin hypothesis, the difference is minuscule. Given three differences in the direction opposed to the hypothesis, and one comparison (admittedly the crucial one) showing virtually no difference, the Cloward–Ohlin hypothesis may be said to be, as judged by the present data, false.[28]

Table 67 / Average Number of Self-Reported Delinquent Acts by Ambition and Family Status—Among Those Agreeing That "The Only Reason to Have a Job Is for Money"

	Family Status			
Ambition	Lower	Semi-Skilled and Skilled Manual	White Collar	Professional
High	1.03 (24)	.76 (53)	.58 (19)	.87 (28)
Low	.98 (48)	.86 (78)	1.44 (28)	1.16 (21)

Commitment to a High-Status Occupation

In contemporary American society, higher education is virtually a necessary condition for a high-status occupation. As the experience of lower-class persons and Negroes shows, however, higher education is by no means a sufficient condition for such occupations.[29] (This fact is poorly communicated to Negro youth, who are likely to see attainment of a "good" education as more difficult than attainment of a "good" job.) In the context of present concerns, the distinction between educational and occupational aspirations is not critical: either should inhibit delinquent activity, since the higher the aspiration, whether educational or occupational, the greater the perceived cost of such activity.

We proceed, then, directly to the strain hypothesis that high occupational aspirations coupled with low occupational expectations generate pressure resulting in delinquency (Table 68).

As was true with respect to educational aspirations, the proportion of students whose occupational aspirations exceed their expectations is small: frustrated occupational ambition cannot be an important cause of delinquency in the present sample. As was also true with respect to educational aspirations, but is even clearer in the present case, *the higher the aspiration, the lower the rate of delinquency, regardless of the student's expectations.* The data are again opposite to the prediction stemming from strain theory.

And, once again, some strain theories are not directly falsified by data such as those shown in Table 68. Cloward and Ohlin, for example, repeatedly affirm that the explanation the person advances for his failure to attain his goal is crucial in determining the reaction that ensues. If he blames himself, the system remains unchallenged, and he is not likely to turn to delinquency. If, however, he perceives (more or less correctly) that the fault lies in social forces over which he has no control, he becomes alienated from the system, rejects its normative patterns, and turns to delinquency.[30]

Many items on the questionnaire deal with the student's perception of the obstacles between him and his desired occupation. If we turn again to the Negro boys, we find items offering a direct contrast between blaming the social system and blaming one's self for failure, especially in light of a specification offered by Cloward and Ohlin: "The efforts of reformers to expose discriminatory practices actually furnish such persons with further justification for withdrawing sentiments in support of the legitimacy of the established norms and free them to attribute legitimacy to alternative norms which may be both legally and morally proscribed by the dominant system." [31]

Table 68 / Average Number of Self-Reported Delinquent Acts by Desired and Expected Occupation

	Job Desired		
Job Expected	Professional	White Collar	Manual
Professional	.66 (565)	— (22)[a]	— (14)[a]
White collar	.53 (34)	.71 (118)	— (16)[a]
Manual	.90 (65)	.93 (32)	.97 (243)

[a] Aspiration-expectation logic suggests that many of the cases in these cells represent response errors, since a student who wants a low-status occupation should be able to get it. Since the occupational questions were relatively complicated, the errors suggested here, few as they are, misrepresent the overall quality of the data.

27 As in most of the tests of control versus some version of strain theory involving three variables, I know the marginal relations in advance of running the three-variable tables. And, as usual, I know that the strain theory is predicting a "specification" in which the original relation reverses in one of the partials. It is not that my operationalizations stack the cards against these theories, but that they explicitly theorize such reversals. The strain theorists would undoubtedly grant that in general the higher the aspiration the lower the delinquency rate; they would also grant that in general the higher the expectation the lower the delinquency rate. Thus the hypothesis that, among those with little expectations, the higher the aspiration the higher the delinquency rate, is a hypothesis which states that, among some sub-group, the relation between some variable and delinquency is opposite to that found in the population as a whole.

28 Cloward and Ohlin do not intend their theory to account for delinquent acts anywhere in the class structure. It is designed to account for lower-class, urban, gang delinquency. Even so these data are relevant to the theory, and their implications for the theory should, I think, be spelled out.

29 Seymour Martin Lipset and Reinhard Bendix, *Social Mobility in Industrial Society* (Berkeley: University of California Press, 1959), pp. 91–101.

30 *Delinquency and Opportunity*, pp. 112, 117–118.

31 *Delinquency and Opportunity*, p. 122.

Table 69 / Average Number of Delinquent Acts by Perceptions of Racial Discrimination and Personal Incompetence as Potential Obstacles to Occupational Success—Negro Boys Only

"Do you think that any of the following things will keep you from getting the kind of job you want to have eventually?"

"Am Not Smart Enough"	Racial Discrimination		
	Yes	Maybe	No
Yes	.88 (48)	.89 (58)	.65 (45)
Maybe	.89 (43)	.83 (156)	1.00 (51)
No	.81 (43)	.91 (147)	.82 (155)

The Negro boy convinced of his own competence and convinced that racial discrimination will prevent him from attaining his goals is, according to this hypothesis, a prime candidate for delinquency. His anticipated failure stems not from personal shortcomings, but from injustice. At another extreme,[32] the Negro boy convinced of his own incompetence and unaware of racial discrimination has no one to blame but himself. He has no excuse for violating the rules of a society prepared to give him all he has earned.

In Table 69, the average number of delinquent acts committed by Negro boys prepared to blame themselves but not racial discrimination for occupational failure is .65; the corresponding average for boys blaming racial discrimination rather than themselves is .81. The general thrust of the results of this test is not, however, in a direction favorable to the Cloward–Ohlin hypothesis. In general, it does not matter whether the boy blames himself or the social system for potential failure; ascription of blame is essentially unrelated to the commission of delinquent acts.

[32] As with any typological independent variable, at least four types are possible and each requires a subtheory. Cloward and Ohlin imply that the "both" and the "neither" cells are empty, that the lower class boy either blames himself or the system.

Social Learning and Deviant Behavior: A Specific Test of a General Theory

Ronald L. Akers, Marvin D. Krohn, Lonn Lanza-Kaduce, and Marcia Radosevich
University of Iowa

A social learning theory of deviant behavior is tested with survey data on adolescent drinking and drug behavior. The theory is strongly supported. The major explanatory variables from that theory, *differential association, differential reinforcement, definitions,* and *imitation* combine to account for 68% of the variance in marijuana use (39% of abuse) and 55% of the variance in alcohol use (32% of abuse) by adolescents. The study demonstrates that central learning concepts are amenable to questionnaire measurement, and the findings indicate that social learning theory will do well when tested with other forms of deviant behavior.

INTRODUCTION

In the last decade we have seen a dramatic shift away from sociological explanations of deviant behavior toward developing theoretical perspectives on societal reactions to and definitions of deviance and crime. Labelling and conflict formulations have become major foci of sociological theorizing as well as the sounding boards for most of the controversy and discourse in the field of deviance. This shift in focus was deemed necessary to redress the previous imbalance of attention to the deviant behavior itself (Akers, 1968), and it clearly has had that effect. Unfortunately, it also has led to the neglect of theoretical developments in the etiology of deviant behavior. Neither labelling nor conflict perspectives has offered a general explanation of deviant behavior, although some conflict theorists have offered preliminary but incomplete efforts in that direction (Taylor, et al., 1973; Spitzer, 1975). There have been other efforts directed toward explaining deviant behavior, but these have been fairly narrow in scope; they have usually been limited either to a specific type of deviant behavior or to a restricted range of substantive variables. For example, a good deal of attention has been paid to the modern resurrection of deterrence theory (Gibbs, 1975; 1977; Waldo and Chiricos, 1972; Tittle, 1975; Silberman, 1976; Erickson et al., 1977; Meier and Johnson, 1977; Geerken and Gove, 1977). The scope of deterrence theory has been changed little, however, since its statement by the classical criminologists two centuries ago and is limited to the actual or perceived certainty, severity, and celerity of formally administered legal sanctions for violations of the criminal law. Another example is Travis Hirschi's (1969) control (social bonding) theory which is a more general explanation of deviance than deterrence theory, but which is, in turn, primarily restricted to informal social control which comes from individuals being bonded to groups and institutions.

The most notable exception to the diminished attention to general explanations of deviant behavior is a form of social learning theory developed first by Robert L. Burgess and Ronald L. Akers as differential association-reinforcement theory (Burgess and Akers, 1966; Akers et al., 1968) and elaborated on later by Akers (1973; 1977). As the name which Burgess and Akers originally chose to apply to this theoretical perspective makes clear, it was constructed as a revision of Edwin H. Sutherland's differential association theory (Sutherland, 1947; Sutherland and Cressey, 1974) in terms of general behavioral reinforcement theory (Skinner, 1953; 1959; Bandura and Walters, 1963; Bandura, 1969; 1977; Staats, 1975).[1] So-

* Direct all communications to: Ronald L. Akers; Department of Sociology; University of Iowa; Iowa City, IA 52242.

The research was conducted while the authors were on the research staff of The Boys Town Center for the Study of Youth Development (Boys Town, Neb.). We gratefully acknowledge the support of the Center and express our appreciation to its director, Dr. Ronald Feldman and his computer, library, and administrative staff for their fine cooperation. We especially thank Matthew Lambert for the fine job he did for us on the project. Appreciation is expressed to the school officials, teachers, and students who cooperated in the survey. We are also appreciative of the parents who agreed to have their sons and daughters take part.

[1] The label *social learning* has been applied to other theories based on reinforcement principles but the Burgess and Akers formulation is the first and only one which ties general learning theory to a long-standing sociological theory and is directed towards specific forms of deviant behavior (crime, delinquency, drug addiction, suicide, etc.). It is to this theory that social learning usually refers when used here. It will be clear from the context when this is not the case.

From *American Sociological Review,* Vol. 44 (August 1979), pp. 636–655. Reprinted by permission of the American Sociological Association and the authors.

cial learning theory as a general perspective in deviance is part of a larger move toward incorporation of modern behaviorism into sociological theory (Homans, 1961; Burgess and Bushell, 1969; Kunkel, 1975; Hamblin et al., 1971; Emerson, 1969; 1972; Kunkel and Nagasawa, 1973; Burgess and Nielsen, 1974; Chadwick-Jones, 1976; for reviews of the relevance of behavioral theory for sociology see Friedrichs, 1974; Tarter, 1973). As such it is a theoretical perspective which is compatible with the more specific forays into the explanation of deviant behavior. Indeed, the major features of such theories as deterrence and control theories (Hirschi, 1969) can be subsumed under the principles of social learning theory (Akers, 1977; Conger, 1976; 1977; Feldman, 1977). However, all too often the relevance for social learning theory of some of the deviance research has been ignored or unrecognized even when the authors employ central learning concepts such as reinforcement (Harris, 1975; 1977; Eaton, 1974; Meier and Johnson, 1977; Hirschi and Hindelang, 1977). This inattention is regrettable for, while other theories delineate the structural variables (class, race, anomic conditions, breakdown in social control, etc.) that yield differential rates of deviance, social learning stresses the behavioral mechanisms by which these variables produce the behavior comprising the rates. As such, social learning is complementary to other sociological theories and could be used to integrate extant formulations to achieve more comprehensive explanations of deviance (in this regard see Akers, 1977:63–8).

The basic learning principles on which this theory is based have received empirical support under laboratory and applied experimental conditions (see Skinner, 1953; Honig, 1966; Ullmann and Krasner, 1969; Bandura, 1969; 1977; McLaughlin, 1971; Staats, 1975). Also, prior research has been supportive of differential association theory (J. Ball, 1957; Short, 1957; Voss, 1964; R. Ball, 1968; Krohn, 1974; Jensen, 1972; Burkett and Jensen, 1975). However, there has been little direct research on learning principles as applied to deviant behavior in natural settings. Akers (1977) has organized a large body of existing research and theory on a wide range of deviant behavior supportive of or consistent with social learning, but his effort is a post hoc application of theoretical principles for he does not present research designed explicitly to test propositions from the theory (in this regard see also Feldman, 1977). The results of other studies are consistent with Akers's social learning approach (Jessor and Jessor, 1975; Thomas et al., 1975), and a couple of studies explicitly testing social learning using secondary data analysis have found support for it (Anderson, 1973; Conger, 1976). However, more crucial and conclusive tests await collecting the relevant primary data in the community. The present study does that. Our purpose here is to report a specific test of social learning theory using standard sociological techniques of data collection and data analysis.

STATEMENT OF SOCIAL LEARNING THEORY

The social learning theory tested here is summarized from Akers (1977:39–68). The primary learning mechanism in social behavior is operant (instrumental) conditioning in which behavior is shaped by the stimuli which follow, or are consequences of the behavior. Social behavior is acquired both through direct conditioning and through *imitation* or modelling of others' behavior. Behavior is strengthened through reward (positive reinforcement) and avoidance of punishment (negative reinforcement) or weakened by aversive stimuli (positive punishment) and loss of reward (negative punishment). Whether deviant or conforming behavior is acquired and persists depends on past and present rewards or punishments for the behavior and the rewards and punishments attached to alternative behavior—*differential reinforcement*. In addition, people learn in interaction with significant groups in their lives evaluative *definitions* (norms, attitudes, orientations) of the behavior as good or bad. These definitions are themselves verbal and cognitive behavior which can be directly reinforced and also act as cue (discriminative) stimuli for other behavior. The more individuals define the behavior as good (positive definition) or at least justified (neutralizing definition) rather than as undesirable (negative definition), the more likely they are to engage in it.

The reinforcers can be nonsocial (as in the direct physiological effects of drugs) as well as social, but the theory posits that the principal behavioral effects come from interaction in or under the influence of those *groups which control individuals' major sources of reinforcement and punishment and expose them to behavioral models and normative definitions*. The most important of these groups with which one is in *differential association* are the *peer-friendship* groups and the *family* but they also include schools, churches, and other groups. Behavior (whether deviant or conforming) results from greater reinforcement, on balance, over punishing contingencies for the same behavior and the reinforcing-punishing contingencies on alternative behavior. The definitions are conducive to deviant behavior when, on balance, the positive and neutralizing definitions of the behavior offset negative definitions of it. Therefore, deviant behavior can be expected to the extent that it has been differentially reinforced over alternative behavior (conforming or other deviant behavior) and is defined as desirable or justified. Progression into more frequent or sustained use and into abuse is also determined by the extent to which a given pattern is sustained by the combination of the reinforcing effects of the substance with social reinforcement, exposure to models, definitions through association with using peers, and by the degree to which it is not deterred through bad effects of the substance and/or the negative sanctions from peers, parents, and the law.

The social learning theory proposes a process which orders and specifies the interrelationships among these variables. Differential association, which refers to interaction and identity with different groups, occurs first. These groups provide the social environments in which exposure to definitions, imitation of models, and social reinforcement for use of or abstinence from any particular substance take place. The definitions are learned through imitation, and social reinforcement of them by members of the groups with whom one is associated, and once learned, these definitions serve as discriminative stimuli for use or abstinence. The definitions in interaction with imitation of using or abstinent models and the anticipated balance of reinforcement produces the initial use or continued abstinence. After the initial use, imitation becomes less important while the effects of definitions should continue (themselves affected by the experience of use). It is at this point in the process that the actual consequences (social and nonsocial reinforcers and punishers) of the specific behavior come into play to determine the probability that use will be continued and at what level. These consequences include the actual effects of the substance at first and subsequent use (the perception of which may, of course, be modified by what effects the person has previously learned to expect) and the actual reactions of others present at the time or who find out about it later, as well as the anticipated reactions of others not present or knowing about the use.

From this depiction of them as aspects of the same learning process, we expect the independent variables to be positively interrelated, and we examine the zero-order relationships among them. Nonetheless, the major variables are conceptually distinct and our measures are empirically distinct enough that we do not expect their interrelationships to preclude separate independent effects. Thus, we also empirically order the independent variables in terms of how much variance is explained in the dependent variables. We test the general hypothesis from the theory that adolescent marijuana and alcohol use and abuse are related to each of the major sets of variables and to all of them combined.

Specifically, we expect that for both alcohol and drugs, the probability of abstinence decreases and the frequency of use increases when there is greater exposure to using rather than to abstinent models, when there is more association with using than with abstinent peers and adults, when use is differentially reinforced (more rewards, fewer punishers) over abstinence, and when there are more positive or neutralizing than negative definitions of use. Similarly, among users the probability of abuse increases with more exposure to abusing rather than moderate or abstinent models, more association with high frequency users or abusers, greater differential reinforcement for abuse over more moderate use, and with more positive and neutralizing rather than negative definitions of use.

RESEARCH ON ADOLESCENT DRUG AND ALCOHOL BEHAVIOR

Adolescent drug and drinking behavior is a particularly strategic area for the current effort for two reasons. First, the area is characterized by the narrow scope of current theories of deviant behavior outlined above. The research has been largely restricted to the prevalence and sociodemographic and social-psychological correlates of teenage drinking and drug use (Abelson et al., 1973; Johnston, 1973; Block et al., 1974; National Commission on Marijuana and Drug Abuse, 1972; Drug Abuse Council, 1975; Rachal et al., 1975; O'Donnell et al., 1976). Little has been done to develop and test explanations of the behavior drawn from general theories. (For a full and comprehensive review of the theory and research literature on adolescent drinking and drug use, see Radosevich et al., forthcoming.) One notable exception to this is the work of the Jessors (Jessor et al., 1968; 1970; 1973; Jessor and Jessor, 1975; 1977; Jessor, 1976) who have built a social-psychological theory of "problem behavior" (deviance) which incorporates part of Rotter's (1954) learning theory (locus of control) and other personality and social variables. Their theory, which is also a version of social learning, consists of three categories of variables—personality, social, and behavioral. Their findings tend to support parts (primarily the social component) of the theory. The Jessors' findings point to the second reason why adolescent drug use and drinking promises to be a fruitful area in which to examine social learning theory; that is, the research on social psychological correlates of drug use and drinking lends support to the relevance of many of the variables in the social learning theory tested here. For instance, research consistently finds that those holding tolerant or positive attitudes toward a substance are much more likely to use it than those holding negative attitudes toward it (Fejer and Smart, 1973; Johnston, 1973; Jessor et al., 1973; Calhoun, 1974; Kendall, 1976). Also, peer and parental influence have been found to be important variables in teenage drug and drinking behavior. Users are more likely than abstainers to associate with peers who are also users and this relationship remains whether friends' use is measured by or independently of the individual's perception of friends' use. (For a review of this research on parental and peer influences see Akers, 1977; recent studies to see are Pearce and Garrett, 1970; Kandel, 1973; 1974; Jessor et al., 1972; O'Donnell et al., 1976; Tec, 1974a; 1974b; Krohn, 1974; Wechsler and Thum, 1973; Kendall, 1976; Lawrence and Velleman, 1974.) Further, the research findings seem to be consistent with the causal ordering of these variables proposed by social learning: the youngster associates with peers who are users, learns definitions favorable to use of the substance, and then uses (Jessor et al., 1973; Krohn, 1974).

METHODOLOGY

Sample and Procedure

Data were collected by administering a self-report questionnaire to 3,065 male and female adolescents attending grades 7 through 12 in seven communities in three midwestern states. A two-stage sample design was followed. First, we selected schools from within each participating school district which were representative in terms of school size and location within the district. In smaller districts this meant selecting all or most of the junior and senior high schools in the district. Secondly, we sampled two to three classrooms (depending on school and average class size) per grade level from among the required or general enrollment classes. Thus, although classrooms were sampled, each student has an approximately equal chance of being included in the sample.[2] The questionnaire (which was pretested in a district not included in the final sample) was administered to all students in attendance in the selected classes on the day of the survey who had obtained written parental permission. The attrition from this parental permission procedure combined with absenteeism on the day of the the survey was not great and 67% of the total number of students enrolled (95% of those with parental permission) in the sampled classes completed the questionnaire.[3]

A small subsample, purposively sampled from among respondents who volunteered in five of the seven districts (n=106, approximately 5% of the sample in these districts), was interviewed two to eight weeks after the administration of the questionnaire. The follow-up interview was intended to serve as a reliability and partial validity check on the questionnaire responses and to provide additional descriptive information. The interviews were conducted individually in private rooms at school during school hours.

Reliability and Validity

Prior research has consistently shown that the self-report questionnaire technique is reliable and valid in measuring adolescent delinquent, drug, and drinking behavior (Hardt and Peterson-Hardt, 1977; Groves, 1974; Block et al., 1974; Single et al., 1975; Whitehead and Smart,

[2] Our primary aim was to test an explanation of drug and drinking behavior and we had no plans to generalize about the prevalence or sociodemographic variations to a wider national or regional population. Therefore, there was no attempt to get a probability sample or to insure that the total sample was regionally or nationally representative. We did plan to report findings to the participating school districts and to generalize findings within each district. Also, we wanted to follow a design which would require the involvement of as few schools and school personnel as possible, which would minimize adjustments needed in the school routine, and which would facilitate administration of the questionnaire to groups of respondents. The sampling of a limited number of classrooms from within each selected school best served these purposes. We believe that being alert to the problem of minimizing interference of the survey into the school routine and proposing the sampling procedure which we followed was a significant element in gaining the approval and cooperation of the school officials. The resultant sample was sufficiently representative within each district that we could make reasonable generalizations about the drug and drinking problem in the district. Whether two or three classes per grade level were sampled from each school depended on the size of the classes. We tried to include enough classes to secure responses from at least 10% of the total school enrollment or a minimum of 100 respondents per school, whichever was greater, to help protect the confidentiality of respondents in the smaller schools.

[3] Overall, 74% of the parental permission forms distributed were returned (the lowest percentage of return in a district was 62% and the highest return rate was 93%). The forms were first distributed by the researchers in the classrooms one week before the survey; then, one more visit was made to the classrooms to remind students to return the forms. For some classes, telephone calls were made to the parents of those students who had not returned the form. Without this call-back procedure, buttressed by telephone calls, the return rate would have been smaller. For the sample as a whole, 95% of those returning forms were granted parental permission to take part in the survey (we asked that the forms be returned whether permission was granted or denied). Ninety-five percent of those attended class and completed the questionnaire on the day of the survey.

1972). Our own checks in the present research confirm this. Internal consistency on interlocking questions was high (Gammas=.91 and higher). In addition, a comparison of the responses to the frequency and quantity of use questions on the questionnaire with responses to the same items given at the time of the interview demonstrated a high degree of reliability (Gammas=.89 and higher). Without exception the interview respondents reported that they believed the researchers assurances of confidentiality and that no one but the researchers would have access to identifiable answers; thus, all said that they felt secure in responding and answered questions both on the questionnaire and in the interview honestly.[4]

Measurement of Variables

Dependent variables. Abstinence-use of alcohol and marijuana is measured by a six-point frequency-of-use scale ranging from nearly every day to never. A quantity frequency (Q-F) scale was also computed but since there is a near perfect correlation between the Q-F scale and the frequency-of-use scale, the analysis here includes only the latter measure.[5]

Abuse among users is measured by combining responses to the frequency questions with responses to a question asking the respondents to check whether or not they had experienced on more than one occasion any of a list of problems while or soon after using alcohol or marijuana.[6] This combination produced a four-point abuse scale ranging from heavy abuse to no abuse.

Independent variables. From the summary of social learning theory presented above it can be seen that the main concepts to be measured are *imitation*, *differential association*, *definitions*, and *differential reinforcement*. For the present analysis, we distinguish between differential reinforcement comprised of social reinforcement combined with non-social reinforcement (experienced or anticipated drug or alcohol effects) and that comprised only of social reinforcement. Each of the resulting five concepts are operationalized by a set of items measuring different aspects of each concept. (The Appendix provides a brief description of the way the five concepts are measured.) These five clusters of variables (a total of 15 variables in the abstinence-use analysis and 16 variables in the abuse analysis) constitute the independent variables in this analysis.[7]

---

[4] Careful steps were taken to protect the rights of both questionnaire and interview respondents and of the school districts. The usual university procedures were followed regarding approval of the project's procedures for protection of the rights of research participants. At the time of the first visit to the classrooms, the students were informed of the survey and each one present was given an envelope containing a letter explaining the purpose and content of the study to the parents and the parental consent form mentioned in fn. 3. The students were told that participation in the study was completely voluntary. It was made clear that no student had to participate as a condition for class credit or any other school requirement and that approval of the study by the district and school officials in no way made participation mandatory. All of the responses were and are held in strictest confidence. In five of the districts, respondents who were willing to be interviewed later were asked to indicate that willingness and to sign their questionnaires. Also, it was possible for anyone to place his or her name on the questionnaire even if not volunteering for an interview (and many did just that). To protect the confidentiality of those volunteering for an interview, all respondents, whether signing the name sheet or not, separated it from the rest of the questionnaire and deposited it in a separate box from the one in which the completed questionnaires were deposited. Only the research staff had and has access to the name lists which, when not in a locked drawer, were kept in a bank safety deposit box. All other respondents in these districts and all respondents in the other two districts where no interviews were conducted were anonymous. At the interview each respondent was again informed of the confidentiality of the information given. Upon completion of the interview, each respondent was paid the previously stipulated amount of $2.50 and signed a sheet acknowledging the voluntary nature of the interview and receipt of the payment. The list of interviewee's names was treated in the same way as the name sheets mentioned above. We also protected the identification of the school districts participating in the study. No community, school district, or school has been or will be identified by name in reports or disseminated findings.

[5] Alcohol use was measured by responses to separate questions on beer, wine, and liquor. The highest percentage of use and most frequent use was reported for beer, and since there is a very high correlation between use of the three forms of alcohol, use of alcohol in this analysis is measured only by reported frequency of use of beer.

[6] The problems included "had an accident," "couldn't remember later what I had done," "used more than I had planned." This is a fairly standard use of "problems associated with" as a nonclinical measure of abuse of some substance. It should not be confused with our measures of positive and negative consequences of use for the differential reinforcement variables. The questions used to measure abuse were asked separately from and never combined with the questions used to measure differential reinforcement.

[7] The concepts are clearly not equal in the scope of concrete empirical phenomena to which each refers. Differential association with family, peer, and other groups exposes the adolescent to using and nonusing models and normative definitions of use. It is in interaction in these groups in which the reactions of others differentially reinforce substance use or abstinent behavior. It is in this sense, then, that the differential association could include empirical referents of each of the other concepts and a general measure of differential association (in addition to being a measure of with whom one interacts), could

Table 1. Zero-Order Correlation Matrix for Variables Included in Alcohol Use Analysis (N = 2,414)*

Variables	1	2	3	4	5	6	7	8	9	10	11	12	13	14	15	16
1. Imitation	1.00															
2. Techniques of Neutralization	.05	1.00														
3. Law abiding/ violating definitions	.11	.40	1.00													
4. Positive/ negative definitions	.19	.39	.39	1.00												
5. Adult norm qualities	.18	.08	.14	.35	1.00											
6. Peer norm qualities	.17	.32	.33	.58	.29	1.00										
7. Differential peer association	.22	.32	.44	.49	.18	.48	1.00									
8. Praise for not using	.09	.19	.22	.24	.16	.24	.29	1.00								
9. Friends' reaction	.16	.32	.32	.41	.17	.45	.46	.26	1.00							
10. Parents' reaction	.14	.11	.11	.29	.33	.19	.27	.24	.26	1.00						
11. Informal deterrence	.03	.19	.18	.19	−.01	.16	.17	.12	.18	.02	1.00					
12. Formal deterrence	.02	.07	.12	.09	.01	.08	.06	.10	.12	−.005	.43	1.00				
13. Interference with activities	.05	.20	.24	.24	.07	.19	.23	.14	.18	10	.19	.14	1.00			
14. Rewards—costs of use	.14	.30	.31	.48	.18	.36	.42	.23	.41	.28	.21	.11	.23	1.00		
15. Reinforcement balance	.15	.36	.39	.47	.18	.37	.46	.21	.38	.23	.20	.09	.27	.44	1.00	
16. Alcohol use	.16	.34	.47	.52	.20	.40	.68	.28	.40	.29	.13	.04	.21	.44	.46	1.00

* In this and in all subsequent tables independent variables have been coded such that positive coefficients indicate the theoretically expected direction.

Method of analysis. Although most of the measures yield ordinal-level data, we will use multiple regression techniques. It has been demonstrated that regression can be confidently employed with ordinal data without introducing bias in the results (Labovitz, 1970; 1971; Kim, 1975). The use of regression techniques provides an overall summary of the explanatory power of the model while also allowing us to examine the unique effects of the five subsets of variables and of each separate variable.

PRESENTATION OF FINDINGS

Explaining Abstinence-Frequency of Use

The zero-order correlation matrices for the alcohol and marijuana use variables are presented in Tables 1 and 2.[8] As expected, most of the independent variables are related in a positive direction with variability in the strength of the relationships. Of particular interest are the relatively weak relationships of the deterrence items to the other variables, especially within the matrix on alcohol behavior. Also, note the strength of the relationships of both alcohol and marijuana use to those variables of associations with and attitudes of peers, to reinforcement balance, and to reward-costs of use, and note the interrelationships among these variables. These zero-order relationships anticipate our findings in the multivariate analysis to which we now turn.

The results of the regression analyses show strong support for the social learning theory of adolescent alcohol and drug behavior.[9] When all the independent variables are incorporated into the full regression equation, the model explains 55% of the variance in drinking behavior (abstinence-frequency of use; Table 3) and 68% of the variance in marijuana behavior (abstinence-frequency of use; Table 4).[10]

The power of the full model including the five subsets of variables, therefore, is demonstrated. But, we are also interested in determining the relative predictive values of the subsets and single variables to see if each part of the theory is supported. We do this in two ways. First, we regress the dependent variables on all variables and each subset of variables in separate regression equations. This provides a partial regression coefficient for each variable in each equation and estimates of the total amount of variance explained by each subset (Tables 3 and 4). Second, we compute the proportion of variance which the remaining subsets explain when each subset in turn is eliminated from the equation. By subtracting each of these values from the proportion of variance explained by the full equation, we have a measure of how much explained variance is lost when a given subset of variables is eliminated. The larger the proportion of explained variance lost (or the smaller the explained variance remaining) when a subset is eliminated, the greater its relative explanatory power (Table 5). By analyzing the data in this fashion, we also circumvent potential problems of multicollinearity among the variables within each subset since our primary concern is with the relative explanatory power of the different subsets of variables and not with the relative power of individual variables within subsets.

With the exception of imitation, each subset explains a substantial proportion of variance in both alcohol and marijuana use. The findings presented in Table 5 show that even when the most predictive subset of variables is eliminated the remaining variables are still able to explain 43% and 56% of the variance in alcohol and marijuana behavior, respectively. The fact that four of the five subsets of variables taken from social learning theory *each* explains a substantial proportion of the variance (and that the fifth is significantly related to the dependent variables in the expected direction) demonstrates that the theory as a whole is supported; its power is not dependent on any single component.

However, the analyses also plainly show that some subsets of variables specified by the theory are more important than others. They are ranked in terms of relative effectiveness in explaining

Table 2. Zero-Order Correlation Matrix for Variables Included in Marijuana Use Analysis (N = 2,395)

Variables	1	2	3	4	5	6	7	8	9	10	11	12	13	14	15	16
1. Imitation	1.00															
2. Techniques of neutralization	.23	1.00														
3. Law abiding/ violating definitions	.26	.23	1.00													
4. Positive/ negative	.39	.45	.53	1.00												
5. Adult norm qualities	.15	.16	.19	.28	1.00											
6. Peer norm qualities	.32	.38	.38	.63	.28	1.00										
7. Differential peer association	.38	.41	.47	.71	.24	.59	1.00									
8. Praise for not using	.15	.25	.24	.32	.13	.30	.32	1.00								
9. Friends' reaction	.32	.37	.39	.55	.18	.52	.59	.29	1.00							
10. Parents' reaction	.12	.10	.13	.20	.18	.13	.18	.09	.18	1.00						
11. Informal deterrence	.18	.24	.28	.38	.08	.31	.33	.18	.32	.11	1.00					
12. Formal deterrence	.11	.18	.22	.22	.01	.17	.18	.12	.20	.10	.49	1.00				
13. Interference with activities	.19	.27	.28	.39	.13	.30	.35	.20	.28	.13	.24	.17	1.00			
14. Rewards—costs of use	.33	.40	.43	.67	.17	.51	.56	.29	.52	.16	.39	.24	.35	1.00		
15. Reinforcement balance	.31	.41	.44	.61	.19	.47	.53	.25	.46	.18	.32	.18	.38	.59	1.00	
16. Marijuana use	.38	.48	.40	.72	.24	.50	.79	.29	.50	.18	.31	.15	.36	.15•	.52	1.00

serve as a general, albeit indirect, index of the combined effects of social reinforcement, imitation, and exposure to normative definitions. But such an index could not distinguish among the specific mechanisms of taking on definitions, imitating, and reinforcing of behavior which occur within the groups with which one is differentially associated. The combined social/nonsocial reinforcement subset obviously includes a wider array of concrete reinforcers than the subset of only social reinforcers. But, while reinforcement is the most abstract concept, the concrete set of events to which our measures here refer makes neither the social/nonsocial reinforcement, nor the social reinforcement subset broader than the definitions subset. Since it refers specifically to observing the behavior of someone else without reference to attitudes toward or consequences of the behavior, the imitation subset represents the most limited range of phenomena.

[8] The zero-order matrices for the abuse variables not presented here are similar to those for use.

[9] The total N in the tables varies because of attrition due to listwise deletion of missing values. The respondents who were eliminated were not significantly different from those included on sociodemographic characteristics and on the dependent variable. We also computed the regression analysis employing pairwise deletion and obtained similar results.

[10] This general level of explained variance and the relationships of the separate independent variables to the dependent variables held when we controlled for such variables as SES and sex (which were not related to the dependent variables) and when we controlled for such variables as grade in school and type of school district (which were related to the dependent variables).

Table 3. Partial Regression Coefficients in Standard Form for Alcohol Use (N = 2,414)

Independent Variables	All Independent Variables	Imitation	Definitions	Differential Association	Differential Reinforcement: Social	Differential Reinforcement: Social/Nonsocial
1. Imitation	−.014	.161				
2. Techniques of neutralization	.040		.086			
3. Law abiding/violating definitions	.142		.288			
4. Positive/negative definitions	.160		.372			
5. Adult norm qualities	.002			.068		
6. Peer norm qualities	−.055			.071		
7. Differential peer association	.458			.629		
8. Praise for not using	.035				.141	
9. Friends' reaction	.008				.290	
10. Parents' reaction	.059				.168	
11. Informal deterrence	−.026				.060	
12. Formal deterrence	−.021				−.045	
13. Interference with activities	−.005				.119	
14. Rewards—costs of use	.067					.326
15. Reinforcement balance	.093					.301
R =	.738	.161	.598	.683	.483	.532
R^2 =	.545	.026	.357	.466	.233	.283

variance in alcohol and marijuana use as follows: (1) differential association, (2) definitions, (3) combined social/nonsocial differential reinforcement, (4) differential social reinforcement, and (5) imitation.[11] Not only does the differential association subset explain the highest proportion of variance, but the differential peer association variable is the most important single variable. The definitions subset accounts for the second highest proportion of variance, and one's positive/negative definitions of the substances is the second most predictive single variable, while one's law-abiding/violating definitions rank third among the single variables. The differential reinforcements variables are next, followed by imitation variables which explain the least amount of variance in the dependent variables.

The fact of peer group influence on substance use comes as no surprise; it is documented by several previous studies. But, previous studies have not shown what the mechanisms are by which peer influence is exerted, and why, therefore, peer group association is so important. Our data show, as predicted by social learning theory, what these mechanisms are—friends provide social reinforcement or punishment for abstinence or use, provide normative definitions of use and abstinence, and, to a lesser extent, serve as admired models to imitate. This is indicated by the fact that these other variables, on their own, explain a substantial amount of the variance in marijuana and alcohol behavior when the effect of the differential peer association variable is removed. The fact that differential interaction explains more variance in the dependent variables than do the reinforcement, definitions, and imitation variables indicates that there may be additional variables at work in interaction beyond those identified by social learning theory, that there are additional effects of the mechanisms specified by our theory which are not captured by our measures of them, or that there are effects of other learning variables which we have not included (e.g., discriminative stimuli in the interactional setting in which reinforcement takes place).

Since social learning theory includes modelling as an important part of the pro-

[11] It is possible that the relative explanatory power of each subset may be due in part to the different number of variables that are contained within each subset. To examine this possibility we selected the most predictive variable from each subset and entered those variables in a multiple regression equation. The result produced no change in the rank ordering of the concepts in either the alcohol or marijuana equation. This also allowed us to examine the possible effects of multicollinearity within subsets on the relative explanatory power of single variables. Again the results were similar to those obtained above, indicating small multicollinearity effects.

Table 4. Partial Regression Coefficients in Standard Form for Marijuana Use (N = 2,395)

Independent Variables	All Independent Variables	Imitation	Definitions	Differential Association	Differential Reinforcement: Social	Differential Reinforcement Social/Nonsocial
1. Imitation	.033	.378				
2. Techniques of neutralization	.016		.070			
3. Law abiding/violating definitions	.054		.123			
4. Positive/negative definitions	.257		.619			
5. Adult norm qualities	.018			.057		
6. Peer norm qualities	−.080			.038		
7. Differential peer association	.550			.751		
8. Praise for not using	.001				.118	
9. Friends' reaction	−.016				.366	
10. Parents' reaction	.006				.063	
11. Informal deterrence	.007				.139	
12. Formal deterrence	−.035				−.044	
13. Interference with activities	.034				.196	
14. Rewards—costs of use	.016					.280
15. Reinforcement balance	.082					.410
R =	.826	.378	.728	.790	.579	.618
R^2 =	.683	.143	.530	.625	.335	.382

cess, the lower levels of variance explained by our imitation measures may seem surprising. However, the relatively weak effect of the imitation subset on our frequency of use and abuse measures was not unexpected. First, imitation refers to the narrowest empirical phenomenon among our measures (see footnote 7) and while, as we have noted, multicollinearity is not a severe problem, the interrelationships specified in the theory would indicate that removing imitation has less effect because its impact is still reflected to some extent in the remaining broader measures. Second, and more important, as indicated in the process outlined in the statement of the theory above, imitation in social learning theory is considered to have its greatest effect in the first acquisition or initial stages of behavior while the associational, reinforcement, and definitional variables are more important in the maintenance of a behavioral pattern. We expect imitation to be more important in first starting to use than we find it to be in explaining frequency of use as analyzed here (but still probably not more important than definitional and reinforcement variables). The analysis here which employs frequency of using as the dependent variable militates against finding a large effect for imitation variables. We would expect imitation to be even less important in accounting for maintenance of abusive patterns of use.

It is evident that social learning theory has been shown to be a powerful explanation of whether youngsters abstain from or are users of alcohol and marijuana. As predicted by the theory, the adolescents in our sample use drugs or alcohol to the extent that the behavior has been differentially reinforced through association in primary groups and defined as more desirable than, or at least as justified as, refraining from use. The next step in testing the validity of this perspective will be to examine how well these same variables account for levels of abuse of alcohol and drugs.

Table 5. Results from Regression Analysis Alternately Eliminating Subsets from the Full Equations for Alcohol and Marijuana Use

	Alcohol Use (N = 2,414)		Marijuana Use (N = 2,395)	
	When Subset Is Eliminated		When Subset Is Eliminated	
Subset Eliminated	R^2 Remaining =	Loss of Explained Variance =	R^2 Remaining =	Loss of Explained Variance =
Differential Association	.427	.118	.561	.122
Definitions	.510	.035	.657	.026
Imitation	.544	.001	.682	.001
Differential Reinforcement: Social	.539	.006	.681	.002
Differential Reinforcement: Social/Nonsocial	.535	.010	.679	.004
Full Equation R^2=	.545		.683	

Explaining Abusive Patterns of Use

The results of the analyses of alcohol and marijuana abuse among adolescents are presented in Tables 6, 7, and 8. For these analyses, only users are included.

The results parallel those of the analyses of abstinence-frequency of use reported above. Both marijuana and alcohol abuse are strongly related to the social learning variables. The proportion of variance explained in use-abuse is well below the explained variance in abstinence-frequency of use but it is still substantial—32% and 39% of the variance in alcohol and marijuana abuse, respectively. The differential association subset again explains the greatest proportion of variance (Tables 6 and 7), but, even without the differential association variables, the other variables in the model do well in accounting for the variance (22% and 30%; Table 8).

The variables are not ordered in terms of relative effectiveness in predicting abuse in the same way they were ranked in explaining abstinence-use. In the analysis of abstinence-use, definitions were the second most effective subset, whereas this subset ranks fourth in accounting for use-abuse while the differential reinforcement variables are ranked higher. In substance abuse the user comes more and more to respond to direct reinforcement, especially from the drug effects themselves; definitions would be expected to play a less significant role. This is shown fairly clearly when we examine the effect of adding an alcohol and marijuana effects variable which was not included in the previous analysis of abstinence-frequency of use. This variable was measured by asking using respondents to report the effects which they usually obtained from smoking marijuana or drinking alcohol.[12] This variable has the largest beta weight among the single variables making up the social/nonsocial differential reinforcement subset and ranks second for marijuana abuse and third for alcohol abuse among the entire set of single variables.

The variable of parental reaction appears to be related to abuse in the direction opposite to that found in the analysis of use. For the latter a lower probability of use is found for those reporting the strongest or harshest parental punishment while for the former a lower probability of abuse is found for those reporting lesser punishment or no parental response. A cross-tabular examination of these relationships reveals a curvilinear relationship between parental reaction and both adolescents' use and abuse of alcohol and marijuana. That is, higher frequency of use and abuse is found with parental response (actual or anticipated) at both the most lenient (encourage or do nothing) and the harshest end of the scale (take some drastic action such as kick the youngsters out of the house or turn them over to the police). The highest probability of abstinence and the lowest levels of use and abuse are found among adolescents who report that their parents have responded or would respond to their use with a moderate negative reaction such as a scolding. Our post hoc interpretation of these relationships is that anticipated parental punishment is a deterrent to use and sustains abstinence. Even after use has begun a reasonable amount of parental punishment holds down the chances of increasing frequency of use or moving into abuse. However, once adolescents have gotten into heavy use or abuse, parental reaction has lost its effect and the increasing abuse of the substances by their children may produce ever harsher reactions by parents in increasingly desperate attempts to do something about it.

While not contradictory to the theory, neither the difference between the amount of variance explained in abstinence-frequency of use and that explained in use-abuse for both alcohol and marijuana behavior nor the difference between the amount of variance explained in alcohol behavior and the amount explained in marijuana behavior was specifically anticipated. The lower level of explained variance in substance abuse than in substance use may be due simply to the fact that the variance in the abuse variables is restricted, thereby producing attenuation in the total variance explained. The differences in the explained variances in alcohol and marijuana behavior may be an artifact of our measurements, may indicate that the stimuli surrounding alcohol behavior are more uniform than those surrounding marijuana behavior, or may point to some real difference in the ability of the theory to account for the two kinds of substance use.

[12] Since abstainers could only report anticipated effects, the question of actual physical effects usually obtained from using the substances could not be included in the analyses of abstinence-frequency of use. Only among users are we able to differentiate between social and nonsocial reinforcement.

Table 6. Partial Regression Coefficients in Standard Form for Alcohol Abuse (N = 1,764)

Independent Variables	All Independent Variables	Imitation	Definitions	Differential Association	Differential Reinforcement: Social	Differential Reinforcement Social/Nonsocial
1. Imitation	.046	.128				
2. Techniques of neutralization	−.005		.007			
3. Law abiding/violating definitions	.094		.220			
4. Positive/negative definitions	.077		.200			
5. Adult norm qualities	.050			.065		
6. Peer norm qualities	−.010			.040		
7. Differential peer association	.351			.474		
8. Praise for not using	.025				.115	
9. Friends' reaction	.042				.123	
10. Parents' reaction	−.130				−.195	
11. Informal deterrence	−.030				.010	
12. Formal deterrence	−.030				−.041	
13. Interference with activities	−.014				.057	
14. Rewards—costs of use	.039					.141
15. Reinforcement balance	−.036					−.047
16. Usual effects of alcohol	.144					.315
R =	.561	.128	.334	.500	.261	.366
R^2 =	.315	.016	.111	.250	.068	.134

Table 7. Partial Regression Coefficients in Standard Form for Marijuana Abuse (N = 948)

Independent Variables	All Independent Variables	Imitation	Definitions	Differential Association	Differential Reinforcement: Social	Differential Reinforcement Social/Nonsocial
1. Imitation	.032	.098				
2. Techniques of neutralization	.036		.106			
3. Law abiding/violating definitions	.098		.182			
4. Positive/negative definitions	.090		.298			
5. Adult norm qualities	.000			.047		
6. Peer norm qualities	−.061			.030		
7. Differential peer association	.384			.533		
8. Praise for not using	−.004				.080	
9. Friends' reaction	.057				.198	
10. Parents' reaction	−.130				−.195	
11. Informal deterrence	−.010				.024	
12. Formal deterrence	−.040				−.067	
13. Interference with activities	.070				.201	
14. Rewards—costs of use	.064					.228
15. Reinforcement balance	−.020					−.022
16. Usual effects of marijuana	.130					.260
R =	.623	.098	.440	.556	.381	.393
R^2 =	.389	.010	.194	.310	.146	.154

SUMMARY AND CONCLUSIONS

In the past decade sociological attention in the study of deviance has shifted to explanations of the control system and away from the equally important task of proposing and testing general explanations of deviant behavior. We have presented a social learning perspective on deviant behavior developed during this same time period which holds promise as a general theory of the process of coming to engage in deviant acts but which had not been tested with primary data collected in the community and subjected to multivariate analysis. We have tested it here on specific forms of adolescent deviance—drug and alchol use and abuse.

The results of the tests support the theory. All of the dependent variables are strongly related to the social learning variables of differential association, definitions, differential reinforcement, and imitation. The most powerful of these independent variables is differential association. The other variables stand on their own, however, and explain substantial portions of variance even without the differential association measures (except for imitation which is the weakest of the variables for use and explains almost none of the variance in abuse).

The strength of empirical support for the theory suggests that the theory will have utility in explaining the use and abuse of other substances by adolescents. These findings also indicate that social learning theory will do well when tested with other forms of deviant behavior in future research. Future research could test the general theory in any number of specific contexts. We believe that our study demonstrates that the central learning concepts are amenable to meaningful questionnaire measurement and that social learning theory can be adequately tested with survey data. This is important given the lack of survey data measuring social learning concepts, and the collection and analysis of cross-sectional data presented here is a necessary step, but a first step, nonetheless. Therefore, the next steps in testing social learning theory not only should include analysis of the use and abuse of stronger and more severely disapproved substances than marijuana and alcohol (stimulants, depressants, psychedelics, and opiates), but also should include the collection of longitudinal data (Jessor and Jessor, 1977; Kandel, 1978). Longitudinal data will allow more adequate testing of the process of learning and temporal-ordering of variables in the theory.

Table 8. Results from Regression Analysis Alternately Eliminating Subsets from the Full Equations for Alcohol and Marijuana Abuse

	Alcohol Abuse (N = 1,764)		Marijuana Abuse (N = 948)	
	When Subset Is Eliminated		When Subset Is Eliminated	
Subset Eliminated	R^2 Remaining =	Loss of Explained Variance =	R^2 Remaining =	Loss of Explained Variance =
Differential Association	.222	.093	.296	.093
Definitions	.302	.013	.372	.017
Imitation	.313	.002	.388	.001
Differential Reinforcement: Social	.292	.023	.364	.025
Differential Reinforcement: Social/Nonsocial	.297	.018	.371	.018
Full Equation R^2=	.315		.389	

REFERENCES

Abelson, H. I., R. Cohen, D. Shrayer, and M. Rappeport
1973 "Drug experience, attitudes and related behavior among adolescents and adults." Pp. 488–867 in Drug Use in America: Problem in Perspective, Vol. 1. Report prepared by the National Commission on Marijuana and Drug Abuse.

Akers, Ronald L.
1968 "Problems in the sociology of deviance: social definitions and behavior." Social Forces 46:455–65.
1973 Deviant Behavior: A Social Learning Approach. Belmont: Wadsworth.
1977 Deviant Behavior: A Social Learning Approach. 2nd ed. Belmont: Wadsworth.

Akers, Ronald L., Robert L. Burgess and Weldon Johnson
1968 "Opiate use, addiction, and relapse." Social Problems 15:459–69.

Anderson, Linda S.
1973 "The impact of formal and informal sanctions on marijuana use: a test of social learning and deterrence." Master's thesis: Florida State University.

Ball, John C.
1957 "Delinquent and non-delinquent attitudes toward the prevalence of stealing." Journal of Criminal Law, Criminology and Police Science 48:259–74.

Ball, Richard A.
1968 "An empirical exploration of neutralization theory." Pp. 255–65 in Mark Lefton, James K. Skipper and Charles H. McCaghy (eds.), Approaches to Deviance. New York: Appleton-Century-Crofts.

Bandura, Albert
1969 Principles of Behavior Modification. New York: Holt, Rinehart and Winston.
1977 Social Learning Theory. Englewood Cliffs: Prentice-Hall.

Bandura, Albert and Richard H. Walters
1963 Social Learning and Personality Development. New York: Holt, Rinehart and Winston.

Block, J. R., N. Goodman, F. Ambellan and J. Revenson
1974 "A self-administered high school study of drugs." Hempstead: Institute for Research and Evaluation.

Burgess, Robert L. and Ronald L. Akers
1966 "A differential association-reinforcement theory of criminal behavior." Social Problems 14:128–47.

Burgess, Robert and Don Bushell (eds.)
1969 Behavioral Sociology. New York: Columbia University Press.

Burgess, Robert L. and Joyce McCarl Nielsen
1974 "An experimental analysis of some structural determinants of equitable and inequitable exchange relations." American Sociologcal Review 39:427–43.

Burkett, Steven and Eric L. Jensen
1975 "Conventional ties, peer influence, and the fear of apprehension: a study of adolescent marijuana use." Sociological Quarterly 16:522–33.

Calhoun, J. F.
1974 "Attitudes toward the sale and use of drugs: a cross-sectional analysis of those who use drugs." Journal of Youth and Adolescence 3:31–47.

Chadwick-Jones, J. K.
1976 Social Exchange Theory: Its Structure and Influence in Social Psychology. New York: Academic Press.

Conger, Rand D.
1976 "Social control and social learning models of delinquent behavior—a synthesis." Criminology 14:17–40.
1977 Rejoinder. Criminology 15:117–26.

Drug Abuse Council, Inc.
1975 Students and Drugs: A Report of the Drug Abuse Council (by Yankelovich, Skelly, and White, Inc.) Washington, D. C.: Drug Abuse Council.

Eaton, William W.
1974 "Mental hospitalization as a reinforcement process." American Sociological Review 39:252–60.

Emerson, Richard M.
1969 "Operant psychology and exchange theory." Pp. 379–405 in Robert L. Burgess and Don Bushell, Jr. (eds.), Behavioral Sociology. New York: Columbia University Press.
1972 "Exchange theory." Pp. 38–87 in Joseph Berger, Morris Zelditch, Jr. and Bo Anderson (eds.), Sociological Theories in Progress, Vol. 2. Boston: Houghton-Mifflin.

Erickson, Maynard L., Jack P. Gibbs and Gary F. Jensen
1977 "The deterrence doctrine and the perceived certainty of legal punishment." American Sociological Review 42:305–17.

Fejer, Dianne and Reginald G. Smart
1973 "The knowledge about drugs, attitudes toward them and drug use rates of high school students." Journal of Drug Education 3:377–88.

Feldman, M. P.
1977 Criminal Behavior: A Psychological Analysis. London: Wiley.

Friedrichs, Robert W.
1974 "The potential impact of B. F. Skinner upon American sociology." The American Sociologist 9:3–8.

Geerken, Michael and Walter R. Gove
1977 "Deterrence, overload, and incapacitation: an empirical evaluation." Social Forces 56:424–47.

Gibbs, Jack P.
1975 Crime, Punishment and Deterrence. New York: Elsevier.
1977 "Social control, deterrence, and perspectives on social order." Social Forces 56:408–23.

Groves, W. Eugene
1974 "Patterns of college student use and lifestyles." Pp. 241–75 in Eric Josephson and Eleanor E. Carrol (eds.), Drug Use: Epidemiological and Sociological Approaches. New York: Wiley.

Hamblin, Robert L., David Buckholdt, Daniel Ferritor, Martin Kozloff and Lois Blackwell
1971 The Humanization Process: A Social Behavioral Analysis of Children's Problems. New York: Wiley.

Hardt, Robert H. and Sandra Peterson-Hardt
1977 "On determining the quality of the delinquency self-report method." Journal of Research in Crime and Delinquency 14:247–61.

Harris, Anthony R.
1975 "Imprisonment and the expected value of criminal choice: a specification and test of aspects of the labeling perspective." American Sociological Review 40:71–87.
1977 "Sex and theories of deviance: toward a functional theory of deviant type-scripts." American Sociological Review 42:3–16.

Hirschi, Travis
1969 Causes of Delinquency. Berkeley and Los Angeles: University of California Press.

Hirschi, Travis and Michael J. Hindelang
1977 "Intelligence and delinquency; a revisionist review." American Sociological Review 42:571–87.

Homans, George C.
1961 Social Behavior: Its Elementary Forms. New York: Harcourt Brace Jovanovich.

Honig, Werner
1966 Operant Behavior: Areas of Research and Application. New York: Appleton-Century-Crofts.

Jensen, Gary F.
1972 "Parents, peers and delinquent action: a test of the differential association perspective." American Journal of Sociology 78:63–72.

Jessor, Richard
1976 "Predicting time of onset of marijuana use: a developmental study of high school youth." Journal of Consulting and Clinical Psychology 44:125–34.

Jessor, R., M. I. Collins and S. L. Jessor
1972 "On becoming a drinker: social-psychological aspects of an adolescent transition." Annals of the New York Academy of Science 197:199–213.

Jessor, R., T. D. Graves, R. C. Hanson and S. L. Jessor
1968 Society, Personality and Deviant Behavior: A Study of a Tri-Ethnic Community. New

York: Holt, Rinehart and Winston.

Jessor, R. and S. L. Jessor
1975 "Adolescent development and the onset of drinking: a longitudinal study." Journal of Studies on Alcohol 36:27–51.
1977 Problem Behavior and Psychosocial Development: A Longitudinal Study of Youth. New York: Academic Press.

Jessor, Richard, Shirley L. Jessor and John Finney
1973 "A social psychology of marijuana use: longitudinal studies of high school and college youth." Journal of Personality and Social Psychology 26:1–15.

Jessor, R., H. B. Young, E. B. Young and G. Tesi
1970 "Perceived opportunity, alienation, and drinking behavior among Italian and American youth." Journal of Personality and Social Psychology 15:215–22.

Johnston, L.
1973 Drugs and American Youth. Ann Arbor: Institute for Social Research.

Kandel, Denise
1973 "Adolescent marijuana use: role of parents and peers." Science 181:1067–70.
1974 "Interpersonal influences on adolescent illegal drug use." Pp. 207–40 in Eric Josephson and Eleanor E. Carrol (eds.), Drug Use: Epidemiological and Sociological Approaches. New York: Wiley
1978 Longitudinal Research on Drug Use. Ed. by D. Kandel. New York: Halsted.

Kendall, Richard Fenwick
1976 The Context and Implications of Drinking and Drug Use among High School and College Students. Ph.D. dissertation, Department of Psychology, New York University.

Kim, Jae-On
1975 "Multivariate analysis of ordinal variables." American Journal of Sociology 81:261–98.

Krohn, Marvin D.
1974 "An investigation of the effect of parental and peer associations on marijuana use: an empirical test of differential association theory." Pp. 75–89 in Marc Reidel and Terrence P. Thornberry (eds.), Crime and Delinquency: Dimensions of Deviance. New York: Praeger.

Kunkel, John H. and Richard H. Nagasawa
1973 "A behavioral model of man: propositions and implications." American Sociological Review 38:530–43.

Kunkel, John R.
1975 Behavior, Social Problems, and Change: a Social Learning Approach. Englewood Cliffs: Prentice-Hall.

Labovitz, Sanford
1970 "The assignment of numbers to rank order categories." American Sociological Review 35:515–24.
1971 "In defense of assigning numbers to ranks." American Sociological Review 36:521–22.

Lawrence, T. S. and J. O. Velleman
1974 "Correlates of student drug use in a suburban high school." Psychiatry 37:129–36.

McLaughlin, Barry
1971 Learning and Social Behavior. New York: Free Press.

Meier, Robert F. and Weldon T. Johnson
1977 "Deterrence as social control: the legal and extralegal production of conformity." American Sociological Review 42:292–304.

National Commission on Marijuana and Drug Abuse
1972 Marijuana: A Signal of Misunderstanding. New York: New American Library.

O'Donnell, John, Harwin L. Voss, Richard R. Clayton, and Robin G. W. Room
1976 Young Men and Drugs—A Nationwide Survey. Rockville: National Institute on Drug Abuse.

Pearce, J. and D. H. Garrett
1970 "A comparison of the drinking behavior of delinquent youth versus non-delinquent youth in the states of Idaho and Utah." Journal of School Health 40:131–5.

Rachal, J. V., J. R. Williams, M. L. Brehm, B. Cavanaugh, R. P. Moore, and W. C. Eckerman
1975 Adolescent Drinking Behavior, Attitudes and Correlates. National Institute on Alcohol Abuse and Alcoholism: U. S. Department of Health, Education and Welfare, Contract No. HSM 42–73–80 (NIA).

Radosevich, Marcia, Lonn Lanza-Kaduce, Ronald L. Akers and Marvin D. Krohn
Forthcoming "The sociology of adolescent drug and drinking behavior: a review of the state of the field: part 1,2." Deviant Behavior: An Interdisciplinary Journal.

Rotter, Julian
1954 Social Learning and Clinical Psychology. Englewood Cliffs: Prentice-Hall.

Short, James F.
1957 "Differential association and delinquency." Social Problems 4:233–9.

Silberman, Matthew
1976 "Toward a theory of criminal deterrence." American Sociological Review 41:442–61.

Single, Eric, Denise Kandel and Bruce D. Johnson
1975 "The reliability and validity of drug use responses in a large scale longitudinal survey." Journal of Drug Issues 5:426–43.

Skinner, B. F.
1953 Science and Human Behavior. New York: Macmillan.
1959 Cumulative Record. New York: Appleton-Century-Crofts.

Spitzer, Steven
1975 "Toward a Marxian theory of deviance." Social Problems 22:638–51.

Staats, Arthur
1975 Social Behaviorism. Homewood: Dorsey Press.

Sutherland, Edwin H.
1947 Principles of Criminology. 4th ed. Philadelphia: Lippincott.

Sutherland, Edwin H. and Donald R. Cressey
1974 Criminology. 9th ed. Philadelphia: Lippincott.

Tarter, Donald E.
1973 "Heeding Skinner's call: toward the development of a social technology." The American Sociologist 8:153–8.

Taylor, Ian, Paul Walton and Jack Young
1973 The New Criminology: for a Social Theory of Deviance. New York: Harper and Row.

Tec, Nechama
1974a Grass Is Green in Suburbia: A Sociological Study of Adolescent Usage of Illicit Drugs. Roslyn Heights: Libra.
1974b "Parent child drug abuse: generational countinuity or adolescent deviancy?" Adolescence 9:351–64.

Thomas, Charles W., David M. Petersen and Matthew T. Zingraff
1975 "Student drug use: a re-examination of the hang-loose ethic hypothesis." Journal of Health and Social Behavior 16:63–73.

Tittle, Charles R.
1975 "Deterrents or labeling?" Social Forces 53:399–410.

Ullmann, Leonard P. and Leonard Krasner
1969 A Psychological Approach to Abnormal Behavior. Englewood Cliffs: Prentice-Hall.

Voss, Harwin
1964 "Differential association and reported delinquent behavior: a replication." Social Problems 12:78–85.

Waldo, Gordon P. and Theodore Chiricos
1972 "Perceived penal sanction and self-reported criminality: a neglected approach to deterrence research." Social Problems 19:522–40.

Wechsler, Henry and Denise Thum
1973 "Teenage drinking, drug use, and social correlates." Quarterly Journal of Studies on Alcohol 34:1220–7.

Whitehead, P. C. and R. G. Smart
1972 "Validity and reliability of self-reported drug use." Canadian Journal of Criminology and Corrections 14:1–8.

APPENDIX

LIST OF SOCIAL LEARNING VARIABLES*

I. Imitation
  1. *Index of Imitation*
     Total of all the "admired" models (parents, friends, other adults, etc.) whom the respondent reports having observed using the substance.

II. Definitions Favorable or Unfavorable to Use
  2. *Techniques of Neutralization Scale*
     A scale of three items measuring Sykes and Matza's (1957) "techniques of neutralization" or definitions justifying or excusing use by "denial of injury," "denial of responsibility," or "condemning the condemnors." Item to scale interrelation for the scale referring to alcohol range from .68 to .76; for marijuana the range is from .68 to .78.
  3. *Scale of Law-Abiding or Law-Violating Definitions*
     A scale of items measuring obedient or violating attitudes toward the law in general and alcohol and drug laws in particular. Item to scale intercorrelations range from .53 to .76.
  4. *Positive or Negative Definitions of Use*
     Respondents' own approval or disapproval of use.

III. Differential Association
  5. *Significant Adults' Norm Qualities*
     Respondents' perception of the approving disapproving attitudes toward use held by adults whose opinions they value.
  6. *Significant Peers' Norm Qualities*
     Respondents' perception of the approving-disapproving attitudes toward use held by other teenagers whose opinions they value.
  7. *Differential Peer Association Scale*
     A scale of three items measuring how many of respondents' best friends, friends with whom they associate most often, and friends whom they have known for the longest time use the substance. Item to scale intercorrelations of the alcohol scale range from .85 to .96; for marijuana the range is from .83 to .96.

IV. Differential Reinforcement: Social
  8. *Praise for Not Using*
     Respondents' report as to whether or not friends, parents or both encouraged them *not* to use.
  9. *Friends' Rewarding or Punishing Reactions*
     Respondents' report of anticipated or actual positive or negative sanctions of friends to respondents' use of the substance, ranging from encouraging their use to turning them

*The variable numbers in this list correspond to the variable numbers in the regression tables. For all items, questions were asked separately for alcohol and marijuana. Copies of the questionnaire and list of concepts measured by questionnaire items are available on request.

in to the authorities.

10. *Parents' Rewarding or Punishing Reactions*
Respondents' report of anticipated or actual positive or negative sanctions of parents for respondents' use of the substance, ranging from encouraging their use to turning them in to the authorities.
11. *Informal Parental Deterrence*
Respondents' perceived probability that their parents would catch them if they used the substance.
12. *Formal Deterrence*
Respondents' perceived probability that the police would catch them if they used the substance.
13. *Interference with Other Important Activities*
Respondents' perception of the extent to which using the substance would interfere with their participation in activities (i.e., school work, athletics, etc.) important to them.

V. Differential Reinforcement: Combined Social/Nonsocial

14. *Index of Social/Nonsocial Rewards Minus Costs of Use*
The total good things from a list of positive drug effects and social outcomes which the using respondent checked as having actually experienced and the nonusing respondents checked as what they perceived they would experience as a result of using the substance *minus* the total bad things checked (there is an equal number of good and bad possible consequences in the list).
15. *Overall Reinforcement Balance*
Respondents' assessment of whether on balance mostly good things (such as "a good high or get along better with others") or mostly bad things (such as "a bad high or get into trouble") would (as perceived by nonusers if they were to use) or did (as reported by users when they used the substance) happen.
16. *Usual Effects Felt When Used*
Respondents' report of the effects the substance usually has on them (from no effect, to mostly good, to mostly bad effects). Asked only of those using more than once.

SECTION FIVE
Summary

The fact that the diverse theories represented in this section are all included as examples of sociological perspectives means that they do share certain fundamental assumptions in common. They all assume (1) that delinquency is not totally random and unpredictable, but rather (2) that it is more likely to occur under some sets of circumstances than others, and (3) that delinquent and law-abiding behaviors are learned behaviors. On the other hand, the theories differ on the circumstances emphasized and on specific views of where in society learning processes facilitate delinquency. Social learning theory has concentrated on the learning process and identified important aspects of the immediate social world that are crucial to the understanding of differential learning.

The theories presented are at odds with one another on a variety of issues, and in fact each typically developed as a partial repudiation of the emphasis in prior theories. Cohen is critical of Merton's illicit means theory and of social-disorganization-control theories. Miller attacks versions of strain theory, and Briar and Piliavin challenge Cohen, Miller, and other "motivational" theorists and construct a theory that focuses on commitments to conformity rather than on motives for delinquency. Matza and Sykes challenge traditional subcultural perspectives as well.

When actually tested, none of the theories has been completely substantiated. Hindelang finds support for some aspects of Travis Hirschi's version of control theory but determines that involvement in conventional activities does not necessarily act as a barrier to delinquency unless the activity considered reflects real commitments (e.g., doing homework). Moreover, unlike Hirschi, he finds that identification with peers does not act as a barrier to delinquency. On the other hand, attachments to conventional people and institutions, commitments to conventional lines of action, and acceptance of conventional moral beliefs do contribute to an explanation of delinquency.

Strain theories have had their problems as well. As Hirschi notes, high aspirations tend to act as a barrier to delinquency, contrary to the strain theorists' view that high aspirations coupled with limited opportunity to realize those aspirations is a cause of delinquency. Moreover, Lerman's study of the values of gang delinquents shows them to be committed to neither an oppositional nor a contracultural value system, nor a distinctively subcultural set of definitions favorable to the violation of the law. Ambivalence and uncertainty appear to be more accurate characterizations. The conception of "drifting" in and out of delinquent episodes is consistent with Matza and Sykes's leisure-class argument. It is also consistent with Briar and Piliavin's control theory in that situational variables play a role in "triggering actual delinquent episodes"; but the probability of a youth's becoming involved in such episodes is determined by the strength of personal commitments to conformity. Thus, the findings fit very well with a social disorganization-social control type of theory.

Cultural conflict or cultural deviance theory posits the existence of subcultural moral standards conducive to lawbreaking that supposedly characterize people with some shared distinguishing characteristic (e.g., a lower-class subculture, a subculture of poverty, a Southern subculture, and so forth). The conduct codes of less powerful groups are presumably in conflict with those of more powerful groups that can impose their standards in the form of laws. The problem with this argument is that there is little actual evidence that identifiable, distinct subgroups define lawbreaking as either acceptable or tolerable behavior. Delinquent youths may be ambivalent about the worth of various forms of conduct, but their ambivalence may reflect a widely shared ambivalence among Americans in general in all status groups. The degree to which youths accept the law as morally binding does help explain delinquency, but no one has demonstrated moral uncertainty or ambivalence to be distinctive to any identifiable socially differential category of Americans.

While the various theories are in conflict with one another on several basic issues, their shared view of delinquency as learned behavior receives considerable support in Akers et al. To a great degree, drug use is a product of learned points of view, imitation, group pressures, and the rewards and punishments of certain important people in a youth's environment. These learning experiences have not been shown to be subculturally structured or more common in some minority groups or status categories than in others. Just exactly how this learning is distributed or most likely to work to encourage delinquency has not been discerned by research sociologists.

SECTION SIX

Social Pressures Impinging on Youth

Human beings, unlike animals, are not born with a set of programmed behaviors or innate instincts that allow them automatically to participate in social life. While ducks may instinctively take to water and honeybees instinctively search for nectar, humans require a long period of preparation before they are able to participate fully in human society. This gradual introduction to social life and social responsibilities, during which individuals learn to become human, is referred to as socialization. While the socialization process is a lifelong task, the most crucial stage occurs in the early years of infancy and childhood, when the basic foundation is laid for later life.

It is important to recognize that while this tedious process of human socialization appears to be terribly slow and inefficient, the relative poverty of human instincts allows us to be far more creative and adaptive than animals. Furthermore, the fact that human society can build on the experiences of past generations results in cultural evolution. Within the animal kingdom, few advances are made from one generation to the next. The strong instinctive drive acts like a straitjacket in preventing creativity or change from one generation to the next. Hence humans create cultures that grow and evolve with changing environmental demands. Human society can advance based on past experiences as people selectively pick and choose among past attempts to solve recurring problems. Incredibly complex social arrangements are possible for our present generation because we can build on the experiences of past generations.

Having just examined some sociological explanations for delinquency, the reader should find it readily apparent that these theories are predicated on the existence of culture, socialization, and social interaction. There may be enormous variations from one sociological theory to the next, but one theme is present in all of them—namely, that delinquency is not inherited biologically but rather is learned or acquired through a series of social interactions. Whether they speak in terms of differential association, status frustration, delinquent subcultures, or unattainable success goals, the crux of these sociological theories is that delinquency is a response to a set of social contigencies. The social environment becomes a crucial background variable in the search for an understanding of how an individual acquires a deviant orientation. People are not born delinquent but are born into social situations or social environments that are conducive to the emergence of delinquent behavior.

An early-twentieth-century social psychologist, Charles Horton Cooley, coined the concept of the "looking-glass self." By this, Cooley intended to convey the notion that society provides a mirror in which we can observe how others react to our behavior. We learn who we are by observing the responses of others. A later social psychologist, George Herbert Mead, elaborated on Cooley's ideas by introducing the notion of the "generalized other." According to Mead, as children move from their families into the world of other children and adults, they begin to develop a generalized picture of what other people expect from them. The attitudes, impressions, and expectations derived from social interactions coalesce to shape a generalized other and serve as a basic guide for future behavior. For both Cooley and Mead, the social self is a social product that slowly unfolds as the child experiences the tugs and pushes of societal demands and expectations. The self is something that develops: it does not exist at birth but arises in the process of social experience.

If some youths are socialized into delinquent tendencies, it becomes of great importance that we examine those agencies of socialization or those structural situations that play a major role in molding human life. While the list of possible agencies of socialization is quite large, we have selected four deemed to be related to delinquency: the family, school, religion, and television. Each of these socializing forces has been accorded a certain degree of importance, but as the readings in this section will show, the research is incomplete and the issues are quite complex.

The family is generally seen as the basic socializing agency in society. It is the place where children first experience emotional ties, learn language, and begin to internalize cultural norms and values. Much of this primary socialization serves as the foundation for later life. Parents make a concerted attempt to teach, discipline, and motivate children in a conscious, deliberate manner. However, as Suzanne Steinmetz and Murray Straus argue, a great deal of socialization into unconventional behavior also takes place in the family. Even though American society professes a commitment to nonviolence, violence in the home is all too common and may provide children with a method of dealing with frustration or aggression in other social settings.

The school is another fundamental agency of socialization. Kenneth Polk sheds light on the ways that school behavior and delinquency can intertwine. Schools have become one of the basic "gatekeepers" of American society. Individuals who successfully pass through the educational system can expect a reasonable degree of success or esteem, while those who drop out or fail have very limited chances of achieving even modest success. Surprisingly little has been written on the relationship between the schools and delinquency, but Polk's discussion serves as a strong indictment of the educational system.

Religion is a very complex social institution that has not been accorded a prominent place in delinquency research. However, Paul Higgins and Gary Albrecht have found some evidence that church attendance and delinquency are inversely related. The confounding issue is that religiosity may not be accorded the same degree of social meaning in different parts of the country.

Finally, the relationship between exposure to television violence and delinquency is explored by Timothy Hartnagel, James Teevan, and Jennie McIntyre. Given that adolescents spend an average of six hours a day viewing shows dealing with murder, robbery, rape, and arson, does this bombardment of violence encourage them to commit violent crimes? Many experimental studies in laboratory settings seem to support the notion that media violence can generate violent behavior in youths. The results of Hartnagel, Teevan, and McIntyre's study are contrary to much popular opinion.

*Hellfire and Delinquency Revisited**

Paul C. Higgins and Gary L. Albrecht
Northwestern University

ABSTRACT

While Hirschi and Stark conclude that religiosity is unrelated to delinquency, their findings and a replication of their study in the Pacific Northwest (Burkett and White) may not be generalizable to other areas of the country. Using self-report data from 1,383 Atlanta tenth graders in 1970, we found a moderate negative relationship between church attendance and delinquent behavior. Our data also suggest a causal structure in which respect for the juvenile court system links church attendance with delinquency. We suspect that church attendance may be a truer reflection of adolescents' religious experience in the South than the West, so accounting for the differences between our findings and those of previous research.

Social scientists have long been interested in the relationship between religiosity and delinquent behavior. Some have argued that religion is a deterrent to delinquency, whereas others assert that religion promotes delinquent behavior due to the perceived insincerity of church leaders, the ethnocentrism of denominationalism, and the identification of the church with society's power structure (Gannon). Research findings have been equally conflicting. Glueck and Glueck, Nye, and Travers and Davis found that children who attended church regularly or had a higher degree of "religious intensity" were less likely to be delinquent than non-attenders or those having a lower degree of religious intensity. On the other hand, Kvaraceus concluded that there were no significant differences between the proportion of delinquents in the general population (New Jersey) and among those who were active church members.

Since these early studies are generally unsophisticated methodologically, they are often inadequate for testing the relationship between religiosity and delinquent behavior. Hirschi and Stark's research does not suffer these same limitations. Their analysis revealed that church attendance was unrelated to delinquent behavior. They concluded that the commonsense notion which regards religion as a deterrent to delinquency is simply wrong. They also found that one set of variables, which they called measures of acceptance of moral values (e.g., respect for the police), was negatively related to delinquency, but unrelated or weakly related to church attendance. Therefore, they argued that previous researchers who did find modest, negative relationships between church attendance and delinquent behavior should have explored possible causal structures that might have linked the two, rather than assuming a simple and direct causal structure.

A recent partial replication (Burkett and White) of Hirschi and Stark's research essentially corroborates their finding of no relationship between religiosity and delinquency. However, church attendance was negatively related to the specific delinquent behaviors of alcohol and marijuana use. Further, Burkett and White found that church attendance was positively related to agreement that alcohol and marijuana use was sinful and the latter was inversely related to alcohol and drug use. Thus a causal mechanism linking church attendance and alcohol and marijuana was demonstrated. Burkett and White conclude that Hirschi and Stark failed to find a negative relation between religiosity and delinquency because the offenses that they measured are condemned not only by churches but also by other secular agencies. They hypothesize that the "relation between religion and delinquency should be stronger in the case of illegal acts traditionally condemned by the churches but no longer condemned by all segments of respectable secular opinion" (406). Victimless crimes such as alcohol and marijuana use fall into that category. In support of Burkett and White's argument, Mauss found that twelfth graders in California who claimed no formal religion were much more likely to use marijuana than were professed Catholics or Protestants.

While Hirschi and Stark's findings may accurately describe the situation in northern California, and here one may include Burkett and White's replication in the Pacific Northwest, there are possible limitations in their investigation which preclude generalization beyond their own research. We feel that their research is methodologically comparable to ours, as we will discuss later. Thus, results can be compared meaningfully. However, our findings differ from theirs. We found a moderate negative relationship between religiosity, as measured by church attendance, and delinquent behavior. Further, our data suggest a causal structure that makes respect for the juvenile court system a link between church attendance and delinquency for three of four sex-by-race groups that we investigated.

METHODS

In 1970, as a part of a larger study of the relationship between respect for the juvenile court system and delinquent behavior, a stratified random sample of 1,410 tenth grade students in six Atlanta high schools completed a lengthy questionnaire. Two items about church attendance and church affiliation were included. More than 98 percent (1,383) of the questionnaires were usable. The *N*s in the tables vary slightly due to nonresponses to specific items.

We take for granted that religiosity is many things and that our two measures tap only part of that domain. The students were asked to indicate which church they usually attended if any, and how often they attended church or religious services. Responses for the latter could vary from "just about never" to "once a week or more." This is similar to Hirschi and Stark's (206) measure of church attendance.

Delinquent behavior was measured by a self-report check list of 17 items which ranged from "skipped school" to "sold narcotics" (see Table 1). Our list of delinquent behaviors include many items which are more serious offenses than the ones included in the Hirschi and Stark study. Students could answer "frequently," "sometimes," "seldom," or "never" to each of the 17 items. A mean frequency score for all 17 items was computed which could range from 0 (never) to 3 (frequently).

Respect for the juvenile court system was assessed through the use of the "good–bad" trait of the semantic differential scale. Using a 7-step scale from "good" to "bad," students were asked to rate how they felt and how they thought their friends felt toward the police, probation officers, juvenile court judges, and the juvenile court. These four items were moderately to highly interrelated, gammas of .40 to .70, for both self and friends. Thus a mean score of responses to these four items was computed to characterize the student's respect and his perception of his friends' respect for the juvenile court system.

*We thank Ed McCabe and two anonymous reviewers for their useful comments on earlier drafts. This research was supported in part by LEAA grant 72–DF–658.

RESULTS

Table 1 indicates that there is a modest to moderately strong negative relationship between frequency of church attendance and each of the 17 delinquent behaviors. Gamma, which is a proportional reduction-in-error statistic and suitable for ordinal data, ranges from −.21 for "run away from home" to −.51 for "used narcotics." (These gammas, as well as the others presented in the paper were computed on collapsed tables so that marginal distributions would not be skewed). Frequency of church attendance is inversely related to delinquent behavior in a consistent pattern; for the composite delinquency measure, gamma is −.48.

Hirschi and Stark suggest that, following common sense, church attendance should reduce delinquent behavior because it fosters acceptance of legitimate legal authority. But they also argue that the finding of a relationship between frequency of church attendance and delinquent behavior should be investigated for some causal structure which links the two. We pursued this idea by investigating the possible causal relationships between religiosity, respect for the juvenile court system, and delinquent behavior.

Table 1. CORRELATIONS BETWEEN CHURCH ATTENDANCE AND DELINQUENCY EXPRESSED IN GAMMAS (N = 1353)

	Frequency of Church Attendance
1. Driving car without a license	−.26
2. Skipped school	−.38
3. Carried a knife, razor, etc.	−.23
4. Run away from home	−.21
5. Reckless or fast driving	−.31
6. Taken things worth over $10.00	−.49
7. Used force to get money from someone	−.29
8. Fight	−.22
9. Car theft (taken a car without the owner's permission)	−.31
10. Bought alcoholic beverage	−.46
11. Drank alcoholic beverage	−.49
12. Sold narcotics	−.44
13. Used narcotics	−.51
14. Sniffed glue	−.24
15. Destroyed property worth over $10.00	−.31
16. Hard to handle at home	−.25
17. Come home later than midnight	−.29

One might expect that church attendance is positively related to respect for the juvenile court system which in turn is negatively related to delinquency. For our total sample, church attendance is positively related, gammas of .21 and .17, to self's and friends' respect for the juvenile court system which in turn are negatively related to the composite measure of delinquency with gammas of −.32 and −.39.

There seems to be a possible causal structure which relates church attendance to delinquency, through the variable of respect for the juvenile court system as measured by both one's own and one's friends' respect. Hirschi and Stark found that one's respect for the police was negatively related to delinquency as did we, but they found only a very weak relation between frequency of church attendance and a respect for the police. But our observed relation between church attendance and respect for the juvenile court system is substantively important and statistically stronger than that found by Hirschi and Stark. However, religiosity (i.e., church attendance) may operate in different ways for whites and nonwhites, males and females. Thus we divided our total sample into four race-by-sex groups, as did Hirschi and Stark, in order to specify further the observed relations among church attendance, respect for the juvenile court system, and delinquency.

Table 2 shows for white males, nonwhite males, and white females that there is a moderate positive relationship between church attendance and one's respect for the juvenile court system. Further, for the latter two groups, there are moderately positive relationships between one's friends' respect for the juvenile court system and church attendance. However the relations between church attendance and one's respect and one's friends' respect for the juvenile court system are weak for nonwhite females. Controlling for religious afffiliation does not affect the relationships. By comparison, Hirschi and Stark found weak relationships between church attendance and respect for the Richmond police for all four sex–race groups.

Table 2. CORRELATION (GAMMAS) BETWEEN FREQUENCY OF CHURCH ATTENDANCE AND ONE'S RESPECT AND ONE'S FRIENDS' RESPECT FOR THE JUVENILE COURT SYSTEM BY RACE × SEX GROUPS

	Self	*N*	*Friend*	*N*
White males	.19	(356)*	.06	(357)
Nonwhite males	.30	(288)	.33	(293)
White females	.38	(350)	.22	(350)
Nonwhite females	.04	(338)	.06	(340)

*The slight variation in *N*s across tables is due to missing data on certain items.

The next step in the potential causal pattern (at least for white males, nonwhite males, and white females) is the relationship between one's respect and one's friends' respect for the juvenile court system and delinquent behavior. According to Table 3, there are moderately strong negative relationships between one's respect for the juvenile court system and delinquent behavior for white males, white females, and nonwhite males. The relationship for nonwhite females is much weaker. For all four race-by-sex groups, one's friends' respect for the juvenile court system is moderately negatively related to delinquency.

Finally, our analysis reveals that church attendance is related on a moderately negative level to delinquency for all four race-by-sex groups: gamma is −.50 for white males, −.31 for nonwhite males, −.43 for white females, and −.31 for nonwhite females. These values are much larger than the ones reported by Hirschi and Stark.

Table 3. CORRELATION (GAMMAS) BETWEEN DELINQUENCY AND ONE'S RESPECT AND ONE'S FRIENDS' RESPECT FOR THE JUVENILE COURT SYSTEM BY RACE × SEX GROUPS

	Self	*N*	*Friend*	*N*
White males	−.57	(362)	−.53	(363)
Nonwhite males	−.36	(301)	−.34	(297)
White females	−.39	(356)	−.54	(356)
Nonwhite females	−.11	(343)	−.37	(345)

DISCUSSION

Not only have we shown a negative relationship between frequency of church attendance and delinquency for four race-by-sex groups, but we have demonstrated a plausible causal pattern linking the two (something which Hirschi and Stark complained had been ignored by previous researchers) for white males, nonwhite males, and white females. Church attendance is positively related to respect for the juvenile court system which in turn is negatively related to delinquency. This causal pattern involves one's respect for the juvenile court system for all three groups, and one's friends' respect for the juvenile court system for nonwhite males and white females. No causal pattern involving respect for the juvenile court system was found for nonwhite females. Other causal pattern(s) must account for the observed inverse relation between church attendance and delinquency for this group. Furthermore, the causal pattern involving respect for the juvenile court system that we have demonstrated for white males, nonwhite males, and white females need not be the only one that links church attendance with delinquency. It may be supplemented by others for which we have no data.

The problem which remains is to reconcile the differences between our findings and Hirschi and Stark's.[1] We accept their data as comparable to our own, but we think certain limitations do not permit them to generalize beyond their own research. An obvious difference between their research and ours is the measurement of respect for the juvenile court system. They used a question asking whether the respondent respected the Richmond police. Our measurement consisted of mean responses to a good–bad semantic differential statement for four groups: police, probation officers, juvenile court judge, and juvenile court. One might argue that this measurement difference led to the difference in outcomes. We do not. A complete separate analysis, using the good–bad semantic trait for the police only, disclosed results similar to those presented in this paper which used a mean response of four good–bad items. Nor do we argue that the several years difference in time between the two data sets accounts for the difference.

More plausibly, the difference in the items used to measure delinquent behavior might help explain the difference in findings. Hirschi and Stark used a 6-item list. We employed a 17-item list which included many serious offenses. Some of the highest correlations between church attendance and delinquency are for those serious offenses that we included in our study but were not included in Hirschi and Stark's. Perhaps, church attendance and religiosity influence only the commission of extremely serious offenses and not the lesser ones that Hirschi and Stark included in their study. However, even this difference in measurement of delinquent behavior probably does not account for the difference between our findings and those of Hirschi and Stark. As one can see from Table 1, those offenses of Hirschi and Stark that we included in our instrument (taking things worth over $10.00;[2] taking a car without the owner's permission; having taken part in a fight) were moderately to highly correlated with church attendance.

The region in which the data were collected, though, may account for the differences in results. Hirschi and Stark collected their data in Western Contra Costra County, particularly the city of Richmond, in northern California. Our data are from Atlanta, Georgia. One might suppose that religion is more of a concern in the South than it is in California, and thus those who go to church in the South are more religiously oriented than those who go to church in California.[3] Hirschi and Stark found that ethical and moral principles related to delinquency were not related to church attendance. Might this be due to the casualness of church attendance in

California? Church attendance in Atlanta might indicate a stronger commitment to general ethical and moral values than does church attendance in California. Though we investigated only one moral value, respect for the juvenile court system, we did find that it was related to delinquency for all four sex and race groups and that it was related to church attendance for three of the four groups. Church attendance was a deterrent to delinquency in Atlanta.

Thus while Hirschi and Stark's conclusion about the lack of a relation between church attendance and delinquency might be true in California, it may not be so for other parts of the country. Similarly, our findings of a relation between church attendance and delinquency and a potential causal pattern involving respect for the juvenile court system need not necessarily apply outside of the South or even outside of Atlanta. As Hirschi and Stark note, religiosity is many things, church attendance being only one part of that domain. Likewise, church attendance means many things to many people, and for some it may be a truer reflection of their religious experience than it is for others.

NOTES

1. The Burkett and White study is basically a corroboration and partial extension of the Hirschi and Stark research. Therefore the discrepancy between findings still holds.
2. Hirschi and Stark used three categories; under $2.00; $2.00–$49.99; $50.00 and over.
3. Burkett and White's replication was done in the Pacific Northwest. One might argue that California and the Pacific Northwest are similar in the meaning that church attendance has for adolescents.

REFERENCES

Burkett, S. R., and M. White. 1974. "Hellfire and Delinquency: Another Look." *Journal for the Scientific Study of Religion* 13(December):455–62.
Gannon, T. M. 1967. "Religious Control and Delinquent Behavior." *Sociology and Social Research* 51(July):418–31.
Glueck, Sheldon, and Eleanor Glueck. 1950. *Unraveling Juvenile Delinquency*. Cambridge: Harvard University Press.
Hirschi, T., and R. Stark. 1969. "Hellfire and Delinquency." *Social Problems* 17(Fall): 202–13.
Kvaraceus, W. C. 1944. "Delinquent Behavior and Church Attendance." *Sociology and Social Research* 28(March–April):284–89.
Mauss, A. L. 1969. "Anticipatory Socialization Toward College as a Factor in Adolescent Marijuana Use." *Social Problems* 16(Winter): 357–64.
Nye, F. Ivan. 1958. *Family Relationships and Delinquent Behavior*. New York: Wiley.
Travers, J. F., and R. G. Davis. 1961. "A Study of Religious Motivation and Delinquency." *The Journal of Educational Sociology* 34(January):205–20.

*Television Violence and Violent Behavior**

Timothy F. Hartnagel
University of Alberta

James J. Teevan, Jr.
University of Western Ontario

Jennie J. McIntyre
University of Maryland

Abstract The relationship between exposure to television violence and violent behavior was examined with questionnaire data obtained from adolescents. It was hypothesized that there would be a positive correlation between these two variables. Only minimal support for this hypothesis was found. Second, it was hypothesized that those adolescents who perceive violence on their favorite television show and those who perceive it as effective would report more violent behavior than adolescents who do not perceive their favorite show in these terms. This hypothesis was supported. Finally, television violence was included with other independent variables in a procedure to predict violent behavior. Television violence was found to be insignificant in comparison to such other variables as sex and grades in school in predicting violent behavior.

In recent years increased concern has been voiced regarding the possible effects of television on the socialization and behavior of children. This concern stems both from the ubiquity and the content of television. Although the most recent, television is now the most popular of the mass media. It has been estimated that 96 percent of American homes have sets and that sets are on an average of six hours and 18 minutes per day (Lyle). Further, a content analysis of commercial television entertainment programs revealed that violence is pervasive, occurring in about 80 percent of all prime time plays (programs neither cartoon nor movie) and the frequency of violence episodes was five per play and eight per hour (Gerbner).

The content of television programming and the extensive exposure to it leads to the question of its possible effects on behavior, attitudes, and beliefs. Many observers feel that the viewer of television violence may be more likely than the nonviewer to engage in criminal or violent behavior. It has also been suggested that violence on television may influence the viewer's perception of the amount of crime and violence in the country, thereby affecting his level of fear and anxiety (President's Commission).

A number of researchers have investigated the effects of TV on behavior.[1] But their conclusions are not consistent. Some researchers have concluded that television has little, if any, effect in causing aggressive or deviant behavior in children. According to this position, when presented with the same television stimuli, aggressive children will be aggressive and adjusted children will not. Schramm has argued, for example, that television interacts with the needs and emotions children bring to it and that the most television can do is feed the malignant impulses that already exist. Bailyn and Haines concur with this view and argue that television has an effect only on susceptible teenagers. According to this position, then, television plays only a minor part in causing deviant behavior since it merely elicits behavior already in the child's repertoire. In addition, Feshbach failed to discover any evidence that exposure to aggressive content in television stimulates or facilitates the acting out of aggressive behavior by adolescent boys.

Other researchers have found that violent television programming does have a significant effect on aggressive behavior. Eron found a positive relationship between violence ratings of

*The research on which this paper is based was conducted under Contract Number HSM 42-70-52 with the National Institute of Mental Health Services and Mental Health Administration, Department of Health, Education and Welfare. W. Andrew Harrell provided useful criticism of an earlier draft.

favorite programs and aggressive behavior among third grade boys, but not girls. Zajonc and Brodbeck found that children will imitate heroes who are successful, whatever means the heroes use. Schramm has summarized the implications of Brodbeck's studies by noting that children may remember, and presumably be able to use, violence even though it is in conflict with their ethics and values. A series of experiments by Bandura and his associates has demonstrated that children learn aggressive behavior from film-mediated models and that they perform this behavior under suitable circumstances (Bandura; Bandura et al., a, b). Similar results were reported by Hicks (a, b). A series of experiments summarized by Berkowitz has shown that catharsis is less likely than arousal of aggressive behavior as a result of observation of aggression. Goranson has concluded that novel aggressive behavior is learned by children through exposure to realistic portrayals of aggression on television and that the performance of such behavior depends largely on the child's belief in the effectiveness of aggression for goal attainment. Finally, demographic comparisons reported in *Mass Media and Violence* (Baker and Ball) indicated a substantial overlap between adults and teenagers who are "violents" with respect to norms and experience with violence; and groups who choose television for relaxation, approve of the kind of violence on television, and prefer violent media content.

Recent analysis has suggested directions in which research on the effects of mass media should move in an attempt to resolve these contradictory findings. Larsen, for example, has argued that the abundance of violent media content and the frequency of exposure to it do not suffice to prove that the mass media can modify attitudes or induce violent behavior. He goes on to state that the question cannot be simply whether the media have an effect. It must be discovered under what conditions, for whom, how much, and what kind of effect the media are likely to have. Furthermore, whatever the effects of the mass media on their audience, these must be assessed in relation to the way other aspects of the larger social system affect these same persons.

The present research was designed to investigate, through survey research, whether exposure to television violence is associated with an increased probability of engaging in violent behavior. The research design differs from previous research in several ways. First, respondents' favorite television shows were the source of the independent variable. Second, the dependent variable consisted of self-reported violent behavior rather than aggressive behavior in a laboratory setting. Third, the respondents were adolescents rather than younger children. Finally, a number of other variables known to be associated with violent behavior were included in order to measure the relative explanatory power of violent television content compared to these other factors.

The mass communications literature suggests that certain distinctions should be made in conceptualizing television violence. At least two elements appear to be crucial: the objective content of television programming and the respondents' subjective perceptions of the content of these programs. It is first necessary to inquire into the objective amount of violence present in the respondents' favorite television shows. Given this objective measure, it must be determined how the respondents perceive this content. For example, is violence perceived to be present and is it seen as effective in achieving goals?

An essential distinction should also be made between attitudes about violence and violent behavior. Although television violence may inculcate norms and values favorable to violent behavior, the performance of such behavior is still problematic. The present analysis will examine the relationship between television violence and violent behavior, while subsequent reports will treat the attitudinal effects of television violence.

Several specific hypotheses were formulated for this research.[2] First, it was hypothesized that exposure to television violence is positively related to violent behavior. Such association is suggested by most laboratory studies of aggression reviewed above.

Second, it was hypothesized that those respondents who perceive television programming as violent and/or perceive the violence as effective means to a goal engage in more violent behavior than those who do not perceive television programming in these terms. This hypothesis is based on the findings of Zajonc and Brodbeck and the mass communications literature on selective perception (Catton; Freidson; Katz; Klapper; Lazarsfeld et al.)

Finally, given the contradictory findings in the literature and Larsen's comments noted above, it was hypothesized that there would be interactions between the objective content of TV programming, the perception of this content, and various demographic and social characteristics of the respondents. However, this phase of the research was exploratory and no specific predictions were made.

Method

The data were collected in 1970 in junior and senior high schools in one Maryland county. (See McIntyre et al. for results of the larger study.) This county was chosen because it includes areas which are quite rural, middle-class and blue-collar suburbs, and some areas which approximate conditions in an inner city. The schools were selected so as to provide a probability sample of students with two restrictions: roughly equal numbers were selected from each grade, seven through twelve, and a predominantly black school was over-sampled to provide sufficient black respondents to enable comparisons.

A questionnaire asked the students to list their four favorite television programs, "the ones you try to watch every time they are on the air." They were then asked to select from that list their single, favorite show. Attention is focused on the favorite shows for two reasons. Respondents cannot be expected to remember and report reliably all programs watched during any time period which would represent their total viewing habits. Favorite programs, on the other hand, can be reported more reliably. Second, favorite programs may be watched more closely and more frequently than other programs.

It should be recognized that no attempt has been made to measure the respondents' total exposure to violent television programming. However, data were collected on the total amount of television viewing (average number of hours spent watching TV daily) in order to control for its possible effect. Furthermore, only the respondents' current program preferences have been measured. We have no data on the respondents' previous exposure to television violence or of its possible cumulative effect. Rather, respondents are categorized on the basis of the violence rating of their currently preferred shows.

A violence rating was assigned to each program and a mean violence rating computed from the ratings of the four favorite shows. These ratings were taken from a survey of television critics (Greenberg and Gordon). Critics' ratings correlated highly with ratings assigned by a general public sample. The definition of violence used to assign the rating was as follows: "By violence I mean how much fighting, shooting, yelling, or killing there usually is in the show." Television programs with variable content, such as Saturday Night at the Movies, could not be coded.

In order to measure perceptions of the violent content, the following statements were presented and the respondents asked to indicate whether they described their favorite show: (1) the main character pushes the others around; (2) the guy who gets rough gets his way. Selection of the first statement indicates that violence is perceived as present and the second that it is rewarded. The measurement of perception was restricted to the most favored show since we felt there was a significant danger of systematic measurement error from response set if the respondents were asked to rate all four shows.

Violent behavior was measured by responses to the following items: (1) got into a serious fight with a student at school; (2) hurt someone badly enough for him to need bandages; (3) took part in a fight where a bunch of your friends were against another bunch.[3] Respondents were instructed to indicate the frequency of occurrence as follows: 1. never 2. once only 3. two or more times. An index of violent behavior was constructed by summing across the three items with two or more counted as two.

Certain background information was also collected. This included data on sex, race, age, father's occupation, educational expectations, family structure, school grades, participation in school activities, and hours spent watching television daily. These variables were selected since the delinquency literature suggests that they are likely to be related to violent behavior, and/or to interact, possibly, with the television violence variables.

Results

The first hypothesis was tested by rank ordering the respondents into low, medium and high categories on both the independent variable of average violence rating of the four favorite shows and the dependent variable of violent behavior. An ordinal measure of association, gamma, was then calculated. Table 1 presents these data. A positive but low correlation (gamma = .16) was found between the average violence rating and violent behavior. Inspection of the percentage differences in Table 1 indicates that while 10 percent of the respondents who were low on the average violence rating were high on violent behavior, only *19* percent of those high on the average violence rating were also high on violent behavior. The Pearson correlation coefficient between these two variables was only .12. Therefore, only minimal support for the first hypothesis was obtained.[4]

The second hypothesis concerns the relationship of the respondents' perception of the content of their favorite show (among the four) to the dependent variable of violent behavior. The first perceptual item concerns perceived violence. It was hypothesized that those respondents who perceived their favorite show as violent would engage in more violent behavior. Referring to Table 2, we observe that respondents who perceive the show as violent engaged in significantly more violent behavior (mean = 2.07) than respondents who did not perceive their favorite show as violent (mean = .95). Hence this hypothesis is supported.

Table 1 Violent Behavior by Average Violence Rating of Favorite Television Shows

	Violent Behavior			
Average Violence Rating	*Low*	*Medium*	*High*	
Low	409 (63%)	179 (28%)	62 (10%)	650
Medium	518 (56%)	255 (28%)	147 (16%)	920
High	280 (50%)	175 (31%)	103 (19%)	558
	1,207	609	312	2,128
Chi square = 28.85	Significant at .001		Gamma = .16	

It was also hypothesized that those respondents who perceived violence on their favorite show as an effective means to a goal would engage in more violent behavior. This hypothesis is also supported by the data in Table 2. Respondents who perceived the violence as effective reported significantly more violent acts (mean = 1.93) than respondents who did not perceive the violence as effective (mean = .94). Perception of television violence, then, appears to be of some significance with respect to violent behavior. It should be noted, however, that only a small proportion of respondents perceive violence on their favorite show. This is surprising since approximately 25 percent of the respondents are in the high category for average violence rating. It is possible that many adolescents have become desensitized to the violence on television through cumulative exposure to it.

The third hypothesis to be tested concerns the interaction between the television variables and various demographic and social characteristics of the respondents. This is the central aspect of the present analysis since a key issue concerns the relationship between television violence and other variables as they relate to violent behavior. The question then becomes which combination of variables will most economically sort respondents into the more and less violent categories.

Table 2 Mean Number of Violent Acts by Perception of Favorite Television Show and Estimated Effectiveness of Violence

Perception of Favorite Show	*Mean Number Violent Acts*	*S.D.*	*N*	*T*
Violent	2.07	2.13	118	5.65*
Not violent	.95	1.45	2138	
Estimated Effectiveness				
Violence effective	1.93	1.94	165	6.44*
Violence not effective	.94	1.45	2092	

*Significant at .001.

The research strategy described by Sonquist and Morgan was used for this analysis. Each category of each predictor variable is scanned to establish the one dichotomy which best explains the variance in the dependent variable. This dichotomized predictor variable is then used to split the original sample. An identical procedure is followed for each of the resulting groups and so on until no further splits can be made according to predetermined criteria.[5] This search strategy, then, stresses the power of predictors in reducing error; and a major advantage is the absence of the restrictive assumptions present in multiple regression techniques.

The following predictors were used in the analysis: sex, age, race, grades in school, educational expectations, hours spent watching TV daily, father's occupation, parents married or divorced, number of school activities engaged in, violence rating of the most favored show, perceived TV violence, and perceived effectiveness of TV violence.

The results of this multivariate analysis are presented in the form of a "tree" diagram (Figure 1) which describes the series of splits made on the dependent variable of violent behavior.[6] The first point to be made about these results is to note the absence of any of the TV violence predictors in the tree. These variables simply do not have sufficient explanatory power, either singly or in combination with other variables, to reduce the amount of unexplained variation in violent behavior when compared to the power of other predictors in reducing error. For the two perceived TV violence variables (but not the objective violence rating), this conclusion should be tempered somewhat by recalling their skewed distribution which could affect the splitting process. However, exposure to TV violence and/or perception of TV violence do not appear to compare in explanatory power with some of the other predictors.

A second point to be noted is that the overall reduction in

Figure 1 Summary of Dichotomized Predictors for Violent Behavior

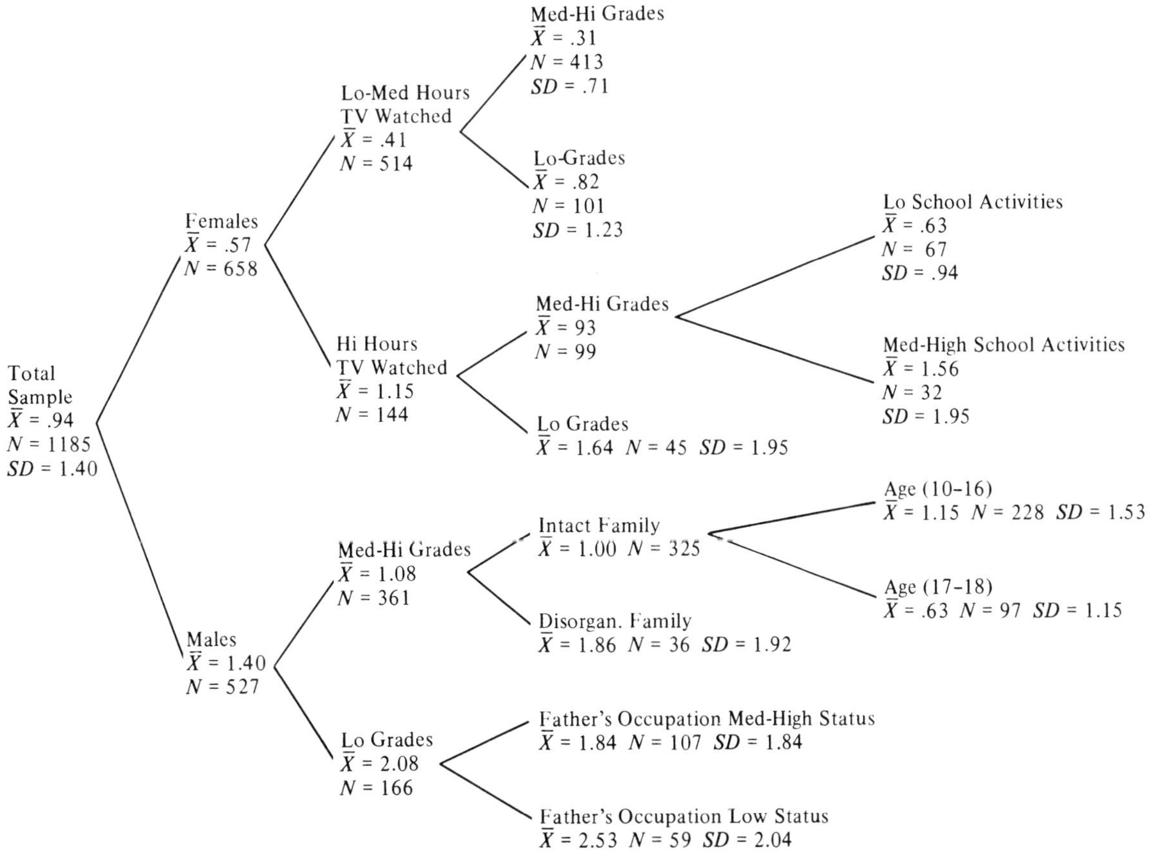

error produced by this analysis (analogous to R^2) is .19. In other words, the set of predictors actually used in the splitting process only explains approximately 20 percent of the variation in violent behavior. This fact is also indicated by the relatively large unexplained variances in many of the final, unsplit, groups. This suggests that other variables in addition to those considered here are needed in order to explain additional variation in violent activity.

Third, this analysis reveals the powerful effects of sex and grades in school on the dependent variable: males engage in more violent conduct than females; and for both males and females those respondents with low grades are more violent.

Other predictors used in the splitting process reveal various interaction effects. For females, amount of time spent watching TV is an important factor, with those females watching a great deal of TV engaging in more violent conduct than those spending lower amounts of time watching TV. But amount of time spent watching TV is not a significant factor in explaining violent activity among males. Further, among females who watch a great deal of TV and who have medium to high grades in school, those who are involved in a larger number of school activities engage in more violent behavior than those who are more minimally involved in such activities. However, the relatively small number of cases in this category (n = 32) cautions against making too much of this finding. Overall, the splitting process for females suggests that watching lower amounts of TV and having medium to high grades in school insulates against involvement in violent behavior. Having low grades, particularly in combination with watching a great deal of TV, is associated with a greater amount of violent conduct.

The effects of father's occupation, family structure, and age on violent behavior interact with sex, being significant explanatory variables only for males. Furthermore, father's occupation appears important only for males with low grades, family structure for males with medium to high grades, and age only for males with medium to high grades living in intact families. Among males with low school grades, having a father with a low-status occupation is associated with greater amounts of violent conduct than with medium- to higher-status occupations. In addition, having medium to high grades, coming from an intact family and being older appears to insulate males from greater involvement in violent behavior.

The present research has not sought to explain violence per se, but rather to assess the relative impact of TV violence, particularly in combination with other variables, on violent behavior. The results indicate that TV violence does not contribute significantly to explaining the variation in violent behavior either over the entire sample or over any of the various subgroups created by the splitting process. We are forced, then, to conclude that the TV violence predictors, both objective and perceived, do not matter significantly in explaining violent behavior.[7]

It is possible that the effects of sex, grades, and the other non-TV predictors on violent conduct are so strong as to mask any effect of TV violence predictors. To test this possibility a two-stage analysis was conducted. All of the demographic and social characteristic variables were placed in the first stage and allowed to explain as much of the variation in the dependent variable as they could (i.e., 19 percent). Then in the second stage of the analysis the TV violence predictors were applied to the remaining unexplained variation (81 percent) from the first stage. However, they did not significantly reduce this unexplained residual. This further supports our general conclusion regarding the relative unimportance of TV violence in explaining violent behavior.

Discussion

The major issue which calls for further discussion is the failure of TV violence in the present research to contribute significantly to explaining the variation in violent behavior while several earlier studies have found such effects. There are several possible explanations for this discrepancy. First, the present research used the actual television shows watched by the respondents while previous research, typically of the laboratory type, has used simulated television shows. While we do not question the internal validity of this earlier work, our results suggest that the external validity (Campbell and Stanley)—i.e., the generalizability—of earlier findings are open to question. Associated with this issue is the possibility that laboratory studies may focus the Ss' attention on the violent content of the simulated show and thereby intensify its effect. But the viewing of actual television shows with violence occurs in a more natural setting along with distractions and perhaps a learned attitude of skepticism, a view of the violent content as unrealistic. Furthermore, laboratory studies use a brief time dimension—the effects of the simulated TV violence on behavior are measured almost immediately after exposure. It is unlikely that the same time dimension exists in the present instance. Also the opportunity to imitate the effects of the simulated TV violence is present immediately within the laboratory setting while such opportunity is much less probable in the case of actual television shows.

Another factor differentiating the present research from many previous studies is the age of the respondents. Laboratory studies have typically used very young children while our respondents were of junior and senior high school age. Adolescents may be less susceptible to the influence of televised violence than are younger children. Alternatively, by the time of adolescence children may have already been exposed to a large quantity of violent television content and have acquired from such exposure a repertoire of violent attitudes and behaviors. The main socializing effects of exposure to television violence may have already occurred by adolescence such that the violent content of current program preferences does not discriminate between those high and low in violent behavior. The general conclusion of this study corresponds to Feshbach's finding that exposure to aggressive content in television did not stimulate aggressive behavior among adolescent boys.

The nature of the violent behavior engaged in is another consideration in explaining differences between our findings and those of earlier work. The dependent variable in this research was actual violent behavior while previous research has typically employed some type of aggression suitable to a laboratory setting. Our results suggest that TV violence does not significantly affect actual violent behavior. Other factors are much more powerful in explaining such activity.

However, we cannot completely dismiss the possibility of effects from TV violence. It is possible that TV violence influences behavior in an indirect fashion, through its impact on learned values and attitudes or through a more general impression that is communicated about the nature of social reality. Values and attitudes or perceptions of the world may be substantially affected by television programming which may, in turn, influence behavior. For example, our finding that only about 5 percent of the respondents perceive violence in their favorite show while approximately 25 percent are in the high category for the average violence rating of favorite shows suggests that television may make viewers so accustomed to violence that they define it as normal. Violent television content may also generate the attitude that violent means for resolving disputes are acceptable, or at least effective; and this attitude may, under appropriate conditions, find expression in the actual use of violent behavior. Exposure to TV violence may also create the impression that the world is a violent place and that the individual should be prepared to confront violence under certain circumstances. In these various ways, then, exposure to TV violence may have important indirect effects upon actual employment of violent behavior.

Notes

1. For more complete reviews of the literature on the effects of television see Goranson; Weiss.
2. Given the design of this study, the hypotheses are stated in correlational rather than causal terms since we are not able to specify the temporal ordering of these variables. It is possible, for example, that engaging in violent behavior causes individuals to select violent TV shows for viewing. However, the presence of a correlation is one of the requirements for establishing a causal relationship (Hyman). Given the absence of correlation we can conclude that no causal relation exists. If a correlation is found we can test for spuriousness by controlling for other variables, which is an additional requirement for establishing a causal relation.
3. These items were included in a conventional self-report delinquency checklist. The present research is concerned solely with the three items pertaining to violent behavior. A self-report measure was used since data were required on all of the violent acts of the above types engaged in by the respondents rather than only those violent acts which produced some official reaction by agencies of social control. The inter-item correlations among these items were: 1 and 2 = .38; 1 and 3 = .43; 2 and 3 = .40. These compare with the average correlation of these items with the remainder of the items as follows: 1 = .17; 2 = .16; 3 = .20.
4. See the analysis for Hypothesis III for an additional test of the effect of television violence with controls for other variables.
5. The maximum allowable number of final groups into which data may be split is 90. The minimum number of observations that must be contained in a group, if that group is to become a candidate for splitting is 25. The best split on a candidate group must reduce the unexplained sum of squares by the proportion .006 of the total sum of squares or that group will not be split.
6. The reduction in the sample size for this analysis is due to two factors. First, about 25 percent of the respondents gave as their favorite show a program which could not be coded for violent content due to variable content (e.g., Saturday Night at the Movies). Second, the computer program for this analysis required that missing data on any one variable resulted in the exclusion of that entire case from the analysis. The cases excluded from this analysis were compared on each of the variables with those cases that were used and no significant differences were found.
7. The same analysis as reported above was conducted using the average violence rating of the four favorite shows with only minor variation in the results. TV violence again did not enter into any of the splits and hence did not significantly contribute to explaining violent conduct. The sample size for this analysis was 1,519.

References

Baker, R. K., and S. J. Ball. 1969. *Mass Media and Violence.* Washington: Government Printing Office.

Bailyn, L. 1959. "Mass Media and Children." *Psychological Monographs* 73:1–48.

Bandura, A. 1965. "Influence of Models' Reinforcement Contingent upon the Acquisition of Imitative Responses." *Journal of Personality and Social Psychology* 1:589–95.

Bandura, A., D. Ross, and S. A. Ross. a:1963. "Imitation of Film-Mediated Aggressive Models." *Journal of Abnormal and Social Psychology* 66:3–11.

———. b:1963. "Vicarious Reinforcement and Imitative Learning." *Journal of Abnormal and Social Psychology* 67:601–7.

Berkowitz, L. 1964. "The Effects of Observing Violence." *Scientific American* 210(February).

Brodbeck, A. J. 1955. "The Mass Media as a Socializing Agency." Paper presented at the annual meeting of the American Psychological Association, San Francisco.

Campbell, D. T., and J. C. Stanley. 1966. *Experimental and Quasi-Experimental Designs for Research.* Chicago: Rand McNally.

Catton, W. R. 1969. "Mass Media as Producers of Effects." In R. K. Baker and S. J. Ball, *Mass Media and Violence.* Washington: Government Printing Office.

Eron, L. D. 1963. "The Relation of T. V. Viewing Habits and Aggressive Behavior in Children." *Journal of Abnormal and Social Psychology* 67:193–6.

Feshbach, S. 1969. "The Catharsis Effect: Research and Another View." In R. K. Baker and S. J. Ball, *Mass Media and Violence.* Washington: Government Printing Office.

Freidson, E. 1953. "Communications Research and the Concept of the Mass." *American Sociological Review* 18:313–7.

Gerbner, G. 1972. "Violence in Television Drama: Trends and Symbolic Functions." In G. A. Comstock and E. A. Rubinstein (eds.), *Television and Social Behavior.* Vol. 1. Washington: Government Printing Office.

Goranson, R. E. 1969. "A Review of Recent Literature on Psychological Effects of Media Portrayals of Violence." In R. K. Baker and S. J. Ball, *Mass Media and Violence.* Washington: Government Printing Office.

Greenburg, B. S., and T. Gordon. 1970. "Critics' and Public Perceptions of Violence in T.V. Programs." East Lansing: Michigan State University. Mimeo.

Haines, W. H. 1955. "Juvenile Delinquency and Television." *Journal of Social Therapy* 1:192–8.

Hicks, D. 1965. "Imitation and Retention of Film-Mediated Aggressive

Peer and Adult Models." *Journal of Personality and Social Psychology* 2:97–100.
———. 1968. "Short and Long Term Retention Affectively Varied Modeled Behavior." *Psychonomic Science* 11:369–70.
Hyman, H. H. 1955. *Survey Design and Analysis.* New York: Free Press.
Katz, E. 1957. "The Two-Step Flow of Communication." *Public Opinion Quarterly* 21(Spring):61–78.
Klapper, J. T. 1960. *The Effects of Mass Communications.* Glencoe: Free Press.
Larsen, O. N. 1969. "Posing the Problem of Effects." In R. K. Baker and S. J. Ball, *Mass Media and Violence.* Washington: Government Printing Office.
Lazarsfeld, P. F., B. Berelson, and J. Gaudet. 1948. *The People's Choice.* New York: Columbia University Press.
Lyle, J. 1972. "Television in Daily Life." In G. A. Comstock and E. A. Rubinstein (eds.), *Television and Social Behavior.* Vol. 4. Washington Government Printing Office.
McIntyre, J. J., J. J. Teevan Jr., and T. F. Hartnagel. 1972. "Television Violence and Delinquency." In G. A. Comstock and E. A. Rubinstein (eds.) *Television and Social Behavior.* Vol. 3. Washington: Government Printing Office.
President's Commission on Law Enforcement and the Administration of Justice. 1967. *The Challenge of Crime in a Free Society.* Washington: Government Printing Office.
Schramm, W. T., J. Lyle, and E. B. Parker. 1961. *Television in the Lives of Our Children.* Stanford: Stanford University Press.
Sonquist, J. A., and J. N. Morgan. 1964. *The Detection of Interaction Effects.* Ann Arbor: Institute for Social Research, University of Michigan.
Weiss, W. 1968. "Effects of the Mass Media of Communication." In G. Lindzey and E. Aronson (eds.), *The Handbook of Social Psychology.* Reading, Mass.: Addison-Wesley.
Zajonc, R. 1954. "Some Effects of the ASpace Serials." *Public Opinion Quarterly* 18:367–74.

Schools and the Delinquency Experience

Kenneth Polk

Any comprehensive discussion of juvenile delinquency must, sooner or later, center on the school. In present-day industrial society, the school has come to occupy a fundamental role in the lives of young people generally—and of delinquents in a particular way. This importance rests on a number of considerations. More is involved here than the fact that schools have become virtual age-based social ghettos, shielding the young from contact with persons at a short distance either older or younger in age (although this segregation is an important feature of the distinctive forms of youthful behavior that are likely to bear such titles as "adolescent subculture" or "teenage society"). Operating within the context of a "credentialed" society, to use the term suggested by Pearl (1972), how well a young person competes in school has enormous consequences for *future* status. The ultimate credential earned in the future is, in fact, the accumulation of countless little credentials in the present and past that take the form of grades, units, and credits. As assumptions about status futures lead to the development of such bureaucratic procedures as curriculum organization, tracking, ability grouping, and grading, these act backward into the status *present* of the child. Who the person is in the present, in the social world of the school, is significantly related to assumptions about who she or he might become. How well the student performs in school, or is seen to perform, comes to provide an important identity "fix" for the establishment of youthful status in school and community. Additionally, a significant part of the social activities provided for the young are organized within and around the school, both formally and informally. Providing a framework for a wide range of social activities (including unconventional and deviant activities), the school extends into the lives of adolescents well beyond the regular school hours.

It would seem only reasonable that the centrality of the school for the adolescent experience generally would extend in the specific form of adolescent behavior we call delinquency. In the sections which follow there will be an examination of a variety of ways that school behavior and delinquency can be seen to intertwine. Describing such interconnections, in other words, will require that a number of features of school behavior be elaborated, rather than one simple feature such as academic performance.

The starting point, however, is delinquency, and the first task is to explicate the meaning, or in this case the meanings, to be given to this term. A starting point is law and legal process. Juvenile delinquency is based in law. Technically, it consists of those persons who have been legally processed and identified as "delinquent youth." As we review literature and data here, then, the search will focus on one definition of delinquency which is grounded in official processing of youth by police and courts.

There are enormous difficulties with such a definition. For one, as Elliott and Voss (1974: 12) observe, it can unwittingly introduce the assumption that there are only two kinds of children—delinquent and nondelinquent. For another, definition based on official processing will contain biases that can be shown to be connected with such processing (for example, see Goldman, 1963). Furthermore, a legal definition based on official processing will combine in unknown and unknowable ways (without considerable additional information) two very different things: some form of *action* on the part of a young person (at least in most instances), combined with some *reaction* on the part of official agents. Hidden in single records are variations in both action and reaction, the result being a label "delinquency" that will suffer from lack of uniformity of meaning. Finally, most theories of youth deviance have a conception of troublesome behavior that do not mesh neatly with simple official records. Virtually all pose processes of alienation, reaction, and rebellion that imply much richer behavior than will ever be available from organizational processing data.

Despite all these difficulties, in these pages one focus of the measure of deviance will be official processing. Juvenile delinquency is a legal term, which, aside from whatever other logical problems are posed, does combine the assumption that some act has occurred with the official response to that act. The logical precision of this definition is clear, whatever the theoretical problems that might follow.

One way to utilize such a definition, and yet come to grips with the resultant problems, is to elaborate an additional conception which permits the inclusion of an additional definition or definitions. That is what is proposed here. At this point some hard decisions must be made. One well-accepted alternative is the utilization of measures of self-report of delinquent activity (for examples, see Elliott and Voss, 1974; Clark and Wenninger, 1962; Short and Nye, 1957-1958; and Short, 1958). These have the virtue of focusing the definition on legal process while avoiding the problem of unknown variations in the reaction process. As Elliott and Voss (1974: 14) observe:

> The point of reference for an operational definition of delinquency must be the legal code, not the conduct norms of particular social groups. The significance of the proscriptions in the legal code is that there is some probability of official response to behavior that violates the statutes. Although official action does not necessarily occur when a delinquent act is detected, it is largely restricted to these acts.

There are yet some difficulties in describing youthful misconduct that are not resolved by definitions, either self-report or official, that remain close to the legal code. Much of the time the theoretical interest in delinquency does not result simply with law-violating behavior, but with a life style that is assumed to be attached to such behavior. One of the clearest illustrations can be found in Cohen's (1955) description of the "delinquency subculture," where the definition evolved around behavior among adolescent groupings characterized by malice, short-run hedonism, nonutilitarian actions, an emphasis on group autonomy, and versatility, all of which evolved among working-class boys through a complex process of reaction formation against their failure in school (and the consequent failure in status aspirations). Another is found in the work of Stinchcombe (1964), who focuses theoretically on issues of rebellion and alienation (among high school youth) as virtually independent phenomena, relegating actual delinquency to a relatively minor role. A characteristic of these theoretical discussions is that what they describe is a general orientation to the world, an orientation imbedded in a set of values and behavior that extends well beyond simple acts of delinquency.

The second definition of delinquency that will be used here will also enter into

AUTHOR'S NOTE: *The research on which this paper is based is supported by funds granted by the National Institute of Mental Health (Grant No. MH14806 "Maturational Reform and Rural Delinquency").*

From *Criminal Justice and Behavior,* Vol. 2 (December 1975), pp. 315–338. "Schools and the Delinquency Experience" by Kenneth Polk is reprinted from *Criminal Justice and Behavior,* Vol. 2, No. 4 (December 1975), pp. 315–338, by permission of the publisher, Sage Publications, Inc.

these murky waters. In general, the intent is to define an orientation, on the part of the young person, which leads to a willingness to engage in forms of behavior, especially peer behavior, which render the individual vulnerable to punishment and sanction by adults. Drawing the boundaries around this set poses problems that cannot be dealt with in the limited space of these pages. What can be done is to assert what are thought to be the major aspects of such an orientation, reserving the elaboration and theoretical justification for another work.

At the core of this troublesome orientation is a set of values and behaviors that evolve around a peer subculture that is in some respects oppositional to standards of behavior established for adolescents by adults. Thus, there is an emphasis on certain forms of behavior either disapproved of or discouraged by adults (drinking, smoking, fighting, and "cruising," to give illustrations), along with the necessary value orientations calling for a rejection of the claims of adults on adolescent behavior, substituting instead peers as the proper persons to establish standards for behavior. Adolescents caught up in this view of the world, in other words, are likely to support peer claims on their behavior and to reject to some degree the attempts of adults (such as parents or teachers) to lay claims on adolescent behavior.

There are two or three aspects of this definition of a "troublesome orientation" that should be clarified. One, it is viewed as being inherently probabilistic. It is not a fixed "thing" which a young person "gets," and, once "got," has forever. It is instead an orientation, a loose way of life, which a youngster may drift into and out of, episodically. Second, it is important to stress the notion of vulnerability. What such an orientation does is, probabilistically, to render the young person vulnerable to adult sanctions. This permits the connection of this perspective to the "labeling" perspective, i.e., a function of the troublesome orientation is to increase the probability that the young person will be vulnerable to a variety of negative labels controlled by adults, especially those organizationally based in the school (slow, emotionally disturbed, noncollege, and the like) or in the juvenile justice system (arrest, probation, adjudication, and the like). Third, this view sees acts of delinquency as episodically imbedded within the troublesome orientation. The young person who drifts into the troublesome orientation may in turn be pressured or drift into specific acts of delinquency, such acts being consistent with this orientation (not a necessary result).

The Meaning of the School Experience

In discussing the relationship between school experience and delinquency, the second definitional problem encountered centers around the meaning of the school experience. At this point, the analysis must become a little complicated. An easy way out would be to focus on a given bit of school behavior—grades or truancy, for example—and show the connection between these and delinquency. Such a procedure has some appeal because it is both easy to do and the results are rather dramatic. The problem is, however, that we must decide what such findings mean, and to do that requires the exposition of some theory, first about school and then about delinquency as it relates to school.

The description of the school experience to be given here starts from the assumption that much of the meaning of what goes on in school is to be found at its termination point: the introduction of the young person into the world of work. It is relatively easy in this society to obtain a ranking of occupations from high to low in terms of a variety of indicators of social and economic status. It is a common sociological observation that in a relatively few decades, this nation (along with many other rapidly industrializing nations) has moved from a system where one inherited her or his occupation from the parent to a condition where one moves into an occupation as a result of a complex negotiation of barriers, notably established in the educational system. Education, in other words, has come to serve a "gatekeeper" function, consigning elite positions to some by means of a complex system of progressive, cumulative credentials, conferring lower status on others through a graded series of progressively lowered credentials.

To take the experience in what is seen here as the *logical* order (which is backward from the *experienced* order), to achieve those positions which consistently score high in the occupational ranking scales—such as judge, physician, lawyer, or college professor—one must negotiate some system of professional and graduate education which leads to a graduate degree (M.D., J.D., or Ph.D.), which in turn requires, in most instances, not only the completion of an undergraduate degree, but the completion of the undergraduate degree with some clear evidence of exemplary merit (indicated both by high levels of academic performance and through letters of recommendation).

Preceding college is the high school experience where the aspiring candidate must have the credentials and the diploma, and further must display evidence of high academic achievement as indicated by the grade point average, but even more, the high achievement must be in the "right" courses, namely those identified as college preparatory. Prior to this is the elementary experience, where the students with high promise are streamed together in the high-ability groups, wherein they receive the requisite educational content to prepare them for the later steps.

The argument here is that this process of sorting out the elites is a basic and fundamental dynamic of the educational system. Much of what happens in school must be understood in terms of this process, including often what appears to be content. Vast numbers of students understand very well—when confronted by paramecia, *Mill on the Floss*, *Beowulf*, or the Articles of Confederation—that what is important is certainly not their interest in these, nor even their understanding, but instead what grade they will receive on the test that covers such topics. Students learn early in the game, in other words, that academic experiences are to be treated *instrumentally* as means to further ends, rather than *intrinsically* in terms of interest or enthusiasm with the substance (this is not to deny that some students, and some teachers, do, in fact, become "involved" in their work).

Further, major features of this system are that there is a tight interlocking between the institutional levels and that much of what happens early is justified and rationalized—by students, teachers, and the organizations—in terms of the destination. Some college courses are designed deliberately to fail large proportions of students, especially in preprofessional programs, in order to sort the wheat from the chaff; tracking of college preparatory students is viewed as necessary both to provide the college bound the requisite academic training and to avoid exposing noncollege students to material which would have no meaning and would, in the view of educators, be beyond them anyway; the ability grouping of elementary students is necessary in order to provide the bright students, again in the view of educators, with the necessary basic academic skills that assure that they will be qualified to take advantage of the college preparatory classes at the secondary level. This grouping/tracking/grading system is relatively tightly linked, and the meaning of the "status flows" that are generated lies in the terminal links with the adult work world.

While this perspective emphasizes the importance of status destination as a fundamental feature of the institutional logic of educational institutions, it does not deny the relevance of status origins. An important aspect of the form of education that has been described is that it is fundamentally competitive: it is designed so that there are both winners and losers. Wins and losses are not randomly distributed, however, and this is where the family background enters the analysis. The first few years of the young person are spent in the family context. One way that the family experience can be viewed is that of making some children more vulnerable to being cast in the role of "loser." Again, this notion of vulnerability emphasizes that the basic reason that children are vulnerable at all is the set of institutional decisions which require that some must fail. The institution creates the categories (in the early years consisting of low-ability groups) that produce the vulnerability. Family background factors then interact to expose some children to such failure, these factors consisting of such things as belonging to a lower social class, being a member of a minority group, speaking a different language, or living in the wrong part of town, to give some of the more traditional sociological variables. The conception of family vulnerability used here goes beyond these basically institutional or structural variables, however, since it is clear that some children in the categories that would appear to be the most vulnerable do in fact succeed, and some that would seem least vulnerable fail. There are operating family and personal "competence" variables whereby young persons even in vulnerable settings have conveyed to them a range of behavioral and attitudinal competences (such as competence in the linguistic style of the school) that permit them to compete effectively, whereas other young persons, even from what would appear to be less vulnerable settings, do not possess such competences and thus are cast in the role of loser.

This conception of the school experience sees the school years as caught between status origins and status destinations, serving as a competitive battleground in the present for the young.

The School Experience and Deviance

Among the many results of this competition, a significant element is that of the potential for the evolution of deviance and deviant careers. The educational system can be viewed as having an explicit concern for the potential for deviance as it relates specifically to the issue of status futures. At a psychological level, for the individual youthful actor, a message is communicated, for example, to the person who is doing well that indicates that engaging or being caught engaging in acts of problematic deviance poses significant threats to the future career. The student planning, say, a career that winds through law school and into the legal profession is confronted with a purely rational constraint either to avoid certain patterns of deviance or at least to be very careful not to get caught. At an institutional level, the school manifests a great concern for idleness and tends to fill up the free time of the promising student with a great variety of activities. The argument is, again, probabilistic. It is not that the high-status potential student will always avoid trouble; rather, there are a variety of personal and institutional constraints operating to restrain entry into deviance and then into deviant careers.

For the student doing poorly, quite a different situation exists. Such students can be explicitly excluded from the social activities of the school by virtue of their low academic output. Once cut away from the school, they encounter a real bind because a majority of the community recreational and social activities provided for the young are monitored through the school system. The poor performer is thusly doubly done in: excluded both from the formal activities of the school and from the legitimate adult community. For such an adolescent, the economic and occupational constraints are not powerful. Whatever the costs of deviance (anxiety, threat to dignity, physical and psychological abuse), the future occupational costs are not operating to the same degree as for the "good" student. Further, the organization is not constraining his time—nor are there clear, legitimate alternatives.

Such a student has one major alternative: involvement in the world of adolescent peers and peer culture. To the extent that this culture provides supports for a range of behavior that runs counter to adult expectations (cruising, drinking, and so on), it can be viewed as increasing the probability that a young person will engage in public acts of deviance and be labeled as deviant by the official control agencies.

Early Adult Life: Achievement and Deviance

The argument here is that these promissory experiences are in fact connected with experiences in early adulthood. Functioning as institutional systems, there evolve over time patterns of institutional career "flows," the consequences of which are clearly observable (or at least these should be) in what happens as young persons move into early adulthood. The "straight" students, who have maintained institutional careers as exemplary students and who have avoided the definition of deviant, should show high levels of access to adult success and low levels of adult criminality. On the other hand, the unsuccessful students, especially those who accumulate over time public definitions as deviants, can be expected to show both high levels of official adult deviance and low levels of access to adult success.

The Promissory and Institutional Character of the Argument

What should be clear by now about this formulation is, first, that it is based on notions of probabilistic promise. The two sets of institutions, socialization and social control, are both seen as being fundamentally based on notions of youthful promise. This is perhaps clearest in the case of the educational work linkage since the process is so clearly based on notions of recruitment, selection, and preparation. But this logic of the status future operates in the social control institutions as well. The contemporary concern about the negative effects of labeling and stigma, and the consequent emphasis on diversion, provides an obvious demonstration of this point. The argument to eliminate these negative processes contains the premise that the alternative need is to protect the interests of the child, especially with respect to the future. In fact, the whole range of status offenses (ungovernable behavior, endangering one's welfare, out of control, being in manifest danger of engaging in lewd or immoral conduct) can be viewed explicitly within this future-oriented, promissory framework. The reason why these statutes are provided is to protect the future interests of the child, to redirect her or him during these youthful years so that "worse problems don't develop later." The concern for the protection of the future of children is so strong, in fact, that the legal system is willing to promulgate unconstitutionally vague conditions for the imposition of the coercive power of the state in order to accomplish the task. Not only is the *intent* of the juvenile justice system to protect (however one may question the effectiveness of such procedures) the futures of children, it also in its *processes* uses as a basic criterion for decision-making the perceived future potential of the child. The child most likely to be either ignored or diverted is the individual who exhibits a multitude of symptoms of success, i.e., if the individual who is doing well in school, who is involved in a lot of legitimate school activities, who is part of the inner circle, and so on happens to be arrested, it is highly likely that the justice system will extend to the limit its capacity to nonintervene. The cases where intervention is likely to be viewed as necessary are instances where there are, instead of indicators of success, symptoms of failure and illegitimacy. It is in such cases that there is likely to be a perceived need for the social control institutions to enter into the scene, quite likely *with the intent of protecting the interests of the child,* i.e., to engage in action to try to improve the status future prospects of the child, at least in terms of the control aspects of status.

A further feature of this status future argument is that the system operates *bureaucratically,* such that *organizational careers* evolve out of the institutional organization of status. In the contemporary world, terms such as "college prep" or "delinquent" derive their basic meaning in bureaucratic process. Interlocking sets of *institutional labels* are generated which derive their logic and meaning in organizational process, and one must sort out issues at the institutional level before discourse about individual issues around labeling can make much sense. Thus, it is important to know how the label exists in the first place, and the role it plays within the institutional context, before it is possible to make sense of the question of how one kind of actor, e.g., the teacher, is able to impose upon another kind of actor, e.g., the student, one or another type of label, e.g., bright or dumb.

Finally, this perspective argues that critical intersections exist between institutional labels in the "socializing" and in the "social control" bureaucracies. The process of building a career definition of a deviant, to give a specific example, is likely to be a slow and cumulative process, involving the building up over time of failure labels in the socializing institutions and "need for control" labels in the social control institutions. The importance of this assumption is that, first, it avoids the mistake of viewing a single negative label event as a catastrophic and transforming experience without reference to the context of other labels. Certainly some experiences which produce labels can lead to basic transformation of identity, e.g., murderer, narc, or spy. It seems likely, however, that a single experience with delinquency, when that experience is contradicted by powerful institutional definitions of success, may have limited impact. The exact same offense, at the exact same time, for another young person with a history of unsuccessful and problematic behavior labels, may have quite different institutional and personal consequences. Second, as illustrated in this last instance, it calls attention to the hypothesis that much of the basis for the imposition of control labels may lie well outside the social control system. If success and nonsuccess have their definition in the institutional intersections of work, school, and family experiences, and if the definition of nonsuccess is a fundamental feature of individuals who ultimately occupy the most persistent and problematic categories of career delinquents, then attempts to alter basic behavior patterns within the context of the social control institutions may be of little consequence. This includes attempts to "radically nonintervene," since the basic features of social vulnerability remain. Putting it another way, for those persons caught most firmly in the intersection of institutional processes that lead to social vulnerability, the presence of the justice system is merely one of a gamut of problematic roles that must be negotiated, however unsuccessfully. However important it may be for social policy to urge and support the limitation of the power of the juvenile justice system, for those young persons who are most vulnerable the critical features of the vulnerability remain: they will possess few educational credentials and have virtually no chance to enter the job market in a satisfying and legitimate role, to give but two features of such vulnerability.

Some Supportive Evidence

The nature of this exercise creates a unique set of demands for a discussion of data. What will be done here will be to examine the key set of institutional intersections and to generate either data drawn from previously published research or new data, depending on the nature of the question and what data are available. The new data will be drawn from an ongoing longitudinal investigation of adolescents in a medium-sized county (1960 population: 120,888) in the Pacific Northwest. A 25% random sample was drawn from a sample frame consisting of all male sophomores enrolled in the schools of the county in 1964. From a total of 309 subjects selected, 284 usable interviews were obtained, giving a response rate of 92%. The one-hour interviews conducted by the project staff members covered a range of demographic, school, family, work, and peer variables. To these data were added grade point average from school transcripts and delinquency reports from juvenile court records. Further description of this study can be found in Polk and Schafer (1972).

The discussion of evidence will be organized by asking a series of questions:

1. Is there evidence of a connection between school performance and adult success? The question is seen as one of the most critical to the argument, since most of the premises are based on the notion of the institutional connection between school and work. Here a variety of supporting evidence can be cited. Census results persistently report that the highest paying occupations are professional and technical positions, i.e., those requiring the most education (Bureau of the Census, 1973a: 1 and 1973b: 213), and, furthermore, these are the occupations with the highest prestige ranking (Miller, 1971: 201). Using as a criterion the amount of lifetime earnings, males with four or more years of college will earn over the course of their lifetime approximately twice the income of persons who do not finish high school, and recent research suggests that this gap is widening over time (U.S. National Center for Educational Statistics, 1975: 22). A strong connection does seem to exist, then, between the educational and work institutions.

2. Is there evidence of a connection between indicators of family power/vulnerability and school performance? Here again, there seems to be wide and general support for the proposition from the literature. Certainly, countless studies have been conducted which show the relationship between class and performance, i.e., to use the language of this argument, that a working-class background, one measure of family vulnerability, renders it more likely that the child will come to be defined as academically unsuccessful (a review, summary, and annotation of a great number of such studies can be found in Squibb, 1973). Using less abstract and

Table 1. Percentage of Troublesome and Delinquent Responses by Social Class Background and Grade Point Average

	Grade Point Average			
	High		Low	
Troublesome Item	(1) White Collar (N = 111)	(2) Blue Collar (N = 77)	(3) White Collar (N = 28)	(4) Blue Collar (N = 44)
"Friends in Trouble"	30	43	75	64
"Drink with Friends"	46	52	75	61
"Enjoy Cruising"	57	61	82	84
"Peers vs. Principal"	52	48	83	70
"Peers vs. Parents"	28	31	65	46
"Peers vs. Police"	59	57	82	79
"Drink Beer"	35	44	64	72
"Like to Fight"	18	20	43	48
"Official Delinquency"	14	21	36	41

Mean Percentage Difference by:

a. Social Class, indicated by comparing columns
1) 1 vs. 2 = 4.2%
2) 3 vs. 4 = 4.2%

b. G.P.A. indicated by comparing columns
1) 1 vs. 3 = 29.6%
2) 2 vs. 4 = 20.9%

Source: Polk, 1969.

less neutral language, Pearl (1965: 92) argues: " 'special ability classes,' 'basic track,' or 'slow learner classes' are various names for another means of systematically denying the poor adequate access to education."

3. Is there evidence of a connection between school performance and deviance? As before, so much evidence exists for this basic premise from earlier research that there is little need for extensive discussion. Considerable data have been gathered showing the relationship between such academic performance variables as grades, tracking or streaming, dropping out, and deviance/delinquency (for examples, see Polk and Schafer, 1972; Stinchcombe, 1964; Hargreaves, 1967; and Elliott and Voss, 1974).

4. Is there evidence of significant independent connections between family background, school performance, and deviance? Now the argument begins to grow more complex. Perhaps it is time to draw upon some actual data, especially to make sense of the earlier distinction between delinquency and the troublesome life style. Extracting part of a table from a previously published study, it can be seen that when the simultaneous effects of class background and academic performance on deviant behavior are examined, both contribute some independent effect, but the strongest effects are a result of academic performance (see Table 1). Persistently, the percentage differences are greater in the contrasts between academic performance categories than is true for the social class categories. Note here that the pattern is the same for the measure of official delinquency as it is for the wider measures of troublesome behavior. We will use this consistency to argue in the tables which follow that there is at least some reason to presume that it may be legitimate to link the specific behavior of official delinquency to a wider troublesome life style. (Making this assumption is necessary both because in some studies to be cited the only measure of deviance available is delinquency and because in other cases the tables would be too complex if a great number of deviance outcome measures were included. Nonetheless, while the empirical measure is based on delinquency, the theoretical conception of delinquency that is being suggested nests such behavior in the context of a wider troublesome life style.)

5. Is there evidence that when academic failure occurs the nature of the involvement with adolescent peers mediates between the deviant and nondeviant experiences? At this point we can draw on some original data. Among those young persons in the Pacific Northwest study who were academically unsuccessful, the level of delinquency involvement varies considerably by involvement in the teenage culture. Using a composite measure of teenage culture suggested by Galvin (1975), students with low grades who had little involvement with teenage culture had low levels of delinquency (14%), while among failing students with high involvement with teenage culture, close to half (46%) became labeled as juvenile delinquents.

Table 2. Percentage of Individuals with Adult Criminal Records by Delinquency Status as Adolescent and by High School Grade Point Average

	Percentage Criminal	
	Delinquent	Non-Delinquent
High G.P.A.	50 (N = 32)	18 (N = 164)
Low G.P.A.	83 (N = 18)	40 (N = 38)

Table 3. Percentage of Young Persons with High Access to Adult Success (Defined by College Attendance) by Academic Performance and Delinquency

	Percentage with High Access to Adult Success	
	Delinquent	Non-Delinquent
High G.P.A.	60	75
Low G.P.A.	26	20

Source: Noblit, 1973.

6. Is there evidence that the connection between educational performance and deviance extends into early adult life? At this point we begin to explore virtually virgin territory, since few previous research findings exist on the link between adolescent or adult school careers and adult criminality. Data from the Pacific Northwest cohort indicate that such a link can be traced. Looking first at high school performance, slightly over half (54%) of individuals with low grade point averages (low meaning in this case below 2.00) had been charged with an adult offense, in contrast with 23% so charged among individuals with higher grade point averages. A similar pattern exists in the case of adult educational attainment. Drawing the line at three years or more of college completed (since some of the successful elements of the cohort are at the time this research is being done still in college), we find low levels of adult criminality (15%) among those with high adult educational attainment, and high levels of criminality (39%) among those with less educational attainment.

7. Is there evidence of a connection between the labels attached by the socializing (school) and the social control (juvenile court) institutions to *adolescent* and *adult* criminality? To get at this question, it is helpful to generate a table (see Table 2); the resultant data indicate strong links between these institutional experiences. Among the small group of individuals who had both delinquent and academically unsuccessful labels, the level of adult criminality was quite high (83%). At the opposite extreme, relatively low levels of adult criminality (18%) were observed among individuals who were both academically successful and nondelinquent as adolescents. Interestingly, if the young person had earned a label of delinquent, in half the cases (50%) even the experience of academic success was not powerful enough to protect against the eventual experience with adult criminal behavior, while 40% of the nondelinquent youth who were academically unsuccessful were pulled toward adult criminality.

8. Is there evidence of a link between the labels attached by the socializing (school) and the social control (juvenile court) institutions to adolescents and adult success? We unfortunately cannot obtain a good test of this question from the Pacific Northwest data, since as of this writing some of the potentially successful elements of the cohort are still in college. Nonetheless, if we use as a temporary measure of potential adult success significant levels of higher education involvement, we can draw upon some previous research to look tentatively at the issue (Noblit, 1974). The findings of that study (see Table 3) indicate that, as might be expected from the earlier discussion, the highest levels of adult success (75% with high educational attainment) are found among young persons with high levels of academic success as adolescents who were not involved with the juvenile justice system. An interesting facet of these findings is that these data are somewhat interactive. What is observed is that the basic factor operating among the most vulnerable is simply academic failure, i.e., among those with low grade point averages the level of success attainment is low, regardless of delinquency involvement (26% of the low g.p.a. delinquents, and 20% of the low g.p.a. nondelinquents being considered as successful adults, the difference between these two categories appearing to be nonsignificant). The barrier to adult success is, apparently, first and foremost academic. Once you have failed, you have little chance to succeed, and the experience of delinquency does not make your chances any worse. Among the academically successful, on the other hand, the experience of delinquency does appear to suppress the level of success (60% achieving high levels of educational attainment, contrasted with the earlier mentioned 75% among the high g.p.a. nondelinquents).

Discussion

By now the case should be taking shape. What is being suggested is that a number of issues must be considered to make sense of the link between the school experience and delinquency. Implied in these terms is an exceptionally complex network of institutional interconnections. Perhaps it would be useful at this point to restate the suggested viewpoint in diagrammatic form (see Figure 1). Starting in the correct temporal sequence, the family can be viewed as establishing the basic support conditions that create either more powerful or more vulnerable young persons (with vulnerability being a result of such considerations as social class, ethnicity, place of residence, family competence variables, and so on). Using a variety of evidence regarding one feature of vulnerability, it does appear that an

Figure 1. Suggested Status Flows among Socializing (family, school, work) and Social Control (police, courts, training schools) Institutions

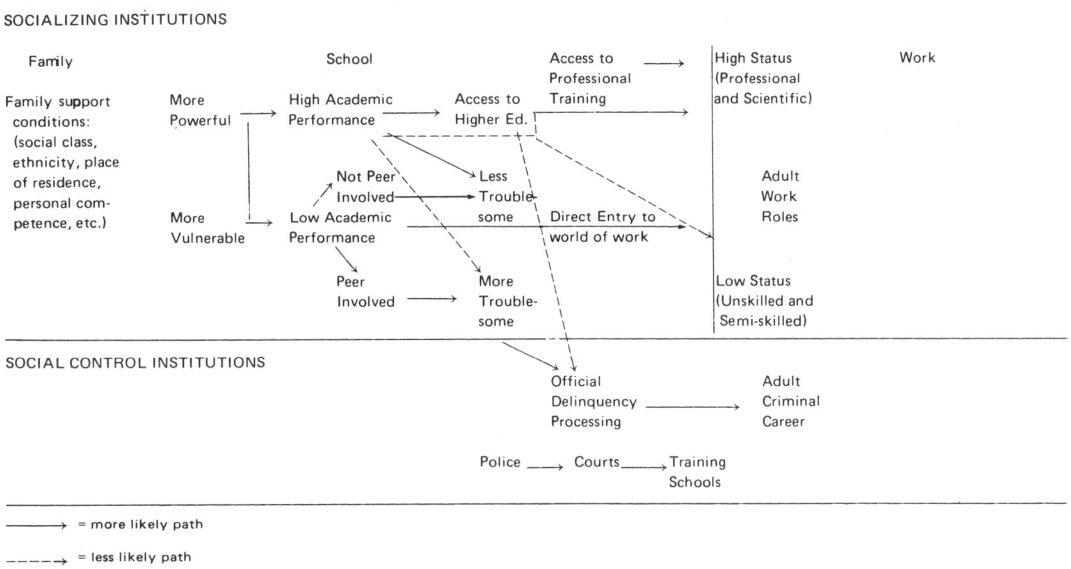

argument can be made that a likely path of the vulnerable youth is low academic success in elementary and secondary school. Once the school has operated in the lives of children for a few years, the evidence suggests that school status may be an important ingredient in setting up the paths to troublesome behavior, with a likely path from high academic achievement being drawn to less troublesome behavior. Among low academic performers, it is suggested that an important condition affecting the flow into deviance may be the quality of the peer experience. If the low performers are not caught up in the supportive teenage culture, the likely path may be to less troublesome behavior. On the other hand, if the unsuccessful youth is surrounded by a supportive peer culture, a likely path may be into a troublesome life style pattern, a feature of which is official delinquency.

At this point, the patterns become complex enough to cause difficulty for simple summarization. On the one hand, the path to adult success seems to be open primarily to those who continue to perform well academically, especially those who avoid the delinquency label, while on the other hand, adult success appears to be closed to the academically unsuccessful, with the probability of success being not much better for the nondelinquents among the school failures. The paths to adult deviancy appear to lead through both the educational and the delinquency labeling processes, with the highest levels of adult criminality occurring where the individual as an adolescent was labeled as both delinquent and failure, while a much less likely path traces through academic success and nondelinquency.

Again, it should be emphasized that these labels are seen, first, as arising out of the bureaucratic and organizational processes. School grades and tracks have their origins and meaning in the process of sorting that leads to the adult work world. Further, the suggested view emphasizes strongly that the labeling experiences are institutionally interconnected and are best understood in terms of specific patterns of interconnections. It simply does not mean much to say that academic achievement is correlated with delinquency. One must have a conception, according to the suggested perspective, regarding what education is about, and then how under particular conditions the level of delinquency may be higher or lower.

As a further note, it should be pointed out that the argument that the ordering derives its meaning from the end points, both in success and deviance careers, refers to the suggested way of analyzing and understanding the order from the viewpoint of the outside analyst. There is some evidence which suggest that the adolescent actors "in the scene" build their understanding from their immediate experiences. For the high school student, the terms college prep or failure have immediate meaning, and the social statuses, however much these are based in institutional futures, are likely to be evaluated by the adolescent actors in terms of their status present (see Elliott and Voss, 1974: 204).

A view has been developed here that suggests that there is a link between the school and delinquency, but that understanding the connection requires explication of the institutional ordering of family-to-school-to-adult work role system. It is in these structural orderings that the basic patterns of vulnerability are created that expose some young persons first to the label of delinquency and then to criminality. These socializing institutions are organized currently in such a way as to assure, even require, that some young persons will come to be labeled in ways that render them socially vulnerable. Seeking the sources of the social vulnerability that are evidenced in delinquency, in other words, necessitates an exploration of features of bureaucratic organization and function, rather than a focus on individual pathology. Furthermore, positive action to address these patterns of vulnerability requires social policies that go well beyond diversion or radical nonintervention, since, as frequently expressed, these make little or no reference to the institutional ordering of the socializing institutions.

References

Clark, J. P. and E. P. Wenniger (1962) "Socio-economic class and area correlates of illegal behavior among juveniles." Amer. Soc. Rev. 27 (December): 826-834.

Cohen, A. K. (1955) *Delinquent Boys.* New York: Free Press.

Elliott, D. S. and H. L. Voss (1974) *Delinquency and Dropout.* Lexington, Mass.: D. C. Heath.

Galvin, J. L. (1975) "Youth culture and adult success." Ph.D. dissertation. University of Oregon, Department of Curriculum and Instruction. September. (unpublished)

Goldman, N. (1963) *The Differential Selection of Juvenile Offenders for Court Appearances.* New York: National Council on Crime and Delinquency.

Hargreaves, D. H. (1967) *Social Relations in a Secondary School.* London: Routledge & Kegan Paul.

Miller, H. P. (1967) *Rich Man, Poor Man.* New York: Thomas Y. Crowell.

Noblit, G. (1973) "Delinquency and access to success: a study of the consequences of the delinquency label." Ph.D. dissertation. University of Oregon, Department of Sociology. (unpublished)

Pearl A. (1972) *Atrocity of Education.* New York: E. P. Dutton.

—— (1965) "Youth in lower class settings," in Muzafer Sherif and Carolyn W. Sherif (eds.) Problems of Youth. Chicago: Aldine.

Polk, K. (1969) "Class, strain, and rebellion among adolescents." Social Problems 17(Fall):214-224.

—— and W. E. Schafer (1972) Schools and Delinquency. Englewood Cliffs, N.J.: Prentice-Hall.

Short, J. F., Jr. (1958) "Differential association with delinquent friends and delinquent behavior." Pacific Soc. Rev. 1:20-25.

—— and F. I. Nye (1957-1958) "Reported behavior as a criterion of deviant behavior." Social Problems 5:207-213.

Squibb, P. G. (1973) "Education and class." Educational Research 15 (June):194-209.

Stinchcombe, A. (1964) *Rebellion in a High School.* Chicago: Quadrangle.

U.S. Bureau of the Census (1973a) Census of the Population: 1970. Subject Reports, Final Report PC (2)-8B, Earnings by Occupation and Education. Washington, D.C.: Government Printing Office.

—— (1973b) Census of the Population: 1970. Subject Reports, Final Report PC (2)-5B Educational Attainment. Washington, D.C.: Government Printing Office.

U.S. National Center for Educational Statistics (1975) Digest of Educational Statistics—1974. Washington, D.C.: Government Printing Office.

The Family as Cradle of Violence

Suzanne K. Steinmetz and Murray A. Straus

Lizzie Borden took an ax
And gave her father 40 whacks.
When the job was neatly done
She gave her mother 41.

Although intrafamily violence like that attributed to Lizzie Borden is occasionally reported, such behavior is considered totally out of the ordinary—families are supposed to be oases of serenity where love and good feeling flow from each parent and child.

Unfortunately, that lovely picture is not accurate. In fact, the grizzly tale of Lizzie Borden may not be unique. Violence seems as typical of family relationships as love; and it would be hard to find a group or institution in American society in which violence is more of an everyday occurrence than it is within the family. Family members physically abuse each other far more often than do nonrelated individuals. Starting with slaps and going on to torture and murder, the family provides a prime setting for every degree of physical violence. So universal is the phenomenon that it is probable that some form of violence will occur in almost every family.

The most universal type of physical violence is corporal punishment by parents. Studies in England and the United States show that between 84 and 97 percent of all parents use physical punishment at some point in their child's life. Moreover, such use of physical force to maintain parental authority is not confined to early childhood. Data on students in three different regions of the United States show that half of the parents sampled either used or threatened their high school seniors with physical punishment.

Of course, physical punishment differs significantly from other violence. But it is violence, nonetheless. Despite its good intentions, it has some of the same consequences as other forms of violence. Research shows that parents who use physical punishment to control the aggressiveness of their children probably increase rather than decrease their child's aggressive tendencies. Violence begets violence, however peaceful and altruistic the motivation.

The violent tendencies thus reinforced may well be turned against the parents, as in the case of Lizzie Borden. Although most intrafamily violence is less bloody than that attributed to Lizzie, some family abuse does go as far as ax murder. Examination of relationships between murderer and victim proves that the largest single category of victim is that of family member or relative.

Homicide at Home

The magnitude of family violence became particularly obvious during the summer heat wave of 1972. Page 1 of the July 22, 1972 *New York Times* carried an article describing the increase in murders during the previous few days of extreme heat in New York City and summarizing the statistics for murder in New York during the previous six months. Page 2 held an article totalling deaths in Northern Ireland during three and a half years of disturbances. About as many people were murdered by their relatives in one six-month period in New York City as had been killed in three and a half years of political upheaval in Northern Ireland.

Murder, though relatively rare, gets far more attention than less violent abuse. Even though more murders

From *Society*, Vol. 10, No. 6, September/October 1973. Published by permission of Transaction, Inc. from *Society*, Vol. 10, No. 6.

are committed on family members than any other type of person, and even though the United States has a high degree of homicide, the rate is still only four or five per 100,000 population. What about non-lethal physical violence between husband and wife? While accurate statistics are hard to find, one way of estimating the magnitude of the phenomenon is through the eyes of the police.

Just as relatives are the largest single category of murder victim, so family fights are the largest single category of police calls. One legal researcher estimates that more police calls involve family conflict than do calls for all criminal incidents, including murders, rapes, nonfamily assaults, robberies and muggings. "Violence in the home" deserves at least as much public concern as "crime in the streets." The police hate and fear family conflict calls for several reasons. First, a family disturbance call lacks the glamour, prestige and public appreciation of a robbery or an accident summons. More important, such calls are extremely dangerous. Many a policeman coming to the aid of a wife who is being beaten has had a chair or a bottle thrown at him or has been stabbed or shot by a wife who suddenly becomes fearful of what is going to happen to her husband, or who abruptly turns her rage from her husband to the police. Twenty-two percent of all police fatalities come from investigating problems between husband and wife or parent and child.

One cannot tell from these data on police calls just what proportion of all husbands and wives have had physical fights, since it takes an unusual combination of events to have the police summoned. The closest published estimate is found in the research of George Levinger and John O'Brien. In studying applicants for divorce, O'Brien found that 17 percent of his cases spontaneously mentioned overt violent behavior, and Levinger found that 23 percent of the middle-class couples and 40 percent of the working-class couples gave "physical abuse" as a major complaint.

Both of these figures probably underestimate the amount of physical violence between husbands and wives because there may well have been violent incidents which were not mentioned or which were not listed as a main cause of divorce. Even doubling the figure, however, leaves us far from knowing the extent of husband-wife violence. First, there is a discrepancy between the O'Brien and the Levinger figures. Second, these figures apply only to couples who have applied for divorce. It may be that there is a lower incidence of physical violence among a cross-section of couples; or it may be, as we suspect, that the difference is not very great.

A survey conducted for the National Commission of the Causes and Prevention of Violence deals with what violence people would approve. These data show that one out of four men and one out of six women approve of slapping a wife under certain conditions. As for a wife slapping a husband, 26 percent of the men and 19 percent of the women approve. Of course, some people who approve of slapping will never do it and some who disapprove *will* slap—or worse. Probably the latter group is larger. If that is true, we know that husband-wife violence at the minimal level of slapping occurs in at least one quarter of American families.

Our own pilot studies also give some indication of the high rate of violence in the family. Richard Gelles of the University of New Hampshire, who has done a series of in-depth case studies of a sample of 80 families, found that about 56 percent of the couples have used physical force on each other at some time.

In a second study, freshman college students responded to a series of questions about conflicts which occurred in their senior year in high school, and to further questions about how these conflicts were handled. Included in the conflict resolution section were questions on whether or not the parties to the disputes had ever hit, pushed, shoved, thrown things or kicked each other in the course of a quarrel.

The results show that during that one year 62 percent of the high school seniors had used physical force on a brother or sister and 16 percent of their parents had used physical force on each other. Since these figures are for a single year, the percentage who had *ever* used violence is probably much greater. How much greater is difficult to estimate because we cannot simply accumulate the 16 percent for one year over the total number of years married. Some couples will never have used violence and others will have used it repeatedly. Nevertheless, it seems safe to assume that it will not always be the same 16 percent. So, it is probably best to fall back on the 56 percent estimate from the 80 earlier interviews.

The fact is that almost all everyday beating, slapping, kicking and throwing things is carried out by normal Americans rather than deranged persons.

Since a vast amount of family violence can be documented, what accounts for the myth of family nonviolence? At least one basis for the rosy, if false, view is that the family is a tremendously important social institution, which must be preserved. In Western countries one supportive device is the ideology of familial love and gentleness, an ideology which helps encourage people to marry and to stay married. It tends to maintain satisfaction with the family system despite the stresses and strains of family life. From the viewpoint of preserving the integrity of a critical social institution, such a mythology is highly useful.

Other simplifications and generalizations also block knowledge and understanding of the nature of violence in the family. The psychopathology myth, the class myth, the sex myth and the catharsis myth must be exposed and examined if the true nature of intrafamily abuse is to emerge.

A growing number of sociologists and psychologists have suggested that a focus on conflict and violence may be a more revealing way of understanding the family than a focus on consensus and solidarity. Most members of this group, however, recognize that family conflict is legitimate, but still consider physical violence only as an abnormality—something which involves sick families. The facts do not support this *psychopathology myth*. According to Richard J. Gelles, only a tiny proportion of those using violence—even child abusers—can be considered mentally ill. Our own studies reveal that physically abusive husbands, wives and children are of overwhelmingly sound mind and body.

The fact that almost all family violence, including everyday beating, slapping, kicking and throwing things, is carried out by normal everyday Americans rather than deranged persons should not lead us to think of violence as being desirable or even acceptable. The important question is, Why is physical violence so common between members of the closest and most intimate of all human groups?

Although social scientists are still far from a full understanding of the causes of violence between family members, evidence is accumulating that family violence is learned—and learned in childhood in the home. This fact does not deny the importance of the human biological heritage. If the capacity for violence were not present in the human organism, learning and social patterning could not produce it.

If a child actually observes and experiences the effects of violence, he will learn to be violent. Husbands, wives and parents play out models of behavior which they learned in childhood from *their* parents and from friends and relatives. Rather than being deviant, they are conforming to patterns learned in childhood. Of course, in most cases they also learned the opposite message—that family violence is wrong. However, a message learned by experience and observation, rather than the message learned Sunday-school-style, has more force, especially when social stresses become great—and family stresses are often very great. The high level of interaction and commitment which is part of the pleasure of family life also produces great tensions.

Another widespread but hard-to-prove belief is the *class myth*, the idea that intrafamily violence occurs mainly in lower- and working-class families. Studying divorce applicants, George Levinger found that 40 percent of the working-class wives and 23 percent of the middle-class wives indicated "physical abuse" as a reason for seeking divorce. If almost one out of four middle-class women can report physical abuse, violence hardly seems absent from middle-class families. The nationwide sample survey conducted for the United States Commission on Violence reveals that over one-fifth of the respondents approve of slapping a spouse under certain conditions. There were no social-class differences in this *approval* of slapping, nor in reports of having ever spanked a child. At the same time, almost twice as many less educated respondents spank *frequently* (42 percent) as more educated respondents (22 percent).

Class Differences

Other research on physical punishment is also contradictory. Most studies report more use of physical punishment by working-class parents, but some find no difference. Howard S. Erlanger undertook a comprehensive review of studies of social-class differences in the use of physical punishment and concluded that, although the weight of the evidence supports the view of less use of this technique among the middle class, the differences are small. Sizeable differences between social classes show up only when the analysis takes into account differences within social classes of such things as race, the sex of the child and of the parent, parental ambition for the child and the specific nature of the father's occupation. Differences *within* social classes are at least as important as differences *between* classes.

Despite the mixed evidence, and despite the fact that there is a great deal of violence in middle-class families, we believe that research will eventually show that intrafamily violence is more common as one goes down the socioeconomic status ladder. Many social scientists attribute this to a lower-class "culture of violence" which encourages violent acts, and to an opposite middle-class culture which condemns violence. Although these cultural elements are well documented, we see them not as a cause, but as a response to fundamental social structural forces which affect families at all social levels but press harder and more frequently on the lower and working classes.

Compensatory Violence

Willingness and ability to use physical violence may compensate for lack of other resources such as money, knowledge and respect. If the social system does not provide an individual with the resources needed to maintain his or her family position, that individual will use violence if he is capable of it. John E. O'Brien asserts that "... there is considerable evidence that ... husbands who ... displayed violent behavior were severely inadequate in work, earner, or family support roles." While lack of the occupational and economic resources needed to fulfill the position of husband in our society is more characteristic of lower-class families than others, it is by no means confined to that stratum. The 1970-72 recession, with its high rates of unemployment among middle-class occupational groups (such as aerospace engineers) provides an opportunity to test this theory. The *resource theory* of violence would predict that unemployed husbands would engage in more intrafamily violence than comparable middle-class husbands who have not lost their jobs.

Some indication that the predicted results might be found is suggested by statistics for Birmingham, England, which showed a sharp rise in wife-beating during a six-month period when unemployment also rose sharply. A 1971 *Parade* report characterized these men as "frustrated, bored, unable to find a satisfying outlet for their energy, Britishers who are reduced to life on the dole meet adversity like men: they blame it on their wives. Then, pow!!!"

In a society such as ours, in which aggression is defined as a normal response to frustration, we can expect that the more frustrating the familial and occupational roles, the greater the amount of violence. Donald McKinley found that the lower the degree of self-direction a man has in his work, the greater the degree of aggressiveness in his relationship with his son. McKinley's data also show that the lower the job satisfaction, the higher the percentage using harsh punishment of children. The same relationship was found within each social class.

> Frustrated, bored, unable to find a satisfying outlet for their energy Britishers who are reduced to life on the dole meet adversity like men: they blame it on their wives. Then, pow!!!

Both husbands and wives suffer from frustration, but since the main avenue of achievement for women has been in the family rather than in occupational roles, we must look within the family for the circumstances that are frustrating to women. Both residential crowding and too many children have been found to be related to the use of physical punishment. As with men, frustrations of this type are more common in the lower class, since lower-class wives are unlikely to have sufficient equipment and money for efficient, convenient housekeeping.

Although intrafamily violence probably is more common among lower-class families, it is incorrect to see it as only a lower-class or working-class phenomenon. What we have called the class myth overlooks the basic structural conditions (such as lack of adequate resources and frustrating life experiences) which are major causes of intrafamily violence and are present at all social levels, though to varying degrees. Some kinds of intrafamily violence are typical of all social classes—such as hitting children—even though the rate may be lower for middle class—while other kinds of intrafamily violence are typical of *neither* class—like severe wife-beating—even though the rate is probably greater for the working class and especially the lower class.

The *sex myth* is the idea that sexual drives are linked to violence by basic biological mechanisms developed in the course of human evolution. Violence in sex is directly related to violence in the family because the family is the main way in which sex is made legitimate. To the extent that there is an inherent connection between sex and violence, it would be part of the biological basis for violence within the family.

There is abundant evidence that sex and violence go together, at least in our society and in a number of others. At the extreme, sex and warfare have been associated in many ways, ranging from societies which view sex before a battle as a source of strength (or in some tribes, as a weakness) to the almost universally high frequency of rape by soldiers, often accompanied by subsequent genital mutilation and murder. In the fighting following the independence of the Congo in the early 1960s, rape was so common that the Catholic church is said to have given a special dispensation so that nuns could take contraceptive pills. More recently, in the Pakistan civil war, rape and mutilation were everyday occurrences. In Vietnam, scattered reports suggest that rapes and sexual tortures have been widespread. Closer to home, we have the romantic view of the aggressive he-man who "takes his woman" as portrayed in westerns and James Bond-type novels. In both cases, sex and gunfights are liberally intertwined.

Sexual Repression

Then there are the sadists and masochists—individuals who can obtain sexual pleasure only by inflicting or receiving violent acts. We could dismiss such people as pathological exceptions, but it seems better to consider sadism and masochism as simply extreme forms of widespread behavior. The sex act itself typically is accompanied at least by mild violence and often by biting and scratching.

Nevertheless, despite all of this and much other evidence which could be cited, we feel that there is little biological linkage between sex and violence. It is true that in our society and in many other societies, sex and violence are linked. But there are enough instances of societies in which this is not the case to raise doubts about the biological linkage. What social conditions produce the association between violence and sex?

The most commonly offered explanation attributes the linkage between sex and violence to rules of the culture which limit or prevent sex. Empirical evidence supporting this sexual repression theory is difficult to establish. Societies which are high in restriction of extramarital intercourse are also societies which tend to be violent—particularly in emphasizing military glory, killing, torture and mutilation of an enemy. But just how this carries over to violence in the sex act is not clear. Our interpretation hinges on the fact that sexual restriction tends to be associated with a definition of sex as intrinsically evil. This combination sets in motion two powerful forces making sex violent in societies having such a sexual code. First, since sex is normally prohibited or restricted, engaging in sexual intercourse may imply license to disregard other normally prohibited or restricted aspects of interpersonal relations. Consequently, aggressively inclined persons will tend to express their aggressiveness when they express their sexuality. Second, since sex is defined as evil and base, this cultural definition of sex may create a label or an expectancy which tends to be acted out.

By contrast, in societies such as Mangaia, which impose minimal sex restrictions and in which sex is defined as something to be enjoyed by all from the time they are first capable until death, sex is nonviolent. In Mangaia, exactly the opposite of the two violence-producing mechanisms just listed seem to operate. First, since sex is a normal everyday activity, the normal standards for control of aggression apply. Second, since sex is defined as an act expressing the best in man, it is an occasion for altruistic behavior. Thus, Donald S. Marshall says of the Mangaia: "My several informants generally agreed that the really important thing in sexual intercourse—for the married man or for his unwed fellow—was to give pleasure to his partner; that her pleasure in orgasm was what gave the male partner a special thrill, separate from his own orgasm."

There is little evidence to show direct linkage between sex and violence. It is true that they are socially linked in many cultures, but there are enough societies where this is not the case to raise doubts about the biological linkage.

Socially patterned antagonism between men and women is at the heart of a related theory which can also account for the association of sex and violence. The sex antagonism and segregation theory suggests that the higher the level of antagonism between men and women, the greater the tendency to use violence in sexual acts. Since, by itself, this statement is open to a charge of circular reasoning, the theory must be backed up by related propositions which account for the sex role antagonism.

In societies such as ours, part of the explanation for antagonism between the sexes is probably traceable to the sexual restrictions and sexual denigration mentioned above. The curse God placed on all women when Eve sinned is the earliest example in our culture of the sexually restrictive ethic, the placing of the "blame" for sex on women, and the resulting negative definition of women—all of which tend to make women culturally legitimate objects of antagonism and aggression. The New Testament reveals much more antipathy to sex than the Old and contains many derogatory (and implicitly hostile) statements about women.

The present level of antagonism between the sexes is probably at least as great as that in biblical times. In novels, biographies and everyday speech, words indicating femaleness, especially in its sexual aspect (such as "bitch"), are used by men as terms of disparagement, and terms for sexual intercourse, such as "screw" and "fuck," are used to indicate an aggressive or harmful act. On the female side, women tend to see men as exploiters and to teach their daughters that men are out to take advantage of them.

It would be a colossal example of ethnocentrism, however, to attribute antagonism between the sexes to the Western Judeo-Christian tradition. Cultural definitions of women as evil are found in many societies. Obviously, more fundamental processes are at work, of which the Christian tradition is only one manifestation.

Catharsis Myth

A clue to a possibly universal process giving rise to antagonism between the sexes may be found in the cross-cultural studies which trace this hostility back to the division of labor between the sexes and other differences in the roles of men and women. This sex role segregation, gives rise to differences in child-rearing practices for boys and girls and to problems in establishing sexual identity. Beatrice Whiting, for example, concludes: "It would seem as if there were a never-ending circle. The separation of the sexes leads to a conflict of identity in the boy children, to unconscious fear of being feminine, which leads to protest masculinity, exaggeration of the differences between men and women, antagonism against and fear of women, male solidarity, and hence back to isolation of women and very young children." This process can also be observed in the matrifocal family of the urban slum and the Caribbean, the relationships between the sexes have been labeled by Jackson Toby as "compulsive masculinity" and vividly depicted in Eldridge Cleaver's "Allegory of the Black Eunuchs." Slightly more genteel forms of the same sexual antagonism are to be found among middle-class men, as illustrated by the character of Jonathan in the movie *Carnal Knowledge*.

Obviously, the linkages between sex and violence are extremely complex, and many other factors probably operate besides the degree of restrictiveness, the cultural definition of sexuality and antagonism between the sexes. But even these indicate sufficiently that it is incorrect to assume a direct connection between sexual drives and violence, since such an assumption disregards the sociocultural framework within which sexual relations take place. These social and cultural factors, rather than sex drives *per se*, give rise to the violent aspects of sexuality in so many societies.

The *catharsis myth* asserts that the expression of "normal" aggression between family members should not be bottled up: if normal aggression is allowed to be expressed, tension is released, and the likelihood of severe violence is therefore reduced. This view has a long and distinguished intellectual history. Aristotle used the term "catharsis" to refer to the purging of the passions or sufferings of spectators through vicarious participation in the suffering of a tragic hero. Both Freud's idea of "the liberation of affect" to enable reexperiencing blocked or inhibited emotions, and the view of John Dollard and his associates that "the occurrence of any act of aggression is assumed to reduce the instigation of aggression" are modern versions of this tradition.

Applying this approach to the family, Bettelheim urges that children should learn about violence in order to learn how to handle it. Under the present rules (at least for the middle class), we forbid a child to hit, yell or swear at us or his playmates. The child must also refrain from destroying property or even his own toys. In teaching this type of self-control, however, Bruno Bettelheim holds that we have denied the child outlets for the instinct of human violence and have failed to teach him how to deal with his violent feelings.

Proof of the catharsis theory is overwhelmingly negative. Exposure to vicariously experienced violence has been shown to increase rather than decrease both aggressive fantasy and aggressive acts. Similarly, experiments in which children are given the opportunity to express violence and aggression show that they express more aggression after the purported cathartic experience than do controls.

Theoretical arguments against the catharsis view are equally cogent. The instinct theory assumptions which underlie the idea of catharsis have long been discarded in social science. Modern social psychological theories—including social learning theory, symbolic interaction theory and labeling theory—all predict the opposite of the catharsis theory: the more frequently an act is performed, the greater the likelihood that it will become a standard part of the behavior repertory of the individual and of the expectations of others for that individual.

Cultural Beliefs

In light of largely negative evidence and cogent theoretical criticism, the sheer persistence of the catharsis theory becomes an interesting phenomenon. There seem to be several factors underlying the persistence of the catharsis myth:

□ *Prestige and influence of psychoanalytic theory.* Albert Bandura and Richard Walters suggest that the persistence of the catharsis view is partly the result of the extent to which psychoanalytic ideas have become part of both social science and popular culture. Granting this, one must also ask why this particular part of Freud's vast writing is unquestioned. After all, much of what Freud wrote has been ignored, and other parts have been dropped on the basis of contrary evidence.

Whenever an element of cultural belief persists in spite of seemingly sound reasons for discarding it, one should look for ways in which the belief may be woven into a system of social behavior. Certain behavior may be least partially congruent with the "false" belief; various social patterns may be justified by such beliefs.

□ *Justification of existing patterns.* Intrafamily violence is a recurring feature of our society, despite the cultural commitment to nonviolence. It is not far-fetched to assume that, under the circumstances, the catharsis theory which in effect justifies sporadic violence will be attractive to a population engaged in occasional violence.

□ *Congruence with the positive value of violence in non-family spheres of life.* Although *familial* norms deprecate or forbid intrafamily violence, the larger value system of American society is hardly nonviolent. In fact, the overwhelming proportion of American parents consider it part of their role to train sons to be tough. The violence commission survey reveals that 70 percent of the respondents believed it is good for boys to have a few fist-fights. Thus, a social theory which justifies violence as being psychologically beneficial to the aggressor is likely to be well received.

□ *Congruence with the way familial violence often occurs.* Given the antiviolence norms, intrafamily physical abuse typically occurs as a climax to a repressed conflict. As Louis Coser points out:

> Closely knit groups in which there exists a high frequency of interaction and high personality involvement of the members have a tendency to suppress conflict. While they provide frequent occasions for hostility (since both sentiments of love and hatred are intensified through frequency of interaction), the acting out of such feelings is sensed as a danger to such intimate relationships, and hence there is a tendency to suppress rather than to allow expression of hostile feelings. In close-knit groups, feelings of hostility tend, therefore, to accumulate and hence to intensify.

At some point the repressed conflict has to be resolved. Frequently, the mechanism which forces the conflict into the open is a violent outburst. This is one of the social functions of violence listed by Coser. In this sense, intrafamily violence does have a cathartic effect. But the catharsis which takes place comes from getting the conflict into the open and resolving it—not the releasing effects of violent incidents *per se*, but on the ability to recognize these as warning signals and to deal with the underlying conflict honestly and with empathy.

□ *Confusion of immediate with long-term effects.* There can be little doubt that a sequence of violent activity is often followed by a sharp reduction of tension, an emotional release and even a feeling of quiescence. To the extent that tension release *is* produced by violence, this immediate cathartic effect is likely to powerfully reinforce the violence which preceded it. Having reduced tension in one instance, it becomes a mode of behavior likely to be repeated later in similar instances. An analogy with sexual orgasm seems plausible. Following orgasm, there is typically a sharp reduction in sexual drive, most obvious in the male's loss of erection. At the same time, however, the experience of orgasm is powerfully reinforcing and has the long-term effect of increasing the sex drive. We believe that violence and sex are similar in this respect. The short-term effect of violence is, in one sense, cathartic; but the long-term effect is a powerful force toward including violence as a standard mode of social interaction.

While the assumptions outlined in this article in some ways contribute to preserving the institution of family, they also keep us from taking a hard and realistic look at the family and taking steps to change it in ways which might correct the underlying problems. Such stereotypes contain a kernel of truth but are dangerous oversimplifications. Although there are differences between social classes in intrafamily violence, the class myth ignores the high level of family violence present in other social strata. The sex myth, although based on historically accurate observation of the link between sex and violence, tends to assume that this link is biologically determined and fails to take into account the social and cultural factors which associate sex and violence in many societies. The catharsis myth seems to have the smallest kernel of truth at its core, and its persistence, in the face of devastating evidence to the contrary, may be due to the subtle justification it gives to the violent nature of American society and to the fact that violent episodes in a family can have the positive function of forcing a repressed conflict into the open for nonviolent resolution.

SECTION SIX

Summary

The four articles included in this section are intended to widen our focus in assessing the relative importance of the different socializing forces that American youth encounter. Some agencies of socialization may play a dominant role in explaining the presence or absence of delinquent behavior, while others, despite their popular appeal, may be of little significance.

The family has historically been accorded a primary position as the cornerstone of society. Many of our values, attitudes, personality characteristics, language patterns, and even personal tastes are developed within the context of the family. The young child learns important cultural norms and values and a vast array of skills that are essential for life from his or her family. But as Steinmetz and Straus point out, not all the learning that takes place within the family is necessarily constructive. Violence in the home—husbands and wives feuding, brothers and sisters quarreling, discipline that hovers close to physical assault—is not uncommon. Furthermore, this open violence cannot be dismissed as the product of mentally ill individuals or lower-class environments. Steinmetz and Straus see family violence as a permanent feature of our society, a situation that may reflect a strong cultural belief in the efficacy of violence. Could it not be the case that the spirit of the "Wild West"—the excitement of a good barroom brawl or a dramatic gun fight—lives on in the twentieth century? Are we as committed to nonviolence as we profess? Are adolescents who engage in acts of violence doing anything different from adults? The discussion on the cradle of violence brings the learning of some forms of delinquent behavior very close to home.

Polk's article on schools and delinquency presents another disturbing element of the socialization of American youth. If we are living in a "credentialed" society, then schools become the major conduits to success. The sorting and filtering that go on in the academic arena might effect the relegation to inferior positions in the social hierarchy of those who do not successfully complete. Polk indicts the school as a major contributor to delinquency for its effective limiting of the success goals of academically poorer students. The causal ordering of events depicted by Polk's diagram at the conclusion of his discussion illustrates the complex interrelationship of family, school, delinquent careers, and adult work roles. What is evident from the diagram is the key role the school plays in facilitating delinquent behavior when academic performance is low. Now the question becomes one of modifying a major agency of socialization. Based on Polk's conclusions, what are some potential ways that positive action or redesigned social policies could weaken the connection between poor academic performance and delinquency?

The Higgins and Albrecht article on the negative relationship between church attendance and delinquency suggests that despite sociologists' almost total neglect of religion, in some situations religion could be a relevant variable. In a previous study, Hirschi and Stark (1969), using data gathered from high-school students in the San Francisco Bay area, found church attendance to be unrelated to delinquency. A few years later, Burkett and White (1974), drawing on students from the Pacific Northwest, found some support for a negative relationship between religion and delinquency. They found that morally ambiguous behavior such as alcohol and marijuana use was inversely related to church attendance. Burkett and White suggested that religious participation could be important in those instances in which secular agencies did not clearly condemn certain forms of behavior. The Higgins and Albrecht selection also shows a strong negative relationship between drug use and church attendance. Thus, it may be that for certain specific acts and for certain religious groups, church attendance is an important consideration. How can this investigation into the potential negative relationship between religious participation and delinquent behavior be further elaborated?

The final selection in this section, which concerns television violence, may be something of a disappointment. It seems logical to assume that there ought to be a relationship between televised violence and aggressive behavior. However, the link has not been clearly established. Is it possible that the impact of televised violence is filtered through other socialization agencies, such as the family and the school? Is it conceivable that children approach the television set with a mental framework that already predisposes them toward or against violent behavior? The Hartnagel, Teevan, and McIntyre reading certainly suggests that this may be the case. After reviewing the discussions by Steinmetz and Straus, and Polk, consider how a stronger test of the role of television violence might be conducted.

REFERENCES

Burkett, S. R., and M. White. 1974. "Hellfire and Delinquency: Another Look." *Journal for the Scientific Study of Religion* 13 (December): 455–62.

Hirschi, T., and R. Stark. 1969. "Hellfire and Delinquency." *Social Problems* 17 (Fall): 202–13.

SECTION SEVEN

Reactions to Delinquency: Deterrence versus Labeling

In Section 1 we encountered two views of the consequences of individuals' contact with the juvenile justice system. In the *Time* article entitled "The Youth Crime Plague," the juvenile court is depicted as an ineffective "kiddies' court" that does nothing to deter youths from further delinquency. From this perspective, it is argued that children are not dealt with harshly enough, so that rather than being deterred from further crime, processed youths come to realize that nothing serious is going to happen to them and commit more offenses. In the article entitled "The Delinquent Nobody Knows," the case study of a boy named Mike is cited, and the author espouses the view that "labels, like the general label juvenile delinquent, beat back the terror of Mike's life for us, but don't help Mike much." From this point of view, exposing youths to the juvenile justice system may be counterproductive–worse than doing nothing at all–and the labels applied in the process are potentially dangerous.

The alleged failure of the juvenile court system has led some critics to advocate tougher policies that would scare youths straight and others to suggest that we leave youths alone whenever possible. These two orientations reflect commitments to two very different views of the legal system's role in maintaining conformity–deterrence theory and labeling theory, respectively. In deterrence theory, conformity with the law is explained, in part, in terms of fear of legal sanctions. Without this fear, the crime rate would presumably increase, and the apprehended offenders would offend again. In contrast, the labeling perspective emphasizes the "boomerang" effects of efforts to deter crime. To paraphrase one of the earliest labeling theorists, Frank Tannenbaum: in the attempt to deter "evil," the evil is dramatized, exaggerated, and compounded.

The juvenile court movement of the 1800s and early 1900s has been depicted as an attempt to shift the emphasis from punishment and deterrence to treatment and rehabilitation. Yet some social historians (see Platt's article in Section 2) argue that justice for juveniles has always been essentially punitive, despite a widespread concern for helping and saving children. Edwin Schur (1973:87) takes the position that the delinquent is in fact "stigmatized, punished and potentially criminalized." Thus, there continues to be strong advocacy of quite contrasting interpretations of exactly how "hard" and how "soft" the juvenile justice system really is and whether variation in official processing deters or increases delinquency. Labeling-oriented critics emphasize a view of the system as tough ("stigmatizing," "punishing," "criminalizing") and feel that the toughness compounds the problem. Deterrence-oriented critics see the system as soft ("lenient," "coddling," "a mere slap on the hand") and take the view that the softness compounds the problem. Neither side sees the system as effective in rehabilitating offenders.

Despite the fact that there is a considerable body of research dealing with the effects of legal sanctions, there is no way at present to declare one or the other side in the controversy to be correct. For example, there is mounting evidence that youths who perceive a high risk of getting caught and punished for lawbreaking are significantly less likely to report involvement in delinquency than are youths who feel they can get away with it. This evidence is relevant to what is called *general deterrence*—that is, the inhibiting effect of fear of punishment in potential offenders. The key argument in the deterrence-versus-labeling-effects debate centers around *specific deterrence*—that is, the inhibiting effect of fear of further punishment in punished offenders. There is evidence suggesting that official processing of juveniles (1) reduces involvement in delinquency, (2) increases involvement in delinquency, and (3) is inconsequential. However, even evidence that the probability of delinquency is decreased by the application of increasingly severe "punishments" would not be clear-cut evidence for specific deterrence. For example, if a study were to show that youths who receive "stiffer" treatment (i.e., detention rather than release; confinement rather than probation, and so on) commit fewer subsequent offenses, this outcome could be attributed to successful *treatment* and called *rehabilitation.* It may or may not be a reflection of fear of further punishment (specific deterrence).

Because there is evidence to support any of these views, some theorists have suggested that all alleged outcomes may in fact occur and that the real puzzle is to identify the variable effects of different reactions to delinquency (whether these are called treatments or punishments) under different circumstances. There are no proved answers to the questions of what is considered to be "punishing" by different groups of juveniles or to the question of whether or not programs construed by the juvenile justice system as "treatments" are perceived by youths as punishing. Are there stigmatizing consequences to juvenile processing? Do wayward youths who have been dealt with by the juvenile justice system differ as a result of their experiences from comparable youths who have avoided detection?

The readings in this section deal with major research issues in the study of reactions to delinquency. The first selection, based on a survey of several thousand high-school students, addresses the issue of general deterrence. It provides support for the hypothesis that the greater the perceived risk of punishment, the lesser the probability of delinquent behavior, especially when a youth's own personal perceptions are considered. Fear of sanctions does appear to be a common concern among American adolescents.

The other three readings deal with the variable consequences of juvenile processing for the youths processed. Anne Mahoney reviews the evidence on the effects of labeling upon (1) subsequent delinquent behavior, (2) community and family reaction, and (3) self-conceptions. The inconsistencies noted in the preceding discussion are summarized, and future research is proposed for dealing with them. The second selection is the final published report on some research discussed by Mahoney—a study of the effects of legal processing on the values and attitudes of youths. It is one of the best studies on the topic because it surveys youths over a four-year period and attempts to identify the subgroups most susceptible to the effects of labeling.

The final selection is included because it endeavors to develop six detailed observations on the *variable* effects of labeling. Rather than viewing labeling theory and deterrence theory as totally incompatible, Bernard Thorsell and Lloyd Klemke propose what many criminologists now accept—that labeling processes can have both reinforcing and deterrent consequences for subsequent involvement in delinquency. This view is likely to govern future research.

REFERENCES

Schur, E. 1973. *Radical Non-Intervention: Rethinking the Delinquency Problem.* Englewood Cliffs, N.J.: Prentice-Hall.

*Perceived Risk of Punishment and Self-Reported Delinquency**

Gary F. Jensen
University of Arizona

Maynard L. Erickson
University of Arizona

Jack P. Gibbs
Vanderbilt University

ABSTRACT

Using data from a survey of students in six Arizona high schools, this paper examines the relation between perceived risk of punishment and self-reported delinquency. Consistent with the deterrence doctrine, the relation is inverse regardless of the location of the schools (metropolitan or small town), type of delinquency, or the kind of measure of perceived risk. However, measures of perceived personal risk (the individual's perception of his or her own risk) provide more consistent support for the deterrence doctrine than measures of perceived aggregate risk (perception of the risk for all juveniles in the same community). Moreover, personal risk is inversely related to delinquency even when social condemnation of delinquent offenses, attachment to conventional persons, and several status characteristics (e.g., age, sex) of the students are taken into account.

The contention that sanctions deter has persisted in legal philosophy, social theory, and folklore for centuries. Moreover, since the late 1960s deterrence has become a major topic in deviance literature along with labeling theory and radical criminology (see surveys by Gibbs, b; Silver; Tittle and Logan; Zimring and Hawkins). Yet our knowledge of deterrence remains very limited. As Tittle and Logan observe: "At this point we can safely say only that sanctions apparently have some deterrent effect under some circumstances. It is now necessary to undertake careful research in an attempt to specify the conditions under which sanctions are likely to be important influences on behavior" (385). Yet despite our limited knowledge, there is appreciable agreement in recent surveys of the literature about priorities for future research. Specifically, research should focus on perceptual properties of punishment in relation to criminal or delinquent behavior in various social settings and control for other sociocultural correlates of crime and delinquency.

Perceptions of Risk

Most deterrence research has focused on objective certainty of punishment,[1] with the measure typically taking the form Np/Nc, where Np is the number of individuals reported in official statistics as having been imprisoned during a stipulated period (e.g., 1961) for a particular type of offense, and Nc is the estimated official incidence of such offenses during a previous period (e.g., 1960). Even though investigators have reported an inverse relation among States between such measures and most offense rates, the findings are hardly compelling evidence of deterrence. Such relations could reflect preventive effects of punishment other than deterrence (such as incapacitation).

More compelling evidence can be realized only by examining the relation between measures of *perceived* certainty of punishment and offense rates. The relation is crucial because the deterrence doctrine is first and foremost a perceptual theory. Indeed, insofar as the doctrine can be reduced to one single assertion, it is as follows: *The more members of a population perceive the punishment for a type of offense as being certain, swift and severe, the lower the rate for that offense in that population.* Given doubts about the importance of the severity and celerity of punishments (Gibbs, b:129–30, 145–216), there is justification for focusing deterrence research on the *perceived certainty* of punishment. That property of punishment has been considered in several studies (Bailey and Lott; Claster; Gold; Grasmick and Milligan; Kraut; Jensen, a; Silberman; Teevan, a, b, c; Waldo and Chiricos), but for reasons described subsequently, each study is subject to criticism.

Measures of Perceived Risk

Most investigations have considered only one measure of the perceived certainty of punishment (henceforth, *perceived risk*). There are, however, several types of measures, depending on the way perceptual questions are worded. For example, Martin Gold used a measure which calls for a *quantitative* answer by survey respondents to a question about perception of *aggregate* risk ("Out of every 10 kids who commit an offense, how many get caught?"). By contrast, Jensen (a) used an aggregate, qualitative measure, based on the degree of agreement by respondents with this statement: "People who break the law are almost always caught and punished." Waldo and Chiricos used items calling for a qualitative response (ranging from "very likely" to "very unlikely") to questions about aggregate risk of apprehension (to "people who commit crimes") and about personal risk (i.e., risk for someone like the respondent). Silberman's questions also pertained to perceptions of personal risk (i.e., "someone like" the respondent). Finally, Teevan has employed questions that pertain to perception of aggregate risk (a) and personal risk (c).

Although each type of measure could be inversely related to the frequency of self-reported offenses, Waldo and Chiricos argue that "perceptions of the certainty of punishment appear most viable as a deterrent when they involve the potential criminal's estimate of his *own chances* for arrest and harsh penalties for a particular crime—independent of the chances for any *generalized other*" (536–7). That argument suggests a possible interpretation of seemingly contradictory results. To illustrate, Gold concluded that his findings "cast serious doubt on deterrence as a treatment for delinquent teenagers and as a preventive lesson to their agemates" (120). Teevan (a) also reports little support for the deterrence doctrine. However, both sets of findings are limited to perceptions of aggregate risk. Waldo and Chiricos, and Silberman reach very different conclusions from findings that pertain to perceptions of personal risk. Those investigators report a close inverse relation between such measures of perceived risk and self-reported offenses. Unfortunately, the sets of findings are for very different populations, and hence alternative measures of risk should be obtained for the *same* populations to reach more definite conclusions.[2]

*This paper is based on data gathered as part of a larger study of "Community Tolerance and Measures of Delinquency" supported by a grant from the National Institute of Mental Health (MH22350). The authors wish to express their gratitude to the entire research staff (especially James Creechan, James Galliher, Grant Stitt, and Karen Wilkinson) for their work in gathering and analyzing these data and to Mark Stafford and Mark Warr for their thoughtful critiques of the manuscript.

Populations Studied

Cynics have characterized sociology as the "science of sophomores," and that indictment fits studies of the perceived risk of punishment during the 1970s. Of the ten studies of perceived risk previously cited, five of the most recent were limited entirely to university students. Waldo and Chiricos interviewed 321 undergraduates at Florida State University, and Teevan (a) surveyed a sample of Canadian university students. Silberman studied an even more select population—174 undergraduates at a small, private university. Kraut used 606 questionnaires returned from 1,500 students living in campus housing at the University of Pennsylvania. Finally, Bailey and Lott administered a questionnaire to 268 students in sociology courses at an urban university in the mid-West.

Of the remaining five studies, Grasmick and Milligan's surveyed 187 adults in a mid-Western city, and the rest pertain to precollege students. Claster's research was based on 42 male inmates in the sixth or higher grades at a training school and 65 eighth and ninth graders in a large East South Central city. Jensen's data (a) pertain to 1,588 white males in grades seven through twelve in the San Francisco Bay area. Gold based his conclusions on data for 522 juveniles (ages13–16) in Flint, Michigan. Teevan's (c) most recent work drew on questionnaires distributed by teachers and mailed back by 421 of 601 Ontario high school students.

Such small and homogeneous samples (college students particularly) cast doubt on all conclusions about the relation between perceived risk of punishment and offense rates, and that is all the more so since investigators have devoted little attention to differences among respondents. Silberman is the only investigator who has considered gender differences, and he concludes that "The deterrent effect of the threat of punishment is clearly specific to males" (448). Yet his sample of 174 undergraduates included only 73 females, and very few of them reported any offense. Moreover, his conclusion is contrary to Tittle and Rowe's experimental findings, which indicate that sanction threats have greater impact on cheating among females than males.

Previous research has considered a very limited range of offenses. Kraut studied only shoplifting, while Waldo and Chiricos considered only petty theft and mar juana use. Grasmick and Milligan studied only traffic violations, and Teevan (c) studied only marijuana and shoplifting. Silberman excluded several serious types of offenses from the analysis because few commissions were reported, and even after excluding several offenses he found: (1) very few males and no females reported assault; (2) only 10 percent reported use of hard drugs; and (3)12 percent reported petty theft. At the other extreme, nearly all reported drinking under age (95 percent), and a sizeable proportion reported marijuana use (63 percent). Despite the limited range of offenses considered, some of the investigators attempted generalizations about the relative deterrability of different offenses.

In sum, most of what we know about the perceived risk of punishment and lawbreaking is limited to small, homogeneous populations and a few types of offenses. Thus, in addition to employing alternative types of measures of perceived risk, there is a pressing need to expand the scope of deterrence research by gathering data on more heterogeneous populations and a far wider range of offenses.

A Particular Evidential Problem

In reviewing the deterrence literature Gibbs (b) points out that an inverse relation between perceived risk and offense rates could be a manifestation of a third variable—differential normative evaluations of offenses; that is, some types of offenses are subject to greater social (extralegal) condemnation than others. It could be that individuals are (1) prone to refrain from acts that are subject to severe social condemnation and (2) perceive punishment of those acts as especially likely for the same reason, meaning that certainty is perceived more in terms of what it *ought to be* rather than what it is in some objective sense (see Erickson et al.). If so, perceived risk and lawbreaking would be inversely related through their mutual association with differential social condemnation. Silberman concluded that the perceived certainty of punishment is related to the frequency of self-reported offenses independently of peer involvement and social condemnation; but, as pointed out previously, his conclusion is based on a very small population and a very limited range of types of offenses.

Spurious or not, the inverse relation between perceived risk and frequency of delicts has never been shown to be truly close. As such, the findings are consistent with the argument that the threat of punishment deters some kinds of persons more than others, but there are several distinct versions of that argument. For example, Zimring and Hawkins argue that punishment threats have the greatest impact where extralegal conditions are conducive to crime. Similarly, Toby maintains that "only the unsocialized (and therefore amoral) individual is deterred from expressing deviant impulses by a nice calculation of pleasures and punishments" (332), which suggests that the behavior of individuals with firm stakes in conformity is determined by extralegal factors alone. By contrast, Tittle argues that "certainty of punishment . . . may be operative primarily in those situations in which negative sanctions are most likely to have implications for the total life circumstances and patterns of interpersonal interaction" (a, 409). From Tittle's perspective, the threat of legal sanctions is *most* important in understanding the behavior of those who are likely to experience stigmatization as a consequence of punishment. Geerken and Gove take a similar position, arguing that those with the most to lose are the most deterrable.

Silberman's findings tend to support Toby, and Zimring and Hawkins' argument, in that the closest inverse relation between perceived certainty and frequency of self-reported offenses was obtained among those expressing the least social condemnation of the offenses. However, since there are such strikingly divergent positions on the issue, it certainly deserves further empirical study.

Research Design

The foregoing review suggests that future deterrence investigators should (1) consider alternative measures of perceived risk; (2) control for a variety of extralegal variables; and (3) employ more representative segments of the population. We take some steps in these directions in the research reported here.

PROCEDURE AND POPULATIONS

The analysis is based on survey data gathered in three metropolitan and three small-town high schools. The metropolitan high schools (one of which is parochial) are located in the Tucson SMSA, which has a population of over 400,000 and one of the highest official crime rates in the United States. The three small-town high schools are located in an adjacent county, and they range in population from 1,200 to 8,000. One of them is a mining town, one a tourist town, and one a farming-ranching center. For some analyses the three Tucson schools are combined as a metropolitan subsample and the other three schools as a small-town subsample.

Data were collected by means of an anonymous questionnaire administered to 1,700 students during the 1973–74 academic year and to 3,145 students in the same schools during 1974–75. With one exception, the 1974–75 sample comprises all students at the school or all students in English and/or Social Studies classes. Thus, between 42 and 86 percent of the student populations were surveyed, with very few refusals and no systematic exclusion of any category of students. Written parental consent was required at one small-town high school, yielding a sample in that school of 42 percent of the available student body. During 1973–74 all small-town schools required written parental consent, while the urban schools allowed the questionnaire to be administered in English and Social Studies classes unless parents withheld their consent. Hence, most of the analysis is based on the 1974–75 sample. Replications by year were conducted to assess the stability of findings.

While the metropolitan schools do not represent a true random sample of schools, the two public schools include students from census tracts with juvenile court referral rates typical for the city. The parochial school draws students from such widely scattered census tracts that a meaningful overall court referral rate cannot be computed, but the rate for the immediate vicinity is not significantly different from that for Tucson as a whole. Each of the small-town schools included is the only high school in the three small-town communities studied.

MEASURES OF PERCEIVED RISK

Three measures of perceived risk are employed. One of them, as in Jensen's research (a), is aggregate and qualitative. It expresses the amount of the students' agreement with statement: "People who break the law are almost always caught and punished."[3] Paralleling Gold, another measure is aggregate and quantitative, being based on students' responses to such questions as: "Out of the last 100 times a juvenile stole something worth more than $100, how many would you guess resulted in an arrest?" Students were asked to give estimates for each of 18 different offenses.[4] The third type of measure is personal and qualitative, expressing the students' assessment of risk in a series of hypothetical situations.[5]

MEASURES OF SELF-REPORTED OFFENSES

The incidence of delinquent behavior was estimated by asking each student how many times he or she had committed each of 18 types of offenses during the last 12 months. A behavioral description of each type of offense was incorporated in each question, and in that part of the questionnaire the students were again assured that the questionnaire information would be anonymous.

Certain parts of the subsequent analysis are based on a delinquency scale or delinquency index, operationalized in the same manner as in recent studies of self-reported delinquency (e.g., Burkett and White; Hindelang; Hirschi; Hirschi and Stark; Jensen, b).[6] That commonly used scale is limited to major and minor property offenses, violence, vandalism, and joyriding. However, the present analysis also extends to a separate treatment of specific types of offenses—burglary, shoplifting, vandalism, and truancy in particular.

MEASURES OF OTHER VARIABLES

As previously suggested, an inverse relation between the perceived risk of punishment and the frequency of self-reported offenses could be a manifestation of extralegal factors that increase perceived risk but decrease the commission of offenses. At present, there is no truly defensible basis for identifying such extralegal variables, but four *possibly* relevant instances are considered here. Normative evaluations of delinquent offenses were assessed by posing questions as to how much a student *condemned* breaking the law in each of four situations pertaining to burglary, shoplifting, vandalism, and truancy.[7] *Ties to conventional society* were assessed by analyzing responses to questions about the relation between a student and his or her parents and teachers.[8] Each measure has been used in previous research and shown to be related to delinquent behavior (Hindelang; Hirschi). *Number of delinquent friends* was introduced as a measure of ties to unconventional society.[9] Finally, students were asked about their *status characteristics*, including sex, age, race, and father's educational status. While variables that might make a difference are seemingly endless, the variables in the present list have been treated as central in delinquency research.[10]

Findings

The first set of findings is summarized in Table 1. The major panel reports the percentage of respondents who reported three or more offenses, and the statistics in the last two columns express the relation between each of three different measures of perceived risk and the delinquency scale. The measure of perceived personal risk is based on the average of student estimates of their own chances of apprehension in three offense situations involving burglary, shoplifting, and vandalism. The aggregate, quantitative measure is the average of student estimates of probability of arrest (any juvenile) for each type of offense in the delinquency index. Since the aggregate, qualitative measure of perceived risk is based on responses to a question about lawbreaking in general, it pertains (in a sense) to all juveniles and all types of offenses. The dependent variable in generating the chi-square tests and gamma coefficients in Table 1 is the general delinquency index.

Table 1. PERCENTAGE OF STUDENTS REPORTING THREE OF MORE OFFENSES BY THREE MEASURES OF PERCEIVED RISK, THREE METROPOLITAN AND THREE SMALL-TOWN HIGH SCHOOLS IN ARIZONA, 1973–74 AND 1974–75

		Kind of Perceived Risk							Summary Statistics*	
Location of School	Period	Personal, Qualitative Perception† (Low)	2	3	4	(High)			Chi-square P	Gamma
Metropolitan	1973-74	53%	30%	15%	6%	3%			.0000	-.38
	1974-75	52%	34%	18%	10%	2%			.0000	-.39
Small town	1973-74	58%	39%	25%	10%	8%			.0000	-.46
	1974-75	56%	40%	18%	14%	6%			.0000	-.40
		Aggregate, Qualitative Perception‡ (Low)	2	3	4	(High)				
Metropolitan	1973-74	31%	20%	13%	13%	11%			.0000	-.20
	1974-75	34%	22%	20%	17%	19%			.0000	-.12
Small town	1973-74	47%	26%	11%	21%	24%			.0001	-.25
	1974-75	43%	26%	22%	18%	25%			.0000	-.15
		Aggregate, Quantitative Perception§ 0-10	11-20	21-30	31-40	41-50	51-60	61+		
Metropolitan	1973-74	33%	23%	21%	19%	13%	11%	20%	.0007	-.11
	1974-75	34%	25%	20%	22%	21%	18%	17%	.0034	-.07
Small town	1973-74	30%	45%	27%	34%	13%	20%	4%	.0066	-.21
	1974-75	34%	30%	28%	25%	17%	14%	18%	.0057	-.14

*Based on the delinquency index trichotomized into zero, one or two, and three or more offenses.

†Based on the average responses to the three criminal choice situations described in note 4, with ordinal designations of the five response categories (1 = "definitely yes" and 5 = "definitely not").

‡"Low" means "strongly disagree" that people who break the law are almost always caught and punished and "high" means "strongly agree."

§An average of all responses to questions about all offenses included in the delinquency index (see text).

Table 2. PERCENTAGE OF STUDENTS REPORTING ONE OR MORE SPECIFIC OFFENSES BY ACT-SPECIFIC PERCEIVED RISK OF PUNISHMENT, THREE METROPOLITAN AND THREE SMALL-TOWN HIGH SCHOOLS IN ARIZONA, 1973–74 AND 1974–75

		Kind of Perceived Risk						Summary Statistics*	
Offense	Period	Personal, Qualitative Perception (Low)	2	3	4	(High)		Chi-Square P	Gamma
Burglary	1973-74	37%	24%	13%	5%	4%		.0000	-.54
	1974-75	34%	23%	12%	7%	6%		.0000	-.48
Vandalism	1973-74	41%	22%	15%	14%	12%		.0000	-.35
	1974-75	40%	26%	18%	13%	10%		.0000	-.37
Shoplifting	1973-74	57%	46%	28%	24%	17%		.0000	-.39
	1974-75	62%	47%	34%	24%	19%		.0000	-.39
Truancy	1973-74	73%	63%	54%	43%	36%		.0000	-.31
	1974-75	77%	68%	55%	42%	36%		.0000	-.37
		Aggregate, Qualitative Perception (Low)	2	3	4	(High)			
Burglary	1973-74	24%	14%	8%	9%	12%		.0000	-.28
	1974-75	25%	14%	10%	8%	11%		.0000	-.28
Vandalism	1973-74	32%	23%	13%	14%	18%		.0000	-.27
	1974-75	34%	23%	19%	18%	16%		.0000	-.21
Shoplifting	1973-74	46%	39%	28%	33%	24%		.0000	-.19
	1974-75	46%	39%	38%	33%	38%		.0000	-.12
Truancy	1973-74	68%	62%	49%	50%	52%		.0000	-.20
	1974-75	68%	60%	56%	51%	55%		.0000	-.13
		Aggregate, Quantitative Perception 0-10	11-20	21-30	31-40	41-50	51+		
Burglary	1973-74	21%	17%	16%	15%	12%	9%	.0198	-.21
	1974-75	23%	14%	12%	14%	12%	9%	.0000	-.22
Vandalism	1973-74	24%	22%	21%	19%	20%	15%	.1978	-.12
	1974-75	26%	22%	21%	21%	18%	20%	.2045	-.10
Shoplifting	1973-74	46%	36%	40%	33%	30%	25%	.0001	-.19
	1974-75	46%	40%	37%	31%	34%	33%	.0000	-.16
Truancy	1973-74	58%	57%	54%	33%	54%	56%	.2441	-.08
	1974-75	58%	64%	46%	65%	56%	53%	.0226	-.07

*For the full range of categories of risk and for each offense dichotomized into "no commissions" and "one or more."

Consistent with the deterrence doctrine, all of the gamma coefficients in Table 1 are negative and each chi-square value is statistically significant beyond the .01 level. Moreover, regardless of the time period or school location (metropolitan–small town), the measure of perceived personal risk is more inversely related to self-reported delinquency than either measure of perceived aggregate risk.

Whereas types of offenses are not distinguished in Table 1, Table 2 reports separate findings for each of four types. Observe particularly that in this case each variable (except the aggregate, qualitative measure of perceived risk for "people who break the law") pertains to a particular offense; and in that sense the analysis is act-specific. The act-specific analysis does not alter the conclusions reached about the data presented in Table 1.[11] All of the gamma coefficients in Table 2 are negative (hence, consistent with the deterrence doctrine), and 19 of 24 of the chi-square values are significant beyond the .01 level. Considerably more support for the deterrence doctrine is again realized in the case of the measure of perceived personal risk. *All* chi-square values for that measure are significant beyond the .01 level, whereas only 3 of 8 values for the aggregate, quantitative measure reach that level of significance. Moreover, each gamma coefficient for the personal measure exceeds the corresponding coefficient for either of the other measures of perceived risk. Finally, there are no conspicuous contrasts in the findings for the two time periods (1973–74, 1974–75).[12]

In summary, three conclusions are suggested by the data. First, there is definitely an inverse relation between perceived risk of punishment and self-reported delinquency. Second, measures of perceived personal risk are more inversely related to self-reported delinquency than are either of the measures of perceived aggregate risk. Third, both of these conclusions hold regardless of location of the schools, the time period considered, or the particular operational procedures used. Thus, internal replications show the findings to be stable at different points in time and in different community settings.

A NOTE ON DETERRABILITY

Few studies have addressed the issue of differential deterrability by type of offense and those which have, either been based on a very limited range of types of offenses, college samples, or both. Assuming petty larceny to be more socially condemned than marijuana use and hence more of a *mala in se* offense than is marijuana use, Waldo and Chiricos' findings led them to conclude that *mala prohibita* offenses are more readily deterred than *mala in se* offenses. However, Silberman gathered data on moral disapproval of types of offenses and concluded just the opposite; that is, the more strongly condemned is a type of offense the greater is the negative correlation between the frequency of the offense and the perceived certainty of punishment.

Table 3. SERIOUSNESS OF ESTIMATED DETERRABILITY, 18 TYPES OF OFFENSES

Type of Offense	Rank Order on Median Seriousness as Evaluated by Students Col. 1	Rank Order on Deterrability[a] Col. 2	Reduction in Number of Offenders* Col. 3
Armed robbery	1	4	-22.6%
Grand theft	2	1	-28.0%
Auto theft	3	5	-20.9%
Robbery	4	2	-25.4%
Burglary	5	3	-25.3%
Assault	6	8	-18.6%
Drugs	7	9	-17.1%
Vandalism	8	6	-19.9%
Petty theft	9	7	-18.9%
Shoplifting	10	11	-13.0%
Marijuana	11	12	-11.9%
Runaway	12	10	-13.3%
Fights	13	13	-11.8%
Drunk	14	14	- 8.2%
Defiance	15	16	- 7.8%
Drinking	16	18	- 6.7%
Truancy	17	17	- 7.8%
Smoking	18	15	- 7.9%

*Based on procedure described in note 14.

In the present study respondents were asked to give magnitude estimates (see Hamblin) of the seriousness of each offense.[13] Their estimates yielded rank ordering that is approximately constant from community to community and by gender. Considering the 4 types of offenses in Table 2, burglary ranks first among the 4 in terms of median seriousness, vandalism second, shoplifting third, and truancy fourth. The 2 most widely examined offenses in deterrence research, marijuana use and shoplifting, ranked tenth and eleventh in a list of 18 offenses. So if deterrability is a function of degree of social condemnation and if social condemnation corresponds to perceived seriousness, marijuana use and petty theft are not strategic types of offenses, for they do not differ appreciably as to degree of social condemnation.

To estimate deterrability, a constant "hypothetical change" was introduced in the perceived certainty of punishment in the sample and then the proportionate reduction in the number of youths committing an offense that would occur given such a change was computed.[14] Among the 4 specific offenses and using act-specific perceptions, there is a perfect direct relation between the rank for seriousness and the rank for deterrability. Burglary ranks first in seriousness and the estimate of deterrability, vandalism ranks second, shoplifting third, and truancy fourth.

Conducting a similar analysis for the 18 offenses shown in Table 3 but using average perceived risk there is a nearly perfect direct relation between seriousness and deterrability, with a *rho* between columns 1 and 2 of +.94. Thus, the greater the perceived seriousness of a type of offense, the greater is the hypothetical impact of a change in the perceived risk of punishment. These findings are consistent with Silberman's conclusion, and they cast doubt on the argument that *mala prohibita* offenses can be more readily deterred than can *mala in se* offenses.

Considering still another distinction, several scholars have argued that instrumental offenses, such as shoplifting, are more readily deterred than expressive offenses, such as assault (Chambliss; Zimring and Hawkins). Overall, the present findings are consistent with that argument. Serious property-oriented offenses appear more deterrable than victimless offenses or status offenses. Yet, there are some apparent exceptions. Vandalism and assault appear more deterrable than either shoplifting or petty theft, but both are commonly depicted as expressive offenses. Similarly, auto theft or joyriding among juveniles is generally viewed as an expressive offense (much like vandalism), but it ranks fairly high in deterrability.

STATUS CHARACTERISTICS

Having found statistical relations that are consistent with the deterrence doctrine, the possibility that those relations are in some sense spurious or contingent on extralegal variables deserves attention. For example, Silberman concluded that the impact of certainty of punishment is specific to males; but, as noted earlier, the nature of his sample and the low frequency of reported offenses cast doubt on that conclusion.

The data in Table 4, panel 1, bear on the hypothesis that the deterrent impact of the perceived risk of punishment is specific to males. In this analysis the data are for 1974–75, and all six schools are combined. The statistics were computed through procedures developed by Goodman (a, b, c) to assess the fit between the observed data and models that either

Table 4. MODELS RELATING THE DELINQUENCY INDEX TO PERCEIVED PERSONAL RISK AND FOUR STATUS CHARACTERISTICS, DATA ON STUDENTS IN SIX ARIZONA HIGH SCHOOLS, 1974–75

Variables	Models*	Chi-square	Degrees of Freedom	Significance Level
Delinquency, risk, gender	1	350.06	5	.0000
	2	173.23	3	.0000
	3	89.42	4	.0000
	4	2.12	2	.3464
Delinquency, risk, age	1	197.08	8	.0000
	2	20.78	6	.0020
	3	181.85	6	.0000
	4	2.00	4	.7350
Delinquency, risk, ethnic status	1	195.73	8	.0000
	2	20.31	6	.0024
	3	181.12	6	.0000
	4	1.56	4	.8158
Delinquency, risk, father's education	1	199.18	11	.0000
	2	36.52	9	.0000
	3	174.86	8	.0000
	4	5.81	6	.4459

*(1) Delinquency is treated as independent of perceived risk of punishment and status, (2) delinquency is treated as dependent on risk but not status, (3) delinquency is treated as dependent on status but not risk, and (4) risk and status each have separable effects on delinquency.

(1) include or exclude interaction between perceived risk and sex *or* (2) assume a spurious relation between perceived risk and delinquency.

Table 4 presents likelihood-ratio chi-square statsitics and the significance levels for four models involving the delinquency index, average perceived risk, and gender. Model 1 specifies that delinquency is independent of both perceived risk and gender. Model 2 specifies that delinquency depends on perceived risk but not on gender. Model 3 specifies that delinquency depends on gender but not on perceived risk. Finally, Model 4 specifies that delinquency is dependent on both gender and perceived risk and that each has a separable effect. When a model yields a significance value *greater than* .05 it will be interpreted as providing an "acceptable fit." If there is more than one acceptable model, models are compared to ascertain whether the difference in chi-square values represents a *significant* improvement in fit. The goal is, of course, to find the simplest acceptable model or the "preferred" model.

The preferred model in this instance is number 4; that is, both gender and perceived risk must be included in the model to provide an acceptable fit and each has a separable effect. The remaining model (the so-called "trivial model") would introduce three-way interaction. The analysis indicates that introducing such an effect would not lead to a significant improvement in fit.[15] This conclusion is further supported by an examination of odds–delinquent (ratio of the number who have committed one or more offenses to the number who have not) for males and females. Among males the odds–delinquent for those low in perceived risk is 2.96 times greater than for those high in perceived risk, as compared to 2.48 for females. Thus, the relation between perceived risk and delinquency is neither specific to males nor spuriously attributable to common links with gender.[16]

Essentially the same results obtained when age, minority status, and father's educational status were introduced into the models. Any deletion of perceived risk led to a significant divergence of observed and expected frequencies, as did the deletion of any status characteristic. In every case, models including both the status characteristic and risk provide the only acceptable fits to the data. Finally, with only one exception (age could be deleted with no significant loss), a replication of the analysis using the 1973–74 data led to the same conclusions.

MORAL AND SOCIAL BONDS

The data in Table 5 bear on the hypothesis that the inverse relation between perceived risk and frequency of self-reported delinquency is simply a manifestation of the social condemnation of offenses. For all four types of offenses and the delinquency scale, *both* personal risk and social condemnation are significantly related to self-reported delinquency. Any model that excludes one or both of those variables departs significantly from the observed data. Models that assume independent relations and no interaction provide an adequate fit. Hence, the findings cast doubt on the argument that the demonstrated inverse relations between perceived personal risk and self-reported delinquency hold only through their mutual association with the social condemnation of delicts.

This conclusion is further supported by an inspection of odds ratios for students expressing different degrees of disapproval of delinquent offenses. There is no indication of interaction of the sort suggested by Silberman. Truancy is the only type of offense characterized by an orderly variation in the relation between perceived risk and frequency of self-reported acts, and even then the relation is closer under conditions of

Table 5. MODELS RELATING PERCEIVED PERSONAL RISK AND SOCIAL CONDEMNATION TO THE DELINQUENCY INDEX AND SPECIFIC OFFENSES, DATA ON STUDENTS IN SIX ARIZONA HIGH SCHOOLS, 1974–75

Dependent Variable (Self-reported Frequency)	Models*	Chi-square	Degrees of Freedom	Significance Level
Delinquency index†	1	364.37	24	.0000
	2	180.15	20	.0000
	3	130.18	20	.0000
	4	15.16	16	.5139
Shoplifting	1	369.10	24	.0000
	2	141.17	20	.0000
	3	165.94	20	.0000
	4	19.43	16	.2472
Burglary	1	280.62	24	.0000
	2	104.54	20	.0000
	3	154.32	20	.0000
	4	20.83	16	.1856
Vandalism	1	225.74	24	.0000
	2	80.12	20	.0000
	3	122.69	20	.0000
	4	17.99	16	.3249
Truancy	1	330.95	24	.0000
	2	110.28	20	.0000
	3	190.74	20	.0000
	4	25.70	16	.0585

*(1) Delinquency treated as independent of risk and condemnation, (2) delinquency treated as dependent on risk but not condemnation, (3) delinquency treated as dependent on condemnation but not risk, and (4) risk and condemnation each have separable effects on delinquency.

†The two independent variables are average perceived personal risk and average seriousness for burglary, shoplifting, and vandalism (see note 4).

marked social condemnation of delinquency (the odds ratio was 5.41 for the highest degree of condemnation as compared to .93 for the lowest).

Similar analyses were conducted by introducing other characteristics of students: (1) number of delinquent friends, (2) attachment to father, (3) attachment to mother, and/or (4) attachment to teachers. As summarized in Table 6, all models that assume independence between the delinquency index and average perceived personal risk can be rejected. The relation cannot be attributed to common associations of the two variables with number of delinquent friends, nor with any measure of attachment to conventional others. Moreover, there is no indication of significant interaction effects between average perceived risk and other variables in relation to delinquency. By contrast, there is an acceptable fit for all models that allow each variable to make a difference.

In the case of specific types of offenses (see Table 7), in only 1 of 16 instances does a model fail to fit at the .05 level. The one exception is vandalism in conjunction with number of delinquent friends. The odds ratios for the one exception suggest that the relation between perceived personal risk and delinquency is closer among students with one or two delinquent friends than among students with no delinquent friends or students with several delinquent friends.

An interesting but unexpected finding is that attachment to father or mother is unrelated to some types of delinquency. Both attachment to father and attachment to mother can be excluded from the model for burglary, and attachment to father can be excluded from the vandalism model. Thus, while some traditional dimensions of the social bond can be eliminated from some models, *perceived risk must be included in every instance examined*.

In a final effort to find evidence of interaction, we analyzed the relation between delinquency and average perceived risk within categories of students distinguished by degree of social condemnation of offenses and number of delinquent friends. Table 8 reports self-reported offenses by

Table 6. MODELS RELATING THE DELINQUENCY INDEX TO PERCEIVED PERSONAL RISK AND ATTACHMENT TO OTHERS, DATA ON STUDENTS IN SIX ARIZONA HIGH SCHOOLS, 1974–75

Variables	Models*	Chi-square	Degrees of Freedom	Significance Level
Delinquency, risk, delinquent friends†	1	368.90	14	.0000
	2	191.42	10	.0000
	3	125.71	10	.0000
	4	12.99	8	.1123
Delinquency, risk, attachment to father†	1	216.16	24	.0000
	2	31.30	20	.0517
	3	191.37	20	.0000
	4	13.59	16	.6294
Delinquency, risk, attachment to mother†	1	223.15	24	.0000
	2	37.79	20	.0095
	3	183.24	20	.0000
	4	14.76	16	.5421
Delinquency, risk, attachment to teacher†	1	243.32	24	.0000
	2	55.45	20	.0000
	3	164.28	30	.0000
	4	10.91	16	.8149

*The models tested are as follows: (1) Delinquency treated as independent of both risk and attachment, (2) delinquency treated as dependent on risk but not attachment, (3) delinquency treated as dependent on attachment but not risk, and (4) risk and attachment each have separable effects on delinquency.

†See notes 8 and 9.

Table 7. MODELS RELATING SPECIFIC TYPES OF OFFENSES TO PERCEIVED RISK AND ATTACHMENT TO OTHERS, DATA ON STUDENTS IN SIX ARIZONA HIGH SCHOOLS, 1974–75

Variables		Preferred Model*	Chi-square	Degrees of Freedom	Significance Level
Offense, risk, delinquent friends	Burglary	4	12.06	8	.1489
	Vandalism	†	0	0	1.0000
	Shoplifting	4	4.71	8	.7881
	Truancy	4	5.56	8	.6976
Offense, risk, attachment to father	Burglary	2	15.75	20	.7316
	Vandalism	2	22.24	20	.3281
	Shoplifting	4	17.76	16	.3385
	Truancy	4	12.42	16	.7148
Offense, risk, attachment to mother	Burglary	2	19.51	20	.4889
	Vandalism	4	19.85	16	.2263
	Shoplifting	4	14.23	16	.5814
	Truancy	4	18.17	16	.3141
Offense, risk, attachment to teacher	Burglary	4	18.96	16	.2711
	Vandalism	4	7.56	16	.9609
	Shoplifting	4	8.28	16	.9401
	Truancy	4	9.17	16	.9063

*Models 1, 2, 3, and 4 were tested in each case. See notes to Table 6 for a description of each of the four models. The particular variables which could be omitted when Model 2 provided an adequate fit are stated in the text.

†In this case the data could not be simplified. Thus, the only acceptable model is the "trivial" model. The trivial model ($x^2 = 0$, df = 0, p = 1.0) includes three-way interaction, is represented by the observed frequencies and is accepted only when simpler models fail to provide an adequate fit as defined in the text.

perceived risk within these two categories. There is a definite negative association between perceived risk and delinquency within every category considered—i.e., both among students with no delinquent peers and a strong tendency to condemn delinquent offenses and students with several delinquent friends and weak disapproval of delinquent offenses. Moreover, gamma coefficients are nearly identical in the two extreme categories (i.e., no delinquent friends, high social condemnation versus three or more delinquent friends, low social condemnation). In short, the evidence suggests that (1) the relation between risk and delinquency is not spurious, (2) the relation is not specific to amoral adolescents, and (3) the relation is not stronger among those most attached to conventional morality.

Conclusions

Overall, the findings are consistent with the deterrent doctrine, and that is particularly the case for the measure of perceived personal risk rather than either measure of perceived aggregate risk. However, there is some confusion in the literature concerning the best measure of risk. For instance, Teevan (b) warns that perceived personal risk is more subject to "contamination" than is perceived aggregate risk (i.e., past deviant behavior may be more likely to affect perceptions of personal risk than aggregate perceptions), and he therefore uses an aggregate measure in his own research. Yet, he also criticizes Claster's use of an aggregate perceptual measure, claiming that it is "irrelevant to the deterrence hypothesis because the subject's actions are determined by their perceptions of the 'risks to themselves and not by perceptions of the risk to others'" (b, 147).

The possibility of contamination is not a justification for excluding

Table 8. DELINQUENT INDEX OFFENSES BY PERCEIVED PERSONAL RISK, SOCIAL CONDEMNATION,* AND DELINQUENT FRIENDS, DATA FOR STUDENTS IN SIX ARIZONA HIGH SCHOOLS, 1974–75

		High Social Condemnation			Low Social Condemnation		
Number of Delinquent Friends	Number of Self-reported Offenses	Low Perceived Risk	Medium Perceived Risk	High Perceived Risk	Low Perceived Risk	Medium Perceived Risk	High Perceived Risk
No delinquent friends	0	42%	52%	68%	23%	31%	48%
	1–2	38%	37%	27%	35%	49%	32%
	3+	20%	11%	5%	42%	20%	19%
	N	385	682	457	78	85	31
	Gamma		−.42			−.33	
One or two delinquent friends	0	30%	38%	41%	12%	33%	22%
	1–2	29%	41%	43%	38%	42%	61%
	3+	41%	21%	16%	50%	26%	17%
	N	170	236	113	58	43	18
	Gamma		−.23			−.40	
Three or more delinquent friends	0	11%	22%	29%	6%	15%	38%
	1–2	25%	42%	48%	27%	32%	38%
	3+	63%	36%	22%	68%	52%	23%
	N	178	132	58	90	40	13
	Gamma		−.45			−.45	

*Perceived personal risk was trichotomized and social condemnation dichotomized in order to maintain a sufficient N in extreme subcategories.

measures of perceived personal risk of punishment. It may be true that perception of personal risk is more influenced by punishment than is perception of aggregate risk, but the relationship between perception and experience is one of the central questions for further work on the deterrence doctrine. The contamination problem might well be solved by longitudinal or experimental data. By eliminating personally relevant measures nothing is gained and perhaps something very important is lost, namely, one of the most significant variables.

The deterrence doctrine is supported by the findings for certain types of offenses more than others, and that conclusion is consistent with what is virtually an article of faith among deterrence investigators—that some kinds of acts are more deterrable than others. However, the contrasts among types of offenses are not clearly consistent with conventional distinctions that are supposedly relevant in contemplating differential deterrability (e.g., that instrumental behavior is supposedly more deterrable than is expressive behavior, or that *mala prohibita* offenses are more deterrable than *mala in se* offenses). Given current evidence it appears that the relevant dimension for differentiating offenses in terms of deterrability is seriousness of the offense. At the very minimum the present findings cast grave doubts on attempts in previous studies to generalize from a few types of offenses.

One interesting finding in Silberman's research (essentially replicated in the current study) is the constancy in findings whether considering specific types of offenses or an index that combines several types of offenses. The absence of sharp and uniform contrasts using scales or specific acts and average or act-specific perceptions could mean that students tend to perceive the risk of punishment in an undifferentiated way and that such beliefs about punishment can deter a wide range of offenses. Overall, the data tend to support Silberman's observation in that the measure of combined perceived risk (i.e., for several types of offenses) is just as persistently related to self-reported commissions of a particular type of offense as is the measure of perceived risk for that specific offense, with no obvious differences in magnitude of the relationships. Thus, there is no empirical basis at present for Teevan's assertion that only act-specific measures of perceived risk are relevant in deterrence research.

Finally, there is no evidence in the present findings that the inverse relation between perceived risk and the self-reported delinquency is contingent on (1) differential social condemnation of offenses, (2) students' attachment to conventional others, (3) students' attachment to unconventional others, or (4) status characteristics of the students (e.g., gender). Thus, the data fail to support Tittle's (a) suggestion that certainty has its greatest impact on those who have a stake in conformity and Toby's claim that only the amoral individual is deterred by a "nice calculation of pleasures and punishments." Moreover, the findings provide no justification for limiting deterrence research to males. Contrary to Silberman's conclusion, perceived risk of punishment is also associated with delinquency among females, and hence it appears that his sample was inadequate for a specification by gender.

The most pressing issue in the study of deterrence is the temporal relation between perception of punishment and law-breaking behavior. There is every reason to assume that beliefs about punishment and behavior are interrelated, that the environmental response to behavior makes a difference for perception or belief, and that perception in turn affects future behavior. Moreover, perceptions of risk may be shaped by a wide range of experiences independent of personal involvement in law-breaking. The process is not untangled here. However, the findings show an association that persists through two time periods for (1) a variety of different measures and forms of analysis, (2) a wide range of offenses and situations, and (3) in comparison with other sociological variables. Hence, it can be concluded with some confidence that there is a stable and persistent relation consistent with the deterrence doctrine. Thus, there is as much empirical support for including beliefs about punishment in theories of crime and delinquency as there is for including variables such as social class, age, gender, and ties to conventional or unconventional others.

Notes

1. Some of the most commonly cited are Bailey et al.; Chiricos and Waldo; Ehrlich; Erickson and Gibbs; Gibbs (a); Gray and Martin; Logan (b); Tittle (a).
2. There are other complexities that should be addressed in subsequent papers as well. For example, Bailey and Lott report very low product–moment coefficients of correlation between perceived personal risk and number of offenses among college students. Waldo and Chiricos report the strongest associations found in the literature, using gamma coefficients and an offender–nonoffender dichotomy. In an article published while this paper was pending, Tittle (c) reports significant relations between perceived personal risk and estimates of the likelihood that a person would commit an offense. The importance of different modes of statistical analysis and different measures or treatments of the dependent variable have yet to be explored.
3. The response categories for this item were "strongly agree," "agree," "uncertain," "disagree," "strongly disagree." Thus, whereas this measure is ordinally scaled, estimates by respondents of the proportion of violations that result in an arrest form an interval scale.
4. The offenses are (1) burglary; (2) grand theft; (3) petty theft; (4) shoplifting; (5) assault; (6) fighting; (7) vandalism; (8) smoking under age; (9) runaway; (10) truancy; (11) auto theft; (12) robbery; (13) armed robbery; (14) defying parents; (15) drinking; (16) drunkenness; (17) marijuana use; and (18) the use of other illicit drugs. All 18 are violations of Arizona criminal statutes and/or juvenile (status) offenses.
5. Students were asked to contemplate the following situations and to indicate whether they thought they could commit the act but not get caught, with the response categories being "definitely yes," "yes," "uncertain," "no," and "definitely not."

Burglary: "Suppose you and your friends were messing around one night and they decided to break into a place to steal some things."
Shoplifting: "Suppose you and your friends were messing around one afternoon and they decided to steal something from a store just for kicks."
Vandalism: "Suppose you and your friends were out one evening and they decided it might be fun to paint some words or signs on the windows at school."
Truancy: "Suppose your friends wanted you to do something with them during school hours when you were supposed to be in school."

Since truancy does not enter into the subsequently described delinquency index (see text), the general index of personal risk used throughout the analysis is an average based on responses to questions about burglary, shoplifting, and vandalism.

6. Note particularly that the scale pertains to the incidence of self-reported delinquency and not to perceptions of the risk of punishment.
7. See note 4 for a description of the situations. Each student was asked, "Would it be wrong to go along?" in each situation with the response categories being "definitely yes," "yes," "uncertain," "no," and "definitely not."
8. The items used were "I feel very close to my father," "I feel very close to my mother," and "I care what my teachers think of me," with the response categories being "strongly agree," "agree," "uncertain," "disagree," and "strongly disagree."
9. Students were asked to "think of those kids you have done things with in your free time during the last month" and then to indicate how many had been in trouble with the police. They were also instructed to "think of the ones that you really enjoy being with" and to indicate how many of those friends had been in trouble with the police. The number of delinquent friends is equated here with the "number of kids" a respondent really enjoyed being with who had been in trouble with the law. Those numbers have been reduced to three categories: no delinquent friends, one or two delinquent friends, and three or more delinquent friends.
10. Most of these variables are also central to claims concerning the specification of deterrence theory. See Gibbs (b); Tittle (b); Zimring and Hawkins for discussions of the many variables which might condition the impact of sanctions.
11. It should be noted that Table 2 is based on an offender–nonoffender dichotomy in order to maintain sufficient cell frequencies for specific acts. Tables 4 through 7 involve such a dichotomy as well.
12. The analysis was extended to each of 7 types of offenses (minor property, major property, violent offense, drinking, illicit drugs, vandalism, joyriding, and juvenile status offenses) for each year and the two types of settings. Again, regardless of school location or year, the relation between perceived risk and self-reported offenses is consistent with the deterrence doctrine and that is especially true for the measure of perceived personal risk. All 84 measures of association are negative, and all pertaining to perceived personal risk are significant beyond the .01 level.
13. Special instructions using illnesses or classroom behavior were used to familiarize students with the technique. Petty theft ("stealing something worth less than $100") was given as a standard (equal to 100) and the students were asked to assign a seriousness score to each of the other offenses. In this study offenses are analyzed in terms of median magnitude estimate of seriousness.
14. There are a number of different ways to examine relative deterrability, depending (among other things) on the particular conception of deterrence. Gibbs (b) differentiates between absolute deterrence (total omission of a type of offense as a result of perceived risk of punishment) and "restrictive deterrence" (limitations on involvement as a result of perceived risk). The *proportion* of a population who have ever committed the offense is the most relevant figure in contemplating absolute deterrence, whereas the *number* of offenses is the most relevant in contemplating restrictive deterrence. While neither acknowledging nor addressing these distinctions, prior research on perceived risk of punishment has focused on absolute deterrence. The dependent variable for Waldo and Chiricos and for most of Silberman's analysis was the proportion offending. Both types of deterrence are considered in the present analysis. Absolute deterrability is estimated by considering the proportionate reduction in the number offending that would occur were the perceptions of subjects manipulated so as to shift 50 percent of the individuals in each perceived risk category into the next higher perceived risk category. Such a hypothetical shift would also reduce the number of offenses, and that reduction is the relevant consideration in contemplating restrictive deterrence. For example, using this procedure such a shift in the act-specific perceived personal risk for shoplifting would reduce the number of shoplifters by 12.6 percent but the number of offenses would be reduced by 24.3 percent. Table 3 summarizes the proportionate reduction in number of offenders for each offense (1) if people could be induced into the next higher category of average perceived risk, (2) exhibited the same offender rate as that category, and (3) the originally observed association is causal. The offenses are ordered nearly the same in terms of proportionate reduction in *number of offenses* as well.
15. The trivial model is represented by the observed frequencies and thus has a chi-square of 0, no degrees of freedom and a p-value of 1.00. The trivial model is accepted when simpler models (in this case models 1 through 4) fail to provide an adequate fit. With one exception (see Table 7), simpler models provide adequate fits in terms of the techniques and significance levels being used.
16. Since our concern in this paper has been with assessing the persistence of the risk-delinquency relationship by act, measure, and sample, we have not generated models summarizing the magnitude of direct and indirect effects nor concentrated on explained variance. In subsequent analysis we hope to address such subjects. The relation between each control variable and the delinquency index can be summarized as follows: (1) females report less delinquency than males; (2) older adolescents report less delinquency than younger adolescents, (3) Anglo adolescents report less delinquency than non Anglo adolescents; (4) the higher the father's educational status, the less the delinquency; and (5) attachment to parents and teachers as well as social condemnation of delinquency are all negatively related to the delinquency index (and to each of the four specific acts examined in Tables 5 and 7), while number of delinquent friends is positively related.

References

Bailey, W. C., J. D. Martin, and L. A. Gray. 1974. "Crime and Deterrence: A Correlational Analysis." *Journal of Research in Crime and Delinquency* 11(July): 124–43.

Bailey, W. C., and R. P. Lott. 1976. "Crime, Punishment and Personality: An Examination of the Deterrence Question." *Journal of Criminal Law and Criminology* 67(March):99–109.

Burkett, S. R., and M. White. 1974. "Hellfire and Delinquency: Another Look." *Journal for the Scientific Study of Religion* 13(December):455–61.

Chambliss, W. J. 1967. "Types of Deviance and the Effectiveness of Legal Sanctions." *Wisconsin Law Review* (Summer):703–19.

Chiricos, T. G., and G. P. Waldo. 1970. "Punishment and Crime: An Examination of Some Empirical Evidence." *Social Problems* 18(Fall):200–17.

Claster, D. S. 1967. "Comparison of Risk Perception Between Delinquents and Nondelinquents." *The Journal of Criminal Law, Criminology and Police Science* 58 (March):80–86.

Ehrlich, I. 1972. "The Deterrent Effect of Criminal Law Enforcement." *Journal of Legal Studies* 1(June):259–76.

Erickson, M. L., and J. P. Gibbs. 1973. "The Deterrence Question: Some Alternative Methods of Analysis." *Social Science Quarterly* 54(December):534–51.

Erickson, M. L., J. P. Gibbs, and G. F. Jensen. 1977. "The Deterrence Doctrine and the Perceived Certainty of Legal Punishments." *American Sociological Review* 42(April):305–17.

Geerkin, M. R., and W. R. Gove. 1975. "Deterrence: Some Theoretical Considerations." *Law and Society Review* 9(Spring):497–513.

Gibbs, J. P. a:1968. "Crime, Punishment and Deterrence." *Southwestern Social Science Quarterly* 48(March):515–30.

______. b:1975. *Crime, Punishment and Deterrence*. New York: Elsevier.

Gold, M. 1970. *Delinquent Behavior in an American City*. Belmont: Brooks/Cole Publishing Company.

Goodman, L. A. a:1972. "A Modified Multiple Regression Approach to the Analysis of Dichotomous Variables." *American Sociological Review* 37(February):28–46.

______. b:1972. "A General Model for the Analysis of Surveys." *American Journal of Sociology* 77:1035–86.

______. c:1973. "Causal Analysis of Data from Panel Studies and Other Kinds of Surveys." *American Journal of Sociology* 78(March):1135–91.

Grasmick, H. G., and H. Milligan, Jr. 1976. "Deterrence Theory Approach to Socioeconomic Demographic Correlates of Crime." *Social Science Quarterly* 57 (December):608–17.

Gray, L. N., and J. D. Martin. 1969. "Punishment and Deterrence: Another Analysis." *Social Science Quarterly* 50(September):389–95.

Hamblin, R. L. 1974. "Social Attitudes: Magnitude Measurement and Theory." In Hubert M. Blalock, Jr. (ed.), *Measurement in the Social Sciences*. Chicago: Aldine-Atherton.

Hindelang, M. J. 1973. "Causes of Delinquency: A Partial Replication and Extension." *Social Problems* 21(Spring):471–87.

Hirschi, T. 1969. *Causes of Delinquency*. Berkeley: University of California Press.

Hirschi, T., and R. Stark. 1969. "Hellfire and Delinquency." *Social Problems* 17(Fall): 202–13.

Jensen, G. F. a:1969. "'Crime Doesn't Pay': Correlates of a Shared Misunderstanding." *Social Problems* 17(Fall):189–201.

______. b:1972. "Delinquency and Adolescent Self-conceptions: A Study of the Personal Relevance of Infraction." *Social Problems* 20(Summer):84–103.

______. c:1972. "Parents, Peers and Delinquent Action: A Test of the Differential Association Hypothesis." *American Journal of Sociology* 78(November):562–75.

Kraut, R. E. 1976. "Deterrent and Definitional Influences on Shoplifting." *Social Problems* 23(February):358–68.

Logan, C. H. a:1971. "On Punishment and Crime (Chiricos and Waldo, 1970): Some Methodological Commentary." *Social Problems* 19(Fall):280–84.

______. b:1972. "General Deterrent Effects of Imprisonment." *Social Forces* 51(September):64–73.

Silberman, M. 1976. "Toward a Theory of Criminal Deterrence." *American Sociological Review* 41(June):442–61.

Silver, M. 1974. "Punishment, Deterrence and Police Effectiveness: A Survey and Critical Interpretation of the Present Econometric Literature." Unpublished manuscript in the form of a report prepared for the Crime Deterrence and Offender Career Project (135 West 78th Street, New York).

Teevan, J. J. a:1973. "Deterrent Effects of Punishment: Subjective Measures Continued." Paper presented at the annual meeting of the Society for the Study of Social Problems, New York.

______. b:1975. "Perceptions of Punishment: Current Research." In Richard L. Henshel and Robert A. Silverman (eds.), *Perception in Criminology*. New York: Columbia University Press.

______. c:1976. "Subjective Perception of Deterrence (Continued)." *Journal of Research in Crime and Delinquency* 13(July):155–64.

Tittle, C. R. a:1969."Crime Rates and Legal Sanction." *Social Problems* 16(Spring): 408–23.

______. b:1975. "Deterrents or Labelling?" *Social Forces* 53(March):399–410.

______. c:1977. "Sanction Fear and the Maintenance of Social Order." *Social Forces* 55(March):579–96.

Tittle, C. R., and C. H. Logan. 1973. "Sanctions and Deviance: Evidence and Remaining Questions." *Law and Society Review* 7(Spring):371–92.

Tittle, C. R., and A. R. Rowe. 1973. "Moral Appeal, Sanction Threat, and Deviance: An Experimental Test." *Social Problems* 20(Spring):488–98.

Toby, J. 1964. "Is Punishment Necessary?" Journal of Criminal Law, *Criminology and Police Science* 55(September):332–37.

Waldo, G. P., and T. G. Chiricos. 1972. "Perceived Penal Sanction and Self-reported Criminality: A Neglected Approach to Deterrence Research." *Social Problems* 19(Spring):522–40.

Zimring, Franklin E., and Gordon Hawkins. 1973. *Deterrence: The Legal Threat in Crime Control*. Chicago: University of Chicago Press.

The Effect of Labeling upon Youths in the Juvenile Justice System: A Review of the Evidence

Anne Rankin Mahoney
University of Denver and IJA-ABA Juvenile Justice Standards Project

AUTHOR'S NOTE: *This essay is drawn from work prepared for the Institute of Judicial Administration — American Bar Association Juvenile Justice Standards Project. The Project is supported by funds from the National Institute of Law Enforcement and Criminal Justice, Andrew W. Mellon Foundation, the American Bar Endowment, the Vincent Astor Foundation and the Herman Goldman Foundation. The latter, in particular, provided support for social science input into the Project.*

The avoidance of the stigma accompanying court appearance was one of the reasons for the development of a specialized court for children. Treatment-oriented reformers had been concerned for many years about the potentially harmful effects upon individuals of arrest, court appearance, and incarceration. As a result, they made efforts in the juvenile court to minimize stigmatization by having informal procedures, hearings closed to the public and press, and limited access to court records. More recently the avoidance of stigma has been used to rationalize the diversion of youths away from the juvenile justice system before they have any contact with it. This heightened concern about stigmatization through juvenile court exeprience flows in part from a growing interest in labeling theory among social scientists.

The common sense notion that stigma results from court contact has been legitimated by its transformation into a "theory." The term "labeling theory" is used frequently among practitioners in the juvenile justice system to justify any effort to minimize court intervention into the lives of children. But, in spite of such general usage, there has been little systematic explication of the applicability of the theory to the juvenile justice system, and little examination of its empirical support. It has been described as "our most widely accepted, untested formulation" (Klein, 1972: 7).

This article attempts to pull together existing empirical evidence about the effects of police and court labeling upon juveniles. Section I is a brief outline of labeling as a theoretical perspective on the etiology of deviant behavior. Section II is a discussion of some of the problems we encounter when we attempt to view the juvenile justice system as a labeling agent. Section III, the main body of the article, is a summary and critical discussion of relevant research on the effects of labeling upon juveniles.

I. LABELING AS A CAUSE OF DEVIANT BEHAVIOR

Until recently, thinking about juvenile delinquency and other deviant behavior focused primarily upon characteristics of the individual deviant or upon his environment (Schur, 1973: 22). Juvenile delinquents, for example, were viewed as children whose problems must be diagnosed and treated, as children whose misbehavior must be punished, or as primarily the products (and thus the victims) of poverty and discrimination. Now, many social scientists are turning their attention to a different aspect of deviance — societal response. Adherents to the societal response (or labeling) perspective are attempting to understand the process through which the response to behavior by community members creates deviance. A deviant is defined by labeling theorists as "one to whom that label has successfully been applied; deviant behavior is behavior that people so label" (Becker, 1963: 9). Adherents to the labeling perspective maintain that the processes of social control, themselves, work to define and produce deviance (Lemert, 1951; Kitsuse, 1964; Tannenbaum, 1938; Scheff, 1970). Community members not only define certain acts as deviant, they stigmatize and negatively sanction a person who is believed to have committed such an act. Social responses to a person who has been labeled may change because of the label, and he or she may become increasingly isolated from other members of the community. As this occurs, the labeled person begins to employ deviant behavior or a role based upon it as a means of defense, attack, or adjustment to the overt or covert problems created by the societal reaction to his behavior. He moves into what Lemert (1951) calls "secondary deviation." The labeled person comes to see himself as outside the community; he becomes committed

From *Law and Society Review,* Vol. 8 (Summer 1974), pp. 583–614. Reprinted by permission of The Law and Society Association, © 1974; *Law and Society Review* is official publication of the Association.

to deviant activities and peers; he comes to see himself as a "deviant."

Under a somewhat simplified version of labeling theory, the process of creating a juvenile delinquent might proceed like this. A youth commits an act, perhaps on a whim or as a reaction to a particular set of circumstances, such as peer pressure or boredom. If the act is not noticed or reacted to by others, it may be denied by the youth as not being part of his usual mode of behavior and not repeated. If he is not labeled, the youth may "grow out" of his delinquent behavior. However, if individuals or institutions in the community respond to his behavior as "bad," the youth may come to define it and eventually himself as "bad." There is a legal and social tendency to define a youth in terms of his acts. Thus a juvenile who is found to have committed delinquent acts is declared by the court to be a "juvenile delinquent." As the labeling process continues, the avenues to law-abiding behavior begin to close for the youth as he is pushed toward the outer boundaries of the "acceptable" community. An official reaction such as court appearance may function as a "degradation ceremony," in which the youth "becomes in the eyes of the witnesses a different person" (Goffman, 1956). As the youth's present behavior is labeled negatively, his *previous* behavior, also, is reviewed through a process of retrospection and redefined negatively to fit his new identity. There is a persistent demand for consistency in character, so the delinquent is defined as bad and is not believed if he is good (Tannenbaum, 1938: ch. 1). Through a process of response and counter-response, the youth moves into a delinquent career.[1]

Such a formulation puts a large part of the responsibility for the development of an individual's deviant career upon the agents of social control who first respond to his initial norm-violating behavior. Thus, the actions of agencies which are attempting to help a youth who has committed an offense may contribute to the development of his deviant identity and to his committing further deviant acts.

Although most labeling theorists would hesitate to attribute all deviance to the effects of labeling (Becker, 1973: 42), it is important to note where the labeling perspective takes us if it is pushed to its logical conclusion. It implies that a youth will stop behaving in a deviant way if he is left alone and not labeled by intervention agencies. In other words, if we ignore delinquency, it will decrease by itself. The delinquent youth is seen in this theory, as in other theories of the etiology of deviant behavior, as an essentially passive participant in the process. Instead of being moved toward deviant acts by socio-economic conditions, psychological forces, or peer pressures, he is pushed outside the law-abiding community by the labeling of the very people who are trying to help him. Labeling theorists do talk about the negotiation process in labeling and about the elements of bargaining and power relations (Schur, 1971: 56-58). Nevertheless, the deviant seems always to be in a "no-win" situation. In criminal court, for example, he can plead guilty to a lesser charge and improve his chances for a suspended sentence, or go to trial and take the increased risk of getting a jail sentence if found guilty. The deviant's bargaining, when it occurs, seems to revolve around the *degree* to which he will be defined as deviant rather than around a fight for a total rejection of the label.

An important question is whether a person, once labeled, can be "delabeled." Theorists usually note that, just as the interaction process leads to a deviant identity, so also can it be reversed and lead to a non-deviant identity. However, there is almost no discussion about the circumstances under which this occurs and the kind of special re-entry problems that might be encountered by an "outsider" coming back in. The lack of discussion about delabeling suggests that the labeled person rarely returns to non-deviant status.[2]

In order to show empirically that the official labeling of a youth increases his delinquent behavior, it is necessary to establish a chain of relationship between official response to a youth's delinquent behavior, his awareness of and reaction to the official label, and modification of his subsequent behavior in the direction of greater delinquency. In accordance with this formulation, we can advance the following propositions: (1) a juvenile who commits an offense and is apprehended is more likely to commit further offenses than a juvenile who commits an offense and is not apprehended. If we assume that the further a youth goes into the juvenile justice system the more seriously the label is taken, then it also follows that (2) the more severe a youth's disposition in the court, the more likely he is to commit additional offenses. If labeling works as hypothesized in the case of the child in juvenile court, the act of labeling (apprehension and/or processing as a juvenile offender) leads to modification of behavior (the commission of increased or more serious offenses). The reaction to the labeling act by (1) the labeled individual, and (2) others who respond to the label, represents two intervening variables which can modify the relationship between the act of labeling and the modification of behavior.

II. THE JUVENILE JUSTICE SYSTEM AS A LABELING AGENT — SOME PROBLEMS

There is a considerable body of literature on labeling theory, but very little deals specifically with juvenile justice. The attempt to apply labeling theory to a particular substantive area such as juvenile delinquency points up many of the problems with the theory and highlights some of the complexities inherent in acts of labeling.

Throughout this review an attempt is made to focus upon the effect on a youth of being labeled by the juvenile justice system. It is difficult to maintain this focus for several reasons. First, it is difficult to isolate the role of the juvenile justice system as a labeling agent; second, it is hard to separate the effects of labeling from the effects of changes in a youth's life circumstances caused by court action; and, third, it is hard to ascertain the subjective meaning of labeling experiences to the youths who are being labeled.

The term "juvenile justice system," as it is used in this review, refers to the entire process of response by police and court to juvenile misbehavior — both status offenses and criminal offenses. It includes responses which range from an unrecorded contact with a police officer through incarceration in an institution.[3]

A. The Role of the Juvenile Justice System as a Labeling Agent

Labeling can be approached on the level of interpersonal interaction or on the level of official decision-making (Bordua, 1967: 151). Most of the commentary and research on stigmatization of juvenile offenders has focused upon official decision-making by courts and police. Wheeler and Cottrell (1967) and Lemert (1967) articulate their concern about police and court actions in their papers for the *Task Force Report: Juvenile*

Delinquency and Youth Crime. They stress that stigma can be one of the consequences of wardship, placement, or commitment to a correctional institution. The official labeling of a misbehaving youth as a "delinquent" clearly places him in a category, and responses to him may be different than they would have been if he had not been so categorized. In this sense, the juvenile court may become a connecting link of a vicious circle in which delinquency causes delinquency. However, in addition to the stigma which may accompany official decisions, a youth may experience stigmatization during interpersonal interactions with peers, guards, judges, lawyers, or social workers as he goes through the juvenile justice system. His contact with the system subjects him to the potential effects of labeling at both the interpersonal and the official level. It is difficult to ascertain whether the effects of labeling, if any appear, come primarily from one level or the other.

A second question regarding the court's role as a labeling agent is whether it initiates labels or rubber-stamps labels previously attached to youths by family, peers, and school officials. Scheff (1964) and Mechanic (1962) found that psychiatric examinations to determine whether an individual should be committed to a mental hospital were often perfunctory, and conducted in a manner clearly indicating that the decision preceded the examination. Emerson (1969: 275) maintains that a similar process operates in the juvenile court. The court "produces delinquents by validating the prior judgments and demands for action of local institutions encountering problems from troublesome youths." The crucial labeling experiences for a juvenile may occur long before he finds his way to court. The court's label represents the end product of a series of institutional reactions to a youth.[4] Whether the court legitimates labels or creates them, its official decision has one uniquely important aspect. The court alone has the power to unleash powerful forces for community interference into a youth's life. The labeling of a youth as "someone whose life the community can tamper with" may be the key labeling act of the juvenile justice system.

B. Separation of Labeling Effects from Other Effects

Labeling itself may lead to changes in behavior, or it may simply accompany other experiences which lead to changes in behavior. Apprehension and processing of a youth by the court not only constitute a series of acts of labeling, but also result in some very real changes in a youth's life. He may be held for hours or months in a detention prison, or removed from his own home and family and placed in a foster home. He may be institutionalized for long periods of time. In the course of his processing through courts and prisons he comes in contact with a wide range of adults and juveniles and has new experiences. These contacts may change him, entirely apart from any effects of labeling.

Nice kids with good work habits, diligence, and high academic achievement rarely acquire a juvenile court record. Youths who do build up a record usually have a lot of problems — family difficulties, school and learning problems, economic hardship. There are a lot of reasons why they might be singled out for juvenile court intervention and a lot of reasons why they might have trouble getting a job, apart from their juvenile court experience. Does an employer refuse to hire a youth because he has a juvenile court record, or does he refuse to hire him because he cannot read, dropped out of school, and is insolent? Does he refuse to hire him because the last three fellows with similar backgrounds whom he hired broke a lot of dishes, and quit after the first day? It's hard to know.

C. Subjective Meaning of the Labeling Experience

Although labeling theory has been used almost exclusively to describe negative experiences, examples of positive labeling abound — graduation ceremonies, weddings, citations for bravery, promotions.[5] Even labeling as a deviant may have positive effects and result in the deterrence of further deviant behavior, as suggested by Thorsell and Klemke (1972: 394). They note that labeling theorists have failed to consider the possibility that the impact of the labeling process may not be uniform in all social settings and across all forms of deviant behavior. Labeling seems to work as a deterrent to deviance in some primary groups where the labeling of deviants creates pressures to bring their behavior back into conformity with group norms.[6]

Court experience might be perceived positively by youths in several different ways. A youth might view his court experience — especially if he is released — as an affirmation of the judge's faith in his basically good nature and his ability to stay out of trouble in the future. Such a view would be in keeping with the rehabilitative, nonthreatening court that many of the early reformers hoped for. Court labeling might be perceived positively for other reasons. Someone who has never received any attention or distinguished himself in any setting before may enjoy the many opportunities provided by the court to enumerate the circumstances of his offenses — real or imagined. For such a youth, the experience may be a positive one, whether the label is or not. Such positive reinforcement of past offenses may result in the committing of further offenses which lead to apprehension and more opportunities for attention.

The court experience may be "positive" for yet another kind of youth. A youth aspiring to membership in a delinquent peer group might view his contact with the court as positive, because to him apprehension and appearance before the court is a symbol of prestige and enhances his status among his peers. If court appearance does give status to a juvenile offender, it may be so only at a certain point in the formation of his delinquent identity — after the labeling process is under way, but before he has acquired full delinquent identity. For a youth in this in-between position, labeling by the court may be extremely damaging and may lead to the changes in behavior hypothesized by labeling theorists.

A common assumption among professionals concerned about juvenile justice is that youths will react positively to a proceeding which is fair. They argue that the youth who is adjudicated delinquent in a proceeding in which his rights have been protected will perceive that he has been treated justly, will feel more positive about the experience, and therefore will be more amenable to rehabilitation. One wonders if anyone who is sentenced to an institution ever *really* believes that his sentence is fair. Justice and fairness look different from in front of the bench than they do from behind the bench. But even if we assume that a youth does believe that the procedure has been fair, does this knowledge have a positive effect upon him? Advocates of the labeling perspective, with their emphasis upon the overriding impact of the label itself, might argue that it does not matter whether we label someone in a fair or unfair manner. What matters is that we label him.

The very fact that a person is labeled by a procedure that

he considers legitimate may have an even greater negative impact on him than it would have had if he had perceived it as illegitimate. A label fairly affixed may be taken more seriously than one attached in a clearly unfair way. An unfair label is easier to deny psychologically. A community that believes its juvenile court is fair is likely to take its judgments seriously. Thus, probably one of the worst things we can do, if we are really concerned about the effects of labeling, is to develop a court that community members and defendants believe is really fair. A just procedure is highly desirable for other reasons, but it will not necessarily decrease the negative effects of labeling.

III. EMPIRICAL RESEARCH

A small but growing body of empirical research on the labeling of juveniles provides some perspective on the theory and the factors we have been discussing. I shall describe and discuss some of the most relevant empirical work on the labeling of juveniles by the juvenile justice system. Relatively few studies are described here because few were found.[7] They all suffer from methodological problems because this is a very hard area in which to conduct precise research. Labeling theory, as it is formulated, gives little guidance to the researcher who wants to test its propositions. Although data on labeled offenders is abundant and relatively easy to find, control data on comparable unlabeled offenders is expensive and difficult to obtain. It is very hard to find similar youths who have committed similar offenses — some of whom have been labeled and some of whom have not. Furthermore, it is hard to find comparable youths who have had different dispositions and thus different degrees of labeling.[8]

The empirical work may be divided into three categories: studies which show the effect of labeling by the juvenile justice system upon a youth's subsequent behavior; studies which show the effect of community and family reaction to a youth's contact with the juvenile justice system and studies which show the effect of labeling upon a youth's self-concept.

A. The Effect of Labeling upon Subsequent Delinquent Behavior

Gold-Williams Study. Gold and Williams (1969) attempt to test the proposition that a youth who is apprehended for an offense will commit more subsequent offenses than a comparable youth who is not apprehended. Data are utilized from a 1967 representative national sample of 847 thirteen to sixteen year old boys and girls who were interviewed as a part of a study of adolescent life. One set of questions in the interview focused on illegal behavior in which the youths had engaged during the three years preceding the study. Interviews recorded information about each offense reported by the youth — its nature, when it was committed, whether it resulted in apprehension, and if so, the disposition of the case. A large majority, 88% of the 847, reported that they had committed illegal acts (Williams and Gold, 1972: 213). A very small number of these youths reported that they were ever apprehended for an act. All the youths who reported a total of four or more offenses and who had ever been apprehended (a total of 74) were selected for the particular study described here. A control group was specified by matching each apprehended offender with an unapprehended offender of the same sex and race, whose age was within six months of the apprehended offender, who had reported an offense within six months of the offense at which his apprehended match had been caught, and who had committed about the same number of offenses prior to the act. With these criteria it was possible to match only 35 of the 74 apprehended youths. The study results are based upon these 35 pairs of matched offenders.

Each pair was compared in terms of the number of offenses committed after the time one youth was apprehended. In 20 of the pairs, the apprehended member committed more offenses than the unapprehended member; in 10 of the pairs, the apprehended offender committed fewer offenses; and in 5 of the pairs, the two youths committed an equal number of offenses.

The authors see their study as providing support for the hypothesis of labeling theorists that apprehension (*i.e.*, official community response to the act) causes further delinquent behavior. However, the study cannot provide very strong support for the hypothesis because of methodological weaknesses. One particular problem is the lack of any control for the seriousness of the reported offenses. Assault, drinking beer at a girl friend's home, and destroying public property are all classified equally. The authors describe no attempt to take into account the seriousness of the offense in the matching of apprehended and unapprehended offenders. Two members of a "matched" pair could thus have very different kinds of offenses. A second problem with the study is the small number of matched pairs. Even though several factors have been controlled through matching, it is difficult to draw conclusions from a sample of 35, especially where the results are 20-15. A third problem with the study, at least in its published version, is the meaning of "more offenses." Were the differences between apprehended and unapprehended youths in most cases a matter of one offense or several? A fourth troubling aspect is the inability of the researchers to match more than half of the apprehended offenders with unapprehended offenders when the pool of unapprehended offenders was so large.

The Gold and Williams study is an example of the kind of research which needs to be done. Its findings suggest that there may be some empirical basis for the labeling perspective, but they hardly provide sufficient support for the labeling hypothesis.

McEachern Study. The study by A. W. McEachern (1968) is designed, according to its author, to assess the relative effectiveness of different dispositions and supervision practices in the probation system. The study is based upon data gathered from 2290 youths who were referred to the probation intake agency in eight California counties over a two month period, and followed for one year. It excludes youths who would have been eighteen within a year of referral because they would pass out of the jurisdiction of juvenile court before the study's one year follow-up period was completed. It also excludes all youths who were committed to institutions (apart from detention before hearing), and all children who were referred for dependency or "minor" traffic violations. Information was obtained on all youths' personal characteristics, delinquent history, school experience, socio-economic status, family history and structure, reason for referral, detention history, court process and initial disposition and placement. All, regardless of initial disposition, were followed for one year. Information was also gathered on individual probation officers' characteristics, positions and caseloads.

Youths in the study are all referred to the probation department for intake interviews. As a result of this initial contact, some are made wards of the court but others are not;

some are "treated" by probation officers, and some are not. Youths were divided into four categories:

1. Not ward of court and no treatment;
2. Not ward of court and treatment;
3. Court ward and no treatment; and
4. Court ward and treatment.

This study can be used to test the labeling proposition that youths with more severe dispositions are more likely to commit further offenses than youths with less severe dispositions. One must, however, assume that being made a court ward and being "treated" are more severe dispositions than not being made a ward of the court and not being contacted by a probation officer.

McEachern created an index of the number and seriousness of offenses over time. He then compared each youth's offense rate for the twelve months prior to inclusion in the study (*i.e.*, prior to his referral to intake) with his offense rate for the twelve months after inclusion. Nearly three quarters of the youths (72%) were *not* referred for delinquent acts during the twelve month follow-up period.

In light of the labeling theory proposition, we would expect to find a variation in offense rate with the court wards and "treated" youths showing a greater incidence of referral during the follow-up year. The offense rate did vary among the four classes of juveniles but not completely in line with labeling theory. Youths who were made wards of the court (*i.e.*, labeled) showed a greater *decrease* in delinquent activity during the follow-up period than the youths who were not made wards of the court. This finding is contrary to labeling theory propositions.

A second finding is that youths who had some contact with a probation officer (whether they were made wards of the court or not) committed *more* offences on the average than the youths who had had no contact with a probation officer. This finding supports the labeling perspective.

The greatest decrease in offenses was recorded for the group of youths who were made wards of the court but were not contacted by a probation officer even though data on the background characteristics of these youths showed that this group contained a disproportionate number of youths who had serious problems.

It is difficult to make sense of these findings from a labeling theory perspective. They would seem to suggest that official labeling action itself is not detrimental, but that contact with treatment agents is. Perhaps the interaction inherent in probation supervision tends to push the youth to an increased self-definition of himself as a delinquent whereas being made a ward of the court without any treatment is a positive labeling experience which enables the youth to define himself as someone the court believes can "stay out of trouble" in the future.

The published report of this study has some serious gaps in information about the decisions by probation officers to contact or not contact youths. Youths were classified as not treated if there was no indication that they were ever contacted by a probation officer. But the reason for this lack of treatment is not clear. Was it a decision by the court or intake officer that none was needed, or was it simply happenstance? One might argue that the results show that decisions about which youths to treat were highly accurate the ones deemed not in need of treatment got into less trouble. However, this is hard to show because the research report includes no qualitative material from the probation officers themselves about how they set priorities within their caseload, and there is no discussion about whether probation was ordered for those youths who were never contacted. The reader is left with the feeling that there must be some important explanatory variables which have been left uncontrolled in this study, but this may reflect our belief that a system which has important effects upon the lives of children must have a rational basis. It may not.

Thornberry Study. Thornberry (1971) also attempts to determine the relationship between legal dispositions and subsequent criminal behavior of youths, but he examines the effect of institutionalization as well as of less severe dispositions. Thornberry's hypothesis, in line with labeling theory, is that as the dispositions become more severe, the impact of the labeling process on the individual is greater, and therefore criminal activity increases.

Thornberry attempted to test this hypothesis through an analysis of the longitudinal data collected by members of the University of Pennsylvania Research Center on all boys born in 1945 who lived in Philadelphia at least between the ages of 10 and 17. The names of these boys were checked in the records of the Philadelphia Police Department and all their offenses and their dispositions were recorded.[9] Thornberry's study is based upon a population of 3,475 boys who committed a total of 9,601 offenses. It includes data on all of each boy's offenses from his first recorded offense to his last recorded offense before he was above the age when he could legally be considered delinquent.

Thornberry uses four dispositional categories. The least severe is *remedial arrest* (6,515 cases) in which the youth is only handled by one agency and the case is resolved in a matter of hours. The next most severe disposition is *adjustment* (1,338 cases) in which the delinquent is dealt with by the Probation Department and occasionally by the court itself as well as by the police. The child may be warned to stay out of trouble and the court may informally "keep tabs" on him. These two dispositions put little or no constraint on the youth's behavior. A more severe disposition is *probation* (1,094 cases). Juveniles have a court hearing and are placed under the direct supervision and guidance of the Probation Department and are required to report regularly to their probation officer. The most severe disposition is *institutionalization* (654 cases) where the youth is incarcerated.

Subsequent criminal behavior is defined in this study in terms of two basic concepts: the volume of recidivism and the seriousness of the offense committed.

The data presented go in the direction hypothesized by labeling theorists in regard to *volume* of subsequent crimes for three groups of youth: white boys, boys of upper socio-economic status, and boys whose initial apprehended offenses were of a less serious nature. For these groups Thornberry found early severe dispositions (short of institutionalization) were more likely than lenient ones to be associated with a greater volume of subsequent crimes. This relationship between severity of disposition and volume of subsequent criminality is not found, however, among youths who are black, of lower socio-economic status, or who initially committed more serious crimes. There was no association between the severity of disposition and the *seriousness* of subsequent crimes, regardless of race, socio-economic status or seriousness of initial offenses.

The most severe disposition, institutionalization, is associated with subsequent criminality in a way that is directly counter to the labeling hypothesis. Youths of all categories who were institutionalized had a *lower* subsequent rate of criminality in terms of both seriousness and volume than the youths who had not received such severe dispositions. The author speculates that the positive effect of institutionalization in decreasing subsequent crime may result from the time spent in incarceration, but he feels that this is unlikely especially since incarceration is also associated with a decrease in the *seriousness* of subsequent offenses and we would not expect a decrease in the seriousness of offenses to be associated with institutionalization. There are three other possible explanations for the finding on the effects of institutionalization. One is that punishment works. Youths who are sent away don't like it and try not to do things which will subject them to such an experience again. A second possible explanation is that youths who are incarcerated learn a lot, become more professional in their delinquency, and consequently don't get caught as often, especially if they are motivated to avoid apprehension because of their extreme distaste for incarceration. This latter argument is not really counter to labeling theory, and may suggest why some propositions are so hard to test empirically. An increase in the actual offense rates of labeled youths may be completely masked by a corresponding increase in expertise in avoiding apprehension. A third explanation, in keeping with labeling theory, is that by the time a youth reaches the point of being institutionalized, he has already moved into secondary deviance and is no longer affected by court labeling. By the time the judge decides to send him to an institution, his definition of himself as a delinquent and the definition of him as delinquent by others may be well established. If this is the case, then the labeling theorist would not expect to find an increase in subsequent offenses as a result of institutionalization. The secondary delinquent, well settled into his delinquent identity and well started on his delinquent career, may reach a point where delinquent activity either stabilizes at a certain level, or becomes less visible because of the delinquent's greater skill in avoiding apprehension. These speculations highlight one assumption which those who test the propositions of labeling theory tend to make. They equate severity of disposition with severity of labeling effect. This may be true only to the point where secondary deviance begins to operate.

Implications. The three studies presented here do not provide very strong support for the proposition that labeling by the juvenile justice system increases subsequent delinquent behavior. They all have methodological weaknesses, which make their findings less definitive than they might otherwise be. Furthermore, the findings are inconsistent with one another. Some support labeling theory; some do not. Clearly, there is a need for more empirical tests of this theory. It is necessary to specify which youths are most susceptible to labeling effects and at what points in the process labeling has its greatest impact.

B. Community and Family Reaction to a Youth's Juvenile Justice Contact

A second category of empirical studies may provide some insight into the short- and long-range consequences of labeling. It deals with the reactions of community members and families to youths who have had contact with the juvenile justice system.

In an effort to minimize stigma, juvenile courts in the United States make an effort to sharply limit the number of community members who have knowledge of a child's contact with the court. Courtrooms are usually closed to visitors and records are confidential. On the one hand the court goes to considerable trouble to avoid the leaking into the community of information about a youth's contact with the court. On the other hand, it involves a youth's family at every level of the proceedings.

Community Reaction. In recent years there has been a growing concern that the privacy protections afforded by the juvenile courts have been inadequate and that court and police records are accessible to employers, the armed forces, and other interested parties (Lemert, 1969). Although laws in some states provide for the expungement of juvenile records after a period of years if no criminal convictions have occurred, such procedures are rarely practical (Baum, 1965; Booth, 1963). A California legislative committee found that the number of routine documents on which a defendant's name may appear from the time his case began until its final disposition often ran over 100. (Lemert, 1969: 383). Thus, it seems clear that interested parties presently have access to information about a juvenile's court and police contact, and will have even greater access in the future as information systems become more efficient and complete.[10]

What effect does this knowledge have? There are possibilities of short-range effects and long-range effects. Some short-range effects have been documented in regard to police and court handling. The youth who is known to the police is more likely to be picked up by the police for questioning about incidents in his neighborhood. He is more likely to be dealt with more harshly by both police and courts if he is apprehended for new acts (Werthman and Piliavin, 1967; Terry, 1967; McEachern and Bauzer, 1967). A youth who has been in juvenile court who subsequently manages to stay out of trouble, and is fortunate enough to not be found in the wrong place at the wrong time may avoid these short-range difficulties, but he may have problems a few years hence when he attempts to get into the Armed Services, get a hack license, or get a civil service job. Some youths may be handicapped by a juvenile court record; other youths may not be. Whether they are or not probably depends in part on luck and on whether the youth aspires to any of the jobs or positions in which his court contact is likely to be discovered and considered a handicap. Goffman (1963) discusses the problems of managing undisclosed discrediting information which faces individuals with what he calls "spoiled identities." The "discreditable" person is one who must face unwitting acceptance of himself by individuals who are prejudiced against persons of the kind he can be revealed to be.

Two empirical studies give some indication of the effects of court contact on job possibilities. Both show that court contact leaves its mark. Prospective employers are loath to hire a person with a record, even if it is only an arrest without a conviction.

Schwartz and Skolnick (1962) tested the effect of an assault charge upon employment possibilities of lower-class unskilled workers through a field experiment. Four employment folders were prepared, the same in all respects except for the criminal court record of the applicant. The first folder indicated that the applicant had been convicted and sentenced for assault; the second that he had been tried for assault and been acquitted; the third indicated that he had been tried for assault and acquitted and included a letter from the judge certifying the finding of not guilty and reaffirming the legal presumption of innocence. The fourth folder made no mention of any criminal record. A sample of one hundred employers was utilized. To each, only one folder was shown and the employer was asked whether he could "use" the man described in the folder. Employers were not given any indication that they were participating in an experiment. Nine of the twenty-five employers shown the "no record" folder gave positive responses. Only one of the twenty-five shown the "convict" folder gave a positive response. Three of the twenty-five approached with the "accused but acquitted" file offered jobs, and six of the twenty-five approached with the applicant whose file included information on his acquittal and a letter from a judge offered a job. Even an acquittal appeared, in this study at least, to decrease the unskilled worker's chances for employment.

The most disturbing finding in this study is the similar reactions by employers to conviction and acquittal. Although the subjects in this study were not identified as juveniles, the findings have some implications for juveniles. One might surmise that the employers who do not distinguish between conviction and acquittal probably would not distinguish between a juvenile court experience and a criminal court experience either. The distinctions so carefully maintained by the legal system may have little importance in the larger community.

A similar study was conducted in the Netherlands by Buikhuisen and Dijkslerhuis (1971) with similar results. In a field experiment, 150 job application letters were sent to 75 large companies in the Netherlands. The letters were identical except for criminal record. One letter included an admission of one conviction for theft, a second included an admission of having temporarily lost a driver's license for drunken driving, and one made no mention of a criminal record. Three comparable companies were matched and each was sent one of the letters. The results showed that both categories of ex-delinquents received significantly fewer positive reactions to their applications than the applicants who made no mention of a previous conviction. Fifty-two percent of the letters with no criminal record received a positive reaction compared to thirty-two percent of the letters mentioning the theft conviction and twenty-six percent of the letters mentioning the license revocation for drunken driving. These two studies show a clear tendency on the part of employers to react less positively to applicants with a known criminal record, than to applicants for whom no criminal record is known.

Balch (1972) studied the reactions to delinquent labels by teachers and students in a junior high school. He randomly assigned 254 ninth graders and 31 teachers to experimental and control groups in which members filled out questionnaires designed to elicit their reactions to five students, each of whom was described in a brief vignette. The questionnaires were identical in every respect but one — in the experimental group each student was identified as a juvenile delinquent. He found that students and teachers alike perceived the labeled boys less favorably than the unlabeled boys. However, contrary to expectations, neither teachers nor students tended to be more punitive toward the delinquents than toward the nondelinquents.

Another study of stigma and deviant careers in school (Fisher, 1972) concludes that a negative association between the status as a delinquent and school performance existed *before* the identification of the juvenile as a delinquent as well as after. Youths were having trouble in school before their teachers knew that they had been labeled as delinquents.

Not all members of the community express equal intolerance of the juvenile who has been in trouble. A mail questionnaire study of public opinion on the definition, reporting, and correction of delinquency by Faust (1970) shows that tolerance varies considerably among members of different racial, status, and age groups. The more tolerant adults tend to be white, middle-class, younger, and better educated.

Family Reaction. Labeling theorists stress the importance of interaction with "significant others" in the labeling process.[11] For the youth who values family members as "significant others," the reaction of his relatives may be one of the key factors in determining whether the court experience will be an important labeling experience for him. Some youths may be punished or ostracized by other family members because of their court experience. Other youths may find a lack of concern among family members or attitudes neutralizing the importance of the court experience. Yet other youths may find family members rallying to their aid and working positively to help them move toward nondelinquent behavior.

The juvenile court tends to operate on the premise, or at least the hope, that the latter positive reaction will occur. Efforts are made to involve the family in the court proceedings as soon as possible. Most guidelines for police handling of juveniles give explicit instructions regarding the prompt notification of a youth's parents if he is apprehended. Probation officers, in preparing intake and pre-disposition reports, may talk to the family, school officials, and other persons with whom the youth may be in contact. The court is committed, at least in theory, to strengthening the family and keeping the child in his home if possible. However, there are youths who have no family, in the sociological sense, although some adult is legally responsible for them and signs the appropriate school and court papers. Blood relationship does not carry, in and of itself, affection and a sense of emotional involvement and responsibility. A child's emotional ties to caretakers, whether they be natural or adoptive parents or others, flow primarily from the psychological and emotional attachments which are built up through years of physical and emotional care and regular contact. The youth who has no real family, blood or adoptive, may be little affected by the labeling of family or community. He may be isolated already from legitimate activities and well into secondary deviation.

Even if a child has a family, the family may be unable or unwilling to help him. Delinquent behavior may pose serious hardship on a family with already dangerously overloaded emotional, social, and economic resources. Such a family may see the delinquent member as evidence of its own failure or as a threat to the well-being and respectability of other family members. Concealment of the delinquency may impose considerable strain on the family and subject members to frustrating role stresses and discomforts (Bryant, 1973). The family may also fear that the official labeling of one of its members will increase the possibility of future official labeling of other family members. In fact, probation reports often cite as negative information about a youth the fact that he or she has a sibling or parent who has also appeared in the court or spent time in an institution. Since each labeling incident of any member is to some extent a labeling of the family, the family may feel threatened by the labeled member and react strongly to isolate him from the family group. Parents often try to minimize the contamination of younger children by an older child who has gotten into trouble. Such a family may be eager to rid itself of its unruly youthful member and may resist efforts to impose responsibility for him or her. On the other hand, parents may resist removal of a child from the home because they see the loss of the child as public evidence of their own failure.

Limited public knowledge of a youth's court appearance may protect the parents more than the youth. Almost everyone who matters to a youth knows about his court appearance and can readily get access to his record — *e.g.*, family, school officials, future employers, probation and institutional workers. Parents, however, may be protected from community knowledge by lack of newspaper publicity, closed courtrooms, and general limiting of community knowledge about the delinquent incident. In fact, the parents' desire for protection from public knowledge of the incident may act as a strong force to keep a child in a family situation when he would be better off out of it. Removal of a child from the home is harder to hide than a court appearance.

Training school staff members who worked on a special project with the families of new arrivals to the Iowa Training School (O'Neil, 1969) noticed that parents tended to feel a sense of guilt about their son's confinement to the institution and a sense of failure in their family relationships. They also felt criticism of themselves by people in the community or members of their own family. Such parental feelings provide the potential for labeling and scapegoating of a delinquent youth. Snyder (1971) found some support for the existence of parental scapegoating of delinquents in her interviews with boys concerning their perceptions about the court hearing. Many of the youths mentioned that their parents' behavior was the thing that made them feel worst during their court hearing, especially such behavior as making negative remarks about them in front of others and crying. Several mentioned that their court experience had made their families feel ashamed.

Foster (1972), in his study of boys' perceptions about the impact of court appearance on their lives, found that 73% of the boys felt that the attitude of their parents towards them had *not* changed as a result of the court appearance. In the majority of cases, parental attitudes toward their children seem pretty well set before court appearance. They either regard their sons as troublesome and are not surprised that they have gotten in trouble or they feel their sons are basically good and will turn out well despite the court appearance. Nevertheless, in at least the remaining 27%, court labeling may have important repercussions on family interaction patterns, and the youth may experience serious changes in his family status as a result of his court experience. It would be interesting to do a follow-up study comparing the subsequent offenses of boys whose parents regarded them as troublesome with the subsequent offenses of boys whose parents thought that they were basically good.

The results of these three studies are inconclusive. There is evidence of parental shame and feelings of failure and some indication of negative interaction between parents and their delinquent offspring. There is also evidence that parent-child interaction patterns are well-established prior to court appearance and that the contact with the juvenile justice system does not substantially modify them.

Given the potentially important labeling role of the family, it is important to acquire empirical information about how a family reacts to a member who has been officially labeled as delinquent. In what kinds of situations does the family join with its deviant member to ward off negative evaluations by the community? In what kinds of cases does the family coalesce with the court agencies to vilify the family member? In what kinds of situations does the family withdraw from the whole affair? If we find that family labeling has a great impact upon at least some youths, then efforts to minimize the stigma attendant upon court appearance or diversion programs should focus upon the family as well as the community. For some youths, removal from the home, if it could be done in a non-stigmatizing way, might result in less labeling than returning the youth to a home where he or she is defined as "bad" or "no good." The problem, at present, is that the alternatives to home are usually detention facilities or institutions which create a whole new set of problems for the youth and do nothing to minimize stigma.

Our traditional assumption that a youth in trouble belongs in his family whenever possible serves a useful purpose for the middle-class, law-abiding community. The ideology that the family unit should be kept intact and that a family should take care of its own, shifts the responsibility for youthful deviant behavior away from the community and locates it in the family. It also makes morally suspect any commitment of public funds to homes and programs which provide alternatives to the family. If the family is regarded as sacred and its preservation is a public goal, then programs providing alternatives to the family may be perceived as morally wrong. Preservation of the family provides a moral justification for providing minimal community and court services to youths in trouble. Such justification will probably continue unless strong empirical evidence is presented to show that many youths really do not have any functioning family unit or that some youths are seriously harmed by family labeling and scapegoating.

C. The Effect of Labeling upon a Youth's Self-Concept

The previous sections dealt with studies which attempted to show a change in behavior as a result of labeling by the juvenile court system and with the reactions of family and community members to the label and the labeled individual. This section deals with the juvenile's own reaction to the labeling experience. Two kinds of studies are included in this section. The first focuses upon the subjective meaning of court appearance to the youths, and the second focuses upon the effect of official labeling upon a youth's self-image.

Impact of Court Hearing upon Youth. Snyder (1971) studied the impact of the juvenile court hearing upon 43 boys, ages 10-16, who had been placed on probation by the court. For 25 of the youths, the experience was a new one; the other 18 had been on probation before. In most cases the actual hearing was observed and the judge and the probation counselor were interviewed. The boys themselves were interviewed a few weeks after the hearing. Snyder found that the most frequently mentioned feeling about the court experience was fear, and the thing that almost all the boys (37 of 43) remembered most vividly was that the judge had placed them on probation instead of sending them away. None of the boys mentioned any feeling of guilt, although a few mentioned that they felt shame during and immediately after the hearing but it diminished with time. Most of the boys denied responsibility for their actions, even though all but one had admitted the offense. Some of the youths did perceive some labeling effect from their court experience. One youth said, "The kids at school find out and look down on you once they know you have been to court" (Snyder, 1971:

488). Youths who had been on probation before felt that once they had been picked up for something, they were suspected of having committed every subsequent offense in their neighborhood.

Baum and Wheeler's study (1966) of 97 boys who had just experienced their first commitment by the juvenile court revealed that the dominant response to the experience of commitment was shock, upset, and unhappiness. Over half of the boys said that they felt that the decision to send them away was fair, and they felt that it would help them by teaching them a lesson, or by breaking a pattern of criminal activity. Most felt that the trouble they were in was their own fault. Some of the boys felt that commitment would have no effect upon them primarily because of what they imagine happens to the "record," *i.e.*, "it is destroyed" or "no one will talk about it when I reach 17." Less than a third of the boys felt that institutionalization would harm them and they were primarily concerned about potential employers and the draft board.

The main concern of the boys in both studies seems to center upon the immediate outcome of the hearing—probation or commitment. The one clear difference in findings between the two studies regards the youth's feelings of responsibility for his behavior. Most of the youths placed on probation denied responsibility for what they had done, while most of the youths committed to institutions blamed themselves for their behavior. It is interesting to speculate whether this difference in response is the result of different interviewing techniques, reflects a factor in the situation which influenced the judge's decision, or whether it is the result of the decision. Perhaps in a hearing in which a boy is committed, a special effort is made to make the boy feel that he has misbehaved and that he, himself, is responsible for his commitment. If this is the case, a court appearance in which a youth is committed may be an important labeling experience because of its emphasis upon the boy's own responsibility for the commitment.

Foster's study of juveniles' perceptions of stigma following public intervention for delinquent behavior (1972), like Snyder's, and Baum and Wheeler's, does not reveal much perception of stigma on the part of the youths involved. His study group consists of 196 delinquent boys from an urban community of 300,000 population — 80 with police dispositions; 115 with juvenile court dispositions. The cases were gathered from the police department and the juvenile court over a period of three months and all subjects were interviewed at home within ten to twenty days after final disposition.

Generally, the youths did not feel that their contact with a law enforcement agency had resulted in any significant social liability in terms of interpersonal relationships. They did not perceive any negative effect whatever upon the attitude of their friends toward them, and there were only a few mentions of slight negative effects upon family relationships. Neither the type of disposition, nor the age nor ethnicity of the subjects significantly altered these responses. The interviewed subjects were asked if they thought what had happened would "create any special difficulty in completing school." Of the 172 boys still in school, 92% felt there would be no special problems. The few who felt otherwise were boys who had been having school problems before getting in trouble with the police. The boys responded with statements such as "what I did had nothing to do with school," or "the teachers don't know about it, so it won't matter." The only spheres about which the boys expressed concern were contact with the police and future employers. Fifty-four percent of the boys expected the police to keep an eye on them once they had been in trouble and forty percent of the boys felt that future employers would hold the incident against them.

None of these three studies provide strong evidence that the juveniles see the court experience as a deeply stigmatizing one. Their concerns seem to be primarily practical ones — hearing outcome, police surveillance and possible job discrimination. As Baum notes, "in the eyes of these youth, commitment to an institution is punishment for misdeeds" (1966: 183). Foster concludes that the results of his study indicate that the extent of perceived stigmatization and social liability that follows police or court intervention seems to be overestimated in the labeling hypothesis. If the deviant believes that his misdeeds are "nothing at all," or that people will soon forget about them, then the long-term implications of the incident are lost from the deviant's perspective, regardless of the real existence of social liability (1972: 208). This perspective is in keeping with the process of neutralization hypothesized by Sykes and Matza (1957) in which the infractious nature of offenses is negated and infraction is converted by the actors into mere action.

Official Labeling and Self-Image. Self-image has at least two components relevant to this discussion of delinquency. One is self-esteem, which has to do with how one feels about oneself and is usually described in qualitative terms as high or low. The second is the image an individual has of himself as a particular kind of person. Measurement of self-esteem or self-image is usually ascertained by some kind of questionnaire or interview in which the individual is asked to choose from a list of words those which he feels best describe him or which he thinks others would use to describe him. Or he may be asked to complete questions such as "I am—" or "My mother thinks I am—," or to agree or disagree with statements about himself. Often a scale of this kind is administered at several points in time so that it is possible to measure a youth's feelings about himself before and after an event such as arrest or institutionalization.

In the first study described here (Jensen, 1972), the relationship between officially-recorded delinquency, self-reported delinquency, self-evaluation as a delinquent, and self-esteem is explored. The study is based upon data gathered in 1964-65 by the Survey Research Center at the University of California, Berkeley, from black and white male students in eleven junior and senior high schools in California. Data are from three sources: school records, a questionnaire completed by the students, and police records.

The most striking finding of the study, relevant to the labeling perspective, is that officially-recorded delinquency is related to self-definition as a delinquent and is more strongly related for white adolescents than for black adolescents. In fact, among youths with a record of two or more offenses, almost twice as many whites as blacks at least sometimes think of themselves as delinquent. White youths are also more likely than black youths to believe that others think of them as delinquent. The tendency of blacks to reject or ignore the label when applied persists in each class context. Among white adolescents, however, there is variation among the status categories. Lower class white boys are more likely to see themselves as delinquent than are the boys whose fathers had some education beyond high school.

The relationship between officially-recorded delinquency and self-esteem showed a different pattern. There appears to be little relationship between official delinquency and self-esteem for white adolescents, but an interesting pattern of relationship by status for black youths. For blacks, officially-recorded delinquency is associated with *high* self-esteem among *lower* status youth and is associated with *low* self-esteem among *higher* status youth.

One difficulty with this study is the lack of a defined time sequence. It is impossible to know whether a youth's low self-esteem or self-definition as delinquent preceded or antedated his first being officially labeled as a delinquent. Unless his self-conception changed after his first brush with the law, it is hard to attribute the effect to labeling. A study by Ageton and Elliott (1973), because it has a longitudinal dimension, provides some data on this point. The study is based upon a secondary analysis of data from 2,617 youths in eight California secondary schools who were interviewed once annually from 9th grade through 12th grade. Those who moved or dropped out of school were included. Self-concept was measured each year by a short form of the Socialization (SO) Scale from the California Psychological Inventory. Data were also obtained from parent interviews, teacher ratings, and school, police, and court records. The results show that, over a four-year period, white (Anglo) youths who had had police contact showed a significant decrease in self-concept when compared with their peers who had had no such contact. Police contact is not a significant factor in accounting for a change in self-concept for any other group (Mexican, black or other). Ageton and Elliott (1973) found, as did Jensen (1972), that it was lower-class white adolescents who were affected by official contact with the juvenile justice system. They found, further, that police apprehension was the most important factor with regard to explaining a decreasing self-concept. Neither self-reported delinquency, nor the delinquency of one's peer group were as important. In other words, a youth's self-concept was influenced by whether he had ever been "caught" by the police rather than by whether he and his friends had ever *done* anything wrong.

One further finding of this study which is particularly interesting in regard to labeling is that the negative effect of police contact seemed to erode over time. Snyder (1971) reports similar findings in her study of adolescents' reaction to court experience. She notes that the youths seemed to develop an awareness and concern for others during and immediately after the hearing, but it subsided markedly with the passing of time. If additional research bears out this tentative finding, that the effect of official labeling wears off, then it is hard to make a case for the effect of labeling experiences upon an individual's future behavior. Exploration in this area could have important implications for the problem of "delabeling," and raises questions about the circumstances under which the effects of labeling wear off. The studies just described provide evidence that official labeling leads to a change in the self-image of some adolescents. White, lower-status boys and upper-status black youths seem to be the most affected by official acts of labeling.

CONCLUSION

The efforts to find out if contact with the juvenile justice system increases a youth's delinquent behavior have lead to conflicting results at best. There is some indication in one of the studies (Thornberry, 1971) that labeling affects white youths more than minority youths, an interesting aspect of labeling which needs to be developed further. Although there is some evidence (O'Neil, 1969; Snyder, 1971) that families sometimes resent or feel shamed by youths who have gotten in trouble with the law, and one can speculate about the potentially serious effects of labeling by family members, there is little empirical research available on the effects of family labeling. What there is (Foster, 1972) indicates that most youths perceive no change in parental attitudes toward them as a result of their court appearance. There is fairly consistent evidence that community members react negatively to youths whom they know have had court contact. Two studies (Schwartz and Skolnick, 1962; Buikhuisen and Dijksterhuss, 1971) showed that a known record of an arrest hurts employment chances. A third study (Balch, 1972) showed that teachers and students react less favorably to a youth who has been to court.

Juveniles themselves don't perceive their court experience as highly stigmatizing. Nevertheless, there is some evidence (Jensen, 1972; Ageton and Elliott, 1973) to suggest that self-definition as a delinquent is related to court contact for some youths, particularly white youths. There is a hint in two of the studies (Snyder, 1971; Ageton and Elliott, 1973) that the labeling effects of court contact may erode over time. In summary, we don't know much about the effects of court labeling upon juveniles. Existing research raises interesting questions about who is affected by labels, which labels have the greatest effect on youths and whether labeling effects have any long-term impact.

Two important policy questions are raised by the conclusions of this survey. One involves diversion and the other involves the court's role regarding the labeling of juveniles. A major argument advanced by proponents of diversion is that diverted individuals are less likely to commit another crime than the individuals who have not been diverted. Part of the basis for this argument is that the official contact with the court (labeling) is detrimental. This would be a strong argument if it were supported by empirical evidence. At this point, it is not. The labeling argument is an appealing argument because it has a certain common sense ring to it, and because it appeals to the liberal reformist belief that the person who comes in contact with the court — whether adult or juvenile — gets a bad deal. It would be unfortunate, however, if we let our concern for labeling effects blind us to some of the less desirable aspects of diversion projects.[12]

A second policy question concerns the proper role of the court regarding community labeling. At least in part, the court responds to labels already given to youths by families, schools, and other community agencies. The court may act primarily to legitimate community labels, or it may question and challenge them. In determining how best to respond to community labels, policy makers need to acquire information about the labeling process:

1. Which agents move juveniles into the justice system? How do they do it?
2. Under what circumstances, if any, is a court applied label crucial to a youth's movement away from or into delinquent behavior?
3. What short-range or long-range effects does court legitimation of community labels have upon youths?
4. Under what circumstances should the court resist the efforts of parents, schools and other community agencies to persuade it to legitimate the labels they have already attached?

In addition to the research which is beginning to be done

on the effects of institutional labeling, there is a need for a study of the dynamics and effects of labeling on the interpersonal level. This review has raised questions about the reactions of a youth's friends and family members to his deviant behavior. How does official labeling of a youth modify his interactions with family and friends? Under what circumstances do family and friends react primarily to a youth's behavior and under what circumstances do they react primarily to the fact that his behavior brings him to the official attention of the community? What kind of congruence is there between the youth's perception of changes in family attitude toward him and his family's perception of changes in their attitudes? Are there different patterns of family reaction to a youth's arrest, and are these patterns related to the extent of a youth's subsequent delinquent behavior?

As the youth goes through the juvenile justice system, what experiences, in addition to the court hearing itself, stand out in his mind as being most important or most demeaning? Does he describe encounters with individuals — police officers, guards, peers, social workers — that modify his image of himself?

Are only some youths affected by court labeling? Are some affected positively while others are affected negatively? If so, what are the characteristics of youths who are affected, and how do those affected positively differ from those affected negatively? How do youths resist or neutralize official labeling experiences? In addition to the study of juveniles who continue to reappear in the court, we need to study juveniles who come into court and then manage to stay out of trouble with the law.

The labeling perspective opens a rich source of insight and research possibilities to us. It focuses our thinking upon the ways in which youths are defined as deviant, the ways in which they are swept into the juvenile justice system, and the effects upon them of other persons' reactions to their behavior. It focuses our thinking also on the youth's perceptions of the process. Perhaps, as research on labeling accumulates and becomes more precise, and as we become better able to raise researchable questions, labeling will emerge as an important causal factor in the etiology of delinquent behavior. Meanwhile, no such evidence exists, and it would be a disservice to both the labeling perspective and the youths in the juvenile justice system to act as if it did.

NOTES

1 This is a very brief and somewhat simplified description of one aspect of labeling theory — the way in which it promotes deviant behavior in an individual labeled "deviant." For more extended discussions about labeling theory in general and about the uses of labels by the dominant society, see Becker, 1973; Downes and Rock, 1971; Erikson, 1962; Scheff, 1966; Schur, 1971; Spitzer, 1971; Warren and Johnson, 1972.

2 Ray's (1961) description of the re-entry problems of ex-heroin addicts highlights some of the problems of "delabeling."

3 This review does not include studies of police decisions to arrest juveniles because such studies focus primarily on the decision about whom to label rather than upon the effects of being labeled. For a review of studies about labeling by police, see Ward, 1971. For some specific studies of police response to juveniles, see Black and Reiss, 1970; Gandy, 1970; Goldman, 1963; Gould, 1969; Hohenstein, 1969; Piliavin and Briar, 1964; Werthman and Piliavin, 1967; and Weiner and Willie, 1971.

4 Young (1972) hypothesized that youths who possess characteristics which are viewed negatively by the dominant society are more likely to be dealt with severely by the juvenile court than other youths who committed similar acts. She found in her study of 2,001 youths in a Utah Juvenile Court that her hypothesis was supported in regard to ethnicity (white-nonwhite), religious activity, and parental income.

5 Rosenthal and Jacobson (1968) found that children who were expected by their teachers to "bloom" intellectually, showed a greater gain in IQ points after one year than other children of equal ability for whom no such expectations were held.

6 *E.g.*, in The Bank Wiring Room, workers who were labeled as "rate busters" were pressured to bring their behavior back within acceptable limits. The experiment also showed that labels applied by members of one's own work group were more effective in changing behavior than labels applied by management representatives. Roethlisberger and Dickson (1939).

7 Wheeler and Cottrell (1966) cite "a variety of social science theory and evidence which suggests that official response to behavior may initiate processes that push the misbehaving juveniles toward further delinquent conduct." But none of these discussions of labeling provide any direct empirical evidence for this hypothesis. See Freidson, 1965; Becker, 1963; Lemert, 1951; Kitsuse, 1964.

8 A recent study on the effectiveness of probation concluded that boys assigned to probation appear to be "better" or "easier" cases than those assigned to other treatment facilities (Scarpitti and Stephenson, 1968).

9 For a detailed description of how these data were gathered and for other interesting findings resulting from the data, see Wolfgang, Figlio, and Sellin, 1972.

10 For a discussion of records in juvenile court, see Lemert (1969).

11 The reaction of "significant others" is an important factor determining the impact of an act of labeling upon an individual. A "significant other" is someone whose opinion the youth values. Whose opinion does a youth value? Tannenbaum (1938: Ch. 1) notes that "[b]ehavior is a matter of choice as to whose approval you want. And whose approval you want may be determined by such invisible and subtle influences as whom you like, who has given you pleasure, and who has commended you."

12 Freed (1974), an early advocate of pre-trial diversion, is now raising some thought-provoking questions about it and urges that diversion legislation be postponed until a more thorough examination of the implications of diversion and diversion procedures is made. Among other unanswered questions, he notes the lack of evidence that diversion reduces recidivism.

REFERENCES

AGETON, Suzanne, and Delbert S. ELLIOTT (1973) "The Effects of Legal Processing on Self-Concept," Boulder: Institute of Behavioral Science, University of Colorado, Unpublished paper.

BALCH, Robert (1972) "Negative Reactions to Delinquent Labels in a Junior High School." Unpublished Ph.D. Dissertation, University of Oregon.

BAUM, Martha and Stanton WHEELER (1966) "Becoming An Inmate," in Stanton WHEELER (ed.) (1968) Controlling Delinquents. New York: John Wiley.

BAUM, Terry (1965) "Wiping Out a Criminal or Juvenile Record," 46 California State Bar Journal 816.

BECKER, Howard S. (1963) Outsiders. New York: Free Press.

.... (1973) "Labeling Theory Reconsidered," in Paul ROCK and Mary McINTOSH (eds.) Deviance and Social Control. New York: Harper & Row.

BLACK, Donald and Albert REISS (1970) "Police Control of Juveniles," 5 American Sociological Review 63.

BOOTH, A. (1963) "The Expungement Myth," 30 Los Angeles Bar Bulletin 63.

BORCHIA, David (1967) "Recent Trends: Deviant Behavior and Social Control," 374 Annals of the American Academy of Political and Social Science 149.

BRIAR, Scott and Irving PILIAVIN (1965) "Delinquency, Situational Inducement and Commitment to Conformity," 13 Social Problems 35.

.... (1964) "Police Encounters with Juveniles," 70 American Journal of Sociology 206.

BRYANT, Clifton D. (1973) "The Concealment of Stigma and Deviancy as a Family Function," in Clifton D. BRYANT and J. Gibson WELLS (eds.) Deviancy and the Family. Philadelphia: F. A. Davis Company.

BUIKHUISEN, Wouter and P. H. DIJKSTERHUSS (1971) "Delinquency and Stigmatization," 11 British Journal of Criminology 185.

CICOUREL, Aaron (1968) The Social Organization of Juvenile Justice. New York: John Wiley.

COHEN, Albert K. (1965) "The Sociology of the Deviant Act: Anomie Theory and Beyond," 30 American Sociological Review 5.

DAVIS, Nanette (1972) "Labeling Theory in Deviance Research: A Critique and Reconsideration," 13 The Sociological Quarterly 447.

DOWNES, David and Paul ROCK (1971) "Social Reaction to Deviance and Its Effects on Crime and Criminal Careers," 22 British Journal of Sociology 351.

DRINAN, Robert F. (1969) "Aftermath of Apprehension: Family Lawyer's Response," 3 Prospectus 31.

EMERSON, Robert (1969) Judging Delinquents. Chicago: Aldine Publishing Co.

ERIKSON, Kai T. (1962) "Notes on the Sociology of Deviance," 9 Social Problems 307.

FAUST, Frederic L. (1970) Dimensions of Delinquency Tolerance: Differential Tolerance of Juvenile Delinquent Behavior by Adult Members of Different Socio-Economic Classes and Racial Groups. Unpublished Ph.D. Dissertation, The Ohio State University.

FISHER, Sethard (1972) "Stigma and Deviant Careers in Schools," 20 Social Problems 78.

FOSTER, Jack D., Simon DINITZ, and Walter C. RECKLESS (1972) "Perceptions of Stigma Following Public Intervention for Delinquent Behavior," 20 Social Problems 202.

FREED, Daniel (1974) Statement on H.R. 9007 and S.798 before the Subcommittee on Courts, Civil Liberties, and Administration of Justice, Committee on the Judiciary, House of Representatives (February 12).

FREIDSON, Eliot (1965) "Disability as Social Deviance," in Marvin B. SUSSMAN (ed.) Sociology and Rehabilitation. Washington: American Sociological Association and Vocational Rehabilitation Administration.

GANDY, John M. (1970) "The Exercise of Discretion by the Police as a Decision-Making Process in the Disposition of Offenders," 8 Osgoode Hall Law Journal 329.

GARFINKEL, Harold (1956) "Conditions of Successful Degradation Ceremonies," 61 The American Journal of Sociology 420. Also in Earl RUBINGTON and Martin WEINBERG (eds.) (1973) Deviance: The Interactionist Perspective. New York: The Macmillan Co.

GIBBS, Jack (1966) "Conceptions of Deviant Behavior: The Old and the New," 9 Pacific Sociological Review 9.

GOFFMAN, Erving (1963) Stigma: Notes on the Management of Spoiled Identity. Englewood Cliffs, New Jersey: Prentice-Hall.

.... (1959) The Presentation of Self in Everyday Life. Garden City, New York: Anchor.

GOLD, Martin and Jay R. WILLIAMS (1969) "National Study of the Aftermath of Apprehension," 3 Prospectus 3.

GOLDMAN, Nathan (1963) The Differential Selection of Juvenile Offenders for Court Appearance. Washington, D.C.: National Council on Crime and Delinquency.

GOULD, Leroy (1969) "Who Defines Delinquency," 16 Social Problems 325.

HOHENSTEIN, William F. (1969) "Factors Influencing the Police Disposition of Juvenile Offenders" in Thorsten SELLIN and Marvin WOLFGANG (eds.) Delinquency: Selected Studies. New York: John Wiley.

JENSEN, Gary F. (1972) "Delinquency and Adolescent Self-Conceptions: A Study of the Personal Relevance of Infraction," 20 Social Problems 84.

KITSUSE, John (1964) "Societal Reaction to Deviant Behavior: Problems of Theory and Method," in Howard BECKER (ed.) The Other Side: Perspectives on Deviance. New York: Free Press.

KLEIN, Malcolm W. (1972) "On the Front End of the Juvenile Justice System," Appendix I in Los Angeles Regional Criminal Justice Planning Board, Juvenile System Rates: Diversion.

LEMERT, Edwin M. (1969) "Records in the Juvenile Court," in Stanton WHEELER (ed.) (1970) On record: Files and Dossiers in American Life. New York: Russell Sage.

.... (1967) "The Juvenile Court — Quest and Realities," in President's Commission on Law Enforcement and Administration of Justice, Task Force Report: Juvenile Delinquency and Youth Crime. Washington: Government Printing Office.

.... (1951) Social Pathology. New York: McGraw-Hill.

MATZA, David (1969) Becoming Deviant. Englewood Cliffs, New Jersey: Prentice-Hall.

McEACHERN, A. W. (1968) "The Juvenile Probation System," 11(3) American Behavioral Scientist 1.

.... and Riva BAUZER (1967) "Factors Related to Disposition in Juvenile Police Contacts," in Malcolm KLEIN (ed.) (1967) Juvenile Gangs in Context: Theory, Research and Action. Englewood Cliffs, New Jersey: Prentice-Hall.

O'NEIL, Carle F. (1969) "Working with Families of Delinquent Boys," 16 Children 198.

MECHANIC, David (1962) "Some Factors in Identifying and Defining Mental Illness," 46 Mental Hygiene 66.

PILIAVIN, Irving and Scott BRIAR (1964) "Police Encounters with Juveniles," 70 American Journal of Sociology 206.

RAY, Marsh (1961) "Abstinence Cycles and Heroin Addicts," 9 Social Problems 132.

ROETHLISBERGER, Fritz and William DICKSON (1939) Management and the Worker. Cambridge: Harvard University Press.

ROSENTHAL, Robert and Lenore JACOBSON (1968) Pygmalion in the Classroom: Teacher Expectation and Pupils' Intellectual Development. New York: Holt, Rinehart and Winston.

SCARPITTI, Frank and Richard STEPHENSON (1968) "A Study of Probation Effectiveness," 59 Journal of Criminal Law, Criminology, and Police Science 361.

SCHEFF, Thomas (1966) Being Mentally Ill. Chicago: Aldine.

.... (1964) "The Societal Reaction to Deviance: Ascriptive Elements in the Psychiatric Screening of Mental Patients in a Midwestern State," 11 Social Problems 401.

.... and E. SANDSTROM (1970) "The Stability of Deviant Behavior Over Time: A Reassessment," 11 Journal of Health and Social Behavior 37.

SCHUR, Edwin M. (1973) Radical Non-Intervention: Rethinking the Delinquency Problem. New York: Prentice-Hall.

.... (1971) Labeling Deviant Behavior: Its Sociological Implications. New York: Harper and Row.

SCHWARTZ, Richard D. and Jerome H. SKOLNICK (1962) "Two Studies of Legal Stigma," 10 Social Problems 133.

SNYDER, Eloise (1971) "The Impact of the Juvenile Court Hearing on the Child" 17 Crime and Delinquency 180.

SPITZER, Steven (1971) Labeling and Deviant Behavior: A Study of Imputation and Reaction in the Definition of Self. Unpublished Ph.D. Dissertation, Indiana University.

STUART, Richard B. (1969) "Aftermath of Apprehension: Social Scientists Response," 3 Prospectus 13.

SYKES, Gresham and David MATZA (1957) "Techniques of Neutralization: A Theory of Delinquency," 22 American Sociological Review 667.

TANNENBAUM, F. (1938) Crime and the Community. New York: Columbia University Press.

TERRY, Robert M. (1967) "The Screening of Juvenile Offenders," 58 Journal of Criminal Law, Criminology and Police Science 173.

THORNBERRY, Terence P. (1971) Punishment and Crime: The Effect of Legal Dispositions on Subsequent Criminal Behavior. Unpublished Ph.D. Dissertation, University of Pennsylvania.

THORSELL, Bernard A. and Lloyd W. KLEMKI (1972) "The Labeling Process: Reinforcement or Deterrent," 6 Law & Society Review 393.

WARD, Richard W. (1971) "The Labeling Theory: A Critical Analysis" 9 Criminology 268.

WARREN, Carol and John JOHNSON (1972) "A Critique of Labeling Theory from the Phenomenological Perspective," in Robert A. SCOTT and Jack DOUGLAS (eds.) Theoretical Perspectives on Deviance. New York: Basic Books.

WEINER, Norman and Charles WILLIE (1971) "Decisions by Juvenile Officers," 77 American Journal of Sociology 199.

WERTHMAN, Carl and Irving PILIAVIN (1967) "Gang Members and The Police," in David BORDUA (ed.) The Police: Six Sociological Essays. New York: John Wiley.

WHEELER, Stanton, Leonard S. COTTRELL, and Anne ROMASCO (1966) "Juvenile Delinquency: Its Prevention and Control," in President's Commission on Law Enforcement and Administration of Justice, Task Force Report: Juvenile Delinquency and Youth Crime. Washington: Government Printing Office.

WILLIAMS, Jay R. and Martin GOLD (1972) "From Delinquent Behavior to Official Delinquency," 20 Social Problems 209.

WOLFGANG, Marvin E., Robert M. FIGLIO and Thorsten SELLIN (1972) Delinquency in a Birth Cohort. Chicago: University of Chicago Press.

YOUNG, Marcella (1972) Dominant Values, Referral Behaviors and Labeling by the Juvenile Court. Unpublished Ph.D. Dissertation, Utah State University.

The Effects of Legal Processing on Delinquent Orientations*

Suzanne S. Ageton and Delbert S. Elliott
University of Colorado

Labelling theorists have long argued that deviant careers and commitments are developed in the process of interaction between individuals and social control agents. A critical issue in this process concerns the effect of official labelling on an individual's subsequent orientation toward delinquency. This study attempts to explicate this process by exploring a number of variables which may intervene in this interaction. Our findings indicate that over a four year period, youth with police contact(s) show a significant increase in delinquent orientations compared with their peers who had no such contact. Such factors as the delinquency level of one's peer group and actual involvement in delinquent behavior as reported by the subjects do not appear to be as important as police contact in explaining the increased orientation toward delinquency. The data also suggest that certain sub-groups (white males, in particular) are more susceptible to the effects of labelling than others.

INTRODUCTION

Traditionally, social theorists have viewed deviance as a unique kind of behavior tied to certain individual characteristics or situational factors. It is only within the last two decades that a process oriented approach known as "labelling" has come to occupy a central place among theories of deviant behavior. Significantly, it has shifted the focus of investigation and analysis from the etiology of deviant behavior to the process whereby individuals come to occupy deviant roles or enter deviant careers. Of major interest here is the labelling theorists' contention that formal interaction with the social control system (legal processing)[1] propels an individual toward a delinquent self-concept. Specifically, it has been suggested that an individual's perception of him or herself as deviant or delinquent is heightened or, in some instances, created by his/her contact with the Juvenile Justice System.

Most social theorists agree that the concept of labelling was first introduced in the work of Tannenbaum (1938), who suggested that once an individual was "tagged" or labelled as deviant, others began to see him/her as such and treat him/her accordingly. However, this idea was not really developed until Lemert (1951) suggested that an individual's self-definition was importantly shaped by his/her particular exposure to the actions of social control agents. He argued that the nature of the social reaction was critical in determining whether the deviation remained primary and situational or became part of a consistent pattern of non-conforming behavior. Lemert referred to the latter outcome as secondary deviation, that which occurs when an individual accepts and internalizes the deviant label society has conferred upon him/her. Other theorists (Garfinkel, 1956; Becker, 1964; Matza, 1964; Lofland, 1969) have supported this theme and placed even greater emphasis on public identification and labelling as critical to the transformation from a non-delinquent to a delinquent self-image. One of the primary consequences of this process, according to the labelling school, is that the individual becomes "caught up" in a delinquent role as a result of the new definition and expectations others have of him/her. From this perspective, then, the operations of the social control system are instrumental to the movement of individuals from non-delinquent to delinquent self-images.

THEORETICAL BACKGROUND

Although the projected relationship between the development of a delinquent self-concept and legal processing is at the heart of the labelling theory, very little empirical research has been undertaken to test it. The research which has been

* The authors are indebted to Richard Jessor for his thoughtful critique of an earlier draft of this paper and to N.C.M.H. for support of this research, MH 2303301.

[1] For the purposes of this research, the term "legal processing" is meant to include any type of interaction with the police, courts and/or correctional or penal institutions. Thus, the term covers all involvement with the Juvenile Justice System, however informal.

From *Social Problems,* Vol. 22 (October 1974), pp. 87–100. Reprinted with the permission of the Society of Social Problems and the authors.

done has centered primarily on the interdependence of self-conceptions and delinquency. The work of Reckless and Dinitz in the late 1950's is the forerunner of much of this research, though it focused specifically on the idea that a favorable self-concept acts as a barrier against environmental pressures conducive to delinquency (Reckless, *et al.*, 1956, 1957). However, there are methodological problems with this research (see Quinney, 1970, and Tangri & Schwartz, 1967) which seriously weaken its conclusions about the relationship between self-conceptions and behavioral patterns (Jensen, 1970).

Other research exploring the interdependence of delinquency and adolescent self-images has discovered that such relationships may vary from context to context. Short and Strodtbeck (1965:140-184) and Hall (1966:146-158) have presented evidence suggesting that the relationship between delinquency and self-conceptions may vary depending on social class standing, the nature of one's peers, and/or orientations towards law-breaking.

The most current empirical work in this area of which we are aware (Jensen, 1972) attempted to assess the idea that the "personal relevance of infraction" (its relation to adolescent self-conceptions) is shaped by the sociocultural context in which it occurs. These findings suggest that while there is variation by class, race, and social standing as to the impact of official labelling on evaluation of self as delinquent, there is overall ". . . a persistent tendency for those who have been officially labelled as delinquent to think of themselves and to feel thought of by others as delinquent more often than those who have not been so labelled."

Though these studies have produced some interesting findings bearing on labelling theory, they have failed to deal with one of the central problems of the whole perspective. Alterations in self-concept are not facile nor immediate. They require the reorganization of a relatively fixed value structure in order to fit the newly acquired self-definition. Such a reorganization takes time and, in the case of labelling theory, involves a move from a conforming to a delinquent orientation. Assuming a population of individuals who have been socialized in a fairly typical manner, it seems realistic to suggest that prior to a self-concept change there must be a period of flux in which the individual is losing his/her old, conforming values and beginning to adopt the new, delinquent ones. Such a period represents a negative socialization, a moving away from a position of conformity into one of delinquency.

While the final result of this period of instability may be the internalization of a delinquent self-concept, it is questionable to relate legal processing and a self-concept change without first demonstrating that legal processing produced the increased orientation toward delinquency which ultimately led to a self-concept alteration. Thus, while it is relevant to test the proposed relationship between legal processing and self-concept change, an important intermediate step would seem to be an examination of the hypothesized link between legal processing and delinquent orientations.

The present research is designed specifically to examine the hypothesized relationship between legal processing and delinquent orientations. It is our contention that the internalization of a delinquent self-image logically follows the acceptance (or at least tolerance) of values and orientations consonant with a delinquent evaluation. Before an individual can accept the label assigned him/her, he/she must readjust his/her orientations to coincide with his/her new identity. Consequently, if legal processing is ultimately to produce a delinquent self-concept as the labelling theorists contend, it must first provoke the shifts in orientations necessary to make the individual susceptible to the delinquent label. In an attempt to ascertain whether in fact legal processing does provoke such changes, the present research was undertaken. Specifically, it is addressed to the following questions:

1) Does legal processing create and/or promote an increased orientation toward delinquency?
2) What effect, if any, do other environmental and behavioral factors such as peer group affiliations and self-reported delinquent behavior play in this process?

Research Objective and Design

Research Outline

While cognizant that labelling may occur in a variety of social settings, i.e., home, school, peer groups, the authors chose to focus upon the Juvenile Justice System, and the police and courts in particular, since they are the agents most frequently discussed in labelling theory.

The overall research design involved a secondary analysis of data previously collected in connection with a six-year longitudinal study of delinquency and dropout in eight California secondary schools (Elliott and Voss, 1971). The study group was composed of 2,617 youth, the entire entering 9th grade class in these schools in September, 1963. This entire group was interviewed once annually from 9th grade through the 12th grade, including those moving or dropping out of school. Over the four year data-gathering period, the mortality (by refusal or loss) was nine percent, the practical result of which was that there was incomplete information on 253 subjects.

Over the four year period, the primary instrument used was a student questionnaire administered once annually to the total cohort. Data derived from this questionnaire included not only basic sociodemographic material but also information on delinquent behavior, friendship nets, feelings about self and significant others, perceived aspirations and opportunities, and involvement in school activities. Aside from minor alterations, the questionnaire was identical for each of the four data-gathering periods. In addition to the student interviews, data from parent interviews, teacher ratings, and school, police and court records were obtained.

Study Variables

The measure of delinquent orientations employed was a short form of the Socialization (SO) Scale from the California Psychological Inventory. Gough (1960) claims that this scale orders individuals along a continuum from asocial to social behavior and forecasts the likelihood that they will transgress the mores established by their particular culture. It is composed of a set of 45 statements (to which the subject responds true or false) designed to discern how the individual views him or herself, as well as how he/she feels about him or herself in relation to others. Examples from the set are such statements as "I hardly ever get excited or thrilled," and "I think that I am stricter about right and wrong than most people." This scale has demonstrated satisfactory validity in distinguishing groups classified as deviant and non-deviant. For example, juvenile delinquents and those with school disciplinary problems score significantly lower on the SO scale than non-delinquent adolescents and students who do not show school disciplinary problems (Gough, 1960). Furthermore, the scale has proved valid in distinguishing degrees of social behavior within a designated group. It was observed by Hetherington and Feldman (1964) that college students who had cheated on course examinations obtained significantly lower SO scores than did their honest peers. Finally, the scale appears to be uninfluenced by such factors as intelligence, socio-economic status, age, or race (Gough, 1965; Donald, 1955; Peterson, Quay & Anderson, 1959). In each of the four years of study, the SO Scale was administered to the total cohort.

Included in the study were several independent variables thought to have some potential for influencing an orientation towards delinquency. Aside from controlling for the sex, class, and race of the respondents, measures of the amount of self-reported delinquent behavior and the involvement of one's friends in delinquency were also obtained and used as controls in the analysis. Both of these variables were considered possible contributors to the development of a delinquent orientation independent of police and/or court contacts.

Since there is reason to believe that police and court records do not accurately reflect an individual's involvement in delinquent behavior (Kobrin, 1951; Perlman, 1949; Short & Nye, 1958; Voss, 1963; Gold, 1970), a self-report measure was employed in an attempt to secure a more realistic picture of each subject's total pattern of delinquent activity. A modification of the Nye-Short (1957) delinquency check list was used with the final scale containing 12 of their original 21 items. The general format of the questions was as follows:

> Have you taken little things (worth less than $2) that did not belong to you?
> ———(1) No
> ———(2) Once or Twice
> ———(3) Several Times
> ———(4) Very Often

Such delinquent acts as auto theft, gang fights, destroying property, grand theft (over $50), and so forth were covered in the 12 items. The cohort received this scale during the initial and final phases of the research study. For the initial phase, respondents were instructed to report on their delinquent activity during the three years of Junior High School, while for the final phase the reporting period covered the three Senior High School years.

In order to secure a measure of the differential exposure to delinquent peer influences, the delinquency involvement of each subject's friends was obtained. A basic sociometric question was asked: "What group of students here at school do you run around with most often?" From responses to this query, a delinquent peer group measure was derived. It reflected the proportion of those persons listed by each subject as friends who either reported serious offenses on the self-report measure or had an official delinquency record, i.e., a police contact, a petition filed, or adjudication by the court.

For the purposes of analysis, both the self-report and delinquent peer group measures were tricotomized, i.e., the entire range of responses was broken into approximate thirds. With each measure having a low, moderate, and high classification, it was possible to discriminate among subjects on the basis of varying involvement with delinquent activities and friends.

Analytic Procedure

The first step was to eliminate all subjects who had had police and/or court contacts prior to the beginning of the study. This procedure insured, as much as possible, that the initial measures on key variables would not be contaminated by prior interaction with the social control system. This sorting process left 2,308 subjects with no known prior police or court encounters.

For each of these subjects a residualized gain score was calculated, representing the positive or negative gain in SO Scale Score over the four year period. While a raw gain score is defined as one's second score minus his/her first, a residual gain score is defined as the difference between the observed second score and a predicted second score based upon the regression of first scores on second scores in the general population. In effect a residual gain score statistically controls or holds constant the effect of one's prior orientation toward delinquency.[2] Following this procedure, the population was stratified into two groups, those having one police encounter and those with multiple police encounters. Finally, an analysis of variance was performed to discover what relationships, if any, existed between the dependent (change in SO Scale Score) and independent (sex, race, class, self-reported delinquency, delinquent peer group, and police/court processing) variables.

A further analysis was conducted within the group having police con-

[2] The formula employed for calculating a residual gain score was

$$\Delta = X_2 - \hat{X}_2 \text{ where } \hat{X} = (X_1 - \overline{X}_1)(r_{12}\,\sigma_2/\sigma_1) + \overline{X}_2$$

For further information regarding residual gain scores, see Lord, 1956, 1958; McNemar, 1958; Manning and Dubois, 1962; Heise, 1970.

tacts to explore the effects of multiple police contacts versus only one such interaction. In addition, we controlled for early (police contact in the first year of the study) or late (police contact after the first year) police processing to assess the impact of labelling over time.

RESULTS

Table 1[3] presents the basic data on the dependent variable by sex, class, and ethnicity. An examination of the table reveals the following general trends: a) males report a greater tendency toward delinquent orientations than females; b) lower-class subjects demonstrate a greater orientation toward delinquency throughout the study than do their upper-class peers. As regards race, the data indicate that initially the minority subjects show a greater delinquent orientation than the non-minority respondents. By the conclusion of the study, however, the SO Scale scores reflect the following changes: for Anglo subjects, a sharp increase in orientation toward delinquency; for Mexican American subjects, a slight decrease in delinquent orientations; and for the black and other respondents, a minor increase in delinquent orientations.

A three-way analysis of variance on sex, class, and race demonstrated that sex was significantly related both to the initial and to the final SO scores.[4] While there was a significant relationship between race and the initial SO score,[5] it was not as strong as the sex variable, nor was it statistically significant in the final year of the study (SO_2). Class was not significant in either time period. Further, there were no significant interaction effects with respect to either SO_1 or SO_2. In both static time frames (SO_1 and SO_2), lower-class, black males demonstrate the greatest orientation toward delinquency.

TABLE 1
THREE-WAY ANALYSIS OF VARIANCE: SO RAW SCORES AND GAIN SCORES BY SEX, CLASS, AND RACE

		SO_1		SO_2		SO_{Gain}	
		N	$\bar{X}$	N	$\bar{X}$	N	$\bar{X}$
Sex	Male	1100	28.795	1002	27.876	997	−.702
	Female	1208	30.670	1131	29.774	1124	+.417
Class	High	948	30.298	896	29.268	893	+.015
	Low	1360	29.413	1237	28.603	1228	−.198
Race	Anglo	1736	32.969	1603	28.912	1593	−.219
	Mexican	300	29.037	281	29.317	280	+.673
	Black	166	27.603	146	27.500	146	−.366
	Other	106	30.491	103	29.194	102	−.073
F Ratios							
Sex			11.8909**		5.5132*		2.4384
Class			1.2406		.7725		.5736
Race			4.5297**		1.1895		.4018
Sex by Class			.8679		.2495		.2788
Sex by Race			.1049		.6339		.0683
Class by Race			.4920		.3063		.3485
Sex by Class by Race			.3667		.6944		.2643

* $p < .05$
** $p < .01$

Although sex and race were related to raw SO Scale Scores, neither was significantly related to residual gain scores derived from these two measures in the three-way analysis of variance. Thus when initial SO Scale Scores were held constant, changes in delinquent orientations were unrelated to sex, race, or class, i.e., there were no significant direct or indirect effects.

Since the initial analysis revealed no significant relationships between SO gain scores and sex, class, and race, these variables were excluded from the analysis presented in Table 2. While we hypothesized that differing levels of involvement in delinquency and exposure to delinquent peers plus legal processing would all affect changes in delinquent orientations, only police contact proved to be significantly related to SO gain scores.[6] Those respondents with police contacts demonstrated substantial negative gains, well in excess of what was expected, given their initial scores. Among the nine strata, there were only two exceptions to this general finding. The first involved those with low levels of delinquency involvement and a low proportion of delinquent friends, and the second involved those with moderate levels of delinquent behavior and a moderate proportion of delinquent friends.

Neither the amount of self-reported delinquency nor the level of delinquency present in the peer group had a significant influence on change in SO scores. However, it is of interest that the only negative gains among the subjects without police encounters came from those with high self-reported delinquency or moderate self-reported delinquency with a highly delinquent peer group. This finding suggests that even without a police contact the combination of moderate to

[3] Traditionally, SO Scale Scores have reflected the number of responses in a delinquent direction. Thus, the higher the score, the more delinquent the self-evaluation, and vice-versa. For this analysis, however, the authors have diverged from this procedure by reverse scoring the scale in order to make the scores more logically consistent (i.e., higher is better) and immediately understandable. Consequently, these scores reflect the mean number of non-delinquent responses for each respective group on the SO Scale. The higher the score, the more positive (i.e., non-deliquent) the self-appraisal and conversely, the lower the score, the more negative or delinquent the self-appraisal. For the gain measure, a negative gain implies a more delinquent position, and a positive gain a more non-delinquent position.

[4] $SO_1 - p < .01$; $SO_2 - p < .05$.

[5] $SO_1 - p < .01$.

[6] The zero-order correlation between delinquent orientations and legal processing is weak, r = .10.

TABLE 2
THREE-WAY ANALYSIS OF VARIANCE: SO GAIN SCORES BY SELF-REPORTED DELINQUENCY, DELINQUENCY OF PEERS, AND POLICE CONTACT

		Police Contact		*No Police Contact*	
		N	$\bar{X}$	*N*	$\bar{X}$
Low S-R Delinq.	Low Delinq. of Peers	23	+1.332	426	+ .863
	Mod. Delinq. of Peers	16	−3.373	128	+ .995
	High Delinq. of Peers	27	−2.129	226	+ .907
Mod. S-R Delinq.	Low Delinq. of Peers	23	−3.329	250	+ .080
	Mod. Delinq. of Peers	12	+ .132	100	+ .139
	High Delinq. of Peers	50	−2.166	182	−1.639
High S-R Delinq.	Low Delinq. of Peers	28	−1.397	101	− .241
	Mod. Delinq. of Peers	17	−1.383	59	+ .593
	High Delinq. of Peers	75	−2.502	210	−1.061

F Ratios	
Self-Reported Delinquency	1.2568
Delinquency of Peers	1.6686
Police Contact	11.8263*
S-R Delinquency by Delinquency of Peers	1.9654
S-R Delinquency by Police Contact	.3717
Delinquency of Peers by Police Contact	.1892
S-R Delinquency by Delinquency of Peers by Police Contact	2.0850

* $p < .01$

high self-involvement in delinquency and a highly delinquent peer group may be sufficient to produce an increase in delinquent orientations. Overall, however, these two independent variables were not significantly related to gain scores either singly or in interaction, although their F values (both joint and three-way interaction) approach significance.

Although the preceding analysis demonstrates the important relationship between some legal processing and delinquent orientations, it does little to help understand such issues as the nature of the process or the extent of its potency. The idea of special vulnerability to the effects of police contact has been generally discussed in the literature (Gould, 1969). Given our initial finding on the generally negative influence of police encounters, it would seem especially relevant to explore the question, for whom, i.e., what socioeconomic, ethnic groups, etc., is legal processing most detrimental regarding negative socialization and the development of a delinquent orientation? In an attempt to answer this question and further explicate the labelling process, we conducted a series of three-way analyses of variance similar to that in Table 2 within each sex, class, and race category to test for possible interaction effects with the police processing and other independent variables.

When the analysis was run separately for males and females, the data indicate that males are more likely to be affected negatively by a police contact than females.[7] Given that much previous delinquency research has suggested that there is a serious sex bias in official police contact reports, i.e., more males than females are contacted, and that males are more likely to have multiple contacts, it is possible that this finding is a consequence of greater exposure to official processing by the police.[8] A further consideration regarding the relationship between sex and the effects of police processing is that there are indications that females tend to be dealt with less harshly than males when processed by the police (Goldman, 1963; Terry, 1967a and 1967b). Taken in combination, the factors of differential exposure and treatment might account for the stronger relationship between police contact and an increased orientation toward delinquency for males than for females.

When the subjects were dichotomized on the basis of class, police contact had a significant effect on the delinquent orientations of both lower- and upper-class youth.[9] Thus within this sample, an increasing orientation toward delinquency does not appear to be class specific. This is a noteworthy finding, given the widely-held belief that lower-class youth have more interaction with the police and, therefore, presumably, greater opportunity for negative outcomes from such encounters. An analysis of variance test for a relationship between class and number of police encounters reinforced the initial finding, however, by indicating that there was no significant difference between the classes with respect to the mean number of police contacts.[10]

In controlling for race, it was somewhat surprising to discover that police contact was a significant factor in accounting for an increasing orientation toward delinquency only for Anglo youth.[11] Police contact was not a significant variable for any of the other racial groups (Mexican American, black or other). Since we had previously suggested and tested the idea that variable exposure to the police might account for the greater negative effect of legal processing for certain groups, we explored that same possibility with regard to race. The results of a one-way analysis of variance between race and number of police contacts indicate that while blacks evidence slightly greater exposure to the police, their rate was not significantly different from the Anglos or Mexican Americans.[12] Since Anglos do not show significantly

[7] For males, $p < .01$; for females, NS.

[8] In fact, it is the case that males have a significantly higher mean number of police contacts than do females. Male $\bar{X} = .269$, female $\bar{X} = .107$; $p < .001$.

[9] For lower and upper class subjects, $p < .05$.

[10] Mean number of police contacts by class: upper class = .170 and lower class = .192, NS.

[11] For Anglo subjects, $p < .001$; for all others, NS.

[12] Mean number of police contacts by race: Anglo = .174; Mexican American = .206; black = .226; other = .194. The overall F value for the above scores was NS.

greater amounts of contact with the police, the idea that variable exposure to the social control system might account for the special vulnerability observed for *Anglo* males is not borne out by this analysis. Furthermore, this finding, in conjunction with the results regarding class, calls into question the entire differential exposure hypothesis, at least for this sample.

In all of the above analyses (i.e., sex, class, and race), neither self-reported delinquency nor the delinquency of one's peer group were important in explaining an increasing orientation toward delinquency, with one notable exception. For the upper-class group, peer delinquency appears to have a direct impact on increases in individual delinquent orientations. The direct effect of this variable approaches a significant level, and in combination with self-reported delinquency and police contact produces a significant F value.[13] Despite this interactive effect, however, our earlier finding (i.e., that police contact is the *most* important of the variables tested with regard to explaining the increases in delinquent orientations) is re-confirmed within sex, class, and race categories.

While the data just examined imply that certain groups (Anglo, males) are more susceptible to the effects of police contact than others, it does not explain why specific individuals within a group are more negatively affected by the legal processing than others. Further, we have not yet made a direct test of the variable amount of exposure hypothesis. Since a continued reinforcement of the negative label may be important to its final internalization by the individual, the question of the effect of multiple police contacts on delinquent orientations seems especially relevant. To get at the issue of differing individual exposure to police contact, several analyses were run just on the group with police contacts. Furthermore, a control for the time of the initial police processing was also employed to determine if the time lag from the point of first police contact to the final measure of delinquency orientation was a factor in the amount and direction of change. Thus, both the number of police contacts and the time of the first encounter were controlled in one-way analyses of variance.

The findings indicate that subjects with multiple police contacts do not display SO gain scores significantly different from those of respondents with only one police encounter.[14] Finally, there is no significant difference on the SO gain scores between the subjects who were processed by the police early in the study and those who were processed later on.[15] These results suggest that not only is the proximity of the initial processing to the final measure of SO score not a factor in explaining increased orientations toward delinquency, but neither is reinforcement of the labelling. The latter finding is especially noteworthy given the emphasis in the labelling literature on the relationship between label reinforcement and a developing orientation toward delinquency.

Discussion

While the results of this study tend to support, at least partially, the proposition that formal interaction with the social control system creates and/or heightens an orientation toward delinquency, caution must be exercised in broadly accepting this conclusion. Although we did observe a statistically significant relationship between delinquent orientations and legal processing, the strength of the association was quite low ($r = .10$). Furthermore, our initial findings suggest that the impact of interaction with the Juvenile Justice System on the development of a delinquent orientation is not as comprehensive as many labelling theorists would have us believe. If as the data imply, certain sub-groups (Anglo males) are more susceptible than others to adverse outcomes from such interaction, then a more detailed analysis is required to sort out the variables which might help explain this special vulnerability. The conjecture that variable exposure to legal processing might account for the unique vulnerability of certain groups to negative outcomes from police contact was not borne out in these analyses, for, in fact, the group which displayed the greatest increase in delinquent orientations (Anglo males) had no greater exposure to the social control system than other ethnic groups.

A possible explanation for the observed vulnerability of Anglos may be that these youth feel more constrained by a system dominated by white secular authorities than do minority youth who may perceive the label as created and applied by "outsiders." The susceptibility of Anglos to negative consequences from police contact is consistent with recent findings by Jensen (1972). His data suggest that contact with official labellers is more detrimental for white youths' self-conceptions as delinquent than for blacks. While his results also imply that attachment to the law does not account for the differential effect of labelling on black and white youth's self-evaluations, he acknowledges methodological problems with this part of his analysis. Thus, the question of general alienation or disposition toward the social control system as a possible explanation for the variable effects of labelling may still be a viable one. Certainly it is one that warrants closer scrutiny.

In addition, the fact that Anglos are the only racial group in our sample to exhibit a negative effect from legal processing may simply reflect the situation that being labelled as delinquent or troublemaker is so common for minority youth that it becomes of little personal relevance to them (Gould, 1969). If everyone assumes you are a "troublemaker" or a "delinquent," the fact that the police do so as well can hardly make much difference!

Our finding that socioeconomic status does not differentiate respondents either with respect to amount or effect of legal processing is interesting on two counts. First, it

[13] Self-reported delinquency by delinquency of peers by police contact, $p < .05$.

[14] Mean SO gain scores by number of police contacts: one police contact = −.168, two or more police contacts = −.309, NS.

[15] Mean SO gain scores by time of first police contact: early processees = −.102 and late processees = −.293, NS.

lends general support to the growing belief that official delinquency is not just a lower-class phenomenon (Voss, 1966; Gold, 1970; Haney and Gold, 1973). On the other hand, it runs counter to some recent research findings which suggest a greater tendency among lower-class youth to be affected negatively by legal processing than among their upper-class peers (Hewitt, 1970; Jensen, 1972). Effectively, the relationship between class and legal processing remains ambiguous; research findings to date have been conflicting and inconsistent. There is a clear need for continued research on this issue, especially since it has such direct relevance for the operation of the social control system.

A further point to consider is the observed effect of peer delinquency on the delinquent orientations of upper-class youth. Though the relationship is not a significant one except in three-way interaction with self-reported delinquent behavior and legal processing, it is strong enough to imply that peer behavior is a factor to be controlled when assessing the delinquent orientations of upper-class youth. Though our data do not shed much light on the nature of the interaction, it may be that for upper-class youth, delinquent peers provide a kind of support for a developing orientation toward delinquency that is not necessary for lower-class youth (given that the latter are more likely to live in an environment generally conducive to an orientation toward delinquency). In essence, the presence or absence of such peers might be a critical factor in explaining an increasing commitment to delinquency when police contact is absent. The entire issue of peer influence regarding delinquency and orientations toward delinquency is certainly in need of further exploration, particularly in light of a recent finding suggesting that youth delinquency occurs in the company of a shifting (rather than stable) number of friends (Haney and Gold, 1970).

In conclusion, it is important to note several limitations of this study. First, of all the variables with possible impact on the development of a delinquent orientation, only a limited number were controlled. Several authors have suggested that the disposition of the individual toward those labelling him/her may determine the effect of the interaction on his/her self-concept (Thorsell and Klemke, 1972; Cameron, 1964; Jensen, 1972). Thus, an individual who expresses alienation towards the social system and displays a lack of commitment to basic societal values may be less susceptible to the labelling process than one who does not. Furthermore, such factors as the nature of the home environment and the actual level of delinquent activity also need to be carefully examined if a more definitive statement about the relationship between legal processing and delinquent orientations is to be made.

In addition, the rather crude distinction between those having and not having police contacts requires refinement. It may well be that the type of police-court contact, i.e., police contact but no court adjudication, court adjudication resulting in probation, etc., has important consequences for the development of an orientation toward delinquency. A classification scheme which reflects these kinds of distinctions seems critical to a more precise understanding of the relationship under study and would permit an analysis of the effects of variable types and lengths of exposure to official processing in the Juvenile Justice System.

Finally, the fact that the present study only measured police contact at two points in time may have produced an excessive time-lag after the police encounters for some of the subjects. A more refined look at the effect of police contact could be achieved with a year-by-year analysis of the data.

References

Becker, Howard S.
1964 The Outsiders. New York: Free Press.

Cameron, Mary O.
1964 The Booster and the Snitch. New York: Free Press.

Donald, E. P.
1955 "Personality scale analysis of new admissions to a reformatory." Unpublished Master's Thesis, Ohio State University.

Elliott, Delbert S. and Harwin L. Voss
1971 Delinquency and Dropout: A Summary Report to the National Institute of Mental Health. Grant numbers: MH 170173 and R01 MH 15285.

Garfinkel, Harold
1956 "Conditions of successful degradation ceremonies." American Journal of Sociology 61(March): 420-24.

Gold, Martin
1970 Delinquent Behavior in an American City. Belmont, California: Wadsworth.

Goldman, Nathan
1963 The Differential Selection of Juvenile Offenders for Court Appearance. New York: National Council on Crime and Delinquency.

Gough, H. G.
1960 "Theory and measurement of socialization." Journal of Consulting Psychology (24):23-30.
1965 "Conceptual analysis of psychological test scores and other diagnostic variables." Journal of Abnormal Psychology (70):294-302.

Gould, Leroy C.
1969 "Who defines delinquency: A comparison of self-reported and officially reported indices of delinquency for three racial groups." Social Problems 16(Winter:325-36.

Hall, Peter M.
1966 "Identification with the delinquent subculture and level of self-evaluation." Sociometry 29(June: 146-158.

Haney, William and Martin Gold
1973 "The juvenile delinquent nobody knows." Psychology Today 7 (September):48-55.

Heise, David R.
1970 "Causal inference from panel data," pp. 3-21 in Edgar F. Borgatta and George W. Bohrnstedt (eds.), Sociological Methodology. San Francisco: Jossey-Bass, Inc.

Hetherington, E. M. and S. E. Feldman
1964 "College cheating as a function of subject and situation variables." Journal of Educational Psychology (50):212-18.

Hewitt, John P.
1970 Social Stratification and Deviant Behavior. New York: Random House.

Jensen, Gary F.
1970 "Containment and delinquency: Analysis of a theory." University of Washington Journal of Sociology

2(November):1-14.
1972 "Delinquency and adolescent self-conceptions: A study of the personal relevance of infraction." Social Problems 20(Summer): 84-103.

Kobrin, Solomon
1951 "The conflict of values in delinquency areas." American Sociological Review 16(October): 653-61.

Lemert, Edwin M.
1951 Social Pathology. New York: McGraw-Hill.

Lofland, John
1969 Deviance and Identity. Englewood Cliffs, New Jersey: Prentice-Hall.

Lord, Frederic M.
1956 "The measurement of growth." Educational and Psychological Measurement 16(Winter): 421-37.
1958 "Further problems in the measurement of growth." Educational and Psychological Measurement 18(Autumn): 437-51.

Manning, W. H. and P. H. Dubois
1962 "Correlational methods in research on human learning." Perceptual and Motor Skills 15 (Monography Supplement No. 15): 287-321.

Matza, David
1964 Delinquency and Drift. New York: Wiley.

McNemar, Quinn
1958 "On growth measurement." Educational and Psychological Measurement 18(Spring): 47-55.

Nye, F. Ivan and James F. Short, Jr.
1957 "Scaling delinquent behavior." American Sociological Review 22(June): 326-31.

Perlman, I. Richard
1964 "Antisocial behavior of the minor in the United States." Federal Probation 28(December): 23-30.

Peterson, D. R., H. C. Quay, and A. C. Anderson.
1959 "Extending the construct validity of a socialization scale." Journal of Consulting Psychology (23):182.

Quinney, Richard
1970 The Social Reality of Crime. Boston: Little, Brown & Company.

Reckless, Walter C., Simon Dinitz, and Ellen Murray
1956 "Self concept as an insulator against delinquency." American Sociological Review 21(December): 144-46.

Reckless, Walter C., Simon Dinitz, and Barbara Kay
1957 "The sub component in potential delinquency and non-delinquency." American Sociological Review 22(October): 566-70.

Short, James F., Jr. and F. Ivan Nye
1958 "Extent of unrecorded juvenile delinquency: Tentative conclusions." Journal of Criminal Law, Criminology and Police Science 49(November-December): 296-302.

Short, James F., Jr. and Fred L. Strodtbeck
1965 Group Processes and Gang Delinquency. Chicago: University of Chicago Press.

Tangri, Sandra S. and Michael Schwartz
1967 "Delinquency and the self-concept variable." Journal of Criminal Law, Criminology, and Police Science 58(June): 182-190.

Tannenbaum, Frank
1938 Crime and the Community. Boston: Ginn.

Terry, Robert M.
1967a "The screening of juvenile offenders." Journal of Criminal Law, Criminology and Police Science 58(June): 173-81.
1967b "Discrimination in the handling of juvenile offenders by social-control agencies." Journal of Research in Crime and Delinquency 4(July): 218-30.

Thorsell, Bernard A. and Lloyd W. Klemke
1972 "The labeling process: Reinforcement and deterrent?" Law and Society Review 6(February): 393-403.

Voss, Harwin L.
1963 "Ethnic differentials in delinquency in Honolulu." Journal of Criminal Law, Criminology and Police Science 54(September): 322-27.
1966 "Socioeconomic status and reported delinquet behavior." Social Problems 13(Winter): 314-324.

The Labeling Process: Reinforcement and Deterrent?

Bernard A. Thorsell
San Fernando Valley State College

Lloyd W. Klemke
Oregon State University

The labeling theory approach to the analysis of deviance depicts stable patterns of deviant behavior as products or outcomes of the process of being apprehended in a deviant act and publicly branded as a deviant person. The involvement of an individual in this process is viewed as depending much less upon what he does or what he is than upon what others do to him as a consequence of his actions. Deviant persons are regarded as having undergone a degradation ceremony with the result that they have been relegated to membership in a deviant group. In the process, they are thought to have come to acquire an inferior social status and to have developed a deviant view of the world and all the knowledges, skills, and attitudes associated with that status.

Labeling analysts make a basic distinction between primary and secondary deviance. This distinction has been clearly formulated by Lemert (1967: 17; 1951: 75). In his view, primary deviance is simply any behavior which might cause an individual to be labeled as a deviant person, whereas secondary deviance is behavior which is generated when an individual is placed in a deviant social role as a result of having been labeled and processed as a deviant person. Labeling analysts attach much greater significance to secondary deviance than to primary deviance, except insofar as other persons react to an act which might be labeled as deviant. They view deviance as a product or outcome of the interaction between the individual who performs the deviant act and those who respond to it by labeling the individual as a deviant person.

Thus, the labeling theory approach to the analysis of deviant behavior typically stresses the importance of the impact of societal reaction on the deviant person rather than focusing upon his psychological or sociological characteristics. Apropos of this, the central issue to which labeling analysts have consistently addressed their inquiries is the consequences of having become the target of a label as a deviant person. The labeling process is depicted as resulting characteristically in the reinforcement and crystallization of deviant behavior as a life style. This *negative* result is attributed to what are considered to be typical sequelae of the labeling process, namely, the isolation of the deviant from nondeviant social relationships and a resultant acceptance of a definition of self as a deviant person.[1]

While readily acknowledging the highly significant contributions that this approach has made to our understanding of deviant behavior, this paper takes special note of the fact that a possibly highly important alternative consequence of the labeling process, namely its *positive* effect on future behavior,[2] has been virtually ignored in the work of labeling analysts. Indeed, the treatment of this issue has been limited almost entirely to a concern for the *negative* effect of the labeling process on future behavior. While labeling analysts have demonstrated that the labeling process appears to reinforce and solidify deviant behavior in many cases, they apparently have not seriously considered the possibility that in other cases it might serve to terminate on-going deviance and to deter future deviant behavior. It is somewhat difficult, at first glance, to understand why labeling analysts have failed to examine, to any appreciable extent, the possibility that the labeling process may have positive or deterrent effects on behavior. It does not appear to be for lack of evidence in the literature or in personal experience. For example, depictions by social scientists of social control techniques often point to labeling as a negative sanction and behavioral deterrent. A good case in point is the Bank Wiring Room experiment in the Western Electric Hawthorne Works studies (Roethlisberger and Dickson, 1939). In that experiment, deviants were sanctioned by their work group by being labeled "rate busters," "speed kings," and so forth, when their work output exceeded the group norm defining "a fair day's work." This treatment by their fellow group members was, on the whole, quite successful in pressuring the deviants to conform to the group norm. Moreover, one's own everyday experiences and observations and common sense all lend support to the general contention that labeling by friends, peers, colleagues, and other associates often does result in a cessation of deviant behavior and can serve to deter future deviance.

The ultimate reasons for the failure of labeling analysts to attend to this dimension of the problem are probably many

AUTHORS' NOTE: *This is a revised version of a paper presented at the Annual Meetings of the American Sociological Association, Washington, D.C., August 31-September 3, 1970.*

From *Law and Society Review*, Vol. 6 (February 1972), pp. 393–403. Reprinted by permission of The Law and Society Association, © 1972; *Law and Society Review* is official publication of the Association.

and varied. Although the determination of these reasons is not the central concern of this paper, it seems appropriate to note in passing that at least one of the roots of the labeling theory approach to the analysis of deviance would seem to lie in a larger perspective on the phenomenon which was established by earlier analysts of deviant behavior, most of whom were criminologists.[3] These analysts sought to identify the social and cultural, as contrasted to the individual and psychological, sources of deviance, particularly crime. Very importantly, they found that the established societal channels for dealing with criminal deviance yielded, on the whole, essentially negative results. The societal agencies and processes involved in apprehension, adjudication, and rehabilitation of the criminal deviant were shown to be largely ineffective in stopping on-going criminal behavior and deterring future crime. Moreover, these agencies and processes were shown to have characteristics which not only failed to rehabilitate the criminal and to deter new criminal behavior, but which actually helped establish and support criminal careers.

This criminological tradition seems to have focused attention almost exclusively on deviance and the labeling process as they take place in an urban, secondary-group-dominated setting where opportunities for personalized observations about behavior are vastly outnumbered by (and thus take second place to) those which are based upon typifications. As a result, it would seem that contemporary labeling analysts, as heirs of this tradition in the study of deviance, have come to center their attention almost exclusively upon the negative outcomes of the labeling process as they typically occur in a mass society setting. Thus, the perspective of contemporary labeling analysts appears to be a carry-over from work within this larger criminological tradition which has been directed at the negative outcomes of the inept and ineffective social control measures characteristic of an urban society.

This approach to deviance and the analytical and empirical results it has produced are highly significant as far as they go. However, it is important to call attention to the fact that it has failed to take into consideration the possibility that the impact of the labeling process may not be uniform in all social settings and across all forms of deviant behavior. For example, there is reason to believe that the effect of the labeling process in a primary group situation may be quite different from that found in a mass society setting. Primary group settings characteristically provide the labeled person much greater exposure to personalized observations by others which may help neutralize the negative stereotypic aspects of the label. Further, as illustrated in the Western Electric Bank Wiring Room research, the effect of labeling in a primary group setting seems to be just the opposite of that observed by labeling analysts in secondary group settings. That is, the labeling process seems to work, for the most part, as a deterrent in the former in sharp contrast to its apparent reinforcing effect upon deviant behavior in the latter. In sum, there is evidence to suggest that the labeling process apparently can function either as a negative, socially disintegrative force or as a positive, socially integrative force, depending upon the social setting and the interpersonal circumstances.

The validity of the currently accepted hypothesis concerning the outcome of the labeling process, therefore, has not to date been completely established. The empirical evidence which lends support to the contention that the labeling process typically results in negative outcomes for future behavior, while significant, is actually very selective in nature and, therefore, satisfies only part of the requirement for the establishment of the validity of this hypothesis. While the data for crime, for example, tend, on the whole, to support the current formulation, it has not been demonstrated that comparably significant data could not be marshalled in support of the converse of the hypothesis with regard to other types of deviant behavior and alternative social settings. Thus, while few, if any, social scientists would contest the idea that the labeling process does in many cases result in negative consequences, it is important to realize that positive outcomes may also be part of the social reality of this phenomenon. The issue is not simply whether the labeling process reinforces or deters future deviance. Rather it is that an examination of the current state of the art in labeling theory forces an increased recognition that both reinforcement *and* deterrence may be outcomes of the labeling process.

At this time, there is no indication that there has been a systematic effort on the part of labeling analysts to evaluate these issues. Moreover, there have been few efforts to undertake the empirical exploration of the implications of labeling theory. In view of this, it seems fair to say that, at this time, the validity of the currently accepted hypothesis that the labeling process typically reinforces deviant behavior seems to rest more upon its repeated assertion by labeling analysts than upon a substantial body of empirical evidence and carefully reasoned conclusions. If this is the case, it seems incumbent upon labeling analysts to entertain the possibility of a systematic empirical exploration of all the possible outcomes of the labeling process.

It is the contention of this paper that the determination of whether the labeling process will result in positive or negative outcomes for future behavior turns upon several conditions of the labeling process which, to date, have received little or no attention from labeling analysts. Several observations regarding these conditions will be examined with the intention of suggesting directions which future research in this area might take.

Observation No. 1: The labeling process seems to have different effects at various stages in a deviant career. Given Lemert's distinction between primary and secondary deviance (1951; 1967), it seems likely that labeling will have fewer effects, positive or negative, after the person has moved into the stage of secondary deviance. The primary deviant seems to be more vulnerable to the direct influence of the labeling process inasmuch as he is still "corruptible." At this stage, the label will either tend to end his deviance or it will serve to push him closer to secondary deviance. Tannenbaum (1938) has emphasized how the youthful troublemaker may be propelled into a delinquent career by being so labeled. On the other hand, Cameron (1964: 165) found that the labeling of the novice pilferer as "shoplifter" usually terminated this activity in her subjects. She points out that the novice pilferer does not think of himself before his arrest as a thief and has no peer group support for such a role. Therefore, being apprehended and labeled as such results in his rejection of that role. In this case, the labeling process serves to terminate the on-going deviant behavior and apparently deters further deviance of this type.

In a recent study (Klemke, 1971) of students who had been officially labeled academic failures by having been dropped for poor scholarship from a large state university, it was found that those attending a local community college did not seem to be caught in a self-fulfilling prophecy of failure. Instead, those who had been stigmatized as failures were found to be earning better grades and to have more favorable attitudes toward their academic work than did the non-failure students. This finding runs counter to the labeling analyst's expectation of a negative outcome in this case and indicates again that there is a need to examine all possible outcomes of the labeling process. Thus, while the primary deviant is still "corruptible," he is also still susceptible to the sanctions of the larger society.

Observation No. 2: When a label is assigned confidentially, and the person so labeled is a non-professional deviant, there appears to be a greater chance that future deviance will be avoided. There is a vast difference between the impact of labeling which is carried out in a limited, confidential manner, as for example, behind the closed doors of a department store manager's office, and that which takes place before a public audience, such as in a court of law. If labeling is done publicly, the processes of alienation and differential treatment, as discussed by Tannenbaum (1938), tend to be set in motion. This outcome would seem to be even more likely if opportunities for acceptance by a deviant subculture were also available. Such acceptance would certainly enhance the probability that the labeled person might move into secondary deviance. However, it must be noted that even when labeling is carried out publicly, it is not inevitable that the labeled person continues or intensifies his deviant behavior. Indeed, most persons so labeled probably do not. Thus, the majority of young males repeatedly labeled in the manner discussed by Tannenbaum do not turn out to be professional criminals. Moreover, in contemporary mass society such public labeling "ceremonies" are increasingly easier to keep secret, and thereby additional negative reactions from others are avoided.

Observation No. 3: When the deviant person has some commitment to and is, therefore, sensitive to the evaluation of the labeler, the effect of the labeling process appears more likely to be positive than negative. Cameron's research, noted earlier, points out that the labeling techniques utilized in handling shoplifting cases worked well to discourage the amateur pilferer but had little success with experienced shoplifters. This points up the importance of subcultural supports which encourage renunciation of the legitimacy of conventional morality. The "techniques of neutralization" provided by the subculture to nullify conventional morality seem to abrogate any effect, positive or negative, that the labeling process might have on the labeled person. This, in turn, suggests that when the labeler is not a member of the "target's" in-group, his evaluation may not carry the same effect as if he were a member. This observation is borne out empirically in the Western Electric Bank Wiring Room experiment noted earlier (Roethlisberger and Dickson, 1939). In that study, labels applied by members of one's own work group were more effective in controlling deviation from group norms than was labeling carried out by management representatives with respect to formal orders contradicting the group norms concerning daily output. Similarly, it has become an increasingly common observation in treatment and correctional settings, such as Synanon and Alcoholics Anonymous, that labeling by one's peers or significant others seems to be more successful in stopping deviant behavior and rehabilitating the deviant than that carried out by non-peers, such as counselors, psychiatrists, or prison guards applying the same labels.

Observation No. 4: If a label can be easily removed, then the probability that the stigmatized person is likely to move toward conforming behavior is greater. In their research on occupational opportunities, Schwartz and Skolnick (1962) found that the revelation of an arrest record, irrespective of conviction or acquittal, markedly reduces the number of job opportunities for the individual, particularly for the lower-class person. In an effort to cope with this problem, some legal authorities for some time have pressed for the expungement of the records of persons placed on probation or parole. In the U.S., this has been limited, for the most part, to juvenile records in cases where the community views the young person as deserving of a "second chance." In Sweden, however, the present policy in this regard is so advanced that it is a cardinal principle of Swedish penal policy to protect and maintain the anonymity of released offenders, especially released murderers (Playfair and Sington, 1957). The released offender is advised to change his name and to take up residence in a community or part of the country different from the one in which his crime was committed. A job and, if necessary, living accommodations are found for him there. The only member of his new community aware of his true identity is his employer who is sworn to secrecy. In short, the released offender has the opportunity to embark on a new life completely free of any evidence from the past that might stigmatize him. Swedish penal officials report that for decades there have been no cases of homicide offenders who have been released under this program repeating their crimes. These results suggest that by making the realistic removal of such labels feasible, it is possible, in many cases, to initiate and to sustain movement away from deviant behavior.

Observation No. 5: The nature of the societal reaction which follows or accompanies the application of a label is of central importance in determining whether the outcome of the process will be positive or negative. In the area of mental illness, the difficulties of the person who has been labeled as "sick" once again becoming perceived as "normal" or "well," has been of interest to labeling analysts.[4] An examination of the ways in which the Hutterites deal with persons exhibiting abnormal behavior was carried out by Eaton and Weil (1953). They found that persons so identified became the objects of extensive efforts on the part of friends and the community in general to aid and support the labeled person in becoming reintegrated into the community. This contrasts sharply with the larger societal reaction to the mentally "sick" person in the United States. In American society, the person so labeled characteristically is regarded as someone to be avoided, rejected, and isolated. Viewed from this perspective, the labeling process is essentially a stimulus which can set off a wide range of societal reactions varying from negative, isolative, and socially disintegrative responses to highly positive, supportive, and socially integrative actions. Where societal reactions are positive, supportive, and socially integrative, the labeling process seems to generate a positive atmosphere in which the effect on future behavior is to move it in the direction of greater conformity.

It is important to distinguish between official, institutionalized reactions to deviant acts and the informal reactions of one's significant others. In the study of academic failures mentioned earlier (Klemke, 1971: 16), it was found that official expulsion from the university was countered by positive, supportive reactions from the student's significant others. These positive reactions were instrumental in encouraging the students to reenter college and try again to succeed academically. They also were significant in maximizing the chances for academic success once the student decided to enter the community college for another try. This finding adds still another dimension to the labeling process and its outcomes which has not been adequately examined by labeling analysts.

Observation No. 6: A liberal assignment of positive labels, within realistic limits, seems to stimulate and increase the prevalence of desirable behavior. In their apparent preoccupation with the negative effects of the labeling process, labeling analysts have paid little attention to the possibility that an increase in desirable behavior might result from the application of positive labels. That positive labeling can function as a stimulus to desirable behavior is shown in the work of Rosenthal and Jacobson (1968) In their study, teachers in an elementary school were led to believe at the beginning of the school year that certain pupils could be expected to show considerable academic improvement during the coming year. The teachers were told that these predictions were based upon intelligence tests which had been administered at the end of the preceding academic year. The children so designated were labeled "spurters" by the investigators in their conversations with the teachers. In reality, the children designated as "spurters" were chosen at random from the roster of students enrolled at the school by using a table of random of numbers. After the school year was in progress, standard intelligence tests were given to all pupils during the year at predetermined intervals. The results indicated clearly that the randomly chosen children labeled as "spurters" improved scholastically considerably more than the rest of the children who were not so designated. Moreover, in addition to depicting the "spurters" as intellectually more alive and autonomous than the other children, their teachers described them as being happier, more interesting, more appealing, and more affectionate, as well as being better adjusted and less in need of social approval. In this case, the application of a positive label clearly generated socially desirable behavior both as perceived by others and as measured by standardized psychological tests.

On the basis of these six observations, it is possible to construct six hypotheses that seem to be amenable to systematic empirical evaluation by the labeling analyst. While there seems to be little doubt that continued observation and reflection could yield additional hypotheses, those suggested here seem sufficient to point the way to a systematic investigation of the converse of the currently accepted hypothesis concerning the outcome of the labeling process. This is the primary purpose of this paper. In order to express the hypotheses as formal statements, it seems to be most convenient to summarize them as follows.

The labeling process is more likely to terminate existing deviant behavior and to deter future deviance:

1. If the labeled person is a primary rather than a secondary deviant.
2. If the labeling is carried out in a confidential setting with the understanding that future deviance will result in public exposure.
3. If the labeling has been carried out by an in-group member or significant other.
4. The more easily the label is removable when the deviant behavior has ceased.
5. The more the labeling results in efforts to reintegrate the deviant into the community.
6. If the label is favorable rather than derogatory.

Empirical evaluation of these hypotheses will do much to expand our knowledge concerning the possible positive effects of the labeling process on both on-going deviance and future conduct. Hopefully, in time it will be possible to amass sufficient empirical evidence so that an objective evaluation of the converse of the currently accepted labeling hypothesis will be possible. All of this will do a great deal to enhance our understanding of the labeling process itself as well as its consequences for future behavior. Moreover, research such as this can begin to provide an objective basis for a systematic evaluation of labeling theory as a general theory of deviant behavior.

FOOTNOTES

[1] See, for example, Becker (1963), Erickson (1962), Kitsuse (1962), Lemert (1951); also Lemert (1967), Scheff (1966).

[2] The terms "positive" and "negative," as used in this context, are utilized only to indicate that deviant behavior is usually regarded negatively by the larger society, whereas a reduction in its frequency or its termination is normally regarded positively. There is no intention of implying that conformity to the norms of the larger society is necessarily better or more desirable than deviance from them. The question as to whether deviance should be discouraged or promoted, while a legitimate and interesting issue, is not at stake here.

[3] The work of pioneering analysts, such as Clemmer, Lemert, Reckless, Sutherland, Taft, Tannenbaum, and others whose work falls within the framework of this general tradition comes to mind here.

[4] See, for example, Scheff (1966).

REFERENCES

BECKER, Howard S. (1963) Outsiders: Studies in the Sociology of Deviances. London: Free Press.

CAMERON, Mary O. (1964) The Booster and the Snitch. London: Free Press.

EATON, Joseph, and Robert J. WEIL (1953) Culture and Mental Disorders. Glencoe: Free Press.

ERICKSON, Kai (1962) "The Sociology of Deviance," 9 Social Problems 307.

KITSUSE, John (1962) "Societal Reaction to Deviant Behavior: Problems of Method and Theory," 9 Social Problems 247.

KLEMKE, Lloyd W. (1971) "Higher Education Failures Coming to a Community College and Labeling Theory." Presented at the 1971 Annual Meeting of the Pacific Sociological Association in Honolulu, Hawaii.

LEMERT, Edwin (1967) Human Deviance, Social Problems and Social Control. Englewood Cliffs, New Jersey: Prentice Hall.

.... (1951) Social Pathology. New York: McGraw Hill Company.

PLAYFAIR, Giles, and Derrick SINGTON (1957) The Offenders: Society and the Atrocious Crime. London: Secker and Warburg.

ROETHLISBERGER, Fritz J., and William J. DICKSON (1939) Management and the Worker. Cambridge: Harvard University Press.

ROSENTHAL, Robert, and Lenore F. JACOBSON (1968) "Teacher Expectations for the Disadvantaged," 218 Scientific American 19.

SCHEFF, Thomas J. (1966) Being Mentally Ill: A Sociological Theory. Chicago: Aldine.

SCHWARTZ, Richard D., and Jerome H. SKOLNICK (1962) "Two Studies of Legal Stigma," 10 Social Problems 133.

TANNENBAUM, Frank (1938) Crime and the Community. Boston: Ginn.

SECTION SEVEN

Summary

The articles in this section might leave the reader with the impression that we can reach no conclusions about either deterrence or labeling effects. However, some tentative observations are justified based on available research, and suggestions for future inquiry are quite consistent. There is mounting evidence that perceived risk of punishment is related to delinquency in a manner consistent with the idea of general deterrence. Numerous studies have reported such a finding: youths who worry about the consequences of juvenile court processing or who think they will get caught if they break the law are less likely to break the law. This finding is appealing to some policymakers because it can be used to argue that manipulating the certainty and severity of punishment will reduce delinquency. The argument may in fact be correct. However, there are a number of problems with this conclusion. First, changes in the nature of law and its enforcement are not necessarily noticed or accorded much importance by the public. Perceptions of risk may affect delinquency, but actual changes in the certainty and severity of punishment may not be perceived. Second, if labeling theorists should be proved correct in predicting boomerang effects, then reductions in delinquency in the general populace through "tougher" law enforcement might be accomplished at the risk of increasing delinquency among those actually subjected to stricter law enforcement. In short, gains in general deterrence *might* be offset by increases in career delinquency due to labeling. The labeling argument has been neither proved to be correct nor shown to be totally erroneous. Of course, claims that offenders can be deterred by the threat of more certain and severe punishments cannot be totally dismissed or totally embraced on the basis of existing evidence, either.

The possibility of boomerang effects is especially important in view of the increasing popularity of programs such as "Scared Straight," in which youths are dramatically confronted with the harsh circumstances of ending up in prison. In this program inmates scare potential offenders straight by convincing them of the horrors of prison life. The approach raises ethical questions concerning limits on treatment. Moreover, the method can be challenged for its use of the threat of illegal sanctions (that is, inmate violence) as a deterrent. It may be true that prison life is horrifying, due in part to the menace of violence and homosexual rape. The prospect of encountering such experiences might scare some youths straight. But labeling theorists challenge us to consider the possibility of alienating and disillusioning consequences from this approach. What happens when the government starts using situations that it is supposed to be attacking (for example, prison violence) to deter delinquency and crime? What happens when "control" becomes more important than "justice"? Prisoners are not supposed to be killing, hurting, and raping. Yet the state now sanctions and approves of programs that throw up illegal behavior of this kind as deterrents. Fear of harm might have immediate specific deterrent effects, and yet the use of this kind of threat might undermine respect for the law and legal authority in the long run.

We must not only consider the possibility of both deterrent and labeling effects but recognize that the labeling process may have quite varying consequences for different categories of youths as well. Those youths most concerned about getting caught and labeled are the least likely to engage in an activity that would make them liable to labeling. However, if they do engage in such an activity for a particular reason (group pressure, necessity, rebellion, and so on), the labeling experience may be particularly consequential for them. In contrast, youths who accord little respect to those laws, people, and institutions involved in the labeling process should not find the labeling experience particularly consequential. The meaning of official processing will vary, depending on the significance of the experience in the juveniles' immediate social worlds, among other things. In short, both deterrence and labeling theory may be correct, and the real chore is to understand the conditions affecting their applicability to people in different social and cultural environments.

SECTION EIGHT

Institutionalization and the Search for Alternatives

While many facets of the juvenile justice system are currently beset by a barrage of criticism, the strongest attack has been on juvenile reform schools and the "warehousing" of juvenile offenders in institutions. Yet the irony is that many of the arguments set forth in this present wave of criticism are similar to those dating back to the early 1800s, when reform-minded critics, campaigning against the inhumane and irrational treatment of offenders, began to demand change and a totally new rationale for institutional confinement. Flogging, mutilation, torture, and capital punishment had been the hallmarks of penal institutions prior to this early reform period. But a new philosophy of humanitarian treatment, underscored by a focus on rehabilitation, ultimately overrode the prevailing concept of punishment.

The emergence of Philadelphia's Walnut Street Jail in 1791 signaled a radically new approach in the treatment of offenders. Prisoners at the jail were housed in private cells that became individual workshops. Through the use of solitary confinement and programs of productive work, prisons were seen as institutions that could facilitate the resocialization of deviants into law-abiding individuals. The Walnut Street Jail served as the basis for massive prison reform under the name "the Pennsylvania System."

A second approach to corrections arose in New York State, based not on solitary confinement but on silence and group workshops. This new model became known as the Auburn System, named after the prison built in 1817 at Auburn, New York. The Auburn System featured group labor under a strictly enforced system of silence during the day and confinement in small, solitary cells at night. A further refinement of the Auburn System was made in 1876 with the opening of the Elmira Reformatory for young offenders. The growing concern on the emphasis of education and trade training for younger prisoners led to the development of the "family reform school." In light of these advances and the emergence of the juvenile court system at the turn of the twentieth century, penal reformers felt confident that they had laid the foundation for significant progress in crime reduction while at the same time advancing the concept of human dignity. Dostoyevsky's remark that "the degree of civilization in a society can be judged by entering its prisons" appeared to express a widespread concern among reformers.

For some sixty years, the entire juvenile justice system was unscathed by criticism or even comment. There appeared to be a pervasive sense of trust in the efficacy of the system, and the buoyant optimism of the early reformers lingered well into the twentieth century. But unfortunately, the optimism of the early reform movement gave way to stark pessimism and outright ridicule of institutional programs. With the advent of the labeling school in the 1950s and 1960s, critics began to cast aspersions on the benign intentions of the juvenile court system. More importantly, a series of task force reports on the police, the courts, and corrections, released in 1967 during the Johnson Administration, exposed the failure of the adult and juvenile justice systems. The particular report entitled "Juvenile Delinquency and Youth Crime" ridiculed the "babelism" of the juvenile courts. New terms had been invented, such as *petition, disposition,* and *treatment,* but the concepts applied remained the same. Children were being arrested, tried, and sentenced in the same way as adults. The task force report charged that the juvenile justice system was neither helpful nor rehabilitative. While the authors did not go so far as to call for jettisoning the system, they did call for sweeping changes.

Following on the heels of the task force reports, a plethora of research findings brought into question the effectiveness of institutional confinement under even the most ideal conditions. Evidence was being marshaled that purported to show that incarceration only heightened juveniles' resistance to change. Captivity was viewed from the perspective of a prisoner-of-war syndrome that generated alienation and hostility. Recidivism rates were not improved, and the financial costs of maintaining these "schools for crime" were escalating at a frighteningly fast pace.

What arose out of this antiinstitutionalization movement was the quest for alternative treatment strategies. In the 1960s and 1970s, a series of intensive community programs was created. The programs involved probation by way of low social worker caseloads, intensive supervision, community-based alternatives, and prevention programs for predelinquents. At first it appeared that progress was being made. However, when evaluation studies were conducted, the new reform efforts did not appear so promising. Perhaps the best that can be said is that they may not have made matters worse by removing offenders from institutions. Success beyond that is dubious.

The four articles that were selected for this section reflect a profound sense of uneasiness. We have attempted to deal with offenders for centuries, but our knowledge of corrections is painfully limited. In the first reading, Charles Tittle criticizes the "myth" of prison failure, arguing that we are unclear as to what we expect prisons to do and that the evidence that prisons do not rehabilitate is not entirely convincing. The reading by Donal MacNamara discusses the controversy between the medical model, which advocates rehabilitation, and the social justice model, which supports the right of society to protect itself. The medical model, as applied to the correctional process, sees the offender as ill, whereas the social justice model opts strictly for punishment. The third selection, by Paul Lerman, questions the effectiveness of alternative treatment approaches but still advocates a humanitarian handling of youthful offenders, whether it is successful or not. Finally, Robert Martinson's famous (or infamous) discussion "What Works?" is a concise review of major treatment approaches. Martinson's conclusions are filled with caveats, and his summary is anything but promising.

Prisons and Rehabilitation: The Inevitability of Disfavor

Charles R. Tittle
Florida Atlantic University

It is argued that widespread belief in the rehabilitative failure of prisons is not justified by the evidence. Reasons for persistence of the myth are suggested. It is argued that the belief in rehabilitative failure will continue even if prison reforms are instituted. The only way in which prisons can escape the onus of failure is by abandoning the rehabilitative mission.

Whether people can be rehabilitated while incarcerated is a question of recurrent interest among academics as well as laymen. In popular literature imprisonment is frequently declare a failure and prisons are often denounced as "schools crime." For example, Ramsey Clark (1970:213) writes:

Jails and prisons in the United States today are more often than not manufacturers of crime. Of those who come to jail undecided, capable either of criminal conduct or of lives free of crime, most are turned to crime.

Similarly, a recent article in the *Intellectual Digest* asserts that "the American prison system is a 200 year old experiment in correction that has failed" (Goldfarb and Singer, 1971:19). And a Federal judge, in outlining a thirteen point reform program, recently declared that "it is all too true that most of our penal institutions prove to be schools for crime" (Edwards, 1972).

Many criminologists also maintain that incarceration has little rehabilitative impact; and some argue that imprisonment reinforces criminal identities or actually produces changes in individuals that contribute to further criminal behavior (Vold, 1954; Westover, 1958; Barnes and Teeters, 1959:584).

Academics and laymen alike constantly criticize the penal system and lament the need for change. It almost seems that prisons have become the favorite "whipping boys," especially after the highly publicized disasters at the Arkansas state prison and at Attica. If a journalist has nothing else to write about, he can seemingly always count on good copy by showing that prisons are non-rehabilitative, just as academics can usually find an outlet for anti-rehabilitative arguments.

The Evidence

Yet, despite widespread belief in the rehabilitative inefficacy of prisons, it is difficult to compile persuasive evidence. The major reason that empirical data concerning the issue are lacking is simply that the concept of "rehabilitation" is ambiguous. Although the word is used often, few people can give more than a vague, generalized statement of what it might mean. Presumably, rehabilitation implies the correction of certain "unhabilitating" defects that characterize offenders. But there is little concrete evidence about what defects might be "unhabilitating" or how to correct them, much less how to determine when they have or have not been corrected.

Recidivism

Because of this ambiguity, many people take a proof-in-the-pudding approach and argue that recidivism is the acid test of rehabilitative success. The assumption is simply that criminal behavior *must* be the result of some personal defect, so that the absence of further criminal behavior must reflect eradication of that defect. The major problem with such an approach, however, is that crime may not be the consequence of a personal defect. Correction of individual deficiencies such as personality or psychic disorders, poor occupational skills, insufficient education, limited moral consciousness, or anti-social attitudes—the kinds of things most people mention when they are forced to specify the shortcomings that prisoners presumably have—may be unrelated to the probability of recidivism (Packer, 1968:56).

From *Social Problems,* Vol. 21, No. 3, 1974, pp. 385–395. Reprinted with the permission of the Society of Social Problems and the author.

There is no reason to believe that psychic disorders necessarily or even usually lead to crime; and most people with rudimentary occupational skills or poor education are in fact law abiding citizens. Furthermore, expanded moral consciousness, instead of inhibiting criminal impulses, often generates feelings of outrage leading to criminal behavior. While incarcerated, a person can be successfully educated, attitudinally reformed, occupationally trained, psychiatrically treated, and religiously converted; yet later engage in unlawful behavior as a result of peer pressures, lack of alternatives, or other situational constraints. After all, it is a major tenet of sociology that crime is as much a function of social conditions and influences as of individual characteristics. In fact, the evidence suggests that most "habilitated" people also violate the law from time to time (Cohen, 1966:24-29).

Furthermore, ex-convicts may lead law abiding lives without having experienced correction of any of their presumed defects. Prison releasees may remain "unhabilitated" but nevertheless refrain from crime because of post prison influences such as family pressures, new opportunities, or the absence of criminal enticements. In addition, they may avoid crime because of prison induced fear of apprehension and reimprisonment. Recidivism, therefore, may be less indicative of the rehabilitative impact of incarceration than of its specific deterrent effect (Andenaes, 1966), or of post prison influences.

Thus, a proof-in-the-pudding approach is not adequate for evaluating rehabilitative success, if rehabilitation implies correction of defects. It might be an appropriate approach if rehabilitation is understood to be *equivalent* to law abiding behavior. According to this alternative conceptualization, criminal behavior is not caused by a personal defect, but rather criminal behavior is the defect. From such a perspective rehabilitation literally means no recidivism. Although many people inadvertently slip into usages that are consistent with this definition, few explicitly embrace it. To do so makes most existing discussions of prison reform or treatment techniques, as well as the concept "rehabilitation," superfluous. The equivalency definition divorces rehabilitation from prison processes altogether. For instance, it is conceivable that confinement per se, independent of any "treatment," might generate fear of being reimprisoned and thereby produce law abiding behavior among some. But would this kind of "rehabilitation be consistent with arguments calling for prison reform? Furthermore, releasees who avoid crime because of post prison occurrences would be classified as rehabilitated—even though what went on while they were incarcerated was irrelevant.

Determining whether people are rehabilitated while in prison, therefore, is rendered exceedingly difficult by the impreciseness of the concept. On one hand, if rehabilitation is taken to mean correcting defects, one is faced with the prospect that the treatment may have no bearing on future crime. On the other hand, if rehabilitation is equated with law abiding behavior, analysis is confused because much "rehabilitation" may be independent of prison processes. In short, arguments based on the extent of recidivism are of dubious value in deciding whether prisons rehabilitate their charges.

But even if conceptual confusion did not exist, and if all could agree that the extent of post prison criminal behavior were an unequivocal indicator of rehabilitative success or failure, the problem of measuring recidivism would make assessment almost impossible. Data adequate to permit accounting of post release behavior are seldom available (Glaser, 1964:13-35; Wilkins, 1969); and many of those which do exist are of questionable validity.

Re-arrest statistics are biased by the differential probability of arrest for ex-convicts, regardless of actual criminal conduct. Arrest may indicate nothing at all about guilt. For example, in an FBI follow-up study of all individuals released from custody in 1963, only 40 percent of those re-arrested within a four-year period of time had been reconvicted at the end of that period (Uniform Crime Reports, 1967:41); and extrapolation suggests that reconviction for the entire population of releases for the indefinite future would not exceed 35 percent.[1] Being arrested does not necessarily signify criminal conduct, just as criminal behavior is frequently undertaken without a resulting arrest. Hence, there is only a tenuous connection between criminality and arrest. Furthermore, persons may be arrested for all sorts of acts, not necessarily of the same type for which they had been previously incarcerated. Arrest for drunkenness is hardly indicative of failure to rehabilitate a burglar.

Although return to prison is probably a better indicator of recidivism than re-arrest, it too falls short. In addition to further criminality, recommitment rates also reflect parole revocation for non-criminal activity, such as failure to hold a job, unmarried cohabitation, or failure to report to the parole supervisor. In addition, return to prison rates are probably inflated because the chance of reconviction is greater for one with a criminal record, independent of actual criminal conduct. Given the pressures for plea bargaining, an ex-convict who is prosecuted probably has little choice but to plead guilty, regardless of his actual guilt or innocence (Newman,

[1] UCR reports a 65 percent re-arrest rate but only a 40 percent conviction rate for those re-arrested during the first four years, or an overall reconviction rate for the entire population of releases of 23 percent. Although it neglects to report convictions for subsequent years, one can extrapolate. In so doing, however, it is necessary to consider the possibility that the number reconvicted may have risen as people arrested during the first four years came to trial after that date and as additional arrests were made. Given that lag time in the judicial process is rarely more than two years, and that most of those re-arrested during the six year follow-up were taken into custody during the first two years (66 percent), it is reasonable to assume that the vast majority of re-arrestees had been tried by the end of the fourth year. If we assume, moreover, that the 40 percent reconviction of arrestees applies only to those arrested during the first two years of the follow-up, and we project this conviction rate to cover all those arrested from the third through the sixth years, we arrive at a total reconviction rate of 26 percent for the original sample of releases. Furthermore, during the fifth and sixth years, an increment of only about two percent per year in additional arrests were added. Hence the reconviction rate of offenders released in 1963 would appear to be well below 35 percent even if one projects the follow-up far beyond the original six years.

1966; Blumberg, 1967). In contrast, it is no doubt true that a great deal of crime by releasees never results in reimprisonment.

Even if these considerations are ignored, basing arguments on rates of recommitment is frustrating because systematic data are almost never kept. The extent to which releasees are returned to prison must be estimated from prison records or from the few career studies that have been undertaken. Estimates based on prison records usually focus on the proportion of prisoners who previously served time. Wilkins has shown that this method seriously exaggerates the degree of recidivism. Because repeat offenders receive longer sentences and are less likely to be paroled, they accumulate in prison and are disproportionately represented in any inmate population (Wilkins, 1969:48–49). Better indication of the rate of recommitment is provided by follow-up studies.

But interestingly enough, many follow-up studies, whether based on recommitment or re-arrest data, can be interpreted favorably toward prison rehabilitation. For example, Glaser's review of recommitment studies, as well as his own study of the Federal system, indicates that incarceration may result in "rehabilitation" in as many as two-thirds of the cases (Glaser, 1964:15–27). A recent three year follow-up using parole disposition, based largely on re-arrest information, classified 56 percent of the releasees as completely clean or associated only with technical parole violations or misdemeanors. (Kassebaum, Ward, and Wilner, 1971:222–223). And the six year FBI follow-up suggests that only about one-third of the prison releasees are reconvicted.[2] Thus recidivism data do not afford an adequate basis for the pessimistic conclusions concerning prison rehabilitation that many have made.

This is even true of the often cited comparisons of rates of recidivism between released incarcerees and offenders not incarcerated. Since those not incarcerated escape exposure to any "rehabilitative" programs, while inmates presumably are "treated," it is argued that if prisons do rehabilitate, then released inmates should have lower subsequent arrest and commitment rates (again assuming that crime is the result of uncorrected personal defects). Because the data are not consistent with this expectation, many conclude that incarceration fails as a rehabilitative process. But even though such comparisons do not support a rehabilitative argument, neither do they contradict one. True enough, probationers appear to have lower recidivism rates than incarcerees (Levin, 1971; Uniform Crime Reports, 1968:38), but this comparison is marred by selectivity that places the best risks on probation (Wilkins, 1969: 14–15). Furthermore, FBI re-arrest data show that incarcerees do have lower re-arrest rates than arrestees who were acquitted, dismissed, or only fined (Uniform Crime Reports, 1968:38).

Institutional Studies

Since the connection between rehabilitation and recidivism is tenuous, and the data are in any case meagre, alternative evidence that might be cited in support of the anti-rehabilitative position are direct measures of the extent to which "unhabilitating" deficiencies are corrected by the institutional experience. Such information consists of pre-incarceration and post-incarceration measures of psychiatric variables, occupational and educational skills, moral commitments, and anti-social attitudes, or of estimations of institutional changes in those variables. Although these data are more straightforward, going directly, as they do, to the question of correcting defects, they are insufficient as a basis for sweeping conclusions. Before and after measurements of occupational and educational skills are almost universally made, but are nowhere systematically published. In some instances psychiatric variables are indexed at various points in time, but the results are not systematically available. Changes in moral commitments and anti-social attitudes can in most cases only be inferred indirectly. Moreover, evaluative research using specific bodies of data of this type suffer from deadly methodological inadequacies (Logan, 1972).

Finally, probably the best known source of data that can be cited in arguing that prisons are anti-rehabilitative is research on institutional living. A series of studies conducted over the past thirty years suggests that living in confinement encourages inmates to cultivate loyalty to each other, to engage in homosexual encounters, to form contra-cultural value systems, and to adopt hostile and rebellious attitudes toward prison officials and programs (Clemmer, 1940; Garabedian, 1963; Giallombardo, 1966; Goffman, 1961; Hayner and Ash, 1939 and 1940; McCorkle and Korn, 1954; Morris and Morris, 1963; Sykes, 1958; Tittle and Tittle, 1964; Tittle, 1969; Ward and Kassebaum, 1965; Weinberg, 1942; Wheeler, 1961; see Messinger, 1969, for a more comprehensive bibliography). It is usually assumed that socialization within a prison culture (prisonization) is equivalent to socialization into a criminal culture.

But only sparce data have actually been reported concerning prison changes in attitudes, values, or behaviors that are directly relevant to life in the outside world (Tittle, 1972a). The conclusion that prison engenders anti-rehabilitative characteristics rests on an assumption that values, attitudes, and behaviors representing antagonism to the official prison regime are indicative of general anti-social characteristics. Contempt for prison rules, inmate cohesion, and disrespect for prison authority are assumed to reflect contempt for law, commitment to the underworld culture, and unwillingness to submit to legal authority. This assumption may be unwarranted. It has yet to be established that anti-prison attitudes and behaviors are predictive of post prison anti-social attitudes or behaviors (see Kassebaum, Ward, and Wilner, 1971:263–264, for an example of failure to find such a linkage).

Indeed, much of the research on institutional living itself provides ample reason to question the relationship between

[2] It is impossible to ascertain this figure exactly, since the reported reconviction rate is for all people released from custody, not just those released from prison. However, since the reconviction rate for the total population of releases was less than 35 percent (see footnote one), and since the re-arrest rate for those under mandatory release or on parole is about average for the entire population of releases (Uniform Crime Reports, 1969:38), it seems reasonable to assume that the reconviction rate for prison releases is also less than 35 percent.

prison related attitudes and behavior and general anti-social characteristics. Some research suggests that anti-staff attitudes and behavior may develop primarily as adaptive responses that weaken and lose salience near time for return to the outside (Wheeler, 1961; Tittle, 1969; Glaser and Stratton, 1961; Ward and Kassebaum, 1965; Garabedian, 1963). Furthermore, the idea that institutional environments create the anti-social characteristics that are manifest in prison has itself been challenged (Irwin and Cressey, 1962; Cline, 1968; Wellford, 1967; Thomas, 1970).

Conclusion

The fact is, it cannot be concluded with confidence, either from recidivism data or research on institutional living, that prisons fail in their rehabilitative efforts, and certainly not that prisons are "schools for crime." The evidence does suggest that many incarcerees are not rehabilitated (however one defines that term), but the evidence can just as easily be interpreted to suggest that many others are rehabilitated. In fact, if taken at face value, much of the data, particularly that concerning recidivism, would demonstrate that prisons do a remarkably good rehabilitative job. Consider in this regard that (1) only 16 percent of the evaluation studies reviewed by Logan concludes that the outcome of correctional application was a "failure," while 44 percent concluded that the degree of success was at least "good" (Logan, 1972), (2) recommitment figures indicate that the majority do not return to prison (Glaser, 1964:26), (3) dispositional data show that most parolees do not return to serious crime (Kassebaum, Ward, and Wilner, 1971:222-223), and (4) the FBI follow-up suggests that far more than half are not reconvicted of another crime (see footnote two). The point is not that the data show that incarceration leads to rehabilitation, but rather that they do not demonstrate a failure to rehabilitate. Yet amost everybody continues to assert in the strongest possible terms that prisons are failures and that rehabilitation is not occurring. It is pertinent to question why unbridled belief in prison failure persists.

Why Persistence

One possibility is that many people have simply been influenced by "authoritative" citation of erroneous, or at best dubious, statistics. Sometimes interesting conclusions are stated in print and "catch on." They are then recited over and over, each writer relying upon the authenticity of the previous citation, until they become "self-evident truths." Reynolds (1966) has documented an outstanding instance of this process in the field of social psychology. A belief that women in the U.S. have greater ability than men to make color discriminations came to be established and widely cited, although it lacked empirical substantiation and even contradicted the available research evidence. If myths can be so easily formed in a "scientific" field, is it any wonder that the same occurs with respect to a topic that is often in the hands of laymen? The frequency with which journalistic sources recite the "fact" that 80 percent of the prison releasees return to crime suggests that the myth making process has been operating.

The belief in prison failure may also reflect application of inappropriate standards for judgment. Since the general crime rate has been increasing steadily for a number of years, it is tempting to many to conclude that efforts at control, including imprisonment are responsible. Since the first line of defense is apprehension and punishment of offenders, an after-the-fact approach, it is almost inevitable that they will be judged failures when crime is such a prevalent public issue, despite any evidence concerning individual rehabilitation. This is especially likely since law enforcement officials insist that the bulk of crime is accounted for by repeaters (Uniform Crime Reports, 1970:37; Clark, 1970).

But it is conceivable, indeed likely, that the prisons could be 100 percent effective in preventing recurrence of crime by releasees, yet have almost no impact on the crime problem. If one is to hold imprisonment responsible for the general crime rate, he should evaluate the extent to which it serves as a general deterrent rather than a specific deterrent. That is, does the fact that some people are imprisoned deter potential criminals from committing crime—not, does imprisonment prevent the individuals who were imprisoned from committing further crime? There is no necessary connection between the two. Imprisonment could logically result in complete specific deterrence but fail totally as a general deterrent, just as it could fail completely as a specific deterrent yet succeed as a general deterrent (Tittle and Logan, 1973; Thorsell and Klemke, 1972). Moreover, Gould and Namenwirth (1971) have shown that it is a logical impossibility for ex-convicts to contribute very much to the crime rate; and in any case, given that so few crimes are "solved," there is no way of accurately estimating how many crimes are committed by repeaters.

Social scientists have always maintained that the causes of crime are multiple and that rising crime rates reflect conditions of life such as urban social organization, changes in age composition, heterogeneity of socialization contexts and normative schemes, and alienation of large segments of populations from collective identity, all of which vary independently of control efforts. To expect prison rehabilitation, or fear of sanctions (deterrence), to bear the responsibility for crime in general is to assume that most crime is committed by ex-convicts or that the only variable influencing crime is fear of punishment. Neither of these assumptions is valid or reasonable. Yet people adhere to them when conceptualizing the crime problem in terms of prison failure.

Another way in which inappropriate criteria of success may contribute to the persistent belief in the failure of prison rehabilitation is by application of unusually stringent standards of success. Regardless of what is meant by rehabilitation, one will find evidence of some failure as well as some success. Whether he decides that the entire enterprise is failing or succeeding will depend upon his criteria of how much individual failure constitutes general failure. Whatever the amount of success, short of 100 percent, some will maintain that it is not good enough and that prisons therefore fail.

Those with deep concern for the condition of mankind and for their society are likely to be dissatisfied when all the sick are not cured, all the ignorant are not educated, and all the prisoners are not rehabilitated. Such people always judge social institutions to be failures and press for reform; and it is they who write much of the material that contributes to a general understanding that prison rehabilitation is not succeeding.

Although myth making and the use of inappropriate standards of judgment contribute to the continuation of a belief in prison failure, the most important reason for persistence is probably that such a belief is functional for many different people and groups. It is difficult to think of anybody who does not benefit in some way by making the argument that prisoners are not rehabilitated. A belief in prison failure has advantages for law enforcement personnel, prison officials, convicts, humanitarians, radicals, ordinary citizens, and others.

For law enforcement personnel, the "inability of prisons to rehabilitate" simply reinforces a prevalent view that criminality is an enduring characteristic of particular individuals. Acknowledging the possibility of rehabilitation contradicts the view that police must mobilize to combat the "criminal element" in attempts to imprison it for long periods of time in the interest of societal protection. In a contrary vein, prison officials admit their own "failure" but do not find it inevitable. Lack of success is, rather, the result of sparce funds, facilities, and personnel. The argument is that rehabilitation is possible but is not being accomplished because of inadequate resources. It, thus, becomes the rationale for budgetary pleas and appeals for public support. To proclaim success would guarantee bureaucratic stagnation, and in the face of widespread belief in failure, would strain credibility.

Convicts argue against the rehabilitative effect of incarceration because it is inconceivable that they could do otherwise. Inmates submit to imprisonment unwillingly and even under the most favorable conditions they usually find it unpleasant (Ward, 1972). Consequently they are likely to feel and openly express resentment and hostility toward the whole program. Given such criticism, it would be contradictory and inconsistent to admit that rehabilitation might occur. Few people can see virtue in something they despise. It is more gratifying and much easier to define the whole experience as unjust, degrading, and useless. Moreover, inmates are usually primarily interested in ameliorating prison deprivations. By invoking an anti-rehabilitative argument, they can sometimes mobilize sympathy in favor of reform to make life easier for the prisoner. Finally, it is sometimes possible for inmates to manipulate prison staffs by complaining of the contradictions between custodial and rehabilitative functions and by criticizing the failure of prisons to live up to their ideas (Mathiesen, 1965; Tittle, 1972b:37).

Those who hold humanitarian views find the "failure of imprisonment" to be consistent with their position that incarceration is brutal and inhumane, while radicals can cite the lack of success for imprisonment as further evidence of the corruption and injustice of society. Both groups would argue that given present arrangements, such "failure" is inevitable, the humanitarian believing that inhumaneness will always elicit response in kind, and the radicals believing that injustice can never generate conforming behavior.

Finally, the ordinary citizen is likely to use "prison failure" as a scapegoat for the rising crime rate. Being unable to comprehend the reasons for lawlessness and feeling helpless to do anything about it, he is likely to find it comforting to hold the prisons responsible, just as he finds it comforting to blame the problems on judges who "coddle" criminals.

Implications

In short, believing that prisons do not rehabilitate is almost all things to all men. And given that the concept of rehabilitation is so confused and the data so poor, people are probably going to continue to believe that prisons do not rehabilitate, regardless of any reforms that are instituted. If the arguments presented here are valid, prisons would still bear the onus of rehabilitative failure, even if their programs, personnel, and treatment approaches were changed. This is not to say that they should not be changed, or that they should not be made more humane or comfortable, but simply that prisons can never win acclaim as successes in the rehabilitative endeavor, even with reform.

Consequently, the only way that prisons can expect to successfully achieve their goals is to abandon the rehabilitative mission altogether (cf. Gould and Namenwirth, 1971; Irwin, 1970). While this may at first sound bizarre, a little thought will reveal the logic of separating rehabilitative and punitive functions. There is no reason why rehabilitation ought to be something reserved for prison inmates or that it is necessarily needed by those convicted of crimes. The community includes many non-offenders who suffer personal defects just as prisons house numerous offenders who do not suffer the defects usually thought in need of correction. Logically, then, rehabilitation ought to be provided, not by prisons, but by community-based institutions which serve anybody in need—including released convicts.

If such institutions did exist, then prisons could perform the job they are suited for—punitive detention for the purpose of implementing vengeance, generating deterrence, or reinforcing normative imperatives. To be sure, prisons might fail in accomplishing these goals, or they might ultimately be declared superfluous institutions, but at least the criteria of evaluation would be clear and the logical possibility of success would exist. Rationality requires that any institutional endeavor have at least that chance.

References

Andenaes, Johs. 1966. "The general preventive effects of punishment." *University of Pennsylvania Law Review* 114:949-983.

Barnes, Harry E., and Negley K. Teeters. 1959. *New Horizons in Criminology.* Englewood Cliffs: Prentice-Hall.

Blumberg, Abraham S. 1967. *Criminal Justice.* Chicago: Quadrangle.

Clark, Ramsey. 1970. *Crime in America.* New York: Simon and Schuster.

Clemmer, Donald. 1940. *The Prison Community.* Boston: Christopher Publishing Company.

Cline, Hugh F. 1968. "The determinants of normative patterns in correctional institutions," pp. 173-184 in *Scandanavian Studies in Criminology,* Vol. 2. Oslo: Universitetsforlaget.

Cohen, Albert K. 1966. *Deviance and Control.* Englewood Cliffs: Prentice-Hall.

Edwards, George. 1972. "Forward–penitentiaries produce no penitents." *Journal of Criminal Law, Criminology and Police Science* 63 (June): 154-161.

Giallombardo, Rose. 1966. *Society of Women: A Study of a Women's Prison.* New York: John Wiley and Sons.

Garabedian, Peter G. 1963. "Social roles and processes of socialization in the prison community." *Social Problems* 11(fall): 139-152.

Glaser, Daniel. 1964. *The Effectiveness of a Prison and Parole System.* Indianapolis, Indiana. Bobbs-Merrill.

Glaser, Daniel, and John Stratton. 1961. "Measuring inmate change in prison," pp. 381-392 in Donald R. Cressey (ed.), *The Prison.* New York: Holt, Rinehart and Winston.

Goffman, Erving. 1961. *Asylums.* Garden City, New York: Doubleday and Company.

Goldfarb, Ronald, and Linda Singer. 1971. "Disaster road: the American prison system." *Intellectual Digest* 2(December): 19-23.

Gould, Leroy, and Zvi Namenwirth. 1971. "Contrary objectives: crime control and rehabilitation of criminals," pp. 237-267 in Jack Douglas (ed.), *Crime and Justice in American Society.* Indianapolis: Bobbs-Merrill.

Hayner, Norman S., and Ellis Ash. 1939. "The prisoner community as a social group." *American Sociological Review* 4(June): 362-369.

———. 1940. "The prison as a community." *American Sociological Review* 5(August): 577-583.

Irwin, John. 1970. *The Felon.* Englewood Cliffs, New Jersey: Prentice-Hall.

Irwin, John, and Donald R. Cressey. 1962. "Thieves, convicts, and the inmate culture." *Social Problems* 10(fall): 142-155.

Kassebaum, Gene, David Ward, and Daniel Wilner. 1971. *Prison Treatment and Parole Survival: An Empirical Assessment.* New York: Wiley.

Levin, Martin A. 1971. "Policy evaluation and recidivism." *Law and Society Review* 6(August): 17-46.

Logan, Charles H. 1972. "Evaluation research in crime and delinquency: a reappraisal." *Journal of Criminal Law, Criminology and Police Science* 63(September): 378-387.

Mathiesen, Thomas. 1965. *The Defenses of the Weak: A Sociological Study of a Norwegian Correctional Institution.* London: Tavistock.

McCorkle, Lloyd W., and Richard Korn. 1954. "Resocialization within walls." *The Annals* 293(May): 88-98.

Messinger, Sheldon. 1969. "Issues in the study of the social system of prison inmates." *Issues in Criminology* 4(No. 2): 133-144.

Morris, Terence, and Pauline Morris. 1963. *Pentonville: A Sociological Study of an English Prison.* London: Routledge and Kegan Paul.

Newman, Donald J. 1966. *Conviction: The Determination of Guilt or Innocence without Trial.* Boston: Little, Brown and Company.

Packer, Herbert L. 1968. *The Limits of the Criminal Sanction.* Stanford: Stanford University Press.

Reynolds, Larry T. 1966. "A note on the perpetuation of a 'scientific' fiction." *Sociometry* 29(March): 85-88.

Sykes, Gresham M. 1958. *The Society of Captives.* Princeton: Princeton University Press.

Thomas, Charles. 1970. "Toward a more inclusive model of the inmate contra-culture." *Criminology* 8(November): 251-262.

Thorsell, Bernard A., and Lloyd W. Klemke. 1972. "The labeling process: reinforcement and deterrent?" *Law and Society Review* 6(February): 393-403.

Tittle, Charles R. 1969. "Inmate organization: sex differentiation and the influence of criminal subcultures." *American Sociological Review* 34(August): 492-505.

———. 1972a. "Institutional living and rehabilitation." *Journal of Health and Social Behavior* 13(September): 263-275.

———. 1972b. *Society of Subordinates: Inmate Organization in a Narcotic Hospital.* Bloomington, Indiana: Indiana University Press.

Tittle, Charles R., and Charles H. Logan. 1973. "Sanctions and deviance: evidence and remaining questions." *Law and Society Review* 6(spring): 371-392.

Tittle, Charles R., and Drollene P. Tittle. 1964. "Social organization of prisoners: an empirical test." *Social Forces* 43(December): 216-221.

Uniform Crime Reports. 1967, 1968, 1970. U.S. Department of Justice, U.S. Government Printing Office, Washington, D.C.

Vold, George B. 1954. "Does the prison reform?" *The Annals* 293(May): 42-50.

Ward, David A. 1972. "Inmate rights and prison reform in Sweden and Denmark." *Journal of Criminal Law, Criminology and Police Science* 63(June): 240-255.

Ward, David A., and Gene G. Kassebaum. 1965. *Women's Prison: Sex and Social Structure.* Chicago: Aldine.

Weinberg, S. Kirson. 1942. "Aspects of the prison's social structure." *American Journal of Sociology* 47(March): 717-726.

Wellford, Charles. 1967. "Factors associated with adoption of the inmate code: a study of normative socialization." *Journal of Criminal Law, Criminology and Police Science* 58(June): 197-203.

Westover, Harry C. 1958. "Is prison rehabilitation successful?" *Federal Probation* 22(March): 3-6.

Wheeler, Stanton. 1961. "Socialization in correctional communities." *American Sociological Review* 26(October): 697-712.

The Medical Model in Corrections

Requiescat in Pace

Donal E. J. MacNamara
John Jay College of Criminal Justice, City University of New York

Abstract

The medical model for corrections, confidently espoused by several generations of behavioral scientists although never empirically validated, is now reeling under attacks from an interdisciplinary (though unorganized) army of critics. Attacking its basic premise (that the offender is "sick" and can be "cured"), the new penologists advocate a justice model based on individual responsibility with uniform penalties consistently imposed for like crimes. Out would go the indeterminate sentence, virtually unlimited judicial discretion, parole, and coerced participation in rehabilitation programs. Deterrence, retribution, and incapacitation would be restored as respectable rationalizations for imprisonment; but in general long prison terms would be reserved only for the habitually violent.

Of all the many correctional shibboleths religiously communicated to their students by professors of sociology, social work, criminology, and corrections, the "medical model" has proved most durable, and strangely so since there has been little, if any, empirical demonstration of its validity. The concept is at once so humane, so modern, so professional, and seemingly so scientific as to commend it to men of good will; and the process of follow-up evaluation so neglected and so fraught with methodological pitfalls as to permit widely disseminated claims of rehabilitative success based on little more than an overly optimistic belief in the ultimate perfectibility of even the most dangerous and recidivistic offenders coupled with a statistical innocence more appropriate to an adolescent interest in batting and fielding averages. Its enduring quality, too, owes not a little to the neanderthal opposition: those who, however valid their overall negative evaluations of the model in practice, couch their countervailing arguments in such discriminatory, punitive, retributive, and unscientific language as to offend the sensibilities and reinforce the basic premises of the reformers and rehabilitators.

In its simplest (perhaps oversimplified) terms, the medical model as applied to corrections assumed the offender to be "sick" (physically, mentally, and/or socially); his offense to be a manifestation or symptom of his illness, a cry for help. Obviously, then, early and accurate diagnosis, followed by prompt and effective therapeutic intervention, assured an affirmative prognosis–rehabilitation. Diagnosis was the function of the presentence investigation (confirmed, expanded, or perhaps corrected during institutional classification); therapeutic intervention was decreed in the sentence and made more specific in the treatment plan devised by the classification committee; and the parole board decided (within certain legal constraints) when the patient was to be discharged back into the community as "cured." Basic to the medical model, although rather surprisingly denied by many of its proponents, is that the criminogenic factors are indigenous to the individual offender and that it is by doing "something" for, to, or with him that rehabilitation can be effected.

There are, to be sure, many illustrative cases to which this model applies: the offender with a glandular imbalance correctable by chemotherapy; the cosmetic elimination of a disfiguring blemish with a consequent minimizing of social discrimination and reactive hostility; even the surgical removal of the testes of an habitual rapist. Somewhat more questionable are the claimed successes for psychiatric interventions; and it is difficult, indeed, since the more credulously religious days of past centuries, to find acceptable examples of moral regeneration. But the medical model school depended less on an affirmative showing that success crowned their programs than on aggressive excuses for failure: rehabilitation was underfunded; treatment was sabotaged by custodial staff; judges and parole boards responded to political and public pressures rather than to treatment imperatives; society had a lust for punishment; even rehabilitated offenders suffered socioeconomic discrimination which drove them back to criminal activity; the brutal, coercive, institutional atmosphere negated therapeutic interventions; "prisonization" (the resocialization of newly incarcerated offenders into the mores and folkways of the inmate community) was contra-rehabilitative; and, among those labelled "radical" criminologists, a retreat position inconsistent with the medical model that denounces the society which defines criminality rather than the offenders who violate society's laws.

The medical model has further implications for criminal justice. It entails wide discretion for the criminal court judiciary, permitting diversion of cases from the criminal justice system; sentencing alternatives ranging from probation to indeterminate sentences of polar dimensions (e.g., one day to life); paroling authorities with in many cases equally liberal alternatives; and to some lesser degree an expanded use of the commutation and pardoning powers of the executive branch. Implicit in the model was the availability of a wide range of treatment alternatives, institutional and community; and anticipated too was an army of professional probation and parole officers, with a department store of social services awaiting referrals, who would not only supervise but service and support manageable caseloads, consisting of clients

From *Criminology,* Vol. 14, No. 4 (February 1977), pp. 439–447, by permission of the publisher, Sage Publications, Inc.

specially selected by judges and parole boards as being of minimal danger to the community and good prospects for societal readjustment. That judicial discretion has been abused and incompetently administered, that the arsenal of treatment alternatives has seldom been provided, that paroling authorities have proved incapable of either resisting pressures or distinguishing dangerous from nondangerous offenders, that probation and parole officers have for a variety of reasons failed either to supervise adequately or provide services and support, that the retributive forces in correction and in the public have inhibited certain rehabilitative approaches, and even that some humane and libertarian proponents of the medical model have, perhaps inconsistently, opposed the more draconian treatment interventions (e.g., behavior modification) may all be accepted as possible explanations for the failure of the rehabilitative ideal. But it is perhaps more likely than not that, even if these negatives could be corrected, the custodial-deterrent-retributive school would be vindicated. For the basic flaw of the medical model is its basic premise: that the offender is "sick" when in fact he is far more likely to be as "normal" as most nonoffenders but inadequately, negatively, or contraculturally socialized, at war with a world he never made, a world in which he has been subjected to abuse, brutalization, discrimination, and exploitation. No program of education, vocational training, medical or psychiatric therapy is relevant to his "cure" and none is likely to reverse his twenty or thirty years of antisocial conditioning. What alternative remains? Incapacitation by custodial control with perhaps some rather speculative deterrent impact on either the offender or on prospective offenders, or both.

Now these views would have earned an academic criminologist naught but contumely less than a decade ago, but correctional fads, fallacies, and fashions change. A proliferating literature, bearing the names of such respectable academicians as Norval Morris, James Q. Wilson, Andrew von Hirsch, Robert Martinson, David Fogel, and Ernst van den Haag, now rejects equally the "tear down the walls" war cry of those who would abolish prisons (in favor of a just society which would eliminate criminogenic factors) and the prison reform movement which campaigns and litigates for smaller, treatment-oriented institutions, court-mandated inmate rights, expansion of community corrections, decriminalization of victimless offenses, and diversion from the criminal justice system for many now subject to its sanctions. The new penologists, if one can so label a quite disparate group, accept prisons as a societal necessity, advocate a narrowing or elimination of judicial discretion in sentencing (flat or definite sentences imposed uniformly and consistently on those convicted of identical crimes), an end to coerced institutional treatment (although they favor voluntary participation by inmates in a variety of educational, vocational, and therapeutic programs), abolition or severe constraints on parole, and acceptance of a deterrent-retributive-punitive rationalization for dealing with offenders. Some implicitly, others more explicitly, justify imprisonment in terms of societal protection by incapacitating for at least the definite period of their confinement those dangerous and habitual offenders who are responsible for the almost paranoid fear of criminals widespread among certain segments of our population and reflected in the increasingly punitive orientation of courts and legislatures.

My colleague, Robert Martinson (and his co-authors Douglas Lipton and Judith Wilks) has perhaps received a less cordial reception for the highly significant monograph, *The Effectiveness of Correctional Treatment* (1975), than has been accorded Morris, Wilson et al.; yet he has furnished us with a more massive and convincing documentation of the irrelevancy and ineffectiveness of therapeutic interventions than have the authors of the more readable polemics. Certainly his book, articles, and lectures have stimulated much of the new and highly controversial correctional dialogue; yet he is actually anti-prison and to a limited extent pro-probation and parole (advocating a transfer of funding which would permit highly intensified, almost one-for-one, supervision or surveillance in the community), thus eliminating the negative impact of imprisonment and at the same time enhancing societal protection against recidivistic crimes by convicted offenders. Martinson advocates the removal of the criminal justice system from the "treatment business," abolishing the indeterminate sentence and parole boards, developing three categories of offenders (suspendees, restrainees, and isolates). *Suspendees* are first offenders to be returned to the community under neither supervision nor coerced treatment, but who are eligible for voluntary services arranged through broker-advocates (not too different from an idealized version of a probation officer) and under the sole injunction that they not be convicted again of a criminal offense. *Restrainees,* either suspendees who recidivate or offenders classified as nondeterrable by mere threat of punishment, would be placed under intensive surveillance within the community ("each *restrainee* will be assigned his own private policeman") by an agent who is unknown to him, with whom he is not to have interpersonal contact, and whose sole function would be to report to the police whenever he observes the restrainee committing a criminal offense. *Isolates,* either suspendees or restrainees who commit new and serious offenses or a small class of first offenders who are convicted of heinous, violent crimes and are too dangerous to be supervised in the community, would be imprisoned in one of a greatly reduced number of existing prisons, with neither treatment, reform, nor rehabilitation as the aim.

Norval Morris, prestigious dean of the University of Chicago Law School, in *The Future of Imprisonment* (1974), argues that prisons are necessary; that they can be made less brutal, corrupt, and dehumanizing; that all rehabilitative and treatment programs be entirely voluntary; that the range of judicial discretion in sentencing be severely constrained; that mandated programs of graduated community release precede parole; that terms of imprisonment be uniform and related to the seriousness of the offense rather than to speculative evaulation of "dangerousness" or potential for recidivism; and that model prisons, not unlike the Danish institution at Herstedvester, be provided for the custody and treatment of such habitually aggressive offenders as recidivistic rapists and murderers.

Ernst van den Haag, prolific polemicist on the faculty of the New School, advocates in *Punishing Criminals: Concerning a Very Old and Painful Question* (1975) a return to the pleasure-pain calculus, balancing temptation with swift and certain punishments, albeit somewhat less harsh than those advocated by many, e.g., day fines (related to the offender's income) for minor crimes; one- or two-year sentences for more serious offenders; longer, indeterminate imprisonment for incorrigibles; and perhaps "exile" for some (i.e., banishment with their families either to special penal communities or to small, isolated villages in which they might be more intensively supervised). This is in fact a feature of Italian penal law, used rather inconsistently as a means of controlling members of the Mafia, and was for centuries a basic penalty in China with the banishment distance in miles correlated to the offense but with the rigors of the climate and type of work available also inputs into the calculus. Van den Haag, probably the essential pragmatist of the new penologists, subordinates even charity and justice to the preservation of social order.

Andrew von Hirsch, of the Rutgers University School of Criminal Justice, in *Doing Justice: The Choice of Punishments* (1976), rejects the medical-rehabilitative model, advocates elimination of both the indeterminate sentence and parole, accepts punishment as the basic rationalization of society's response to criminality, opts for somewhat harsher sentences than does van den Haag (a five-year maximum, for all crimes except murder, which—although von Hirsch does not mention it—has been established by psychological research as the outer parameter of the human ability to project into the future), and emphasizes that offenders "deserve" to be punished in proportion to the gravity of their crime(s) against society.

James Q. Wilson, Harvard political scientist, has unlike the great majority of his disciplinary colleagues devoted much of his attention to the criminal justice system, forcefully dissenting from *The Challenge of Crime in a Free Society* (Ruth et al., 1971) and publishing an insightful study, *Varieties of Police Behavior* (1968). In a collection of essays, *Thinking About Crime* (1975), Wilson comes down hard on the side of prisons and punishments as mechanisms to reduce crime incidence substantially. Seeing the habitual, career criminal as responsible for a high proportion of serious criminality, he call for incarceration, and holds out hope that imprisonment might additionally have some deterrent impact on others not yet committed to a life of crime. He, too, feels that swift and certain short terms of imprisonment (up to two years) can be effective, perhaps more effective than the much harsher maximum penalties provided for in the statutes but rarely imposed and even more rarely served. Wilson strongly implies that the failure of the prison population to increase proportionately to the significantly higher crime incidence after World War II was itself a cause of the increased criminality. And finally, he has short shrift for rehabilitation ("whatever it means") which he avers has no role in the prison sanction.

David Fogel's name has become synonymous with the rehabilitation of the "flat" or definite sentence and the "justice model" for corrections. While commissioner of corrections in Minnesota and later as director of the Illinois Law Enforcement Commission, he expressed very clearly his belief that rehabilitation and therapists have nothing to do with justice and safety, that rehabilitation should have nothing to do with whether an offender is sentenced to prison or when an offender should be released, and that the justice model must include justice for the victim (which led to his establishing the Minnesota restitution program). Fogel's sentencing recommendations divided crimes into categories based on degree of seriousness and provided limited judicial discretion (sentences could vary by as much as 20% if there were mitigating or aggravating factors); and, importantly, only offenders who were clearly dangerous to society would go to prison (e.g., he believes that all or most property offenders, many of whom now get committed to penal institutions, can be safely supervised within the community). Fogel's ineptly titled *We Are the Living Proof: The Justice Model for Corrections* (1975) is a clear and forceful presentation of his views and an especially convincing argument in favor of limiting the sentencing discretion of America's criminal court judges.

Finally, mention must be made of *Prison Without Walls* (1975), the report on parole in New York State by the Citizens' Inquiry on Parole and Criminal Justice (of which the author was a member and a consultant). Ramsey Clark and Herman Schwartz, both of whom might well be classified as prison abolitionists, headed the inquiry, and Jack Himmelstein, David Rothman, Richard Cloward, David Fogel, Michael Meltsner, Tom Wicker, Edward Bennet Williams, and William vanden Heuvel were among the better known students and practitioners of criminal justice lending their expertise. *Prison Without Walls* recommends that parole be abolished (as has Attorney General Edward Levi) because it is an adjunct of a sentencing process that attempts to reconcile elements of law, justice, and societal protection with considerations of rehabilitation and treatment. The result is an uneasy amalgam, as unfair to the offender as it is ineffective in the achievement of society's goals. Prisons do not "treat" offenders; they do not rehabilitate. Parole boards have little demonstrated competence in distinguishing dangerous from nondangerous inmates. Predictions of postinstitutional behavior, based largely on adjustment to the abnormal routines of institutional life, have proved disastrously inaccurate (in a California study, almost 90% so). The parole decision-making process is itself inequitable, if not unconstitutional (arbitrary and without empirically derived guidelines, subject to whim and pressure). In addition to concluding that the parole board be abolished, the report made both long-term and transitional recommendations, including elimination of compulsory community supervision, shorter sentences within a much narrower range of judicial discretion, development of rational criteria for early release, development of new alternatives to incarceration, public scrutiny of correctional decision-making, a wide range of voluntary programs to be offered to offenders before, during, and after incarceration, a specific code of inmate rights in parole board proceedings, shifting the burden of proof to parole boards in denying parole, open hearings, one year maximum on parole supervision in the community, simplification of the parole contract, abolition of the law enforcement function of parole agents (revocation to be based only on a new crime), financial assistance for parolees, extensive social services, and crediting of time on conditional release toward maximum sentence. *Prison Without Walls,* though somewhat different in its genesis and orientation, fits comfortably into the matrix of justice model studies; and better than many documents its far-reaching and quite controversial conclusions are fortified with persuasive data from the official archives but, even more importantly, from the client population.

The new penologists posit a basic conflict between a medical model maintaining that crime is the product of individual defects and disorders that can be corrected in a program of medical, psychiatric, and social rehabilitation and a readjusted or reformed offender returned to his rightful place in society *versus* a justice model based on the more classic doctrine of the free moral agent and of individual responsibility for one's criminal behavior. The controversy is somewhat complicated by reform and pragmatic considerations–reformers who want not to abolish prisons but rather to make them more humane and their rehabilitation programs more effective, and realists who insist that society has a right to protect itself from predatory elements by confining them in prisons, whether or not this leads to their rehabilitation and in fact irrespective of whether it contributes to their further criminality after release. The battle lines involve power dynamics as well as ideological conflicts. Judges wish to retain the tremendous discretion with which the medical model has invested them over the past half-century, and parole board members fight valiantly to retain their posts of power and prestige; both probation and parole officers are defending their jobs and their careers; program staff members in institutions (educators, vocational training specialists, therapists) see themselves threatened by making inmate participation voluntary; custodial elements scent victory over the hated headshrinkers; law and order politicians and some punitive-retributive legislators and pressure groups misread Morris, Wilson, Martinson, Fogel, von Hirsch and van den Haag as "lock 'em up and throw the key away" neanderthals; and the general public, ill-served by the communications media, is confused and unhappy. Perhaps least perturbed is the target population, offenders in or out of prisons. To a man they see this conflict as a charade . . . they *know* from past experience that nothing good ever happens to them. They have every expectation that no matter how things change, justice for them will remain very much the same.

REFERENCES

Citizens' Inquiry on Parole and Criminal Justice (1975) Prison Without Walls. New York: Praeger.

FOGEL, D. (1975) We Are the Living Proof: The Justice Model for Corrections. Cincinnati: W. H. Anderson.

LIPTON, D., R. MARTINSON, and J. WILKS (1975) The Effectiveness of Correctional Treatment. New York: Praeger.

MORRIS, N. (1974) The Future of Imprisonment. Chicago: Univ. of Chicago Press.

RUTH, H. et al. (1971) The Challenge of Crime in a Free Society. New York: Da Capo.
van den HAAG, E. (1975) Punishing Criminals: Concerning a Very Old and Painful Question. New York: Basic Books.
von HIRSCH, A. (1976) Doing Justice: The Choice of Punishments. New York: Hill & Wang.
WILSON, J. Q. (1975) Thinking About Crime. New York: Basic Books.
--- (1968) Varieties of Police Behavior: The Management of Law and Order in Eight Communities. Cambridge: Harvard Univ. Press.

Evaluative Studies of Institutions for Delinquents: Implications for Research and Social Policy

Paul Lerman

Most evaluative studies of institutions for delinquents try to measure organizational successes. This is a misleading approach since reliance is usually placed on indications of renewed delinquent involvement—a measure of potential organizational failure. When all sources of potential failure are taken into account, it is found that private residential treatment centers are as likely to be associated with failure as are their nonselective public counterparts.

Evaluative research is usually undertaken for the purpose of gathering evidence of a program's success in achieving its avowed goals.[1] This approach can be questioned, however, unless a more basic question has first been answered in the affirmative: Is there any empirical evidence that the program under consideration is more likely to be associated with success than with failure? It is not sufficient merely to assume that assessing success is the relevant evaluative problem. One must be willing to face the possibility that the program is associated with high rates of failure. Instead of the success of a program, it might be more relevant to evaluate its failure.

This point of view can be applied to any program of interest to social workers. It is especially appropriate in studying institutions that seek to transform delinquents into law-abiding youths. This paper will provide evidence that supports the following conclusion: Regardless of the type of program investigated, residential institutions for delinquents (under 18 years of age) are characterized by high rates of potential failure. On the basis of this evidence, it will be argued that researchers interested in evaluating new programs should focus on the problem of whether (and how) failure rates have been reduced—not whether an institution can claim success. In addition, this paper will propose that the issue of humanitarianism be considered apart from the ideologies of treatment and success.

Paul Lerman, DWS, *is Assistant Professor, Columbia University School of Social Work, New York, New York.*

What Is Organizational Failure?

It has become virtually a custom in the delinquency field to measure the success of correctional organizations by determining whether boys released from custody have refrained from known law violations.[2] From an evaluative perspective this approach is quite misleading. Boys released from a residential institution who are not "renoticed" by the legal system *might* be regarded as successes, but it still must be demonstrated that their success is attributable to the organization. Boys can be successful in this respect for many reasons that have little to do with their residential experiences. It is the task of evaluative research to demonstrate that the organization was actually responsible for the boys' achievement.[3]

The crucial difference between potential and actual organizational success becomes even clearer when the boys who *are* renoticed are examined. Residential organizations will not readily agree that renoticed boys constitute evidence of the organizations' *actual* failure to rehabilitate. Rather, they argue (and correctly so) that the failure may be due to many factors—some of which may be beyond the power of the institution to control. Without further evidence, it is no less unfair to attribute the failures to the organization than to credit it with the successes. But organizations cannot claim unnoticed boys as their successes without also claiming renoticed boys as their failures. Again, it is the task of evaluative research to demonstrate that the organization was responsible for the boys' failure or success.

From *Social Work,* Vol. 13 (July 1968), pp. 55–64. Copyright 1968, National Association of Social Workers, Inc. Reprinted with permission from *Social Work,* Vol. 13, No. 3 (July 1968), pp. 55–64.

At the stage of formulating the evaluative problem to be investigated, interest is in estimating *potential* organizational failures. To carry out this purpose, *all the boys whom the organization cannot reasonably claim as evidence of success must be identified.*

Recontact with the criminal justice system constitutes one measure of potential failure. Although this is a crude measure, it is difficult to deny its social utility. If it is granted that there is social utility in assessing failure by indications of renewed delinquent activity, it is still appropriate to question the usual measure utilized in evaluation studies. Most delinquency studies rely on recidivist data—the reinstitutionalization of released boys. This type of measure implies that boys who are known to the police and/or courts but who were not reinstitutionalized should be counted as successes, which is a dubious practice. Sophisticated criminologists are well aware that indications of delinquency or criminality decrease in reliability as the level of enforcement takes one further away from the offense itself. Sellin, the dean of American criminology, states this position as follows:

The difficulty with statistics drawn from later stages in the administrative process is that they may show changes or fluctuations which are not due to changes in criminality but to variations in the policies or the efficiencies of administrative agencies.[4]

In classifying boys as potential successes or failures, it is important that one avoid confounding the issue of renewed delinquent behavior with discretionary reactions to that behavior by court personnel. Whenever possible, studies must be analyzed to obtain indications of failure regardless of whether boys were reinstitutionalized. In brief, the notion of counting as successes boys whose behavior indicates that the institution has probably failed is rejected.

The importance of making these distinctions explicit can be highlighted by reviewing the results of a major current study.[5] For the past 6½ years the California Youth Authority's research department has been continually engaged in evaluating the Community Treatment Project, in which since September 1961 first-commitment youths have been randomly assigned to experimental services in their own communities or to a control situation that involves residence in an institution away from home. As of March 31, 1966, 241 in the experimental group and 220 in the control group had been paroled to Sacramento and Stockton, the two major sources of the sample; the former had been on parole for an average of 16.4 months and the latter for an average of 17.9 months. As of May 1967, 33 percent of the experimentals and 55 percent of the controls had violated parole (i.e., the boys' parole was officially revoked, they were recommitted, or they had received an unfavorable discharge from the youth authority). A more detailed analysis sustains this difference, but regardless of the refinement, the findings are quite misleading about the behavior of the two groups.

The difference in parole violation figures suggests that the experimentals as a group were less delinquent in their behavior than the controls, but this is not the case. As a matter of fact, the experimentals had more known delinquent offenses per boy than the controls (2.81 to 1.61).[6] When the seriousness of the offenses is considered, then the rates for "low serious" offenses are 1.56 per boy for the experimentals and .52 for the controls; for "medium serious" offenses, .61 per boy for the experimentals and .45 for the controls; and for "high serious" offenses, .64 per boy for both groups.[7] The authors present convincing evidence that the parole officers of the experimentals were much more likely to know about their boys' offenses than the parole officers of the controls.[8] In effect, they argue that the delinquent *behavioral output* was probably the same, but that the *rate of being noticed* was different.

Table 1 Rates of Parole Violation per Offense Category for Experimentals and Controls, California Community Treatment Project

Seriousness of Offense[a]	Experimentals		Controls	
	Number	Rate	Number	Rate
Low	376	.02	114	.17
Medium	146	.10	100	.40
High	156	.37	140	.44

[a]Seriousness-of-offense ratings are those used in the CTP study, but they have been trichotomized to highlight the trends. The low category includes California Youth Authority ratings 1–2, medium includes ratings 3–1, and high includes ratings 5–10.

Source: Marguerite Q. Warren, Virginia V. Neto, Theodore B. Palmer, and James K. Turner, "Community Treatment Project: An Evaluation of Community Treatment for Delinquents," CTP Research Report No. 7 (Sacramento: California Youth Authority, Division of Research, August 1966), (Mimeographed.) These rates do not appear in the report but are easily derived by using Tables 6 and 15.

The report could go a step further: It could demonstrate that the noticed offenses were reacted to differently by the experimental and control organizations. The parole violation rates differ because the modes of reacting to and handling the offenses are different. Table 1 compares the experimental and control groups by the seriousness of the offenses officially known; using known offenses as the base, the table then indicates the proportion of parole violations for each offense category for experimentals and controls. The table attempts to answer the following questions: Are noticed offenses of varying degrees of severity more or less likely to be judged parole violations when committed by the experimental group?

As the table clearly shows, the chance that an experimental boy's offense will be handled by revocation of parole is lower than for a control boy if the offense is low or moderate in seriousness; experimentals are judged similarly to the controls *only* when the offenses are of high seriousness. It is difficult not to conclude that the experimental boys have a lower parole violation rate because offenses of low and medium seriousness are evaluated differently by adults according to organizational context.

Instead of the misleading conclusion derived from using only parole violation differences, it appears that the potential rates of failure of the two programs are similar (at this point in time). The behavioral outputs of the experimentals and controls are probably the same; however, the experimentals' parole agents notice more of this behavior and therefore give the impression that the experimentals are more delinquent. But even though the behavior of experimentals attracts more notice, it is not evaluated in the same way as the behavior of the controls. This important study may have exercised excellent control over the random selection of boys; unfortunately, the ideology of treating boys in the community spilled over into the postexperimental phase. The experimental and control groups appear to differ in the behavior of the parole agents with respect to revocation of parole—not in the delinquent behavior of the boys.

In addition to officially noticed delinquent actions that are not regarded as parole violations, there is another measure of potential failure that has been disregarded: boys who do not "complete treatment." The following section will describe this additional source of measurement; a subsequent section will then provide data from published and unpublished studies that highlight the importance of measuring *all* the potential failures.

Counting All Outcomes

Before measurement of this other type of failure is discussed, the social bookkeeping of institutions must be understood. The literature on delinquency reveals a curious bookkeeping habit: Boys who do not complete treatment are usually *not counted* in evaluations of organizational effectiveness. These boys are treated statistically as if they never existed; in a sense they are dealt with as Orwellian "no-persons." It is difficult to think of such outcomes as successes, but organizations do not like to count them as failures. Therefore, these boys are set aside and ignored. If this group were small, this accounting fiction might be accepted; unfortunately, it is not. The rate of no-persons in an institutional population can exceed 30 percent. Discarding a third of an agency' budget as nonaccountable would never be tolerated; should one tolerate discarding a third of its clients?

The problem of how to count boys who are labeled as not completing treatment is especially acute in the private sector. Although private institutions for delinquents are heavily subsidized by public funds, they have been permitted an enormous amount of discretion in controlling the population they treat, especially with regard to intake and maintenance. These agencies choose the boys who will enter into residence and those who will remain in residence and complete treatment (and, of course, those who will not do so). By contrast, most public institutions, unless they are special experimental programs, are forced to accept into residence all boys the private institutions reject at intake; even if the boys do not "work out," they are usually maintained in the institution, since there are few if any other places that will take them. State training schools rarely have reason to use the classification "not completing treatment."

One private residential center in New York State studied by the author controls its population to the extent of rejecting seventeen boys for every one accepted for residential treatment. This institution (hereafter referred to as "Boysville") considers many nonpsychological factors in exercising discretion at intake, i.e., age, previous record, ethnicity, space in the cottages. Having exercised this population control at intake, Boysville then proceeds to use its freedom to reject boys who "resist treatment." An unpublished study by the author of Boysville found that 31 percent (51 out of 164) of the boys in the study sample released from the institution were classified as not completing treatment. Most of these boys (40) were sent to state training schools. The average length of their stay at the private institution was sixteen months, far exceeding the customary remand period of ninety days. Had these boys been sent to nearby "Statesville" at intake, their average stay would have been only nine months.

This outcome was not unique to the specific time chosen for the Boysville study. The administrative staff was so surprised by the findings that they examined their records for a different time period. This unusual replication—conducted surreptitiously—revealed an almost identical rate of boys classified as not completing treatment released from the institution (33 percent).

Nor is this problem unique to private nonsectarian organizations in New York State; it is just more acute at Boysville. A study of Highlights, a special public organization located in New Jersey, reveals that 18 percent of the population released did not complete treatment.[9] A study of another special public program located in Michigan reveals a rate of 18 percent.[10] An unpublished study of a sectarian residential treatment center in New York State disclosed a rate of 25 percent.[11] Street, Vinter, and Perrow comment that in one treatment institution "many boys were screened out in the first three months."[12] These organizations share one characteristic: each exercised control at intake and was able to "get rid of" boys who were "untreatable." In a less sophisticated period these boys might have been called "incorrigible."

This shift in semantic labels should suggest to the researcher the need to seek his own definition of this outcome. It is suggested that boys classified as not completing treatment have been granted "dishonorable discharges" from the institution, whereas those who have completed treatment are released as "honorably discharged." Only the latter boys can reasonably be conceived of as contributing to an organization's potential success. Redefining boys not completing treatment as dishonorably discharged permits counting of *all* the boys admitted to an institution in evaluating its success. Once this is done, it is clear that institutions yield two types of potential failures:

1. *Internal potential failures*—boys released from residential institutions via the route of a dishonorable discharge.
2. *External potential failures*—boys released with an honorable discharge who later engage in criminal or delinquent violations.

Internal failures can easily be identified in the everyday records of residential institutions. However, the type of discharge will not be stamped on the folders. Of the fifty-one boys in the Boysville sample who did not receive the usual honorable discharge—release to aftercare—forty were reinstitutionalized in state training schools, five were sent to mental hospitals, and six were purportedly "released to the community," but were actually runaways who could not be found. All these boys are classifiable as dishonorably discharged; they should be counted as the institution's potential internal failures. Certainly it is unreasonable to view them as potential successes.

Adding Up Failures

The profound differences that can ensue when *all* boys regardless of discharge status are counted are clearly shown in Table 2. When internal failures are taken into account, the minimum estimate of the total potential failures of Boysville is 51 percent. (If this group of boys had been followed for a longer period of time, there is little doubt that the total failure rate would have been higher.) If the usual custom of "not counting" internal failures in either the numerator or the denominator had been followed, the estimate would have been 34 percent. Which social bookkeeping method is used obviously matters; the distinction is not just academic.

Table 2 Potential Failures of Boysville Residential Treatment Center by Two Counting Methods (percentage)

Type of Failure	*All Boys Released (n = 164)*	*Honorable Discharges Only (n = 113)*
Internal	31	0
External[a]	23	34
Total	54	34

[a]Refers to boys officially rated as having violated the law between six and twenty-four months after their release to one of the five boroughs of New York City. Institutional records and the state files at Albany furnished the data.

Table 3 Comparison of Potential Failures of Two New Jersey Public Institutions (percentage)

Type of Failure	*Highfields (n = 229)*	*Annandale (n = 116)*
Internal	18	3
External	34	59
Total	52	62

[a]The external failures include all law violators, both institutionalized and noninstitutionalized, who had been released for at least eight months.

Source: H. Ashley Weeks, *Youthful Offenders at Highfields* (Ann Arbor: University of Michigan Press, 1958), pp. 46-50, 52, 60. This table does not appear in Weeks but is derived from data appearing in the cited pages.

Although Boysville differs in many ways from its public neighbor, Statesville, the total potential failure rates for the two institutions are quite comparable for similar postrelease periods. The major difference between them is that Boysville's potential failure rate is derived from both internal and external sources; Statesville has an internal failure rate of only 3 percent. The total rates are similar even though Boysville and Statesville differ in their relative power to control intake and maintenance of population in addition to treatment modalities.

Is this estimate of comparable failure rates a unique finding? Reanalysis of the best evaluation study available in the literature indicates that it is not.[13] In Table 3 data obtained from Weeks's comparison of Highfields, a special public program, and Annandale, a typical state training school—both of which are located in New Jersey—are presented.

The rates of total potential failures differ by only 10 percent. However, the two institutions differed in their treatment services; Highfields boys worked away from their residence, received "guided group interaction," and stayed only four months; Annandale boys were incarcerated on a routine twenty-four-hour basis and stayed twelve months. The similarity of the failure rates is even more striking when the initial differences between the populations are taken into account: Annandale boys were likely to have come from urban centers rather than suburban towns, were more likely to be Negro, and had longer and more intense careers as delinquents; Highfields boys tended to be younger and to have completed more years of schooling. In addition to these initial population differences, Highfields was composed of first offenders only; although the Annandale sample was also composed of first offenders, the institution itself contained knowledgeable multiple offenders. Annandale had little control over the maintenance of membership and initial recruitment, while Highfields had a great deal.

Furthermore, the two populations were exposed to different types of parole (or aftercare) services. Highfields parole officers encouraged boys to enlist in the armed services; twenty-seven Highfields boys and only seven Annandale boys entered the armed forces and thus were removed from the risk of failure. Also, Highfields boys, unlike their peers from Annandale, were discharged from postprogram supervision "within only a few months after their release."[14] More Annandale than Highfields boys were actually reinstitutionalized because of parole violations; had these boys not been under longer supervision they might not have been so easily renoticed. In general, Weeks presents an image of the Highfields population as more advantaged before, during, and after treatment. Despite these differences, the total potential failure rates are not too dissimilar and in both cases involve a majority of the boys.

Comparability of Control Groups

In investigating potential failure, it is not necessary to measure boys "before" and "after." Attempting to assess attitudinal change that can be attributed to an organizational experience is a complex affair; if the potential rates of failure are high, there is scant justification for expending money, personnel, and creative energy in this direction. However, there is one feature of the usual approach to evaluation that cannot be set aside so easily in assessing potential failure: if two organizations are being compared, then it is crucial that the population of boys be quite similar. The Highfields study by Weeks exhibits sensitivity to this requirement; unfortunately, a more recent study indicates that this sensitivity has not yet been translated into a norm of evaluative research.

In 1965, Jesness released a study, sponsored by the California Youth Authority, that attempted to compare "outcomes with small versus large living groups in the rehabilitation of delinquents."[15] The design of the study called for random assignment of 10–11-year-old boys at Fricot Ranch to either the experimental twenty-boy lodge or the control fifty-boy lodge. For unknown reasons, random processes did not appear to be operating in the actual assignments. Instead of being comparable, the two populations were discovered to have significant background differences: the experimentals were 73 percent white and the controls only 55 percent, 35 percent of the experimentals and 50 percent of the controls came from the poorest homes, and 67 percent of the experimentals were from households in which the father was the main provider as compared with only 52 percent of the controls.[16]

Using revocation of parole as a measure of failure, Jesness found that the experimentals were less likely to fail than the controls up until after thirty-six months of exposure to parole. The rates are as follows: 32–48 percent after twelve months, 42–58 percent after fifteen months, and 61–70 percent after twenty-four months. After thirty-six months the rates were virtually the same—76 and 78 percent respectively.[17] Jesness concludes that the "effects of the experimental program tend to fade as the exposure period increases."[18] This may be so, but it seems even more likely that the higher failure rates of the controls reflect the fact that they were actually a higher-risk group at the outset of parole, since the group was comprised of more Negroes and Mexican-Americans and came from poorer homes than the experimentals (and probably poorer neighborhoods, too). Unless Jesness presents evidence that these critical background variables, when used as analytical controls, do not change the differential outcomes after twelve or fifteen months of parole exposure, his inference cannot be accepted. These background variables, for which Jesness does not control, have usually been strongly associated with delinquency and recidivism and these, not the institutional experiences, probably account for the differences in failure. In the language of multivariate analysis, Jesness' findings on early failure are probably spurious (i.e., the result of a third, uncontrolled variable).

Institutional Interests

Organizational personnel have a major stake in any evaluative outcome. They want to be associated with potential success, not failure. Researchers are not likely to have a similar stake in the outcome. Although researchers do not purposefully

Table 4 Successes and Failures as Reported by William McCord and Joan McCord (percentage)

Type of Outcome[a]	*Wiltwyck (n = 65)*	*"New England State" (n = 228)*
Complete success	43	48
Partial success	28	5
Complete failure	29	33
Don't know	0	13

[a]For definitions of categories *see* text.

Source: William McCord and Joan McCord, "Two Approaches to the Cure of Delinquents," in Sheldon Glueck, ed., *The Problem of Delinquency* (Boston: Houghton-Mifflin Co., 1959), pp. 735–736.

seek to devalue people or organizations, their motto is much more likely to be: "Let's find out the truth and let the chips fall where they may." Their reference group is the scientific community and their ethics are ideally guided accordingly. Administrators, on the other hand—the persons who hire researchers—usually want the evaluators to demonstrate that their operations are successful and worthy of the external community's moral and financial support. Rather than deny this conflict of interest, one ought to be aware of its existence and make sure that biases do not influence empirical studies and written reports.

Biases influenced by organizational interests are especially likely to develop when researchers give up their independence and seek ways to demonstrate program success. Consider the evaluative study of Wiltwyck reported by William and Joan McCord.[19] Employed as the institution's resident psychologists, the McCords seemed so eager to prove its success that they defined one type of *failure* as "partial success." Table 4 presents the data as reported by the McCords for Wiltwyck and "New England State School."

From the McCord text it is learned that "partial success" refers to boys who actually appeared in court for law violations but were not reinstitutionalized; "complete failures" were both noticed and reinstitutionalized. The McCords do not seem to be bothered by this odd use of labels, for they claim that Wiltwyck had a *combined* success rate of 71 percent whereas New England, a state institution, had a rate of only 53 percent. A fair appraisal of the data would suggest that there is no appreciable difference between these institutions in potential success, using this writer's definition; the 5 percent difference—in favor of New England—is small. If all law violations are counted as potential failure, regardless of court disposition, it appears that *both* institutions are characterized by high external failure.

A subtle form of bias can be found in a study reported by Black and Glick.[20] The population of primary interest was composed mainly of Jewish boys sentenced to Hawthorne Cedar Knolls School, a sectarian-sponsored residential treatment institution. Both researchers were regular employees of the Jewish Board of Guardians, the sponsoring agency. In a monograph reporting their results, the investigators describe the selection of their sample as follows: "For purposes of this study the followup period was computed from the date of discharge from after-care."[21] Not surprisingly, Black and Glick report that Hawthorne Cedar Knolls had a higher success rate than a neighboring state school. They excluded from their sample not only all of the internal failures, but also all of the external failures occurring during the period of aftercare. Since the bulk of postrelease failures take place within the first two years, the researchers thus eliminated the chance of finding many failures. In effect, all this study can hope to describe is the potential success rate of an unknown population that has been selectively screened for boys who might be failures. Since the researchers have gone to such lengths to minimize their potential failures, it is reasonable to conclude that they were unwilling to face up to the possibility that their organization, like the state school, is characterized by a high rate of internal and/or external failure.

Implications for a Humanitarian Policy

The consistent finding that treatment programs have not yet been proved to have an appreciable impact on failure rates should not be misinterpreted. For even though institutions for delinquents are probably not highly successful—regardless of treatment type—there is no reason to go back to harsher methods of child handling. It can be argued, rather, that even when boys are kept for only four months and treated with trust (as at Highfields), there is no evidence that this "coddling" will yield greater failure rates.

The case for a humanitarian approach needs to be divorced from any specific mode of treatment. People can be nice to boys with and without engaging in psychotherapy. This point is implicit in the recent work by Street, Vinter, and Perrow.[22] But we should not delude ourselves into adopting the unsubstantiated position that a humanitarian organization for delinquent boys yields lower rates of potential failures. With our present state of knowledge, it makes more sense to advocate a more humanitarian approach on the ground that it does not increase the *risk* of potential failure.

If it is decided to advocate humanitarianism in its own right, the social policy issue becomes much clearer. Given the fact that social work is still unable to influence appreciably the rates of failure of institutions for court-sentenced delinquents, should not ways be sought to make the total criminal-delinquent system more humane? In the name of treatment, boys have actually been sentenced for two and a half years (as at Boysville) for offenses that might bring an adult a sentence of only thirty, sixty, or ninety days. Surely it is time that youths were dealt with as humanely, and with similar regard for equity and due process of law, as adults.[23]

If lighter sentences do not increase the risk of failure, then why not be more humane and equitable? Keeping boys in the community is undoubtedly a lighter sentence than sending them away. But California has found that this probably does not increase the risk of failure. Actually, the California Community Treatment Program has evolved a series of graded punishments. If youngsters in this program misbehave or do not obey the youth officer, they are *temporarily* confined. During the first nineteen months of the program, 57 of 72 experimental cases were placed in temporary confinement a total of 183 times; this was an average of three times each, with an average length of stay of twelve days per confinement.[24] As earlier analysis disclosed, the risk of postprogram failure is not increased by using this kind of approach. It is even conceivable—although this has not been demonstrated—that keeping these boys out of all long-term institutions in itself constitutes treatment and that this treatment may have a payoff much later, when the boys become adults. Spending less time in an all-delinquent community might yield more conforming adults.

Even if communities are not willing to follow the California community approach, one can still argue for shorter "lock-ups." Highfields kept first offenders for only four months, yet the risk of failure was not increased. As long as society is still determined to "teach boys a lesson" by locking them up (or sending them away), why not extend the idea of shorter confinements to a series of graded punishments for offenses? Adults are sentenced for thirty, sixty, or ninety days—why not children? Perhaps we might even come to advocate taking the institutional budgets allocated for food, beds, and clothing (based on lengthy stays) and spending them on boys and their families in their own homes. It is doubtful whether this would add to the risks, but the program would be a great deal more fun to study and run than the old failures.

Whether one embraces the perspective offered here, it is certainly time to address the problem of social accountability, regardless of the type of program. Social welfare institutions are too heavily subsidized, indirectly and directly, for social workers not to take the responsibility for knowing what has happened to the people served. A good start can be made by keeping track of all the people not completing treatment, discontinuing service, dropping out of programs, and running away. Rigorous and nondeceptive social bookkeeping may yield discomforting facts about agency success and reputation. It is hoped that we will be aware of defensive reactions and remind ourselves that we entered social work to serve *people* in trouble—not established agencies, ideologies, and methods.

---

[1]Herbert H. Hyman, Charles R. Wright, and Terrence K. Hopkins, *Application of Methods of Evaluation: Four Studies of the Encampment for Citizenship* (Berkeley and Los Angeles: University of California Press, 1962), pp. 3-88.

[2]For example, *see* Bernard C. Kirby, "Measuring Effects of Treatment of Criminals and Delinquents," *Sociology and Social Research*, Vol. 38, No. 6 (July-August 1954), pp. 368-375; Vernon Fox, "Michigan Experiment in Minimum Security Penology," *Journal of Criminal Law and*

Criminology, Vol. 41, No. 2 (July-August 1950), pp. 150–166; William McCord and Joan McCord. "Two Approaches to the Cure of Delinquents," in Sheldon Glueck, ed., *The Problem of Delinquency* (Boston: Houghton-Mifflin Co., 1959): Bertram J. Black and Selma J. Glick, *Recidivism at the Hawthorne Cedar Knolls School,* Research Monograph No. 2 (New York: Jewish Board of Guardians, 1952); H. Ashley Weeks, *Youthful Offenders at Highfields: An Evaluation of the Effects of the Short-Term Treatment of Delinquent Boys* (Ann Arbor: University of Michigan Press, 1958).

[3] This type of research demands careful attention to design to provide evidence that the experimental program had a greater impact on attitudes and values that, in turn, influenced postrelease behavior. This requires control groups and "before-after" measures. At the level of evaluative research herein referred to, in which *potential* outcomes are being assessed, attitudinal measures before and after are *not* necessary. As noted later on, comparability of groups continues to be important at *all* levels of evaluative research. *See* Hyman, Wright, and Hopkins, *op. cit.,* for a general statement of the problems. *See* Weeks, *op. cit.,* for the best-detailed example of evaluative research regarding institutions for delinquents.

[4] Thorstein Sellin, "The Significance of Records of Crime," in Marvin E. Wolfgang, Leonard Savitz, and Norman Johnston, eds., *The Sociology of Crime and Delinquency* (New York: John Wiley & Sons, 1962), p. 64.

[5] Marguerite Q. Warren, Virginia V. Neto, Theodore B. Palmer, and James K. Turner, "Community Treatment Project: An Evaluation of Community Treatment for Delinquents," CTP Research Report No. 7 (Sacramento: California Youth Authority, Division of Research, August 1966). (Mimeographed.)

[6] *Ibid.,* p. 64.

[7] *See ibid.,* Table 15, p. 68. For an explanation of the ranking of offenses by seriousness on which these figures are based, *see* Table 1 of this article.

[8] *Ibid.,* p. 65.

[9] Weeks, *op. cit.*

[10] Fox, *op. cit.*

[11] Personal communication from Robert Ontell, former study director of Mobilization For Youth's Reintegration of Juvenile Offenders Project, 1962.

[12] David Street, Robert D. Vinter, and Charles Perrow, *Organization for Treatment: A Comparative Study of Institutions for Delinquents* (New York: Free Press, 1966), p. 196. This information is presented in a parenthetical comment about "Inland," a private institution. How many of the boys released as not completing treatment are actually excluded or included in this study is difficult to estimate. This study focuses on the attitudes of institutionalized boys about their experiences in residence. It would have been extremely valuable to know whether the screened-out boys differed in their responses to the attitudinal questions. It would also have been valuable to know whether the runaways also differed. Such information might have provided evidence that the attitudinal measures had validity. Presumably boys "resisting treatment" (i.e., those who were screened out or ran away) should have responded differently to questions about themselves and the institutional staff. These kinds of missing data are quite central to the argument concerning the institutional "effectiveness" of Inland.

[13] Weeks, *op. cit.,* pp. 41–62.

[14] *Ibid.,* p. 61.

[15] Carl F. Jesness, "The Fricot Ranch Study: Outcomes with Small vs. Large Living Groups in the Rehabilitation of Delinquents." Research Report No. 47 (Sacramento: California Youth Authority, Division of Research, October 1, 1965). (Mimeographed.)

[16] *Ibid.,* p. 52.

[17] *Ibid.,* pp. 85–90.

[18] *Ibid.,* p. 89.

[19] McCord and McCord, *op. cit.* The Wiltwyck sample is composed only of Negro boys between the ages of 8 and 12 (at intake) who presented no "deep-seated psychiatric problems." "New England," on the other hand, is much more heterogeneous and has older boys. The data regarding the Wiltwyck sample can be found in Lois Wiley, "An Early Follow-up Study for Wiltwyck School." Unpublished master's thesis, New York School of Social Work, 1941.

[20] Black and Glick, *op. cit.*

[21] *Ibid.,* p. 4.

[22] *Op. cit.*

[23] *See* David Matza's insightful description of youthful appraisals of the juvenile court system in the discussion of the "Sense of Injustice," in Matza, *Delinquency and Drift* (New York: John Wiley & Sons, 1964).

[24] Marguerite Q. Grant, Martin Warren, and James K. Turner, "Community Treatment Project: An Evaluation of Community Treatment of Delinquents," CTP Research Report No. 3 (Sacramento: California Youth Authority, Division of Research, August 1, 1963), p. 38. (Mimeographed.)

What Works? "The Martinson Report"

Robert Martinson

IN THE PAST SEVERAL YEARS, AMERICAN PRISONS have gone through one of their recurrent periods of strikes, riots, and other disturbances. Simultaneously, and in consequence, the articulate public has entered another one of its sporadic fits of attentiveness to the condition of our prisons and to the perennial questions they pose about the nature of crime and the uses of punishment. The result has been a widespread call for "prison reform," i.e., for "reformed" prisons which will produce "reformed" convicts. Such calls are a familiar feature of American prison history. American prisons, perhaps more than those of any other country, have stood or fallen in public esteem according to their ability to fulfill their promise of rehabilitation.

One of the problems in the constant debate over "prison reform" is that we have been able to draw very little on any systematic empirical knowledge about the success or failure that we have met when we *have* tried to rehabilitate offenders, with various treatments and in various institutional and non-institutional settings. The field of penology has produced a voluminous research literature on this subject, but until recently there has been no comprehensive review of this literature and no attempt to bring its findings to bear, in a useful way, on the general question of "What works?." My purpose in this essay is to sketch an answer to that question.

THE TRAVAILS OF A STUDY

In 1966, the New York State Governor's Special Committee on Criminal Offenders recognized their need for such an answer. The Committee was organized on the premise that prisons could rehabilitate, that the prisons of New York were not in fact making a serious effort at rehabilitation, and that New York's prisons should be converted from their existing custodial basis to a new rehabilitative one. The problem for the Committee was that there was no available guidance on the question of what had been shown to be the most effective means of rehabilitation. My colleagues and I were hired by the committee to remedy this defect in our knowledge; our job was to undertake a comprehensive survey of what was known about rehabilitation.

In 1968, in order to qualify for federal funds under the Omnibus Crime Control and Safe Streets Act, the state established a planning organization, which acquired from the Governor's Committee the responsibility for our report. But by 1970, when the project was formally completed, the state had changed its mind about the worth and proper use of the information we had gathered. The Governor's Committee had begun by thinking that such information was a necessary basis for any reforms that might be undertaken; the state planning agency ended by viewing the study as a document whose disturbing conclusions posed a serious threat to the programs which, in the meantime, they had determined to carry forward. By the spring of 1972—fully a year after I had re-edited the study for final publication—the state had not only failed to publish it, but had also refused to give me permission to publish it on my own. The document itself would still not be available to me or to the public today had not Joseph Alan Kaplon, an attorney, subpoenaed it from the state for use as evidence in a case before the Bronx Supreme Court.[1]

During the time of my efforts to get the study released, reports of it began to be widely circulated, and it acquired something of an underground reputation. But this article is the first published account, albeit a brief one, of the findings contained in that 1,400-page manuscript.

What we set out to do in this study was fairly simple, though it turned into a massive task. First we undertook a six-month search of the literature for any available reports published in the English language on attempts at rehabilitation that had been made in our corrections systems and those of other countries from 1945 through 1967. We then picked from that literature all those studies whose findings were interpretable—that is, whose design and execution met the conventional standards of social science research. Our criteria were rigorous but hardly esoteric: A study had to be an evaluation of a treatment method, it had to employ an independent measure of the improvement secured by that method, and it had to use some control group, some untreated individuals with whom the treated ones could be compared. We excluded studies only for methodological reasons: They presented insufficient data, they were only preliminary, they presented only a summary of findings and did not allow a reader to evaluate those findings, their results were confounded by extraneous factors, they used unreliable measures, one could not understand their descriptions of the treatment in question, they drew spurious conclusions from their data, their samples were undescribed or too small or provided no true comparability between treated and untreated groups, or they had used inappropriate statistical tests and did not provide enough information for the reader to recompute the data. Using these standards, we drew from the total number of studies 231 acceptable ones, which we not only analyzed ourselves but summarized in detail so that a reader of our analysis would be able to compare it with his independent conclusions.

These treatment studies use various measures of offender improvement: recidivism rates (that is, the rates at which offenders return to crime), adjustment to prison life, vocational success, educational achievement, personality and attitude change, and general adjustment to the outside community. We included all of these in our study; but in these pages I will deal only with the effects of rehabilitative treatment on recidivism, the phenomenon which reflects most directly how well our present treatment programs are performing the task of rehabilitation. The use of even this one measure brings with it enough methodological complications to make a

[1]Following this case, the state finally did give its permission to have the work published. [Eds.: the book *The Effectiveness of Correctional Treatment* by Douglas Lipton, Robert Martinson and Judith Wilks was published by Praeger in 1975].

clear reporting of the findings most difficult. The groups that are studied, for instance, are exceedingly disparate, so that it is hard to tell whether what "works" for one kind of offender also works for others. In addition, there has been little attempt to replicate studies; therefore one cannot be certain how stable and reliable the various findings are. Just as important, when the various studies use the term "recidivism rate," they may in fact be talking about somewhat different measures of offender behavior—i.e., "failure" measures such as arrest rates or parole violation rates, or "success" measures such as favorable discharge from parole or probation. And not all of these measures correlate very highly with one another. These difficulties will become apparent again and again in the course of this discussion.

With these caveats, it is possible to give a rather bald summary of our findings: *With few and isolated exceptions, the rehabilitative efforts that have been reported so far have had no appreciable effect on recidivism.* Studies that have been done since our survey was completed do not present any major grounds for altering that original conclusion. What follows is an attempt to answer the questions and challenges that might be posed to such an unqualified statement.

EDUCATION AND VOCATIONAL TRAINING

1. *Isn't it true that a correctional facility running a truly rehabilitative program—one that prepares inmates for life on the outside through education and vocational training—will turn out more successful individuals than will a prison which merely leaves its inmates to rot?*

If this *is* true, the fact remains that there is very little empirical evidence to support it. Skill development and education programs are in fact quite common in correctional facilities, and one might begin by examining their effects on young males, those who might be thought most amenable to such efforts. A study by New York State (1964)[2] found that for young males as a whole, the degree of success achieved in the regular prison academic education program, as measured by changes in grade achievement levels, made no significant difference in recidivism rates. The only exception was the relative improvement, compared with the sample as a whole, that greater progress made in the top seven per cent of the participating population—those who had high I.Q.'s, had made good records in previous schooling, and who also made good records of academic progress in the institution. And a study by Glaser (1964) found that while it was true that, when one controlled for sentence length, more attendance in regular prison academic programs slightly decreased the subsequent chances of parole violation, this improvement was not large enough to outweigh the associated disadvantage for the "long-attenders": Those who attended prison school the longest also turned out to be those who were in prison the longest. Presumably, those getting the most education were also the worst parole risks in the first place.[3]

Studies of special education programs aimed at vocational or social skill development, as opposed to conventional academic education programs, report similarly discouraging results and reveal additional problems in the field of correctional research. Jacobson (1965) studied a program of "skill re-education" for institutionalized young males, consisting of 10 weeks of daily discussions aimed at developing problem-solving skills. The discussions were led by an adult who was thought capable of serving as a role model for the boys, and they were encouraged to follow the example that he set. Jacobson found that over all, the program produced no improvement in recidivism rates. There was only one special subgroup which provided an exception to this pessimistic finding: If boys in the experimental program decided afterwards to go on to take three or more regular prison courses, they did better upon release than "control" boys who had done the same. (Of course, it also seems likely that experimental boys who did *not* take these extra courses did *worse* than their controls.)

Zivan (1966) also reported negative results from a much more ambitious vocational training program at the Children's Village in Dobbs Ferry, New York. Boys in his special program were prepared for their return to the community in a wide variety of ways. First of all, they were given, in sequence, three types of vocational guidance: "assessment counseling," "development counseling," and "preplacement counseling." In addition, they participated in an "occupational orientation," consisting of role-playing, presentations via audio-visual aids, field trips, and talks by practitioners in various fields of work. Furthermore, the boys were prepared for work by participating in the Auxiliary Maintenance Corps, which performed various chores in the institution; a boy might be promoted from the Corps to the Work Activity Program, which "hired" him, for a small fee, to perform various artisans' tasks. And finally, after release from Children's Village, a boy in the special program received supportive after-care and job placement aid.

None of this made any difference in recidivism rates. Nevertheless, one must add that it is impossible to tell whether this failure lay in the program itself or in the conditions under which it was administered. For one thing, the education department of the institution itself was hostile to the program; they believed instead in the efficacy of academic education. This staff therefore tended to place in the pool from which experimental subjects were randomly selected mainly "multi-problem" boys. This by itself would not have invalidated the experiment as a test of vocational training for this particular type of youth, but staff hostility did not end there; it exerted subtle pressures of disapproval throughout the life of the program. Moreover, the program's "after-care" phase also ran into difficulties; boys who were sent back to school before getting a job often received advice that conflicted with the program's counseling, and boys actually looking for jobs met with the frustrating fact that the program's personnel, despite concerted efforts, simply could not get businesses to hire the boys.

We do not know whether these constraints, so often found in penal institutions, were responsible for the program's failure; it might have failed anyway. All one can say is that this research failed to show the effectiveness of special vocational training for young males.

The only clearly positive report in this area comes from a study by Sullivan (1967) of a program that combined academic education with special training in the use of IBM equipment. Recidivism rates after one year were only 48 per cent for experimentals, as compared with 66 per cent for controls. But when one examines the data, it appears that this difference emerged only between the controls and those who had successfully *completed* the training. When one compares the control group with all those who had been *enrolled* in the program, the difference disappears. Moreover, during this study the random assignment procedure between experimental and control groups seems to have broken down, so that towards the end, better risks had a greater chance of being assigned to the special program.

In sum, many of these studies of young males are extremely hard to interpret because of flaws in research design. But it can safely be said that they provide us with no clear evidence that education or skill development programs have been successful.

TRAINING ADULT INMATES

When one turns to adult male inmates, as opposed to young ones, the results are even more discouraging. There have been six studies of this type; three of them report that their programs, which ranged from academic to prison work experience, produced no significant differences in recidivism rates, and one—by Glaser (1964)—is almost impossible to interpret because of the risk differentials of the prisoners participating in the various programs.

Two studies—by Schnur (1948) and by Saden (1962)—*do* report a positive difference from skill development programs. In one of them, the Saden study, it is questionable whether the experimental and control groups were truly comparable. But what is more interesting is that both these "positive" studies dealt with inmates incarcerated prior to or during World War II. Perhaps the rise in our educational standards as a whole since then has lessened the differences that prison education or training can make. The only other interesting possibility emerges from a study by Gearhart (1967). His study was one of those that reported vocational education to be non-significant in affecting recidivism rates. He did note, however, that when a trainee succeeded in finding a job related to his area of training, he had a slightly higher chance of becoming a successful parolee. It is possible, then, that skill development programs fail because what they teach bears so little relationship to an

[2] All studies cited in the text are referenced in the bibliography which appears at the conclusion of this article.

[3] The net result was that those who received *less* prison education—because their sentences were shorter or because they were probably better risks—ended up having better parole chances than those who received more prison education.

offender's subsequent life outside the prison.

One other study of adults, this one with fairly clear implications, has been performed with women rather than men. An experimental group of institutionalized women in Milwaukee was given an extremely comprehensive special education program, accompanied by group counseling. Their training was both academic and practical; it included reading, writing, spelling, business filing, child care, and grooming. Kettering (1965) found that the program made no difference in the women's rates of recidivism.

Two things should be noted about these studies. One is the difficulty of interpreting them as a whole. The disparity in the programs that were tried, in the populations that were affected, and in the institutional settings that surrounded these projects make it hard to be sure that one is observing the same category of treatment in each case. But the second point is that despite this difficulty, one can be reasonably sure that, so far, educational and vocational programs have not worked. We don't know why they have failed. We don't know whether the programs themselves are flawed, or whether they are incapable of overcoming the effects of prison life in general. The difficulty may be that they lack applicability to the world the inmate will face outside of prison. Or perhaps the type of educational and skill improvement they produce simply doesn't have very much to do with an individual's propensity to commit a crime. What we do know is that, to date, education and skill development have not reduced recidivism by rehabilitating criminals.

THE EFFECTS OF INDIVIDUAL COUNSELING

2. *But when we speak of a rehabilitative prison, aren't we referring to more than education and skill development alone? Isn't what's needed some way of counseling inmates, or helping them with the deeper problems that have caused their maladjustment?*

This, too, is a reasonable hypothesis; but when one examines the programs of this type that have been tried, it's hard to find any more grounds for enthusiasm than we found with skill development and education. One method that's been tried—though so far, there have been acceptable reports only of its application to young offenders—has been individual psychotherapy. For young males, we found seven such reported studies. One study, by Guttman (1963) at the Nelles School, found such treatment to be ineffective in reducing recidivism rates; another, by Rudoff (1960), found it unrelated to *institutional* violation rates, which were themselves related to parole success. It must be pointed out that Rudoff used only this indirect measure of association, and the study therefore cannot rule out the possibility of a treatment effect. A third, also by Guttman (1963) but at another institution, found that such treatment was actually related to a slightly *higher* parole violation rate; and a study by Adams (1959b and 1961b) also found a lack of improvement in parole revocation and first suspension rates.

There were two studies at variance with this pattern. One by Persons (1967) said that if a boy was judged to be "successfully" treated—as opposed to simply being subjected to the treatment experience—he did tend to do better. And there was one finding both hopeful and cautionary: At the Deuel School (Adams, 1961a), the experimental boys were first divided into two groups, those rated as "amenable" to treatment and those rated "non-amenable." Amenable boys who got the treatment did better than non-treated boys. On the other hand, "non-amenable" boys who were treated actually did *worse* than they would have done if they had received no treatment at all. It must be pointed out that Guttman (1963), dealing with younger boys in his Nelles School study, did not find such an "amenability" effect, either to the detriment of the non-amenables who were treated *or* to the benefit of the amenables who were treated. But the Deuel School study (Adams, 1961a) suggests both that there is something to be hoped for in treating properly selected amenable subjects and that if these subjects are *not* properly selected, one may not only wind up doing no good but may actually produce harm.

There have been two studies of the effects of individual psychotherapy on young incarcerated *female* offenders, and both of them (Adams 1959a, Adams 1961b) report no significant effects from the therapy. But one of the Adams studies (1959a) does contain a suggestive, although not clearly interpretable, finding: If this individual therapy was administered by a psychiatrist or a psychologist, the resulting parole suspension rate was almost two-and-a-half times *higher* than if it was administered by a social worker without this specialized training.

There has also been a much smaller number of studies of two other types of individual therapy: counseling, which is directed towards a prisoner's gaining new insight into his own problems, and casework, which aims at helping a prisoner cope with his more pragmatic immediate needs. These types of therapy both rely heavily on the empathetic relationship that is to be developed between the professional and the client. It was noted above that the Adams study (1961b) of therapy administered to girls, referred to in the discussion of individual psychotherapy, found that social workers seemed better at the job than psychologists or psychiatrists. This difference seems to suggest a favorable outlook for these alternative forms of individual therapy. But other studies of such therapy have produced ambiguous results. Bernsten (1961) reported a Danish experiment that showed that socio-psychological counseling combined with comprehensive welfare measures—job and residence placement, clothing, union and health insurance membership, and financial aid—produced an improvement among some short-term male offenders, though not those in either the highest-risk or the lowest-risk categories. On the other hand, Hood, in Britain (1966), reported generally non-significant results with a program of counseling for young males. (Interestingly enough, this experiment *did* point to a mechanism capable of changing recidivism rates. When boys were released from institutional care and entered the army directly, "poor risk" boys among both experimentals *and* controls did better than expected. "Good risks" did worse.)

So these foreign data are sparse and not in agreement; the American data are just as sparse. The only American study which provides a direct measure of the effects of individual counseling—a study of California's Intensive Treatment Program (California, 1958a), which was "psychodynamically" oriented—found no improvement in recidivism rates.

It was this finding of the failure of the Intensive Treatment Program which contributed to the decision in California to de-emphasize individual counseling in its penal system in favor of group methods. And indeed one might suspect that the preceding reports reveal not the inadequacy of counseling as a whole but only the failure of one *type* of counseling, the individual type. *Group* counseling methods, in which offenders are permitted to aid and compare experiences with one another, might be thought to have a better chance of success. So it is important to ask what results these alternative methods have actually produced.

GROUP COUNSELING

Group counseling has indeed been tried in correctional institutions, both with and without a specifically psychotherapeutic orientation. There has been one study of "pragmatic," problem-oriented counseling on *young* institutionalized males, by Seckel (1965). This type of counseling had no significant effect. For adult males, there have been three such studies of the "pragmatic" and "insight" methods. Two (Kassebaum, 1971; Harrison, 1964) report no long-lasting significant effects. (One of these two did report a real but short-term effect that wore off as the program became institutionalized and as offenders were at liberty longer.) The third study of adults, by Shelley (1961), dealt with a "pragmatic" casework program, directed towards the educational and vocational needs of institutionalized young adult males in a Michigan prison camp. The treatment lasted for six months and at the end of that time Shelley found an improvement in attitudes; the possession of "good" attitudes was independently found by Shelley to correlate with parole success. Unfortunately, though, Shelley was not able to measure the *direct* impact of the counseling on recidivism rates. His two separate correlations are suggestive, but they fall short of being able to tell us that it really is the counseling that has a direct effect on recidivism.

With regard to more professional group *psychotherapy,* the reports are also conflicting. We have two studies of group psychotherapy on young males. One, by Persons (1966), says that this treatment did in fact reduce recidivism. The improved recidivism rate stems from the improved performance only of those who were clinically judged to have been "successfully" treated; still, the overall result of the treatment was to improve recidivism rates for the experimental group as a whole. On the other hand, a study by Craft (1964) of young males designated "psychopaths," comparing "self-government" group psychotherapy with "authoritarian" individual counseling, found that the "group therapy" boys afterwards committed *twice* as many new offenses as the individually treated ones. Perhaps some forms of group psychotherapy work for some types of offenders but not others; a reader must draw his own conclusions, on the basis of sparse evidence.

With regard to young females, the results are just as equivocal. Adams, in his study of females (1959a), found that there was no improvement to be gained from treating girls by group rather than individual methods. A study by Taylor of borstal (reformatory) girls in New Zealand (1967) found a similar lack of any great improvement for group therapy as opposed to individual therapy or even to no therapy at all. But the Taylor study does offer one real, positive finding: When the "group therapy" girls *did* commit new offenses, these offenses were less serious than the ones for which they had originally been incarcerated.

There is a third study that does report an overall positive finding as opposed to a partial one. Truax (1966) found that girls subjected to group psychotherapy and then released were likely to spend less time reincarcerated in the future. But what is most interesting about this improvement is the very special and important circumstance under which it occurred. The therapists chosen for this program did not merely have to have the proper analytic training; they were specially chosen for their "empathy" and "non-possessive warmth." In other words, it may well have been the therapists' special personal gifts rather than the fact of treatment itself which produced the favorable result. This possibility will emerge again when we examine the effects of other types of rehabilitative treatment later in this article.

As with the question of skill development, it is hard to summarize these results. The programs administered were various; the groups to which they were administered varied not only by sex but by age as well; there were also variations in the length of time for which the programs were carried on, the frequency of contact during that time, and the period for which the subjects were followed up. Still, one must say that the burden of the evidence is not encouraging. These programs seem to work best when they are new, when their subjects are amenable to treatment in the first place, and when the counselors are not only trained people but "good" people as well. Such findings, which would not be much of a surprise to a student of organization or personality, are hardly encouraging for a policy planner, who must adopt measures that are generally applicable, that are capable of being successfully institutionalized, and that must rely for personnel on something other than the exceptional individual.

TRANSFORMING THE INSTITUTIONAL ENVIRONMENT

3. *But maybe the reason these counseling programs don't seem to work is not that they are ineffective per se, but that the institutional environment* outside *the program is unwholesome enough to undo any good work that the counseling does. Isn't a truly successful rehabilitative institution the one where the inmate's whole environment is directed towards true correction rather than towards custody or punishment?*

This argument has not only been made, it has been embodied in several institutional programs that go by the name of "milieu therapy." They are designed to make every element of the inmate's environment a part of his treatment, to reduce the distinctions between the custodial staff and the treatment staff, to create a supportive, non-authoritarian, and non-regimented atmosphere, and to enlist peer influence in the formation of constructive values. These programs are especially hard to summarize because of their variety; they differ, for example, in how "supportive" or "permissive" they are designed to be, in the extent to which they are combined with other treatment methods such as individual therapy, group counseling, or skill development, and in how completely the program is able to control all the relevant aspects of the institutional environment.

One might well begin with two studies that have been done of institutionalized adults, in regular prisons, who have been subjected to such treatment; this is the category whose results are the most clearly discouraging. One study of such a program, by Robison (1967), found that the therapy did seem to reduce recidivism after one year. After two years, however, this effect disappeared, and the treated convicts did no better than the untreated. Another study by Kassebaum, Ward, and Wilner (1971), dealt with a program which had been able to effect an exceptionally extensive and experimentally rigorous transformation of the institutional environment. This sophisticated study had a follow-up period of 36 months, and it found that the program had no significant effect on parole failure or success rates.

The results of the studies of youth are more equivocal. As for young females, one study by Adams (1966) of such a program found that it had no significant effect on recidivism; another study, by Goldberg and Adams (1964), found that such a program *did* have a positive effect. This effect declined when the program began to deal with girls who were judged beforehand to be worse risks.

As for young males, the studies may conveniently be divided into those dealing with juveniles (under 16) and those dealing with youths. There have been five studies of milieu therapy administered to juveniles. Two of them—by Laulicht (1962) and by Jesness (1965)—report clearly that the program in question either had no significant effect or had a short-term effect that wore off with passing time. Jesness does report that when his experimental juveniles did commit new offenses, the offenses were less serious than those committed by controls. A third study of juveniles, by McCord (1953) at the Wiltwyck School, reports mixed results. Using two measures of performance, a "success" rate and a "failure" rate, McCord found that his experimental group achieved both less failure *and* less success than the controls did. There have been two positive reports on milieu therapy programs for male juveniles; both of them have come out of the Highfields program, the milieu therapy experiment which has become the most famous and widely quoted example of "success" via this method. A group of boys was confined for a relatively short time to the unrestrictive, supportive environment of Highfields; and at a follow-up of six months, Freeman (1956) found that the group did indeed show a lower recidivism rate (as measured by parole revocation) than a similar group spending a longer time in the regular reformatory. McCorkle (1958) also reported positive findings from Highfields. But in fact, the McCorkle data show, this improvement was not so clear: The Highfields boys had lower recidivism rates at 12 and 36 months in the follow-up period, but not at 24 and 60 months. The length of follow-up, these data remind us, may have large implications for a study's conclusions. But more important were other flaws in the Highfields experiment: The populations were not fully comparable (they differed according to risk level and time of admission); different organizations—the probation agency for the Highfield boys, the parole agency for the others—were making the revocation decisions for each group; more of the Highfields boys were discharged early from supervision, and thus removed from any risk of revocation. In short, not even from the celebrated Highfields case may we take clear assurance that milieu therapy works.

In the case of male youths, as opposed to male juveniles, the findings are just as equivocal, and hardly more encouraging. One such study by Empey (1966) in a residential context did not produce significant results. A study by Seckel (1967) described California's Fremont Program, in which institutionalized youths participated in a combination of therapy, work projects, field trips, and community meetings. Seckel found that the youths subjected to this treatment committed *more* violations of law than did their non-treated counterparts. This difference could have occurred by chance; still, there was certainly no evidence of relative improvement. Another study, by Levinson1964), also found a lack of improvement in recidivism rates—but Levinson noted the encouraging fact that the treated group spent somewhat more time in the community before recidivating, and committed less serious offenses. And a study by the State of California (1967) also shows a partially positive finding. This was a study of the Marshall Program, similar to California's Fremont Program but different in several ways. The Marshall Program was shorter and more tightly organized than its Fremont counterpart. In the Marshall Program, as opposed to the Fremont Program, a youth could be ejected from the group and sent back to regular institutions before the completion of the program. Also, the Marshall Program offered some additional benefits: the teaching of "social survival skills" (i.e., getting and holding a job), group counseling of parents, and an occasional opportunity for boys to visit home. When youthful offenders were released to the Marshall Program, either directly or after spending some time in a regular institution, they did no better than a comparable regularly institutionalized population, though both Marshall youth and youth in regular institutions did better than those who were directly released by the court and given no special treatment.

So the youth in these milieu therapy programs at least do no worse than their counterparts in regular institutions and the special programs may cost less. One may therefore be encouraged—not on grounds of rehabilitation but on grounds of cost-effectiveness.

WHAT ABOUT MEDICAL TREATMENT?

4. *Isn't there anything you can do in an institutional setting that will reduce recidivism, for instance, through strictly medical treatment?*

A number of studies deal with the results of efforts to change the behavior of offenders through drugs and surgery. As for surgery, the one experimental study of a plastic surgery program—by Mandell (1967)—had negative results. For non-addicts who received plastic surgery, Mandell purported to find improvement in performance on parole; but when one reanalyzes his data, it appears that surgery alone did not in fact make a significant difference.

One type of surgery does seem to be highly successful in reducing recidivism. A twenty-year Danish study of sex offenders, by Stuerup (1960), found that while those who had been treated with hormones and therapy continued to commit both sex crimes (29.6 per cent of them did so) and non-sex crimes (21.0 per cent), those who had been castrated had rates of only 3.5 per cent (not, interestingly enough, a rate of zero; where there's a will, apparently there's a way) and 9.2 per cent. One hopes that the policy implications of this study will be found to be distinctly limited.

As for drugs, the major report on such a program—involving tranquilization—was made by Adams (1961b). The tranquilizers were administered to male and female institutionalized youths. With boys, there was only a slight improvement in their subsequent behavior; this improvement disappeared within a year. With girls, the tranquilization produced worse results than when the girls were given no treatment at all.

THE EFFECTS OF SENTENCING

5. *Well, at least it may be possible to manipulate certain gross features of the existing, conventional prison system—such as length of sentence and degree of security—in order to affect these recidivism rates. Isn't this the case?*

At this point, it's still impossible to say that this is the case. As for the degree of security in an institution, Glaser's (1964) work reported that, for both youth and adults, a less restrictive "custody grading" in American federal prisons was related to success on parole; but this is hardly surprising, since those assigned to more restrictive custody are likely to be worse risks in the first place. More to the point, an American study by Fox (1950) discovered that for "older youths" who were deemed to be good risks for the future, a minimum security institution produced better results than a maximum security one. On the other hand, the data we have on youths under 16—from a study by McClintock (1961), done in Great Britain—indicate that so-called Borstals, in which boys are totally confined, are more effective than a less restrictive regime of partial physical custody. In short, we know very little about the recidivism effects of various degrees of security in existing institutions; and our problems in finding out will be compounded by the probability that these effects will vary widely according to the particular *type* of offender that we're dealing with.

The same problems of mixed results and lack of comparable populations have plagued attempts to study the effects of sentence length. A number of studies—by Narloch (1959), by Bernsten (1965), and by the State of California (1956)—suggest that those who are released earlier from institutions than their scheduled parole date, or those who serve short sentences of under three months rather than longer sentences of eight months or more, either do better on parole or at least do no worse.[4] The implication here is quite clear and important: Even if early releases and short sentences produce no improvement in recidivism rates, one could at least maintain the same rates while lowering the cost of maintaining the offender and lessening his own burden of imprisonment. Of course, this implication carries with it its concommitant danger: the danger that though shorter sentences cause no worsening of the recidivism rate, they may increase the total amount of crime in the community by increasing the absolute number of potential recidivists at large.

On the other hand, Glaser's (1964) data show not a consistent linear relationship between the shortness of the sentence and the rate of parole success, but a curvilinear one. Of his subjects, those who served less than a year had a 73 per cent success rate, those who served up to two years were only 65 per cent successful, and those who served up to three years fell to a rate of 56 per cent. But among those who served sentences of *more* than three years, the success rate rose again—to 60 per cent. These findings should be viewed with some caution since Glaser did not control for the pre-existing degree of risk associated with each of his categories of offenders. But the data do suggest that the relationship between sentence length and recidivism may not be a simple linear one.

More important, the effect of sentence length seems to vary widely according to type of offender. In a British study (1963), for instance, Hammond found that for a group of "hard-core recidivists," shortening the sentence caused no improvement in the recidivism rate. In Denmark, Bernsten (1965) discovered a similar phenomenon: That the beneficial effect of three-month sentences as against eight-month ones disappeared in the case of these "hard-core recidivists." Garrity found another such distinction in his 1956 study. He divided his offenders into three categories: "pro-social," "anti-social," and "manipulative." "Pro-social" offenders he found to have low recidivism rates regardless of the length of their sentence; "anti-social" offenders did better with short sentences; the "manipulative" did better with long ones. Two studies from Britain made yet another division of the offender population, and found yet other variations. One (Great Britain, 1964) found that previous offenders—but not first offenders—did better with *longer* sentences, while the other (Cambridge, 1952) found the *reverse* to be true with juveniles.

To add to the problem of interpretation, these studies deal not only with different types and categorizations of offenders but with different types of institutions as well. No more than in the case of institution type can we say that length of sentence has a clear relationship to recidivism.

DECARCERATING THE CONVICT

6. *All of this seems to suggest that there's not much we know how to do to rehabilitate an offender when he's in an institution. Doesn't this lead to the clear possibility that the way to rehabilitate offenders is to deal with them outside an institutional setting?*

This is indeed an important possibility, and it is suggested by other pieces of information as well. For instance, Miner (1967) reported on a milieu therapy program in Massachusetts called Outward Bound. It took youths 15½ and over; it was oriented toward the development of skills in the out-of-doors and conducted in a wilderness atmosphere very different from that of most existing institutions. The culmination of the 26-day program was a final 24 hours in which each youth had to survive alone in the wilderness. And Miner found that the program did indeed work in reducing recidivism rates.

But by and large, when one takes the programs that have been administered in institutions and applies them in a non-institutional setting, the results do not grow to encouraging proportions. With casework and individual counseling in the community, for instance, there have been three studies; they dealt with counseling methods from psycho-social and vocational counseling to "operant conditioning," in which an offender was rewarded first simply for coming to counseling sessions and then, gradually, for performing other types of approved acts. Two of them report that the community-counseled offenders did no better than their institutional controls, while the third notes that although community counseling produced fewer arrests per person, it did not ultimately reduce the offender's chance of returning to a reformatory.

The one study of a non-institutional skill development program, by Kovacs (1967), described the New Start Program in Denver, in which offenders participated in vocational training, role playing, programmed instruction, group counseling, college class attendance, and trips to art galleries and museums. After all this, Kovacs found no significant improvement over incarceration.

There have also been studies of milieu therapy programs conducted with youthful male probationers not in actual physical custody. One of them found no significant improvement at all. One, by Empey (1966), did say that after a follow-up of six months, a boy who was judged to have "successfully" completed the milieu program was less likely to recidivate afterwards than was a "successful" regular probationer. Empey's "successes" came out of an extraordinary program in Provo, Utah, which

[4] A similar phenomenon has been measured indirectly by studies that have dealt with the effect of various parole policies on recidivism rates. Where parole decisions have been liberalized so that an offender could be released with only the "reasonable assurance" of a job rather than with a definite job already developed by a parole officer (Stanton, 1963), this liberal release policy has produced no worsening of recidivism rates.

aimed to rehabilitate by subjecting offenders to a non-supportive milieu. The staff of this program operated on the principle that they were *not* to go out of their way to interact and be empathetic with the boys. Indeed, a boy who misbehaved was to be met with "role dispossession": He was to be excluded from meetings of his peer group, and he was not to be given answers to his questions as to why he had been excluded or what his ultimate fate might be. This peer group and its meetings were designed to be the major force for reform at Provo; they were intended to develop, and indeed did develop, strong and controlling norms for the behavior of individual members. For one thing, group members were not to associate with delinquent boys outside the program; for another, individuals were to submit to a group review of all their actions and problems; and they were to be completely honest and open with the group about their attitudes, their states of mind, their personal failings. The group was granted quite a few sanctions with which to enforce these norms: They could practice derision or temporary ostracism, or they could lock up an aberrant member for a weekend, refuse to release him from the program, or send him away to the regular reformatory.

One might be tempted to forgive these methods because of the success that Empey reports, except for one thing. If one judges the program not only by its "successful" boys but by all the boys who were subjected to it—those who succeeded and those who, not surprisingly, failed—the totals show *no* significant improvement in recidivism rates compared with boys on regular probation. Empey did find that both the Provo boys and those on regular probation did better than those in regular reformatories—in contradiction, it may be recalled, to the finding from the residential Marshall Program, in which the direct releases given no special treatment did *worse* than boys in regular institutions.

The third such study of non-residential milieu therapy, by McCravey (1967), found not only that there was no significant improvement, but that the longer a boy participated in the treatment, the *worse* was likely to do afterwards.

PSYCHOTHERAPY IN COMMUNITY SETTINGS

There is some indication that individual psychotherapy may "work" in a community setting. Massimo (1963) reported on one such program, using what might be termed a "pragmatic" psychotherapeutic approach, including "insight" therapy and a focus on vocational problems. The program was marked by its small size and by its use of therapists who were personally enthusiastic about the project; Massimo found that there was indeed a decline in recidivism rates. Adamson (1956), on the other hand, found no significant difference produced by another program of individual therapy (though he did note that arrest rates among the experimental boys declined with what he called "intensity of treatment"). And Schwitzgebel (1963, 1964), studying other, different kinds of therapy programs, found that the programs *did* produce improvements in the attitudes of his boys—but, unfortunately, not in their rates of recidivism.

And with *group* therapy administered in the community, we find yet another set of equivocal results. The results from studies of pragmatic group counseling are only mildly optimistic. Adams (1965) did report that a form of group therapy, "guided group interaction," when administered to juvenile gangs, did somewhat reduce the percentage that were to be found in custody six years later. On the other hand, in a study of juveniles, Adams (1964) found that while such a program did reduce the number of contacts that an experimental youth had with police, it made no ultimate difference in the detention rate. And the attitudes of the counseled youth showed no improvement. Finally, when O'Brien (1961) examined a community-based program of group psychotherapy, he found not only that the program produced no improvement in the recidivism rate, but that the experimental boys actually did worse than their controls on a series of psychological tests.

PROBATION OR PAROLE VERSUS PRISON

But by far the most extensive and important work that has been done on the effect of community-based treatments has been done in the areas of probation and parole. This work sets out to answer the question of whether it makes any difference how you supervise and treat an offender once he has been released from prison or has come under state surveillance in lieu of prison. This is the work that has provided the main basis to date for the claim that we do indeed have the means at our disposal for rehabilitating the offender or at least decarcerating him safely.

One group of these studies has compared the use of probation with other dispositions for offenders; these provide some slight evidence that, at least under some circumstances, probation may make an offender's future chances better than if he had been sent to prison. Or, at least, probation may not worsen those chances.[5] A British study, by Wilkins (1958), reported that when probation was granted more frequently, recidivism rates among probationers did not increase significantly. And another such study by the state of Michigan in 1963 reported that an expansion in the use of probation actually improved recidivism rates—though there are serious problems of comparability in the groups and systems that were studied.

One experiment—by Babst (1965)—compared a group of parolees, drawn from adult male felony offenders in Wisconsin, and excluding murderers and sex criminals, with a similar group that had been put on probation; it found that the probationers committed fewer violations if they had been first offenders, and did no worse if they were recidivists. The problem in interpreting this experiment, though, is that the behavior of those groups was being measured by separate organizations, by probation officers for the probationers, and by parole officers for the parolees; it is not clear that the definition of "violation" was the same in each case, or that other types of uniform standards were being applied. Also, it is not clear what the results would have been if subjects had been released directly to the parole organization without having experienced prison first. Another such study, done in Israel by Shoham (1964), must be interpreted cautiously because his experimental and control groups had slightly different characteristics. But Shoham found that when one compared a suspended sentence plus probation for first offenders with a one-year prison sentence, only first offenders under 20 years of age did better on probation; those from 21 to 45 actually did *worse*. And Shoham's findings also differ from Babst's in another way. Babst had found that parole rather than prison brought no improvement for recidivists, but Shoham reported that for recidivists with four or more prior offenses, a suspended sentence was actually *better*—though the improvement was much less when the recidivist had committed a crime of violence.

But both the Babst and the Shoham studies, even while they suggest the possible value of suspended sentences, probation, or parole for some offenders (though they contradict each other in telling us *which* offenders), also indicate a pessimistic general conclusion concerning the limits of the effectiveness of treatment programs. For they found that the personal characteristics of offenders—first-offender status, or age, or type of offense—were more important than the form of treatment in determining future recidivism. An offender with a "favorable" prognosis will do better than one without, it seems, no matter how you distribute "good" or "bad," "enlightened" or "regressive" treatments among them.

Quite a large group of studies deals not with probation as compared to other dispositions, but instead with the type of treatment that an offender receives once he is *on* probation or parole. These are the studies that have provided the most encouraging reports on rehabilitative treatment and that have also raised the most serious questions about the nature of the research that has been going on in the corrections field.

Five of these studies have dealt with youthful probationers from 13 to 18 who were assigned to probation officers with small caseloads or provided with other ways of receiving more intensive supervision (Adams, 1966—two reports; Feistman, 1966; Kawaguchi, 1967; Pilnick, 1967). These studies report that, by and large, intensive supervision does work—that the specially treated youngsters do better according to some measure of recidivism. Yet these studies left some important questions unanswered. For instance, was this improved performance a function merely of the number of contacts a youngster had with his probation officer? Did it also depend on the length of time in treatment? Or was it the quality of supervision that was making the difference, rather than the quantity?

INTENSIVE SUPERVISION: THE WARREN STUDIES

The widely-reported Warren studies (1966a, 1966b, 1967) in California constitute an ex-

[5]It will be recalled that Empey's report on the Provo program made such a finding.

tremely ambitious attempt to answer these questions. In this project, a control group of youths, drawn from a pool of candidates ready for first admission to a California Youth Authority institution, was assigned to regular detention, usually for eight to nine months, and then released to regular supervision. The experimental group received considerably more elaborate treatment. They were released directly to probation status and assigned to 12-man caseloads. To decide what special treatment was appropriate within these caseloads, the youths were divided according to their "interpersonal maturity level classification," by use of a scale developed by Grant and Grant. And each level dictated its own special type of therapy. For instance, a youth might be judged to occupy the lowest maturity level; this would be a youth, according to the scale, primarily concerned with "demands that the world take care of him. . . . He behaves impulsively, unaware of anything except the grossest effects of his behavior on others." A youth like this would be placed in a supportive environment such as a foster home; the goals of his therapy would be to meet his dependency needs and help him gain more accurate perceptions about his relationship to others. At the other end of the three-tier classification, a youth might exhibit high maturity. This would be a youth who had internalized "a set of standards by which he judges his and others' behavior. . . . He shows some ability to understand reasons for behavior, some ability to relate to people emotionally and on a long-term basis." These high-maturity youths could come in several varieties—a "neurotic acting out," for instance, a "neurotic anxious," a "situational emotional reactor," or a "cultural identifier." But the appropriate treatment for these youths was individual psychotherapy, or family or group therapy for the purpose of reducing internal conflicts and increasing the youths' awareness of personal and family dynamics.

"Success" in this experiment was defined as favorable discharge by the Youth Authority; "failure" was unfavorable discharge, revocation, or recommitment by a court. Warren reported an encouraging finding: Among all but one of the "subtypes," the experimentals had a significantly lower failure rate than the controls. The experiment did have certain problems: The experimentals might have been performing better because of the enthusiasm of the staff and the attention lavished on them; none of the controls had been *directly* released to their regular supervision programs instead of being detained first; and it was impossible to separate the effects of the experimentals' small caseloads from their specially designed treatments, since no experimental youths had been assigned to a small caseload with "inappropriate" treatment, or with no treatment at all. Still, none of these problems were serious enough to vitiate the encouraging prospect that this finding presented for successful treatment of probationers.

This encouraging finding was, however, accompanied by a rather more disturbing clue. As has been mentioned before, the experimental subjects, when measured, had a lower *failure* rate than the controls. But the experimentals also had a lower *success* rate. That is, fewer of the experimentals as compared with the controls had been judged to have successfully completed their program of supervision and to be suitable for favorable release. When my colleagues and I undertook a rather laborious reanalysis of the Warren data, it became clear why this discrepancy had appeared. It turned out that fewer experimentals were "successful" because the experimentals were actually committing more offenses than their controls. The reason that the experimentals' relatively large number of offenses was not being reflected in their failure rates was simply that the experimentals' probation officers were using a more lenient revocation policy. In other words, the controls had a higher failure rate because the controls were being revoked for less serious offenses.

So it seems that what Warren was reporting in her "failure" rates was not merely the treatment effect of her small caseloads and special programs. Instead, what Warren was finding was not so much a change in the behavior of the experimental youths as a change in the behavior of the experimental *probation officers*, who knew the "special" status of their charges and who had evidently decided to revoke probation status at a lower than normal rate. The experimentals continued to commit offenses; what was different was that when they committed these offenses, they were permitted to remain on probation.

The experimenters claimed that this low revocation policy, and the greater number of offenses committed by the special treatment youth, were *not* an indication that these youth were behaving specially badly and that policy makers were simply letting them get away with it. Instead, it was claimed, the higher reported offense rate was primarily an artifact of the more intense surveillance that the experimental youth received. But the data show that this is not a sufficient explanation of the low failure rate among experimental youth; the difference in "tolerance" of offenses between experimental officials and control officials was much greater than the difference in the rates at which these two systems detected youths committing new offenses. Needless to say, this reinterpretation of the data presents a much bleaker picture of the possibilities of intensive supervision with special treatment.

"TREATMENT EFFECTS" VS. "POLICY EFFECTS"

This same problem of experimenter bias may also be present in the predecessors of the Warren study, the ones which had also found positive results from intensive supervision on probation; indeed, this disturbing question can be raised about many of the previously discussed reports of positive "treatment effects."

This possibility of a "policy effect" rather than a "treatment effect" applies, for instance, to the previously discussed studies of the effects of intensive supervision on juvenile and youthful probationers. These were the studies, it will be recalled, which found lower recidivism rates for the intensively supervised.[6]

One opportunity to make a further check on the effects of this problem is provided, in a slightly different context, by Johnson (1962a). Johnson was measuring the effects of intensive supervision on youthful *parolees* (as distinct from probationers). There have been several such studies of the effects on youths of intensive parole supervision plus special counseling, and their findings are on the whole less encouraging than the probation studies; they are difficult to interpret because of experimental problems, but studies by Boston University in 1966, and by Van Couvering in 1966, report no significant effects and possibly some bad effects from such special programs. But Johnson's studies were unique for the chance they provide to measure both treatment effects and the effect of agency policy.

Johnson, like Warren, assigned experimental subjects to small caseloads and his experiment had the virtue of being performed with two separate populations and at two different times. But in contrast with the Warren case, the Johnson experiment did not engage in a large continuing attempt to choose the experimental counselors specially, to train them specially, and to keep them informed about the progress and importance of the experiment. The first time the experiment was performed, the experimental youths had a slightly lower revocation rate than the controls at six months. But the second time, the experimentals did *not* do better than their controls; indeed, they did slightly worse. And with the experimentals from the first group—those who *had* shown an improvement after six months—this effect wore off at 18 months. In the Johnson study, my colleagues and I found, "intensive" supervision did *not* increase the experimental youths' risk of detection. Instead, what was happening in the Johnson experiment was that the first time it had been performed—just as in the Warren study—the experimentals were simply revoked less often per number of offenses committed, and they were revoked for offenses more serious than those which prompted revocation among the controls. The second time around, this "policy" discrepancy disappeared; and when it did, the "improved" performance of the experimentals disappeared as well. The enthusiasm guiding the project had simply worn off in the absence of reinforcement.

One must conclude that the "benefits" of intensive supervision for youthful offenders may stem not so much from a "treatment" effect as from a "policy" effect—that such supervision, so far as we now know, results not in rehabilitation but in a decision to look the other way when an offense is committed. But there is one major modification to be added to this conclusion. Johnson performed a further measurement (1962b) in his parole experiment: He rated all the supervising agents according to the "adequacy" of the supervision they gave. And he found that an "adequate" agent, whether he was working in a small *or* a large caseload, produced a relative improvement in his charges. The converse was not true: An *in*adequate agent was more likely to produce youthful "failures" when he was given a *small* caseload to supervise. One can't much help a "good" agent, it seems, by reducing his caseload size; such reduction can

[6]But one of these reports, by Kawaguchi (1967), also found that an intensively supervised juvenile, by the time he finally "failed," had had more previous *detentions* while under supervision than a control juvenile had experienced.

only do further harm to those youths who fall into the hands of "bad" agents.

So with youthful offenders, Johnson found, intensive supervision does not seem to provide the rehabilitative benefits claimed for it; the only such benefits may flow not from intensive supervision itself but from contact with one of the "good people" who are frequently in such short supply.

INTENSIVE SUPERVISION OF ADULTS

The results are similarly ambiguous when one applies this intensive supervision to adult offenders. There have been several studies of the effects of intensive supervision on adult parolees. Some of these are hard to interpret because of problems of comparability between experimental and control groups (general risk ratings, for instance, or distribution of narcotics offenders, or policy changes that took place between various phases of the experiments), but two of them (California, 1966; Stanton, 1964) do not seem to give evidence of the benefits of intensive supervision. By far the most extensive work, though, on the effects of intensive supervision of adult parolees has been a series of studies of California's Special Intensive Parole Unit (SIPU), a 10-year-long experiment designed to test the treatment possibilities of various special parole programs. Three of the four "phases" of this experiment produced "negative results." The first phase tested the effect of a reduced caseload size; no lasting effect was found. The second phase slightly increased the size of the small caseloads and provided for a longer time in treatment; again there was no evidence of a treatment effect. In the fourth phase, caseload sizes and time in treatment were again varied, and treatments were simultaneously varied in a sophisticated way according to personality characteristics of the parolees; once again, significant results did not appear.

The only phase of this experiment for which positive results were reported was Phase Three. Here, it was indeed found that a smaller caseload improved one's chances of parole success. There is, however, an important caveat that attaches to this finding: When my colleagues and I divided the whole population of subjects into two groups—those receiving supervision in the North of the state and those in the South—we found that the "improvement" of the experimentals' success rates was taking place primarily in the North. The North differed from the South in one important aspect: Its agents practiced a policy of returning both "experimental" and "control" violators to prison at relatively high rates. And it was the North that produced the higher success rate among its experimentals. So this improvement in experimentals' performance was taking place only when accompanied by a "realistic threat" of severe sanctions. It is interesting to compare this situation with that of the Warren studies. In the Warren studies, experimental subjects were being revoked at a relatively *low* rate. These experimentals "failed" less, but they also committed more new offenses than their controls. By contrast, in the Northern region of the SIPU experiment, there was a policy of *high* rate of return to prison for experimentals; and here, the special program *did* seem to produce a real improvement in the behavior of offenders. What this suggests is that when intensive supervision *does* produce an improvement in offenders' behavior, it does so not through the mechanism of "treatment" or "rehabilitation," but instead through a mechanism that our studies have almost totally ignored—the mechanism of *deterrence*. And a similar mechanism is suggested by Lohman's study (1967) of intensive supervision of probationers. In this study intensive supervision led to higher total violation rates. But one also notes that intensive supervision combined the highest rate of technical violations with the lowest rate for *new* offenses.

THE EFFECTS OF COMMUNITY TREATMENT

In sum, even in the case of treatment programs administered outside penal institutions, we simply cannot say that this treatment in itself has an appreciable effect on offender behavior. On the other hand, there is one encouraging set of findings that emerges from these studies. For from many of them there flows the strong suggestion that even if we can't "treat" offenders so as to make them do better, a great many of the programs designed to rehabilitate them at least did not make them do *worse*. And if these programs did not show the advantages of actually rehabilitating, some of them did have the advantage of being less onerous to the offender himself without seeming to pose increased danger to the community. And some of these programs—especially those involving less restrictive custody, minimal supervision, and early release—simply cost fewer dollars to administer. The information on the dollar costs of these programs is just beginning to be developed but the implication is clear: *that if we can't do more for (and to) offenders, at least we can safely do less.*

There is, however, one important caveat even to this note of optimism: In order to calculate the true costs of these programs, one must in each case include not only their administrative cost but also the cost of maintaining in the community an offender population increased in size. This population might well not be committing new offenses at any greater rate; but the offender population might, under some of these plans, be larger in absolute *numbers*. So the total number of offenses committed might rise, and our chances of victimization might therefore rise too. We need to be able to make a judgment about the size and probable duration of this effect; as of now, we simply do not know.

DOES NOTHING WORK?

7. *Do all of these studies lead us irrevocably to the conclusion that nothing works, that we haven't the faintest clue about how to rehabilitate offenders and reduce recidivism? And if so, what shall we do?*

We tried to exclude from our survey those studies which were so poorly done that they simply could not be interpreted. But despite our efforts, a pattern has run through much of this discussion—of studies which "found" effects without making any truly rigorous attempt to exclude competing hypotheses, of extraneous factors permitted to intrude upon the measurements, of recidivism measures which are not all measuring the same thing, of "follow-up" periods which vary enormously and rarely extend beyond the period of legal supervision, of experiments never replicated, of "system effects" not taken into account, of categories drawn up without any theory to guide the enterprise. It is just possible that some of our treatment programs *are* working to some extent, but that our research is so bad that it is incapable of telling.

Having entered this very serious caveat, I am bound to say that these data, involving over two hundred studies and hundreds of thousands o individuals as they do, are the best available and give us very little reason to hope that we have in fact found a sure way of reducing recidivism through rehabilitation. This is not to say that we found no instances of success or partial success; it is only to say that these instances have been isolated, producing no clear pattern to indicate the efficacy of any particular method of treatment. And neither is this to say that factors *outside* the realm of rehabilitation may not be working to reduce recidivism—factors such as the tendency for recidivism to be lower in offenders over the age of 30; it is only to say that such factors seem to have little connection with any of the treatment methods now at our disposal.

From this probability, one may draw any of several conclusions. It may be simply that our programs aren't yet good enough—that the education we provide to inmates is still poor education, that the therapy we administer is not administered skillfully enough, that our intensive supervision and counseling do not yet provide enough personal support for the offenders who are subjected to them. If one wishes to believe this, then what our correctional system needs is simply a more full-hearted commitment to the strategy of treatment.

It may be, on the other hand, that there is a more radical flaw in our present strategies—that education at its best, or that psychotherapy at its best, cannot overcome, or even appreciably reduce, the powerful tendency for offenders to continue in criminal behavior. Our present treatment programs are based on a theory of crime as a "disease"—that is to say, as something foreign and abnormal in the individual which can presumably be cured. This theory may well be flawed, in that it overlooks—indeed, denies—both the normality of crime in society and the personal normality of a very large proportion of offenders, criminals who are merely responding to the facts and conditions of our society.

This opposing theory of "crime as a social phenomenon" directs our attention away from a "rehabilitative" strategy, away from the notion that we may best insure public safety through a series of "treatments" to be imposed forcibly on convicted offenders. These treatments have on occasion become, and have the potential for becoming, so draconian as to offend the moral order of a democratic society; and the theory of crime as a social phenomenon suggests that such treatments may be not only offensive but ineffective as well. This theory points, instead, to decarceration for low-risk offenders—and, presumably, to keeping high-risk offenders in prisons which are nothing more (and aim to be nothing more) than custodial institutions.

But this approach has its own problems. To begin with, there is the moral dimension of crime and punishment. Many low-risk offenders have committed serious crimes (murder, sometimes) and even if one is reasonably sure they will never commit another crime, it violates our sense of justice that they should experience no significant retribution for their actions. A middle-class banker who kills his adulterous wife in a moment of passion is a "low-risk" criminal; a juvenile delinquent in the ghetto who commits armed robbery has, statistically, a much higher probability of committing another crime. Are we going to put the first on probation and sentence the latter to a long-term in prison?

Besides, one cannot ignore the fact that the punishment of offenders is the major means we have for *deterring* incipient offenders. We know almost nothing about the "deterrent effect," largely because "treatment" theories have so dominated our research, and "deterrence" theories have been relegated to the status of a historical curiosity. Since we have almost no idea of the deterrent functions that our present system performs or that future strategies might be made to perform, it is possible that there is indeed something that works—that to some extent is working right now in front of our noses, and that might be made to work better—something that deters rather than cures, something that does not so much reform convicted offenders as prevent criminal behavior in the first place. But whether that is the case and, if it is, what strategies will be found to make our deterrence system work better than it does now, are questions we will not be able to answer with data until a new family of studies has been brought into existence. As we begin to learn the facts, we will be in a better position than we are now to judge to what degree the prison has become an anachronism and can be replaced by more effective means of social control.

BIBLIOGRAPHY OF STUDIES REFERRED TO BY NAME

Adams, Stuart. "Effectiveness of the Youth Authority Special Treatment Program: First Interim Report." Research Report No. 5. California Youth Authority, March 6, 1959. (Mimeographed.)

Adams, Stuart. "Assessment of the Psychiatric Treatment Program: Second Interim Report." Research Report No. 15. California Youth Authority, December 13, 1959. (Mimeographed.)

Adams, Stuart. "Effectiveness of Interview Therapy with Older Youth Authority Wards: An Interim Evaluation of the PICO Project." Research Report No. 20. California Youth Authority, January 20, 1961. (Mimeographed.)

Adams, Stuart. "Assessment of the Psychiatric Treatment Program, Phase I: Third Interim Report." Research Report No. 21. California Youth Authority, January 31, 1961. (Mimeographed.)

Adams, Stuart. "An Experimental Assessment of Group Counseling with Juvenile Probationers." Paper presented at the 18th Convention of the California State Psychological Association, Los Angeles, December 12, 1964. (Mimeographed.)

Adams, Stuart, Rice, Rogert E., and Olive, Borden. "A Cost Analysis of the Effectiveness of the Group Guidance Program." Research Memorandum 65–3. Los Angeles County Probation Department, January 1965. (Mimeographed.)

Adams, Stuart. "Development of a Program Research Service in Probation." Research Report No. 27 (Final Report, NIMH Project MH007 18.) Los Angeles County Probation Department, January 1966. (Processed.)

Adamson, LeMay, and Dunham, H. Warren. "Clinical Treatment Of Male Delinquents. A Case Study in Effort and Result," *American Sociological Review,* XXI, 3 (1956), 312–320.

Babst, Dean V., and Mannering, John W. "Probation versus Imprisonment for Similar Types of Offenders: A Comparision by Subsequent Violations," *Journal of Research in Crime and Delinquency,* II, 2 (1965), 60–71.

Bernsten, Karen, and Christiansen, Karl O. "A Resocialization Experiment with Short-term Offenders," *Scandinavian Studies in Criminology,* I (1965), 35–54.

California, Adult Authority, Division of Adult Paroles. "Special Intensive Parole Unit, Phase I: Fifteen Man Caseload Study." Prepared by Walter I. Stone. Sacramento, Calif., November 1956. (Mimeographed.)

California, Department of Corrections. "Intensive Treatment Program: Second Annual Report." Prepared by Harold B. Bradley and Jack D. Williams. Sacramento, Calif., December 1, 1958. (Mimeographed.)

California, Department of Corrections. "Special Intensive Parole Unit, Phase II: Thirty Man Caseload Study." Prepared by Ernest Reimer and Martin Warren. Sacramento, Calif., December 1958. (Mimeographed.)

California, Department of Corrections. "Parole Work Unit Program: An Evaluative Report." A memorandum to the California Joint Legislative Budget Committee, December 30, 1966. (Mimeographed.)

California, Department of the Youth Authority. "James Marshall Treatment Program: Progress Report." January 1967. (Processed.)

Cambridge University, Department of Criminal Science. *Detention in Remand Homes.* London: Macmillan, 1952.

Craft, Michael, Stephenson, Geoffrey, and Granger, Clive. "A Controlled Trial of Authoritarian and Self-Governing Regimes with Adolescent Psychopaths," *American Journal of Orthopsychiatry,* XXXIV, 3 (1964), 543–554.

Empey, LeMar T. "The Provo Experiment: A Brief Review." Los Angeles: Youth Studies Center, University of Southern California. 1966. (Processed.)

Feistman, Eugene G. "Comparative Analysis of the Willow-Brook-Harbor Intensive Services Program, March 1, 1965 through February 28, 1966." Research Report No. 28. Los Angeles County Probation Department, June 1966. (Processed.)

Forman, B. "The Effects of Differential Treatment on Attitudes, Personality Traits, and Behavior of Adult Parolees." Unpublished Ph.D. dissertation, University of Southern California, 1960.

Fox, Vernon. "Michigan's Experiment in Minimum Security Penology," *Journal of Criminal Law, Criminology, and Police Science,* XLI, 2 (1950), 150–166.

Freeman, Howard E., and Weeks, H. Ashley. "Analysis of a Program of Treatment of Delinquent Boys," *American Journal of Sociology,* LXII, 1 (1956), 56–61.

Garrity, Donald Lee. "The Effects of Length of Incarceration upon Parole Adjustment and Estimation of Optimum Sentence: Washington State Correctional Institutions." Unpublished Ph.D. dissertation, University of Washington, 1956.

Gearhart, J. Walter, Keith, Harold L., and Clemmons, Gloria. "An Analysis of the Vocational Training Program in the Washington State Adult Correctional Institutions." Research Review No. 23. State of Washington, Department of Institutions, May 1967. (Processed.)

Glaser, Daniel. *The Effectiveness of a Prison and Parole System.* New York: Bobbs-Merrill, 1964.

Goldberg, Lisbeth, and Adams, Stuart. "An Experimental Evaluation of the Lathrop Hall Program." Los Angeles County Probation Department, December 1964. (Summarized in: Adams, Stuart. "Development of a Program Research Service in Probation," pp. 19–22.)

Great Britain. Home Office. *The Sentence of the Court: A Handbook for Courts on the Treatment of Offenders.* London: Her Majesty's Stationery Office, 1964.

Guttman, Evelyn S. "Effects of Short-Term Psychiatric Treatment on Boys in Two California Youth Authority Institutions." Research Report No. 36. California Youth Authority, December 1963. (Processed.)

Hammond, W. H., and Chayen, E. *Persistent Criminals: A Home Office Research Unit Report.* London: Her Majesty's Stationery Office, 1963.

Harrison, Robert M., and Mueller, Paul F. C. "Clue Hunting About Group Counseling and Parole Outcome." Research Report No. 11. California Department of Corrections, May 1964. (Mimeographed.)

Havel, Joan, and Sulka, Elaine. "Special Intensive Parole Unit: Phase Three." Research Report No. 3. California Department of Corrections, March 1962. (Processed.)

Havel, Joan. "A Synopsis of Research Report No. 10, SIPU Phase IV—The High Base Expectancy Study." Administrative Abstract No. 10. California Department of Corrections, June 1963. (Processed.)

Havel, Joan. "Special Intensive Parole Unit—Phase Four: 'The Parole Outcome Study.'" Research Report No. 13. California Department of Corrections, September 1965. (Processed.)

Hood, Roger. Homeless Borstal Boys: *A Study of Their After-Care and After-Conduct.* Occasional Papers on Social Administration No. 18. London: G. Bell & Sons, 1966.

Jacobson, Frank, and McGee, Eugene. "Englewood Project: Re-education: A Radical Correction of Incarcerated Delinquents." Englewood, Colo.: July 1965. (Mimeographed.)

Jesness, Carl F. "The Fricot Ranch Study: Outcomes with Small versus Large Living Groups in the Rehabilitation of Delinquents." Research Report No. 47 California Youth Authority, October 1, 1965. (Processed.)

Johnson, Bertram. "Parole Performance of the First Year's Releases, Parole Research Project: Evaluation of Reduced Caseloads." Research Report No. 27. California Youth Authority, January 31, 1962. (Mimeographed.)

Johnson, Bertram. "An Analysis of Predictions of Parole Performance and of Judgments of Supervision in the Parole Research Project," Research Report No. 32. California Youth Authority, December 31, 1962. (Mimeographed.)

Kassebaum, Gene, Ward, David, and Wilnet, Daniel. *Prison Treatment and Parole Survival: An Empirical Assessment.* New York: Wiley, 1971.

Kawaguchi, Ray M., and Siff, Leon, M. "An Analysis of Intensive Probation Services—Phase II." Research Report No. 29. Los Angeles County Probation Department, April 1967. (Processed.)

Kettering, Marvin E. "Rehabilitation of Women in the Milwaukee County Jail: An Exploration Experiment." Unpublished Master's Thesis, Colorado State College, 1965.

Kovacs, Frank W. "Evaluation and Final Report of the New Start Demonstration Project." Colorado Department of Employment, October 1967. (Processed.)

Lavlicht, Jerome, et al., in *Berkshire Farms Monographs,* I, 1 (1962), 11–48.

Levinson, Robert B., and Kitchenet, Howard L. "Demonstration Counseling Project." 2 vols. Washington, D.C.: National Training School for Boys, 1962–1964. (Mimeographed.)

Lohman, Joseph D., et al., "The Intensive Supervision Caseloads: A Preliminary Evaluation." The San Francisco Project: A Study of Federal Probation and Parole. Research Report No. 11. School of Criminology, University of California, March 1967. (Processed.)

McClintock, F. H. *Attendance Centres.* London. Macmillan, 1961.

McCord, William and Joan. "Two Approaches to the Cure of Delinquents," *Journal of Criminal Law, Criminology, and Police Science,* XLIV, 4 (1953), 442–467.

McCorkle, Lloyd W., Elias, Albert, and Bixby, F. Lovell. The Highfields Story: *An Experimental Treatment Project for Youthful Offenders.* New York: Holt, 1958.

McCravy, Newton, Jr., and Delehanty, Dolores S. "Community Rehabilitation of the Younger Delinquent Boy, Parkland Non-Residential Group Center." Final Report, Kentucky Child Welfare Research Foundation, Inc., September 1, 1967. (Mimeographed.)

Mandell, Wallace, *et al.* "Surgical and Social Rehabilitation of Adult Offenders." Final Report. Montefiore Hospital and Medical Center, With Staten Island Mental Health Society. New York City Department of Correction, 1967. (Processed.)

Massimo, Joseph L., and Shore, Milton F. "The Effectiveness of a Comprehensive Vocationally Oriented Psychotherapeutic Program for Adolescent Delinquent Boys," *American Journal of Orthopsychiatry,* XXXIII, 4 (1963), 634–642.

Minet, Joshua, III, Kelly, Francis J., and Hatch, M. Charles. "Outward Bound Inc.: Juvenile Delinquency Demonstration Project, Year End Report." Massachusetts Division of Youth Service, May 31, 1967.

Narloch, R. P., Adams, Stuart, and Jenkins, Kendall J. "Characteristics and Parole Performance of California Youth Authority Early Releases." Research Report No. 7. California Youth Authority, June 22, 1959. (Mimeographed.)

New York State, Division of Parole, Department of Correction. "Parole Adjustment and Prior Educational Achievement of Male Adolescent Offenders, June 1957-June 1961." September 1964. (Mimeographed.)

O'Brien, William J. "Personality Assessment as a Measure of Change Resulting from Group Psychotherapy with Male Juvenile Delinquents." The Institute for the Study of Crime and Delinquency, and the California Youth Authority, December 1961. (Processed.)

Persons, Roy W. "Psychological and Behavioral Change in Delinquents Following Psychotherapy," *Journal of Clinical Psychology,* XXII, 3 (1966), 337–340.

Persons, Roy W. "Relationship Between Psychotherapy with Institutionalized Boys and Subsequent Community Adjustment," *Journal of Consulting Psychology,* XXXI, 2 (1967), 137N141.

Pilnick, Saul, *et al.* "Collegefields: From Delinquency to Freedom." A Report . . . on Collegefields Group Educational Center. Laboratory for Applied Behavioral Science, Newark State College, February 1967. (Processed.)

Robison, James, and Kevotkian, Marinette. "Intensive Treatment Project: Phase II. Parole Outcome: Interim Report." Research Report No. 27. California Department of Corrections, Youth and Adult Correctional Agency, January 1967. (Mimeographed.)

Rudoff, Alvin. "The Effect of Treatment on Incarcerated Young Adult Delinquents as Measured by Disciplinary History." Unpublished Master's thesis, University of Southern California, 1960.

Saden, S. J. "Correctional Research at Jackson Prison," *Journal of Correctional Education,* XV (October 1962), 22–26.

Schnur, Alfred C. "The Educational Treatment of Prisoners and Recidivism," *American Journal of Sociology,* LIV, 2 (1948), 142–147.

Schwitzgebel, Robert and Ralph. "Therapeutic Research: A Procedure for the Reduction of Adolescent Crime." Paper presented at meetings of the American Psychological Association, Philadelphia, Pa., August 1963.

Schwitzgebel, Robert and Kolb, D. A. "Inducing Behavior Change in Adolescent Delinquents," *Behavior Research Therapy, I* (1964), 297–304.

Seckel, Joachim P. "Experiments in Group Counseling at Two Youth Authority Institutions." Research Report No. 46. California Youth Authority, September 1965. (Processed.)

Seckel, Joachim P. "The Fremont Experiment, Assessment of Residential Treatment at a Youth Authority Reception Center." Research Report No. 50. California Youth Authority, January 1967. (Mimeographed.)

Shelley, Ernest L. V., and Johnson, Walter F., Jr. "Evaluating an Organized Counseling Service for Youthful Offenders," *Journal of Counseling Psychology,* VIII, 4 (1961), 351–354.

Shoham, Shlomo, and Sandberg, Moshe. "Suspended Sentences in Israel: An Evaluation of the Preventive Efficacy of Prospective Imprisonment," *Crime and Delinquency,* X, 1 (1964), 74–83.

Stanton, John M. "Delinquencies and Types of Parole Programs to Which Inmates are Released." New York State Division of Parole, May 15, 1963. (Mimeographed.)

Stanton, John M. "Board Directed Extensive Supervision." New York State Division of Parole, August 3, 1964. (Mimeographed.)

Stuerup, Georg K. "The Treatment of Sexual Offenders," *Bulletin de la societe internationale de criminologie* (1960), pp. 320–329.

Sullivan, Clyde E., Mandell, Wallace. "Restoration of Youth Through Training: A Final Report." Staten Island, New York: Wakoff Research Center, April 1967. (Processed.)

Taylor, A. J. W. "An Evaluation of Group Psychotherapy in a Girls' Borstal," *International Journal of Group Psychotherapy,* XVII, 2 (1967), 168–177.

Truax, Charles B., Wargo, Donald G., and Silber, Leon D. "Effects of Group Psychotherapy with High Adequate Empathy and Nonpossessive Warmth upon Female Institutionalized Delinquents," *Journal of Abnormal Psychology,* LXXI, 4 (1966), 267–274.

Warren, Marguerite. "The Community Treatment Project after Five Years." California Youth Authority, 1966. (Processed.)

Warren, Marguerite, *et al.* "Community Treatment Project, an Evaluation of Community Treatment for Delinquents: a Fifth Progress Report." C.T.P. Research Report No. 7. California Youth Authority, August 1966. (Processed.)

Warren, Marguerite, *et al.* "Community Treatment Project, an Evaluation of Community Treatment for Delinquents: Sixth Progress Report." C.T.P. Research Report No. 8. California Youth Authority, September 1967. (Processed.)

Wilkins, Leslie T. "A Small Comparative Study of the Results of Probation," *British Journal of Criminology,* VIII, 3 (1958), 201–209.

Zivan, Morton. "Youth in Trouble: A Vocational Approach." Final Report of a Research and Demonstration Project, May 31, 1961-August 31, 1966. Dobbs Ferry, N.Y., Children's Village, 1966. (Processed.)

SECTION EIGHT

Summary

After reading these four discussions of imprisonment and treatment alternatives, one feels quite ready to despair and throw up his or her hands in total confusion. It seems that imprisonment is inherently evil but that any alternative is doomed to failure. We are approaching the twenty-first century with more questions than answers!

In one sense, it is indeed the case that we know very little about effectively dealing with offenders. Putting youthful offenders into institutions does not seem to solve many problems, but virtually every other alternative yields equally disappointing results. Yet this is not to say that we know nothing about corrections, because our knowledge is advanced even when we come up with negative findings. For example, it is becoming painfully obvious that we are not able to change behaviors that may have been learned over a period of years. Rehabilitation does not occur in a brief encounter. Furthermore, there may be forces operating in the social milieu that are exerting pressure on offenders. The individual's behavior may be unchangeable in light of the social context. Rehabilitation is not simply a matter of dealing with attitudes or motivations. The entire social environment may come into play.

Tittle's discussion of the meaning of rehabilitation raises many questions. The data that have been gathered on correctional outcomes are not sensitive enough to the multidimensional aspect of rehabilitation. How does one define success or failure? How can it be proved that prisons do not rehabilitate? Perhaps the most perplexing issue in Tittle's presentation is that we may never have good answers to these questions because we cannot experiment with human subjects as we can with animal subjects. If we could randomly assign subjects to treatment groups and control groups without being confronted with basic issues of due process and human rights, we could learn a great deal. But there is a limit to human experimentation, and consequently our knowledge will remain limited.

MacNamara's discussion taps another controversial aspect of correctional philosophy. Are we attempting to change behaviors by treating offenders, or are we really extracting retribution and punishment? Even if the medical model does not work, could it not be the case that punishment of offenders serves some sort of a cathartic social need? Could it not be argued that since crime is unjust, the punishment due will probably also be unjust to a certain degree? MacNamara's "new penologists" may reflect an antirehabilitation philosophy that simply argues for societal protection. Is incapacitation a sufficient justification for imprisonment?

Lerman's discussion of the success or failure of alternative treatment programs poses a problem similar to Tittle's nagging question of what is meant by rehabilitation. When one adds up internal and external failures and carefully considers the "social bookkeeping" method used, there is little evidence that alternative programs are more effective than traditional institutionalization. However, Lerman is quick to point out that humanitarian considerations may be the overriding concern. How does one reconcile Lerman's recommendation with the social justice model discussed by MacNamara?

The final reading selection by the late Robert Martinson has received widespread publicity. The article is based on a monumental study of correctional treatment. Martinson's review of treatment types is quite extensive, but his conclusions are not encouraging. Some instances of success have been found, but overall no clearly effective method of treatment emerges. Martinson's concluding section should be read very carefully. There are still many unexplained issues regarding rehabilitation, but what we do know is disturbing. Once again, we are confronted with the question of rehabilitation versus retribution, incapacitation, or deterrence. Are we dealing with an unresolvable problem? Why bother at all with delinquent offenders if the outcome is failure?

SECTION NINE

Diverting Offenders from the Juvenile Court

Diversion refers to the process of turning offenders away from the formal justice system toward community-based alternatives that are less punitive and less stigmatizing (though the term has also been used to describe a form of discretion in police screening and a process of reducing the exposure of offenders to formal court proceedings). Many of the initial arguments justifying the need for the diversion of juveniles away from the justice system toward alternative treatment programs in the community have been derived from the principles of labeling and differential association theories.

Proponents of labeling theory argued that the juvenile court should be an agency of last resort and popularized the concept of "judicious nonintervention" (Lemert, 1967). Those who subscribed to differential association theory saw institutions for youthful offenders as "schools for crime" where petty noncriminal offenders were grouped with serious delinquent offenders. Both schools of thought argued that the juvenile court had become as much of a social work agency as a court of law. It had become too powerful, too indiscriminate, and above all too heavy-handed in dealing with youths. Something of a reform movement arose in the 1960s, centering on alternative approaches to juvenile justice: it rode the coattails of the civil rights movement, the growing frustration with rapidly rising delinquency rates, and an emerging sense of due process of law considerations for juveniles. At present, diversion is in effect a social movement that has received strong endorsement from all sectors of society.

There are several conceivable advantages to a juvenile diversion program. First, it promotes alternative processing of offenders by referring youths to existing community treatment programs in lieu of the traditional juvenile justice system. Second, the diversion of status offenders allows the juvenile court system to focus its attention on hard-core criminal offenders. Third, formal diversion programs that establish clear standards and precise alternatives introduce an element of procedural regularity and reduce arbitrary decisionmaking by law enforcement officials. Finally, the diversion of noncriminal offenders to alternative programs should result in considerable financial savings by reducing the sheer number of offenders that appear in the juvenile courts.

On the other hand, a number of disadvantages to diversion might offset the apparent advantages. For example, the application of diversion principles may result in a "widening of the net." In other words, more offenders may be pulled into the system with the expansion of services for noncriminal offenses. Similarly, ambiguity arising from the various meanings of *diversion* may lead to questionable practices, particularly as the term relates to due process of law considerations. There is also some evidence that diversion programs decrease rather than increase community tolerance by giving inordinate attention to noncriminal offenders. Last, as discussed in the previous section on alternatives, there is scant evidence that diversion programs are effective.

The three readings that follow underscore the uncertainties that shroud the issue of diversion. Frederick Howlett's discussion examines the use of the Youth Service Bureau (YSB) as a diversion agency. The conclusion is that the YSB may not significantly advance the rights of children. The article by Bruce Bullington et al. suggests that diversion programs are potentially as abusive as the juvenile courts themselves: the authors find most of the programs naive and impracticable. Dean Rojek's discussion argues that, in the shifting of juvenile offenders from the public sector to the private, a new array of problems may arise. While the juvenile court system is riddled with questionable practices, the potential for abuse is far greater when juvenile offenders are turned over to community agencies. All three readings cast doubt on the wisdom of the total acceptance of diversion as the solution to current problems of the juvenile court system.

Is the Youth Service Bureau All It's Cracked Up to Be?*

Frederick W. Howlett

For every social wrong there must be a remedy. But the remedy can be nothing less than the abolition of the wrong. Halfway measures, mere ameliorations and secondary reforms, can at any time accomplish little, and can in the long run avail nothing. Our charities, our penal laws, our restrictions and prohibitions by which with so little avail we endeavor to assuage poverty and check crime, what are they, at the very best, but the device of the clown who, having put the whole burden on his ass in one pannier, sought to enable the poor animal to walk straight by loading up the other pannier with stones.[1]

Even as he wrote this, Henry George was besieged with calls from newspapers and churches for contributions to fresh-air funds which, at best, removed children from their tenement homes for a short time.

The 1966 study of the President's Commission on Law Enforcement and Administration of Justice, recognizing the myriad problems facing the juvenile courts of America, suggested the creation of youth service bureaus, which it envisioned as "central coordinators of all community services for young people . . . [which] would also provide services lacking in the community or neighborhood, especially ones designed for less seriously delinquent youth."[2]

Despite the vagueness of this definition and the lack of knowledge or agreement concerning either the desirability of or the necessity for youth service bureaus, the concept became tremendously popular throughout the nation. When the Commission's report was published in February 1967, there were only about a half-dozen organizations operating as youth service bureaus. In the next three years more than 40 of the 55 states and territories established agencies so labeled, and, by 1971, more than 150 such organizations were operating throughout the country. Federal, state, local, and private funds amounting to well over $21 million were expended to support them. In March 1973, when this was written, I was not able to locate anyone who knew how many youth service bureaus there were or how much they were costing.

In 1967, coincident with the Commission's suggestions for alleviating the juvenile courts' caseloads, NCCD adopted a goal of diverting from the juvenile court all cases that community programs could handle more effectively.[3] In 1970 the mechanism of the youth service bureau (YSB) as a means of diverting children from the justice system was made a national program priority by the NCCD Board of Trustees.[4]

Throughout the history of children-centered services in America, promising ideas have been altered in practice with diastrous results for the child. Because of this and because of the mushroom-like growth of youth service bureaus without due consideration or either philosophical underpinnings of probable consequences to the community, the YSB concept and strategy of "noncoercive intervention" must be questioned.

THE YSB: A FUNCTIONAL DEFINITION

When the community intervenes in the life of a child, the degree and substance of that intervention should relate directly to the child's rights as well as to his needs. Therefore, in an effort to determine ways in which children may be provided assistance without legal intervention, NCCD has studied the concept of the youth service bureau for over five years. In March 1972, NCCD published the first definitive work dealing with the concept, approach, and problem areas associated with youth service bureaus. Designed to help communities address their needs in concert with their children's, *The Youth Service Bureau: A Key to Delinquency Prevention* defines the youth service bureau as "a noncoercive, independent public agency

*Adapted from a paper presented May 18, 1971, at the National Conference on Social Welfare Dallas, Texas.

SOURCE: Frederick W. Howlett, "Is the YSB All It's Cracked Up to Be," from *Crime and Delinquency,* Volume 91, No. 4, October, 1973, pp. 485–492. Reprinted with permission of the National Council on Crime and Delinquency.

[1]Henry George, "First Principles," *Social Problems* (New York: Doubleday, Page, 1906), p. 81.

[2]President's Commission on Law Enforcement and Administration of Justice, *The Challenge of Crime in a Free Society* (Washington, D.C.: U.S. Government Printing Office, 1967), p. 83.

[3]National Council on Crime and Delinquency, "Goals and Recommendations" (New York: NCCD, n.d.), p. 7.

[4]National Council on Crime and Delinquency, Minutes of the Meeting of the Executive Committee of the Board of Trustees, New York, June 1970, p. 4 (mimeo).

Reprinted with permission of the National Council on Crime and Delinquency from Frederick W. Howlett, "Is the YSB All It's Cracked Up to Be?" *Crime and Delinquency,* October 1973, pp. 485–492.

established to divert children and youth from the justice system by (1) mobilizing community resources to solve youth problems; (2) strengthening existing youth resources and developing new ones; and (3) promoting positive programs to remedy delinquency-breeding conditions."[5]

NCCD's definition of the YSB implies three distinct functions:

1. Organization sufficient to "mobilize" community resources.

2. Resource modification to provide existing community agencies with the means to provide the services for which they were established.

3. Resource development, or the creation of new agencies designed to meet the unmet needs of youth.

Two additional functions are not definitionally implied:

4. Service brokerage, through which the YSB acts both as referral agent for children in need of service and as advocate for the child to insure that he receives the services for which he was referred.

5. Direct service to children in those instances where their problems may be quickly resolved (through purchase, crisis counseling, etc.).

HISTORICAL ANTECEDENTS

Diversion of children from the criminal justice system is not a new idea. Probably the first legally recognized attempt to divert children was the enactment of the Illinois Juvenile Court Act in 1899. Like the youth service bureau of today, the purpose of this early legislation was to decriminalize children. In reality, the problem of the errant child was transferred, magnified, and expanded. *All* children would be "treated," regardless of their acts or desires, separately from the treatment of adults.

A "new" system was developed. Vacated jails became "juvenile detention homes"; "guards" became "youth supervisors"; a system of prisons for children, carefully labeled "state reform schools," "industrial schools," or, more recently, "treatment centers," was established, and children, many of them not charged with criminal acts, soon filled them up.

Texas, for example, considered by some authorities as having one of the most expansive systems of state training schools in the nation, is plagued by an inordinately

Table 1[a]

COMMITMENTS TO TEXAS STATE TRAINING SCHOOLS, 1966–1970

	1966	1967	1968	1969	1970
Total	2746	3033	2547	2328	2713
Noncriminal commitments[b]	805	891	826	776	942
Percentage of total commitments	29.3%	29.4%	32.4%	33.3%	34.7%

[a] SOURCE: *Annual Report of the Texas Youth Council to the Governor* (1966-1970).
[b] Limited to truant, runaway, ungovernable, vagrant/bad associates, malicious mischief (vandalism).

Table 2[a]

NEW YORK DISPOSITIONS: PINS V. DELINQUENT CHILDREN COMMITTED OR PLACED IN STATE TRAINING SCHOOLS, 1966-1970

	1966	1967	1968	1969	1970
Total	1761	1677	1601	1545	1312
Delinquent	1103	1007	919	913	679
PINS	658	670	682	632	633
Percentage of total (PINS)	37.4%	40.0%	42.6%	40.9%	48.2%

[a] SOURCE: *Report of the New York State Judicial Conference,* 1966-1970.

high number of nondelinquent juvenile commitments. Over one-third of the total juvenile commitments in 1970 were for acts of truancy, running away, ungovernability, vagrancy/bad associates, and malicious mischief (randalism). Further, the proportion of noncriminal juvenile commitments to the state training schools seems to be increasing (see Table 1).

The essential characteristic distinguishing the juvenile court from its adult counterpart was and in many respects continues to be the absence of constitutional rights, which were routinely afforded adults charged with criminal offenses.

The magnificent experiment caught on, and the result, exemplified in Table 1, was quite predictable. The juvenile court broadened its scope, and its umbrella opened to shelter virtually every child who walked the streets. It brought more and more children into its system through its all-encompassing definition of delinquency. Its resources—the probation departments, detention homes, and training schools—soon became congested.

To alleviate the congestion—and again in the spirit of justice—another definitional concept was created. The Person in Need of Supervision (PINS) came into being. Originally the PINS concept was designed to deal with the child who, though delinquent in the sense that he had misbehaved, had not actually committed a criminal act. PINS legislation clearly stated that these children would not be committed to state training schools.

As with other attempts to process noncriminal children through the court rather than address the fundamental problem, however, the PINS approach put even more strain on the system. Eager to assume the parental role, the courts, police, and probation departments zealously exercised jurisdiction over children at the mere whim of parents or legal guardians, thereby relieving them of their parental responsibility. Children were still arrested, charged and, in an extremely loose sense, "tried," but this was accepted because they were no longer being labeled delinquent.

After processing by the courts and "treatment" by largely untrained and unqualified probation staffs, nondelinquent children were still placed in state training schools along with delinquents. Violation of court-ordered terms of "supervision" is, after all, contempt of court and therefore a delinquent act.

New York State, one of the earliest to initiate PINS legislation, provides a classic example of the point made here: over 40 percent of *all* commitments or placements to state training schools in recent years have been PINS children, as shown in Table 2. Over 80 percent of all female commitments or placements in New York State training schools from 1966 to 1970 were PINS children.

And now we have the youth service bureau. The question of its desirability and relevance must be raised. In haste to provide a helpful service to children trapped in situations beyond their control, the community has often failed to recognize the dangers inherent in the well-meaning services it creates.

[5] Sherwood Norman, *The Youth Service Bureau: A Key to Delinquency Prevention* (Paramus, N.J.: National Council on Crime and Delinquency, 1972), p. 8.

FLAWS IN THE CONCEPT

As conceived in the 1967 report of the President's Commission on Law Enforcement and Administration of Justice, the youth service bureau was to function as both advocate for the child and resource for the agency faced with troubled children whose problems could not appropriately be addressed by the Juvenile court. It would receive both delinquent and nondelinquent children referred by the police, the juvenile court, parents, schools, and other sources.

Diversion does not respond to the denial of certain basic rights of individuals—the rights to associate with those of their choice and to engage voluntarily in acts that harm no one but themselves. The drunk who clogs our courts should have the right to get drunk; the homosexual, of age to exercise his judgment, should have the right to do so behind his apartment door; the prostitute and her client should not have to answer to the law for an act that is their personal decision. The misbehaving child likewise has a fundamental right to be a child, and if he has committed no act that would be considered criminal were he an adult, why seek recourse through the courts and why create another agency to divert him from the courts?

Diversion, as it is presently conceived, is not based upon consideration of the fundamental rights of children but is another in a series of responses to the economic needs of a juvenile justice system so inadequately formulated that it has become inoperable. Diversion of children through the mechanism of the youth service bureau may be a counterproductive response to the problem caused by a humanitarian but misdirected attempt to cure the ills of all mankind.

As with other attempts to divert from the justice system those who ought not be its objects in the first place, the youth service bureau, though laudable in intent, may fail if it is viewed as freeing the polity and its agencies from direct confrontation with problems engendered through structural and social inequities which, historically, have tended to obstruct the rights of children. Rubin has pointed out that our system of handling children is designed to protect and nourish them. To this end, they are surrounded by protective statutes. As a result the child is restricted in his daily living; he is not permitted to enter into contracts, buy liquor, read certain types of books, attend certain events, or express himself sexually. On the other hand, he must attend school, he must register for the draft, and he must obey his parents. Indeed, are children considered people?[6]

Are we creating still another agency to relieve existing community agencies and parents of their responsibility to children as people? More important, will the YSB continue to interfere with the mature child's right to determine his own destiny?

Conceptually, the youth service bureau views diversion of children to nonjudicial resources as an extra-legal solution to economic problems now confronting the juvenile justice system—a solution that will enable the community to continue to control and constrain its youthful population.

Will further development of the youth service bureau broaden the umbrella of ineffective services for children?

We must seriously ask whether the youth service bureau is necessary in a society which many authorities feel has already gone too far in transferring family problems and responsibilities to the public domain. Is the YSB desirable in those communities that thus far have relegated both social and academic education to inadequate school systems; mental and emotional health to psychiatry; religion to churches; recreation to the boys' clubs; and welfare to the state? Is it not conceivable that the youth service bureau, through creation and development of more agencies, will contribute to even further disintegration of the family unit which, for decades, has been society's whipping boy for the deliquency problem?

There are some who maintain that the youth service bureau effectively precludes the illegitimate exercise of authority over its youthful clients. The rationale for this position (that the problem lies not with the concept of the YSB, but with the community's interpretation and application of the concept) neatly sidesteps the basic issue.[7] The same rationale could be applied to juvenile court and PINS legislation. Analytically this is a sound argument; pragmatically, however, kids continue to be adjudicated delinquent or in need of supervision and end up prisoners in training schools or other "treatment" agencies. We cannot separate the concept from its application in real life. If the concept allows for such gross misinterpretation and misapplication, as do the juvenile court and PINS concepts, then it should be revised or abandoned.

Klapmuts raises a question concerning the validity of the YSB's "noncoercive" nature:

> If referral by the agency or Bureau for services or treatment in the community is backed by the threat of referral to court, then the allegedly nonpenal agency is really an adjunct of the justice system and "diversion" a verbal fiction. On the other hand, if the agency's powers are based on nothing more than the ability of personnel to *persuade* a youth to accept services, then the Youth Service Bureau would seem to be an excellent means of insuring both the right of the individual to receive treatment and his right to refuse services he does not view as helpful or necessary.[8]

It is difficult to understand how "persuasion" of an eight- or ten-year-old child (probably referred to a youth service bureau by a uniformed, badge-wearing, pistol-packing policeman) to accept services could amount to anything but coercion.

There is the distinct possibility that the presence of the youth service bureau will also rid existing community agencies of their responsibilities. In 1971, when we originally raised this issue, our concern centered in the routine use of the youth service bureau by schools and law enforcement agencies as a convenient catchall for their problems. Since then we have provided consultation and evaluation services to youth service bureaus in five states and have found, without exception, that YSB's eagerly direct truants to counselors or tutors; we have yet to succeed in persuading the schools to modify their programing, which, in all probability, contributes to the truancy problem.

We have also found that the YSB's provide police officers (potentially the most influential "social workers" on the contemporary scene) with an easy way to avoid exercising their discretion. Where policemen previously returned most errant children to their homes—a procedure which to some extent required the parents to deal with them—they are now sending them to the youth service bureau. Such children immediately become the subject

[6]Sol Rubin, "Children as Victims of Institutionalization," a paper given at the Central Regional Conference of the Child Welfare League of America, Indianapolis, Ind., March 31, 1971.

[7]Nora Klapmuts, "Children's Rights—The Legal Rights of Minors in Conflict with Law of Social Custom," *Crime and Delinquency Literature,* September 1972, p. 473.

[8]*Ibid.*

of a file and, in the more sophisticated YSB's (those with diagnostic or clinical services immediately available), become labeled as some sort of mild deviate, but deviate nonetheless.

Labeling notwithstanding, youth service bureaus require referrals in order to survive. The routine and often inappropriate use of the youth service bureau by any number of agencies fosters the illusion that something constructive is being done for the community's children and tends to perpetuate the YSB by providing it with statistical justification for its continued existence.

In one midwestern community, for example, continued funding of the youth service bureau was justified by a local law enforcement department's assertion that fully one-third of its juvenile contacts were referred to the bureau. The department's annual statistical report for the preceding year, however, showed a comparable drop in the number of children released to the family. There is reason to suspect that in this instance the YSB actually discouraged police officers from returning children to their homes.

The agency-oriented approach utilized by existing YSB's only rationalizes a need for more agencies to address problems after the fact rather than preventing them in the first place. By so doing, the YSB may also spare the community the task of addressing the problems where they originate: the home and the school—the basic structure of contemporary society.

Will the YSB provide a cop-out for the community, its polity, and its children, or can it provide services to kids who heretofore have received short shift, not only in the legal arena but in the social as well?

Before rushing to treat or "help" a person outside the justice system, should not the community first consider the alternative of doing nothing? Should it not recognize the child's right, as a person, to nontreatment and noninterference by an outside authority? In response to our original paper in 1971, upon which this article is based, a youth service bureau director wrote:

> Those people engaged in creating a working model for diverting young people from the juvenile justice system must heed an even greater *caveat* than Mr. Howlett's. In order for a Youth Services Bureau to be effective within a community (if in fact it is necessary for it to be in the community initially) the staff must be aware of creating their own reason for existence. That is, as so many other social service agencies have done, the Youth Services Bureau must not seek out problems to solve and must not continuously attempt to justify its being for the sake of security. By definition, a Youth Services Bureau should be created to be destroyed. There should be a self-destruct mechanism built into the structure of every Youth Services Bureau whether it is a success or a failure. If a Youth Services Bureau is a success, the community—with time—will accept its responsibility, redefine its guidelines of acceptable behavior, and assimilate into its strength those elements which the Youth Services Bureau proves can work; if a Youth Services Bureau is a failure it should be abandoned as one would abandon a doomed ship.[9]

CONCLUSION

Intolerant of behavior that does not comply with its present, immovable norms, America has chosen to try changing that behavior. In attempting to identify and "treat" the most venial forms of deviance, many of which neither require nor are amenable to treatment, the community blinds itself to its inability to tolerate, absorb, or modify its concept of deviance.

The youth service bureau, as presently conceived and operating, appears to be another manifestation of the child-saving movement described by Platt in 1969:

> The child-saving movement further illustrates that corrections may be understood historically as a succession of reforms. Academics have demonstrated a remarkably persistent optimism about reform, and operate on the premise that they can have a humanitarian influence on correctional administration. . . .
>
> There is little evidence to support this faith in the ultimate wisdom of policy-makers in corrections.
>
> Nevertheless, the optimism continues, and . . . [present] . . . correctional policy consists of "A redoubling of efforts in the face of persistent failure."[10]

The same may be said for child-service planners. They are required to accommodate current community definitions of deviance. Child-service administrators, in turn, are required to manage the child-victims of popular "curative" fads and fashions. Neither planner nor administrator has substantial influence on legislators, much less law enforcement and other community agencies. There is no clear mandate issued by any accountable agency or individual other than "Help children."

Unfortunately, the community is forced to live and deal with its proven failures. As an inevitable result, the child-service planners and administrators "are doomed to annual investigations, blue-ribbon commissions, ephemeral research studies, and endless volumes of propaganda and muckraking. They live with the inevitability of professional mediocrity, poor salaries, uncomfortable living conditions, ungrateful 'clients' and tenuous links with established institutions."[11]

The community clearly must redefine its limits of acceptable behavior. It cannot economically or morally continue to create new intrusive enterprises supplying comprehensive prophylaxis. It must learn to accept much of the deviance that may not be in accord with its life styles, moralistic beliefs, or concepts of social justice.

---

[9]Ed Underwood, Director, San Angelo (Texas) Youth Services Bureau.

[10]Anthony Platt, "The Rise of the Child Saving Movement," *Annuals*, January 1969, p. 37.

[11]*Id.*, p. 38.

A Critique of Diversionary Juvenile Justice

Bruce Bullington, James Sprowls, Daniel Katkin, and Mark Phillips

The increasingly zealous support today for diversion of youth from the juvenile justice system is a consequence of several widely held notions: (1) Traditional strategies for dealing with juvenile offenders have not worked; (2) informal diversion is used both widely and effectively now; and (3) the most humane treatment of troubled youth is based upon the parens patriae philosophy of justice. Yet, the authors contend, diversion may be seen as potentially dangerous and harmful, and they present several arguments against expansion of diversionary services: (1) The concept's ambiguity allows many to promote expansion of the juvenile justice system in the form of diversion "to" other programs, while true diversion "from" the system is nonexistent; (2) the goals of diversionary programs—such as elimination of stigmatizing labels and formal duplication of existing informal processes—are unattainable; (3) formal diversion is incompatible with due process ideals. Until these difficulties have been resolved, diversionary options should be viewed with caution.

The atmosphere of juvenile justice systems today is charged with talk of diversion.[1] Professionals are planning diversionary programs and worrying about the feasibility of implementation.[2] Books, monographs, and articles are being rushed into publication.[3] Research projects are being funded.[4] Diversion is widely advertised as a panacea not only for delinquency but also for the inequities and imperfections of the juvenile justice system.[5] The National Advisory Commission on Criminal Justice Standards and Goals, for example, was sufficiently convinced about the worth of diversionary programs to suggest that the rate of delinquency cases coming to court should be reduced by 70 percent between 1973 and 1983.[6]

Several considerations underlie this "faddish" interest in diversion: (1) widespread dissatisfaction with the inequities and failures of traditional strategies for the treatment and prevention of delinquency; (2) recurring observations that the well-established practice of informal, unofficial diversion has great social utility; and (3) continuing concern for the effective and humane resolution of the problems of troubled children. While agreeing that these motives combine to create a compelling justification for reform, our purpose in this paper is to argue *against* the widespread development of diversionary programs. We believe that these programs are impracticable, that they are fraught with potential for inequity and abuse, and that they involve implicit renunciation of the civil libertarian values articulated in Supreme Court decisions such as *In re Gault*.[7] Before developing these objections it will be useful to explore in detail the reasons behind the contemporary interest in diversion.

BRUCE BULLINGTON is Associate Professor, Division of Community Development, College of Human Development, Pennsylvania State University. JAMES SPROWLS is Instructor, Division of Community Development, College of Human Development, Pennsylvania State University. DANIEL KATKIN is Associate Professor of Law, College of Human Development, Pennsylvania State University. MARK PHILLIPS is a doctoral candidate, Community Systems Planning and Development Program, Pennsylvania State University.

1. The term *diversion* is generally used to refer to the policy of processing youngsters accused of misbehavior away from the juvenile justice system's formal mechanisms of adjudication and institutional care. Donald R. Cressey and Robert A. McDermott, *Diversion from the Juvenile Justice System* (Washington, D.C.: National Institute of Law Enforcement and Criminal Justice, 1974), pp. 3-4, observe: "If 'true' diversion occurs, the juvenile is safely out of the official realm of the juvenile justice system and he is immune from incurring the delinquent label or any of its variations—predelinquent, delinquent tendencies, bad guy, hard core, unreachable. Further, when he walks out the door from the person diverting him, he is technically free to tell the diverter to go to hell. We found very little 'true' diversion in the communities studied." In the absence of "true" diversion, professionals have been developing diversionary programs which seek to process misbehaving youngsters away from juvenile courts, reform schools, and the stigmatizing labels associated with official delinquency. Diversionary programs, however, generally require some degree of participation in structured treatment of one type or another. We focus our attention in this paper on diversionary programs rather than on the pure, but generally unimplemented, concept of "true" diversion.

2. See, for example, Pennsylvania Department of Public Welfare, *Juvenile Justice: A Stance for Cooperation* (Harrisburg, Pa.: Pennsylvania Department of Public Welfare, December 1974).

3. See, for example, the following books: Robert M. Carter and Malcolm W. Klein, *Back on the Street: The Diversion of Juvenile Offenders* (Englewood Cliffs, N.J.: Prentice-Hall, 1976); Daniel Katkin, Drew Hyman, and John Kramer, *Delinquency and the Juvenile Justice System* (North Scituate, Mass.: Duxbury Press, 1976). Monographs include: Cressey and McDermott, *Diversion from the Juvenile Justice System*; Raymond T. Nimmer, *Diversion: The Search for Alternative Forms of Prosecution* (Chicago: American Bar Foundation, 1974); Edwin M. Lemert, *Instead of Court: Diversion in Juvenile Justice* (Chevy Chase, Md.: National Institute of Mental Health, Center for Studies of Crime and Delinquency, 1971). See also the following articles: Thomas H. Kelley, Judy L. Schulman, and Kathleen Lynch, "Decentralized Intake and Diversion," *Juvenile Justice*, February 1976, pp. 3-11; Phillip Z. Cole, "Diversion and the Juvenile Court: Competition or Cooperation," *Juvenile Justice*, February 1976, pp. 33-37; Michael Wald, "State Intervention on Behalf of Neglected Children: A Search for Realistic Standards," *Stanford Law Review*, April 1975, pp. 985-1040; "A Symposium: Juveniles and the Law," *American Criminal Law Review*, Summer 1974, pp. 1-189; John Stratton, "Crisis Intervention Counseling and Police Diversion from the Juvenile Justice System: A Review of the Literature," *Juvenile Justice*, May 1974, pp. 44-53; Sanford J. Fox, "The Reform of Juvenile Justice: The Child's Right to Punishment," *Juvenile Justice*, August 1974, pp. 2-9.

4. See, for example, Cressey and McDermott, *Diversion from the Juvenile Justice System*.

5. See, for example, National Advisory Commission on Criminal Justice Standards and Goals, *A National Strategy to Reduce Crime* (Washington, D.C.: U.S. Govt. Printing Office, 1973), pp. 23-25.

6. The commission recommended that juvenile status offenses be removed from the jurisdiction of juvenile courts and that the rate of nonstatus delinquency cases (those involving acts which would be crimes if committed by adults) be cut to half the 1973 rate. Ibid.

7. In re Gault, 387 U.S. 1 (1967).

Reprinted with permission of the National Council on Crime and Delinquency from Bruce Bullington et al., "A Critique of Diversionary Juvenile Justice," *Crime and Delinquency*, January 1978, pp. 59–71.

RATIONALE FOR DIVERSION

Dissatisfaction with Present System

During the past twenty years the juvenile justice system has been subjected to scathing denunciations by journalists, scholars, judges, politicians, administrators, and concerned citizens.[8] For example, so reputable an authority as Dean Roscoe Pound described the juvenile court as a tribunal more awesome in its abuse of power than the star chamber.[9] Between 1965 and 1971 the constitutionality of juvenile court procedures received four major challenges: On three occasions the Supreme Court found that the rights of children were being violated.[10] In *Kent* v. *U.S.* the Court observed:

> Some juvenile courts . . . lack the personnel, facilities and techniques to perform adequately as representatives of the State in a *parens patriae* capacity, at least with respect to children charged with law violation. There is evidence, in fact, that there may be grounds for concern that the child receives the worst of both worlds: That he gets neither the protections afforded adults nor the solicitous care and regenerative treatment postulated for children.[11]

Mixed with criticism of the juvenile courts is widespread dissatisfaction with the quality of, treatment programs available for adjudicated delinquents. In *In re Gault* the Supreme Court went so far as to suggest that the term *reform school* is little more than a euphemism for prison:

> However euphemistic the title, a "receiving home" or an "industrial school" for juveniles is an institution of confinement in which the child is incarcerated for a greater or lesser time. His world becomes "a building with white-washed walls, regimented routine and institutional laws. . . ." Instead of mother and father and sisters and brothers and friends and classmates, his world is peopled by guards, custodians, state employees, and "delinquents" confined with him for anything from waywardness to rape and homicide.[12]

Christian Science Monitor editor Howard James and Philadelphia Judge Lisa Richette, to cite only two examples, have argued that institutions for delinquents are among the least humane in the nation.[13] Numerous investigative reporters are loudly voicing the same view.[14] Senator Birch Bayh contends:

> Too many young people are thrown into custodial institutions . . . [which are characterized by] punishment, isolation, neglect, and abuse . . . [including] harassment, affront to human dignity, and the gross denial of human rights.[15]

A picture of the formal structures of juvenile justice has begun to emerge which paints them not as agencies for the protection of children but rather as agencies from which children need to be protected. This picture has been reinforced by growing acceptance of propositions derived from labeling theory[16] —namely, that the imposition of stigmatizing labels such as "delinquent" may propogate deviant self-concepts and exacerbate patterns of lawbreaking behavior. The National Advisory Commission on Criminal Justice Standards and Goals observed:

> People . . . tend to become what they are told they are. The stigma of involvement with the criminal justice system, even if only in the informal processes of juvenile justice, isolates persons from lawful society and may make further training or employment difficult.[17]

To the extent that this is true, the juvenile justice system may be characterized not merely as "unfair," "inadequate," or "unresponsive," but also as a cause of delinquency. Even such an established figure as Milton Luger, head of the delinquency division of the Law Enforcement Assistance Administration and formerly director of juvenile correction for New York State and chairman of the National Association of State Juvenile Delinquency Program Administrators, has conceded:

> With the exception of a relatively few youths it [would be] better for all concerned if young delinquents were not detected, apprehended, or institutionalized. Too many of them get worse in our care.[18]

Criticism such as this, public dismay about the high cost of institutional services,[19] and increasingly militant minority groups—whose members are disproportionately likely to be singled out for delinquent labels and treatment[20] —have driven juvenile justice professionals to search for alternatives. That diversion has emerged as an attractive alternative is due, in part, to recurring observations that many misbehaving youngsters are already diverted from the formal mechanisms of juvenile justice with apparently beneficial results.

Diversion: The Rule

To appreciate the extent to which diversion already exists, one must recognize the pervasiveness of what might be considered delinquent behavior. Delinquency studies using self-reports of previous behavior indicate that almost 90 percent of all young people commit offenses for which they could be adjudicated delinquent.[21] Obviously, most of these youngsters never come to the attention of the police. In Pennsylvania, for example, it is estimated that there are 1.4 million children whose behavior would sustain a finding of delinquency[22]; yet, in 1971, only 92,000 were taken into custody by agents of any of the state's more than 4,000 police jurisdictions.[23] That doesn't mean that the other 1.3 million were actively diverted; most, quite likely, were never detected by anyone. In many other cases, the delinquencies were noticed by parents, neighbors, shopkeepers, teachers, social workers, and even policemen—who decided not to invoke the formal processes of law.[24] That is true diversion.

Diversion of youngsters from the formal processes of adjudication continues in police-juvenile interaction:

> Of 92,000 children against whom proceedings were initiated by the police in Pennsylvania in 1971, 47,000 (52 percent) were released without further referral. It is conceivable, but improbable, that the police decided that more than half of their juvenile arrests were made without cause. It is more likely that police divert known juvenile offenders as frequently as they detain them.[25]

This diversionary process does not stop with the police. In many states, statutes specifically authorize pretrial hearings at which probation officers attempt "informal adjustment" of cases.[26] In Pennsylvania, only one-third of the cases sent by the police to juvenile court result in findings of delinquency or neglect.[27] Some of the other 30,000 cases are resolved on the basis of factual innocence; most, however, appear to be instances of diversion.[28]

Even among the 15,000 formally adjudicated Pennsylvania youngsters, only about one-fourth are institutionalized.[29] If this is not a form of true diversion, it is at least an example of a closely related concept: "minimization of penetration."[30]

It can be argued, then, that juvenile justice systems are already in the business of diverting young offenders from formal adjudication and institutional treatment. The recent interest in expanded systems of diversionary justice seems to be motivated by three beliefs: (1) Diverted youngsters are less likely than institutionalized juveniles to persist in delinquent careers[31]; (2) the benefits of current diversionary practices are disproportionately likely to be

8. See, for example, Howard James, *Children in Trouble: A National Scandal* (New York: McKay, 1970); Francis A. Allen, "Criminal Justice, Legal Values and the Rehabilitative Ideal," *Journal of Criminal Law, Criminology and Police Science*, September-October 1959, pp. 226-32; Orman Ketcham, "The Unfulfilled Promise of the American Juvenile Court," in *Justice for the Child*, M. Rosenheim, ed. (New York: Free Press, 1962); Lisa Richette, *The Throwaway Children* (Philadelphia: Lippincott, 1969).
9. Roscoe Pound, "Foreword," *Social Treatment in Probation and Delinquency*, Pauline Young (New York: McGraw-Hill, 1937), p. xxvii.
10. Kent v. United States, 383 U.S. 541 (1966); In re Gault, 387 U.S. 1 (1967); In re Winship, 397 U.S. 358 (1970); McKeiver v. Pennsylvania, 403 U.S. 528 (1971) (finding against the right to a jury trial in juvenile court).
11. Kent v. United States 383 U.S. 541, 555-6 (1966).
12. In re Gault, 387 U.S. 1, 27 (1967).
13. James, *Children in Trouble*, and Richette, *The Throwaway Children*.
14. See, for example, the 1971 documentary by the National Broadcasting Corporation: *This Child Is Rated X*.
15. U.S., Congress, Senate, Committee on the Judiciary, Subcommittee to Investigate Juvenile Delinquency, 92d Cong., 1st sess., May 3-18, 1971.
16. See Katkin, Hyman, and Kramer, *Delinquency and the Juvenile Justice System*, pp. 57-66.
17. National Advisory Commission, *National Strategy to Reduce Crime*, p. 23.
18. Quoted in James, *Children in Trouble*, p. 108.
19. See Robert D. Vinter, George Downs, and John Hall, *Juvenile Corrections in the States: Residential Programs and Deinstitutionalization* (Ann Arbor, Mich.: National Assessment of Juvenile Corrections, November 1975), pp. 20-29.
20. See, for example, Melvin P. Sikes, *The Administration of Injustice* (New York: Harper & Row, 1975); and Irving Piliavin and Scott Brier, "Police Encounters with Juveniles," *American Journal of Sociology*, September 1964, pp. 206-14.
21. See, for example, Martin Gold, *Delinquent Behavior in an American City* (Belmont, Calif.: Brooks/Cole, 1970); National Council on Crime and Delinquency Survey, *A Feasibility Study of Regional Juvenile Detention* (Hackensack, N.J.: NCCD, 1971).
22. Katkin, Hyman, and Kramer, *Delinquency and the Juvenile Justice System*, p. 133.
23. Ibid.
24. Ibid., pp. 134, 175-79. See also Sophia Robinson, *Can Delinquency Be Measured?* (New York: Columbia University Press, 1936).
25. Katkin, Hyman, and Kramer, *Delinquency and the Juvenile Justice System*, p. 135.
26. See, for example, Pennsylvania Juvenile Act of 1972, Section 18.
27. Katkin, Hyman, and Kramer, *Delinquency and the Juvenile Justice System*, p. 136.
28. Ibid.
29. Ibid., p. 137.
30. This term is used by Cressey and McDermott, *Diversion from the Juvenile Justice System*, to describe programs which do not qualify as "true" diversion but which operate to minimize the use of formal sanctions.
31. See Katkin, Hyman, and Kramer, *Delinquency and the Juvenile Justice System*, pp. 396-400.

bestowed upon white or affluent youths[32]; and (3) social services from community agencies are purchased by many of the offenders now diverted from the juvenile justice system; these should be augmented and publicly subsidized to meet the needs of a new class of diverted youngsters.[33]

With the possible exception of differential treatment based upon race and income, little evidence is available to support these beliefs.[34] Nevertheless, advocates of diversionary programs contend with certainty that families and social service agencies are currently providing advocacy and other services to large numbers of young offenders and that those offenders and the larger community benefit from the arrangement.[35]

In short, dissatisfaction with the formal mechanisms of juvenile justice *combined* with uninformed interest in traditional informal practices has produced this enthusiasm for diversion.

Diversion and Parens Patriae Justice

The widespread popularity of diversionary programs is due to the fact that they offer the appearance of significant reform without any major modification of values. The extension of "benign," "helping," community-based services to a larger population of youngsters is altogether compatible with the traditional parens patriae values of juvenile justice—namely, that treatment for juveniles should be therapeutic and nonpunitive and that procedures should be informal and nonstigmatizing.

These values have dominated the juvenile justice system since the turn of the century when zealous reformers created children's courts to "divert" young offenders from the stigmatizing and punitive processes of the criminal justice system.[36] Most planners and practitioners involved in developing diversionary programs subscribe to these values, whose attractiveness derives from the fact that they seek to introduce humanitarian aims and social scientific principles into the law, and whose power derives from the fact that they have broad constituencies among liberals, social scientists, and helping professionals. Diversionary programs appear to aid in "reforming" institutions without so much as suggesting a need to reassess objectives.

THE ARGUMENT AGAINST DIVERSION

Three related concerns underlie our opposition to diversionary programs: (1) The concept of diversion is dangerously ambiguous; (2) the goals of these programs may be unattainable; and (3) diversionary efforts may be incompatible with concepts of due process and fundamental fairness.

Definitional Ambiguity

In general usage the word *diversion* has two meanings. We may speak of diversion *from* something or of diversion *to* something. Diversion of youngsters from the juvenile justice system implies that the system will be limited in scope and authority. This makes sense in light of the persistent criticism that the processes of juvenile justice are unfair, stigmatizing, and dysfunctional.[37] But to achieve diversion from the juvenile justice system, no new "programs" are necessary. Increasing the number of programs for juvenile offenders is incompatible with the idea of diversion from the system: New programs, however we label them, are certainly a part of the overall system for responding to delinquency, and sending youngsters to those programs cannot fairly be characterized as keeping them out of the system. Diversion from the system—true diversion, as it is sometimes called—suggests that resources for the treatment of deviant youngsters ought to be reduced. If there are fewer programs, there will be room for fewer youngsters, and more will have to be diverted.[38] From this perspective, the phrase *diversionary program* is a contradiction. When new programs are proposed it can only be because it is hoped that youngsters will be diverted *to* them, thus remaining within the overall system.

At present, the term *diversion* is used, somewhat self-servingly, as if its two meanings were entirely compatible. Thus, critics of the juvenile justice system describe it as dehumanizing, argue that its caseload should be reduced, and call for diversion *to* new programs. In the name of diverting youngsters from the system, communities are asked to make additional resources available so that new treatment modalities can be created for youngsters who might otherwise be left alone.

The confusion between diverting children *from* the system and diverting them to new parts of it might be pardonable if it were clear that these new programs would provide humane, nonstigmatizing, helpful treatment for young offenders who had been fairly and equitably determined to need it. However, the evidence that new diversionary efforts will be more equitable or more effective than the traditional programs of juvenile courts, probation departments, and reform schools is not there.

Impracticable Goals

Advocates of diversionary programs are committed to the notion that services provided outside the aegis of the formal mechanisms of the juvenile justice system will be superior. They argue that these new programs will be less stigmatizing than traditional treatment and will provide services similar to those currently received by youngsters now informally diverted out of the system. Neither argument is persuasive.

There is no reason to believe that the labels imposed by Youth Service Bureaus and other instruments of diversion will be nonstigmatizing. The term *delinquent*, it should be remembered, was coined by turn-of-the-century reformers who wished to spare youngsters the stigma of criminality. It did not take long for popular language to catch up with this professional euphemism; Americans have known for a long time that delinquent is a nice way of saying "young hoodlum." Of course, it is possible to shift euphemisms again, but to believe that the public will not catch on and that the new terms *(child in need of supervision*, or *person in need of services)* will not convey stigma is naive. True diversion from the juvenile justice system might save children from the negative impact of stigmatizing labels; creating new labels by new programs will have little effect on the labeling process or on the secondary deviance labeling is thought to engender.[39]

Advocates of diversionary programs argue that youngsters currently adjudicated delinquent would benefit from the types of informal, supportive services available to youngsters who are currently being diverted. Indeed, it can be argued that adjudicated delinquents are a population discriminated against and deprived because they lack the resources to *purchase* the humane, effective support services available to middle- and upper-class children. It is hoped that if informal, community-based services are made available to more young offenders, fewer youths will be adjudicated. While the argument is attractive, there is little evidence to support its assumptions. Do affluent youngsters and their families actually purchase the types of services that will be provided through diversionary programs? Have such services been effective in preventing the eventual adjudication of offenders purchasing them? We do not know.

Furthermore, the argument that the present system of informal diversion can be effectively expanded through diversion programs is based upon the assumption that informal processes can be duplicated as part of a formal system. Is there any reason to believe that publicly supported programs, staffed by professionals or civil service employees, can actually function in the same manner as parents and others who are currently involved in informal diversion? Parents are permitted—perhaps even expected—to conceal their youngsters' actions in order to protect the children's interests; public employees cannot do that without seriously compromising themselves. Parents are expected to advocate their children's interests unfalteringly; formal programs will always be under some pressure to protect the community by identifying youngsters who seem to be failing. Professionals' concern with maintaining a program may interfere with their willingness to engage in advocacy on behalf of potentially dangerous youngsters whose trouble-making behavior might compromise that program's recidivism statistics. Advocates in the informal system are free of those types of constraints. To believe that services which are effective as part of an informal process of diversion can be bureaucratized with no loss of effectiveness is simply naive.

Formalized Diversion and Due Process

The nature of diversionary programs is that they involve disposition without adjudication. Services are to be provided outside the justice system without

32. See, for example, Nathan Goldman, *The Differential Selection of Juveniles for Court Appearance* (New York: National Research and Information Center, NCCD, 1963).

33. See, for example, Sherwood Norman, *The Youth Service Bureau: A Key to Delinquency Prevention* (Paramus, N.J.: NCCD, 1972).

34. For a discussion of these issues, see Katkin, Hyman, and Kramer, *Diversion from the Juvenile Justice System*, pp. 167-85, 406-50. See also J. A. Seymour, The Current Status of Youth Services Bureaus (unpub. manuscript, University of Chicago Law School, Center for Studies in Criminal Justice).

35. See, for example, George G. Killinger and Paul F. Cromwell, Jr., *Corrections in the Community* (St. Paul, Minn.: West, 1974), pp. 1-60.

36. See Anthony Platt, "The Rise of the Child Saving Movement: A Study in Social Policy and Correctional Reform," *Annals of the American Academy of Political and Social Science*, January 1969.

37. Ibid., pp. 1-4.

38. This argument is well made by Kai T. Erikson, *Wayward Puritans* (New York: Wiley, 1966), pp. 13-18.

39. See Edwin M. Schur, *Labeling Deviant Behavior* (New York: Harper & Row, 1971).

the stigmatizing processes of judicial or even quasi-judicial decision making. Those "stigmatizing" procedures, however, are also the core of a legal system which seeks to protect innocent people from unwanted intrusions into their lives. The history of the juvenile court testifies to the dangers of dispensing with procedural regularity in order to facilitate helpful treatment.

Juvenile courts, dominated by the parens patriae philosophy of justice, have always conceived of themselves as seeking to provide children in trouble with the type of care and custody they might receive at the hands of "wise" parents. Procedures have always been informal because it was thought to be obvious that the relationship between a parent and child—even an erring child—cannot be regulated by the same rules that apply in adult adjudication. Due process safeguards were generally considered unnecessary and potentially harmful: unnecessary because due process is a safeguard against unfair punishment and juvenile courts were never intended to be punitive; harmful because legalistic rules might interfere with the therapeutic process. As one appellate court put it:

> The natural parent needs no [due] process [of law] to temporarily deprive his child of liberty by confining it in its own home, to save it and to shield it from the consequences of persistence in a career of waywardness, nor is the state, when compelled, as *parens patriae*, to take the place of the father for the same purpose required to adopt . . . [due] process as a means of placing its hands upon the child to lead it into one of its courts.[40]

Such decisions freed the nation's juvenile courts from traditional due process restraint and set the stage for an experiment in informal justice. Lawyers, juries, Fifth Amendment rights, and traditional standards of notice and proof were excluded from delinquency hearings so that attention could focus on issues of treatment rather than on questions about factual and legal guilt.[41] Unfortunately, this "experimental" system has not fared well. It has been characterized by inequity, abuse, and unfairness. Consider, for example, the case of fifteen-year-old Gerald Gault, whose adjudication of delinquency for an alleged obscene telephone call made constitutional history. Gerald's trial took place without any notice of the specific charges against him ever having been given either to him or to his parents. The family was never advised of a right to counsel. The woman to whom the obscene call had allegedly been made was not present in court and could not be cross-examined. Gerald was interrogated by the judges without having been advised of the privilege against self-incrimination. An adult guilty of the same offense could have received a maximum punishment of two months' imprisonment or a fine of up to fifty dollars; Gault, however, was committed for treatment at a state industrial school for a period to extend until he was "cured" or until his twenty-first birthday, whichever came first.

Appalled by such cavalier deprivations of liberty, the United States Supreme Court ruled that any youngster charged with a delinquent act which could result in deprivation of liberty must be accorded "the essentials of due process and fair treatment."[42] The *Gault* decision has been hailed as a victory for civil libertarian values. Professionals in the juvenile system, who generally see themselves as liberal, are typically willing to admit that an unchecked system of parens patriae justice is potentially dangerous, and that *Gault* was a necessary corrective. Yet the concept of diversion, which permits intervention into children's lives with no formal process, has been enthusiastically embraced.

The juvenile justice system has come full circle. The juvenile court, once the informal mechanism of diversion from the stigmatizing and punitive processes of criminal justice, is now the legalistic tribunal from which children are to be diverted. The informal practices of parens patriae justice are being abandoned in juvenile courts only to be re-created in innovative diversion programs. Reformers in the field of juvenile justice do not seem to have learned much from history: They do not yet recognize the basic incompatibility of informality and justice, nor do they recognize that benign intentions are inadequate safeguards of individual liberties.

SUMMARY AND CONCLUSION

The idea that institutional confinement serves to rehabilitate deviants has lost much of its credibility in recent years. In juvenile justice, mental health, and even in adult correction,[43] one finds increasing support for the view that institutions serve the interests neither of society nor of its "deviants." Opposition to the warehousing of human beings in prisons, mental hospitals, and reform schools has become so widespread that it may no longer be fanciful to suggest that the demise of large state institutions is at hand.

It is incumbent upon would-be reformers to develop alternatives to institutionalization which will avoid (or at least minimize) the inequity and waste which have too often characterized current practices. While critics of juvenile justice have been convincingly articulate in documenting the brutality, futility, and injustice of existing programs for the care and custody of delinquents, they have been imprecise and unconvincing in attempts to formulate alternatives. Indeed, a central theme in this paper is that diversionary programs currently in vogue are potentially as abusive as the programs they seek to reform. Innovations being advertised as alternatives to incarceration may prove to be merely alternative forms of incarceration. It is essential that the professional literature stop describing the idea of diversion in optimistic generalities and begin to address itself to serious and difficult questions about the concept's practicability.

Who Is to Be Served?

While all of the talk today suggests that clients in diversionary programs will be youngsters who would otherwise penetrate deeply into the system, the practice may not follow these good intentions. Police officials, probation officers, and courts may use innovative diversionary programs for youngsters who might otherwise have been institutionalized, but they may also use them for youngsters who might otherwise have been ignored or released to the custody of their families. Unless safeguards are built into the system, diversionary programs intended to narrow the domain of the juvenile justice system and promote less restrictive alternatives may result in the official and semi-official processing of larger numbers of young people than ever before. Research on existing "experimental" programs ought to focus on the question of where clients come from: Are they in fact youngsters who would otherwise have been incarcerated or are they often youngsters who might have been left alone? To prevent the possibility of an unintended expansion of the juvenile justice system's confinement capacity, it may prove necessary to close institutional facilities at the same time as opening new programs; otherwise, we will be left with both.

Procedural Safeguards

Current discussion of diversion indicates that none of the recently won rights of juveniles will be applicable in diversionary hearings. One can anticipate hearing familiar justifications for the denial of notice, counsel, cross-examination, and other constitutional rights in informal, treatment-oriented diversion hearings.

The reputedly therapeutic, nonpunitive nature of diversionary programs should not be permitted to serve as an excuse for the abridgement of fundamental constitutional freedoms. Placing properly adjudicated delinquents in these programs may be a commendable alternative to incarceration, but it would be a serious step backward to permit diversionary placements without legal safeguards which assure that the community has a sound basis for any intervention at all. It will be a sad irony, indeed, if the Supreme Court is compelled to observe, some twenty or thirty years hence: "However euphemistic the title, a diversionary program or community treatment facility for juveniles is an agency for the deprivation of liberty. . . ." Research on existing diversionary programs ought to assess the extent to which "voluntary" participation is actually a result of plea bargaining away constitutional rights to minimize the chances of institutional confinement.

The Stigma

As long as institutional confinement is a commonly invoked sanction, lesser sanctions can be expected to be less stigmatizing. In the event that diversionary programs become widespread, with a concomitant reduction in the use of institutions, diverted youngsters may come to be seen as the "most

40. Commonwealth v. Fisher, 213 Pa. 48, 53, 62 At. 198, 200 (1905).

41. For an excellent discussion, see W. V. Stapleton and L. E. Teitelbaum, *In Defense of Youth* (New York: Russell Sage Foundation, 1972), pp. 1-55.

42. In re Gault, 387 U.S. 1, 41 (1967).

43. See, for example, the following discussions of the inadequacies and injustices of current institutional practices: Erving Goffman, *Asylums* (New York: Doubleday, 1961); David J. Rothman, *The Discovery of the Asylum* (Boston: Little, Brown, 1971); Nicholas N. Kittrie, *The Right to Be Different* (Baltimore, Md.: Johns Hopkins Press, 1971); Thomas S. Szasz, *Law, Liberty and Psychiatry: An Inquiry into the Social Uses of Mental Health Practices* (New York: Macmillan, 1963); Thomas S. Szasz, *The Manufacture of Madness* (New York: Harper & Row, 1970); American Friends Service Society, *Struggle for Justice* (New York: Hill & Wang, 1971).

deviant," and participation in diversionary programs may carry a considerable stigma.[44] There is little reason to expect that current efforts will be any more successful than the efforts of the juvenile court reformers who coined the term *delinquent* to avoid the stigma of criminal classification.

Impact on the Poor and on Minorities

The criminal justice and social work professions share a long-standing bias against lower-class and minority lifestyles and social institutions.[45] The capacity of the black family, in particular, to function as a vehicle for socialization and social control is repeatedly questioned by these professions.[46] Diversionary programs are advertised as promoting interactions such as might be found in middle-class white families. Thus, such programs may come to be seen by judges and probation officers as particularly appropriate for youngsters from lower-class and minority cultures. There is no reason to believe that minority group and poor children will not continue to be overrepresented both in the populations of diverted youngsters and in the residual population of institutionalized juveniles.

One overwhelmingly clear lesson is to be learned from the history of juvenile justice in America: namely, that the path to hell is paved with good intentions. If this lesson is lost on the current generation of reformers, today's innovations may well become tomorrow's abuses. Reform of juvenile justice is necessary. It may have to involve bolder and more daring changes in our assumptions about juvenile justice than proponents of diversionary programs apparently perceive.

44. See Kai T. Erickson, *Wayward Puritans*, p. 11.

45. For a critical discussion of this bias, see, for example, Eleanor Bunke Leacock, ed., *The Culture of Poverty: A Critique* (New York: Simon and Schuster, 1971); and Charles A. Valentine, *Culture and Poverty* (Chicago: University of Chicago Press, 1968).

46. Daniel P. Moynihan, *The Negro Family: The Case for National Action* (Washington, D.C.: U.S. Department of Labor, 1965) has probably had the greatest influence on recent policy in the field.

Juvenile Diversion: A Study of Community Cooptation *

Dean G. Rojek

The evolution of the juvenile justice system has been described by some as a series of futile attempts to reinvent the wheel. The Common Law tradition of extending a concerted degree of care and solicitous concern for youthful offenders was seen as empty rhetoric that led to the development of houses of refuge in the early nineteenth century. However, within a few short decades, these houses of refuge became warehouses "for the youthful wastage of a rapidly growing metropolis" (Finestone, 1976: 30). In 1899, the house of refuge movement gave way to the creation of a new judicial system, the juvenile court, that purported to be a kindly parent (Murphy, 1974). Unfortunately, this new system of justice has not been immune from criticism. Commenting on the Supreme Court's first major ruling in 1966 on the juvenile court's disregard for due process of law guarantees, Mr. Justice Fortas stated: "There is evidence, in fact, that there may be grounds for concern that the child receives the worst of both worlds; that he gets neither the protection accorded to adults nor the solicitous care and regenerative treatment postulated for children (*Kent* v. *United States,* 1966). Presently, there is a pervasive sense of disillusionment with the juvenile justice system, prompting David Rothman (1971) to suggest that the tendency to regard major societal innovations as reforms is not only bad logic but bad history.

Our most recent "reform" tactic in juvenile justice is subsumed under the rubric of *diversion*. Because of the multidimensional meanings of the word *diversion,* ambiguity is rife, for different definitions reflect different objectives. For example, for some, "true" diversion is simply the process of turning offenders away from the traditional juvenile justice system. For others, *diversion* connotes not only a turning away but also a referral to a community alternative. Finally, to confound the concept even more, diversion has also been described as an attempt to "minimize penetration into the juvenile justice system" (Cressey and McDermott, 1973). Yet, as confusing and ambiguous as the term *diversion* is, diversion is emerging as one of the most fashionable reform movements in public policy.

Amitai Etzioni, commenting on what he perceives to be the faddist nature of public policy, observed, "Collective amnesia seems to be at work, insuring that each new generation of policy-makers learns little from past mistakes and is as ready as the last to be lured by a new fashion's flashing promise and untested payoff" (1976: 9). And later in this same article, arguing against society's wholesale deinstitutionalization of the mentally ill in referring them to community-based services or providing no services at all, Etzioni concludes, "The sick and the weak are vulnerable enough, without adding to their afflictions the need to adapt to mercurial fashions' (1976: 10). In essence, Etzioni is apprehensive of what may be a reckless and frantic surge to remove individuals from institutions without careful examination of whether placing them in the community affords a significant improvement in their quality of life.

In the area of juvenile justice, diversion is being heralded as more humane and more cost-efficient than the traditional processing of offenders through the juvenile court. Diversion programs redirect the juvenile away from the traditional processing machinery of the juvenile court to a purportedly less stigmatizing and less punitive community-based system. Proponents of diversion also argue that diversion is only about one-tenth as expensive as regular processing, resulting in a savings of approximately $1.5 billion (Gemignani, 1973). Yet, as promising as diversion may be, there is growing apprehension that this form of alternative treatment may not necessarily be inherently benign or efficacious. Beyond the ambiguity that shrouds the concept of diversion, there is mounting concern that there may be a basic incompatibility with highly discretionary or informal decisionmaking and procedural safeguards for due process of law considerations. The history of the juvenile court underscores the fallacy that "benign intentions are inadequate safeguards of individual liberties"

* The research was supported by Grant #79-JN-AX-0026 from the National Institute for Juvenile Justice and Delinquency Prevention, Law Enforcement Assistance Administration, U.S. Department of Justice.

(Bullington et al., 1978). The purpose of this discussion is to investigate the potential dangers of diversionary programs, which may allow the community the right to abridge certain fundamental freedoms of youthful offenders under the guise of helping.

A Case Study of Diversionary Juvenile Justice

The Juvenile Justice and Delinquency Prevention Act of 1974 called for the development of a series of deinstitutionalization programs for status offenders. In 1976, two-year grants were awarded to eleven jurisdictions across the country for the development of community-based alternatives for status offenders. Specifically, the legislative intent of this act was to remove status offenders from detention and correctional institutions in the eleven program sites, to evaluate the impact on the juvenile justice system and the local community, and to determine the relative success or failure of such a deinstitutionalization program. Because of the conceptual ambiguity surrounding this undertaking, the grant awarded to the Pima County, Arizona, Juvenile Court was viewed by the program administrators to be a diversion rather than a deinstitutionalization project. Since the juvenile court had de facto deinstitutionalized status offenders several years prior to the advent of this program, the logical conclusion was that the grant would facilitate the next phase of diversion programs. Armed with over a million-dollar grant, the juvenile court set out to elicit community support for this undertaking.

The objective of this diversion program was for the juvenile court to divest itself of all status offenders by soliciting community agencies to act as service centers for those status offenders in need of assistance. Based on initial screening, a youthful offender might simply be sent home or referred to a community-based program. The juvenile court acted as a service contractor and diversion unit, although status offenders could be referred to the program by any person or agency in the community. The court imposed few restrictions in its request for proposals from local community groups and individuals so as to encourage a high degree of creativity and service diversification. In all a total of twenty community-based diversion programs and one court-based diversion unit were funded during the two-year grant period.

This diversion program was organized in such a way that any of the twenty-one service providers could function as an intake unit. However, most status offenders were referred to the juvenile court. A diversion unit was created within the juvenile court to funnel status offenders out of the formal juvenile justice system. Because of the need to divert offenders out of the processing machinery as soon as possible, it became necessary to allow this diversion unit to function in the field. Thus there emerged the notion of a mobile diversion unit that had the capability of rendering an immediate on-the-spot field adjustment, with no referral for any additional service. In the diversion literature, this is referred to as "true" diversion, in that youth are simply deflected from the official system and sent home. The other option, when some form of treatment or service was warranted was to refer juveniles to a community-based diversion agency.

Figure 1 attempts to illustrate the diversion process as it evolved in the Pima County project. A major change in the source of referrals is reflected in the reduction of police input and the emergence of new referral sources. Prior to the diversion program, upwards of 95 percent of all referrals to the juvenile court came from the law enforcement sector. With the advent of diversion, the police made fewer referrals, while community agencies and institutions became exceptionally active. Specifically, 20.6 percent of referrals came directly from parents, 10.5 percent from schools, and 11.5 percent from community agencies. Further, a new concept was invented—that of "self-referral." Slightly over 10 percent of all diversion clients appeared of their own accord and requested a service. In most instances, these self-referrals were simply the result of diversion agencies actively soliciting any clients who expressed an interest in a particular program. Such new sources of referral may constitute a certain widening of the net, posing a grave danger to the diversion movement. Unless each program is carefully monitored, the community can use diversion agencies as new dumping grounds, replacing the juvenile court. Whereas the police screen virtually all clients sent to the juvenile court, many diversion strategies allow the community to refer juveniles directly to a program. The potential for flagrant violation of human rights needs to be carefully assessed before conduits are built that bypass the police or juvenile court personnel.

As shown in Figure 1, 4,982 juveniles were admitted into the two-year Pima County diversion program. At program intake each youth was either administered some form of crisis intervention (equivalent to true diversion) or else was referred for additional services. Of the total number of clients, 44.4 percent were diverted and 55.6 percent were diverted and referred to a community-based program. The entry point into the diversion program was the critical determinate of which route the client took. Of those diverted ($N = 2,210$), over 95 percent were initially processed by the court's mobile diversion unit (M.D.U.), whereas the twenty community agencies accounted for less than 5 percent of diverted cases. Conversely, of those youth referred for services ($N = 2,772$), mobile diversion accounted for 30.8 percent and the community agencies for 69.2 percent. In other words, the court-based diversion unit tended to reflect more of a non-interventionist perspective than the community-based agencies.

Finally, Figure 1 purports to show the diversion route a juvenile took if he or she were referred for services. If the mobile diversion unit was the initial point of entry and a referral was made, 95.2 percent of these clients were referred to some agency other than this diversion unit itself. Only 4.8 percent were referred to the unit itself (self-referral). On the other hand, if a community agency served as the entry point and a referral was made, 93.4 percent were simply "referred" to the same agency that functioned as an intake unit. Less than 7 percent were referred to some other diversion agency. Once again there looms an imminent danger, when agencies tend to coopt a reform movement for self-aggrandizement.

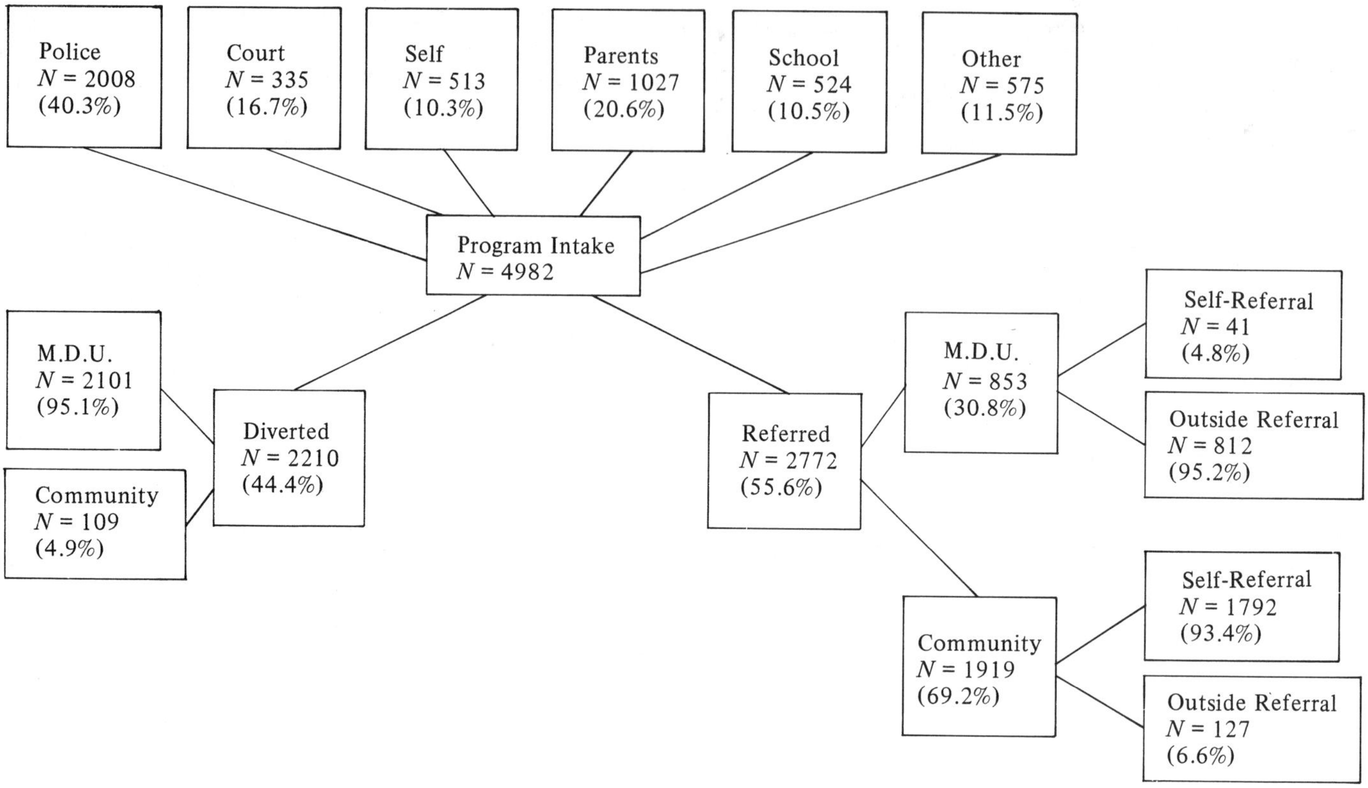

Diversion programs that attempt to closely align themselves with community agencies may become distorted and "diverted" by unintended operational biases.

Table 1 serves to amplify the preliminary findings from Figure 1. In Table 1 the offense committed is cross-tabulated with the diversion service assigned. The twenty-one diversion agencies offered basically six types of services. Crisis intervention without any additional service is a surrogate for true diversion. As indicated in Table 1, 44.4 percent of youths were assigned only crisis intervention. Counseling, shelter care, education, employment, recreation, and "other" (legal services, advocacy, and medical services) constituted a referral for services. Counseling was the most highly utilized referral service, followed by shelter care, recreational activities, educational programs, and employment opportunities.

This diversion project was intended solely for status offenders; but as is indicated in Table 1, slightly over 17 percent of the clients were non-status offenders. Some were placed in the program despite having no offenses (*N* = 361); others were labeled potential runaways (*N* = 257); and still others were termed health and welfare cases (*N* = 163). Although delinquents were clearly not eligible for this program, a small number (*N* = 82) was still admitted. Although this is not shown on Table 1, nearly all the non-status offenders were admitted into the diversion program by one of the community agencies, not the court's mobile diversion unit.

As is indicated in Table 1, each of the various types of programs tended to render services for all types of offenders. It was originally envisioned that shelter care facilities would offer services exclusively for runaways. However, only 27.7 percent were actual runaways, while 19.5 percent were potential runaways and the remaining 52.8 percent represented other forms of delinquent behavior. Similarly, although educational programs were initially created for truants, nearly 80 percent of the clients assigned to an educational program were non-truants. What is imbedded in Table 1 and in fact surfaced as an unintended consequence is the high degree of competition that arose among the various community-based diversion agencies. Slots left unfilled were viewed as programmatic failures. Clients appearing for services became a valued commodity for future funding. Hence all community agencies vied for clients, whether the form of service or treatment was appropriate or not.

Length of Stay in Diversion Programs

Diversion is being touted as a significant advancement in juvenile justice reform because it represents more humane and more cost-efficient treatment. Rather than languishing in the juvenile court process, youthful offenders are administered short-term services in a community setting. Whether any of these assumptions is correct is subject to debate. If diversion represents a widening-of-the-net phenomenon, then more juveniles are being identified as deviant, a situation that could lead to more punitive treatment than that in effect prior to the advent of diversion programs. Similarly, if community-based programs are reluctant to terminate services predicated on agency survival rather than client needs, then the argument for cost effectiveness may also be suspect. True diversion approaches Schur's (1973) objective of non-intervention, but diversion coupled with a referral may be tantamount to Klein's (1976) concept of alternative encapsulation.

In Table 2, the nine offense categories are cross-tabulated with the length of stay in the diversion program. The unit of analysis in Table 2 is the individual (N = 3,283), whereas the unit of analysis in Figure 1 and Table 1 was the number of referrals to the diversion program (N = 4,982). The range of time spent in a diversion program varied from less than a day to a maximum of two years, the actual duration of the grant time period. Examining first the marginal distribution of the length of stay in Table 2, we find that slightly over 50 percent of all diverted youths spent less than one day in the diversion process. Another 18.4 percent spent between one to thirty days, 8.1 percent spent thirty-one to sixty days, and 22.1 percent spent in excess of two months in the program. As shown in Table 2, nearly 10 percent of all offenders spent over six months receiving some form of treatment in a community-based agency. Within this latter group, seventy-three diverted offenders were receiving services for nearly twenty-four months. Table 2 is partially misleading because it does not take into consideration the ceiling effect on length of services provided by the termination of the grant at the end of two years. In a reexamination of the termination dates for clients, it was found that 458 were summarily terminated when the grant expired. The suggestion is that the longer the diversion program was operational, the longer clients would have been receiving services.

A cursory inspection of the cell frequencies in Table 2 reveals some perplexing patterns. Runaway offenders were initially considered the most suitable clients for a referral to a community-based agency such as a shelter care facility. In point of fact, runaway offenders had one of the lowest lengths of stay (66.3 percent terminated in less than one day; $\bar{x}$ = 16.1 days), whereas truancy cases accounted for the longest stays (11.9 percent terminated in less than one day; $\bar{x}$ = 102.1 days).[1] It is also of interest to note that while two out of three actual runaways were terminated in less than twenty-four hours, only one out of five potential runaways was terminated in the same time span. On the average, clients labeled potential runaways spent twice as much time in the program as actual runaways ($\bar{x}$ runaways = 16.1 days, $\bar{x}$ potential runaways = 32.3 days).

The average number of days spent in a diversion program by offense is given at the bottom of Table 2. The overall average number of days spent in a program was 38.5, but this varies from a low of 11.4 days for alcohol-related offenses to a high of 102.1 days for truancy. The intensity of the treatment is not accurately reflected in these data, but Table 2 does convey two distinct ideas. First, diversion is not necessarily synonymous with non-intervention. Nearly 50 percent

[1]While it is possible to argue that the average length of stay for runaway offenders is suppressed because they ran away from the community-based agency, the data do not support this conjecture. The successful completion rate for runaways (79 percent) was in fact slightly higher than for non-runaway offenders (71 percent). The normal "treatment" regimen for runaway offenders called for a twenty-four- to forty-eight-hour stay at a shelter care facility, followed by one or two follow-up counseling sessions. The services for non-runaway offenders often called for daily or weekly involvement at the community agency for an extended period of time.

Table 1 Diversion Service Assigned by Offense at Intake

Offense	*Crisis Intervention*	*Counseling*	*Shelter Care*	*Education*	*Employment*	*Recreation*	*Other*	*Total*	
Runaway	551 (40.2%)	279 (20.3%)	380 (27.7%)	35 (2.6%)	39 (2.8%)	49 (3.6%)	39 (2.8%)	1372 (100.0%)	(27.5%)
Ungovernable	837 (54.7%)	262 (17.1%)	175 (11.5%)	49 (3.2%)	48 (3.1%)	95 (6.2%)	63 (4.1%)	1529 (100.0%)	(30.7%)
Truancy	198 (38.3%)	89 (17.2%)	7 (1.4%)	101 (19.5%)	36 (7.0%)	61 (11.8%)	25 (4.8%)	517 (100.0%)	(10.4%)
Curfew	101 (36.1%)	85 (30.4%)	15 (5.4%)	15 (5.4%)	9 (3.2%)	39 (13.9%)	16 (5.7%)	280 (100.0%)	(5.6%)
Alcohol	180 (42.8%)	167 (39.7%)	8 (1.9%)	11 (2.6%)	12 (2.9%)	20 (4.8%)	23 (5.5%)	421 (100.0%)	(8.5%)
No offense	175 (48.5%)	59 (16.3%)	21 (5.8%)	26 (7.2%)	17 (4.7%)	38 (10.5%)	25 (6.9%)	361 (100.0%)	(7.2%)
Potential R/A	81 (31.5%)	46 (17.8%)	50 (19.5%)	21 (8.2%)	25 (9.7%)	21 (8.2%)	13 (5.1%)	257 (100.0%)	(5.2%)
Health & welfare	69 (42.3%)	29 (17.8%)	10 (6.1%)	19 (11.7%)	13 (8.0%)	11 (6.7%)	12 (7.4%)	163 (100.0%)	(3.3%)
Delinquent	18 (22.0%)	23 (28.0%)	5 (6.1%)	9 (11.0%)	2 (2.4%)	10 (12.2%)	15 (18.3%)	82 (100.0%)	(1.6%)
Total	2210 (44.4%)	1039 (20.9%)	671 (13.5%)	286 (5.7%)	201 (4.0%)	344 (6.9%)	231 (4.6%)	4982 (100.0%)	(100.0%)

Table 2 Length of Stay in Diversion Program by Offense

Length of Stay	*Runaway*	*Ungovernable*	*Truancy*	*Curfew*	*Alcohol*	*No Offense*	*Potential R/A*	*Health & Welfare*	*Delinquent*	*Total*
Less than 1 day	497 (66.3%)	379 (51.1%)	47 (11.9%)	138 (65.6%)	254 (84.9%)	100 (22.3%)	22 (21.8%)	205 (69.0%)	9 (20.0%)	1651 (51.5%)
1–30 days	176 (23.5%)	147 (19.8%)	49 (12.7%)	7 (3.3%)	20 (6.7%)	109 (24.3%)	54 (53.5%)	50 (16.8%)	11 (25.0%)	623
31–60 days	23 (3.0%)	59 (8.0%)	49 (12.7%)	8 (3.9%)	8 (2.5%)	99 (22.0%)	7 (6.9%)	11 (3.7%)	7 (15.0%)	271 (8.1%)
61–120 days	23 (3.0%)	44 (5.9%)	89 (22.8%)	16 (7.8%)	8 (2.5%)	60 (13.3%)	12 (11.9%)	11 (3.7%)	9 (20.0%)	272 (8.0%)
121–180 days	8 (1.1%)	36 (4.9%)	49 (12.7%)	23 (11.0%)	4 (1.3%)	22 (4.9%)	5 (4.9%)	8 (2.7%)	2 (5.0%)	157 (4.8%)
181 or more	23 (3.0%)	77 (10.4%)	106 (27.2%)	18 (8.4%)	6 (2.1%)	59 (13.3%)	1 (1.0%)	12 (4.0%)	7 (15.0%)	309 (9.3%)
Total	750 (22.8%) (100.0%)	742 (22.6%) (100.0%)	389 (11.8%) (100.0%)	210 (6.4%) (100.0%)	300 (9.1%) (100.0%)	449 (13.7%) (100.0%)	101 (3.1%) (100.0%)	297 (9.0%) (100.0%)	45 (1.4%) (100.0%)	3283 (100.0%)
Average days	16.1	40.1	102.1	42.8	11.4	59.2	32.3	20.3	67.4	38.5

of all diverted offenders received some form of a service that was administered over an extended period of time, ranging from one day to two years. Second, from the perspective of efficiency, considerable program time was devoted to petty offenses and, in some instances, to youths with no recorded arrest. In this instance, diversion represents a substantial investment of resources in questionable acts of deviance.

Multivariate Analysis of Diversion Decisionmaking

Table 3 examines the diversion process controlling for basic demographic and offense variables as well as the type of diversion agency. Of the three demographic variables, age was coded as an interval variable (range eight to eighteeen years of age), sex was dummy-coded (0 = male and 1 = female), and race-ethnicity was also dummy-coded (0 = white and 1 = black or Hispanic). The status offenses and other types of recorded offenses were dummy-coded (0 = not charged and 1 = charged offense). Runaway offenses were deleted in this analysis of variance framework and will serve as the comparison group for the remaining offense categories. Through use of police statistics, the total number of prior arrests was tabulated for each diverted offender ("total arrests" in Table 3). A self-reported delinquency survey was also administered to each diverted juvenile shortly after admission to the diversion program. The juvenile was asked to indicate the number of times during the past six months he or she committed a total of twenty-seven possible felony, misdemeanor, or status offenses. This variable is labeled "total self-reports" in Table 3. Finally, the twenty-one diversion agencies were dichotomized into court-based = 0, and non-court-based or community agency = 1.

Three dependent variables were created: diverted clients, referred clients, and total days in the diversion program. The first two dependent variables were dummy variables (diverted, 0 = no and 1 = yes; referred, 0 = no and 1 = yes). Because the assumptions of homoscedasticity and normal distributions are violated when one uses dummy variables, the Grizzle, Starmer, and Koch (GSK) modification was applied, which substitutes a chi-square test for an F-test. When the GSK modification is used, the interpretation of the coefficients is virtually synonymous with ordinary least-squares regression.

Examining the first regression model in Table 3, we find that the decision to divert is not contingent on any of the three demographic variables, any of the offense variables, the prior arrest record, or self-reported delinquency involvement. The only prediction variable significant in the decision to divert is whether or not the intake agency was the mobile diversion unit or a community-based diversion agency. The probability of some form of true diversion was determined solely by the nature of the intake agency. The court's mobile diversion unit had a very high diversion rate, while the community agencies displayed a marked aversion to true diversion.

The second column of Table 3 examines the decision to refer clients for further survices. Females had a significantly higher referral rate than males, but neither age nor race nor ethnicity were significant prediction variables. The offense

Table 3 Analysis of Variance

Independent Variables	*Diverted*[1]	*Referred*[1]	*Total Days*[2]
Age	-.01	-.00	-.96
Sex	-.04	.15**	1.31*
Race-ethnicity	.00	-.02	.11
Ungovernable	.12	-.03	12.39**
Truant	-.01	.01	23.15***
Curfew	-.02	.04	8.76**
Alcohol	.00	.01	-1.22
No offense	.06	-.03	11.88**
Potential R/A	-.11	.00	8.26**
Health & Welfare	.03	.01	2.49
Delinquent	-.14	.10	21.39**
Total arrests	.00	.00	.05
Total self-reports	.00	.00	.12
Diversion agency	-.62***	.45***	29.63***

*.05 sig. level
**.01 sig. level
***.001 sig. level
[1]Grizzle, Starmer, Koch method.
[2]Ordinary least squares method.

variables are not significant, indicating no difference between any offense in Table 3 and the omitted category of runaway. Finally, prior delinquency involvement, whether measured by police or self-report data, is also nonsignificant. However, the type of diversion agency involved at intake rises into great prominence. The twenty non-court-based agencies had a significantly higher referral rate than the single court-based unit. Thus, the decision to divert or refer was not predicated on any offense or prior record of delinquency involvement but was attributed mainly to the intake agency.

The third column of Table 3 represents the parameter effects influencing the length of stay in the diversion program. Females tended to receive services longer than males, but neither age nor the race-ethnicity variable is significant. Once again the omitted offense is runaway, the juvenile act most eligible for a referral service. As seen in Table 3, ungovernable, truant, curfew, no offense, potential runaway, and delinquent acts have highly significant positive coefficients, indicating a longer term of treatment than for runaway. Only an alcohol-related offense has a negative coefficient. The irony of this finding is that the runaway offense has been construed as the most serious of all status offenses, and one requiring some form of service at a shelter care facility. Based on the findings in Table 3, runaway offenses accounted for nearly the shortest length of stay. Neither the total number of prior arrests nor the total number of self-reported delinquent acts appears to exert any influence on the length of time spent in a diversion program.

Finally, the dichotomized diversion agency variable is positive and highly significant. As in the two other regression models in Table 3, the point of entry into the diversion program is highly predictive of the length of stay. Controlling for the three demographic variables, eight offense variables, and two prior offense variables, community-based intake added nearly thirty days to the length of stay, as compared to the court-based diversion unit.

Summary and Conclusion

An examination of a juvenile diversion program with multiple intake points indicated that community-based agencies tended to be more reactive to juvenile offenders than a court-based intake unit. In theory, diversion is perceived to be a process of deflecting offenders away from the traditional juvenile justice system. However, there is strong evidence that this deflection may result in another form of encapsulation. The reason behind diversion versus referral is not predicated on the seriousness of the offense or the juvenile's deviant career but perhaps simply on the need for agency survival and funding justification. Despite the popular image of the juvenile court, the court's diversion intake unit appeared to take a non-interventionist stance as compared with community-based agencies. Based on the length of stay, it could also be argued that the court's diversion unit was less punitive than the twenty community-based agencies.

Much of the legislative intent surrounding deinstitutionalization and diversion entails a progressive moment from the public to the private sector. As stated by Spergel (1976: 89), "Diversion out of one system requires increasing the absorptive capacity of another or reciprocal system." The assumption has long been that private welfare systems in the local community are more efficacious than the public welfare system. Yet, the evidence presented in this study suggests that the private welfare sector may have normative standards that are more rigorous than the public or official welfare sector.

Clearly, the move to divest the juvenile court of jurisdiction over a certain range of deviant acts, such as status offenses, may be premature. The court has long been criticized for its disregard of procedural regularity. However, whether a youthful offender is accorded greater solicitous care in a community-based agency is debatable. In many ways, community agencies are more vulnerable to social pressures than are official agencies. Often the incessant demand for secure funding gives some community agencies a chameleonlike quality as they struggle to adapt to new demands or expectations. Diversion may not be the hoped-for panacea for the juvenile court, if it results in the creation of a new juvenile process that is more punitive and intervention-oriented than the system it was intended to replace.

References

Bullington, B., J. Sprowls, D. Katkin, and M. Phillips. 1978. "A Critique of Diversionary Juvenile Justice." *Crime and Delinquency* 24 (January): 59–71.

Cressey, D., and R. McDermott. 1973. *Diversion from the Juvenile Justice System.* Ann Arbor, Mich.: National Assessment of Juvenile Corrections.

Etzioni, A. 1976. "Deinstitutionalization: A Public Policy Fashion." *Evaluation* 3: 9–10.

Finestone, H. 1976. *Victims of Change.* Westport, Conn.: Greenwood Press.

Gemignani, R. 1973. "Diversion of Juvenile Offenders from the Juvenile Justice System." In P. Lejins, ed., *Criminal Justice Monograph: New Approaches to Diversion and Treatment of Juvenile Offenders.* Washington, D.C.: U.S. Government Printing Office.

Kent v. *United States.* 1966. 383 U.S. 541.

Klein, M., et al. 1976. "The Explosion in Police Diversion Programs: Evaluating the Structural Dimensions of a Social Fad." In M. Klein, ed., *The Juvenile Justice System.* Beverly Hills, Calif.: Sage.

Murphy, P. T. 1974. *Our Kindly Parent: The State.* New York: Viking Press.

Rothman, D. J. 1971. *The Discovery of the Asylum.* Boston: Little, Brown.

Schur, E. M. 1973. *Radical Non-intervention: Rethinking the Delinquency Problem.* Englewood Cliffs, N.J.: Prentice-Hall.

Spergel, I. A. 1976. "Interactions between Community Structure, Delinquency and Social Policy." In M. W. Klein, ed., *The Juvenile Justice System.* Beverly Hills, Calif.: Sage.

SECTION NINE

Summary

It should now be apparent that the concept of diversion is multi-faceted. In some cases diversion represents a viable alternative to exposure to the juvenile justice system, but in others it becomes another method of institutionalizing juvenile offenders. Until diversion is rigorously defined and operationalized, it is doubtful whether any meaningful discussion or conclusion is possible. Despite the laudable intentions of theoreticians and practitioners, diversion may be as abusive as the juvenile court itself.

The thrust of Howlett's criticism of the Youth Service Bureau is that the agency amounts to a form of alternative encapsulation. If we create an agency that serves simply as a new dumping ground for troublesome youths, are we really addressing the problems of adolescent misbehavior? Howlett states in no uncertain terms that a YSB is a "cop-out" for the community. Is his assessment accurate? Is there a role for a YSB, or should it be totally eliminated?

The reading by Bullington et al. is an elaboration of Howlett's critique. It appears that the emergence of diversion programs is similar to the reinvention of the wheel. All the negative aspects of the current juvenile justice system are only magnified with the development of diversion alternatives. Bullington, Sprowls, Katkin, and Phillips go so far as to say that diversion may be another form of denial of basic human rights to juveniles. They call for a more fundamental change in the juvenile justice machinery. Based on their critique of diversion and traversing "the path of hell that is paved with good intentions," is there anything to commend diversion? Is Howlett's assessment of the basic concept of diversion itself more favorable than the evaluation of Bullington, Sprowls, Katkin, and Phillips?

The section's last reading, by Rojek, conveys the notion that community-based treatment may not be more beneficial or more humane than juvenile court processing. As community agencies vie for clients and funds, youthful offenders may get caught in a highly competitive market for organizational survival. How convincing is the argument that the juvenile justice system is inherently bad in light of the alternatives? How might community organizations be regulated so as to instill a strong sense of due process of law while still retaining their separation from the formal court process?

It appears that diversion, like so many other reform movements, has benefitted from a certain bandwagon effect that accompanies anything that is new or innovative. Unfortunately, in our haste to plug a few leaks, we could sink the ship! Nearly everyone is quick to agree that youths need to be diverted from the juvenile justice system, but this is not tantamount to saying that kids should be left alone. The original philosophy behind diversion called for nonintervention, not additional treatment. It may be that "pure" diversion is simply too radical a concept and that the juvenile justice system as we presently know it will remain with us for many years. In some ways it is ironic that approximately one hundred years after the founding of the original child-saving movement, another juvenile reform movement is building. The rhetoric of the two movements and their solution to the problem are very similar. Is it conceivable that we are just tinkering with a few parts instead of overhauling the complete engine?

SECTION TEN

Prevention

The juvenile justice system was created supposedly to divert juveniles from the harsh realities of the adult criminal justice system. However, after eight decades, the same arguments that were used to advocate the establishment of a separate juvenile justice system are the basis for the recommendation of diversion from the juvenile justice system itself. Recent efforts to divert youthful offenders are also subject to criticism, since they involve assumptions about the distinctiveness of the status offenders that are not true. Moreover, the diversion movement has been accompanied by the development of new diversion alternatives that compete for scarce status offenders but that do not differ significantly from previously applied alternative "treatments." The fact that the juvenile court system has not been able to demonstrate convincingly that its dispositions have their intended effect has led to new proposals that call for far more fundamental changes in policies for dealing with delinquency. These proposals most often involve another popular but vague concept—prevention.

Of course, all the programs described in the preceding two sections are, in a sense, prevention programs: they attempt to check further delinquency among youths brought to the juvenile courts. Similarly, proposals that we can reduce delinquency by increasing the severity of punishment—that by "getting tough" we can "nip-it-in-the-bud"—are concerned with preventing delinquency. However, the term *prevention* is generally used to refer to policies, proposals, or programs that purport to reduce the probability of delinquency by modifying characteristics of the social environment thought to be the "seedbed" of crime and delinquency. It has generally been associated with calls for social reform, alterations in the economy, and changes in the quality of life.

Like the concept of diversion, the idea of prevention is by no means new. It has been repeatedly advocated, "reborn," and presented as if it were revolutionary for at least a century. However, the persistent and widespread advocacy of prevention has not been accompanied by very specific ideas about *what* should be changed in order to prevent delinquency or how to bring change about once a target has been identified.

When we look at prevention programs actually initiated, we find considerable variation in their targets and techniques. Some have been aimed at individuals and have centered around personalized counseling. For example, the "early identification and intensive treatment programs" reviewed in the first article in this section are based on the assumption that youths headed for trouble can be identified and provided some form of individualized treatment that will help prevent wrongdoing. The emphasis is on changing the individual and, with parental involvement, manipulating some features of his or her social world. The underpinnings of this approach are primarily psychological, and the techniques used draw heavily on clinical psychological ideas about helping people.

Instead of focusing on individuals, several programs have attempted to prevent delinquency by providing some form of work. The job corps and neighborhood youth corps programs are based on the premise that the provision of work and training not only reduces the amount of time available for youths to get into trouble but additionally leads to the development of new skills and new bonds to conventional activities. By paying youths for their efforts, these programs presume that possible economic motives for delinquency will be inhibited as well. The second selection in this section summarizes an evaluation of two such programs—one in Detroit and one in Cincinnati.

While job corps programs have attempted to enhance the economic well-being and future prospects of youths, other programs have been directed specifically toward modifying their educational prospects. One such effort, described and evaluated in the third selection, was a school-based delinquency prevention program. Specifically, it provided "predelinquent" youths, youths on probation, and youths released from institutions with "advocates" who intervened on their behalf at school and in the community. The advocates' role was to create an environment conducive to the completion of schooling.

Sociologists interested in prevention have generally criticized prevention programs for either (1) focusing on the individual and using individual-centered techniques or (2) addressing only limited and minor aspects of a youth's social-cultural world. There have been attempts—in Chicago, Boston, and Seattle—to implement prevention programs that eliminate both of these potential weaknesses. The Chicago Area Projects attempted to increase cohesiveness within neighborhoods, promote the idea of community leadership, and hence reduce the degree of social disorganization characterizing neighborhoods with high crime rates. In central Seattle, caseworkers sought to organize young black males into groups and worked with the boys, their families, and the schools to lower the risk of delinquency. In Boston a comprehensive program known as the Midcity Project worked toward strengthening local citizens' groups and youth agencies, furnishing intensive psychiatric casework for problem families, and assigning social workers to provide guidance for street gangs. The Midcity Project was based on the idea that the orderly application of a wide range of techniques had more promise than the use of any one technique. The fourth article in this section is a report on the Midcity Project.

Some sociologists view the prevention programs that have been implemented as far too limited and insignificant to have much impact on delinquency. To replace the mere tinkering with the system, such critics call for basic social reform or fundamental changes in the position of youths in American society. Jackson Toby has advocated fuller youth participation in major institutions. In the last selection, Herman and Julia Schwendinger argue that a problem such as delinquency reflects the "marginal" status of youth in American society. They believe that "piece-meal and accommodative social policies" are doomed to failure and advocate long-term strategies that modify society's entire economic structure. Their specific proposal is that the best possibilities for solving the problem of marginality rest with socialism. This recommendation will upset many readers because it raises the emotionally charged issue of competing political ideologies. Nevertheless, it is important that we present and examine it, because the view is consistent with theories that attribute the delinquency problem to weaknesses in the organization and operation of our social, political, and economic systems. Short-term strategies and limited reforms appear to be of little or no consequence, and arguments that far more basic changes are required make sense to many people.

An Evaluation of Early Identification and Intensive Treatment Programs for Predelinquents*

Jackson Toby
Rutgers University

The "early identification and intensive treatment" approach to delinquency control is breathtakingly plausible. A plausible argument is not necessarily correct, as Columbus showed those who believed that the world was flat. "Early identification and intensive treatment," though probably not as erroneous as the flat-world theory, is more a slogan or a rallying cry than a realistic assessment of the difficulties that delinquency control programs must overcome. This paper points out the need for sharper definition of the implicit assumptions of "early identification and intensive treatment" programs and then examines two of the best-known early identification programs in the light of this need.

Early identification programs are based on either of two logically distinct principles: extrapolation or circumstantial vulnerability. The principle of extrapolation assumes that predelinquents are youngsters in the early stages of a delinquent way of life; the principle of circumstantial vulnerability assumes that youngsters who have been exposed to circumstances believed to cause delinquency are likely to become delinquent. The Cambridge-Somerville Youth Study emphasized the extrapolative approach to prediction. "Difficult boys" and "average boys" were nominated by teachers and policemen. The expectation of adolescent delinquency was based primarily on quasi-delinquent behavior during preadolescence. Although the three raters on the Cambridge-Somerville research team made a clinical assessment of each case and made predictions on a variety of family and personal circumstances, the great majority of the predictions were that difficult boys would remain difficult and average boys, average.[1] Early identification meant in short that anti-social tendencies would persist and develop further —unless checked by outside intervention. This is quite different from identifying potential delinquents by a theory of delinquency which holds that youngsters exposed to certain sociocultural conditions will become delinquent. Yet the latter is also called "early identifi-

* A preliminary version of this paper was published in *Social Work*, 6 (July, 1961), pp. 3-13. The research on which it is based was financed by the Ford Foundation.

1 Professor Robert Stanfield found in his re-analysis of the Cambridge-Somerville data that 81 to 84 per cent of the "difficult" referrals were given a *delinquent* prognosis; 59 to 68 per cent of the "average" referrals were given a *nondelinquent* prognosis. (Personal communication, March 24, 1965.) Nevertheless, the extent to which the raters were influenced by the source and nature of the referrals is not clear. The seeming extrapolations might be accounted for by systematic differences in the environmental circumstances of "difficult" and "average" boys. The three raters themselves claimed to give considerable weight to the nature of the neighborhood and the family situation. See Donald W. Taylor, "An analysis of Predictions of Delinquency Based on Case Studies," *Journal of Abnormal and Social Psychology*, 42 (January, 1947), pp. 45-46. Recall, however, that the design of the study was such that the raters started with a bimodal universe: boys identified by teachers and policemen as troublesome and boys identified as law-abiding. Although the ratings ranged from minus 5 (most delinquent) to plus 5 (most nondelinquent), comparatively few borderline ratings (zero) were made. In characterizing the predictions as extrapolative, I am assuming that a troublesome boy was predicted to be more or less delinquent depending on his family and neighborhood situation and a law-abiding boy was predicted to be more or less nondelinquent, but troublesome boys did not usually get into the nondelinquent prediction range nor law-abiding boys into the delinquent range by virtue of their family and neighborhood situations. In Tables 1 and 2, any prediction from minus five to minus one was considered a prediction of delinquency, and any prediction from plus five to plus one was considered a prediction of nondelinquency. Zero predictions were eliminated from the analysis. See also the discussion in Edwin Powers and Helen Witmer, *An Experiment in the Prevention of Delinquency: The Cambridge-Somerville Youth Study*, New York: Columbia University Press, 1951, pp. 29-36.

From *Social Problems*, Vol. 13 (Fall 1965), pp. 160–175. Reprinted with the permission of the Society of Social Problems and the author.

cation." Criminologists Sheldon and Eleanor Glueck claim to be able to predict delinquency on the basis of factors distinct from the child's early behavior: (1) affection of mother for the boy; (2) affection of father for the boy; (3) discipline of boy by father; (4) supervision of boy by mother; and (5) family cohesiveness.[2] The New York City Youth Board has attempted to test this claim by applying the Glueck prediction table to a sample of 223 boys who in 1952 entered the first grade of two New York City schools in high delinquency neighborhoods. Note that the Cambridge-Somerville approach to prediction is less ambitious than the Youth Board-Glueck approach. One can extrapolate without knowing much about causes. One presumably ought to know a great deal about the causes of delinquency if one hopes to make accurate predictions on the basis of the sociocultural circumstances to which the child is exposed.

This distinction between an extrapolative prediction and a circumstantial prediction, though clear in theory, is often obscured in practice. Diagnostic interviews or self-rating scales (like the Minnesota Multiphasic Personality Inventory) combine the youngster's reports about his own antisocial behavior and/or attitudes with his reports about his family and neighborhood environment. Thus, in many attempts at early identification, the basis for the prediction of future delinquency is not clear.[3] Of course, it can be contended that a better prediction can be made if it is based *both* on the child's early behavior and on his exposure to known deleterious influences. Possibly so. However, such predictions emerge like sausages from a sausage machine but without real insight into *why* they are correct. The drawback of predictions made without theory becomes all too evident when treatment is attempted. Since the prediction is mechanical and does not imply an understanding of the causes of delinquency, it provides no guidance for treatment. "Treatment" becomes an umbrella word meaning all things to all men. A therapeutic program based on family casework is not the same thing as one based on individual psychotherapy, the improvement of reading skills, participation in organized sports, or vocational counseling.

Predictions made without a theory of delinquency causation can be matched with a treatment program that is similarly eclectic. Sometimes it is very difficult indeed to find out what "intensive treatment" consists of. The therapist may contend that each case is unique and that treatment is tailored to the individual case. One might well be suspicious of such vagueness. Vagueness can conceal two kinds of ignorance: ignorance as to what is causing the antisocial behavior and ignorance of the best strategy of intervention. In any case, most "individual treatment" programs and programs claiming to "co-ordinate" community resources are in practice not genuinely eclectic. They implicitly answer the question, "What kind of treatment?" by selecting resources ideologically congenial to the agency. For example, the same predelinquent child may be treated through casework techniques if he comes to the attention of one agency and through group work techniques if he comes to the attention of another. Presumably the type of treatment selected should be governed by the etiological factor involved in the youngster's predelinquency. The type of treatment selected by practitioners of "individual treatment" seems more closely related to the practitioners' preconceptions than to the child's problems. This is said, not to condemn efforts to treat predelinquency, but to point out that in the present state of knowledge the frequently invoked analogy between medical practice and delinquency control is misleading. Whereas medical practice aims at precise diagnosis and specific treatment, early identification and intensive treatment of delinquency usually address themselves to an unknown problem with an unproved technique. Is it any wonder that the few treatment programs that have been rigorously evaluated reveal disappointingly small effects? For instance, the Cambridge-Somerville Youth Study offers little support to proponents of "early identification and intensive treatment" as an approach to delinquency control. Whereas 41 per cent of the 253 boys in the treatment group subsequently were convicted of at least one major crime in a state or federal court, 37 per cent of the 253 boys in the control group were so convicted. Considering (a) that treatment began by age 10 for 121 boys and by age 13 for the remaining 132, and (b) that treatment lasted for four years or more for 171 boys, *more* criminality in the treatment group is rather surprising. The McCords point out that only 12 of the 253 boys had intensive therapy (according to their quite reasonable criteria of "intensive"), and they suggest that for this reason intensive treatment was not really tested. Perhaps so. On the other hand, hardly a probation or parole system in the United States gives as intense supervision as was given routinely in the course of the Cambridge-Somerville Youth Study. The case loads of Cambridge-Somerville workers were 34 youngsters per counselor at the beginning of the study and even fewer when the boys grew older.[4]

Tacit Assumptions of Early Identification and Intensive Treatment Programs

Presumably the rationale of early identification is to economize treatment efforts. Otherwise, society would expose all youth to whatever resources are available for delinquency control. But in order to achieve economy, the predictions must be accurate. If delinquency occurs in too many cases where nondelinquency was predicted or *fails* to occur in too many cases where it *was* predicted, economy may not be realized. Once the predictions are found to be sufficiently accurate, greater intensity of treatment efforts is possible because youngsters not in danger of becoming delinquent can be ignored.

The conditions under which accurate predictions may be anticipated are therefore important. For the occurrence of adolescent delinquency to be predicted accurately from either preadolescent behavior or preadolescent circumstances, no crucial etiological factors should make their appearance after the original predictions have been made. For instance, in the New York City Youth Board project, the ratings of the family backgrounds of the 223 boys were made when they were 6 years old. If family relations are the major factor in delinquency and if family relations change appreciably in the course of the study, the predictions ought not

---

[2] Sheldon and Eleanor Glueck, *Unraveling Juvenile Delinquency,* New York: Commonwealth Fund, 1950; Sheldon and Eleanor Glueck, *Predicting Delinquency and Crime,* Cambridge, Massachusetts: Harvard University Press, 1959; Eleanor T. Glueck, "Efforts to Identify Delinquents," *Federal Probation,* 24 (June, 1960), pp. 49-56.

[3] D. H. Stott, "The Prediction of Delinquency from Non-Delinquent Behavior," *British Journal of Delinquency,* 10 (January, 1960), pp. 195-210.

[4] See Powers and Witmer, *op. cit.,* pp. 85, 88; William and Joan McCord, *Origins of Crime: A New Evaluation of the Cambridge-Somerville Youth Study,* New York: Columbia University Press, 1959, pp. 20, 26, 29, 38-39.

to be very accurate.[5] Peer group relations are even more prone to change than family relations. Since studies of adolescent street-corner groups reveal that youngsters who join such groups are more likely to commit delinquent acts than youngsters who do not join such groups and since delinquent groups rarely recruit members younger than 10, preadolescent ratings of school misbehavior or family background ought not to predict delinquency during adolescence very accurately. Of course, if we assume that early childhood experiences are so important that they establish a differential vulnerability for all subsequent experiences, early predictions might be accurate despite later changes in family and peer relations. Freudian psychiatrists subscribe to this assumption of the disproportionate importance of early socialization; sociologists, on the other hand, believe that socialization continues throughout life and that the course of a child's life can be radically changed by subsequent experiences.

Correct identification of youngsters who will ultimately become delinquent is the first step of "early identification and intensive treatment" programs. The second step is to upset these initially correct predictions by an effective treatment program. It is usually assumed by the proponents of "early identification and intensive treatment" that treatment is effective merely by being intensive. This is not necessarily so. The focusing of treatment efforts on youngsters most likely to become delinquent necessarily involves special handling for them. It is extremely difficult for a focused treatment program to avoid stigmatizing the recipients of the "benefits" of the program. Early identification does not necessarily imply early stigmatization, but early *discriminatory* treatment seems to. Thus, it is conceivable that a boomerang effect will occur and that greater intensity of exposure to treatment will be *less* effective than less intense but less discriminatory exposure. Suppose, for instance, that a community has an organized recreational program for *all* children up to the age of 16. Someone convinces the city fathers that organized recreation can prevent delinquency, and the program is changed to focus on identified predelinquents. Instead of 1,000 boys using the facilities occasionally, 200 boys use them frequently. Before leaping to the conclusion that these 200 boys are less likely to become delinquent, let us consider what the impact of their segregation is on "predelinquents." We know from experience with ability groupings in the schools that the evaluations of the adult world cannot be concealed from youngsters. Just as the children in the "dumb" classes know that they are not in the "smart" classes, these 200 boys are unlikely to think of themselves as the pride of the community. It is possible that less intensive recreational participation would have been more effective in arresting their delinquent tendencies than the more intensive—and incidentally more stigmatizing—exposure.[6]

The Cambridge-Somerville Youth Study and the New York City Youth Board Prediction Study did not assess the effect of neighborhood, ethnic background, or socio-economic status on the *accuracy* of their predictions. As a result, they missed an opportunity to clarify the conditions under which predisposing personal or family factors eventuate in delinquency. I propose to examine both studies in the light of these omissions in order to demonstrate that explicit consideration of the social context is necessary for further progress in delinquency *prediction* and ultimately control.

The Cambridge-Somerville Youth Study

Table 1 shows a positive relationship between the original predictions of delinquency or nondelinquency made in 1937-38 and the outcomes as of 1956.[7] Insofar as errors of prediction occurred, they were mainly overpredictions of delinquency. That is, of the 305 boys for whom delinquency was predicted, 191 turned into "good" boys (63 per cent); but only 18 of the 150 for whom *nondelinquency* was predicted subsequently committed offenses (12 per cent). Bear in mind that the Cambridge-Somerville Youth Study assumed that, unless the service program were successful, preadolescent boys who manifested antisocial behavior would continue such behavior in adolescence. In point of fact, the majority of identified predelinquents did *not* persist in their delinquent activities. The obvious question is: Why not?

It might be possible to find out why delinquency was overpredicted and, hopefully, the conditions making for more accurate predictions if the data in Table 1 were partitioned into meaningful subsamples. For example, various ethnic groups are represented in the study population: "Italian," "Other Latin," "Negro," "Eastern European," "Western European," and "Native American."[8] If predictions were more accurate for Italian boys than, say, for native American boys, this might throw light on the relationship between cultural values and delinquency.[9] Similarly, several socioeconomic levels were represented in the study population. If predictions were more accurate for slum-dwelling youngsters than for boys living in better residential neighborhoods, this might throw light

[5] Professor Isidor Chein of New York University suggested that the Youth Board rate the family situations of the 223 boys *again* several years after the original ratings were made. How well would the two sets of ratings correlate with one another? If the later ratings were less closely related to outcome than the earlier ratings, this would tend to support the Glueck hypothesis that the early family situation is the major factor in delinquency. If the later ratings were more closely related to outcome than the earlier ratings, this would suggest that the contemporary situation—familial and extrafamilial—is more important in the genesis of delinquency than the Gluecks think.

[6] Proponents of early identification and intensive treatment might argue that stigmatization occurs but that it is helpful in preventing delinquency (by nipping the deviant tendency in the bud). Law enforcement officials sometimes use this argument, but they usually talk in terms of "punishment" rather than "treatment." Social workers and psychiatrists seem unwilling to face the logical possibility that well-intentioned "treatment" can do more harm than good. For an analysis of the comparative consequences of punishment and treatment, see Jackson Toby, "Is Punishment Necessary?" *Journal of Criminal Law, Criminology and Police Science,* 55 (September, 1964), pp. 332-337.

[7] The unpublished tabulations in Tables 1 and 2 were made available to me through the graciousness of Professor William McCord of Stanford University, Professor Gordon W. Allport of Harvard University, Dr. Stanton Wheeler of the Russell Sage Foundation, and Professor Robert Stanfield of the University of Massachusetts. Note that these tabulations include boys from both treatment and control groups. Since the treatment program proved ineffective, the exclusion of treatment cases from the analysis was unnecessary.

[8] The ethnic data relating to the study population do not appear in *Origins of Crime* but are found in a second volume, which explored the causes of alcoholism rather than crime. For information on ethnic groupings, see William and Joan McCord, *Origins of Alcoholism,* Stanford, California: Stanford University Press, 1960, p. 38.

[9] See Jackson Toby, "Hoodlum or Business Man: An American Dilemma," in Marshall Sklare, ed., *The Jews,* Glencoe, Ill.: The Free Press, 1958, pp. 542-550, for a discussion of the relationship between ethnic background and delinquency.

TABLE 1
COMPARISON OF ORIGINAL PREDICTIONS AND FINAL OUTCOMES OF BOYS IN THE CAMBRIDGE-SOMERVILLE YOUTH STUDY

	Outcomes		
Predictions	Delinquent	Nondelinquent	Total
Delinquent	114	191*	305
Nondelinquent	18*	132	150
Total	132	323	455

* Errors of prediction.

TABLE 2
PARTITION OF CAMBRIDGE-SOMERVILLE YOUTH STUDY CASES BY NEIGHBORHOOD OF RESIDENCE

Predictions	Outcomes					
	In Slum Neighborhoods			In Better Neighborhoods		
	Delinquent	Non-delinquent	Total	Delinquent	Non-delinquent	Total
Delinquent	90	126*	216	24	65*	89
Nondelinquent	12*	62	74	6*	70	76
Total	102	188	290	30	135	165

* Errors of prediction.

on the relationship between social class and delinquency. Table 2 explores the latter question by breaking down the data of Table 1 into subsamples of neighborhoods. What does Table 2 reveal about the effect of the socioeconomic milieu?

Facts

1. Predictions of delinquency were more likely to be made in slum neighborhoods than in better residential neighborhoods. Seventy-five per cent of the 290 boys from slum neighborhoods were predicted by the raters to become delinquent as compared with 54 per cent of boys from better neighborhoods.
2. Predictions of delinquency were more likely to be correct in slum neighborhoods than in better neighborhoods. Forty-two per cent of the 216 boys predicted delinquent from slum neighborhoods actually became so as compared with 27 per cent of the 89 boys predicted delinquent in better neighborhoods.
3. Predictions of *nondelinquency* were more likely to be correct in better residential neighborhoods than in slum neighborhoods. Ninety-two per cent of the boys predicted nondelinquent from better neighborhoods remained law-abiding as compared with 84 per cent of the boys predicted nondelinquent in slum neighborhoods.
4. The differences between the later delinquency rates of troublesome and conforming preadolescents are striking. In slum neighborhoods, 42 per cent of the troublesome preadolescents, as contrasted with 16 per cent of the conformists, subsequently committed offenses. In the better residential neighborhoods, 27 per cent of the troublesome preadolescents, as contrasted with 8 per cent of the conformists, subsequently committed offenses.

Interpretation

1. Predictions of delinquency could have varied by neighborhood for either one of two reasons (or a combination of both):
   a. Because preadolescent misbehavior at school and in the community is more common in slum neighborhoods than in better residential neighborhoods.
   b. Because preadolescent misbehavior was likely to be discounted by the Cambridge-Somerville raters on the basis of favorable family situations, and such situations are more frequent in better residential neighborhoods. That is to say, the raters were more likely to predict nondelinquency or to assign an undecided (zero) rating if the troublesome preadolescent came from a "good" neighborhood.

2. The greater tendency of predictions of delinquency to come true and predictions of nondelinquency to be incorrect in slum neighborhoods may be explained by differing neighborhood traditions of delinquency. Precisely how these traditions originate and are sustained is not clear. One relevant factor is a concentration of disorganized families exercising ineffective control over children, especially over adolescent boys.[10] Another is the proliferation of highly visible street-corner groups that are frequently delinquent. Sociologists have suggested that the weakness of family control and the influence of the peer group are different sides of the same coin.[11]

3. The negligible tendency of *conforming* preadolescents to become delinquent in later years—in both slum neighborhoods and in better residential neighborhoods—may mean that boys controlled effectively by their parents in preadolescence continue to be controlled effectively in adolescence and young adulthood. External controls, however, may not be so crucial as the conforming preadolescent develops a nondelinquent self-conception that insulates him from involvement in delinquent peer groups.[12] Thus, the delinquent peer group is likely to have a quite different impact on troublesome and on conforming preadolescents. Not only were the differences between the delinquency records of the troublesome and the conforming preadolescents substantial in later years. The conforming preadolescents from slum neighborhoods had a less delinquent record than the troublesome preadolescents from the better neighborhoods.

4. The reason or reasons for the overprediction of delinquency are not clear. An obvious possibility is that a considerable amount of delinquency goes unrecorded.[13] If this "hidden delinquency" could somehow be put into the record, the predictions might well seem more accurate. Another possibility

[10] Jackson Toby, "The Differential Impact of Family Disorganization," *American Sociological Review,* 22 (October, 1957), pp. 505-512.

[11] Frederick M. Thrasher, *The Gang,* Chicago: University of Cricago Press, 1927; William Foote Whyte, "Social Organization in the Slums," *American Sociological Review,* 8 (February, 1943), pp. 34-39.

[12] Walter C. Reckless, Simon Dinitz, and Ellen Murray, "Self-Concept as an Insulator Against Delinquency," *American Sociological Review,* 21 (December, 1956), pp. 744-747; Simon Dinitz, Frank R. Scarpitti, and Walter C. Reckless, "Delinquency Vulnerability: A Cross Group and Longitudinal Analysis," *American Sociological Review,* 27 (August, 1962), pp. 515-517.

[13] Fred J. Murphy, Mary M. Shirley, and Helen L. Witmer, "The Incidence of Hidden Delinquency," *American Journal of Orthopsychiatry,* 16 (October, 1946), pp. 286-296.

TABLE 3

DELINQUENCY AMONG TREATMENT BOYS AND CONTROL BOYS IN THE CAMBRIDGE-SOMERVILLE YOUTH STUDY, BY TYPE OF NEIGHBORHOOD

Type of Neighborhood	% of Convictions in Treatment Group (N = 233)	% of Convictions in Control Group (N = 250)
Good	38	26
Fair	37	33
Poor	40	44
Worst	46	49

TABLE 4

A COMPARISON AMONG THE YOUTH BOARD TWO- OR THREE-FACTOR TABLE, THE GLUECK FIVE-FACTOR TABLE, AND A SINGLE FACTOR (PUBLIC ASSISTANCE) IN PREDICTING DELINQUENCY

1952 Predictions	Outcomes, 7 Years Later		
	Delinquent	Nondelinquent	Total
Based on Five Factors			
Probably delinquent	17	50*	67
Probably nondelinquent	4*	152	156
Total	21	202	223
Based on Two or Three Factors			
Probably delinquent	13	24*	37
Probably nondelinquent	8*	178	186
Total	21	202	223
Based on Single Factor (Economic Status of Family When Boy Entered School in 1952)			
Public assistance	13	39*	52
No public assistance	8*	163	171
Total	21	202	223

* Errors of prediction.

is that delinquent tendencies were somehow "nipped in the bud." Troublesome preadolescents were salvaged. The difficulty with this interpretation is that the planned program of intervention did not result in a lower delinquency rate in the treatment group as compared with the control group. As a matter of fact, Table 3 suggests more strongly than the overall treatment group-control group comparison that a boomerang effect might have occurred.[14] The difference between the treatment group and the control group in the "good" neighborhoods was greater than the difference in the "worst" neighborhoods. This difference can be explained by sampling peculiarities. On the other hand, it is clear that the program of intervention was not *more* successful in the better residential neighborhoods. Since delinquent peer group influences are relatively weak in better residential neighborhoods, one would expect a program of delinquency prevention to have a *better* chance in such neighborhoods. The planned treatment program of the Cambridge-Somerville Youth Study staff may have been ineffectual; yet there is still the possibility that unplanned circumstances intervened to arrest delinquent tendencies. For example, parents may have moved to more wholesome communities to escape the delinquent influences of the slum. (The neighborhood ratings in the Cambridge-Somerville files date from the start of the study; they do not take into account subsequent moves.) The possible benefits of movement into low-delinquency neighborhoods is, unfortunately, pure speculation.

NEW YORK CITY YOUTH BOARD PREDICTION STUDY

The New York City Youth Board Prediction Study differed from the Cambridge-Somerville Youth Study in important respects. In the first place, all the boys for whom delinquency predictions were made came from two high-delinquency neighborhoods. Second, the predictions were based on home visits by social workers when the youngsters entered the first grade. They gave negligible weight to a factor particularly stressed in the Cambridge-Somerville Youth Study, the boy's own behavior. The critical question, of course, is: By what mechanism do "bad" family situations lead to delinquency in high-delinquency neighborhoods? Consider two quite different mechanisms by which a bad family situation might lead to delinquency:

1. Parental rejection and neglect damage the personality of the developing child. Lack of impulse control results from pathological socialization.[15] The psychopathic or neurotic boy reacts with violence to trivial provocations, sets fires, and steals purposelessly.

2. Parental inadequacy and neglect, by reducing family control, thereby orient the boy toward his agemates in the neighborhood.[16] (The family and the peer group are in a sense competing for the allegiance of boys in high-delinquency neighborhoods.) If the peer group is delinquent, a boy's desire for acceptance by his peers tempts him to participate in delinquent activities.

The Youth Board researchers do not make clear which of these mechanisms they suspect has greater influence. Although both are probably at work, mutually reinforcing one another to produce delinquency, a delinquency control program cannot do all things at once; hence it would seem desirable to be explicit about suspected etiological mechanisms. In point of fact, the intensive treatment program undertaken by the Youth Board addressed psychiatric problems; a clinic was set up in one of the two schools, and treatment was offered by a team consisting of psychologists, psychiatrists, and social workers to all of the boys predicted delinquent by the original Glueck scale.[17] The boys who were likewise predicted delinquent in the other school were to serve as a control group. Although the experimental program lasted four years, it failed in its objective. As in the Cambridge-Somerville Youth Study, members of the treatment group were no less likely to

[14] William and Joan McCord, *Origins of Crime,* pp. 71, 204.

[15] Kate Friedlander, *The Psychoanalytic Approach to Juvenile Delinquency,* New York: International Universities Press, 1944.

[16] Thrasher, *op. cit.*

[17] New York City Youth Board, Research Department, *A Study in Variance from Predicted Delinquency: A Study of 20 Negro Boys Who Were Overpredicted,* mimeographed, 1962, ch. 4.

become delinquent than members of the control group.[18] A possible explanation for the failure is that the treatment program was predicated on the first mechanism whereas the second mechanism may have been more relevant to the delinquency of these underprivileged boys. Let us examine the relationship between predictions and outcomes in the light of this hypothesis.

Table 4 reports the relationship between 1952 predictions and 1959 outcomes utilizing three different prediction techniques:

(1) the five-factor scale designated by the Youth Board at the beginning of the research as the official prediction device;[19]

(2) a two- and three-factor scale developed late in the research to adapt the Glueck scale to the ethnic groups represented in the Youth Board population (especially Negroes);[20]

(3) a single-item predictive device (based on whether or not the family was receiving welfare assistance in 1952), the purpose of which is to provide a basis for comparing the predictive power of the Youth Board scales with predictions based on a readily available socioeconomic datum.

Note that the original five-factor prediction table made 54 errors, more than the 47 errors made by the table based on the public assistance criterion alone. The two- and three-factor table did considerably better: only 32 errors. But *why* did the two- and three-factor table do better than the five? What factors were eliminated? The revised scale used "mother's supervision" and "cohesiveness of the family" supplemented by "father's discipline" in those cases "where a father or father substitute has been in the home a sufficient length of time to have had an influence in the boy's life."[21] From this improvement of prediction resulting from the elimination of "affection of mother for the boy" and of "affection of the father for the boy," it might be inferred that these factors are not important to the etiology of delinquency in this population. (Bear in mind that the universe consists of boys from *high-delinquency* neighborhoods.) Eleanor Glueck assures skeptics that "this is not the case."[22] She explains the greater accuracy of the two- and three-factor table as compared with the original five-factor table as due to inconsistency of ratings of parental affection by social workers of different intellectual persuasions and to the difficulty of making ratings for families where the father has long been out of the home. To me this argument is not convincing. Only 28 of 224 boys lacked fathers (or father substitutes) in the home for a major portion of their lives, and presumably the absence of mothers or mother substitutes was rarer.[23] Why was "affection of the *Mother*" not a useful predictive item? Mrs. Glueck's argument is essentially that parental affection is etiologically important but that the Youth Board researchers were unable to measure parental affection reliably. An alternative interpretation is that parental *affection* is less closely correlated with delinquency in high-delinquency neighborhoods than is parental *control.* The explanation of the greater accuracy of the shorter scale as compared with the five-factor scale may simply be that mother's supervision, family cohesiveness, and father's discipline are more closely related to parental control than are affection of the mother and affection of the father.

Is there any other evidence in favor of the hypothesis that parental control is the crucial variable affecting the accuracy of the Youth Board predictions? The Youth Board itself provided such evidence in a study of 20 Negro boys who were predicted delinquent by the five-factor Glueck prediction table and failed to become so in the subsequent eight years.[24] In a chapter entitled, "Mother's Supervision Counteracting Peer Group Environment," the author of the Youth Board monograph (Dr. Philip W. Furst) emphasizes the role of the mother or mother-substitute in preventing gang membership or defining it as undesirable (dangerous). "She uses various means: exhortation, reason, rewards, example, tongue-lashing, threats, discipline, manipulation of the environment, coaxing, cajoling. And this process goes on with ever broadening content into the middle teens and beyond."[25] *Seven* of these 20 boys had been rated in 1952 as effectively supervised by the mother—as contrasted with *two* of 14 Negro boys predicted delinquent who confirmed the prediction.[26] Four additional boys "were saved in the school years by mothers' supervision even though the mothers' original supervision ratings were poor. . . ."[27] In another four cases, recognition of the *grandmother's* part in supervision and in the cohesiveness of the family might have led to a more hopeful prediction. For instance, one of the two boys out of the 20 considered to have the *highest* probability of becoming delinquent had little contact with his parents. "What the interviewer did not grasp in 1952 . . . was the fact that the person who really counted in those children's lives was the marvelous grandmother in whose home the family was living."[28] Thus, 15 of the 20 incorrect predictions of delinquency might have been avoided by emphasizing parental control more strongly.

Those mothers and mother-substitutes who were concerned about supervising the activities of their sons may have been distressed at the growing crime problems of their neighborhoods.

18 Based on a personal conversation with Mrs. Maude Craig, research director of the Youth Board. To the best of my knowledge the New York City Youth Board has not published a full account of this experiment, apparently on the assumption that something went wrong in the execution of the experiment that did not reflect on its underlying assumptions. This attitude strikes me as dubious, particularly in view of the Youth Board's awareness of the similar results of a project in Washington, D.C., which also used the Glueck scale to identify predelinquents and which also attempted clinical treatment. *Ibid.*, p. 58.

19 Sheldon and Eleanor Glueck, *Unraveling Juvenile Delinquency,* New York: Commonwealth Fund, 1950.

20 Further modifications of the Glueck scales occurred after eight years. Instead of getting rater agreement on total scores, the Youth Board researchers insisted now on rater agreement on each factor going into the score. Second, aware of the fact that the scales were overpredicting delinquency, the Youth Board researchers reviewed some cases and reclassified them from probably delinquent to probably nondelinquent. These changes were seemingly made for cogent research considerations. Unfortunately though, they were made long after the research began and could no longer be regarded as uncontaminated "prospective predictions." For a history of these changes, see New York City Youth Board, *An Experiment in the Use of the Glueck Social Prediction Table as a Prognosticator of Potential Delinquency,* mimeographed, October, 1961.

21 *Ibid.*, p. 10.

22 Eleanor T. Glueck, *op. cit.*, pp. 55-56.

23 New York City Youth Board, *op. cit.*, 1961, p. 13. Note that the total of 224 boys includes one Puerto Rican youngster not included in earlier reports I have examined and therefore not included in Tables 4 or 5.

24 New York City Youth Board, *op. cit.*, 1962.

25 *Ibid.*, pp. 28-29.

26 *Ibid.*, p. S6.

27 *Ibid.*, p. S15.

28 *Ibid.*, p. 36. See also pp. 63-68.

TABLE 5

DIFFERENTIAL IMPACT OF A "BAD" FAMILY SITUATION ON ECONOMICALLY DEPENDENT AND ON SELF-SUFFICIENT WHITE, NEGRO, AND PUERTO RICAN FAMILIES

Ethnic Background	1952 Predictions Two- and Three-Factor Table	1959 Outcomes: For 1952 Public Assistance Families: Delinquent	Nondelinquent	Total	For 1952 Self-sufficient Families: Delinquent	Nondelinquent	Total
White	Probably delinquent	1	2*	3	0	1*	1
	Probably nondelinquent	0*	0	0	0*	49	49
	Total	1	2	3	0	50	50
Negro	Probably delinquent	4	9*	13	4	11*	15
	Probably nondelinquent	4*	19	23	3*	77	80
	Total	8	28	36	7	88	95
Puerto Rican	Probably delinquent	3	1*	4	1	0*	1
	Probably nondelinquent	1*	8	9	0*	25	25
	Total	4	9	13	1	25	26
All	Probably delinquent	8	12*	20	5	12*	17
	Probably nondelinquent	5*	27	32	3*	151	154
	Total	13	39	52	8	163	171

* Errors of prediction.

Although the schools were selected by the Youth Board in 1952 because they lay in high-delinquency neighborhoods, the delinquency rates in the two neighborhoods increased over the ten-year period of the study. Three families moved from the Bronx to rural areas, at least one for the express purpose of providing better child supervision.[29] Bear in mind that choice of neighborhoods was limited for these 20 Negro families. Furthermore, half of them were receiving public assistance at some time during the study, reflecting economic disabilities that must have also reduced their opportunities to relocate. Nevertheless, eight of the twenty families had moved by 1961 to better neighborhoods. Perhaps it is only a coincidence, but four of the seven families where the mother's supervision was rated effective in 1965 had relocated into neighborhoods with lower delinquency rates—as compared with four of the 13 families where the mother's supervision was poor.

Residential mobility was not confined to Negro families; 29 of the 53 white boys in the Youth Board study were Jewish, and other studies have shown that Jewish families move readily to better neighborhoods when their old communities deteriorate.[30] Mobility is not motivated exclusively by a concern for the upbringing of children, important though this is; population flow is to be expected in a large city. The Youth Board researchers have complained about the difficulty of keeping track of 61 boys scattered by 1961 in out-of-town schools in 12 states, Puerto Rico, and Malta.[31] And of course moves occurred within New York City. Regardless of the motivation for residential moves, however, an important consequence is to provide a new environment for children. Of 14 boys predicted *nondelinquent* in 1952 whose families moved to a *better* neighborhood, none became delinquent; of 31 boys with exactly the same prediction score whose families moved to neighborhoods with the *same* or *worse* levels of delinquency, 7 became delinquent.[32] The Youth Board has not yet analyzed the moves of all the families in the study in relation to prediction scores and outcomes. Hence, it is not known whether boys predicted *delinquent* in 1952 were less likely to become so if their families moved to better neighborhoods. It sounds plausible.

If indeed weak family control predisposes a boy living in a high-delinquency neighborhood to become delinquent, it would be helpful to know the ethnic and socioeconomic circumstances that reinforce this tendency. The question is not *whether* the various prediction tables predict delinquency but *how* both successful and unsuccessful predictions provide clues to underlying causes and ultimately to programs of intervention. As an illustration of this approach Table 5 breaks down the relationship between the two- and three-factor prediction table and delinquent outcomes (shown in Table 4) for three ethnic groups and two socioeconomic statuses.[33] What does Table 5 reveal about the reinforcing effect of the social milieu?

Facts

1. Predictions of delinquency were more likely to be made for Negro boys than for Puerto Rican or white boys. Twenty-one per cent of the 131 Negro boys were given better than a 50-50 chance of becoming delinquent—as contrasted with 13 per cent of the 39 Puerto Rican boys and 8 per cent of the 53 white boys. To look at the data in another way, of the 37 boys predicted delinquent, 33 were Negro or Puerto Rican.

2. Although the number of cases in some categories were very small, e.g., only four *white* boys and five *Puerto*

[29] *Ibid.*, pp. S7-8.

[30] *Ibid.*, p. 4; Nathan Glazer and Daniel Patrick Moynihan, *Beyond the Melting Pot: The Negroes, Puerto Ricans, Jews, Italians, and Irish of New York City*, Cambridge, Massachusetts, M.I.T. Press, 1963, pp. 53-67, 160-163.

[31] New York City Youth Board, *op. cit.*, 1961, p. 15.

[32] New York City Youth Board, Research Department, *A Study of Mobility and Delinquency in a Sample of Boys in Glueck Project*, mimeographed, February, 1963, p. 6.

[33] Mrs. Maude Craig, research director of the Youth Board, graciously provided unpublished data on the economic status and the ethnic backgrounds of the 223 boys in the study.

Ricans predicted delinquent, predictions of delinquency were more likely to be correct and predictions of nondelinquency to be wrong for Negroes and Puerto Ricans than for whites. Whereas one out of four of the white boys predicted delinquent became so, 36 per cent of the Negroes and Puerto Ricans predicted delinquent fulfilled the prediction. None of the 49 white boys predicted non-delinquent became delinquent but 8 per cent of the Negro and Puerto Rican boys did within seven years.

3. Predictions of delinquency were more likely to be made for boys from public assistance families than for boys from self-sufficient families. Thirty-eight per cent of the 52 public assistance boys were given better than a 50-50 chance of becoming delinquent—as contrasted with 10 per cent of the 171 boys from self-sufficient families.

4. Predictions of delinquency were more likely to be correct and predictions of nondelinquency more likely to be wrong for public assistance families than for self-sufficient families. This tendency was characteristic of white, Negro, and Puerto Rican families looked at separately; the fact of public assistance had an adverse effect on outcomes regardless of ethnicity.

Interpretation

1. Since the predictions of delinquency were based on pathological family situations, the greater tendency for predictions of delinquency to be made in Negro and Puerto Rican families must be due mainly to the greater incidence of family disorganization in these ethnic groups. This disorganization is highly correlated with dependency and, very likely, with employment opportunities. Note, for example, that only 16 per cent of the boys from self-sufficient Negro families were predicted delinquent—as contrasted with 36 per cent from dependent Negro families.

2. Recall that in the Cambridge-Somerville Youth Study the greater tendency for predictions of delinquency to come true and predictions of nondelinquency to be wrong in slum neighborhoods was interpreted as due to differing neighborhood traditions of delinquency. In the Youth Board study we see again a greater tendency for predictions of delinquency to come true and predictions of nondelinquency to be incorrect in disadvantaged segments of the population, this time among Negroes and Puerto Ricans and among the children of welfare recipients rather than among boys from poorer neighborhoods. Part of the explanation here may be that ethnic traditions of delinquency are analogous to neighborhood traditions of delinquency. Obviously, however, differing ethnic traditions of delinquency cannot explain the fact that boys from public assistance families were more likely to become delinquent within the same ethnic group and the same Glueck prediction category. It is unlikely that public assistance families constitute a community within a community and that the children of such families have a distinct tradition of delinquency. Possibly boys from economically dependent families are more likely to be *recorded* as delinquents than boys from self-sufficient families who are behaving similarly; this assumes that the police know the welfare status of the family and discriminate against the most deprived. This seems to me far-fetched. More likely, economic disadvantage has adverse effects on the school adjustment and (ultimately) on the occupational opportunities of public assistance children.[34] Their greater proneness to delinquency may stem from their lesser hopes for and commitments to legitimate enterprises.[35]

3. Bear in mind that all of the preadolescent boys followed up in the Youth Board Prediction Study came from two high delinquency neighborhoods characterized by considerable gang activity. Yet those members of the Study population *predicted non-delinquent,* i.e., closely supervised by their parents, usually avoided delinquent associates and bore out the prediction. Exceptions to this generalization are Negro boys from public assistance families predicted nondelinquent; 17 per cent of them became delinquent within seven years. Perhaps the double disadvantage of race prejudice and poor economic prospects reduced their stake in conformity.[36]

4. One reason for the overprediction of delinquency is that Table 5 does not include *all* delinquencies committed by the boys in the study from 1952 to 1959; some delinquent acts were undetected or unrecorded. Another reason for the overprediction of delinquency in Table 5 is that some boys became delinquent for the first time *after* 1959. But there remains the possibility that many of the prophecies of delinquency were defeated because deliberate as well as unintentional interventions occurred in the lives of these boys. Families moved to neighborhoods with fewer delinquent gangs; boys joined boys' clubs or the Boy Scouts; social agencies helped the families to solve their problems and thereby improved parental supervision; the schools offered remedial education to slow learners.

Conclusion

The problem of delinquency control has long been the subject of jurisdictional disputes among sociologists, psychologists, social workers and psychiatrists—not to mention lawyers and the police. Recently, "early identification and intensive treatment of predelinquents" has attracted much interest, and it seemed at first that this approach offered a relatively uncontroversial technique of delinquency control.

Careful analysis of two notable experiments in early identification and intensive treatment of predelinquents shows that intellectual confusion lurks beneath the surface plausibility of early identification and intensive treatment. The following issues have not been resolved:

1. Does early identification depend on extrapolating antisocial tendencies already observable in the preadolescent boy or girl into adolescence? Or does early identification consist of locating youngsters who have been exposed to family or community experiences known to cause delinquency?
2. Can *early* identification be accurate? The issue of accuracy is essentially a theoretical problem. Accurate early identification is possible only (a) if no crucial etiological factors make their appearance *after* the predictions are made or (b) if early experiences establish a differential vulnerability for all subsequent experiences.

34 Richard A. Cloward and Lloyd E. Ohlin, *Delinquency and Opportunity,* Glencoe, Ill.: The Free Press, 1960.

35 Larry Karacki and Jackson Toby, "The Uncommitted Adolescent: Candidate for Gang Socialization," *Sociological Inquiry,* 32 (Spring, 1962), pp. 203-215.

36 Jackson Toby, "Social Disorganization and Stake in Conformity: Complementary Factors in the Predatory Behavior of Young Hoodlums," *Journal of Criminal Law, Criminology and Police Science,* 48 (May-June, 1957), pp. 12-17. Arthur L. Stinchcombe, *Rebellion in a High School,* Chicago: Quadrangle Books, 1964, chs. 3 and 4.

3. What *kind* of intensive treatment should be given? Does the type of treatment have to be individualized according to the problem of the youngster? Or are all types of treatment equally effective with all types of delinquents providing treatment is "intensive"?
4. How intensive must "intensive treatment" be and how early must it start in order to satisfy the early identification and intensive treatment formula? (The McCords have dismissed the negative results of the Cambridge-Somerville Youth Study as irrelevant to the validity of the early identification and intensive treatment approach because the treatment program was not sufficiently intensive.)
5. How can early identification and intensive treatment programs avoid "self-fulfilling prophecies"? If the treatment program concentrates its efforts on youngsters who are especially vulnerable to delinquency, how can it justify its discriminatory policy except by stigmatizing predelinquents? And may not the delinquency-producing effects of the stigmatization equal or exceed the delinquency-preventing benefits of the treatment?
6. Finally, is it likely that an effective approach to delinquency control can emerge without clarification of the underlying intellectual issues in the etiology of delinquency? Although they approached early identification of predelinquents in theoretically distinct ways, both the Cambridge-Somerville Youth Study and the New York City Youth Board Prediction Study show that attention to the social context can improve the accuracy of predictions. The neighborhood of residence in the Cambridge-Somerville Youth Study and the dependency status of the family and its ethnicity in the New York City Youth Board Prediction Study were relevant to later outcomes. However, in neither study is it clear *why* predictions of delinquency were more likely to be correct and predictions of nondelinquency wrong for youngsters of disadvantaged social origins. The relationship among social origin, family functioning, individual self-conception, and peer group influence was ignored. Can a theoretically blind prediction technique provide the basis for effective intervention?

Anti-Poverty Programs and Delinquency

Gerald D. Robin

The provision of jobs, training, or work experience is an important component in many anti-poverty programs, frequently being the base around which the entire program is structured and developed. Within this work-oriented milieu the program participants are offered services in the form of counseling, remedial education, and job supervision. The dialogue supporting such programs has increasingly emphasized their contribution toward reducing delinquency and youth crime by inculcating more positive and socially acceptable attitudes and values in the youths and by constructively occupying leisure time through employment activities, thereby reducing the inclination and opportunity of its recipients to engage in behavior which would make them the objects of law enforcement attention. Examples of serious scientific attempts to explore empirically the hypothesis that such programs reduce delinquency are not only isolated but virtually nonexistent in the literature. Because of this, because the anti-poverty program evaluated in the present study was the in-school Neighborhood Youth Corps—one of the largest and best known federally created and subsidized programs, reaching hundreds of thousands of ghetto youths in their natural milieu and at a time when they are highly susceptible to contacts with the police—and because it was possible to establish a control group of unassailable quality, the findings presented in this paper are particularly relevant.

The in-school Neighborhood Youth Corps (NYC) program provides jobs to students 16 through 21 years of age who come from poor families.[1] During the school term these students are permitted to work as many as fifteen hours a week and up to thirty-two hours a week during the summer, at a standard rate of $1.25 per hour; a majority of the in-school NYC projects are operated (sponsored) by school boards and educational institutions.[2] At their employment sites the student "enrollees" are under the direction of a work supervisor and are also assigned NYC counselors who periodically meet with them to discuss their problems, progress in the program, the role and value of education, and the need to complete high school.

The Groups Studied

Exploration of the hypothesis that participation in anti-poverty programs reduces delinquency is explored here by an analysis of the police records of random samples of Negro youths interviewed in the summer of 1966 who, as of the time of sample selection (1) were actively enrolled and working in the in-school Neighborhood Youth Corps program operated by the Public Board of Education in Cincinnati—hereafter referred to as *year-round* enrollees, (2) were about to enter the Cincinnati NYC program for the first time—hereafter referred to as *summer-only* enrollees, and (3) had applied for enrollment and been found eligible but were not accepted into the program in order that they might be used as a control group. The larger study of which the police contact analysis is but a part was a longitudinal survey that involved interviewing NYC and control youths three times over a one-year period, with the first phase of interviewing conducted at the start of the 1966 summer and the last wave in March 1967, a month after the collection of the police contact data. The fact that the police record analysis is based upon those youths who were originally interviewed rather than upon the entire sample of names selected from the NYC records is not a serious limitation because at least four-fifths of the youths in each sample of names selected were in fact interviewed; in addition, virtually all of the non-respondents were uninterviewed because they could not be located within the time available rather than because of refusals or other more substantial factors associated with self-selection.

On June 2, 1966, two-hundred names stratified by sex within school were randomly selected from the active NYC files containing the names of all youths (723) who were enrolled in the program at that point, of which 167 (84%) were interviewed. Because this group had worked in the Neighborhood Youth Corps for at least some part of that school year, they are referred to, for convenience and in order to distinguish them from the second experimental sample to be described below, as *year-round* enrollees. This does not mean that, as of the time their names were drawn from the active files, they were enrolled in the program for an entire school year, school term or for a total of one year overall. The *summer-only* group consisted of youths who were to enter the NYC for the first time in the 1966 summer program and who were to be terminated at its conclusion, because of a reduction in the number of authorized jobs which would be available in the fall of 1967—this in contrast to the year-round youths who were not summarily terminated from the NYC at a particular point but rather were permitted to remain in the program and were subject to voluntary and involuntary departure for any number of reasons over a long period of time; in fact, fully half of this group were still working in the NYC when the police record data were collected in February 1967. The summer-only enrollees, on the other hand, were exposed to the NYC for a maximum period of 8 to 11 weeks, depending upon their summer assigment; many of them had assigments that lasted 6 to 8 weeks or may have left the project before its completion. While the utilization of two treatment groups, the year-round and summer-only enrollees, with which to compare the controls has certain advantages which will become apparent in the analysis, one which may be mentioned at this point is the variation in the length of program participation which they introduce: the summer-only youths were in the NYC for an average of 8 weeks, while the average length of participation for the year-round enrollees, at the time of the police record determination, was 14 months. Findings based upon the year-round sample may suggest that there is a critical minimal period of program exposure which must obtain before the program's effect on reducing delinquency becomes manifest and that such exposure is not satisfied by a summer's experience in the program.

The summer-only and control groups were established from the 351 names of youths who, as of June 1966, were on the "waiting list" for entrance into the summer program; that is, there were 351 youths in Cincinnati who had applied for admission to the NYC prior to June 1966, had been screened and found eligible, and who had never worked in the program before. These "waiting list" names were arranged alphabetically and randomly assigned to the summer-only or control

From *Journal of Criminal Law, Criminology, and Police Science*, Vol. 60 (Fall 1969), pp. 323–331.

groups. This procedure led to the creation of an eligible universe of 136 summer-only names (130 of whom were interviewed) and 173 control names (136 of whom were interviewed). As part of their cooperation and participation in the study, the NYC administrators agreed not to accept any of the controls into the program until all field phases of the investigation were completed, and to terminate all new summer-only (SO) enrollees at the end of the 1966 summer program, this latter group also to be excluded from re-entering until all field phases were completed. It is singularly important to note that the control and summer-only groups were experimentally created specifically for research purposes and were established by a chance termination of *which* "waiting list" youths were to be admitted to the program. This random assignment of youths to the control or treatment (SO) group eliminated bias associated with self-selection, a serious shortcoming in some recent anti-poverty studies which have utilized "no shows"—applicants who do not enroll in programs after being accepted—as a control group.[3] Those who *reject* program participation are likely to be considerably different from enrollees, particularly with respect to motivation and associated variables that may be criteria for measuring program effectiveness. No such compromise was required to identify and utilize a control group in the present study in Cincinnati: their exclusion from the Neighborhood Youth Corps was determined by fortuitous circumstances in which the youths themselves played no part and by a methodologically unassailable procedure which could not have resulted in systematic differences between the control and summer-only, or indeed year-round (YR) enrollees.[4]

Because almost all of the youths in the samples were Negroes, cases of white youths were excluded from the study. Thus, the number of Negro youths who were interviewed in each sample and who therefore constitute the groups on which the police record analysis is based is 138 year-round enrollees (82 males, 56 females), 109 summer-only enrollees (50 males, 59 females), and 119 controls (54 males, 65 females).

Source of Police Contact Data

Identification on all of the youths originally interviewed and accompanying data collection forms were submitted to law enforcement authorities in Cincinnati in order to ascertain whether they had any juvenile or adult record of police contacts, and if so, to record the date and charges entered against the youths for each police contact. After the Master Record File—the central register from which juvenile police contacts were abstracted—had been inspected for this purpose, the forms were sent to the Adult Division of the police department, since at the time of offense record determination many of the "youths" were officially adults, and all *criminal* charges against them were entered on the forms. The Master Record File in the Juvenile Division contained all recorded police contacts which a youth had with the law, regardless of the precinct of origination. Thus, despite the nature of the police contact—of its severity or triviality, and of the location of the offense and the original jurisdiction of police administration over the case—if the police contact was recorded at any level it was routinely processed and entered into the juvenile Master Record File. Furthermore, the Master Record File had been maintained for a sufficiently long period such that it was in operation before any of the youths in the present study were seven years of age, so that it contained all of the ever-recorded delinquencies committed by the youths. Thus, the complete history of recorded juvenile, as well as adult, police contacts was collected. Because a majority of the youths in each sample were 16 years old when they enrolled in or applied to the program, and because approximately nine-tenths of them were between 16 and 18 years of age at the time the police contact data were collected, youths with offense records will frequently be referred to as delinquents, although it is recognized that technically individuals who incur their first police contact after juvenile status are considered criminals.

The Findings

Delinquency patterns and prevalence are primarily an expression of, or at least largely predictable from, socioeconomic status, sex, race and age; because all of the subjects in the study were Negroes of approximately the same age who were living in poverty and because the police record analysis was of course performed separately for males and females, in both experimental groups the distribution and *interaction* of these and other variables associated with Negro poverty were very closely matched with that of the controls. The serious limitation in the summer-only sample in the present analysis is the very brief period of their participation in the Neighborhood Youth Corps, thus constituting a severe restriction on one of the most important "follow-up" police contact exposure periods—the reader will recall that the average duration in the program for the summer-only group was 8 weeks, while that for the year-round enrollees at the time that the delinquency data were collected was approximately 14 months. Obviously, the greater the interval, the more likely that offenses will be committed which result in officially reported police contacts. This variable, however, has been "equated" in the year-round and control groups through natural conditions resulting from the fact that these two groups of youths tended to apply for admission and to enroll in the program over essentially the same time period, and were therefore characterized by the same police contact exposure intervals, *e.g.*, the average length of NYC participation for the year-round youths, at the time the offense data were collected, was 13.6 months while the functionally and analytically equivalent follow-up period for the controls—the interval between their application to the program and the date the offense records were checked—was 12.8 months.

The analysis which follows is based upon the identification of carefully constructed and meaningful time periods in relation to program enrollment and program participation for the year-round and summer-only youths, and the date of application for the controls.[5] Thus, the police contact profile for the experimental youths has been delineated, inspected, and calculated for the periods *before* they enrolled in the Neighborhood Youth Corps, *while* they were working in the program, and from the point of *enrollment to the date of the offense record check*. The second time period mentioned—*while* the youths were actively enrolled in the program—constitutes perhaps the most relevant temporal base for testing the relationship between NYC participation and delinquency—whereas the last period alluded to combines the *in-program* (*while* the youths were active in the NYC) with the *after program* period (the interval between termination from the NYC and the date of the offense record check) in order to ascertain whether there was any *overall* change in the enrollees' delinquency proneness prior to entering the NYC as contrasted with that which obtained from the time they joined until the offense record data were collected. In the case of the controls, the temporal frame of reference was dichotomized into *before application* (equivalent to the pre-enrollment period of the experimental youths) and *after application*, *i.e.*, from the point of application to the date of the offense record check (approximating the interval between enrollment and the offense record check for both experimental groups and equivalent to the time *while* the YR enrollees were working in the program). The terms "prior" or "previous" will refer to the period before enrollment or application, and the term "subsequent" to the period after enrollment or application to the date of the offense record check. With the preceding comments by way of introduction, the findings may now be presented.

Prior to enrollment/application among the males, a significantly[6] larger proportion of the controls (63%) than of the experimental samples (38% YR, 34% SO) had committed serious offenses, the latter defined as acts against the person or property violations and hereafter referred to interchangeably as felonies, personal/property offenses, or serious offenses; 37% of the year-round and 39% of the control youths had incurred minor or non-serious police contacts of the misdemeanor variety, while 49% YR, 54% SO and two-thirds of the controls had an offense record of some kind. Among the females in this time period, twice as many controls (19%) as year-round youths (7%), and the same proportion of summer-only youths (19%) had committed serious offenses, twice as many controls (23%) as year-round or summer-only enrollees (10–11%) had incurred minor police contacts, and 37% of the control females had an offense record before applying to the program, compared with only 16% of the year-round and one-fifth of the summer-only females before enrolling, significant differences which place the control females at a "disadvantage" in relation to the year-round females.

Moreover, the average number of felonies,

misdemeanors, or any offenses committed by all of the controls before application and by all of the experimental youths before enrollment was either virtually identical, or greater among the controls than the enrollees; the same was true concerning the number of offenses of a given typology committed by those who had such charges against them. For example, among all males, the mean number of felony police contacts incurred by the controls before application to the NYC was 1.2, compared with 0.7 for each of the year-round and summer-only groups. Among the male youths who were charged with felonies before enrollment/application to the program, the average number of such charges for this subgroup of control youths was 1.9 compared with 2.0 for the year-round enrollees and 2.2 for the summer-only enrollees. Similarly, the mean number of total police contacts prior to application was 3.3 for the male controls, 3.0 for the male year-round youths, and 3.5 for the male summer-only enrollees. The same trend of results obtained for the females and for the distribution of misdemeanors in the "before" period. Furthermore, because differences in the average number of felony charges, misdemeanor charges, or any police contacts incurred by the total group of control and experimental youths, as well as by those specific subgroups of youths who committed the respective kinds of offenses, generally approached zero and rarely exceeded .3 in all of the tables generated for the delinquency analysis, continued reference to the number of acts or offenses will be avoided, since these differences could hardly be more inconsequential.

Thus, both the control males and females in Cincinnati were noticeably more delinquent in their police contact typology in the pre-application period than were the corresponding experimental youths, and this difference was greatest between the controls and the year-round sample—the experimental group which offered the most critical opportunity for testing the effect of NYC participation on delinquency and youth crime.

While they were in the NYC the proportion of year-round males who incurred police contacts represented a 33% reduction from the proportion who had an offense record prior to joining the program (from 49% to 33%), but the proportion of control males who committed offenses after applying for admission—encompassing a follow-up exposure period which was equivalent to that of the year-round males—was 39% less than the proportion who were offenders prior to trying to join the NYC (from 67% to 41%). Similarly, the male YRs charged with serious offenses decreased from 38% before enrollment to 17% *while* in the program—a 55% reduction in those who committed felonies while working in the NYC—whereas the proportion of control males with offenses against the person/property decreased by 68% (from 63% before to 20% after application). Thus, despite the fact that the control males were more serious offenders prior to application than were the year-round males prior to enrollment, the latter were equally as likely to commit serious offenses while they were active in the NYC program as were the control males after application, nor were there any significant differences in the proportion of the year-round versus control males in this same time period who committed misdemeanors or who had any offenses charged to their record. *Accordingly, there is no evidence that NYC participation reduced delinquency among its enrollees while they were working in the program, a somewhat unexpected finding if for no reason other than that the program utilized approximately 1,000 hours of what would otherwise have been leisure time and therefore opportunity for misbehavior.* Nor was program participation related to delinquency prevention after termination from the NYC: the YR males had worked in the NYC fully six times as long as the SO males (11.5 months versus 8.3 weeks), and the exposure period after termination was shorter for the year-round (3.6 months) than for the SO males (5.3 months); yet, the proportion of both groups who committed offenses after leaving the program was the same (23% YR and 20% SO). In the interval between enrollment/application and the offense record check—which was twice as long for the controls (13 months) as for the summer-only enrollees (7 months)—there were no significant differences between the male controls and either of the experimental samples in the proportion of youths who were charged with serious, minor, or any offenses; indeed, with one exception, the proportions were virtually identical: 21% YR, 20% C and 12% SO were charged with felonies, 29% YR, 28% C and 26% SO with misdemeanors, and 39% YR, 41% C and 36% SO with any offenses.

The above analysis is based upon the *gross* effects of the program in reducing anti-social behavior without identifying specific subgroups of youths with records and determining whether these individuals benefited from program participation as reflected in their police contact profiles in appropriate follow-up periods. The crucial test of the NYC's effect on youth crime is its ability to insulate those youths who were delinquent prior to enrollment from continuing to commit offenses *while* they are working in the program, as well as from the point of entrance to the program throughout the subsequent exposure period (*i.e.*, up to the point of the offense record check)—thus yielding the program's *net* rather than *gross* effects on delinquency; exclusive focus on the latter approach has serious shortcomings, not noted by the author of a recent study of the effects of the out-of-school Neighborhood Youth Corps program on police contacts, which purported to demonstrate that *that* program reduced delinquency among the female enrollees.[7]

Among the youths who had serious police contacts prior to enrollment/application, the proportion of year-round males who committed serious offenses while they were working in the NYC was identical to that of the male controls charged with offenses against person/property subsequent to application (one-quarter). Similarly, among those with misdeamenor offenses or any record previously, there were no significant differences in the proportion of year-round versus control males who had minor or any police contacts charged against them *while* in the NYC and *after* application, respectively. Finally, holding constant police contact typology prior to enrollment/application, there were no significant differences subsequently between the control and the experimental males: (1) of those with serious previous offenses, 29% YR, 24% SO and 25% C incurred serious police contacts subsequently, (2) of those with minor offenses previously, 37% YR, 33% SO and 35% C continued to commit such offenses subsequently, and (3) of those with any previous offense record, 48% YR, 48% SO and 50% C were offenders subsequently. As indicated earlier, the difference in the *number* of police contacts which characterized the individual samples was so small that a routine presentation of this information is unwarranted. Illustrative of this point is that among those with felony changes prior to enrollment/application, the average number of serious charges incurred subsequently was 0.3 for the year-round, 0.3 for the controls and 0.4 for the summer-only males; similarly, disregarding previous records, the average number of felonies committed by those charged with such acts in the subsequent period was 1.3 for the year-round, 1.3 for the controls and 1.7 for the summer-only males; this same pattern of differences in the number of police contacts approaching zero obtained for the remaining typological subgroups (number of misdemeanors and number of any police contacts) of youths.

Up to this point the analysis has been concerned with whether NYC participation tended to insulate youths who prior to enrollment had committed serious offenses from continuing to do so once they started to work in the program, those who were minor offenders previously from continuing to commit or engage in misdemeanant behavior, and youths who had known records of previous contacts from incurring subsequent police contacts. Another related aspect of this analysis, however, is whether NYC participation prevented youths who prior to enrollment had no serious charges against them from committing felonies after they entered the program, as well as those who had no previous misdemeanors from incurring minor police contacts subsequently. On both of these criteria, NYC participation continued to demonstrate no effect on reducing criminality: of the 51 year-round males who had no felony charges prior to enrollment, 12% were charged with serious offenses while they were working in the NYC, while in the functionally equivalent time period 10% of the control males who had no serious offense records prior to application acquired one after application; similarly, 19% of the year-round and 23% of the control males who had no misdemeanor police contacts before enrollment/application were charged with minor offenses while in the NYC and after they applied to the program. Moreover, when the interval between enrollment and the date of the offense record check is used for the enrollees—a period directly comparable with the subsequent time period for the controls—the proportion of the year-round males who committed their first serious offense during this time was 16% (12% did so in the shorter exposure period *while* in the program) and the proportion who committed their first minor offense was 25% (19% did so *while* in the program), compared with the same statistics reported above for the control males of 10% and 23% who, after application to the program, committed their first serious and minor offenses, respectively.

Of perhaps equal importance as the indices of "delinquency reduction" utilized above in studying the relationship between NYC participation and police contacts is the program's effect on discouraging youths who were *non-delinquent* prior to enrolling from *becoming* delinquent after entering. That is, it may be more reasonable to expect that NYC participation would be more successful in *preventing* delinquency than in *reducing* it. While it is obviously a less demanding and more modest task to prevent youths who have not become the objects of police action and attention from doing so than it is to discourage already delinquent youths from persisting in their misconduct, the former accomplishment would nonetheless be substantial. Unfortunately, however, there was no evidence that this occurred as a result of the Neighborhood Youth Corps: of the year-round males without an offense record prior to enrollment, 24% acquired one, *i.e., became* delinquent *while* working in the NYC, the very same proportion as the previously non-delinquent control males who became delinquent after applying to the program. With respect to the previously non-delinquent females, 98% of the year-round enrollees continued to be non-delinquent while in the NYC as did 98% of the control females after application. Finally, among both males and females who were non-delinquent prior to enrollment/application, there were no significant differences in the proportion who became delinquent subsequently: among the males, one-third YR (31%), 24% C and 22% SO did so, while among the females less than 3% of any sample subsequently became delinquent.

The Detroit Data

An analysis of the police records similar to the above was performed for the same typology of random samples of interviewed Negroes (after excluding a small number of white cases) who were enrolled in and applied to the Detroit in-public school Neighborhood Youth Corps program: 161 year-round enrollees (51 males, 110 females), 239 summer-only enrollees (132 males, 107 females),[8] and 124 controls (38 males, 86 females). There are three reasons that less confidence should be placed in the Detroit than in the Cincinnati data, two of which deal with the control group and the other with the Master Record File, discussed below.

First, because a sample of financially eligible applicants not admitted to the NYC was not available in Detroit, applicants who, prior to the date of sample selection in the summer of 1966, had been rejected because of over-income were utilized as the control subjects. It was desirable to use the smallest possible over-income cutoff point that would identify an adequate sample size of controls in order to minimize serious poverty status differences between them and the experimental (YR and SO) youths, who of course had met the financial eligibility criteria. A family over-income of $1,500 as the cutoff point yielded 245 names of applicants who were utilized as the control sample in Detroit. While the control group in Detroit represents a slight compromise, the average family income by which they exceeded the financial eligibility requirements of the Neighborhood Youth Corps was only $648, confirming that the financial background of the two experimental groups—year-round and summer-only enrollees—was not substantially less than that of the control group in Detroit. Family income differentials would only be serious if they were such as to identify distinct social class categories, because of the known and documented class-related variation in behavior patterns. It is submitted that discrepancies in financial background of what amounts to a few hundred dollars annually are not likely to cause or account for differentials in the present criterion and that, therefore, no injury has been done by accepting the minimally over-income Detroit youths as valid controls. It would indeed be difficult to argue, for example, that the Detroit controls from 6-member households whose annual family income exceeded the eligibility requirement by $673 were, in their behavior, attitudes, motivation, values, etc., discernably different and presumably "better" than those from even less fortunate families. Even when the average family over-income of the Detroit controls was related to size of household, it never reached as much as $1,000.

Secondly, out of the population of 245 controls, only 140, or 57%, were interviewed.[9] While the completion rate for the Detroit control group is admittedly low, it should be noted that it represents the entire eligible universe rather than a sample proper selected from a larger population; thus the interview-to-universe ratio is quite high for the controls in Detroit: 1 out of less than every 2 controls in the population was interviewed. In addition, almost without exception the reason for not obtaining interviews with the Detroit controls was that they could not be located in time or had moved and were therefore physically inaccessible—reasons which, a priori, would not distinguish the uninterviewed controls from those who were. Thus, despite a low completion *rate*, a high interview/population ratio and the absence of self-selection factors served to maximize the representativeness of those controls in Detroit who were interviewed.

Finally, the charges listed in the juvenile Master Record File in Detroit did not contain all known recorded police contacts but only those—presumably representing the more serious offenses—which were filtered through the individual police precincts after they had been recorded in the latter's record. Thus, in Detroit all of the charges recorded at the precinct level, for one reason or another, were not routinely made known to and incorporated into the Master Record File, which was the source of data collection in the present study. However, the structure of the present analysis is less concerned with the absolute number of police contacts or delinquency typology than it is with the comparative profile of police contacts among the controls and experimental youths, to which the same procedural limitations were applicable. Thus, since there is no reason to believe that the under-recording of the number of juvenile police contacts and their typology is not randomly distributed among the experimental and control groups, *i.e.*, since there is no systematic bias in recording juvenile police contacts among the youth samples, the utilization of this data in Detroit is not viewed as problematic. With the preceding remarks by way of introduction and qualification, the Detroit findings may now be summarized below.

Because the number of youths in each group type in Detroit who had a known offense record was initially restricted because of this last mentioned procedural consideration, segmentation of data—holding constant offense status and typology prior to enrollment/application in order to measure change in subsequent periods—was limited. *The gross effects in Detroit, however, are the same as those in Cincinnati, revealing no effect of program participation on reducing or preventing delinquency.* Among the males, prior to enrolling in the Neighborhood Youth Corps 17% YR, 21% SO and 21% C had been charged with felonies, 2% YR, 10% SO and 18% C with misdemeanors, and 17% YR, 24% SO and 29% C had an offense record. In other words, in the pre-enrollment/application period the controls were equally as, if not more, delinquent than the experimental youths. Yet, the proportion of control males who committed felonies (11%), misdemeanors (5%) or any offenses (13%) after application was no different from that of the year-round males who committed the same offenses *while* working in the NYC, or from the proportion of summer-only males who incurred this typology of offenses after enrolling in the program.

Among the females in Detroit, there were no significant differences in the proportion who previously were charged with serious offenses (7% YR, 17% SO, 9% C), with misdemeanors (5% YR, 18% SO, 7% C) or with any offenses (10% YR, 26% SO, 14% C). Nor were there any salient differences in the proportion of controls who subsequently committed felonies (4%), misdemeanors (none) or any offenses (4%) compared with year-round females who were charged with felonies (2%), misdemeanors (2%), or any offenses (4%) *while* working in the NYC, or compared with summer-only females (5% felonies, 8% misdemeanors, 11% any offenses) after entering the program. Among both male and female youths in Detroit who were non-delinquent prior to enrollment/application, almost all of them continued to remain free of an offense record subsequently: among the males, 92% YR *while* in the program and in the entire subsequent period, 93% controls and 92% of the summer-only after joining the program did so; and among the females 97% while in the program, 99% controls and 90% of the summer-only after joining the program continued to remain non-delinquent.

Summary

Separate analyses of the police records of year-round and summer-only enrollees who worked in the in-school Neighborhood Youth Corps programs in Cincinnati and Detroit compared with those of control youths who applied to the program revealed that NYC participation, among both males and females, was unrelated to delinquency prevention or reduction. Examination of the gross and net effects of program participation disclosed no evidence that working in the program made enrollees with a previous offense record less likely to continue to commit offenses while they were working in the program, in any way had a positive effect on particular types of offenders, or reduced overall the number of police contacts or specific kinds of offensive behavior. Nor, among enrollees who had no previous offense record prior to enrollment, did the program dissuade them from entering the ranks of delinquency more so than was the case with the controls in the absence of program participation. In neither city was there any indication that NYC participation had an effect on reducing criminality on the part of enrollees while the youths were working in the program or after they left it.

Assuming that police contacts are a valid index of variation in illegal behavior, then the putative importance of anti-poverty programs that consist largely of the creation of work opportunities in reducing criminality among juveniles and young people may be more illusive than real.

---

[1] The *out-of-school* Neighborhood Youth Corps program provides "full time" employment to youths who have dropped out of school; one of the out-of-school program's main objectives is to encourage the enrollees to return to school in order to complete their high school education.

[2] These conditions were in effect at the time the present study was conducted. More recently, there have been efforts to lower the entrance age to 14 years and to provide for a pay *scale* rather than a fixed rate of compensation.

[3] PETERSON, AN EVALUATION OF THE CONCEPT OF TRAINEE CAMPS FOR UNEMPLOYED YOUTH.

[4] Despite the random distribution of waiting list youths into control and summer-only subjects, this procedure did not in any way affect the *total* number of youths who worked in the program, since the 1966 Cincinnati summer program quota could not accommodate all eligible applicants. Thus, while the specific individuals on the waiting list who were admitted to the program were guided and determined by research considerations, the *sum total of services* offered in the 1966 summer program was completely unaffected by the study design.

[5] The dates on which the year-round youths *applied* to the program were not available.

[6] The term "significant" refers to statistically significant differences in proportions at at least .05 level of confidence.

[7] WALTHER & MAGNUSSON, A RETROSPECTIVE STUDY OF THE EFFECTIVENESS OF OUT-OF-SCHOOL NEIGHBORHOOD YOUTH CORPS PROGRAMS IN FOUR URBAN SITES 116–124. In addition, these authors utilize a highly questionable approach in inferring program effects on youth crime, one based upon changes in the *number* of police contacts and changes in the proportion of total police contacts which were serious. For example, Walther and Magnusson report that before application to the program the 115 experimental youths had a total of 294 police contacts compared with only 15 police contacts after application; these figures compare with 250 police contacts incurred by the 115 controls before application and 23 police contacts after application, and apparently take some consolation in the "greater" reduction in the police contacts of the enrollees. Stated somewhat differently, these figures indicate that the experimental youths were charged with an average of 2.6 police contacts before applying to the NYC and 0.1 after application; in the same time periods the average number of police contacts for the controls went from 2.2 to 0.2. Similarly, the authors make much of the "finding" that before application 49% of all police contacts incurred by the enrollees were serious ones (*143 out of 294*) and that after application only 20% (*3 out of 15*) were. By contrast, so the authors reason, before application 38% of the total police charges against the controls were serious ones (96 out of 250), which increased to 48% after application (*11 out of 23*). Thus, Walther and Magnusson infer positive program effect on the basis that the proportion of serious charges in relation to total police contacts decreased from 49% to 20% among the NYC participants and increased from 38% to 48% among the controls. This approach is open to serious criticism on the basis of its logic and meaningfulness alone, not to mention that by using a measure of central tendency, the same figures reveal that the average number of serious offenses committed by the experimental youths before application was 1.2 compared with 0.0 after application, while among the controls the mean reduction in serious police contacts was from 0.8 to 0.1. What these statistics on serious police contacts suggest much more strongly than program effect is that after applying to the out-of-school Neighborhood Youth Corps virtually none of the youths in either group were charged with serious offenses.

[8] The summer-only sample consisted of Negroes who worked in the 1966 summer program operated by Total Action against Poverty, rather than by the Detroit Public Board of Education, because the latter sponsor did not anticipate a reduction in their Fall 1967 quota which would make it necessary to terminate a substantial number of the enrollees who worked in the NYC during their 1966 summer program.

[9] All of the eligible summer-only enrollees and 70% of the sample of year-round names selected were interviewed.

Evaluation and Case Study of a School-Based Delinquency Prevention Program

The Minnesota Youth Advocate Program

Paul S. Higgins

The Program emphasized counseling and advocacy for returnees from correctional institutions. Grades, attendance, offenses, and institutionalizations were compared for 66 E returnees to Advocate-served school-attendance areas and 40 C returnees to non-Advocate areas. Both groups showed similar community-adjustment gains and school-adjustment declines. At study's end, however, Es more than Cs were school-enrolled (often in "alternative schools") and outside institutions ($p < .05$). The Program probably had a small positive impact on delinquents. Suggested Program improvements include policy changes, greater Advocate "follow-through," and greater attention to returnee anxiety differences. The Program's 1972-1976 development was guided by funding availability, Advocate-administrator relations, and lobbying effectiveness, not by evaluations.

Juvenile delinquency has been an intractable social problem. The Minnesota Youth Advocate Program, begun in January 1972, stands in a long line of programs providing an adult to aid the adjustment of delinquents (e.g., Powers and Witmer, 1951; Berleman and Steinburn, 1967). Unfortunately, for most antidelinquency and corrections programs there is little reliable evidence that subjects receiving counseling or other "treatment" fared better than nontreated subjects.

Reviews of evaluative research concerning delinquency prevention efforts consistently conclude that (a) only a small fraction of such efforts are ever evaluated; (b) available evaluation studies usually have serious methodological flaws and frequently do not even clearly describe the treatment; and (c) the more adequate the research design, the less likely is the conclusion of a large treatment effect (e.g., Bailey, 1966; Lundman et al., 1976; Wright and Dixon, 1977).

The Minnesota Youth Advocate Program differs from many antidelinquency programs in being school-based and in its emphasis on school as well as community adjustment.

Each Youth Advocate has been a certified teacher, school social worker, or guidance counselor specially trained to perform a new role in the school—that of aiding a delinquent's transition from a correctional institution to the public school.

The most recent views of antidelinquency research (e.g., Lundman et al., 1976; Wright and Dixon, 1977) have emphasized the need for closer coordination between practitioners, researchers, and theorists in the design of new delinquency prevention programs.

Practitioners—particularly in the field of child welfare (as distinguished from the more narrow field of youth corrections), and particularly since federally funded reports, con-

AUTHOR'S NOTE: The evaluation and doctoral dissertation on which this paper is based were funded under a grant to the Project Evaluation Unit, Minnesota Governor's Commission on Crime Prevention and Control. The author gratefully acknowledges the help of Joseph Dotson, Ann Higgins, Marilyn Roelike, Paul Uhler, and the Youth Advocates in collecting data; and Judy Bolduc, Kathy Soukup, and Diane Boardman in providing clerical support. During the conduct of the evaluation, the author received the support and advice of many others, including David Lykken, John Bostad, Charles MacDonald, Cynthia Turnure, Doug Frisbie, and R. W. Faunce. Requests for reprints should be sent to the author, now with the Research and Evaluation Department, Minneapolis Public Schools, at the following address: 4904 13th Ave. So., Minneapolis, MN 55417.

From *Evaluation Quarterly*, Vol. 2 (May 1978), pp. 215-235. "Evaluation and Case Study of a School-Based Delinquency Prevention Program" by Paul S. Higgins is reprinted from *Evaluation Quarterly*, Vol. 2, No. 2 (May 1978), pp. 215-235, by permission of the publisher, Sage Publications, Inc.

ferences, and congressional activity of the late 1960s and early 1970s—currently emphasize the need for child advocacy. Child advocacy implies "going to bat" for children with agencies and systems. To be called an Advocate, a person must do more than provide direct service to an individual child (for discussions of youth advocacy, see, for example, Knitzer, 1976, and Polier, 1977).

Most researchers now agree that one-to-one counseling, as ordinarily practiced, is generally ineffective in preventing delinquency. One encouraging conclusion of recent research reviewers, however, is that treatment of offenders in the community is at least as effective, and often less expensive, than institutionalization (e.g., Wright and Dixon, 1977).

Recently, theorists (e.g., Polk, 1975; Schuchter, 1975; Elliott, 1966) have discussed the high correlation between delinquency and school failure, and most of these theorists attribute delinquency in part to enlightened school programs and policies.

These theorists differ, however, in their beliefs concerning the role schools can realistically be expected to play in delinquency prevention.

Polk, for example, implies the need for school reforms that would lessen competition for success-versus-failure labels and give more students a stake in both the social and academic life of the school. Schuchter believes that schools are unlikely to change and that alternate paths to adult success, that bypass the schools, should be created. Elliott asserts that dropping out of school leads to at least a short-run decline in delinquency. However, the long-run frustration of career aspirations caused by lack of a diploma may be a factor leading to adult criminality, particularly among dropouts of moderate and high intelligence (Hathaway et al., 1969). Furthermore, the creation of nonschool paths to adult occupational success may be a task at least as difficult as the reform of schools.

In summary, the basic approach of the Youth Advocate Program—that of keeping delinquents in school and in the community, while providing them emotional support and advocacy in dealing with school and criminal justice systems—is a strategy not inconsistent with much current delinquency-prevention thinking.

The purposes of this paper are:

1. to present a brief chronology of the Youth Advocate Program, from the time the first Advocates entered the schools in January 1972, through 1976. This narrative includes the decision made in early spring 1974 to end the program in Minneapolis and Duluth.
2. to present my evaluation of the 1972-1973 operation of the Program. This evaluation included quasi-experimental tests of the Program's effectiveness, as well as discussion of Advocate and delinquent-returnee differences accounting for differences in returnee adjustment.
3. to discuss obstacles to evaluation as a basis for improving and funding social action programs, using examples from the case study of the Advocate Program.

Purposes 1 and 3 may not at first seem appropriate for a journal article. I feel it important, however, for professional evaluators to share information on the social context of their evaluations. For this social context determines whether a program will be evaluated, how it will be evaluated, and how the results will be used.

A Chronology of the Youth Advocate Program, 1971-1976

Background Factors Leading to Proposal

During 1971 a combination of factors led planners in the Minnesota Department of Education and the Governor's Commission on Crime Prevention and Control to develop the first grant proposal for a Youth Advocate Program.

1. the possibility of creating full-time school positions by matching state special education money with federal Law Enforcement Assistance Administration (LEAA) money;
2. the knowledge that only about half the school-age boys and girls released from Minnesota correctional institutions to Minnesota cities returned to school;
3. the desire by corrections officials to cooperate with public schools toward improved prerelease educational planning for returnees—one institution had even hired its own "school liaison."

The Program's Golden Age: 1972-1973

During the 1972-1973 school year, the Program was extended to St. Paul (6 Advocates), making a total of 25 Advocates (including 13 in Minneapolis and 6 in Duluth). This second year of operation was characterized by high morale and unclouded by financial concerns. The 1972-1973 Program budget was about $400,000, half of which was spent in Minneapolis alone. Most felt Program funding was assured for at least three years, the Crime Commission's customary period of financial commitment to viable programs.

During this "zenith" year, I was hired to conduct a quasi-experimental evaluation of the Program. The Crime Commission had been dissatisfied with the largely anecdotal, testimonial nature of the first-year evaluation, and now wanted "hard" data on Program effectiveness.

Decline and Fall: 1973-1974

With the end of the 1973-1974 school year, the Program ended in Minneapolis and Duluth. In both cities, the following three factors—tight budgets, personal conflict, and poor lobbying efforts—led to termination of the Program.

In both Minneapolis and Duluth, 1973-1974 was the third and final expected year for LEAA funding. In both cities the special education departments that housed the Advocate Program did not lobby hard for continuation of the Program with local funds. Educators experience little external pressure to provide services specifically for delinquents. Almost by definition, and unlike other special education students, delinquents have no parent advocacy organized on their behalf.

In "going to bat" for delinquents with principals, Advocates did not always help their own cause. Reenrollment of returnees who had been discipline problems was often difficult. "What are you doing here?" was the principal's greeting to one returnee. When unable to place students in a regular public school, Advocates, especially in Minneapolis, often referred students to privately funded alternative schools serving hard-to-handle or poorly achieving adolescents. Yet the same principals who barred the schoolhouse door also complained when their state-aided budgets were reduced by students enrolling in private schools. In short, Advocates were often in a "no-win" situation with their principals. And when top administrators of the Minneapolis schools met in February 1974 to discuss the 1974-75 budget, they could report only a few principals who actively supported the Program.

The St. Paul Remnant: 1974-1976

The Advocate Program survives in St. Paul to the present day, despite a cutoff of LEAA funds after the 1974-1975 school year. As of 1975-1976 there had been no attrition among the original six Advocates; and in addition, two Advocates had been added to the St. Paul complement since 1972. Furthermore, the Advocate Program seems likely to continue in St. Paul indefinitely.

Unlike Minneapolis, St. Paul found a new source of funds for Advocate salaries in a new state law funding community corrections programs. Also, St. Paul's Director of Special Education has invested his own time and professional stature in a campaign to develop public and public-school support for the Program; and to make the Program a permanent part of the special education spectrum of services. The skill of St. Paul's Advocate supervisor in mediating conflicts between Advocates and other professionals has apparently been another factor helping the Program survive.

Evaluation of the 1972-1973 Advocate Program's Success in Meeting Its Objectives

The specific objectives of Advocates with returnees were: (a) increased school persistence (as measured by enrollment and attendance), (b) improved school performance (grades and graduation), (c) reduced recidivism (new offenses and severity of offenses), and (d) reduced reinstitutionalization (returns to correctional institutions).[1]

While the program was aimed primarily at returnees, the grant proposals allowed each Advocate to work with boys and girls either on probation or "predelinquent." During the 1972-1973 school year, Advocates reportedly worked "in depth" with 1,310 youths. This total consisted of 336 returnees, 451 probationers, and 523 predelinquents.

The evaluation studied the work of Advocates with returnees, since returnees were the primary target population of the Program. A research follow-up was conducted on 216 returnees eligible for Advocate service and on a comparison group of 40 returnees to school areas not served by Advocates. The evaluation provided answers to five questions about the operation, effectiveness, and improvement of the Program.

(1) What Was the Advocate's Role?

Based on a day I observed each Advocate, Advocates spent about one-third of their time counseling (including "rapping") with delinquency-prone youth. Advocates' second most time-consuming activity was sharing of information regarding delinquents with other youth-serving persons, most frequently teachers.

Other activities included: serving young people in tangible ways (e.g., driving delinquents to job interviews), providing a place for youths to relax between class periods, advocating for the delinquents (e.g., "going to bat" for the delinquent in disputes with adults; helping the youth reenroll in school), and being an "expert" on youth during the planning of youth-serving programs (e.g., drug education, sex education, curriculum reform).

Three Advocates were observed in activities judged inappropriate for this antidelinquency program; for example, planning educational programs for the whole school, disciplining students, checking lockers and lavatories for drugs and smoking activity. Six Advocates maintained little contact with returnees. For several Advocates, a low rate of area delinquency explains this lack of emphasis on returnees. Several other Advocates, however, seemed negligent in their pursuit of returnees.

When they first entered the schools, some Advocates experienced role conflict with school administrators, parole officers, probation officers, and other youth-serving professions and agencies. The term "Youth Advocate" was an affront to several professionals who also regarded themselves as "advocating" for youth. Most Advocates and these other professionals eventually found themselves in complementary roles, however. For example, parole and probation officers saw Advocates as a unique resource in their detailed knowledge of returnees' educational opportunities.

(2) What Percent of Eligible Returnees to the Attendance Areas of Advocate Schools Actually Received Advocate Service?

Each Advocate was asked to list all contracted returnees and to describe the breadth and persistence of services rendered to each. For each city, the number of served returnees was compared with the total number eligible for Advocate service.

In brief, *service-eligible* returnees were those boys and girls released from a state or county correctional institution in 1972, whom Advocates could reasonably have been expected to serve, from release through March 1973. Service-eligible returnees were of secondary-school age (under 18) and grade-placement. They were committed from, and released to, the same city. They were also released at a time when the current Advocate was serving the returnee's school attendance-area. Using this definition, there were 216 service-eligible returnees in the three cities.

Of these eligibles, 154 (or 71%) were also *served* returnees. A served returnee was a service-eligible returnee with whom the Advocate had initiated at least one in-person contact. In Minneapolis alone, 154 returnees were eligible for service (and eligible for research follow-up); 70% of these 154 were seen at least once by an Advocate. In St. Paul, 74% of 38 service-eligible returnees were served. In Duluth, 75% of the 24 service-eligible returnees were seen at least once.

In general, Advocates did a good job of seeking out returnees. Most nonserved returnees probably had no intention of setting foot in school again. Nevertheless, such youths should have been contacted once to determine what, if any, help might be rendered.

Service breadth and service persistence were the two measures of Advocate service for each returnee. Service breadth was measured by the Advocate's performance of six services. The three most frequently performed services were encouraging the returnee to attend school, counseling the returnee, and coordinating academic program-planning for the returnee. Somewhat less frequently performed were the activities of visiting the returnee in the institution, aiding returnees in their dealings with adults and social agencies, and helping the returnee find educational and vocational opportunities outside the Advocate's homebase school.

In general, Advocates performed each of the six services for at least half of their served returnees. Returnees were more likely to receive services that could be rendered in the school than services requiring the Advocate's presence in an institution or the community.

Service persistence for each returnee was the percent of months—from one month before the first service-eligible release through March 31, 1973—that the Advocate served the returnee twice. Advocates performed a role-prescribed service on two separate occasions during approximately 40% of the months for Minneapolis returnees, 70% for St. Paul returnees, and 60% for Duluth returnees. St. Paul Advocates, most recently hired on the average, also tended to have the greatest service persistence. Their returnees had less time to drift away from the school and Advocate service.

(3) Was the Program Effective in Meeting Its Objectives?

Quasi-experimental tests were conducted between two groups of returnees, an "Advocate" (E) group and a "non-Advocate" (C) group. Returnees in both groups resided in Minneapolis secondary-school attendance areas roughly comparable in "socio-educational disadvantagement." These areas could be described as "moderately deprived." The use of only moderately deprived areas was dictated by the lack of an adequate match for four highly deprived Advocate-school areas. Although a number of moderately deprived school areas did not have an Advocate, all highly deprived school areas in Minneapolis were assigned an Advocate.

The dependent variables for this control group comparison were those most relevant to Program objectives: school attendance, grades, offenses, and commitments to correctional institutions.

There were 66 service-eligible returnees (48 boys, 18 girls) to experimental (Advocate) attendance areas of Minneapolis, and 40 returnees (27 boys, 13 girls) to control (non-Advocate) attendance areas. These E and C groups consisted of *all* returnees to these 15 moderately deprived school areas during specified periods in 1972. Seven of 66 experimental-area returnees never met their Advocate; they were, nevertheless, included in the E group. Correspondingly, several of the 40 control-area returnees *were* served by Advocates and were included in the C group so as to avoid sample-selection bias. The E-C comparisons therefore may be conservative, since a few "non-Advocate" returnees were served.

Table 1 shows all available data on pre- and postrelease adjustment for all E and C returnees. Unfortunately, however, complete pre- and postdata on the four measures of school-community adjustment were obtainable for only about 70% of the returnees, regardless of group and sex. Table 2 shows school-community adjustment for only those returnees with complete data.

Tables 1 and 2 show that E and C groups were generally well matched in their prerelease adjustment (before the Advocate Program). E girls with complete adjustment data, however, appeared somewhat better in their prerelease adjustment than C girls. Complete-data E girls had slightly lower average offense rates and periods of institutionalization during the prerelease period than complete-data C girls. The prerelease period for each returnee was one-year long. The prerelease period ended on the first 1972 release date when the returnee could have been served by an Advocate (for C returnees, the prerelease period ended on the first 1972 release date).

Another mismatch occurred because E boys were somewhat less well adjusted in school grades and attendance during the prerelease period than C boys.

Table 1 shows that during the postrelease period—ending for each returnee on March 31, 1973—returnees to the experimental (Advocate-served) attendance areas were better adjusted than returnees to control (non-Advocate) attendance areas on every measure of postrelease adjustment employed. These results obtained for both boys and girls, taken separately. (The adjustment of boys and girls was analyzed separately because boys, as a group, had higher offense rates—reflecting more frequent and more serious officially recorded offenses—than girls during both pre- and post-release periods.)

Table 2, however, based solely on returnees with complete adjustment data, suggests little or no difference between E and C boys in postrelease adjustment.

If one compares prerelease and postrelease scores on each of the four adjustment variables—percent of noninstitutionalized school days attended, grade point average (GPA), offense rate, and percent of time spent in correctional institutions—the following pattern emerges (see Table 2): for both E and C returnees, school adjustment (attendance and grades) generally declined, while community adjustment (offenses and institutionalization) generally improved, from the prerelease to the postrelease period.

For each of the four variables and for each sex taken separately, there was little evidence that E returnees made

Table 1 Pre- and Postrelease School-Community Adjustment of Service-Eligible Returnees to Experimental (Advocate) and Control (Non-Advocate) Attendance Areas of Minneapolis

Adjustment variable	*Male*												*Female*											
	Experimental						*Control*						*Experimental*						*Control*					
	Pre			*Post*			*Pre*			*Post*			*Pre*			*Post*			*Pre*			*Post*		
	M	*SD*	*N*	*M*	*SD*	*N*	*M*	*SD*	*N*	*M*	*SD*	*N*	*M*	*SD*	*N*	*M*	*SD*	*N*	*M*	*SD*	*N*	*M*	*SD*	*N*
School Persistence Score (% of non-institutionalized school days attended)	52	30	36	36	34	47	62	25	20	34	35	27	50	28	13	35	37	17	51	29	8	16	22	13
School Performance Score (grade-point-average)[a]	.9	.8	36	.8	1.0	47	1.1	.7	20	.5	.8	27	.6	.7	13	.8	1.0	18	.9	.9	8	.2	.4	13
Offense Score (yearly rate, each offense weighted by its severity)[b]	14	11	46	10	11	48	15	10	25	14	15	27	8	5	16	6	6	18	12	6	13	9	15	13
Institutionalization Score (% of days in a State or County correctional institution)	34	25	48	12	20	48	41	30	27	24	28	27	41	35	18	8	21	18	42	29	13	14	22	13
Index of School-Community Adjustment (mean of = scores for the 4 variables above)	.08	.60	36	17	68	48	.17	.61	18	−.17	.78	27	.25	.43	12	.36	.74	18	.09	.68	8	−.15	.66	13

[a]Grade point average was computed by assigning numbers to letter grades as follows: A = 4, B = 3, C = 2, D = 1, F = 0.

[b]Severity of offense was generally determined by the severity rank of the punishment prescribed by the Minnesota Criminal Code of 1963, As Amended (State of Minnesota, 1971), had the offense been committed by an adult. The ratings used in this study for each offense were: 6 = felony-type offenses involving death or great bodily harm, 5 = other felony-type offenses, 4 = gross misdemeanor-type offenses, 3 = misdemeanor-type offenses, 2 = juvenile status offenses and petty misdemeanor-type offenses, 1 = violations of technical rules *only*, while returnee was on parole or probation supervision.

greater gains than C returnees. Only one of eight gain differences between E and C returnees was reliable at conventional significance levels: E boys appear to have declined less in grade point average than C boys. Yet grades for all returnee groups were generally near failing (D on the average) during both the pre- and postrelease periods.

For each of those 70% of returnees with complete adjustment data, indices of school-community adjustment were computed for the prerelease and postrelease periods. For each periods, this index of school-community adjustment was the mean of the four adjustment variables—percent of noninstitutionalized school days attended, grade point average, offense rate, and percent of time spent in correctional institutions—after the original scores on these variables had been converted to z scores.

The difference for each returnee between the preindex and the post-index of school-community adjustment was called the adjustment gain score. This adjustment gain score was the statistic used to summarize the overall impact of the Advocate Program on the four principal measures of returnee adjustment.

Table 2 shows that both E boys and E girls showed a slight overall adjustment gain from the pre- to postrelease period, while their C counterparts showed a slight adjustment decline. The differences in mean adjustment gain score between E and C boys, or E and C girls, were not reliable at conventional significance levels, however.

School-community Status, Both Sexes Combined. Another index of adjustment was the returnee's school-community status as of the last date of the follow-up period—March 31, 1973. E returnees were more likely to be enrolled in school on this date than C returnees (41% of Es versus 25% of Cs), and this difference was significant ($p < .05$, one-tailed z-test for the difference between two proportions). C returnees were more likely than Es to be in correctional institutions on this date (30% versus 12%, $p < .05$). In addition, E returnee-attenders were more likely to be in an "alternative-type" school. Over half of the E attenders were in alternative schools.

The Importance of Alternative Schools. Minneapolis has a large number of alternative schools. As just noted, over half of the E attenders (15 of 27) were in an alternative school as of March 31, while only 3 of 10 control attenders were in alternative schools.

What are the characteristics of these alternative schools that make them magnets for returnees? First, in alternative schools the curriculum is flexible and geared to the needs of the students. The alternatives attended by returnees offered basic reading and math, plus elective areas (e.g., poetry writing, ecology, Indian history, humanistic psychology) not emphasized in the regular public school curriculum.

Second, school operation is relatively democratic. Students and teachers share responsibility for the planning of

Table 2 Quasi-Experimental Tests Comparing the School-Community Adjustment of Service-Eligible Returnees to Experimental (Advocate) and Control (Non-Advocate) Attendance Area Minneapolis, Based on Returnees With Complete Pre- and Postrelease Data

Adjustment variable	*Male*													*Female*											
	Experimental (N = 36)						*Control (N = 18)*						*Difference between E-C mean differences*	*Experimental (N = 12)*						*Control (N = 8)*					
	Pre		*Post*		*Difference*		*Pre*		*Post*		*Difference*			*Pre*		*Post*		*Difference*		*Pre*		*Post*		*Difference*	
	M	*SD*	*M*	*SD*	*M*	*SD*	*M*	*SD*	*M*	*SD*	*M*	*SD*		*M*	*SD*	*M*	*SD*	*M*	*SD*	*M*	*SD*	*M*	*SD*	*M*	*SD*
School Persistence Score (% of noninstitutionalized school days attended)	52	30	36	34	−16	42	65	22	39	38	−26	29	10.1	53	26	36	38	−18	35	51	29	11	17	40	30
School Performance Score (grade-point average)[a]	.9	.8	.8	.9	.1	1.1	1.2	.7	.6	.9	.7	.9	.5*	.7	.7	.7	1.0	.0	1.0	.9	.9	.2	.4	−.7	.9
Offense Score (yearly rate, each offense weighted by its severity)[b]	13	10	9	11	4	16	17	11	9	9	8	15	3.7	7	3	4	4	3	6	11	6	12	18	−1	17
Institutionalization Score (% of days in a State or County correctional institution)	29	20	12	21	16	31	32	23	13	21	18	28	1.8	25	21	9	26	16	42	35	24	20	26	15	40
Index of School-Community Adjustment (mean of z scores for the 4 variables above)	.08	.60	.17	.69	.09	.93	.17	.61	.12	.59	−.05	.59	.14	25	.43	.33	.78	.08	.92	.09	.68	−.32	.76	−.41	1.10

a, b See notes a and b for Table 1.

*p = .05, one tailed t-test for independent means.

Note: For all difference scores, a plus sign indicates improved adjustment. For differences between E-C mean differences, therefore, a plus sign means greater improvements in adjustment by the experimental (Adv than by the control (non-Advocate) group.

educational activities. Formal lectures are rare; individualized assignments are common. Attendance requirements are liberal, implicitly if not explicitly, and yet most returnees in these schools were attending at least three of every five school days.[2]

Students in alternative schools for adolescents seem to represent a wide range of scholastic aptitude and social status. A majority, however, seemed educationally deprived. A number of enrollees were "pushouts," who had been encouraged to leave regular public schools where they had been disruptive.

The larger proportion of E returnees than C returnees attending alternative schools seems attributable to the Advocate Program. Very few returnees in either group attended alternative schools during the prerelease period. Referral to an alternative school by an Advocate seemed crucial to a returnee's enrollment in that type of school. For example, three control public schools had affiliated alternative schools ("pocket schools"). Yet, only two returnees to control areas were attending one of these easily accessible alternatives. One of the most popular alternatives for E returnees was located next to a control school, but was attended by no C returnees. Yet, several Advocates successfully referred returnees to this school.

School-community Adjustment of Returnees to St. Paul, to Duluth, and to Highly Deprived Attendance Areas of Minneapolis. In addition to E and C returnees from moderately deprived areas of Minneapolis, I also studied the adjustment of all returnees to other areas of Minneapolis and all *served* returnees to the cities of St. Paul and Duluth (see Higgins, 1974a and 1974b, for adjustment data on these returnees not involved in E-C comparisons).

The "Average" Metropolitan Returnee. Data on returnees from all three cities were used to construct a profile of an "average" returnee. This returnee was a boy, 15-years-old at the time of his first studied release during the summer (fall for St. Paul) of 1972, who was entering the tenth grade. He stood a fairly even chance of being committed to the State Department of Corrections, by March 31, 1973.

From the preinstitutionalization to the postrelease period, his school attendance dropped (except in Duluth), his GPA stayed near the D level, and his rate of officially charged offenses declined. He may have gone back to the institution for one or more usually brief stays. During the prerelease period he was committing offenses at the rate of three felony-type offenses (e.g., car theft, major burglary, robbery) or five misdemeanor-type offenses (e.g., minor theft, or shoplifting; marijuana or other minor drug charge; auto tampering; vandalism; lurking) per year. During the postrelease period he committed felony-type offenses at the rate of two per year or misdemeanor-type offenses, three per year.

If he was in school, he probably attended fewer than three of every five school days. If he was out of school, a prospect more likely, he tended to be unemployed. If a Minneapolis resident and a school attender, he probably went to an alternative school where his attendance was better than 50%.

Summary of Results Concerning Program Effectiveness. Comparisons between E and C returnees suggest that returnees to Advocate-served areas made a very slight gain in an overall index of school-community adjustment from the pre- to postrelease period. Returnees to non-Advocate areas declined very slightly in adjustment. However, the difference between the two groups in adjustment gain was not reliably different from zero.

Both experimental and control returnees showed poorer school adjustment and better community adjustment during the postrelease period, compared to the preinstitutionalization period.

On individual measures comprising the postrelease adjustment index—namely, school attendance, grades, offenses, and time spent in correctional institutions—the experimental returnee girls were consistently, but not significantly, better adjusted than the control girls. Experimental boys had reliably higher (yet only D average) grades than control males during the postrelease period; on the other three adjustment measures, these two groups were nearly indistinguishable.

E returnees were clearly favored over C returnees in their school-community status at the end of the follow-up period. E returnees were over 1½ times more likely than C returnees to be in school; C returnees were 2½ times more likely to be in institutions.

In short, the Advocate Program seems to have had a small favorable impact on adjustment. This impact was seen more in returnees' location at the end of the follow-up period than in their adjustment throughout that period.

(4) Did Selected Individual Differences, Both Advocate Differences and Returnee Differences, Account for Differing Degrees of Program Effectiveness?

Determinants of returnee adjustment were sought via case study of Advocates and returnees: 10 Advocates were dichotomized into those having greater and lesser adjustment gains among their served returnees; 34 returnees were dichotomized into those showing better and poorer overall postrelease adjustment.

Advocate characteristics correlated with returnee gains included: assertiveness in seeking out returnees; knowledge of school and job opportunities; direct, tangible help in finding a school or job; liking for, and open communication with, returnees; and persistent monitoring of returnees' adjustment progress. Returnee characteristics correlated with poor postrelease adjustment included low anxiety, avoidance of adults, deprived families, poor reading, and external-control beliefs. (The procedures used to select Advocates and returnees for case study, to interview those selected, and to arrive at the preceding conclusions are described in Higgins, 1974a, 1974b. Case studies of advocates and returnees are also presented.)

Anxiety Differences Among Case-study Returnees. Each case-study returnee completed the activity preference questionnaire (APQ; Lykken and Katzenmeyer, 1968), a measure of physical and social fear. Among the present sample of case-study returnees, total APQ scores and physical anxiety scores for Minneapolis boys correlated -.35 to -.53 with offense rate and institutionalization rate during the postrelease period. That is, lower anxiety was associated with higher offense and institutionalization rates (for boys only).

Further analysis indicated that less anxious boys were charged with more serious crimes during the postrelease period. While high- and low-anxiety case-study boys had similar offense patterns before their first-studied institutionalization, these two groups differed in delinquency after release. Six of 11 boys above median in anxiety had *no* chargeable offense during the postrelease period; only 2 of 12 lower-anxiety boys had no chargeable offense. In fact, 9 of the 12 lower-anxiety boys were charged with a felony-type or gross misdemeanor-type offense during the post-release period. In summary, these lower-anxiety boys seem not to have profited from adverse experiences in the criminal justice system.

Several low anxiety returnees required a disproportionate share of the Advocate's time, yet were extremely frustrating to help. During the 1972-1973 school year, one such returnee to an Advocate's school on separate occasions (a) broke into the school, (b) was critically injured after a high-speed chase in a stolen car, and (c) despite his recent injuries, attempted an acrobatic burglary of a corner grocery. The Advocate spent days seeking educational, medical, and legal help for this returnee. The Advocate even provided temporary food and shelter.

A low "anxiety IQ" is probably a great handicap in school and community adjustment. Low anxiety could, however, be turned into an asset in a delinquent's rehabilitation. Low anxiety delinquents should make a good adjustment in jobs that reward their willingness to take physical and social risks.[3]

(5) What Recommendations Should Be Made Concerning the Improvement and Refunding of the Program?

Recommendations included (a) Advocates' involvement in school policy-and-program planning affecting delinquents; (b) Advocates' notification of prerelease staffings and Advocates' involvement in prerelease educational planning; (c) greater efforts to recruit Advocates among those already effective with delinquents; (d) recruitment of Native American Advocates, to serve the sizable numbers of Native American returnees; (e) greater emphasis in Advocate training on alternative schools and job programs; and (f) improved interprofessional relations (e.g., with police).

Given recommended improvements, the Program was, in my opinion, worthy of refunding as one of few antidelinquency efforts with a demonstrable (although generally small) impact on the behavior of delinquents (i.e., on school enrollment, and, in the case of some highly competent Advocates, on school-community adjustment).

Pitfalls on the Path to An Experimenting Society

The findings and recommendations of the 1972-1973 evaluation were not used as a basis for decisions to refund or terminate the Program. Nor was the evaluation used as a basis for improving Program operation, except possibly in St. Paul.

For example, my evaluation was given apparent, but not real, consideration during a meeting of a panel screening Twin Cities area requests for LEAA funds. One of the panel members was a nationally recognized expert in the evaluation of correctional programs; and more importantly, an outspoken critic of one-to-one treatment programs for offenders. This panel member seized upon a finding of small overall effectiveness of the Program as evidence that the Program was unworthy of refunding. This panel member totally ignored (a) findings suggesting conditions under which effective Advocate service was rendered and (b) recommendations that could have improved the operation and possibly the effectiveness of the Program. In fact, the review panel on this occasion was probably involved in a pro forma exercise: the proposal requested a fourth year of LEAA funding. Very few human services programs for offender rehabilitation in Minnesota have obtained LEAA funding past the third year.

In the chronology presented earlier, the demise of the Program in Minneapolis and Duluth was attributed to the Program's "soft money" support, to the lack of an effective lobby on behalf of delinquents, and to personal conflicts between Advocates and school administrators. Correspondingly, the Program's survival in St. Paul was probably due to effective lobbying, a successful search for alternative funding, and effective human relations work by the Advocate supervisor.

In his 1969 article, Campbell provided a classic statement of both methodological and nonmethodological aspects of evaluation. After my experience as an evaluator for the Youth Advocate Program, I am convinced that the nonmethodological factors which one might call "the social context of evaluation research" deserve frequent formal discussion.

This paper has presented an evaluation approach that may be useful to others who study social action programs serving youth. This paper is also a case study to show that social, nonmethodological aspects of evaluation can easily rival methodological inadequacies as pitfalls on the path to Campbell's "experimenting society."

In the case of the Youth Advocate Program, the well-established educational and criminal justice systems that were aloof stepparents of the Program were given little incentive to adopt recommendations that could possibly have made the Program more effective. In short, the social context of this evaluation was unfavorable for direct and immediate utilization of the evaluation results. The development and decline of the Program in each city was guided more by the availability of federal and state funds than by social scientific feedback concerning the Program's strengths and weaknesses in helping delinquents meet important behavioral objectives.

Notes

1. This section summarizes my evaluation of the 1972–1973 Program which operated in Minneapolis, St. Paul, and Duluth. Readers who wish a more detailed presentation are referred to the original evaluation reports (Higgins, 1974a, 1974b).
2. The words of an E group girl summarize some attractive characteristics of these schools: "I've had no hassles since coming here. I can't stand sitting in a class and listening to a teacher. I'd rather teach myself. Here you have tutors when you need help. You can smoke, drink pop, get snacks. In a regular school, you just work.
3. Case-study returnees were asked to name the occupation they would most enjoy if they had complete freedom to choose. They were also asked the occupation they would actually pursue after they left school for good. Lower-anxiety boys tended more than higher-anxiety boys to aspire to those challenging and risky jobs that might be called "the moral equivalent of crime." Many of the ideal job choices of lower-anxiety boys involved physical danger (e.g., pilot, dirt-bike racer) or social risk (e.g., politician, lawyer, actor, "boss," company president). Nearly all involved freedom from coercive supervision (e.g., artist, car designer). The ideal job choices of the higher-anxiety male returnees were somewhat more likely to involve routine, onerous, and carefully supervised activity (e.g., rubbish hauler, bodyshop worker, janitor, local truck driver).

Although differing in job aspirations, higher- and lower-anxiety boys were *similar* in their actual job expectations. Irrespective of their APQ standing, most boys believed they would actually seek routine, coercively supervised jobs offering little physical or social challenge (e.g., assembly work, warehouse stockboy, factory worker).

The long-range success of antidelinquency efforts like the Youth Advocate Program may depend in part on these programs' capacity to find low-anxiety clients school settings low in authoritarian discipline, and the career opportunities that reward their propensity to take physical and social risks.

References

Bailey, W. C. (1966) "Correctional outcome: An evaluation of 100 reports." J. of Criminal Law, Criminology and Police Sci. 57:153–160.

Berleman, W. C. and T. W. Steinburn (1967) "The execution and evaluation of a delinquency prevention program." Social Problems 14:413–423.

Campbell, D. T. (1969) "Reform as experiments." Amer. Psychologist 24:409–429.

Elliott, D. S. (1966) "Delinquency, school attendance and dropout." Social Problems 13:307–314.

Hathaway, S. R., P. C. Reynolds, and E. D. Monachesi (1969) "Follow-up of the later careers and lives of 1,000 boys who dropped out of high school." J. of Consulting and Clinical Psychology 33:370–380.

Higgins, P. S. (1974a) "Evaluation of the Minnesota youth-advocate delinquency-rehabilitation program." Ph.D. dissertation, University of Minnesota.

——. (1974b) The Minnesota Youth Advocacy Corps: An Evaluation. St. Paul: Minnesota Governor's Commission on Crime Prevention and Control.

Knitzer, J. E. (1976) "Child advocacy: a perspective." Amer. J. of Orthopsychiatry 46:200–216.

Lundman, R. J., P. T. McFarlane, and F. R. Scarpitti (1976) "Delinquency prevention: a description and assessment of projects reported in the professional literature." Crime and Delinquency 22:297–308.

Lykken, D. T. and C. G. Katzenmeyer (1968) Manual for the Activity Preference Questionnaire (APQ). Minneapolis: University of Minnesota, Department of Psychiatry, Research Laboratories (Report PR-68-3).

Polier, J. W. (1977) "External and internal roadblocks to effective child advocacy." Child Welfare 61:497–508.

Polk, K. (1975) "Schools and the delinquency experience." Criminal Justice and Behavior 2:315–338.

Powers, E. and H. Witmer (1951) An Experiment in the Prevention of Delinquency: The Cambridge-Somerville Youth Study. New York: Columbia Univ. Press.

Schuchter, A. (1975) "Schools and delinquency prevention strategies." Criminal Justice and Behavior 2:339–345.

State of Minnesota (1971) Minnesota Criminal Code of 1963 (as amended). St. Paul: Documents Section, Minnesota Department of Administration.

Wright, W. E. and M. C. Dixon (1977) "Community prevention and treatment of juvenile delinquency: A review of evaluation studies." J. of Research in Crime and Delinquency 14:35–67.

The Impact of a 'Total Community' Delinquency Control Project

Walter B. Miller

The Midcity Project: Methods and Client Population

The Midcity Project conducted a delinquency control program in a lower-class district of Boston between the years 1954 and 1957. A major objective of the Project was to inhibit or reduce the amount of illegal activity engaged in by resident adolescents. Project methods derived from a "total community" philosophy which has become increasingly popular in recent years, and currently forms the basis of several large-scale delinquency control programs.[1] On the assumption that delinquent behavior by urban lower-class adolescents, whatever their personality characteristics, is in some significant degree facilitated by or actualized through certain structural features of the community, the Project executed "action" programs directed at three of the societal units seen to figure importantly in the genesis and perpetuation of delinquent behavior—the community, the family, and the gang.

The community program involved two major efforts: 1) the development and strengthening of local citizens' groups so as to enable them to take direct action in regard to local problems, including delinquency, and 2) an attempt to secure cooperation between those professional agencies whose operations in the community in some way involved adolescents (e.g., settlement houses, churches, schools, psychiatric and medical clinics, police, courts and probation departments, corrections and parole departments). A major short-term objective was to increase the possibility of concerted action both among the professional agencies themselves and between the professionals and the citizens' groups. The ultimate objective of these organizational efforts was to focus a variety of diffuse and uncoordinated efforts on problems of youth and delinquency in a single community so as to bring about more effective processes of prevention and control.[2]

Work with families was conducted within the framework of a "chronic-problem-family" approach; a group of families with histories of repeated and long-term utilization of public welfare services were located and subjected to a special and intensive program of psychiatrically-oriented casework.[3]

Work with gangs, the major effort of the Project, was based on the detached worker or area worker approach utilized by the New York Youth Board and similar projects.[4] An adult worker is assigned to an area, group, or groups with a mandate to contact, establish relations with, and attempt to change resident gangs. The application of this method by the Midcity Project incorporated three features not generally included in earlier programs: 1) All workers were professionally trained, with degrees in case work, group work, or both; 2) Each worker but one devoted primary attention to a single group, maintaining recurrent and intensive contact with group members over an extended time period; 3) Psychiatric consultation was made available on a regular basis, so that workers were in a position to utilize methods and perspectives of psychodynamic psychiatry in addition to the group dynamics and recreational approaches in which they had been trained.

Between June 1954 and May 1957, seven project field workers (five men, two women) maintained contact with approximately 400 youngsters between the ages of 12 and 21, comprising the membership of some 21 corner gangs. Seven of these, totaling 205 members, were subjected to intensive attention. Workers contacted their groups on an average of 3.5 times a week; contact periods averaged about 5 or 6 hours; total duration of contact ranged from 10 to 34 months. Four of the intensive service groups were white males (Catholic, largely Irish, some Italians and Canadian French); one was negro male,

[1] The principal current example is the extensive "Mobilization for Youth" project now underway in the Lower East Side of Manhattan. Present plans call for over 30 separate "action" programs in four major areas of work, education, community, and group service. The project is reported in detail in "A Proposal for the Prevention and Control of Delinquency by Expanding Opportunities," New York City: Mobilization for Youth, Inc. (December, 1961), and in brief in "Report on Juvenile Delinquency," Washington: Hearings of the Subcommittee on Appropriations, 1960, pp. 113-116.

[2] See Lester Houston and Lena DiCicco, "Community Development in a Boston District," on file United Community Services of Boston, 1956.

[3] See David M. Austin, "The Special Youth Program Approach to Chronic Problem Families," *Community Organization Papers*, New York City: Columbia University Press, 1958. Also, Joan Zilbach, "Work with Chronic Problem Families: A Five Year Appraisal," Boston: on file Judge Baker Guidance Center, 1962.

[4] A brief description of the background of this method appears on p. 406 of Walter B. Miller, "The Impact of a Community Group Work Program on Delinquent Corner Groups," *The Social Service Review*, 31 (December, 1957), pp. 390-406.

From *Social Problems*, Vol. 10 (Fall 1962), pp. 168–191. Reprinted with the permission of the Society of Social Problems and the author.

one white female, and one negro female. All groups "hung out" in contiguous neighborhoods of a single district of Midcity—a fairly typical lower-class "inner-city" community.[5]

The average size of male groups was 30, and of female 9. All intensive service groups, as well as most of the other known groups, were "locality-based" rather than "emergent" or "situationally organized" groups.[6] This meant that the groups were indigenous, self-formed, and inheritors of a gang tradition which in some cases extended back for fifty years or more. This kind of gang system in important respects resembled certain African age-class systems in that a new "class" or corner-group unit was formed every two or three years, recruiting from like-aged boys residing in the vicinity of the central "hanging" locale.[7] Thus the total corner aggregate in relatively stable residential areas generally consisted of three to five age-graded male groups, each maintaining a sense of allegiance to their corner and/or traditional gang name, and at the same time maintaining a clear sense of identity as a particular age-graded unit within the larger grouping.

Girls groups, for the most part, achieved their identity primarily through their relations with specific boys units, which were both larger and more solidary. Each locality aggregate thus included several female groups, generally bearing a feminized version of the male group name (Bandits-Bandettes; Kings-Queens).

Action Methods with Corner Gangs

The methods used by Project workers encompassed a wide range of techniques and entailed work on many levels with many kinds of groups, agencies and organizations.[8] Workers conceptualized the process of working with the groups as a series of sequential phases, on the model of individual psychotherapy. Three major phases were delineated—roughly, relationship establishment, behavior modification, and termination. In practice workers found it difficult to conduct operations according to the planned "phase" sequence, and techniques seen as primarily appropriate to one phase were often used during another. There was, however, sufficiently close adherence to the phase concept as to make it possible to consider specific techniques as primarily associated with a given phase.

Phase I: Contact and Relationship Establishment. During this phase workers sought out and located resident corner gangs and established an acceptable role-identity. Neither the location of the groups nor the establishment of a viable basis for a continued relationship entailed particular difficulties.[9] This phase included considerable "testing" of the workers; the youngsters put on display a wide range of their customary behaviors, with particular stress on violative forms—watching the worker closely to see whether his reactions and evaluative responses fell within an acceptable range. The workers, for their part, had to evince sufficient familiarity with and control over the basic subcultural system of lower class adolescents and its component skills as to merit the respect of the groups, and the right to continued association.

A major objective in gaining entree to the groups was to establish what workers called a "relationship." Influenced in part by concepts derived from individual psychotherapy, Project staff felt that the establishment of close and meaningful relationships with group members was a major device for effecting behavior change, and was in fact a necessary precondition of all other direct service methods. The workers' conception of a "good" relationship was complex, but can be de-

---

[5] The term "lower class" is used in this paper to refer to that sector of the population in the lowest educational and occupational categories. For the purposes of Project statistical analyses, those census tracts in Midcity were designated as "lower class" in which 50% or more of the adult residents had failed to finish high school, and 60% or more of resident males pursued occupations in the bottom five occupational categories delineated by the 1950 United States Census. Nineteen of the 21 census tracts in Midcity were designated "lower class" by these criteria. Within lower class, three levels were distinguished. "Lower-class 3" included census tracts with 80% or more of adult males in the bottom five occupational categories and 70% or more of the adults in the "high-school non-completion" category; "Lower-class 2" included tracts with 70-80% males in low occupations and 60-70% adults not having completed high school; "Lower-class 1," 60-70% low occupation males, 50-60% high school non-completion. Of the 6,500 adolescents in Midcity, 17.5% lived in Lower-class 3 tracts; 53.1% in Lower-class 2, and 20.4% in Lower-class 1. The remaining 8.8% were designated "middle class." Project gangs derived primarily from Lower-class 2 and 3 areas; studied gangs comprised approximately 16% of the adolescent (13-19) Lower-class 2 and 3 population of the study area—roughly 30% of the males and 4% of the females.

[6] Beyond this crude distinction between "locality-based" gangs and "other" types, a more systematic typology of Midcity gangs cannot be presented here. Karl Holton also distinguishes a locality-based gang ("area gang") as one type in Los Angeles County, and includes a classic brief description which applies without modification to the Midcity type. Karl Holton, "Juvenile Gangs in the Los Angeles Area," in Hearings of the Subcommittee on Juvenile Delinquency, 86th Congress, Part 5, Washington, D. C.: (November, 1960), pp. 886-888. The importance of the "locality-based" typological distinction in this context is to emphasize the fact that Project gangs were *not* "emergent" groups organized in response to some common activity interest such as athletics, or formed around a single influential "magnetic" youngster, or organized under the influence of recreational or social work personnel. The gang structure pre-existed the Project, was coordinate with and systematically related to the kinship structure, and was "multi-functional" and "versatile" in that it served as a staging base for a wide range of activities and served a wide range of functions, both practical and psychological, for its members.

[7] The age-class system of Midcity closely resembles that of the Otoro of Central Sudan as described by Asmarom Legesse, "[Some East African Age-] Class Systems," Special Paper, Graduate School of Education, Harvard University, May 1961 and S. F. Nadel, *The Nuba,* London: Oxford University Press, 1947, pp. 132-146. The Otoro age-class system, "one of the simplest . . . in eastern Africa" is in operation between the ages of 11 and 26 (in contrast to other systems which operate during the total life span), and comprises five classes formed at three-year intervals (Class I, 11-14; II, 14-17; III, 17-20; IV, 20-23; V, 23-26). The Midcity system, while less formalized, operates roughly between the ages of 12 and 23, and generally comprises four classes with new classes forming every two to four years, depending on the size of the available recruitment pool, density of population, and other factors. (Class I [Midgets] 12-14; II [Juniors] 14-16; III [Intermediates] 16-19; IV [Seniors] 19-22.) Otoro age classes, like Midcity's, are "multi-functional" in that they form the basis of athletic teams, work groups, and other types of associational unit.

[8] Project "action" methods have been described briefly in several published papers; David M. Austin, "Goals for Gang Workers," *Social Work,* 2 (October 1957), pp. 43-50; Ethel Ackley and Beverly Fliegel, "A Social Work Approach to Street-Corner Girls," *Social Work,* 5 (October 1960), pp. 27-36; Walter B. Miller, "The Impact of a Community Group Work Program on Delinquent Corner Groups," *op. cit.;* and "Preventive Work with Street-Corner Groups: Boston Delinquency Project," *The Annals of the American Academy of Political and Social Science,* 322 (March 1959), pp. 97-106, and in detail in one unpublished report, David Kantor and Lester Houston, *Methods of Working with Street Corner Youth,* 1959, mimeo, 227 pp., on file Harvard Student Volunteers Project.

[9] Extensive discussion of the specific techniques of contact, role-identity establishment and relationship maintenance is included in Kantor and Houston, *ibid.*

scribed briefly as a situation in which both worker and group defined themselves as contained within a common orbit whose major conditions were mutual trust, mutual affection, and maintenance of reciprocal obligations. The workers in fact succeeded in establishing and maintaining relationships of just this type. Considering the fact that these alliances had to bridge both age (adult-adolescent) and social status (lower class-middle class) differences, they were achieved and maintained with a surprising degree of success.[10]

Phase II: Behavior Modification via Mutual Activity Involvement. The behavior modification phase made the greatest demands on the skills, resourcefulness, and energy of the workers. Workers engaged in a wide variety of activities with and in behalf of their groups. The bulk of these activities, however, centered around three major kinds of effort: 1) Organizing groups and using these as the basis of involvement in organized activities; 2) Serving as intermediary between group members and adult institutions; 3) Utilizing techniques of direct influence.

The workers devoted considerable effort to changing group relational systems from the informal type of the street gang to the formal type of the club or athletic team, and involving the groups so reorganized in a range of activities such as club meetings, athletic contests, dances, and fund-raising dinners. In most cases this effort was highly successful. Clubs formed from the corner groups met regularly, adopted constitutions, carried out extensive and effective club activities. Athletic teams moved from cellar positions to championships in city athletic leagues. One group grossed close to a thousand dollars at a fund-raising dance.

Project use of the "organized group and planned activities" method was buttressed by rationale which included at least five premises. 1) The experience of learning to operate in the "rule-governed" atmosphere of the formal club would, it was felt, increase the group members' ability to conduct collective activities in an orderly and law-abiding fashion. 2) The influence of the more lawfully-oriented leaders would be increased, since authority-roles in clubs or teams would be allocated on different bases from those in the corner gang. 3) The need for the clubs to rely heavily on the adult worker for advice and facilitation would place him in a strategic position to influence group behavior. 4) The need for clubs to maintain harmonious relations with local adults such as settlement house personnel and dance hall owners in order to carry out their activity program, as well as the increasing visibility of the organized group, would put a premium on maintaining a public reputation as non-troublesome, and thus inhibit behavior which would jeopardize this objective. 5) Active and extensive involvement in lawful and adult-approved recreational activities would, it was felt, substantially curtail both time and energy potentially available for unlawful activity. This devil-finds-work premise was taken as self-evidently valid, and was reinforced by the idleness-boredom explanation frequently forwarded by group members themselves—"We get in trouble because there's nuthin to do around here." On these grounds as well as others, the use of this method appeared amply justified.[11]

In performing the role of intermediary, workers proceeded on the premise that gang members were essentially isolated within their own adolescent slum world and were either denied, or lacked the ability to seek out, "access" to major adult institutions. This blocked access, it was felt, prevented the youngsters from seeking prestige through "legitimate" channels, forcing them instead to resort to "illegitimate" forms of achievement such as thievery, fighting, and prostitution. On this assumption, the Project aimed deliberately to open up channels of access to adult institutions—particularly in the areas of education and employment.

In the world of work, Project workers arranged appointments with employment agencies, drove group members to job interviews, counseled them as to proper demeanor as job applicants and as employees, urged wavering workers not to quit their jobs. Workers also contacted business firms and urged them to hire group members. In the area of education, workers attempted to solidify the often tenuous bonds between group members and the schools. They visited teachers, acted to discourage truancy, and worked assiduously—through means ranging from subtle persuasion to vigorous argument—to discourage the practice of dropping-out of school at or before the legally-permissible age. Workers arranged meetings with school personnel and attempted to acquaint teachers and other school staff with the special problems of corner youngsters. Every effort was made to arrange scholarships (generally athletic) for those group members for whom college seemed a possibility.

Workers also acted as go-between for their youngsters and a variety of other institutions. They arranged for lawyers in the event of court appearances, and interceded with judges, probation officers, correctional officials and parole personnel. They obtained the use of the recreational facilities and meeting places in settlement houses and gyms which would not have considered admitting the rough and troublesome gang members in the absence of a responsible adult sponsor. They persuaded local storekeepers and businessmen to aid the groups in their money-raising efforts. They arranged for the use or rental of dance halls, and solicited radio stations to provide locally-famous disc-jockeys to conduct record hops. They organized meetings between gang members and local policemen during which both sides were given the opportunity to air their mutual grievances.

During later stages of the Project, workers brought together the clubs of the corner gangs and the adult organizations formed by the Project's Community Organization program, and gang members and community adults served together on joint committees working in the area of community improvement. One such committee exerted sufficient pressure on municipal authorities to obtain a $60,000 allocation for the improvement of a local ball field; another committee instituted an annual "Sports Night" during which most of the community's gangs—some of whom were active gang-fighting enemies—attended a large banquet in which city officials and well-known sports figures made speeches and presented awards for meritorious athletic achievement.

Thus, as a consequence of the work-

---

[10] Research methods for categorizing worker-group relationships according to intensity and intimacy will be cited in future reports.

[11] Further elaboration of the rationale behind the "group-organization-and-activity" method, as well as some additional detail on its operation, is contained in David Austin, "Goals for Gang Workers," *op. cit.*, p. 49, and Walter B. Miller, "*The Place of the Organized Club in Corner-Group Work Method*, Boston: on file Special Youth Program, mimeo, 7 pp. (November, 1956).

ers' activities, gang members gained access to a wide variety of legitimate adult institutions and organizations—schools, business establishments, settlement houses, municipal athletic leagues, public recreational facilities, guidance services, health facilities, municipal governmental agencies, citizens groups, and others. It could no longer be said that the groups were isolated, in any practical sense, from the world of legitimate opportunity.[12]

While Project methods placed major stress on changing environmental conditions through organization, activity involvement, and opening channels of access, workers were also committed to the use of methods designed to induce personality change. The training of most workers had involved exposure to the principles of, and some practice in the techniques of, psychodynamic psychotherapy, and serious consideration was given to the possibility of attempting some form of direct application of psychotherapeutic principles, or techniques based on "insight" therapy. After much discussion workers decided that the use of techniques appropriate to the controlled therapist-patient situation would not be practicable in the open and multi-cliented arena of the corner gang world, and arrangements were made to utilize this approach through indirect rather than direct means.

Psychodynamic methods and individual treatment approaches were utilized in two ways. First, a contract was made with a well-known child-psychiatry clinic, and workers consulted with psychodynamically trained psychiatrists on a regular basis. During these sessions the psychiatrists analyzed individual cases on the basis of detailed case summaries, and recommended procedures for the workers to execute. In this way the actual operating policies of the workers were directly influenced by the diagnostic concepts and therapeutic procedures of psychodynamic psychiatry. Second, in cases where the workers or the psychiatric consultants felt that more direct or intensive therapy for group members or their families was indicated, arrangements were made to refer these cases either to the psychiatric clinic or to local casework or family-service agencies.

Another type of direct influence technique utilized by the workers was "group-dynamics"—a method which combined approaches of both psychodynamic and small-group theory. As adult advisors during club meetings, during informal bull-sessions, and in some instances during specially-arranged group-therapy sessions, workers employed the specific techniques of persuasion and influence developed out of the group-dynamics approach (indirect suggestion, non-directive leadership, permissive group guidance, collective reinforcement). Sessions based on the group-therapy model were generally geared to specific emergent situations—such as an episode of sexual misbehavior among the girls or an upsurge of racial sentiment among the boys.[13]

The direct-influence technique which operated most consistently, however, was simply the continued presence with the group of a law-abiding, middle-class-oriented adult who provided active support for a particular value position. This value stance was communicated to the youngsters through two principal devices—advice and exemplification. The worker served as counsellor, advisor, mentor in a wide range of specific issues, problems and areas of behavioral choice as these emerged in the course of daily life. Should I continue school or drop-out? Can we refrain from retaliatory attack and still maintain our honor? How does one approach girls? How does one handle an overly-romantic boy? Should I start a pimping operation? In all these issues and many more—sometimes broached by the worker, more frequently by the youngsters—the workers put their support—often subtle but nonetheless consistent—behind the law-abiding versus the law-violating choice, and, to a lesser extent, the middle-class-oriented over the lower-class-oriented course of action in regard to long-term issues such as education, occupation, and family life.[14]

But the continued association of worker and group engaged a mechanism of influence which proved in many ways more potent than advice and counsel. The fact of constant association, and the fact that workers became increasingly accepted and admired, meant that they were in a particularly strategic position to serve as a "role-model," or object of emulation. A strong case can be made for the influencive potency of this device. Adolescents, as they move towards adult status, are often pictured as highly sensitive to, and in search of, models of estimable adult behavior, and to be particularly susceptible to emulation of an adult who plays an important role in their lives, and whom they respect and admire. It appeared, in fact, that gang members were considerably more impressed by what the workers *were* than by what they said or did. The youngsters were particularly aware that the workers were college people, that they were responsible spouses and parents in stable mother-father families, that they were conscientious workers under circumstances which afforded maximum opportunities for goofing-off. The workers' statuses as college people, "good" family people, and responsible workers constituted an implicit endorsement of these statuses, and the course of action they implied.

In some instances the admiration of group members for their worker approached hero-worship. One group set up a kind of shrine to their worker after his departure; on a shelf in the corner store where they hung out they placed his photograph, the athletic trophies they had won under his aegis, and a scrap-book containing accounts of the many activities they had shared together. Vistors who knew the worker were importuned to relay to him a vital message—"Tell him we're keepin' our noses clean. . . ."

Phase III: Termination. Since the Project was set up on a three-year "demonstration" basis, the date of final

[12] Project research data made it possible to determine the relative amount of worker effort devoted to various types of activity. The frequency of 12 different kinds of activity engaged in by workers toward or in behalf of group members ("worker functions") was tabulated for all 7 workers. Of 9958 recorded worker functions, 3878 were executed in connection with 22 organizations or agencies. Of these "institutionally-oriented" functions, workers acted in the capacity of "intermediary" for group members 768 times (19.8%), making "intermediation" the second most frequent type of "institutionally-oriented" worker function. The most frequent function was the exercise of "direct influence" (28.7%), to be discussed in the next section. Thus about one-half of all institutionally-oriented worker activity involved two functions—acting as intermediary and engaging in direct influence efforts. Of the 768 intermediary functions, 466 (60.7%) were exercised in connection with 6 kinds of organizations or groups—business organizations, schools, social welfare agencies, families, and other gangs.

[13] A description of the use of group-dynamics techniques by Project workers is included in A. Paul Hare, "Group Dynamics as a Technique for Reducing Intergroup Tensions," Cambridge: Harvard University, unpublished paper, 1957, pp. 14-22.

[14] For the frequency of use of "direct influence" techniques, see footnote 12.

contact was known well in advance. Due largely to the influence of psychodynamic concepts, workers were very much concerned about the possibly harmful effects of "termination," and formulated careful and extensive plans for effecting disengagement from their groups. During the termination phase the workers' efforts centered around three major areas; scheduling a gradual reduction in the frequency of contact and "services" so as to avoid an abrupt cut-off; preparing the groups emotionally for the idea of termination by probing for and discussing feelings of "desertion" anger and loss; and arranging for community agencies to assume as many as possible of the services workers had provided for the groups (e.g., recreational involvement, counseling, meeting places for the clubs).

Despite some difficult moments for both workers and group members (one worker's car was stolen during the tearful farewell banquet tendered him by his group the night before he was to leave for a new job in another city; group members explained this as a symbolic way of saying "Don't leave Midcity!"), termination was effected quite successfully; workers moved off to other involvements and the groups reassumed their workerless position within the community.

In sum, then, the methods used in the Project's attempt to inhibit delinquent behavior were based on a sophisticated rationale, utilized both sociocultural and psychological concepts and methods, encompassed an unusually wide range of practice techniques, and were executed with care, diligence and energy by competent and professionally trained workers. It was impossible, of course, to execute all planned programs and methods as fully or as extensively as might have been desired, but in overall perspective the execution of the Project showed an unusually close degree of adherence to its ambitious and comprehensive plan of operation.[15] What, then, was the impact of these efforts on delinquent behavior?

The Impact of Project Efforts

The Midcity Project was originally instituted in response to a community perception that uncontrolled gang violence was rampant in Midcity. Once the furor attending its inception had abated, the Project was reconceptualized as a "demonstration" project in community delinquency control.[16] This meant that in addition to setting up methods for effecting changes in its client population, the Project also assumed responsibility for testing the efficacy of these methods. The task of evaluating project effectiveness was assigned to a social science research staff which operated in conjunction with the action program.[17] Since the major effort of the Project was its work with gangs, the evaluative aspect of the research design focused on the gang program, and took as a major concern the impact of group-directed methods on the behavior of target gangs. However, since the focal "client" population of the group-work program (gang members) was a subpopulation of the larger client population of the overall project ("trouble"-prone Midcity adolescents), measures of change in the gangs also constituted a test of the totality of control measures utilized by the Project, including its community organization and family-service programs.

The broad question—"Did the Project have any impact on the behavior of the groups it worked with?"—has, in effect, already been answered. The above description of Project methods shows that workers became actively and intensively involved in the lives and activities of the groups. It is hardly conceivable that relatively small groups of adolescents could experience daily association with an adult—especially an adult committed to the task of changing their behavior—without undergoing some substantial modification. But the fundamental *raison d'etre* of the Project was not that of demonstrating the possibility of establishing close relationships with gangs, or of organizing them into clubs, or of increasing their involvement in recreational activities, or of providing them with access to occupational or educational opportunities, or of forming citizens' organizations, or of increasing inter-agency cooperation. These objectives, estimable as they might be, were pursued not as ends in themselves but as means to a further and more fundamental end—the inhibition and control of criminal behavior. The substantial effects of the Project on non-violative forms of behavior will be reported elsewhere; this paper addresses itself to a central and critical measure—the impact of the Project on specifically violative behavior.[18]

The principal question of the evaluative research was phrased as follows: *Was there a significant measurable inhibition of law-violating or morally-disapproved behavior as a consequence of Project efforts?* For purposes of research procedure this question was broken down into two component questions: 1) To what extent was there a measurable reduction in the actual or expected frequency of violative behavior by Project group members during or after the period of Project contact? and 2) To what extent could observed changes in violative behavior be attributed to Project activity rather than to other possible "causative" factors such as maturation or police activity?[19] Firm affirmative answers to

[15] A previous report, "Preventive Work with Street-Corner Groups: Boston Delinquency Project," *op. cit.*, p. 106, cited certain factors which made it difficult to execute some project methods as fully as might have been desired. With greater perspective, derived both from the passage of time and increased knowledge of the experience of other projects, it would now appear that the Midcity Project was relatively less impeded in this regard than many similar projects, especially in regard to difficulties with police, courts, and schools, and that from a comparative viewpoint the Project was able to proceed relatively freely to effect most of its major methods.

[16] Events attending the inception of the Midcity Project are cited in "The Impact of a Community Group Work Program on Delinquent Corner Groups," *op. cit.*, and in Walter B. Miller, "Inter-Institutional Conflict as a Major Impediment to Delinquency Prevention," *Human Organization*, 17 (Fall 1958), pp. 20-23.

[17] Research methods were complex, utilizing a wide range of techniques and approaches. A major distinction was made between "evaluative" (measurement of impact) and "informational" (ethnographic description and analysis) research. No detailed account of research methods has been published, but brief descriptions appear in "The Impact of a Community Group Work Program on Delinquent Corner Groups," *op. cit.*, pp. 392-396, and "Preventive Work with Street-Corner Groups: Boston Delinquency Project," *op. cit.*, pp. 99-100, *passim*. A somewhat more detailed description of one kind of content analysis method used in an earlier pilot study, and modified for use in the larger study, appears in Walter B. Miller, Hildred Geertz and Henry S. G. Cutter, "Aggression in a Boys' Street-Corner Group," *Psychiatry*, 24 (November 1961), pp. 284-285.

[18] Detailed analyses of changes in "non-violative" forms of behavior (e.g., frequency of recreational activities, trends in "evaluatively neutral" behaviors) as well as more generalized "change-process" analyses (e.g., "structural" changes in groups—factions, leadership; overall patterning of change and relations between changes in violative and non-violative patterns) will appear in Walter B. Miller, *City Gangs: An Experiment in Changing Gang Behavior*, John Wiley and Sons, in preparation.

[19] The "study population" toward which these questions were directed was the 205 members of the seven corner gangs subjected to "intensive service" by workers. (See

the first question would necessarily have to precede attempts to answer further questions such as "Which methods were most effective?"; the value of describing what the workers did in order to reduce delinquency would evidently depend on whether it could be shown that delinquency had in fact been reduced.

Following sections will report three separate measures of change in patterns of violative behavior. These are: 1) Disapproved forms of customary behavior; 2) Illegal behavior; 3) Court appearance rates. These three sets of measures represent different methods of analysis, different orders of specificity, and were derived from different sources. The implications of this for achieved results will be discussed later.

Trends in Disapproved Behavior

A central form of "violative" behavior is that which violates specific legal statutes (e.g., theft, armed assault). Also important, however, is behavior which violates "moral" norms or ethical standards. Concern with such behavior is of interest in its own right (Was there a reduction in morally-violative behavior?) as well as in relation to illegal behavior (Were developments in the areas of illegal and immoral behavior related or independent?). The relationship between immoral and illegal behavior is highly complex; most behavior which violates legal norms also violates moral norms (overtime parking is one example of an exception), but much immoral behavior seldom results in legal action (homosexual intimacy between women; failure to attempt to rescue a drowning stranger).

Designating specific forms of behavior as "illegal" presents a relatively simple task, since detailed and fairly explicit criminal codes are available; designating behavior as "immoral" is far more difficult, both because of the multiplicity of moral codes in American society, and because many important moral norms are not explicitly codified.[20] In addressing the question—"Did the Project bring about a decrease in morally-violative behavior?", at least four sets of moral codes are of relevance—those of middle class adults, of middle class adolescents, of lower class adults, and of lower class adolescents.[21] While there are large areas of concordance among these sets, there are also important areas of non-correspondence. The method employed in this area was as follows:

A major source of data for Project research was a large population of "behavior sequences" engaged in by group members during the study period. These were derived from a variety of sources, the principal source being the detailed descriptive daily field reports of the workers.[22] All recorded behavioral events involving group members were extracted from the records and typed on separate data cards. These cards were coded, and filed in chronological order under 65 separate categories of behavior such as drinking behavior, sexual behavior, and theft. A total of 100,000 behavior sequences was recorded, coded, and filed.

Fourteen of the 65 behavior categories were selected for the purpose of analyzing trends in immoral behavior.[23] These were: theft, assault, drinking, sex, mating, work, education, religion, and involvement with courts, police, corrections, social welfare, family, and other gangs. Seventy-five thousand behavioral sequences were included under these fourteen categories.

A separate set of evaluative standards, based primarily on the workers' own values, was developed for each of the fourteen areas. The workers as individuals were essentially oriented to the value system of middle class adults, but due largely to their training in social work, they espoused an "easier" or more permissive version of these standards. In addition, as a result of their experiences in the lower class community, their standards had been further modified to accommodate in some degree those of the adolescent gangs. The workers' standards thus comprised an easier baseline against which to measure change since they were considerably less rigid than those which would be applied by most middle class adults.

Listings were drawn up for each of the fourteen areas which designated as "approved" or "disapproved" about 25 specific forms of behavior per area. A distinction was made between "actions" (behavioral events observed to occur) and "sentiments" (attitudes or intentions).[24] Designations were based on three kinds of information; evaluative statements made by the workers concerning particular areas of behavior; attitudes or actions workers had supported or opposed in actual situations, and an attitude questionnaire administered to each worker. Preliminary listings were submitted to the workers to see if the items did in fact reflect the evaluative standards they felt themselves to espouse; there was high agreement with the listings; in a few instances of disagreement modifications were made.

A total of 14,471 actions and sentiments were categorized as "approved," "disapproved," or "evaluatively-neutral." While these data made possible detailed and extensive analysis of differential patterns of behavior change in various areas and on different levels, the primary question for the most general purposes of impact measurement was phrased as—"Was there a significant reduction in the relative frequency of *disapproved actions* during the period of worker contact?" With some qualifications, the answer was "No."

Each worker's term of contact was divided into three equal phases, and the relative frequency of disapproved actions during the first and third phase was compared.[25] During the full study

pp. 169-170.) Unless otherwise specified, the term "Project Groups" will be used to refer to this population.

20 A brief discussion of the complexities of the "multiple-moral-norm" system of the United States is contained in William C. Kvaraceus, Walter B. Miller, *et al, Delinquent Behavior: Culture and the Individual,* Washington: National Education Association of the United States, 1959, pp. 46-49.

21 This four-type distinction is very gross; a range of subsystems could be delineated within each of the four cited "systems."

22 8870 pages of typescript records were subjected to coding. Of these, 6600 pages were self-recorded field reports by workers; 690 pages were worker reports to the Project Director; 640 were field reports and interviews by research staff; 150 were tape-recorded transcriptions of group interaction. A brief description of the principles of the data-coding system, based on the concept of the "object-oriented-behavior-sequence," is included in Ernest Lilienstein, James Short, *et al,* "Procedural Notes for the Coding of Detached Worker Interviews," Chicago: University of Chicago Youth Studies Program (February 1962), pp. 2-7.

23 These 14 were selected because they included the largest numbers of recorded events, and because they represented a range of behaviors along the dimension "high violative potential" (theft, assault) through "low violative potential" (church, family-oriented behavior).

24 Examples of approved and disapproved actions and sentiments in the area of drinking are as follows: *Approved action;* "refusal to buy or accept liquor": *disapproved action;* "getting drunk, going on a drinking spree": *approved sentiment;* "stated intention to discontinue or reduce frequency of drinking": *disapproved sentiment;* "bragging of one's drinking prowess."

25 Selected findings in regard only to disapproved actions are reported here. Future reports will present and analyze trends in both actions and sentiments, and in approved, disapproved and evaluatively-neutral forms, and the relations among these.

period, the 205 members of the seven intensive analysis groups engaged in 4518 approved or disapproved actions. During the initial phase, 785 of 1604 actions (48.9%) were disapproved; during the final phase, 613 of 1364 (44.9%)—a reduction of only 4%.

Of the fourteen behavior areas, only one ("school-oriented behavior") showed a statistically significant reduction in disapproved actions. Of the remaining 13, ten showed decreases in disapproved actions, one no change, and two (church- and social-agency-oriented behavior) showed increases. Of the seven analysis groups, only one (white, male, younger, higher social status) showed a statistically significant reduction. Of the remaining six, five showed decreases in disapproved actions, one no change, and one (white, male, older, lower social status) an increase.[26]

The unexpected degree of stability over time in the ratio of approved to disapproved actions is all the more noteworthy in view of the fact that one might have expected the area of moral behavior to have felt the most direct impact of the workers' presence. One clue to the stability of the change figures lies in the fact that there was a good correspondence between the degree of change in disapproved actions and the social status of the group; in general, the lower the group's social status, the smaller the reduction in disapproved actions.[27]

Trends in Illegal Acts

The central question to be asked of a delinquency control program is—"Does it control delinquency?" One direct way of approaching this question is to focus on that "target" population most directly exposed to program action methods and ask "Was there a decrease in the frequency of crimes committed by the target population during the period of the program?" Under most circumstances this is difficult to answer, owing to the necessity of relying on records collected by police, courts, or other "official" agencies. The drawbacks of utilizing official incidence statistics as a measure of the actual occurrence of criminal behavior have frequently been pointed out; among these is the very complex process of selectivity which governs the conversion of committed crimes into official statistics; many crimes are never officially detected; many of those detected do not result in an official arrest; many arrests do not eventuate in court action, and so on. At each stage of the conversion process, there is a multiplicity of factors relatively independent of the commission of the crime itself which determines whether or not a crime will be officially recorded, and in what form.

The Midcity Project was able to a large extent to overcome this difficulty by the nature of its base data. Because of their intimate daily association with gang members, workers were in a position both to observe crimes directly, and to receive reports of crimes shortly after they occurred. The great majority of these never appeared in official records.[28]

The research question in the area of illegal behavior was phrased: "Was there a significant decrease in the frequency of statute violations committed by Project group members during the period of worker contact?" As in the case of disapproved actions, the answer was, with some qualifications, "No." Methods and results were as follows.

Every statute-violating act committed by a Project group member during the course of the contact period was recorded on an individual record form. While the bulk of recorded acts were derived from the workers' field reports, information was obtained from all available sources, including official records. Very few of the crimes recorded by official agencies were not also recorded by the Project; many of the crimes recorded by the Project did not appear in official records. During the course of the Project, a total of 1005 legally violative acts was recorded for members of the seven intensive analysis groups. Eighty-three per cent of the 205 Project group members had committed at least one illegal act; 90% of the 150 males had been so involved. These figures alone show that the Project did not prevent crime, and there had been no expectation that it would. But did it "control" or "inhibit" crime?

Offenses were classified under eleven categories: theft, assault, alcohol violations, sex offenses, trespassing, disorderly conduct, truancy, vandalism, gambling violations, and "other" (e.g., strewing tacks on street, killing cats).[29] Each worker's term of contact was divided into three equal phases, and the frequency of offenses during the initial and final phase was compared.

Seven hundred and fifty-two of the 1005 offenses were committed during the initial and final phases. Of these, 394 occurred during the initial phase, and 358 during the final—a reduction of 9.1%. Considering males only, however, 614 male crimes accounting for 81.6% of all offenses showed an *increase* of 1.3% between initial and final phases. In order to localize areas of greater and lesser change, a distinction was made between "major" and "minor" types of offense, in which theft, assault, and alcohol offenses, accounting for 70.5% of all male offenses, were categorized as "major." On these major offenses the male groups showed an increase of 11.2%—the older male groups showing an increase of 4.7%, and the younger an increase of 21.8%.

In sum, then, it could not be said that there was any significant reduction in the frequency of known crimes during the course of the Project. The modest decrease shown by the total sample was accounted for largely by the girls and by minor offenses; major offenses by boys, in contrast, increased

[26] Chi-square was used to test significance. For all fourteen behavior areas for all seven groups, chi-square was 4.57 (one d.f.), which was significant between the .02 and .05 level. However, almost all the "change" variance was accounted for by the single area which showed a significant reduction (chi-square for "school" was 14.32, significant beyond the .01 level). The other 13 behavior areas, accounting for 91.6% of the evaluated actions, showed a reduction of only 2.3%. Chi-square was 1.52 (one d.f.) which fails of significance. Chi-square for the one significant change group (Junior Outlaws) was 9.21, significant at the .01 level. However, omitting the one "significant change" behavior area (school) from consideration, chi-square for the remaining 90% of Junior Outlaws behavior areas was 3.19—which fails of significance at the .05 level.

[27] Rank-difference correlation between "reduction in disapproved actions" and "lower social status" was −.82. The fact that this kind of association (the lower the social status the less change) appeared frequently in analyses of specific forms of behavior attests to the strength of the influence of group social status on patterns of delinquency and vulnerability to change efforts.

[28] The availability to the Project of both official and unofficial statistics on crime frequency made it possible to derive "conversion ratios" showing the proportion of crimes recorded by official agencies to those recorded by the Project. These ratios will be reported in greater detail in *City Gangs, op. cit.;* in brief, ratios of "Project-recorded" to "court-appeared" offenses were as follows. For all categories of offense for both sexes, 15% of known crimes resulted in court action. For males only this ratio was 16%; fewer than 1% of recorded female crimes were court processed. The highest ratio was in the case of theft-type offenses by males; about 25% were court processed. About 10% of male drinking and assaultive offenses resulted in court appearance.

in frenquency during the course of the Project, and major offenses by younger boys increased most of all.[30]

Trends in Court Appearances

The third major index to Project impact was based on court appearance statistics. The principal research question in this area was phrased: "Did the Project effect any decrease in the frequency with which Project group members appeared in court in connection with crimes?"[31] The use of court-appearance data made it possible to amplify and strengthen the measurement of impact in three major ways. 1) It permitted a considerable time-extension. Previous sections describe trends which occurred during the actual period of worker contact. Sound determination of impact makes it necessary to know how these "during" trends related to trends both preceding and following the contact period. Post-contact trends become particularly important in light of the "negligible change" findings of the "during-contact" period, which raise the possibility that the real impact of the Project may have occurred following the workers' departure, as a kind of delayed reaction response. 2) The data were compiled by agencies which were essentially independent of the Project. Although the Project made every attempt to recognize, accommodate to, and correct for the possibility of in-project bias,[32] exclusive reliance on data collected primarily by those in the employ of the Project would admit the possibility that the objectives or values of Project staff would in some way prejudice results. Despite some contact between Project and court personnel, the operations of the courts were essentially independent of those of the Project, and the likelihood that the various courts in which group members appeared would be influenced in any consistent way by Project values or objectives was extremely small. 3) It made possible the application of time-trend measures to groups other than those taken by the Project as objects of change. The inclusion of a control population as part of the basic evaluative design was of vital importance. Despite the detail obtainable through the continued and intimate contact of group and worker, it would have been difficult to know, without a control population, the extent to which the experience of Project group members during the contact period was a response to worker influence rather than a variety of other possible influencing factors.

Court-appearance data were processed in three different ways. The first made these data directly comparable with the other "during-contact" measures by asking—"Was there a significant decrease in the frequency with which Project group members appeared in court in connection with crimes during the contact period?" The second exploited the time-extension potentialities of the data by asking—"How did the frequency of court appearance during the contact period compare with frequency preceding and following this period?" The third utilized a control population and asked—"Did the court-appearance experience of gang members worked with by a delinquency control project for various periods between the ages of 14 and 19 differ significantly from the experience of similar gang members not so worked with?"

Contact Period Trends: Names of the 205 members of the Project's intensive contact groups were submitted to the state's central criminal records division. Court appearance records were returned for all group members with court experience. These records contained full court appearance and correctional commitment data for the 16 year period from 1945 to 1961—at which time older group members averaged 23 years of age, and younger, 21. It was thus possible to process the full sample as an age cohort in regard to court experience between the ages of 7 and 23, and including the period of Project contact. Each appearance in court on a new count for all male group members was tabulated.[33] "During-contact" appearance trends were analyzed in the same fashion as disapproved and illegal actions. The contact term for each group was divided into three equal phases, and the frequency of appearances during the initial and final phase was compared.

Trends in court-appeared offenses were essentially the same as trends in illegal actions. Group members appeared in court in connection with 144 offenses during the contact period. Fifty-one appearances occurred during the initial period and 48 during the final—a decrease of 5.8%. However, categorizing offenses as "major" and "minor" as was done in the case of illegal actions showed that for major offenses (theft, assault, alcohol), 31 appearances occurred during the initial phase and 35 during the final—an increase of 12.9%.[34] There was, therefore, no significant decrease in the frequency with which group members appeared in court during the term of worker contact. Neither the slight decrease in all-offense trends nor the in-

[29] Determination of illegality was based on the offense classifications of the Massachusetts Penal Code. The complexities of definition of the various offense categories cannot be detailed here, but most categories represent higher level generality definitions than those of the code. For example, the category "theft" is used here to include all forms of unlawful appropriation of property, thus subsuming the more than 30 distinctions of the Penal code, e.g., robbery, armed, unarmed; larceny, grand, petty, burglary, etc.). Non-theft auto violations are included under "other" since so few were recorded; similarly, narcotics violations, a major form of crime from a "seriousness" point of view, are included under "other" since virtually no instances were recorded.

[30] None of these changes proved significant on the basis of chi-square. Chi-square for the largest change, the increase of 21.8% for the younger males, was 3.32, which is just below the .05 level. More detailed analyses of these trends, broken down according to type of offense, sex, age, etc., will be presented in *City Gangs, op. cit.*

[31] Phrasing the question in this way was one of the devices used to accommodate the difficulties in using statistics compiled by official agencies. This phrasing takes the court appearance itself as an essentially independent index of impact; it does not assume any systematic connection between frequency of court appearance and frequency of criminal behavior. Having separate measures of Project-recorded and court processed crimes (See footnote 28) makes possible separate computations of these ratios. Further, since court-appeared crime rather than committed crime can be seen, from one perspective, as the more serious social problem, Project impact on the likelihood of appearance itself can be taken as one relatively independent measure of effectiveness.

[32] The technical and methodological devices for accommodating to or correcting for the possibility of in-project bias will be detailed in future reporting.

[33] Out of 145 "during-contact" court appearances, only one involved a girl. Since 155 illegal acts involved females, this supports the frequently reported finding that females are far less likely to be subjected to official processing for crimes than males. All following figures, therefore, refer to males only.

[34] Neither of these changes was statistically significant, testing with chi-square and Fisher's Exact Test. The three "major" offenses showed differing trends—with "theft" showing some decrease (23 to 19), "assault" remaining about the same (5 to 6) and "Alcohol" showing a considerable increase (3 to 10). "Minor" crimes decreased from 20 to 13. These trends will be reported and analyzed more fully in future reports.

TABLE I

NUMBER OF COURT APPEARANCES PER YEAR*: AGES 7 - 23

PROJECT AND CONTROL GROUPS

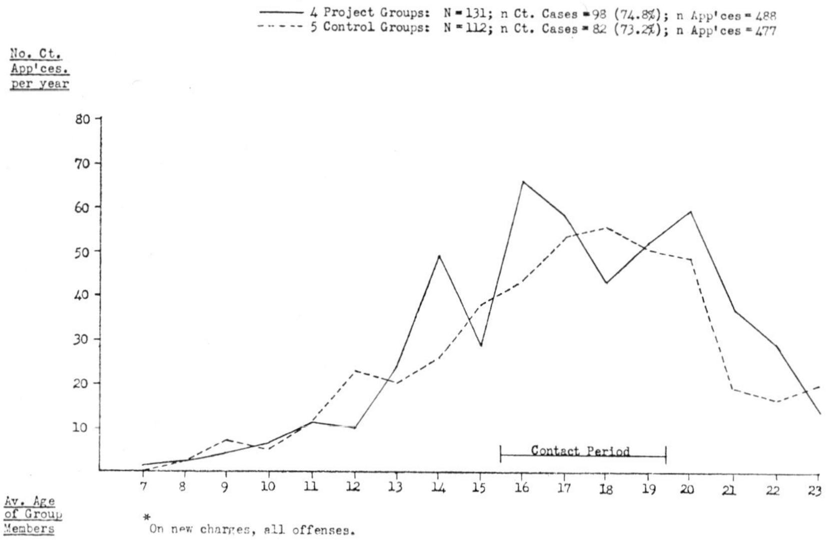

* On new charges, all offenses.

crease in major offense trends proved statistically significant. The fact that these "during-contact" court appearance trends, involving 155 offenses, closely paralleled illegal act trends, involving 1005 offenses, served to corroborate both sets of trends, and to reinforce the finding of "negligible change" in legally-violative behavior for the period of worker contact.

Before-During-After Trends: Project Groups: In order to place the "during-contact" offense trends in a broader time-perspective, it was necessary to compare them to rates preceding and following the contact period. Since group members were of different ages during the contact period, data were processed so as to make it possible to compare the court experience of the several groups at equivalent age periods. The average age of each group was determined, and the number of court appearances per group for each six month period between the ages of 7 and 23 was tabulated. One set of results is shown in Table 1. The frequency curve of yearly court appearances resembled a normal distribution curve, skewed to the right. Appearance frequency increased gradually between the ages of 7 and 16, maintained a high level between 16 and 20, and dropped off quite rapidly after 20.

The period of maximum frequency of court appearances coincided, in general, with the period of worker contact. Although no single group remained in contact with a worker during the full period between ages 16 and 20, each of the groups experienced contact for periods ranging from one to two and a half years during this period. It could not be said, then, that frequency of court appearance during the contact period was appreciably lower than during the pre-contact period; on the contrary, groups achieved a peak of appearance frequency during the period of Project service efforts.

Another way of describing these trends is by examining appearance frequency by six month periods. During the six months preceding contact there were 21 appearances; during the first six months of contact there were 29, and during the last, 27. In the six months following termination appearances rose to 39, dropped to 20 for the next six months, and rose to 39 for the next. Thus, 18 months after project termination, appearance frequency was at its highest point for the total adolescent period.

The yearly appearance curve (Table 1) does, however, show two rather prominent dips—one at age 15, the other at 18. The dip at 15 could not have been related to the Project, since contact had not yet begun. The dip at 18, however, occurred at a time when each of the three older groups was in contact with workers, and thus admits the possibility of worker influence.[35] It is also possible that the post-twenty decline may have represented a delayed-action effect. Thus, looking at the period of worker contact as one phase within the overall period of adolescence, it would appear that the presence of the workers did not inhibit the frequency of court appearances, but that a dip in appearance frequency at age 18 and a drop in frequency after age twenty may have been related to the workers' efforts.

Comparison of Project and Control Group Trends: Extending the examination of offense trends from the during-contact period to "before" and "after" periods, while furnishing important additional information, also raised additional questions. Was it just coincidental that the 16 to 19 peak in court appearances occurred during the contact period—or could the presence of the workers have been in some way responsible? Was the sharp decline in frequency of appearances after age 20 a delayed action result of worker effort? To clarify these questions it was necessary to examine the court appearance experience of a control population—a set of corner gangs as similar as possible to Project gangs, but who had *not* been worked with by the Project. The indexes reported so far have provided information as to whether significant change occurred, but have been inconclusive as to the all-important question of cause-and-effect (To what extent were observed trends related to the workers' efforts?). The use of a control population entailed certain risks—primarily the possibility that service and control populations might not be adequately matched in some respects—but the unique potency of the control method as a device for furnishing evidence in the vital area of "cause" outweighed these risks.

Each of the Project's seven intensive service groups was matched with a somewhat smaller number of members of similarly organized corner gangs of similar age, sex, ethnic status, and social status. Most of these groups hung out in the same district as did Project groups, and their existence and membership had been ascertained during the course of the Project. Since the total membership of the Control groups was not known as fully as that of Project groups, it was necessary in some instances to match one Project group with two Control groups of

[35] This "dip" phenomenon—a lowering of the frequency of violative behavior during the "middle" phase of worker contact—was also noted in connection with a somewhat different kind of processing of illegal acts reported in "Preventive Work with Street-Corner Groups: Boston Delinquency Project," *op. cit.*, p. 100. Currently available data make it possible to amplify and modify the interpretation presented in the earlier paper.

TABLE II

NUMBER OF INDIVIDUALS APPEARING IN COURT PER YEAR*: AGES 7 - 23

PROJECT AND CONTROL GROUPS

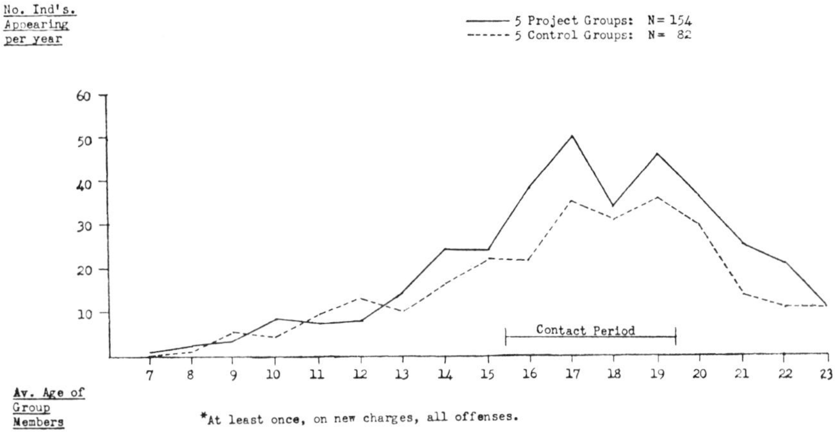

*At least once, on new charges, all offenses.

similar status characteristics. By this process, a population comprising 172 members of 11 corner gangs was selected to serve as a control population for the 205 members of the seven project gangs. Court appearance data on Control groups were obtained, and the groups were processed as an age cohort in the same manner as Project groups.

The court appearance frequency curves for Project and Control groups are very similar (See Table 1). If the two dips in the Project curve are eliminated by joining the peaks at 14, 16 and 20, the shape of the two curves becomes almost identical. Both curves show a gradual rise from ages 7 to 16 or 17, maintain a high level to age 20, and drop rapidly between 20 and 23. Table 2 compares Project and Control groups according to the number of *individuals* per year per group to appear in court, rather than according to the number of *appearances* per year per group. On this basis, the similarity between Project and Control curves becomes even more marked. The dip at age 14 in the Project appearance curve (Table 1) flattens out, and both Project and Control groups show a dip at age 18, making the Project and Control curves virtually identical.[36]

The unusual degree of similarity between the court appearance curves of Project and Control groups constitutes the single most powerful piece of evidence on Project impact obtained by the research. The fact that a group of similar gangs not worked with by the Project showed an almost identical decrease in court appearance frequency between ages 20 and 23 removes any reasonable basis for attributing the post-20 decline of Project groups to worker efforts. Indeed, the high degree of overall similarity in court appearance experience between "served" and "unserved" groups makes it most difficult to claim that anything done by the Project had any significant influence on the likelihood of court appearance.

Project and Control groups show equally striking similarities in regard to three additional measures—the proportion of individuals who had appeared in court by age 23, the proportion who had re-appeared, and the number of appearances per individual. Of 131 members of four male Project groups, 98, or *74.8%,* had appeared in court at least once by age 23. The fact that 75% of the members of gangs worked with by social workers had nevertheless appeared in court by age 23 would in itself appear to indicate very limited Project impact. This finding, however, still admits the possibility that appearance frequency might have been even higher in the absence of the workers, or conversely, that the high figure was in some way a consequence of the workers' efforts. Both of these possibilities are weakened by the Control cohort figures. Of 112 members of five male groups *not* worked with by the Project, 82, or *73.2%,* had appeared in court by age 23—almost exactly the same percentage shown by Project groups.[37]

The possibility still remains that Project group members, once having appeared in court, would be less likely than Control members to *reappear.* This was not the case. Of 98 members of Project groups who appeared in court at least once, 72, or *73.5%,* appeared at least once again; of 82 Control group members who appeared at least once, 61, or *74.3%,* appeared at least once more. A further possibility exists that while similar proportions of *individuals* might have appeared in court, Project group members might have made fewer *appearances* per individual. However, Project and Control groups were also similar in this respect. Ninety-eight Project members who appeared in court between the ages of 7 and 23 appeared 488 times, or 5.0 appearances per individual. Eighty-two Control males appeared 447 times, or 5.4 appearances per individual. These figures, while not as close to identity as the outcome figures, fail to show a statistically significant difference. The unusual degree of closeness in all these court appearance measures for male Project and Control groups provides a firm basis for concluding that Project impact on the likelihood of court appearance was negligible.

Summary of "Impact" Findings

It is now possible to provide a definite answer to the principal evaluative research question—"Was there a significant measurable inhibition of law-violating or morally-disapproved behavior as a consequence of Project efforts?" The answer, with little necessary qualification, is "No." All major measures of violative behavior—disapproved actions, illegal actions, during-contact court appearances, before-

36 The implications of these court-appearance frequency trends transcend their utility as a technique for "controlling" for worker influence. One implication will be cited in footnote 43; more detailed interpretation and analysis, with special attention to the relative influence of worker activity and subcultural forces on the shape of the curves will be included in *City Gangs, op. cit.* Also included will be greater detail on the process of locating, selecting, matching and processing the control population.

37 The finding of negligible difference in court appearance frequency between Project and Control groups parallels the findings of the Cambridge-Somerville Youth Study —one of the few delinquency control projects to report findings of careful evaluative research (Edwin Powers and Helen Witmer, *An Experiment in the Prevention of Delinquency,* New York: Columbia University Press, 1951). It was found that 29.5% of a 325 boy treatment group had appeared in court by the time the oldest boys were 21, as compared with 28.3% of a 325 boy control group (p. 326). Despite differences in methods (Cambridge-Somerville used primarily individually-focused counseling) and client populations (Cambridge-Somerville boys were less delinquent), the degree of similarity between the two projects in treatment and control outcomes is striking.

during-after appearances, and Project-Control group appearances—provide consistent support for a finding of "negligible impact."

There was a modest decrease, during the period of worker contact, in the frequency of disapproved actions in 14 areas of behavior—but much of this reduction was due to a decrease in a single area—school-oriented behavior. The overall change in the other 13 areas was only −2.3%.[38] The total number of illegal actions engaged in by group members also decreased slightly, though not significantly, during the course of the Project. Most of this reduction, however, was accounted for by minor offenses; major offenses showed a slight increase. Similarly, while there was a small decrease in the frequency of all categories of court-appeared offenses, major offenses showed an increase. Examining the group members' court-appearance trends between the ages 7 and 23 showed that court appearances were most frequent during the age-period when Project workers were with the groups. The possibility that a pronounced decrease in court-appearance frequency after age 20 represented a delayed response to the Project was weakened by the fact that a similar decline occurred in the case of a set of similar gangs not worked with by the Project, and which, in fact, showed extremely similar court appearance trends both before, during, and after the age period during which Project groups were in contact with workers.

The fact that the various measures of impact are mutually consistent increases confidence in the overall "negligible impact" finding. Not only do the several indexes delineate similar trends in regard to the direction and magnitude of change (e.g., "during-period" change in disapproved actions, −4.0%; in illegal actions, −9.1%; in court appearance frequency, −5.8%), but also show a high degree of internal consistency in other respects. For example, the rank position of the five male groups in the degree of reduction in violative behavior shown by the three major indexes was very similar.[39]

Two previous papers reporting impact findings of the Midcity Project conveyed the impression of a limited but definite reduction in delinquency.[40] Why does the present report support a different conclusion? In the first place, present findings are based on new data not available in 1957 and '59, as well as on more extensive analysis of data then available. Both previous papers stated that reported results were preliminary, and cited the possibility of modification by future analysis.[41] Second, present data focus more directly on the specific experience of a specific target population; some of the previous impact findings were based on less focused indexes of general community trends, in which the behavior of the Project's target groups was not as directly distinguishable. Third, the "before" and "after" time extension made possible by the use of court data show some previously reported trends to have been relatively temporary fluctuations. Fourth, the use of a control population made it possible to anchor results more firmly by showing that important observed trends were common to both Project and non-Project groups, thus making possible a better determination of the extent to which "during" Project variation was in fact related to the workers' efforts.

THE EFFICACY OF PROJECT CONTROL METHODS

Which of the Project's methods were "tested" by the "negligible impact" findings? This complex question can be addressed only briefly here. It is evident that it was those methods which were most extensively employed or successfully executed which were shown most directly to have been least effective in inhibiting delinquency. Fifteen separate methods or techniques were cited earlier in connection with the three major programs (Community Organization, Family Service, Gang Work) of the Midcity Project. Of these, seven could be designated as extensively employed or successfully executed: establishment of district citizens' council; locating and contacting adolescent corner gangs; establishing relationships with gang members; effecting formal organization and involvement in organized recreational activity; provision of access to adult institutions; provision of adult role-model. It is to these seven methods that the "negligible impact" finding applies most directly. Of these, "recreation" is already recognized quite widely to be of limited effectiveness as an exclusive method; "relationship" is still seen in many quarters as quite effective; "adult role-model" was also found, by the Cambridge-Somerville Project, to have had little effect. Of two aspects of "access-provision"—enabling youngsters to avail themselves of existing opportunities, and altering larger societal institutions so as to create new opportunities—the Project achieved the former but exerted limited systematic effort in regard to the latter, so that this aspect of access-provision was only minimally tested.

Six methods could be characterized as less extensively employed or implemented with only moderate success: formation of citizens' groups; coordination of efforts of youth groups and adult citizens' groups; coordination of family-service agencies; treatment of "chronic problem" families; psychodynamic counseling and therapy; group dynamics. Some of these programs continued beyond the Project's three year demonstration period, but there is as yet no evidence available that any of these have had an impact on delinquency substantially different from that of the "best-tested" methods.

Two final methods—effecting concerted effort between citizens' groups and professional agencies, and coordinating the varied efforts of professional agencies themselves—were implemented only minimally. It is to these methods, then, that the "negligible impact" finding has least applicability. However, this failure of effectuation, especially in the area of inter-agency-cooperation, was achieved only after extensive expenditure of effort, which might suggest that the cost of implementing this type of method, whose potential impact on delinquency is as

---

[38] It is possible that the decrease in disapproved school-oriented actions was due largely to a decrease in the frequency of truancy brought about by the fact that many of the earlier period truants had, by Project termination, passed the age at which school attendance was compulsory, thus ending their truancy. This possibility will be tested as part of a detailed analysis of change trends in each behavior area.

[39] Rank-difference correlation coefficients were as follows: disapproved acts and illegal acts +.80; disapproved acts and court appearances +.87; illegal acts and court appearances, +.97. Even with the small N of 5, the good correspondence between disapproved acts and court appearances is impressive, since the data for the two rank series were derived from completely independent sources.

[40] "The Impact of a Community Group Work Program on Delinquent Corner Groups," *op. cit.*, pp. 390-406, and "Preventive Work with Street-Corner Groups: Boston Delinquency Project," *op. cit.*, pp. 97-106.

[41] It is similarly possible that some of the results cited here will be modified in the final Project report, especially in areas where more extensive internal analysis will enable fuller interpretations of reported trends.

yet undetermined, might not be commensurate with the degree of delinquency-reduction it could perhaps produce.

In addition, granting that some of the Project's methods were tested less fully than others, the fact that all 15 (and others) were applied concurrently and in concert also constituted a test of the "synergism" concept—that the simultaneous and concerted application of multiple and diverse programs on different levels will produce an impact greater than the summed impact of the component programs. Thus the total-community-multiple-programs approach, as executed by the Midcity Project, also fell within the category of methods best tested by the finding of "negligible impact."

In evaluating the significance of these "negligible impact" findings three considerations should be borne in mind. The first concerns the scope and nature of the question to which "negligible impact" is an answer, the second the level on which the answer is presented, and the third the value of the Project to delinquency control as a larger enterprise.

The phrasing of the principal evaluative research question tests the effectiveness of the Project against a single and central criterion—the measurable inhibition of explicitly violative behavior of a designated target population. The Project had considerable impact in other areas. To cite only two of these; the establishment of the control project and the spread of knowledge as to its existence had a calming effect on the adult community. Pre-Project gang activities in Midcity had activated a sense of fear among many adults, and a feeling of helplessness in the face of actual and potential violence. Simple knowledge of the existence of the Project served to alleviate the community's sense of threat, in that there was now an established locus of responsibility for gang crime. The fact that *something* was being done was in itself important quite independent of the possible effectiveness of what was being done.

The Project was also instrumental in establishing new delinquency-control organizations, and left the community a legacy of organizations and programs which it had either brought into being or taken primary responsibility for. Among these were the District Community Council organized by Project staff, the project for providing direct service to "chronic problem" families, an annual sports award dinner for the youth of the community, and a permanent program of area work administered by the municipal government. The organizational plan of this latter enterprise was drawn up before Project termination, so that the municipal delinquency control bureau, once established, was able to extend the general approach of the Project to the entire municipal area.[42] While the value of these organized enterprises must also be measured against the same "impact on delinquency" criterion which was applied to the Project, it is clear that their existence was one tangible product of the Project.

A second consideration concerns the "level" of the reported findings. Data presented in connection with each of the major indexes to impact are at the most gross analytical level—that is, they neither specify nor analyze systematically the internal variation of the reported trends in three important respects—variations among the several groups, variations among the several behavior areas, and finer fluctuations over time. The finding of "negligible impact" encompasses, most accurately, *all* analyzed forms of behavior of *all* analyzed groups for extended periods. Internal analyses not reported here show that some groups showed considerable change in some areas, and that some areas showed considerable change for some groups. Further, while initial and final levels of violative behavior in many instances showed little difference, a good deal of turbulence or fluctuation characterized intervening periods. The flat "negligible impact" statement, then, by concealing a considerable degree of internal variability, obscures the fact that there was differential vulnerability to change in different areas and for different groups. Fuller analyses of these variations, along with the methods associated with greater and lesser vulnerability, will furnish specific policy guides to more and less strategic points of intervention.

A final consideration concerns the "value" of the Project in the face of its "negligible inhibition of delinquent behavior" outcome. There can be an important distinction, obscured by the term "evaluation" between the "effect" of an enterprise and its "value." The Midcity Project was established to test the possible effectiveness of its several approaches. These were in fact tested, and the Project was thus successful in the achievement of its "demonstration" objective. The evaluation model used here, based on multiple indexes to change, and using the "behavioral event" as a primary unit of analysis, can be applied in other instances where the impact of a specific change enterprise is at issue. Even more important, perhaps, is the fact that the process of gathering and analyzing the great bulk of data necessary to furnish a sound answer to the question of impact also produced a large volume of information of direct relevance to basic theoretical questions as to the origins of gangs and of gang delinquency. These findings also bear directly on a further question of considerable importance—"Why did the Project have so little impact on delinquency?"—a question to be addressed in some detail in future reports.[43]

---

[42] See D. Austin, "Recommendations for a Municipal Program of Delinquency Prevention," mimeo, 7 pp., United Community Services of Boston, 1957.

[43] Factors accounting for the limited impact of Project efforts will be treated in detail in *City Gangs, op. cit.* The explanatory analysis will forward the thesis that culturally-derived incentives for engaging in violative behavior were far stronger than any counterpressures the Project could bring to bear. This explanation will derive from a general theory of gang delinquency whose central proposition, to be expanded at length, will be that patterned involvement in violative behavior by gangs of the Midcity type occurs where four cultural "conditions" exist concurrently—*maleness, adolescence, urban residence,* and *low-skill laboring class status.* Each of these conditions is conceptualized as a particular type of subcultural system—each of whose "demanded" sets of behavior, taken separately, contribute some element of the motivation for engagement in gang delinquency, and whose concerted operation produces a subcultural milieu which furnishes strong and consistent support for customary involvement in criminal behavior. Data on "impact" presented here document the influence of two of these conditions—age status and social status. Court-appearance frequency trends (Tables I and II) would appear to indicate that the single most important determinant of the frequency of that order of criminal behavior which eventuated in court appearance for Midcity male gangs was *age,* or more specifically, movement through a series of age-based subcultural stages. Commission of criminal acts of given types and frequency appeared as a required concomitant of passing through the successive age-stages of adolescence and a prerequisite to the assumption of adult status. The influence of these age-class demands, on the basis of this and other evidence, would appear to exceed that of other factors—including conditions of the family, school, neighborhood or job world; police arrest policies, sentencing, confinement, probation and parole policies, and others. Data on *social status* (e.g., footnote 27, passim) along with much additional data not reported here, indicate a systematic relation-

ship between social status *within* the lower class, and delinquency. 1. Within the 21 gang sample of the Midcity study, crime was both more prevalent and more serious among those whose social status, measured by occupational and educational indexes, was lowest. 2. Relatively small differences in status were associated with relatively large differences in patterned behavior; as lower status levels were approached, delinquency incidence increased exponentially rather than linearly; this indicates the necessity of making refined intra-class distinctions when analyzing the social "location" of criminal behavior. 3. Groups of lower social status showed the least reduction in violative forms of behavior; this lower vulnerability to change efforts would indicate that violative behavior was more entrenched, and thus more central to the subcultural system.

Marginal Youth and Social Policy

Herman Schwendinger and Julia R. Schwendinger
University of Nevada, Las Vegas

Marginalization of a portion of American youth is described as a result of the structure of the major socialization agencies, the family and the school, in contemporary capitalist society. The family and other agencies mediate the process of marginalization created by economy. To eliminate marginalization, social policies must change the economic structure of society.

THE PROCESSES OF MARGINALIZATION

Whether it includes behavior inside or outside of school, the most sustained official reactions to delinquency usually involve a marginal population of youth, that has existed since the early centuries of capitalism. In those early centuries, however, many marginal youth were integrated within a larger population, composed of unemployed or subemployed laborers and debt-ridden artisans and farmers (Schwendinger and Schwendinger, 1976). Prior to the 19th century, marginals were originally produced and then "chastized for their enforced transformation into vagabonds and paupers," before manufacturing establishments could absorb their labor power (Marx, 1959:731-734). The process of marginalization subsequently annihilated urban artisanry and filled the debtors prisons with artisans bankrupted by the rise of pre-industrial manufactories and the domestic cottage industries. Afterward, the expansion of industrialism marginalized the toilers who had worked within the cottage industries. Simultaneously, this expansion absorbed millions of other marginals while it was producing a relative surplus population. With the rise of monopoly-capitalism, this population was generally restricted to the secondary labor market.

Long-term trends toward stagnation, also a characteristic of modern capitalist societies, inevitably occur and have only been overcome periodically. In colonial and semi-colonial capitalist societies, the effects of these trends on marginalization are particularly evident. Marginals in Venezuela, for instance, constitute almost one third of the population. The agrarian marginals live on subsistence payments or work without explicit wages. On the edges of the cities, rural migrants and urban marginals, who are underemployed, intermittently employed, and just plain unemployed, live in rat-infested slums. Some of these persons are employed in part-time or otherwise unproductive jobs, largely concentrated in the inflated tertiary sector (Hein and Stenzal, 1973). These persons are the menial "service workers" or the "penny capitalists," who desperately shift for themselves by scavenging, huckstering, working at odd jobs, and performing a variety of personal services for minimal payments.

The United States is also beset by long-term trends toward stagnation. The American economy no longer expands sufficiently to absorb most of its technologically displaced labor force—much less the new generations of workers. The rate of absorption has only surged for short periods during wartime or during a post-war boom. Generally the younger, the older, and the most oppressed workers have been excluded from the labor market. Millions have become marginal. From an economic standpoint, these persons at any given time are either absolutely or relatively superfluous.

Advanced capitalism prolongs the dependent status of youth. This prolongation elevates

From *Social Problems,* Vol. 24 (December 1976), pp. 84–91. Reprinted with the permission of the Society of Social Problems and the authors.

the theoretical importance of certain factors in the socialization agencies, which include the family, yet center on the modern school. These factors, as we shall see, uniquely recreate the process of marginalization *within* the socialization agencies themselves.

Analysis of the family and the school indicates that significant economic functions, which undoubtedly effect delinquent relations, are performed by these agencies. Most socialization agencies concentrate on youth who will generally become proletarians and who, therefore, require certain types of services for the production of their labor power. These services are largely provided by parents and by teachers, whose efforts are exerted in the family and the school. With regard to the reproduction of their labor power both socialization agencies seem to operate separately while, in fact, they are quite interdependent.

Various kinds of interdependent relations characterize these agencies: obviously, a child's success in school is dependent upon other family relations. Empirical studies also indicate that the family is a stronger determinant of the child's eventual "success" as a labor force participant. But *determination* of individual success cannot be equated with *domination* of the general standards which regulate successful striving. The family is forced to regulate its own productive relations according to the meritocratic and technical standards exerted by the school. For the long-term reproduction of labor power, therefore, the school is the dominating agency.

The reproductive relations in the school are in turn largely dominated by industrial relations. Social scientists have clearly demonstrated that educational standards "correspond" to the hierarchical and segmented organization of the labor force (Bowles and Gintis, 1973). The standards used to reward and punish a student's behavior within the school, therefore, are synchronized with the standards that are used by managers to control workers.

The reproductive relations within the family are also dominated by industry, but this form of domination is partly mediated by the school. As indicated, the school, in spite of appearances, essentially organizes its production relations around industrially related standards. By dominating production relations within the family, the school as well as industry imposes these standards upon parents and children.

At least two general consequences flow from these serial relations of domination. First, the reproductive relations within socialization agencies are synchronized with the alienated social relations that generally characterize commodity production. These synchronized relations are not confined to the youngsters who are in the process of acquiring the power to labor. They include both the parents and the teachers, who are involved in the long-term production of this commodity.

Second, these dominating relations are expressed in the same general laws of investment and profit maximization which culminate in the uneven development of various groups and nations (Bluestone, 1972). This means investments in the development of the labor force are allocated unevenly. Such investments concentrate on those groups of persons considered to have a greater potentiality for meeting the meritocratic criteria prevailing in educational institutions. Conversely, unless political struggles broaden educational policies, the investments of private or public resources—calculable in terms of money, equipment, facilities, faculties, and even in the teacher's time, attention, and expectations—will be minimal for the development of those groups of persons who do not appear to meet these criteria.

Consequently, the allocation of educational resources favors the youth who have already been the recipients of superior resources. They are recipients because of the advantages that are passed on to the members of certain ethnic, racial, or occupational strata, or because of the compensatory time and energy expended on them by self-sacrificing parents. During the elementary school period, a mutually reinforcing relationship is established between the activities of youth who show the productive signs of superior familial investments, and the patterns for selectively allocating resources within educational institutions. Throughout the child's formative period, educational capital continuously builds on the most favored students.

Simultaneously, the competitive position of the least favored students deteriorates and a process, analogous to marginalization within the economy, occurs in the context of the school and the family. This inherently contradictory trend results in anarchic behavior patterns, created by students who are not strongly motivated to achieve, and who do not make any disciplined effort to achieve. These are also the students who actually do not achieve the cognitive and non-cognitive traits that generally favor sustained labor force participation in the future. Although their chances for future employment are somewhat independent of their status in socialization agencies, these children manifest early in life the adaptive characteristics that evolve in capitalism among numerous owners of the least valuable forms of labor power.

Thus, the relations that favor the uneven development of labor power early in life generate a youthful population of *prototypic* marginals, whose status is not actually determined directly by economic institutions. The members of this population are not usually counted among "the employed" or "the unemployed." Instead, they are usually regarded as students and, during most of their adolescent years, workaday life is very far from their minds.

Within communities across the United States, adolescents speak about these prototypic marginals. Such names as Greaser, Vato, Dude, Honcho, Hodad, and Hood appear whenever they are mentioned in conversations. These metaphors refer to individual marginals and, among other social regularities in their personal behavior, to their conduct, carriage, attitudes, gestures, grooming, argot, clothing, and delinquent acts.

The marginalization process under discussion is not directly determined by labor market relations. Here the term "marginal" simply refers to the "prototypic" rather than labor force marginal. The effects of this process will therefore be reflected in family and school relationships, but they are not classified by any official economic category.

It is taken for granted that certain types of family conflicts or "breakdowns" will definitely enhance the possibilities of marginalization. But these possibilities are also mediated by parental resources. Wealthy families can employ such "absorption mechanisms" as psychiatric counseling, boarding school, and the tutorial trip abroad to cushion the effects of family disturbance on the child. If these mechanisms are unsuccessful, then their wealth further provides children who are becoming marginalized with a second chance later in life. Some of these children, in fact, never have to concern themselves with labor market activity: they can be sustained by inherited property.

By contrast, working class families are exposed to greater hardships and difficulties. Absorption mechanisms are relatively unavailable and family problems directly influence the parents' and child's active contribution to the production of the child's labor power. They interact with the already disadvantaged competitive relations engendered by the school.

Consequently, traditional socio-economic attributes, such as the parents' income, education, and property, which represent the most widespread family characteristics, directly effect the likelihood of marginalization. Because of the long-term effects of the uneven development of capital, a greater proportion of marginal youth can be expected among lower status families. Alternatively, marginalization can certainly be expected among *higher* status families (or among "middle class" families), but to a lesser degree. This observation is important, because the literature on "middle class" delinquency has glossed over the differences between marginal "middle class" delinquents and *other* types of delinquents.

Let us now consider youth who, from the standpoint of the school, represent the most highly developed forms of labor power. As high academic achievers, they strikingly epitomize the division of labor among mental and manual workers in capitalist societies. They are usually very articulate, and some have broad interests in politics, culture, and science. Others, noted for their narrow academic and technical interests, symbolize how much young personalities have been influenced by the extreme labor force segmentation among mental workers. Their personal interests are "overspecialized," and they are organized largely by experiences based on the appropriation and dispensation of technical knowledge.

In this work, the term "prototypic intellectuals" will be used to characterize the youth mentioned above. The word "intellectual" classifies those persons who devote their occupational activities to the formulation of ideas, to the creation of artistic representations of ideas, or to the application of ideas, such as the application of scientific-technical knowledge to human affairs. The development of modern intellectuals can be traced back to the early capitalist period. But this development has been accelerated enormously by expansion of monopoly capitalism and the modern state (Schwendingers, 1974:143-158, 360-361). Today the category of intellectuals includes writers, artists, librarians, social workers, city planners, teachers, and scientists.

The prototypic intellectual, on the other hand, refers to youth showing the personal interests and characteristics generated among adults by the developments mentioned above. Historically, educational institutions have played a very important role in regulating the formation of this particular population. Certain families, however, have contributed candidates disproportionately. Bourgeois families, including the small farmers as well as independent professions, have supplied the greatest proportions. In recent years, the established families of such "mental workers" as teachers, technicians, and scientists, also contribute relatively higher numbers of prototypic intellectuals.

On the other hand, because of bourgeois educational policies and the intergenerational effects of uneven investment, young women, youth of both sexes who belong to racially oppressed groups, and children of unskilled workers become candidates to a less degree. It has been chiefly the white families of higher socio-economic status that have established a mutually dependent relation with the school. The children of families that *have* more *get* more, because the public educational system converts human beings into potential commodities and builds upon *that* human material which already has considerable investment.

In communities across the United States, one finds that metaphors for this latter youth also appear in peer conversations. Included among these names are Intellectual, Brain, Pencil-Neck, Egg Head, Book Worm, and Walking Encyclopedia (See Schwendingers, forthcoming). For now, it should be noted that by contrast with many marginals, these youth are paragons of virtue. In fact, they are foremost members of the least delinquent population in a local society of youth.

SOCIAL POLICY

What social policies are required for the elimination of marginalization, uneven development and delinquency? Unfortunately, a theory of fundamental causes cannot provide either quick or direct answers to this question. Social policy formulation requires more than a causal theory. The level of the productive forces and hence the actual resources available in a given society must be considered. Conflicts over resources are also important. In fact, among the general determinants of social policies, class forces and political conflicts over control of these resources are most important.

In our opinion, an examination of both fundamental causes and social policy determinants lead to but one conclusion. The best possibilities for eliminating marginalization, uneven development, and delinquency exist in socialist societies. This conclusion, however, cannot be applied universally because socialist nations diverge in the course of their development, and the divergences have retrogressive as well as progressive consequences. Furthermore, some socialist nations, such as Yugoslavia, still retain anarchic market systems, which produce marginalization. Nevertheless, genuine socialist developments are numerous and they counter marginalization, uneven development, and delinquency.

As socialist societies overcome the anarchy of the market through economic planning, then marginalization and delinquency are curtailed sharply. The virtual elimination of unemployment and subemployment enormously decreases the numbers of adolescent marginals, and the size and stability of their delinquent group formations. (In capitalist societies, these groups are concentrated in slums and ghettos.) Walter O'Connor (1972:93), a liberal scholar, reports,

> Soviet delinquents tend to commit their offenses in groups . . . these groups, however, are generally rather small in number and fluid in composition, bearing little resemblance to the organized fighting gangs of large American cities in the 1950's. On the whole, it seems doubtful that we can speak of 'gangs' at all in the Soviet case. The instances of Soviet delinquents acting in concert frequently seem to reflect a spontaneous and temporary coming together for the purpose of some relatively specific act.

China provides additional illustrations of the decrease in marginalization and delinquency. American journalists have been struck by the relative absence of crime in the People's Republic of China today. This absence cannot be due to cultural differences between the Eastern and the Western hemispheres, because the differences between "liberated China" and "nationalist China" were discerned long ago by American observors. William Hinton (1970:19), for instance, worked during the post war years in China as a representative of the United Nations Relief and Rehabilitation Administration. He observed that in 1947,

> The most striking thing about the [communist] towns was the absence of beggars . . . It was unbelievable but true. The same went for prostitutes: there did not seem to be any. I was never opportuned even though I wandered day and night in the main streets and back alleys of the biggest towns in the area. In Nationalist-held Peking, on the other hand, clerks and roomboys in the main hotels doubled as pimps, while little children touted for their sisters on the sidewalks.

Futher illustrations can be obtained from Cuba and the German Democratic Republic. In the pre-revolutionary period, Havana was the center of organized crime in the Carribean. In addition, Cuba, like other Latin American countries, had an enormous population of marginals. Today, marginalization and organized crime, and their effects on children and adolescents, have disappeared from Cuba. Additional comparisons referring to unemployment that favor socialism can be made between the German Democratic Republic and the Federal Republic of Germany. With regard to crime, there has been a long-term decreasing trend in ordinary crime within the German Democratic Republic, but no comparable decline in West Germany. Again, since similar national groups are involved, such differences are due to their social orders.

The complete elimination of marginalization and delinquency depends upon advanced socialist changes. Socialism does not emerge full grown from the womb of class societies; it bears the imprint of thousands of years of class developments. Under socialism, school and family relations continue to reproduce the labor force, and some of these reproductive relations are not changed radically because certain bourgeois rights are maintained in industry. Such rights include equal pay for equal units of work; hence, they also include differentials in pay resulting from variations in individual skills, talents, and physical abilities. Consequently, since the products of labor are distributed during this transitional period "from each according to his or her ability; to each according to work performance," certain pre-existing socialization functions, social distinctions, and competitive relations are sustained. They are gradually eliminated, however, as their material basis is transformed, and the prevailing distributive principle becomes " . . . to each according to need." Consequently, as the state becomes a genuine expression of workers' power, and as the economy becomes regulated by "a settled plan," and as the creative powers of labor are devoted to social needs, then the social inequalities between town and country, between intellectual and manual workers, and between sexes, races, and nationalities will be eliminated. Marginalization, uneven development and delinquency will finally disappear.

Obviously, the formation of social policy planning in the United States is generally organized around different possibilities. The United States remains a capitalist society and, consequently, policy makers underwrite capital accumulation. They defend multinational interests through C.I.A. activity in Latin American countries and they enrich commercial interests through urban renewal programs in North American cities. By developing educational-industrial, police-industrial, and other social-industrial complexes, they exploit domestic problems to maintain profits (O'Connor, 1974; McLaughan, 1975). Such developments undermine attempts to prevent marginalization, uneven development and delinquency.

Because of the domination by capital, social policy planning usually avoids conflict with essential structural relations, but this accomodation is self-defeating. Since they are subordinated to the very forces that cause these problems, social policy planners cannot deal with the problems successfully. Instead, they attack the problems piece-meal without regard to long-term strategies for structural changes. Although direct intervention into the immediate causes of marginalization, uneven development and delinquency is required even for the *amelioration* of these problems, such intervention is rarely attempted.

Take the numerous manpower training programs, which have concentrated on black marginals. The programs have failed to make any improvement in black communities, because they do not lower unemployment directly. Surveys report, therefore, that

> without a direct transformation and augmentation of the demand for their labor, significant improvement in the economic situation of ghetto dwellers is unlikely. Attempts to change the worker himself—whether to remedy his personal 'defects' or to move him to a 'better' environment—have not worked up until now, and the [several sources of data reported] in this study provide little if any evidence to support the belief that such attempts will be sufficient in the future (Harrison, 1975:159-160).

Thus, without significant attempts to expand and stabilize the labor market directly through public works, the socialization of industries, and economic planning, the social investment in reducing marginalization through manpower training is irrational.

As indicated, such manpower programs are not integrated with policies that change structural relations in the economy; hence, their effects on marginalization are negligible. Similar relations apply to the school. Since compensatory education policies are also restricted by capital, they are not related to strategies that change structural relations in either the school or economy. Hence their effects on the equalization of school achievement are very limited.

While compensatory education has some positive effects on racial, ethnic, or economic groups that have higher proportions of prototypic marginal youth, the relative magnitude of these effects is questionable. Martin Carnoy's (1975:233-242) survey of studies about teacher performance indicates that compensatory programs have strikingly similar results.

> They generally show a positive relationship between so-called higher 'quality' characteristics of teachers and exam score. They also show significantly different teacher input-school output relationships for different ethnic groups and, in Puerto Rico, for different class groups. Finally, they show that even if increasing teacher quality results in higher achievement, average achievement scores will at best bring them only part of the way toward equality with presently high scoring groups . . . even if substantially higher-quality teaching is made available to the low-scoring than to the high-scoring students, the change would result in only a partial reduction of exam-score difference between the two. In the case of ethnic and racial minorities in the United States, the reduction may well be negligible.

Such findings are not surprising. Social investments do effect student development, but the combined effects of intergenerational and governmental investments, generally favoring groups with higher statuses, far outweigh social investments into compensatory education. Consequently, the effects of that education are, of necessity, limited, and they cannot neutralize the tendencies toward uneven development. Furthermore, certain other limitations of compensatory education policies are not revealed by studies of isolated programs. The most severe test of these policies would be made if they were instituted everywhere. Under such conditions, various mechanisms (e.g., grading by the "thirds," or by other standardized scores) would maintain the same competitive and hierarchical school relationships, despite the fluctuations in average levels of individual productivity. Hence, marginal youth would still be produced, but with a higher achievement score than before.

With regard to the labor market, value-determining and price-making mechanisms accomplish similar ends. The distribution of educational investments has improved considerably over the last three decades. But, Carnoy (1975:369-370) points out,

> the payoff to schooling changes in a way that makes lower levels of schooling worth less over time relative to higher levels. Thus, the number of people who receive secondary schooling has increased markedly in the United States between 1939 and 1959, but the payoff to that level actually fell. So just as the poor begin to get higher levels of schooling, the relative value to the labor market of those levels falls. Even when a society invests more in schooling for the poor, therefore, the labor market values that schooling less than before the poor were getting it.

The same dismal pattern characterizes delinquency policies. Numerous studies indicate that piece-meal and accommodative social policies have insignificant effects on delinquency. The failure of these policies, which involve counseling, job training, or diversion programs, simply reinforces the necessity for socialist strategies for change. To be successful, short-term programmatic solutions must be part of long-term strategies which support working-class movements that are primary agents of fundamental structural change. The linkage between short-term programs and these long-term strategies represents the central challenge to social policy analysts. There will be no magical solutions by professionals working to eliminate marginalization, uneven development, and delinquency, as long as structural relations in our society are disregarded.

REFERENCES

Bluestone, Barry
1972 "Capitalism and poverty in America: A discussion." Monthly Review 2:64-71.

Bowles, Samuel and Herbert Gintis
1973 "I.Q. in the U.S. class structure." Social Policy 3:65-96.

Bremner, Robert H.
1970 Children and Youth in America, A Documentary History, I. Cambridge, Massachusetts: Harvard University Press.

Carnoy, Martin
1975 Schooling in a Corporate Society, the Political Economy of Education in America. Second Edition. New York: David McKay Company, Inc.

Carson, Robert B.
1972 "Youthful labor surplus in disaccumulationist capitalism." Socialist Revolution 2:15-44.

The Editors
1975 "Capitalism and unemployment." Monthly Review 27:1-13.

Harrison, Bennett
1975 "Education and underemployment in the urban ghetto." Pp. 133-60 in Martin Carnoy (ed.), Schooling in a Corporate Society. New York: David McKay Company, Inc.

Hein, Wolfgang and Konrad Stenzal
1973 "The capitalist state and underdevelopment in Latin America–the case of Venezuela." Kapitalistate 2:31-48.

Hinton, William
1970 Iron Oxen. New York: Monthly Review Press.

Marx, Karl
1959 Capital, I. Moscow: Foreign Languages Publishing House.

McLaughlan, Gregory
1975 "LEAA: A case study in the development of the social industrial complex." Crime and Social Justice 4:15-23.

O'Connor, James
1973 The Fiscal Crisis of the State. New York: St. Martin's Press.

O'Connor, Walter D.
1972 Deviance in Soviet Society, Crime, Delinquency, and Alcoholism. New York: Columbia University Press.

Reich, Michael, David M. Gordon and Richard C. Edwards
1973 "A theory of labor market segmentation," American Economic Review 63:359-365.

Schwendinger, Herman and Julia R. Schwendinger
1974 The Sociologists of the Chair, A Radical Analysis of the Formative Years of North American Sociology (1883-1922). New York: Basic Books.
1976 "The collective varieties of youth." Crime and Social Justice 5:7-25.
Forthcoming The Collective Varieties of Youth Book.

SECTION TEN

Summary

Without a doubt, many who have read the preceding selections will be confused, frustrated, and upset. Nothing seems to work! In fact, the selections *should be upsetting,* because they challenge and overturn common beliefs about what needs to be done. The assumptions behind the various programs evaluated strike many people as reasonable. They are based on ideas so commonly advanced by scientists, social workers, politicians, and concerned citizens that it is shocking when they do not work.

How should we respond to the research? It is tempting simply to dismiss it on the grounds that a few studies do not prove anything. However, in this case the few studies do not yield conclusions different from any reached in reviews of comparable studies conducted over several decades.

Another response might be to argue that a program failed because more time and more resources were needed. There are several problems with this response as well. The programs described in the selections were neither trivial nor poorly planned. They were carried out with commitment, dedication, and intensity. Moreover, why is it that there are limits on time and resources? Why is it that programs are carried out in an atmosphere of conflict and competition? The Boston Midcity Project was impeded by conflict among the people and agencies involved. The Minnesota Advocate Program generated hostility and conflict between school principals and youth advocates. There may be agreement on general ideas, like "An ounce of prevention is worth a pound of cure" and "Youths need to be given more responsibility and a stake in the system." Yet when attempts are made to act on these beliefs, we find hidden reservations that call for serious qualifications: "Providing that vested interests are not unduly upset. . . ." More dramatic and far-reaching proposals can be made, but the considerable resistance to small-scale programs should suggest even more opposition and greater barriers to the implementation of grander schemes.

If neither revolutionary change nor a "war on crime" is acceptable, there are other responses worthy of consideration. Earlier readings testing theories of delinquency have implications for the designing of new responses to delinquency. For example, tests of social control theory suggest that school experiences are particularly crucial for explaining delinquency. The greater a student's achievement, the lesser his or her involvement in delinquency. While criminologists cannot specify exactly how to improve achievement, directing efforts toward that end could have the side benefit of decreasing delinquency. However, the Schwendingers point out that past efforts to enhance achievement have met with limited success. Without changes in the labor market, increased achievement may not eliminate marginalization. Rather, it could result in more able marginal youths.

The test of social learning theory in Section Five has implications for "personal policies" of prevention. The research shows delinquency to be learned in a process that involves imitation, differential reinforcement, differential association, and normative learning. We tend to ask what the government can do to prevent delinquency, often forgetting that each of us is part of the learning process. What each of us does has an impact on others. We should be concerned with whether we do what we tell others to do. We should ask ourselves whether we *encourage* delinquency through some of our own actions and inactions. Can we continue to smoke and drink while condemning drug use among the young? Can we take shortcuts, use loopholes, and excuse our own behavior while pointing to others as less worthy? Social learning theory suggests that what *we do* has to be considered in the explanation of delinquency.

We should also consider the possibility that the traditional rationales for directing an inordinate amount of attention toward delinquency prevention rather than toward the direct prevention of *adult crime* are misleading. The most common rationale is the simplistic notion that the best way to solve a problem is to "nip it in the bud." Texts on delinquency typically begin with a presentation of alarming statistics on juvenile crime, together with claims to the effect that most serious criminals get their start as delinquents. The prevention of delinquency is depicted as America's best hope for reducing crime.

Each of these claims can be challenged. The most commonly cited statistics on "serious" crimes do not include data for serious adult-dominated offenses and do not weight offenses by degrees of graveness. The statistics show juveniles to be disproportionately involved in direct attacks on other people's property, while young adults dominate arrest data for interpersonal violence and older adults prevail in the most lucrative crimes. Moreover, it can be argued that adult crime is a cause of delinquency in the sense that adult values, attitudes, and behavior affect what the young do. Since nip-it-in-the-bud programs have failed, we might consider more direct, concerted attacks on adult crime, especially those forms that have not been given much attention.

Actually, in making these statements, we have come full circle. This book of readings began with a presentation of examples of the delinquency problem and a discussion of its dramatic aspects. We have found the problem to involve more than merely the objective behavioral realities of delinquency. Haney and Gold point out that our delinquency programs are based on myths, and Chambliss illustrates how differences in observer reactions to different groups of boys contributes to the problem. In our concluding comments, we are suggesting that both taken-for-granted assumptions about where attention should be directed, and the priority of delinquency as a social problem, be questioned as well. Perhaps future texts will note with alarm the powerful impact of adult crime on the young and propose that we "prevent the flower from going to seed" by turning our attention to adult transgression.

1 2 3 4 5 6 7 8 9 0